THE PUBLIC GENERAL ACTS

AND GENERAL SYNOD MEASURES

1976

[IN THREE PARTS]

PART I
(Chapters 1–52)

with
Lists of the Public General Acts,
Local Acts and General Synod Measures
and an Index

LONDON
HER MAJESTY'S STATIONERY OFFICE
£46.00 net

ISBN 0 11 840159 9*

THIS PUBLICATION

relates to

the Public General Acts

and General Synod Measures

which received the Royal Assent in 1976

in which year ended the TWENTY-FOURTH

and began the TWENTY-FIFTH YEAR

of the Reign of HER MAJESTY

QUEEN ELIZABETH THE SECOND

and

ended the Second Session

and began the Third Session

of the Forty-Seventh Parliament of the

United Kingdom of Great Britain

and Northern Ireland.

371556

d

Printed by BERNARD M. THIMONT,
Controller of Her Majesty's Stationery Office and
Queen's Printer of Acts of Parliament

CONTENTS

PART I

PART II

PART III

TABLE I

Alphabetical List of the Public General Acts of 1976

TABLE II

Chronological List of the Public General Acts of 1976

Chapter		Part	Page
1	National Coal Board (Finance) Act	I	1
2	Consolidated Fund Act	I	4
3	Road Traffic (Drivers' Ages and Hours of Work) Act	I	5
4	Trustee Savings Banks Act	I	21
5	Education (School-Leaving Dates) Act	I	56
6	Solicitors (Scotland) Act	I	59
7	Trade Union and Labour Relations (Amendment) Act	I	71
8	Prevention of Terrorism (Temporary Provisions) Act	I	77
9	Water Charges Act	I	95
10	Post Office (Banking Services) Act	I	100
11	Housing (Amendment) (Scotland) Act	I	103
12	Statute Law Revision (Northern Ireland) Act ...	I	105
13	Damages (Scotland) Act	I	132
14	Fatal Accidents and Sudden Deaths Inquiry (Scotland) Act	I	139
15	Rating (Caravan Sites) Act	I	148
16	Statute Law (Repeals) Act	I	155
17	Land Drainage (Amendment) Act	I	185
18	Licensing (Amendment) Act	I	205
19	Seychelles Act	I	206
20	Education (Scotland) Act	I	211
21	Crofting Reform (Scotland) Act	I	221
22	Freshwater and Salmon Fisheries (Scotland) Act ...	I	251
23	Atomic Energy Authority (Special Constables) Act ...	I	265
24	Development Land Tax Act	I	269
25	Fair Employment (Northern Ireland) Act	I	461
26	Explosives (Age of Purchase &c.) Act	I	517
27	Theatres Trust Act	I	518
28	Congenital Disabilities (Civil Liability) Act	I	523
29	Representation of the People (Armed Forces) Act ...	I	527
*30	Fatal Accidents Act	I	531
*31	Legitimacy Act	I	537
*32	Lotteries and Amusements Act	I	545
*33	Restrictive Practices Court Act	I	576
*34	Restrictive Trade Practices Act	I	583

* Consolidation Act.

* Consolidation Act.

TABLE III

Alphabetical List of the Local and Personal Acts of 1976

TABLE IV

Chronological List of

the General Synod Measures of 1976

Measures passed by the General Synod of the Church of England which received the Royal Assent during the year 1976

THE PUBLIC GENERAL ACTS OF 1976

National Coal Board (Finance) Act 1976

1976 CHAPTER 1

An Act to increase the limit on the borrowing powers of the National Coal Board; to provide for reimbursing to the Board out of public money certain expenditure of theirs in respect of the mineworkers' pension scheme; and to extend the purposes for which grants may be made, under section 7 of the Coal Industry Act 1973, towards the cost of stock-piling coal and coke.

[4th March 1976]

BE IT ENACTED by the Queen's most Excellent Majesty, by and with the advice and consent of the Lords Spiritual and Temporal, and Commons, in this present Parliament assembled, and by the authority of the same, as follows:—

Borrowing powers of National Coal Board. 1965 c. 82.

1.—(1) In section 1(3) of the Coal Industry Act 1965 (which, as substituted by section 2 of the 1973 Act, limits the aggregate of sums borrowed by the Board and its wholly-owned subsidiaries to a sum not exceeding £550 million or such greater sum not exceeding £700 million as the Secretary of State may by order specify), for " £550 million " and " £700 million " there shall be substituted respectively " £1,100 million " and " £1,400 million ".

S.I. 1974 No. 1296.

(2) The Coal Industry (Borrowing Powers) Order 1974 (which increased the borrowing limit to £700 million) is hereby revoked.

Payments towards mineworkers' pension scheme deficiency.

2.—(1) If the Board, in any of their financial years 1975–76 to 1994–95 (both inclusive), have incurred expenditure towards reducing or eliminating deficiencies of the mineworkers' pension scheme, then subject to the provisions of this section the Secretary of State may, if he thinks fit, reimburse to the Board (in whole or in part) so much of that expenditure as appears to him to relate to current and contingent liabilities of the scheme to and in respect of persons whose service in the coal industry was terminated (by death, retirement or otherwise) before 6th April 1975.

(2) In determining the amounts to be reimbursed to the Board under this section, the Secretary of State shall disregard any extent to which the scales and rates of pensions and other benefits, paid or to be paid in discharge of those liabilities, have been uprated since that date otherwise than for the purpose only of maintaining their real value from time to time.

(3) Any payments by the Secretary of State under this section shall be made from money provided by Parliament: and the maximum aggregate of such payments shall not exceed—

(*a*) in respect of the Board's financial year 1975–76, £18 million less the total amount of any payments made by him to the Board in respect of that year under section 5 of the 1973 Act (contributions towards increased pensions); and

(*b*) in respect of any subsequent financial year up to and including 1994–1995, £18 million.

(4) The Secretary of State may by order in a statutory instrument direct that, in respect of the Board's financial year in which the order is made and any subsequent financial year, subsection (3) above shall apply with the substitution in paragraph (*b*) of an increased (or further increased) maximum sum specified by the order; but—

(*a*) no such order shall be made unless the Treasury consent nor unless a draft of it has been laid before the House of Commons and approved by a resolution of that House;

(*b*) before laying a draft order, the Secretary of State shall review the overall financial position of the Board; and

(*c*) with the draft order he shall lay a statement explaining (by reference to the result of his review and to the matters mentioned in subsections (1) and (2) of this section) the considerations which have led him to conclude that the order should be made.

(5) The expenditure of the Board referred to in subsection (1) above does not include any which is relevant expenditure for the purposes of section 3 of the 1965 Act (pit closures), as amended.

(6) As from 1st April 1976, no further payment shall be made by the Secretary of State under section 5 of the 1973 Act; and that section is hereby repealed with effect from that date.

3.—(1) The costs in respect of which the Secretary of State may make grants to the Board under section 7 of the 1973 Act (building up and maintaining stocks of coal or coke) shall include those incurred in the financial year 1975–76 in enabling such stocks to be built up and maintained by the following of the Board's customers namely, the Central Electricity Generating Board, the South of Scotland Electricity Board and the British Steel Corporation. Costs of stock-piling coal and coke.

(2) In applying subsection (2) of that section (Board's own stocks to be taken into account only within lower limit determined by the Secretary of State and upper limit of 30 million tonnes), so much of the stocks held at any time by those customers as has been supplied by the Board but not paid for is to be treated as, or as having been, owned at that time by the Board.

(3) If an order of the Secretary of State comes into force under subsection (3) of that section (extension of grant to the Board's financial years 1976–77 and 1977–78), the reference in subsection (1) above to the financial year 1975–76 is also amended to include those two financial years of the Board.

4.—(1) This Act may be cited as the National Coal Board (Finance) Act 1976. Citation, interpretation and extent.

(2) The Coal Industry Acts 1946 to 1973, the Coal Industry Act 1975 and this Act may be cited together as the Coal Industry Acts 1946 to 1976. 1975 c. 56.

(3) In this Act—

" the 1965 Act " means the Coal Industry Act 1965; 1965 c. 82.

" the 1973 Act " means the Coal Industry Act 1973; 1973 c. 8.

" the Board " means the National Coal Board; and

" the mineworkers' pension scheme " means the scheme established by that name in pursuance of regulations made under section 37 of the Coal Industry Nationalisation Act 1946. 9 & 10 Geo. 6. c. 59.

(4) This Act does not extend to Northern Ireland.

Consolidated Fund Act 1976

1976 CHAPTER 2

An Act to apply certain sums out of the Consolidated Fund to the service of the years ending on 31st March 1975 and 1976. [25th March 1976]

Most Gracious Sovereign,

WE, Your Majesty's most dutiful and loyal subjects, the Commons of the United Kingdom in Parliament assembled, towards making good the supply which we have cheerfully granted to Your Majesty in this Session of Parliament, have resolved to grant unto Your Majesty the sums hereinafter mentioned; and do therefore most humbly beseech Your Majesty that it may be enacted, and be it enacted by the Queen's most Excellent Majesty, by and with the advice and consent of the Lords Spiritual and Temporal, and Commons, in this present Parliament assembled, and by the authority of the same, as follows:—

Issue out of the Consolidated Fund for the year ending 31st March 1975.

1. The Treasury may issue out of the Consolidated Fund of the United Kingdom and apply towards making good the supply granted to Her Majesty for the service of the year ending on 31st March 1975 the sum of £12,737,351·80.

Issue out of the Consolidated Fund for the year ending 31st March 1976.

2. The Treasury may issue out of the Consolidated Fund of the United Kingdom and apply towards making good the supply granted to Her Majesty for the service of the year ending on 31st March 1976 the sum of £951,518,000.

Short title.

3. This Act may be cited as the Consolidated Fund Act 1976.

Road Traffic (Drivers' Ages and Hours of Work) Act 1976

1976 CHAPTER 3

An Act to amend the Road Traffic Act 1972 in so far as it relates to drivers' licences and the minimum age for driving certain classes of vehicles and to amend Part VI of the Transport Act 1968 and for connected purposes. [25th March 1976]

BE IT ENACTED by the Queen's most Excellent Majesty, by and with the advice and consent of the Lords Spiritual and Temporal, and Commons, in this present Parliament assembled, and by the authority of the same, as follows:—

Amendment of Road Traffic Act 1972 as to drivers' licences and the minimum age of drivers 1972 c. 20.

1.—(1) Section 4 of the Road Traffic Act 1972 (offence of driving under age) is hereby repealed and Part III of that Act (ordinary driving licences) shall, subject to Schedule 2 to this Act, have effect with the substitution for section 96 (disqualification of persons under age) of the following—

"Disqualification of persons under age.

96.—(1) A person is disqualified for holding or obtaining a licence to drive a motor vehicle of a class specified in the following Table if he is under the age specified in relation thereto in the second column of that Table.

TABLE

Class of motor vehicle	*Age (in years)*
1. Invalid carriage	16
2. Motor cycle...	16

Class of motor vehicle	*Age (in years)*
3. Small passenger vehicle or small goods vehicle	17
4. Agricultural tractor	17
5. Medium-sized goods vehicle	18
6. Other motor vehicles	21

(2) The Secretary of State may by regulations provide that subsection (1) above shall have effect as if for the classes of vehicles and the ages specified in the Table thereto there were substituted different classes of vehicles and ages or different classes of vehicles or different ages.

(3) Subject to sub-paragraph (4) below, regulations under subsection (2) above may—

(*a*) apply to persons of a class specified in or under the regulations;

(*b*) apply in circumstances so specified;

(*c*) impose conditions or create exemptions or provide for the imposition of conditions or the creations of exemptions;

(*d*) contain such transitional and supplemental provisions (including provisions amending section 110, 124 or 188(3) of this Act as the Secretary of State considers necessary or expedient.

(4) For the purpose of defining the class of persons to whom, the class of vehicles to which, the circumstances in which or the conditions subject to which regulations under subsection (2) above are to apply where an approved training scheme for drivers is in force, it shall be sufficient for the regulations to refer to a document which embodies the terms (or any of the terms) of the scheme or to a document which is in force in pursuance of the scheme.

(5) In subsection (4) above—

"approved" means approved for the time being by the Secretary of State for the purpose of regulations under subsection (2) above;

"training scheme for drivers" means a scheme for training persons to drive vehicles of a class in relation to which the age which is in force under this section but apart from any such scheme is 21 years;

but no approved training scheme for drivers shall be amended without the approval of the Secretary of State."

(2) Schedule 1 to this Act (which contains consequential and other amendments including amendments about heavy goods vehicle drivers' licences) shall have effect.

(3) Schedule 1 to this Act shall be treated, in so far as it amends sections 85, 107 and 110 of the Road Traffic Act 1972, as having had effect since the beginning of 1976— 1972 c. 20.

(*a*) for authorising the grant of driving licences authorising the driving of motor vehicles of any class since that time by reference to the classes of vehicles and the ages specified in section 96 of that Act as substituted by subsection (1) above; and

(*b*) for the interpretation of such licences;

and any regulations made by virtue of those amendments may have effect accordingly.

(4) Schedule 2 to this Act (which contains saving provisions) shall also have effect.

(5) The enactments specified in Part I of Schedule 3 to this Act (which includes some which are spent) are hereby repealed to the extent specified in the third column of that Schedule.

Amendment of Transport Act 1968 about drivers' hours. 1968 c. 73.

2.—(1) In Part VI of the Transport Act 1968 (drivers' hours)—

(*a*) in section 103(1), for the definition of " the international rules " there shall be substituted the words " ' the applicable Community rules ' means any directly applicable Community provision for the time being in force about the driving of road vehicles ";

(*b*) in section 103(1), in the appropriate places in alphabetical order, there shall be inserted the following definitions—

" ' the domestic drivers' hours code ' has the meaning given by section 96(13) of this Act ";

" ' relevant Community provision ' means any Community provision for the time being in force about the driving of road vehicles, whether directly applicable or not ";

(*c*) for the words " the international rules " wherever occurring in that Part, there shall be substituted the words " the applicable Community rules ";

(*d*) in section 95(1), there shall be inserted after the words " proper hours " the words " or periods " and there shall be substituted, for the words after " fatigue " (about the adaptation of that Part to take account of Community provisions relating to international journeys), the following words—

" but the Secretary of State may by regulations make such provision by way of substitution for or adaptation of the provisions of this Part, or supplemental or incidental to this Part, as he considers necessary or expedient to take account of the operation of any relevant Community provision.

(1A) Regulations under subsection (1) above may in particular—

(*a*) substitute different requirements for the requirements of the domestic drivers' hours code or add to, make exceptions from or otherwise modify any of the requirements of that code;

(*b*) apply to journeys and work to which no relevant Community provision applies;

(*c*) include provision as to the circumstances in which a period of driving or duty to which a relevant Community provision or the domestic drivers' hours code applies is to be included or excluded in reckoning any period for purposes of the domestic drivers' hours code or any relevant Community provision respectively; and

(*d*) may contain such transitional, supplemental or consequential provisions as the Secretary of State thinks necessary or expedient ";

(*e*) in section 96(11), for the words from " subsections (1) to (6) " to " (10) thereof " there shall be substituted the words " the domestic drivers' hours code ";

(*f*) after section 96(12) there shall be added the following subsection—

" (13) In this Part of this Act " the domestic driver's hours code " means the provisions of subsections (1) to (6) of this section as for the time being in force (and, in particular, as modified, added to or substituted by or under any instrument in force under section 95(1) of this Act or subsection (10) or (12) of this section) ";

(*g*) in section 98, for the words " books and records " in subsection (2) and the words " books or records " in subsection (4), there shall be substituted the words " books, records or documents "; and

(*h*) in section 99, in subsection (1)(*d*), the word " corresponding " shall be omitted and in subsection (5) for the words " book or register kept " there shall be substituted the words " book, register or document kept or carried ";

(*i*) in section 101, in subsection (3), after the words " (except regulations made " there shall be inserted the words " under section 95(1) or " and after that subsection there shall be inserted the following subsection—

" (3A) No regulations shall be made under section 95(1) of this Act unless a draft of the regulations has been laid before, and approved by a resolution of, each House of Parliament."

(2) In the following enactments in the Transport Act 1968, that is to say, in section 35(2)(*b*), 62(4)(*b*) and 64(2)(*c*) and paragraph 2(5) of Schedule 9, any reference to Part VI of that Act shall be deemed to include a reference to the applicable Community rules (within the meaning of that Part). 1968 c. 73.

(3) In the following enactments, that is to say section 11(1)(*a*) of the Road Haulage Wages Act 1938, section 19(3)(*b*) of the Wages Councils Act 1959 and Schedule 2 to the Road Traffic (Foreign Vehicles) Act 1972, for the words " the international rules " there shall be substituted the words " the applicable Community rules ". 1938 c. 44. 1959 c. 69. 1972 c. 27.

(4) The enactment specified in Part II of Schedule 3 to this Act is hereby repealed.

(5) Nothing in subsection (1) above shall invalidate any regulations made under the said section 95(1) and those regulations shall have effect as if they had been made under that subsection as substituted by paragraph (*d*) of subsection (1) above.

Extension of jurisdiction over offences about drivers' hours.

3. For section 103(7) of the Transport Act 1968 (which confers jurisdiction over an offence about drivers' hours on any court having jurisdiction in the place where the person charged with the offence is for the time being) there shall be substituted the following—

" (7) An offence under this Part of this Act may be treated for the purpose of conferring jurisdiction on a court (but without prejudice to any jurisdiction it may have apart from this subsection) as having been committed in any of the following places, that is to say—

(*a*) the place where the person charged with the offence was driving when evidence of the offence first came to the attention of a constable or vehicle examiner;

(*b*) the place where that person resides or is or is believed to reside or be at the time when the proceedings are commenced; or (*c*) the place where at that time that person or, in the case of an employee-driver, that person's employer or, in the case of an owner-driver, the person for whom he was driving, has his place or principal place of business or his operating centre for the vehicle in question.

In this subsection " vehicle examiner " means an officer within the meaning of section 99 of this Act."

Citation, commencement and extent.

4.—(1) This Act may be cited as the Road Traffic (Drivers' Ages and Hours of Work) Act 1976.

(2) The provisions of this Act shall come into force as follows—

(*a*) with the exception of the provisions specified in paragraph (*b*) below, sections 1, 3 and 4 shall come into force on the passing of this Act;

(*b*) in Schedule 1, paragraph 8 and (except so far as it has effect for purposes of section 119 of the Road Traffic Act 1972) paragraph 11, and, in Schedule 2, subparagraphs (1), (2), (3) and (7) of paragraph 3 shall come into force on the appointed day;

(*c*) section 2 shall come into force on the appointed day.

(3) The Secretary of State may by order made by statutory instrument appoint a day for the coming into force of the provisions of this Act falling within paragraph (*b*) or (*c*) of subsection (2) above and different days may be appointed under this subsection for different provisions of section 2.

(4) In this Act " appointed day ", in relation to any provision of it, means the day appointed under subsection (3) above for that provision to come into force.

(5) This Act does not extend to Northern Ireland.

SCHEDULES

SCHEDULE 1

Section 1.

Consequential and Other Amendments

1. In section 84 of the Road Traffic Act 1972 (in this Schedule referred to as " the principal Act ") the following amendments shall be made— 1972 c. 20.

(*a*) in subsection (2) (offence of employing a person to drive without an ordinary driving licence), for the words " employ a person " there shall be substituted the words " cause or permit another person " and for the words " if the person employed " there shall be substituted the words " if that other person ";

(*b*) in subsection (3) there shall be substituted, for the words " a person may, without holding a licence " the words " it shall be lawful for a person who is not the holder of a licence, to " and for the words " a person may employ " the words " for a person to cause or permit "; and

(*c*) in subsection (4) there shall be substituted, for the words " a person may at any time drive or employ ", the words " it shall be lawful for a person to drive or cause or permit ".

2. In section 85(1) of the principal Act (conditions of entitlement to driving licences) after the words " as to provisional licences " there shall be inserted the words " and to the provisions of any regulations made by virtue of section 107(1)(*f*) of this Act ".

3. In section 88 of the principal Act, in subsection (3) (matters to be stated in driving licence), for paragraph (*b*), there shall be substituted—

" (*b*) specify the restrictions on the driving of vehicles of any class in pursuance of the licence to which its holder is subject by virtue of the provisions of section 96 of this Act; "

and in subsection (4) (restrictions on classes of vehicles which may be driven as if driven under a provisional licence), for paragraph (*a*), there shall be substituted—

" (*a*) a vehicle of a class for the driving of which he could not, by reason of the provisions of section 96 of this Act, lawfully hold a licence, or ".

4. In section 107(1) of the principal Act (general power to make regulations about ordinary driving licences), there shall be inserted after paragraph (*e*) the following paragraphs—

" (*f*) the effect of a change in the classification of motor vehicles for the purposes of this Part of this Act on licences then in force or issued or on the right to or the granting of licences thereafter; ".

(*g*) the enabling of a person—

(i) whose entitlement to the grant of a licence to drive a class of motor vehicle is preserved by regulations under paragraph (*f*) above, and

(ii) who satisfies such conditions as may be prescribed to drive (and be employed in driving) that class of motor vehicle while he applies for the licence to be granted to him, "

Section 1.

5. In section 110 of the principal Act (definitions for purposes of provisions about ordinary driving licences) there shall be inserted in the appropriate places the following definitions—

" 'agricultural tractor' means a tractor used primarily for work on land in connection with agriculture";

" 'articulated goods vehicle' means a motor vehicle which is so constructed that a trailer designed to carry goods may by partial superimposition be attached thereto in such a manner as to cause a substantial part of the weight of the trailer to be borne by the motor vehicle, and 'articulated goods vehicle combination' means an articulated goods vehicle with a trailer so attached;"

" 'maximum gross weight', in relation to a motor vehicle or trailer, means the weight of the vehicle laden with the heaviest load which it is constructed or adapted to carry;"

" 'maximum train weight', in relation to an articulated goods vehicle combination, means the weight of the combination laden with the heaviest load which it is constructed or adapted to carry;"

" 'medium-sized goods vehicle' means a motor vehicle which is constructed or adapted to carry or to haul goods and is not adapted to carry more than 9 persons inclusive of the driver and the permissible maximum weight of which exceeds 3·5 but not 7·5 tonnes;"

" 'permissible maximum weight', in relation to a goods vehicle (of whatever description), means—

(*a*) in the case of a motor vehicle which neither is an articulated goods vehicle nor is drawing a trailer, the relevant maximum weight of the vehicle;

(*b*) in the case of an articulated goods vehicle—

(i) when drawing only a semi-trailer, the relevant maximum train weight of the articulated goods vehicle combination;

(ii) when drawing a trailer as well as a semi-trailer, the aggregate of the relevant maximum train weight of the articulated goods vehicle combination and the relevant maximum weight of the trailer;

(iii) when drawing a trailer but not a semi-trailer, the aggregate of the relevant maximum weight of the articulated goods vehicle and the relevant maximum weight of the trailer;

(iv) when drawing neither a semi-trailer nor a trailer, the relevant maximum weight of the vehicle;

(*c*) in the case of a motor vehicle (not being an articulated goods vehicle) which is drawing a trailer, the aggregate of the relevant maximum weight of the motor vehicle and the relevant maximum weight of the trailer;"

"'relevant maximum weight', in relation to a motor vehicle or trailer, means—

(*a*) in the case of a vehicle to which regulations under section 45 of this Act apply which is required by regulations under section 40 of this Act to have a maximum gross weight for the vehicle marked on a plate issued by the Secretary of State under regulations under the said section 40, the maximum gross weight so marked on the vehicle;

(*b*) in the case of a vehicle which is required by regulations under section 40 of this Act to have a maximum gross weight for the vehicle marked on the vehicle and does not also have a maximum gross weight marked on it as mentioned in paragraph (*a*) above, the maximum gross weight marked on the vehicle;

(*c*) in the case of a vehicle on which a maximum gross weight is marked by the same means as would be required by regulations under the said section 40 if those regulations applied to the vehicle, the maximum gross weight so marked on the vehicle;

(*d*) in the case of a vehicle on which a maximum gross weight is not marked as mentioned in paragraph (*a*), (*b*) or (*c*) above, the notional maximum gross weight of the vehicle, that is to say, such weight as is produced by multiplying the unladen weight of the vehicle by the number prescribed by the Secretary of State for the class of vehicle into which that vehicle falls;"

"'relevant maximum train weight', in relation to an articulated goods vehicle combination, means—

(*a*) in the case of an articulated goods vehicle to which regulations under section 45 of this Act apply which is required by regulations under section 40 of this Act to have a maximum train weight for the combination marked on a plate issued by the Secretary of State under regulations under the said section 40, the maximum train weight so marked on the motor vehicle;

(*b*) in the case of an articulated goods vehicle which is required by regulations under section 40 of this Act to have a maximum train weight for the combination marked on the vehicle and does not also have a maximum train weight marked on it as mentioned in paragraph (*a*) above, the maximum train weight marked on the motor vehicle;

(*c*) in the case of an articulated goods vehicle on which a maximum train weight is marked by the same means as would be required by regulations under section 40 of this Act if those regulations applied to the vehicle, the maximum train weight so marked on the motor vehicle;

(*d*) in the case of an articulated goods vehicle on which a maximum train weight is not marked as mentioned in paragraph (*a*), (*b*) or (*c*) above, the notional maximum gross weight of the combination, that is to say, such weight as is produced by multiplying the sum of the unladen

SCH. 1

weights of the motor vehicle and the semi-trailer by the number prescribed by the Secretary of State for the class of articulated goods vehicle combination into which that combination falls; "

" ' semi-trailer ', in relation to an articulated goods vehicle, means a trailer attached to it in the manner described in the definition of articulated goods vehicle; "

" ' small goods vehicle ' means a motor vehicle (other than a motor cycle or invalid carriage) which is constructed or adapted to carry or to haul goods and is not adapted to carry more than 9 persons inclusive of the driver and the permissible maximum weight of which does not exceed 3·5 tonnes; "

" ' small passenger vehicle ' means a motor vehicle (other than a motor cycle or invalid carriage) which is constructed solely to carry passengers and their effects and is adapted to carry not more than 9 persons inclusive of the driver; ".

6. In section 111(1) of the principal Act, for the words " be employed in driving " there shall be substituted the words " for a person to cause or permit the holder of such a licence to drive ".

7. In section 112 of the principal Act the following amendments shall be made—

(*a*) in subsection (2) (offence of employing a person to drive without a heavy goods vehicle drivers' licence), for the word " employ ", there shall be substituted the words " cause or permit ";

(*b*) in subsection (3), for the words from " as the case " to " employed " there shall be substituted the words " shall make it unlawful for a person who is not so licensed to act or, as the case may be, for a person to cause or permit such a person "; and

(*c*) in subsection (4), for the word " employment ", there shall be substituted the words " causing or permitting ".

8. In section 114(1) of the principal Act (conditions precedent to grant of heavy goods vehicle drivers' licences), for the words from " Subject " to "Act " there shall be substituted the words " Subject to the provisions of any regulations made by virtue of section 119(1)(*l*) of this Act ".

9. In section 114(4) of the principal Act (offence of employing a person under 21 to drive heavy goods vehicles in contravention of conditions of licence), for the word " employ " there shall be substituted the words " cause or permit ".

10. In section 119(1) of the principal Act (general power to make regulations about heavy goods vehicle drivers' licences) the following amendments shall be made—

(*a*) in paragraph (*b*), after the word " conduct " there shall be inserted the words " and, if the applicant is to be authorised to drive vehicles of any class at an age below the normal minimum age for driving vehicles of that class, with respect to participation in an approved training scheme for drivers) ";

(*b*) there shall be inserted after paragraph (*k*) the following paragraph—

" (*l*) make provision about the effect of a change in the meaning of heavy goods vehicle or in the classification of heavy goods vehicles for the purposes of this Part of this Act on heavy goods vehicle drivers' licences then in force or issued or on the granting of such licences thereafter;"

11. In section 124 of the principal Act (definitions for purposes of provisions about heavy goods vehicle drivers' licences) the following amendments shall be made, that is to say—

(*a*) for the definition of " heavy goods vehicle " there shall be substituted the following definition—

" ' heavy goods vehicle ' means any of the following vehicles—

(*a*) an articulated goods vehicle;

(*b*) a large goods vehicle, that is to say, a motor vehicle (not being an articulated goods vehicle) which is constructed or adapted to carry or to haul goods and the permissible maximum weight of which exceeds 7·5 tonnes;"

(*b*) the following new definitions shall be inserted at the appropriate places—

(i) " ' approved training scheme for drivers' means a training scheme for drivers (within the meaning of section 96(4) of this Act) approved for the time being by the Secretary of State for the purposes of regulations under section 119 of this Act ";

(ii) " ' normal minimum age for driving ', in relation to the driving of vehicles of any class, means the age which is in force under section 96 of this Act (but apart from any approved training scheme for drivers) in relation to that class of vehicle; " '.

(*c*) there shall be inserted at the end the following paragraph—

" and ' articulated goods vehicle ' and ' permissible maximum weight ' have the same meanings as they have for the purposes of Part III of this Act ".

12. In section 188(3) of the principal Act (minimum age restrictions not to apply to the driving of vehicles of armed forces), for the words preceding " shall not apply " there shall be substituted the words " Subject to regulations made under subsection (2) of section 96 of this Act, that section (in so far as it prohibits persons under 21 from holding or obtaining a licence to drive motor vehicles or persons under 18 from holding or obtaining a licence to drive medium-sized goods vehicles) ".

13. In section 196(2) of the principal Act (interpretation of " class ") after the word " defined " there shall be inserted the words " or described ".

Sch. 1

14. In section 198(4) of the principal Act, for the word " section " there shall be substituted the words " sections 96 and ".

15. In Part I of Schedule 4 to the principal Act (punishment of offences) in column 2 of the entries relating to section 84(2), 112(2) and 114(4), there shall be substituted for the word " Employing " the words " Causing or permitting ".

1967 c. 76. 16. In section 104(2) of the Road Traffic Regulation Act 1967 (interpretation of " class "), after the word " defined " there shall be inserted the words " or described ".

Section 1.

SCHEDULE 2

Saving Provisions

Saving for existing regulations about minimum ages for driving

1972 c. 20. 1. Notwithstanding the repeal by section 1 of this Act of section 4 of the Road Traffic Act 1972 (in this Schedule referred to as " the principal Act ") any instrument made or having effect as if made under the said section 4 shall have effect (with the appropriate adaptation of references) as if made under subsection (2) of section 96 of the principal Act as substituted by section 1 of this Act and may be varied or revoked accordingly.

Saving in relation to certain motor cars for holders of driving licences and similar persons

2.—(1) This paragraph applies to a person who immediately before 1st January 1976 fulfilled any of the following conditions, that is to say—

(*a*) he held a licence (whether full or provisional) authorising him to drive a motor car;

(*b*) he was entitled to obtain a licence (other than a provisional licence) authorising him to drive a motor car or, having previously held a provisional licence, was entitled to obtain a provisional licence authorising him to drive a motor car or would have been (in either case) so entitled but for a current disqualification imposed by order of a court;

(*c*) he would have been the holder of a valid licence authorising him to drive a motor car but for a current disqualification imposed by order of a court;

(*d*) he was treated by virtue of regulations under subsection (5) of section 84 of the principal Act as being the holder of a licence authorising him to drive a motor car for the purposes of subsections (1) and (2) of that section or would have been so treated but for a current disqualification imposed by order of a court.

(2) Subject to sub-paragraph (3) below, a person to whom this paragraph applies shall not, by reason only of the provisions of section 96 of the principal Act as substituted by section 1 of this Act, be disqualified for holding or obtaining a licence authorising him to drive motor vehicles falling within the class described in paragraph 5 or 6 of the Table set out in subsection (1) of the said section 96.

(3) A person shall not be treated, by virtue of sub-paragraph (2) above, as entitled to the grant of a licence authorising him to drive a goods vehicle the permissible maximum weight of which exceeds 10 tonnes or a motor vehicle constructed solely for the carriage of passengers and their effects which is adapted to carry more than 15 passengers inclusive of the driver. SCH. 2

(4) This paragraph shall be construed as if it were contained in Part III of the principal Act but in sub-paragraph (1) " licence " includes a licence to drive motor vehicles granted under Part I of the Road Traffic Act (Northern Ireland) 1970. 1970 c. 2 (N.I.).

Saving in relation to certain goods vehicles for holders of driving licences and similar persons

3.—(1) This paragraph applies to—

(*a*) a goods vehicle which has by virtue of this Act become classified as a heavy goods vehicle, that is to say a motor car which—

(i) is, by virtue of paragraph 11 of Schedule 1 to this Act, a heavy goods vehicle for the purposes of Part IV of the principal Act (not having been a heavy goods vehicle for those purposes before the passing of this Act); and

(ii) is not an articulated goods vehicle (within the meaning of that Part);

(*b*) a person who, immediately before the passing of this Act, fulfilled any of the following conditions, that is to say—

(i) he held a driving licence (whether full or provisional) authorising him to drive a goods vehicle to which this paragraph applies;

(ii) he was entitled to obtain a driving licence (other than a provisional licence) authorising him to drive a goods vehicle to which this paragraph applies or, having previously held a provisional licence, was entitled to obtain a provisional licence authorising him to drive a goods vehicle to which this paragraph applies or would have been (in either case) so entitled but for a current disqualification imposed by order of a court;

(iii) he would have been the holder of a valid driving licence authorising him to drive a goods vehicle to which this paragraph applies but for a current disqualification imposed by order of a court.

(2) Nothing in section 112(1) or (2) of the principal Act (offences arising out of driving without heavy goods vehicle drivers' licence) shall apply to or in relation to the driving by a person to whom this paragraph applies of a goods vehicle to which this paragraph applies during 1976.

(3) Nothing in section 114(1) of the principal Act (restriction on grant of heavy goods vehicle drivers' licences) shall prevent the licensing authority from granting a full licence to drive a heavy goods vehicle if—

(*a*) the application for the grant of the licence is made during 1976 by a person to whom this paragraph applies;

SCH. 2

(*b*) the licensing authority is satisfied that in the course of any 12 consecutive months between the beginning of 1975 and the relevant appointed day the applicant had been in the habit during any period or periods of, or amounting in the aggregate to, six months of driving a goods vehicle to which this paragraph applies of a qualifying weight;

but any licence which the licensing authority grants by virtue of this sub-paragraph shall restrict the person to whom it is granted to the driving of a heavy goods vehicle which is not an articulated goods vehicle (within the meaning of Part IV of the principal Act) and the permissible maximum weight of which does not exceed 10 tonnes.

(4) The reference in sub-paragraph (3) above to the driving of a goods vehicle in any period between the beginning of 1975 and the relevant appointed day does not include a reference to the driving of a goods vehicle of a prescribed class or of a goods vehicle while it is being used in prescribed circumstances.

(5) The Secretary of State may by regulations restrict the class of goods vehicles to which this paragraph applies for the driving of which a licence may be granted by virtue of sub-paragraph (3) above by reference to the class of vehicle which the applicant for the licence was driving during any period between the beginning of 1975 and the relevant appointed day.

(6) In this paragraph—

" driving licence " means a licence to drive a motor vehicle granted under Part III of the principal Act or under Part I of the Road Traffic Act (Northern Ireland) 1970;

1970 c. 2 (N.I.).

" goods vehicle " and " motor car " have the same meanings as they have in the principal Act;

" licensing authority " and " permissible maximum weight " have the same meanings as they have in Part IV of that Act;

" prescribed " means prescribed by regulations made by the Secretary of State;

" provisional licence " has the same meaning as it has in Part III of the principal Act or, as the case requires, in Part I of the Road Traffic Act (Northern Ireland) 1970;

" qualifying weight ", in relation to a goods vehicle, means that the vehicle has an unladen weight of 3 tons or less and a permissible maximum weight in excess of 7·5 tonnes;

" relevant appointed day " means the appointed day for paragraph 11 of Schedule 1 to this Act.

(7) Any reference in this paragraph to a driving licence authorising a person to drive a goods vehicle to which this paragraph applies shall, in relation to a driving licence granted under Part I of the Road Traffic Act (Northern Ireland) 1970, be construed as a reference to a licence so granted authorising him to drive a goods vehicle of a class which—

(*a*) is, by virtue of any provision having effect in Northern Ireland and corresponding with paragraph 11 of Schedule 1 to this Act, a heavy goods vehicle for the purposes of sections 66 to 72 and 74 of the Road Traffic Act (Northern Ireland) 1970 (not having been a heavy goods vehicle for those purposes before the coming into force of that provision); and SCH. 2

(*b*) is not an articulated goods vehicle within the meaning of section 74 of that Act.

(8) This paragraph shall be treated, for the purposes of section 199 of the principal Act (exercise and Parliamentary control of regulation-making powers), as if it were contained in that Act.

4. Notwithstanding section 38(2) of the Interpretation Act 1889 (repeals not to affect accrued liabilities and proceedings therefor), no person shall be convicted (whether in proceedings instituted before or in proceedings instituted after the passing of this Act) of an offence under section 4 or any provision of Part III of the principal Act by reason of his having at any time since the beginning of 1976 driven a motor vehicle of any class on a road under the age which by or under the said section 4 is the minimum age for driving a motor vehicle of that class if at that time he was the holder of a driving licence issued before the passing of this Act authorising him to drive a motor vehicle of that class and had attained the minimum age specified in the licence for driving that class of vehicle. 1889 c. 63.

SCHEDULE 3

Sections 1 and 2.

ENACTMENTS REPEALED

PART I

Chapter	Short Title	Extent of Repeal
1972 c. 20.	The Road Traffic Act 1972.	Section 4. In section 107, in subsections (1) and (2), the words " section 4 or ". In section 110, the words " and section 4 thereof ". Section 122. In section 124, the words " and Schedule 5 thereto ". In section 198(1), the word " 4 ". In Schedule 4, in Part I, the entries relating to section 4(4). Schedule 5.
1972 c. 68.	The European Communities Act 1972.	In Schedule 4, in paragraph 9, sub-paragraph (1).
1974 c. 50.	The Road Traffic Act 1974.	Section 15(1).

PART II

Chapter	Short Title	Extent of Repeal
1972 c. 68.	The European Communities Act 1972.	In Schedule 4, in paragraph 9, sub-paragraph (3).

Trustee Savings Banks Act 1976

1976 CHAPTER 4

An Act to establish a Trustee Savings Banks Central Board; to confer wider powers on trustee savings banks; to transfer to the Registrar of Friendly Societies certain functions previously exercised by other persons; and for purposes connected therewith.

[25th March 1976]

BE IT ENACTED by the Queen's most Excellent Majesty, by and with the advice and consent of the Lords Spiritual and Temporal, and Commons, in this present Parliament assembled, and by the authority of the same, as follows:—

PART I

THE TRUSTEE SAVINGS BANKS CENTRAL BOARD

The Trustee Savings Banks Central Board

Establishment and functions of the Central Board.

1.—(1) There shall be established a Board to be called the Trustee Savings Banks Central Board (hereafter in this Act referred to as " the Central Board ").

(2) The provisions in Schedule 1 to this Act shall have effect in relation to the Central Board.

(3) The Central Board—

(*a*) may give directions of a general character to the trustee savings banks as to the carrying on by the trustee savings banks of their activities ;

(*b*) may provide banking services for the trustee savings banks ;

PART I

(*c*) may provide other common services for the trustee savings banks including (without prejudice to the generality of the foregoing) data processing services and the formation, management and operation of unit trusts ;

(*d*) may give directions to the trustee savings banks as to the equipment and procedures to be adopted by them in the operation of banking services, the manner in which funds are to be raised, expended, allocated to reserve and invested and the rates of interest to be paid on deposits ;

(*e*) shall give directions to the trustee savings banks as to the conditions of service of persons employed by the banks ; any directions given under this paragraph shall be in accordance with the terms of any settlement which may have been reached or award which may have been made by virtue of paragraph 18 of Schedule 1 to this Act ;

(*f*) may exercise such other powers and shall perform such other duties as may be conferred on them by this Act.

(4) The powers conferred on—

(*a*) the Inspection Committee by the following sections of the Act of 1969 that is to say—

1969 c. 50.

(i) section 9(3) and (4) (power of Inspection Committee in relation to appointment and removal of custodian trustees),

(ii) section 58(1) (power of Inspection Committee to appoint inspectors), and

(iii) section 85(2) (power of Inspection Committee in relation to keeping of books), and

(*b*) the National Debt Commissioners by the following enactments, that is to say—

(i) section 61(1) of the Act of 1969 (assent of Commissioners as to amalgamations), and

1948 c. 38.

1960 c. 22 (N.I.).

(ii) section 399(8) of the Companies Act 1948 (power of Commissioners to petition for the winding up of a trustee savings bank) and section 349(8) of the Companies Act (Northern Ireland) 1960 (which makes corresponding provision for Northern Ireland),

shall be exercisable by the Central Board, and accordingly, references in those enactments to the Inspection Committee and the National Debt Commissioners shall be construed as references to the Central Board.

PART I

(5) The Central Board shall have power to carry on all such activities as may appear to them to be requisite, advantageous or convenient for them to carry on for or in connection with the discharge of their powers and duties under subsections (3) and (4) above.

(6) The Central Board shall have power to enter into any transaction (whether or not involving the expenditure of money, the investment of money, the borrowing of money, the acquisition of any property or rights or the disposal of any property or rights) which in their opinion is calculated to facilitate the exercise of their powers or performance of their duties under this Act or is incidental or conducive to the exercise of their powers or performance of their duties.

(7) Notwithstanding the provisions of this section, the Central Board shall not be taken as satisfying the conditions mentioned in paragraphs *(a)* to *(c)* of section 112(1) of the Fair Trading Act 1973 (provisions as to certain associations). 1973 c. 41.

Financial provisions

Revenue of Central Board and subsidiaries to cover outgoings and allocations to reserves.

2.—(1) The Central Board shall exercise their powers and perform their duties under this Act and exercise control over their subsidiaries so as to secure that taking one year with another, the combined revenues of the Central Board and their subsidiaries are not less than sufficient—

(a) to meet the total outgoings of the Central Board and their subsidiaries properly chargeable to revenue account, and

(b) to enable the Central Board and their subsidiaries to make such allocations to reserves as the Central Board consider adequate.

(2) The reserves of the Central Board shall be applied for such purposes as the Central Board may determine.

Power to levy contributions on trustee savings banks.

3.—(1) The Central Board may, from time to time, for the purpose of financing their expenditure in exercising the powers and performing the duties conferred on them by or by virtue of sections 1 and 2 of this Act, require each trustee savings bank to pay to them such sum as the Central Board may determine.

(2) On determining the sum to be paid by each trustee savings bank under subsection (1) above, the Central Board shall send to each trustee savings bank a notice stating the sum required to be paid and each trustee savings bank shall within one month of the date of the notice pay over to the Central Board the sum so required.

PART II

THE TRUSTEE SAVINGS BANKS

General Provisions

Duty to comply with directions.

4.—(1) It shall be the duty of each trustee savings bank to comply with such directions as may be given to it by the Central Board in the exercise of their powers and performance of their duties under this Act.

(2) If a trustee savings bank fails to comply with any directions of the Central Board, that Board may give notice in writing to the bank to remedy the non-compliance within a specified time and, if the trustee savings bank does not comply within that time, the Central Board may—

- (*a*) appoint a person to conduct an inquiry into the conduct of the trustee savings bank and to report his findings to the Central Board ;
- (*b*) report the non-compliance to the Registrar of Friendly Societies with a request that an examination be made under section 59 of the Act of 1969 (appointment of commissioner to examine affairs of trustee savings banks) into the affairs of the trustee savings bank ; [1969 c. 50.]
- (*c*) withdraw any or all of the banking services or other common services provided by the Central Board as that Board may determine until the bank complies.

(3) A person appointed under subsection (2)(*a*) above need not be an officer of the Central Board ; and the trustee savings bank concerned shall give all due facilities for enabling the inquiry to be made.

Scheme for appointment and removal of trustees.

5.—(1) Subject to subsection (5) below, by such date as the Central Board may direct, each trustee savings bank shall submit to the Central Board, for that Board's approval, a scheme providing for the appointment of trustees and for their removal by its depositors.

(2) When such a scheme has been approved, with or without modifications, by the Central Board the trustee savings bank shall within six months of the date of approval alter its rules in accordance with the provisions of the scheme.

(3) If a trustee savings bank fails to alter its rules in accordance with the scheme approved by the Central Board by the expiry of the period of six months mentioned in subsection (2) above, the Central Board may give a direction to the bank to so alter its rules within such time as may be specified in the direction.

(4) If a trustee savings bank fails to submit a scheme for approval by the date by which it is due, the Central Board may

make a scheme on behalf of the bank and give a direction to that bank to alter its rules in accordance with the provisions of that scheme within such time as may be specified in the direction.

(5) In the application of this section to a trustee savings bank whose formation has been promoted by a local authority, the scheme submitted under subsection (1) above shall provide for the appointment and removal of that bank's trustees by the local authority.

6.—(1) A person who has attained the age of 70 shall cease to be a trustee of a trustee savings bank. Age limit for trustees.

(2) Subsection (1) above shall apply to a person who is a trustee of a trustee savings bank on the commencement of that subsection, with the substitution of the word " 75 " for the word " 70 ".

(3) Any person who is appointed or to his knowledge proposed to be appointed a trustee of a trustee savings bank shall give notice of his age to the bank.

7. Whenever a person becomes or ceases to be a trustee of a trustee savings bank, the bank shall within one month give notice thereof to the Central Board and to the Registrar of Friendly Societies and shall furnish such particulars of that person as the Central Board may direct. Notification of changes of trustees.

8.—(1) Section 2 of the Act of 1969 (requirements as to bank rules) shall be amended as set out in the following subsections. Requirements as to bank rules. 1969 c. 50.

(2) For subsection (1) there shall be substituted—

" (1) A savings bank shall not have the benefit of this Act nor of the Trustee Savings Banks Act 1976 unless the rules of the bank expressly provide for the matters set out in Schedule 1 to this Act nor unless those rules—

(*a*) have been certified by the Registrar in pursuance of this section, and

(*b*) have been entered in a book to be kept by an officer of the bank appointed for that purpose which is to open at all proper times for inspection by depositors."

(3) In subsection (4) for the words " deposited by the Registrar with the Commissioners " there shall be substituted the words " retained by the Registrar ".

(4) For Schedule 1 to the Act of 1969 (matters to be covered by the rules of a bank which is to have the benefit of the Act) there shall be substituted the Schedule set out in Schedule 2 to this Act.

PART II

Powers of trustee savings banks

Power to carry on business of banking.

9.—(1) Subject to the provisions of this Act, each trustee savings bank shall have power to carry on the business of banking.

(2) Any expenditure properly incurred by a trustee savings bank in carrying on the business of banking shall be deemed to be necessary expenses of management for the purposes of section 1 of the Act of 1969 (conditions under which a savings bank may obtain the benefit of the Act).

Provisions relating to the purchase and disposal of property, the erection of buildings, etc.

1969 c. 50.

10.—(1) The power conferred on the trustees of a trustee savings bank by section 11 of the Act of 1969 (power to purchase and dispose of property etc.) shall cease to be subject to the consent of the National Debt Commissioners; and, accordingly, in subsection (1) of that section the words " , with the consent of the Commissioners," and " with the like consent ", and in subsection (3) of that section, the words " , or consent of the Commissioners to,", and subsection (4) of that section shall cease to have effect.

(2) The trustees of a trustee savings bank shall have power to purchase land or erect buildings jointly with one or more other trustee savings banks for their joint purposes.

1889 c. 63.

(3) Without prejudice to section 38 of the Interpretation Act 1889 (effect of repeals) any certificate issued under section 11(4) of the Act of 1969 before the commencement of this section shall continue to be conclusive evidence of the matters mentioned in that subsection.

Power to pay trustees.

11. A trustee savings bank shall have power to pay to its trustees such remuneration by way of fees and expenses as it may with the approval of the Central Board determine.

General financial provisions relating to trustee savings banks

Ordinary deposits.

12.—(1) Moneys deposited with the trustees of a trustee savings bank as ordinary deposits to be placed to the credit of a current account shall not be required to be invested with the National Debt Commissioners in accordance with the provisions of section 12(1) of the Act of 1969 (investment of deposits).

(2) Moneys deposited with the trustees of a trustee savings bank for investment as ordinary deposits to be placed to the credit of a savings account shall not be required to be invested with the National Debt Commissioners in accordance with the provisions of section 12(1) of the Act of 1969 (investment of deposits).

PART II

(3) Each trustee savings bank shall give notice to the persons who have savings account deposits with the bank that those deposits will be transferred to another kind of account with the bank, together with interest accrued thereon in accordance with section 15(1) of the Act of 1969 (payment of interest on ordinary deposits) from the date on which interest was last computed under subsection (2) of that section to the date on which the deposit is so transferred.

1969 c. 50.

(4) For section 32(2) of the Act of 1969 (investment of ordinary deposits) there shall be substituted—

" (2) Subsection (1) above shall not apply to such percentage, as the National Debt Commissioners may, after consultation with the Treasury, specify of such sums of money as represents the bank's liabilities to its depositors."

Trustee savings bank liabilities as banker to be matched by cash and liquid assets.

13.—(1) It shall be the duty of each trustee savings bank to secure that at any time—

(*a*) such proportion of the aggregate of the sums owed by it to its depositors as the Treasury may from time to time determine is matched by assets of the trustee savings bank of one or more of the classes specified in Part I of Schedule 3 to this Act ; and

(*b*) the residue of that aggregate is matched by assets of the trustee savings bank of one or more of the classes specified in Part II of that Schedule.

(2) The Treasury may from time to time determine the amount which may be invested by a trustee savings bank in any class of assets specified in or designated by virtue of Schedule 3 to this Act as a proportion of the total amount invested by the bank in all classes of assets specified in or designated by virtue of that Schedule.

Revenue of trustee savings bank to cover outgoings and allocations to reserves.

14. It shall be the duty of each trustee savings bank to conduct its business so as to secure that, taking one year with another, its revenue is not less than sufficient—

(*a*) to meet the total outgoings of the bank properly chargeable to revenue account, and

(*b*) to enable the bank to make such allocations to reserves as it may consider adequate and as may be necessary to comply with any directions given by the Central Board under section 1 above.

Financing of capital expenditure.

15. Sections 51 to 54 of the Act of 1969 (provisions relating to the defraying of expenditure in the acquisition of land and equipment) shall cease to have effect but without prejudice to any advance made under sections 53 and 54 of that Act before the commencement of this section.

PART II

The Fund for the Banks for Savings

The Fund for the Banks for Savings.

16.—(1) The Fund for the Banks for Savings shall be closed.

(2) Until the commencement of subsection (1) above the following provisions of this section shall apply in relation to the Fund.

(3) The National Debt Commissioners shall repay to each trustee savings bank such amount standing to that bank's credit in the Fund as represents the current account deposits of that bank, together with interest accrued thereon in accordance with section 35(1) of the Act of 1969 (interest on sums in the Fund) from the date on which the interest was last credited under subsection (2) of that section to the date of repayment of the amount.

(4) The Treasury may by order fix a limit on the sums which may be withdrawn in any period of six months ending on 20th November or 20th May by a trustee savings bank from the amount standing to the bank's credit in the Fund in respect of the savings account deposits of that bank.

(5) At the end of the period of six months ending on 20th November or, as the case may be, on 20th May immediately preceding the commencement of subsection (1) above, the National Debt Commissioners shall pay to each trustee savings bank the amount (if any) standing to its credit in the Fund, together with any interest accrued thereon under section 35(1) of the Act of 1969 (interest on sums in the Fund) from the date on which interest was last credited under subsection (2) of that section to the date of payment.

(6) After paying each bank in accordance with subsection (5) above, the National Debt Commissioners shall pay any surplus amount remaining in the Fund into the Consolidated Fund.

(7) The power to make an order under this section shall be exercisable by statutory instrument which shall be subject to annulment in pursuance of a resolution of either House of Parliament; and includes power to vary or revoke a previous order.

Provisions as to accounts, audit and returns by trustee savings banks

Provisions as to accounts and balance sheets.

17.—(1) Each trustee savings bank shall—

(*a*) keep proper accounts and proper records in relation to the accounts; and

(*b*) prepare in respect of each financial year a statement of accounts in such form as the Central Board may direct, being a form which shall conform to the best commercial accounting practice.

PART II

(2) Each statement of accounts shall include—

(*a*) a balance sheet giving a true and fair view of the state of affairs of the bank at the end of the financial year; and

(*b*) an income and expenditure account of the bank giving a true and fair view of the income and expenditure of the bank for the financial year.

(3) The accounts prepared in pursuance of this section shall be supported by—

(*a*) schedules or notes to the accounts, including a statement of the accounting policies adopted by the bank, giving such information as is necessary for a proper understanding of the accounts; and

(*b*) a statement with respect to the state of affairs of the bank listing the principal activities of the bank in the course of the financial year and indicating any significant change in those activities in that year.

Right to receive copies of accounts.

18.—(1) A copy of the audited accounts shall be sent by each trustee savings bank to the Central Board and to the Registrar of Friendly Societies within four months of the end of each financial year, and shall be accompanied by a statement of the trustees of the bank giving such particulars as the Central Board may direct.

(2) Each depositor of a trustee savings bank shall be entitled, on demand and without charge to be furnished with a copy of the last audited accounts of the bank.

Appointment and qualifications of auditors.

19.—(1) Each trustee savings bank shall at the beginning of each financial year appoint a qualified auditor or qualified auditors to audit its accounts.

(2) A person shall not be qualified to be an auditor of a trustee savings bank, unless he is a member of one or more of the following bodies—

(*a*) the Institute of Chartered Accountants in England and Wales;

(*b*) the Institute of Chartered Accountants of Scotland;

(*c*) the Association of Certified Accountants;

(*d*) the Institute of Chartered Accountants in Ireland;

(*e*) any other body of accountants established in the United Kingdom and for the time being recognised for the purposes of section 161(1)(*a*) of the Companies Act 1948 or section 155(1)(*a*) of the Companies Act (Northern Ireland) 1960,

1948 c. 38.
1960 c. 22 (N.I.).

or a person who is for the time being authorised under section 161(1)(*b*) of the said Act of 1948 or section 155(1)(*b*) of the

PART II

said Act of 1960 as being a person with similar qualifications obtained outside the United Kingdom.

(3) None of the following persons shall be qualified to be an auditor of a trustee savings bank—

(*a*) a trustee, officer or servant of the bank ;

(*b*) a person who is a partner of or in the employment of a trustee, officer or servant of the bank ;

(*c*) a body corporate.

(4) References in subsection (3) above to an officer or servant shall be construed as not including an auditor.

(5) Notwithstanding anything in this section, a Scottish firm shall be qualified to act as auditor of a trustee savings bank if all the partners are qualified so to act.

Periodic returns.
1969 c. 50.

20.—(1) For section 55 of the Act of 1969 (which provides for weekly returns to be submitted to the National Debt Commissioners) there shall be substituted—

" Periodic returns to National Debt Commissioners.

55. The trustees of each trustee savings bank shall transmit such periodic returns to the Commissioners in such form and containing such particulars as the Commissioners may from time to time direct.".

(2) Each trustee savings bank shall transmit to the Central Board such periodic returns in such form and containing such particulars as the Central Board may from time to time require.

Mutual assistance

Repeal of sections 62 and 63 of the Act of 1969.

21.—(1) Section 62 of the Act of 1969 (advances by trustee savings banks for development) shall cease to have effect but without prejudice to any advance made under that section before the commencement of this section.

(2) Section 63 of the Act of 1969 (grants by trustee savings banks for benefit of other trustee savings banks) shall cease to have effect and any sum standing to the credit of the mutual assistance account by virtue of that section shall be paid over to the Central Board, together with interest accrued thereon in accordance with subsection (3) of that section from the date on which interest was last credited to the date of payment.

Closing of trustee savings banks

Closing of trustee savings banks.

22. For sections 64 and 65 of the Act of 1969 (closing of trustee savings banks) there shall be substituted the following sections—

" Procedure for closing of bank.

64. It shall not be lawful for the trustees of a trustee savings bank to close, or dissolve, the bank or cease to carry on the business of the bank or carry on business only for the purposes of winding up its affairs unless—

(a) the approval of the Central Board has been obtained and, then, only in the manner prescribed by the bank's rules, or

(b) the bank is ordered to be wound up in pursuance of section 399 of the Companies Act 1948 (which makes provision for the winding up of unregistered companies) or of section 349 of the Companies Act (Northern Ireland) 1960 (which makes corresponding provision for Northern Ireland).

1948 c. 38.

1960 c. 22. (N.I.).

Disposal of surplus money on closing of a bank.

65. When a trustee savings bank is finally closed, the trustees shall pay over to the Central Board any surplus moneys remaining in the hands of the trustees, after providing for the sums due to depositors and for any expenses authorised by the bank's rules; and the Central Board may distribute the moneys among such other trustee savings banks as the Central Board think fit."

Closed banks fund.

1969 c. 50.

23.—(1) The closed banks fund, within the meaning of section 65(3) of the Act of 1969 (which makes provision regarding the proceeds of the sale of property on the closing of a bank), shall be closed and as soon as may be thereafter the National Debt Commissioners shall pay over to the Central Board any moneys standing to the credit of that fund.

(2) The moneys received by the Central Board by virtue of subsection (1) above shall be subject to any claims that may thereafter be substantiated on account of any depositor in a bank up to the amount of money (if any) carried in the fund on account of the bank.

PART III

MISCELLANEOUS PROVISIONS

Powers and duties of Registrar of Friendly Societies

Transfer of functions under the Act of 1969 to the Registrar of Friendly Societies.

24.—(1) The power conferred on the National Debt Commissioners by section 1(2) of the Act of 1969 (conditions under which a savings bank may obtain the benefit of the Act) shall be exercisable by the Registrar of Friendly Societies.

(2) The duties conferred on the National Debt Commissioners by section 10 of the Act of 1969 (register of and certificates as to custodian trustees and property) shall be performed by the

PART III Registrar of Friendly Societies; and accordingly section 10 of that Act shall be amended in accordance with subsection (3) below.

(3) In subsections (1) and (3) of section 10 of the Act of 1969 for the word " Commissioners " in each place there shall be substituted the word " Registrar "; and in subsection (2) for the words from " Comptroller General " to " Office " there shall be substituted the word " Registrar ".

(4) The powers conferred on the National Debt Commissioners by section 55 (as originally enacted and as substituted by section 20 of this Act) of the Act of 1969 (which provides for returns to be transmitted to the National Debt Commissioners) shall be exercisable by the Registrar of Friendly Societies; and accordingly the references in that section to the Commissioners shall be construed as references to the Registrar.

1969 c. 50.

(5) The powers conferred on the Treasury by section 59 of the Act of 1969 (appointment of commissioner to examine affairs of trustee savings bank) shall be exercisable by the Registrar of Friendly Societies after consultation with the Treasury; and accordingly in subsections (1) and (5) of that section for the word " Treasury " in each place there shall be substituted the words " Registrar, after consultation with the Treasury,".

Advertising

Power to control advertising.

25.—(1) If, with respect to any trustee savings bank, the Chief Registrar of Friendly Societies considers it expedient to do so in the interests of persons who may invest or deposit money with the bank, he may with the consent of the Treasury serve on the trustees of the bank a notice giving a direction under this section.

(2) A direction given to the trustees under this section may do all or any of the following things—

(*a*) prohibit the issue by the bank of advertisements of any description specified in the direction, or

(*b*) prohibit the issue by the bank of any advertisements which are, or are substantially, repetitions of an advertisement which has been issued and which is specified in the direction, or

(*c*) require the bank to take all practical steps to withdraw any advertisement, or any description of advertisement, specified in the direction which is on display in any place.

PART III

(3) If a trustee savings bank contravenes a direction under this section, it shall be liable—

(*a*) on summary conviction to a fine not exceeding £400, or

(*b*) on conviction on indictment to a fine ;

and every trustee who knowingly authorises or permits a contravention of a direction under this section shall be liable—

(i) on summary conviction to a fine not exceeding £400, or

(ii) on conviction on indictment to a fine or to imprisonment for a term not exceeding two years, or to both.

(4) Any direction under this section may be varied or revoked at any time by a subsequent direction thereunder.

Supplementary provisions as to directions under section 25.

26.—(1) Not less than one week before giving a direction under section 25 of this Act to a trustee savings bank, the Chief Registrar of Friendly Societies shall serve on the bank, and on every trustee of the bank, a notice stating that he proposes to give the direction.

(2) A notice served on a trustee savings bank under subsection (1) above shall specify the considerations which have led the Chief Registrar of Friendly Societies to conclude that it would be in the interests of persons who may invest or deposit money with the bank to give the direction.

(3) The Chief Registrar of Friendly Societies shall consider any representations with respect to the notice which may be made to him by the trustee savings bank within the period of one week from the date on which the bank is served with the notice, and, if the bank so requests, shall afford to it an opportunity of being heard by him within that period.

(4) On giving a direction under section 25 of this Act the Chief Registrar of Friendly Societies shall serve on the trustee savings bank, and on every trustee of the bank, a notice of the giving of the direction, and shall serve on the bank a notice specifying the considerations which have led him to conclude that it is expedient to give the direction in the interests of persons who may invest or deposit money with the bank ; and the Chief Registrar of Friendly Societies shall not have power to give a direction under section 25 of this Act unless all the considerations so specified were those, or were among those which were specified in the notice served on the bank under subsection (1) above.

PART III

General control of advertisements and other communications.

27.—(1) The Chief Registrar of Friendly Societies may, with the consent of the Treasury, make regulations with respect to the nature and form of any kind of communication which a trustee savings bank may issue or cause to be issued, and in particular—

(*a*) of any kind of advertisement, or

(*b*) of any kind of invitation, whether or not addressed to particular persons, to invest in or lend money to a trustee savings bank.

(2) Regulations under this section may in particular—

(*a*) require that in any specified kind of advertisement or invitation to invest in or lend money to a trustee savings bank, there shall be included in the prescribed form information concerning the general financial position of the trustee savings bank or giving any particular information with respect to the affairs of the bank;

(*b*) require a trustee savings bank to take prescribed steps to withdraw advertisements which are on display in public places and which do not comply with the requirements of the regulations.

(3) Any regulations made under this section—

(*a*) may make different provision for different cases, and

(*b*) may contain such transitional, supplementary and incidental provisions as appear to the Chief Registrar of Friendly Societies to be desirable.

(4) If a trustee savings bank contravenes any provisions contained in regulations under this section it shall be liable—

(*a*) on summary conviction to a fine not exceeding £400, or

(*b*) on conviction on indictment to a fine;

and every trustee who knowingly contravenes or authorises or permits a contravention of any provisions contained in regulations under this section shall be liable—

(i) on summary conviction to a fine not exceeding £400, or

(ii) on conviction on indictment to a fine or to imprisonment for a term not exceeding two years, or to both.

(5) If an employee of a trustee savings bank knowingly contravenes any provision contained in regulations under this section he shall be liable—

(*a*) on summary conviction to a fine not exceeding £400, or

(*b*) on conviction on indictment to a fine or to imprisonment for a term not exceeding two years, or to both.

PART III

(6) In this section " prescribed " means prescribed by regulations under this section.

(7) The power conferred by this section to make regulations shall be exercisable by statutory instrument which shall be subject to annulment in pursuance of a resolution of either House of Parliament.

(8) The Statutory Instruments Act 1946 shall apply to the power to make statutory instruments under this section as if the Chief Registrar of Friendly Societies were a Minister of the Crown. 1946 c. 36.

Defence available to persons charged with offences.

28. In any proceedings under sections 25 and 27 of this Act it shall be a defence for the person charged to prove that he took all reasonable precautions and exercised all due diligence to avoid the commission of such an offence by himself or any person under his control.

Time limit for commencement of summary proceedings.

29.—(1) Summary proceedings in England, Wales and Northern Ireland for any offence under sections 25 and 27 of this Act may, subject to subsection (4) below, be commenced by the Chief Registrar of Friendly Societies at any time within the period of one year beginning with the date on which evidence, sufficient in the opinion of the Chief Registrar to justify a prosecution for the offence, comes to his knowledge.

(2) Summary proceedings in Scotland for any offence under sections 25 and 27 of this Act may, subject to subsection (4) below, be commenced at any time—

(*a*) within the period of one year beginning with the date on which evidence, sufficient in the opinion of the Lord Advocate to justify proceedings, comes to his knowledge, or

(*b*) where such evidence was reported to him by the Chief Registrar of Friendly Societies within one year after the date on which it came to the knowledge of the Chief Registrar,

and subsection (3) of section 331 of the Criminal Procedure (Scotland) Act 1975 shall apply for the purposes of this section as it applies for the purposes of that section. 1975 c. 21.

(3) In relation to summary proceedings in Scotland this section shall have effect as if any reference to the Chief Registrar of Friendly Societies included a reference to the Assistant Registrar of Friendly Societies for Scotland, and the period of one year referred to in subsection (2)(*b*) above shall run from the time when evidence as aforesaid first came earliest to the knowledge of either.

PART III

(4) Nothing in this section shall authorise the commencement of proceedings for any offence at a time more than three years after the date on which the offence was committed.

(5) For the purposes of subsection (1) above, a certificate, purporting to be signed by or on behalf of the Chief Registrar of Friendly Societies as to the date on which sufficient evidence as is mentioned in that subsection came to his knowledge, shall be conclusive evidence of that date.

(6) For the purposes of subsection (2) above, a certificate, purporting to be signed by or on behalf of the Lord Advocate or of the Chief Registrar of Friendly Societies or of the Assistant Registrar of Friendly Societies for Scotland as to the date on which sufficient evidence as is mentioned in that subsection came to his knowledge, shall be conclusive evidence of that date.

Superannuation

Superannuation schemes.

30.—(1) The Central Board shall direct the trustee savings banks—

(*a*) to pay such pensions, allowances, gratuities or other benefits to or in respect of such of the employees of the banks as that Board may determine;

(*b*) to make such payments towards the provision of such pensions, allowances, gratuities or other benefits as may be so determined.

(2) The Central Board shall make and administer such schemes (whether contributory or not) for the payment of such pensions, allowances, gratuities or other benefits to be paid to or in respect of employees of the trustee savings banks as may be determined by the Central Board.

(3) Any scheme under subsection (2) above may amend or revoke any previous scheme made thereunder.

(4) No scheme under subsection (2) above shall make any provision which would have the effect of reducing the amount of any pension, allowance, gratuity or other benefit in so far as that amount is calculated by reference to service rendered before the coming into operation of the scheme, or of reducing the length of any reckonable service so rendered.

(5) Notwithstanding any repeal made by this Act of the existing superannuation provisions, that is to say, sections 75, 76, 78 to 82 of the Act of 1969 the said sections and any instruments made thereunder in so far as those instruments apply to trustee savings banks shall, with the necessary adaptations and modifications, have effect as from the commencement of this section as if they constituted a scheme under subsection (2) above coming into effect on the said commencement and may be revoked or amended accordingly.

1969 c. 50.

PART III

(6) The repeal of the enactments mentioned in subsection (5) above shall not affect any pension, allowance, gratuity or other benefit granted or any contribution paid or any other thing done under or by virtue of those enactments before the commencement of this section.

Superannuation reserve established under section 80 of the Act of 1969.

31. The National Debt Commissioners shall pay to each trustee savings bank the sum representing the assets of that bank's superannuation reserve invested with them under section 80(6) of the Act of 1969, together with interest accrued thereon from the date on which it was last credited in accordance with that subsection to the date of payment.

The Inspection Committee

Dissolution of the Inspection Committee and preservation of pensions.

32.—(1) The Inspection Committee shall cease to exist and all property, rights and liabilities to which the Inspection Committee is entitled or subject shall be transferred to the Central Board.

(2) The repeal by this Act of sections 77 and 82 of the Act of 1969 (provisions as respects superannuation for officers of the inspection committee) shall not affect any pension, allowance, gratuity or other benefit granted or any thing done under or by virtue of those sections before the commencement of this section.

National Savings Stock Register

Provisions with respect to National Savings Stock Register.

33.—(1) There shall not be registered in those parts of the National Savings Stock Register kept by trustees of trustee savings banks any description of government stock, within the meaning of section 15 of the National Debt Act 1972, which has not, immediately preceding the commencement of this subsection, been registered in those parts.

1972 c. 65.

(2) The Treasury may by order provide for stock registered in such parts of the National Savings Stock Register as are kept by the trustees of trustee savings banks to be transferred to that part of the Register kept by the Director of Savings on such day as may be specified in the order.

(3) Each trustee savings bank shall send to the Director of Savings a list containing full particulars of all holdings of relevant stock registered in that part of the Register kept by it immediately before such day as may be specified by an order made under subsection (2) above.

(4) An order under this section may make different provision for different cases.

(5) The power to make an order under this section shall be exercisable by statutory instrument which shall be subject to

PART III

annulment in pursuance of a resolution of either House of Parliament; and includes power to vary or revoke a previous order before the day specified thereby.

Execution of documents by custodian trustees

Amendment of section 9 of the Act of 1969 to provide for custodian trustees to execute documents under seal. 1969 c. 50.

34.—(1) For subsection (9) of section 9 of the Act of 1969 (which makes provision as respects bank property) there shall be substituted—

"(9) Schedule 1A to this Act shall have effect with respect to the execution of documents by the custodian trustees of a trustee savings bank."

(2) The Schedule set out in Schedule 4 to this Act shall be inserted as Schedule 1A to the Act of 1969.

PART IV

GENERAL

Interpretation.

35.—(1) In this Act, unless the context otherwise requires—

"the Act of 1969" means the Trustee Savings Banks Act 1969;

"advertisement" means an advertisement in any medium inviting business or making known the activities of a trustee savings bank, and includes any circular or hand bill inviting business or making known the bank's activities;

"current account deposit" has the meaning assigned to it by section 13(4) of the Act of 1969;

"enactment" includes an enactment of the Parliament of Northern Ireland or of the Northern Ireland Assembly, and an Order in Council having the same effect as such an enactment;

"financial year" means in relation to a trustee savings bank the period in respect of which an income and expenditure account of the trustee savings bank is made up, whether that period is a year or not;

"the Fund" has the meaning assigned to it by section 33(1) of the Act of 1969;

"Inspection Committee" means the committee established under section 4 of the Act of 1969;

"land" includes hereditaments and chattels real and in Scotland heritable subjects of any description;

"the Registrar of Friendly Societies" means, in relation to any trustee savings bank in Scotland, the Assistant Registrar of Friendly Societies for Scotland and, in

PART IV

relation to any trustee savings bank in England and Wales, Northern Ireland, the Isle of Man or the Channel Islands, the Central Office of the Registry of Friendly Societies;

" savings account deposit " has the meaning assigned to it by section 13(4) of the Act of 1969;

" subsidiary " has the meaning assigned to it by section 154 of the Companies Act 1948 or section 148 of the Companies Act (Northern Ireland) 1960; 1948 c. 38. 1960 c. 22 (N.I.)

" trustee " in relation to a trustee savings bank does not include a custodian trustee;

" trustee savings bank " means a bank certified under the Trustee Savings Banks Act 1969, the Trustee Savings Banks Act 1954 or the Trustee Savings Banks Act 1863. 1969 c. 50. 1954 c. 63. 1863 c. 87.

(2) Any reference in this Act to any enactment is, except where the context otherwise requires, a reference to it as amended by or under any other enactment, including this Act.

Consequential and minor amendments and repeals.

36.—(1) The enactments mentioned in Schedule 5 to this Act shall be amended in accordance with that Schedule.

(2) The enactments specified in Schedule 6 to this Act are hereby repealed to the extent specified in the third column of that Schedule.

Application to Isle of Man and Channel Islands.

37.—(1) This Act shall extend to the Isle of Man and the Channel Islands and shall have effect in those islands subject to such adaptations and modifications as Her Majesty may by Order in Council specify.

(2) Any Order in Council made under subsection (1) above may be varied or revoked by a subsequent Order in Council so made.

Short title, citation, commencement and extent.

38.—(1) This Act may be cited as the Trustee Savings Banks Act 1976.

(2) The Trustee Savings Banks Act 1969 and this Act may be cited together as the Trustee Savings Banks Acts 1969 and 1976.

(3) This Act shall come into force on such day as the Treasury may by order made by statutory instrument appoint and different days may be so appointed for, or for different purposes of, any one or more of the provisions of this Act, including, in the case of section 36 of this Act, the amendment or repeal of the different enactments specified in Schedule 5 or 6 to this Act or of different provisions of any enactment so specified.

PART IV

(4) Any reference in this Act to the commencement of any provision of this Act shall be construed as a reference to the day appointed under this section for the coming into operation of that provision.

(5) An order under this section may make such transitional, incidental, supplementary and consequential provisions as the Treasury may consider necessary or expedient in connection with the provisions of this Act which are thereby brought (wholly or in part) into force.

(6) Any order under this section may be varied or revoked at any time before the day appointed thereby.

(7) This Act extends to Northern Ireland.

SCHEDULES

SCHEDULE 1

Section 1.

PROVISIONS AS TO THE TRUSTEE SAVINGS BANKS CENTRAL BOARD

Corporate Status

1. The Central Board shall be a body corporate.

Membership of Board

2.—(1) The Central Board shall consist of—

(*a*) persons appointed by eligible trustee savings banks, each of which shall appoint one member ;

(*b*) the chief officer and deputy chief officer for the time being of the Board ;

(*c*) the persons acting as alternate members by virtue of paragraph 14(3) of this Schedule, and

(*d*) the persons appointed under sub-paragraph (2) below.

(2) The Central Board shall have power to appoint not more than four persons to be members of the Board.

(3) The person to be appointed a member of the Central Board by an eligible trustee savings bank shall be either one of the trustees or the general manager of the bank.

(4) In this paragraph " eligible trustee savings bank " means—

(*a*) as respects the first members of the Central Board appointed under sub-paragraph (1)(*a*) above, a trustee savings bank which has satisfied the Chief Registrar of Friendly Societies immediately before the commencement of section 1 of this Act that its cash liabilities to its depositors exceed £100 million ;

(*b*) as respects the appointment of members under sub-paragraph (1)(*a*) above other than the first members, a trustee savings bank which satisfies the Central Board that its cash liabilities to its depositors exceed £100 million or such other sum as the Board may from time to time determine.

Terms of office of members of Board

3.—(1) The first members of the Central Board (other than the chief officer and the deputy chief officer) shall come into office on the day on which the Board comes into existence or in the case of such a member for any reason appointed after that day, on the day on which the appointment is made.

(2) A member, other than the chief officer or the deputy chief officer, shall hold office in accordance with the terms of his appointment.

SCH. 1

Vacation of office by members

4. A member of the Central Board may resign his office.

5. A member of the Central Board shall vacate his office if—

(*a*) he ceases to be a trustee or, as the case may be, the general manager of the trustee savings bank which appointed him,

(*b*) the trustee savings bank which appointed him ceases to be an eligible trustee savings bank as defined in paragraph 2(4)(*b*) of this Schedule.

First meeting of the Board

6. The first meeting of the Central Board shall be held on such day, and at such time and place, and shall be convened by such person, as may be determined by the National Debt Commissioners.

Chairman

7.—(1) The chairman of the Central Board shall be elected by the Board from the members of the Board.

(2) The chief officer and the deputy chief officer shall not be eligible for election as chairman.

8. The election of the chairman shall be the first business of the first meeting of the Central Board.

9. Subject to the provisions of paragraphs 10 and 11 of this Schedule and of any standing orders made under paragraph 13(1)(*b*) of this Schedule, the chairman shall hold office for a period of 3 years from the date of his appointment but shall be eligible for reappointment.

10. If the chairman ceases to be a member of the Central Board he shall cease to be chairman.

11. The chairman may resign as such without resigning his membership of the Central Board.

Meetings and proceedings of the Board and committees

12.—(1) The Central Board may appoint such committees for any such purpose as the Board consider necessary or desirable.

(2) The Central Board may delegate to a committee appointed under this paragraph, with or without restrictions or conditions, as the Board think fit, any of the functions of the Board.

(3) Members of committees appointed under this paragraph need not be members of the Central Board.

(4) The number of members of a committee appointed under this paragraph and the terms of office of the members thereof shall be fixed by the Central Board.

(5) The proceedings of the Central Board or of any committee appointed under this paragraph shall not be invalidated by any vacancy in their number.

13.—(1) The Central Board may make standing orders with respect to—

(*a*) the proceedings and conduct (including quorum, voting, place of meeting and notices to be given of meetings) of the Board or of any committee appointed by the Board under paragraph 12 of this Schedule ; and

(*b*) subject to paragraphs 7, 10 and 11 of this Schedule, the appointment and removal of a chairman of the Board or of a chairman of any committee.

(2) Subject to any standing orders made under this paragraph, the proceedings of any committee appointed under paragraph 12 of this Schedule shall be such as the committee may determine.

14.—(1) A trustee savings bank may, in respect of the member appointed by it, appoint a person (being a trustee or the general manager of the bank) to perform the duties of that member in his absence.

(2) A person appointed under sub-paragraph (1) above may take part in the proceedings of the Central Board and of any committee in the absence of the member in respect of whom he was appointed or as provided by sub-paragraph (3) below, but not otherwise.

(3) If a member dies or vacates his office (otherwise than by virtue of paragraph 5(*b*) of this Schedule), his alternate may act as member in his place until a new person is appointed to fill his office as member.

(4) A person appointed as an alternate member shall hold office in accordance with the terms of his appointment and shall not act as an alternate member until his appointment as such has been notified in writing to the chief officer of the Central Board and any such appointment shall have effect either in relation to meetings during a stated period or until the appointment is revoked.

(5) A person appointed as an alternate member may resign his office and shall vacate his office if the member for whom he is an alternate vacates his office by virtue of paragraph 5(*b*) of this Schedule.

Authentication of documents

15.—(1) The application of the seal of the Central Board shall be authenticated by the signature of the chairman of the Board or of any member of the Board authorised by them either generally or specially to act for that purpose.

(2) Any document purporting to be a document duly executed under the seal of the Central Board shall be received in evidence and shall, unless the contrary is proved, be deemed to be so executed.

Officers

16.—(1) The Central Board shall appoint a chief officer and a deputy chief officer but no appointment of a chief officer shall be made except with the approval of the Treasury.

SCH. 1 (2) The Central Board may appoint such number of other officers as the Board may determine.

Remuneration and allowances for members and officers

17.—(1) The Central Board shall pay each member or alternate member of the Board, other than the chief officer and the deputy chief officer, such fees and allowances as the Board may determine.

(2) The Central Board shall pay to the officers of the Board such remuneration and allowances as the Board may determine.

(3) The Central Board shall—

(*a*) pay such pensions, allowances or gratuities to or in respect of their officers;

(*b*) make such payments towards the provision of such pensions, allowances and gratuities; or

(*c*) provide and maintain such schemes (whether contributory or not) for the payment of such pensions, allowances or gratuities

as the Board may determine.

18.—(1) Except in so far as the Central Board consider adequate machinery exists for achieving the purposes of this paragraph, the Board shall seek consultation with such independent trade unions as appear to the Board to be appropriate with a view to the conclusion between the Board and any such trade union of agreements to establish and maintain machinery for—

(*a*) the settlement by negotiation of terms and conditions of employment of persons employed by the Board, the Board's subsidiaries and trustee savings banks, with provision for reference to arbitration in default of such settlement in such cases as may be determined by or under the agreements; and

(*b*) consultation between the Board and independent trade unions on matters of common interest to the Board, the persons employed by the Board and the Board's subsidiaries and persons employed by trustee savings banks.

(2) In this paragraph the expression " independent trade union " has (throughout the United Kingdom) the meaning assigned to it by section 30(1) of the Trade Union and Labour Relations Act 1974. **1974 c. 52.**

Accounts and audit practice

19.—(1) The Central Board shall keep proper accounts and proper records in relation to the accounts and shall prepare in respect of each financial year a statement of accounts in a form which shall conform to the best commercial accounting practice.

(2) Each statement of accounts shall include—

(*a*) a balance sheet giving a true and fair view of the state of affairs of the Central Board at the end of the financial year; and

(*b*) a consolidated balance sheet in respect of the Central Board and the Board's subsidiaries giving a true and fair view of the state of affairs of the Board and the Board's subsidiaries at the end of the financial year; and Sch. 1

(c) a consolidated income and expenditure account of the Central Board and the Board's subsidiaries giving a true and fair view of the income and expenditure of the Board and the Board's subsidiaries for the financial year.

(3) The accounts prepared in pursuance of this paragraph shall be supported by—

(a) schedules or notes to the accounts, including a statement of the accounting policies adopted by the Central Board and the Board's subsidiaries, giving such information as is necessary for a proper understanding of the accounts; and

(b) a statement with respect to the state of affairs of the Central Board and the Board's subsidiaries listing the names of the persons who at any time during the financial year were members of the Board, the principal activities of the Board and the Board's subsidiaries in the course of the year and indicating any significant change in those activities in that year.

(4) A copy of the audited accounts shall be transmitted to the Registrar of Friendly Societies within four months of the end of each financial year.

Appointment and qualifications of auditors

20.—(1) The Central Board shall at the beginning of each financial year appoint a qualified auditor or qualified auditors to audit the accounts of the Board and the Board's subsidiaries.

(2) A person shall not be qualified to be an auditor of the Central Board, unless he is a member of one or more of the following bodies—

(a) the Institute of Chartered Accountants in England and Wales;

(b) the Institute of Chartered Accountants of Scotland;

(c) the Association of Certified Accountants;

(d) the Institute of Chartered Accountants in Ireland;

(e) any other body of accountants established in the United Kingdom and for the time being recognised for the purposes of section 161(1)(a) of the Companies Act 1948 or section 155(1)(a) of the Companies Act (Northern Ireland) 1960. 1948 c. 38. 1960 c. 22 (N.I.).

or a person who is for the time being authorised under section 161(1)(b) of the said Act of 1948 or section 155(1)(b) of the said Act of 1960 as being a person with similar qualifications obtained outside the United Kingdom.

(3) None of the following persons shall be qualified to be an auditor of the Central Board—

(a) a member, officer or servant of the Central Board;

(b) a person who is a partner of or in the employment of a member, officer or servant of the Central Board;

(c) a body corporate.

SCH. 1

(4) References in sub-paragraph (3) above to an officer or servant shall be construed as not including an auditor.

(5) Notwithstanding anything in this paragraph, a Scottish firm shall be qualified to act as auditor of the Central Board if all the partners are qualified so to act.

Status of Board and its property

21. The Central Board shall not be regarded as the servant or agent of the Crown or as enjoying any status, privilege or amenity of the Crown and the property of the Board shall not be regarded as property of or property held on behalf of the Crown.

Interpretation

22. In this Schedule "financial year" means in relation to the Central Board the period in respect of which a consolidated income and expenditure account of the Board and the Board's subsidiaries is laid before the Board, whether that period is a year or not.

Section 8.

SCHEDULE 2

1969 c. 50.

SCHEDULE TO BE SUBSTITUTED FOR SCHEDULE 1 TO THE TRUSTEE SAVINGS BANKS ACT 1969

"SCHEDULE 1

MATTERS TO BE COVERED BY THE RULES OF A BANK WHICH IS TO HAVE THE BENEFIT OF THIS ACT

The rules of a trustee savings bank must expressly provide for the following matters.

1. The manner of appointment and removal of the trustees of the bank.

2. The manner of appointment and removal of any committee of management of the bank.

3. The manner of appointment of auditors.

4. The calling and holding of meetings of trustees and the procedure to be followed at such meetings.

5. The manner in which security is to be given by officers of the bank or in which insurance is to be effected against losses due to acts of default of officers of the bank.

6. The manner in which the bank is to be closed or dissolved."

SCHEDULE 3

Section 13.

Classes of Assets to be Held by a Trustee Savings Bank to Match its Liabilities to Depositors

Part I

Classes of Assets to Match a Proportion, Determined under Section 13(1)(*a*) of this Act, of Sums Due to Depositors

1. Cash.

2. Deposits in the Fund for the Banks for Savings.

3. Money held on current account by other bankers (including the Central Trustee Savings Bank Limited) on behalf of the trustee savings bank.

4. Deposits in accounts with other bankers (including the Central Trustee Savings Bank Limited) repayable at not longer than 7 days' notice.

5. Loans of either of the kinds mentioned in paragraph 9 of Part II of Schedule 1 to the Trustee Investments Act 1961, being loans repayable within one month. 1961 c. 62

6. Treasury Bills payable not more than ninety-one days from date ; bills so payable issued by Her Majesty's Government in Northern Ireland and by local authorities in the United Kingdom.

7. Marketable fixed interest securities, issued by Her Majesty's Government in the United Kingdom or Her Majesty's Government in Northern Ireland, being securities within one year of the final redemption date.

8. Marketable fixed interest securities the payment of interest on which is guaranteed by Her Majesty's Government in the United Kingdom, or Her Majesty's Government in Northern Ireland, being securities within one year of the final redemption date.

9. Assets of such other classes as may from time to time be designated by the Treasury for the purposes of this Part of this Schedule.

Part II

Classes of Assets to be Held to Match the Residue of Sums due to Depositors

10. Cash.

11. Deposits in the Fund for the Banks for Savings.

12. Money held as mentioned in paragraph 3 above.

13. Deposits in accounts with other bankers (including the Central Trustee Savings Bank Limited).

14. Sterling Certificates of Deposit.

15. Treasury Bills ; bills issued by Her Majesty's Government in Northern Ireland.

SCH. 3 16. Marketable fixed interest securities, issued by Her Majesty's Government in the United Kingdom, Her Majesty's Government in Northern Ireland or the Government of the Isle of Man.

17. Marketable fixed interest securities the payment of interest on which is guaranteed by Her Majesty's Government in the United Kingdom, Her Majesty's Government in Northern Ireland or the Government of the Isle of Man.

18. Loans of either of the kinds mentioned in paragraph 9 of
1961 c. 62. Part II of Schedule 1 to the Trustee Investments Act 1961.

19. Fixed interest securities of the kinds mentioned in paragraphs 3, 5 and 9 of Part II of Schedule 1 to the Trustee Investments Act 1961.

20. Debentures of the kind mentioned in paragraph 8 of Part II of Schedule 1 to the Trustee Investments Act 1961.

21. Capital assets acquired under the provisions of section 11
1969 c. 50. of the Trustee Savings Banks Act 1969 as amended by section 10 of this Act.

22. Assets of such other classes (including loans to a depositor or customer of the trustee savings bank) as may, from time to time, be designated by the Treasury for the purposes of Part I of this Schedule or for the purposes of this Part of this Schedule.

Section 34.

SCHEDULE 4

SCHEDULE TO BE INSERTED AFTER SCHEDULE 1 TO THE TRUSTEE SAVINGS BANKS ACT 1969

"SCHEDULE 1A

EXECUTION OF DOCUMENTS BY CUSTODIAN TRUSTEES

1.—(1) The custodian trustees of every trustee savings bank shall have an official seal which shall be officially and judicially noticed.

(2) The seal shall be authenticated by the signatures of one of the custodian trustees and of an officer of the trustee savings bank authorised by the custodian trustees to act on their behalf.

2. Every document purporting to be a document executed by the custodian trustees and to be sealed with the seal of the custodian trustees and authenticated in the manner provided by paragraph 1(2) above shall be received in evidence and be deemed to be such a document without further proof, unless the contrary is proved."

SCHEDULE 5

Section 36(1)

CONSEQUENTIAL AND MINOR AMENDMENTS

The Mineral Workings Act 1951 c. 60

1. In section 2(3) of the Mineral Workings Act 1951 for the words " for savings banks funds " there shall be substituted the words " for ordinary deposits with the National Savings Bank ".

The Companies Act (Northern Ireland) 1960 c. 22

2. In section 348 of the Companies Act (Northern Ireland) 1960 for the words " or the Trustee Savings Banks Act, 1954 ", there shall be substituted the words " the Trustee Savings Banks Act 1954 or the Trustee Savings Banks Act 1969 ".

The Crown Estate Act 1961 c. 55

3. In section 3(4) of the Crown Estate Act 1961 in paragraph (*b*) for the words from " for the investment " to " Savings " there shall be substituted the words " as investments for ordinary deposits with the National Savings Bank ".

The Protection of Depositors Act 1963 c. 16

4. In section 2(2) of the Protection of Depositors Act 1963 at the end there shall be inserted the words " or trustee savings bank ".

5. In section 27(1) of that Act there shall be inserted at the appropriate place—

' " trustee savings bank " means a trustee savings bank within the meaning of section 95(1) of the Trustee Savings Banks Act 1969,'.

The Protection of Depositors Act (Northern Ireland) 1964 c. 22

6. In section 2(2) of the Protection of Depositors Act (Northern Ireland) 1964 at the end there shall be inserted the words " or trustee savings bank ".

7. In section 27(1) of that Act, there shall be inserted at the appropriate place—

' " trustee savings bank " means a trustee savings bank within the meaning of section 95(1) of the Trustee Savings Banks Act 1969 ; '.

The Trustee Savings Banks Act 1969 c. 50

8.—(1) In section 1 of the Trustee Savings Banks Act 1969—

(*a*) in subsection (1) after the words " this Act ", where first occurring, there shall be inserted the words " and of the Trustee Savings Banks Act 1976 ", and the words in brackets shall be omitted ;

(*b*) in subsection (2) after the words " this Act " there shall be inserted the words " nor of the Trustee Savings Banks Act 1976 " ;

SCH. 5

(*c*) in subsection (2) for the words from " by the National Debt Commissioners " to " Office " there shall be substituted the words " by the Registrar " ;

(*d*) after subsection (3) there shall be inserted the following subsection—

" (4) The provisions of subsection (3)(*c*) above shall not be construed as requiring the return to a depositor of the produce of any deposit standing to the credit of an account in his name on which no interest is paid."

(2) The amendment to subsection (2) set out in sub-paragraph (1)(*c*) above shall not apply to any savings bank formed before the commencement of section 24(1) of this Act.

9. In section 6(4) of that Act, for the words " deposited by the Registrar with the Commissioners " there shall be substituted the words " retained by the Registrar ".

10. In section 7 of that Act—

(*a*) in subsection (1) the word " , managers " shall be omitted ;

(*b*) in subsection (2) for the words " transmitted under this Act to the Commissioners " there shall be substituted the words " certified under this Act by the Registrar " ; and for the words " so transmitted " there shall be substituted the words " so certified ".

11. In section 28 of that Act—

(*a*) in subsection (1) for the words from " a trustee savings bank " onwards there shall be substituted the words " respect of savings account deposits in a trustee savings bank " ;

(*b*) in subsection (2) for the word " shall " there shall be substituted the word " may ".

12. In section 58(1) of that Act—

(*a*) in subsection (1) after the words " this Act " there shall be inserted the words " and of the Trustee Savings Banks Act 1976 " ; and the words from " and of the rules " to " unnecessary " shall be omitted ; and

(*b*) subsections (2) to (10) shall be omitted.

13. In section 59 of that Act—

(*a*) in subsection (1), after the word " Commissioners " there shall be inserted the words " or the Central Board " ;

(*b*) in subsection (5), after the word " depositors ", there shall be inserted the words " or by the Central Board ".

14. In section 69 of that Act—

(*a*) in subsection (1)—

(i) the words " or manager " shall be omitted ;

(ii) in paragraph (*b*) the words from " the maintenance " to " accounts " shall be omitted ;

(iii) for paragraph (*c*) there shall be substituted—

"(*c*) for knowingly authorising or permitting a contravention of a direction under section 25 of the Trustee Savings Banks Act 1976, or

(*d*) for knowingly authorising or permitting a contravention of any provisions contained in regulations under section 27 of the Trustee Savings Banks Act 1976." ;

(*b*) subsection (2) shall be omitted.

15. In section 95(1) of that Act—

(*a*) the definitions of " the Association ", " charges scheme ", " closed banks fund ", " current account ", " current account deposit ", " current account service ", " the Fund ", " Inspection Committee ", " ordinary deposit ", " penny savings bank ", " reserves ", " savings account deposit " and " special investment " shall be omitted ;

(*b*) the following definition shall be inserted at the appropriate place—

'" the Central Board " means the Central Board established under section 1 of the Trustee Savings Banks Act 1976 ; ' ;

(*c*) for the definition of " Registrar " there shall be substituted the following—

'" Registrar " means, in relation to any trustee savings bank in Scotland, the assistant registrar of Friendly Societies for Scotland ; in relation to any trustee savings bank in Northern Ireland, the Chief Registrar of Friendly Societies or a deputy appointed by him ; and in relation to any trustee savings bank in England and Wales, the Isle of Man or the Channel Isles, the Central Office of the Registry of Friendly Societies ; '.

16. In section 98(1) of that Act for the words " section 16 of this Act or any other " there shall be substituted the word " any ".

The Pensions (Increase) Act 1971 *c.*56

17. Section 19(2)(*b*) of the Pensions (Increase) Act 1971 shall be omitted ; but the omission shall not affect any pension which begins (as defined in section 17(1) of that Act) before the commencement of section 30 of this Act.

18. In Part III of Schedule 2 to that Act paragraph 65 shall be omitted ; but the omission shall not affect any pension which begins before the commencement of section 30 of this Act.

The National Debt Act 1972 *c.*65

19. In section 3 of the National Debt Act 1972—

(*a*) in subsection (1)—

(i) for the words " The appropriate authority " there shall be substituted the words " The Treasury " ;

Sch. 5

(ii) the words from " and separate regulations " onwards shall be omitted ;

(*b*) subsection (3) shall be omitted.

20. In section 7 of that Act—

(*a*) in subsection (1)—

(i) the words from ", and " to " Commissioners ", shall be omitted ;

(ii) for the words " the appropriate authority " in each place there shall be substituted the words " the Director of Savings " ;

(*b*) in subsection (2) for the words " the appropriate authority and the National Debt Commissioners " there shall be substituted the words " the Director of Savings " ;

(*c*) subsection (3) shall be omitted.

SCHEDULE 6

Section 36(2).

REPEALS

Chapter	Short Title	Extent of Repeal
34 & 35 Vict. c. 36.	The Pensions Commutation Act 1871.	In section 6, the words " and the Trustee Savings Banks Act 1863, or either of such Acts ".
1961 c. 62.	The Trustee Investments Act 1961.	In Schedule 1, in Part I, in paragraph 2 the words " ordinary deposits in a trustee savings bank ", in Part II, paragraph 11, and in Part IV, in paragraph 4 the definitions of " ordinary deposits " and " special investment ".
1969 c. 50.	The Trustee Savings Banks Act 1969.	In section 1(1), the words in brackets. In section 2, in subsection (2), the words " and managers ", and subsection (5). Section 4. In section 7(1), the word " , managers ". Section 8. In section 11, in subsection (1) the words " with the consent of the Commissioners ", and the words " with the like consent ", in subsection (3) the words " or consent of the Commissioners to ", and subsection (4). Sections 12 to 26. In section 27(1), the words " and managers ". Section 28(1). Section 30. Sections 32 to 54. Sections 56 and 57. In section 58, in subsection (1) the words from " and of the rules " to " unnecessary ", and subsections (2) to (10). Section 60. In section 61(1), the words " , on the recommendation of the Inspection Committee,". Sections 62 and 63. Sections 66 and 67. In section 68(1), the words " and managers ". In section 69, in subsection (1) the words " or manager ", and in paragraph (*b*) the words from " the maintenance " to " accounts ", and subsection (2).

SCH. 6

Chapter	Short Title	Extent of Repeal
1969 c. 50—*cont.*	The Trustee Savings Banks Act 1969—*cont.*	In section 71, the words " and three managers ", and the words " or managers " in every place. Sections 73 to 84. Section 91. Section 93(3). Section 94. In section 95(1), the definitions of "the Association", " charges scheme ", " closed banks fund", "current account ", " current account deposit ", " current account service ", " the Fund ", " Inspection Committee", " ordinary deposit ", " penny savings bank ", " reserves ", " savings account deposit " and " special investment ". Section 96(3), (5) and (6). Schedule 2.
1971 c. 56.	The Pensions (Increase) Act 1971.	Section 19(2)(*b*), except in relation to any pension beginning before the commencement of section 30 of this Act. In Schedule 2, in Part III, paragraph 65, except in relation to any pension beginning before the commencement of section 30 of this Act.
1972 c. 11.	The Superannuation Act 1972.	In Schedule 6, paragraphs 75 and 76.
1972 c. 65.	The National Debt Act 1972.	In section 2(2), the words from " , except " to " banks, ". In section 3, in subsection (1) the words from " and separate regulations " onwards, and subsection (3). In section 5, in subsection (1) the words " or the trustees of a trustee savings bank " and in subsection (2) the words " or trustees ". In section 7, in subsection (1) the words from " , and " to " Commissioners,", and subsection (3). In section 11, in subsection (1), in paragraph (*b*) the words " trustee savings bank or ", and in subsection (2) the words " trustee savings bank and ". Section 14.

SCH. 6

Chapter	Short Title	Extent of Repeal
1972 c. 65—*cont.*	The National Debt Act 1972—*cont.*	In section 15(3), the words from " and " onwards. In section 16(3), the words " trustee savings bank and ".
1976 c. 4.	The Trustee Savings Banks Act 1976.	Section 12(4). In Schedule 5, paragraph 11(*a*).

Education (School-leaving Dates) Act 1976

1976 CHAPTER 5

An Act to make further provision with respect to school-leaving dates; and for connected purposes.
[25th March 1976]

BE IT ENACTED by the Queen's most Excellent Majesty, by and with the advice and consent of the Lords Spiritual and Temporal, and Commons, in this present Parliament assembled, and by the authority of the same, as follows:—

Alteration of summer school-leaving date. 1962 c. 12.

1.—(1) For subsections (3) and (4) of section 9 of the Education Act 1962 (under which a person who attains the age of 16 between the end of January and the beginning of September is deemed to attain the upper limit of compulsory school age at the end of the summer term) there shall be substituted—

"(3) If he attains that age after the end of January but before the next May school-leaving date, he shall be deemed not to have attained that age until that date.

(4) If he attains that age after the May school-leaving date and before the beginning of September next following that date, he shall be deemed to have attained that age on that date."

(2) After subsection (7) of that section there shall be added—

"(8) In this section " the May school-leaving date " means the Friday before the last Monday in May."

Family allowances and social security. 1965 c. 53.

2.—(1) The power to make regulations under section 13 of the Family Allowances Act 1965 shall include power to provide that a person who has attained the upper limit of compulsory school age for the purposes of that Act shall be treated for those purposes as being under that limit until such date as may be specified in the regulations; and regulations made by virtue of this subsection may make different provision for different cases.

(2) In section 2(2)(*a*) of the said Act of 1965 for the words from " the age that is for the time being " onwards there shall be substituted the words " the age of sixteen ".

(3) For the purposes of section 56(7) of the Social Security Act 1975 (injury benefit) a person shall be treated as not having attained school-leaving age if he would be treated as being under the upper limit of compulsory school age for the purposes of the Family Allowances Act 1965.

1975 c. 14.

1965 c. 53.

(4) In sections 4(2)(*a*), 7(1) and 8(1) of the said Act of 1975 (contributions) for the words " over school-leaving age " there shall be substituted the words " over the age of 16 ".

Citation, repeals, commencement and extent.

3.—(1) This Act may be cited as the Education (School-leaving Dates) Act 1976.

(2) The Education Acts 1944 to 1975 and this Act may be cited together as the Education Acts 1944 to 1976.

(3) The enactments mentioned in the Schedule to this Act (which include provisions that are spent in consequence of the Raising of the School Leaving Age Order 1972) are hereby repealed to the extent specified in the third column of that Schedule.

S.I. 1972 No. 444.

(4) Section 21(2) of the Child Benefit Act 1975 (repeals consequential on the introduction of child benefit) shall have effect as if section 2(1) to (3) above were included among the enactments mentioned in Part I of Schedule 5 to that Act.

1975 c. 61.

(5) Section 2(4) above and so much of the Schedule to this Act as relates to the Social Security Act 1975 shall not come into force until 6th April 1976.

(6) This Act does not extend to Northern Ireland; and section 1 above does not extend to Scotland.

Section 3(3).

SCHEDULE

REPEALS

Chapter	Short Title	Extent of Repeal
7 & 8 Geo. 6. c. 31.	The Education Act 1944.	Section 38(1). In section 114, in subsection (1) in the definition of " compulsory school age" the words " subject to the provisions of section thirty-eight of this Act " and subsection (6).
10 & 11 Eliz. 2. c. 12.	The Education Act 1962.	In section 9, the proviso to subsection (5), subsection (6) and in subsection (7) the definition of " the appropriate summer term " (together with the word " and " immediately preceding it) and the words " or month of September (as the case may be) ".
1964 c. 82.	The Education Act 1964.	Section 2. In section 5(3) and (6) the words " and 2 ".
1965 c. 53.	The Family Allowances Act 1965.	Section 2(2)(*b*).
1967 c. 90.	The Family Allowances and National Insurance Act 1967.	Section 2(1) and (2).
1973 c. 38.	The Social Security Act 1973.	In Schedule 27, paragraph 22
1975 c. 14.	The Social Security Act 1975.	In Schedule 20, the definition of " school-leaving age ".
1975 c. 61.	The Child Benefit Act 1975.	In Schedule 4, in paragraph 38, the words " and ' School-leaving age ' " (in the opening passage) and the definitions of " School-leaving age " and " The upper limit of compulsory school age ". In Schedule 5 the repeal in the Education Act 1962, the repeal of section 2(1) and (2) of the Family Allowances and National Insurance Act 1967 and the repeal of the definition of " School-leaving age " in Schedule 20 to the Social Security Act 1975.

Solicitors (Scotland) Act 1976

1976 CHAPTER 6

An Act to make provision as to the powers of the Law Society of Scotland to intervene in the professional practice and conduct of solicitors; to make provision for the appointment of a lay observer to examine the Society's treatment of complaints about solicitors and the appointment of lay members of the Scottish Solicitors Discipline Tribunal; to extend the powers of that Tribunal; to make provision as to the indemnity of solicitors against professional liability; to amend the Solicitors (Scotland) Acts 1933 to 1965; and for connected purposes. [25th March 1976]

BE IT ENACTED by the Queen's most Excellent Majesty, by and with the advice and consent of the Lords Spiritual and Temporal, and Commons, in this present Parliament assembled, and by the authority of the same, as follows:—

PART I

PROFESSIONAL PRACTICE AND CONDUCT OF SOLICITORS

Extension and alteration of power of Society to deal with property under the control of certain solicitors

Power of Council of Society to deal with property in hands of solicitor dying or ceasing to practise.

1. Where a solicitor who is practising as a solicitor under his own name or as a sole solicitor under a firm name dies or ceases to practise for any reason other than being struck off the roll of solicitors or being suspended from practice and the Council of the Society are not satisfied that suitable arrangements have been made for making available to his clients or to some other

PART I

solicitor or solicitors instructed by his clients or on their behalf—

(*a*) all deeds, wills, securities, papers, books of accounts, records, vouchers and other documents in his or his firm's possession or control which are held on behalf of his clients or which relate to any trust of which he is sole trustee or co-trustee only with one or more of his clerks or servants; and

(*b*) all sums of money due from him or his firm or held by him or his firm on behalf of his clients or subject to any such trust as aforesaid;

the provisions of paragraphs 5 and 6 of Schedule 6 to the Act of 1949 (which relate to the production or delivery of documents by and to payments out of any bank account in the name of a solicitor in certain circumstances) shall apply in relation to any such solicitor notwithstanding that the Council may not have reasonable cause to believe that he has been guilty of any such dishonesty as is mentioned in subsection (2) of section 22 of that Act.

Power of Society to deal with client accounts of solicitor incapacitated.

2.—(1) Where the Council of the Society are satisfied that a solicitor who is practising as a solicitor under his own name or as a sole solicitor under a firm name is incapacitated by illness or accident to such an extent as to be unable to operate on or otherwise deal with any client account in name of the solicitor or his firm and no other arrangements acceptable to the Council have been made, the right to operate on or otherwise deal with such account shall notwithstanding any enactment or any rule of law to the contrary vest solely in the Society so long, but only so long, as the Council are satisfied that such incapacity and absence of other acceptable arrangements continues.

(2) In this section "client account" has the same meaning as in section 3 of the Act of 1965.

Society entitled to recover expenses incurred.

3. At the end of section 3 of the Act of 1965 (on death of a solicitor practising on his own account Society to deal with banking accounts of practice) the following subsection shall be inserted—

"(3) In a case where the Society have operated on or otherwise dealt with a client account under this section the Society shall be entitled to recover from the estate of the solicitor who has died such reasonable expenses as the Society have thereby incurred."

PART I

Extension of power of Council to apply for appointment of judicial factor on estate of solicitor.

4. In section 15 of the Act of 1958 (power of Council to apply for appointment of judicial factor on estate of solicitor in certain cases) in paragraph (*b*) the word " either " shall be omitted and at the end of sub-paragraph (ii) there shall be inserted the word " or " and the following sub-paragraph—

" (iii) there is reasonable ground for apprehending that a claim on the Guarantee Fund may ensue,".

Extension of power of Council to make rules regarding certain accounts.

5.—(1) The duties to make rules imposed on the Council of the Society by section 20(1)(*a*) of the Act of 1949 (Council of Society to make rules with respect to bank accounts etc.) shall be duties to make rules requiring solicitors to open and keep accounts only with the Bank of England, a Trustee Savings Bank within the meaning of section 95 of the Trustee Savings Bank Act 1969, the National Savings Bank and any company as to which the Secretary of State is satisfied that it ought to be treated as a banking company or as a discount company for the purposes of the Protection of Depositors Act 1963 as amended by the Companies Act 1967 ; and the rules may specify the location of the banks' or companies' branches at which the accounts are to be kept.

1969 c. 50.
1963 c. 16.
1967 c. 81.

(2) In section 20(1) of the Act of 1949 (Council of Society to make rules with respect to bank accounts etc.)—

(*a*) after paragraph (*a*) there shall be inserted the following paragraph—

" (*aa*) as to the opening and keeping by solicitors of—

(i) a deposit or share account with a building society designated under section 1 of the House Purchase and Housing Act 1959, or

(ii) an account showing sums on loan to a local authority,

being in either case for a client whose name is specified in the title of the account ".

(*b*) at the end there shall be inserted the following—

" In this subsection " local authority " means a local authority within the meaning of the Local Government Act 1972 or the Local Government (Scotland) Act 1973 ".

(3) Section 3(2) of the Act of 1965 shall have effect as if there were included in the meaning of client account a reference to the accounts mentioned in section 20 of the Act of 1949 as amended by subsections (1) and (2) above.

PART I

Power of Council in investigating complaints.

6.—(1) If a complaint is made to the Society that there has been undue delay on the part of a solicitor in dealing with any matter in which he or his firm is or has been concerned in a professional capacity or any matter relating to a trust of which he is or was the sole trustee or co-trustee only with one or more of his partners, clerks or servants, and the Council are of opinion that the delay ought to be investigated, they may by notice in writing at any time and from time to time require the solicitor to give an explanation of the delay.

(2) The notice given by the Council may specify a period, not being less than twenty-one days, within which they require an explanation to be furnished and if within that period the solicitor does not reply or fails to furnish an explanation which the Council regard as sufficient and satisfactory and he is so informed in writing, the provisions of paragraphs 5 and 6 of Schedule 6 to the Act of 1949 (which relate to the production or delivery of documents by and to payments out of any banking account in the name of a solicitor or his firm in certain circumstances) shall apply in relation to that solicitor and his firm but only in so far as they relate to documents or payments connected with the matter complained of and shall so apply notwithstanding that the Council may not have reasonable cause to believe that the solicitor has been guilty of any such dishonesty as is mentioned in subsection (2) of section 22 of that Act.

Lay observer

Investigation by lay observer of Society's treatment of complaints.

7.—(1) The Secretary of State, if he thinks fit, may, after consultation with the Lord President, appoint a person (in this section referred to as " the lay observer ") to examine any written allegation made by or on behalf of a member of the public concerning the Society's treatment of a complaint about a solicitor or an employee of a solicitor made to the Society by that member of the public or on his behalf.

(2) No solicitor or advocate shall be appointed as the lay observer.

(3) The lay observer shall hold and vacate his office in accordance with the terms of his appointment and shall, on ceasing to hold office, be eligible for re-appointment.

(4) The Secretary of State may give general directions to the lay observer about the scope and discharge of his functions, and shall publish any such directions.

(5) The Society shall consider any report or recommendation which it receives from the lay observer and shall notify him of any action which it has taken in consequence.

(6) The Secretary of State may appoint staff for the lay observer.

PART I

(7) Remuneration for the lay observer and his staff and any other expenses of the lay observer shall be paid out of money provided by Parliament.

(8) In determining the terms of employment and remuneration of the lay observer and his staff, the number of his staff and any amount payable by way of expenses under subsection (7) above the Secretary of State shall act only with the approval of the Minister for the Civil Service.

(9) The Society shall furnish the lay observer with such information as he may from time to time reasonably require.

(10) The Secretary of State shall direct the submission to him of an annual report by the lay observer on the discharge of the functions conferred on him by this section.

(11) The Secretary of State shall lay a copy of any report under subsection (10) before each House of Parliament.

(12) In Part III of Schedule 1 to the House of Commons Disqualification Act 1975 (offices disqualifying for membership) there shall be inserted at the appropriate place in alphabetical order the entry " Lay observer appointed under section 7 of the Solicitors (Scotland) Act 1976 ". 1975 c. 24.

Indemnity of Solicitors against Professional Liability

Arrangements for professional indemnity.

8.—(1) The Council may make rules with the concurrence of the Lord President concerning indemnity for solicitors and former solicitors against any class of professional liability and the rules may for the purpose of providing such indemnity do all or any of the following things, namely—

(*a*) authorise or require the Society to establish and maintain a fund or funds ;

(*b*) authorise or require the Society to take out and maintain insurance with any person permitted under the Insurance Companies Act 1974 to carry on liability insurance business or pecuniary loss insurance business ; 1974 c. 49.

(*c*) require solicitors or any specified class of solicitors to take out and maintain insurance with any person permitted under the Insurance Companies Act 1974 to carry on liability insurance business or pecuniary loss insurance business.

(2) The Society shall have power, without prejudice to any of its other powers, to carry into effect any arrangements which it considers necessary or expedient for the purpose of the rules.

(3) Without prejudice to the generality of subsections (1) and (2) above, the rules—

(*a*) may specify the terms and conditions on which indemnity is to be available, and any circumstances in which the right to it is to be excluded or modified ;

PART I

(*b*) may provide for the management, administration and protection of any fund maintained by virtue of subsection (1)(*a*) above and require solicitors or any class of solicitors to make payments to any such fund ;

(*c*) may require solicitors or any class of solicitors to make payments by way of premium on any insurance policy maintained by the Society by virtue of subsection (1)(*b*) above ;

(*d*) may prescribe the conditions which an insurance policy must satisfy for the purposes of subsection (1)(*c*) above ;

(*e*) may authorise the Society to determine the amount of any payments required by the rules subject to such limits, or in accordance with such provisions, as may be prescribed by the rules ;

(*f*) may specify circumstances in which, where a solicitor for whom indemnity is provided has failed to comply with the rules, proceedings in respect of sums paid by way of indemnity in connection with a matter in relation to which he has failed to comply may be taken against him by the Society or by insurers ;

(*g*) may specify circumstances in which solicitors are exempt from the rules ;

(*h*) may empower the Council to take such steps as they consider necessary or expedient to ascertain whether or not the rules are being complied with ; and

(*i*) may contain incidental, procedural or supplementary provisions.

(4) Failure to comply with rules made under this section may be treated as professional misconduct for the purposes of the provisions of the Act of 1958 relating to discipline, and any person may make a complaint in respect of that failure to the Scottish Solicitors Discipline Tribunal.

(5) In this section " professional liability " means any civil liability incurred by a solicitor or former solicitor in connection with his practice or in connection with any trust of which he is or formerly was a trustee.

Apprentices

Limitation on taking apprentices by certain solicitors.

9. In section 25 of the Act of 1949 (provisions as to taking apprentices)—

(*a*) after subsection (1) there shall be inserted the following subsection—

" (1A) If the Council of the Society after such inquiry as they may think fit as regards the practice

PART I

of a solicitor decide that he would be unable to fulfil the proper obligations of the master in a contract for a legal apprenticeship either in relation to a particular application or generally they shall intimate their decision to the solicitor and the solicitor notwithstanding that he satisfies the provisions of subsection (1) of this section shall not thereafter take any apprentice without the special leave in writing of the Council." ;

(*b*) at the end of the section there shall be inserted the following subsection—

" (5) Any person aggrieved by a decision of the Council under subsection (1A) of this section may, within twenty-one days of the date of intimation of the decision, appeal to the Court and on any such appeal the Court may give such directions, including directions as to the expenses of the proceedings before the Court, as they think fit ".

The Roll of Solicitors

Additional provision as regards keeping of the roll.

10. In section 17 of the Act of 1958 (provisions as to the keeping of the roll)—

(*a*) in subsection (1)—

(i) in paragraph (*b*) the word " and " at the end thereof shall be deleted ; and there shall be inserted the following paragraph—

" (*bb*) to send any solicitor enrolled thereon, who has for at least three years been so enrolled in pursuance of regulations made by the Council under section 1 of this Act on an undertaking by him to serve a post-qualifying year of practical training which the Council are not satisfied that he has implemented, a letter enquiring whether he intends to fulfil that undertaking and intimating that unless a reply which the Council regard as satisfactory is received within the period of six months beginning with the date of the posting of the letter, his name may be removed from the roll ; and " ; and

(ii) in paragraph (*c*) after the word " reply " in the second place where that word occurs there shall be inserted the words " or in the case of a letter sent under paragraph (*bb*) of this subsection a reply which the Council of the Society do not regard as

PART I

satisfactory " and after the words " paragraph (*b*) " there shall be inserted the words " or paragraph (*bb*) ";

(*b*) in subsection (3) for the reference to section 7 there shall be substituted a reference to subsection (2) of section 3.

Practising Certificates

Addition to discretion of registrar as regards practising certificates.

11. In Schedule 5 to the Act of 1949 (provisions with respect to practising certificates etc.) in sub-paragraph (1) of paragraph 2 there shall be inserted at the end of item (*e*) the word " or " and the following items—

" (*f*) when, after a complaint has been made

(i) relating to his conduct of the business of a client his attention has been drawn by the Council to the matter, and he has not replied or has not furnished a reply in respect thereof which would enable the Council to dispose of the matter, or

(ii) of delay in the disposal of the business of a client he has not completed that business within such period as the Council may fix as being a reasonable period within which to do so,

and in either case he has been notified in writing by the Council accordingly; or

(*g*) where he has still to serve a post qualifying obligatory year of practical training in terms of an undertaking by him to that effect in his indenture of apprenticeship; ".

Solicitors acting as consultants to hold practising certificates.

12. Any solicitor who not being in partnership with a solicitor or with other solicitors causes or permits his name to be associated with the name of that solicitor or with the firm name of those other solicitors, whether he is described as a consultant or adviser or in any other way, shall be deemed to be practising as a solicitor and the provisions of the Act of 1949 relating to practising certificates and to the Guarantee Fund shall apply to him accordingly:

Provided that the Council of the Society may if they think fit in any particular case exempt such a solicitor from all or any of the provisions of the said Act relating to the Guarantee Fund.

Employment by solicitor of person struck off the roll or suspended.

13.—(1) No solicitor shall, in connection with his practice as a solicitor, without the written permission of the Council of the Society which may be given for such period and subject to such conditions as the Council thinks fit, employ or remunerate any person who to his knowledge is disqualified from practising as a solicitor by reason of the fact that his name has been struck off the roll or that he is suspended from practising as a solicitor.

(2) A solicitor aggrieved by the refusal of the Council to grant any such permission as aforesaid or by any conditions attached by the Council to the grant thereof may appeal to the Court, and on any such appeal the Court may give such directions in the matter as they think fit.

(3) If any solicitor acts in contravention of the provisions of this section or of the conditions subject to which any permission has been given thereunder his name shall be struck off the roll or he shall be suspended from practice for such period as the Discipline Tribunal, or in the case of an appeal the Court, may think fit.

PART II

DISCIPLINE

The Scottish Solicitors Discipline Tribunal.

14.—(1) The Discipline Committee constituted under section 24 of the Act of 1933 shall be known as " The Scottish Solicitors Discipline Tribunal " and references in any enactment or instrument shall be construed accordingly.

(2) In this section " enactments " includes any regulations or rules made under any enactment.

Discipline Tribunal to include lay members.

15. In section 24 of the Act of 1933 (constitution of Discipline Tribunal)—

(*a*) in subsection (1) after the word " Scotland " in the second place where that word occurs there shall be inserted the words " and of two members (referred to in this section as lay members) who are neither solicitors nor advocates " and at the end of the subsection there shall be added the words " or, as the case may be, by the appointment of a lay member." ;

(*b*) for subsection (4) there shall be substituted the following subsection—

" (4) The Tribunal shall be deemed to be properly constituted if—

(*a*) at least four members are present ; and

(*b*) at least one lay member is present ; and

(*c*) the number of solicitor members present exceeds the number of lay members present." ;

(*c*) there shall be added the following subsection—

" (5) There shall be paid to the lay members out of money provided by Parliament such fees and allowances as the Secretary of State may, with the approval of the Minister for the Civil Service, determine.".

PART II

Power of Society to deal with client account of solicitor struck off roll or suspended.

16.—(1) Where a solicitor who is practising as a solicitor under his own name or as a sole solicitor under a firm name has been struck off the roll of solicitors or has been suspended from practice, there shall, notwithstanding any enactment or any rule of law to the contrary, vest thereupon in the Society to the exclusion of any other person the right to operate on or otherwise deal with any client account in name of the solicitor or his firm.

(2) In this section the expression " client account " has the same meaning as in section 3 of the Act of 1965.

Power of Discipline Tribunal to order decision to take effect on intimation, and to impose conditions on practising certificates.

17. In the Act of 1958 after section 5 there shall be inserted the following section—

" 5A.—(1) In any case in which the Discipline Tribunal decide to order that a solicitor be struck off the roll or suspended they may order that the decision shall take effect on the date on which it is intimated to the solicitor and it shall take effect accordingly.

(2) Unless on an application to the Court under subsection (2) of section 7 of this Act the Court orders otherwise, an order made under subsection (1) of this section shall continue to have effect notwithstanding that any matter before the Court under the said section 7 has not been finally determined.

(3) In any case in which the Tribunal have exercised the power conferred by section 5 of this Act to censure or impose a fine on a solicitor or both to censure and impose a fine the Tribunal may order that his practising certificate shall be issued subject to such terms and conditions as they may direct and the registrar shall give effect to the order of the Tribunal accordingly.".

Appeal from decision of Discipline Tribunal.

18.—(1) At the end of section 7 of the Act of 1958 the following subsection shall be inserted—

" (2) Where the Discipline Tribunal have exercised the power conferred by subsection (1) of section 5A of this Act to order that their decision shall take effect on the date on which it is intimated to the solicitor concerned, that solicitor may within twenty-one days of that date apply to the Court for an order to vary or quash the order of the Discipline Tribunal in so far as it relates to the date of taking effect and on such an application the Court may make the order applied for or such other order with respect to the matter as the Court may think fit.".

PART II

(2) In subsection (2) of section 9 of the Act of 1958 (power of Council of Society to deal with property in the hands of solicitor struck off roll or suspended) for paragraph (*b*) there shall be substituted the following paragraph—

" (*b*) the last date on which

(i) an appeal against that order may be lodged or an application may be made to the Court under subsection (2) of section 7 of this Act, or

(ii) an appeal against a decision of the Council under section 3 of this Act may be lodged ; ".

PART III

GENERAL

Name of solicitor whose name is removed from roll also to be removed from roll of notaries public.

19. The provisions of section 11 of the Act of 1958 (removal of notaries public from roll of notaries public) shall apply in the case of a solicitor who is also a notary public whose name is removed from the roll of solicitors in pursuance of the provisions of section 17 of that Act in like manner as the said provisions of section 11 apply in the case of a solicitor struck off the roll of solicitors under the provisions of that Act relating to discipline or having his name removed from the said roll at his own request under section 19 of the Act of 1933.

Agreements between solicitors as to sharing fees.

20. In section 41 of the Act of 1933 (agreements between solicitors as to sharing fees) for the words from " whom he discloses " to the end of the section there shall be substituted the words " whether or not he discloses that client shall be liable to any other solicitor employed by him for the fees and outlays of that other solicitor unless at the time of the employment he expressly disclaims such liability.".

Amendment of requirements relating to termination of suspension of solicitor.

21. In section 3 of the Act of 1958 (power of Council of Society to withdraw practising certificate on failure to comply with Accounts Rules) in subsection (1) the words " for some other competent reason " shall be omitted.

Alteration of fees payable by solicitors.

22.—(1) In section 2 of the Act of 1958 (fee payable on admission as solicitor) the words " not exceeding five pounds " shall be omitted.

(2) In Schedule 6 to the Act of 1949 (provisions with respect to the Scottish Solicitors' Guarantee Fund)—

(*a*) in sub-paragraph (1) of paragraph 1 for the words " five pounds " there shall be substituted the words " twenty five pounds ", and

(*b*) in item (*b*) of the proviso to sub-paragraph (4) of paragraph 1 for the words " ten pounds " there shall be substituted the words " twenty five pounds ".

PART III

Amendment of Schedule 1 to Act of 1958.

23. In Schedule 1 to the Act of 1958 in sub-paragraph (4) of paragraph 4—

(*a*) after the word " fined " there shall be inserted the words " or in the case of a decision under section 5A of this Act which has not been varied or quashed by the Court ",

(*b*) before the word " send " there shall be inserted the word " immediately ", and

(*c*) after the words " roll of solicitors " in the third place where those words occur there shall be inserted the words " and to any terms and conditions directed by the Tribunal under subsection (3) of section 5A of this Act ".

Definition of Discipline Tribunal.

24. In section 50 of the Act of 1933 (interpretation of terms) the definition of " Discipline Committee " shall cease to have effect and after the definition of " General Council " there shall be inserted—

" Discipline Tribunal " means the Scottish Solicitors Discipline Tribunal constituted in terms of this Act.

Interpretation.

25.—(1) In this Act except where the context otherwise requires—

1933 c. 21. " The Act of 1933 " means the Solicitors (Scotland) Act 1933.

1949 c. 63. " The Act of 1949 " means the Solicitors (Scotland) Act 1949.

1958 c. 28. " The Act of 1958 " means the Solicitors (Scotland) Act 1958.

1965 c. 29. " The Act of 1965 " means the Solicitors (Scotland) Act 1965.

(2) Save where the context otherwise requires, references in this Act to any enactment shall be construed as references to that enactment as amended, extended or applied by or under any other enactment, including any enactment contained in this Act.

Citation, construction and extent.

26.—(1) This Act may be cited as the Solicitors (Scotland) Act 1976 and shall be construed as one with the Solicitors (Scotland) Acts 1933 to 1965 and those Acts and this Act may be cited together as the Solicitors (Scotland) Acts 1933 to 1976.

(2) This Act except in so far as it relates to the amendment

1975 c. 24. of the House of Commons Disqualification Act 1975 extends to Scotland only.

Trade Union and Labour Relations (Amendment) Act 1976

1976 CHAPTER 7

An Act to repeal (in whole or in part), replace or amend sections 5, 6, 7, 8, 13, 29 and 30 of the Trade Union and Labour Relations Act 1974 and paragraph 6 of Schedule 1 to that Act and to provide for a charter on matters relating to the freedom of the press. [25 March 1976]

BE IT ENACTED by the Queen's most Excellent Majesty, by and with the advice and consent of the Lords Spiritual and Temporal, and Commons, in this present Parliament assembled, and by the authority of the same, as follows:—

1. The following provisions and passages of the Trade Union and Labour Relations Act 1974 (hereafter in this Act referred to as " the principal Act ") are hereby repealed, that is to say— Repeals of the principal Act. 1974 c. 52.

(*a*) section 5 (rights of workers as to arbitrary or unreasonable exclusion or expulsion from trade union);

(*b*) section 6 (provisions as to rules of trade unions and employers' associations);

(*c*) in section 8(6) (power of Registrar of Friendly Societies to remove name of organisation from list of trade unions or list of employers' associations), the words " or that its rules do not comply with the provisions of this Act ";

(*d*) in section 29(3) (trade disputes relating to matters occurring outside Great Britain), the words from " so long as " onwards ;

(*e*) in paragraph 6(5) of Schedule 1 (cases where dismissal is to be regarded as fair), the words " or on any reasonable grounds to being a member of a particular trade union."

Freedom of the press.

2. After section 1 of the principal Act there shall be inserted the following section: —

" Charter on freedom of the press.

1A.—(1) If before the end of the period of twelve months beginning with the passing of the Trade Union and Labour Relations (Amendment) Act 1976, there is agreed among parties including employers of journalists (or employers' associations representing such employers), editors (or editors' organisations) and trade unions representing journalists, a charter containing practical guidance for employers, trade unions and editors and other journalists on matters relating to the freedom of the press, the Secretary of State shall lay before both Houses of Parliament a draft of that charter.

(2) For the purposes of subsection (1) above, practical guidance on matters relating to the freedom of the press must include guidance on the avoidance of improper pressure to distort or suppress news, comment, or criticism, the application of union membership agreements to journalists (and in particular the right of editors to discharge their duties and to commission and to publish any article) and the question of access for contributors.

(3) If no such charter has been agreed as mentioned above, or if a draft charter laid before Parliament (under subsection (1) above or this subsection) is not approved by resolution of each House of Parliament as mentioned in subsection (6) below, the Secretary of State shall after consultation with the Press Council and such of the parties referred to in subsection (1) above, such organisations representing workers and such organisations representing employers, as he thinks fit, prepare in draft a charter, as follows: —

(*a*) where, or so far as, there appears to the Secretary of State to be agreement among the parties referred to in subsection (1) above on any matter relating to the freedom of the press, he shall incorporate in the draft charter such practical guidance as he thinks appropriate to give effect to that agreement;

(*b*) where, so far as there appears to the Secretary of State to be no such agreement on any of the particular matters referred to in subsection (2) above, he shall incorporate in the draft charter such practical guidance on that matter as he thinks fit,

and the Secretary of State shall lay the draft charter before both Houses of Parliament.

(4) A charter agreed as mentioned in subsection (1) above, or prepared by the Secretary of State in accordance with subsection (3) above, shall define its field of operation.

(5) A charter agreed as mentioned in subsection (1) above, or prepared by the Secretary of State in accordance with subsection (3) above, shall provide for the constitution of a body which shall have the functions of—

(*a*) hearing any complaint by a person aggrieved by a failure on the part of any other person to observe any provision of the charter;

(*b*) issuing to the parties a declaration as to whether such a complaint is well-founded; and

(*c*) securing the publication of its decision.

(6) If a draft laid under subsection (1) or (3) above is approved by a resolution of each House of Parliament, the Secretary of State shall issue the charter in the form of the draft.

(7) A charter for the time being in force under this section may be revised from time to time by agreement between such parties as are referred to in subsection (1) above, and the Secretary of State shall lay a draft of the revised charter before both Houses of Parliament.

(8) If a draft laid under subsection (7) above is approved by a resolution of each House of Parliament, the Secretary of State shall issue the revised charter in the form of the draft.

(9) On issuing a charter or revised charter under subsection (6) or (8) above the Secretary of State shall make by statutory instrument an order specifying the date on which the charter or revised charter is to come into effect.

(10) A failure on the part of any person to observe any provision of a charter which is for the time being in force under this section shall not of itself render him liable to any proceedings, but in any proceedings—

(*a*) any such charter shall be admissible in evidence, and

(*b*) any provision of such a charter which appears to the court or tribunal to be relevant to any question arising in those proceedings shall be taken into account by the court or tribunal in determining that question."

Amendments of the principal Act.

3.—(1) For section 7 of the principal Act (right to terminate membership of trade union) there shall be substituted the following section:—

"Right to terminate membership of trade union.

7. In every contract of membership of a trade union, whether made before or after the passing of this Act, there shall be implied a term conferring a right on the member, on giving reasonable notice and complying with any reasonable conditions, to terminate his membership of the union."

(2) For section 13(1) of the principal Act (inducing or threatening breach of a contract of employment in contemplation or furtherance of a trade dispute) there shall be substituted the following subsection:—

"(1) An act done by a person in contemplation or furtherance of a trade dispute shall not be actionable in tort on the ground only—

(*a*) that it induces another person to break a contract or interferes or induces any other person to interfere with its performance; or

(*b*) that it consists in his threatening that a contract (whether one to which he is a party or not) will be broken or its performance interfered with, or that he will induce another person to break a contract or to interfere with its performance."

(3) In section 30(1) of the principal Act (interpretation), in paragraph (*c*) of the definition of " union membership agreement ",—

(*a*) for the words " of requiring the terms and conditions of employment of every employee of that class to include a condition that he must " there shall be substituted the words " in practice of requiring the employees for the time being of the class to which it relates (whether or not there is a condition to that effect in their contract of employment) to " ; and

(*b*) for the word " appropriate " there shall be substituted the word " specified,"

and at the end of that definition there shall be inserted the words " and references in this definition to a trade union include references to a branch or section of a trade union ; and a trade union is specified for the purposes of, or in relation to, a union membership agreement if it is specified in the agreement or is accepted by the parties to the agreement as being the equivalent of a union so specified ".

(4) After section 30(5) of the principal Act there shall be inserted the following subsection:—

" (5A) For the purposes of this Act employees are to be treated, in relation to a union membership agreement, as belonging to the same class if they have been identified as such by the parties to the agreement, and employees may be so identified by reference to any characteristics or circumstances whatsoever.".

(5) In paragraph 6(5) of Schedule 1 to the principal Act (cases where dismissal is to be regarded as fair) for the words " all the employees of that employer or all employees " there shall be substituted the words " employees for the time being ".

(6) In paragraph 6(9) of Schedule 1 to the principal Act (definitions), after the word " paragraph " there shall be inserted the words " unless the context otherwise requires, references to a trade union include references to a branch or section of a trade union, and ".

4.—(1) This Act may be cited as the Trade Union and Labour Relations (Amendment) Act 1976. **Short title, citation and transitional provisions.**

(2) The principal Act and this Act may be cited together as the Trade Union and Labour Relations Acts 1974 and 1976.

(3) Section 1(*e*) above and subsections (3), (5) and (6) of section 3 above shall not apply in relation to a case where a person is dismissed and the effective date of termination falls before the passing of this Act.

Prevention of Terrorism (Temporary Provisions) Act 1976

1976 CHAPTER 8

An Act to repeal and re-enact with amendments the provisions of the Prevention of Terrorism (Temporary Provisions) Act 1974. [25th March 1976]

BE IT ENACTED by the Queen's most Excellent Majesty, by and with the advice and consent of the Lords Spiritual and Temporal, and Commons, in this present Parliament assembled, and by the authority of the same, as follows:—

PART I

PROSCRIBED ORGANISATIONS

1.—(1) Subject to subsection (6) below, if any person— *Proscribed organisations.*

(*a*) belongs or professes to belong to a proscribed organisation;

(*b*) solicits or invites financial or other support for a proscribed organisation, or knowingly makes or receives any contribution in money or otherwise to the resources of a proscribed organisation; or

(*c*) arranges or assists in the arrangement or management of, or addresses, any meeting of three or more persons (whether or not it is a meeting to which the public are admitted) knowing that the meeting is to support or to further the activities of, a proscribed organisation.

PART I

or is to be addressed by a person belonging or professing to belong to a proscribed organisation,

he shall be liable—

(i) on summary conviction to imprisonment for a term not exceeding six months or to a fine not exceeding £400, or both, or

(ii) on conviction on indictment to imprisonment for a term not exceeding five years or to a fine, or both.

(2) Any organisation for the time being specified in Schedule 1 to this Act is a proscribed organisation for the purposes of this Act; and any organisation which passes under a name mentioned in that Schedule shall be treated as proscribed, whatever relationship (if any) it has to any other organisation of the same name.

(3) The Secretary of State may by order add to Schedule 1 to this Act any organisation that appears to him to be concerned in terrorism occurring in the United Kingdom and connected with Northern Irish affairs, or in promoting or encouraging it.

(4) The Secretary of State may also by order remove an organisation from Schedule 1 to this Act.

(5) In this section " organisation " includes an association or combination of persons.

(6) A person belonging to a proscribed organisation shall not be guilty of an offence under this section by reason of belonging to the organisation if he shows that he became a member when it was not a proscribed organisation and that he has not since he became a member taken part in any of its activities at any time while it was a proscribed organisation.

In this subsection the reference to a person becoming a member of an organisation shall be taken to be a reference to the only or last occasion on which he became a member.

(7) The court by or before which a person is convicted of an offence under this section may order the forfeiture of any money or other property which, at the time of the offence, he had in his possession or under his control for the use or benefit of the proscribed organisation.

Display of support in public for a proscribed organisation.

2.—(1) Any person who in a public place—

(*a*) wears any item of dress, or

(*b*) wears, carries or displays any article,

in such a way or in such circumstances as to arouse reasonable apprehension that he is a member or supporter of a proscribed organisation, shall be liable on summary conviction to imprisonment for a term not exceeding six months or to a fine not exceeding £400, or both.

(2) A constable may arrest without warrant a person whom he reasonably suspects to be a person guilty of an offence under this section.

(3) In this section "public place" includes any highway and any other premises or place to which at the material time the public have, or are permitted to have, access whether on payment or otherwise.

PART II
EXCLUSION ORDERS

Exclusion orders: general.

3.—(1) The Secretary of State may exercise the powers conferred on him by this Part of this Act in such way as appears to him expedient to prevent acts of terrorism (whether in the United Kingdom or elsewhere) designed to influence public opinion or Government policy with respect to affairs in Northern Ireland.

(2) An order under section 4, 5 or 6 of this Act is referred to in this Act as an "exclusion order".

(3) An exclusion order may be revoked at any time by a further order made by the Secretary of State.

Orders excluding persons from Great Britain.

4.—(1) If the Secretary of State is satisfied that any person—

(*a*) is or has been concerned (whether in Great Britain or elsewhere) in the commission, preparation or instigation of acts of terrorism, or

(*b*) is attempting or may attempt to enter Great Britain with a view to being concerned in the commission, preparation or instigation of acts of terrorism,

the Secretary of State may make an order against that person prohibiting him from being in, or entering, Great Britain.

(2) In deciding whether to make an order under this section against a person who is ordinarily resident in Great Britain, the Secretary of State shall have regard to the question whether that person's connection with any territory outside Great Britain is such as to make it appropriate that such an order should be made.

(3) An order shall not be made under this section against a person who is a citizen of the United Kingdom and Colonies and who—

(*a*) is at the time ordinarily resident in Great Britain, and has then been ordinarily resident in Great Britain throughout the last 20 years, or

(*b*) was born in Great Britain and has, throughout his life, been ordinarily resident in Great Britain, or

(*c*) is at the time subject to an order under section 5 of this Act.

PART II

Paragraph (*a*) shall be construed in accordance with Schedule 2 to this Act.

Orders excluding persons from Northern Ireland.

5.—(1) If the Secretary of State is satisfied that any person—

(*a*) is or has been concerned (whether in Northern Ireland or elsewhere) in the commission, preparation or instigation of acts of terrorism, or

(*b*) is attempting or may attempt to enter Northern Ireland with a view to being concerned in the commission, preparation or instigation of acts of terrorism,

the Secretary of State may make an order against that person prohibiting him from being in, or entering, Northern Ireland.

(2) In deciding whether to make an order under this section against a person who is ordinarily resident in Northern Ireland, the Secretary of State shall have regard to the question whether that person's connection with any territory outside Northern Ireland is such as to make it appropriate that such an order should be made.

(3) An order shall not be made under this section against a person who is a citizen of the United Kingdom and Colonies and who—

(*a*) is at the time ordinarily resident in Northern Ireland, and has then been ordinarily resident in Northern Ireland throughout the last 20 years, or

(*b*) was born in Northern Ireland and has, throughout his life, been ordinarily resident in Northern Ireland, or

(*c*) is at the time subject to an order under section 4 of this Act.

Paragraph (*a*) shall be construed in accordance with Schedule 2 to this Act.

Orders excluding persons from the United Kingdom.

6.—(1) If the Secretary of State is satisfied that any person—

(*a*) is or has been concerned (whether in the United Kingdom or elsewhere) in the commission, preparation or instigation of acts of terrorism, or

(*b*) is attempting or may attempt to enter Great Britain or Northern Ireland with a view to being concerned in the commission, preparation or instigation of acts of terrorism,

the Secretary of State may make an order against that person prohibiting him from being in, or entering, the United Kingdom.

(2) In deciding whether to make an order under this section against a person who is ordinarily resident in the United Kingdom, the Secretary of State shall have regard to the

question whether that person's connection with any territory outside the United Kingdom is such as to make it appropriate that such an order should be made.

(3) An order shall not be made under this section against a person who is a citizen of the United Kingdom and Colonies.

Right to make representations etc. to Secretary of State.

7.—(1) As soon as may be after the making of an exclusion order, notice of the making of the order shall be served on the person against whom it is made, and the notice shall—

(*a*) set out the rights afforded to him by this section, and

(*b*) specify the manner in which those rights are to be exercised.

(2) Subsection (1) above shall not impose an obligation to take any steps to serve a notice on a person at a time when he is outside the United Kingdom.

(3) If a person served with notice of the making of an exclusion order objects to the order, he may within 96 hours of service of the notice—

(*a*) make representations in writing to the Secretary of State setting out the grounds of his objection, and

(*b*) include in those representations a request for a personal interview with the person or persons nominated by the Secretary of State under subsection (4) below.

(4) Where representations are duly made under this section, the Secretary of State shall, unless he considers the grounds to be frivolous, refer the matter for the advice of one or more persons nominated by him.

(5) Where a matter is referred for the advice of one or more persons nominated by the Secretary of State and the person against whom the order was made—

(*a*) included in his representations a request under subsection (3)(*b*) above, and

(*b*) has not been removed, with his consent, from Great Britain, Northern Ireland or the United Kingdom, as the case may be, under section 8 of this Act,

that person shall be granted a personal interview with the person or persons so nominated.

(6) After receiving the representations and the report of the person or persons nominated by him under subsection (4) above, the Secretary of State shall, as soon as may be, reconsider the case.

(7) Where representations are duly made under this section the Secretary of State shall, if it is reasonably practicable, notify the person against whom the order was made of any decision he takes as to whether or not to revoke the order.

PART II

Powers of removal.

8. Where a person is subject to an exclusion order and notice of the order has been served on him, the Secretary of State may have him removed from Great Britain, Northern Ireland or the United Kingdom, as the case may be, if—

(*a*) he consents, or

(*b*) no representations have been duly made by him under section 7 of this Act, or

(*c*) where such representations have been duly made by him, he has been notified of the Secretary of State's decision not to revoke the order.

Offences under Part II.

9.—(1) If any person who is subject to an exclusion order fails to comply with the order at a time after he has been, or has become liable to be, removed under section 8 of this Act from Great Britain, Northern Ireland or the United Kingdom, as the case may be, he shall be guilty of an offence.

(2) If any person—

(*a*) is knowingly concerned in arrangements for securing or facilitating the entry into Great Britain, Northern Ireland or the United Kingdom of, or

(*b*) in Great Britain, Northern Ireland or the United Kingdom knowingly harbours,

a person whom he knows, or has reasonable cause to believe, to be a person who is subject to an exclusion order and who has been, or has become liable to be, removed from there under section 8 of this Act, he shall be guilty of an offence.

(3) A person guilty of an offence under subsection (1) or subsection (2) above shall be liable—

(*a*) on summary conviction to imprisonment for a term not exceeding six months, or to a fine not exceeding £400, or both, or

(*b*) on conviction on indictment to imprisonment for a term not exceeding five years, or to a fine, or both.

PART III

GENERAL AND MISCELLANEOUS

Contributions towards acts of terrorism.

10.—(1) If any person—

(*a*) solicits or invites any other person to give or lend, whether for consideration or not, any money or other property, or

PART III

(*b*) receives or accepts from any other person, whether for consideration or not, any money or other property,

intending that the money or other property shall be applied or used for or in connection with the commission, preparation or instigation of acts of terrorism to which this section applies, he shall be guilty of an offence.

(2) If any person gives, lends or otherwise makes available to any other person, whether for consideration or not, any money or other property, knowing or suspecting that the money or other property will or may be applied or used for or in connection with the commission, preparation or instigation of acts of terrorism to which this section applies, he shall be guilty of an offence.

(3) A person guilty of an offence under subsection (1) or subsection (2) above shall be liable—

(*a*) on summary conviction to imprisonment for a term not exceeding six months, or to a fine not exceeding £400, or both, or

(*b*) on conviction on indictment to imprisonment for a term not exceeding five years or to a fine, or both.

(4) A court by or before which a person is convicted of an offence under subsection (1) above may order the forfeiture of any money or other property—

(*a*) which, at the time of the offence, he had in his possession or under his control, and

(*b*) which, at that time, he intended should be applied or used for or in connection with the commission, preparation or instigation of acts of terrorism to which this section applies.

(5) This section and section 11 of this Act apply to acts of terrorism occurring in the United Kingdom and connected with Northern Irish affairs.

Information about acts of terrorism.

11.—(1) If a person who has information which he knows or believes might be of material assistance—

(*a*) in preventing an act of terrorism to which this section applies, or

(*b*) in securing the apprehension, prosecution or conviction of any person for an offence involving the commission, preparation or instigation of an act of terrorism to which this section applies,

fails without reasonable excuse to disclose that information as soon as reasonably practicable—

(i) in England and Wales, to a constable, or

PART III

(ii) in Scotland, to a constable or the procurator fiscal, or

(iii) in Northern Ireland, to a constable or a member of Her Majesty's forces,

he shall be guilty of an offence.

(2) A person guilty of an offence under subsection (1) above shall be liable—

(*a*) on summary conviction to imprisonment for a term not exceeding six months, or to a fine not exceeding £400, or both, or

(*b*) on conviction on indictment to imprisonment for a term not exceeding five years, or to a fine, or both.

(3) Proceedings for an offence under this section may be taken, and the offence may for the purpose of those proceedings be treated as having been committed, in any place where the offender is or has at any time been since he first knew or believed that the information might be of material assistance as mentioned in subsection (1) above.

Powers of arrest and detention.

12.—(1) A constable may arrest without warrant a person whom he reasonably suspects to be—

(*a*) a person guilty of an offence under section 1, 9, 10 or 11 of this Act;

(*b*) a person who is or has been concerned in the commission, preparation or instigation of acts of terrorism;

(*c*) a person subject to an exclusion order.

(2) A person arrested under this section shall not be detained in right of the arrest for more than 48 hours after his arrest; but the Secretary of State may, in any particular case, extend the period of 48 hours by a further period not exceeding 5 days.

(3) The following provisions (requirement to bring arrested person before a court after his arrest) shall not apply to a person detained in right of the arrest.

The said provisions are—

1952 c. 55. Section 38 of the Magistrates' Court Act 1952,

1969 c. 54. Section 29 of the Children and Young Persons Act 1969,

1975 c. 21. Section 321(3) of the Criminal Procedure (Scotland) Act 1975,

1964 c. 21 (N.I.). Section 132 of the Magistrates' Courts Act (Northern Ireland) 1964, and

1968 c. 34 (N.I.). Section 50(3) of the Children and Young Persons Act (Northern Ireland) 1968.

(4) In Scotland section 295(1) of the Criminal Procedure (Scotland) Act 1975 (chief constable may in certain cases accept

bail) shall not apply to a person detained in right of an arrest under this section. PART III

(5) The provisions of this section are without prejudice to any power of arrest conferred by law apart from this section.

Control of entry and procedure for removal.

13.—(1) The Secretary of State may by order provide for—

(*a*) the examination of persons arriving in, or leaving, Great Britain or Northern Ireland, with a view to determining—

(i) whether any such person appears to be a person who is or has been concerned in the commission, preparation or instigation of acts of terrorism, or

(ii) whether any such person is subject to an exclusion order, or

(iii) whether there are grounds for suspecting that any such person has committed an offence under section 9 or 11 of this Act,

(*b*) the arrest and detention of persons subject to exclusion orders, pending their removal pursuant to section 8 of this Act, and

(*c*) arrangements for the removal of persons pursuant to section 8 of this Act.

(2) An order under this section may confer powers on examining officers (appointed in accordance with paragraph 1(2) of Schedule 3 to this Act), including—

(*a*) the power of arresting and detaining any person pending—

(i) his examination,

(ii) the taking of a decision by the Secretary of State as to whether or not to make an exclusion order against him, or

(iii) his removal pursuant to section 8 of this Act,

(*b*) the power of searching persons, of boarding ships or aircraft, of searching in ships or aircraft, or elsewhere and of detaining articles—

(i) for use in connection with the taking of a decision by the Secretary of State as to whether or not to make an exclusion order, or

(ii) for use as evidence in criminal proceedings.

Supplemental provisions.

14.—(1) In this Act, unless the context otherwise requires—

" aircraft " includes hovercraft,

" captain " means master (of a ship) or commander (of an aircraft),

PART III

"exclusion order" has the meaning given by section 3(2) of this Act,

"port" includes airport and hoverport,

"ship" includes every description of vessel used in navigation,

"terrorism" means the use of violence for political ends, and includes any use of violence for the purpose of putting the public or any section of the public in fear.

(2) The powers conferred by Part II and section 13 of this Act shall be exercisable notwithstanding the rights conferred by section 1 of the Immigration Act 1971 (general principles regulating entry into and staying in the United Kingdom).

1971 c. 77.

(3) Any reference in a provision of this Act to a person's having been concerned in the commission, preparation or instigation of acts of terrorism shall be taken to be a reference to his having been so concerned at any time, whether before or after the coming into force of that provision.

(4) When any question arises under this Act whether or not a person is exempted from the provisions of section 4, 5 or 6 of this Act, it shall lie on the person asserting it to prove that he is.

(5) The provisions of Schedule 3 to this Act shall have effect for supplementing sections 1 to 13 of this Act.

(6) Any power to make an order conferred by section 1, 13 or 17 of this Act shall be exercisable by statutory instrument and shall include power to vary or revoke any order so made.

(7) An order made under section 13 of this Act varying or revoking a previous order so made may contain such transitional provisions and savings as appear to the Secretary of State to be necessary or expedient.

(8) An order made under section 13 of this Act shall be subject to annulment in pursuance of a resolution of either House of Parliament.

(9) No order under section 1 or 17 of this Act shall be made unless—

(*a*) a draft of the order has been approved by resolution of each House of Parliament, or

(*b*) it is declared in the order that it appears to the Secretary of State that by reason of urgency it is necessary to make the order without a draft having been so approved.

PART III

(10) Every order under section 1 or 17 of this Act (except such an order of which a draft has been so approved)—

(*a*) shall be laid before Parliament, and

(*b*) shall cease to have effect at the expiration of a period of 40 days beginning with the date on which it was made unless, before the expiration of that period, the order has been approved by resolution of each House of Parliament, but without prejudice to anything previously done or to the making of a new order.

In reckoning for the purposes of this subsection any period of 40 days, no account shall be taken of any period during which Parliament is dissolved or prorogued or during which both Houses are adjourned for more than 4 days.

Financial provisions.

15. Any expenses incurred by the Secretary of State under, or by virtue of, this Act shall be paid out of money provided by Parliament.

Power to extend to Channel Islands and Isle of Man.

16.—(1) Her Majesty may by Order in Council direct that any of the provisions of this Act shall extend, with such exceptions, adaptations and modifications, if any, as may be specified in the Order, to any of the Channel Islands and the Isle of Man.

(2) An Order in Council under this section may be varied or revoked by a further Order in Council.

Duration, expiry and revival of Act.

17.—(1) The provisions of—

sections 1 to 13 of this Act,

section 14 of this Act except in so far as it relates to orders under subsection (2)(*a*) or (*b*) below,

subsection (2)(*c*) below, and

Schedules 1 to 3 to this Act

shall remain in force until the expiry of the period of twelve months beginning with the passing of this Act and shall then expire unless continued in force by an order under subsection (2)(*a*) below.

(2) The Secretary of State may by order provide—

(*a*) that all or any of the said provisions which are for the time being in force (including any in force by virtue of an order under this paragraph or paragraph (*c*) below) shall continue in force for a period not exceeding twelve months from the coming into operation of the order;

PART III

(*b*) that all or any of the said provisions which are for the time being in force shall cease to be in force ; or

(*c*) that all or any of the said provisions which are not for the time being in force shall come into force again and remain in force for a period not exceeding twelve months from the coming into operation of the order.

1889 c. 63.

(3) On the expiration of any provision of this Act, section 38(2) of the Interpretation Act 1889 (effect of repeals) shall apply as if that provision of this Act was then repealed by another Act.

Repeal of Act of 1974.
1974 c. 56.

18.—(1) The Prevention of Terrorism (Temporary Provisions) Act 1974 (in this section referred to as " the Act of 1974 ") is hereby repealed.

(2) In so far as any order made, direction given or other thing done under any of the provisions of the Act of 1974 could have been made, given or done under a corresponding provision of this Act, it shall not be invalidated by the repeal but shall have effect as if made, given or done under that corresponding provision ; and anything begun under that Act may be continued under this Act as if begun under this Act.

(3) The repeal shall not affect the operation of any Order in Council made under the Act of 1974 extending that Act, with such exceptions, adaptations and modifications (if any) as may be specified in the Order, to any of the Channel Islands or the Isle of Man ; but any such Order may be revoked by an Order in Council under this Act as if made under this Act.

1889 c. 63.

(4) Nothing in this section shall be taken as prejudicing the operation of section 38(2) of the Interpretation Act 1889 (effect of repeals).

Short title and extent.

19.—(1) This Act may be cited as the Prevention of Terrorism (Temporary Provisions) Act 1976.

(2) Part I of this Act shall not extend to Northern Ireland.

SCHEDULES

SCHEDULE 1

Section 1.

PROSCRIBED ORGANISATIONS

Irish Republican Army

SCHEDULE 2

Sections 4 and 5

EXCLUSION ORDERS: CALCULATION OF PERIOD OF RESIDENCE

1.—(1) It is hereby declared that a person is not to be treated—

(*a*) as ordinarily resident in Great Britain for the purpose of the exemption in section 4(3)(*a*) of this Act, or

(*b*) as ordinarily resident in Northern Ireland for the purpose of the exemption in section 5(3)(*a*) of this Act,

at a time when he is there in breach of—

(i) an exclusion order;

(ii) the Immigration Act 1971; or 1971 c. 77.

(iii) any law for purposes similar to that Act which is or was for the time being (before or after the passing of this Act) in force in any part of the United Kingdom.

(2) In each of those exemptions " the last 20 years " is to be taken as a period amounting in total to 20 years exclusive of any time during which the person claiming exemption was undergoing imprisonment or detention by virtue of a sentence passed for an offence on a conviction in the United Kingdom and Islands, and the period for which he was imprisoned or detained by virtue of the sentence amounted to six months or more.

2. In this Schedule—

(*a*) " sentence " includes any order made on conviction of an offence;

(*b*) two or more sentences for consecutive (or partly consecutive) terms shall be treated as a single sentence;

(*c*) a person shall be deemed to be detained by virtue of a sentence—

(i) at any time when he is liable to imprisonment or detention by virtue of the sentence, but is unlawfully at large; and

(ii) during any period of custody by which under any relevant enactment the term to be served under the sentence is reduced;

(*d*) " Islands " means the Channel Islands and the Isle of Man.

Sch. 2

1967 c. 80. 1962 c. 15.

3. In paragraph 2(*c*)(ii) above " relevant enactment " means section 67 of the Criminal Justice Act 1967 (or before that section operated, section 17(2) of the Criminal Justice Administration Act 1962) and any similar enactment which is for the time being or has (before or after the passing of this Act) been in force in any part of the United Kingdom or Islands.

Section 14.

SCHEDULE 3

Supplemental Provisions for Sections 1 to 13

Part I

Orders under Section 13

1.—(1) In this Part of this Schedule references to an order are to an order made under section 13 of this Act.

(2) An order shall provide for the appointment as examining officers of—

(*a*) constables,

1971 c. 77. (*b*) immigration officers appointed for the purposes of the Immigration Act 1971 under paragraph 1 of Schedule 2 to that Act, and

(*c*) officers of customs and excise who are the subject of arrangements for their employment as immigration officers, made by the Secretary of State under the said paragraph 1.

(3) In Scotland persons employed by a police authority for the assistance of constables under section 9 of the Police (Scotland) Act 1967 may perform such functions conferred on examining officers as are specified in the order.

1967 c. 77.

(4) In Northern Ireland members of Her Majesty's forces may perform such functions conferred on examining officers as are specified in the order.

(5) Where, by virtue of subsection (2)(*b*) of section 13, an order confers powers of search and of detaining articles on an examining officer, the order may also confer power on the examining officer to authorise any other person to exercise, on his behalf, any of the powers conferred by virtue of that subsection.

(6) An order may—

(*a*) in the case of ships and aircraft—

(i) coming to Great Britain from the Republic of Ireland, Northern Ireland, the Channel Islands or the Isle of Man, or

(ii) going from Great Britain to any other of those places,

restrict the ports, areas or places in Great Britain which they may use, and

Sch. 3

(*b*) in the case of ships and aircraft—

(i) coming to Northern Ireland from the Republic of Ireland, Great Britain, the Channel Islands or the Isle of Man, or

(ii) going from Northern Ireland to any other of those places,

restrict the ports, areas or places in Northern Ireland which they may use, and

(*c*) provide for the supply and use of—

(i) landing cards by passengers disembarking in Great Britain or Northern Ireland from ships or aircraft, and

(ii) embarkation cards by passengers boarding ships or aircraft about to leave either of those places.

(7) The persons on whom duties may be imposed by the order shall include persons arriving in, or leaving, Great Britain or Northern Ireland whether as passengers or otherwise, and captains, owners or agents of ships or aircraft.

(8) Without prejudice to the generality of section 13 or of the preceding provisions of this paragraph, an order may contain such supplemental or incidental provisions as appear to the Secretary of State to be expedient, and may contain provisions comparable to those contained in or made under the following administrative provisions of the Immigration Act 1971, that is to say, section 33(3) (designation of ports of entry and exit) and the following paragraphs of Schedule 2:— 1971 c. 77.

Paragraph	
4	Duties of persons being examined, and powers to search them and their belongings.
5	Orders about landing and embarkation cards.
8, 10 and 11 ...	Arrangements for the removal of persons.
16, 17 and 18(3) ...	Detention of persons liable to examination or removal.
26 and 27	Supplemental duties of those connected with ships or aircraft or with ports.

(9) A person who knowingly contravenes or fails to comply with an order shall be guilty of an offence, and shall be liable on summary conviction to a fine not exceeding £200, or to imprisonment for not more than three months, or both.

(10) Examining officers appointed in pursuance of sub-paragraph (2) above shall exercise their functions under this Act in accordance with such instructions as may from time to time be given them by the Secretary of State.

2. An order may make such provision as appears to the Secretary of State expedient as respects persons who enter or leave Northern Ireland by land, or who seek to do so.

SCH. 3

PART II

OFFENCES, DETENTION, ETC.

Prosecution of offences

3. Proceedings shall not be instituted—

(*a*) in England and Wales for an offence under section 1, 2, 9, 10 or 11 of this Act, except by or with the consent of the Attorney General, or

(*b*) in Northern Ireland for an offence under section 9, 10 or 11 of this Act, except by or with the consent of the Attorney General for Northern Ireland.

Search warrants

4.—(1) If a justice of the peace is satisfied that there is reasonable ground for suspecting that—

(*a*) evidence of the commission of an offence under section 1, 9, 10 or 11 of this Act, or

(*b*) evidence sufficient to justify the making of an order under section 1 of this Act or an exclusion order,

is to be found at any premises or place, he may grant a search warrant authorising entry to the premises or place.

(2) An application for a warrant under sub-paragraph (1) above shall be made by a member of a police force of a rank not lower than the rank of an inspector, and he shall give his information to the justice on oath.

(3) The warrant shall authorise the applicant, and any other member of any police force, to enter the premises or place, if necessary by force, and to search the premises or place and every person found therein and to seize anything found on the premises or place, or on any such person, which any member of a police force acting under the warrant has reasonable grounds for suspecting to be evidence falling within sub-paragraph (1) above.

(4) If a member of a police force of a rank not lower than the rank of superintendent has reasonable grounds for believing that the case is one of great emergency and that in the interests of the State immediate action is necessary, he may by a written order signed by him give to any member of a police force the authority which may be given by a search warrant under this paragraph.

(5) Where any authority is so given, particulars of the case shall be notified as soon as may be to the Secretary of State.

(6) No woman shall, in pursuance of a warrant or order given under this paragraph, be searched except by a woman.

(7) In the application of this paragraph to Scotland, for any reference to a justice of the peace there shall be substituted a reference to a sheriff or a magistrate or justice of the peace; and for any reference to information on oath there shall be substituted a reference to evidence on oath.

(8) In the application of this paragraph to Northern Ireland references to a police force shall be substituted as follows— SCH. 3

(*a*) for the reference in sub-paragraph (2) and the first reference in sub-paragraph (4) there shall be substituted references to the Royal Ulster Constabulary, and

(*b*) for all other references there shall be substituted references to the Royal Ulster Constabulary, including the Royal Ulster Constabulary Reserve.

Detention : supplemental provisions

5.—(1) A person may be detained—

(*a*) in right of an arrest under section 12 of this Act, or

(*b*) under any provision contained in or made under section 13 of this Act, or Part I of this Schedule,

in such place as the Secretary of State may from time to time direct (when not detained in accordance with an order under section 13 of this Act on board a ship or aircraft).

(2) A person shall be deemed to be in legal custody at any time when he is so detained.

(3) Where a person is so detained, any examining officer, constable or prison officer, or any other person authorised by the Secretary of State, may take all such steps as may be reasonably necessary for photographing, measuring or otherwise identifying him.

Powers of search without warrant

6.—(1) In any circumstances in which a constable has power under section 12 of this Act to arrest a person, he may also, for the purpose of ascertaining whether he has in his possession any document or other article which may constitute evidence that he is a person liable to arrest, stop that person, and search him.

(2) Where a constable has arrested a person under the said section, for any reason other than for the commission of a criminal offence, he, or any other constable, may search him for the purpose of ascertaining whether he has in his possession any document or other article which may constitute evidence that he is a person liable to arrest.

(3) No woman shall in pursuance of this paragraph be searched except by a woman.

Evidence in proceedings

7.—(1) Any document purporting to be an order, notice or direction made or given by the Secretary of State for the purposes of any provision contained in or made under this Act and to be signed by him or on his behalf shall be received in evidence, and shall, until the contrary is proved, be deemed to be made or given by him.

(2) Prima facie evidence of any such order, notice or direction may, in any legal proceedings, be given by the production of a document bearing a certificate purporting to be signed by or on

Sch. 3 behalf of the Secretary of State and stating that the document is a true copy of the order, notice or direction; and the certificate shall be received in evidence, and shall, until the contrary is proved, be deemed to be made or issued by the Secretary of State.

Scheduled offences

8. Offences under sections 9, 10 and 11 of this Act shall be scheduled offences for the purposes of the Northern Ireland (Emergency Provisions) Act 1973 (1973 c. 53.); and accordingly in Part I of Schedule 4 to that Act there shall be inserted after the paragraph 13 inserted there by paragraph 7 of Schedule 2 to the Northern Ireland (Emergency Provisions) (Amendment) Act 1975 (1975 c. 62.) the following paragraph:—

"*Prevention of Terrorism (Temporary Provisions) Act* 1976

13A. Offences under the following provisions of the Prevention of Terrorism (Temporary Provisions) Act 1976—

(*a*) section 9 (breach of exclusion orders);

(*b*) section 10 (contributions towards acts of terrorism);

(*c*) section 11 (information about acts of terrorism)."

Water Charges Act 1976

1976 CHAPTER 9

An Act to make provision for the refund of certain charges made by water authorities in England and Wales in respect of the financial years 1974–75 and 1975–76 and as to the scope of the powers of such authorities to make charges. [25th March 1976]

BE IT ENACTED by the Queen's most Excellent Majesty, by and with the advice and consent of the Lords Spiritual and Temporal, and Commons, in this present Parliament assembled, and by the authority of the same, as follows:—

1.—(1) On 1st April 1976 it shall become the duty of every water authority to refund— Duty of water authorities to refund certain charges.

(*a*) all charges for sewerage or sewage disposal paid in pursuance of the Water Authorities (Collection of Charges) Order 1974 or the Water Authorities (Collection of Charges) Order 1975 in respect of any hereditament which was without sewerage on the relevant date, together with any associated legal costs, and S.I. 1974 No. 448. S.I. 1975 No. 396.

(*b*) all water rates or charges paid for the financial year 1974–75 or the financial year 1975–76 in respect of any hereditament for which on the relevant date no supply of water was made available by them.

(2) In subsection (1)(*a*) above " associated legal costs " means any costs awarded in relation to a summons under Part VI of the General Rate Act 1967 issued solely in respect of non-payment of a general services charge under one or other of the orders mentioned in that paragraph or in relation to the 1967 c. 9.

obtaining of a warrant of distress under the said Part VI in respect of such a non-payment.

(3) It is hereby declared that, in calculating sums to be refunded for the financial year 1974–75 under subsection (1) above, a water authority may deduct, in respect of any such charges or water rates as are mentioned in that subsection, amounts which by reason of rate relief were not paid by the person who would otherwise have been liable to pay them, and may retain any such amounts.

(4) Subject to subsection (5) below, the relevant date for the determination of entitlement to a refund for either of the financial years mentioned in subsection (1) above is the beginning of the year in question.

(5) If a hereditament was not liable to be rated at the beginning of one of those financial years, the relevant date for the determination of entitlement to a refund for that year is the date on which it was first so liable.

(6) A water authority may recover the aggregate amount of sums refunded under subsection (1)(*a*) above from persons liable to be rated in respect of hereditaments with sewerage at any time in the financial year 1976–77 and the aggregate amount of sums refunded under subsection (1)(*b*) above from persons liable to be rated in respect of hereditaments for which a supply of water is made available by them at any time in that year.

(7) Sums falling to be so recovered may be recovered by the
1973 c. 37. imposition of charges under section 30 of the Water Act 1973 as if they were payable in respect of services performed for the persons mentioned in subsection (6) above during the financial year 1976–77.

(8) A hereditament is without sewerage for the purposes of this section—

(*a*) if the following conditions are satisfied in relation to it, namely—

(i) it is not drained by a sewer or drain connecting, either directly or through an intermediate sewer or drain, with a public sewer provided for foul water or surface water or both, and

(ii) the person liable to be rated in respect of the hereditament does not have the use, for the benefit of the hereditament, of facilities which drain to a sewer or drain so connecting, or

(*b*) if it is subject to special rating and is of a description specified for the purposes of this section by an order
1972 c. 70. under section 254 of the Local Government Act 1972.

(9) At the end of paragraph 5(2)(*cc*) of Schedule 6 to the Water Act 1973 (which was added to paragraph 5(2) of that

Schedule by paragraph 14 of Schedule 7 to the Local Government Act 1974) there shall be inserted the following paragraphs:— 1974 c. 7.

"(*cca*) as to the making by a local authority on behalf of a water authority of refunds under the Water Charges Act 1976;

(*ccb*) specifying for the purposes of section 1 of the Water Charges Act 1976 any description of hereditament which is subject to special rating, as defined in that Act;

(*ccc*) for the calculation by a local authority of amounts to be refunded under the said Act of 1976;

(*ccd*) as to the basis or bases on which such amounts are to be calculated (including, without prejudice to the generality of this paragraph, a special basis or bases for the calculation of refunds in respect of hereditaments specified by virtue of paragraph (*ccb*) above);".

Water authorities' power to charge. 1973 c. 37.

2.—(1) The following subsections shall be substituted for section 30(1) of the Water Act 1973:—

"(1) Subject to the provisions of this Act, a water authority shall have power to fix such charges for the services performed, facilities provided or rights made available by them (including separate charges for separate services, facilities or rights or combined charges for a number of services, facilities or rights) as they think fit, and to demand, take and recover such charges—

(*a*) for services performed, facilities provided or rights made available in the exercise of any of their functions, from persons for whom they perform the services, provide the facilities or make the rights available, and

(*b*) without prejudice to paragraph (*a*) above,—

(i) for services performed, facilities provided or rights made available in the exercise of functions under section 14 above, from persons liable to be rated in respect of hereditaments to which this sub-paragraph applies, and

(ii) for services performed, facilities provided or rights made available in the exercise of functions specified in subsection (1B) below, from all persons liable to be rated in respect of hereditaments in their area or particular classes of such persons.

(1A) Subsection (1)(*b*)(i) above applies to a hereditament if—

(*a*) it is drained by a sewer or drain connecting, either directly or through an intermediate sewer or drain, with a public sewer provided for foul water or surface water or both, or

(*b*) the person liable to be rated in respect of the hereditament has the use, for the benefit of the hereditament, of facilities which drain to a sewer or drain so connecting, or

(*c*) it is subject to special rating.

(1B) The functions mentioned in subsection (1)(*b*)(ii) above are functions under—

(*a*) the Rivers (Prevention of Pollution) Acts 1951 to 1961;

(*b*) sections 20, 21 and 22 of the Water Act 1973 (recreation, nature conservation and amenity):

(*c*) the Control of Pollution Act 1974;

(*d*) the Salmon and Freshwater Fisheries Act 1975;

(*e*) any local statutory provision conferring functions analogous to those mentioned in paragraphs (*a*) to (*d*) above; and

(*f*) any local statutory provision conferring functions with respect to navigation ".

(2) The following subsection shall be added at the end of the said section 30:—

" (11) In this section—

" hereditament " has the meaning assigned to it by section 115(1) of the General Rate Act 1967, and

" special rating " means rating under any enactment contained in sections 31 to 34 of the General Rate Act 1967 or under section 52 of the Post Office Act 1969, and includes rating under any order made by virtue of section 19 of the Local Government Act 1974 amending any of those sections.".

(3) It is hereby declared that the powers conferred on a water

1973 c. 37. authority by section 30 of the Water Act 1973 have always included power to charge all persons liable to be rated in respect of hereditaments in their area or particular classes of such persons for any services performed, facilities provided or rights made available in the exercise of functions specified in subsection (1B) of that section.

(4) At the end of paragraph 5(2) of Schedule 6 to the Water Act 1973 there shall be added the following sub-paragraph:—

" (3) Without prejudice to the generality of sub-paragraph (2)(*c*) above, an order may include provision for calculations on a special basis or bases of amounts payable in respect of hereditaments specified by virtue of sub-paragraph (2)(*ccb*) above.".

3.—(1) This Act may be cited as the Water Charges Act 1976. Citation etc.

(2) The Water Act 1973 and this Act may be cited together as the Water Acts 1973 and 1976.

(3) In this Act—

" hereditament " has the meaning assigned to it by section 115(1) of the General Rate Act 1967; 1967 c. 9.

" public sewer " has the meaning assigned to it by section 38(1) of the Water Act 1973; and 1973 c. 37.

" special rating " means rating under any enactment contained in sections 31 to 34 of the General Rate Act 1967 or under section 52 of the Post Office Act 1969 and includes 1969 c. 48. rating under any order made by virtue of section 19 of the Local Government Act 1974 amending any of those 1974 c. 7. sections.

(4) Except in so far as the context otherwise requires, any reference in this Act to an enactment shall be construed as a reference to that enactment as amended, applied or extended by or under any other enactment, including this Act.

(5) This Act extends to England and Wales only.

Post Office (Banking Services) Act 1976

1976 CHAPTER 10

An Act to extend the powers of the Post Office to provide banking services; to make capital available for the provision of those services; to reduce the capital debt of the Post Office; and for connected purposes.

[25th March 1976]

BE IT ENACTED by the Queen's most Excellent Majesty, by and with the advice and consent of the Lords Spiritual and Temporal, and Commons, in this present Parliament assembled, and by the authority of the same, as follows:—

Extension of power of Post Office to provide banking services.

1969 c. 48.

1963 c. 16.

1964 c. 22 (N.I.).

1.—(1) In section 7(1)(*b*) of the Post Office Act 1969 (power to provide a banking service of the kind commonly known as a giro system) for the words from " a banking service " to " giro system " there shall be substituted the words " banking services ".

(2) The words " or the Post Office " shall be added at the end of section 2(2) of the Protection of Depositors Act 1963 and of section 2(2) of the Protection of Depositors Act (Northern Ireland) 1964 (exemption from restriction on advertisements for deposits).

Financial objective.

2. The Secretary of State may from time to time determine, after consultation with the Post Office and with the concurrence of the Treasury, financial objectives to be achieved by the Post Office in providing banking services; and the duty of the Post Office to achieve those objectives shall be in addition to the duty imposed on it by section 31(1) of the Post Office Act 1969 (revenue to be sufficient to meet charges properly chargeable to revenue account).

Government investment in Post Office's banking services.

3.—(1) The Secretary of State may from time to time pay to the Post Office out of moneys provided by Parliament such sums, to be used by it for the purposes of its banking services, as he thinks fit.

(2) Sums received by the Post Office under subsection (1) of this section are in this section referred to as public dividend capital and shall be treated for the purposes of section 36(2) of the Post Office Act 1969 (aggregate limit of indebtedness) as being part of the aggregate mentioned therein. 1969 c. 48.

(3) In consideration of receiving public dividend capital the Post Office shall make to the Secretary of State for each accounting year (except any with respect to which the Post Office satisfies him that it would be inappropriate to make a payment under this subsection) payments (in this section referred to as public dividends) of such amounts as may be proposed by the Post Office and agreed by the Secretary of State or such other amounts as the Secretary of State may determine after consultation with the Post Office.

(4) In proposing, agreeing or determining the amounts of public dividends the Post Office and the Secretary of State shall have regard to the financial results of the banking services provided by the Post Office.

(5) The Secretary of State shall pay any public dividends received by him under this section into the Consolidated Fund.

(6) For the purposes of this section the Post Office shall be deemed to have received on 1st April 1975 public dividend capital of the amount of £13 million.

(7) References in this section to the Secretary of State are references to him acting with the approval of the Treasury.

Reduction of capital debt of Post Office.

4.—(1) The liability of the Post Office in respect of—

(*a*) the commencing capital debt assumed by it under section 33(1) of the Post Office Act 1969; and

(*b*) any debt incurred by it before 1st April 1975 under section 35(2) of that Act (power to borrow for purposes for which capital moneys are properly applicable);

is hereby reduced by £29·7 million; and accordingly the assets of the National Loans Fund are hereby reduced by the same amount.

(2) Of the amount by which the liability of the Post Office is reduced by virtue of this section £8·48 million shall be treated as reducing its commencing capital debt and the remainder as reducing the principal of moneys borrowed under section 35(2) of the Post Office Act 1969.

(3) The reduction under this section of the liability of the Post Office and of the assets of the National Loans Fund shall be deemed to have been effected on 1st April 1975.

1972 c. 79.

(4) Section 1(2) of the Post Office (Borrowing) Act 1972 is hereby repealed.

Accounts.

5. In section 39 of the Post Office Act 1969 (accounts of Secretary of State) the word " and " after " section 37 of this Act " shall be omitted, and after the words " that section " there shall be inserted the words " and of sums paid or received by him under the Post Office (Banking Services) Act 1976 ".

Short title and extent.

6.—(1) This Act may be cited as the Post Office (Banking Services) Act 1976.

(2) This Act extends to the whole of the United Kingdom, the Channel Islands and the Isle of Man.

Housing (Amendment) (Scotland) Act 1976

1976 CHAPTER 11

An Act to amend section 25(1) of the Housing (Financial Provisions) (Scotland) Act 1968. [13th April 1976]

BE IT ENACTED by the Queen's most Excellent Majesty, by and with the advice and consent of the Lords Spiritual and Temporal, and Commons, in this present Parliament assembled, and by the authority of the same, as follows:—

Increase in limit on aggregate amount of advances to Scottish Special Housing Association.

1.—(1) In proviso (i) to section 25(1) of the Housing (Financial Provisions) (Scotland) Act 1968, as amended by section 1(2) of the Housing (Amendment) (Scotland) Act 1970, for the words " two hundred and thirty million pounds or such greater sum, not exceeding two hundred and ninety million pounds " there shall be substituted the words " three hundred and seventy five million pounds or such greater sum, not exceeding five hundred million pounds ". 1968 c. 31.

(2) The Housing (Amendment) (Scotland) Act 1970 is hereby repealed. 1970 c. 5.

Citation.

2.—(1) This Act may be cited as the Housing (Amendment) (Scotland) Act 1976.

(2) The Housing (Scotland) Acts 1966 to 1975 and this Act may be cited together as the Housing (Scotland) Acts 1966 to 1976.

Statute Law Revision (Northern Ireland) Act 1976

1976 CHAPTER 12

An Act to revise the statute law of Northern Ireland by repealing obsolete, spent, unnecessary or superseded enactments. [13th April 1976]

BE IT ENACTED by the Queen's Most Excellent Majesty, by and with the advice and consent of the Lords Spiritual and Temporal, and Commons, in this present Parliament assembled, and by the authority of the same, as follows:—

1. The enactments specified in the Schedule to this Act (which to the extent specified in column 3 of that Schedule are obsolete, spent or unnecessary or have been superseded by other enactments) are hereby repealed to that extent. Repeals.

2.—(1) This Act may be cited as the Statute Law Revision (Northern Ireland) Act 1976. Short title, extent, etc.

(2) This Act extends to Northern Ireland only.

(3) In this Act " enactment " includes an Act of the Parliament of Northern Ireland and a Measure of the Northern Ireland Assembly.

Section 1.

SCHEDULE

Enactments Repealed

Part I

Administration of Justice

Chapter	Short Title	Extent of Repeal
54 Geo. 3. c. 159.	The Harbours Act 1814.	In section 26, the words " or justice of the peace ".
60 Geo. 3 & 1 Geo. 4. c. 4.	The Pleading in Misdemeanour Act 1819.	In section 1, the words " either by information or " and " or information " wherever they occur. In section 2, the words " or information ". In section 8, the words " or solicitor " and " information or ". In section 9, the words " or solicitor " (twice).
6 Geo. 4. c. 51.	The Assizes (Ireland) Act 1825.	In section 4, the words " found by any grand jury of such county of a city, county of a town, or town corporate ", " or inquisition ", " and inquisitions " and " or inquisitions ". Section 5. In section 6, the words " by such grand jury as aforesaid ". In section 7, the words from " or any inquisition " to " offences aforesaid " and the words " or to remove such inquisition into " and " or on the trial of such inquisition ". In section 9, the words " or inquisition " and " or to return any inquisition ".
1 & 2 Vict. c. 28.	The Bread (Ireland) Act 1838.	In section 13, the words from " and shall moreover " to " be sooner paid and discharged ". In section 23, the words from " where any distress " onwards.
6 & 7 Vict. c. 96.	The Libel Act 1843.	In section 6, the words " or information " wherever they occur. In section 7, the words " or information ".
7 & 8 Vict. c. 81.	The Marriages (Ireland) Act 1844.	In section 51, the words " or solicitor general ". In section 77, the words from " and if on the conviction " onwards.

Chapter	Short Title	Extent of Repeal
8 & 9 Vict. c. 20.	The Railways Clauses Consolidation Act 1845.	In section 152, the words from " and on nonpayment " onwards.
8 & 9 Vict. c. 37.	The Bankers (Ireland) Act 1845.	In section 29, the words " or solicitor general ".
8 & 9 Vict. c. 109.	The Gaming Act 1845.	In section 4, the words from " and on nonpayment " to " convicting justices ". In section 8, the words " or justices ". In section 11, the words " or any two justices of the peace " and " or justices " (twice). In section 12, the words from " or two justices " to " kept by such person ". In section 14, the words " or any two justices of the peace ".
10 & 11 Vict. c. 14.	The Markets and Fairs Clauses Act 1847.	Section 55.
10 & 11 Vict. c. 15.	The Gasworks Clauses Act 1847.	Section 42.
10 & 11 Vict. c. 16.	The Commissioners Clauses Act 1847.	Section 105.
10 & 11 Vict. c. 27.	The Harbours, Docks, and Piers Clauses Act 1847.	Section 94.
10 & 11 Vict. c. 34.	The Towns Improvement Clauses Act 1847.	Section 212.
10 & 11 Vict. c. 65.	The Cemeteries Clauses Act 1847.	Section 64.
14 & 15 Vict. c. 93.	The Petty Sessions (Ireland) Act 1851.	Section 48.
17 & 18 Vict. c. 38.	The Gaming Houses Act 1854.	In sections 1 and 3, the words from " together with " to " and costs " and from " in the first instance " to " seem fit ". Section 7.
20 & 21 Vict. c. 60.	The Irish Bankrupt and Insolvent Act 1857.	Sections 81 and 90. In section 116, the words " as well copy or customary-hold as freehold ". Sections 151 to 177. In section 268, the words " (except copy or customary hold,) ". In section 319, the words " or to the Court of Directors of the East India Company " and " or of the secretary of said Court of Directors ". Sections 395 and 398. Schedule (C).

Chapter	Short Title	Extent of Repeal
22 & 23 Vict. c. 35.	The Law of Property Amendment Act 1859.	In section 24, the words from " or, in case that office " to "Majesty's Solicitor General" and the words " or the Solicitor General (as the case may be) ".
22 & 23 Vict. c. 66.	The Sale of Gas Act 1859.	In section 22, the words " justices of the peace ", "justices" and " they or ".
24 & 25 Vict. c. 97.	The Malicious Damage Act 1861.	Section 65. In section 76, the words " two or more justices of the peace, or ".
24 & 25 Vict. c. 100.	The Offences Against the Person Act 1861.	In section 76, the words "two or more justices of the peace, or ".
35 & 36 Vict. c. 58.	The Bankruptcy (Ireland) Amendment Act 1872.	In section 4, the definition of " Trader ". In section 13, the words from " at the time " to " said offices ". Section 19. In section 21(3), the words " or suffered himself to be outlawed ". Section 67.
39 & 40 Vict. c. 78.	The Juries Procedure (Ireland) Act 1876.	In section 11, the words " or information ".
40 & 41 Vict. c. 57.	The Supreme Court of Judicature Act (Ireland) 1877.	In section 3, the definitions of " Crown cases reserved " and " Registration of Voters Acts ". In section 36, each paragraph (1), paragraph (3) and the words " (3) and ".
48 & 49 Vict. c. 69.	The Criminal Law Amendment Act 1885.	In section 13, the paragraph beginning " Any person on being ".
1 & 2 Geo. 5. c. 28.	The Official Secrets Act 1911.	In section 12, in the definition of " Attorney General ", the words " or Solicitor ".
4 & 5 Geo. 5. c. 58.	The Criminal Justice Administration Act 1914.	Section 41. In section 43(1), the words from " sections one " to " twelve inclusive " and the words from " subsection (2) of section twenty-five " onwards.
10 & 11 Geo. 5. c. 26.	The Sheriffs (Ireland) Act 1920.	In section 1(3), the words " an existing under-sheriff, or ". In section 2, in subsection (1), the words from " (including " to " returning officer) " and in subsection (2), the words from " and in connection " to " assizes or commissions ". In section 11, the definition of " existing ".

Chapter	Short Title	Extent of Repeal
14 & 15 Geo. 5. c. 27 (N.I.).	The Illegitimate Children (Affiliation Orders) Act (Northern Ireland) 1924.	Section 7(2).
25 & 26 Geo. 5. c. 13 (N.I.).	The Summary Jurisdiction and Criminal Justice Act (Northern Ireland) 1935.	Sections 61 and 64.
1945 c. 15 (N.I.).	The Criminal Justice Act (Northern Ireland) 1945.	In section 47(2), the words " and section thirty-four ".
1953 c. 14 (N.I.).	The Criminal Justice Act (Northern Ireland) 1953.	Section 26. Schedule 1. In Schedule 2, the amendments of the Refreshment Houses (Ireland) Act 1860 and section 11 of the Firearms Act 1920.
1953 c. 19 (N.I.).	The Juries Act (Northern Ireland) 1953.	In section 1(5), the words from the beginning to " Parliament but ". Section 3. In section 4, in subsection (1), the words from " after " to " fifty-three " and the words " after that date " (twice) and subsections (2) and (3). In section 5, the words from the beginning to " fifty-three ". In section 9(1) and (2), the words from " after " to " fifty-three,". Schedule 1.
1954 c. 9 (N.I.).	The Administration of Justice Act (Northern Ireland) 1954.	Section 6. Section 7(4) and (5). Section 8(2) and (3). In section 12(4), the words from " so however " onwards. Section 19(1).
1954 c. 27 (N.I.).	The Charitable Trusts (Validation) Act (Northern Ireland) 1954.	Section 4(3).
1958 c. 9 (N.I.).	The Summary Jurisdiction and Criminal Justice Act (Northern Ireland) 1958.	In section 2, the words " (in this Act referred to as ' the Act of 1851 ') ". In section 39, the definitions of " Act of 1851 " and " Act of 1935 ".
1959 c. 25 (N.I.).	The County Courts Act (Northern Ireland) 1959.	Section 146(9). In Schedule 4, the amendments of the Agricultural Marketing Act (Northern Ireland) 1933, the Excessive Rents (Prevention) Act (Northern Ireland) 1941 and the Adoption of Children Act (Northern Ireland) 1950.
1961 c. 18 (N.I.).	The Rights of Light Act (Northern Ireland) 1961.	Section 3.

Chapter	Short Title	Extent of Repeal
1964 c. 16 (N.I.).	The Clean Air Act (Northern Ireland) 1964.	Section 2. Section 41(1).
1964 c. 36 (N.I.).	The Business Tenancies Act (Northern Ireland) 1964.	In Schedule 2, paragraph 1.

In column 3 of this Part of this Schedule any reference to an enactment includes a reference to it as applied by or incorporated with any other enactment.

PART II

AGRICULTURE AND FISHERIES

Chapter	Short Title	Extent of Repeal
62 & 63 Vict. c. 50.	The Agriculture and Technical Instruction (Ireland) Act 1899.	Section 2(1)(*a*), (*c*), (*e*), (*f*) and (*h*) and (2). Section 17(1). Sections 25 and 28. In section 30, the definitions of " the purposes of sea fisheries ", " public body ", " the Irish Church Temporalities Fund ", " the Albert Institution " and " the Munster Institution ". Section 33.
1949 c. 2 (N.I.).	The Agriculture Act (Northern Ireland) 1949.	In section 21(1), the words from " or, where " onwards.
1952 c. 5 (N.I.).	The Foyle Fisheries Act (Northern Ireland) 1952.	Section 2(3) to (5). Sections 7 and 20. In section 22(1), the words from the beginning to " 1952, and " and the word " subsequent ". Section 26.
1952 c. 24 (N.I.).	The Exported Animals (Compensation) Act (Northern Ireland) 1952.	In Schedule 1, in paragraph 1, sub-paragraph (*a*) and in sub-paragraph (*b*), the words " in the case of every member subsequently appointed ".
1959 c. 2 (N.I.).	The Agriculture (Miscellaneous Provisions) Act (Northern Ireland) 1959.	Section 1. Section 2(6). Section 3.
1960 c. 19 (N.I.).	The Agriculture (Miscellaneous Provisions) Act (Northern Ireland) 1960.	Sections 1 and 7. The Schedule.
1964 c. 25 (N.I.).	The Pig Production Development Act (Northern Ireland) 1964.	In the Schedule, in Part I, paragraph 3(4).
1966 c. 17 (N.I.).	The Fisheries Act (Northern Ireland) 1966.	Section 36.

Chapter	Short Title	Extent of Repeal
1967 c. 21 (N.I.).	The Livestock Marketing Commission Act (Northern Ireland) 1967.	In the Schedule, in Part II, paragraph 1(2).
1968 c. 31 (N.I.).	The Fisheries (Amendment) Act (Northern Ireland) 1968.	Section 5(1).

PART III

APPROPRIATION AND CONSOLIDATED FUND ENACTMENTS

Acts

Chapter	Short Title	Extent of Repeal
1956 c. 1 (N.I.).	The Consolidated Fund Act (Northern Ireland) 1956.	The whole Act.
1967 c. 4 (N.I.).	The Consolidated Fund Act (Northern Ireland) 1967.	The whole Act.
1967 c. 19 (N.I.).	The Appropriation Act (Northern Ireland) 1967.	The whole Act.
1967 c. 26 (N.I.).	The Appropriation (No. 2) Act (Northern Ireland) 1967.	The whole Act.
1968 c. 3 (N.I.).	The Consolidated Fund Act (Northern Ireland) 1968.	The whole Act.
1968 c. 15 (N.I.).	The Appropriation Act (Northern Ireland) 1968.	The whole Act.
1968 c. 22 (N.I.).	The Appropriation (No. 2) Act (Northern Ireland) 1968.	The whole Act.
1969 c. 1 (N.I.).	The Consolidated Fund Act (Northern Ireland) 1969.	The whole Act.
1969 c. 17 (N.I.).	The Appropriation Act (Northern Ireland) 1969.	The whole Act.
1969 c. 31 (N.I.).	The Appropriation (No. 2) Act (Northern Ireland) 1969.	The whole Act.
1970 c. 8 (N.I.).	The Consolidated Fund Act (Northern Ireland) 1970.	The whole Act.
1970 c. 27 (N.I.).	The Appropriation Act (Northern Ireland) 1970.	The whole Act.
1970 c. 34 (N.I.).	The Appropriation (No. 2) Act (Northern Ireland) 1970.	The whole Act.
1971 c. 11 (N.I.).	The Consolidated Fund Act (Northern Ireland) 1971.	The whole Act.

Chapter	Short Title	Extent of Repeal
1971 c. 26 (N.I.).	The Appropriation Act (Northern Ireland) 1971.	The whole Act.
1971 c. 39 (N.I.).	The Appropriation (No. 2) Act (Northern Ireland) 1971.	The whole Act.
1972 c. 14 (N.I.).	The Consolidated Fund Act (Northern Ireland) 1972.	The whole Act.

Orders in Council

Number	Short Title	Extent of Repeal
S.I. 1972/671 (N.I. 2).	The Appropriation (Northern Ireland) Order 1972.	The whole Order.
S.I. 1972/1071 (N.I. 8).	The Appropriation (No. 2) (Northern Ireland) Order 1972.	The whole Order.
S.I. 1972/1812 (N.I. 18).	The Appropriation (No. 3) (Northern Ireland) Order 1972.	The whole Order.
S.I. 1973/413 (N.I. 4).	The Appropriation (Northern Ireland) Order 1973.	The whole Order.
S.I. 1973/1227 (N.I. 15).	The Appropriation (No. 2) (Northern Ireland) Order 1973.	The whole Order.
S.I. 1973/2094 (N.I. 23).	The Appropriation (No. 3) (Northern Ireland) Order 1973.	The whole Order.

PART IV

CONSTITUTIONAL

Acts

Chapter	Short Title	Extent of Repeal
10 Geo. 4. c. 7.	The Roman Catholic Relief Act 1829.	In section 12, the words " or the office of lord lieutenant of Ireland ".
33 & 34 Vict. c. 90.	The Foreign Enlistment Act 1870.	In section 19, the words from " or such chief " to " Act mentioned ". In section 23, the words " or the chief executive authority " and " or chief executive authority " (wherever they occur).

Chapter	Short Title	Extent of Repeal
33 & 34 Vict. c. 90—*cont.*	The Foreign Enlistment Act 1870—*cont.*	In section 24, the words " or chief executive authority " (wherever they occur). In section 25, the words " or the chief executive authority ". In section 26, the words from " and such powers " to " Lord Lieutenant ". In section 29, the words " , nor shall the chief executive authority ".
14 & 15 Geo. 5. c. 11 (N.I.).	The Ministers (Temporary Exercise of Powers) Act (Northern Ireland) 1924.	In section 1, the words from " any Parliamentary Secretary " to " head, or " and the words " Parliamentary Secretary or ".
1968 c. 24 (N.I.).	The Legislative Procedure Act (Northern Ireland) 1968.	Section 1.

Orders in Council

Number	Short Title	Extent of Repeal
S.I. 1972/538 (N.I. 1).	The Prosecution of Offences (Northern Ireland) Order 1972.	Article 3(1).
S.I. 1972/730 (N.I. 3).	The Explosives (Northern Ireland) Order 1972.	Article 3(3).
S.I. 1972/963 (N.I. 6).	The Employer's Liability (Defective Equipment and Compulsory Insurance) (Northern Ireland) Order 1972.	Article 3.
S.I. 1972/1072 (N.I. 9).	The Electricity Supply (Northern Ireland) Order 1972.	Articles 3 and **51**.
S.I. 1972/1100 (N.I. 11).	The Finance (Northern Ireland) Order 1972.	Article 3.
S.I. 1972/1263 (N.I. 12).	The Education and Libraries (Northern Ireland) Order 1972.	Article 2(3).
S.I. 1972/1265 (N.I. 14).	The Health and Personal Social Services (Northern Ireland) Order 1972.	Article 3.
S.I. 1972/1633 (N.I. 16).	The Rates (Northern Ireland) Order 1972.	Article 5.
S.I. 1972/1634 (N.I. 17).	The Planning (Northern Ireland) Order 1972.	Article 2(3).
S.I. 1972/1996 (N.I. 19).	The Building Regulations (Northern Ireland) Order 1972.	Articles 2(4) and **14**.
S.I. 1973/69 (N.I. 1).	The Drainage (Northern Ireland) Order 1973.	Article 2(3).

Number	Short Title	Extent of Repeal
S.I. 1973/70 (N.I. 2).	The Water and Sewerage Services (Northern Ireland) Order 1973.	Article 2(3).
S.I. 1973/414 (N.I. 5).	The Financial Provisions (Northern Ireland) Order 1973.	Articles 2(2) and 9.
S.I. 1973/415 (N.I. 6).	The Firearms (Amendment) (Northern Ireland) Order 1973.	Article 2(3).
S.I. 1973/416 (N.I. 7).	The Museums (Northern Ireland) Order 1973.	Articles 2(2) and 12.
S.I. 1973/601 (N.I. 9).	The Fire Services (Northern Ireland) Order 1973.	Article 2(3).
S.I. 1973/961 (N.I. 12).	The Recreation and Youth Service (Northern Ireland) Order 1973.	Article 2(3).
S.I. 1973/1229 (N.I. 17).	The Road Traffic (Amendment) (Northern Ireland) Order 1973.	Articles 2(3) and 16.
S.I. 1973/1896 (N.I. 21).	The Land Acquisition and Compensation (Northern Ireland) Order 1973.	Articles 3 and 71.

PART V

ELECTIONS

Acts

Chapter	Short Title	Extent of Repeal
15 & 16 Vict. c. 57.	The Election Commissioners Act 1852.	The whole Act, so far as unrepealed.
31 & 32 Vict. c. 125.	The Parliamentary Elections Act 1868.	Sections 3, 15 and 56.
32 & 33 Vict. c. 21.	The Corrupt Practices Commission Expenses Act 1869.	The whole Act, so far as unrepealed.
46 & 47 Vict. c. 51.	The Corrupt and Illegal Practices Prevention Act 1883.	The whole Act, so far as unrepealed.
12 & 13 Geo. 5. c. 50.	The Expiring Laws Act 1922.	In Schedule 1, in Part I, the entry relating to the Corrupt Practices Commission Expenses Act 1869.
1946 c. 27 (N.I.).	The Local Government Elections (Validation) Act (Northern Ireland) 1946.	The whole Act.
1962 c. 14 (N.I.).	The Electoral Law Act (Northern Ireland) 1962.	In section 118(1), the words from " or if it was " to " two years after the offence was committed ". In section 130(1), the definition of " election commissioners ".

Orders in Council

Number	Short Title	Extent of Repeal
S.I. 1972/1264 (N.I. 13).	The Electoral Law (Northern Ireland) Order 1972.	Article 2(3). Article 5. In Article 7, in paragraph (1), the words " in the year 1973 and " and the words from " subsequent " to " in that ", in paragraph (3), the words " in the year 1973 and " and "subsequent" paragraphs (4) and (5) and in paragraph (6), the words " or (5).". Article 15. In Article 16(3), in sub-paragraph (*a*) the words " in the year 1973 and " and " subsequent " and sub-paragraph (*c*).
S.I. 1972/1998 (N.I. 21).	The Local Government (Postponement of Elections and Reorganisation) (Northern Ireland) Order 1972.	In Schedule 1, in Part I, in the amendment of the Electoral Law (Northern Ireland) Order 1972, the word " 5 ".

PART VI
EXPENSES
Acts

Chapter	Short Title	Extent of Repeal
1951 c. 5 (N.I.).	The Administrative and Financial Provisions Act (Northern Ireland) 1951.	Section 8.
1954 c. 5 (N.I.).	The Agriculture (Poisonous Substances) Act (Northern Ireland) 1954.	Section 8.
1954 c. 31 (N.I.).	The Agriculture (Temporary Assistance) Act (Northern Ireland) 1954.	Section 3.
1955 c. 13 (N.I.).	The Public Health and Local Government (Miscellaneous Provisions) Act (Northern Ireland) 1955.	Section 25.
1957 c. 3 (N.I.).	The Agriculture (Temporary Assistance) (Amendment) Act (Northern Ireland) 1957.	Section 2.
1958 c. 3 (N.I.).	The Housing Associations Act (Northern Ireland) 1958.	Section 2.
1958 c. 27 (N.I.).	The Food and Drugs Act (Northern Ireland) 1958.	Section 69(1).

Chapter	Short Title	Extent of Repeal
1958 c. 31 (N.I.).	The Marketing of Milk Products Act (Northern Ireland) 1958.	In section 14(1), the words from the beginning to " Parliament and ".
1961 c. 15 (N.I.).	The Mental Health Act (Northern Ireland) 1961.	Section 95.
1961 c. 17 (N.I.).	The Aid to Industry Act (Northern Ireland) 1961.	Section 6(1).
1962 c. 13 (N.I.).	The Agricultural Produce (Meat Regulation and Pig Industry) Act (Northern Ireland) 1962.	In section 21, the words from the beginning to " Parliament and ".
1963 c. 2 (N.I.).	The Terms and Conditions of Employment Act (Northern Ireland) 1963.	Section 10.
1963 c. 4 (N.I.).	The Development of Tourist Traffic (Amendment) Act (Northern Ireland) 1963.	Section 11(1).
1964 c. 6 (N.I.).	The Administrative and Financial Provisions Act (Northern Ireland) 1964.	Section 10.
1964 c. 8 (N.I.).	The Marketing of Potatoes Act (Northern Ireland) 1964.	In section 14, the words from the beginning to " Parliament and ".
1964 c. 18 (N.I.).	The Industrial Training Act (Northern Ireland) 1964.	Section 18.
1964 c. 27 (N.I.).	The Private Streets Act (Northern Ireland) 1964.	Section 37(1).
1965 c. 3 (N.I.).	The Agriculture (Miscellaneous Provisions) Act (Northern Ireland) 1965.	Section 21.
1965 c. 9 (N.I.).	The Amenity Lands Act (Northern Ireland) 1965.	Section 23.
1965 c. 12 (N.I.).	The Administrative and Financial Provisions Act (Northern Ireland) 1965.	Section 11.
1965 c. 21 (N.I.).	The Slaughter-houses Act (Northern Ireland) 1965.	Section 6.
1965 c. 22 (N.I.).	The Seeds Act (Northern Ireland) 1965.	Section 13.
1966 c. 15 (N.I.).	The Horticulture Act (Northern Ireland) 1966.	Section 34.
1966 c. 26 (N.I.).	The Office and Shop Premises Act (Northern Ireland) 1966.	Section 76(1).
1966 c. 34 (N.I.).	The Tourist Traffic (Amendment) Act (Northern Ireland) 1966.	Section 9.
1966 c. 38 (N.I.).	The Local Government Act (Northern Ireland) 1966.	Section 26.
1967 c. 6 (N.I.).	The Weights and Measures Act (Northern Ireland) 1967.	Section 39.
1967 c. 7 (N.I.).	The Diseases of Fish Act (Northern Ireland) 1967.	Section 7(2).

Chapter	Short Title	Extent of Repeal
1968 c. 12 (N.I.).	The Poultry Improvement Act (Northern Ireland) 1968.	In section 13, the words from the beginning to " Parliament, and ".
1968 c. 14 (N.I.).	The Ulster College Act (Northern Ireland) 1968.	Section 10.
1968 c. 26 (N.I.).	The Welfare Foods Act (Northern Ireland) 1968.	Section 4.
1968 c. 30 (N.I.).	The Local Government and Roads Act (Northern Ireland) 1968.	Section 15.
1968 c. 33 (N.I.).	The New Towns (Amendment) Act (Northern Ireland) 1968.	Section 3.
1969 c. 14 (N.I.).	The Motor Vehicles and Refuse (Disposal) Act (Northern Ireland) 1969.	Section 13.
1969 c. 33 (N.I.).	The Marketing of Eggs (Amendment) Act (Northern Ireland) 1969.	Section 8.
1970 c. 1 (N.I.).	The Harbours Act (Northern Ireland) 1970.	Section 33(3).
1970 c. 2 (N.I.).	The Road Traffic Act (Northern Ireland) 1970.	Section 186(3).
1970 c. 20 (N.I.).	The Agriculture (Miscellaneous Provisions) Act (Northern Ireland) 1970.	Section 13.
1971 c. 3 (N.I.).	The Statistics of Trade (Amendment) Act (Northern Ireland) 1971.	Section 5(*b*).
1971 c. 5 (N.I.).	The Housing Executive Act (Northern Ireland) 1971.	Section 23.
1971 c. 15 (N.I.).	The Aerodromes Act (Northern Ireland) 1971.	Section 18.
1971 c. 17 (N.I.).	The Historic Monuments Act (Northern Ireland) 1971.	Section 26.
1971 c. 22 (N.I.).	The Industries Development Act (Northern Ireland) 1971.	Section 8(1).
1972 c. 4 (N.I.).	The Fish Industry Act (Northern Ireland) 1972.	Section 10.

Orders in Council

Number	Short Title	Extent of Repeal
S.I. 1972/1073 (N.I. 10).	The Superannuation (Northern Ireland) Order 1972.	Article 21.
S.I. 1972/1997 (N.I. 20).	The Development of Tourist Traffic (Northern Ireland) Order 1972.	Article 11.
S.I. 1972/1999 (N.I. 22).	The Local Government &c. (Northern Ireland) Order 1972.	Article 10(1).

Number	Short Title	Extent of Repeal
S.I. 1973/600 (N.I. 8).	The Births, Deaths and Marriages Registration (Northern Ireland) Order 1973.	Article 8.

PART VII

FINANCIAL

Chapter	Short Title	Extent of Repeal
5 & 6 Vict. c. 82.	The Stamp Duties (Ireland) Act 1842.	Section 13.
3 & 4 Geo. 5. c. 3.	The Provisional Collection of Taxes Act 1913.	The whole Act, so far as unrepealed.
13 & 14 Geo. 5. c. 14.	The Finance Act 1923.	In section 13(6), the words from " and the Commissioners " onwards.
1953 c. 23 (N.I.).	The Finance Act (Northern Ireland) 1953.	Section 4.
1954 c. 33 (N.I.).	The Interpretation Act (Northern Ireland) 1954.	Section 14(3).
1957 c. 9 (N.I.).	The Midgley (Pension) Act (Northern Ireland) 1957.	The whole Act.
1959 c. 23 (N.I.).	The Consolidated Fund (Miscellaneous Provisions) Act (Northern Ireland) 1959.	The whole Act, so far as unrepealed.
1963 c. 22 (N.I.).	The Finance Act (Northern Ireland) 1963.	Section 18. Section 20. In section 22(6), the words " (except section 18 thereof) ".
1967 c. 20 (N.I.).	The Finance Act (Northern Ireland) 1967.	In section 17, in subsection (1), the words from " the following " to the word " and " following paragraph (*d*) and subsection (2).
1968 c. 25 (N.I.).	The Financial Provisions Act (Northern Ireland) 1968.	Section 4.
1969 c. 18 (N.I.).	The Finance Act (Northern Ireland) 1969.	Section 14(4).
1971 c. 6 (N.I.).	The Financial Provisions Act (Northern Ireland) 1971.	Section 8. In Schedules 1 and 2, the entry relating to the Water Supplies and Sewerage Act (Northern Ireland) 1945.

Part VIII

Housing

Chapter	Short Title	Extent of Repeal
53 & 54 Vict. c. 70.	The Housing of the Working Classes Act 1890.	Sections 71 and 84. Section 86(1). In section 92, the words "district", "and 'local rate'", " respectively ", " areas " and " and rates ". In section 93, the definition of " superior court ". Section 98(3) and (10). In Schedule 1, the headings " District " (twice) and " Local Rates " (twice), the entries relating to those headings and the Note. Schedule 2.
62 & 63 Vict. c. 44.	The Small Dwellings Acquisition Act 1899.	Section 14(6) and (7).
1943 c. 9 (N.I.).	The Rent Restriction Law (Amendment) Act (Northern Ireland) 1943.	Section 1.
1948 c. 9 (N.I.).	The Housing Act (Northern Ireland) 1948.	Section 3.
1956 c. 10 (N.I.).	The Housing (Miscellaneous Provisions) and Rent Restriction Law (Amendment) Act (Northern Ireland) 1956.	In section 1, in subsection (1), the words from " Subject " to " submit to " and from " in such form " onwards and subsection (2). Section 22. In section 30(2)(*b*), the words from " and power " onwards. Section 43(1)(*c*) to (*e*) and (4)(*b*). In Schedule 4, paragraphs 2(*b*) and (*c*) and 4.
1962 c. 7 (N.I.).	The Administrative and Financial Provisions Act (Northern Ireland) 1962.	Section 16.
1963 c. 26 (N.I.).	The Housing Act (Northern Ireland) 1963.	Section 36(1)(*a*),(*b*) and (*d*). Section 37.
1964 c. 6 (N.I.).	The Administrative and Financial Provisions Act (Northern Ireland) 1964.	Section 9.
1965 c. 12 (N.I.).	The Administrative and Financial Provisions Act (Northern Ireland) 1965.	Section 9.
1967 c. 34 (N.I.).	The Housing Act (Northern Ireland) 1967.	Section 30(3).
1971 c. 16 (N.I.).	The Housing Act (Northern Ireland) 1971.	Section 51(3).

Part IX

Local Government

Chapter	Short Title	Extent of Repeal
6 & 7 Will. 4. c. 116.	The Grand Jury (Ireland) Act 1836.	Section 110. In section 174, the words from "the schedules" to "further; and that". Schedule (S).
3 & 4 Vict. c. 108.	The Municipal Corporations (Ireland) Act 1840.	In section 215, the definition of "parish".
35 & 36 Vict. c. 69.	The Local Government Board (Ireland) Act 1872.	Sections 3 and 4.
61 & 62 Vict. c. 37.	The Local Government (Ireland) Act 1898.	Section 4(2). Section 6. In section 27, in subsection (5), the words "urban county" and "rural" and in subsection (7), the words "or county". Section 30. In section 69(5), the words from "shall continue to be clerk of the Crown, and" to "amalgamated". Section 83(1) to (11) and (14). Section 92. Section 96(2) and (3). In section 101(2), the words "the Lord Lieutenant or". Section 101(3). Section 102(1) and (2). In section 108(1)(*c*), the words from "so far as" onwards. In section 109(1), the definitions of "town", "mayor", "judge of assize", "existing", "local financial year" and "Registration Acts".
63 & 64 Vict. c. 63.	The Local Government (Ireland) Act 1900.	Sections 4 and 6. The Schedule.
1949 c. 4 (N.I.).	The Finance (Miscellaneous Provisions) Act (Northern Ireland) 1949.	Sections 5, 6 and 7(2).
1957 c. 5 (N.I.).	The Revaluation (Amendment and Consequential Provisions) Act (Northern Ireland) 1957.	Section 4.
1958 c. 1 (N.I.).	The Local Government (Finance) Act (Northern Ireland) 1958.	The whole Act.
1971 c. 9 (N.I.).	The Local Government (Boundaries) Act (Northern Ireland) 1971.	Sections 2 and 3. Section 4(1) to (4). Schedules 2 and 3.

PART X
PROPERTY

Chapter	Short Title	Extent of Repeal
1 & 2 Will. 4. c. 32.	The Game Act 1831.	In section 2, the words from " and the words " onwards.
3 & 4 Will. 4. c. 74.	The Fines and Recoveries Act 1833.	In section 1, in the definition of " lands ", the words " (except copy of court roll) " and the words from " but when " to " undivided share thereof " and in the definition of " money subject to be invested in the purchase of lands ", the words " to lands held by copy of court roll, and also ". In section 58, the words " not held by copy of court roll ". In section 59, the words " not held by copy of court roll " and the words from " and every deed by which " onwards. Section 66. In section 67, the words from " shall apply to " to " court roll, but " and the word " other " where it last appears. In section 71, the words " except copy of court roll ", the words from " and shall, in the case of " to " copyhold, and were actually purchased and settled " and the words from " in regard to " onwards.
4 & 5 Will. 4. c. 92.	The Fines and Recoveries (Ireland) Act 1834.	In section 38, the words from " and if " onwards. Section 43. Sections 68 to 75 and 81.
7 Will. 4 & 1 Vict. c. 26.	The Wills Act 1837.	In section 1, in the definition of " real estate " the words " customary freehold, tenant right ". In section 3, the words " upon the heir at law or customary heir of him, or, if he became entitled by descent, of his ancestor, or ", the words from " to all real estate of the nature " to " made; and also " and the words "whether there shall or shall not be any special occupant thereof " and " customary freehold, tenant right ". Sections 4, 5 and 8.
1 & 2 Vict. c. 109.	The Tithe Rentcharge (Ireland) Act 1838.	Section 25.

Chapter	Short Title	Extent of Repeal
5 & 6 Vict. c. 94.	The Defence Act 1842.	Section 8. In section 10, the words " feoffees or ", " husbands ", " femes covert ", " surrender" and " enfranchisements, surrenders ". In sections 12, 13 and 14, the word " surrender " (wherever occurring) and in section 14 the word " surrendered ". In section 15, the words from " or, being femes covert " to " that purpose) " and the words " discovert at ". In section 18, the words " feoffees or ", " husbands ", " femes covert ", " surrender " and " surrenders ". In section 25 the words " enfranchisement of any copyhold or ".
8 & 9 Vict. c. 18.	The Lands Clauses Consolidation Act 1845.	In section 7, the words " tenants in tail or for life, married women seised in their own right or entitled to dower ", " or feoffees in trust ", " married women entitled to dower, or ", " sole and ", " wives " and " femes covert ". In section 8, the words from the beginning to " therewith, and ". In section 11, the words " with costs of suit, by action of debt ". In section 69, the words " married woman seised in her own right or entitled to dower ". In section 70, the words from " in the purchase of " to " real securities ". In sections 71 and 72, the words " coverture " and " husbands ". In section 77, the words from " the cashier " to " paid in; and ". In section 78, the words " by petition " and " in a summary way, as to such court shall seem fit ". In section 81, the words " estates tail, and all other ". In section 83, the words " upon petition in a summary way " and the words from

Chapter	Short Title	Extent of Repeal
8 & 9 Vict. c. 18.—*cont.*	The Lands Clauses Consolidation Act 1845.—*cont.*	" or the same " to " other cases of costs ". In section 86, the words from " and upon such deposit " onwards. In section 87, the words " by petition " and " in bank annuities or government securities ". In section 89, the words " with costs, by action ". In section 107, the words " by an order to be made upon petition ". Section 126. Section 143.
8 & 9 Vict. c. 106.	The Real Property Act 1845.	In section 3, the words " not being copyhold " (twice). In section 6, the words from " and every such disposition " onwards.
10 & 11 Vict. c. 32.	The Landed Property Improvement (Ireland) Act 1847.	In section 23, the words from " nor shall any proceeding " onwards. In section 49, the words " in a summary manner " and " in a summary way ". In section 51, the words " by petition in a summary way " and " or to the husband of such person being a feme covert ".
12 & 13 Vict. c. 105.	The Renewable Leasehold Conversion Act 1849.	In sections 17 and 22, the words " feme covert " and " husband ". In section 24, the word " husband " (twice). In section 35, the words " feoffee or " (twice), " or as a special occupant of an estate pour autre vie " (twice), " or quasi in tail " and the words from " and where a feme covert " to " feme sole ".
13 & 14 Vict. c. 28.	The Trustee Appointment Act 1850.	In section 1, the words " copyhold, or customary " wherever they occur. Section 2.
17 & 18 Vict. c. 112.	The Literary and Scientific Institutions Act 1854.	In section 1, the words " and in any manor or ", " or enfranchise " and " manor or ". In section 4, the words " or manor ". In section 5, the words " manor or ". In section 6, the words " justices of the peace ".

Chapter	Short Title	Extent of Repeal
17 & 18 Vict. c. 112.—*cont.*	The Literary and Scientific Institutions Act 1854.—*cont.*	" parochial ", " or enfranchise " and " justices " and the words from " Provided also " to " convey the same ". In section 7, the words " other than parochial trustees " and the words from " and the justices " onwards. In section 13, the words " [*add if necessary*, enfranchise] " and the words from "And no bargain " onwards. Sections 14 and 34.
18 & 19 Vict. c. 39.	The Leasing Powers Act for Religious Worship in Ireland 1855.	In section 3, paragraph (5) and in paragraph (10), the words " and feoffees ".
18 & 19 Vict. c. 117.	The Ordnance Board Transfer Act 1855.	In section 2, the words from " nevertheless " onwards. In section 4, the words " feoffees or ", " husbands " and " surrender ".
20 & 21 Vict. c. 57.	The Married Women's Reversionary Interests Act 1857.	The whole Act.
21 & 22 Vict. c. 72.	The Landed Estates Court (Ireland) Act 1858.	In section 1, in the definition of " owner " the words " or quasi fee tail ". In section 73, the words " or married woman ", " and husband ", the words from " but a married woman " to " feme sole " and the words from " and where the Court " onwards.
23 & 24 Vict. c. 112.	The Defence Act 1860.	In section 11, the words " feoffees or ", the words from " and all tenants " to " of any such lands " and the words " husbands " and " femes covert ".
28 & 29 Vict. c. 43.	The Married Women's Property (Ireland) Act 1865.	Section 1.
30 & 31 Vict. c. 44.	The Chancery (Ireland) Act 1867.	In section 2, the words " ' agent ' and " and " agent or ". In section 111, the words " married women ". Section 113. In section 117, the words from " and where " onwards. In section 123, the words " to such married woman and her husband " and the words " married woman " wherever else they occur.
32 & 33 Vict. c. 42.	The Irish Church Act 1869.	In section 22, the words " notwithstanding the statutes of mortmain ".

Chapter	Short Title	Extent of Repeal
33 & 34 Vict. c. 46.	The Landlord and Tenant (Ireland) Act 1870.	Section 60. In section 61, the words from " and where such Civil Bill " onwards.
39 & 40 Vict. c. 17.	The Partition Act 1876.	In section 6, the words " married woman " and " next friend ".
40 & 41 Vict. c. 18.	The Settled Estates Act 1877.	Sections 50 and 51. In section 52, the words " Subject to such examination as aforesaid ".
42 & 43 Vict. c. 50.	The Bills of Sale (Ireland) Act 1879.	In section 11, the words from " Provided, that " to "eighty " (in the second place where it occurs).
44 & 45 Vict. c. 41.	The Conveyancing Act 1881.	In section 2(xiii), the words " inclosure award ". In section 3(6), the words " inclosure awards " and " court rolls ". In section 65(2)(i), the words from " but, in case " onwards. Section 69(8).
44 & 45 Vict. c. 49.	The Land Law (Ireland) Act 1881.	Section 38(4).
44 & 45 Vict. c. 65.	The Leases for Schools (Ireland) Act 1881.	Section 2(*d*).
45 & 46 Vict. c. 38.	The Settled Land Act 1882.	Section 2(10)(vi). In section 3(ii), the words " or the freehold and inheritance of any copyhold or customary land, parcel of the manor " and " in every such case ". In section 20(1), the words " copyhold or customary or ". Section 61.
45 & 46 Vict. c. 39.	The Conveyancing Act 1882.	In section 1(4), the words " and in the Schedule thereto ". Section 7.
45 & 46 Vict. c. 75.	The Married Women's Property Act 1882.	Sections 6 to 10. Section 13. Sections 18 and 19. In section 24, the words from the beginning to " or administration ".
54 & 55 Vict. c. 48.	The Purchase of Land (Ireland) Act 1891.	Sections 8, 15, 16, 27, 28 and 33. In section 42, the definitions of " prescribed ", " Consolidated Fund ", " consolidated annuities ", " rateable value ", " population " and " Irish Church Temporalities Fund ".
56 & 57 Vict. c. 63.	The Married Women's Property Act 1893.	The whole Act.
7 Edw. 7. c. 18.	The Married Women's Property Act 1907.	Section 2. In section 4(4), the words " and 1893 ".

Chapter	Short Title	Extent of Repeal
1 & 2 Geo. 5. c. 37.	The Conveyancing Act 1911.	Section 7.
3 & 4 Geo. 5 c. 20.	The Bankruptcy (Scotland) Act 1913.	In section 97(3), the words " copyhold," (twice), " enrolment," (wherever it occurs) and "enrolled,".
1 Edw. 8 & 1 Geo. 6. c. 9 (N.I.).	The Law Reform (Miscellaneous Provisions) Act (Northern Ireland) 1937.	Section 12(1)(*a*).

In column 3 of this Part of this Schedule any reference to an enactment includes a reference to it as applied by or incorporated with any other enactment.

Part XI

Transport

Chapter	Short Title	Extent of Repeal
30 & 31 Vict. c. 50.	The Bridges (Ireland) Act 1867.	The whole Act, so far as unrepealed.
36 & 37 Vict. c. 76.	The Railway Regulation Act (Returns of Signal Arrangements, Workings, &c.) 1873.	The whole Act, so far as unrepealed.
38 & 39 Vict. c. 46.	The Bridges (Ireland) Act 1875.	The whole Act, so far as unrepealed.
11 & 12 Geo. 5. c. 55.	The Railways Act 1921.	The whole Act, so far as unrepealed.
1 Edw. 8 & 1 Geo. 6. c. 17 (N.I.).	The Finance (No. 2) Act (Northern Ireland) 1937.	The whole Act, so far as unrepealed.
1948 c. 28 (N.I.).	The Roads Act (Northern Ireland) 1948.	Section 15(5).
1954 c. 1 (N.I.).	The Inland Navigation Act (Northern Ireland) 1954.	Section 10(3) and (4). Sections 11 and 12. Section 13(1) and (3) to (6).
1955 c. 15 (N.I.).	The Lough Neagh and Lower Bann Drainage and Navigation Act (Northern Ireland) 1955.	Section 14(1) and (2).
1967 c. 37 (N.I.).	The Transport Act (Northern Ireland) 1967.	In section 23(1), the words " 24 and ". Sections 24, 30, 71 and 72. Section 75(3) and (4). Section 77.

Part XII

Miscellaneous

Acts

Chapter	Short Title	Extent of Repeal
41 & 42 Vict. c. 52.	The Public Health (Ireland) Act 1878.	Sections 34 and 66. In section 122, the words " or constabulary acting within the district of the defaulting authority " and " or constabulary " (in the second place where they occur). Section 262.
46 & 47 Vict. c. 14.	The Constabulary and Police (Ireland) Act 1883.	Section 2. In section 3, in subsection (1), the words from " who became " to " sixty-six, or ", paragraphs (*a*), (*b*) and (*d*) and the word " and " preceding paragraph (*d*), subsection (2)(*a*), in subsection (3), the words " and gratuities " and subsections (5) and (6). In section 4, subsections (2), (3) and (5) and in subsection (6), the words " or children ". In section 6, subsections (1) to (3) and in subsection (5) the words from " requiring " to " forfeiting or ". Sections 8, 10 and 11. In Schedule 2, paragraph (1), in paragraph (2), sub-paragraph (*d*), the word " and " preceding it, and the proviso, in paragraphs (3) and (4), sub-paragraph (*c*), the word "and" preceding it, and the proviso, in paragraph (5), the words from " and if " onwards, paragraph (6), in paragraph (9), the words " and the allowances to his children ", sub-paragraph (*b*) and the word " and " preceding it, paragraphs (10), (11) and (13) and in paragraph (14), the words " gratuity, or allowance ", in sub-paragraph (*a*), the words " or gratuity ", in sub-paragraph (*b*), the words " or gratuity " and " and an allowance or gratuity to a child ", sub-paragraph (*d*) and the words " and allowances ".

Chapter	Short Title	Extent of Repeal
53 & 54 Vict. c. 59.	The Public Health Acts Amendment Act 1890.	In section 1, the words " Part II.—Telegraph &c. wires " and " Part V.—Stock ". In section 2, the words " Two " and " Four, and Five ". Section 3(5)(*b*). In section 11(3), the words " surveyor ", " lands " and " premises ". In section 12(7), the words " eighty-four, one hundred and sixteen, one hundred and seventeen ", " one hundred and fifty-eight ", " two hundred and twenty-nine, two hundred and thirty ", " and three hundred and six ", " ninety-five, one hundred and thirty-two, one hundred and thirty-three ", " forty-two ", " two hundred and thirty-two, two hundred and thirty-three " and the words from " and two hundred and seventy-two " onwards. Section 12(11).
7 Edw. 7. c. 53.	The Public Health Acts Amendment Act 1907.	In section 1, the words from " IV " to " lodging-houses " and the words " IX.—Sky signs ". In section 3(4) the words " and Part IX (Sky Signs) ". In section 13, the definition of " infectious disease ". Section 14(2) and (5). In the Schedule, the entries relating to sections 77, 78, 86, 88, 124, 126, 132, 157, 158, 175, 176 and 186 of the Public Health Act 1875 and the corresponding sections of the Public Health (Ireland) Act 1878.
13 & 14 Geo. 5. c. 6 (N.I.).	The Companies (Reconstitution of Records) Act (Northern Ireland) 1923.	The whole Act.
18 & 19 Geo. 5. c. 5 (N.I.).	The Legitimacy Act (Northern Ireland) 1928.	Section 1(4).
1 Edw. 8 & 1 Geo. 6. c. 9 (N.I.).	The Law Reform (Miscellaneous Provisions) Act (Northern Ireland) 1937.	In section 19(1), the definitions of " Personal representatives " and " Will ".
1950 c. 7 (N.I.).	The Probation Act (Northern Ireland) 1950.	Section 12(3). In section 17(1), the definitions of " quarter sessions " and " statutory period ". Section 18.

Chapter	Short Title	Extent of Repeal
1950 c. 11 (N.I.).	The Civil Defence Act (Northern Ireland) 1950.	In section 9(1), in the definition of " police forces " the words " and the Ulster Special Constabulary ".
1953 c. 3 (N.I.).	The Summary Jurisdiction Act (Northern Ireland) 1953.	Section 49(1).
1955 c. 24 (N.I.).	The Administration of Estates Act (Northern Ireland) 1955.	Section 41(2). In Schedule 2, the amendments of the Real Property Limitation Act 1833, section 72 of the Probates and Letters of Administration (Ireland) Act 1857 and the County Officers and Courts (Ireland) Act 1877.
1960 c. 22 (N.I.).	The Companies Act (Northern Ireland) 1960.	Section 380(1)(*a*).
1961 c. 13 (N.I.).	The Museum Act (Northern Ireland) 1961.	Section 9.
1962 c. 12 (N.I.).	The Public Health and Local Government (Miscellaneous Provisions) Act (Northern Ireland) 1962.	Sections 30 and 31.
1963 c. 16 (N.I.).	The Aid to Aircraft Industry Act (Northern Ireland) 1963.	In section 1, the definition of " the ' Belfast ' Air Freighter project ".
1964 c. 28 (N.I.).	The Petroleum (Production) Act (Northern Ireland) 1964.	In section 12, the words " the year 1965 and in " and " succeeding ".
1964 c. 29 (N.I.).	The Lands Tribunal and Compensation Act (Northern Ireland) 1964.	In Schedule 1, in Part I, the amendments of the Transport Act (Northern Ireland) 1948.
1966 c. 28 (N.I.).	The Supplementary Benefits &c. Act (Northern Ireland) 1966.	Sections 16, 22 and 39. Section 40(2). In Schedule 6, paragraphs 1 and 2.
1967 c. 5 (N.I.).	The Administration of Estates (Small Payments) Act (Northern Ireland) 1967.	In Schedule 3, the amendments of the Building Societies Act 1874, the Industrial and Provident Societies Act 1893 and the Friendly Societies Act 1896.
1967 c. 31 (N.I.).	The Building Societies Act (Northern Ireland) 1967.	In Schedule 8, paragraph 2.
1967 c. 33 (N.I.).	The Expiring Laws Continuance Act (Northern Ireland) 1967.	The whole Act.
1968 c. 23 (N.I.).	The Expiring Laws Continuance Act (Northern Ireland) 1968.	The whole Act.
1968 c. 34 (N.I.).	The Children and Young Persons Act (Northern Ireland) 1968.	In Schedule 7, paragraphs 8, 9 and 25.

Chapter	Short Title	Extent of Repeal
1969 c. 6 (N.I.).	The Mines Act (Northern Ireland) 1969.	Section 70(2) and (4)(*a*). Sections 147 and 153. In section 164(1), the words from " made before " to " operation at, the commencement of this Act ". In section 168(1), the words " 147 ".
1969 c. 16 (N.I.).	The Theft Act (Northern Ireland) 1969.	In Schedule 2, the amendments of the Road Traffic Act (Northern Ireland) 1955 and the Road Traffic Act (Northern Ireland) 1967.
1969 c. 28 (N.I.).	The Age of Majority Act (Northern Ireland) 1969.	In Schedule 1, in Part I, the entry relating to the Friendly Societies Act 1896.
1969 c. 35 (N.I.).	The Mineral Development Act (Northern Ireland) 1969.	In Schedule 3, paragraph 3.
1970 c. 9 (N.I.).	The Police Act (Northern Ireland) 1970.	In Schedule 3, the amendment of the Jury Laws Amendment Act (Northern Ireland) 1926.
1970 c. 11 (N.I.).	The Nurses and Midwives Act (Northern Ireland) 1970.	Section 2(2). Section 53.
1971 c. 8 (N.I.).	The Family Income Supplements Act (Northern Ireland) 1971.	Section 14. Section 15(2).
1972 c. 5 (N.I.).	The Water Act (Northern Ireland) 1972.	Sections 27 and 29.

Orders in Council

Number	Short Title	Extent of Repeal
S.I. 1972/731 (N.I. 4).	The Northern Ireland Finance Corporation (Northern Ireland) Order 1972.	Article 2(3). In Article 10(1), sub-paragraph (*a*) and the words from " in the " (where they first occur) to " paragraph (*b*) ", the words " mentioned in that paragraph " and in sub-paragraph (*b*), the word " subsequent ". Article 13.

Number	Short Title	Extent of Repeal
S.I. 1972/1998 (N.I. 21).	The Local Government (Postponement of Elections and Reorganisation) (Northern Ireland) Order 1972.	Article 5(3). In Schedule 1, in Part I, the entry relating to the Water Act (Northern Ireland) 1972.
S.I. 1973/1228 (N.I. 16).	The Enterprise Ulster (Northern Ireland) Order 1973.	Article 2(3). In Article 10(1), sub-paragraph (*a*) and the words from " in the " (where they first occur) to " paragraph (*b*) ", the words " mentioned in that paragraph " and in sub-paragraph (*b*), the word " subsequent ". Article 13.

Damages (Scotland) Act 1976

1976 CHAPTER 13

An Act to amend the law of Scotland relating to the damages recoverable in respect of deaths caused by personal injuries; to define the rights to damages in respect of personal injuries and death which are transmitted to an executor; to abolish rights to assythment; to make provision relating to the damages due to a pursuer for patrimonial loss caused by personal injuries whereby his expectation of life is diminished; and for purposes connected with the matters aforesaid. [13th April 1976]

BE IT ENACTED by the Queen's most Excellent Majesty, by and with the advice and consent of the Lords Spiritual and Temporal, and Commons, in this present Parliament assembled, and by the authority of the same, as follows:—

Rights of relatives of a deceased person.

1.—(1) Where a person dies in consequence of personal injuries sustained by him as a result of an act or omission of another person, being an act or omission giving rise to liability to pay damages to the injured person or his executor, then, subject to the following provisions of this Act, the person liable to pay those damages (in this section referred to as " the responsible person ") shall also be liable to pay damages in accordance with this section to any relative of the deceased, being a relative within the meaning of Schedule 1 to this Act.

(2) No liability shall arise under this section if the liability to the deceased or his executor in respect of the act or omission has been excluded or discharged (whether by antecedent agreement or otherwise) by the deceased before his death, or is excluded by virtue of any enactment.

(3) The damages which the responsible person shall be liable to pay to a relative of a deceased under this section shall (subject to the provisions of this Act) be such as will compensate the relative for any loss of support suffered by him since the date of the deceased's death or likely to be suffered by him as a result of the act or omission in question, together with any reasonable expense incurred by him in connection with the deceased's funeral.

(4) If the relative is a member of the deceased's immediate family (within the meaning of section 10(2) of this Act) there shall be awarded, without prejudice to any claim under subsection (3) above, such sum of damages, if any, as the court thinks just by way of compensation for the loss of such non-patrimonial benefit as the relative might have been expected to derive from the deceased's society and guidance if he had not died; and a sum of damages such as is mentioned in this subsection shall be known as a " loss of society award ".

(5) In assessing for the purposes of this section the amount of any loss of support suffered by a relative of a deceased no account shall be taken of—

(*a*) any patrimonial gain or advantage which has accrued or will or may accrue to the relative from the deceased or from any other person by way of succession or settlement;

(*b*) any insurance money, benefit, pension or gratuity which has been, or will be or may be, paid as a result of the deceased's death;

and in this subsection—

" benefit " means benefit under the Social Security Act 1975 or the Social Security (Northern Ireland) Act 1975, and any payment by a friendly society or trade union for the relief or maintenance of a member's dependants; **1975 c. 14. 1975 c. 15.**

" insurance money " includes a return of premiums; and

" pension " includes a return of contributions and any payment of a lump sum in respect of a person's employment.

(6) In order to establish loss of support for the purposes of this section it shall not be essential for a claimant to show that the deceased was, or might have become, subject to a duty in law to provide or contribute to the support of the claimant; but if any such fact is established it may be taken into account in determining whether, and if so to what extent, the deceased, if he had not died, would have been likely to provide or contribute to such support.

(7) Except as provided in this section no person shall be entitled by reason of relationship to damages (including damages by way of solatium) in respect of the death of another person.

Rights transmitted to executor in respect of deceased person's injuries.

2.—(1) Subject to subsection (3) below there shall be transmitted to the executor of a deceased person the like rights to damages in respect of personal injuries sustained by the deceased as were vested in him immediately before his death ; and for the purpose of enforcing any such right the executor shall be entitled to bring an action or, if an action for that purpose had been brought by the deceased before his death and had not been concluded before then, to be sisted as pursuer in that action.

(2) For the purpose of subsection (1) above an action shall not be taken to be concluded while any appeal is competent or before any appeal timeously taken has been disposed of.

(3) There shall not be transmitted to the executor of a deceased person any right to damages in respect of personal injuries sustained by the deceased and vested in the deceased as aforesaid, being a right to damages—

(*a*) by way of solatium ;

(*b*) by way of compensation for patrimonial loss attributable to any period after the deceased's death,

and accordingly the executor shall not be entitled to bring an action, or to be sisted as pursuer in any action brought by the deceased before his death, for the purpose of enforcing any such right.

Certain rights arising on death of another not transmissible.

3. There shall not be transmitted to the executor of a deceased person any right which has accrued to the deceased before his death, being a right to—

(*a*) damages by way of solatium in respect of the death of any other person, under the law in force before the commencement of this Act ;

(*b*) a loss of society award,

and accordingly the executor shall not be entitled to bring an action, or to be sisted as pursuer in any action brought by the deceased before his death, for the purpose of enforcing any such right.

Executor's claim not to be excluded by relatives' claim: and *vice versa.*

4. A claim by the executor of a deceased person for damages under section 2 of this Act is not excluded by the making of a claim by a relative of the deceased for damages under section 1 of this Act; nor is a claim by a relative of a deceased person for damages under the said section 1 excluded by the making of a claim by the deceased's executor for damages under the said section 2; but this section is without prejudice to section 5 of this Act.

Provisions for avoidance of multiplicity of actions.

5.—(1) This section applies to any action in which, following the death of any person from personal injuries, damages are claimed—

(*a*) by the executor of the deceased, in respect of the relevant injuries;

(*b*) in respect of the death of the deceased, by any relative of his;

and in this section, in relation to any such action,—

(i) " the relevant injuries " means the injuries from which the deceased died, and

(ii) " connected person " means a person, not being a party to the action, who (apart from this section) would have a title, whether as the executor of the deceased or as a relative of his, to sue the same defender in another such action based on the relevant injuries, or, as the case may be, on the death.

(2) Where an action to which this section applies has been raised any connected person shall be entitled to be sisted as a pursuer in that action, and except as provided in subsection (5) below every connected person shall be barred from suing the same defender in another such action (whether in the same or any other court) based on the relevant injuries, or, as the case may be, on the death.

(3) A connected person shall not be entitled to be sisted as a pursuer in accordance with subsection (2) above unless he has served notice on all other parties to the action of his application so to be sisted.

(4) Nothing in subsection (2) above shall prevent a court from exercising any power it may have apart from this section to sist any person as a party to an action.

(5) Where an action to which this section applies has been raised nothing in subsection (2) above shall prevent a connected person from suing the same defender in another such action if in that other action he satisfies the court that by reason of lack of knowledge that the first-mentioned action had been raised or for any other reasonable cause he was unable to make an application under the said subsection in that action.

(6) Where an action to which this section applies has been raised it shall be the duty of the pursuer to serve notice of the action on every connected person of whose existence and connection with the action the pursuer is aware or could with reasonable diligence have become aware; and if in any action it appears to the court that the pursuer has failed to implement the duty imposed on him by this subsection the court may, if it thinks fit, dismiss the action.

(7) A notice under subsection (6) above shall contain a statement of the effect of subsection (2) above.

Limitation of total amount of liability.

6.—(1) Where in any action to which section 5 of this Act applies, so far as directed against any defender, it is shown that by antecedent agreement, compromise or otherwise, the liability arising in relation to that defender from the personal injuries in question had, before the deceased's death, been limited to damages of a specified or ascertainable amount, or where that liability is so limited by virtue of any enactment, nothing in this Act shall make the defender liable to pay damages exceeding that amount; and accordingly where in such an action there are two or more pursuers any damages to which they would respectively be entitled under this Act apart from the said limitation shall, if necessary, be reduced *pro rata*.

(2) Where two or more such actions are conjoined, the conjoined actions shall be treated for the purposes of this section as if they were a single action.

Amendment of references in other Acts.

7. In any Act passed before this Act, unless the context otherwise requires, any reference to solatium in respect of the death of any person (however expressed) shall be construed as a reference to a loss of society award within the meaning of section 1 of this Act; and any reference to a dependant of a deceased person, in relation to an action claiming damages in respect of the deceased person's death, shall be construed as including a reference to a relative of the deceased person within the meaning of this Act.

Abolition of right of assythment.

8. After the commencement of this Act no person shall in any circumstances have a right to assythment, and accordingly any action claiming that remedy shall (to the extent that it does so) be incompetent.

Damages due to injured person for patrimonial loss caused by personal injuries whereby expectation of life is diminished.

9.—(1) This section applies to any action for damages in respect of personal injuries sustained by the pursuer where his expected date of death is earlier than it would have been if he had not sustained the injuries.

(2) In assessing, in any action to which this section applies, the amount of any patrimonial loss in respect of the period after the date of decree—

(*a*) it shall be assumed that the pursuer will live until the date when he would have been expected to die if he had not sustained the injuries (hereinafter referred to as the " notional date of death ");

(*b*) the court may have regard to any amount, whether or not it is an amount related to earnings by the pursuer's own labour or other gainful activity, which in its opinion the pursuer, if he had not sustained the injuries in question, would have received in the period up to his notional date of death by way of benefits in money or money's worth, being benefits derived from sources other than the pursuer's own estate;

(*c*) the court shall have regard to any diminution of any such amount as aforesaid by virtue of expenses which in the opinion of the court the pursuer, if he had not sustained the injuries in question, would reasonably have incurred in the said period by way of living expenses.

Interpretation.

10.—(1) In this Act, unless the context otherwise requires—

"loss of society award" has the meaning assigned to it by section 1(4) of this Act;

"personal injuries" includes any disease or any impairment of a person's physical or mental condition;

"relative", in relation to a deceased person, has the meaning assigned to it by Schedule 1 to this Act.

(2) References in this Act to a member of a deceased person's immediate family are references to any relative of his who falls within subparagraph (*a*), (*b*) or (*c*) of paragraph 1 of Schedule 1 to this Act.

(3) References in this Act to any other Act are references to that Act as amended, extended or applied by any other enactment, including this Act.

Repeals.

11. The enactments specified in Schedule 2 to this Act are hereby repealed to the extent specified in relation thereto in the third column of that Schedule.

Citation, application to Crown, commencement and extent.

12.—(1) This Act may be cited as the Damages (Scotland) Act 1976.

(2) This Act binds the Crown.

(3) This Act shall come into operation on the expiration of one month beginning with the day on which it is passed.

(4) Nothing in this Act affects any proceedings commenced before this Act comes into operation.

(5) This Act extends to Scotland only.

SCHEDULES

Section 1.

SCHEDULE 1

Definition of "Relative"

1. In this Act "relative" in relation to a deceased person includes—

(*a*) any person who immediately before the deceased's death was the spouse of the deceased;

(*b*) any person who was a parent or child of the deceased;

(*c*) any person not falling within paragraph (*b*) above who was accepted by the deceased as a child of his family;

(*d*) any person who was an ascendant or descendant (other than a parent or child) of the deceased;

(*e*) any person who was, or was the issue of, a brother, sister, uncle or aunt of the deceased; and

(*f*) any person who, having been a spouse of the deceased, had ceased to be so by virtue of a divorce;

but does not include any other person.

2. In deducing any relationship for the purposes of the foregoing paragraph—

(*a*) any relationship by affinity shall be treated as a relationship by consanguinity; any relationship of the half blood shall be treated as a relationship of the whole blood; and the step-child of any person shall be treated as his child; and

(*b*) an illegitimate person shall be treated as the legitimate child of his mother and reputed father.

Section 11.

SCHEDULE 2

Repeals

Chapter	Short Title	Extent of Repeal
3 & 4 Geo. 6. c. 42.	Law Reform (Miscellaneous Provisions) (Scotland) Act 1940.	Section 2.
11 & 12 Geo. 6. c. 41.	Law Reform (Personal Injuries) Act 1948.	Section 2(5A).
1 & 2 Eliz. 2. c. 7.	Law Reform (Personal Injuries) (Amendment) Act 1953.	The whole Act.
10 & 11 Eliz. 2. c. 42.	Law Reform (Damages and Solatium) (Scotland) Act 1962.	The whole Act.
1972 c. 33.	Carriage by Railway Act 1972.	Section 3(2).

Fatal Accidents and Sudden Deaths Inquiry (Scotland) Act 1976

1976 CHAPTER 14

An Act to make provision for Scotland for the holding of public inquiries in respect of fatal accidents, deaths of persons in legal custody, sudden, suspicious and unexplained deaths and deaths occurring in circumstances giving rise to serious public concern.

[13th April 1976]

BE IT ENACTED by the Queen's most Excellent Majesty, by and with the advice and consent of the Lords Spiritual and Temporal, and Commons, in this present Parliament assembled, and by the authority of the same, as follows:—

Investigation of death and application for public inquiry.

1.—(1) Subject to the provisions of any enactment specified in Schedule I to this Act and subsection (2) below, where—

(*a*) in the case of a death to which this paragraph applies—

(i) it appears that the death has resulted from an accident occurring in Scotland while the person who has died, being an employee, was in the course of his employment or, being an employer or self-employed person, was engaged in his occupation as such ; or

(ii) the person who has died was, at the time of his death, in legal custody ; or (*b*) it appears to the Lord Advocate to be expedient in the public interest in the case of a death to which this paragraph applies that an inquiry under this Act should be held into the circumstances of the death on the ground that it was sudden, suspicious or unexplained, or has occurred in circumstances such as to give rise to serious public concern,

the procurator fiscal for the district with which the circumstances of the death appear to be most closely connected shall investigate those circumstances and apply to the sheriff for the holding of an inquiry under this Act into those circumstances.

(2) Paragraph (*a*) of subsection (1) above applies to a death occurring in Scotland after the commencement of this Act (other than such a death in a case where criminal proceedings have been concluded against any person in respect of the death or any accident from which the death resulted, and the Lord Advocate is satisfied that the circumstances of the death have been sufficiently established in the course of such proceedings), and paragraph (*b*) of that subsection applies to a death occurring there at any time after the date 3 years before such commencement.

(3) An application under subsection (1) above—

(*a*) shall be made to the sheriff with whose sheriffdom the circumstances of the death appear to be most closely connected ;

(*b*) shall narrate briefly the circumstances of the death so far as known to the procurator fiscal ;

(*c*) may, if it appears that more deaths than one have occurred as a result of the same accident or in the same or similar circumstances, relate to both or all such deaths.

(4) For the purposes of subsection (1)(*a*) (ii) above, a person is in legal custody if—

(*a*) he is detained in, or is subject to detention in, a prison, remand centre, detention centre, borstal institution, or young offenders institution, all within the meaning of
1952 c. 61. the Prisons (Scotland) Act 1952 ; or

(*b*) he is detained in a police station, police cell, or other similar place ; or

(*c*) he is being taken—

(i) to any of the places specified in paragraphs (*a*) and (*b*) of this subsection to be detained therein ; or

(ii) from any such place in which immediately before such taking he was detained.

2.—(1) The procurator fiscal may, for the purpose of carrying out his investigation under section 1(1) of this Act, cite witnesses for precognition by him, and this section shall be sufficient warrant for such citation. **Citation of witnesses for precognition.**

(2) If any witness cited under subsection (1) above—

(*a*) fails without reasonable excuse and after receiving reasonable notice to attend for precognition by the procurator fiscal at the time and place mentioned in the citation served on him ; or

(*b*) refuses when so cited to give information within his knowledge regarding any matter relevant to the investigation in relation to which such precognition is taken,

the procurator fiscal may apply to the sheriff for an order requiring the witness to attend for such precognition or to give such information at a time and place specified in the order ; and the sheriff shall, if he considers it expedient to do so, make such an order.

(3) If the witness fails to comply with the order of the sheriff under subsection (2) above, he shall be liable to be summarily punished forthwith by a fine not exceeding £25 or by imprisonment for any period not exceeding 20 days.

3.—(1) On an application under section 1 of this Act being made to him, the sheriff shall make an order— **Holding of public inquiry.**

(*a*) fixing a time and place for the holding by him of an inquiry under this Act (hereafter in this Act referred to as " the inquiry "), which shall be as soon thereafter as is reasonably practicable in such courthouse or other premises as appear to him to be appropriate, having regard to the apparent circumstances of the death ; and

(*b*) granting warrant to cite witnesses and havers to attend at the inquiry at the instance of the procurator fiscal or of any person who may be entitled by virtue of this Act to appear at the inquiry.

(2) On the making of an order under subsection (1) above, the procurator fiscal shall—

(*a*) intimate the holding of the inquiry and the time and place fixed for it to the wife or husband or the nearest known relative and, in a case where the inquiry is being held in respect of such a death as is referred to in section 1(1)(*a*)(i) of this Act, to the employer, if any, of the person whose death is the subject of the inquiry, and to such other person or class of persons as may be prescribed in rules made under section 7(1)(*g*) of this Act ; and (*b*) give public notice of the holding of the inquiry and of the time and place fixed for it.

(3) Where an application under section 1 of this Act relates to more than one death, the order made under subsection (1) above shall so relate; and in this Act references to a death shall include references to both or all deaths or to each death as the case may require, and in subsection (2)(*a*) above the reference to the person whose death is the subject of the inquiry shall include a reference to each person whose death is the subject of the inquiry.

Conduct of public inquiry.

4.—(1) At the inquiry, it shall be the duty of the procurator fiscal to adduce evidence with regard to the circumstances of the death which is the subject of the inquiry.

(2) The wife or husband, or the nearest known relative, and, in a case where the inquiry is being held in respect of such a death as is referred to in section 1(1)(*a*)(i) of this Act, the employer, if any, of the person whose death is the subject of the inquiry, an inspector appointed under section 19 of the Health and Safety at Work etc. Act 1974 and any other person who the sheriff is satisfied has an interest in the inquiry may appear and adduce evidence at the inquiry.

1974 c. 37.

(3) Subject to subsection (4) below, the inquiry shall be open to the public.

(4) Where a person under the age of 17 is in any way involved in the inquiry, the sheriff may, at his own instance or on an application made to him by any party to the inquiry, make an order providing that—

(*a*) no report of the inquiry which is made in a newspaper or other publication or a sound or television broadcast shall reveal the name, address or school, or include any particulars calculated to lead to the identification of that person;

(*b*) no picture relating to the inquiry which is or includes a picture of that person shall be published in any newspaper or other publication or televised broadcast.

(5) Any person who contravenes an order made under subsection (4) above shall be guilty of an offence and shall be liable on summary conviction to a fine not exceeding £250 in respect of each offence.

(6) The sheriff may, either at his own instance or at the request of the procurator fiscal or of any party who may be entitled by virtue of this Act to appear at the inquiry, summon any person having special knowledge and being willing to do so, to act as an assessor at the inquiry.

(7) Subject to the provisions of this Act and any rules made under section 7 of this Act, the rules of evidence, the procedure and the powers of the sheriff to deal with contempt of court and to enforce the attendance of witnesses at the inquiry shall be as nearly as possible those applicable in an ordinary civil cause brought before the sheriff sitting alone.

Criminal proceedings and compellability of witnesses.

5.—(1) The examination of a witness or haver at the inquiry shall not be a bar to criminal proceedings being taken against him.

(2) No witness at the inquiry shall be compellable to answer any question tending to show that he is guilty of any crime or offence.

Sheriff's determination etc.

6.—(1) At the conclusion of the evidence and any submissions thereon, or as soon as possible thereafter, the sheriff shall make a determination setting out the following circumstances of the death so far as they have been established to his satisfaction—

(*a*) where and when the death and any accident resulting in the death took place;

(*b*) the cause or causes of such death and any accident resulting in the death;

(*c*) the reasonable precautions, if any, whereby the death and any accident resulting in the death might have been avoided;

(*d*) the defects, if any, in any system of working which contributed to the death or any accident resulting in the death; and

(*e*) any other facts which are relevant to the circumstances of the death.

(2) The sheriff shall be entitled to be satisfied that any circumstances referred to in subsection (1) above have been established by evidence, notwithstanding that that evidence is not corroborated.

(3) The determination of the sheriff shall not be admissible in evidence or be founded on in any judicial proceedings, of whatever nature, arising out of the death or out of any accident from which the death resulted.

(4) On the conclusion of the inquiry—

(*a*) the sheriff clerk shall send to the Lord Advocate a copy of the determination of the sheriff and, on a request being made to him, send to any Minister or Government Department or to the Health and Safety Commission, a copy of

(i) the application made under section 1 of this Act;

(ii) the transcript of the evidence;

(iii) any report or documentary production used in the inquiry;

(iv) the determination of the sheriff, and

(*b*) the procurator fiscal shall send to the Registrar General of Births, Deaths and Marriages for Scotland the name and last known address of the person who has died and the date, place and cause of his death.

(5) Upon payment of such fee as may be prescribed in rules made under paragraph (i) of section 7(1) of this Act, any person—

(*a*) may obtain a copy of the determination of the sheriff;

(*b*) who has an interest in the inquiry may, within such period as may be prescribed in rules made under paragraph (*j*) of the said section 7(1), obtain a copy of the transcript of the evidence,

from the sheriff clerk.

Rules.

7.—(1) The Lord Advocate may, by rules, provide in relation to inquiries under this Act—

(*a*) as to the form of any document to be used in or for the purposes of such inquiries;

(*b*) for the representation, on such conditions as may be specified in the rules, of any person who is entitled by virtue of this Act to appear at the inquiry;

(*c*) for the authorisation by the sheriff of the taking and holding in safe custody of anything which it may be considered necessary to produce;

(*d*) for the inspection by the sheriff or any person authorised by him of any land, premises, article, or other thing;

(*e*) that written statements and reports may, on such conditions as may be specified in the rules, be admissible in lieu of parole evidence;

(*f*) as to the duties, remuneration and other conditions of appointment of any assessor summoned under section 4 of this Act, and for keeping of lists of persons willing to act as such;

(*g*) as to intimation of the holding of the inquiry;

(*h*) as to the payment of fees to solicitors and expenses to witnesses and havers;

(*i*) as to the payment of a fee by a person obtaining a copy of the determination of the sheriff or a copy of the transcript of the evidence;

(*j*) as to the period within which a person entitled may obtain a copy of the transcript of the evidence at the inquiry;

(*k*) as to such other matters relating to procedure as the Lord Advocate thinks appropriate.

(2) The power to make rules conferred by any provision of this Act shall be exercisable by statutory instrument.

(3) Rules made by the Lord Advocate under this Act may contain such incidental, consequential and supplemental provisions as appear to him to be necessary or proper for bringing the rules into operation and giving full effect thereto.

Minor and consequential amendments and repeals.

8.—(1) The enactments mentioned in Schedule 1 to this Act shall have effect subject to the amendments respectively specified in that Schedule, being minor amendments and amendments consequential on the provisions of this Act.

(2) The enactments set out in Schedule 2 to this Act are hereby repealed to the extent specified in column 3 of that Schedule.

Application to continental shelf.

9. For the purposes of this Act a death or any accident from which death has resulted which has occurred—

(*a*) in connection with the exploration of the sea bed or subsoil or the exploitation of their natural resources; and

(*b*) in that area, or any part of that area, in respect of which it is provided by Order in Council under section 3(2) of the Continental Shelf Act 1964 that questions arising out of acts or omissions taking place therein shall be determined in accordance with the law in force in Scotland, 1964 c. 29.

shall be taken to have occurred in Scotland.

Interpretation, transitional, citation, commencement and extent.

10.—(1) Any reference in this Act to any other enactment shall be construed as a reference to that enactment as amended by or under any other enactment including this Act.

(2) Any inquiry instituted under the Fatal Accidents Inquiry (Scotland) Act 1895 or the Fatal Accidents and Sudden Deaths Inquiry (Scotland) Act 1906 or section 25(2) of the Prisons (Scotland) Act 1952 and continuing at the commencement of this Act may be continued under that Act as if this Act had not been passed. 1895 c. 36. 1906 c. 35. 1952 c. 61.

(3) Where, before the date appointed under subsection (5) below, a death has occurred in respect of which an inquiry is required to be held under the said Act of 1895 or the said section

25(2) but that inquiry has not been instituted before that appointed date, an inquiry shall take place, but shall be held under this Act as if the death was one in respect of which application is required to be made under section 1(1) of this Act.

(4) This Act may be cited as the Fatal Accidents and Sudden Deaths Inquiry (Scotland) Act 1976.

(5) This Act, except this section, shall come into force on such date as the Lord Advocate may by order made by statutory instrument appoint.

(6) This Act, other than subsections (4) and (5) of section 4 and section 9 of this Act, extends to Scotland only.

SCHEDULES

SCHEDULE 1

Section 8(1).

Minor and Consequential Amendments

The Gas Act 1965

1965 c. 36

1. In section 17(4) (accidents), for the words " Inquiry (Scotland) Act 1895 " there shall be substituted the words " and Sudden Deaths Inquiry (Scotland) Act 1976.".

The Merchant Shipping Act 1970

1970 c. 36.

2. In section 61(4) (inquiries into death of crew members and others), for the words from " Inquiry (Scotland) Act 1895 " to the end there shall be substituted the words " and Sudden Deaths Inquiry (Scotland) Act 1976.".

The Mineral Workings (Offshore Installations) Act 1971

1971 c. 61.

3. At the end of section 6 (safety regulations), there shall be added the following subsection—

> " (5) If an inquiry is held in pursuance of regulations under this Act into an accident which causes the death of any person, no inquiry with regard to that death shall, unless the Lord Advocate otherwise directs, be held in pursuance of the Fatal Accidents and Sudden Deaths Inquiry (Scotland) Act 1976.".

The Health and Safety at Work Etc. Act 1974

1974 c. 37.

4. In section 14(7) (which provides that no inquiry under the Fatal Accidents Inquiry (Scotland) Act 1895 is to be held into a death which is the subject of an inquiry under section 14(2)(*b*) of the said Act of 1974 unless the Lord Advocate otherwise directs), for the words " Inquiry (Scotland) Act 1895 " there shall be substituted the words " and Sudden Deaths Inquiry (Scotland) Act 1976 ".

The Petroleum and Submarine Pipe-lines Act 1975

1975 c. 74.

5. In section 27(5) (inspectors), for the words " Inquiry (Scotland) Act 1895 " there shall be substituted the words " and Sudden Deaths Inquiry (Scotland) Act 1976 ".

SCHEDULE 2

Section 8(2).

Repeals

Chapter	Short Title	Extent of Repeal
58 & 59 Vict. c. 36.	The Fatal Accidents Inquiry (Scotland) Act 1895.	The whole Act.
6 Edw. 7 c. 35.	The Fatal Accidents and Sudden Deaths Inquiry (Scotland) Act 1906.	The whole Act.
1933 c. 41.	The Administration of Justice (Scotland) Act 1933.	Section 38.
15 & 16 Geo. 6 & 1 Eliz. 2. c. 61.	The Prisons (Scotland) Act 1952.	Section 25(2).

Rating (Caravan Sites) Act 1976

1976 CHAPTER 15

An Act to allow for the valuation and rating as a single unit in certain cases of caravan sites or portions of caravan sites inclusive of parts separately occupied by caravanners and of their caravans; and for purposes connected therewith. [13th April 1976]

BE IT ENACTED by the Queen's most Excellent Majesty, by and with the advice and consent of the Lords Spiritual and Temporal, and Commons, in this present Parliament assembled, and by the authority of the same, as follows:—

Provisions for England and Wales

Rating of caravan sites in England and Wales.

1967 c. 9.

1.—(1) Where in a caravan site in England or Wales having an area of not less than 400 square yards pitches for leisure caravans are separately occupied by persons other than the site operator so that a pitch so occupied is a separate hereditament for purposes of rating within the meaning of the General Rate Act 1967, the valuation officer, if he thinks fit, may in the valuation list treat all or any of those pitches as forming a single hereditament together with so much, if any, of the site as is in the occupation of the site operator.

(2) For purposes of this section a caravan pitch (and any area comprising it) shall be taken as including the caravan for the time being on the pitch if, but only if, apart from this section, the caravan would be included as part of a rateable hereditament.

(3) Where any area of a caravan site is under subsection (1) above treated as a single hereditament, it shall, for the purposes

of rating (within the meaning of the General Rate Act 1967), be deemed to be a single hereditament in the occupation of the site operator. 1967 c. 9.

(4) In relation to that hereditament section 19(2) of the General Rate Act 1967 (which makes special provision as to ascertaining rateable value in the case of hereditaments consisting of one or more houses or other non-industrial buildings) shall not in any case apply; but in determining whether the hereditament is a mixed hereditament for purposes of section 48 of that Act (under which the rates on dwelling houses and mixed hereditaments are to be reduced by reference to the domestic element of the rate support grant) any caravan pitches which are separately occupied by persons other than the site operator but are included in the hereditament by virtue of this section shall be treated as used for purposes of private dwellings notwithstanding the exclusion by section 48(5) of sites for movable dwellings.

Where by virtue of this subsection a hereditament is for purposes of section 48 of the General Rate Act 1967 a mixed hereditament as at the 1st April in any year, it shall be treated as being a mixed hereditament throughout the rating year beginning with that date, notwithstanding that it appears to the rating authority or is determined to have ceased to be one.

(5) For purposes of any proposal for the alteration of the valuation list made by the valuation officer by virtue of subsection (1) above the hereditament shall be treated as in the occupation of the site operator, and in section 70(2) of the General Rate Act 1967 (which confers on owners and occupiers the right to object to a proposal) the reference to any part of the hereditament shall be omitted.

(6) Where a valuation list is altered by virtue of subsection (1) above so as to include an area of a caravan site as a single hereditament, any item comprised in that hereditament and separately entered in the list may be deleted from the list without any proposal being made to delete it; and a deletion so made shall have effect as from the same date as the alteration of the list to include the single hereditament.

(7) Where any area of a caravan site is under subsection (1) above treated as a single hereditament, or where the valuation officer has made a proposal for the alteration of the valuation list in order that it shall be so treated, a proposal for there to be omitted from the hereditament and entered separately in the valuation list a caravan pitch occupied by a person other than the site operator may be made by that person if the pitch would fall to be separately entered in the list but for this section; and in the General Rate Act 1967 section 69(4) and (5) and sections 70 to 74 shall apply in relation to a proposal under this subsection as they apply in relation to a proposal under section 69.

1930 c. 44.

(8) Where at the date on which a drainage rate is made under Part IV of the Land Drainage Act 1930 for any internal drainage district or sub-district land situated wholly or partly within the district or sub-district is included in the valuation list as a single hereditament by virtue of subsection (1) above, that land or the part so situated may be treated as a single hereditament for purposes of the drainage rate; and as regards any period for which an area of a caravan site is rated as a single hereditament by virtue of this subsection, the site operator for the time being shall be deemed to be the occupier of that area for purposes of sections 24 to 31 of the Land Drainage Act 1930 and any other enactment referring to drainage rates under that Act, including Schedule 3 to that Act (which relates to qualification of electors to and members of internal drainage boards).

1967 c. 9.

(9) This section shall have effect for any rate period (within the meaning of the General Rate Act 1967) beginning after the end of March 1976; and any proposal of the valuation officer made during the year beginning with the 1st April 1976, if it could have been made on that date had this section been then in force, may be made so as to have effect as of that date, and section 79 of the General Rate Act 1967 (which relates to the effect of alterations in the valuation list) shall apply accordingly.

Information for caravanners about rating of caravan sites mentioned in s. 1.

2.—(1) Where the valuation officer makes a proposal for the alteration of the valuation list in order that an area of a caravan site shall be treated as a single hereditament under section 1(1) above, and there is not already an area of that site so treated, he shall within one month after the date on which the proposal is made give written notice to the site operator stating how many caravans occupied by persons other than the site operator are included in the hereditament proposed to be entered in the valuation list and how much of the rateable value proposed for the hereditament he attributes to those caravans, together with their pitches.

(2) After receiving a notice under subsection (1) above the site operator shall display a notice on the site from the beginning of April to the end of October in every year so long as the proposal is current or the site or part of it is treated as a single hereditament under section 1(1) above (but starting with the April following the receipt of the notice under subsection (1), if it is received in October), and shall state in the notice so displayed—

(*a*) the part of the site included in the hereditament by the proposal or in the valuation list (or that the whole site is so included);

(*b*) the facts stated in the notice under subsection (1); and

(*c*) the rate in the pound at which the general rate for the rating area is charged under the General Rate Act 1967 in respect of the period during which the notice is for the time being displayed.

(3) If at any time it appears to the valuation officer that the facts stated in a notice under subsection (1) above or under this subsection are no longer accurate, he shall give to the site operator a further written notice bringing the facts so stated up to date; and the notice or last notice received by the site operator under this subsection shall after his receipt of it (or, if it is received in October, then from the beginning of the following April) take the place of the notice under subsection (1) for purposes of subsection (2)(*b*) above.

(4) The notice required by subsection (2) above shall be displayed at some conspicuous place where it is likely to attract the attention of persons occupying pitches for leisure caravans which are included in the hereditament by the proposal or in the valuation list.

(5) If so requested by a person occupying any such pitch as aforesaid, the site operator shall give him in writing the information required by subsection (2) above to be given by a notice under that subsection as the subsection would apply at the time of the request if a notice were required to be displayed at all times after receipt of a notice under subsection (1) and to take account of any notice received under subsection (3).

(6) If a site operator fails without reasonable excuse to display and keep displayed a notice as required by subsections (2) and (4) above, or to give information to a person as required by subsection (5) within one month after a written request from that person, he shall be liable on summary conviction to a fine not exceeding £50.

Provisions for Scotland

Valuation and rating of caravan sites in Scotland.

3.—(1) Where in a caravan site in Scotland having an area of not less than 400 square yards pitches for leisure caravans are separately occupied by persons other than the site operator so that a pitch so occupied is a separate unit of lands and heritages for purposes of valuation and rating, the assessor shall as respects the year 1976–77 and subsequent years for the aforesaid purposes treat all those pitches together with so much, if any, of the site as is in the occupation of the site operator as forming a single unit of lands and heritages in the occupation of the site operator; and the assessor shall make up the valuation roll or alter the valuation roll for the time being in force accordingly, and send a copy of the relevant entry therein to the rating authority.

(2) Any alteration in the valuation roll under subsection (1) above shall have effect as from the beginning of the year in which the alteration is made or as from the date on which the caravan site becomes treated as a single unit of lands and heritages under the said subsection, whichever is the later:

Provided that any such alteration which is made during the year 1976–77, in a case where the caravan site would have been treated as such a single unit of lands and heritages as from 1st April 1976 if this Act had been in force on that date, shall have effect as from that date.

(3) Where as respects any year the valuation roll has been altered under subsection (1) above the rate for that year shall be levied accordingly.

(4) For purposes of valuation and rating, the proprietor or tenant of a caravan site which is treated as a single unit of lands and heritages under subsection (1) above shall be deemed to be the proprietor or tenant of the said single unit.

(5) For purposes of this section a caravan pitch shall be taken

(*a*) as including the caravan for the time being on the pitch if, but only if, apart from this section, the caravan would be included as part of lands and heritages; and

1956 c. 60. (*b*) as excluding a caravan thereon which is any such structure as is mentioned in section 8(1) of the Valuation and Rating (Scotland) Act 1956 (which relates to structures for the use of persons suffering from certain disabilities).

(6) In relation to the said single unit subsections (2) and (6) of section 6 of the said Act of 1956 (which make provision as to ascertaining rateable value in the case of lands and heritages consisting of one or more dwelling-houses or other non-industrial buildings) shall not in any case apply.

(7) Where there are in a caravan site which is treated as a single unit of lands and heritages under subsection (1) above

1966 c. 51. caravan pitches to which subsection (3) of section 7 of the Local Government (Scotland) Act 1966 applies (reduction of rates on dwellings by reference to the domestic element), subsection (4) of that section shall have effect as if—

(*a*) the references to the rateable value to be determined thereunder and to the occupier of the premises were references respectively to the rateable value of all the said pitches as a single sum and to the site operator;

(*b*) the words " gross annual value and " were omitted.

(8) Section 22 of the said Act of 1966 (complaints regarding omissions from the valuation roll) shall have effect as if in subsection (1)—

(*a*) after the word " effect " there were inserted the word " (*a*) ";

(*b*) after the words " so included " there were inserted the words " or (*b*) that lands and heritages consisting of a pitch for a caravan have been treated as part of a single unit of lands and heritages by virtue of section 3(1) of the Rating (Caravan Sites) Act 1976 and ought to be separately entered in such valuation roll; ".

(9) Expressions used in this section and in the previous Valuation Acts shall have the same meanings in this section as in those Acts; and this Act, as it applies to Scotland, and the previous Valuation Acts may be cited together as the Valuation Acts.

In this subsection " the previous Valuation Acts " means the Lands Valuation (Scotland) Act 1854, the Acts amending that Act and any other Act relating to valuation, including the Local Government (Scotland) Act 1975.

1854 c. 91.
1975 c. 30.

(10) In this section " rate " includes a domestic water rate and " rating " shall be construed accordingly.

Information for caravanners about rating of caravan sites mentioned in s. 3.

4.—(1) Where the assessor alters the valuation roll under section 3(1) above, he shall include in the notice of deletion which he sends in pursuance of section 3(3) of the Local Government (Scotland) Act 1975 to each person named in the valuation roll as the occupier of a pitch for a leisure caravan, the following additional information—

(*a*) the name and location of the caravan site on which the pitch is situated;

(*b*) a statement that the assessor has deleted from the valuation roll the entry relating to the pitch because, for the purposes of valuation and rating, he is treating the caravan site including the pitch as a single unit in the occupation of the site operator;

(*c*) the number of such pitches which the assessor is including in the said single unit;

(*d*) the amount of the rateable value of the said single unit which the assessor attributes to such pitches; and

(*e*) the rate in the pound (as reduced under section 7(1) of the Local Government (Scotland) Act 1966) at which rates are levied within the area in which the site is situated for the first year in which the site and pitches thereon are assessed as a single unit.

1966 c. 51.

(2) Subsections (5) and (9) of section 3 above shall apply for the purposes of this section as they apply for the purposes of that section.

Transitional provision for Scotland.

5.—(1) Where before the passing of this Act an agreement is entered into, relating to the payment of rent, between the site operator and the occupier of lands and heritages which consist of a pitch for a leisure caravan on the site and which foı the year 1975–76 are separately entered in the valuation roll, the site operator may recover from that occupier during the currency of such agreement, in addition to the rent payable thereunder, a sum which represents the amount of rates payable by the site operator in respect of the site which is reasonably attributable to the pitch of such occupier and which but for the enactment of section 3 above would not be payable by the site operator.

(2) Subsections (5), (9) and (10) of section 3 above shall apply for the purposes of this section as they apply for the purposes of that section.

General

Interpretation.

6. For purposes of this Act—

1960 c. 62.

(*a*) " caravan " has the same meaning as it has for purposes of Part I of the Caravan Sites and Control of Development Act 1960;

(*b*) " caravan site " means any land in respect of which a site licence is required under Part I of that Act, or would be so required if paragraph 4 and paragraph 11 of Schedule 1 to the Act (exemption of certain land occupied and supervised by organisations concerned with recreational activities and of land occupied by local authorities) were omitted;

(*c*) a caravan pitch is a " pitch for a leisure caravan " if in accordance with any licence or planning permission regulating the use of the caravan site a caravan stationed on the pitch is not allowed to be used for human habitation throughout the year;

(*d*) " site operator " means the person who is for purposes of Part I of that Act the occupier of the caravan site.

Short title and extent.

7.—(1) This Act may be cited as the Rating (Caravan Sites) Act 1976.

(2) This Act does not extend to Northern Ireland.

Statute Law (Repeals) Act 1976

1976 CHAPTER 16

An Act to promote the reform of the statute law by the repeal, in accordance with recommendations of the Law Commission and the Scottish Law Commission, of certain enactments which (except in so far as their effect is preserved) are no longer of practical utility, and to make other provision in connection with the repeal of those enactments. [27th May 1976]

BE IT ENACTED by the Queen's most Excellent Majesty, by and with the advice and consent of the Lords Spiritual and Temporal, and Commons, in this present Parliament assembled, and by the authority of the same, as follows:—

1.—(1) The enactments mentioned in Schedule 1 to this Act are hereby repealed to the extent specified in column 3 of that Schedule.

Repeals and associated amendments.

(2) The enactments mentioned in Part I of Schedule 2 to this Act shall have effect with the amendments there specified (which are consequential on or otherwise made in connection with certain of the repeals in Part II (Alcoholism) of Schedule 1 to this Act) and the enactments mentioned in Part II of Schedule 2 to this Act shall have effect with the amendments there specified (which are consequential on other repeals made by this Act).

Savings. 1924 c. 3. 1926 c. 62.

2.—(1) Notwithstanding the repeal by this Act (Schedule 1 Part XIII) of the Irish Free State Land Purchase (Loan Guarantee) Act 1924 and the East Africa Loans Act 1926—

(*a*) there shall continue to be charged on and issued out of the Consolidated Fund any sums required by the Treasury for fulfilling the guarantees given under the said Acts and there shall continue to be paid into the Consolidated Fund any sums received by way of repayment of any sums so issued; and

(*b*) the Treasury shall continue to be under a duty to lay before both Houses of Parliament an account of any sums issued out of the Consolidated Fund for the purpose of the guarantee given under the said Act of 1924 as soon as may be after any sum is so issued.

1959 c. 71.

(2) Notwithstanding the repeal by this Act (Schedule 1 Part XIII) of the Colonial Development and Welfare Act 1959—

1965 c. 38.

(*a*) any schemes under that Act in force at the commencement of this Act shall, so far as then in force (that is to say, by virtue of section 1(3) of the Overseas Development and Service Act 1965, so far as they make provision for the payment out of money provided by Parliament of pensions, allowances or other benefits in respect of injuries or diseases, or aggravation of diseases, incurred by persons engaged in activities carried on for the purposes of such schemes) continue in force; and

(*b*) there shall continue to be paid into the Consolidated Fund any sums received by way of interest on, or in repayment of, any outstanding loans under that Act.

1967 c. 69. 1967 c. 76. 1967 No. 1900. 1975 No. 1949.

(3) The repeal by this Act (Schedule 1 Part XVI) of section 25 of the Civic Amenities Act 1967 and of the amendment of that section in Schedule 6 to the Road Traffic Regulation Act 1967 shall not affect the operation of the Removal and Disposal of Vehicles (Alteration of Enactments) Order 1967 or the Removal and Disposal of Vehicles (Alteration of Enactments) (Amendment) Order 1975 and accordingly sections 20, 52 and 53 of the Road Traffic Regulation Act 1967 shall continue to have effect as amended by those orders.

Extent.

3.—(1) This Act extends to Northern Ireland.

(2) This Act does not repeal any enactment so far as the enactment forms part of the law of a country outside the United Kingdom, but Her Majesty may by Order in Council provide that the repeal by this Act of any enactment specified in the Order shall on a date so specified extend to any of the Channel Islands or the Isle of Man or any colony for whose external relations the United Kingdom is responsible.

Short title.

4.—This Act may be cited as the Statute Law (Repeals) Act 1976.

SCHEDULES

SCHEDULE 1

Section 1.

ENACTMENTS REPEALED

PART I

ADMINISTRATION OF JUSTICE

Chapter	Short title	Extent of repeal
57 Geo. 3. c. 93.	Distress (Costs) Act 1817.	Section 7.
3 & 4 Will. 4. c. 74.	Fines and Recoveries Act 1833.	In section 67, including that section as applied by any other Act, the words from " and in case any action of trespass " to " special matter in evidence ".
6 & 7 Will. 4. c. 19.	Durham (County Palatine) Act 1836.	The whole Act.
33 & 34 Vict. c. 30.	Wages Attachment Abolition Act 1870.	The whole Act.
36 & 37 Vict. c. 81.	Langbaurgh Coroners Act 1873.	The whole Act.
36 & 37 Vict. c. 88.	Slave Trade Act 1873.	In section 18, the words from " or given " onwards.
45 & 46 Vict. c. 31.	Inferior Courts Judgments Extension Act 1882.	In section 2, in the definition of " inferior courts " the words " and the Court of Bankruptcy ".
4 & 5 Geo. 5. c. 78.	Courts (Emergency Powers) Act 1914.	The whole Act.
6 & 7 Geo. 5. c. 13.	Courts (Emergency Powers) (Amendment) Act 1916.	The whole Act.
6 & 7 Geo. 5. c. 18.	Courts (Emergency Powers) (No. 2) Act 1916.	The whole Act.
18 & 19 Geo. 5. c. 26.	Administration of Justice Act 1928.	In section 20(5), the words from " A copy of " onwards. In Schedule 1, in Part I the amendments of sections 118 and 167 of the Supreme Court of Judicature (Consolidation) Act 1925.
22 & 23 Geo. 5. c. 2.	Expiring Laws Act 1931.	The whole Act.
7 & 8 Geo. 6. c. 7.	Prize Salvage Act 1944.	Section 1(2).
12, 13 & 14 Geo. 6. c. 63.	Legal Aid and Solicitors (Scotland) Act 1949.	In Schedule 7, in the third column the entries relating to sections 9 and 26 to 28 of the Solicitors (Scotland) Act 1933.
2 & 3 Eliz. 2. c. 36.	Law Reform (Limitation of Actions, &c.) Act 1954.	Sections 5 and 7. Section 8(2) except the words " this Act extends to Great Britain only ".

SCH. 1

Chapter	Short title	Extent of repeal
7 & 8 Eliz. 2. c. 65.	Fatal Accidents Act 1959.	Section 3(5) except the words " this Act does not extend to Scotland or Northern Ireland ".
1965 c. 72.	Matrimonial Causes Act 1965.	Section 38.

PART II

ALCOHOLISM

Chapter	Short title	Extent of repeal
42 & 43 Vict. c. 19.	Habitual Drunkards Act 1879.	The whole Act.
51 & 52 Vict. c. 19.	Inebriates Act 1888.	The whole Act.
61 & 62 Vict. c. 60.	Inebriates Act 1898.	The whole Act except section 30 and Schedule 1. In Schedule 1, the entries relating to the Refreshment Houses (Ireland) Act 1860, the Dublin Police Act 1842 and the Licensing (Ireland) Act 1836.
62 & 63 Vict. c. 35.	Inebriates Act 1899.	The whole Act.
63 & 64 Vict. c. 28.	Inebriates Amendment (Scotland) Act 1900.	The whole Act.
2 Edw. 7. c. 28.	Licensing Act 1902.	In section 2, in subsection (1) the words " with or without hard labour " and, in subsection (3), the words " and in section sixty of the Licensing Act 1872 ". Section 3.
12, 13 & 14 Geo. 6. c. 47.	Finance Act 1949.	In Schedule 8, paragraph 4 of Part II.
7 & 8 Eliz. 2. c. 72.	Mental Health Act 1959.	In Schedule 7, the entry relating to the Habitual Drunkards Act 1879.
8 & 9 Eliz. 2. c. 61.	Mental Health (Scotland) Act 1960.	In Schedule 4, the entry relating to the Habitual Drunkards Act 1879.

PART III

SCH. 1

ANIMALS

Chapter	Short title	Extent of repeal
6 Edw. 7. c. 32.	Dogs Act 1906.	Sections 8(*c*) and 9(*a*).
1 & 2 Geo. 5. c. 27.	Protection of Animals Act 1911.	Section 17.
6 & 7 Eliz. 2. c. 43.	Horse Breeding Act 1958.	Section 17(1), (6) and (7).
1963 c. 11.	Agriculture (Miscellaneous Provisions) Act 1963.	Section 15.
1963 c. 43.	Animal Boarding Establishments Act 1963.	Sections 6 and 7(2).
1964 c. 70.	Riding Establishments Act 1964.	Sections 7 and 8.
1967 c. 46.	Protection of Birds Act 1967.	Sections 1 and 2. In section 3, subsection (1), in subsection (2) the word " Accordingly ", and subsection (3). In section 12(3), the words from " so much " to " principal Act ".
1973 c. 57.	Badgers Act 1973.	In section 11, in the definition of " local authority " paragraph (*a*), and in paragraph (*b*) the words " on and after 1st April 1974 ".

PART IV

ARMED FORCES

Chapter	Short title	Extent of repeal
53 Geo. 3. c. 154.	Kilmainham Hospital (Pensions Commutation) Act 1813.	The whole Act.
7 Geo. 4. c. 16.	Chelsea and Kilmainham Hospitals Act 1826.	Sections 4, 6, 7, 8 and 9. In section 10, the words " or Kilmainham ". Section 12. In section 13, the words " or through the commissioners or governors of Kilmainham Hospital ". Section 22. In section 24, the words " or Kilmainham " and the words, wherever occurring, " of either of the said hospitals ", " into

Sch. 1

Chapter	Short title	Extent of repeal
7 Geo. 4. c. 16 —*cont.*	Chelsea and Kilmainham Hospitals Act 1826—*cont.*	either of the said hospitals ", and " either of the said hospitals ". Section 26. In section 27, the words " either " and " or Kilmainham ". Section 33.
11 Geo. 4 & 1 Will. 4. c. 41.	Army Pensions Act 1830.	The whole Act.
2 & 3 Vict. c. 51.	Pensions Act 1839.	The whole Act.
10 & 11 Vict. c. 4.	Chelsea Pensions (Abolition of Poundage) Act 1847.	The whole Act.
28 & 29 Vict. c. 73.	Naval and Marine Pay and Pensions Act 1865.	In section 4, the words " or by a person entitled to any marine half pay," and the words " or half pay ". Section 7.
28 & 29 Vict. c. 89.	Greenwich Hospital Act 1865.	In section 5, the words " half pay ". Section 8.
47 & 48 Vict. c. 44.	Naval Pensions Act 1884.	Section 3.
47 & 48 Vict. c. 55.	Pensions and Yeomanry Pay Act 1884.	In the title, the words " and to the pay and pensions of the Yeomanry ". In section 2(1), the words " and to the pay and pensions of the Yeomanry "; and the words from " both such pay " onwards except the word " pensions ". Section 6.
61 & 62 Vict. c. 24.	Greenwich Hospital Act 1898.	The whole Act except section 1 as that section applies to Northern Ireland.
4 & 5 Geo. 5. c. 83.	Army Pensions Act 1914.	In section 1, the words in the proviso from " this section " to " and that ".
7 & 8 Geo. 5. c. 51.	Air Force (Constitution) Act 1917.	Section 6(2).
14 & 15 Geo. 5. c. 15.	Auxiliary Air Force and Air Force Reserve Act 1924.	The whole Act.
24 & 25 Geo. 5. c. 5.	Air Force Reserve (Pilots and Observers) Act 1934.	The whole Act.
12, 13 & 14 Geo. 6. c. 96.	Auxiliary and Reserve Forces Act 1949.	Section 7. In section 8, the words " or as part of the short title of the Auxiliary Air Force and Air Force Reserve Act 1924 ". Sections 14, 15 and 16(1).
14 Geo. 6. c. 33.	Air Force Reserve Act 1950.	Section 29.

SCH. 1

Chapter	Short title	Extent of repeal
14 & 15 Geo. 6. c. 23.	Reserve and Auxiliary Forces (Training) Act 1951.	The whole Act.
1 & 2 Eliz. 2. c. 50.	Auxiliary Forces Act 1953.	Sections 45 and 46(6).
2 & 3 Eliz. 2. c. 10.	Navy, Army and Air Force Reserves Act 1954.	The whole Act.
1966 c. 30.	Reserve Forces Act 1966.	In Schedule 1, paragraph 31.
1969 c. 23.	Army Reserve Act 1969.	The whole Act.

PART V

CIVIL DEFENCE

Chapter	Short title	Extent of repeal
1 & 2 Geo. 6. c. 6.	Air-Raid Precautions Act 1937.	The whole Act.
2 & 3 Geo. 6. c. 31.	Civil Defence Act 1939.	Parts I to IV. Part V except sections 36, 37 and 39. In section 36(2), the proviso. Part VI. Part VIII except section 62. In section 62, in subsection (1)(*b*) the words " (as defined in the Act of 1937) ", and subsection (5). Sections 74, 75, 81 and 82. In section 83, subsection (1), the proviso to subsection (4), and subsection (5). Sections 85 to 89. In section 90(1), the definition of " Annual value ", in the definition of " Civil defence functions " the words " the Act of 1937 or ", and the definitions of " Diminution in the annual value ", " Electricity undertakers ", " Fire authority ", " Lease ", " Owner ", and " Public air-raid shelter ". Section 91 except subsections (20), (21), (28) and (34). In section 91(20), the words from the beginning to " sixty-eight and ". In section 91(21), the words " and to section five of the Act of 1937 ", the word " re-

SCH. 1

Chapter	Short title	Extent of repeal
2 & 3 Geo. 6. c. 31—*cont.*	Civil Defence Act 1939—*cont.*	spectively ", and the words from " and to subsection (9) " onwards. In section 91(34), the words " of the Act of 1937 or ". Schedule 2.
9 & 10 Geo. 6. c. 12.	Civil Defence (Suspension of Powers) Act 1945.	The whole Act.
9 & 10 Geo. 6. c. 49.	Acquisition of Land (Authorisation Procedure) Act 1946.	In Schedule 4, the entries relating to the Air-Raid Precautions Act 1937 and the Civil Defence Act 1939.
9 & 10 Eliz. 2. c. 64.	Public Health Act 1961.	In Part III of Schedule 1, the entry relating to the Civil Defence Act 1939.
1963 c. 33.	London Government Act 1963.	In section 49, in subsection (1) the words " of the Civil Defence Acts 1937 and 1939 or " and the words " in the said Acts of 1937 and 1939 and ", and subsections (5) and (6).
1967 c. 76.	Road Traffic Regulation Act 1967.	In Schedule 6, the entry relating to the Civil Defence Act 1939.
1969 c. 48.	Post Office Act 1969.	In Schedule 4, in paragraph 36(1), the words from "other than " onwards.
1970 c. 38.	Building (Scotland) Act 1970.	In Part II of Schedule 1, paragraph 3.
1973 c. 65.	Local Government (Scotland) Act 1973.	In Schedule 27, the entries relating to the Air-Raid Precautions Act 1937 and the Civil Defence Act 1939.

PART VI

CUSTOMS AND EXCISE

Chapter	Short title	Extent of repeal
23 & 24 Vict. c. 90.	Game Licences Act 1860.	In section 16, the words " and Dublin ". Sections 17 and 18.
13 & 14 Geo. 5. c. 14.	Finance Act 1923.	In section 39(1) the words from " so far as ", where first occurring, to " excise ", where first occurring.
14 & 15 Geo. 5. c. 21.	Finance Act 1924.	In section 17, in subsection (1) the words " or a gun licence ", the word " respectively " in both places, the words " and gun licences " in both places

SCH. 1

Chapter	Short title	Extent of repeal
14 & 15 Geo. 5. c. 21—*cont.*	Finance Act 1924—*cont.*	and the words " or licence ", in subsection (2) the words " and gun licences ", and in subsection (3) the words from " and the expression ' gun licence ' " onwards.
18 & 19 Geo. 5. c. 17.	Finance Act 1928.	In section 35(1), the words from " and the expression " onwards.
15 & 16 Geo. 6 & 1 Eliz. 2. c. 44.	Customs and Excise Act 1952.	In section 237(2), the words from " and to licences " onwards.
1963 c. 25.	Finance Act 1963.	Section 2.
1970 c. 24.	Finance Act 1970.	In section 2(9), the words from " for " onwards.

PART VII

INDIA

Chapter	Short title	Extent of repeal
6 & 7 Vict. c. 98.	Slave Trade Act 1843.	Section 4(2).
28 & 29 Vict. c. 63.	Colonial Laws Validity Act 1865.	In section 1, the words "British India ".
31 & 32 Vict. c. 37.	Documentary Evidence Act 1868.	Section 5(2).
33 & 34 Vict. c. 52.	Extradition Act 1870.	Section 23.
33 & 34 Vict. c. 90.	Foreign Enlistment Act 1870.	In section 30, the words " as respects India, mean the Governor General and ".
36 & 37 Vict. c. 88.	Slave Trade Act 1873.	In section 2, in the definition of " governor ", the proviso.
37 & 38 Vict. c. 27.	Courts (Colonial) Jurisdiction Act 1874.	In section 2, the words " British India ". Section 2A.
40 & 41 Vict. c. 59.	Colonial Stock Act 1877.	In section 26, the words " and not forming part of British India ".
41 & 42 Vict. c. 73.	Territorial Waters Jurisdiction Act 1878.	In section 7, the words " as respects India, means the Governor General and ".
47 & 48 Vict. c. 31.	Colonial Prisoners Removal Act 1884.	Section 14A. In section 18, the words " and subject, as respects India, to the provisions of section fourteen A of this Act ", and in the definition of " British possession ", the words " which are not part of India ".

SCH. 1

Chapter	Short title	Extent of repeal
48 & 49 Vict. c. 25.	East India Unclaimed Stock Act 1885.	In section 2, the definitions of " Government director " and " Indian railway company ". Sections 17 to 24.
53 & 54 Vict. c. 27.	Colonial Courts of Admiralty Act 1890.	In section 4, the words " This section shall not apply to Indian laws ".
57 & 58 Vict. c. 60.	Merchant Shipping Act 1894.	Section 368.
8 Edw. 7. c. 51.	Appellate Jurisdiction Act 1908.	Section 2.
5 & 6 Geo. 5. c. 57.	Prize Courts Act 1915.	In section 4(1), the words from " as respects any prize court in India " to " its principal seat or ".
9 & 10 Geo. 5. c. 101.	Government of India Act 1919.	The whole Act, so far as unrepealed by the Government of India Act 1935.
10 & 11 Geo. 5. c. 75.	Official Secrets Act 1920.	In section 11(1)(*a*), the word " India ".
11 & 12 Geo. 5. c. 58.	Trusts (Scotland) Act 1921.	In section 2, the definition of " East India Stock ".
17 & 18 Geo. 5. c. 40.	Indian Church Act 1927.	The whole Act.
19 & 20 Geo. 5. c. 8.	Appellate Jurisdiction Act 1929.	The whole Act.
25 & 26 Geo. 5. c. 42.	Government of India Act 1935.	The whole Act.
26 Geo. 5 & 1 Edw. 8. c. 1.	Government of India (Reprinting) Act 1935.	The whole Act.
26 Geo. 5 & 1 Edw. 8. c. 2.	Government of India Act 1935.	The whole Act except sections 1 and 311(4) and (5).
1 Edw. 8 & 1 Geo. 6. c. 9.	India and Burma (Existing Laws) Act 1937.	The whole Act.
2 & 3 Geo. 6. c. 66.	Government of India Act (Amendment) Act 1939.	The whole Act.
3 & 4 Geo. 6. c. 5.	India and Burma (Miscellaneous Amendments) Act 1940.	The whole Act.
3 & 4 Geo. 6. c. 33.	India and Burma (Emergency Provisions) Act 1940.	The whole Act.
4 & 5 Geo. 6. c. 44.	India and Burma (Postponement of Elections) Act 1941.	The whole Act.
5 & 6 Geo. 6. c. 7.	India (Federal Court Judges) Act 1942.	The whole Act.
5 & 6 Geo. 6. c. 39.	India and Burma (Temporary and Miscellaneous Provisions) Act 1942.	The whole Act.
7 & 8 Geo. 6. c. 14.	India (Attachment of States) Act 1944.	The whole Act.
7 & 8 Geo. 6. c. 38.	India (Miscellaneous Provisions) Act 1944.	The whole Act.
8 & 9 Geo. 6. c. 7.	India (Estate Duty) Act 1945.	The whole Act.

Sch. 1

Chapter	Short title	Extent of repeal
9 & 10 Geo. 6. c. 2.	Indian Franchise Act 1945.	The whole Act.
9 & 10 Geo. 6. c. 5.	Indian Divorce Act 1945.	The whole Act.
9 & 10 Geo. 6. c. 23.	India (Proclamations of Emergency) Act 1946.	The whole Act.
9 & 10 Geo. 6. c. 39.	India (Central Government and Legislature) Act 1946.	The whole Act.
10 & 11 Geo. 6. c. 30.	Indian Independence Act 1947.	Sections 2 to 5. Section 6(1) to (3) and (6). Sections 8 to 12. In section 14, in subsection (2), the words from " or as applying " onwards; and subsections (3) and (4). In section 15(3), the words from " and any legal proceedings " onwards. Section 16. Section 18(3) to (5). Section 19. Schedules 1 and 2.
12, 13 & 14 Geo. 6. c. 92.	India (Consequential Provision) Act 1949.	In section 1(1), the words " and subject to the provisions of subsection (3) of this section " Section 1(3) and (4).
	Church Assembly Measure	
17 & 18 Geo. 5. No. 1.	Indian Church Measure 1927.	The whole Measure.

Part VIII

Local Government

Chapter	Title or short title	Extent of repeal
33 Geo. 3. c. 124 (1793).	An Act for rebuilding the Tron Church of the City of Glasgow; for opening certain streets, for removing obstructions in Trongate Street; for building a bridge over the River Clyde, opposite the Salt Market Street; for regulating the weight and measure of coals and the mode of carrying wood and timber in the streets of the said city; for enlarging the gaol or tol-	The whole Act.

SCH. 1

Chapter	Title or short title	Extent of repeal
Geo. 3. c. 124 (1793)—*cont.*	booth there; and for selling part of the High or Calton Green, and also the Glebe belonging to the Inner High Church and Parish of Glasgow.	
6 & 7 Will. 4. c. 87.	Liberties Act 1836.	The whole Act.
20 & 21 Vict. c. 63.	Dunbar Harbour Loan Act 1857.	The whole Act.
34 & 35 Vict. c. 68 (1871).	An Act to determine the boundaries of the Barony and Regality of Glasgow for the purposes of registration.	The whole Act.
45 & 46 Vict. c. 50.	Municipal Corporations Act 1882.	Sections 193, 225, 228, 229, 232 and 245.
52 & 53 Vict. c. 50.	Local Government (Scotland) Act 1889.	The whole Act.
56 & 57 Vict. c. 73.	Local Government Act 1894.	Section 25(7).
8 Edw. 7. c. 62.	Local Government (Scotland) Act 1908.	Sections 29 to 31.
19 & 20 Geo. 5. c. 17.	Local Government Act 1929.	Sections 57(4), 85 and 127. In section 134, the definition of " Classified road ".
10 & 11 Geo. 6. c. 43.	Local Government (Scotland) Act 1947.	Section 377(6). In section 379(1), the definitions of " alteration of area ", " classified road ", " delegate ", " ecclesiastical charity ", " educational endowment ", " educational establishment ", " General Board of Control ", " grant-aided school ", " grants under Part III of the Local Government (Scotland) Act, 1929 ", " gross annual valuation ", " landward area ", " large burgh ", " local government elector " or " elector ", " magistrates ", " property", " public body ", " Public Health Acts ", " refer ", " Registration of Births, Deaths and Marriages Acts ", " Roads and Bridges Acts ", " senior bailie ", " small burgh " and " statutory undertakers ".
11 & 12 Geo. 6. c. 26.	Local Government Act 1948.	Section 68.
1 & 2 Eliz. 2. c. 26.	Local Government (Miscellaneous Provisions) Act 1953.	Sections 15 to 17. Section 19(3) from the beginning to the words " as aforesaid ".

SCH. 1

Chapter	Title or short title	Extent of repeal
2 & 3 Eliz. 2. c. 13.	Local Government (Financial Provisions) (Scotland) Act 1954.	The whole Act.
4 & 5 Eliz. 2. c. 36.	Local Authorities (Expenses) Act 1956.	The whole Act.
6 & 7 Eliz. 2. c. 64.	Local Government and Miscellaneous Financial Provisions (Scotland) Act 1958.	In section 21(1), the definitions of the expressions "Act of 1954" and "relevant expenditure". In Schedule 4, paragraphs 10 and 11. Schedule 5.
7 & 8 Eliz. 2. c. 62.	New Towns Act 1959.	Sections 9(1) and 10.
9 & 10 Eliz. 2. c. 43.	Public Authorities (Allowances) Act 1961.	The whole Act.
10 & 11 Eliz. 2. c. 36.	Local Authorities (Historic Buildings) Act 1962.	Section 3.
1963 c. 46.	Local Government (Financial Provisions) Act 1963.	In section 5, the words "including an enactment contained in this Act". Section 13. In section 14(1), the words from "(except sections" to "thereof)" and the words "(except as aforesaid)". In section 15(1), the definition of "the Act of 1948".
1965 c. 27.	Lost Property (Scotland) Act 1965.	The whole Act as from 1st January 1980.
1966 c. 42.	Local Government Act 1966.	In Schedule 5, paragraphs 4 and 8.
1966 c. 51.	Local Government (Scotland) Act 1966.	Section 1.
1967 c. 18.	Local Government (Termination of Reviews) Act 1967.	The whole Act.

PART IX

LONDON

Chapter	Title or short title	Extent of repeal
7 Geo. 3. c. 23 (1766).	An Act to prevent frauds and abuses in the admeasurement of coals, sold by wharf measure, within the City of London, and the liberties thereof; and between Tower Dock and Limehouse Hole in the county of Middlesex.	The whole Act.

SCH. 1

Chapter	Title or short title	Extent of repeal
10 Geo. 3. c. 53 (1770).	An Act to repeal an Act passed in the 31st year of the reign of His late Majesty King *George* the Second, intituled, *An Act for the relief of coal-heavers working upon the River Thames; and for enabling them to make provision for such of themselves as shall be sick, lame or past their labour, and for their widows and orphans;* and to regulate the price of their labour; to prevent fraud and impositions on such labourers; and for their further relief.	The whole Act.
17 Geo. 3. c. 13 (1776).	An Act for continuing for a limited time [the Act 7 Geo. 3. c. 23].	The whole Act.
26 Geo. 3. c. 83 (1786).	An Act to explain and amend [the Act 7 Geo. 3. c. 23].	The whole Act.
29 & 30 Vict. c. 31.	Superannuation (Metropolis) Act 1866.	The whole Act.
41 & 42 Vict. c. 14.	Baths and Washhouses Act 1878.	The whole Act.
52 & 53 Vict. c. 17.	London Coal Duties Abolition Act 1889.	The whole Act.
2 Edw. 7. c. 41.	Metropolis Water Act 1902.	Section 24(4). In section 47(8), the words from " or of any " to " by this Act,".
25 & 26 Geo. 5. c. lxxxiv.	Metropolitan Water Board Act 1935.	In section 66, in subsection (1) the definition of " the Act of 1866 ", in subsection (2)(*a*) the words " Notwithstanding anything contained in the Act of 1866 as applied to the Board by the Act of 1902 ", and in subsection (4) the words " in the Act of 1866 as applied to the Board by the Act of 1902 or ".
1963 c. 33.	London Government Act 1963.	Sections 64, 65, 78(4) and (5). In section 89(1), the definition of " county review area ".
1970 c. 57.	Town and Country Planning Regulations (London) (Indemnity) Act 1970.	The whole Act.

PART X

MEDICINE

Chapter	Short title	Extent of repeal
55 Geo. 3. c. 194.	Apothecaries Act 1815.	Section 5. In section 8, the words " or by the five apothecaries hereinafter mentioned, or the major part of them present ". In section 9, the words from " and such court ", where secondly occurring, onwards. In section 17, the words " or by five apothecaries so to be appointed as hereinafter is mentioned " and " or from the said five apothecaries ". Sections 18, 20 and 21. In section 22, the words " or the said five apothecaries so to be appointed for any county or counties as aforesaid " and " or to and for the said five apothecaries in any county or counties as aforesaid ". Sections 25, 26 and 27.
2 & 3 Will. 4. c. 75.	Anatomy Act 1832.	In section 6, the words from " and an annual return " onwards.
37 & 38 Vict. c. 34.	Apothecaries Act Amendment Act 1874.	Section 5.
38 & 39 Vict. c. 43.	Medical Act (Royal College of Surgeons of England) 1875.	In section 1, the first proviso and in the second proviso the word "also ". Section 2.
39 & 40 Vict. c. 41.	Medical Act 1876.	The whole Act.
49 & 50 Vict. c. 48.	Medical Act 1886.	Section 25.
14 & 15 Geo. 6. c. 39.	Common Informers Act 1951.	In the Schedule, the entry relating to the Apothecaries Act 1815.

PART XI

MONEY

Chapter	Short title	Extent of repeal
5 & 6 Will. & Mar. c. 20.	Bank of England Act 1694.	Section 28.

SCH. 1

Chapter	Short title	Extent of repeal
9 Geo. 4. c. 24.	Bills of Exchange (Ireland) Act 1828.	Sections 15 and 16.
17 & 18 Vict. c. 90.	Usury Laws Repeal Act 1854.	The whole Act.
36 & 37 Vict. c. 57.	Consolidated Fund (Permanent Charges Redemption) Act 1873.	In section 7, in the definition of " limited owner ", the words " a married woman entitled in her own right ".
9 & 10 Geo. 6. c. 27.	Bank of England Act 1946.	In section 5(*b*), the words from " not being " onwards. In Schedule 2, the proviso to paragraph 2, and paragraph 7.
4 & 5 Eliz. 2. c. 6.	Miscellaneous Financial Provisions Act 1955.	Section 1(2).
1964 c. 9.	Public Works Loans Act 1964.	Section 8.
1969 c. 43.	Air Corporations Act 1969.	In section 1(1), paragraph (*a*). In Schedule 1, Part I.

PART XII

OBSOLETE COUNCILS IN ENGLAND AND WALES

Chapter	Short title	Extent of repeal
13 & 14 Geo. 5. c. 18.	War Memorials (Local Authorities' Powers) Act 1923.	In section 4, the words " county borough, metropolitan " and the words " or other borough, or of an urban ".
1 Edw. 8 & 1 Geo. 6. c. 46.	Physical Training and Recreation Act 1937.	In section 9, the words " county borough, metropolitan " and the word " county " in the expression " county district ".
1 Edw. 8 & 1 Geo. 6. c. 70.	Agriculture Act 1937.	In section 32, in the definition of " Local authority " the words " metropolitan " and " county borough " and the word " county " in the expression " county district ".
2 & 3 Geo. 6. c. 73.	Housing (Emergency Powers) Act 1939.	In section 3(1A), the words "county boroughs and county" and " metropolitan ".
4 & 5 Geo. 6. c. 41.	Landlord and Tenant (War Damage) (Amendment) Act 1941.	In section 1(10), in the definition of " local authority ", the words " metropolitan " and " the council of a county borough " and the word " county " in the expression " county district ".

Chapter	Short title	Extent of repeal
5 & 6 Geo. 6. c. 9.	Restoration of Pre-War Trade Practices Act 1942.	In section 11(1), in the definition of " local authority ", the words " county borough, county" and "metropolitan".
8 & 9 Geo. 6. c. 43.	Requisitioned Land and War Works Act 1945.	In section 59(1), in the definition of " local authority " the words " county borough, metropolitan " and the word " county " in the expression " county district ".
12, 13 & 14 Geo. 6. c. 84.	War Damaged Sites Act 1949.	In section 17(1), in the definition of " local authority ", the words " metropolitan borough, county " and the word " county " in the expression " county district ".
1 & 2 Eliz. 2. c. 26.	Local Government (Miscellaneous Provisions) Act 1953.	In section 18(1), the words " county borough, metropolitan " and the word " county " in the expression " county district ".
1 & 2 Eliz. 2. c. 37.	Registration Service Act 1953.	In section 21(2)(*b*), the word " metropolitan ".
3 & 4 Eliz. 2. c. 18.	Army Act 1955.	In section 163, the words " county borough, county " and " metropolitan ".
3 & 4 Eliz. 2. c. 19.	Air Force Act 1955.	In section 163, the words " county borough, county " and " metropolitan ".
6 & 7 Eliz. 2. c. 34.	Litter Act 1958.	In section 1(2), the words " county borough, metropolitan ", and the words " non-county borough, urban district, rural ".
7 & 8 Eliz. 2. c. 53.	Town and Country Planning Act 1959.	In section 27, in subsection (3)(*a*) the words " county borough " and " metropolitan " and in subsection (3)(*b*) the word " county " in both places.
10 & 11 Eliz. 2. c. 36.	Local Authorities (Historic Buildings) Act 1962.	In section 1(4), the words " county borough, metropolitan " and the word " county " in the expression " county district ".

SCH. 1

PART XIII

OVERSEAS FINANCIAL AID

Chapter	Short title	Extent of repeal
12 & 13 Geo. 5. c. 13.	Empire Settlement Act 1922.	The whole Act.
15 & 16 Geo. 5. c. 3.	Irish Free State Land Purchase (Loan Guarantee) Act 1924.	The whole Act.
16 & 17 Geo. 5. c. 62.	East Africa Loans Act 1926.	The whole Act.
20 & 21 Geo. 5. c. 5.	Colonial Development Act 1929.	Section 4.
21 & 22 Geo. 5. c. 21.	East Africa Loans (Amendment) Act 1931.	The whole Act.
22 & 23 Geo. 5. c. 17.	Tanganyika and British Honduras Loans Act 1932.	The whole Act.
1 Edw. 8 & 1 Geo. 6. c. 18.	Empire Settlement Act 1937.	The whole Act.
5 & 6 Eliz. 2. c. 6.	Ghana Independence Act 1957.	Section 3.
5 & 6 Eliz. 2. c. 54.	Tanganyika Agricultural Corporation Act 1957.	The whole Act.
5 & 6 Eliz. 2. c. 60.	Federation of Malaya Independence Act 1957.	Section 2(1)(*c*).
7 & 8 Eliz. 2. c. 71.	Colonial Development and Welfare Act 1959.	The whole Act.
10 & 11 Eliz. 2. c. 1.	Tanganyika Independence Act 1961.	Section 4.
1963 c. 40.	Commonwealth Development Act 1963.	Section 2. Section 3(3).
1963 c. 54.	Kenya Independence Act 1963.	Section 5.
1963 c. 55.	Zanzibar Act 1963.	In Schedule 1, paragraph 14.
1964 c. 65.	Zambia Independence Act 1964.	In Schedule 1, paragraph 12.
1965 c. 38.	Overseas Development and Service Act 1965.	Section 1. Section 3(2).
1966 c. 21.	Overseas Aid Act 1966.	Section 1(3) to (5). Section 5.
1966 c. 23.	Botswana Independence Act 1966.	In the Schedule, paragraph 11.
1966 c. 24.	Lesotho Independence Act 1966.	In the Schedule, in paragraph 12, the words " the Colonial Development and Welfare Act 1959 ".
1967 c. 31.	Commonwealth Settlement Act 1967.	The whole Act.
1968 c. 13.	National Loans Act 1968.	In section 10(3), the words from " loans " to " or of ".
1968 c. 56.	Swaziland Independence Act 1968.	In the Schedule, paragraph 12.
1970 c. 22.	Tonga Act 1970.	In the Schedule, paragraph 10.
1975 c. 26.	Ministers of the Crown Act 1975.	In Schedule 2, the entries relating to the Colonial Development and Welfare Act 1959 and the Commonwealth Development Act 1963.

Sch. 1

Part XIV
Overseas Territories

Chapter	Short title	Extent of repeal
5 Geo. 3. c. 26.	Isle of Man Purchase Act 1765.	The whole Act.
59 Geo. 3. c. 38.	North American Fisheries Act 1819.	The whole Act.
6 & 7 Vict. c. 22.	The (Colonies) Evidence Act 1843.	The whole Act.
16 & 17 Vict. c. 48.	Coinage (Colonial Offences) Act 1853.	The whole Act.
35 & 36 Vict. c. 45.	Treaty of Washington Act 1872.	The whole Act.
40 & 41 Vict. c. 23.	Colonial Fortifications Act 1877.	The whole Act.
47 & 48 Vict. c. 31.	Colonial Prisoners Removal Act 1884.	Section 17.
4 Edw. 7. c. 33.	Anglo-French Convention Act 1904.	The whole Act.
9 Edw. 7. c. 9.	South Africa Act 1909.	The whole Act.
9 Edw. 7. c. 18.	Naval Establishments in British Possessions Act 1909.	The whole Act.
11 & 12 Geo. 6. c. 27.	Palestine Act 1948.	In Schedule 2, paragraph 3.
14 & 15 Geo. 6. c. 39.	Common Informers Act 1951.	In the Schedule, the entry relating to the North American Fisheries Act 1819.
1 & 2 Eliz. 2. c. 30.	Rhodesia and Nyasaland Federation Act 1953.	The whole Act.
3 & 4 Eliz. 2. c. 5.	Cocos Islands Act 1955.	The whole Act.
6 & 7 Eliz. 2. c. 10.	British Nationality Act 1958.	Section 1.
6 & 7 Eliz. 2. c. 25.	Christmas Island Act 1958.	The whole Act.
10 & 11 Eliz. 2. c. 23.	South Africa Act 1962.	In Schedule 3, paragraph 1.

Part XV
Property

Chapter	Short title	Extent of repeal
17 & 18 Vict. c. 112.	Literary and Scientific Institutions Act 1854.	The following provisions as they apply to Great Britain— In section 1, the words " of and " where they first occur, the words " manor or " in both places, the words " of freehold, copyhold, or customary tenure " and the words " or enfranchise ".

SCH. 1

Chapter	Short title	Extent of repeal
17 & 18 Vict. c. 112—*cont.*	Literary and Scientific Institutions Act 1854 —*cont.*	In section 2, the words " or enfranchise " and " or enfranchised ". In section 3, the words " or enfranchise ". In section 5, the words " manor or ". In section 6, the words " or enfranchise ". In section 13, the words "[*add if necessary*, enfranchise]" and the words from " And no bargain and sale " onwards.
18 & 19 Vict. c. 117.	Ordnance Board Transfer Act 1855.	The following provisions as they apply to Great Britain— In section 2, including that section as applied by any other Act, the words from " nevertheless " onwards. In section 4, the words " feoffees or ", the words from " tenants for life " to " curators ", and the word " surrender ".
20 & 21 Vict. c. 26.	Registration of Long Leases (Scotland) Act 1857.	In section 15, the words " and being subscribed by the keeper of the register ".
23 & 24 Vict. c. 112.	Defence Act 1860.	The following provisions as they apply to Great Britain— In section 11, the words " feoffees or ", the words from " tenants for life " to " committees, and ", and the words from " femes covert " to " idiots, or ".
28 & 29 Vict. c. 89.	Greenwich Hospital Act 1865.	Section 43, as it applies to Northern Ireland. Section 45.
38 & 39 Vict. c. 25.	Public Stores Act 1875.	Section 17.
61 & 62 Vict. c. 24.	Greenwich Hospital Act 1898.	Section 1, as it applies to Northern Ireland.
15 & 16 Geo. 5. c. 33.	Church of Scotland (Property and Endowments) Act 1925.	Sections 3 to 6. Section 10. Schedules 3 and 4.
2 & 3 Eliz. 2. c. 56.	Landlord and Tenant Act 1954.	In Schedule 9, paragraphs 1, 2, 7, 9 and 10.
5 & 6 Eliz. 2. c. 61.	Winfrith Heath Act 1957.	The whole Act.
1967 c. 88.	Leasehold Reform Act 1967.	Section 39(3).
1969 c. 62.	Rent (Control of Increases) Act 1969.	The whole Act.

PART XVI

ROAD TRAFFIC: CIVIC AMENITIES

Chapter	Short title	Extent of repeal
1967 c. 69.	Civic Amenities Act 1967.	Section 25.
1967 c. 76.	Road Traffic Regulation Act 1967.	In Schedule 6, the amendment of section 25 of the Civic Amenities Act 1967.
1968 c. 73.	Transport Act 1968.	In Schedule 14, in Part VI, paragraphs 14, 25 and 26.
1973 c. 65.	Local Government (Scotland) Act 1973.	In Schedule 14, paragraph 68.

PART XVII

ROAD TRAFFIC: GENERAL

Chapter	Short Title	Extent of Repeal
1 & 2 Will. 4. c. 22.	London Hackney Carriage Act 1831.	In section 4, the proviso. Section 18. In section 27, the words from " and for want of sufficient distress " onwards. In section 28, the words from " and for want of sufficient distress " to " justice shall direct ". In section 35, the words " and having thereon any of the numbered plates required by this Act to be fixed on hackney carriages ". In section 36, the words from " and in default " onwards. In section 41, the words from " and upon the refusal " onwards. In section 51, the words from " shall stand or ply " to " hackney carriage; or if any such proprietor or driver ", and the words " or other person ". In section 56, the words from " and in default of payment " to " house of correction ". In section 57, the words from " and in default of payment " onwards. Sections 62, 63, 68, 70 and 71.

Sch. 1

Chapter	Short title	Extent of repeal
6 & 7 Vict. c. 86.	London Hackney Carriages Act 1843.	In section 2, the definitions of "metropolitan stage carriage", "conductor", and "passenger"; and in the definition of "proprietor", the words "or any metropolitan stage carriage", wherever occurring. Section 7. In section 8, the words "or as driver or as conductor of metropolitan stage carriages (as the case may be)"; the words from "respectively" to "sixteen years of age"; and the words "or conductor" and "conductor", wherever occurring. In section 10, the words from the beginning to "and also"; the words "or as driver or as conductor of any metropolitan stage carriage"; and the words "or conductor", wherever occurring. Section 15. In section 17, the word "conductor", wherever occurring. In section 20, the words "or for the driver or the conductor of a metropolitan stage carriage"; and the words from "such imprisonment" to "as the court shall think fit". In section 21, the words "and of every metropolitan stage carriage"; the words "or of a metropolitan stage carriage"; and the words "or conductor", wherever occurring. In section 22, the words "or metropolitan stage carriage"; and the words "or conductor", wherever occurring. In section 23, the words "or conductor", wherever occurring; and the words "or metropolitan stage carriage". In section 24, the words "or conductor", wherever occurring; and the words from "and payment" to "by such justice". In section 25, the word "conductor", wherever occurring.

Chapter	Short title	Extent of repeal
6 & 7 Vict. c. 86—*cont.*	London Hackney Carriages Act 1843—*cont.*	In section 27, the words (wherever occurring) " or conductor ", " or as conductor " and " or as a conductor "; the words " or as driver or conductor of any metropolitan stage carriage "; and the words " or as driver or conductor of such metropolitan stage carriage ". In section 28, the words " or driver or conductor of a metropolitan stage carriage "; the word " conductor "; the words " with or without hard labour, as the justice shall direct "; the words " or metropolitan stage carriage "; and the words " or conductor ", wherever occurring. Section 30. In section 33, the words from " and also " to " place provided for him "; and the words from " and every driver or conductor " (where last occurring) to " upon such carriage ". In section 35, the words " or the driver or the conductor of any metropolitan stage carriage "; and the words " or conductor " and " and conductor ", wherever occurring. Sections 36 and 37. In section 38, the words from " except such " to "this Act ". In section 39, the words from " and in case of nonpayment " onwards. Sections 40, 41, 42 and 43. In section 44, the words " or metropolitan stage carriage ". Sections 45 and 46. The Schedule.
16 & 17 Vict. c. 33.	London Hackney Carriage Act 1853.	In section 2, the words " metropolitan stage and " and " metropolitan stage or ". Section 11. In section 12, the words "metropolitan stage carriages or ". In section 13, the words "metropolitan stage carriages or " and " and at places where metropolitan stage carriages usually call or ply for hire ".

SCH. 1

Chapter	Short title	Extent of repeal
16 & 17 Vict. c. 33—*cont.*	London Hackney Carriage Act 1853—*cont.*	Sections 14 and 15. In section 17, the words " The driver or conductor of any metropolitan stage carriage, or ", " respectively ", and " or in default of payment to imprisonment ". In section 19, the words " or in default of payment be imprisoned ".
16 & 17 Vict. c. 127.	London Hackney Carriage (No. 2) Act 1853.	In section 16, the words " or metropolitan stage carriage ".
30 & 31 Vict. c. 134.	Metropolitan Streets Act 1867.	Section 17.
32 & 33 Vict. c. 115.	Metropolitan Public Carriage Act 1869.	Section 5. In sections 6 and 7, the words " and stage " and " or stage ", wherever occurring. In section 8, the words from " and no stage carriage " to " Secretary of State "; the words " or stage ", wherever occurring; the words " in the case of a hackney carriage "; the words " and in the case of a stage carriage, that the conductor or driver, as the case may require "; and the words " or conductor ". In section 9, the words " or stage ", wherever occurring. In section 15, the words " and metropolitan stage carriages".
7 Edw. 7. c. 55.	London Cab and Stage Carriage Act 1907.	Section 1(2). Sections 3 and 5. In section 6(2), the words " stage carriages, metropolitan stage carriages ", " stage carriage ", and " metropolitan stage carriage ".
23 & 24 Geo. 5. c. 14.	London Passenger Transport Act 1933.	Section 51.
24 & 25 Geo. 5. c. 50.	Road Traffic Act 1934.	Section 41(8).
15 & 16 Geo. 6. & 1 Eliz. 2. c. 39.	Motor Vehicles (International Circulation) Act 1952.	Section 3.
1967 c. 76.	Road Traffic Regulation Act 1967.	In section 21(6), the words from " and references " onwards. Section 110(1). Schedule 7. In Schedule 8, paragraph 4.
1969 c. 60.	Transport (London) Amendment Act 1969.	The whole Act.

PART XVIII
STAMP DUTIES

SCH. 1

Chapter	Short title	Extent of repeal
54 & 55 Vict. c. 39.	Stamp Act 1891.	In Schedule 1, the heading " Faculty or Dispensation of any other kind ".
59 & 60 Vict. c. 28.	Finance Act 1896.	In section 39, the words from " Part Three " to " 1891 ".
10 & 11 Geo. 5. c. 18.	Finance Act 1920.	Section 36.
1 & 2 Geo. 6. c. 46.	Finance Act 1938.	Section 51.
2 & 3 Geo. 6. c. 41.	Finance Act 1939.	In section 35(2), the words " and shall be exempt from stamp duty ".
10 & 11 Geo. 6. c. 35.	Finance Act 1947.	Section 56.
11 & 12 Geo. 6. c. 49.	Finance Act 1948.	Section 75.
12, 13 & 14 Geo. 6. c. 47.	Finance Act 1949.	Section 34.
7 & 8 Eliz. 2. c. 58.	Finance Act 1959.	In section 30, in subsection (4), paragraphs (*a*) and (*b*) and the words " and the said ", and subsection (5). Section 32.
1969 c. 48.	Post Office Act 1969.	Sections 115 and 116.
	Acts of Parliament of Northern Ireland	
1948 c. 15 (N.I.).	Finance Act (Northern Ireland) 1948.	Sections 7 and 8.
1954 c. 3 (N.I.).	Finance (Miscellaneous Provisions) Act (Northern Ireland) 1954.	Section 5.
1959 c. 9 (N.I.).	Finance Act (Northern Ireland) 1959.	In section 5, in subsection (4), paragraphs (*a*) and (*b*) and the words " and the said ", and subsection (5).

PART XIX
SUPERVISORY POWERS OF SUPERIOR COURTS

Chapter	Short title	Extent of repeal
54 Geo. 3. c. 159.	Harbours Act 1814.	Section 23.
1 Geo. 4. c. 100.	Militia (City of London) Act 1820.	Section 48.
9 Geo. 4. c. 69.	Night Poaching Act 1828.	Section 7.
1 & 2 Will. 4. c. 32.	Game Act 1831.	Section 45.
1 & 2 Will. 4. c. 37.	Truck Act 1831.	Section 17

SCH. 1

Chapter	Short Title	Extent of Repeal
1 & 2 Will. 4. c. 55.	Illicit Distillation (Ireland) Act 1831.	Section 49.
1 & 2 Vict. c. 28.	Bread (Ireland) Act 1838.	In section 23, the words from the beginning to " record at Dublin; and ".
3 & 4 Vict. c. 97.	Railway Regulation Act 1840.	Section 17.
7 & 8 Vict. c. 81.	Marriages (Ireland) Act 1844.	Section 80.
8 & 9 Vict. c. 16.	Companies Clauses Consolidation Act 1845.	Section 158, including that section as incorporated in any other Act.
8 & 9 Vict. c. 20.	Railways Clauses Consolidation Act 1845.	Section 156, including that section as incorporated in any other Act.
8 & 9 Vict. c. 109.	Gaming Act 1845.	Section 25.
10 & 11 Vict. c. 84.	Vagrancy (Ireland) Act 1847.	Section 6.
14 & 15 Vict. c. 92.	Summary Jurisdiction (Ireland) Act 1851.	Section 24.
16 & 17 Vict. c. 119.	Betting Act 1853.	Section 14.
17 & 18 Vict. c. 38.	Gaming Houses Act 1854.	Section 11.
17 & 18 Vict. c. 103.	Towns Improvement (Ireland) Act 1854.	Section 96, including that section as incorporated in any other Act.
22 & 23 Vict. c. 66.	Sale of Gas Act 1859.	Section 24.
24 & 25 Vict. c. 97.	Malicious Damage Act 1861.	Section 69.
24 & 25 Vict. c. 100.	Offences against the Person Act 1861.	Section 72.
25 & 26 Vict. c. 114.	Poaching Prevention Act 1862.	Section 5.
35 & 36 Vict. c. 50.	Railway Rolling Stock Protection Act 1872.	Section 7.
41 & 42 Vict. c. 52.	Public Health (Ireland) Act 1878.	Section 261.
26 Geo. 5 & 1 Edw. 8. c. 16.	Coinage Offences Act 1936.	Section 4(4).

PART XX

WAR AND EMERGENCY

Chapter	Short title	Extent of repeal
9 & 10 Geo. 5. c. 33.	Treaty of Peace Act 1919.	The whole Act.
2 & 3 Geo. 6. c. 75.	Compensation (Defence) Act 1939.	In section 17(1), in the definition of " emergency powers " paragraph (*a*) and the word " or " immediately preceding paragraph (*c*).

Chapter	Short title	Extent of repeal
7 & 8 Geo. 6. c. 5.	Landlord and Tenant (Requisitioned Land) Act 1944.	In section 5, in the definition of " Emergency powers ", paragraphs (*a*) and (*b*).
7 & 8 Geo. 6. c. 34.	Validation of War-time Leases Act 1944.	The whole Act.
1 & 2 Eliz. 2. c. 47.	Emergency Laws (Miscellaneous Provisions) Act 1953.	In section 2, the words from " and accordingly " onwards. Section 3(5). Section 5(1) from the beginning to the words " Regulation but ". Sections 9 and 11. In section 12, in subsections (1) and (2) the words " or the Minister of Transport ", and in subsection (3) the word " four ". In section 13, the words " nine and eleven ", the words from " and paragraphs " to " thereto " and the words from " and Part II " onwards. Section 14(2). Schedule 3.
1 & 2 Eliz. 2. c. 52.	Enemy Property Act 1953.	The whole Act except sections 4(1) and (2), 16 and 18.
1969 c. 20.	Foreign Compensation Act 1969.	Section 1(6).

PART XXI

MISCELLANEOUS

Chapter	Title, short title or subject	Extent of repeal
27 Geo. 2. c. 19 (1754).	(Bedford Level).	Section 49.
59 Geo. 3. c. 7.	Cutlery Trade Act 1819.	The whole Act.
4 Geo. 4. c. 46 (1823).	An Act for repealing the capital punishments inflicted by several Acts of the 6th and 27th years of King George the Second; and of the 3rd, 4th and 22nd years of King George the Third; and for providing other punishments in lieu thereof, and in lieu of the punishment of frame breaking under an Act of the 28th year of the same reign.	The whole Act.

SCH. 1

Chapter	Title, short title or subject	Extent of repeal
3 & 4 Vict. c. 97.	Railway Regulation Act 1840.	Section 21.
23 & 24 Vict. c. 37 (1860).	An Act to levy an assessment in the county of Inverness to discharge a debt on the Castle Stewart and Nairn Road in the said county.	The whole Act.
35 & 36 Vict. c. 94.	Licensing Act 1872.	In section 39, the words " or confirm ". In section 75, the words from " and in construing " onwards.
37 & 38 Vict. c. 40.	Board of Trade Arbitrations &c. Act 1874.	In section 4, the words from "An order " onwards.
50 & 51 Vict. c. 51.	Valuation of Lands (Scotland) Amendment Act 1887.	The whole Act.
12, 13 & 14 Geo. 6. c. 68.	Representation of the People Act 1949.	In section 64(2)(*b*)(i), the words from " (other than " to " electoral areas) ".
8 & 9 Eliz. 2. c. 64.	Building Societies Act 1960.	In section 72(2), the words " ' director ' and ".
1969 c. 15.	Representation of the People Act 1969.	In section 8(1)(*b*)(i), the words from " (other than " to " electoral areas) ".
1973 c. 56.	Land Compensation (Scotland) Act 1973.	Section 81(2).
1975 c. 24.	House of Commons Disqualification Act 1975.	In Part III of Schedule 1, the words " Local government officers, the following:—".
1975 c. 25.	Northern Ireland Assembly Disqualification Act 1975.	In Part III of Schedule 1, the words " Local government officers, the following:—".

SCHEDULE 2

AMENDMENTS

PART I

ALCOHOLISM AMENDMENTS

The Inebriates Act 1898 1898 c. 60.

In section 30 of the Inebriates Act 1898, for the words from " shall be " onwards substitute—

" the First Schedule to this Act shall have effect for the purposes of the following enactments, namely—

the Licensing Act 1902, section 6,

the Licensing (Scotland) Act 1903, section 71, and

the Licensing (Scotland) Act 1959, section 160,

(being enactments which operate by reference to the list of offences set out in the Schedule).".

The Licensing Act 1902 1902 c. 28.

In section 6(1) of the Licensing Act 1902, for the words from the beginning to " shall " substitute—

" Where a person is convicted of an offence mentioned in the First Schedule to the Inebriates Act 1898 and such person has, during the period of twelve months immediately preceding the date of the offence, been convicted on three occasions of an offence mentioned in the said Schedule, the court may ".

The Licensing (Scotland) Act 1903 1903 c. 25

In section 73 of the Licensing (Scotland) Act 1903—

(*a*) for the words " section three of the Habitual Drunkards Act, 1879 " substitute " subsection (2) below "; and

(*b*) at the end add—

" (2) In this section " habitual drunkard " means a person who, not being a person suffering from mental disorder within the meaning of the Mental Health (Scotland) Act 1960, is notwithstanding, by reason of habitual intemperate drinking of intoxicating liquor, at times dangerous to himself or to others, or incapable of managing himself and his affairs.".

SCH. 2

PART II

OTHER AMENDMENTS

1939 c. 31

The Civil Defence Act 1939

After section 62(1) of the Civil Defence Act 1939 insert—

"(1A) In subsection (1)(*b*) above 'local authority', in the first place where it occurs—

(*a*) in the case of England and Wales, includes any authority having power to levy a rate as defined for the purposes of the General Rate Act 1967, or for whose expenses a precept may be issued for the levying of such a rate, and any combination or joint committee of any such authorities;

(*b*) in the case of Scotland, means a regional, islands or district council.".

1953 c. 52.

The Enemy Property Act 1953

In section 4(1) of the Enemy Property Act 1953 after "custodian" in the first place where it occurs insert "of enemy property appointed under section 7 of the Trading with the Enemy Act 1939 (hereinafter referred to as 'the Act of 1939')".

1955 c. 6 (4 & 5 Eliz. 2).

The Miscellaneous Financial Provisions Act 1955

In section 1(3) of the Miscellaneous Financial Provisions Act 1955 for "the said proviso" substitute "the proviso to subsection (1) of the said section three".

1967 c. 46.

The Protection of Birds Act 1967

In the Protection of Birds Act 1967—

(*a*) in section 3(2), for "the said section 6(1)" substitute "section 6(1) of the principal Act";

(*b*) in section 12(2), for the words "This Act shall be construed as one with the principal Act" substitute "In this Act 'the principal Act' means the Protection of Birds Act 1954; and this Act shall be construed as one with that Act".

Land Drainage (Amendment) Act 1976

1976 CHAPTER 17

An Act to amend the Land Drainage Act 1930, the Land Drainage Act 1961, Part IV of the Agriculture (Miscellaneous Provisions) Act 1968 and related enactments. [27th May 1976]

BE IT ENACTED by the Queen's most Excellent Majesty, by and with the advice and consent of the Lords Spiritual and Temporal, and Commons, in this present Parliament assembled, and by the authority of the same, as follows:—

1. In this Act " the 1930 Act " means the Land Drainage Act 1930, " the 1961 Act " means the Land Drainage Act 1961, " the 1968 Act " means the Agriculture (Miscellaneous Provisions) Act 1968 and " the Minister " means the Minister of Agriculture, Fisheries and Food.

Definitions. 1930 c. 44. 1961 c. 48. 1968 c. 34.

2.—(1) In paragraph 2 of Part I of Schedule 3 to the 1930 Act (under which the number of votes to which an elector at an election of members of an internal drainage board is entitled depends upon the rateable value of the property in respect of which he is entitled to vote) the reference to rateable value shall be taken as a reference to—

Voting entitlement and qualifications for election at elections of members of internal drainage boards.

(*a*) in the case of any land as respects which a drainage rate levied at the relevant date would, in accordance with section 24(4) of the 1930 Act, be assessable by reference to annual value (as determined for drainage rates purposes), the value on which such a drainage rate would be assessable ;

(*b*) in the case of any land as respects which a drainage rate levied at the relevant date would, in accordance with section 22(4) of the 1961 Act, be assessable by reference to rateable value, the value on which such a rate would be assessable if there were then in force a resolution that section 1 of the Drainage Rates Act 1962 should apply for the purposes of drainage rates made by the board (whether or not there is in fact such a resolution then in force).

1962 c. 39.

(2) In paragraph 1 of Part II of Schedule 3 to the 1930 Act (under which one of the qualifications for election as a member of an internal drainage board is framed by reference to the annual value of land in the electoral district owned or occupied by the candidate, and another is framed by reference to the annual value of such land owned by a person nominating the candidate) the references to annual value shall be taken as references to—

(*a*) in the case of any land as respects which a drainage rate levied at the relevant date would (in accordance with section 24(4) of the 1930 Act) be assessable by reference to annual value (as determined for drainage rates purposes), that value;

(*b*) in the case of any land as respects which a drainage rate levied at the relevant date would, in accordance with section 22(4) of the 1961 Act, be assessable by reference to rateable value, the value arrived at by applying to the rateable value (within the meaning of that section) the relative fraction applied for the purposes of that section in respect of the last drainage rate made before the relevant date (whether that fraction was applied in respect of value or in respect of poundage).

(3) In subsection (2)(*b*) above the reference to the relative fraction is a reference to the fraction arrived at in accordance with section 23 of the 1961 Act.

(4) In this section "the relevant date" means the date as at which, in accordance with rules made under section 33 of the 1930 Act, the voting entitlement of electors at the election in question or, as the case may be, the qualifications of candidates for the election in question are determined.

Petitions and appeals under the Land Drainage Act 1961.

3.—(1) Subsection (2) below shall have effect in substitution for the concluding paragraph (the words from "In relation to" to the end of the subsection) of subsection (2) of section 52 of the 1961 Act (number of qualified persons sufficient for purposes of making a petition or appeal under that Act in relation to an internal drainage district).

(2) In relation to land assessed by reference to rateable value, in accordance with section 22(4) of the 1961 Act, the references in paragraph (*c*) of section 52(2) of the 1961 Act to the annual value shall be construed as references to the value arrived at by applying to the rateable value (within the meaning of the said section 22) the relative fraction applied for the purposes of the said section 22 in respect of the drainage rate referred to in that paragraph (whether that fraction was applied in respect of value or in respect of poundage).

(3) Section 2(3) above applies to the reference to the relative fraction in subsection (2) above as it applies to that reference in section 2(2)(*b*) above.

Powers of entry of internal drainage boards.

4.—(1) The following provisions of this section, which reproduce with minor amendments, and with an increase in the penalty for obstruction, the powers of entry of internal drainage boards provided by section 43 of the 1930 Act and section 40 of the 1961 Act, shall have effect in substitution for the provisions of those sections; and any document expressed as an authority to enter for the purposes of those sections or either of them shall have effect accordingly.

(2) Without prejudice to any other enactment conferring powers of entry, a person authorised by an internal drainage board may, after producing, if so required, a duly authenticated document showing his authority, at all reasonable times—

(*a*) enter any land for the purpose of exercising any function of the board;

(*b*) without prejudice to paragraph (*a*) above, enter and survey any land (including the interior of any mill through which water passes or in connection with which water is impounded) and take levels of the land and inspect the condition of any drainage work on it; and

(*c*) inspect and take copies of any Acts of Parliament, awards or other documents in the possession of any internal drainage board or navigation authority which relate to land drainage and confer any powers or impose any duties on that board or authority.

(3) A person entitled under this section to enter any land may take with him such other persons and such equipment as may be necessary and if the land is unoccupied he shall, on leaving it, leave it as effectually secured against trespassers as he found it.

(4) Except in an emergency, admission to any land shall not be demanded as of right under this section unless notice

in writing of the intended entry has been given to the occupier and, if the land is used for residential purposes or the demand is for admission with heavy equipment, has been given not less than seven days before the demand is made.

(5) Section 34(3) of the 1930 Act shall extend to any injury sustained by any person by reason of the exercise of a power conferred by this section.

(6) If any person intentionally obstructs or impedes any person exercising a power conferred by this section he shall be liable on summary conviction to a fine not exceeding £200.

(7) This section shall not apply in relation to land belonging to Her Majesty in right of the Crown or the Duchy of Lancaster, in relation to land belonging to the Duchy of Cornwall or in relation to land belonging to a government department.

Powers of entry of local authorities for land drainage purposes.

5.—(1) Subsections (2) to (7) of section 4 above shall apply in relation to local authorities, and in relation to their functions under the 1930 Act and the 1961 Act, as they apply in relation to, and to the functions of, internal drainage boards.

(2) The powers of entry conferred on local authorities by subsection (1) above are in substitution for the powers of entry exercisable by such authorities under section 51 of the 1930 Act and by virtue of section 30(9) and 34(1) of the 1961 Act.

(3) In this section "local authorities" means any of the following, namely, the council of a county, district or London borough, the Common Council of the City of London and the Greater London Council.

Meaning of agricultural buildings for purposes of drainage charges and drainage rates.

1967 c. 9.

6. For the avoidance of doubt it is hereby declared that in section 16 of the 1961 Act (which, as amended by section 116(6) of the General Rate Act 1967, contains, for the purposes of the provisions of the 1961 Act relating to drainage charges, a definition of agricultural buildings by reference to the meaning given to that expression by section 26(4) of the said Act of 1967) and in section 22(2) of the 1961 Act (which equates agricultural buildings with agricultural land for the purposes of assessing drainage rates, and which, as amended by section 116(6) of the General Rate Act 1967, also defines agricultural buildings by reference to the meaning given to that expression by section 26(4) of the said Act of 1967) the reference to the General Rate Act 1967 is a reference to that Act as amended by the Rating Act 1971.

1971 c. 39.

Compensation for loss of office, etc.

7.—(1) The provisions of subsections (2) to (6) below shall have effect in substitution for section 67 of the 1930 Act.

(2) The Minister shall by regulations provide for the payment, subject to such exceptions or conditions as may be specified in the regulations, of compensation to any officer or other employee of a relevant authority who suffers loss of employment or loss or diminution of emoluments which is attributable to—

(*a*) a scheme under section 4 of the 1930 Act;

(*b*) an order under section 11 of the 1930 Act; or

(*c*) an agreement under section 25 of the 1961 Act.

(3) For the purposes of subsection (2) above the relevant authorities are—

(*a*) in cases falling within paragraph (*a*) of that subsection, drainage authorities within the meaning of the 1930 Act; and

(*b*) in cases falling within paragraph (*b*) or (*c*) of that subsection, internal drainage boards.

(4) Any compensation payable by virtue of this section shall be paid—

(*a*) in the case of compensation for loss attributable to a scheme under section 4(1)(*a*) or an order under section 11 of the 1930 Act, by the water authority to whom the transfer effected by the scheme or order is made;

(*b*) in the case of compensation for loss attributable to an agreement under section 25 of the 1961 Act, by the internal drainage board with whom the agreement is made; and

(*c*) in the case of compensation for loss attributable to a scheme under section 4(1)(*b*) of the 1930 Act, by such water authority as may be specified for this purpose in the scheme or such internal drainage board or boards as may be so specified.

(5) Regulations under this section—

(*a*) may make different provision in relation to different classes of persons;

(*b*) may include provision as to the manner in which and the persons to whom any claim for compensation by virtue of this section is to be made, and for the determination of all questions arising under the regulations.

(6) Regulations under this section shall be made by statutory instrument and shall be subject to annulment in pursuance of a resolution of either House of Parliament.

8.—(1) The amendments in Schedule 1 to this Act shall have effect (being amendments for increasing the fines payable in respect of offences created by the 1930 Act, the 1961 Act and Offences.

Part IV of the 1968 Act and for removing inconsistencies at present existing as between certain offences of a similar nature created by those Acts).

(2) For the avoidance of doubt it is hereby declared that section 50(4) of the 1968 Act (offences committed by body corporate) does not apply in relation to offences under the enactments applied for the purposes of section 26 of that Act by subsection (3) of the said section 26.

Minor amendments and repeals.

9.—(1) Schedule 2 to this Act, which makes minor amendments to the 1930 Act, the 1961 Act, the 1968 Act and related enactments, including amendments consequential on the foregoing provisions of this Act, shall have effect.

(2) The enactments and instruments specified in Schedule 3 to this Act (which include certain spent enactments) are hereby repealed to the extent specified in the third column of that Schedule.

Construction etc.

10.—(1) Except in so far as the context otherwise requires, any reference in this Act to an enactment is a reference to that enactment as amended, extended or applied by or under any other enactment, including any enactment contained in this Act.

(2) Without prejudice to subsection (1) above, references in this Act to land assessed in accordance with section 22(4) of the 1961 Act (assessment of land for drainage rates by reference to rateable value) include references to land assessed in accordance with the said section 22(4) by virtue of a determination under section 31 of the 1968 Act (which provides for assessment by reference to an apportioned rateable value in certain cases), and references to rateable value shall be construed accordingly.

(3) There shall be paid out of money provided by Parliament any increase attributable to this Act in the sums so payable under any other Act.

(4) This Act may be cited as the Land Drainage (Amendment) Act 1976.

(5) This Act shall come into force on such day as the Minister may by order made by statutory instrument appoint.

SCHEDULES

SCHEDULE 1

Section 8.

Increase of Penalties and Harmonisation of Certain Offences

1. In section 10(3) of the 1930 Act (fine for obstructing or impeding a person authorised by a water authority to inspect and to take copies of documents of an internal drainage board) for " five pounds " substitute " two hundred pounds ".

2.—(1) In section 26(4A) of the 1930 Act (failing to provide information, or providing false information, with respect to name and address of occupier of hereditament for drainage rates purposes)—

(*a*) for " require " substitute " serve a notice on " and after " levied " insert " requiring him " ;

(*b*) after " fails " insert " without reasonable excuse " ;

(*c*) after " knowingly " insert " or recklessly " ;

(*d*) for " false statement " substitute " statement that is false in a material particular " ; and

(*e*) for " five pounds " substitute " two hundred pounds ".

(2) After section 26(4A) of that Act insert—

" (4B) Where a person is convicted under subsection (4A) above in respect of a failure to comply with a notice and the failure continues after the conviction, then, unless he has a reasonable excuse for the continuance of the failure, he shall be guilty of a further offence under that subsection and may, on summary conviction, be punished accordingly.".

3. In section 44(4) of the 1930 Act (fine for unlawfully obstructing a watercourse) for " one hundred pounds " substitute " four hundred pounds ", and in section 44(5) of that Act (daily fine for failure to obey court order to remove the obstruction) for " five pounds " substitute " forty pounds ".

4. In section 47(8) of the 1930 Act (fine for contravention of or failure to comply with a byelaw and daily fine for continued contravention or failure) for " fifty pounds " substitute " four hundred pounds " and for " five pounds " substitute " forty pounds ".

5. In section 12 of the 1961 Act (failure to provide information, or providing false information, with respect to name and address of occupiers of land)—

(*a*) for " require " substitute " serve a notice on " and after " area " insert " requiring him " ;

(*b*) after " fails " insert " without reasonable excuse " ;

(*c*) after " knowingly " insert " or recklessly " ;

(*d*) for " misstatement " substitute " statement that is false in a material particular " ;

Sch. 1

(*e*) for " five pounds " substitute " two hundred pounds " ; and

(*f*) renumber the section as subsection (1) of the section and add—

" (2) Where a person is convicted under subsection (1) above in respect of a failure to comply with a notice and the failure continues after the conviction, then, unless he has a reasonable excuse for the continuance of the failure, he shall be guilty of a further offence under that subsection and may, on summary conviction, be punished accordingly.".

6. In subsection (5) of section 28 of the 1961 Act (which, with modifications, applies to notices under that section the provisions of section 290(2) to (7) of the Public Health Act 1936) insert after " subsection (6) " in paragraph (*c*) " for the words ' five pounds ' there shall be substituted ' two hundred pounds ' and ".

1936 c. 49.

7. In section 26 of the 1968 Act (which, as amended by the General Rate Act 1967, applies, in respect of a failure to give information, or giving false information, under that section, the provisions of section 82(4) and (5) of the General Rate Act 1967, and of section 82(6) so far as it provides for a fine) add at the end " but so that, in their application for the purposes of this section, the fines under section 82(4) and (6) shall, instead of being, respectively, twenty pounds and one hundred pounds, be in both cases two hundred pounds ".

1967 c. 9.

Section 9(1).

SCHEDULE 2

Minor Amendments

1930 c. 44.

The Land Drainage Act 1930

1. In section 4 of the 1930 Act (schemes for re-organisation) subsection (1A) (which was inserted by paragraph 21(4) of Schedule 8 to the Water Act 1973) shall (without prejudice to the duty of a water authority, under section 19(1) of the Water Act 1973, to delegate their functions under the said section 4 to their regional land drainage committee) be omitted.

1973 c. 37.

2. In sections 7(3), 36(3), 42(5) and 44(5) of the 1930 Act (recovery of expenses by water authorities and internal drainage boards) omit the words " summarily as a civil debt ".

3. In section 8 of the 1930 Act (power to vary awards) subsection (1A) (which was inserted by paragraph 22(2) of Schedule 8 to the Water Act 1973) shall (without prejudice to the duty of a water authority, under section 19(1) of the Water Act 1973, to delegate their functions under the said section 8 to their regional land drainage committee) be omitted.

4. In section 9(1) of the 1930 Act (commutation by water authority of obligations to repair by reason of tenure etc.) after " work " insert " in the area of the authority ".

5. In section 10(3) of the 1930 Act (obstructing or impeding person authorised by water authority to inspect and to take copies of documents of internal drainage board) after " who " insert " intentionally ". SCH. 2

6. In section 11 of the 1930 Act (transfer of functions of internal drainage boards) subsection (2) (which was added by paragraph 23 of Schedule 8 to the Water Act 1973) shall (without prejudice to the duty of a water authority, under section 19(1) of the Water Act 1973, to delegate their functions under the said section 11 to their regional land drainage committee) be omitted.

7. In section 13 of the 1930 Act (provisions with respect to the making and validity of orders)—

(*a*) after " all orders " insert " by the Minister ";

(*b*) for " provisional only " substitute " subject to special parliamentary procedure ";

(*c*) after " shall ", in the third place where that word occurs, insert " except as provided by paragraph 5 thereof ";

(*d*) for the words " such orders under this Part of this Act as are not confirmed by Parliament " substitute " all orders made by the Minister under this Part of this Act ".

8. In section 22(3) of the 1930 Act (precepts issued by water authorities to internal drainage boards) for " in a form to be prescribed by the Minister " substitute " in such form as the Minister may direct ".

9. In section 23 of the 1930 Act (amounts due from local authorities to water authorities under the Water Act 1973) after subsection (1) insert—

" (1A) Any amount due to a water authority from the council of a London borough under the Water Act 1973 shall be defrayed as the council, having regard to the benefit, if any, derived by various areas, think just and equitable as general expenses or as special expenses chargeable on such part or parts of the London borough within the water authority's area as the council think fit.". 1973 c. 37.

10. In the proviso to subsection (3) of section 24 of the 1930 Act (owner deemed to be in occupation of unoccupied land for drainage rating purposes) after " Act " insert " and Part I of the Third Schedule to this Act "; and in subsection (6) of that section (differential drainage rates) omit the words from " So long as any such order " to the end of the subsection.

11.—(1) In section 26(4) of the 1930 Act (incidence of drainage rates) omit " or is deemed to be " in each place where those words occur and omit " or is deemed to have been ".

(2) In paragraph (*c*) of the said section 26(4) after " shall " insert " (subject to any agreement to the contrary) ".

(3) In paragraph (*e*) of the said section 26(4) for the words from " in respect of " to " paragraph (*d*) of this subsection " substitute " the full amount of an occupier's rate ", for the words " so much of

SCH. 2 any sum so paid in excess " substitute " such sum " and for the words " the said paragraph (*d*) " substitute " paragraph (*d*) of this subsection ".

12. In section 27(2) of the 1930 Act (publication of drainage rate) after " Any such notice " insert " must state the amount of the rate, the relative fraction for the purposes of section 23 of the Land Drainage Act 1961 applicable in respect thereof, and the date on which the rate was made and ".

1961 c. 48.

13. In section 29 of the 1930 Act—

(*a*) in subsection (3) (notice of apportionment of annual value for drainage rates purposes) after " decision " where it first occurs insert " together with a statement in writing of the rights of appeal conferred by this section " ;

(*b*) in subsection (4) (power of internal drainage boards to get information from inland revenue authorities) for " surveyors of taxes " substitute " inspector of taxes ", omit " in force " and at the end add " (being the annual value for the purposes of Schedule A shown in the assessments for that year signed and allowed under section 35 of the Income Tax Act 1952 or, in cases where appeals were made against the assessments, the annual values for those purposes as finally determined in the proceedings on or in consequence of the appeals) ".

14. In section 30(1) of the 1930 Act (appeal against drainage rates) and section 31(3) of that Act (recovery of drainage rates) after " section 29(3) of this Act " insert " or section 32 of the Agriculture (Miscellaneous Provisions) Act 1968 ".

1968 c. 34.

15. In section 34 of the 1930 Act (general drainage powers of drainage boards)—

(*a*) in subsection (3) (compensation for injury sustained by reason of the exercise of powers under the section) after " under this section " insert " or under section 6(2) above " ; and

(*b*) in subsection (4) (nothing in the section to be taken as authorising entry on land except for the purpose of maintaining existing works) after " this section " insert " or section 6(2) above ".

16. In section 35(14) of the 1930 Act (maintenance of watercourses) before " this section " insert " subsections (11) and (12) of " before " the main river " insert " any watercourse forming part of " and at the end add " and in the said subsection (11) ' local authority ' means any of the following, namely, the council of a county, district or London borough, the Common Council of the City of London and the Greater London Council ".

17. In section 37(1) of the 1930 Act (commutation by drainage board of obligations to repair by reason of tenure etc.) after " work " where that word first occurs insert " in the district of the board ".

18. In section 41(1) of the 1930 Act (power to vary navigation rights) for the words " in the case of a navigation authority which "

substitute " it appears to the Minister that a navigation authority ", after " vested in it," insert " and ", and for " any navigation authority " substitute " the navigation authority ". Sch. 2

19. In section 42(2) and in section 42(4) of the 1930 Act (power of drainage board to levy navigation tolls) insert " subsection (1) of " before " this section " and in paragraph (ii) of the said section 42(2) for the words from " provisional only " to the end of the paragraph substitute " subject to special parliamentary procedure ".

20. In section 44 of the 1930 Act (obstructions in watercourses)—

(*a*) in subsection (3) for " the person by whom the said obstruction has been erected or raised or otherwise altered " substitute " such person as is specified in subsection (7) of this section " ;

(*b*) for subsection (7) substitute—

" (7) The person upon whom a notice may be served under subsection (3) of this section is—

(*a*) in a case where the person by whom the obstruction has been erected or raised or otherwise altered has, at the time when the notice is served, power to remove the obstruction, that person ;

(*b*) in any other case, any person having power to remove the obstruction.".

21. For section 45 of the 1930 Act (power of internal drainage boards to acquire and dispose of land) substitute the following (which reproduces with minor amendments the said section 45 and the enactments applied by that section):—

" Powers of internal drainage boards to acquire and dispose of land.

45.—(1) An internal drainage board may, for any purpose in connection with the performance of any of their functions, acquire by agreement or, if authorised by the Minister, compulsorily, any land, whether inside or outside their area.

(2) An internal drainage board may exercise the powers conferred by subsection (1) above so as to acquire interests in or rights over land by way of securing the creation of new interests or rights in their favour (as well as by acquiring interests or rights already in existence).

(3) Where an internal drainage board exercise their powers under this section so as to acquire compulsorily an interest in or right over land by way of securing compulsorily the creation in their favour of a new interest or right, the enactments relating to compensation for the compulsory purchase of land shall, in their application to such acquisition, have effect with the necessary modifications and the Acquisition of Land (Authorisation Procedure) Act 1946 and the Compulsory Purchase Act 1965 shall, in their application to any such acquisition, have effect with such modifications as may be prescribed.

1946 c. 49.
1965 c. 56.

SCH. 2

(4) Where an internal drainage board propose to acquire by agreement any land belonging to Her Majesty in right of the Duchy of Lancaster, the Chancellor and Council of that Duchy may sell the land to the board and the land may be granted to them and the proceeds of sale shall be paid and dealt with as if the land had been sold under the authority of the Duchy of Lancaster Lands Act 1855.

1855 c. 58.

(5) Nothing in this section shall authorise the compulsory acquisition of any land belonging to Her Majesty in right of the Crown or the Duchy of Lancaster, or of any land belonging to the Duchy of Cornwall or a government department.

(6) Subject to subsections (7) to (9) below, an internal drainage board may dispose of land held by them in any manner they wish.

(7) Except with the consent of the Minister, an internal drainage board shall not dispose of land under this section, otherwise than by way of a short tenancy, for a consideration less than the best that can reasonably be obtained.

(8) Except with the consent of the Minister, an internal drainage board shall not dispose under this section, otherwise than by way of a short tenancy, of land which (whether before or after the commencement of this Act) has been acquired by the board compulsorily, or acquired by them by agreement at a time when they were authorised to acquire it compulsorily.

(9) For the purposes of this section a disposal of land is a disposal by way of a short tenancy if it consists of the grant of a term not exceeding 7 years, or the assignment of a term which at the date of the assignment has not more than 7 years to run.".

22. In section 48 of the 1930 Act (appointment of officers of internal drainage boards) for the words from " appoint " to the end of the section substitute " pay to persons employed by them such reasonable remuneration as they think fit ".

23. In section 50(2) of the 1930 Act (general drainage powers of local authorities) before " drainage boards " insert " internal ".

24. In section 53 of the 1930 Act (expenses and borrowing of county and London borough councils) the references to that Act shall include references to the 1961 Act ; and in subsection (1) of that section (which, as amended by paragraph 1 of Schedule 14 to the London Government Act 1963 and paragraph 25(5) of Schedule 29 to the Local Government Act 1972, makes provision with respect to the expenses of county councils, London borough councils and the Common Council of the City of London) omit the reference to the Common Council of the City of London.

1963 c. 33.
1972 c. 70.

25. In section 55(1) of the 1930 Act (grants in respect of drainage works)— SCH. 2

(*a*) omit the words " under this Act " ;

(*b*) insert " drainage " before " works ", in both places where that word occurs ;

(*c*) in paragraph (*a*) of the proviso after " is being " insert " or has been ".

26. In section 59 of the 1930 Act (power of Minister to authorise landowners to execute drainage works)—

(*a*) at the end of subsection (6) add " and after receiving the report of such inquiry he shall proceed as provided by subsection (5) above " ;

(*b*) in the proviso to subsection (7), for the words from " no entry " onwards substitute " every person interested in the land (other than any person who is one of those authorised to execute the works) shall be entitled to compensation for any injury suffered by him in respect of that interest by reason of the works " ;

(*c*) after subsection (7) insert—

" (7A) In case of dispute as to the amount of any compensation payable under subsection (7) above, the amount shall be determined by the Lands Tribunal.".

27. In section 70 of the 1930 Act (expenses of Minister) omit the words " to such an amount as the Treasury may sanction ".

28. For section 72 of the 1930 Act (power of the Minister to hold inquiries) there shall be substituted—

" 72.—(1) The Minister may cause to be held such inquiries as he considers necessary or desirable for the purposes of the Land Drainage Acts.

(2) The provisions of section 250(2) to (5) of the Local Government Act 1972 (which relate to the giving of evidence at and defraying the cost of local inquiries) shall apply for the purposes of any inquiry held pursuant to subsection (1) above or any other provision of the Land Drainage Acts, but with the omission of the word " local " from subsection (4). 1972 c. 70.

(3) In subsection (1) above " the Land Drainage Acts " means this Act, the Land Drainage Act 1961, Part IV of the Agriculture (Miscellaneous Provisions) Act 1968 and Part V of the Agriculture Act 1970.".

29. In section 74(1) of the 1930 Act (power of the Minister to make regulations) the second reference to that Act shall include a reference to the 1961 Act, Part IV of the 1968 Act and Part V of the Agriculture Act 1970.

30. In section 75 of the 1930 Act (notices) after " this Act " insert " the Land Drainage Act 1961 or Part IV of the Agriculture (Miscellaneous Provisions) Act 1968 " and after " any person " insert " shall be in writing and ".

SCH. 2

31. In section 81 of the 1930 Act (interpretation)—

(*a*) in the definition of " drainage " after " water ", where it first occurs, insert " (including sea water) ", after " irrigation " insert " other than spray irrigation " and omit " and the supply of water " ; and

(*b*) at the end of the section add the following paragraph—

" References in this Act to the execution of drainage works include references to the improvement of drainage works, and in section 7 the reference includes also reference to the maintenance of drainage works.".

32. In section 82(2) of the 1930 Act (exercise of local Act powers where drainage boundaries are altered), for " a drainage district or drainage area " substitute " an internal drainage district ", for " drainage board of the district or area " substitute " internal drainage board of the district " and omit " or area " in the second place where those words occur.

33. In Part III of Schedule 2 to the 1930 Act (validity of orders). in paragraph 5 (which was added by the Statutory Orders (Special
1949 No. 2393. Procedure) (Substitution) Order 1949) omit the words " paragraphs 2 to 4 of " and for " those provisions " substitute " paragraphs 2 to 4 of this Part of this Schedule ".

34. In paragraph 1 of Part I of Schedule 3 to the 1930 Act (persons to vote at election of members of internal drainage board) after " land " where it first occurs insert " in a board's district ", and in paragraph 2 of the said Part I in the first column for " exceeds £1000 " substitute " amounts to £1000 or more ".

The Drainage Rates Act 1958

35.—(1) Sub-paragraph (2) below shall have effect in substitution
1958 c. 37. for subsections (2) to (6) of section 1 of the Drainage Rates Act 1958 (annual value for purposes of drainage rates) and the reference
1963 c. 10. to that section in section 1(2)(*a*) of the Drainage Rates Act 1963 shall be construed accordingly.

(2) For the purposes of section 1(1) of the said Act of 1958 the annual value of any land for the purposes of Schedule A as determined for the purposes of the year of assessment 1962-63, is its annual value for the purposes of Schedule A as shown in the assess-
1952 c. 10. ment for that year signed and allowed under section 35 of the Income Tax Act 1952 or, in any case where an appeal was made against the assessment, its annual value for those purposes as finally determined in the proceedings on or in consequence of the appeal.

1961 c. 48. *The Land Drainage Act* 1961

36. In subsection (1) (power of water authority to raise revenue by means of general drainage charges) of section 1 of the 1961 Act (as
1973 c. 37. substituted by paragraph 12(1) of Schedule 5 to the Water Act 1973) after " district " insert " in their area ".

37. In section 1A of the 1961 Act (which is one of the sections substituted for section 1 of that Act by paragraph 12 of Schedule 5 to the

Water Act 1973, and makes provision with respect to the amount of general drainage charges) after subsection (3) insert the following subsection— Sch. 2

" (3A) An order under this section shall be made by statutory instrument, shall be subject to annulment in pursuance of a resolution of either House of Parliament, and may be varied or revoked by a subsequent order under this section.".

38. Section 3 of the 1961 Act (designation of watercourses and special drainage charge) shall (without prejudice to the duty of a water authority, under section 19(1) of the Water Act 1973, to delegate their functions under the said section 3 to their regional land drainage committee) have effect as though the amendments to the said section 3 contained in paragraph 72(1) and (2) of Schedule 8 to the Water Act 1973 had not been made, and shall have effect also as though the last amendment to subsection (9) contained in paragraph 25(1) of Schedule 29 to the Local Government Act 1972 (substitution of certain words for " it ") had not been made.

39. In paragraph (*c*) of section 5(4) o fthe 1961 Act after " may " insert " (subject to any agreement to the contrary) ".

40. In section 6(2) of the 1961 Act (publication of drainage charges) for " that area " substitute " the area in respect of which the charge was raised ".

41. In section 8 of the 1961 Act (amendments as respects drainage charge) after subsection (3) add—

" (4) Where an amendment is made in pursuance of this section any amount overpaid shall be repaid or allowed and any amount underpaid may be recovered as if it were arrears of the charge.".

42. In section 11 of the 1961 Act (agreements for assessment to and recovery of drainage charge)—

(*a*) at the end of subsection (2) insert " and, in relation to any water authority, any chargeable land " ;

(*b*) omit subsection (3) (which was inserted by paragraph 25(2) of Schedule 29 to the Local Government Act 1972). 1972 c. 70.

43. In section 23(2) of the 1961 Act (notice of relative fraction for drainage rates purposes) for the words from the beginning to " the notice ", in the second place where those words occur, substitute " The notice of the rate given under section 27 of the Act of 1930 and stating, in accordance with that section, the relative fraction ".

44.—(1) In paragraph (*b*) of section 23(4) of the 1961 Act (annual value for the purposes of that section) for the words from " (apportioned " to the end of the paragraph substitute " or in any case where an appeal was made against the assessment, its annual value under Schedule A as finally determined in the proceedings on or in consequence of the appeal (apportioned where the hereditament forms part only of any land in respect of which an assessment to income tax was made under Schedule A for the year of assessment 1962-63).".)

SCH. 2 (2) Omit section 23(5) of the 1961 Act (power of internal drainage board to obtain information from tax authorities).

45. In section 25(4) of the 1961 Act (whereby agreements entered into by an internal drainage board under that section may provide for amending the constitution of the board) after " appoint members of the board " insert " in addition to the elected members ".

46. In section 28 of the 1961 Act (removal of obstruction from watercourses)—

(*a*) after subsection (5)(*b*) insert—

" (*bb*) in subsection (5) the words 'the part of the watercourse where the impediment occurs or land adjoining that part' shall be substituted for the words 'the premises in question' ; " ;

(*b*) at the end of subsection (5)(*c*) add " and after the words 'and he shall be liable' there shall be inserted 'on summary conviction' " ;

(*c*) at the end of subsection (6) add " (but no other provision of the said Act of 1936 shall apply in relation to the said section two hundred and ninety as applied by this section) ".

47. In section 30(9) of the 1961 Act (schemes for drainage of small areas) before " drainage board " insert " internal ", before " the Act of 1930 " insert " sections 34 and 38 of ", after " restrictions " insert " and liabilities " and for " that Act " substitute " those sections ".

48. In section 34 of the 1961 Act (power of local authorities to undertake drainage works against flooding)—

(*a*) in subsection (2B) (which was inserted by paragraph 22(4) of
1973 c. 70. Schedule 5 to the Water Act 1973) for the words from the beginning to " shall " substitute " A council other than the Greater London Council shall not " ;

(*b*) in subsection (4) for " expenses for special county purposes " substitute " special expenses chargeable on the district in respect of which they were incurred ".

49. For section 38(3) of the 1961 Act substitute—

" (3) The council of a county or London borough, the Common Council and, as respects the main metropolitan watercourses (as defined in Schedule 14 to the London Government Act 1963), the Greater London Council, may by agreement with any person execute within the council's area, at his expense (excluding the amount of any grant paid under this subsection), any drainage works which that person is entitled to execute ; and the Minister may, with the approval of the Treasury, make grants to a council in respect of the cost of any works executed by the council in pursuance of this subsection.

For the purposes of this subsection the area of the Common Council shall include the Inner Temple and the Middle Tempe.".

The London Government Act 1963 Sch. 2

50. In Schedule 14 to the London Government Act 1963 (functions of local authorities in London in respect to land drainage)— 1963 c. 33.

(*a*) in paragraph 1 after " the City ", in both places, insert " and the Temples " ;

(*b*) in paragraph 3 omit the words from " and without prejudice " onwards ;

(*c*) in paragraph 13 for the words from " under section 23 " onwards substitute " (in like manner as under section 23(1A) of the Act of 1930) " ;

(*d*) in paragraph 15(1) at the end of the definition of " local enactment " add " or, where the watercourse is a metropolitan watercourse by virtue of an order under sub-paragraph (2)(*a*) below, such enactments as may be specified in relation thereto by the order " and in the first column of paragraph (2A) of the Table (the paragraph inserted by section 7(4)(*d*) of the Greater London Council (General Powers) Act 1968) omit the words from " and any other watercourse " onwards ; 1968 c. xxxix.

(*e*) after paragraph 15(2) insert—

" (2A) An order under sub-paragraph (2)(*a*) above shall specify the local enactments that are to be the local enactments for the purposes of this Schedule in relation to the watercourse or part of a watercourse dealt with by the order.".

The Agriculture (Miscellaneous Provisions) Act 1968 1968 c. 34.

51. The special drainage charge raised by a water authority for any year shall be of such amount as may, subject to subsection (1) of section 23 of the 1968 Act, be determined by the authority's regional land drainage committee ; and accordingly, that subsection shall be amended by substituting for the words " being an amount which exceeds " the words " and such amount shall be determined by the authority's regional land drainage committee but shall exceed ".

52. In section 37(4) of the 1968 Act (grants in respect of the cost of works executed by agreement with other persons) after " water authority " insert " or internal drainage board ".

The Agriculture Act 1970 1970 c. 40.

53. In subsection (4) of section 88 of the Agriculture Act 1970 (power of Greater London Council to provide flood warning system) for the words " section 51 of the Land Drainage Act 1930 and section 40 of the Land Drainage Act 1961 " substitute " section 4 of the Land Drainage (Amendment) Act 1975 ", and for paragraph (i) of that subsection substitute—

" (i) in the case of the said section 4, in relation to, and to the functions under this subsection of, the Greater London Council as it applies in relation to, and to the functions of, an internal drainage board, or ".

SCH. 2

The Local Government Act 1972

1972 c. 70.

1961 c. 48.

54. In paragraph 25 of Schedule 29 to the Local Government Act 1972 (amendments of Land Drainage Act 1961)—

(*a*) in sub-paragraph (1) omit the words from " and for the word " to the end of the sub-paragraph ; and

(*b*) in sub-paragraph (2) omit the words from " and at the end " to the end of the sub-paragraph.

1973 c. 37.

The Water Act 1973

55. In section 6(3) of the Water Act 1973 after " charges " insert " applying for a charges option order pursuant to section 19(7) below ".

56. In section 19(1) of that Act (discharge of water authority's functions by their regional land drainage committee) for " making " substitute " raising " and after " precepts " insert " the making of an application for a charges option order ".

57. In paragraph 11 of Schedule 5 to that Act (precepts by water authorities to local authorities)—

(*a*) in sub-paragraph (11) (carrying forward excesses or deficiencies to the next financial year) for " the next financial year " substitute " the financial year following that in which the determination is made or (at the option of the water authority) the next financial year after that following financial year ", and for the words " that next financial year " substitute " the financial year to which it is brought forward " ; and

(*b*) in sub-paragraph (13) (definitions) at the end of the definition of " relevant expenditure " insert " and this shall be taken to include an appropriate proportion of the administrative expenses of the authority, of the expenses of their research and related activities, of any amount allocated by them to reserve pursuant to paragraph 31(1) of Schedule 3 to this Act ; and of any payment to the Council pursuant to paragraph 33 of that Schedule ".

SCHEDULE 3

Section 9(2).

Repeals

Acts

Chapter	Short Title	Extent of Repeal
11 & 12 Geo. 5. c. lxxxviii.	The Lancashire County Council (Drainage) Act 1921.	The whole Act.
13 & 14 Geo. 5. c. xcviii.	The West Riding of Yorkshire County Council (Drainage) Act 1923.	The whole Act.
20 & 21 Geo. 5. c. 44.	The Land Drainage Act 1930.	Section 4(1A). In section 8(1), the words " subject to subsection (1A) below ". Section 8(1A). In section 16, the words from the beginning to " and ". Section 11(2). Section 43. Section 51. Section 67.
9 & 10 Geo. 6. c. 49.	The Acquisition of Land (Authorisation Procedure) Act 1946.	In Schedule 4, the entry relating to the Land Drainage Act 1930.
6 & 7 Eliz. 2. c. 37.	The Drainage Rates Act 1958.	Section 1(2) to (6).
9 & 10 Eliz. 2. c. 48.	The Land Drainage Act 1961.	Section 3(1A). Section 11(3). In section 34(1), the words " forty-three " and the words from " and section forty " onwards. Section 40. In section 43, the words from " and the provision " onwards. In section 52(2), the concluding paragraph. In Schedule 1, paragraphs 17(2) and 18.
1963 c. 33.	The London Government Act 1963.	In Schedule 14, in paragraph 2 the words " and section 51 " and in paragraph 7(*c*) the words from " or by virtue " onwards.
1968 c. 34.	The Agriculture (Miscellaneous Provisions) Act 1968.	In section 36(2), the words from " section 75 " to " and ".
1972 c. 70.	The Local Government Act 1972.	In Schedule 29, in paragraph 25(1) the words from " and for the word " onwards and in paragraph 25(2) the words from " and at the end " onwards.
1973 c. 37.	The Water Act 1973.	In Schedule 8, paragraphs 21(4), 22, 23, 72(1) and (2) and 74.

SCH. 3

INSTRUMENTS

No.	Title	Extent of Repeal
1971 No. 1732.	The Temples Order 1971.	Paragraph (*a*) of Article 5(4).
1974 No. 595.	The Local Authorities etc. (Miscellaneous Provisions) (No. 2) Order 1974.	Article 3(5).

Licensing (Amendment) Act 1976

1976 CHAPTER 18

An Act to amend the law relating to premises for which special hours certificates may be granted under the Licensing Act 1964. [27th May 1976]

BE IT ENACTED by the Queen's most Excellent Majesty, by and with the advice and consent of the Lords Spiritual and Temporal, and Commons, in this present Parliament assembled, and by the authority of the same, as follows:—

Repeal of section 76(5) of Licensing Act 1964.

1964 c. 26.

1. Subsection (5) of section 76 of the Licensing Act 1964 (which excludes any bar from premises in respect of which any special hours certificate may be granted under that Act) is hereby repealed.

Short title, citation and extent.

2.—(1) This Act may be cited as the Licensing (Amendment) Act 1976.

(2) The Licensing Acts 1964 and 1967 and this Act may be cited together as the Licensing Acts 1964 to 1976.

(3) This Act does not extend to Scotland or Northern Ireland.

Seychelles Act 1976

1976 CHAPTER 19

An Act to make provision for, and in connection with, the attainment by Seychelles of fully responsible status as a Republic within the Commonwealth.

[27th May 1976]

BE IT ENACTED by the Queen's most Excellent Majesty, by and with the advice and consent of the Lords Spiritual and Temporal, and Commons, in this present Parliament assembled, and by the authority of the same, as follows:—

Fully responsible status of Seychelles

1.—(1) On and after 29th June 1976 (in this Act referred to as " the appointed day ") Her Majesty's Government in the United Kingdom shall have no responsibility for the government of Seychelles.

(2) No Act of the Parliament of the United Kingdom passed on or after the appointed day shall extend, or be deemed to extend, to Seychelles as part of its law.

Power to provide for constitution of Seychelles as Republic.

2. Her Majesty may by Order in Council (to be laid before Parliament after being made) make provision for the constitution of Seychelles as a Republic on the appointed day.

Consequential modifications of British Nationality Acts.

1948 c. 56.

3.—(1) On and after the appointed day the British Nationality Acts 1948 to 1965 shall have effect as if in section 1(3) of the British Nationality Act 1948 (Commonwealth countries having separate citizenship) there were added at the end the words " and Seychelles ".

(2) Except as provided by section 4 of this Act, any person who immediately before the appointed day is a citizen of the United Kingdom and Colonies shall on that day cease to be such a citizen if he becomes on that day a citizen of Seychelles.

(3) Section 6(2) of the British Nationality Act 1948 (registration as citizens of the United Kingdom and Colonies of women who have been married to such citizens) shall not apply to a woman by virtue of her marriage to a person who on the appointed day ceases to be such a citizen under subsection (2) of this section or who would have done so if living on the appointed day. 1948 c. 56.

(4) In accordance with section 3(3) of the West Indies Act 1967, it is hereby declared that this and the next following section extend to all associated states. 1967 c. 4.

Retention of citizenship of the United Kingdom and Colonies by certain citizens of Seychelles.

4.—(1) Subject to subsection (4) of this section, a person shall not cease to be a citizen of the United Kingdom and Colonies under section 3(2) of this Act if he, his father or his father's father—

(*a*) was born in the United Kingdom or in a colony or an associated state ; or

(*b*) is or was a person naturalised in the United Kingdom and Colonies ; or

(*c*) was registered as a citizen of the United Kingdom and Colonies ; or

(*d*) became a British subject by reason of the annexation of any territory included in a colony.

(2) The references to a colony in subsection (1) of this section shall be construed as not including any territory which, on the appointed day, is not a colony for the purposes of the British Nationality Act 1948 as that Act has effect on that day, and accordingly do not include Seychelles.

(3) Subject to subsection (4) of this section, the reference in subsection (1)(*b*) of this section to a person naturalised in the United Kingdom and Colonies shall include a person who would, if living immediately before the commencement of the British Nationality Act 1948, have become a person naturalised in the United Kingdom and Colonies by virtue of section 32(6) of that Act (persons given local naturalisation in a colony or protectorate before the commencement of that Act).

(4) Subsection (1) of this section shall not apply to a person by virtue of any certificate of naturalisation granted or registration effected by the Governor or Government of a territory which by virtue of subsection (2) of this section is excluded from the references to a colony in subsection (1) of this section

or which on the appointed day is not a protectorate or protected state for the purposes of the British Nationality Act 1948 as that Act has effect on that appointed day.

1948 c. 56.

(5) A woman who is the wife of a citizen of the United Kingdom and Colonies shall not cease to be such a citizen under section 3(2) of this Act unless her husband does so.

(6) Part III of the British Nationality Act 1948 (supplemental provisions) as in force at the passing of this Act shall have effect for the purposes of this section as if this section were included in that Act.

Operation of existing law.

5.—(1) Subject to subsection (3) of this section, all law to which this section applies, whether being a rule of law or a provision of an Act of Parliament or of any other enactment or instrument whatsoever, which is in force on the appointed day, or, having been passed or made before that day, comes or has come into force thereafter, shall, unless and until provision to the contrary is made by Parliament or some other authority having power in that behalf, have the same operation in relation to Seychelles, and persons and things belonging to or connected with Seychelles, as it would have had apart from this subsection if there had been no change in the status of Seychelles.

(2) This section applies to law of, or any part of, the United Kingdom, the Channel Islands and the Isle of Man and, in relation only to any enactment of the Parliament of the United Kingdom or any Order in Council made by virtue of any such enactment whereby any such enactment applies in relation to Seychelles, to law of any other country or territory to which that enactment or Order extends.

(3) Notwithstanding anything in subsections (1) and (2) of this section, the provisions set out in Appendix C in Schedule 1 to the Immigration Act 1971 (whereby a person becoming a citizen of the United Kingdom and Colonies by registration is in certain circumstances required to take an oath of allegiance) shall have effect in relation to citizens of Seychelles as if subsection (1) of this section had not been enacted.

1971 c. 77.

Pending appeals to Her Majesty in Council.

6.—(1) This section applies to appeals to Her Majesty in Council from any court having jurisdiction for Seychelles in relation to which before the appointed day leave to appeal has been granted by that court or special leave to appeal has been granted by Her Majesty in Council.

(2) In respect of appeals to which this section applies, or in respect of any class of such appeals, Her Majesty may by Order

in Council (to be laid before Parliament after being made) confer on the Judicial Committee of the Privy Council such jurisdiction as appears to Her Majesty to be appropriate in the circumstances for the purposes of enabling them to be continued before and disposed of by that Committee.

(3) An Order in Council under this section may, if Her Majesty thinks fit, direct that any appeal continued before the Judicial Committee of the Privy Council in pursuance of the Order shall abate on a date specified in the Order unless it has been heard by the Committee before that date; and an Order containing such a direction may contain provisions to facilitate the hearing of any such appeal before that date, including provisions as to the sittings of the Committee and provisions for expediting the steps to be taken by the parties preliminary to the hearing of an appeal.

(4) An Order in Council under this section may determine the practice and procedure to be followed on any appeal continued before the said Committee in pursuance of the Order, and, in particular, may include provisions as to the form of any report or recommendation to be made by that Committee in the exercise of the jurisdiction conferred on that Committee by the Order, as to the authority to whom any such report or recommendation is to be transmitted and as to the manner in which it is to be transmitted to that authority.

(5) Except so far as otherwise provided by an Order in Council under this section, and subject to such modifications as may be so provided, the Judicial Committee Act 1833 shall apply in relation to appeals continued before the Judicial Committee of the Privy Council under this section as it applied in relation to those appeals before the appointed day. **1833 c. 41.**

Consequential modifications of other enactments.

7.—(1) On and after the appointed day the provisions specified in the Schedule to this Act shall have effect subject to the amendments specified respectively in that Schedule.

(2) Subsection (1) of this section, and the Schedule to this Act, shall not extend to Seychelles as part of its law.

Interpretation.

8.—(1) In this Act, and in any amendment made by this Act in any other enactment, " Seychelles " means the territories which immediately before the appointed day constitute the Colony of Seychelles.

(2) References in this Act to any enactment are references to that enactment as amended or extended by or under another enactment.

Short title.

9. This Act may be cited as the Seychelles Act 1976.

Section 7.

SCHEDULE

Amendments not affecting the Law of Seychelles

Diplomatic immunities

1961 c. 11. 1. In section 1(5) of the Diplomatic Immunities (Conferences with Commonwealth Countries and Republic of Ireland) Act 1961, before the word " and " in the last place where it occurs there shall be inserted the word " Seychelles ".

The Services

2. In the definitions—

1955 c. 18. 1955 c. 19. (*a*) of " Commonwealth force " in section 225(1) of the Army Act 1955 and section 223(1) of the Air Force Act 1955, and

1957 c. 53. (*b*) of " Commonwealth country " in section 135(1) of the Naval Discipline Act 1957,

at the end there shall be added the words " or Seychelles ".

Visiting forces

1933 c. 6. 3. In the Visiting Forces (British Commonwealth) Act 1933, section 4 (attachment and mutual powers of command) shall apply in relation to forces raised in Seychelles as it applies to forces raised in Dominions within the meaning of the Statute of Westminster 1931.

1931 c. 4. (22 & 23 Geo. 5.).

1952 c. 67. 4. In the Visiting Forces Act 1952, in section 1(1)(*a*) (countries to which the Act applies) at the end there shall be added the words " Seychelles or ".

5. Until express provision with respect to Seychelles is made by an Order in Council under section 8 of that Act (application to visiting forces of law relating to home forces), any such Order for the time being in force shall be deemed to apply to visiting forces of Seychelles.

Ships

1894 c. 60. 1949 c. 43. 6. In section 427(2) of the Merchant Shipping Act 1894, as set out in section 2 of the Merchant Shipping (Safety Convention) Act 1949, before the words " or in any " there shall be inserted the words " or Seychelles ".

1934 c. 49. 7. In the Whaling Industry (Regulation) Act 1934, the expression " British ship to which this Act applies " shall not include a British ship registered in Seychelles.

Commonwealth Institute

1925 c. xvii. 1958 c. 16. 8. In section 8(2) of the Imperial Institute Act 1925, as amended by the Commonwealth Institute Act 1958 (power to vary the provisions of the said Act of 1925 if an agreement for the purpose is made with the governments of certain territories which for the time being are contributing towards the expenses of the Commonwealth Institute) at the end there shall be added the words " and Seychelles ".

ELIZABETH II

Education (Scotland) Act 1976

1976 CHAPTER 20

An Act to make further provision with respect to school commencement and leaving dates and the supply of milk in schools; to provide for the remuneration of members of Independent Schools Tribunals; to make provision with respect to the construction of educational endowment schemes; to make minor amendments to the Education (Scotland) Act 1962 and the Education (Scotland) Act 1969; and for connected purposes. [10th June 1976]

BE IT ENACTED by the Queen's most Excellent Majesty, by and with the advice and consent of the Lords Spiritual and Temporal, and Commons, in this present Parliament assembled, and by the authority of the same, as follows:—

Commencement of school attendance. 1962 c. 47.

1. The following section shall be substituted for section 33 of the Education (Scotland) Act 1962:—

"Dates for commencement of school attendance.

33.—(1) Subject to subsection (7) below, an education authority shall fix a date or dates (any such fixed date being hereinafter referred to as a " school commencement date ") for the commencement of attendance at primary schools in their area ; and any such date may be either a calendar date or fixed by reference to the occurrence of a particular annual event.

(2) Subject to subsection (7) below, an education authority may, under subsection (1) above—

(*a*) fix different school commencement dates for different primary schools in their area ;

(*b*) at any time fix a different school commencement date in substitution for any date previously fixed by them under the said subsection (1).

(3) A child who does not attain the age of five years on a school commencement date shall, for the purposes of section 32 of this Act, be deemed not to have attained that age until the school commencement date next following the fifth anniversary of his birth.

(4) Subject to subsection (7) below, an education authority shall, in respect of each school commencement date fixed by them under subsection (1) above and applicable to a public primary school, fix the latest following date (any such fixed date being hereinafter referred to as an " appropriate latest date ") on or before which a child must attain the age of five years in order to come within the category of children whom the authority consider of sufficient age to commence attendance at a public primary school at that school commencement date.

(5) Subject to subsection (7) below, an education authority may, under subsection (4) above—

(*a*) where a school commencement date is applicable to more than one public primary school in their area, fix in respect of that school commencement date different appropriate latest dates for those different schools ;

(*b*) at any time fix a different appropriate latest date in substitution for any date previously fixed by them under the said subsection (4).

(6) The education authority shall carry out their duty under section 1 of this Act as if a child who is under school age on a school commencement date, but who will attain the age of five years on or before the next following appropriate latest date fixed in respect of the school commencement date, has attained the age of five years on the school commencement date ; but nothing in this subsection or in subsection (4) above shall, in respect of a child under school age,—

(*a*) impose any duty on his parent ; or

(*b*) require an education authority to take any action under section 36 or 37 of this Act.

(7) The period between an appropriate latest date applicable to a school and the next following school commencement date applicable to that school (whether or not the school commencement date is that in respect of which the appropriate latest date is fixed) shall not, except with the approval of the Secretary of State on an application to him by the education authority, exceed six months by more than seven days:

Provided that no such application shall be made, nor approval given, in respect of any such period which commences after 31st December 1979.

(8) In relation to any child, " school commencement date "—

(*a*) in subsection (3) above—

(i) means, where the child is a pupil in attendance at a primary school, a school commencement date of that school;

(ii) in any other case has the same meaning as in subsection (6) above;

(*b*) in subsection (6) above means a school commencement date of the public primary school to which a child of his religious denomination and from his place of residence would normally be admitted.

(9) In this section, " primary school " does not include a nursery school or a nursery class.".

School leaving dates. 1962 c. 47.

2. The following section shall be inserted after section 33 of the Education (Scotland) Act 1962:—

" School leaving dates.

33A.—(1) The last day of May (hereinafter referred to as the " summer leaving date ") and the appropriate day in December (hereinafter referred to as the " winter leaving date ") shall be the school leaving dates in each year.

(2) Subject to subsection (4) below, for the purposes of section 32 of this Act a person shall, if the date of his attaining the age of sixteen years is—

(*a*) on or after 1st March but before the next summer leaving date, be deemed not to have attained that age until the summer leaving date;

(*b*) after the summer leaving date but before 1st October next following that date, be deemed to have attained that age on the summer leaving date ;

(*c*) on or after 1st October but before the next winter leaving date, be deemed not to have attained that age until the winter leaving date ;

(*d*) after the winter leaving date but before 1st March next following that date, be deemed to have attained that age on the winter leaving date.

(3) In subsection (1) above, " the appropriate day in December " means—

(*a*) in the case of a person who is a pupil in attendance at a school, the first day of the Christmas holiday period ;

(*b*) in any other case, 21st December,

and in paragraph (*a*) of this subsection, " Christmas holiday period " means a period of consecutive days which includes 25th December and in which the school does not meet for the purpose of providing school education.

(4) A person who attains the age of sixteen years—

(*a*) before the date of commencement of section 2 of the Education (Scotland) Act 1976 and who has not ceased to be of school age before that date ; or

(*b*) on or after the said date but before 1st October or 1st March (whichever is the earlier) next following such commencement,

shall be deemed not to be over school age until such date (being the said commencement date or a date thereafter) as the Secretary of State may by order made by statutory instrument prescribe ; and different dates may be prescribed for different categories of such persons.".

School milk. 1971 c. 74.

3. In section 2(2) of the Education (Milk) Act 1971 (which makes provision for enabling education authorities to provide milk but for the expense to be defrayed by the pupils or their parents) the words from " but " onwards are hereby repealed.

Remuneration of members of Independent Schools Tribunals.

4. The Secretary of State may, out of monies provided by Parliament, pay to the members of Independent Schools Tribunals such remuneration and allowances as he may, with the consent of the Minister for the Civil Service, determine.

5. After the date of commencement of this section any reference in a scheme made or approved under Part VI of the Education (Scotland) Act 1946 or under Part VI of the Education (Scotland) Act 1962 (reorganisation of educational endowments)— Construction of educational endowment schemes. 1946 c. 72. 1962 c. 47.

(*a*) to a certificated teacher shall be construed as a reference to a teacher registered under the Teaching Council (Scotland) Act 1965; 1965 c. 19.

(*b*) to a children's committee shall be construed as a reference to a social work committee established under section 2(1) of the Social Work (Scotland) Act 1968; 1968 c. 49.

(*c*) to the Scottish Counties of Cities Association or to the Association of County Councils in Scotland shall be construed as a reference to the Convention of Scottish Local Authorities.

6.—(1) The enactments specified in Schedule 1 to this Act shall have effect subject to the amendments specified in that Schedule (being minor amendments or amendments consequential on the preceding provisions of this Act). Amendments and repeals.

(2) The enactments specified in Schedule 2 to this Act are hereby repealed to the extent shown in column 3 of that Schedule.

7.—(1) This Act may be cited as the Education (Scotland) Act 1976, and this Act and the Education (Scotland) Acts 1939 to 1974 may be cited together as the Education (Scotland) Acts 1939 to 1976. Citation, commencement, construction and extent.

(2) This Act (except this section) shall come into force on such date as the Secretary of State may by order made by statutory instrument appoint and different dates may be appointed for, or for different purposes of, different provisions.

(3) Any reference in this Act or in any other Act to the commencement of any provision of this Act shall be construed as a reference to the day when that provision comes into force.

(4) Any reference in this Act to any other enactment shall be construed as a reference to that enactment as amended by or under any other enactment, including this Act.

(5) This Act shall extend to Scotland only.

SCHEDULES

SCHEDULE 1

Section 6(1).

MINOR AND CONSEQUENTIAL AMENDMENTS

The Children Act 1958 (*c.* 65)

1. In section 17, (interpretation) in the definition of " compulsory school age ", for the words " Acts, 1939 to 1956 " there shall be substituted the words " Act 1962 ".

The Mental Health (Scotland) Act 1960 (*c.* 61)

2. In section 12(1)(*b*), (training of mental defectives) for the words " the age of sixteen " there shall be substituted the words " school age within the meaning of the Education (Scotland) Act 1962 ".

The Factories Act 1961 (*c.* 34)

3. In section 176(1), (interpretation) in the definition of " child ", for the word " 1946 " there shall be substituted the word " 1962 ".

The Education (Scotland) Act 1962 (*c.* 47)

4. In section 6, (social activities, physical education etc.)—

(*a*) for paragraph (*a*) of subsection (1) there shall be substituted the following paragraph—

" (*a*) establish, maintain and manage—

(i) camps, outdoor centres, playing fields, and swimming pools ;

(ii) play areas and centres ;

(iii) sports halls, centres and clubs ;

(iv) youth, community and cultural centres and clubs,

and other places at which any such facilities as aforesaid are available." ;

(*b*) for paragraphs (*a*) and (*b*) of subsection (2) there shall be substituted the following words—

" (*a*) may assist any body whose objects include ;

(*b*) shall, so far as practicable, co-operate with local authorities and with voluntary societies or bodies whose objects include,

the provision or promotion of social, cultural and recreative activities and physical education and training or the facilities for such activities, education and training."

5. In section 13, (provision of hostels) for the words from " day " to the end there shall be substituted the words " educational establishments in their area.".

6. For section 32, (school age) there shall be substituted the following section—

" School Age.

32. Subject to sections 33(3) and 33A(2) and (4) of this Act, a person is of school age if he has attained the age of five years and has not attained the age of sixteen years.".

7. In section 42, (reasonable excuses)— Sch. 1

(*a*) in subsection (1)(*a*)(i), after the word " fifty " there shall be inserted the words " or fifty-one " ;

(*b*) in subsection (3), for the words " of the education authority " there shall be substituted the words " of the appropriate Health Board " ;

(*c*) in subsection (4), at the end there shall be added the words " ; and " the appropriate Health Board " in relation to any child, means—

(*a*) where an attendance order is in force in respect of the child, the Health Board in whose area the school named in the order is situated ;

(*b*) in any other case, the Health Board in whose area the place of residence of the child is situated.".

8. In section 58, (medical inspection, supervision and treatment of pupils and young persons)—

(*a*) in subsection (2) after the words " made by the " there shall be inserted the word " appropriate " ;

(*b*) at the end there shall be added the following subsection—

" (3) In this section, " the appropriate Health Board ", in relation to any pupil or young person, means the Health Board in whose area is situated the school, junior college or other educational establishment at which the pupil or young person is in attendance.".

9. In section 58A, (dental inspection and supervision of pupils and young persons)—

(*a*) in subsection (2), after the words " made by the " there shall be inserted the word " appropriate " ;

(*b*) at the end there shall be added the following subsection—

" (4) In this section " the appropriate Health Board " has the same meaning as in section 58 of this Act.".

10. In section 61, (power to ensure cleanliness)—

(*a*) in subsection (1), for the words " Health Board for the area " there shall be substituted the words " appropriate Health Board " ;

(*b*) at the end there shall be added the following subsection—

" (8) In this section " the appropriate Health Board " has the same meaning as in section 58 of this Act.".

11. In section 81 (power of Secretary of State to make regulations with respect to certain institutions providing further education)—

(*a*) in subsection (1) after paragraph (v) there shall be added the following paragraph—

" (vi) provide that the governing body of such a college shall comply with any direction given by the Secretary of State, after consultation with them, as to the

SCH. 1

discontinuance of any course of instruction provided in the college or the number of students of different categories to be admitted to the college in any period.";

(*b*) in subsection (2), for the words from " provision with " to " (v), of " there shall be substituted the words " such provision and prescribe such matters with respect to such institutions as may be provided or prescribed with respect to grant-aided colleges in regulations made under " ;

(*c*) at the end of subsection (2) there shall be added the following words " ; and regulations under this subsection may make different provision in relation to different classes of institution or different institutions.";

(*d*) at the end of subsection (3) there shall be added the following words "and such regulations may provide—

(*a*) for the transfer of the staff of such a college to, and

(*b*) that the property, rights, liabilities and obligations of the college shall be transferred to and vest in,

such institution established by regulations under subsection (2) above or grant-aided college as may be specified in the regulations on such conditions as to the use and disposal of the property so transferred as may be so specified:

Provided that any property transferred by virtue of such regulations shall remain subject to any trust or condition (whether contained in a scheme made or approved under Part VI of this Act or otherwise) to which it was subject immediately before such transfer." ;

(*e*) in subsection (4) after the words " subsection (1) " there shall be inserted the words " or (3) ".

12. In section 124(1), (accounts and audit of educational endowments) for the words " the provisions of subsection (2) of section one hundred and ninety-six of the Local Government (Scotland) Act 1947, apply " there shall be substituted the words " section 106(1) of the Local Government (Scotland) Act 1973 applies ".

13. In section 145, (interpretation)—

(*a*) in subsection (17)(iii), for the words " apply in writing to " there shall be substituted the words " have obtained the consent of " and for the words " for the club or centre to be " there shall be substituted the words " to the club or centre being " ;

(*b*) after subsection (22) there shall be inserted the following subsection—

" (22A) " Health Board " means a Health Board constituted under section 13 of the National Health Service (Scotland) Act 1972." ;

(*c*) for subsection (43) there shall be substituted the following subsection— **Sch. 1**

" (43) " School age " shall be construed in accordance with section 32 of this Act.".

The Social Work (Scotland) Act 1968 (*c.* 49)

14. In section 94(1), (interpretation) for the definition of " school age " there shall be substituted—

" " school age " shall be construed in accordance with section 32 of the Education (Scotland) Act 1962.".

The Education (Scotland) Act 1969 (*c.* 49)

15. In section 16(3), (age of retirement of teachers) for the words " as references to a post which attracts a responsibility allowance in terms of " there shall be substituted the words " in accordance with ".

SCHEDULE 2

Section 6(2).

Repeals

Chapter	Short Title	Extent of Repeal
10 & 11 Eliz II c. 47.	The Education (Scotland) Act 1962.	In section 1(2)(*a*)(i) the words " , for the purpose of school attendance,". Section 72. In section 116(1), the words from " and as to the payment " to the end.
1969 c. 49.	The Education (Scotland) Act 1969.	Section 8. In Part I of Schedule 2, paragraph 16.
1971 c. 74.	The Education (Milk) Act 1971.	In section 2(3), the words " Subject to subsection (2) above ". Section 3(2).

Crofting Reform (Scotland) Act 1976

1976 CHAPTER 21

An Act to confer new rights on crofters and cottars to acquire subjects tenanted or occupied by them; to confer rights on crofters to share in the value of land resumed by landlords or taken possession of compulsorily; to protect the interests of crofters and cottars from planning blight; to make further provision as to financial assistance for crofters, cottars and certain owner-occupiers of certain land; to make further provision as to the removal of land from crofting tenure; to amend the law with respect to common grazings; to extend the powers of the Scottish Land Court; to make provision for pensions and compensation for members of the Crofters Commission; and for connected purposes. [10th June 1976]

BE IT ENACTED by the Queen's most Excellent Majesty, by and with the advice and consent of the Lords Spiritual and Temporal, and Commons, in this present Parliament assembled, and by the authority of the same, as follows:—

New rights of crofters and cottars to acquire their subjects.

1.—(1) A crofter may, failing agreement with the landlord as to the acquisition by the crofter of croft land tenanted by him, apply to the Land Court for an order authorising him to make such acquisition.

(2) A crofter shall be entitled to a conveyance of the site of the dwelling-house on or pertaining to the croft tenanted by him, and a cottar shall be entitled to a conveyance of the site of the dwelling-house on or pertaining to his subject, and the crofter or cottar may, failing agreement with the landlord, apply to the Land Court for an order requiring the landlord to grant such a conveyance.

(3) In this Act " croft land " includes any land being part of a croft, other than—

(*a*) the site of the dwelling-house on or pertaining to the croft;

(*b*) any land, comprising any part of a common grazing, unless the land has been apportioned under section 27(4) of the Act of 1955 and is either—

(i) adjacent or contiguous to any other part of the croft, or

(ii) arable machair;

(*c*) any right to mines, metals or minerals or salmon fishings (not being salmon fishings in Orkney or Shetland) pertaining to the croft.

(4) In this Act, " the site of the dwelling-house " includes any building thereon and such extent of garden ground as, failing agreement with the landlord, may be determined by the Land Court by order under section 4(1) of this Act to be appropriate for the reasonable enjoyment of the dwelling-house as a residence but does not include—

(*a*) any right to mines, metals or minerals pertaining thereto; or

(*b*) where there is more than one dwelling-house on or pertaining to a croft or, as the case may be, the subject of a cottar, the site of more than one dwelling-house; or

(*c*) where the site of the dwelling-house on or pertaining to a croft has been acquired by the crofter after the passing of this Act, the site of any dwelling-house erected after such acquisition on or pertaining to the remainder of the croft.

Authorisation by Land Court of acquisition of croft land.

2.—(1) The Land Court, on an application made to them under section 1(1) of this Act, may make an order—

(*a*) authorising the crofter to acquire such croft land as may be specified in the order, subject to such terms and conditions as, failing agreement with the landlord, may be so specified, and requiring the landlord to convey the land to the crofter or his nominee in accordance with such terms and conditions; or

(*b*) refusing the application.

(2) The Land Court shall not make an order in accordance with subsection (1)(*a*) above where they are satisfied by the landlord as to either or both of the following matters—

(*a*) that, in all the circumstances pertaining to the landlord and having regard to the extent of land owned by him to which the Act of 1955 applies, the making of such an order would cause a substantial degree of hardship to the landlord;

(*b*) that the making of such an order would be substantially detrimental to the interests of sound management of the estate of the landlord of which the croft land to which the application relates forms part.

(3) The Land Court, in making an order in accordance with subsection (1)(*a*) above, may provide that the authorisation to acquire is conditional on the crofter granting a lease to the landlord of the shooting rights over or the fishing rights pertaining to the croft land and shall so provide where they are satisfied that if such a lease were not granted the interests of the landlord in the shooting or fishing rights of which the rights being acquired by the crofter form part would be materially affected; and any such lease shall be at such nominal annual rent, for such period of not less than 20 years and subject to such other terms and conditions as the Land Court may specify.

(4) The Land Court, in making an order in accordance with subsection (1)(*a*) above, may include the condition that the crofter shall grant a standard security in favour of the landlord to secure any sum which may become payable to him or his personal representative under section 3(3) of this Act in the event of disposal of the croft land or any part thereof.

(5) Where the Land Court propose to make an order authorising the crofter to acquire—

(*a*) land comprising any part of a common grazing which has been apportioned under section 27(4) of the Act of 1955; or

(*b*) land held runrig which has been apportioned under section 27(7) of that Act,

and they are satisfied that the apportionment has been made subject to conditions imposed by the Commission under section 15(5) of the Act of 1961, or, as the case may be, the said section 27(7), they shall have regard to the conditions so imposed.

Consideration payable in respect of acquisition of croft land.

3.—(1) Where the Land Court make an order in accordance with section 2(1)(*a*) of this Act and the crofter and the landlord have failed to reach agreement about the consideration payable in respect of the acquisition, the consideration shall, subject to subsection (3) below, be the crofting value of the croft land specified in the order as determined by the Land Court under subsection (2) below.

(2) The crofting value of the croft land, as determined by the Land Court for the purposes of subsection (1) above, shall be 15 years' purchase of such amount as the Land Court may determine to be the proportion attributable to the croft land of

the current rent payable for the croft of which the croft land forms part:

Provided that the Land Court, on an application made to them by the landlord at any time before they make a final order under section 2(1) of this Act, may determine a fair rent for the croft which shall be deemed to be the current rent for the purposes of this subsection; and section 5(4) of the Act of 1955 shall apply for the purposes of this proviso as if for the word " parties " there were substituted the words " landlord and the crofter ".

(3) If the person who has acquired croft land by virtue of section 2(1) of this Act (" the former crofter ") or a member of the former crofter's family who has obtained the title to that land either—

(i) as the nominee of the former crofter, or

(ii) from the former crofter or his nominee,

disposes of that land or any part of it (" the relevant land ") to anyone who is not a member of the former crofter's family, by any means other than by a lease for crofting or agricultural purposes, forthwith or at any time within five years of the date of its acquisition by the former crofter then, subject to subsection (6) below, the person disposing of the relevant land shall pay to the landlord referred to in the said section 2(1) or to his personal representative a sum equal to one half of the difference between—

(*a*) the market value of the relevant land (on the date of such disposal) which, failing agreement between the parties concerned, shall be as determined by the Land Court under subsection (4) below on the application of such landlord or personal representative; and

(*b*) the consideration which was paid under subsection (1) above in respect of the relevant land.

(4) The market value of the relevant land as determined by the Land Court shall be the amount which the land, if sold in the open market by a willing seller (not being an authority as 1975 c. 77. defined in section 1(1)(*b*) of the Community Land Act 1975), might be expected to realise assuming that on the date of the disposal—

(*a*) there were no improvements on the land which, if the land were let to a crofter, would be permanent improvements in respect of which the crofter would be entitled to compensation under section 14 of the Act of 1955 on renunciation of the tenancy of the croft of which the land formed part;

(*b*) no other development had been carried out on the land (not being development carried out on the land, when it was subject to the tenancy of the former crofter or any of his predecessors in the tenancy, by a person other than that crofter or any of such predecessors); and

(*c*) no development of the land which consisted of the making of such an improvement as is referred to in paragraph (*a*) above were or would be permitted in pursuance of the Town and Country Planning (Scotland) Act 1972. 1972 c. 52.

(5) If the relevant land comprises only part of the land which was acquired under section 2(1) of this Act, the Land Court may, failing agreement between the parties concerned, on an application made to them by the person disposing of the relevant land or the landlord referred to in the said section 2(1) or his personal representative, determine for the purposes of subsection (3)(*b*) above the proportion of the amount of the consideration which was paid under subsection (1) above in respect of the relevant land.

(6) No payment shall be made under subsection (3) above in respect of the disposal of the relevant land in a case where payment is made in respect of such disposal in accordance with an agreement entered into between the landlord and the person disposing of that land.

Determination by Land Court of terms and conditions for conveyance of the site of the dwelling-house.

4.—(1) The Land Court, on an application made to them under section 1(2) of this Act, may make an order requiring the landlord to convey the site of the dwelling-house to the crofter or cottar or his nominee with such boundaries and subject to such terms and conditions as, failing agreement, may be specified in the order.

(2) Where the parties have failed to reach agreement about the consideration payable in respect of the conveyance the consideration shall be—

(*a*) the amount as determined by the Land Court which the site, if sold in the open market by a willing seller, might be expected to realise assuming that—

(i) there were or would be no buildings on the site;

(ii) the site were available with vacant possession;

(iii) the site were not land to which the Crofters (Scotland) Acts 1955 and 1961 apply; and

(iv) no development of the site were or would be permitted in pursuance of the Town and Country Planning (Scotland) Act 1972;

and in addition, in a case where the landlord has provided fixed equipment on the site—

(*b*) an amount equal to one half of the proportion attributable to that fixed equipment, as determined by the Land Court, of the value of the site, such value being the amount as so determined which the site, if sold as aforesaid, might be expected to realise making the assumptions referred to in sub-paragraphs (ii), (iii) and (iv) of paragraph (*a*) above.

(3) The Land Court in making an order under subsection (1) above may determine that any of the expenses of the conveyance of the site and other expenses necessarily incurred by the landlord in relation thereto shall be borne by the crofter or cottar:

Provided that where the order relates to the conveyance of the site of the dwelling-house on or pertaining to a croft, any such determination shall be subject to the condition that the conveyance is not included in a deed which also provides for the conveyance of croft land.

(4) Failing agreement between the parties as to the amount of such expenses, the auditor of the Land Court may, on the application of either party, determine such amount; and may determine that the expenses of taxing such expenses shall be borne by the parties in such proportion as he thinks fit.

Provisions relating to conveyance.

1845 c. 19.

5.—(1) A landlord shall have power to execute a valid conveyance in pursuance of the foregoing provisions of this Act, notwithstanding that he may be under any such disability as is mentioned in section 7 of the Lands Clauses Consolidation (Scotland) Act 1845.

(2) Where the Land Court are satisfied, on the application of the crofter or cottar or his nominee that the landlord has failed to execute a conveyance of land in favour of such person in compliance with an order under section 2(1) or 4(1) of this Act within such time as the Land Court consider reasonable, they shall make an order authorising their principal clerk to execute the conveyance and such other deeds as adjusted at his sight as may be necessary to give effect to the order; and a conveyance executed by the principal clerk under this subsection shall have the like force and effect in all respects as if it had been executed by the landlord.

(3) Where the principal clerk of the Land Court has executed a conveyance in pursuance of subsection (2) above, the Land Court may make such order as they think fit with regard to the payment of the consideration in respect of the conveyance and in particular providing for the distribution of the sum comprised in the consideration according to the respective estates or interests of persons making claim to such sum.

(4) Notwithstanding that the Land Court have made an order under section 2(1) or 4(1) of this Act determining the terms and conditions on which land is to be conveyed, the crofter or, as the case may be, the cottar and the landlord may arrange for the conveyance of the land on any other terms and conditions that they may agree.

(5) Where a person other than the landlord is infeft in the subjects to be conveyed, the second references in sections 1(2) and 2(1) of this Act and the reference in the said section 4(1) and in the foregoing provisions of this section to the landlord shall be construed as references to the landlord and such other person for their respective rights.

(6) The Land Court in specifying in an order under the said section 2(1) or 4(1) the terms and conditions on which land is to be conveyed shall have regard to any existing land obligations as defined in section 1(2) of the Conveyancing and Feudal Reform (Scotland) Act 1970 relating to such land. **1970 c. 35.**

(7) Where the landlords are the National Trust for Scotland, they shall not be required to convey land by an order of the Land Court under the said section 2(1) or 4(1) otherwise than by a grant in feu; but section 4(2) of the Order confirmed by the National Trust for Scotland Order Confirmation Act 1947 (which requires the consent of the Lord Advocate to grants in feu by the Trust exceeding 20 acres) shall not apply to such a grant. **1947 cxxxviii.**

(8) Where the Land Court are satisfied, on the application of the landlord, that the crofter or his nominee has failed to execute a standard security in favour of the landlord in compliance with a condition imposed by the Land Court under section 2(4) of this Act within such time as the Land Court consider reasonable, they shall make an order authorising their principal clerk to execute the standard security; and a standard security executed by the principal clerk under this subsection shall have the like force and effect in all respects as if it had been executed by the crofter or his nominee.

Provisions supplementary to sections 2 and 4.

6.—(1) An order of the Land Court under section 2(1)(*a*) or 4(1) of this Act shall have effect for a period of two years from the date of intimation of the order or for such other period as may at any time be agreed to in writing by the crofter or, as the case may be, the cottar and the landlord or as may be determined by the Land Court on the application of either party.

(2) Where an order has been made by the Land Court under the said section 2(1)(*a*) or 4(1) in relation to croft land or the site of the dwelling-house on or pertaining to a croft or under the

said section 4(1) in relation to the site of the dwelling-house on or pertaining to the subject of a cottar, then, so long as the order has effect—

(*a*) the crofter shall not be entitled under section 14(1) of the Act of 1955 to compensation for any permanent improvement made on the croft land or site; and

(*b*) the landlord of the croft shall not be entitled under section 14(6) of that Act to recover from the crofter compensation for any deterioration of, or damage to, any fixed equipment provided by the landlord in respect of the croft land or site; or

(*c*) the cottar shall not be entitled under section 28(1) of that Act to compensation for any permanent improvement made on the site,

being compensation to which the crofter and the landlord or, as the case may be, the cottar would be entitled but for this subsection.

(3) Any condition or provision to the effect that—

(*a*) the superior of any feu shall be entitled to a right of pre-emption in the event of a sale thereof or any part thereof by the proprietor of the feu, or

(*b*) any other person with an interest in land shall be entitled to a right of pre-emption in the event of a sale thereof or of any part thereof by the proprietor for the time being,

shall not be capable of being enforced where the sale is by a landlord to a crofter or his nominee of croft land or to a crofter or a cottar or his nominee of the site of the dwelling-house on or pertaining to the croft or the subject of the cottar in pursuance of an order under the said section 2(1) or, as the case may be, 4(1).

(4) Where the landlords are the National Trust for Scotland, the Land Court, in making an order under the said section 2(1) or 4(1), shall have regard to the purposes of the Trust.

(5) A compulsory purchase order which authorises the compulsory purchase of land, being land which was held inalienably by the National Trust for Scotland on the date of the passing of this Act and was acquired from the Trust by a crofter in pursuance of an order under section 2(1) or 4(1) of this Act, shall in so far as it so authorises be subject to special parliamentary procedure in any case where an objection has been
1947 c. 42 duly made by the Trust under the Acquisition of Land (Authorisation Procedure) (Scotland) Act 1947 and has not been withdrawn; and in this subsection " held inalienably " has the same meaning as in section 7(1) of the said Act of 1947.

(6) Where the site of the dwelling-house on or pertaining to a croft has been acquired after the passing of this Act by a person, who immediately before the acquisition was the tenant of the croft, that person and the wife or husband of that person may, so long as either of them continues to occupy the subjects conveyed, enjoy any right to cut and take peats for the use of those subjects which that person enjoyed immediately before the acquisition.

(7) Any person acquiring croft land shall, unless and until the land ceases to be a croft by a direction of the Commission under section 16(9) of the Act of 1955, be required to give notice to the Commission of the change of ownership of the land.

Adjustment of rent for remainder of croft where part conveyed to crofter.

7. Where a crofter acquires the site of the dwelling-house on or pertaining to his croft or any croft land forming part of his croft, then, notwithstanding that it is less than seven years since the term at which the existing rent for the croft first became payable, the Land Court may, on the application of the crofter or his landlord, determine a fair rent for the part of the croft which remains subject to the tenancy of the crofter, and accordingly subsections (3) and (4) of section 5 of the Act of 1955 shall apply for the purposes of such a determination as if the provisos to subsection (3) were omitted; but thereafter the said provisos shall apply to a rent so determined.

Provisions relating to existing loans and heritable securities.

8.—(1) Where—

(*a*) a crofter who acquires the site of the dwelling-house on or pertaining to his croft is on the date of the acquisition under any liability to the Secretary of State or the Highlands and Islands Development Board, or

(*b*) a cottar who acquires the site of the dwelling-house on or pertaining to his subject is on the date of the acquisition under any liability to the Secretary of State,

in respect of any loan, the amount outstanding in respect of such liability shall be deemed, as from the last day on which the crofter or cottar was liable to pay rent in respect of that site or on which the cottar was entitled to occupy the site as a cottar, to be a loan by the Secretary of State to the crofter or cottar or, as the case may be, by the Board to the crofter, and the provisions of Schedule 3 to the Act of 1955 (provisions as to security, etc., of loans) shall apply in relation to any such loan by the Secretary of State and, subject to any necessary modifications, to any such loan by the Board.

(2) Any question arising under subsection (1) above as to the day from which the outstanding amount is deemed to be a loan shall be determined by the Land Court.

(3) Any rights of the Board created under subsection (1) above shall be postponed to any rights, whensoever constituted, of the Secretary of State under that subsection; and such rights of the Secretary of State and the Board shall have priority over any other loan in respect of which the crofter or the cottar or his nominee as owner of the site of the dwelling-house is under any liability and shall be postponed only to such items as are referred to in heads (i), (ii) and (iii) of paragraph 4(*b*) of Schedule 2 to the Housing (Scotland) Act 1969.

1969 c. 34.

(4) Any heritable security which immediately before the execution of a conveyance in pursuance of the foregoing provisions of this Act burdened the subjects conveyed shall, as from the date of recording of the conveyance in the Register of Sasines—

(*a*) in the case of a conveyance in feu, cease to burden the *dominium utile* of the subjects conveyed and burden only the superiority thereof;

(*b*) in the case of a conveyance otherwise than in feu where the heritable security burdened only the subjects conveyed, cease to burden those subjects;

(*c*) in the case of a conveyance otherwise than in feu where the heritable security also burdened other land, burden only that other land;

and, unless the creditors in right of any such security otherwise agree, the landlord shall pay to them according to their respective rights and preferences any sum paid to him by the crofter or cottar as consideration for the subjects conveyed.

Crofter's right to share in value of land resumed by landlord.

9.—(1) Where the Land Court authorise the resumption of a croft or a part thereof under section 12 of the Act of 1955, the crofter shall be entitled to receive from the landlord, in addition to any compensation payable to him under that section, a share in the value of the land so resumed the amount whereof shall be one half of the difference between, subject to subsection (5) below, the market value of the land (on the date on which resumption thereof is so authorised) as determined by the Land Court in accordance with subsections (2) and (3) below (less any compensation payable as aforesaid) and the crofting value thereof.

(2) Where the resumption of the land is so authorised for some reasonable purpose which has been or is to be carried out by the landlord or by any person not being an authority possessing compulsory purchase powers, the market value for the purposes of subsection (1) above shall be a sum equal to

the amount which the land, if sold in the open market by a willing seller (not being an authority as defined in section 1(1)(*b*) of the Community Land Act 1975) might be expected to realise. **1975 c. 77.**

(3) Where the resumption is so authorised for some reasonable purpose which has been or is to be carried out by an authority possessing compulsory purchase powers (not being the landlord) on the acquisition by them of the land so resumed, the market value for the purposes of subsection (1) above shall be a sum equal to the amount of compensation payable by the authority to the landlord in respect of the acquisition:

Provided that, where the land so resumed forms part only of the land acquired from the landlord by the authority, the market value shall be a sum equal to such amount as the Land Court may determine to be the proportion of the amount of compensation so payable by the authority which relates to the land so resumed.

(4) Where the land so resumed forms or forms part of a common grazing, the share of the value of that land payable to the crofters sharing in the common grazing shall be apportioned among such crofters according to the proportion that the right in the common grazing of each such crofter bears to the total of such rights; and any sum so apportioned to such a crofter shall be deemed to be the share in the value of such land resumed to which he is entitled under subsection (1) above.

(5) For the purposes of this section, where any development has been carried out by any person, other than the crofter or any of his predecessors in the tenancy, on the land which the Land Court have authorised the landlord to resume before such authorisation, there shall be deducted from the market value such amount thereof as, in the opinion of the Land Court, is attributable to that development.

(6) In this section—

"crofting value", in relation to land resumed, has the same meaning as it has in section 3 of this Act in relation to croft land;

"reasonable purpose" has the same meaning as in section 12(2) of the Act of 1955.

Crofter's right to share in value of land taken possession of compulsorily.

10.—(1) Where in pursuance of any enactment providing for the acquisition and taking of possession of land compulsorily by any person (in this section referred to as an "acquiring authority"), an acquiring authority acquire and take possession of a croft or a part thereof from a crofter, the crofter shall be entitled to receive from the acquiring authority, in addition to any compensation payable to him under section 114 of the

1845 c. 19. Lands Clauses Consolidation (Scotland) Act 1845, a share in the value of the land of which possession has been taken, the amount whereof shall be one half of the difference between, subject to subsection (4) below, the market value of the land (on the date on which such possession is taken) as determined by the Land Court in accordance with subsection (2) below (less any compensation payable as aforesaid) and the crofting value thereof.

(2) The market value for the purposes of subsection (1) above shall be a sum equal to the amount which the land, if sold in the open market by a willing seller (not being an authority as defined in section 1(1)(*b*) of the Community Land Act 1975) might be expected to realise assuming that the land were not land to which the Crofters (Scotland) Acts 1955 and 1961 apply.

1975 c. 77.

(3) Section 9(4) of this Act shall apply to land which has been taken possession of compulsorily by an acquiring authority as it applies to land of which the Land Court have authorised resumption.

(4) For the purposes of this section, where any development has been carried out by any person, other than the crofter or any of his predecessors in the tenancy, on the land referred to in subsection (1) above before the land has been acquired by and taken possession of by the acquiring authority, there shall be deducted from the market value such amount thereof as, in the opinion of the Land Court, is attributable to that development.

(5) In this section " crofting value ", in relation to land which has been taken possession of compulsorily, has the same meaning as it has in section 3 of this Act in relation to croft land.

Protection of interests of crofters and cottars from planning blight.

1972 c. 52.

1973 c. 56.

11. The interests qualifying for protection under sections 181 to 196 of the Town and Country Planning (Scotland) Act 1972 and sections 64 to 77 of the Land Compensation (Scotland) Act 1973 (planning blight) shall include the interest of a crofter in his croft or a cottar in his subject; and accordingly the aforesaid enactments shall have effect subject to the amendments set out in Schedule 1 to this Act.

Financial assistance to crofters, cottars and certain owner-occupiers.

12.—(1) The Secretary of State may provide assistance under section 22(2) of the Act of 1955 but not in respect of buildings other than dwelling-houses to—

(*a*) a person, being a crofter who has acquired the site of the dwelling-house on or pertaining to his croft after the passing of this Act;

(*b*) the nominee of such a person, being a member of his family, to whom the site was conveyed by the landlord of the croft;

(*c*) a member of such a person's family who has acquired the title to the site from that person or such nominee;

(*d*) a person, being a cottar who has acquired the site of the dwelling-house on or pertaining to his subject after the passing of this Act;

for a period of seven years from the date of the acquisition from the landlord.

(2) The Secretary of State may provide assistance under the said section 22(2) or under section 31(1) of the Act of 1955 (building grants and loans to owner-occupiers of like economic status as crofters) towards the provision or improvement of roads, or water or electricity or gas supplies.

(3) The provisions of Schedule 3 to the Act of 1955 (provisions as to security etc. of loans) shall apply in relation to any loan made under the said section 22(2) by virtue of subsection (1) above.

(4) Where a person other than the landlord was infeft in the site of the dwelling-house immediately before the conveyance, the reference in subsection (1)(*b*) above to the landlord shall be construed as a reference to the landlord and such other person for their respective rights.

(5) If any person, for the purpose of obtaining for himself or any other person, a grant or loan under a scheme made under section 22(1) of the Act of 1955 or under the said section 22(2), knowingly or recklessly makes a false statement he shall be liable on summary conviction to a fine not exceeding £400.

(6) Any scheme made under the said section 22(1) may be varied or revoked by a subsequent scheme made in like manner.

Provision as respects removal of land from crofting tenure.

13.—(1) For subsection (7) of section 16 of the Act of 1955 (vacant crofts) there shall be substituted the following subsection—

"(7) Where a croft has, in consequence of the making of an order under section 17(1) of this Act, become vacant and has remained unlet for a period of six months beginning with the date on which the croft so became vacant, the Commission shall, if the landlord at any time within three months after the expiry of the period aforesaid gives notice to the Commission requiring them to do so, direct that the croft shall cease to be a croft; and if the landlord within one month after the issuing of such a direction gives notice to the Secretary of State requiring him to purchase the buildings on the croft, the Secretary of State shall purchase such buildings."

(2) For subsection (9) of the said section 16 there shall be substituted the following subsections—

" (9) Where a croft is vacant, the Commission may, on the application of the landlord, direct that the croft shall cease to be a croft or refuse to grant the application; and if the Commission direct under this subsection or under subsection (7) above that a croft shall cease to be a croft, the provisions of this Act and, subject to subsection (9A) below, the Crofters (Scotland) Act 1961 shall cease to apply to the croft, without prejudice, however, to the subsequent exercise of any powers conferred by any enactment for the enlargement of existing crofts.

(9A) The coming into effect of a direction given by the Commission by virtue of section 16A(4) of this Act shall not affect the powers contained in the proviso to section 13(3) of the said Act of 1961 (subleases).".

(3) After the said section 16 there shall be inserted the following section—

" Provisions supplementary to s. 16(9).

16A.—(1) The Commission shall give a direction under section 16(9) of this Act that a croft shall cease to be a croft if—

(*a*) subject to subsection (2) below, they are satisfied that the applicant has applied for the direction in order that the croft may be used for or in connection with some reasonable purpose within the meaning of section 12(2) of this Act and that the extent of the land to which the application relates is not excessive in relation to that purpose; or

(*b*) the application is made in respect of a part of a croft, which consists only of the site of the dwelling-house on or pertaining to the croft and in respect of which a crofter is entitled at the time of the application, or has been entitled, to a conveyance by virtue of section 1(2) of the Crofting Reform (Scotland) Act 1976, and they are satisfied that the extent of garden ground included in that part is appropriate for the reasonable enjoyment of the dwelling-house as a residence.

(2) Without prejudice to subsection (1)(*b*) above, the Commission, in determining whether or not to give such a direction, shall have regard to the general interest of the crofting community in the district in which the croft is situated and in particular to the demand, if any, for a tenancy of the croft from persons who might reasonably be

expected to obtain that tenancy if the croft were offered for letting on the open market on the date when they are considering the application.

(3) Where the Commission give such a direction on being satisfied as mentioned in subsection (1)(*a*) above, they may in the direction impose such conditions as appear to them requisite for securing that the land to which the direction relates is used for the proposed use; and if at any time they are satisfied that there has been a breach of any such condition, they may make a further direction that the land in respect of which there has been such a breach shall be a vacant croft.

(4) The Commission may, on the application of a crofter who is proposing to acquire croft land or the site of the dwelling-house on or pertaining to his croft, give a direction under the said section 16(9) as if the land were a vacant croft and the application were made by the landlord, that in the event of such acquisition of the land it shall cease to be a croft, or refuse the application; but such a direction shall not have effect until the land to which it relates has been acquired by the crofter or his nominee and unless the acquisition is made within five years of the date of the giving of the direction.

(5) A direction under the said section 16(9) may be given taking account of such modification of the application in relation to which the direction is given as the Commission consider appropriate.

(6) The Commission shall advertise all applications under the said section 16(9) or subsection (4) above (except an application made in respect of a part of a croft consisting only of the site of the dwelling-house on or pertaining to the croft) in one or more newspapers circulating in the district in which the croft to which the application relates is situated, and before disposing of such an application shall, if requested by the applicant, afford a hearing to the applicant and to such other person as they think fit.

(7) The Commission shall give notice in writing to the applicant of their proposed decision on an application made to them under the said section 16(9) or subsection (4) above, specifying the nature of and the reasons for such decision.

(8) The applicant may within 21 days of receipt of the notice under subsection (7) above, and the

owner of land to which a further direction under subsection (3) above relates may within 21 days of the making of that further direction, appeal against the proposed decision or further direction to the Land Court who may hear or consider such evidence as they think fit in order to enable them to dispose of the appeal.

(9) The Commission shall give effect to the determination of the Land Court on an appeal under subsection (8) above.".

Extension of section 3 of Act of 1955.

14. Section 3 of the Act of 1955 (definition of croft and crofter) shall have effect as if for subsection (5) there were substituted the following subsections—

" (5) For the purposes of this Act, the Crofters (Scotland) Act 1961 and the Crofting Reform (Scotland) Act 1976, any right in pasture or grazing land held or to be held by the tenant of a croft, whether alone or in common with others, and any land comprising any part of a common grazing which has been apportioned for the exclusive use of a crofter under section 27(4) of this Act and any land held runrig which has been apportioned under section 27(7) of this Act, shall be deemed to form part of the croft.

(6) For the purposes of the aforesaid Acts, where—

(*a*) a crofter has acquired his entire croft other than any such right or land as is referred to in subsection (5) above, or

(*b*) any person, not being a crofter, has obtained an apportionment of any land under the said section 27,

then the person referred to in paragraph (*a*) or (*b*) above shall be deemed to hold the right or land referred to therein in tenancy until held otherwise and that right or land shall be deemed to be a croft.".

Assignation of croft.

15.—(1) Section 8 of the Act of 1955 (assignation of croft) shall apply to a part of a croft, being a part consisting of any right in pasture or grazing land deemed by virtue of section 3(5) of that Act to form part of a croft, as it applies to a croft.

(2) A crofter, who proposes to assign his croft or such a part as is referred to in subsection (1) above to a member of his family, shall not, if he obtains the consent of his landlord, be required to obtain the consent of the Commission under the said section 8; and a landlord who has given such consent shall notify the Commission of the assignation and the name of the assignee.

16.—(1) At the end of section 24 of the Act of 1955 (appointment, etc., of grazings committee) there shall be added the following subsection— **Amendment of law with respect to common grazings.**

"(9) A grazings committee shall pay such annual remuneration to the clerk appointed under subsection (6) or (8) of this section as they may determine; and they may recover from the crofters sharing in the common grazings all expenditure incurred by them in paying such remuneration.".

(2) Nothing in paragraph *(a)* or *(b)* of section 25(1) of the Act of 1955 shall preclude a grazings committee from performing the duties therein specified on land other than the common grazings.

(3) After subsection (1) of the said section 25 there shall be inserted the following subsections—

"(1A) The grazings committee shall give notice to each crofter sharing in the common grazings of any proposals to carry out works in pursuance of the duty imposed by subsection (1)*(b)* above and the proposed allocation of the expenditure to be incurred in respect of those works among such crofters; and any such crofter may within one month of the date of such notice make representations in respect of the proposals or the proposed allocation to the Commission who may approve the proposals or proposed allocation with or without modifications or reject them.

(1B) Notwithstanding section 13(2) of the Act of 1961 (which provides that where a right in common grazings is sublet the subtenant comes in place of the crofter in relation to any matter which concerns such right), subsection (1A) above shall have effect in a case where such a right is sublet as if any reference to a crofter included a reference to a crofter in whose place a subtenant has come; but no liability to meet expenditure incurred by a grazings committee in the performance of the duties imposed on them by subsection (1)*(b)* above shall be imposed on such a crofter in respect of any period during which such a subtenancy subsists.".

(4) For section 26(2)*(b)* of the Act of 1955 (common grazings regulations) there shall be substituted the following paragraph—

"*(b)* the recovery by the grazings committee from such crofters of all expenses incurred by the committee in the performance of the duties imposed on them by section 25(1)*(b)* of this Act according to the proposed allocation of expenditure referred to in subsection (1A) of the said section 25 or, as the case may be, that allocation as approved or modified by the Commission under that subsection;".

(5) Section 27(7) of the said Act (apportionment by the Commission of lands held runrig) shall have effect as if after the word " manner " there were inserted the words " and subject to such conditions ".

Extension of powers of Land Court.

1911 c. 49.

17.—(1) An order or determination of the Land Court may be enforced as if it were a decree of the sheriff having jurisdiction in the area in which the order or determination is to be enforced; and accordingly section 25(6) of the Small Landholders (Scotland) Act 1911 (enforcement of Land Court orders) shall cease to have effect.

1886 c. 29.

(2) The books called the " Crofters Holdings Book " and the " Landholders Holdings Book " kept in pursuance of section 27 of the Crofters Holdings (Scotland) Act 1886 shall be kept by the principal clerk of the Land Court; and accordingly the said section 27 shall cease to have effect.

Pensions and compensation for members of Commission.

18. Schedule 1 to the Act of 1955 (provisions as to the Crofters Commission) shall have effect as if after paragraph 4 there were inserted the following paragraphs—

" 4A. The Secretary of State shall, in the case of any member of the Commission to whom he may with the approval of the Minister for the Civil Service determine that this paragraph applies, pay such pension, allowance or gratuity to or in respect of the member on his retirement or death, or make such payments towards the provision of such a pension, allowance or gratuity, as he may, with the like approval, determine.

4B. If a person ceases to be a member of the Commission and it appears to the Secretary of State that there are special circumstances which makes it right that that person should receive compensation he may, with the approval of the said Minister, pay to that person a sum of such amount as he may, with the like approval, determine.".

Application of Act to Crown.

19.—(1) This Act shall apply to land an interest in which belongs to Her Majesty in right of the Crown and land an interest in which belongs to a government department or is held in trust for Her Majesty for the purposes of a government department; but in its application to any land an interest in which belongs or is held as aforesaid this Act shall have effect subject to such modifications as may be prescribed by regulations made by the Secretary of State.

(2) Any regulations made by the Secretary of State under this section shall be embodied in a statutory instrument which shall be subject to annulment in pursuance of a resolution of either House of Parliament.

20.—(1) There shall be paid out of moneys provided by Parliament any increase attributable to this Act in the sums payable out of moneys so provided under section 3(10) of the Small Landholders (Scotland) Act 1911 and the Act of 1955. Financial provisions. 1911 c. 49.

(2) All sums received by the Secretary of State by virtue of this Act shall be paid into the Consolidated Fund.

21.—(1) Expressions used in this Act and the Act of 1955 have the same meanings in this Act as in that Act. Interpretation.

(2) In this Act—

"the Act of 1955" means the Crofters (Scotland) Act 1955; 1955 c. 21.

"the Act of 1961" means the Crofters (Scotland) Act 1961; 1961 c. 58.

"authority possessing compulsory purchase powers" has the same meaning as in the Town and Country Planning (Scotland) Act 1972; 1972 c. 52.

"cottar" has the same meaning as in section 28 of the Act of 1955;

"croft land" has the meaning assigned to it by section 1(3) of this Act;

"development" has the same meaning as in section 19 of the Town and Country Planning (Scotland) Act 1972, except that it includes the operations and uses of land referred to in paragraphs (*a*) and (*e*) of subsection (2) of that section;

"landlord", in relation to the site of the dwelling-house on or pertaining to the subject of a cottar, means—

(*a*) where the cottar is the tenant of the subject, the landlord thereof, and

(*b*) where the cottar is the occupier of the subject who pays no rent, the owner thereof;

"National Trust for Scotland" means the National Trust for Scotland for Places of Historic Interest or Natural Beauty incorporated by the Order confirmed by the National Trust for Scotland Order Confirmation Act 1935; 1935 c. ii.

"the site of the dwelling-house" has the meaning assigned to it by section 1(4) of this Act.

(3) Any reference in this Act to a member of a person's or crofter's or former crofter's family is a reference to the wife or husband of that person or crofter or former crofter or his son-in-law or daughter-in-law or anyone who would be, or would in any circumstances have been, entitled to succeed to his estate on intestacy by virtue of the Succession (Scotland) Act 1964. 1964 c. 41.

(4) Any reference in this Act to any other enactment shall, unless the context otherwise requires, be construed as a reference to that enactment as amended, extended or applied by any other enactment including this Act.

Minor and consequential amendments, repeals and savings.

22.—(1) The enactments mentioned in Schedule 2 to this Act shall have effect subject to the amendments respectively specified in that Schedule, being minor amendments or amendments consequential on the provisions of this Act.

(2) The enactments set out in Schedule 3 to this Act are hereby repealed to the extent specified in the third column of that Schedule.

(3) The repeal by this Act of part of section 17 of the Act of 1955 and of sections 18 of that Act and 7 of the Act of 1961 shall not affect anything done or any right established under any such provision before the passing of this Act.

Short title and extent.

23.—(1) This Act may be cited as the Crofting Reform (Scotland) Act 1976.

(2) This Act extends to Scotland only.

SCHEDULES

SCHEDULE 1

Section 11.

AMENDMENT OF ENACTMENTS CONSEQUENTIAL ON SECTION 11

The Town and Country Planning (Scotland) Act 1972 1972 c. 52.

1. At the end of section 182 (power to serve blight notice), there shall be added the following subsection—

" (5) Where the claimant is a crofter or cottar, this section shall have effect as if—

(*a*) in subsection (1)(*c*) for the word " sell " there were substituted the word " assign ";

(*b*) in subsection (1)(*d*) for the words from " sell it " to " to sell " there were substituted the words " assign it except at a price substantially lower than that for which he might reasonably have expected to assign it ";

(*c*) in subsections (1) and (4) for the word " purchase " there were substituted the words " take possession of ".".

2. In section 184 (reference of objections to Lands Tribunal), in subsection (6) after the word " treat " there shall be inserted the words " or, in a case where the claimant is a crofter or cottar, notice of entry ".

3. At the end of section 185 (effect of valid blight notice), there shall be added the following subsection—

" (5) Where the claimant is a crofter or cottar, this section shall have effect as if in subsections (1) and (3) for the words from " acquire " to " respect thereof " there were substituted the words " require the crofter or cottar to give up possession of the land occupied by him and to have served a notice of entry in respect thereof under paragraph 3 of Schedule 2 to the Acquisition of Land (Authorisation Procedure) (Scotland) Act 1947.".

4. At the end of section 188 (effect on powers of compulsory acquisition of counter-notice disclaiming intention to acquire), there shall be added the following subsection—

" (5) Where the claimant is a crofter or cottar, this section shall have effect as if in subsections (2) and (4) for the words from " or by " to " claimant in " there were substituted the words " to require the crofter or cottar to give up possession of ".".

5. In section 192(4) (meaning of " owner's interest "), after the words " interest of " there shall be inserted the word " (*a*) " and after the word " years " there shall be inserted the words " and (*b*) a crofter or cottar therein ".

6. In section 196(1) (general interpretation), after the definition of " the claimant " there shall be inserted the following definitions—

" " cottar " has the same meaning as in section 28(4) of the Crofters (Scotland) Act 1955 ; 1955 c. 21.

SCH. 1

"crofter" has the same meaning as in section 3(2) of the Crofters (Scotland) Act 1955".

1973 c. 56.

The Land Compensation (Scotland) Act 1973

7. At the end of section 68 (land affected by orders relating to new towns), there shall be added the following subsection—

"(6) This section shall have effect where the service of the blight notice by virtue of subsection (1) above is by a crofter or cottar as if—

(*a*) in subsection (4) for the words "acquire compulsorily any interest in land" and "acquires an interest" there were substituted respectively the words "take possession of any land occupied by the crofter or cottar" and "takes possession" and in paragraphs (*a*) and (*b*) for the word "interest" there were substituted the word "possession";

(*b*) in subsection (5) for the words from "acquisition of" to "acquisition were" there were substituted the words "taking of possession of land by the Secretary of State under subsection (4) above as if the taking of possession were"."

8. At the end of section 74 (blight notice requiring purchase of whole agricultural unit), there shall be added the following subsection—

"(3) This section shall have effect where the blight notice is served by a crofter or cottar as if for subsection (1)(*b*) there were substituted the following paragraph—

"(*b*) a requirement that the appropriate authority shall take possession of the whole of the unit or, as the case may be, the whole of the part of it to which the notice relates."."

9. At the end of section 76 (effect of blight notice requiring purchase of whole agricultural unit), there shall be added the following subsection—

"(9) Where the claimant is a crofter or cottar this section shall have effect as if—

(*a*) in subsections (2) and (4) for the words from "acquire compulsorily" to "interest" and for the words "to treat in respect thereof" there were substituted respectively the words "take possession compulsorily of the land" and the words "of entry in respect of that land under paragraph 3 of Schedule 2 to the Acquisition of Land (Authorisation Procedure) (Scotland) Act 1947";

(*b*) in subsection (4)(*a*) for the word "acquire" there were substituted the words "take possession of"."

SCHEDULE 2

Section 22(1).

MINOR AND CONSEQUENTIAL AMENDMENTS

The Small Landholders (Scotland) Act 1911

1911 c. 49.

1. In section 32(14) (provisions as to statutory small tenants), for the words " twenty, and section twenty-seven " there shall be substituted the words " and section twenty ".

The Land Settlement (Scotland) Act 1919

1919 c. 97.

2. At the end of section 6 (duty of Secretary of State with respect to sale or lease of land), there shall be added the following subsection—

" (6) Subsections (3) and (4) above shall not apply to crofts as defined in section 3 of the Crofters (Scotland) Act 1955.".

The Acquisition of Land (Authorisation Procedure) (Scotland) Act 1947

1947 c. 42.

3. In Schedule 1 (procedure for authorising compulsory purchases), in paragraph 4(1) after the word " aforesaid " there shall be inserted the words " or if no objection is duly made by the National Trust for Scotland in a case where the land comprised in the order was held inalienably by the Trust on the date of the passing of the Crofting Reform (Scotland) Act 1976 and was acquired from the Trust by a crofter as defined in section 3 of the Crofters (Scotland) Act 1955 in pursuance of an order under section 2(1) or 4(1) of the said Act of 1976 ".

The Crofters (Scotland) Act 1955

1955 c. 21.

4. At the end of section 1(1) (constitution and general functions of the Commission), there shall be added the words " and the Crofting Reform (Scotland) Act 1976.".

5. In section 2 (particular powers and duties of the Commission)—

(*a*) in subsection (1)(*d*), after the word " Act " there shall be inserted the words " and the Crofting Reform (Scotland) Act 1976 ";

(*b*) in subsection (3), for the words " sheriff-clerk " there shall be substituted the words " principal clerk of the Land Court ", and the words from " and the provisions " to the end shall cease to have effect ;

(*c*) in subsection (4), after the word " Act " there shall be inserted the words " and the Crofting Reform (Scotland) Act 1976."

6. In section 8 (assignation of croft)—

(*a*) for subsections (1) and (2) there shall be substituted the following subsections—

" (1) A crofter shall not assign his croft—

(*a*) to a member of his family unless he obtains the consent in writing of his landlord or, failing such consent, the consent in writing of the Commission on an application made to them ;

SCH. 2

(*b*) to a person other than a member of his family unless he obtains the consent in writing of the Commission on an application made to them.

(2) A landlord who has given his consent in pursuance of subsection (1)(*a*) above shall notify the Commission of the assignation and the name of the assignee." ;

(*b*) in subsection (5), after the word "Commission" where it first occurs there shall be inserted the words "in a case where he is required to obtain such consent in pursuance of subsection (1) above" ;

(*c*) at the end there shall be added the following subsections—

"(7) Any reference in this section to a croft shall include a reference to a part of a croft, being a part consisting of any right in pasture or grazing land deemed by virtue of section 3(5) of this Act to form part of a croft.

(8) In this section "member of his family", in relation to a crofter, has the same meaning as "member of the crofter's family" has in section 10(7) of this Act."

7. In section 15(1) (Commission to obtain information and to compile register of crofts)—

(*a*) for the word "acreage" there shall be substituted the word "extent" ;

(*b*) at the end there shall be added the words "and the Crofting Reform (Scotland) Act 1976."

8. In section 16 (vacant crofts)—

(*a*) in the proviso to subsection (4), for the words from "an application" to the end there shall be substituted the words "the Secretary of State is considering an application made to him under subsection (3) above for consent to let, or the Commission are considering an application made to them under subsection (9) below for a direction that the croft shall cease to be a croft" ;

(*b*) in subsection (8), after the words "section or" there shall be inserted the words "by the landlord to the Secretary of State" ;

(*c*) in subsections (11A) and (13), after the word "section" there shall be inserted the words "and section 16A of this Act" ;

(*d*) at the end of the section there shall be added the following subsection—

"(14) For the avoidance of doubt it is hereby declared that this section has effect (and shall be deemed always to have had effect since 27th August 1961) as if—

(*a*) a person who has become the owner-occupier of a croft were required under subsection (1) above within one month of the date on which he became such owner-occupier to give notice thereof to the Commission ; and (*b*) any reference in the section other than in subsection (1) above to a landlord included a reference to an owner-occupier." Sch. 2

9. In section 17(1)(*a*) (absentee crofters), for the words "ten miles" there shall be substituted the words "sixteen kilometres".

10. In section 22(5) (power of Secretary of State to give financial assistance to crofters), after the word "building" there shall be inserted the words "or towards the provision or improvement of roads, or water or electricity or gas supplies" and for the words "such erection, improvement or rebuilding" there shall be substituted the words "the works in question".

11. In section 27(1) (common grazings), for the words "forty shillings" and "five shillings" there shall be substituted respectively the words "£10" and "50 pence".

12. In section 30(4) (provisions as to entry and inspection), for the words "five pounds" there shall be substituted the word "£10".

13. In section 31(2) (building grants and loans to owner-occupiers of like economic status as crofters), for paragraph (*b*) there shall be substituted the following paragraph—

"(*b*) is either—

(i) a holding of which the area does not exceed 30 hectares, or

(ii) a holding of which the annual rent, if it were a croft let to a crofter under this Act and the Crofters (Scotland) Act 1961, would not in the opinion of the Secretary of State exceed £100, or

(iii) a holding which exceeds 30 hectares and of which the annual rent if it were a croft so let would in the opinion of the Secretary of State exceed £100, but which in the opinion of the Secretary of State is not substantially larger than 30 hectares or is capable of being let as a croft at an annual rent not substantially in excess of £100;".

14. In section 34(1) (determination of disputes, etc.) after the word "Act" there shall be inserted the words "or the Crofting Reform (Scotland) Act 1976".

15. In Schedule 3 (provisions as to security, etc., of loans)—

(*a*) in paragraph 1, for the words "bond which shall be a charge on" there shall be substituted the words "heritable security over";

(*b*) in paragraph 4, for the word "bond" there shall be substituted the words "heritable security".

The Valuation and Rating (Scotland) Act 1956 1956 c. 60.

16. In section 7 (provisions relating to agricultural lands and heritages and dwelling-houses occupied in connection therewith)—

(*a*) in subsection (6)(*b*) for the words "fifty pounds" there shall be substituted the word "£100";

SCH. 2

(*b*) at the end of subsection (8)(*b*) there shall be added the words " and

(*c*) to a dwelling-house, comprised in a conveyance of the site of the dwelling-house on or pertaining to a croft or the subject of a cottar obtained after the passing of the Crofting Reform (Scotland) Act 1976 by a person who is the crofter of the croft or, as the case may be, the cottar of the subject of which the dwelling-house then forms part, and occupied by that person or the husband or wife of that person."

1961 c. 58.

The Crofters (Scotland) Act 1961

17. In section 2 (new crofts, enlarged crofts and common grazings)—

(*a*) subsection (1), and in subsection (5) the words from the beginning to " section, and " shall cease to have effect;

(*b*) in subsections (2)(*a*) and (*b*) and (3) for the words " and this Act " there shall be substituted the words " this Act and the Crofting Reform (Scotland) Act 1976 ";

(*c*) in subsection (2)(*b*)—

(i) for the words " seventy-five acres " and " fifty pounds " there shall be substituted respectively the words " 30 hectares " and " £100 ",

(ii) for the words " Secretary of State ", " him " and " he makes " there shall be substituted respectively the words " Commission ", " them " and " they make ";

(*d*) after subsection (2) there shall be inserted the following subsection—

" (2A) The Commission shall make a direction under subsection (2) above only if they are satisfied that such a direction—

(*a*) would be of benefit to the croft; and

(*b*) would not result in the croft as enlarged by the land referred to in that subsection being substantially larger than 30 hectares or capable of being let as a croft at an annual rent substantially in excess of £100."

18. At the end of section 3(2) (Commission to maintain register of crofts), there shall be added the following proviso—

" Provided that the Commission shall not be required under this subsection to send a copy of any new entry or of any entry altered by them or to intimate the omission of any entry to any person who has to any extent assisted the Commission in the performance of their duties of inserting or, as the case may be, altering or omitting an entry by the furnishing of information to them.".

19. In section 4 (determination of questions by Land Court), in subsections (1) and (2), after the words " or this Act " and " and this Act " wherever they occur there shall be inserted respectively the words " or the Crofting Reform (Scotland) Act 1976 " and " and the Crofting Reform (Scotland) Act 1976 ".

20. In section 12(10)(*c*) (subletting of crofts not adequately used), for the words " one acre " there shall be substituted the words " one half hectare ". Sch. 2

21. In section 13 (subleases of crofts), in the proviso to subsection (3) after the words " one month " where they first occur there shall be inserted the words " or such longer period not exceeding three months as the Commission may in all the circumstances think reasonable ", and after the words " one month " where they subsequently occur there shall be inserted the words " or the said longer period ".

22. In section 14(1) (amendment of powers of Secretary of State with respect to giving of financial assistance in crofting counties)—

(*a*) in paragraph (*b*), for the words " seventy-five acres " and " fifty pounds " there shall be substituted respectively the words " 30 hectares " and " £100 " ;

(*b*) after paragraph (*b*) there shall be inserted the following paragraph—

" (*bb*) for occupiers of holdings, other than crofts situated in the crofting counties which exceed 30 hectares (exclusive of any common pasture or grazing held therewith) and of which the annual rent if they were crofts so let would in the opinion of the Secretary of State exceed £100, but which in the opinion of the Secretary of State are not substantially larger than 30 hectares (exclusive of any common pasture or grazing held therewith) or are capable of being so let at an annual rent not substantially in excess of £100, being occupiers who in the opinion of the Secretary of State are of substantially the same economic status as a crofter ; and ".

23. In section 15 (amendment of law with respect to common grazings)—

(*a*) in subsection (2)—

(i) for the words " paragraph (*b*) of the said subsection " there shall be substituted the words " such of the crofters referred to in paragraph (*b*) of that subsection as are liable to pay any expenses in accordance with a proposed allocation of expenditure referred to in subsection (1A) of section 25 of that Act or, as the case may be, such a proposed allocation as approved or modified by the Commission under that subsection " ;

(ii) for the words from " discharge " to the end there shall be substituted the words " performance of the duties imposed on them by paragraphs (*a*) and (*b*) respectively of section 25(1) of that Act." ;

(*b*) in subsection (6) for the words " and of this Act " and " either " there shall be substituted respectively the words " this Act and the Crofting Reform (Scotland) Act 1976 " and " any ".

SCH. 2

1967 c. 86.

The Countryside (Scotland) Act 1967

24. In section 13 (access agreements)—

(*a*) in subsection (9)(*a*), after the word " either " there shall be inserted the word " (i) ", and for the words from " with the consent " to " Commission " there shall be substituted the words " (ii) subject to subsection (9A) below " ;

(*b*) after subsection (9) there shall be inserted the following subsection—

" (9A) A grazings committee to whom such a payment as is referred to in paragraph (*a*) of subsection (9) above has been made and who are proposing to apply the payment in carrying out works in accordance with head (ii) of that paragraph shall give notice in writing to each crofter sharing in the common grazings of their proposals ; and any such crofter may within one month of the date of such notice make representations in respect of the proposals to the Crofters Commission who may approve them with or without modifications or reject them."

1968 c. 34.

The Agriculture (Miscellaneous Provisions) Act 1968

25. For section 11(8) (certain payments to tenant farmers), there shall be substituted the following subsection—

" (8) The provisions of the Small Landholders (Scotland) Acts 1886 to 1931 with regard to the Scottish Land Court shall, with any necessary modifications, apply for the purpose of the determination of any matter referred to them under subsection (7) of this section as they apply for the purpose of the determination by them of matters referred to them under those Acts.".

SCHEDULE 3

Section 22(2).

Repeal of Enactments

Chapter	Short Title	Extent of Repeal
49 & 50 Vict. c. 29.	The Crofters Holdings (Scotland) Act 1886.	Section 27.
1 & 2 Geo. 5. c. 49.	The Small Landholders (Scotland) Act 1911.	Section 25(6).
3 & 4 Eliz. 2. c. 21.	The Crofters (Scotland) Act 1955.	In section 2 (3), the words from "and the provisions" to the end. In section 12(4), the words "the constitution of new crofts or". In section 16, subsection (2), in subsection (4) the words from the beginning of paragraph (*a*) to "case" in paragraph (*b*). In section 17, subsections (4) to (8), in subsection (9) the words from the beginning to "foregoing subsection" and subsection (10). Section 18. In section 22, subsections (4)(*d*) and (8). In section 25(1), the proviso. In Schedule 3, in paragraph 4, the word "appropriate".
9 & 10 Eliz. 2. c. 58.	The Crofters (Scotland) Act 1961.	In section 2, subsection (1), in subsection (5) the words from the beginning to "section, and" and subsection (7). In section 6, in subsection (2) the words "as a separate croft" and in subsection (3) the words "or paragraph (*a*) of subsection (9) of section 19 of that Act". Section 7. Section 8(3)(*e*).

Freshwater and Salmon Fisheries (Scotland) Act 1976

1976 CHAPTER 22

An Act to make new provision with respect to freshwater and salmon fisheries in Scotland; and for connected purposes. [10th June 1976]

BE IT ENACTED by the Queen's most Excellent Majesty, by and with the advice and consent of the Lords Spiritual and Temporal, and Commons, in this present Parliament assembled, and by the authority of the same, as follows:—

Increased availability of, and protection for, freshwater fishing.

1.—(1) Where the Secretary of State is satisfied that, if proposals submitted to him under this section were implemented, there would be a significant increase in the availability of fishing for freshwater fish in inland waters to which the proposals relate, he may, subject to subsection (3) below, make an order (in this Act referred to as a " protection order ").

(2) A protection order shall—

(*a*) be made in relation to such area as the Secretary of State may prescribe, which shall be the catchment area or such part thereof, as the Secretary of State thinks appropriate, of any river ; and

(*b*) prohibit persons without legal right or without written permission from a person having such right from fishing for or taking freshwater fish in the inland waters in the prescribed area.

(3) The Secretary of State shall not make a protection order unless—

(*a*) he has received proposals in writing from or on behalf of an owner of land, to which pertains a right of fishing for freshwater fish in any inland waters in the area to which the proposals relate, or an occupier of such right, in relation to the improvement of, or the giving or availability of access to, fishings ; and

(*b*) he has consulted a body which in his opinion is representative of persons wishing to fish for freshwater fish in inland waters in Scotland ; and (*c*) he is satisfied that, if such proposals were implemented, fishing for freshwater fish in the area to be prescribed by him in the protection order would be available—

(i) to a degree, which he considered reasonable having regard in particular to what is, in his opinion, the demand, by persons who are neither owners nor occupiers of a right of fishing for freshwater fish in the waters to which the proposals relate nor members of a club which is such an owner or occupier in those waters, for fishing in that area, and

(ii) on such terms and conditions as he considered reasonable ; and

(*d*) he has taken into consideration the need for conservation of any species of fish and has carried out such consultations in this regard as he considers necessary.

(4) Proposals referred to in subsection (3)(*a*) above shall specify—

(*a*) the limits of the waters to which they relate ;

(*b*) the extent to which, and the places with regard to which, it is proposed to grant leases or permits in respect of fishing for freshwater fish in those waters, and any terms and conditions (including charges) relating to such leases or permits ;

(*c*) any operations which it is proposed to carry out for the purpose of improving such fishing in those waters ;

(*d*) such matters as the Secretary of State may at any time in relation to the proposals direct ;

and the person submitting such proposals to the Secretary of State may at any time withdraw them or, after consultation with him, modify them.

(5) In deciding for the purposes of subsection (3)(*c*) above whether the terms and conditions referred to therein are reasonable, the Secretary of State may have regard to the circumstances in which fishing is made available in any waters other than those to which the proposals relate in respect of the following matters—

(*a*) the amount of charges ;

(*b*) the permitted methods of fishing or tackle ;

(*c*) the maximum number of fish that may be caught ;

(*d*) the permitted maximum number of rods ;

(*e*) the permitted times of fishing ;

(*f*) the permitted minimum size of fish which may be taken ;

(*g*) the number of persons permitted to fish who are neither owners nor occupiers of a right of fishing for freshwater fish in those waters nor members of a club which is such an owner or occupier in those waters ; and (*h*) any other matters which the Secretary of State considers relevant.

(6) The Secretary of State may at any time require an owner or occupier of a right of fishing for freshwater fish in a prescribed area to furnish him with information regarding the implementation in that area of proposals in so far as they relate to that right.

(7) A protection order may provide that it shall cease to have effect on a date specified therein ; but if on that date the Secretary of State has received no complaints concerning the implementation of proposals, or if, in his opinion, the complaints received by him are insignificant or frivolous, he may make a protection order renewing that protection order without further procedure, except that paragraph 7 of Schedule 1 to this Act shall apply to such an order.

(8) Any person contravening a prohibition contained in a protection order shall be guilty of an offence and liable on summary conviction to a fine not exceeding £25 or, in the case of a second or subsequent conviction, not exceeding £50.

(9) Without prejudice to the operation of section 312(*o*) of the Criminal Procedure (Scotland) Act 1975, any person who attempts to commit or does any act preparatory to the commission of such an offence as is referred to in subsection (8) above shall be guilty of an offence and shall be punishable in like manner as for the said offence. **1975 c. 21.**

(10) A protection order shall be made by statutory instrument and may be varied or revoked by a subsequent order so made ; and, subject to subsection (7) above, Schedule 1 to this Act shall have effect as to the procedure in the making, variation and revocation of a protection order.

(11) In subsections (1), (3)(*c*), (6) and (7) above " proposals " means proposals as originally submitted to the Secretary of State or, as the case may be, as modified under subsection (4) above.

Appointment of wardens to secure compliance with protection order.

2.—(1) For the purpose of securing compliance with a protection order, the Secretary of State may appoint as wardens such persons as he thinks fit from among persons nominated to him by or on behalf of an owner of land to which a right of fishing for freshwater fish pertains or by or on behalf of an occupier of such a right in any inland waters in the prescribed area.

(2) A warden appointed under subsection (1) above or a constable may—

(*a*) make enquiry as to the legal right or written permission of any person to fish for or take freshwater fish in any waters in the prescribed area where he has reasonable cause to suspect that that person has no such right or permit and may require that person to produce written evidence of such right or permission within 14 days ;

(*b*) if he has reasonable cause to suspect that a contravention of a prohibition contained in a protection order has taken place, within the prescribed area seize any instrument or article used or calculated to be of use in such contravention.

Powers of entry and obstruction of wardens etc.

3.—(1) A warden shall have a right to enter any land—

(*a*) in the vicinity of any waters in the prescribed area for the purpose of exercising any of the powers conferred on him by section 2(2) of this Act;

(*b*) for the purpose of affixing or maintaining a copy of any order or notice which he is required to affix or maintain by any provision of Schedule 1 to this Act;

(*c*) in the vicinity of any waters in the prescribed area and remain there during any period for the purpose of preventing a breach of a protection order or of detecting any person contravening a protection order; and no warden remaining on such land for such a purpose shall be deemed to be a trespasser on that land.

(2) Any person duly authorised in writing by the Secretary of State under the said Schedule 1 shall have a right to enter land for the purpose of affixing or maintaining a copy of any notice or order which he is required to affix or maintain by any provision of that Schedule.

(3) Any person who wilfully obstructs or refuses to allow—

(*a*) a warden to exercise any of the powers conferred on him by section 2(2) of this Act or subsection (1) above; or

(*b*) any person referred to in subsection (2) above to exercise the powers conferred on him by that subsection,

shall be guilty of an offence and liable on summary conviction to a fine not exceeding £50, or, in the case of a second or subsequent conviction, to a fine not exceeding £100 or to imprisonment for a term not exceeding 3 months.

(4) The production of the instrument of appointment of a warden purporting to be signed by or on behalf of the Secretary of State or of the authorisation by the Secretary of State of any person referred to in subsection (2) above shall be sufficient warrant for the exercise of any power which has been conferred on that warden or such a person.

(5) In this section " land " does not include any building thereon.

Legal status of right of freshwater fishing.

4. Notwithstanding any rule of law to the contrary, any contract entered into in writing for a consideration and for a period of not less than a year whereby an owner of land to which a right of fishing for freshwater fish in any inland waters pertains or the occupier of such a right authorises another person to so fish shall be deemed to be a lease to which the Leases Act 1449 applies, and the right of fishing so authorised shall, for the purposes of succession to that right, be deemed to be heritable property. 1449 c. 6.

Exchequer contributions towards organisations developing freshwater fisheries.

5. The Secretary of State may, in accordance with arrangements made by him with the approval of the Treasury, make payments out of money provided by Parliament of such amount and subject to such conditions as he may determine to any organisation approved by him and having as their object, or one of their principal objects, the development and improvement of freshwater fisheries and the making of such fisheries available for letting or fishing by persons authorised to fish.

Penalties for offences against fisheries enactments.

6.—(1) Schedule 2 to this Act shall have effect with respect to the penalties for offences against the enactments relating to salmon and freshwater fisheries specified in column 1 of that Schedule (of which a rough description is given in column 2 thereof) in place of the penalties in force for such offences at the passing of this Act: and in that Schedule—

(*a*) column 3 shows whether the offence is punishable on summary conviction (in that column referred to as summarily) or on indictment or either in one way or the other;

(*b*) columns 4 and 5 show the maximum penalty by way of fine or imprisonment which may be imposed on the summary conviction of a person for a first offence and a second or subsequent offence respectively; and

(*c*) column 6 shows the maximum penalty by way of fine or imprisonment which may be imposed on a person convicted of the offence on indictment.

(2) Nothing in this section shall affect the penalty which may be imposed on conviction of an offence against any of the said enactments committed before the passing of this Act.

Fish farmers not to be guilty of contravention of certain enactments.

7.—(1) Subject to subsection (2) below, a person shall not be guilty of a contravention of any of the enactments specified in Part I of Schedule 3 to this Act in respect of any act or omission if he carries out the act or the omission takes place within a fish farm in the course of the operation of a fish farm.

(2) There shall be no contravention of paragraph (*b*) or (*c*) of section 4 of the Salmon and Freshwater Fisheries (Protection) (Scotland) Act 1951, by virtue of subsection (1) above, in respect of an act referred to in the said paragraph (*b*) or (*c*) only if the act is carried out with the consent of the Secretary of State. 1951 c. 26.

(3) For the purposes of subsection (1) above, the act of selling or exporting fish by or on behalf of a person who has reared the fish in a fish farm shall be deemed to be an act carried out within a fish farm in the course of the operation of that farm.

(4) In any proceedings for an offence under any of the enactments specified in Part II of Schedule 3 to this Act in relation to a boat or other thing mentioned in any such enactment which is not in a fish farm, it shall be a defence for the person charged with such offence to prove that the act or omission complained of was necessary for the purpose of the operation of a fish farm.

Application of Act to Crown.

8.—(1) This Act shall apply to land an interest in which belongs to Her Majesty in right of the Crown and land an interest in which belongs to a government department or is held in trust for Her Majesty for the purposes of a government department; but in its application to any land an interest in which belongs or is held as aforesaid this Act shall have effect subject to such modifications as may be prescribed by regulations made by the Secretary of State.

(2) Any regulations made by the Secretary of State under this section shall be embodied in a statutory instrument which shall be subject to annulment in pursuance of a resolution of either House of Parliament.

Interpretation.

9.—(1) In this Act, unless the context otherwise requires—

"fish farm" has the same meaning as in section 10(1) of the Diseases of Fish Act 1937; (1937 c. 33.)

"freshwater fish" has the same meaning as in section 24(1) of the Salmon and Freshwater Fisheries (Protection) (Scotland) Act 1951; (1951 c. 26.)

"inland waters" includes all rivers (other than their tidal parts) and their tributary streams, and all waters, watercourses and lochs whether natural or artificial which drain or drain to some extent into the sea;

"land" includes land covered by water;

"prescribed area" means the area prescribed in a protection order;

(2) References to an occupier of a right of fishing for freshwater fish are references to a person who is in possession of that right as tenant under a lease of land to which such a right pertains or under a contract which by virtue of section 4 of this Act is deemed to be a lease, and, for the purposes of this subsection, "tenant" and "lease" include "subtenant" and "sublease" respectively.

Short title and extent.

10.—(1) This Act may be cited as the Freshwater and Salmon Fisheries (Scotland) Act 1976.

(2) This Act extends to Scotland only.

SCHEDULES

SCHEDULE 1

Section 1.

Provisions as to Making, Variation and Revocation of Protection Orders

Making of protection order

1. Before the Secretary of State makes a protection order he shall require a person from whom he has received proposals under section 1(3)(*a*) of this Act to give notice in such form as the Secretary of State may direct—

(*a*) stating the general effect of those proposals ;

(*b*) naming a place or places where a copy of the proposals and any map accompanying the proposals may be inspected free of charge at all reasonable hours ; and

(*c*) specifying the time (not being less than 28 days from the date of the first publication of the notice) within which, and the manner in which, representations or objections with respect to the proposals may be made.

2. The notice to be given under paragraph 1 above shall be given by publication in the Edinburgh Gazette and in such number of such newspapers as the Secretary of State may direct.

3. The Secretary of State may direct that, in addition to publication of the notice as required by paragraph 2 above, a copy or copies of it shall be affixed by a person duly authorised in writing by the Secretary of State to some conspicuous object or objects on the banks of any waters to which the proposals relate or of such other waters as the Secretary of State may direct and at such number of places as he may direct.

4. If no representations or objections are duly made, or if any so made are withdrawn, the Secretary of State may make a protection order.

5.—(1) If any representation or objection duly made is not withdrawn, the Secretary of State may, after considering the same, forthwith make a protection order or may cause a local inquiry to be held.

(2) The Secretary of State shall appoint a person to hold the inquiry and to report thereon to him.

(3) Notification of the time when and the place where the inquiry is to be held shall be sent to any person who has duly made and has not withdrawn representations or objections to the proposals, and shall be published in such newspaper or newspapers as the Secretary of State may direct.

(4) The person appointed to hold the inquiry may, on the motion of any party thereto or on his own motion, serve a notice in writing on any person requiring him to attend at the time and place set forth in the notice to give evidence or to produce any books or

SCH. 1 documents in his custody or under his control which relate to any matter in question at the inquiry ;

Provided that—

(i) no person shall be required in obedience to such a notice to attend at any place which is more than ten miles from the place where he resides unless the necessary expenses are paid or tendered to him ; and

(ii) nothing in this sub-paragraph shall empower the person appointed to hold the inquiry to require any person to produce any book or document or to answer any question which he would be entitled, on the ground of privilege or confidentiality, to refuse to produce or to answer if the inquiry were a proceeding in a court of law.

(5) The person appointed to hold the inquiry may administer oaths and examine witnesses on oath and may accept, in lieu of evidence on oath by any person, a statement in writing by that person.

(6) Any person who refuses or wilfully neglects to attend in obedience to a notice under sub-paragraph (4) above or to give evidence or who wilfully alters, suppresses, conceals, destroys, or refuses to produce, any book or document which he may be required to produce by any such notice shall be liable on summary conviction to a fine not exceeding £20 or to imprisonment for a period not exceeding 3 months.

(7) The Secretary of State may make orders as to the expenses incurred by him in relation to the inquiry (including such reasonable sum as he may determine for the services of the person appointed to hold the inquiry) and as to the expenses incurred by the parties to the inquiry and as to the parties by whom such expenses shall be paid.

(8) Any order of the Secretary of State under sub-paragraph (7) above requiring any party to pay expenses may be enforced in like manner as a recorded decree arbitral.

6. After considering the report of the person appointed to hold the inquiry in pursuance of paragraph 5 above and any representations or objections which were duly made, the Secretary of State may make a protection order.

7. As soon as may be after a protection order has been made—

(*a*) the Secretary of State shall publish the making of the order in the Edinburgh Gazette and in such number of local newspapers circulating in the area to which the order relates as he thinks fit ; and

(*b*) a person duly authorised in writing by the Secretary of State or a warden shall affix and maintain a copy or copies of the order and such other notice as the Secretary of State may consider necessary of the incidence of the order to some conspicuous object or objects, at such places as the Secretary of State may direct, on the banks of any waters to which the order relates or elsewhere.

Variation of protection order

SCH. 1

8. Paragraph 7 above shall apply to an order varying a protection order as it applies to a protection order.

Revocation of protection order

9.—(1) Before the Secretary of State makes an order revoking a protection order, he may by notice make such publication as he thinks fit of the general effect of the proposed revocation and specify a time within which, and the manner in which, representations or objections with respect to the proposed revocation may be made.

(2) The Secretary of State may cause a copy or copies of the notice referred to in sub-paragraph (1) above to be affixed by a person duly authorised by him in writing to some conspicuous object or objects on the banks of such waters at such places as the Secretary of State may direct.

(3) If no representations or objections are duly made, or if any so made are withdrawn, the Secretary of State may make the order revoking the protection order.

(4) If any representation or objection duly made is not withdrawn, the Secretary of State may forthwith make the order or may cause a local inquiry to be held.

(5) Sub-paragraphs (2) to (8) of paragraph 5 above shall apply in relation to an inquiry under this paragraph as they apply in relation to an inquiry under that paragraph, but as if in sub-paragraph (3) of that paragraph for the word " proposals " there were substituted the words " proposed revocation ".

(6) Paragraphs 6 and 7 above shall apply in relation to an order revoking a protection order as they apply in relation to a protection order, but as if in paragraph 6 for the reference to paragraph 5 above there were substituted a reference to this paragraph.

Publication of Orders

10. The Secretary of State shall cause to be published each year a list of prescribed areas which are the subject of protection orders.

Section 6.

SCHEDULE 2

Penalties for Offences against Enactments relating to Salmon and Freshwater Fisheries

1 Provision of enactment creating the offence	2 Rough description of offence	3 Mode of prosecution	4 Penalty for first offence on summary conviction	5 Penalty for second and subsequent offence on summary conviction	6 Penalty for conviction on indictment
The Salmon Fisheries (Scotland) Act 1868 (*c.* 123).					
Section 15(1)... ...	Fishing for salmon in annual close season, other than by rod and line.	Summarily.	£100.	£200.	—
Section 15(2)...	(*a*) Fishing in weekly close time (other than by rod and line). (*b*) Fishing on Sundays by rod and line. (*c*) Contravention of any bye-law relating to weekly close time.	Summarily.	£100.	£200.	—
Section 15(3)... ...	Fishing for salmon by rod and line during close season contrary to bye-law provisions.	Summarily.	£50.	£100.	—
Section 15(4)... ...	Using a net with a mesh contrary to bye-law provisions.	Summarily.	£50.	£100.	—
Section 15(5)... ...	Using a net to catch salmon at falls etc.	Summarily.	£100.	£200.	—
Section 15(6)... ...	Preventing the passage of or catching salmon at fish passes.	Summarily.	£100.	£200.	—
Section 15(8)... ...	Contravention of any bye-law.	Summarily.	£100.	£200.	—
Section 18	Buying, selling or possessing salmon roe.	Summarily.	£50.	£100.	—
Section 19	Buying, selling or possessing young salmon; disturbing spawn etc.	Summarily.	£50.	£100.	—

1	2	3	4	5	6
Provision of enactment creating the offence	Rough description of offence	Mode of prosecution	Penalty for first offence on summary conviction	Penalty for second and subsequent offence on summary conviction	Penalty for conviction on indictment
Section 20	Buying, selling, taking or possessing unclean or unseasonable salmon.	Summarily.	£50.	£100.	—
Section 21	Buying or selling or having in possession salmon taken in close season.	Summarily.	£50.	£100.	—
Section 23	Failing to remove boats, nets, etc. in close season.	Summarily.	£100.	£200.	—
Section 24	Failing to observe weekly close time arrangements for nets.	Summarily.	£100.	£200.	—
The Freshwater Fish (Scotland) Act 1902 (*c.* 29).					
Section 1	Fishing for or having possession of trout in close season.	Summarily.	£50.	£100.	—
The Trout (Scotland) Act 1933 (*c.* 35).					
Section 2	Purchase or sale of trout under 8 inches or between 1st September and 31st March.	Summarily.	£50.	£100.	—
The Salmon and Freshwater Fisheries (Protection) (Scotland) Act 1951 (*c.* 26).					
Section 1	Fishing for salmon without legal right or written permission.	Summarily.	£50.	£100.	—
Section 2	Fishing by illegal methods.	Summarily.	£100.	£200.	—
Section 3	Illegal fishing by two or more persons acting together.	(*a*) Summarily.	£200 or 3 months imprisonment.	£400 and/or 6 months imprisonment.	—
		(*b*) On indictment.	—	—	Unlimited fine and/or 2 years imprisonment.

1 Provision of enactment creating the offence	2 Rough description of offence	3 Mode of prosecution	4 Punishment for first offence on summary conviction	5 Punishment for second and subsequent offence on summary conviction	6 Punishment for conviction on indictment
Section 4	Use of explosives, poisons and electrical devices.	(*a*) Summarily.	£200 or 3 months imprisonment.	£400 and/or 6 months imprisonment.	—
		(*b*) On indictment.	—	—	Unlimited fine and/or 2 years imprisonment.
Section 6	Unauthorised removal of dead salmon or trout.	Summarily.	£100.	£200.	—
Section 10(6)... ...	Obstruction of a water bailiff, constable etc.	Summarily.	£100 and/or 3 months imprisonment.	£100 and/or 3 months imprisonment.	—
Section 13 ...	(*a*) Fishing for salmon in the weekly close time (other than by rod and line). (*b*) Fishing for salmon on Sundays by rod and line.	Summarily.	£100.	£200.	—
Section 15(2)... ...	Refusing or neglecting to provide statistics.	Summarily.	£100.	£100.	—
Section 16	Contravention of regulations relating to the packing of salmon and trout.	Summarily.	£50.	£100.	—

SCHEDULE 3

Section 7.

Enactments to Which Section 7 Applies

Part I

Enactments to which subsection (1) applies

1. In the Solway Act 1804
   (*a*) section I (imposition of close time);
   (*b*) section II (requirement to remove boats, etc.);
   (*c*) section XI (selling fish out of season, and having fish in possession);
   (*d*) section XV (regulation of size of mesh of nets).

2. In the Tweed Fisheries Act 1857—
   (*a*) section XLV (prohibition against use of any pout net or net during close season);
   (*b*) section LXXII (requirement to return unclean fish to river);
   (*c*) section LXXIV (prohibition against destruction of spawn or fry).

3. In the Tweed Fisheries Amendment Act 1859—
   (*a*) section VI (offence of fishing in close season);
   (*b*) section X (offence of having in possession during close season salmon taken or caught in the river);
   (*c*) section XI (boats, nets etc. to be removed in close season);
   (*d*) section XIII (prohibits drawing or using in the river nets with mesh less than prescribed size).

4. Section 3 of the Salmon Acts Amendment Act 1863 (export of unclean salmon, or salmon caught during certain times, prohibited). 1863 c. 10.

5. In the Salmon Fisheries (Scotland) Act 1868— 1868 c. 123.
   (*a*) section 15(1) (fishing for salmon in close season other than by rod and line);
   (*b*) section 15(2) (fishing for salmon in weekly close time);
   (*c*) section 15(4) (fishing for salmon with a net having a mesh contrary to any byelaw);
   (*d*) section 20 (buying, selling, taking or possessing unclean or unseasonable salmon);
   (*e*) section 21 (buying, selling, exposing for sale or having in possession salmon taken in close season);
   (*f*) section 23 (boats, nets etc., to be removed in close season).

6. In the Freshwater Fish (Scotland) Act 1902, section 1 (fishing for or having possession of trout in close season). 1902 c. 29.

7. In the Trout (Scotland) Act 1933, section 2 (purchase or sale of trout under 8″ or between 1 September and 31 March). 1933 c. 35.

SCH. 3

1951 c. 26. 8. In the Salmon and Freshwater Fisheries (Protection) (Scotland) Act 1951—

(*a*) section 2 (fishing for salmon and freshwater fish by illegal methods);

(*b*) paragraphs (*b*) and (*c*) of section 4 (prohibition against using poisons and electrical devices for destruction of fish);

(*c*) section 13 (fishing for salmon in weekly close time).

PART II

Enactments to which subsection (4) applies

9. In the Solway Act 1804, section II (requirement to remove boats, etc.).

10. In the Tweed Fisheries Amendment Act 1859, section XI (boats, nets, etc. to be removed in close season).

1868 c. 123. 11. In the Salmon Fisheries (Scotland) Act 1868, section 23 (boats, nets, etc. to be removed in close season).

Atomic Energy Authority (Special Constables) Act 1976

1976 CHAPTER 23

An Act to extend the powers relating to firearms of special constables appointed on the nomination of the United Kingdom Atomic Energy Authority; to extend the property in respect of which, and the places where, they may exercise those and their other powers; to make certain minor amendments about their powers; and for connected purposes. [10th June 1976]

BE IT ENACTED by the Queen's most Excellent Majesty, by and with the advice and consent of the Lords Spiritual and Temporal, and Commons, in this present Parliament assembled, and by the authority of the same, as follows:—

Extension of powers of special constables as regards firearms. 1968 c. 27.

1.—(1) For the purposes of—

(*a*) section 54 of the Firearms Act 1968 (application to Crown servants and treating the police as being in the service of Her Majesty), and

(*b*) any rule of law whereby any provision of that Act does not bind the Crown,

an Authority constable shall be deemed to be a person in the service of Her Majesty.

(2) In the application by virtue of subsection (1) above of subsection (2) (*a*) of the said section 54 (acquisition by persons in such service of firearms for the public service without certificate) the reference to the public service shall be deemed to be a reference to use by any Authority constable in exercising his functions as such.

Extension of property in respect of which special constables may exercise their powers.
1965 c. 57.
1971 c. 11.
1923 c. 11.

2.—(1) In Schedule 1 to the Nuclear Installations Act 1965 (which is set out in the Schedule to the Atomic Energy Authority Act 1971) the following sub-paragraph shall be added at the end of paragraph 4 (which extends section 3 of the Special Constables Act 1923 so as to provide for the appointment of persons nominated by the Authority to be special constables in and within 15 miles of premises under the control of specified bodies corporate)—

> " (3) For the purposes of section 2 of the Metropolitan Police Act 1860 (which limits the use of the powers of special constables to property of the Crown in certain circumstances) any property of the specified body corporate shall be deemed to be property of the Crown ; and in this sub-paragraph property of the specified body corporate includes property which (though not owned by them) is in their possession or under their control and property which has been unlawfully removed from their possession or control ".

(2) Accordingly, in section 19(1) of the Atomic Energy Authority Act 1971 (application to designated companies of security provisions set out in the Schedule to that Act) after the words " set out in the Schedule to this Act " there shall be inserted the words " and as amended by section 2(1) of the Atomic Energy Authority (Special Constables) Act 1976 ".

1954 c. 32.

(3) In Schedule 3 to the Atomic Energy Authority Act 1954, after the words " For the purposes of section two of the Metropolitan Police Act, 1860, any property of the Authority shall be deemed to be property of the Crown " there shall be added the words " ; and in this paragraph property of the Authority includes property which (though not owned by them) is in their possession or under their control and property which has been unlawfully removed from their possession or control."

Extension of places where special constables may exercise their powers.

3.—(1) An Authority constable may exercise the powers and privileges, and shall be liable to the duties and responsibilities, of such a constable in any place where it appears to him expedient to go—

(*a*) in order to safeguard any nuclear matter which is being carried or is being stored incidentally to its carriage before its delivery at its final destination and which is owned by the Crown or is owned by, or (though not so owned) is in the possession or under the control of, the Authority, a specified body corporate or a designated company ;

(*b*) in order to pursue, arrest, place in the custody of the police, or take to the limits within which the constable was appointed to act as an Authority constable, a person who the constable reasonably believes has unlawfully removed or attempted to remove from the possession or control of the Crown, the Authority, a specified body corporate or a designated company any nuclear matter being safeguarded by the constable.

(2) An Authority constable acting in pursuance of paragraph (*a*) or (*b*) of subsection (1) above may not exercise his powers and privileges as such a constable in respect of any property other than such nuclear matter as is mentioned in the paragraph concerned.

(3) In this section " nuclear matter " means—

(*a*) any fissile material in the form of uranium metal, alloy or chemical compound, or of plutonium metal, alloy or chemical compound, and any other fissile material which may be prescribed ; and

(*b*) any radioactive material produced in, or made radioactive by exposure to the radiation incidental to, the process of producing or utilising any such fissile material as aforesaid.

(4) In subsection (3)(*a*) above " prescribed " means prescribed by regulations made by the Secretary of State ; and any such regulations shall be made by statutory instrument and be subject to annulment in pursuance of a resolution of either House of Parliament.

Citation, interpretation, minor amendments and extent.

4.—(1) This Act may be cited as the Atomic Energy Authority (Special Constables) Act 1976.

(2) In this Act—

" Authority " means the United Kingdom Atomic Energy Authority ;

" Authority constable " means a person appointed under section 3 of the Special Constables Act 1923 to be a special constable on the nomination of the Authority ; 1923 c. 11.

" specified body corporate " means a body corporate specified in an order made under section 2(1B) of the Nuclear Installations Act 1965 (under which special provisions apply in relation to such a body which has a permit to undertake certain operations involving irradiated matter or uranium) ; and 1965 c. 57.

" designated company " means a company designated under section 19 of the Atomic Energy Authority Act 1971 (under which certain of those special provisions apply in relation to a company so designated as they apply in relation to a specified body corporate). 1971 c. 11.

(3) Except in so far as the context otherwise requires, a reference in this Act to any other enactment is a reference to

it as amended, and includes a reference to it as extended or applied, by or under any other enactment, including one contained in this Act.

1860 c. 135. (4) In the application of the proviso to section 2 of the Metropolitan Police Act 1860 (restriction of powers of constables when outside certain yards etc.) to the powers and privileges of Authority constables, for the words from " yards " to " service " there shall be substituted the words " premises (but within the limits) within which they were appointed to act as constables " and the words from " or of persons " to " discipline " shall be omitted.

(5) This Act does not extend to Northern Ireland.

Development Land Tax Act 1976

1976 CHAPTER 24

An Act to impose a new tax on the realisation of the development value of land; to provide for the termination of the charges on capital gains from land imposed by Chapters I and II of Part III of the Finance Act 1974; and for connected purposes. [22nd July 1976]

Most Gracious Sovereign,

WE, Your Majesty's most dutiful and loyal subjects, the Commons of the United Kingdom in Parliament assembled, towards raising the necessary supplies to defray Your Majesty's public expenses, and making an addition to the public revenue, have freely and voluntarily resolved to give and grant unto Your Majesty the new tax hereinafter mentioned and to make such other provision as is hereinafter contained; and do therefore most humbly beseech Your Majesty that it may be enacted, and be it enacted by the Queen's most Excellent Majesty, by and with the advice and consent of the Lords Spiritual and Temporal, and Commons, in this present Parliament assembled, and by the authority of the same, as follows:—

The charge to tax

Development land tax.

1.—(1) A tax, to be called development land tax, shall be charged in accordance with the provisions of this Act in respect of the realisation of the development value of land in the United Kingdom.

(2) Subject to the provisions of this Act, a person shall be chargeable to development land tax on the realised development value, determined in accordance with this Act, which accrues to him on the disposal by him on or after the appointed day

of an interest in land in the United Kingdom, and shall be so chargeable whether or not he is resident (for purposes of income tax or otherwise) in the United Kingdom.

(3) Subject to section 13 below, the rate of development land tax shall be 80 per cent.

Deemed disposals at start of material development.

2.—(1) Immediately before a project of material development is begun on any land, every major interest then subsisting in that land shall be deemed for the purposes of this Act to be disposed of for a consideration equal to its market value at that time and to be immediately reacquired at that value.

(2) Part I of Schedule 1 to this Act shall have effect for determining what is a project of material development, what land is comprised in such a project and at what time such a project is to be treated for the purposes of this Act as begun, and Part II of that Schedule shall have effect with respect to deemed disposals and reacquisitions.

(3) Subject to section 28(6) below, for the purposes of this Act an interest in land comprised in a project of material development is a major interest unless—

(*a*) as to all the land in which it subsists, it is in reversion (at law or in equity) on one or more long leases or (in Northern Ireland) it is the interest of a person entitled for the time being to the rent payable under a grant in fee farm, and the rent or the aggregate of the rents and of any premium or premiums to which, under or by virtue thereof, the owner of the interest is entitled does not, and cannot be made to, reflect the value or any part of the value of the development concerned; or

(*b*) its market value on the date on which the project is begun is less than £5,000 and—

(i) if the land is in England, Wales or Northern Ireland, the interest does not confer, either absolutely or conditionally, and whether on that date or at any later time, a right to possession, as defined in section 205(1) of the Law of Property Act 1925; and

1925 c. 20.

(ii) if the land is in Scotland, the interest is not the estate or interest of the proprietor of the *dominium utile*, or, in the case of property other than feudal property, of the owner, or an interest under a lease.

(4) For the purposes of paragraph (*a*) of subsection (3) above, a lease is a long lease unless, on the date on which the project referred to in that subsection is begun, the unexpired term of

the lease does not exceed thirty-five years; and in the application of that subsection to Scotland, that paragraph shall have effect with the omission of the words " (at law or in equity) ".

(5) For the purposes of this section, the following leases shall be treated as granted for terms not exceeding thirty-five years, namely,—

(*a*) a lease of land in Northern Ireland which is a lease for life or lives or for any terms of years determinable with life or lives and is not a lease in perpetuity, within the meaning of section 1 of the Renewable Leasehold Conversion Act 1849, or a lease to which section 37 of that Act applies; and

1849 c. 105.

(*b*) a lease of land in England and Wales which is, or takes effect as if, granted for a term exceeding thirty-five years and which is determinable by notice (whether by the lessor or otherwise) at a time after the death of the lessor or any other person or of the survivor of two or more persons; and

(*c*) a lease of land in Scotland which is determinable on the death of any person.

(6) The provisions of Part III of Schedule 1 to this Act (being provisions corresponding to subsections (1)(*b*), (*c*) and (*d*) and (2) to (3A) of section 84 of the Income and Corporation Taxes Act 1970) shall have effect in ascertaining for the purposes of this section when the term of a lease will expire.

1970 c. 10.

Part disposals.

3.—(1) Subject to section 8 below, references in this Act to a disposal of an interest in land include references to a part disposal thereof, and for the purposes of this Act there is a part disposal of an interest in land—

(*a*) where the owner of that interest grants a lease or other interest in land out of, or by virtue of his ownership of, his interest; or

(*b*) where the owner of that interest grants to another his interest in some but not all of the land in which that interest subsisted before the grant.

(2) Without prejudice to subsection (1) above, there is for the purposes of this Act a part disposal of an interest in land by the owner thereof where any sum is derived from his ownership of that interest and that sum is neither rent payable under a lease nor otherwise attributable to the acquisition (at any time) by the person paying that sum of an interest in that land, and this subsection applies in particular to—

(*a*) sums received by way of compensation for any kind of damage to land in which that interest subsists or for any depreciation or risk of depreciation of that interest;

(*b*) sums received in return for forfeiture or surrender of, or refraining from exercising, rights which are vested in the owner of the interest by virtue of his ownership thereof; and

(*c*) sums received as consideration for use or exploitation of the land in which that interest subsists or of any assets, other than minerals, in, on or under that land;

and for the purposes of this Act such a part disposal shall be deemed to take place, subject to subsection (3) below, at the time at which the sum in question is received.

(3) In any case where—

(*a*) there is a part disposal of an interest in land falling within subsection (2) above, and

(*b*) before the sum in question is received but after the right to receive it has accrued, there is a disposal, other than a deemed disposal, of that interest or of an interest of which it is a part for the purposes of Part I of Schedule 2 to this Act,

the part disposal shall be deemed for the purposes of this Act to take place immediately before the disposal referred to in paragraph (*b*) above.

(4) In subsection (2) above " sum " means money or money's worth.

(5) In relation to a part disposal of an interest in land,—

(*a*) references in this Act to the retained interest are references to that interest in land which, by virtue of his previous ownership of the interest disposed of, the chargeable person has immediately after the disposal; and

(*b*) references in this Act to the granted interest apply only in the case of a disposal falling within subsection (1) above and, in such a case, are references to the interest granted as mentioned in paragraph (*a*) or paragraph (*b*) of that subsection.

Realised development value.

4.—(1) Subject to the following provisions of this Act, the realised development value accruing to a person on the disposal by him of an interest in land shall be the amount (if any) by which the net proceeds of the disposal exceed the relevant base value of that interest.

(2) In this Act, in relation to a disposal of an interest in land, " the chargeable person " means the person making the disposal.

(3) References in this Act to the net proceeds of the disposal of an interest in land are references to the consideration for the disposal, less the incidental costs to the chargeable person of making the disposal.

(4) The provisions of Schedule 2 to this Act shall have effect for supplementing this section and sections 5 to 7 below and, for the purpose of determining the realised development value accruing on a disposal occurring on or after the appointed day, those provisions shall be taken to have had effect in relation to events before, as well as on or after, that day.

(5) Subject to any express provision contained in this Act, for the purpose of determining the realised development value accruing to a person on the disposal of an interest in land, any necessary apportionment shall be made of any consideration, expenditure or value and the method of apportionment adopted shall be such as appears to the Board or, on an appeal, to the Commissioners concerned to be just and reasonable.

(6) In determining the amount of any realised development value for the purposes of this Act, no deduction shall be allowable under any provision of this Act more than once from any amount or from more than one amount.

5.—(1) Subject to the provisions of this section, on the disposal of an interest in land the relevant base value of that interest is that one of the following which gives the highest figure, namely,— Relevant base value.

(*a*) the aggregate of—

(i) the cost of the chargeable person's acquisition of the interest, and

(ii) any expenditure on relevant improvements, and

(iii) the amount by which the current use value of the interest at the time of the disposal exceeds the current use value of the interest at the time of its acquisition or on 6th April 1965, whichever is the later, and

(iv) where section 6 below applies, the special addition provided for by subsection (2) of that section, and

(v) where subsection (5) below applies, the amount of the further addition referred to in that subsection ;

(*b*) the aggregate of 110 per cent. of the current use value of the interest at the time of the disposal and of any expenditure on relevant improvements ;

(*c*) 110 per cent. of the aggregate of the cost of the chargeable person's acquisition of the interest and of any expenditure on improvements ;

and in this Act the three bases specified in paragraphs (*a*) to (*c*) above are referred to as " base A ", " base B " and " base C " respectively.

(2) For the purposes of this Act, the cost of a person's acquisition of an interest in land means, subject to subsection (4) below, the amount or value of the consideration given by him or on his behalf wholly and exclusively for the acquisition of the interest, together with the incidental costs to him of the acquisition.

(3) Part I of Schedule 3 to this Act shall have effect—

(*a*) for determining, in relation to a disposal by any person of an interest in land, the amount of any expenditure on improvements and of any expenditure on relevant improvements; and

(*b*) with respect to matters consequential upon that determination.

(4) For the purposes of this section there shall be deducted from the amount which on the disposal of an interest in land would, apart from this subsection, be the amount of any consideration falling within subsection (2) above or of any expenditure on improvements or relevant improvements, so much of that consideration or expenditure as has been or is to be provided or met, directly or indirectly, by the Crown or a government or public or local authority, whether in the United Kingdom or elsewhere.

(5) If in the aggregate amount which constitutes base A of an interest in land an amount is included by virtue of both sub-paragraph (ii) and sub-paragraph (iv) of paragraph (*a*) of subsection (1) above, a further addition determined in accordance with Part II of Schedule 3 to this Act shall be included in that aggregate by virtue of sub-paragraph (v) of that paragraph.

(6) Subject to subsection (7) below, on the disposal of an interest in land which the chargeable person acquired—

(*a*) within the period of twelve months ending on the date of the disposal, and

(*b*) as a result of a disposal made by a person who, at the time of that disposal, was connected with him for
1965 c. 25. the purposes of Part III of the Finance Act 1965 (capital gains tax),

subsection (1) above shall have effect for determining the relevant base value of that interest as if—

(i) in paragraph (*a*), sub-paragraph (iv) were omitted; and

(ii) in paragraph (*c*), the words " 110 per cent. of " were transferred from the beginning of the paragraph to follow the word " and " and the word " of ", in the last place where it occurs were omitted.

(7) Subsection (6) above does not apply to the disposal of an interest in land where—

(*a*) the disposal is made by personal representatives in the course of administering the deceased's estate, or

(*b*) on the death of any person the interest is treated for the purposes of this Act as being disposed of by the deceased to the person becoming entitled to it on his death.

Special addition to base A.

6.—(1) Subject to subsection (4) below, the provisions of this section apply for the purpose of determining base A on the disposal of an interest in land (in this section referred to as " the relevant interest ") where the chargeable person acquired that interest before 1st May 1977.

(2) Subject to subsection (5) below, where this section applies, there shall be included in the calculation of the base value of the relevant interest a special addition of an amount equal to D×E per cent. of the cost of the chargeable person's acquisition of the relevant interest, where—

D is the number of years, subject to a maximum of four, in the period beginning at the time of the chargeable person's acquisition of the relevant interest and ending at the time of the disposal ; and

E is 15, if the chargeable person acquired the relevant interest before 13th September 1974, and 10 in any other case.

(3) For the purposes of subsection (2) above a year is a period of twelve months beginning on, or on an anniversary of, the date of acquisition of the relevant interest by the chargeable person and if, apart from this subsection, D referred to in subsection (2) above would consist of either a part of a year or one or more whole years and a part of a year, that part shall be treated for the purposes of this section as a whole year.

(4) Subject to subsection (5) below, where there is a deemed disposal and reacquisition of an interest in land, this section shall not apply to a disposal which occurs after the deemed reacquisition if—

(*a*) that later disposal is either a disposal of the interest which was the relevant interest in relation to the deemed disposal or would be such a disposal if there had been no previous disposal of that interest since the time of the deemed disposal ; and

(*b*) the cost of acquisition of the interest which is the relevant interest in relation to that later disposal is the cost established on the occasion of the deemed reacquisition or, by virtue of any provision of Part II of Schedule 2 to this Act, is in any way derived from the cost so established.

(5) Subject to subsection (8) below, where there is a deemed disposal and reacquisition of an interest in land and on that disposal (in the following provisions of this section referred to as " the deemed disposal ") the amount which is base A of the relevant interest exceeds the net proceeds of the disposal, this section shall apply on the occasion of a disposal—

(*a*) which occurs after the deemed disposal, and

(*b*) which is a disposal of the interest which was the relevant interest in relation to the deemed disposal, and

(*c*) in relation to which paragraph (*b*) of subsection (4) above applies,

subject to the modifications specified in subsection (6) below; and in subsection (6) below the disposal which falls within paragraphs (*a*) to (*c*) above is referred to, in relation to the deemed disposal, as " the subsequent disposal ".

(6) In the application of this section to the subsequent disposal in accordance with subsection (5) above—

(*a*) references to the time at which the chargeable person acquired the relevant interest shall be construed as references to the time (prior to the deemed disposal) at which he acquired that interest, otherwise than on the occasion of a deemed disposal and reacquisition;

(*b*) the reference in subsection (2) above to the cost of the chargeable person's acquisition of the relevant interest shall be construed as a reference to the relevant fraction of the amount which would have been that cost on a notional disposal by him of the relevant interest occurring immediately after the time at which he acquired that interest as mentioned in paragraph (*a*) above; and

(*c*) D referred to in subsection (2) above shall be treated as reduced by the number of years (ascertained in accordance with subsection (3) above) in the period beginning at the time at which the chargeable person acquired the interest as mentioned in paragraph (*a*) above and ending at the time of the deemed disposal.

(7) Subject to subsection (8) below, the relevant fraction referred to in subsection (6) (*b*) above is—

$$\frac{BV - PD}{BV}$$

where—

" PD " is the net proceeds of the deemed disposal; and

" BV ", subject to subsection (8) below, is the amount which is base A of the relevant interest on the deemed disposal.

(8) In a case where paragraph 11 of Schedule 1 to this Act applies in determining the market value of the relevant interest for the purposes of the deemed disposal, references in subsections (5) and (7) above to the amount which is base A of that interest on the deemed disposal shall be construed as references to what that amount would be if paragraph 18(1) of Schedule 2 to this Act did not apply.

(9) In any case where—

(*a*) this section has applied in relation to a disposal of an interest in land subject to the modifications in subsection (6) above, and

(*b*) that disposal was itself a deemed disposal, and

(*c*) on that deemed disposal the amount which was base A of the relevant interest exceeded the net proceeds of the disposal,

then, in the application of subsections (5) to (7) above on the occasion of a disposal which, in relation to that deemed disposal, is the subsequent disposal for the purposes of subsection (6) above, the relevant fraction referred to in paragraph (*b*) of that subsection shall be whichever is the less of the fraction determined under subsection (7) above and the fraction which was the relevant fraction in the application of that paragraph on the occasion of that deemed disposal.

Market value, current use value and material development.

7.—(1) For the purposes of this Act, the market value at any time of an interest in land is the consideration which that interest might reasonably be expected to fetch on a sale at that time in the open market; but that consideration shall not be assumed to be reduced on the ground that the interest in all of the land in question is to be placed on the market at one and the same time.

(2) Subject to the following provisions of this section, for the purposes of this Act, the current use value of an interest in land at any time is the market value of that interest at that time calculated on the assumption—

(*a*) that, subject to Part I of Schedule 4 to this Act, planning permission would be granted for any development of the land which is development of a class specified in the relevant planning Schedule; and

(*b*) that it is at that time and will continue to be unlawful to carry out any material development of the land other than development which—

(i) is development for which, by virtue of paragraph (*a*) above, it is assumed at that time that planning permission would be granted; or

(ii) was comprised in a project of material development begun before that time.

(3) In subsection (2)(*a*) above " the relevant planning Schedule " means—

(*a*) in relation to England and Wales, Schedule 8 to the Town and Country Planning Act 1971 ;

1971 c. 78.

1972 c. 52.

(*b*) in relation to Scotland, Schedule 6 to the Town and Country Planning (Scotland) Act 1972 ; and

1965 c. 23 (N.I.).

(*c*) in relation to Northern Ireland, Schedule 1 to the Land Development Values (Compensation) Act (Northern Ireland) 1965.

(4) In determining the realised development value accruing to the chargeable person on the disposal of an interest in land which is a part disposal resulting from the receipt of any such sum as is referred to in section 3(2) above, the current use value of that interest at the time of that disposal shall be taken to be what it would have been at that time if the circumstances which caused the sum to be received had not arisen.

(5) In determining the market value or current use value of an interest in land at any time, the interest shall be treated as being sold free from any interest or right which exists by way of security in or over the land concerned.

(6) In determining the current use value of an interest in land at the time of a disposal thereof where—

(*a*) the disposal is to an authority possessing compulsory powers, and

(*b*) immediately before the disposal the land concerned, or any part of it, had an unexpended balance of established development value for the purposes of Part VII of the Town and Country Planning Act 1971 or, as the case may require, the Town and Country Planning (Scotland) Act 1972,

no account shall be taken of the operation, in relation to the acquisition or sale to which the disposal gives effect, of any provision of that Part providing for the reduction or extinguishment of such a balance on the acquisition of land under compulsory powers.

(7) For the purposes of this Act " material development " means any development other than—

(*a*) development for which planning permission—

(i) is granted by a general development order for the time being in force, or

(ii) would be so granted but for a direction given under the order or a condition imposed in any planning permission granted or deemed to be granted otherwise than by such an order, and which is carried out so as to comply with any condition or limitation subject to which planning permission is or would be so granted ; and

(*b*) development which is excluded from being material development by Part II of Schedule 4 to this Act ;

and in paragraph (*a*) above " general development order " means a development order made as a general order applicable (subject to such exceptions as may be specified therein) to all land in England and Wales, to all land in Scotland or to all land in Northern Ireland, as the case may be.

Options to acquire interests in land etc.

8.—(1) Notwithstanding anything in section 3(1) above, for the purposes of this Act the grant of an option to acquire an interest in land, including an interest which is not in existence at the time of the grant,—

(*a*) shall be treated as the disposal of a newly created interest in land, namely the option, and

(*b*) shall not be treated as a part disposal of any other interest in land, and

(*c*) where no consideration is given for the grant, shall be treated for the purposes of section 10 below as an interest acquired in circumstances where consideration was given for the acquisition,

and in the following provisions of this section any reference to the option is a reference to such an option as is referred to above and any reference to the grantor is a reference to the person by whom the option was granted or the person who is for the time being obliged to give effect to the option if it is exercised.

(2) In relation to the person who is for the time being the owner of an option, the exercise or abandonment of the option shall not be treated for the purposes of this Act as the disposal of an interest in land by that person.

(3) If an option is exercised, then, in relation to the grantor of the option, the grant of the option and the disposal made by him in fulfilment of his obligations under the option shall be treated for the purposes of this Act as a single transaction taking place at the time the option is exercised and, accordingly,—

(*a*) the consideration for the option shall be treated as part of the consideration for the disposal of the interest acquired in pursuance of the option ; and

(*b*) any development land tax paid in respect of realised development value which accrued on the grant of the option shall be treated as paid on account of any development land tax which is chargeable on the disposal.

(4) If, after an option is exercised, the person by whom it was exercised disposes of the interest acquired in pursuance of the option (in this subsection referred to as " the substantive interest ") or of any interest of which the substantive interest is a part for the purposes of Part I of Schedule 2 to this Act, then,—

(*a*) for the purpose of determining the cost of acquisition of the interest disposed of, and

(*b*) for the purpose of the application of paragraph 7 or paragraph 8 of that Schedule,

the option and the substantive interest shall be treated for the purposes of that Part as two separate interests together making up the substantive interest.

(5) Without prejudice to subsection (1) above but subject to subsection (6) below, a disposal consisting of the grant of a lease containing an option shall be treated for the purposes of this Act as the disposal of two separate interests (namely the lease and the option) and if no part of the consideration for the disposal is separately attributable to the option, the option shall be treated for the purposes of this Act as having been acquired for a consideration of £1.

(6) Nothing in subsection (1) or subsection (5) above shall apply in relation to an option to renew a lease where the obligation under the option touches and concerns the land or, in accordance with section 142 of the Law of Property Act 1925 or (in Northern Ireland) section 11 of the Conveyancing Act 1881, is annexed and incident to the reversionary estate, and such an option shall not be treated for the purposes of this Act as an interest in land separate from the lease itself.

1925 c. 20.
1881 c. 41.

In the application of this subsection to Scotland, the words from " in accordance " to " 1881 " shall be omitted.

(7) This section shall apply in relation to—

(*a*) a forfeited deposit of money for the purchase of an interest in land, or

(*b*) other money paid by way of consideration for a prospective purchase of an interest in land which is abandoned,

as if that deposit or other money were consideration given for the grant of an option to acquire that interest.

(8) This section shall not apply in relation to options granted for a lease solely relating to the carrying out of material development consisting of the winning or working of minerals.

Devolution on death.

9.—(1) For the purposes of this Act, the devolution of an interest in land on the personal representatives of the person by whom it was held immediately before his death shall be treated neither as a disposal by the deceased nor as an acquisition by the personal representatives but, for the purposes of this Act, anything done by the deceased shall be treated as having been done (at the time it was in fact done) by the personal representatives and, accordingly,—

(a) the acquisition by the deceased shall be treated as if it had been the acquisition by the personal representatives; and

(b) any expenditure incurred by the deceased shall be treated as having been incurred by the personal representatives.

(2) For the purposes of this Act, the personal representatives of a deceased person shall be treated as being a single and continuing body of persons distinct from the persons who may from time to time be the personal representatives.

(3) In any case where, on the death of any person, an interest in land held by him devolves, otherwise than by virtue of any beneficial entitlement thereto, on a person other than his personal representatives, any reference in this Act to his personal representatives shall be construed, in relation to that interest, as being or, as the case may require, as including a reference to that person.

Interests in land acquired by gift or, in certain cases, at an under value.

10.—(1) Subsection (2) below shall apply in determining the realised development value accruing to the chargeable person on the disposal of an interest in land (in this section referred to as " the relevant interest ") in any case where no consideration was given for the chargeable person's acquisition of that interest; and in the following provisions of this section—

(a) " the material disposal " means the disposal of the relevant interest referred to above;

(b) " the previous disposal " means the disposal as a result of which the chargeable person acquired the relevant interest; and

(c) " the donor's interest " means the interest disposed of by the previous disposal (that is to say, except where that disposal was a part disposal, the relevant interest).

(2) For the purpose of determining the relevant base value of the relevant interest on the material disposal—

(a) the chargeable person's cost of acquisition of the relevant interest shall be taken to consist of an amount equal to that which was taken as the cost of acquisition of the donor's interest in determining the relevant base value of that interest on the previous disposal, together with any incidental costs to the chargeable person of the acquisition of the relevant interest;

(b) to the amount which, apart from this section, would be the amount of expenditure on improvements or on relevant improvements there shall be added an amount equal to that which was taken as the amount of expenditure on improvements or, as the case may be, on relevant improvements for the purpose of determining the relevant base value of the donor's interest on the previous disposal;

(*c*) the current use value of the relevant interest at the time of its acquisition or on 6th April 1965 shall be taken to be equal to the value which, for the purpose of determining the relevant base value of the donor's interest on the previous disposal, was taken as the current use value of that interest at the time of its acquisition or on 6th April 1965, whichever was the later; and

(*d*) section 6 above shall not apply but—

(i) if that section applied for the purpose of determining base A of the donor's interest on the previous disposal, sub-paragraph (iv) of paragraph (*a*) of section 5(1) above shall have effect in relation to the material disposal as if it referred to the amount which, for that purpose, was the special addition provided for in relation to the previous disposal; and

(ii) if in relation to the previous disposal sub-paragraph (iv) of paragraph (*a*) of section 5(1) above had effect as referring to the amount specified in sub-paragraph (i) above, it shall have effect as referring to the like amount in relation to the material disposal;

and if the previous disposal occurred before the appointed day it shall be assumed for the purposes of this subsection that that day fell (and this Act was in force) before the previous disposal occurred.

(3) For the purposes of the application of this Act in Scotland,—

(*a*) where, on the death of an heir of entail in possession, the entailed estate devolves on a person as the succeeding heir of entail, the estate shall be treated as being disposed of by the deceased on his death to that person, and

(*b*) where, on the death of a person, an interest in land, of which the deceased was not at the time of his death competent to dispose, devolves on another person in accordance with the terms of a special destination contained in a deed, the interest in land shall be treated as being disposed of by the deceased on his death to that person, and accordingly, where an interest is treated as being disposed of to any person by virtue of paragraph (*a*) or paragraph (*b*) above, that person's acquisition shall be treated as a case where no consideration is given for the acquisition of the interest in question.

(4) For the purposes of the application of this Act in Northern Ireland, where immediately before his death a person holds an interest in land which, on his death, vests in a person other than his personal representatives, that interest shall be treated as having been disposed of by the deceased on his death to the person beneficially entitled thereto and accordingly that person's acquisition of the interest shall be treated as a case where no consideration was given for the acquisition.

(5) For the purpose of determining the realised development value accruing to the chargeable person on the disposal of an interest in land where—

(*a*) the chargeable person is either a charity or a body specified in paragraph 12 of Schedule 6 to the Finance Act 1975 (for purposes of capital transfer tax, transfers of value to certain bodies to be exempt transfers), and 1975 c. 7.

(*b*) the chargeable person did not acquire that interest otherwise than for value, but acquired it for a consideration less than that which it might reasonably have been expected to fetch in the open market, and

(*c*) the application of subsection (2) above would give a higher relevant base value of the interest disposed of than would be available if that subsection were not applied,

this Act shall apply as if no consideration were given for the chargeable person's acquisition of that interest.

(6) Subject to subsection (7) below, if—

(*a*) the incidental costs of the disposal of an interest in land are borne by the person acquiring the interest or by any other person (other than the chargeable person), and

(*b*) no other consideration is given for the acquisition of that interest,

this Act shall apply as if no consideration were given for the acquisition of that interest.

(7) In any case where by virtue of any provision of this Act an amount falls to be added to the amount which, apart from that provision, would be the cost of acquisition of an interest in land then, notwithstanding that no consideration is in fact given for the acquisition of that interest, the acquisition shall not be

treated for the purposes of this Act as being an acquisition for which no consideration was given.

Exemptions, reduced rate and deferments

Bodies totally exempt from development land tax.

11.—(1) On the disposal of an interest in land, development land tax shall not be chargeable on any realised development value accruing to—

1975 c. 77.

(*a*) an authority, as defined in relation to England, Scotland or Wales by section 1(1) of the Community Land Act 1975 or a joint board established under section 2 of that Act ; or

(*b*) a body corporate established under section 50 of that Act (bodies to exercise reserve powers) ; or

1973 c. 65.

(*c*) the council of a district in Scotland which is within the district of a general planning authority, within the meaning of Part IX of the Local Government (Scotland) Act 1973 ; or

(*d*) the council of a county or district in Wales ; or

(*e*) a parish council, parish meeting or the trustees of a parish or, in Wales, a community council ; or

1964 c. 48.
1967 c. 77.

(*f*) any combined police authority constituted as mentioned in section 3 of the Police Act 1964 or a joint police committee constituted in accordance with a scheme under sections 19 to 21A of the Police (Scotland) Act 1967 ; or

1947 c. 41.

(*g*) a joint committee constituted in accordance with an administration scheme, as defined in subsection (3) of section 36 of the Fire Services Act 1947 (schemes for providing in Scotland fire services in certain combined areas) ; or

(*h*) any of the bodies specified in subsection (2) below ; or

(*i*) a relevant Northern Ireland authority, as defined in subsection (3) below.

(2) The bodies referred to in subsection (1)(*h*) above are:—

(*a*) the Commission for the New Towns ;

(*b*) the Highlands and Islands Development Board ;

(*c*) the Lee Valley Regional Park Authority ;

(*d*) the Letchworth Garden City Corporation ;

(*e*) the North Eastern Housing Association ;

(*f*) the Scottish Development Agency ;

(*g*) the Scottish Special Housing Association ; and

(*h*) the Welsh Development Agency.

(3) The relevant Northern Ireland authorities referred to in subsection (1)(*i*) above are:—

1965 c. 13 (N.I.).

(*a*) a new town commission established under the New Towns Act (Northern Ireland) 1965 ;

(*b*) the Police Authority for Northern Ireland established under the Police Act (Northern Ireland) 1970; 1970 c. 9 (N.I.).

(*c*) the Northern Ireland Housing Executive established under the Housing Executive Act (Northern Ireland) 1971; 1971 c. 5 (N.I.).

(*d*) a district council established under the Local Government Act (Northern Ireland) 1972; 1972 c. 9 (N.I.).

(*e*) an Education and Library Board established under the Education and Libraries (Northern Ireland) Order 1972; and S.I. 1972/1263 (N.I. 12).

(*f*) the Fire Authority for Northern Ireland established under the Fire Services (Northern Ireland) Order 1973. S.I. 1973/601 (N.I. 9).

Exemption for first £10,000 of development value.

12.—(1) Subject to the provisions of this section, if the total amount of realised development value which accrues to any person in a financial year and on which, apart from this section, that person would be chargeable to development land tax does not exceed £10,000, development land tax shall not be chargeable on any of that realised development value.

(2) If subsection (1) above does not apply to any person in respect of a financial year, then, subject to the following provisions of this section, the sum of £10,000 shall be deducted from the amount of realised development value on which, apart from this subsection, that person would be chargeable to development land tax in that financial year.

(3) If, in a case where subsection (2) above applies in relation to any person in respect of a particular financial year, the realised development value accruing to that person in that year is made up of two or more separate amounts accruing on two or more separate disposals, the sum of £10,000 referred to in that subsection shall be set against those separate amounts in the order of the disposals on which they accrued until the whole sum is exhausted.

(4) If in a financial year realised development value accrues to any person on a disposal to which, by virtue of subsection (5) or subsection (6) below, this subsection applies, then, subject to subsection (7) below,—

(*a*) development land tax shall be chargeable on that realised development value as if subsections (1) to (3) above had not been enacted; but

(*b*) no account shall be taken of that realised development value in determining, for the purposes of subsections (1) to (3) above, the total amount of realised development value which accrues to that person in any financial year.

(5) Subsection (4) above applies to a disposal to which subsection (6) of section 5 above applies and to any other disposal

of an interest in land which, subject to subsection (10) below, is made otherwise than by an individual where the chargeable person acquired that interest—

(*a*) after 12th September 1974 and within the period of six years ending on the date of the disposal; and

(*b*) for a consideration less than it might reasonably have been expected to fetch in the open market; and

(*c*) as a result of a disposal made by a person who, at the time of that disposal, was connected with him for the 1965 c. 25. purposes of Part III of the Finance Act 1965 (capital gains tax).

(6) If in a financial year realised development value accrues to any person on the disposal of an interest in land (in this subsection and subsection (7) below referred to as " the relevant interest ") and the circumstances are such that—

(*a*) the disposal is one to which Part I of Schedule 2 to this Act applies, and

(*b*) if, in place of the disposal of the relevant interest, there were a separate disposal of each part of the relevant interest, within the meaning of that Part, subsection (4) above would apply by virtue of subsection (5) above to the realised development value which accrued on the disposal of one of those parts (in this subsection and subsection (7) below referred to as " the material part "),

subsection (4) above shall apply to the disposal of the relevant interest subject to the modifications in subsection (7) below.

(7) Where subsection (4) above applies to the disposal of the relevant interest by virtue of subsection (6) above, the references in paragraphs (*a*) and (*b*) of subsection (4) above to the realised development value which accrues on the disposal shall be construed as references to so much only of that realised development value as is equal to the amount of realised development value which would accrue to the chargeable person if—

(*a*) the material part existed as a separate entity; and

(*b*) in place of the disposal of the relevant interest there were a disposal at market value of the material part; and

(*c*) on that disposal the relevant base value of the material part were derived from that one of the three bases specified in section 5(1) above which in fact gives the relevant base value of the relevant interest;

and if there is more than one part of the relevant interest, within the meaning of Part I of Schedule 2 to this Act, which is capable of being the material part, paragraphs (*a*) to (*c*) above shall have effect as if any reference therein to the material part were a reference to each of those parts and the reference in paragraph (*c*) above to the disposal of the material part were a reference to the several disposals of those parts.

(8) In any case where, by virtue of any provision of this Act, any liability to development land tax in respect of the realised development value accruing to any person on a deemed disposal of an interest in land is deferred until the occasion of a subsequent actual disposal or other event, the realised development value shall nevertheless be regarded for the purposes of this section as accruing at the end of the financial year in which the earlier deemed disposal occurred.

(9) Subject to subsection (10) below, where two or more persons carry on a trade or business in partnership, then, for the purposes of the preceding provisions of this section,—

(*a*) notwithstanding anything in section 31 below, the firm shall be treated as a single individual and all disposals by the firm of interests in land forming part of the assets of the partnership shall be treated as made by that individual ; and

(*b*) a change in the persons carrying on the trade or business shall be disregarded if, assuming an election under section 154(2) of the Income and Corporation Taxes Act 1970 to have been duly made, the trade or business would not by virtue of section 154(1) of that Act be treated as discontinued by reason of the change. 1970 c. 10.

(10) Notwithstanding anything in subsection (9) above, a disposal falling within paragraph (*a*) of that subsection shall be treated for the purposes of subsection (5) above as made otherwise than by an individual.

Reduced rate during interim financial years.

13.—(1) The provisions of this section shall have effect with respect to chargeable realised development value accruing to any person on the disposal of an interest in land on or before 31st March 1979 ; and in this Act any financial year which ends on or before that date is referred to as an " interim financial year ".

(2) If the total amount of chargeable realised development value which accrues to any person in an interim financial year does not exceed £150,000, the rate of development land tax applicable to that chargeable realised development value shall be 66⅔ per cent.

(3) If the total amount of chargeable realised development value which accrues to any person in an interim financial year exceeds £150,000, development land tax shall be charged at the rate of 66⅔ per cent. on the first £150,000 of chargeable realised development value which accrues to him in that year.

(4) If in an interim financial year development land tax is, by virtue of subsection (4) of section 12 above, chargeable on any realised development value as mentioned in paragraph (*a*) of that subsection, it shall be so chargeable as if subsections (2) and (3) above had not been enacted.

(5) Subsection (8) of section 12 above shall apply for the purposes of this section as it applies for the purposes of that.

(6) Where two or more persons carry on a trade or business in partnership, then, for the purposes of subsections (1) to (3) above,—

(*a*) notwithstanding anything in section 31 below, the firm shall be treated as a single individual and all disposals by the firm of interests in land forming part of the assets of the partnership shall be treated as made by that individual; and

(*b*) a change in the persons carrying on the trade or business shall be disregarded if, assuming an election under section 154(2) of the Income and Corporation Taxes Act 1970 to have been duly made, the trade or business would not by virtue of section 154(1) of that Act be treated as discontinued by reason of the change.

1970 c. 10.

Private residences.

14.—(1) Subject to the provisions of this section, where realised development value accrues to an individual on the disposal of an interest in land which is or includes the whole or any part of his private residence, development land tax shall not be chargeable on that realised development value except to the extent (if any) that that value is attributable to land which does not form part of his private residence.

(2) For the purposes of this section an individual's " private residence " means—

(*a*) land comprising a dwelling-house which, at the time of the disposal in question, is that individual's only or main residence; and

(*b*) land which at that time he has for his own occupation and enjoyment with that dwelling-house as its garden or grounds up to an area which, when aggregated with the area of the site of that dwelling-house, does not exceed one acre or such larger area as the Commissioners concerned may in any particular case determine on being satisfied that, regard being had to the size and character of the dwelling-house, the larger area is required for the reasonable enjoyment of it as a residence;

and where part of the land occupied with a dwelling-house forms part of an individual's private residence and part does not, then (up to the permitted area) the part which is to be taken as included in his private residence is that which, if the remainder were separately occupied, would be most suitable for occupation and enjoyment with the dwelling-house.

(3) At the time of the disposal by an individual of an interest in land, a dwelling-house shall be regarded as that individual's only or main residence if and only if his period of ownership of it is not less than six months and it has been his only or main residence—

(*a*) where his period of ownership is two years or more, throughout at least twelve of the twenty-four months ending at the time of the disposal ; and

(*b*) where his period of ownership is less than two years, throughout at least half that period or throughout a period of six months, whichever is the greater.

(4) If realised development value accrues to an individual on the disposal of an interest in land which comprises a dwelling-house which is or forms part of his private residence but which is used in part exclusively for the purposes of a trade or business or of a profession, vocation, office or employment, the realised development value shall be apportioned and subsection (1) above shall apply in relation to the part of that value apportioned to the part which is not exclusively used for those purposes.

(5) If at any time—

(*a*) within the period of ownership, and

(*b*) within the period of twenty-four months ending at the time of the disposal,

there is a change in what is occupied as the individual's residence, whether on account of a reconstruction or conversion of a building or for any other reason, or there have been changes as regards the use of part of his private residence for the purpose of a trade or business or of a profession, vocation, office or employment, or for any other purpose, the relief given by this section may be adjusted in such manner as appears to the Board or, on an appeal, to the Commissioners concerned to be just and reasonable.

(6) Subject to subsection (10) below, this section shall also apply in relation to realised development value accruing to trustees on the disposal of an interest in land which is a disposal of settled property (or which is treated as such by virtue of section 30(4) below) if—

(*a*) the land in which that interest subsists includes the whole or any part of an individual's private residence ; and

(*b*) that individual is entitled under the terms of the settlement either to occupy the dwelling-house concerned or to the whole of the income derived from, or from the proceeds of sale of, that interest;

and in this section as so applied, except in relation to the occupation of a dwelling-house, references to the individual shall be taken as references to the trustees.

(7) In any case where—

(*a*) realised development value accrues to the personal representatives of a deceased person on the disposal, within the period of two years beginning on the date of the deceased's death, of an interest in land forming part of his estate, and

(*b*) if the deceased had disposed of that interest immediately before his death the preceding provisions of this section would have applied to the whole or any part of the realised development value accruing to him on that disposal,

this section shall apply to the like extent to the realised development value referred to in paragraph (*a*) above as it would have applied to the realised development value referred to in paragraph (*b*) above.

(8) In determining whether, and to what extent, any provisions of this section would have applied in the circumstances specified in subsection (7)(*b*) above—

(*a*) subsection (3) above shall have effect with the omission of the words " his period of ownership of it is not less than six months and " and, in paragraph (*b*) of that subsection, with the omission of the words from " or throughout " to the end of the paragraph; and

(*b*) if the deceased died before the appointed day, it shall be assumed that that day fell (and this Act was in force) before his death.

(9) If an individual makes a claim with respect to realised development value which accrues to him on the disposal of an interest in land which is or includes the whole or any part of the private residence of a dependent relative of the claimant, provided rent-free and without any other consideration, such relief shall be given under this section in respect of that dwelling-house as would be so given if it had been the claimant's only or main residence during the period it was his dependent relative's private residence: and where such a claim is made—

(*a*) any such relief shall be given in addition to any relief available under this section apart from this subsection; and

(*b*) for the purpose of determining any such relief, not more than one dwelling-house shall be assumed by virtue of this subsection to be the claimant's only or main residence at any one time.

(10) The preceding provisions of this section shall not apply in relation to realised development value accruing to any person on the disposal of an interest in land if that interest or an interest which is a part of that interest for the purposes of Part I of Schedule 2 to this Act was acquired wholly or partly for the purpose of realising any of that development value by the disposal.

(11) In this section " dwelling-house " includes a part of a dwelling-house and " period of ownership ", in relation to the disposal by an individual of an interest in land, means the period—

(*a*) beginning at the time at which that individual acquired that interest or any other interest conferring on him a right to immediate possession of, or of any part of, that land ; and

(*b*) ending at the time of the disposal ;

and for the purpose of paragraph (*a*) above any acquisition on the occasion of a deemed disposal and reacquisition shall be disregarded.

Exemption for certain dwelling-houses built for owner occupation, etc.

15.—(1) Subject to the provisions of this section, on the deemed disposal of an interest in land (in this section referred to as " the relevant interest ") development land tax shall not be chargeable on any realised development value accruing to the person (in this section referred to as " the owner ") who is the owner of the relevant interest at the time of the disposal if—

(*a*) on 12th September 1974 the owner owned the relevant interest or an interest which, in relation to the deemed disposal, is a part of the relevant interest, within the meaning of Part I of Schedule 2 to this Act ; and

(*b*) the material development comprised in the project, the beginning of which is the occasion of the deemed disposal, consists exclusively of the building of a single dwelling-house, with or without any related development ; and

(*c*) at the time of the deemed disposal, the owner or a dependent relative of his or a person who, though not a dependent relative, is an adult member of his family intends to occupy the dwelling-house as his sole or main residence.

(2) No individual shall be entitled to exemption under subsection (1) above in respect of more than two projects of material development to which paragraph (*b*) of that subsection applies ; and the exemption under that subsection shall apply to two such

projects if, and only if, the dwelling-house concerned in one of those projects is built on land in the curtilage of a dwelling-house owned and occupied by the individual on 12th September 1974.

(3) For the purposes of this section a person is an adult member of the owner's family at any time if, at that time, that person—

(*a*) is the owner's wife or husband ; or

(*b*) is a son or daughter of the owner or of the owner's wife or husband, and has attained the age of eighteen at the time of the deemed disposal ; or

(*c*) is the father or mother of the owner or of the owner's wife or husband.

(4) In subsection (3) above—

(*a*) any reference to the owner's wife or husband includes a reference to any divorced wife or husband of the owner ;

(*b*) any reference to a person's son or daughter includes a reference to any stepson or stepdaughter, any adopted son or daughter and any illegitimate son or daughter of that person ; and

(*c*) any reference to a person's father or mother includes a reference to any stepfather or stepmother, any adoptive father or mother and (if that person is illegitimate) the natural father or mother of that person.

(5) In subsection (1)(*b*) above, in relation to development consisting of the building of a single dwelling-house, " related development " means the construction or laying out of any garage, outbuilding, garden, yard, court, forecourt or other appurtenance for occupation with, and for the purposes of, the dwelling-house.

Land held as stock in trade.

16.—(1) If realised development value accrues to any person on the disposal of an interest in land (in this section referred to as " the relevant disposal ") and—

(*a*) that interest was acquired by him on or before 12th September 1974 (disregarding for this purpose any acquisition on the occasion of a deemed disposal and reacquisition) and on that date was held by him as stock in trade, and

(*b*) on that date there was in force planning permission authorising any development (in this section referred to as " authorised development ") of the whole or any part of that land,

he shall not be chargeable to development land tax on so much of that realised development value as, in accordance with this section, is determined to be attributable to the authorised development.

(2) The realised development value attributable to any authorised development is that amount of realised development value which would have accrued to the chargeable person on the relevant disposal if—

(*a*) it was at the time of the disposal and would continue to be unlawful to carry out any material development of the land other than authorised development; and

(*b*) where the relevant disposal was a deemed disposal occurring immediately before a project of material development was begun, so much of the material development comprised in the project as was not authorised development were not so comprised; and

(*c*) where paragraph (*b*) above does not apply, the consideration for the disposal were the market value (on the basis set out in paragraph (*a*) above) of the interest which is the subject-matter of the disposal or, in the case of a part disposal, of the granted interest.

(3) In any case where—

(*a*) a person (in this subsection referred to as " the donee ") acquires an interest in land for no consideration, and

(*b*) the circumstances are such that if the person from whom the donee acquired that interest (in this subsection referred to as " the donor ") had disposed of it at market value immediately before he disposed of it to the donee, subsections (1) and (2) above would have had effect in relation to any realised development value accruing to the donor on that disposal,

that donee shall be treated for the purposes of this section and paragraph 7 of Schedule 2 to this Act as if he and the donor were one and the same person (and, accordingly, as if the disposal by the donor and the acquisition by the donee had not occurred).

(4) In any case where—

(*a*) on the death of any person, an interest in land held by him devolves on his personal representatives, and

(*b*) the circumstances are such that if the deceased had disposed of that interest at market value immediately before his death, subsections (1) and (2) above would have had effect in relation to any realised development value accruing to him on that disposal,

the personal representatives shall be treated for the purposes of this section and paragraph 7 of Schedule 2 to this Act as if they and the deceased were one and the same person.

(5) In any case where the time of the hypothetical disposal referred to in paragraph (*b*) of subsection (3) or subsection (4)

above falls before the appointed day, it shall be assumed, in determining whether the circumstances are such as fall within that paragraph, that the appointed day fell (and this Act was in force) before that time.

(6) For the purposes of this section an interest in land was held by a person as stock in trade on 12th September 1974 if, had he sold that interest on that date, the proceeds of sale would have been taken into account in computing the profits or gains of a trade carried on by him.

(7) For the purposes of the application of this section to Northern Ireland, planning permission shall be treated as in force on 12th September 1974 if—

(*a*) it was in force on 31st August 1974; and

(*b*) it would have been in force on 12th September 1974 but for the operation of paragraph 6 of Schedule 5 to the Planning (Northern Ireland) Order 1972.

S.I. 1972/1634 (N.I. 17).

(8) For the purposes of this section—

(*a*) notwithstanding anything in section 45(2)(*a*) below, an interest in land acquired by any person under a conditional contract entered into on or before 12th September 1974 shall be treated as held by him on that date; and

(*b*) the provisions of Schedule 5 to this Act shall have effect for determining the nature and extent of any planning permission and the development authorised by it.

Minerals.

17.—(1) If realised development value accrues to any person on the deemed disposal of an interest in land comprised in a project of material development and that material development consists of or includes the winning or working of minerals, development land tax shall not be chargeable on so much of that realised development value as, in accordance with subsection (2) below, is determined to be attributable to the winning or working of minerals.

(2) In a case where subsection (1) above applies, the realised development value attributable to the winning or working of minerals is the amount by which the realised development value which accrues to the chargeable person on the deemed disposal exceeds the realised development value (if any) which would have accrued to him on that disposal if there were excluded from the project of material development concerned any development which—

(*a*) consists of the winning or working of minerals; and

(*b*) is authorised by planning permission in force at the time of the disposal.

(3) Subject to subsection (6) below, for the purpose of determining—

(*a*) the amount of realised development value which accrues on the disposal, other than a deemed disposal, of an interest in land at a time when there is in force, as regards that land or any part of it, planning permission authorising material development consisting of the winning or working of minerals, and

(*b*) in relation to the person to whom that disposal is made, the cost of acquisition on that disposal of the interest disposed of or, in the case of a part disposal, of the granted interest,

the amount which, apart from this section, would be the consideration for the disposal (in this section referred to as " the gross consideration ") shall be deemed to be reduced to the sum determined under subsection (4) below.

(4) Subject to subsection (5) below, the sum referred to in subsection (3) above is the aggregate of the following amounts, namely—

(*a*) the market value, immediately after the disposal, of the interest which is the subject matter of the disposal or, in the case of a part disposal, of the granted interest, determined on the assumption that it was at that time, and would continue to be, unlawful to carry out material development consisting of the winning or working of minerals on any of the land in which that interest subsists ; and

(*b*) one half of the amount by which the gross consideration exceeds the market value referred to in paragraph (*a*) above.

(5) If the disposal referred to in subsection (3) above is a part disposal consisting of the grant of a lease, any reference in subsection (4) above to the market value of the granted interest shall be construed as a reference to the consideration which, at the time of the disposal, might reasonably have been obtained in the open market for the grant of a lease—

(*a*) which does not permit the carrying out of any material development consisting of the winning or working of minerals but permits the land in question to be used for any other purpose which is authorised by planning permission for the time being in force, or for which planning permission might reasonably be expected to be obtained ; and

(*b*) which (except as to rent and any other consideration given or agreed to be given) is in other respects similar, so far as the nature of the case allows, to the lease which was in fact granted.

(6) Notwithstanding anything in subsection (3) above, in the case of a disposal of an interest in land which consists of the grant of a mineral lease or agreement, within the meaning of
1970 c. 24. section 29 of the Finance Act 1970 (taxation of mineral royalties),—

(*a*) if any part of the gross consideration is not mineral royalties, within the meaning of that section, the amount which, apart from this subsection, would by virtue of subsection (3) above be the amount of realised development value which accrues on the disposal shall be taken to be reduced by multiplying it by the fraction of which the denominator is the gross consideration and the numerator is so much of that consideration as does not consist of mineral royalties (within the meaning of that section); and

(*b*) in any other case, no realised development value shall be taken to accrue on the disposal.

(7) In the preceding provisions of this section the expression " winning or working ", in relation to minerals, includes—

(*a*) the grading, washing, grinding and crushing of minerals; and

(*b*) the carrying out of any operations ancillary to the winning or working of minerals or to any of the activities specified in paragraph (*a*) above.

Exemption for projects begun within three years of acquisition of land.

18.—(1) On the deemed disposal of an interest in land (in this section referred to as " the relevant interest ") development land tax shall not be chargeable on any realised development value accruing to the person (in this section referred to as " the owner ") who is the owner of the relevant interest at the time of the disposal if the Board are satisfied that the conditions in subsection (2) below are fulfilled.

(2) The conditions referred to in subsection (1) above are—

(*a*) that the owner acquired the relevant interest within the period of three years ending on the date of the deemed disposal (disregarding for this purpose any acquisition on the occasion of an earlier deemed disposal and reacquisition); and

(*b*) that if the project, the beginning of which is the occasion of the deemed disposal, had been begun immediately after the relevant interest was so acquired, no significant amount of realised development value would have accrued to the owner on the deemed disposal occurring immediately before the project began;

and, for the purposes of paragraph (*b*) above, in any case where the owner acquired the relevant interest before the appointed day.

it shall be assumed that the appointed day fell (and this Act was in force) before the time of his acquisition.

(3) In any case where—

(*a*) it is proposed that a project of material development should be begun on any land, and

(*b*) before that project is begun, the owner of an interest in that land makes an application to the Board in that behalf and furnishes to the Board such information as they may require with respect to the proposed project and to such other matters as may be material to the exercise of the Board's functions under this section,

the Board shall notify the owner whether, if the project were to be begun forthwith, they would or would not be satisfied that the conditions in subsection (2) above would be fulfilled with respect to that interest and that project.

(4) A notification under subsection (3) above that the Board would be satisfied as mentioned in that subsection shall specify—

(*a*) the name of the person to whom the notification is given;

(*b*) the interest to which the notification relates and the date on which the person concerned acquired that interest; and

(*c*) the project to which the notification relates.

(5) Where—

(*a*) such a notification as is referred to in subsection (4) above has been given, and

(*b*) the project to which the notification relates is begun within the period of three years beginning on the date specified in accordance with subsection (4)(*b*) above, and

(*c*) immediately before the beginning of that project, there is a deemed disposal of the interest to which the notification relates,

then, subject to subsection (6) below, development land tax shall not be chargeable on any realised development value accruing to the person specified in the notice or to his personal representatives on the deemed disposal referred to in paragraph (*c*) above.

(6) If any of the information furnished to the Board under subsection (3)(*b*) above was not such as to make full and accurate disclosure of all facts and considerations which were material to enable the Board properly to exercise their functions under this section with respect to the interest and project concerned, any such notification as is referred to in subsection (4) above

which has been given with respect to that interest and project shall be of no effect for the purposes of subsection (5) above.

Development for industrial use.

19.—(1) Subject to section 20 below if, in a case where realised development accrues to the chargeable person on the deemed disposal of an interest in land (in this section referred to as " the relevant interest "),—

(*a*) the chargeable person carries on a trade, and

(*b*) the project of material development, the beginning of which is the occason of the deemed disposal, relates to a building or other land to be used, in whole or in part, for the industrial purposes of that trade,

then, subject to the following provisions of this section, liability for development land tax on such proportion of that realised development value as is properly attributable to property to be used for the industrial purposes of a trade carried on by the chargeable person shall be deferred until the occasion of the first subsequent disposal of the relevant interest which is neither—

(i) a deemed disposal ; nor

(ii) a disposal to which either section 20(1) below or subsection (1) or subsection (4) of section 22 below applies ; nor

(iii) a disposal which forms part of a sale and lease-back transaction.

(2) For the purposes of this section, a building or other land constitutes property used for the industrial purposes of a trade carried on by any person if and to the extent that—

(*a*) it is used in the course of such a trade for the carrying on of any process for or incidental to any of the purposes specified in paragraph (*a*) of Class E in paragraph 7 of Schedule 4 to this Act or for or incidental to the generation of electricity, or

(*b*) it is used, otherwise than as a dwelling-house, for the welfare of workers employed in such a trade,

and any reference to property to be used for such purposes shall be construed accordingly.

(3) For the purposes of this section, premises which—

(*a*) are used or designed for use for providing services or facilities ancillary to the use of other premises which, in accordance with subsection (2) above, constitute property used for the industrial purposes of a trade, and

(*b*) are or are to be comprised in the same building or the same curtilage as those other premises,

shall themselves be treated as falling within paragraph (*a*) or paragraph (*b*) of subsection (2) above.

(4) In any case where it appears to the Board or, on an appeal, to the Commissioners concerned that a project of material development falling within paragraph (*b*) of subsection (1) above relates exclusively to property to be used for the industrial purposes of a trade carried on by the chargeable person, the proportion of realised development value referred to in that subsection shall be 100 per cent., but, in any other case—

(*a*) the proportion properly attributable to the property to be used for the industrial purposes of such a trade, and

(*b*) the method of apportionment adopted,

shall be such as appears to the Board or, on an appeal, to the Commissioners concerned to be just and reasonable.

(5) Subject to subsection (6) and section 20 below, if—

(*a*) the whole or any part of a building or other land to which a project of material development falling within subsection (1)(*b*) above relates ceases at any time, otherwise than on the occasion of a disposal of the relevant interest, to constitute property used by the chargeable person referred to in subsection (1)(*a*) above for the industrial purposes of a trade for the time being carried on by him, and

(*b*) at that time or at a subsequent time either that person ceases to carry on any trade at all or a non-qualifying use is established for the building or other land or part thereof to which paragraph (*a*) above applies,

the relevant interest or, if paragraph (*a*) above applies to part only of the building or other land, so much of the relevant interest as subsists in that part shall be treated for the purposes only of subsection (1) above and section 27 below as having been disposed of at the time when the condition in paragraph (*b*) above is fulfilled.

(6) Subject to section 20 below, for the purposes of subsection (5) above, a non-qualifying use is established for any building or other land or part thereof if, for at least half of any continuous period of twenty-four months, it is used in such circumstances that it does not constitute property used for the industrial purposes of a trade carried on by the chargeable person ; and accordingly the non-qualifying use shall be taken to be established at the expiry of the 365th day in that period on which the building or other land or part thereof is so used.

(7) For the purposes of this section a disposal of the relevant interest (in the following provisions of this section referred to as " the primary disposal ") forms part of a sale and lease-back transaction if—

(*a*) it is either a disposal of the whole of the relevant interest or a part disposal of that interest which falls within paragraph (*b*) of subsection (1) of section 3 above; and

(*b*) it forms part of a transaction whereby, at or immediately after the time at which the relevant interest or, in the case of a part disposal, the granted interest is acquired as a result of the primary disposal, the person by whom that interest is so acquired grants a lease to the person who was the chargeable person in relation to the primary disposal; and

(*c*) the lease subsists in the whole or any part of the land in which the relevant interest or, as the case may be, the granted interest subsists.

(8) If, after the primary disposal, there is a disposal of the lease referred to in paragraph (*c*) of subsection (7) above, subsection (5) above shall have effect as if, at the time of that disposal, the conditions in paragraphs (*a*) and (*b*) of that subsection were fulfilled with respect to so much of any building or other land as is the subject matter of the lease.

(9) If, in a case where the primary disposal is such a part disposal as is referred to in subsection (7)(*a*) above, there is a subsequent disposal of the interest which is the retained interest in relation to that part disposal, subsection (1) above and section 27 below shall apply as if in place of, but to the like effect as, that subsequent disposal there were a part disposal of the relevant interest.

(10) For the purposes of subsections (1) and (5)(*a*) above, a disposal shall be treated as a disposal of the relevant interest if it is a disposal of an interest in land of which the relevant interest is a part for the purposes of Part I of Schedule 2 to this Act.

Groups of companies.

20.—(1) Subject to the provisions of this section, every disposal of an interest in land (whether before, on or after the appointed day) by a member of a group of companies to another member of the group shall be treated for the purposes of this Act as a disposal (and acquisition) for which no consideration is given.

(2) Subsection (1) above does not apply—

(*a*) to a disposal to a non-resident member of a group of companies by a resident member of the group, or

(*b*) to a disposal to a body which is exempt from development land tax by virtue of section 11 above by a company which is a member of the same group of companies as that body but which is not so exempt,

but a disposal shall not be regarded as one to which that subsection does not apply by reason only that it is in fact a disposal for which no consideration is given.

(3) Where section 10 above has effect in a case where the previous disposal is one to which subsection (1) above applies,—

(*a*) the chargeable person shall be treated for the purposes of section 5(6) and, subject to paragraph (*c*) below, section 6 above as having acquired the relevant interest at the time which was the date of acquisition of the donor's interest for the purposes of the previous disposal, and

(*b*) paragraph (*d*) of subsection (2) of section 10 above shall not apply, and

(*c*) section 6 above shall not apply where the material disposal is itself a disposal to which subsection (1) above applies,

and expressions to which a meaning is assigned by subsection (1) of section 10 above have in this subsection the meaning assigned by that subsection.

(4) For the purposes of section 18 above—

(*a*) where the person who is defined as the owner in subsection (1) of that section is a member of a group of companies, any reference in subsection (2) of that section to the owner shall be construed as a reference to the owner or any other member of the group; and

(*b*) where the person making an application under subsection (3) of that section is a member of a group of companies, the reference in subsection (4)(*b*) of that section to the person concerned and the reference in subsection (5) of that section to the person specified in the notice shall be construed as a reference to that person or any other member of the group.

(5) For the purposes of section 19 above, where the chargeable person is a member of a group of companies—

(*a*) paragraph (*a*) of subsection (1) of that section shall have effect as if the reference to the chargeable person were a reference to any member of the group;

(*b*) any reference in paragraph (*a*) of subsection (5) of that section to the chargeable person referred to in subsection (1)(*a*) thereof shall be construed as a reference to any member of the group;

(*c*) the reference in paragraph (*b*) of subsection (5) of that section to the chargeable person ceasing to carry on any trade at all at a particular time shall be construed as a reference to the members of the group ceasing to carry on their trades, and for the purposes of that subsection the time at which the members of the group cease to carry on their trades is the time at which the last of the members to do so ceases to carry on its trade; and (*d*) the reference in subsection (6) of that section to the chargeable person shall be construed as a reference to any member of the group.

Company ceasing to be a member of a group.

21.—(1) The provisions of this section apply where a company (in this section referred to as " the chargeable company ") ceases on or after the appointed day to be a member of a group of companies and, at the time when it so ceases (in this section referred to as " the time of severance "), it holds an interest in land (in this section referred to as " the relevant interest "); and references in this section to a company ceasing to be a member of a group of companies do not apply to cases where a company ceases to be a member of a group by being wound up or dissolved or in consequence of another member of the group being wound up or dissolved.

(2) Subject to subsection (3) below, if after 12th September 1974 and within the period of six years ending at the time of severance, the chargeable company acquired the relevant interest or a part thereof from another company which, at the time of the acquisition, was a member of the group, the chargeable company shall be treated for the purposes of this Act as having sold and immediately reacquired the relevant interest immediately after the time of severance for a consideration equal to that which the relevant interest might reasonably have been expected to fetch on a sale at that time in the open market.

(3) In any case where—

(*a*) the chargeable company is one of two or more associated companies which cease to be members of a group at the same time, and

(*b*) the relevant interest or part thereof acquired by the chargeable company as mentioned in subsection (2) above was acquired from one of the other associated companies,

subsection (2) above shall not apply unless, after 12th September 1974 and within the period referred to in that subsection, one of those associated companies acquired the relevant interest or, as the case may be, that part from a company which is not one of those associated companies but which at the time of the acquisition was a member of the group.

(4) For the purposes only of section 19(1) above and section 27 below the sale provided for by subsection (2) above shall constitute a disposal of every part of the relevant interest as well as a disposal of the relevant interest itself.

(5) If, in a case where subsection (2) above applies in relation the relevant interest,—

(*a*) there has been a deemed disposal and reacquisition of an interest in land (in the following provisions of this section referred to as " the material interest "), and (*b*) at the time of the deemed disposal and reacquisition of the material interest it was held by the chargeable company or another company which at that time was a member of the group, and

(*c*) section 19(1) above applied in relation to the whole or any part of the realised development value which accrued on that deemed disposal, and

(*d*) the material interest is neither the relevant interest nor a part of it (so that subsection (2) above does not apply in relation to the material interest) but the relevant interest subsists in the whole or part of the building or other land (with or without additional land) in which the material interest subsisted, and

(*e*) at the time of severance liability for all or any of the development land tax accruing on the deemed disposal of the material interest has not yet arisen,

then, subject to subsection (6) below, for the purposes only of section 19(1) above and section 27 below, the chargeable company shall be treated as owning the material interest at the time of severance and as disposing of it at that time by the grant of an interest in land corresponding, as near as may be, to the relevant interest, so far as that interest subsists in the building or other land referred to in paragraph (*d*) above.

(6) If, before the time of severance, there has been a part disposal of the material interest or of an interest of which the material interest was a part for the purposes of Part I of Schedule 2 to this Act and that disposal is the operative disposal for the purposes of section 27 below, the disposal which is treated as occurring at the time of severance by virtue of subsection (5) above shall be deemed for the purposes of that section to be a further disposal falling within subsection (5) thereof.

(7) For the purposes of this section—

(*a*) two or more companies are associated companies if, by themselves, they would form a group of companies; and

(*b*) a " part ", in relation to the relevant interest, means an interest in land which, on the sale of the relevant interest provided for by subsection (2) above, constitutes a part thereof for the purposes of Part I of Schedule 2 to this Act.

Amalgamations and reconstructions, etc.

22.—(1) Subject to subsection (2) below, where—

(*a*) any scheme of reconstruction or amalgamation involves the transfer of the whole or part of the business of a company (in this section referred to as " the first company ") to another company (in this section referred to as " the second company "), and (*b*) the first company receives no part of the consideration for the transfer (otherwise than by the second company taking over the whole or part of the liabilities of the business), and

(*c*) as part of the transfer the first company disposes of an interest in land to the second company,

the disposal referred to in paragraph (*c*) above shall be treated for the purposes of this Act as a disposal (and acquisition) for which no consideration is given.

(2) Subsection (1) above does not apply—

(*a*) if the first company is resident in the United Kingdom and the second company is not; or

(*b*) if the second company is a body which is exempt from development land tax by virtue of section 11 above and the first company is not.

(3) In subsection (1) above " scheme of reconstruction or amalgamation " means a scheme for the reconstruction of any company or companies or the amalgamation of any two or more companies.

(4) If in the course of, or as part of, a union or amalgamation of two or more registered industrial and provident societies, or a transfer of engagements from one registered industrial and provident society to another, there is a disposal of an interest in land by one society (in this section referred to as " the first society ") to another (in this section referred to as " the second society "), that disposal shall be treated for the purposes of this Act as a disposal (and acquisition) for which no consideration is given.

(5) Any reference in subsection (4) above to a registered industrial and provident society includes a reference to a body which—

(*a*) is a co-operative association for the purposes of section 340 of the Income and Corporation Taxes Act 1970; and

1970 c. 10.

(*b*) is established and resident in the United Kingdom; and

(*c*) has as its object or primary object to assist its members in the carrying on of agricultural or horticultural businesses on land occupied by them in the United Kingdom or in the carrying on of businesses consisting in the catching or taking of fish or shell-fish.

(6) In this section " registered industrial and provident society " means a society registered or deemed to be registered under the Industrial and Provident Societies Act 1965 or under the Industrial and Provident Societies Act (Northern Ireland) 1969.

1965 c. 12.
1969 c. 24 (N.I.).

(7) Where section 10 above has effect in a case where the previous disposal is one to which either subsection (1) or subsection (4) above applies,—

(*a*) the chargeable person shall be treated for the purposes of section 5(6) and, subject to paragraph (*c*) below, section 6 above as having acquired the relevant interest at the time which was the date of acquisition of the donor's interest for the purposes of the previous disposal, and

(*b*) paragraph (*d*) of subsection (2) of section 10 above shall not apply, and

(*c*) section 6 above shall not apply where the material disposal is itself a disposal to which subsection (1) above applies,

and expressions to which a meaning is assigned by subsection (1) of section 10 above have in this subsection the meaning assigned by that subsection.

(8) For the purposes of section 18 above—

(*a*) where the person who is defined as the owner in subsection (1) of that section is the second company or the second society, any reference in subsection (2) of that section to the owner shall be construed as a reference to the owner or, as the case may require, the first company or the first society; and

(*b*) where the person making an application under subsection (3) of that section is the second company or the second society, the reference in subsection (4)(*b*) of that section to the person concerned shall be construed as a reference to either the first company or the second company or, as the case may require, either the first society or the second society; and

(*c*) where a notification under subsection (3) of that section is given to the first company or the first society, the reference in subsection (5) of that section to the person specified in the notice shall be construed as a reference to either the first company or the second company or, as the case may require, either the first society or the second society.

23.—(1) If, on the deemed disposal of an interest in land held by statutory undertakers (in this section referred to as " the relevant interest ")— Statutory undertakers.

(*a*) realised development value accrues to the statutory undertakers, and

(*b*) the project of material development, the start of which is the occasion of the deemed disposal, relates to a building or other land to be used in whole or in part for the purpose of a statutory undertaking,

then, subject to the following provisions of this section, liability for development land tax on such proportion of that realised development value as is properly attributable to property to be used by statutory undertakers shall be deferred until the occasion of the first subsequent disposal of the relevant interest which is neither—

(i) a deemed disposal, nor

(ii) a disposal to which either section 20(1) or section 22(1) above applies, nor

(iii) a disposal which forms part of a sale and lease-back transaction.

(2) For the purposes of subsection (1) above a disposal shall be treated as a disposal of the relevant interest if it is a disposal of an interest in land of which the relevant interest is a part for the purposes of Part I of Schedule 2 to this Act.

(3) For the purposes of this section, a building or other land constitutes property used by statutory undertakers if and to the extent that—

(*a*) it is used solely by statutory undertakers for the purpose of carrying on the statutory undertaking, and

(*b*) the use by the statutory undertakers is not for a purpose which, in the area in which the building or other land is situated, is more akin to the purpose for which other persons use buildings or other land in that area than the purpose, or one of the purposes, for which the statutory undertaking exists,

or if and to the extent that it is used, otherwise than as a dwelling-house, for the welfare of persons employed by statutory undertakers; and any reference to property to be used by statutory undertakers shall be construed accordingly.

(4) Any question arising under this section as to whether or to what extent a building or other land is or is to be used as mentioned in paragraphs (*a*) and (*b*) of subsection (3) above shall be determined by the appropriate Minister.

(5) In any case where it appears to the Board or, on an appeal, to the Commissioners concerned that a project of material development falling within paragraph (*b*) of subsection (1) above relates exclusively to property to be used by statutory undertakers, the proportion of realised development value referred to in that subsection shall be 100 per cent., but in any other case—

(*a*) the proportion properly attributable to the property to be used by statutory undertakers, and (*b*) the method of apportionment adopted,

shall be such as appears to the Board or, on an appeal, to the Commissioners concerned to be just and reasonable.

(6) No account shall be taken for the purposes of subsection (1) above or any provision of section 27 below of a disposal by statutory undertakers of an interest in land which—

(*a*) is a part disposal falling within paragraph (*a*) of section 3(1) above ; and

(*b*) is made to such a person and for such a purpose as in the opinion of the appropriate Minister is consistent with furthering the purposes of the statutory undertaking.

(7) In any case where—

(*a*) it appears to the appropriate Minister that the whole or any part of a building or other land to which a project of material development falling within paragraph (*b*) of subsection (1) above relates has ceased at any time, otherwise than on the occasion of such a disposal as is referred to in that subsection, to constitute property used or to be used by statutory undertakers, and

(*b*) the appropriate Minister certifies that, with effect from such date as may be specified in the certificate, this subsection is to have effect in relation to the whole, or such part as may be specified in the certificate, of that building or other land,

the relevant interest or, if only part of the building or other land is specified in the certificate, so much of the relevant interest as subsists in that part shall be treated for the purposes of subsection (1) above and section 27 below as having been disposed of on the date specified in the certificate.

(8) Subsections (7) and (9) of section 19 above shall apply for the purposes of this section as they apply for the purposes of that section, except that, in the application of those subsections for the purposes of this section,—

(*a*) any reference to the relevant interest shall be construed in accordance with subsection (1) of this section ; and

(*b*) the reference to subsection (1) of that section shall be construed as a reference to subsection (1) of this section.

(9) If after the primary disposal, within the meaning of subsection (7) of section 19 above, as that subsection has effect by virtue of subsection (8) above, there is a disposal of the lease referred to in subsection (7)(*c*) of that section, so much of the relevant interest as subsists in the building or other land which is the subject matter of the lease shall be treated for the purposes

of subsection (1) above and section 27 below as having been disposed of on the date of the disposal of the lease.

(10) In this section " statutory undertakers " means—

(*a*) the persons and bodies specified in paragraphs (*a*) and (*b*) of subsection (1) of section 5 of the Community Land Act 1975 ; [1975 c. 77.]

(*b*) the British Broadcasting Corporation ;

(*c*) the British Steel Corporation ;

(*d*) the Independent Broadcasting Authority ;

(*e*) the United Kingdom Atomic Energy Authority ; and

(*f*) any regional water authority to the extent that it does not fall within paragraph (*a*) above ;

and " statutory undertaking " shall be construed accordingly.

(11) In this section " the appropriate Minister "—

(*a*) in relation to the British Airports Authority, means the Secretary of State for Trade ; and

(*b*) in relation to any other statutory undertakers who are also statutory undertakers for the purposes of any provision of Part XI of the Town and Country Planning Act 1971 or of the Town and Country Planning (Scotland) Act 1972, has the same meaning as in that Part ; and [1971 c. 78. 1972 c. 52.]

(*c*) in relation to any other statutory undertakers, means such Minister (including, in relation to statutory undertakers in Northern Ireland, the head of a Northern Ireland Department) as may be determined for the purposes of this section by the Treasury.

(12) In the application of this section to Northern Ireland, the provisions of section 5 of the Community Land Act 1975 referred to in subsection (10)(*a*) above shall have effect as if—

(*a*) any reference therein to an enactment included a reference to an enactment of the Parliament of Northern Ireland or of the Northern Ireland Assembly ; and

(*b*) the reference therein to the Town and Country Planning Act 1971 included a reference to the Planning (Northern Ireland) Order 1972. [S.I. 1972/1634 (N.I. 17).]

Charities: interests in land held on 12th September 1974.

24.—(1) Development land tax shall not be chargeable on any realised development value accruing to a charity on the disposal of an interest in land which—

(*a*) was held by the charity on 12th September 1974 ; or

(*b*) was held by another charity on that date and has at no time between that date and the time of the disposal been held otherwise than by a charity ; or (*c*) is the retained interest or the granted interest in relation to a previous disposal of an interest in land which, immediately before that disposal, fell within paragraph (*a*) or paragraph (*b*) above or this paragraph and which has at no time between the time of its acquisition and the time at which it is disposed of been held otherwise than by a charity ;

and for the purposes of this section an interest in land shall be treated as held by a charity on 12th September 1974 if, under the will of a person who died before that date, the charity would on that date have been absolutely entitled to that interest if the administration of the deceased's estate had been completed.

(2) Subject to subsection (3) below, in any case where—

(*a*) on 12th September 1974 a lease was held by a charity, and

(*b*) subsequent to that date, but without its ever having been held otherwise than by a charity, the lease became merged in another interest (in this subsection and subsection (3) below referred to as " the greater interest "), and

(*c*) after the merger the greater interest was acquired by another charity, without its ever having been held otherwise than by a charity,

paragraph 8 of Schedule 2 to this Act shall have effect on a disposal of the greater interest by a charity which acquired it as mentioned in paragraph (*c*) above as if, immediately before the acquisition of the greater interest by the charity,—

(i) the lease continued to exist as a separate entity, and

(ii) the charity acquired the lease for an appropriate proportion of the consideration given by it for the acquisition of the greater interest,

so that the lease constitutes a part of the relevant interest for the purposes of the said paragraph 8.

(3) Subsection (2) above shall cease to apply in relation to a lease at such time as the lease would have come to an end had it not become merged in another interest and, for the purposes of that subsection, references (other than in paragraph (*b*) thereof) to the greater interest include references to an interest in land of which, on a disposal thereof by a charity, the greater interest was a part for the purposes of Part I of Schedule 2 to this Act.

(4) In any case where—

(*a*) on 12th September 1974 a charity held an option falling within section 8(1) above, and

(*b*) the option was subsequently exercised, without it ever having been held otherwise than by a charity, and (*c*) the interest acquired by virtue of the exercise of the option (in this subsection and subsection (5) below referred to as " the substantive interest ") was subsequently acquired by another charity, without its ever having been held otherwise than by a charity,

paragraph 8 of Schedule 2 to this Act shall have effect on a disposal of the substantive interest by a charity which acquired it as mentioned in paragraph (*c*) above as if—

(i) the option had not been exercised at the time of that acquisition and the charity had acquired the option instead of the substantive interest, and

(ii) immediately after its acquisition of the option the charity had acquired the substantive interest in exercise of the option,

so that the option constitutes a part of the relevant interest for the purposes of the said paragraph 8.

(5) References in subsection (4) above to the substantive interest include references to an interest in land of which, on a disposal thereof by a charity, the substantive interest was a part for the purposes of Part I of Schedule 2 to this Act.

(6) If, at any time after the disposal of an interest in land falling within any of paragraphs (*a*) to (*c*) of subsection (1) above, the body which made the disposal ceases to be a charity, then, immediately after it so ceases, an amount of realised development value equal, subject to subsection (7) below, to that in respect of which the exemption in subsection (1) above applied on the disposal shall be treated for the purposes of this Act as accruing to that body, as on the disposal of an interest in land.

(7) The amount of realised development value which is treated as accruing to a body under subsection (6) above shall not exceed the market value of the property (if any) which—

(*a*) is held by that body immediately before the time at which it ceases to be a charity, and

(*b*) is not immediately after that time held for charitable purposes by another body,

and for the purposes of this subsection section 7(1) above shall apply in relation to the market value of any property other than an interest in land as it applies in relation to the market value of an interest in land.

(8) Notwithstanding anything in section 45(2)(*a*) below, an interest in land acquired by a charity under a conditional contract entered into on or before 12th September 1974 shall be treated for the purposes of this section as held by the charity on that date.

Charities: development on land acquired after 12th September 1974.

25.—(1) If, on the deemed disposal of an interest in land to which subsection (1) of section 24 above does not apply (in this section referred to as " the relevant interest "),—

(*a*) realised development value accrues to a charity, and

(*b*) the project of material development, the beginning of which is the occasion of the deemed disposal, relates to a building or other land to be used in whole or in part for the purposes of the charity,

then, subject to the following provisions of this section, liability for development land tax on such proportion of that realised development value as is properly attributable to property to be used by the charity shall be deferred until the occasion of the first subsequent disposal of the relevant interest which is neither—

(i) a deemed disposal, nor

(ii) if the relevant interest is a lease, a disposal which forms part of a transaction by which one lease is surrendered and a new lease is granted of the whole, or substantially the whole, of the land in which the relevant interest subsisted.

(2) For the purposes of this section, a building or other land constitutes property used by a charity if and to the extent that—

(*a*) it is occupied solely by the charity for its own use ; or

(*b*) it is otherwise used solely for carrying out the charitable purposes of the charity ;

and any reference to property to be used by a charity shall be construed accordingly.

(3) In any case where it appears to the Board or, on an appeal, to the Commissioners concerned that a project of material development falling within paragraph (*b*) of subsection (1) above relates exclusively to property to be used by a charity, the proportion of realised development value referred to in that subsection shall be 100 per cent., but, in any other case,—

(*a*) the proportion properly attributable to the property to be used by the charity, and

(*b*) the method of apportionment adopted,

shall be such as appears to the Board or, on an appeal, to the Commissioners concerned to be just and reasonable.

(4) If both subsection (1) above and subsection (2) or subsection (4) of section 24 above apply in relation to the realised development value which accrues to a charity on the deemed disposal of an interest in land, then,—

(*a*) in the first instance subsection (3) above shall apply, without regard to section 24 above, to determine the proportion of that realised development value which is properly attributable to the property to be used by the charity; and

(*b*) for the purpose of determining the amount of realised development value on which liability for development land tax is deferred in accordance with this section, the proportion determined as mentioned in paragraph (*a*) above shall be applied only to so much of the realised development value which accrues to the charity as remains after deducting therefrom the amount on which, by virtue of section 24 above, the charity is not chargeable to development land tax.

(5) Immediately after a disposal of the relevant interest which forms part of a transaction falling within paragraph (ii) of subsection (1) above, that subsection, this subsection and section 27 below shall have effect as if the new lease were itself the relevant interest.

(6) Subject to subsection (7) below, if—

(*a*) the whole or any part of a building or other land to which a project of material development falling within subsection (1)(*b*) above relates ceases at any time, otherwise than on the occasion of a disposal of the relevant interest, to constitute property used by a charity, and

(*b*) at that time or at a subsequent time either the relevant interest ceases to be held by a charity or a non-qualifying use is established for the building or other land or part thereof to which paragraph (*a*) above applies,

the relevant interest or, if paragraph (*a*) above applies to part only of the building or other land, so much of the relevant interest as subsists in that part shall be treated for the purposes only of subsection (1) above and section 27 below as having been disposed of at the time when the condition in paragraph (*b*) above is fulfilled.

(7) For the purposes of subsection (6) above, a non-qualifying use is established for any building or other land or part thereof if, for at least half of any continuous period of twenty-four months, it is used in such circumstances that it does not constitute property used by a charity; and accordingly the non-qualifying use shall be taken to be established at the expiry of the 365th day in that period on which the building or other land or part thereof is so used.

(8) No account shall be taken for the purposes of subsection (1) above or any provision of section 27 below of a disposal of an interest in land which—

(*a*) is a part disposal falling within paragraph (*a*) of section 3(1) above; and (*b*) is made on such terms as to secure that the land is used for the charitable purposes of the charity.

(9) For the purposes of subsections (1) and (6)(*a*) above, a disposal shall be treated as a disposal of the relevant interest if it is a disposal of an interest in land of which the relevant interest is a part for the purposes of Part I of Schedule 2 to this Act.

The Housing Corporation and certain housing associations.

26.—(1) Development land tax shall not be chargeable on any realised development value accruing to—

(*a*) an approved co-operative housing association, or

(*b*) a self-build society,

on the deemed disposal of an interest in land by that association or society.

(2) If, on the deemed disposal of an interest in land by—

(*a*) the Housing Corporation, or

(*b*) a registered housing association which is neither an approved co-operative housing association nor a self-build society,

realised development value accrues to the Corporation or that association, liability to development land tax on that realised development value shall be deferred until the occasion of the first subsequent disposal of that interest which is neither a disposal to which subsection (3) below applies nor a deemed disposal; and for the purposes of this subsection a disposal shall be treated as a disposal of that interest if it is a disposal of an interest in land of which that interest is a part for the purposes of Part I of Schedule 2 to this Act.

(3) Subject to subsections (4) and (5) below, every disposal of an interest in land by a body specified in subsection (1) or subsection (2) above to a body so specified shall be treated for the purposes of this Act as a disposal (and acquisition) for which no consideration is given.

(4) Subsection (3) above does not apply—

(*a*) to a deemed disposal, or

(*b*) to a disposal occurring before the appointed day, or

(*c*) to a disposal to an unregistered self-build society,

but a disposal shall not be regarded as one to which that subsection does not apply by reason only that it is in fact a disposal for which no consideration is given.

(5) Where section 10 above has effect in a case where the previous disposal is one to which subsection (3) above applies, paragraph (*d*) of subsection (2) of that section shall not apply but—

(*a*) the chargeable person shall be treated as having acquired the relevant interest at the time which was the time of acquisition of the donor's interest for the purposes of the previous disposal, and

(*b*) section 6 above shall not apply where the material disposal is itself a disposal to which subsection (3) above applies,

and expressions to which a meaning is assigned by subsection (1) of section 10 above have in this subsection the meaning assigned by that subsection.

(6) Any reference in this section to a registered housing association includes a reference to a charity—

(*a*) which is an exempt charity, within the meaning of the Charities Act 1960; and

1960 c. 58.

(*b*) which is a housing association; and

(*c*) which satisfies any criteria for the time being established as mentioned in section 13(4) of the Housing Act 1974 for housing associations seeking registration.

1974 c. 44.

(7) In this section—

"approved co-operative housing association" means an association which is for the time being approved for the purposes of, and in accordance with, section 341 of the Income and Corporation Taxes Act 1970;

1970 c. 10.

"housing association" has, in England and Wales, the meaning assigned to it by section 189(1) of the Housing Act 1957 and, in Scotland, the same meaning as in section 208(1) of the Housing (Scotland) Act 1966 and, in Northern Ireland, the same meaning as in section 12 of the Housing and Local Government (Miscellaneous Provisions) Act (Northern Ireland) 1946;

1957 c. 56.
1966 c. 49.
1946 c. 4 (N.I.).

"registered", "registration" and "unregistered" have, except in Northern Ireland, the same meaning as in the Housing Act 1974;

"self-build society" means a housing association whose object is to provide, for sale to or occupation by its members, dwellings built or improved principally by the use of its members' own labour, and for this purpose "dwelling" has, in England and Wales and in Northern Ireland, the meaning assigned to it by subsection (1) of section 129 of the Housing Act 1974 and, in Scotland, means a house within the meaning of section 208(1) of the Housing (Scotland) Act 1966; and

"unregistered self-build society" means a self-build society which is not a registered housing association.

(8) In the application of this section to Northern Ireland, "registered", in relation to a housing association, means a housing association approved for the purposes of this section by the Department of the Environment for Northern Ireland and "unregistered" shall be construed accordingly.

Deferred liability for development land tax.

27.—(1) The provisions of this section shall have effect in any case where, by virtue of any provision of this Act, liability for development land tax on any realised development value (in this section referred to as "the accrued development value") which accrued to any person on the deemed disposal of an interest in land (in this section referred to as "the deemed disposal") is deferred until the occasion of a subsequent disposal (in this section referred to as "the operative disposal") of the interest which was the subject matter of the deemed disposal.

(2) In a case where the provisions of this section have effect,—

(*a*) no liability for development land tax on the accrued development value shall be taken to arise on the deemed disposal; and

(*b*) at the time of the operative disposal, the person who is the chargeable person in relation to that disposal (in this section referred to as "the relevant person") shall become liable in accordance with this section for development land tax on the accrued development value (in addition to being liable for development land tax on any realised development value which accrues to him on the operative disposal).

(3) Subject to subsection (4) below, the development land tax for which the relevant person becomes liable as mentioned in subsection (2) above in respect of the accrued development value is the amount by which—

(*a*) the development land tax for which, if that liability had not been deferred, the person who was the chargeable person in relation to the deemed disposal would have been liable in the financial year in which the deemed disposal occurred

exceeds

(*b*) the development land tax for which that person was in fact liable in that financial year, disregarding (if the operative disposal also occurred in that financial year) any development land tax in respect of the accrued development value.

(4) If the operative disposal is only a part disposal of the interest which was the subject matter of the deemed disposal, the relevant person shall become liable as mentioned in subsection (2) above for only such proportion of the amount of development land tax determined under subsection (3) above as

appears to the Board or, on an appeal, to the Commissioners concerned to be just and reasonable.

(5) Where subsection (4) above has had effect in relation to a part disposal of the interest which was the subject matter of the deemed disposal and there is a further disposal which is neither a deemed disposal nor a disposal to which section 20(1) above applies but which is a disposal of an interest—

(*a*) in the whole or any part of the land which was comprised in the project of material development the beginning of which was the occasion of the deemed disposal, and

(*b*) which is, or is derived through any one or more disposals from, the interest which was the subject matter of the deemed disposal,

then, subject to subsection (6) below, the person who is the chargeable person in relation to that further disposal shall, at the time of that disposal, become liable for such further proportion (if any) of the amount of development land tax determined under subsection (3) above as appears to the Board or, on an appeal, to the Commissioners concerned to be just and reasonable (in addition to being liable for development land tax on any realised development value which accrues to him on that further disposal).

(6) The aggregate of the development land tax apportioned under subsections (4) and (5) above shall not exceed the total of the amount of development land tax determined under subsection (3) above.

(7) Any reference in this section to a disposal of the interest which was the subject matter of the deemed disposal includes a reference to a disposal to which Part I of Schedule 2 to this Act applies and in relation to which that interest is a part of the relevant interest for the purposes of that Part.

Trusts, settled property, partnerships, mortgagees and liquidators

Property held on a bare trust.

28.—(1) At any time when an interest in land is held on trust—

(*a*) for a person absolutely entitled as against the trustees, or

(*b*) for a person who would be so entitled but for being an infant or other person under disability,

this Act shall apply as if the interest were vested in, and the acts of the trustees in relation to the interest were the acts of, the person referred to in paragraph (*a*) or paragraph (*b*) above (acquisitions from or disposals to the trustees by that person being disregarded accordingly).

(2) If at any time—

(a) an interest in land becomes held on trust as mentioned in subsection (1) above, and

(b) immediately before it came to be so held the interest in land was settled property,

then, for the purposes of this Act, the interest shall at that time be deemed to have been disposed of by the trustees as settled property and immediately reacquired by them as an interest held on trust as mentioned in subsection (1) above; and for those purposes the disposal and reacquisition by the trustees shall be assumed to have been made for no consideration (so that section 10 above applies).

(3) For the purposes of this section, an interest in land is held on trust for a person absolutely entitled as against the trustees where that person has the exclusive right, subject only to satisfying any outstanding charge, lien or other right of the trustees to resort to the interest for payment of duty, taxes, costs or other outgoings, to direct how that interest shall be dealt with.

In the application of this subsection to Scotland, the words from " subject " to " outgoings " shall be omitted.

(4) Any reference in this section to a person absolutely entitled as against the trustees or to a person who would be so entitled but for being an infant or other person under disability includes a reference to two or more persons who are or would be so entitled jointly; and in this subsection the expression " entitled jointly ",—

(a) except in the application of this subsection to Scotland, means entitled as joint tenants, tenants in common or as coparceners; and

(b) in the application of this subsection to Scotland, means entitled as joint owners or owners in common.

(5) In this Act—

(a) an interest in land which is held on trust as mentioned in subsection (1) above is referred to as being held on a bare trust; and

(b) in relation to an interest so held, any reference to the beneficiary or the beneficiaries is a reference to the person or persons for whom the interest is for the time being so held; and

(c) in relation to an interest in land (in Northern Ireland) which is settled land for the purposes of the Settled Land Act 1882 by virtue of section 59 of that Act 1882 c. 38.

(infant absolutely entitled to be as tenant for life) any reference to the trustees includes a reference to any person entitled to exercise the powers of a tenant for life by virtue of an order under section 60 of that Act (powers of infant tenant for life to be exercised by trustees of the settlement or persons ordered by the court).

(6) If, immediately before a project of material development is begun on any land, an interest in that land which is held on a bare trust is a major interest, the interest of a beneficiary in that land is not a major interest for the purposes of this Act.

Disposal of beneficial interests under bare trusts.

29.—(1) The provisions of this section apply if, where an interest in land is held on a bare trust, the beneficiary or one of the beneficiaries disposes of his interest in the property held on trust.

(2) For the purposes of this Act, in any case where the interest in land held on a bare trust forms part only of the property which is held on trust as mentioned in subsection (1) of section 28 above,—

(*a*) the interest of a beneficiary in that property shall be treated as an interest in land only ; but

(*b*) any consideration for the disposal of that interest shall be treated as reduced to such amount as appears to the Board or, on an appeal, to the Commissioners concerned to be just and reasonable, having regard to the value of that portion of the trust property which consists of property other than an interest in land.

(3) In the following provisions of this section the interest in land held on a bare trust is referred to as " the legal interest " and the interest disposed of as mentioned in subsection (1) above is referred to as " the beneficial interest ".

(4) Without prejudice to section 28(1) above, if there is only one beneficiary for whom the legal interest is held on trust, then, for the purposes of this Act,—

(*a*) the disposal by the beneficiary of the beneficial interest shall be treated as a corresponding disposal by him of the legal interest ; and

(*b*) the interest acquired by the person to whom the disposal is made shall be treated as the legal interest or, in the case of a part disposal, as the interest which would be the granted interest in relation to that corresponding disposal of the legal interest.

(5) Subject to subsections (6) and (7) below, where there is more than one beneficiary for whom the legal interest is held

on trust then, in the application of the provisions of this Act in relation to the disposal of the beneficial interest,—

(*a*) the cost of acquisition, the market value and the current use value of the beneficial interest at any time, and

(*b*) the expenditure on improvements or on relevant improvements, in relation to the beneficial interest,

shall (before taking account, where the disposal is a part disposal, of any provision of this Act applicable to part disposals) be taken to be the relevant fraction of the amounts which would be that cost, value or expenditure in relation to a disposal (not being a part disposal) of the legal interest occurring at the same time as the disposal of the beneficial interest.

(6) The relevant fraction referred to in subsection (5) above is that of which the numerator is the market value of the beneficial interest at the time of the disposal and the denominator is the aggregate of that market value and the market value at that time of the interest or interests of the other beneficiary or beneficiaries; and subsection (5) above shall not have effect to determine the market value of any interest for the purposes of this subsection.

(7) In any case where the beneficiary acquired the whole or any part of the beneficial interest from a person who was a beneficiary at the time of the acquisition, subsection (5) above shall not apply to determine the cost of acquisition of the beneficial interest or, as the case may be, the part so acquired; and for the purposes of this subsection any reference to a part of the beneficial interest is a reference to an interest which, in relation to the disposal of the beneficial interest, is such a part for the purposes of Part I of Schedule 2 to this Act.

(8) In any case where—

(*a*) there is a disposal of an interest in land held on a bare trust (in this subsection referred to as " the relevant interest "), and

(*b*) one of the beneficiaries acquired the whole or part of his interest in the land as mentioned in subsection (7) above, and

(*c*) that beneficiary makes a claim in that behalf,

then, for the purposes of determining the amount of realised development value which accrues on the disposal and the liability of each beneficiary in respect of that realised development value, the disposal (but not the acquisition) of the relevant interest shall be treated as a contemporaneous disposal of each of the beneficial interests and the consideration for the disposal shall be apportioned accordingly; but nothing in this subsection shall affect the operation of section 12 of this Act in relation to the disposal.

Settled property.

30.—(1) Subject to subsection (8) below, in this Act " settled property " means an interest in land which is held on trust for any person or persons in such circumstances that it is not held on a bare trust, and, subject to the following provisions of this section, in relation to settled property, the trustees of the settlement shall for the purposes of this Act be treated as a single and continuing body of persons, distinct from the persons who may from time to time be the trustees.

(2) In relation to settled property which, in England and Wales or in Northern Ireland, is settled land,—

(*a*) the tenant for life or statutory owner for the time being, and

(*b*) the trustees of the settlement (so far as not comprised in the expression " statutory owner "),

shall be treated for the purposes of this Act as constituting and, in so far as they act separately, as acting on behalf of a single and continuing body of trustees distinct from the persons of whom that body is for the time being composed.

(3) In subsection (2) above—

(*a*) in its application in England and Wales, " settled land " and other expressions to which a meaning is assigned by the Settled Land Act 1925 have the same meaning as in that Act ; and

1925 c. 18.

(*b*) in its application in Northern Ireland " settled land " and other expressions to which a meaning is assigned by the Settled Land Act 1882 have the same meaning as in that Act and references to a statutory owner shall be construed as references to any person having under section 58 of that Act the powers of a tenant for life.

1882 c. 38.

(4) For the purposes of this Act, in any case where land in Northern Ireland is settled land within the meaning of the Settled Land Act 1882 but, under the settlement, any estate or interest in land stands for the time being limited to any persons by way of succession without the interposition of any trust (and, accordingly, without being settled property, within the meaning of this Act,—

(*a*) the tenant for life and the trustees of the settlement (if any) shall nevertheless be treated as constituting a single and continuing body of trustees ; and

(*b*) any disposal of an interest in land which is effected in exercise of the powers conferred by that Act or of any such additional or larger powers as are referred to in section 57 of that Act or which is otherwise effected by the tenant for life and could have been effected in exercise of those powers shall be treated as a disposal of settled property by that body of trustees ; and (*c*) any realised development value which accrues on such a disposal shall be treated as accruing to that body of trustees ;

and expressions used in this subsection to which a meaning is assigned by section 2 of the Settled Land Act 1882 have the same meaning in this subsection as in that Act. 1882 c. 38.

(5) In the case of a settlement falling within subsection (4) above, the settled property which is treated as being the subject of a disposal falling within paragraph (*b*) of that subsection shall be deemed for the purposes of this Act to be the legal estate in fee simple or other interest which, by virtue of the settlement referred to in that subsection, stands limited to any persons by way of succession.

(6) Subject to subsection (7) below, if and so long as any land in Northern Ireland remains settled land, within the meaning of the Settled Land Act 1882, and subject to a settlement falling within subsection (4) above, neither—

(*a*) the beneficial interest of the tenant for life referred to in subsection (4) above, nor

(*b*) any estate or interest in reversion or remainder which is comprised in the subject of the settlement for the purposes of that Act, nor

(*c*) any other interest arising under the settlement,

shall be treated for the purposes of this Act as an interest in land.

(7) In any case where, by virtue of the disposal to him of one or more interests falling within subsection (6) above and not by virtue of a disposal effected under the powers conferred by the Settled Land Act 1882, a person becomes entitled to an interest in land (in this subsection referred to as " the relevant interest ") which, in his hands, is not settled land, within the meaning of the Settled Land Act 1882, then,—

(*a*) if he acquired the relevant interest or any part of it otherwise than for value, he shall be treated for the purposes of this Act as having so acquired the interest or part from the settlor by the disposal of an interest in land ; and

(*b*) if he acquired the whole or any part of the relevant interest for value, the disposal by virtue of which he acquired that interest or part shall be treated for the purposes of this Act as the disposal of an interest in land, notwithstanding that, immediately before the disposal, the interest disposed of was an interest falling within subsection (6) above ;

and for the purposes of this subsection a part of the relevant interest means an interest which, disregarding the provisions of subsection (6) above, would be such a part for the purposes of the application of Part I of Schedule 2 to this Act to a disposal of the relevant interest.

(8) In this Act " settled property " does not include an interest in land held by a person as trustee or assignee in bankruptcy or under a deed of arrangement or, as respects Scotland, as trustee on a sequestrated estate or as a judicial factor who has powers or duties corresponding to those possessed by such a trustee, or as trustee for behoof of creditors.

(9) Subsections (2) and (3) above do not extend to Scotland and subsections (4) to (7) above extend to Northern Ireland only.

Partnerships.

31. Where two or more persons carry on a trade or business in partnership—

(*a*) any partnership dealings shall be treated as dealings by the partners and not by the firm as such ; and

(*b*) development land tax in respect of realised development value accruing to the partners on the disposal of an interest in land or for which the partners otherwise become liable at any time shall, in Scotland as well as elsewhere in the United Kingdom, be charged on them separately.

Enforcement of security by mortgagees and other creditors.

32.—(1) Subject to subsection (3) below, where a person entitled to a security in any land or to the benefit of a charge or incumbrance affecting any land deals with an interest in that land for the purpose of enforcing or giving effect to his security, charge or incumbrance, his dealings with the interest in land shall be treated for the purposes of this Act as if they were done by him as bare trustee for the person entitled to that interest in land subject to the security, charge or incumbrance.

(2) Subsection (1) above shall apply to the dealings of any person appointed to enforce or give effect to the security, charge or incumbrance referred to in that subsection, whether as receiver and manager or judicial factor, as it applies to the dealings of the person entitled as mentioned in that subsection.

(3) Where, as a result of an order for foreclosure, or, in Scotland, of the recording of an extract of a decree of foreclosure, an interest in land becomes vested beneficially in a creditor, that interest shall be treated as having been disposed of by the borrower and acquired by the creditor for a consideration equal to the amount of principal, interest and costs, payment of which in due time would have prevented the foreclosure becoming absolute, or, in Scotland, the granting of the decree of foreclosure.

(4) If a foreclosure is reopened after an order absolute, such adjustments, whether by way of a further assessment or the discharge or repayment of tax or otherwise, shall be made as may be required in consequence.

(5) Any reference in this section to a security in any land is a reference to an interest falling within paragraph (*a*) or paragraph (*b*) of subsection (2) of section 46 below.

(6) In relation to Scotland, in subsection (3) above " decree of foreclosure " includes a decree granted under section 8 of the Heritable Securities (Scotland) Act 1894 and subsection (4) above does not apply. 1894 c. 44.

(7) Subsections (3) and (4) above do not apply to Northern Ireland.

Liquidators and trustees in bankruptcy, etc.

1948 c. 38.
1960 c. 22 (N.I.).

33.—(1) Where any property belonging to a company or held by trustees on behalf of a company is vested in a liquidator under section 244 of the Companies Act 1948 or section 226 of the Companies Act (Northern Ireland) 1960 or otherwise, this Act shall have effect as if any interest in land comprised in that property were vested in, and the acts of the liquidator in relation to that interest were the acts of, the company (acquisitions from or disposals to the liquidator by the company being disregarded accordingly).

(2) Subject to subsections (3) and (4) below, at any time when an interest in land is held by a person as trustee or assignee in bankruptcy or under a deed of arrangement or, as respects Scotland, by a trustee for behoof of creditors, the provisions of this Act shall apply as if the interest were vested in, and the acts of the trustee or assignee in relation to the interest were the acts of, the bankrupt or debtor (acquisitions from or disposals to him by the bankrupt or debtor being disregarded accordingly), and development land tax in respect of any realised development value which accrues to any such trustee or assignee shall be assessable on and recoverable from the trustee or assignee.

(3) If, at the death of a bankrupt or debtor, an interest in land is held by a trustee or assignee in bankruptcy or under a deed of arrangement or, as respects Scotland, by a trustee for behoof of creditors, then, in relation to events after the death, subsection (2) above shall not apply and the provisions of this Act shall have effect as if—

(*a*) the interest had been held by the bankrupt or debtor immediately before his death and had devolved on his death upon the trustee or assignee ; and

(*b*) the trustee or assignee were a personal representative of the deceased.

(4) Where an interest in land is acquired by a trustee in bankruptcy after the death of the bankrupt or debtor, subsection (2) above shall not apply and the provisions of this Act shall have effect as if the trustee were a personal representative of the deceased.

(5) In the application of this section to Scotland, " trustee in bankruptcy " means a trustee on a sequestrated estate and includes a judicial factor who has powers and duties corresponding to those possessed by a trustee on a sequestrated estate.

Other taxes

Interaction of development land tax with other taxes.

34.—(1) The provisions of Schedule 6 to this Act shall have effect where development land tax falls to be charged on the realisation of development value which is also brought into account, in whole or in part, for the purposes of—

(*a*) tax on chargeable gains ;

(*b*) tax on profits or gains of a trade ;

(*c*) estate duty ;

(*d*) capital transfer tax ;

1970 c. 10.

(*e*) section 80 or section 82 of the Income and Corporation Taxes Act 1970 (certain capital sums to be taxable as rent) ; or

1974 c. 30.

(*f*) Chapter I of Part III of the Finance Act 1974 (development gains from land).

(2) Without prejudice to subsection (1) above, payments of development land tax shall not be available as a deduction in computing the amount of the profits or gains of a trade or the amount of a chargeable gain.

(3) In Schedule 6 to this Act—

(*a*) a " CGT disposal " means a disposal, for the purposes of tax on chargeable gains, of an asset consisting of an interest in land ;

(*b*) a " DLT disposal " means a disposal (within the meaning of this Act) of an interest in land, other than a disposal for which no consideration is given ;

(*c*) a " trading disposal " means a disposal of an interest in land where the proceeds of the disposal or the market value of the interest disposed of fell or falls to be included in the computation of the profits or gains of a trade carried on by any person ; and

(*d*) a " CTT transfer " means a transfer of value, for the purposes of capital transfer tax,—

(i) on the occasion of which an interest in land is acquired by any person, and

(ii) which, subject to subsection (5) below, gives rise to liability for capital transfer tax,

or a capital distribution, as defined in section 51(1) of the Finance Act 1975, made on the occasion of a transaction on which an interest in land is acquired by any person. 1975 c. 7.

(4) If, by virtue of any provision of this Act, liability for development land tax on any realised development value which accrues on a deemed disposal is deferred until a subsequent disposal or other event, then, without prejudice to the operation of section 12(8) of this Act, for the purposes of Schedule 6 to this Act and, in particular, for the purpose of determining whether any chargeable realised development value accrues on that deemed disposal and, if so, the amount of that chargeable realised development value, the liability shall be assumed not to have been deferred.

(5) In any case where the whole or any part of the land in which the interest referred to in sub-paragraph (i) of paragraph (*d*) of subsection (3) above subsists is designated as property to which section 34 of the Finance Act 1975 applies (conditional exemption for certain buildings etc., on death) it shall be assumed for the purpose only of determining whether the condition in sub-paragraph (ii) of that paragraph is fulfilled that tax has become chargeable with respect to that land or part thereof in accordance with subsection (7) of that section.

(6) Subsections (2) and (2A) of section 51 of the Finance Act 1975 (construction of references to transfer of value and the value transferred by chargeable transfers) shall have effect in relation to the provisions of subsection (3)(*d*) above and paragraphs 18 to 24 of Schedule 6 to this Act as if those provisions were included in Part III of the Finance Act 1975.

(7) For the purposes of Schedule 6 to this Act, a person (in this subsection referred to as " A ") who makes a disposal of an interest in land (in this subsection referred to as " the relevant interest ") claims for DLT purposes through another person (in this subsection referred to as " B ") if—

(*a*) no consideration was given for A's acquisition of the relevant interest, and

(*b*) B has made a disposal of an interest in land for which no consideration was given, and

(*c*) in the application of subsection (2) of section 10 above for the purpose of determining the relevant base value of the relevant interest on the disposal in question, the disposal referred to in paragraph (*b*) above is the previous disposal,

and in any case where, by virtue of the preceding provisions of this subsection, B himself claimed for DLT purposes through another person in relation to the making of the disposal referred to in paragraph (*b*) above, A also claims for DLT purposes through that other person.

Termination of tax on development gains.

1974 c. 30.

35.—(1) Subject to subsection (2) and sections 36 and 37 below, no part of a chargeable gain which accrues to any person on the disposal of an interest in land on or after the appointed day shall be a development gain by virtue of Chapter I of Part III of the Finance Act 1974 (in this section referred to as " the enactment relating to development gains ").

(2) Nothing in section 45 below shall be taken as affecting the time at which an interest in land is disposed of for the purposes of tax on chargeable gains (or the enactment relating to development gains) and in any case where the disposal of an interest in land occurs—

(*a*) before the appointed day for the purposes of liability to development land tax, and

(*b*) on or after that day for the purposes of tax on chargeable gains,

subsection (1) above shall not affect the application of the enactment relating to development gains in relation to that disposal.

(3) In the following provisions of Schedule 3 to the Finance Act 1974, namely,—

(*a*) sub-paragraphs (1) and (6) of paragraph 11 (computation of development gain in respect of disposal of interest in land after material development has been carried out),

(*b*) sub-paragraphs (1) and (4) of paragraph 12 (computation of development gain in respect of disposal of interest in land reflecting expenditure on enhancement), and

(*c*) sub-paragraphs (1) and (2) of paragraph 13 (provisions supplementary to paragraphs 11 and 12),

after the words " 17th December 1973 ", in each place where they occur, there shall be inserted the word " and " and after the words " acquired the interest ", in each place where they occur, there shall be added or, as the case may require, inserted the words " but before the appointed day, within the meaning of the Development Land Tax Act 1976 ".

(4) In this section " disposal " has the same meaning as it has for the purposes of tax on chargeable gains.

Exclusion of s. 35 in certain cases where development began before appointed day.

36.—(1) In any case where,—

(*a*) after 17th December 1973 and before the appointed day, material development was begun on any land, and

(*b*) in the period beginning immediately before the date on which that development was begun and ending immediately before the appointed day any material interest in the land comprised in the development was not subject to a disposal excluding, for this purpose, a no gain/no loss disposal,

section 35(1) above shall not affect the application of the enactment relating to development gains in relation to the first disposal of that material interest which occurs on or after the appointed day and is not a no gain/no loss disposal.

(2) Part I of Schedule 3 to the Finance Act 1974 shall have effect to determine for the purposes of this section what is material development and the date on which any such development is to be taken to be begun, and for the purposes of this section— 1974 c. 30.

(*a*) " material interest ", in relation to the land comprised in any material development, means any interest which was in existence immediately before the development began or which came into existence in the period referred to in subsection (1)(*b*) above; and

(*b*) on the occasion of a disposal within that period of part of a material interest, only the interest which is acquired by the person to whom the disposal is made shall be taken to have been subject to a disposal.

(3) If, on or after the appointed day,—

(*a*) there is a no gain/no loss disposal of a material interest which has not previously been the subject of a chargeable disposal, and

(*b*) as a result of that disposal an interest in land comes into being which, apart from this subsection, would not be a material interest,

the interest referred to in paragraph (*b*) above shall be treated for the purposes of subsections (1) and (2) above and subsection (4) below as if it were itself a material interest falling within subsection (1)(*b*) above.

(4) In any case where—

(*a*) a material interest was not the subject of a chargeable disposal before the appointed day, and

(*b*) the first disposal of that interest which occurs on or after the appointed day and is not a no gain/no loss disposal is a disposal of part only of that interest,

the part of the interest which remains after the disposal shall be treated for the purposes of subsections (1) to (3) above as if it were itself a material interest falling within subsection (1)(*b*) above.

(5) For the purposes of the enactment relating to development gains, in any case where—

(*a*) by virtue of the preceding provisions of this section that enactment applies in relation to the disposal of an interest in land on or after the appointed day, and

(*b*) the amount which for the purposes of that enactment is the net proceeds of the disposal would, apart from this subsection, be greater than the amount which for those purposes is the current use value of the interest disposed of at the time of the disposal,

the net proceeds of the disposal shall be taken to be an amount equal to that current use value.

(6) For the purposes of this section—

(*a*) " chargeable disposal ", in relation to an interest in land on which material development was begun as mentioned in subsection (1)(*a*) above, means a disposal which occurs on or after the date on which that development was begun and is a disposal to which the enactment relating to development gains applies;

(*b*) " disposal " has the meaning which it has for the purposes of tax on chargeable gains;

(*c*) " the enactment relating to development gains " has the meaning assigned to it by section 35(1) above; and

(*d*) a " no gain/no loss disposal " of an interest in land means a disposal on which, by virtue of any enactment, the person making the disposal and the person to whom the disposal is made fall to be treated for the purposes of tax on chargeable gains as if the latter's acquisition were for a consideration of such amount as would secure that, on the disposal, neither a gain nor a loss would accrue to the person making the disposal.

Exclusion of s. 35 in case of certain interests acquired before appointed day.

37.—(1) In any case where—

(*a*) after 17th December 1973 and before the appointed day, a person acquired an interest in land (in this subsection and subsections (2) to (4) below referred to as " the relevant interest ") on the occasion of a no gain/no loss disposal, and

(*b*) that no gain/no loss disposal was not a disposal to which section 20(1) above applied, and

(*c*) in the period beginning immediately after that acquisition and ending immediately before the appointed day, there has been no disposal of the relevant interest, other than a no gain/no loss disposal,

section 35(1) above shall not affect the application of the enactment relating to development gains in relation to the first disposal of the relevant interest which occurs on or after the appointed day and is not a no gain/no loss disposal.

(2) If, in a case where subsection (1) above applies, there occurs within the period specified in paragraph (*c*) of that subsection a disposal of part of the relevant interest, then,—

(*a*) this section shall have effect as if the part which remains were itself the relevant interest; and

(*b*) if that disposal is a no gain/no loss disposal, this section shall also have effect as if the interest acquired as a result of the disposal were itself another interest to which paragraphs (*a*) to (*c*) of subsection (1) above apply.

(3) If, on or after the appointed day,—

(*a*) there is a no gain/no loss disposal of the relevant interest, and

(*b*) that disposal is a disposal of part only of the relevant interest, and

(*c*) there has not previously (but on or after the appointed day) been a disposal of the relevant interest to which the enactment relating to development gains applies,

not only the part of the relevant interest which remains after the disposal but also the interest acquired as a result of the disposal shall be treated for the purposes of this section as an interest to which paragraphs (*a*) to (*c*) of subsection (1) above apply.

(4) If, in a case where subsection (1) above applies, the first disposal of the relevant interest which occurs on or after the appointed day and is not a no gain/no loss disposal is a disposal of part only of the relevant interest, this section shall have effect in relation to the part which remains as if it were a separate interest to which paragraphs (*a*) to (*c*) of subsection (1) above apply.

(5) In any case where—

(*a*) a lease was granted after 17th December 1973 and before the appointed day, and

(*b*) in the period beginning immediately after the grant of the lease and ending immediately before the appointed day there has been no disposal, other than a no gain/no loss disposal, of the interest in land out of which the lease was granted (in this subsection and the following provisions of this section referred to as " the reversion "),

section 35(1) above shall not affect the application of the enactment relating to development gains in relation to the first disposal of the reversion which occurs on or after the appointed day and is not a no gain/no loss disposal.

(6) If, in a case where subsection (5) above applies, there occurs within the period specified in paragraph (*b*) of that subsection a disposal of part of the reversion, then,—

(*a*) this section shall have effect as if the part which remains were itself the reversion ; and

(*b*) if that disposal is a no gain/no loss disposal, this section shall also have effect as if the interest acquired as a result of the disposal were itself an interest in land out of which a lease falling within paragraph (*a*) of subsection (5) above was granted.

(7) If, on or after the appointed day,—

(*a*) there is a no gain/no loss disposal of the reversion, and

(*b*) that disposal is a disposal of part only of the reversion, and

(*c*) there has not previously (but on or after the appointed day) been a disposal of the reversion to which the enactment relating to development gains applies,

not only the part of the reversion which remains after the disposal but also the interest acquired as a result of the disposal shall be treated for the purposes of this section as an interest in land out of which a lease falling within paragraph (*a*) of subsection (5) above was granted.

(8) If, in a case where subsection (5) above applies, the first disposal of the reversion which occurs on or after the appointed day and is not a no gain/no loss disposal is a disposal of part only of the reversion, this section shall have effect in relation to the part which remains as if it were a separate interest in land out of which a lease falling within paragraph (*a*) of subsection (5) above was granted.

(9) For the purposes of this section,—

(*a*) " disposal " has, except in subsection (1)(*b*) above, the meaning which it has for the purposes of tax on chargeable gains ;

(*b*) " the enactment relating to development gains " has the meaning assigned to it by section 35(1) above ; and

(*c*) a " no gain/no loss disposal " of an interest in land means a disposal on which, by virtue of any enactment, the person making the disposal and the person to whom the disposal is made fall to be treated for the purposes of tax on chargeable gains as if the latter's acquisition were for a consideration of such amount as would secure that, on the disposal, neither a gain nor a loss would accrue to the person making the disposal.

38.—(1) On and after the appointed day, no interest in land shall be deemed to be disposed of and immediately reacquired by virtue of, and for the purposes of the provisions specified in, section 45(1) of the Finance Act 1974 (first letting charge) unless the relevant development relating to the chargeable building in question was begun before 18th May 1976.

Termination of first letting charge.

1974 c. 30.

(2) In subsection (1) above the expressions "chargeable building" and "the relevant development" have the meaning assigned to them by section 46 of the Finance Act 1974, and paragraph 9 of Schedule 3 to that Act shall have effect to determine the date on which the relevant development is to be taken to be begun.

(3) In any case where, on or after the appointed day, an interest in land is deemed to be disposed of and immediately reacquired as mentioned in subsection (1) above, nothing in section 35(1) above shall affect the operation of Chapter I of Part III of the Finance Act 1974 (development gains) in relation to the disposal.

Deduction, administration and collection of development land tax

39.—(1) Subject to subsection (2) below, on the disposal of an interest in land to—

Deduction of development land tax from consideration in case of certain disposals to exempt bodies.

(*a*) a body specified in any of paragraphs (*a*) to (*d*) of subsection (1) of section 11 above, or

(*b*) any other exempt body which, in relation to the disposal of that interest, is an authority possessing compulsory powers,

the body shall, on paying any amount by way of consideration for the disposal, make a deduction in accordance with this section on account of any development land tax for which the chargeable person may be liable on the disposal.

(2) Subsection (1) above does not apply to a disposal of an interest in land by a body which is itself an exempt body.

(3) In this section and in Schedule 7 to this Act—

(*a*) a "material disposal" means a disposal falling within subsection (1) above; and

(*b*) in relation to a payment of consideration and in relation to a material disposal in respect of which there is only one payment of consideration, the " DLT deduction " means the amount of the deduction made from that payment in accordance with subsection (1) above, and in relation to a material disposal in respect of which there is more than one payment of consideration the " DLT deduction " means the aggregate of the DLT deductions made in respect of each of those payments.

(4) Where, in connection with a material disposal, an exempt body makes a payment of consideration from which it deducts a DLT deduction, the body shall furnish to the chargeable person a statement in writing showing—

(*a*) what the amount of that payment would be if no deduction were made in accordance with this section;

(*b*) the amount of the DLT deduction; and

(*c*) the amount actually paid by way of consideration;

and a statement under this subsection shall be either in a form prescribed by the Board or in a form authorised by them for use in substitution for the form prescribed and containing a statement that it has been so authorised.

(5) Where, in connection with a material disposal, the chargeable person is furnished with a statement under subsection (4) above, he shall be treated for all purposes—

(*a*) as having received (in addition to any consideration actually paid) an amount by way of consideration for the disposal equal to the DLT deduction shown in the statement; and

(*b*) as having paid to the Board, in respect of the disposal, an amount of development land tax equal to that DLT deduction.

(6) If an amount of development land tax, in addition to that represented by the DLT deduction, is payable by the chargeable person in respect of the realised development value which accrues on a material disposal, the amount of any development land tax so paid shall be payable by the Board to the exempt body to whom the disposal is made.

(7) Any amount which is treated as having been paid to the Board by virtue of subsection (5)(*b*) above or which is payable by the Board to an exempt body by virtue of subsection (6) above shall be regarded—

(*a*) as not forming part of the gross revenues which the Board are required, under section 10 of the Exchequer and Audit Departments Act 1866 (gross revenues to be paid to Exchequer), to pay to the account referred to in that section; and

1866 c. 39.

(b) as not being included in the money and securities collected or received as mentioned in section 1(2) of the Public Accounts and Charges Act 1891 (money collected by the Board to be paid or remitted to a special account at the Bank). 1891 c. 24.

(8) The provisions of Schedule 7 to this Act shall have effect for supplementing the provisions of this section and, in particular with respect to—

(a) the notices and information to be given to and by the Board;

(b) the determination of the amount of the DLT deduction in any case;

(c) the procedure for making the DLT deduction and accounting for it to the Board;

(d) interest on sums deducted;

(e) the inspection of books, accounts and other documents and records on behalf of the Board; and

(f) the finalisation of the liability of the chargeable person for development land tax in respect of realised development value accruing on a material disposal.

(9) The Board may by regulations made by statutory instrument make further provision with respect to the matters specified in paragraphs (b), (c) and (f) of subsection (8) above, and in connection with any such provision may by such regulations make incidental or consequential amendments of Schedule 7 to this Act and—

(a) no regulations containing provisions with respect to the matter specified in paragraph (b) of that subsection shall be made unless a draft of the regulations has been laid before and approved by a resolution of the Commons House of Parliament; and

(b) a statutory instrument containing any other regulations under this subsection shall be subject to annulment in pursuance of a resolution of the Commons House of Parliament.

(10) In this section and Schedule 7 to this Act " exempt body " means—

(a) a body which, on the disposal by it of an interest in land, would not be chargeable to development land tax by virtue of section 11 above; or

(b) a Minister of the Crown or government department, including a department of the Government of Northern Ireland.

Deduction on account of development land tax from consideration for disposals by non-residents.

40.—(1) If at any time a person whose usual place of abode is outside the United Kingdom disposes of an interest in land in the United Kingdom which, at that time, is development land and the disposal is not a disposal falling within section 39(1) above, then, subject to and in accordance with this section, the person to whom the disposal is made shall, on paying the consideration or any part of the consideration for his acquisition of the interest disposed of or, as the case may be, the granted interest, make a deduction on account of any liability of the chargeable person for development land tax on the disposal.

(2) Subsection (1) above does not apply to a disposal if the consideration for the disposal, or so much of that consideration as is payable within the period of seven years beginning on the date of the disposal, does not exceed £10,000 ; and in the case of a disposal which consists of the grant of a lease, paragraphs 26 to 28 of Schedule 2 to this Act shall not apply to determine whether subsection (1) above applies to the disposal.

(3) No deduction shall be made by virtue of this section—

(*a*) from any payment of rent, or

(*b*) from any other instalment of consideration which falls to be paid after the expiry of the period of eight years beginning on the date of the disposal,

but the deduction to be made from any other payment of consideration for a disposal to which subsection (1) applies shall be one half of the amount which would be payable apart from this section.

(4) On making a payment from which a deduction is made by virtue of this section, the person making the payment shall forthwith remit the amount deducted to the Board and furnish to the Board and to the chargeable person a certificate in a form prescribed by the Board identifying the disposal and the person by whom it was made and showing—

(*a*) what the payment would have been if no deduction had been made by virtue of this section ;

(*b*) the amount deducted ; and

(*c*) the amount actually paid.

(5) Where, in connection with a disposal to which subsection (1) above applies, a certificate is furnished to the chargeable person in accordance with subsection (4) above, he shall be treated for all purposes—

(*a*) as having received (in addition to any payment actually made) a payment of consideration in respect of that disposal equal to the amount deducted, as stated in the certificate ; and (*b*) as having paid to the Board, in respect of any liability of his for development land tax on the disposal, an amount equal to the amount deducted, as stated in the certificate.

(6) If any person who is required to make a deduction from a payment by virtue of this section fails to remit to the Board the amount required to be so deducted or, if it is greater, the amount certified as being deducted in accordance with subsection (4) above, a sum of that amount shall be recoverable from him by the Board as if it were an amount of development land tax accruing due from him on the date on which he made the payment from which the deduction fell to be made.

(7) The Board may by regulations made by statutory instrument make provision for supplementing the provisions of this section and, in particular,—

(*a*) make exceptions, in circumstances specified in the regulations, from the requirement to make a deduction under subsection (1) above ;

(*b*) vary the amount required to be deducted by virtue of this section in particular cases ; and

(*c*) make provision with respect to the interest to be allowed to the chargeable person where a deduction required to be made under subsection (1) above is made before the reckonable date ;

and a statutory instrument containing any such regulations shall be subject to annulment in pursuance of a resolution of the Commons House of Parliament.

(8) For the purposes of subsection (1) above, land is development land at the time of a disposal of an interest in it if—

(*a*) there is in force at that time planning permission authorising any material development of the whole or any part of the land ; and

(*b*) the material development referred to in paragraph (*a*) above was not comprised in any project of material development begun before that time.

Administration of development land tax.

41.—(1) For the purposes of—

(*a*) placing development land tax under the care and management of the Board, and

(*b*) the application of the provisions of the Taxes Management Act 1970 in relation to development land tax, 1970 c. 9.

that Act shall be amended in accordance with Part I of Schedule 8 to this Act.

(2) In Schedule 8 to this Act—

(*a*) Part II shall have effect with respect to the notices and information to be given for the purposes of this Act and the penalties for failure to give such notices and information;

(*b*) Part III shall have effect with respect to the payment of development land tax; and

(*c*) Part IV shall have effect for supplementing the provisions of this section and the preceding provisions of that Schedule.

Supplementary

Priority of development land tax in bankruptcy and winding up.

42.—(1) In a bankruptcy or winding up under the law of any part of the United Kingdom development land tax shall have the same priority as income tax.

(2) In the application of this Act to Northern Ireland the reference in subsection (1) above to priority in bankruptcy includes a reference to any other priority given to income tax under the Bankruptcy Acts (Northern Ireland) 1857 to 1964.

(3) In the enactments relating to priority of debts, as those enactments have effect in relation to development land tax by virtue of subsection (1) above, the reference to one year's assessment shall be construed as a reference to the amount of development land tax the liability for which arose in one financial year.

(4) The enactments relating to priority of debts referred to in subsection (3) above are:—

1913 c. 20. (*a*) section 118(1)(*a*) of the Bankruptcy (Scotland) Act 1913;

1914 c. 59. (b) section 33(1)(*a*) of the Bankruptcy Act 1914;

1948 c. 38. (*c*) section 319(1)(*a*)(ii) of the Companies Act 1948;

1960 c. 22 (N.I.). (*d*) section 287(1)(*a*)(ii) of the Companies Act (Northern Ireland) 1960; and

1964 c. 32 (N.I.). (*e*) section 1(1)(*a*)(ii) of the Preferential Payments (Bankruptcies and Arrangements) Act (Northern Ireland) 1964.

Use of capital money to pay development land tax.

1925 c. 18.
1925 c. 20.
1925 c. 24.

43.—(1) In relation to England and Wales,—

(*a*) the purposes authorised for the application of capital money by section 73 of the Settled Land Act 1925, by that section as applied by section 28 of the Law of Property Act 1925 in relation to trusts for sale and by section 26 of the Universities and College Estates Act 1925, and

(*b*) the purposes authorised by section 71 of the Settled Land Act 1925, by that section as applied by section

28 of the Law of Property Act 1925 in relation to trusts for sale and by section 30 of the Universities and College Estates Act 1925 as purposes for which money may be raised by mortgage, 1925 c. 20. 1925 c. 24.

shall include the discharge of any sum payable in respect of development land tax, other than a sum payable by way of interest under Schedule 8 to this Act.

(2) In relation to Scotland, for the purposes of discharging any sum payable in respect of development land tax, other than a sum payable by way of interest under Schedule 8 to this Act, a trustee, a proper liferenter or an heir of entail in possession shall have power to expend capital money and to sell, or to borrow money on the security of, the estate or any part thereof, heritable as well as moveable.

(3) In relation to Northern Ireland,—

(*a*) the purposes authorised for the application of capital money by section 21 of the Settled Land Act 1882, and 1882 c. 38.

(*b*) the purposes authorised by section 11 of the Settled Land Act 1890 as purposes for which money may be raised by mortgage, 1890 c. 69.

shall include the discharge of any sum payable in respect of development land tax, other than a sum payable by way of interest under Schedule 8 to this Act.

Duration of leases: effect of extensions, terminations and variations.

44.—(1) Where the terms of a lease include provision for the extension of the lease beyond a given date by notice given by the tenant, it shall be assumed for the purposes of this Act, other than section 2 thereof, that the term of the lease will extend for as long as it can be extended by the tenant.

(2) If a lease comes to an end on a day before its presumed expiry date (whether by agreement between the parties, by forfeiture or for any other reason) it shall be assumed for the purposes of this Act, other than this subsection, that the tenant has on that day surrendered the lease to the landlord.

(3) In subsection (2) above " presumed expiry date ", in relation to a lease, means the date on which the term of the lease will expire in accordance with the grant or, where subsection (1) above applies, by virtue of that subsection.

(4) Where there is a material variation of the terms and conditions of a lease, it shall be assumed for the purposes of this Act, other than this subsection,—

(*a*) that the tenant has surrendered the lease to the landlord immediately before the time at which the variation comes into force ; and (*b*) that the landlord, by a part disposal of his interest, has granted to the tenant a new lease taking effect immediately after that time and, so far as that assumption allows, on the terms and conditions of the lease then in force.

(5) For the purposes of subsection (4) above, there is a material variation of the terms and conditions of a lease where—

(*a*) there is a variation of any terms and conditions which, on a disposal, would be relevant to determine the duration of the lease for the purposes of this Act, other than section 2 above; or

(*b*) the terms and conditions are varied by the release or modification of a covenant or agreement restricting the material development of any of the land in which the lease subsists.

Time of disposal and acquisition of interests in land.

45.—(1) The provisions of this section shall have effect for determining the time at which, for the purposes of liability to development land tax, an interest in land is to be taken to be disposed of or acquired.

(2) Subject to subsections (2) and (3) of section 3 above and the following provisions of this section, where under a contract an interest in land is disposed of and that interest or, in the case of a part disposal, the granted interest is acquired, then,—

(*a*) if the contract is conditional (and, in particular, if it is conditional on the exercise of an option) the time at which the disposal and acquisition is made is the time when the condition is satisfied; and

(*b*) in any other case, the time at which the disposal and acquisition is made is the time the contract is made and not, if it is different, the time at which the interest is conveyed or transferred.

(3) For the purposes of this Act where, at the time a person holds an interest in land, there is a deemed disposal and reacquisition of that interest, then, except in so far as any provision of this Act otherwise provides, the time at which that person acquired that interest is the time of the reacquisition (or, if there is more than one deemed disposal and reacquisition of the interest, the time of the last such reacquisition).

(4) Subject to subsections (5) and (8) below, where an interest in land is acquired compulsorily by an authority possessing compulsory powers, the time at which the disposal and acquisition is made is the time at which the compensation for the acquisition is agreed or otherwise determined (variations on appeal being disregarded for this purpose) or, if earlier, the time when the authority enter on the land in pursuance of their powers.

(5) Subject to subsection (8) below, where an interest in land is acquired—

(*a*) in England, Scotland or Wales by virtue of a general vesting declaration, within the meaning of Schedule 3 to the Town and Country Planning Act 1968 or, in Scotland, Schedule 24 to the Town and Country Planning (Scotland) Act 1972, or 1968 c. 72. 1972 c. 52.

(*b*) in Northern Ireland by way of a vesting order,

the time at which the disposal and acquisition is made is the end of the period specified in the declaration or, in Northern Ireland, the time at which the vesting order becomes operative.

(6) Subject to subsection (9) below, if the disposal of an interest in land under a conditional contract entered into before 13th September 1974 is made for a consideration not depending wholly or mainly on the value of the interest at the time the condition is satisfied, then for the purposes of subsection (2) above the contract shall be treated (on the condition being satisfied) as if it had never been conditional.

(7) Subject to subsection (9) below, where an owner of an interest in land had before 13th September 1974 arranged (without entering into a binding contract) to dispose of that interest to another person and—

(*a*) the arrangement was made in writing or is evidenced by a memorandum or note thereof so made before that date, and

(*b*) he disposes of the interest to that other person under a contract which is entered into within the period of twelve months beginning on the appointed day and of which the terms do not differ materially from the terms of the arrangement or, if they so differ, are not more beneficial to the owner,

the contract, if not conditional, shall be treated for the purposes of subsection (2)(*b*) above as made before the appointed day and, if conditional, shall be treated for the purposes of subsection (6) above as entered into before 13th September 1974.

(8) Subject to subsection (9) below, where an interest in land is disposed of on or after the appointed day to an authority possessing compulsory powers then, if notice to treat in respect of that interest was (or is by virtue of any enactment deemed to have been served before 13th September 1974 on the person making the disposal, the disposal shall be treated for the purposes of this Act as having been made before the appointed day.

(9) Nothing in subsections (6) to (8) above shall apply to determine the time at which an interest in land is to be taken to be acquired.

Interests in land.

46.—(1) Subject to subsection (2) below, except where the context otherwise requires, in this Act the expression " interest in land " means any estate or interest in land, any right in or over land or affecting the use or disposition of land, and any right to obtain such an estate, interest or right from another which is conditional on the other's ability to grant the estate, interest or right in question.

(2) Notwithstanding anything in subsection (1) above, the expression " interest in land " does not in this Act include—

(*a*) the interest of a creditor (other than a creditor in respect of a rent charge) whose debt is secured by way of a mortgage or charge of any kind over land or an agreement for any such mortgage or charge ; or

(*b*) in Scotland, the interest of a creditor in a charge or security of any kind over land (other than a creditor in a contract of ground annual) ; or

(*c*) the interest of a beneficiary in any settled property.

(3) Without prejudice to paragraphs (*a*) and (*b*) of subsection (2) above, the conveyance or transfer by way of security of an interest in land (including a re-conveyance or re-transfer on redemption of the security) shall not be treated for the purposes of this Act as constituting a disposal or acquisition of that interest.

(4) For the avoidance of doubt, it is hereby declared that, in a case where an interest in land is held on a bare trust, the interest of a beneficiary in the proceeds of sale of that interest (as well as the interest of a beneficiary in the land itself) is for the purposes of this Act an interest in land.

(5) In this Act the expression " lease " does not include any interest which, by virtue of subsection (2) above, is not an interest in land, but, subject to that, that expression—

(*a*) comprehends any leasehold tenancy, whether in the nature of a head lease, sub-lease or underlease, and

(*b*) includes an agreement to grant any such leasehold tenancy,

and, in their application to a lease which consists of such an agreement as is referred to in paragraph (*b*) above, expressions appropriate to a lease which has been granted (such as " landlord ", " reversion ", " tenant " and " term ") shall be construed accordingly.

Interpretation.

47.—(1) In this Act, unless the context otherwise requires,—

" appointed day " means such day as the Treasury may by order made by statutory instrument appoint ;

" authority possessing compulsory powers " means, in relation to a disposal of an interest in land, a person acquiring the interest compulsorily, or who has been or could be authorised to acquire it compulsorily for the purposes for which it is acquired, or for whom another person has been or could be authorised so to acquire it;

"beneficiary", in relation to an interest in land held on a bare trust, shall be construed in accordance with section 28(5) of this Act;

"the Board" means the Commissioners of Inland Revenue;

"building" includes any structure or erection, and any part of a building, as so defined, but does not include plant or machinery comprised in a building;

"chargeable gain" has the same meaning as in Part III of the Finance Act 1965; 1965 c. 25.

"chargeable person" has the meaning assigned to it by section 4(2) of this Act;

"chargeable realised development value" means realised development value on which development land tax is in fact chargeable;

"charity" has the same meaning as in section 360 of the Income and Corporation Taxes Act 1970; 1970 c. 10.

"company" means any body corporate or unincorporated association, other than a partnership;

"consideration" means consideration in money or money's worth;

"cost", in relation to a person's acquisition of an interest in land, shall be construed in accordance with section 5(2) of this Act;

"current use value" shall be construed in accordance with section 7 of this Act;

"deed of arrangement" means a deed of arrangement to which the Deeds of Arrangement Act 1914 or any 1914 c. 47. corresponding enactment forming part of the law of Northern Ireland applies;

"deemed disposal", in relation to an interest in land, means a disposal of that interest which is deemed to occur by virtue of section 2 of this Act and "deemed reacquisition", in relation to an interest of which there has been a deemed disposal, means the reacquisition of that interest which is provided for by that section;

"dependent relative", in relation to an individual, means—

(*a*) a relative of the individual, or of his or her wife or husband, who is incapacitated by old age or infirmity from maintaining himself, or (*b*) the mother of the individual or of his or her wife or husband, if the mother is widowed or living apart from her husband or, in consequence of dissolution or annulment of marriage, a single woman;

" development " and " development order " have the meaning assigned to them by the relevant planning enactment;

" easement ", in relation to Scotland, means servitude;

" enactment " includes an enactment of the Parliament of Northern Ireland or of the Northern Ireland Assembly;

" expenditure on improvements " and " expenditure on relevant improvements " shall be construed in accordance with Schedule 3 to this Act;

" granted interest " shall be construed in accordance with section 3(5)(*b*) of this Act;

" incidental costs " shall be construed in accordance with Part VI of Schedule 2 to this Act;

" infant ", in relation to Scotland, means a person under the age of eighteen;

" interest in land " shall be construed in accordance with section 46 of this Act;

" interim financial year " has the meaning assigned to it by section 13(1) of this Act;

" land ", except in relation to Scotland, means any corporeal hereditament, including a building, and in relation to Scotland includes land covered with water and any building;

" lease " shall be construed in accordance with section 46(5) of this Act;

" major interest " has the meaning assigned to it by section 2(3) of this Act;

" market value " has the meaning assigned to it by section 7(1) of this Act;

" material development " has the meaning assigned to it by section 7(7) of this Act;

" minerals " includes all minerals and substances in or under land of a kind ordinarily worked for removal by underground or surface working;

" net proceeds " in relation to the disposal of an interest in land, shall be construed in accordance with section 4(3) of this Act;

" part disposal " shall be construed in accordance with section 3 of this Act;

" personal representatives " means, in relation to the estate of a deceased person—

(*a*) in relation to England and Wales, his personal representatives as defined by section 55 of the Administration of Estates Act 1925 ; and 1925 c. 22.

(*b*) in relation to Scotland, the executor of that person or the judicial factor on his estate ; and

(*c*) in relation to Northern Ireland, his personal representatives as defined by section 45(1) of the Administration of Estates Act (Northern Ireland) 1955 ; and 1955 c. 24 (N.I.).

(*d*) in relation to any other country, the persons having in relation to the deceased under the law of that country any functions corresponding to the functions for administration purposes under the law of England and Wales of personal representatives as so defined ;

" planning permission " has the meaning assigned to it by the relevant planning enactment ;

" project of material development " has the meaning assigned to it by paragraph 1 of Schedule 1 to this Act ;

" realised development value " shall be construed in accordance with section 4(1) of this Act ;

" the reckonable date ", in relation to the liability of any person for an amount of development land tax, means the date on which expires the period of three months beginning with the date of the disposal or other event which gives rise to his liability or, in the case of a person who would not be liable but for his being assessed and charged, by virtue of any enactment, in the name or otherwise in the place or on the default of another person, to that other person's liability ;

" relevant base value ", " base A ", " base B " and " base C " shall be construed in accordance with section 5(1) of this Act ;

" the relevant planning enactment " means—

(*a*) in relation to land in England and Wales, section 290(1) of the Town and Country Planning Act 1971 ; 1971 c. 78.

(*b*) in relation to land in Scotland, section 275(1) of the Town and Country Planning (Scotland) Act 1972 ; and 1972 c. 52.

(*c*) in relation to land in Northern Ireland, Article 2 of the Planning (Northern Ireland) Order 1972 ; S.I. 1972/1684 (N.I. 17).

"retained interest" shall be construed in accordance with section 3(5)(*a*) of this Act;

"reversion", in relation to Scotland, means the interest of the landlord in land subject to a lease or, as the case may be, the interest of the lessee of land who is the landlord under a sub-lease;

"settled property" has the meaning assigned to it by section 30 of this Act;

"trade", "profession", "vocation", "office" and "employment" have the same meaning as in the Income Tax Acts.

1970 c. 10. (2) Section 272 of the Income and Corporation Taxes Act 1970 (groups of companies: definitions) shall have effect in relation to this Act with the omission of subsections (1)(*a*) and (2) (restriction to companies resident in the United Kingdom) but otherwise as if the provisions of this Act were included among the sections of Chapter II of Part XI of that Act (companies' capital gains) which follow that section.

(3) Unless the contrary intention appears, any reference in this Act to any other enactment shall be construed as referring to that enactment as amended by or under any other enactment, including this Act.

Short title and extent.

48.—(1) This Act may be cited as the Development Land Tax Act 1976.

(2) This Act extends to Northern Ireland.

SCHEDULES

SCHEDULE 1

Section 2.

Projects of Material Development

Part I

General Provisions

1. For the purposes of this Act a "project of material development" is any project or scheme in pursuance of which any material development is, or is to be, carried out.

2.—(1) Subject to the following provisions of this Part of this Schedule, for the purposes of this Act a project of material development shall be taken to be begun at the earliest time at which any specified operation comprised in the project is begun.

(2) In this Schedule "specified operation" means any of the following, that is to say—

(*a*) any work of construction in the course of the erection of a building;

(*b*) the digging of a trench which is to contain the foundations, or part of the foundations, of a building;

(*c*) the laying of any underground main or pipe to the foundations, or part of the foundations, of a building or to any such trench as is mentioned in paragraph (*b*) above;

(*d*) any operation in the course of laying out or constructing a road or part of a road;

(*e*) any operation in the course of winning or working minerals, within the meaning of section 17 of this Act;

(*f*) any change in the use of any land, where that change constitutes development.

(3) Notwithstanding anything in sub-paragraph (1) above, where an operative notice of a project of material development is given under paragraph 36(1) of Schedule 8 below specifying a date (in this sub-paragraph referred to as "the specified starting date") as the date on which the project is to be or has been begun, then for the purposes of this Act the project shall be taken to be begun on the specified starting date unless—

(*a*) the Board are informed by or on behalf of the person by whom the notice was given that the project was not in fact started, or will not be started, on the specified starting date, or

(*b*) the Board notify that person that they consider that the specified starting date is materially different from the date on which the project would be taken to be begun, having regard to sub-paragraphs (1) and (2) above, or

SCH. 1

(*c*) notice is given by the Board under paragraph 6(6) below with respect to the whole or any part of the material development specified in the notice of the project,

and accordingly, in any case falling within paragraphs (*a*) to (*c*) above, the date on which for the purposes of this Act the project is to be taken to be begun shall be determined without regard to the date specified in the notice under paragraph 36(1) of Schedule 8 below.

(4) Notwithstanding anything in sub-paragraph (1) above, where, in relation to a project of material development, the Board determine the date on which the project should be taken to be begun and serve notice of their determination under paragraph 36(5) of Schedule 8 below, the project shall be taken for the purposes of this Act to be begun on that date.

3. Without prejudice to the preceding provisions of this Schedule, where—

(*a*) any material development is carried out on land in accordance with planning permission granted after 12th September 1974 for a limited period, and

(*b*) subsequently planning permission is granted for the retention on the land of any building or works authorised by the planning permission referred to in paragraph (*a*) above or, as the case may be, for the continuance of a use so authorised,

then, for the purposes of this Act, the retention or continued use referred to in paragraph (*b*) above shall be treated as constituting a project of material development consisting of a material change in the use of the land to which the planning permission referred to in that paragraph relates and that project shall be taken to be begun at the end of the period specified in the planning permission referred to in paragraph (*a*) above.

4.—(1) Subject to the following provisions of this Part of this Schedule, in determining for the purposes of this Act what is at any time comprised in a project of material development—

(*a*) all the development (whether material development or not) which is to be, or has before that time been, carried out in pursuance of the project and all operations in the course of the clearing of the land which are to be, or have before that time been, so carried out shall be taken to be comprised in the project ; and

(*b*) all land which is to be, or has before that time been, developed or cleared in pursuance of the project (but no other land) shall be taken to be land comprised in the project.

(2) Notwithstanding anything in sub-paragraph (1) above, but subject to the following provisions of this Part of this Schedule, where—

(*a*) notice relating to a project of material development has been given under paragraph 36 of Schedule 8 below, and (*b*) that notice was either— SCH. 1

(i) an operative notice under sub-paragraph (1) of that paragraph, or

(ii) a notice given by the Board under sub-paragraph (5) of that paragraph, and

(*c*) in a case falling within paragraph (*b*)(i) above, no notice has been given under paragraph 6(6) below with respect to the whole or any part of the material development specified in the notice referred to in paragraph (*a*) above,

then, for the purposes of this Act, no development which does not fall within the nature and scope of the project as specified in the notice referred to in paragraph (*a*) above shall be taken to be development comprised in the project ; and no land which does not form part of the land specified in that notice shall be taken to be land comprised in the project.

(3) Notwithstanding anything in sub-paragraph (1) above, but subject to the following provisions of this Part of this Schedule, where, in relation to a project of material development, an operative notice has been given under sub-paragraph (1) of paragraph 36 of Schedule 8 below or a notice has been given by the Board under sub-paragraph (5) of that paragraph and notice of the variation of that project has been given under sub-paragraph (7) of that paragraph, then, for the purposes of this Act,—

(*a*) no development which does not fall within the nature and scope of the project as specified in the notice of the variation shall be taken to be or to have been comprised in the project ; and

(*b*) no land which does not form part of the land specified in the notice of the variation shall be taken to be or to have been comprised in the project ;

and, if it appears to the Board to be appropriate, the amount of realised development value accruing to any person on the deemed disposal of an interest in land comprised in the project shall be redetermined accordingly and such adjustment, whether by way of discharge or repayment of tax or otherwise, shall be made as is required in consequence.

(4) Where a project of material development consists of or includes the erection of one or more buildings, the land comprised in the project shall be taken to include (in so far as it would not do so apart from this sub-paragraph) the site of any garage, outbuilding, garden, yard, court, forecourt or other appurtenance which is to be, or has been, constructed or laid out for occupation with, and for the purposes of, that building or those buildings, as the case may be.

(5) In the case of a project of material development which does not include any development other than a material change in the use of the whole or part of a hereditament, the land comprised in the project shall for the purposes of this Act be taken to be that hereditament.

(6) In sub-paragraph (5) above " hereditament " in relation to a project of material development, means the aggregate of the land which, at the date on which that project is begun, forms the subject of

SCH. 1 a single entry in the valuation list or, in Scotland, the valuation roll for the time being in force for a rating area.

(7) In the case of development comprising a material change of use of a building and alteration or improvement works to be carried out for the purpose of that change of use, the change of use together with the alteration and improvement works shall be taken to comprise a single project of material development.

5.—(1) Notwithstanding anything in paragraph 4(1) above, but subject to paragraph 6 below, in relation to a project of material development which is begun but not completed before the appointed day, no material development shall be taken to be comprised in the project unless it was on that day authorised by planning permission then in force.

(2) In determining for the purposes of sub-paragraph (1) above what material development of any land was authorised by planning permission in force on the appointed day, only such development of the land as on that day—

(*a*) was authorised by that permission without any requirement as to subsequent approval, or

(*b*) was not so authorised but had been approved in the manner applicable to that planning permission,

shall for those purposes be taken to have been authorised by that permission on that day.

(3) In a case where sub-paragraph (1) above applies to restrict the development comprised in a project, on the first occasion on or after the appointed day on which a specified operation is begun which is referable only to development not comprised in the project, a new project of material development shall be taken to be begun.

6.—(1) The provisions of this paragraph shall have effect where a project of material development (in this paragraph referred to as " the original project ") is carried out so as to include material development (in this paragraph referred to as " the additional development ") which is not comprised in the project in accordance with the preceding provisions of this Part of this Schedule.

(2) In any case where—

(*a*) the Board receive an operative notice of the additional development under paragraph 37(1) of Schedule 8 below, and

(*b*) it appears to the Board that the whole or any part of the additional development constitutes a separate project of material development, having regard to all relevant matters, including in particular the nature and scope of the original project, and

(*c*) by notice given for the purposes of this sub-paragraph not later than sixty days after the date on which the Board receive the notice referred to in paragraph (*a*) above, the Board so direct with respect to development specified in the notice,

the provisions of this Act, other than this paragraph, shall have effect as if the development specified in the notice given by the Board were comprised in a separate project of material development.

(3) In any case where—

(*a*) in relation to the additional development the Board give notice under paragraph 37(5) of Schedule 8 below, and

(*b*) it appears to the Board that the whole or any part of the additional development constitutes a separate project of material development, having regard to all relevant matters, including in particular the nature and scope of the original project, and

(*c*) by the notice referred to in paragraph (*a*) above, the Board so direct with respect to the whole or such part as may be specified in the notice of the development to which that notice relates,

the provisions of this Act, other than this paragraph, shall have effect as if the development to which the direction relates were comprised in a separate project of material development.

(4) Where any additional development consists of development on land which was not comprised in the original project, then, to the extent that that development is not specified in a direction given by the Board under sub-paragraph (2) or sub-paragraph (3) above, it shall be taken for the purposes of this Act to constitute a separate project of material development.

(5) If any additional development is not comprised in a separate project of material development for the purposes of this Act, it shall be treated for those purposes as always having been comprised in the original project and, if it appears to the Board to be appropriate, the amount of realised development value accruing to any person on the deemed disposal of an interest in land comprised in the project shall be redetermined accordingly and such adjustment, whether by way of a further assessment to tax or otherwise, shall be made as is required in consequence.

(6) In any case where,—

(*a*) after the date on which the original project is begun, an operative notice of another project of material development (in this sub-paragraph referred to as " the subsequent notice ") is given under paragraph 36(1) of Schedule 8 below, and

(*b*) the date which is specified in the subsequent notice as the date on which the project referred to in the notice is to be or has been begun falls within the period of three years beginning with the date on which the original project began, and

(*c*) it appears to the Board that the whole or any part of the material development specified in the subsequent notice constitutes a part of the original project, having regard to all relevant matters, including in particular the nature and scope of that project,

the Board may, by notice given for the purposes of this sub-paragraph not later than sixty days after the date on which the Board receive the subsequent notice, direct that the whole or such part

SCH. 1 as may be specified in the notice of the material development specified in the subsequent notice forms part of the original project.

(7) In any case where—

(*a*) after the date on which the original project is begun, notice relating to another project of material development (in this sub-paragraph referred to as "the subsequent notice") is given by the Board under paragraph 36(5) of Schedule 8 below, and

(*b*) the date which is specified in the subsequent notice as the date on which the project referred to in the notice is to be taken to be begun falls within the period of three years beginning with the date on which the original project began, and

(*c*) it appears to the Board that the whole or any part of the material development to which the subsequent notice relates constitutes a part of the original project, having regard to all relevant matters, including in particular the nature and scope of that project,

the Board may, by the subsequent notice referred to in paragraph (*a*) above, direct that the whole or such part as may be specified in the notice of the material development to which that notice relates forms part of the original project.

(8) Where a direction is given by the Board under sub-paragraph (6) or sub-paragraph (7) above, the material development to which the direction relates—

(*a*) shall be treated for the purposes of this Act as additional development falling within sub-paragraph (5) above; and

(*b*) shall be deemed not to be included in the project of material development to which the subsequent notice refers.

(9) On an appeal against an assessment to development land tax, the Special Commissioners shall have jurisdiction to review any decision taken by the Board under sub-paragraph (2)(*b*), sub-paragraph (3)(*b*), sub-paragraph (6)(*c*) or sub-paragraph (7)(*c*) above.

7. In the preceding provisions of this Schedule, any expression to which a meaning is assigned by the relevant planning enactment and which is not otherwise defined for the purposes of this Act has the same meaning as in that enactment.

PART II

SUPPLEMENTARY PROVISIONS RELATING TO DEEMED DISPOSALS AND REACQUISITIONS

8.—(1) In determining for the purposes of this Act the market value of an interest in land immediately before a project of material development is begun,—

(*a*) it shall be assumed—

(i) that it is lawful for the project to be carried out, and

(ii) that planning permission would not be and has not been granted for any development of that land which constitutes material development, which is not comprised in the project and which has not been carried out or begun before the time at which the project is begun ; Sch. 1

(*b*) account shall be taken of any conditions imposed on any grant of planning permission for all or any of the development comprised in the project ; and

(*c*) to the extent that it would restrict the doing of anything comprised in the project, no account shall be taken of any other interest which is an incumbrance falling within sub-paragraph (2) below.

(2) The incumbrances referred to in sub-paragraph (1)(*c*) above are the following, so far as they subsist immediately before the project of material development is begun and affect any of the land comprised in the project, namely,—

(*a*) any easement ;

(*b*) any restrictive covenant ;

(*c*) any covenant or agreement restrictive of the use or development of land which, having been made between a lessor and a lessee, forms part of the terms and conditions of an interest in that land ;

(*d*) any land obligation within the meaning of section 1(2) of the Conveyancing and Feudal Reform (Scotland) Act 1970 ; and 1970 c. 35.

(*e*) any mining lease.

(3) In determining, for the purposes of a deemed disposal and reacquisition, the market value or the current use value of an interest in land which is held on a bare trust, it shall be assumed that the interest can be sold in the open market free from the interests of the beneficiaries (whether or not the interest which is held on the bare trust is in fact capable of being so sold, by virtue of a trust for sale, a statutory power or otherwise).

9.—(1) Without prejudice to paragraph 8 above, where there is a deemed disposal of a major interest in land, the chargeable person shall be treated as having assumed, as part of the disposal, a contingent liability in respect of the incumbrances which fall within paragraph 8(2) above.

(2) If at any time after the project of material development in question is begun, a person who is treated as having assumed a contingent liability under sub-paragraph (1) above incurs any expenditure in consideration of a disposal of an incumbrance which falls within paragraph 8(2) above, that expenditure shall be treated for the purposes of this Act as incurred by him in pursuance of that contingent liability.

10.—(1) The provisions of this paragraph apply where, by virtue of the beginning of a project of material development,—

(*a*) there is a deemed disposal of a major interest which is an interest falling within paragraph 8(2) above (in this paragraph referred to as " the incumbrance ") ; and

SCH. 1

(*b*) there is a deemed disposal of another major interest on which the chargeable person is treated, by virtue of paragraph 9(1) above, as having assumed a contingent liability in respect of the incumbrance.

(2) Where realised development value accrues to the holder of the incumbrance on the deemed disposal referred to in sub-paragraph (1)(*a*) above, liability for development land tax on that realised development value shall be deferred until the occasion of the first subsequent disposal of the incumbrance which is not a deemed disposal.

(3) In its application to a liability for development land tax which is deferred by virtue of this paragraph, section 27 of this Act shall have effect with the omission of subsections (4) to (6) and, in subsection (3), of the words " Subject to subsection (4) below ".

11. Without prejudice to paragraph 8 above, where—

(*a*) there is a deemed disposal of a major interest in land, and

(*b*) the land in which the interest subsists includes both the land comprised in the project of material development in question (in this paragraph referred to as " the project land ") and other land,

it shall be assumed for the purpose only of determining the market value of that interest immediately before the project is begun that that interest subsists only in the project land.

12. Where there is a deemed disposal and reacquisition of an interest in land, then, notwithstanding anything in section 2(1) of this Act, for the purpose of determining the current use value of that interest at the time of the deemed reacquisition, it shall be assumed that the reacquisition occurred immediately after the beginning of the project of material development which gave rise to the deemed disposal.

PART III

MAJOR INTERESTS: DURATION OF LEASES

13. This Part of this Schedule shall have effect in ascertaining whether, on the date on which a project of material development is begun, the unexpired term of a lease exceeds thirty-five years.

14.—(1) Where any of the terms of the lease (whether relating to forfeiture or to any other matter) or any other circumstances render it unlikely that the lease will continue beyond a date falling before the expiry of the term of the lease and any premium was not substantially greater than it would have been (on the assumptions required by paragraph 15 below) had the term been one expiring on that date, the lease shall not be treated as having been granted for a term longer than one ending on that date.

(2) Where the terms of the lease include provision for the extension of the lease beyond a given date by notice given by the tenant,

account may be taken of any circumstances making it likely that the lease will be so extended. SCH. 1

(3) Where the tenant, or a person connected with him, within the meaning of section 533 of the Income and Corporation Taxes Act 1970, is or may become entitled to a further lease or the grant of a further lease (whenever commencing) of the same premises or of premises including the whole or part of the same premises, the term of the lease may be treated as not expiring before the term of the further lease. 1970 c. 10.

15.—(1) Paragraph 14 above shall be applied by reference to the facts which are known or ascertainable at the time at which the project of material development is begun.

(2) In applying paragraph 14 above, it shall be assumed that all parties concerned, whatever their relationship, act as they would act if they were at arm's length.

(3) Where, by the lease or in connection with the granting of it,—

(*a*) benefits were conferred other than vacant possession and beneficial occupation of the premises or the right to receive rent at a reasonable commercial rate in respect of them, or

(*b*) payments were made which would not be expected to be made by parties acting at arm's length if no other benefits had been so conferred,

then, unless it is shown that the benefits were not conferred or the payments made for the purpose of securing a tax advantage in the application of Part III of the Income and Corporation Taxes Act 1970 (Schedule A and associated charges), it shall be further assumed, in applying paragraph 14 above, that the benefits would not have been conferred nor the payments made had the lease been for a term ending at the date mentioned in sub-paragraph (1) of that paragraph.

16. Where the Board have reason to believe that a person has information relevant to the ascertainment of the duration of a lease in accordance with this Part of this Schedule, the Board may by notice in writing require him to give, within a time specified in the notice, such information on the matters specified in the notice as is in his possession ; but a solicitor shall not be so required to do more, in relation to anything done by him on behalf of a client, than state that he is or was acting on behalf of a client and give the name and address of his client.

17.—(1) In this Part of this Schedule—

" premises " includes any land ;

" premium " shall be construed in accodance wih sub-paragraphs (5) and (6) below ; and

" term ", in relation to Scotland, where referring to the duration of a lease, means " period ".

SCH. 1

(2) For the purposes of this Part of this Schedule any sum (other than rent) paid on or in connection with the granting of a lease shall be presumed to have been paid by way of premium, except in so far as other sufficient consideration for the payment is shown to have been given.

(3) Where sub-paragraph (3) of paragraph 14 above applies, the premium or an appropriate part of the premium payable for or in connection with either lease mentioned in that sub-paragraph may be treated as having been required under the other.

(4) References in this paragraph to a sum shall be construed as including the value of any consideration, and references to a sum paid or payable or to the payment of a sum shall be construed accordingly.

(5) In this Part of this Schedule "premium" includes any like sum, whether payable to the immediate or a superior landlord or to a person connected, within the meaning of section 533 of the Income and Corporation Taxes Act 1970, with the immediate or a superior landlord.

1970 c. 10.

(6) In the application of this Part of this Schedule to Scotland "premium" includes in particular a grassum payable to any landlord or intermediate landlord on the creation of a sub-lease; and in this sub-paragraph "intermediate landlord" means, where an occupying lessee is a sub-lessee, any person for the time being holding the interest of landlord under a sub-lease which comprises the property of which the occupying lessee is sub-lessee, but does not include the immediate landlord.

Section 4.

SCHEDULE 2

REALISED DEVELOPMENT VALUE: SUPPLEMENTARY PROVISIONS

PART I

DISPOSALS OUT OF ASSEMBLED LAND

The assembly and its parts

1.—(1) Subject to sub-paragraph (2) and paragraph 2 below, this Part of this Schedule applies in any case where there is a disposal of an interest in land (in this Part of this Schedule referred to as "the relevant interest") and the chargeable person did not acquire the whole of the rights which make up the relevant interest in a single transaction but acquired at different times two or more different interests (whether those interests were different in nature or were in different pieces of land or both) which together make up the relevant interest.

(2) Except in so far as it may be necessary, in accordance with any provision of paragraph 11 or paragraph 12 below, to establish, on a subsequent disposal of the retained interest referred to in that paragraph,—

(*a*) the expenditure on improvements referable to that interest, or (*b*) the current use value of that interest as at the time of its acquisition or on 6th April 1965, whichever is the later,

this Part of this Schedule does not apply where the interest disposed of is the retained interest in relation to a previous part disposal of an interest in land.

(3) Any reference in this Part of this Schedule to a part of the relevant interest is a reference to an interest in land—

(*a*) which was acquired by the chargeable person at a particular time, or

(*b*) which is the retained interest in relation to a previous part disposal by him,

and which, taken together with one or more other interests falling within paragraph (*a*) or paragraph (*b*) above, makes up the relevant interest.

(4) If before the disposal of the relevant interest, the chargeable person acquired a lease which (at the time of its acquisition or otherwise) became merged in another part of the relevant interest, the lease shall continue to be regarded for the purposes of this Part of this Schedule as a part of the relevant interest until the date on which it would have expired if the merger had not occurred.

2.—(1) If and so far as a lease of any land is lawfully granted by a landlord who has a different interest in one part of the land as compared with another (as where he is the lessee under one lease of a part of the land and the lessee under a different lease of another part)—

(*a*) the interests by virtue of which the landlord grants the lease shall not be treated as a single interest in land to which paragraph 1 above applies ; and

(*b*) the grant of the lease shall be treated for the purposes of this Act as being carried out by separate disposals of the landlord's interest in each part of the land.

(2) For the purposes of the operation of sub-paragraph (1)(*b*) above, an apportionment shall be made under section 4(5) of this Act of the consideration for the grant of the lease and of any other matters necessary to secure that the grant is treated as resulting from separate part disposals of the different interests of the landlord.

Time and cost of acquisition

3.—(1) For the purposes of this Act, the time of acquisition of the relevant interest shall be treated, subject to paragraph 5 below, as the time at which the chargeable person last acquired a part of the relevant interest and the cost of his acquisition of the relevant interest shall be the aggregate of the costs of his acquisition of the several parts of the relevant interest.

(2) If the chargeable person acquired a part of the relevant interest in such circumstances that, if that part continued to exist as a separate entity, section 10 of this Act would apply in determining

SCH. 2

the realised development value accruing to the chargeable person on a disposal of it, then, for the purposes of sub-paragraph (1) above, the cost of the chargeable person's acquisition of that part (in this Part of the Schedule referred to as " the material interest ") shall be the amount which, if there were a separate disposal of the material interest, would be determined under paragraph (*a*) of subsection (2) of section 10 of this Act.

(3) Nothing in sub-paragraph (1) above shall affect the construction of any reference in the following provisions of this Part of this Schedule to the time of acquisition of any part of the relevant interest.

Expenditure on improvements

4.—(1) Notwithstanding anything in paragraph 3 above, for the purposes of determining the relevant base value of the relevant interest, the expenditure on improvements or, as the case may be, on relevant improvements shall be the aggregate of the amounts which, if there were a separate disposal of each part of the relevant interest, would be the amount of that expenditure in determining the relevant base value of each part.

(2) For the purpose of the determination referred to in sub-paragraph (1) above, the separate disposals shall be assumed to take place at the same time as the actual disposal of the relevant interest.

Determination of base A

5.—(1) Subject to sub-paragraphs (2) and (3) below, for the purpose of determining base A of the relevant interest,—

(*a*) a separate current use value, as at the time of its acquisition or on 6th April 1965, whichever is the later, shall be established for each part of the relevant interest; and

(*b*) the aggregate of the current use values of the several parts established in accordance with paragraph (*a*) above shall be treated as the current use value of the relevant interest at the time of its acquisition or on 6th April 1965, whichever is the later ; and

(*c*) if the chargeable person acquired any part of the relevant interest before 1st May 1977, section 6 of this Act shall apply, subject to paragraph (*d*) below, on the disposal of the relevant interest (whether or not the time of acquisition of that interest, as determined under paragraph 3 above, is before that date) ; and

(*d*) where section 6 of this Act applies on the disposal of the relevant interest, it shall be applied separately with respect to each part of that interest (taking account of the time of acquisition of each part) and, in determining base A of the relevant interest, the special addition provided for by that section shall be taken to be the aggregate of the special additions determined for the several parts of the relevant interest in accordance with this sub-paragraph.

(2) In a case where paragraph 3(2) above applies to determine the cost of acquisition of the material interest— Sch. 2

(*a*) the separate current use value of the material interest required to be established under sub-paragraph (1)(*a*) above, shall be taken to be the value which, if there were a separate disposal of the material interest, would be determined under paragraph (*c*) of subsection (2) of section 10 of this Act; and

(*b*) if section 6 of this Act falls to be applied as mentioned in sub-paragraph (1)(*d*) above, it shall not be applied with respect to the material interest; and

(*c*) if, on a separate disposal of the material interest, paragraph (*d*) of subsection (2) of section 10 of this Act would apply, the amount of the special addition referred to in that paragraph shall be treated for the purposes of sub-paragraph (1)(*d*) above as the special addition determined for the material interest in accordance with that provision.

(3) In any case where—

(*a*) section 6 of this Act falls to be applied as mentioned in sub-paragraph (1)(*d*) above, and

(*b*) the chargeable person acquired a part of the relevant interest in such circumstances that, if that part continued to exist as a separate entity, subsection (1) of section 5 of this Act would have effect subject to subsection (6) of that section in determining the relevant base value of that part on a separate disposal of it,

section 6 of this Act shall not be applied with respect to that part.

(4) For the purposes of sub-paragraphs (2) and (3) above, the separate disposal of the material interest or, as the case may be, the part in question shall be assumed to take place at the same time as the actual disposal of the relevant interest.

Determination of base C where section 5(6) applies to a part

6.—(1) For the purpose of determining base C of the relevant interest in a case where paragraph 5(3)(*b*) above applies in relation to a part thereof (in this paragraph referred to as " the material part ") there shall be determined the amount which would be base C of the material part on a separate disposal of that part taking place at the same time as the actual disposal of the relevant interest—

(*a*) on the basis that subsection (1) of section 5 of this Act has effect subject to subsection (6) of that section; and

(*b*) on the basis that subsection (6) of that section does not apply.

(2) From the amount which, apart from this paragraph, would be base C of the relevant interest there shall be deducted an amount equal to the difference between base C of the material

SCH. 2 part determined as mentioned in paragraph (*a*) of sub-paragraph (1) above and base C of that part determined as mentioned in paragraph (*b*) of that sub-paragraph.

Part acquired as stock in trade

7.—(1) The provisions of this paragraph apply if the chargeable person acquired a part of the relevant interest (in this paragraph referred to as " the stock in trade interest ") in such circumstances that, if the stock in trade interest continued to exist as a separate entity, section 16 of this Act would have effect in relation to any realised development value which accrued on a disposal of it.

(2) Where this paragraph applies, there shall be ascertained the amount which, for the purposes of section 16 of this Act, would be the realised development value attributable to the authorised development (within the meaning of that section) if—

(*a*) the stock in trade interest existed as a separate entity ; and

(*b*) in place of the disposal of the relevant interest there were a disposal at market value of the stock in trade interest ; and

(*c*) on that disposal the relevant base value of the stock in trade interest were derived from that one of the three bases specified in section 5(1) of this Act which in fact gives the relevant base value of the relevant interest.

(3) Subject to sub-paragraph (4) below, on the disposal of the relevant interest the chargeable person shall not be chargeable to development land tax on so much of the realised development value which accrues on that disposal as is equal to the amount ascertained under sub-paragraph (2) above.

(4) Where the disposal of the relevant interest is a deemed disposal and the amount ascertained under sub-paragraph (2) above exceeds the realised development value which accrues on the disposal,—

(*a*) the amount so ascertained shall be treated for the purposes of sub-paragraph (3) above as equal to the amount of that realised development value ; and

(*b*) the amount of the excess shall be carried forward to a subsequent disposal of the relevant interest in accordance with sub-paragraph (5) below.

(5) On the first disposal of the relevant interest occurring after the deemed disposal referred to in sub-paragraph (4) above, sub-paragraph (3) above shall have effect as if—

(*a*) this Part of this Schedule applied on that disposal ; and

(*b*) the condition in sub-paragraph (1) above applied ; and

(*c*) for the reference to the amount ascertained under sub-paragraph (2) above there were substituted a reference to the amount of the excess referred to in sub-paragraph (4)(*b*) above.

(6) In any case where—

(*a*) the disposal to which sub-paragraph (5) above applies is itself a deemed disposal, and (*b*) the amount of the excess referred to in paragraph (*c*) of that sub-paragraph exceeds the realised development value which accrues on that disposal, Sch. 2

then, in relation to a subsequent disposal of the relevant interest, sub-paragraph (5) above and, if it is a deemed disposal, this sub-paragraph shall apply in relation to the excess referred to in paragraph (*b*) above as if it were the excess referred to in sub-paragraph (4)(*b*) above, and so on, where there is a succession of deemed disposals, until the whole of the original excess referred to in sub-paragraph (4)(*b*) above is exhausted.

Charities : part acquired on or before 12th September 1974

8.—(1) The provisions of this paragraph apply if the chargeable person is a charity and acquired a part of the relevant interest (in this paragraph referred to as " the material interest ") in such circumstances that, if the material interest continued to exist as a separate entity, section 24(1) of this Act would have effect in relation to any realised development value which accrued on a disposal of it.

(2) Where this paragraph applies, there shall be ascertained the amount of realised development value which would accrue to the chargeable person if—

(*a*) the material interest existed as a separate entity ; and

(*b*) in place of the disposal of the relevant interest there were a disposal at market value of the material interest ; and

(*c*) on that disposal the relevant base value of the material interest were derived from that one of the three bases specified in section 5(1) of this Act which in fact gives the relevant base value of the relevant interest.

(3) Subject to sub-paragraph (4) below, on the disposal of the relevant interest the chargeable person shall not be chargeable to development land tax on so much of the realised development value which accrues on that disposal as is equal to the amount ascertained under sub-paragraph (2) above.

(4) Sub-paragraphs (4) to (6) of paragraph 7 above shall apply in relation to this paragraph as they apply in relation to that.

Part II

Part Disposals

9. The provisions of this Part of this Schedule shall have effect where there is a part disposal of an interest in land (in this Part of this Schedule referred to as " the relevant interest ") ; and in the following provisions of this Part of this Schedule—

(*a*) any reference to the disposal is a reference to the part disposal of the relevant interest ; and

(*b*) any reference to relevant base value is a reference to that value of the relevant interest for the purposes of the disposal ; and

SCH. 2

(*c*) any reference to the base values is a reference to base A, base B and base C of the relevant interest for the purposes of the disposal (regardless of which of those bases gives the relevant base value) ; and

(*d*) any reference to chargeable realised development value is a reference to the chargeable realised development value which accrues on the disposal.

10.—(1) Subject to paragraph 11 below, for the purpose of determining the base values and the amount of chargeable realised development value, the amounts which, apart from this sub-paragraph, would be—

(*a*) the cost of the chargeable person's acquisition of the relevant interest (in this paragraph referred to as " A "), and

(*b*) the expenditure on relevant improvements or, in relation to base C, on improvements (in this paragraph referred to as " RI " and " I " respectively), and

(*c*) where section 6 of this Act applies on the disposal, the amount of the special addition (in this paragraph referred to as " S ") provided for by subsection (2) of that section, and

(*d*) the realised development value (if any) on which, by virtue of any exempting provision, the chargeable person is not chargeable to development land tax (in this paragraph referred to as " E "),

shall each be reduced by applying to them the fraction—

$$\frac{PD}{PD + MR}$$

where—

PD is, subject to sub-paragraph (2) below, the net proceeds of the disposal ; and

MR is the market value of the retained interest immediately after the disposal.

(2) Where the disposal is a disposal—

(*a*) otherwise than for value, or

(*b*) for a consideration less than that which might reasonably have been obtained in the open market,

the net proceeds of the disposal shall be determined for the purposes of sub-paragraph (1) above as if the consideration for the disposal were the consideration that might reasonably have been obtained in the open market.

(3) Where sub-paragraph (1) above applies on the disposal, then, for the purposes of this Act,—

(*a*) so much of A as remains after deducting the amount which, by virtue of that sub-paragraph, was the cost of the chargeable person's acquisition of the relevant interest shall be taken to be the cost of acquisition of the retained interest ; and (*b*) the time of acquisition of the retained interest shall be taken, subject to sub-paragraph (5) below, to be the time of acquisition of the relevant interest, but if section 6 of this Act did not apply on the disposal of the relevant interest it shall not apply on a subsequent disposal of the retained interest; and

(*c*) on a subsequent disposal of the retained interest, development land tax shall not be chargeable on an amount of realised development value equal to the difference between E and the amount on which, by virtue of sub-paragraph (1) above and any exempting provision, the chargeable person was not chargeable to development land tax on the disposal.

(4) If, having regard to sub-paragraph (3)(*b*) above, section 6 of this Act applies in relation to a subsequent disposal of the retained interest, then, for the purposes of this Act,—

(*a*) in the application of that section, D referred to in subsection (2) of that section shall be treated as reduced by the number of years (ascertained in accordance with subsection (3) of that section) in the period beginning at the time of the acquisition of the relevant interest and ending at the time of the disposal; and

(*b*) to the amount (if any) of the special addition determined in accordance with paragraph (*a*) above in relation to the subsequent disposal of the retained interest there shall be added so much of S as remains after deducting the amount which, by virtue of sub-paragraph (1) above, was the amount, for the purpose specified in that sub-paragraph, of the special addition so provided for.

(5) Subject to sub-paragraphs (6) and (7) below, where sub-paragraph (1) above applies on the disposal, then, for the purposes of determining the amount of any expenditure on improvements or, as the case may be, on relevant improvements in relation to a subsequent disposal of the retained interest, the time of acquisition of that interest shall be taken to be the time of the disposal of the relevant interest.

(6) To the amount which, by virtue of sub-paragraph (5) above, is the amount of expenditure on improvements in relation to a subsequent disposal of the retained interest there shall be added a sum equal to so much of I as remains after deducting the amount which, by virtue of sub-paragraph (1) above, was the expenditure on improvements for the purpose specified in that sub-paragraph.

(7) To the amount which, by virtue of sub-paragraph (5) above, is the amount of expenditure on relevant improvements in relation to a subsequent disposal of the retained interest there shall be added a sum equal to so much of RI as remains after deducting the amount which, by virtue of sub-paragraph (1) above, was the expenditure on relevant improvements for the purpose specified in that sub-paragraph.

(8) In this paragraph "exempting provision" means paragraph 7 or paragraph 8 above or sub-paragraph (3)(*c*) above.

SCH. 2

11.—(1) In any case where—

(*a*) the disposal of the relevant interest falls within section 3(1)(*b*) of this Act, and

(*b*) the relevant interest is an interest to which paragraph 1 above applies, and

(*c*) the granted interest is part of the relevant interest for the purposes of the application of Part I above to the disposal or is the aggregate of two or more such parts,

paragraph 10 above shall have effect with the omission of paragraphs (*a*) and (*c*) of sub-paragraph (1), paragraphs (*a*) and (*b*) of sub-paragraph (3) and sub-paragraph (4).

(2) Subject to paragraph 10(5) above, where sub-paragraph (1) above applies,—

(*a*) the cost and time of acquisition of the relevant interest shall be taken to be the cost and time of acquisition of the granted interest ; and

(*b*) if section 6 of this Act applies on the disposal, the amount of the special addition shall be determined by reference to the cost and time of acquisition of the granted interest.

(3) If, in a case where sub-paragraph (1) above applies, the granted interest consists of more than one such part as is referred to in paragraph (*c*) of that sub-paragraph, Part I above shall have effect for the purpose of determining—

(*a*) the cost and time referred to in sub-paragraph (2)(*a*) above, and

(*b*) where appropriate, the special addition referred to in sub-paragraph (2)(*b*) above,

as if the granted interest were " the relevant interest " within the meaning of that Part.

(4) If, in a case where sub-paragraph (1) above applies, the retained interest consists of more than one such part of the relevant interest as is referred to in paragraph (*c*) of that sub-paragraph, Part I above shall have effect for the purpose of determining, in relation to a subsequent disposal of the retained interest,—

(*a*) the cost and time of acquisition of that interest, and

(*b*) the special addition (if any) applicable under section 6 of this Act,

as if the retained interest were " the relevant interest ", within the meaning of that Part, and not a retained interest.

(5) If in a case where the disposal falls within section 3(1)(*b*) of this Act, the expenditure on improvements referable to the land in which the granted interest subsists is, without reference to sub-paragraphs (1)(*b*) and (5) to (7) of paragraph 10 above, identifiable separately from the expenditure on improvements referable to the rest of the land in which the relevant interest subsists immediately

before the disposal, those sub-paragraphs shall not have effect in relation to the disposal and, for the purposes of this Act,— Sch. 2

(a) the expenditure referable to the land in which the granted interest subsists shall be treated as the expenditure on improvements to be taken into account in determining the relevant base value referred to in paragraph 9(b) above; and

(b) the expenditure on improvements referable to the retained interest shall be separately determined on a subsequent disposal of that interest.

12.—(1) Subject to sub-paragraph (4) below, for the purpose of determining the relevant base value, the amount (in this paragraph referred to as "CW") which, apart from this paragraph, would be the current use value of the relevant interest at the time of the disposal shall be reduced by deducting therefrom an amount (in this paragraph referred to as "CR") equal to the current use value immediately after that time of the retained interest.

(2) Subject to sub-paragraph (5) below, for the purpose of determining base A of the relevant interest the amount which, apart from this paragraph, would be the current use value of the relevant interest at the time of its acquisition by the chargeable person or on 6th April 1965, whichever is the later, shall be reduced by applying to it the fraction $\frac{CW-CR}{CW}$.

(3) Where sub-paragraph (2) above applies on the disposal, then, in relation to a subsequent disposal of the retained interest, so much of the amount referred to in that sub-paragraph as remains after deducting from it the fraction thereof referred to in that sub-paragraph shall be deemed for the purposes of this Act to be the current use value of the retained interest at the time of its acquisition by the chargeable person or on 6th April 1965, whichever is the later.

(4) If the current use value, as at the time of the disposal, of the granted interest is identifiable without reference to sub-paragraph (1) above, that sub-paragraph shall not apply and, for the purposes of the disposal, that current use value shall be treated as the current use value of the relevant interest at that time.

(5) In a case where sub-paragraph (1) of paragraph 11 above applies sub-paragraphs (2) and (3) above shall not apply and—

(a) for the purpose of the disposal the current use value of the relevant interest as at the time of its acquisition or on 6th April 1965, whichever is the later, shall be taken to be the current use value of the granted interest as at the time of its acquisition or on 6th April 1965, whichever is the later; and

(b) if sub-paragraph (3) of paragraph 11 above applies for the purpose of determining the cost and time of acquisition of the granted interest, Part I above shall have effect as

SCH. 2

mentioned in that sub-paragraph for the purpose of determining the current use value referred to in paragraph (*a*) above ; and

(*c*) on a subsequent disposal of the retained interest, a separate current use value shall be established for that interest as at the time of its acquisition or on 6th April 1965, whichever is the later ; and

(*d*) if sub-paragraph (4) of paragraph 11 above applies for the purposes of determining the cost and time of acquisition of the retained interest (in relation to a subsequent disposal of that interest) Part I above shall have effect as mentioned in that sub-paragraph for the purpose of determining the current use value referred to in paragraph (*c*) above.

PART III

ADDITIONAL PROVISIONS APPLICABLE TO LEASES AND REVERSIONS ON LEASES

13.—(1) In determining the realised development value accruing to the chargeable person on the part disposal of an interest in land which consists of the grant of a lease out of that interest, from the amounts which, apart from this sub-paragraph, would be the market value and the current use value of the retained interest there shall be deducted an amount equal to the value immediately after the grant of the landlord's rights under the lease.

(2) Any reference in this Part of this Schedule to the value at any time of the landlord's rights under a lease is a reference to the value at that time of the rights of the landlord under the lease exclusive of the right to recover possession at the expiry of the term.

14.—(1) The provisions of this paragraph shall have effect where there is a part disposal of a lease and, where that part disposal consists of the grant of another lease out of that lease, shall have effect in addition to paragraph 13(1) above.

(2) To the amounts which, apart from this sub-paragraph, would be the market value and the current use value of the retained interest, there shall be added a sum equal to the value of the landlord's rights under the lease immediately after the part disposal.

(3) In determining the current use value of the lease at the time of the part disposal or of its acquisition or on 6th April 1965, no account shall be taken of any liability of the tenant under the lease other than the obligation to deliver up possession on the expiry of the term.

(4) If, at the time of the part disposal, the unexpired term of the lease does not exceed 50 years,—

(*a*) base C shall not be available as the relevant base value of the lease, and

(*b*) paragraph (*a*) of section 5(1) of this Act shall have effect as if, from the aggregate of the items specified in that paragraph, there were required to be deducted the amount (if any) by which the current use value of the lease at the time of its acquisition or on 6th April 1965, whichever is the later, exceeds the current use value of the lease at the time of the part disposal.

15.—(1) Subject to sub-paragraphs (2) and (3) below, for the purposes of this Act, in the case of the disposal of an interest in land which, immediately before the disposal, consists of the reversion on a lease, an amount equal to the value immediately before the disposal of the landlord's rights under the lease shall be deducted—

(*a*) from the amount which, apart from this paragraph, would be the net proceeds of the disposal; and

(*b*) from the amount which, apart from this paragraph, would be the current use value of that interest at the time of the disposal; and

(*c*) from the amount which apart from this paragraph would, in relation to the person acquiring that interest, be his cost of acquisition on the occasion of the disposal.

(2) In the application of sub-paragraph (1) above to a part disposal which falls within section 3(1)(*b*) of this Act—

(*a*) paragraph (*c*) of that sub-paragraph shall have effect with the substitution of a reference to the cost of acquisition of the granted interest for the reference to the cost of acquisition of the interest disposed of; and

(*b*) the deduction from the amounts referred to in paragraphs (*a*) and (*c*) of that sub-paragraph shall be limited to so much of the value of the landlord's rights under the lease as, immediately after the part disposal, is attributable to the granted interest.

(3) In the application of sub-paragraph (1) above to a part disposal falling within section 3(2) of this Act, paragraphs (*a*) and (*c*) of that sub-paragraph shall be omitted.

(4) Where there is a part disposal of a reversion on a lease, from the amounts which, apart from this sub-paragraph, would be the market value and the current use value of the retained interest there shall be deducted an amount equal to the value of the landlord's rights under the lease immediately after the part disposal, so far as those rights are attributable to the retained interest.

(5) If, in the case of such a disposal as is referred to in sub-paragraph (1) above, the interest disposed of was also a reversion on a lease at the time of its acquisition or on 6th April 1965, whichever is the later, then, for the purpose of determining base A of that interest on the disposal, an amount equal to what was then the value of the landlord's rights under the lease shall be deducted from the amount which, apart from this paragraph, would then be the current use value of that interest.

16.—(1) References in this paragraph to a disposal of a lease do not include references to a part disposal thereof but, subject to that, this paragraph shall have effect in determining—

(*a*) the realised development value accruing to the chargeable person on the disposal of a lease, and

SCH. 2

(*b*) in relation to the person acquiring the lease, his cost of acquisition on the occasion of the disposal,

and, where that lease is itself the reversion on another lease, shall have effect in addition to paragraph 15 above.

(2) To the amounts which, apart from this sub-paragraph, would be—

(*a*) the net proceeds of the disposal of a lease, and

(*b*) in relation to the person acquiring the lease, his cost of acquisition on the occasion of the disposal,

there shall be added a sum equal to the value immediately before the disposal of the landlord's rights under the lease.

(3) In determining the current use value of a lease at the time of its disposal or of its acquisition or on 6th April 1965, no account shall be taken of any liability of the tenant under the lease, other than the obligation to deliver up possession at the expiry of the term.

(4) Where, at the time of the disposal, the unexpired term of the lease does not exceed 50 years, paragraphs (*a*) and (*b*) of sub-paragraph (4) of paragraph 14 above shall apply as they apply where there is a part disposal of a lease to which that sub-paragraph applies.

17.—(1) The provisions of this paragraph apply where there is a material variation, for the purpose of subsection (4) of section 44 of this Act, of the terms and conditions of a lease ; and in this paragraph—

"the disposal of the original lease" means the surrender of the lease which, by virtue of paragraph (*a*) of that subsection is assumed to occur ;

"the grant of the new lease" means the part disposal of the landlord's interest which, by virtue of paragraph (*b*) of that subsection is assumed to occur ; and

"the cost of acquisition of the new lease" means the amount which, for the purpose of determining the realised development value accruing on an assignment by the tenant referred to in that subsection of the new lease referred to in paragraph (*b*) thereof, would be the cost of his acquisition.

(2) If, apart from this sub-paragraph, realised development value would accrue to the chargeable person on the disposal of the original lease, then, for the purposes of this Act, other than this sub-paragraph,—

(*a*) if the amount which, apart from this paragraph, would be the cost of acquisition of the new lease equals or exceeds the amount of that realised development value, the cost of acquisition of the new lease shall be treated as reduced or, as the case may be, as extinguished by deducting therefrom the amount of that realised development value and, accordingly, no realised development value shall be taken to accrue on the disposal of the original lease ; and

(*b*) if the amount of that realised development value exceeds the amount which, apart from this paragraph, would be the cost of acquisition of the new lease, only the excess shall be treated as realised development value accruing on the disposal of the original lease and the cost of acquisition of the new lease shall be treated, except for the purposes of section 10 of this Act, as nil.

(3) Any consideration given by the tenant for the variation referred to in sub-paragraph (1) above shall be treated for the purposes of this Act as referable to the grant of the new lease and not to the disposal of the original lease and any consideration given by the landlord for that variation shall be treated for the purposes of this Act as referable to his acquisition on the disposal of the original lease.

(4) Subject to sub-paragraph (5) below if, on the disposal of the original lease, the amount which is base A of the interest disposed of exceeds the net proceeds of the disposal, then, to the amount which, apart from this sub-paragraph, would be the cost of acquisition of the new lease there shall be added an amount equal to that excess.

(5) In any case where, for the purpose of determining base A on the disposal of an interest in land, subsection (2) of section 6 of this Act applies to determine the amount of a special addition by reference to the whole or any part of the cost of acquisition of the new lease, sub-paragraph (4) above shall not have effect in relation to that cost for the purposes of that determination.

PART IV
PROJECTS OF MATERIAL DEVELOPMENT

18.—(1) Where paragraph 11 of Schedule 1 to this Act applies in determining the market value of an interest in land immediately before a project of material development is begun, then, for the purpose of determining the relevant base value of that interest on the deemed disposal thereof which occurs at that time, it shall be assumed that that interest subsists only in the project land (within the meaning of that paragraph) and all necessary apportionments shall be made under section 4(5) of this Act of—

(*a*) the cost of the chargeable person's acquisition of that interest,

(*b*) the amount of any expenditure on improvements or on relevant improvements,

(*c*) the current use value of that interest at the time of its acquisition or on 6th April 1965 and at the time of the disposal, and

(*d*) where any provision of Part III of this Schedule applies, the value which, for the purposes of that Part, is the value at any time of the landlord's rights under the lease concerned.

(2) In a case where sub-paragraph (1) above applies there shall also be determined the amount which, if that sub-paragraph did not apply, would be base A of the interest concerned on the deemed disposal referred to in that sub-paragraph, and to the amount which, apart from this sub-paragraph, would be the market value of that interest for the purposes of the immediately following deemed reacquisition there shall be added an amount equal to that by which base A of that interest determined in accordance with this

SCH. 2 sub-paragraph exceeds base A of that interest determined on the assumption and in accordance with the apportionments provided for by sub-paragraph (1) above.

19. In any case where, on the deemed disposal of an interest in land, the amount which is base A of that interest exceeds the net proceeds of that disposal, to the amount which, apart from this paragraph, would be the market value of that interest for the purposes of the immediately following deemed reacquisition there shall be added an amount equal to that excess.

PART V

CONSIDERATION

Preliminary

20. This Part of this Schedule shall have effect with respect to the determination of the consideration both for the disposal and for the acquisition of an interest in land; and, except where the context otherwise requires, any reference in the following provisions of this Part of this Schedule to the consideration for the disposal of an interest in land shall be construed, in relation to the person to whom the disposal is made, as a reference to the consideration given for the acquisition.

General rules

21.—(1) Subject to the following provisions of this Part of this Schedule, for the purposes of this Act, the consideration for a disposal shall be brought into account—

(*a*) without any discount for postponement of the right to receive any part of it, and

(*b*) in the first instance, without regard to a risk of any part of the consideration being irrecoverable.

(2) If any part of the consideration brought into account in accordance with sub-paragraph (1) above is subsequently shown to the satisfaction of the Board to be irrecoverable, such adjustment, whether by way of discharge or repayment of tax or otherwise, shall be made as is required in consequence.

(3) Where the relief obtainable under sub-paragraph (2) above requires a discharge or repayment of tax, it shall be given on a claim to the Board and such a claim may be made at any time.

22.—(1) In determining for the purposes of this Act the consideration for the disposal of an interest in land, no account shall be taken, in the first instance, of any contingent liability assumed by the chargeable person, by the person acquiring the interest or by any other person.

(2) If it is subsequently shown to the satisfaction of the Board that a contingent liability which was not taken into account in determining the consideration for a disposal has become enforceable and is being or has been enforced, such adjustment, whether by way of a further assessment or the discharge or repayment of tax or otherwise, shall be made as is required in consequence.

(3) Where the relief obtainable under sub-paragraph (2) above requires a discharge or repayment of tax, it shall be given on a claim to the Board and such a claim may be made at any time. SCH. 2

23.—(1) From the amount which, apart from this paragraph, would be the consideration for the disposal of an interest in land there shall be deducted an amount equal to any tax which is chargeable on that disposal under the law of a country outside the United Kingdom and which is borne by the chargeable person.

(2) Notwithstanding anything in paragraph 20 above, the deduction in sub-paragraph (1) above shall not apply in determining the amount of the consideration for the acquisition of the interest disposed of.

24.—(1) For the purposes of this Act, other than this paragraph, where—

(*a*) an interest in land is disposed of subject to a mortgage or charge, and

(*b*) the consideration for the disposal is less than it would be if the mortgage or charge were not continuing after the disposal, and

(*c*) by virtue of section 7(5) of this Act the mortgage or charge is not taken into account in determining the current use value of that interest at the time of the disposal,

to the amount which, apart from this paragraph, would be the consideration for the disposal there shall be added an amount equal to the principal which, at the time of the disposal, is outstanding under the mortgage or charge.

(2) In this paragraph " mortgage or charge " means an interest falling within paragraph (*a*) or paragraph (*b*) of subsection (2) of section 46 of this Act.

25. Notwithstanding that, by virtue of his ownership of any such interest as falls within any of paragraphs (*a*) to (*c*) of subsection (2) of section 46 of this Act, a person becomes entitled to an interest in land, no part of any consideration given for the first-mentioned interest shall be treated for the purposes of this Act as consideration given as mentioned in section 5(2) of this Act for the acquisition of the interest in land.

Rents and other income payments

26. For the purposes of this Act, in the case of a disposal consisting of the grant of a lease, the consideration for the disposal shall be taken to be the aggregate of the market values at the time of the disposal of—

(*a*) the right to receive the rent (if any) which, in accordance with the terms of the grant, is payable in respect of the lease ; and

(*b*) any other consideration which in accordance with those terms is given or agreed to be given for the grant of the lease, whether to the grantor or to any other person.

SCH. 2 27. In calculating for the purposes of this Act the market value at any time of a right to receive rent payable in respect of a lease and the market value of any such consideration as is referred to in paragraph 26(*b*) above,—

(*a*) paragraph 21(1)(*a*) above shall not apply ; and

(*b*) it shall be assumed that the lessee under the lease will always pay the rent when it falls due and will perform his other obligations under the lease.

28. Without prejudice to paragraphs 26 and 27 above, if the whole or any part of the consideration for the disposal of an interest in land consists of a rent-charge, ground annual or any other series of payments in the nature of income, then, for the purposes of this Act, that consideration or part thereof shall be taken to be the market value at the time of the disposal of the right to receive that rent-charge, ground annual or other series of payments ; and for this purpose paragraph 21(1)(*a*) above shall not apply.

Compulsory acquisition : deduction for disturbance element

29.—(1) In the case of a disposal of an interest in land to an authority possessing compulsory powers, the amount which, apart from this paragraph, would be the consideration for the disposal shall be treated for the purposes of this Act as reduced by the amount which, in accordance with this paragraph, is determined to be the disturbance element.

(2) In the case of a disposal falling within sub-paragraph (1) above, there shall be determined the amount of compensation which would have been payable by the authority concerned in respect of the acquisition of the interest acquired on the disposal if—

(*a*) no planning permission for the carrying out of any material development of the land in question were in force at the time of the disposal, and

(*b*) it were to be assumed that no such planning permission would be granted,

and the disturbance element referred to in sub-paragraph (1) above is so much of that compensation as would have been attributable to disturbance.

(3) If the disposal referred to in sub-paragraph (1) above is a disposal in pursuance of an agreement and not in pursuance of a notice to treat, sub-paragraph (2) above shall have effect as if the acquisition referred to in that sub-paragraph were in pursuance of a notice to treat served at the time of the agreement.

(4) In the application of this paragraph to Northern Ireland, sub-paragraph (3) above shall have effect as if—

(*a*) for the words " notice to treat ", in each place where they occur, there were substituted the words " vesting order " ; and

(*b*) for the word " served " there were substituted the word " made ".

Insurance money

SCH. 2

30. If, in the case of a disposal of an interest in land which is a part disposal falling within subsection (2) of section 3 of this Act,—

(*a*) the sum which is derived as mentioned in that subsection is a sum—

(i) received under a policy of insurance of the risk of any kind of damage to, or the loss of, a building, or

(ii) obtained under the Criminal Injuries to Property (Compensation) Act (Northern Ireland) 1971, or under any enactment repealed by that Act, as compensation in respect of damage to, or the loss of, a building, or 1971 c. 38 (N.I.).

(iii) obtained under any enactment or the common law as compensation in respect of damage to or the loss of land or building as a result of a riot or an unlawful assembly, and

(*b*) that sum exceeds the amount which, for the purpose of determining the relevant base value of the interest disposed of, is by virtue of paragraph 12(1) above the current use value of that interest.

then, for the purposes of this Act, the consideration for the part disposal shall be taken to be reduced to a sum equal to the amount of the current use value referred to in paragraph (*b*) above.

Distribution in kind

31. Where there is a disposal of an interest in land by way of distribution from a company in respect of shares in the company, the consideration for the disposal shall be taken for the purposes of this Act to be an amount equal to the consideration which, at the time of that disposal, that interest might reasonably have been expected to fetch on a sale in the open market.

PART VI
INCIDENTAL COSTS

32.—(1) For the purposes of this Act, the incidental costs to a chargeable person of the acquisition of an interest in land or of its disposal shall consist of expenditure falling within sub-paragraph (2) below and wholly and exclusively incurred by him for the purposes of the acquisition or, as the case may be, the disposal.

(2) The expenditure referred to in sub-paragraph (1) above is expenditure on fees, commission or remuneration paid for the professional services of any legal adviser, surveyor, valuer, auctioneer, accountant or agent, and any other costs of conveyance or transfer (including stamp duty) together—

(*a*) in the case of the acquisition of an interest in land, with costs of advertising to find a seller, and

(*b*) in the case of the disposal of an interest in land, with costs of advertising to find a buyer and costs reasonably incurred in making any valuation or apportionment required for the purposes of determining the realised development value accruing to the chargeable person on the disposal, including in particular expenses reasonably incurred in ascertaining market value where required for the purposes of that determination.

Section 5.

SCHEDULE 3

PART I

IMPROVEMENTS

1.—(1) For the purposes of this Act, in relation to a disposal by any person of an interest in land (in this Part of this Schedule referred to as " the relevant interest "), expenditure on improvements means, subject to the following provisions of this Part of this Schedule, any expenditure incurred by that person or on his behalf—

(*a*) in enhancing the value of the relevant interest, being expenditure reflected in the state of the land in which that interest subsists or the market value of that interest at the time of the disposal ; or

(*b*) in establishing, preserving or defending his title to that interest or his enjoyment of the land by virtue of that interest.

(2) Notwithstanding anything in sub-paragraph (1) above, expenditure incurred in, or in respect of, the carrying out of any work of maintenance, repair or decoration or any similar work of a recurrent nature is not expenditure on improvements.

(3) Where any expenditure incurred as mentioned in sub-paragraph (1) above did not relate exclusively to the land in which the relevant interest subsists, only that proportion of that expenditure which inured for the benefit of that land shall be treated as expenditure on improvements.

(4) Notwithstanding anything in sub-paragraph (1) above, if—

(*a*) there is a deemed disposal and reacquisition of an interest in land, and

(*b*) the time of acquisition—

(i) of the relevant interest, or

(ii) of an interest which, on the disposal of the relevant interest, is a part of the relevant interest for the purposes of Part I of Schedule 2 to this Act,

is the time of that reacquisition,

expenditure which, on the deemed disposal referred to in paragraph (*a*) above or on an earlier deemed disposal of an interest in land, was reflected in the relevant base value of the interest disposed of is not expenditure on improvements in relation to the disposal of the relevant interest.

2. For the purposes of this Act, in relation to the disposal of the relevant interest, expenditure on relevant improvements is that part of the expenditure on improvements which remains after deducting therefrom a sum equal to the amount by which, at the time of the disposal, the current use value of the relevant interest has increased as a result of the expenditure on improvements.

3.—(1) Subject to paragraph 5 below, this paragraph applies where, after the time of acquisition of the relevant interest or of an interest which is a part of the relevant interest for the purposes of

Part I of Schedule 2 to this Act, planning permission for the development of the land in which that interest subsists or subsisted has been granted subject to a condition regulating the development or use of other land in which, at the time of the grant, the chargeable person held an interest (in this paragraph referred to as " the affected interest"). SCH. 3

(2) In this paragraph " the material time " means whichever is the earlier of—

(*a*) the time of the disposal of the relevant interest ; and

(*b*) the earliest time after the grant of the planning permission concerned at which there is a disposal, other than a deemed disposal, of the affected interest or of an interest of which the affected interest is a part for the purposes of Part I of Schedule 2 to this Act.

(3) Where this paragraph applies—

(*a*) there shall be ascertained the amount that would have been the current use value of the affected interest at the material time if the condition referred to in sub-paragraph (1) above had not been imposed ; and

(*b*) on the disposal of the relevant interest the amount (if any) by which the current use value determined under paragraph (*a*) above exceeds or exceeded the actual current use value of the affected interest at the material time shall be treated for the purposes of this Act as expenditure incurred as mentioned in paragraph 1(1) above.

(4) In any case where the material time is the time of a part disposal of the affected interest any reference in sub-paragraph (3) above to a current use value of the affected interest at that time is a reference to what that current use value would have been had the disposal been an outright disposal of the affected interest.

4.—(1) Where paragraph 3 above applies, the amount which, apart from this paragraph, would be taken as the cost of acquisition of the affected interest on a disposal of that interest (or of an interest of which it is a part for the purposes of Part I of Schedule 2 to this Act) shall be reduced for the purposes of this Act by whichever is the smaller of the following amounts, namely,—

(*a*) the amount which, by virtue of paragraph 3(3)(*b*) above, was or will be treated as mentioned in that paragraph on the disposal of the relevant interest ; and

(*b*) the amount (if any) by which the current use value of the affected interest at the time of its acquisition or on 6 April 1965, whichever is the later, exceeds the current use value of that interest at the time of the disposal.

(2) In this paragraph " the affected interest " has the same meaning as in paragraph 3 above.

5.—(1) If, in a case where paragraph 3 above applies, the condition referred to in sub-paragraph (1) of that paragraph is varied at any time before the expiry of the period of six years beginning at

SCH. 3 the time of the disposal of the relevant interest, that paragraph shall be taken always to have applied with the condition in the form in which it is as varied.

(2) If, in a case where paragraph 3 above applies, the condition referred to in sub-paragraph (1) of that paragraph is removed at any such time as is mentioned in sub-paragraph (1) above, paragraph 3 above shall be taken never to have applied in the case in question.

(3) All such adjustments with respect to liability to development land tax shall be made as may be necessary in consequence of the provisions of sub-paragraphs (1) and (2) above.

6.—(1) Where, after the time of acquisition of the relevant interest or of an interest which is a part of the relevant interest for the purposes of Part I of Schedule 2 to this Act,—

(*a*) planning permission was granted for the development of any of the land in which that interest subsists or subsisted, and

(*b*) as part of an arrangement relating to the grant of that permission, the chargeable person enters into an agreement falling within sub-paragraph (2) below which contains a condition restricting or otherwise regulating the development or use of other land in which, at the time of the making of the agreement, the chargeable person held an interest,

paragraphs 3 to 5 above shall apply as if the condition referred to in paragraph (*b*) above were a condition subject to which the planning permission referred to in paragraph (*a*) above was granted and, accordingly, as if the interest referred to in paragraph (*b*) above were the affected interest, as defined in paragraph 3 above.

(2) An agreement is one to which sub-paragraph (1) above applies if—

(*a*) a public body is a party to it, and

(*b*) it does not result in the receipt of any such sum as is referred to in section 3(2) of this Act and does not otherwise form part of the consideration for the disposal of an interest in land, and

(*c*) it is enforceable, by or under any enactment, by the public body referred to in paragraph (*a*) above against persons deriving title under the chargeable person in respect of the land to which the agreement relates.

(3) In this paragraph " public body " means—

(*a*) a body specified in any of paragraphs (*a*) to (*d*) of subsection (1) of section 11 of this Act ; or

(*b*) a Minister of the Crown or government department, including a department of the Government of Northern Ireland ; or

(*c*) a statutory undertaker, within the meaning of section 23 of this Act.

7.—(1) Sub-paragraph (2) below shall apply if, in the case of the acquisition of an interest in land (in this paragraph referred to as "the acquired interest") by an authority possessing compulsory powers,— SCH. 3

(a) a deduction falls to be made in calculating the compensation or purchase price on account of betterment of an interest in other land (in this paragraph referred to as "the bettered interest"); and

(b) a sum equal to 110 per cent. of the current use value of the acquired interest exceeds the amount of the compensation or purchase price.

(2) Where this sub-paragraph applies, an amount equal to the excess referred to in sub-paragraph (1)(b) above shall be treated for the purposes of this Act as expenditure on improvements which—

(a) is incurred immediately after the acquisition of the acquired interest; and

(b) relates exclusively to the bettered interest; and

(c) consists of expenditure on relevant improvements.

(3) In sub-paragraph (1)(a) above "betterment" means any increase in the value of an interest in other land which,—

(a) for the purpose of assessing compensation in respect of a compulsory acquisition falls to be taken into account by virtue of—

(i) section 7 of the Land Compensation Act 1961 or section 14 of the Land Compensation (Scotland) Act 1963 (effect of certain actual or prospective development of adjacent land in same ownership), or 1961 c. 33. 1963 c. 51.

(ii) any such local enactment as is mentioned in subsection (5) or any such enactment as is specified in subsection (7) of section 8 of the said Act of 1961 or, as the case may require, of section 15 of the said Act of 1963 (special cases where the enactments in paragraph (i) above do not apply), or

(iii) any enactment which, in relation to land in Northern Ireland, provides (in whatever terms) that, in assessing compensation in respect of compulsory acquisition thereunder, account shall be taken of any increase in the value of an interest in contiguous or adjacent land; or

(b) in the case of a sale which is not a compulsory acquisition, is an increase which would have fallen to be so taken into account if the sale had been a compulsory acquisition.

(4) For the purpose of sub-paragraph (1)(b) above, the current use value of the acquired interest means the amount which, for the purpose of determining the relevant base value of the interest disposed of, was taken as its current use value for the purpose of the disposal by which the authority acquired the acquired interest.

SCH. 3

PART II

FURTHER ADDITION TO BASE A

8.—(1) In determining base A of an interest in land in a case where subsection (5) of section 5 of this Act applies, the further amount referred to in that subsection is that given by the formula—

$$RI \times \frac{A}{C}$$

where " RI ", " A ", and " C " have the meanings assigned to them by sub-paragraph (2) below.

(2) The constituents of the formula in sub-paragraph (1) above are derived from the several amounts which, in accordance with paragraph (*a*) of subsection (1) of section 5 of this Act, are included in the aggregate referred to in that paragraph, so that—

" C " is the amount so included by virtue of sub-paragraph (i) of that paragraph;

" RI " is the amount so included by virtue of sub-paragraph (ii) of that paragraph; and

" A " is the amount so included by virtue of sub-paragraph (iv) of that paragraph.

Section 7.

SCHEDULE 4

CURRENT USE VALUE AND MATERIAL DEVELOPMENT

PART I

LIMITATIONS ON ASSUMPTIONS AS TO PLANNING PERMISSION IN DETERMINING CURRENT USE VALUE

1. The provisions of this Part of this Schedule shall have effect notwithstanding anything in paragraph (*a*) of subsection (2) of section 7 of this Act (in this Schedule referred to as " the relevant planning provision ") and in this Part of this Schedule—

(*a*) " the relevant land " means the land in which subsists the interest of which the current use value falls to be determined;

(*b*) " the relevant planning Schedule " has the meaning assigned to it by section 7(3) of this Act; and

(*c*) " the operative time " means the time at which the current use value referred to in paragraph (*a*) above falls to be determined.

2. It shall not be assumed by virtue of the relevant planning provision that planning permission would be granted, in respect of the relevant land, for development of any class specified in Part II or, in Northern Ireland, any provision of the relevant planning Schedule, if it is development for which planning permission was refused before the operative time and compensation became payable in respect of that refusal under—

(*a*) section 169 of the Town and Country Planning Act 1971 ; or SCH. 4

(*b*) section 158 of the Town and Country Planning (Scotland) Act 1972 ; or 1971 c. 78. 1972 c. 52.

(*c*) section 29 of the Land Development Values (Compensation) Act (Northern Ireland) 1965. 1965 c. 23 (N.I.).

3. Where, before the operative time, planning permission was granted in respect of the relevant land for development of any class specified in Part II or, in Northern Ireland, any provision of the relevant planning Schedule, but was so granted subject to conditions, and compensation became payable in respect of the imposition of the conditions under any of the enactments specified in sub-paragraphs (*a*) to (*c*) of paragraph 2 above, it shall not be assumed by virtue of the relevant planning provision that planning permission for that development, in respect of the relevant land, would be granted otherwise than subject to those conditions.

4. Where, before the operative time, an order was made in respect of the relevant land under—

(*a*) section 51 of the Town and Country Planning Act 1971, or

(*b*) section 49 of the Town and Country Planning (Scotland) Act 1972,

requiring the removal of any building or the discontinuance of any use, and compensation became payable in respect of that order under section 170 of the said Act of 1971 or, as the case may require, section 159 of the said Act of 1972, it shall not be assumed by virtue of the relevant planning provision that planning permission would be granted, in respect of the relevant land, for the rebuilding of that building or the resumption of that use.

PART II

DEVELOPMENT EXCLUDED FROM MATERIAL DEVELOPMENT

5.—(1) To the extent that any of the following activities constitutes development, they do not constitute material development for the purposes of this Act, namely,—

(*a*) the carrying out of works for the maintenance, improvement, enlargement or other alteration of any building, so long as the cubic content of the original building is not exceeded by more than one-tenth ;

(*b*) the carrying out of works for the rebuilding, as often as occasion may require, of any building which was in existence at the relevant time, or of any building which was in existence in the period of ten years immediately preceding the day on which that time falls but was destroyed or demolished before the relevant time, so long as (in either case) the cubic content of the original building is not exceeded by more than one-tenth ;

(*c*) the carrying out on any land used for the purposes of agriculture or forestry of any building or other operations required for the purposes of that use ;

SCH. 4

(*d*) the carrying out of operations on land for, or the use of land for, the display of an advertisement ;

(*e*) the carrying out of operations for, or the use of land for, car parking, provided that such use shall not exceed six years ;

(*f*) in the case of a building or other land which at the relevant time was used for a purpose falling within any class specified in paragraph 7 below or which, being unoccupied at that time, was last used for any such purpose, the use of that building or other land for any other purpose falling within the same class ;

(*g*) in the case of a building or other land which at the relevant time was in the occupation of a person by whom it was used as to part only for a particular purpose, the use for that purpose of any additional part of the building or land not exceeding one-tenth of the cubic content of the part of the building used for that purpose at the relevant time or, as the case may be, one-tenth of the area of the land so used at that time ;

(*h*) in the case of land which at the relevant time was being temporarily used for a purpose other than the purpose for which it was normally used, the resumption of the use of the land for the last-mentioned purpose ; and

(*i*) in the case of land which was unoccupied at the relevant time, the use of the land for the purpose for which it was last used before that time.

(2) Any reference in sub-paragraph (1) above to the relevant time shall be construed as follows:—

(*a*) in any case where the question whether development is or is not material development is relevant in determining whether a project of material development is begun on any land, any such reference is a reference to the time at which any specified operation, within the meaning of Schedule 1 to this Act, is begun on that land or any part of it ; and

(*b*) in any case where that question is relevant to the determination of any matter on the occasion of a disposal, acquisition, variation of the terms and conditions of a lease or other event, any such reference is a reference to the time of that disposal, acquisition, variation or other event.

(3) For the purposes of paragraphs (*a*) and (*b*) of sub-paragraph (1) above,—

(*a*) where any development extends to two or more buildings within the same curtilage, those buildings may be regarded as a single building ; and

(*b*) where two or more buildings within the same curtilage result from the carrying out of development of a single building, the new buildings may together be regarded as a single building.

6.—(1) In determining for the purposes of sub-paragraph (1)(*a*) or sub-paragraph (1)(*b*) of paragraph 5 above whether or not the cubic content of the original building has been exceeded by more than one-tenth, the cubic content of the building after the carrying out of the work in question shall be treated as reduced by the amount (if any) by which so much of that cubic content as is attributable to one or more of the matters mentioned in sub-paragraph (2) below exceeds so much of the cubic content of the original building as was attributable to one or more of the matters so mentioned. SCH. 4

(2) The matters referred to in sub-paragraph (1) above are the following, that is to say,—

(*a*) means of escape in case of fire ;

(*b*) car-parking or garage space ;

(*c*) accommodation for plant providing heating, air-conditioning or similar facilities ; and

(*d*) lifts and staircases.

(3) In relation to a building erected after 12th September 1974, being a building resulting from the carrying out of any such works as are described in sub-paragraph (1)(*a*) or sub-paragraph (1)(*b*) of paragraph 5 above, any reference in this Schedule to the original building is a reference to the building in relation to which those works were carried out and not to the building resulting from the carrying out of those works.

7. The classes of purposes mentioned in paragraph 5(1)(*f*) above are the following:—

Class A—Use as a dwelling-house or for the purpose of any activities which are wholly or mainly carried on otherwise than for profit, except use for a purpose falling within Class B, C or E:

Class B—Use as an office or retail shop:

Class C—Use as a hotel, boarding-house or guest-house, or as premises licensed for the sale of intoxicating liquors for consumption on the premises:

Class D—Use for the purpose of any activities wholly or mainly carried on for profit, except—

(*a*) use as a dwelling-house or for the purposes of agriculture or forestry ; and

(*b*) use for a purpose falling within Class B, C or E:

and

Class E—Use for any of the following purposes, namely,—

(*a*) the carrying on of any process for or incidental to any of the following purposes, namely—

(i) the making of any article or of any part of any article, or the production of any substance,

(ii) the altering, repairing, ornamenting, finishing, cleaning, washing, freezing, packing or canning, or adapting for sale, or breaking up or demolishing of any article, or

(iii) without prejudice to sub-paragraphs (i) and (ii) above, the getting, dressing or treatment of minerals,

SCH. 4

being a process carried on in the course of a trade or business other than agriculture or forestry, but excluding any process carried on at a dwelling-house or retail shop;

(*b*) storage purposes (whether or not involving use as a warehouse or repository) other than storage purposes ancillary to a purpose falling within Class B or C.

8. In determining for the purposes of sub-paragraph (1)(*g*) of paragraph 5 above what part of a building or other land was used by a person for a particular purpose at any time, there shall be disregarded any part of that building or land which was not used for that purpose on 12th September 1974 or the date on which any part of that building or land first began to be used for that purpose, whichever is the later.

9.—(1) In this Part of this Schedule, unless the context otherwise requires—

"article" means an article of any description;

"forestry" includes afforestation;

"retail shop" includes any premises of a similar character where retail trade or business (including repair work) is carried on;

"substance" means any natural or artificial substance or material, whether in solid or liquid form or in the form of a gas or vapour.

(2) Any reference in this Part of this Schedule to the cubic content of a building is a reference to that content as ascertained by external measurement.

(3) In this part of this Schedule, any expression to which a meaning is assigned by the relevant planning enactment and which—

(*a*) is not defined in sub-paragraph (1) above, and

(*b*) is not otherwise defined for the purposes of this Act,

has the same meaning as in that enactment.

Section 16.

SCHEDULE 5

AUTHORISED DEVELOPMENT ETC.

1.—(1) For the purpose of determining what planning permission was in force on 12th September 1974 with respect to any land in England, Scotland or Wales, a determination made by the Secretary of State before the time of the relevant disposal and after 12th September 1974—

(*a*) on an application referred to him on or before that date by virtue of a direction under the calling-in provision, or

(*b*) on an appeal under the appeals provision against a decision of a planning authority made (or, for the purpose of the appeal, treated as made) on or before that date,

shall be treated for the purposes of the principal section as having been made immediately before that date.

Sch. 5

(2) For the purpose of determining what planning permission was in force on 12th September 1974 with respect to any land in Northern Ireland—

(*a*) a determination made by the Department of the Environment for Northern Ireland before the time of the relevant disposal and after 12th September 1974 on an application in relation to which a notice was served on or before that date under the calling-in provision, and

(*b*) a determination made by the Planning Appeals Commission before the time of the relevant disposal and after 12th September 1974 on an appeal under the appeals provision against a decision of the Department of the Environment for Northern Ireland made (or, for the purpose of the appeal, treated as made) on or before that date,

shall be treated for the purposes of the principal section as having been made immediately before that date.

(3) For the purpose of determining what planning permission was in force on 12th September 1974 in a case where—

(*a*) by virtue of the default provision, the appeals provision applies in relation to an application as if the permission or approval to which the application relates had been refused on or before that date, and

(*b*) the applicant does not exercise the right of appeal given to him by virtue of the default provision but makes a further application which does not differ in any significant respect from the application referred to in paragraph (*a*) above,

a decision of a planning authority or, in Northern Ireland, of the Department of the Environment for Northern Ireland made after that date on the application referred to in paragraph (*b*) above shall be treated for the purposes of the principal section and the preceding provisions of this paragraph as having been made immediately before that date.

(4) In the application of the preceding provisions of this paragraph in England and Wales, any reference to a planning authority shall be construed as a reference to a local planning authority and as if this paragraph were included in the Town and Country Planning Act 1971. 1971 c. 78.

(5) In sub-paragraphs (1) to (3) above " the calling-in provision ", " the appeals provision " and " the default provision " mean—

(*a*) in England and Wales, sections 35, 36, and 37 respectively of the Town and Country Planning Act 1971 ;

(*b*) in Scotland, sections 32, 33 and 34 respectively of the Town and Country Planning (Scotland) Act 1972 ; and 1972 c. 52.

(*c*) in Northern Ireland, Articles 22, 23 and 24 respectively of the Planning (Northern Ireland) Order 1972. S.I. 1972/1634 (N.I. 17).

2.—(1) Where planning permission in force on 12th September 1974 was outline planning permission only, then, for the purposes of

SCH. 5

the principal section, the development of the land concerned which is to be treated as authorised by that permission is any development which—

(*a*) on that date was authorised by that permission without any requirement as to subsequent approval, or

(*b*) was not so authorised on that date but was either—

(i) development for which, at the time of the relevant disposal, approval had been granted in the manner applicable to that planning permission, or

(ii) development for which, on 12th September 1974, approval might reasonably have been expected to be granted in that manner, not being development for which, at the time of disposal, approval had been refused in that manner.

(2) In sub-paragraph (1) above "outline planning permission" has,—

(*a*) in England and Wales, the meaning assigned to it by section 42 of the Town and Country Planning Act 1971; 1971 c. 78.

(*b*) in Scotland, the meaning assigned to it by section 39 of the Town and Country Planning (Scotland) Act 1972; and 1972 c. 52.

(*c*) in Northern Ireland, the meaning assigned to it by Article 26 of the Planning (Northern Ireland) Order 1972. S.I. 1972/1634 (N.I. 17).

3.—(1) On the disposal of an interest in land for which planning permission granted for a limited period was in force on 12th September 1974, that permission shall be treated, for the purposes of the principal section, as having ceased to be in force before that date unless it was also in force at the time of disposal.

(2) In sub-paragraph (1) above "planning permission granted for a limited period" has the meaning assigned to it by the relevant planning enactment.

4. In this Schedule—

"the principal section" means section 16 of this Act; and

"the relevant disposal" has the same meaning as in the principal section.

Section 34.

SCHEDULE 6

INTERACTION OF DEVELOPMENT LAND TAX WITH OTHER TAXES

PART I

DLT DISPOSAL PRECEDES OR IS CONTEMPORANEOUS WITH CGT DISPOSAL OR TRADING DISPOSAL

Reduction of chargeable gain on contemporaneous disposal

1.—(1) If chargeable realised development value accrues to any person on a DLT disposal and that disposal is also a CGT disposal then, subject to the provisions of this Part of this Schedule, a sum equal to the amount of that chargeable realised development value shall be available as a deduction in accordance with sub-paragraph (2) below. SCH. 6

(2) If a chargeable gain accrues (or would but for this Part of this Schedule accrue) on the CGT disposal referred to in sub-paragraph (1) above, then, for the purposes of capital gains tax or, as the case may require, corporation tax on chargeable gains, the sum available as a deduction by virtue of that sub-paragraph shall be deducted from the amount which, apart from this Part of this Schedule, would be the amount of the chargeable gain.

(3) Where chargeable realised development value accrues to any person on a DLT disposal and, by virtue of Part II of this Schedule, the amount of development land tax chargeable in respect of that value is reduced by an amount which is the credit for other tax paid, within the meaning of that Part, then, for the purposes of this Part of this Schedule, the amount of chargeable realised development value which accrues on that DLT disposal shall be taken to be reduced by an amount equal, subject to sub-paragraph (4) below, to the amount of the notional reduction in liability, within the meaning of that Part, relevant to the calculation of that credit.

(4) Where sub-paragraph (1) of paragraph 14 below applies to the DLT disposal referred to in sub-paragraph (3) above and the case is one to which sub-paragraph (2) of that paragraph applies, the reference in sub-paragraph (3) above to the amount of the notional reduction in liability relevant to the calculation of the credit for other tax paid shall be construed as follows—

(*a*) except where paragraph 15 below applies, the reference shall be construed as a reference to the aggregate of the amounts of the notional reductions in liability determined in relation to each of the relevant CGT disposals, as defined in paragraph 14(2) below ; and

(*b*) where paragraph 15 below applies, the reference shall be construed as a reference to the relevant proportion of the amount which was the notional reduction in liability for the purpose of determining, in accordance with sub-paragraph (2) of that paragraph, the amount of the gross credit referred to in sub-paragraph (1) of that paragraph ;

and, for the purposes of paragraph (*b*) above, the relevant proportion is the proportion which the credit for other tax paid appropriate to the DLT disposal referred to in sub-paragraph (3) above bears to the total of the gross credit referred to in paragraph (*b*) above.

(5) The deduction from the amount of a chargeable gain which is provided for by sub-paragraph (2) above shall be applied to the amount of that gain—

(*a*) before making any reduction under section 34 of the Finance Act 1965 (transfer of business on retirement) or under any other enactment providing for relief by reference to the aggregate of a loss and a gain or of two or more gains or losses, and 1965 c. 25.

SCH. 6

(*b*) before making any adjustment under section 38(2) of that Act (unit trusts: in certain cases only one-tenth of gains to be chargeable gains), under the proviso to section 208(2)

1970 c. 10. of the Income and Corporation Taxes Act 1970 (partially approved superannuation funds: part of gain not to be

1970 c. 24. chargeable gain) or under section 21(7) of the Finance Act 1970 (investments held partially for purposes of certain retirement benefit schemes: part of gain not to be chargeable gain), and

1972 c. 41. (*c*) before making any reduction under section 93 of the Finance Act 1972 (reduction in amount of chargeable gains to be included in company's total profits),

but after taking account of any other provision affecting the determination of the amount of any chargeable gain.

(6) Subject to the following provisions of this Part of this Schedule, in any case where, apart from this sub-paragraph, the sum available as a deduction as mentioned in sub-paragraph (1) above would be greater than the amount from which, by virtue of sub-paragraph (2) above, it falls to be deducted, that sum shall be treated for the purposes of those sub-paragraphs as equal to that amount.

Reduction where DLT disposal precedes CGT disposal

2.—(1) Subject to sub-paragraph (2) below, if chargeable realised development value accrues to any person on a DLT disposal which is a deemed disposal and, accordingly, does not constitute a CGT disposal of the interest in question and that deemed disposal is followed by a CGT disposal (in this paragraph referred to as " the subsequent disposal ") of that interest or any part of it, then,—

(*a*) if the subsequent disposal is not also a DLT disposal, it shall be treated as such for the purposes of paragraph 1 above ; and

(*b*) whether or not paragraph (*a*) above applies, the chargeable realised development value which accrued on the earlier deemed DLT disposal shall be treated for the purposes of paragraph 1 above as accruing on the subsequent DLT disposal (in addition to any chargeable realised development value which in fact accrues or is otherwise treated as accruing on that disposal).

(2) Sub-paragraph (1) above does not apply if, in the period between the earlier deemed DLT disposal and the subsequent disposal, the interest which is the subject matter of the subsequent disposal was acquired in circumstances falling within section 24(1)

1965 c. 25. of the Finance Act 1965 (for capital gains tax purposes, personal representatives acquire deceased's assets at market value but without there being a CGT disposal).

Part disposals

3.—(1) The provisions of this paragraph apply if, in a case where paragraph 1(1) above applies,—

(*a*) chargeable realised development value accrues to any person on a DLT disposal which is a part disposal consisting of the grant of a lease ; or (*b*) if paragraph 2 above also applies, the subsequent disposal referred to in that paragraph is a part disposal; Sch. 6

and in the following provisions of this paragraph the part disposal referred to in paragraph (*a*) or, as the case may be, paragraph (*b*) above is referred to as " the principal disposal " (and references to the principal DLT disposal and the principal CGT disposal shall be construed accordingly) and the interest of which the principal disposal is a part disposal is referred to as " the relevant interest ".

(2) If, in a case where this paragraph applies, the principal disposal consists of the grant of a lease and, apart from this sub-paragraph, paragraph 2 of Schedule 8 to the Finance Act 1965 (premiums for leases) would not apply to the principal disposal by reason only that no premium is required as mentioned in sub-paragraph (1) of that paragraph, it shall be assumed for the purposes of the application of this Part of this Schedule that the payment of a premium of £1 was required under the lease and, accordingly, that the principal disposal is such a CGT disposal as is referred to in the said paragraph 2. 1965 c. 25

(3) Where this paragraph applies in a case falling within sub-paragraph (1)(*b*) above, then, for the purposes of the following provisions of this paragraph, the consideration for the principal DLT disposal shall be taken to be the aggregate of—

(*a*) the consideration for the earlier deemed DLT disposal referred to in paragraph 2 above; and

(*b*) the amount which would be the amount of expenditure on improvements for the purposes of a DLT disposal of the relevant interest, assuming that DLT disposal to occur contemporaneously with the principal disposal.

(4) If, in a case where this paragraph applies, the consideration for the principal DLT disposal (in this paragraph referred to as " CD ") exceeds the consideration for the principal CGT disposal, as determined for the purposes of tax on chargeable gains, paragraph 1(1) above shall have effect as if the reference therein to a sum equal to the amount of the chargeable realised development value which accrues on the DLT disposal were a reference to a sum equal to that fraction of that value of which the numerator is the consideration for the CGT disposal, as so determined, and the denominator, subject to sub-paragraph (5) below, is CD.

(5) If, in a case where paragraph 1(1) above has effect in accordance with sub-paragraph (4) above,—

(*a*) the relevant interest is itself a lease, and

(*b*) the principal disposal is the grant of a sub-lease,

the denominator in the fraction referred to in that sub-paragraph shall be $CD-(HR \times F)$ where—

" HR " is the amount which, for the purposes of Part III of Schedule 2 to this Act, is the value at the time of the principal disposal of the rights of the landlord under the relevant interest; and

SCH. 6

"F" is the fraction which, under sub-paragraph (1) of paragraph 10 of that Schedule is applied (or would but for paragraph 11 of that Schedule be applied) to the matters specified in paragraphs (*a*) to (*d*) of that sub-paragraph for the purpose of determining the amount of chargeable realised development value which accrues on the principal DLT disposal.

(6) Subject to sub-paragraph (9) below,—

(*a*) where paragraph 1(1) above has had effect in accordance with sub-paragraph (4) above in relation to the principal disposal, and

(*b*) there is a subsequent disposal (in this paragraph referred to as "the later disposal") of the balance of the relevant interest which is either a CGT disposal alone or both a DLT disposal and a CGT disposal,

then, if the later disposal is not also a DLT disposal, it shall be treated as such for the purposes of this paragraph and paragraph 1 above and (in every case) there shall be treated, for the purposes of paragraph 1 above, as accruing on the later disposal, in addition to any chargeable realised development value which in fact accrues on that disposal, such part of the chargeable realised development value which accrued on the principal disposal as is represented by the difference between the fraction of that value appropriate to the later disposal and the fraction of that value appropriate to the last preceding disposal of the relevant interest (whether that is the principal disposal or a subsequent disposal of the balance of the relevant interest).

(7) For the purposes of this paragraph a disposal of the balance of the relevant interest means—

(*a*) a disposal of the interest which was the retained interest in relation to the principal disposal, or

(*b*) a disposal which would fall within paragraph (*a*) above if, in the period beginning immediately after the principal disposal and ending immediately before the disposal in question, no disposal had occurred which falls within either paragraph (*a*) above or this paragraph.

(8) For the purposes of this paragraph, in relation to the chargeable realised development value which accrued on the principal disposal, the fraction appropriate to that disposal is the fraction applied under sub-paragraph (4) above, and the fraction appropriate to any subsequent disposal of the balance of the relevant interest is the fraction of which the denominator is the amount which is the denominator in the fraction appropriate to the principal disposal and the numerator is CA, where "CA" is the aggregate of the following, as determined for the purposes of tax on chargeable gains, namely,—

(*a*) the consideration for the principal disposal ;

(*b*) the consideration for the subsequent disposal ; and

(c) the consideration for any disposal of the balance of the relevant interest which occurred between the principal disposal and the subsequent disposal. Sch. 6

(9) On the occasion of the first disposal of the balance of the relevant interest where the fraction which, in accordance with sub-paragraph (8) above, is appropriate to the disposal is or exceeds unity, sub-paragraph (6) above shall have effect in relation to the disposal as if for the words " as is represented by the difference between the fraction of that value appropriate to the later disposal and " there were substituted the words " as remains after deducting therefrom "; and thereafter the preceding provisions of this paragraph shall no longer apply in relation to any part of the chargeable realised development value which accrued on the principal disposal.

(10) In determining for the purposes of this paragraph the consideration for a CGT disposal, no account shall be taken of the exclusion of any amount from any consideration by virtue of sub-paragraph (1) or sub-paragraph (4) of paragraph 5 of Schedule 8 to the Finance Act 1965 (where, by reference to any premium, 1965 c. 25. income tax becomes chargeable under section 80 or section 82 of the Income and Corporation Taxes Act 1970 on any amount, that 1970 c. 10. amount is to be excluded from the consideration brought into account for the purpose of computing any chargeable gain).

Modifications where part of premium, etc. taxable as income

4.—(1) If, in a case where paragraph 1(1) above applies on the disposal of an interest in land,—

(a) the CGT disposal is such that, by virtue of any provision of paragraph 5 of Schedule 8 to the Finance Act 1965, an amount (in this paragraph referred to as " the income element ") falls to be excluded either from the consideration brought into account in making a computation under Schedule 6 to that Act or from any gain accruing on the disposal, and

(b) by virtue of section 80 or section 82 of the Income and Corporation Taxes Act 1970, the income element falls to be taxable as rent or is chargeable to tax under Case VI of Schedule D,

paragraph 1(2) above shall have effect in accordance with sub-paragraph (2) below.

(2) Where sub-paragraph (1) above applies, paragraph 1(2) above shall have effect as if—

(a) the reference to the amount of the chargeable gain were a reference to the aggregate of the income element and the amount of the chargeable gain ; and

(b) the reference to capital gains tax included a reference to income tax ; and

SCH. 6

(*c*) in the phrase " corporation tax on chargeable gains " the words " on chargeable gains " were omitted.

(3) If, in a case where sub-paragraph (1) above applies, the sum available as a deduction as mentioned in paragraph 1(1) above is less than the aggregate referred to in sub-paragraph (2)(*a*) above, the deduction provided for by paragraph 1(2) above shall be made in the first instance from the amount which, apart from this Part of this Schedule, would be the income element, so that only if the sum so available exceeds that amount will the balance of that sum fall to be deducted from the amount which, apart from this Part of this Schedule, would be the amount of the chargeable gain.

(4) In determining in any case—

(*a*) the amount excluded from any consideration or chargeable gain by virtue of any provision of paragraph 5 of Schedule 8 to the Finance Act 1965, or

1965 c. 25.

(*b*) the amount of any deduction under section 83 or section 134 of the Income and Corporation Taxes Act 1970 (deduction for other tax purposes where tax has become chargeable under any provision of sections 80 to 82 of that Act),

1970 c. 10.

no account shall be taken of any deduction made by virtue of any provision of this Schedule on account of any chargeable realised development value.

(5) If, in a case where sub-paragraph (1) above applies, the DLT disposal (in this paragraph referred to as " the material disposal ") which gives rise to the sum available as a deduction as mentioned in paragraph 1(1) above occurs in an interim financial year, it shall be ascertained whether the person who is the chargeable person in relation to the material disposal has, within the meaning of this paragraph, a deficiency of tax for the year of assessment in which the income element is brought into account as mentioned in sub-paragraph (1)(*b*) above, or would be so brought into account apart from the provisions of this Part of this Schedule.

(6) A person has, within the meaning of this paragraph, a deficiency of tax for a year of assessment if—

(*a*) had the sum referred to in sub-paragraph (5) above not been deducted in accordance with paragraph 1(2) and sub-paragraph (3) above, the amount of income tax which would be payable by him in respect of his total income for that and each preceding material year of assessment

exceeds

(*b*) the aggregate of—

(i) the income tax payable in respect of his total income for that and each preceding material year of assessment, having regard to the operation of paragraph 1 and sub-paragraphs (2) and (3) above, and

(ii) the appropriate proportion of the development land tax payable in respect of the chargeable realised development value which accrued on the material disposal;

and in the following provisions of this paragraph a year of assessment in which there is such an excess is referred to as an " affected year " and the amount of that excess is referred to as " the deficiency " for that year. SCH. 6

(7) For the purposes of this paragraph a year of assessment is a material year of assessment if it is, or begins after, a year of assessment in which account is taken (for the purposes of income tax) of the deduction referred to in sub-paragraph (3) above, either directly or by virtue of the making of any claim.

(8) The appropriate proportion referred to in sub-paragraph (6)(*b*)(ii) above shall be determined as follows:—

(*a*) if the amount which, apart from this Part of this Schedule, would be the income element equals or exceeds the sum referred to in sub-paragraph (5) above, the appropriate proportion is 100 per cent. ; and

(*b*) in any other case, the appropriate proportion is that which the amount which, apart from this Part of this Schedule, would be the income element bears to the sum referred to in sub-paragraph (5) above.

(9) Where a person has a deficiency of tax for an affected year—

(*a*) he shall be treated as having received in that year a payment chargeable under Case VI of Schedule D of an amount such that income tax thereon at the basic rate for that year is equal to the deficiency for that year ; and

(*b*) any payment which a person is treated by virtue of paragraph (*a*) above as having received in any year shall not on that account constitute income of his for any of the purposes of the Income Tax Acts other than the charge to tax by virtue of that paragraph and, in particular, no part of any such payment shall constitute profits or gains brought into charge for income tax for the purposes of section 52 of the Income and Corporation Taxes Act 1970 (payments out of profits or gains brought into charge to income tax). 1970 c. 10.

Modifications where roll-over relief applies on CGT disposal

5.—(1) If, in a case where paragraph 1(1) above applies on the disposal of an interest in land,—

(*a*) section 33 of the Finance Act 1965 (replacement of business assets) applies in relation to the CGT disposal in such circumstances that the interest disposed of constitutes or is included among the old assets, and 1965 c. 25.

(*b*) the chargeable realised development value referred to in that paragraph is greater than the chargeable gain, if any, which, apart from this Schedule, would accrue on the disposal,

paragraph 1(6) above shall not apply and, subject to sub-paragraph (2) below, the amount by which that chargeable realised development value exceeds that chargeable gain (in this paragraph referred to as " the unapplied balance of chargeable development value ") shall be carried forward from the disposal and applied in accordance with the provisions of this paragraph.

SCH. 6

(2) If, in a case falling within sub-paragraph (1) above, the chargeable realised development value referred to in paragraph 1(1) above exceeds what would be the amount of the chargeable gain accruing
1965 c. 25. on the disposal in question if section 33 of the Finance Act 1965 did not apply, the chargeable realised development value shall be treated for the purposes of sub-paragraph (1) above and the following provisions of this paragraph as equal to that amount.

(3) Subject to sub-paragraph (4) below, the unapplied balance of chargeable development value shall be set off against the amount of any chargeable gain which (apart from this paragraph) would accrue on a subsequent CGT disposal of the new assets and, if the unapplied balance is greater than the amount of any such chargeable gain, the remainder shall again be carried forward to set off against subsequent chargeable gains accruing on the disposal of further replacement assets, and so on until the whole of the balance is exhausted.

(4) If, in a case falling within sub-paragraph (1) above, section 33 of the Finance Act 1965 has effect subject to the provisions of para-
1969 c. 32. graph 16 of Schedule 19 to the Finance Act 1969 (depreciating assets) in such circumstances that the whole or any part of the chargeable gain referred to in sub-paragraph (2) of that paragraph accrues in accordance with that sub-paragraph,—

(*a*) the unapplied balance of chargeable development value shall be set off against the amount of any chargeable gain which accrues as mentioned in that sub-paragraph ; and

(*b*) if the unapplied balance is greater than the amount of any such chargeable gain and part of the postponed gain is carried forward to asset No. 3 under sub-paragraph (3) of that paragraph, the remainder of the unapplied balance shall be dealt with under sub-paragraph (3) above.

(5) In any case where, by virtue of sub-paragraph (3) or sub-paragraph (4) above, the unapplied balance of chargeable development value or any part of it falls to be set off against the amount of a chargeable gain, a sum equal to that unapplied balance or part thereof shall be deducted from the amount which, apart from this paragraph, would be the amount of the chargeable gain and, if the unapplied balance or part thereof exceeds that amount, the chargeable gain shall be extinguished.

(6) In this paragraph " the old assets " and " the new assets " have the same meaning as in section 33 of the Finance Act 1965 and " asset No. 3 " has the same meaning as in paragraph 16 of Schedule 19 to the Finance Act 1969.

Reduction of profits or gains on contemporaneous disposal

6.—(1) If chargeable realised development value accrues to any person on a DLT disposal and that disposal is also a trading disposal, then, subject to the following provisions of this paragraph, a sum equal to the amount of that chargeable realised development value shall be allowable as a deduction in accordance with sub-paragraph (2) below in computing the profits or gains of the trade in question.

SCH. 6

(2) For the purpose of determining the year of assessment or accounting period in which account is to be taken of the deduction referred to in sub-paragraph (1) above, that deduction shall be treated as if it were a trading expense incurred on the date on which occurred the trading disposal referred to in that sub-paragraph.

(3) If the DLT disposal (in this paragraph referred to as " the material disposal ") which gives rise to the deduction referred to in sub-paragraph (1) above occurs in an interim financial year and income tax is chargeable in respect of the profits or gains of the trade in question for a year of assessment in which account is taken of the deduction by virtue of sub-paragraph (2) above, it shall be ascertained whether the person who is the chargeable person in relation to the material disposal has, within the meaning of this paragraph, a deficiency of tax for that year of assessment.

(4) If sub-paragraph (3) above does not apply in relation to a year of assessment by reason only that a loss is sustained in the trade in question, it shall be ascertained whether, as a result of relief given under any provision of the Income Tax Acts in respect of the whole or any part of that loss, the person referred to in sub-paragraph (3) above has, within the meaning of this paragraph, a deficiency of tax for that or any other year of assessment.

(5) A person has, within the meaning of this paragraph, a deficiency of tax for a year of assessment if—

(*a*) had the sum referred to in sub-paragraph (1) above not been allowable as a deduction as mentioned in that sub-paragraph, the amount of income tax which would be payable by him in respect of his total income for that and each preceding material year of assessment

exceeds

(*b*) the aggregate of—

(i) the income tax payable in respect of his total income for that and each preceding material year of assessment, having regard to the operation of sub-paragraph (1) above ; and

(ii) the development land tax payable in respect of the chargeable realised development value which accrued on the material disposal ;

and in the following provisions of this paragraph a year of assessment in which there is such an excess is referred to as an " affected year " and the amount of that excess is referred to as " the deficiency " for that year.

(6) For the purposes of this paragraph a year of assessment is a material year of assessment if it is, or begins after, a year of assessment in which account is taken of the deduction referred to in sub-paragraph (3) above, either directly or by virtue of the making of any claim.

(7) A person who has a deficiency of tax for an affected year shall be treated as having received in respect of that year a payment chargeable under Case VI of Schedule D of an amount such that income tax thereon at the basic rate for the year of assessment in

SCH. 6 which, by virtue of sub-paragraph (8) below, the payment is treated as being received is equal to the deficiency for that affected year.

(8) Where, by virtue of any provision of the Income Tax Acts, income tax under Schedule D in respect of the profits or gains of a trade for any year of assessment is to be computed by reference to the amount of the profits or gains of some other period and, as a result, more than one year of assessment is, by virtue of the preceding provisions of this paragraph, an affected year by reason of the same deduction under sub-paragraph (1) above, the payments which are treated as having been received as mentioned in sub-paragraph (7) above in respect of each of those affected years shall be treated as all being received in the last of those affected years ; but in any other case a payment so treated as having been received in respect of an affected year shall be treated as having been received in that year.

(9) Any payment which a person is treated by virtue of sub-paragraphs (7) and (8) above as having received in any year shall not on that account constitute income of his for any of the purposes of the Income Tax Acts other than the charge to tax by virtue of those sub-paragraphs and, in particular, no part of any such payment shall constitute profits or gains brought into charge for
1970 c. 10. income tax for the purposes of section 52 of the Income and Corporation Taxes Act 1970 (payments out of profits or gains brought into charge to income tax).

Reduction where DLT disposal precedes trading disposal

7. If chargeable realised development value accrues to any person on a DLT disposal which is a deemed disposal and, accordingly, does not constitute a trading disposal of the interest in question and that deemed DLT disposal is followed by a trading disposal (in this paragraph referred to as " the subsequent disposal ") of that interest or any part of it, then,—

(*a*) if the subsequent disposal is not also a DLT disposal, it shall be treated as such for the purposes of paragraph 6 above ; and

(*b*) whether or not paragraph (*a*) above applies, the chargeable realised development value which accrued on the earlier deemed DLT disposal shall be treated for the purposes of paragraph 6 above as accruing on the subsequent DLT disposal (in addition to any chargeable realised development value which in fact accrues or is otherwise treated as accruing on that disposal).

Part disposals

8.—(1) The provisions of this paragraph apply if, in a case where paragraph 6(1) applies,—

(*a*) chargeable realised development value accrues to any person on a DLT disposal which is a part disposal consisting of the grant of a lease ; or

(*b*) if paragraph 7 above also applies, the subsequent DLT disposal referred to in that paragraph is a part disposal,

and in the following provisions of this paragraph the part disposal referred to in paragraph (*a*) or, as the case may be, paragraph (*b*) above is referred to as " the principal disposal " (and references to the principal DLT disposal and the principal trading disposal shall be construed accordingly) and the interest of which the principal DLT disposal is a part disposal is referred to as " the relevant interest ".

(2) If in a case where this paragraph applies, the principal disposal consists of the grant of a lease and, apart from this sub-paragraph, the principal disposal would not be a trading disposal by reason only that no part of the consideration would fall to be included in the computation of the profits or gains of the trade in question, then, for the purposes of this paragraph and paragraphs 6 and 7 above, the disposal shall be treated as a trading disposal and the sum of £1 shall be taken to be the consideration for the disposal which falls to be included in the computation of those profits or gains.

(3) Where this paragraph applies in a case falling within sub-paragraph (1)(*b*) above, then, for the purposes of the following provisions of this paragraph, the consideration for the principal DLT disposal shall be taken to be the aggregate of—

(*a*) the consideration for the earlier deemed disposal referred to in paragraph 7 above ; and

(*b*) the amount which would be the amount of expenditure on improvements for the purposes of a DLT disposal of the relevant interest, assuming that DLT disposal to occur contemporaneously with the principal disposal.

(4) If, in a case where this paragraph applies, the consideration for the principal DLT disposal (in this paragraph referred to as " CD ") exceeds the consideration for the principal trading disposal (in this paragraph referred to as " CT ") as brought into account in computing the profits or gains of the trade in question, paragraph 6(1) above shall have effect as if the reference therein to a sum equal to the amount of the chargeable realised development value which accrues on the DLT disposal were a reference to a sum equal to that fraction of that value of which the numerator is CT and the denominator, subject to sub-paragraph (5) below, is CD.

(5) Sub-paragraphs (5) to (9) of paragraph 3 above shall have effect in relation to the preceding provisions of this paragraph as if, in those sub-paragraphs,—

(*a*) any reference to paragraph 1 or paragraph 1(1) above were a reference to paragraph 6 or paragraph 6(1) above ;

(*b*) any expression to which a meaning is assigned by the preceding provisions of this paragraph had that meaning ;

(*c*) any reference to sub-paragraph (4) of paragraph 3 above were a reference to sub-paragraph (4) of this paragraph ; and

(*d*) any reference to a CGT disposal were a reference to a trading disposal ;

and as if, in sub-paragraph (8) of paragraph 3 above, for the words " as determined for the purposes of tax on chargeable gains " there were substituted the words " as brought into account in computing the profits or gains of the trade in question."

SCH. 6

Realised development value charged at 66⅔ per cent.: effect on apportionment of income of close companies

9.—(1) In this paragraph "development value charged at the lower rate" means so much of the chargeable realised development value which—

(*a*) accrues on a DLT disposal in relation to which paragraph 1(2) above has effect in accordance with paragraph 4(2) above, or

(*b*) accrues on a DLT disposal to which paragraph 6(1) above applies,

as, by virtue of section 13 of this Act, is chargeable to development land tax at the rate of 66⅔ per cent.

(2) Subject to sub-paragraph (4) below, where any sum—

(*a*) which is available as a deduction in accordance with paragraph 1(2) above, as that paragraph has effect by virtue of paragraph 4(2) above, or

(*b*) which is allowable as a deduction in accordance with paragraph 6(2) above,

is derived, in whole or in part, from an amount of chargeable realised development value which accrued on a particular disposal and is or includes development value charged at the lower rate, then, in relation to that sum, the related development value charged at the lower rate is—

(i) in a case where that sum is equal to the whole of, or to an aggregate which includes the whole of, the chargeable realised development value which accrued on that disposal, all the development value charged at the lower rate which accrued on that disposal; and

(ii) where that sum is equal to part only of, or to an aggregate amount which includes part only of, the chargeable realised development value which accrued on that disposal, the relevant fraction of the development value charged at the lower rate which accrued on that disposal.

(3) In relation to a particular disposal, the relevant fraction referred to in paragraph (ii) of sub-paragraph (2) above is that of which the numerator is the sum referred to in that paragraph and the denominator is the total amount of chargeable realised development value which accrued on that disposal.

(4) In any case where the sum which is available as a deduction as mentioned in sub-paragraph (2)(*a*) above exceeds the amount of the income element, as defined in paragraph 4 above, the amount which, apart from this sub-paragraph, would be the related development value charged at the lower rate shall be reduced by multiplying it by the fraction of which the numerator is the income element, as so defined, and the denominator is that sum.

(5) In the following provisions of this paragraph the expression "net", in relation to any development value charged at the lower rate refers to the amount of that development value less the development land tax charged on it.

(6) For the purposes of Schedule 16 to the Finance Act 1972 (apportionment of income, etc. of close companies) for any accounting period of a company in which— SCH. 6 1972 c. 41.

(*a*) account is taken of the income element, as defined in paragraph 4 above, and by virtue of paragraphs 1 and 4 above a sum falls to be deducted from the aggregate referred to in paragraph 4(2)(*a*) above, or

(*b*) by virtue of paragraph 6 above a sum allowable as a deduction is treated as a trading expense,

and in relation to that sum there is related development value charged at the lower rate, sub-paragraph (1) of paragraph 9 of that Schedule (maximum amount of " relevant income ") shall have effect as if, to the amount which by virtue of that sub-paragraph is the limit of the company's relevant income, there were added, subject to sub-paragraph (8) below, 30 per cent. of the net related development value charged at the lower rate.

(7) In any case where, for any accounting period of a company, sub-paragraph (1) of paragraph 9 of Schedule 16 to the Finance Act 1972 has effect in accordance with sub-paragraph (6) above,—

(*a*) any reference in paragraph 8(1) (determination of " relevant income ") or paragraph 9(2) (adjustment of amounts of estate or trading income by reference to certain maximum and minimum amounts) of that Schedule to the estate or trading income of the company for that accounting period shall be construed as a reference to the aggregate of that income and the net related development value charged at the lower rate which is referred to in sub-paragraph (6) above; and

(*b*) an amount equal to that net related development value shall be added to the aggregate of the amounts specified in sub-paragraphs (i) to (iii) of paragraph 10(2)(*a*) of that Schedule (definition of " distributable profits ").

(8) In any case where—

(*a*) for any accounting period of a company, paragraph 9(1) of Schedule 16 to the Finance Act 1972 has effect in accordance with sub-paragraph (6) above, and

(*b*) the relevant income (within the meaning of that Schedule) of the company for that accounting period falls to be calculated in accordance with paragraph 13 of that Schedule (company ceasing to trade, etc.),

sub-paragraph (6) above shall have effect in relation to that accounting period as if for the words " 30 per cent." there were substituted the words " 60 per cent.".

PART II

CGT DISPOSAL OR TRADING DISPOSAL PRECEDES DLT DISPOSAL

Set-off of tax on chargeable gains against liability to development land tax

10.—(1) In any case where—

(*a*) before, on or after the appointed day, a chargeable gain accrues to any person on a CGT disposal (in this Part of this Schedule referred to as " the primary CGT disposal ") which does not constitute a DLT disposal, and

Sch. 6

(*b*) within the period of twelve years beginning on the date of the primary CGT disposal the person who made that disposal or a person claiming through him for DLT purposes makes a DLT disposal (in this Part of this Schedule referred to as "the subsequent disposal") of the interest in land which was the subject-matter of the primary CGT disposal, and

(*c*) chargeable realised development value accrues on the subsequent disposal, and

(*d*) the person making the subsequent disposal makes a claim in that behalf to the Board,

then, subject to paragraph 13 below, the amount of development land tax to which, apart from this Part of this Schedule, he would be chargeable in respect of the chargeable realised development value referred to in paragraph (*c*) above shall be reduced by an amount (in this Part of this Schedule referred to as "the credit for other tax paid") determined in accordance with the following provisions of this Part of this Schedule.

(2) If the primary CGT disposal occurred before the appointed day it shall be assumed for the purposes of—

(*a*) determining whether that disposal also constitutes a DLT disposal, and

(*b*) making any determination required by the following provisions of this Part of this Schedule in relation to a DLT disposal occurring at the same time as the primary CGT disposal,

that the appointed day fell (and this Act was in force) before the primary CGT disposal occurred.

(3) In a case where a CGT disposal is, for the purposes of tax on chargeable gains, a part disposal only, any reference in this Part of this Schedule to the interest in land which was the subject matter of that CGT disposal is a reference to the interest which is acquired by the person to whom that disposal is made.

11.—(1) Where paragraph 10 above applies there shall be determined the amount of chargeable realised development value which, subject to sub-paragraph (2) below, would have accrued on the primary CGT disposal if that disposal had also been a DLT disposal for a consideration equal to that which, for the purposes of tax on chargeable gains, was the consideration for the primary CGT disposal.

(2) For the purposes of the determination referred to sub-paragraph (1) above, it shall be assumed that section 12 of this Act had not been enacted.

(3) Where paragraph 10 above applies there shall also be determined, subject to the following provisions of this Part of this Schedule, the amount of capital gains tax or, as the case may be, corporation tax for which the person who made the primary CGT disposal would have been liable for the material year of assessment or financial year if the amount of the chargeable gain which accrued on that disposal had been reduced by an amount equal to—

(*a*) the chargeable realised development value determined under sub-paragraph (1) above, or (*b*) the chargeable realised development value which accrues on the subsequent disposal, SCH. 6

whichever is the less, and in this Part of this Schedule the reduction provided for by this sub-paragraph is referred to as " the notional reduction in liability ".

(4) Sub-paragraph (5) of paragraph 1 above shall have effect in relation to the notional reduction in liability as it has effect in relation to the deduction provided for by sub-paragraph (2) of that paragraph.

(5) In any case where, apart from this sub-paragraph, the amount of the notional reduction in liability would be greater than the amount of the chargeable gain to which the reduction is to be applied, it shall be treated for the purposes of sub-paragraph (3) above as equal to the amount of that chargeable gain.

(6) In this paragraph and paragraph 12 below, in relation to the person who made the primary CGT disposal,—

(*a*) the material year of assessment means the year of assessment in which that disposal occurred, and

(*b*) the material financial year means the financial year or years in which falls the whole or any part of the accounting period in which that disposal occurred.

The credit for other tax paid

12.—(1) Subject to the following provisions of this Part of this Schedule, where paragraph 10 above applies the credit for other tax paid which is allowable by reference to the primary CGT disposal is the amount determined under sub-paragraph (2) below.

(2) The amount referred to in sub-paragraph (1) above is that by which the capital gains tax or, as the case may be, corporation tax for which the person who made the primary CGT disposal was actually liable for the material year of assessment or accounting period exceeds the amount determined under paragraph 11(3) above.

Application of credit to later DLT disposals

13.—(1) Subject to the following provision of this paragraph, where the preceding provisions of this Part of this Schedule have had effect in relation to a DLT disposal falling within paragraph 10(1)(*b*) above (in the following provisions of this Part of this Schedule referred to as " the first relevant DLT disposal ") no credit for other tax paid shall be allowable by reference to the primary CGT disposal on any later disposal of the interest which was the subject-matter of that CGT disposal.

(2) Subject to paragraph 15 below, in any case where—

(*a*) the first relevant DLT disposal was a part disposal only, and

(*b*) in relation to the first relevant DLT disposal, the amount of the nominal reduction in liability was that specified in paragraph 11(3)(*b*) above, and

(*c*) within the period of twelve years beginning on the date of the primary CGT disposal, the person who made the first

SCH. 6

relevant DLT disposal or a person claiming through him for DLT purposes makes a later material DLT disposal, and

(*d*) paragraph 10 above applies in relation to the later material DLT disposal referred to in paragraph (*c*) above,

sub-paragraph (1) above shall not apply but paragraphs 11 and 12 above shall have effect in relation to that later material DLT disposal (in this paragraph referred to as the " later relevant DLT disposal ") subject to the following provisions of this paragraph.

(3) For the purposes of this paragraph and paragraph 15 below, a DLT disposal is a material disposal if it is—

(*a*) a disposal of the interest which was the retained interest in relation to the first relevant DLT disposal, or

(*b*) a disposal which would fall within paragraph (*a*) above if, in the period beginning immediately after the first relevant DLT disposal and ending immediately before the disposal in question, no DLT disposal had occurred which falls within either paragraph (*a*) above or this paragraph.

(4) Subject to sub-paragraph (5) below, where sub-paragraph (2) above applies in relation to a later relevant DLT disposal,—

(*a*) paragraph 11(3)(*b*) above shall have effect as if it referred to the aggregate of the chargeable realised development value which accrued on the first relevant DLT disposal and the chargeable realised development value which accrues on the later relevant DLT disposal ; and

(*b*) sub-paragraph (2) of paragraph 12 above shall have effect as if from the excess referred to in that sub-paragraph there were required to be deducted the amount which was the credit for other tax paid in relation to the first relevant DLT disposal.

(5) Where sub-paragraph (2) above has applied in relation to a later relevant DLT disposal and again falls to be applied in relation to such a disposal,—

(*a*) to the aggregate referred to in sub-paragraph (4)(*a*) above there shall be added the chargeable realised development value which accrued on the later relevant DLT disposal or disposals in relation to which sub-paragraph (2) above has already applied ; and

(*b*) the amount to be deducted in accordance with sub-paragraph (4)(*b*) above shall be the aggregate of the credit for other tax paid in relation to the first relevant DLT disposal and the credit or credits for other tax paid in relation to the later relevant DLT disposal or disposals in relation to which sub-paragraph (2) above has already applied.

(6) If, in relation to a later relevant DLT disposal, the amount of the notional reduction in liability is, by virtue of the preceding provisions of this paragraph, that specified in paragraph 11(3)(*a*) above, sub-paragraph (2) above shall not again apply in relation to any later relevant DLT disposal.

Assembly of interests after primary CGT disposal

14.—(1) In any case where—

(*a*) there is a CGT disposal which falls within paragraph (*a*) of sub-paragraph (1) of paragraph 10 above, and

(*b*) within the period of twelve years beginning on the date of that CGT disposal there is a DLT disposal which is one to which Part I of Schedule 2 to this Act applies, and

(*c*) the interest which was the subject matter of the CGT disposal referred to in paragraph (*a*) above is, in relation to the DLT disposal referred to in paragraph (*b*) above, a part of the relevant interest for the purposes of Part I of Schedule 2 to this Act,

the DLT disposal shall be treated as falling within paragraph (*b*) of sub-paragraph (1) of paragraph 10 above, notwithstanding that it is a disposal of a greater interest than that which was the subject matter of the primary CGT disposal.

(2) If, in a case where paragraph 10 above applies by virtue of sub-paragraph (1) above, there is more than one CGT disposal which—

(*a*) is of an interest which, in relation to the subsequent disposal, is a part of the relevant interest for the purposes of Part I of Schedule 2 to this Act, and

(*b*) is capable of constituting the primary CGT disposal in relation to the subsequent disposal,

paragraphs 11 and 12 above shall have effect subject to the following provisions of this paragraph ; and in those provisions and paragraph 15 below the CGT disposals falling within paragraphs (*a*) and (*b*) above are referred to as " the relevant CGT disposals ".

(3) Where sub-paragraph (2) applies, sub-paragraph (1) of paragraph 11 above shall be applied separately in relation to each of the relevant CGT disposals and, subject to sub-paragraph (4) below,—

(*a*) sub-paragraphs (3) to (6) of paragraph 11 and paragraph 12(2) above shall also be applied separately in relation to each of the relevant CGT disposals ; and

(*b*) sub-paragraph (1) of paragraph 12 above shall have effect as if the reference therein to the amount determined under sub-paragraph (2) of that paragraph were a reference to the aggregate of the amounts so determined.

(4) If the aggregate of the amounts of chargeable realised development value determined under paragraph 11(1) above in relation to each of the relevant CGT disposals is greater than the chargeable realised development value which accrues on the subsequent disposal then, for the purposes of sub-paragraphs (3) to (6) of paragraph 11 and paragraph 12 above (as applied by paragraphs (*a*) and (*b*) of sub-paragraph (3) above), each of those amounts of chargeable realised development value shall be treated as reduced proportionately so that the aggregate of them is equal to the chargeable realised development value which accrues on the subsequent disposal.

SCH. 6

(5) In any case where—

(*a*) a CGT disposal is a disposal which is deemed to occur by virtue of subsection (1) of section 45 of the Finance Act 1974 (first letting charge), and

1974 c. 30.

(*b*) by virtue of any provision of sub-paragraph (2) of paragraph 2 of Schedule 9 to that Act, that subsection does not apply to a person's interest in so much of the land occupied by him as is referred to in that sub-paragraph,

any reference in the preceding provisions of this paragraph to the interest which was the subject matter of the CGT disposal shall be construed as a reference to what that interest would have been but for the operation of the provision referred to in paragraph (*b*) above.

Part disposals out of assemblies

15.—(1) In a case falling within sub-paragraph (2) of paragraph 14 above, sub-paragraphs (2) and (4) to (6) of paragraph 13 above shall not apply, but if, in such a case,—

(*a*) the subsequent disposal was a part disposal only, and

(*b*) sub-paragraph (4) of paragraph 14 above also applies, and

(*c*) within the period of twelve years beginning on the date of the first of the relevant CGT disposals, the person who made the first relevant DLT disposal or a person claiming through him for DLT purposes makes a later material DLT disposal, and

(*d*) paragraph 10 above applies in relation to the later material DLT disposal referred to in paragraph (*c*) above,

there shall be determined the amount (in this paragraph referred to as " the credit carried forward ") by which the gross credit determined under sub-paragraph (2) below exceeds the amount which was the credit for other tax paid in relation to the first relevant DLT disposal.

(2) The gross credit referred to in sub-paragraph (1) above is the amount which would have been the credit for other tax paid in relation to the first relevant DLT disposal if, in paragraph 14 above, sub-paragraph (4) (and the reference thereto in sub-paragraph (3)) were omitted.

(3) Where sub-paragraph (1) above applies, paragraphs 11 and 12 above shall not apply to the later DLT disposal referred to in paragraph (*c*) of that sub-paragraph (in this paragraph referred to as the " later relevant DLT disposal ") but, subject to sub-paragraph (5) below, the credit for other tax paid which is appropriate to the later relevant DLT disposal shall be determined by the formula—

$$A \times \frac{B}{C\text{-}D}$$

where, subject to sub-paragraph (4) below,—

" A " is the credit carried forward ;

"B" is the chargeable realised development value which accrues on the later relevant DLT disposal ; Sch. 6

"C" is the aggregate of the amounts chargeable realised development value referred to in paragraph 14(4) above ; and

"D" is the chargeable realised development value which accrued on the first relevant DLT disposal.

(4) Where sub-paragraph (1) above has applied in relation to a later relevant DLT disposal and again falls to be applied in relation to such a disposal, then, in the formula set out in sub-paragraph (3) above,—

"A" is the credit carried forward less the amount of the credit or credits for other tax paid appropriate to the later relevant DLT disposal or disposals in relation to which sub-paragraph (1) above has already applied ; and

"D" is the aggregate of the chargeable realised development value which accrued on the first relevant DLT disposal and the chargeable realised development value which accrued on that later disposal or, as the case may be, those later disposals.

(5) If, in relation to any later relevant DLT disposal, the fraction $\frac{B}{C-D}$ in the formula set out in sub-paragraph (3) above, would (apart from this sub-paragraph) be greater than unity, it shall be treated for the purposes of this paragraph as unity.

(6) If, in relation to any later relevant DLT disposal, the fraction referred to in sub-paragraph (5) above is unity (whether by virtue of that sub-paragraph or otherwise) sub-paragraph (3) above shall not thereafter have effect in relation to any further DLT disposal which falls within sub-paragraph (1)(*c*) above.

Set-off of tax on development gains against liability to development land tax

16.—(1) The provisions of this paragraph apply if, in a case where paragraph 10 above applies, a development gain as well as a chargeable gain accrues on the primary CGT disposal or, where paragraph 14(2) above applies, on any of the relevant CGT disposals as defined in that paragraph.

(2) Where this paragraph applies, sub-paragraph (3) of paragraph 11 above shall have effect in relation to a CGT disposal on which a development gain accrues—

(*a*) as if the reference to the amount of capital gains tax were a reference to the aggregate of capital gains tax and income tax ; and

(*b*) as if the reference to the amount of the chargeable gain were a reference to the aggregate of the chargeable gain and the development gain ; and

SCH. 6

(*c*) as if the notional reduction in liability were applied, in the first instance, exclusively to the development gain, so that only if the amount of the reduction exceeds the amount of the development gain is the balance of the reduction applied to the amount of the chargeable gain.

(3) Where sub-paragraph (3) of paragraph 11 above has effect in relation to a CGT disposal in accordance with sub-paragraph (2) above, then, in relation to that CGT disposal—

(*a*) sub-paragraphs (4) and (5) of that paragraph shall have effect as if the reference to the notional reduction in liability were a reference to the balance of that reduction referred to in sub-paragraph (2)(*c*) above ; and

(*b*) sub-paragraph (2) of paragraph 12 above shall have effect as if the reference to capital gains tax were a reference to the aggregate of capital gains tax and income tax.

(4) In a case where sub-paragraph (2) of paragraph 14 above applies, the modifications provided for by sub-paragraphs (2) and (3) above shall have effect in addition to those provided for by sub-paragraphs (3) and (4) of that paragraph.

1974 c. 30.

(5) In this paragraph " development gain " has the same meaning as in Part III of the Finance Act 1974.

Set-off of tax on profits or gains against liability to development land tax

17. Paragraphs 10 to 15 above shall apply in relation to trading disposals as they apply in relation to CGT disposals subject to the following modifications:—

(*a*) for " CGT ", wherever occurring, there shall be substituted " trading ";

(*b*) for the words " capital gains tax ", wherever occurring, there shall be substituted the words " income tax " ;

(*c*) in paragraph 10(1)(*a*) for the words " a chargeable gain accrues to any person on a CGT disposal " there shall be substituted the words " there is a trading disposal ";

(*d*) sub-paragraph (3) of paragraph 10, sub-paragraph (4) of paragraph 11 and sub-paragraph (5) of paragraph 14 shall be omitted ;

(*e*) in sub-paragraph (1) of paragraph 11 for the words from " consideration equal to " to the end of the sub-paragraph there shall be substituted the words " consideration equal to the amount (in this paragraph referred to as ' the proceeds of the disposal ') which was brought into account in respect of the trading disposal in computing the profits or gains of the trade in question " ; and

(*f*) in sub-paragraph (3) of paragraph 11 for the words " amount of the chargeable gain which accrued on that disposal " and in sub-paragraph (5) of that paragraph for the words " amount of the chargeable gain " there shall be substituted the words " proceeds of the disposal ".

PART III

Sch. 6

LIABILITY FOR CAPITAL TRANSFER TAX OR ESTATE DUTY PRECEDES CHARGE TO DEVELOPMENT LAND TAX

Set-off of capital transfer tax against chargeable realised development value

18.—(1) Subject to sub-paragraphs (2) and (3) below, in any case where—

(*a*) before, on or after the appointed day, an interest in land (in this Part of this Schedule referred to as " the relevant interest ") is acquired by any person on the occasion of a CTT transfer (in this Part of this Schedule referred to as " the primary CTT transfer "), and

(*b*) the disposal as a result of which the relevant interest is acquired as mentioned in paragraph (*a*) above is not a DLT disposal, and

(*c*) within the period of twelve years beginning on the date of the primary CTT transfer, the person who acquired the relevant interest as mentioned in paragraph (*a*) above or a person claiming through him for DLT purposes makes a DLT disposal (in this paragraph and paragraphs 19 to 23 below referred to as " the subsequent disposal ") of the relevant interest, and

(*d*) chargeable realised development value accrues, or would but for this Part of this Schedule accrue, on the subsequent disposal, and

(*e*) the person making the subsequent disposal makes a claim in that behalf to the Board,

then, subject to paragraph 21 below, the amount which, apart from this Part of this Schedule, would be the chargeable realised development value accruing on the subsequent disposal shall be reduced by an amount (in this Part of this Schedule referred to as " the capital transfer tax deduction ") determined in accordance with the following provisions of this Part of this Schedule.

(2) In any case where the primary CTT transfer arises by virtue of section 22 of the Finance Act 1975 (transfer on death) and the whole or any part of the land in which the relevant interest subsists is designated as property to which section 34 of that Act applies (conditional exemption for certain buildings etc. on death), then,— 1975 c. 7.

(*a*) where the whole of that land is so designated and capital transfer tax becomes chargeable at any time in accordance with subsection (7) or subsection (8) of section 34 of the Finance Act 1975 with respect to that land (or any of it), sub-paragraph (1) above shall have effect as if the period referred to in paragraph (*c*) thereof began immediately before that time ; and

(*b*) where part only of that land is so designated and capital transfer tax becomes chargeable at any time as mentioned in paragraph (*a*) above with respect to the part of the land which is so designated (or any of it) sub-paragraph (1) above

SCH. 6

shall have effect in relation to that capital transfer tax as if the period referred to in paragraph (*c*) thereof began immediately before that time;

but nothing in paragraph (*b*) above shall affect the operation of this Part of this Schedule in relation to any capital transfer tax paid in respect of the value of the part of the land which is not so designated.

(3) In any case where the disposal as a result of which the relevant interest was acquired as mentioned in sub-paragraph (1)(*a*) above is a DLT disposal so that the condition in sub-paragraph (1)(*b*) above is not fulfilled but—

(*a*) the consideration for that acquisition was less than that which the relevant interest might reasonably have been expected to fetch in the open market, and

(*b*) the person by whom the relevant interest was acquired bore some or all of the capital transfer tax chargeable on the value transferred by the primary CTT transfer,

then, for the purposes of this Part of this Schedule (other than this sub-paragraph), the condition in sub-paragraph (1)(*b*) above shall be taken to be fulfilled.

(4) If the primary CTT transfer occurred before the appointed day it shall be assumed for the purpose of—

(*a*) determining whether that transfer also constitutes a DLT disposal, and

(*b*) making any determination required by the following provisions of this Part of this Schedule in relation to a DLT disposal occurring at the same time as the primary CTT transfer,

that the appointed day fell (and this Act was in force) before the primary CTT transfer occurred.

(5) If, after the amount of chargeable realised development value accruing on a DLT disposal has been ascertained, having regard to the amount of the capital transfer tax deduction applicable under this Part of this Schedule, the amount of capital transfer tax which is payable by any person by virtue of a CTT transfer taken into account in determining that deduction is varied, such adjustment, whether by way of a further assessment to development land tax or the discharge or repayment of development land tax or otherwise, shall be made as is required in consequence.

19.—(1) Where paragraph 18 above applies there shall be determined the amount of chargeable realised development value which, subject to sub-paragraph (2) below, would have accrued on the primary CTT transfer if that transfer had also been a DLT disposal of the relevant interest for a consideration equal to the price which the relevant interest might have been expected to fetch if sold in the open market at the time of the primary CTT transfer.

(2) For the purposes of the determination referred to in sub-paragraph (1) above, it shall be assumed that section 12 of this Act had not been enacted.

(3) Where paragraph 18 above applies, there shall be determined the amount of the capital transfer tax chargeable on the value transferred by the primary CTT transfer which is attributable to the value of the relevant interest as ascertained for the purposes of capital transfer tax, and, subject to sub-paragraph (5) below, in this Part of this Schedule "the relevant amount of tax" means the amount of tax so attributable.

(4) For the purpose of sub-paragraph (3) above, the amount of tax chargeable as mentioned in that sub-paragraph which is attributable to the value of the relevant interest shall not include tax chargeable on any part of the value transferred which is represented by any such liability for capital transfer tax as is mentioned in paragraph 1(2) of Schedule 10 to the Finance Act 1975 (value transferred to include transferor's liability for tax on the value transferred). 1975 c. 7.

(5) If, in a case where this Part of this Schedule applies by virtue of sub-paragraph (3) of paragraph 18 above, the person referred to in paragraph (*b*) of that sub-paragraph did not bear the whole of the amount of capital transfer tax which is attributable, as mentioned in sub-paragraph (3) above, to the value of the relevant interest, the amount which, apart from this sub-paragraph, would be the relevant amount of tax shall be reduced to the amount of the capital transfer tax so attributable which was borne by that person.

The capital transfer tax deduction

20.—(1) Subject to the following provisions of this Part of this Schedule, where paragraph 18 applies the capital transfer tax deduction which is allowable by reference to the primary CTT transfer is the amount determined under sub-paragraph (2) below.

(2) The amount referred to in sub-paragraph (1) above is that given by the formula—

$$\frac{A \times C}{B}$$

where—

"A" is the chargeable realised development value determined under paragraph 19(1) above or the chargeable realised development value which accrues on the subsequent disposal, whichever is the less;

"B" is the amount taken as the consideration for the DLT disposal referred to in paragraph 19(1) above; and

"C" is the relevant amount of tax.

Application of deduction to later DLT disposals

21.—(1) Subject to the provisions of this paragraph, where the preceding provisions of this Part of this Schedule have had effect in relation to a DLT disposal falling within paragraph 18(1)(*c*) above (in this paragraph and paragraphs 22 and 23 below referred to as "the first relevant DLT disposal") no capital transfer tax deduction shall be allowable by reference to the primary CTT transfer on any later disposal of the relevant interest.

SCH. 6

(2) Subject to paragraph 23 below, in any case where—

(*a*) the first relevant DLT disposal was a part disposal only, and

(*b*) in relation to the first relevant DLT disposal, " A " in the formula specified in paragraph 20(2) above was the chargeable realised development value which accrued on that disposal, and

(*c*) within the period of twelve years referred to in paragraph 18(1)(*c*) above, the person who made the first relevant DLT disposal or a person claiming through him for DLT purposes makes a later material DLT disposal, and

(*d*) paragraph 18 above applies in relation to the later material disposal referred to in paragraph (*c*) above,

sub-paragraph (1) above shall not apply but paragraphs 19 and 20 above shall have effect in relation to that later material DLT disposal (in this paragraph referred to as the " later relevant DLT disposal ") subject to the following provisions of this paragraph.

(3) For the purposes of this paragraph a DLT disposal is a material disposal if it is—

(*a*) a disposal of the interest which was the retained interest in relation to the first relevant DLT disposal, or

(*b*) a disposal which would fall within paragraph (*a*) above if, in the period beginning immediately after the first relevant DLT disposal and ending immediately before the disposal in question, no DLT disposal had occurred which falls within paragraph (*a*) above or this paragraph.

(4) Subject to sub-paragraph (5) below, where sub-paragraph (2) above applies in relation to a later relevant DLT disposal,—

(*a*) in the definition of " A " in paragraph 20(2) above the reference to the chargeable realised development value which accrues on the subsequent disposal shall have effect as a reference to the aggregate of the chargeable realised development value which accrued on the first relevant DLT disposal and the chargeable realised development value which accrues on the later relevant DLT disposal ; and

(*b*) from the amount which, apart from this sub-paragraph, would be the capital transfer tax deduction there shall be subtracted the amount which was the capital transfer tax deduction in relation to the first relevant DLT disposal.

(5) Where sub-paragraph (2) has applied in relation to a later relevant DLT disposal and again falls to be applied in relation to such a disposal,—

(*a*) to the aggregate referred to in sub-paragraph (4)(*a*) above there shall be added the chargeable realised development value which accrued on the later relevant DLT disposal or disposals in relation to which sub-paragraph (2) above has already applied ; and

(*b*) the amount to be subtracted in accordance with sub-paragraph (4)(*b*) above shall be the aggregate of the capital transfer tax deduction in relation to the first relevant DLT disposal and the capital transfer tax deduction or deductions in relation to the later relevant DLT disposal or disposals in relation to which sub-paragraph (2) above has already applied. SCH. 6

(6) If, by virtue of the preceding provisions of this paragraph, in relation to a later relevant DLT disposal " A " in the formula specified in paragraph 20(2) above is the chargeable realised development value determined under paragraph 19(1) above, sub-paragraph (2) above shall not again apply in relation to any later disposal.

Assembly of interests after primary CTT transfer

22.—(1) In any case where—

(*a*) there is a CTT transfer which falls within paragraphs (*a*) and (*b*) of sub-paragraph (1) of paragraph 18 above, and

(*b*) within the period of twelve years referred to in paragraph (*c*) of that sub-paragraph there is a DLT disposal which is one to which Part I of Schedule 2 to this Act applies, and

(*c*) for the purposes of Part I of Schedule 2 to this Act, the relevant interest is, in relation to the DLT disposal referred to in paragraph (*b*) above, a part of the interest which is the subject matter of that disposal,

the DLT disposal shall be treated as falling within paragraph (*c*) of sub-paragraph (1) of paragraph 18 above, notwithstanding that it is a disposal of an interest greater than the relevant interest.

(2) If, in a case where paragraph 18 above applies by virtue of sub-paragraph (1) above, there is more than one CTT transfer—

(*a*) on the occasion of which a person acquires an interest in land which for the purposes of Part I of Schedule 2 to this Act is, in relation to the subsequent disposal, a part of the interest which is the subject matter of that disposal, and

(*b*) which is capable of constituting the primary CTT transfer in relation to the subsequent disposal,

paragraphs 19 and 20 above shall have effect subject to the following provisions of this paragraph ; and in those provisions and paragraph 23 below the CTT transfers falling within paragraphs (*a*) and (*b*) above are referred to as " the relevant CTT transfers ".

(3) Subject to sub-paragraph (4) below, where sub-paragraph (2) above applies—

(*a*) paragraphs 19 and 20(2) above shall be applied separately in relation to each of the relevant CTT transfers, and

(*b*) sub-paragraph (1) of paragraph 20 above shall have effect as if the reference therein to the amount determined under sub-paragraph (2) of that paragraph were a reference to the aggregate of the amounts so determined.

(4) If the aggregate of the amounts of chargeable realised development value determined under paragraph 19(1) above in relation to

SCH. 6

each of the relevant CTT transfers is greater than the chargeable realised development value which accrues on the subsequent disposal then, for the purpose of paragraph 20(2) above (as applied by sub-paragraph (3) above), each of those amounts of chargeable realised development value shall be treated as reduced proportionately so that the aggregate of them is equal to the chargeable realised development value which accrues on the subsequent disposal.

Part disposals out of assemblies

23.—(1) In a case falling within sub-paragraph (2) of paragraph 22 above, such-paragraphs (2) and (4) to (6) of paragraph 21 above shall not apply, but if, in such a case—

(*a*) the subsequent disposal was a part disposal only, and

(*b*) sub-paragraph (4) of paragraph 22 above applies, and

(*c*) within the period of twelve years beginning on the date of the first of the relevant CTT transfers, the person who made the first relevant DLT disposal or a person claiming through him for DLT purposes makes a later DLT disposal which is a material disposal, as defined in paragraph 21(3) above, and

(*d*) paragraph 18 above applies in relation to the later DLT disposal referred to in paragraph (*c*) above,

there shall be determined the amount (in this paragraph referred to as " the balance carried forward ") by which the gross deduction determined under sub-paragraph (2) below exceeds the amount which was the capital transfer tax deduction in relation to the first relevant DLT disposal.

(2) The gross deduction referred to in sub-paragraph (1) above is the amount which would have been the capital transfer tax deduction in relation to the first relevant DLT disposal if, in paragraph 22 above, sub-paragraph (4) (and the reference thereto in sub-paragraph (3)) were omitted.

(3) Where sub-paragraph (1) applies, paragraphs 19 and 20 above shall not apply to the later DLT disposal referred to in paragraph (*c*) of that sub-paragraph (in this paragraph referred to as the " later relevant DLT disposal ") but, subject to sub-paragraph (5) below, the capital transfer tax deduction which is appropriate to the later relevant DLT disposal shall be determined by the formula—

$$A \times \frac{B}{C-D}$$

where, subject to sub-paragraph (4) below—

" A " is the balance carried forward ;

" B " is the chargeable realised development value which accrues on the later relevant DLT disposal ;

" C " is the aggregate of the amounts of chargeable realised development value referred to in paragraph 22(4) above ; and

" D " is the chargeable realised develoment value which accrued on the first relevant DLT disposal.

(4) Where sub-paragraph (1) above has applied in relation to a later relevant DLT disposal and again falls to be applied in relation to such a disposal, then, in the formula set out in sub-paragraph (3) above,— SCH. 6

" A " is the balance carried forward less the amount of the capital transfer tax deduction or deductions appropriate to the later relevant DLT disposal or disposals in relation to which sub-paragraph (1) above has already applied ; and

" D " is the aggregate of the chargeable realised development value which accrued on the first relevant DLT disposal and the chargeable realised development value which accrued on that later disposal or, as the case may be, those later disposals.

(5) If, in relation to any later relevant DLT disposal, the fraction $\frac{B}{C-D}$ in the formula set out in sub-paragraph (3) above would (apart from this sub-paragraph) be greater than unity, it shall be treated for the purposes of this paragraph as unity.

(6) If, in relation to any later relevant DLT disposal, the fraction referred to in sub-paragraph (5) above is unity (whether by virtue of that sub-paragraph or otherwise) sub-paragraph (3) above shall not thereafter have effect in relation to any further DLT disposal which falls within sub-paragraph (1)(*c*) above.

Capital transfer tax charged at higher rate because of death of transferor

24.—(1) In any case where—

(*a*) account has been taken under any of the preceding provisions of this Schedule of an amount of capital transfer tax chargeable on the value transferred by a CTT transfer, and

(*b*) that amount was in fact charged at a rate or rates applicable under the Second Table set out in subsection (3) of section 37 of the Finance Act 1975 (the Table applicable to gifts inter vivos etc.), and 1975 c. 7.

(*c*) as a result of the death of the transferor within three years of the CTT transfer, the amount of capital transfer tax chargeable on the value transferred by that transfer falls to be recalculated by reference to a rate or rates applicable under the First Table set out in the said subsection (3),

any deduction for capital transfer tax paid which, in whole or in part, is derived from the amount of capital transfer tax chargeable on the value transferred by the CTT transfer shall be redetermined accordingly and such adjustment, whether by way of repayment of development land tax or otherwise, shall be made as is required in consequence.

(2) If, in a case where the disposal as a result of which the relevant interest was acquired as mentioned in paragraph 18(1)(*a*) above was a DLT disposal,—

(*a*) account has not been taken as mentioned in sub-paragraph (1)(*a*) above of an amount of capital transfer tax chargeable

SCH. 6

on the value transferred by a CTT transfer by reason only that the condition in paragraph 18(3)(*b*) above was not fulfilled, and

(*b*) the conditions in paragraphs (*b*) and (*c*) of sub-paragraph (1) above are fulfilled with respect to the amount of capital transfer tax referred to in paragraph (*a*) above, and

(*c*) the additional capital transfer tax falling to be paid as a result of the recalculation referred to in sub-paragraph (1)(*c*) above is borne by the person by whom the relevant interest was acquired as mentioned in paragraph 18(1)(*a*) above,

sub-paragraph (1) above shall apply on the basis that the condition in paragraph (*b*) of sub-paragraph (3) of paragraph 18 above was fulfilled with respect to £1 of the capital transfer tax referred to in that paragraph.

Set-off of estate duty against chargeable realised development value

25.—(1) In any case where—

(*a*) before the appointed day a person acquired an interest in land (in this Part of this Schedule referred to as " the material interest ") either on the death of a person (in this Part of this Schedule referred to as " the deceased ") or by a disposition made before the deceased's death but at such time and in such circumstances that the interest fell to be included in the property passing on the deceased's death for the purposes of estate duty, and

(*b*) an amount of estate duty was payable on the material interest (as part of the property comprised in the deceased's estate), and

(*c*) within the period of six years beginning on the date of the relevant event the person who acquired the material interest as mentioned in paragraph (*a*) above or a person claiming through him for DLT purposes makes a DLT disposal (in the following provisions of this Part of this Schedule referred to as " the subsequent disposal ") of the material interest, and

(*d*) chargeable realised development value accrues, or would but for this Part of this Schedule accrue, on the subsequent disposal, and

(*e*) the person making the subsequent disposal makes a claim in that behalf to the Board,

then, subject to paragraph 28 below, the amount which, apart from this Part of this Schedule, would be the chargeable realised development value accruing on the subsequent disposal shall be reduced by an amount (in this Part of this Schedule referred to as " the estate duty deduction ") determined in accordance with the following provisions of this Part of this Schedule.

(2) In sub-paragraph (1)(*c*) above and the following provisions of this Part of this Schedule " the relevant event " means the death or disposition on the occasion of which the material interest was acquired as mentioned in sub-paragraph (1)(*a*) above.

(3) For the purpose of making any determination required by the following provisions of this Part of this Schedule in relation to a DLT disposal occurring at the same time as the relevant event, it shall be assumed that the appointed day fell (and this Act was in force) before the relevant event occurred. SCH. 6

(4) If, after the amount of chargeable realised development value accruing on a DLT disposal has been ascertained, having regard to the amount of the estate duty deduction applicable under this Part of this Schedule, the amount of estate duty payable in respect of the material interest and taken into account in determining that deduction is varied, such adjustment, whether by way of a further assessment to development land tax or the discharge or repayment of development land tax or otherwise, shall be made as is required in consequence.

26.—(1) Where paragraph 25 above applies there shall be determined the amount of chargeable realised development value which, subject to sub-paragraphs (2) and (3) below, would have accrued if, at the time of the relevant event, there had been a DLT disposal by the deceased of the material interest for a consideration equal to the principal value for estate duty of the material interest on the deceased's death.

(2) Where the relevant event is such a disposition as is referred to in paragraph 25(1)(*a*) above and that disposition was made by a person other than the deceased, the reference in sub-paragraph (1) above to a DLT disposal by the deceased shall be construed as a reference to a DLT disposal by that other person.

(3) For the purposes of the determination referred to in sub-paragraph (1) above, it shall be assumed that section 12 of this Act had not been enacted.

The estate duty deduction

27.—(1) Subject to the following provisions of this Part of this Schedule, where paragraph 25 above applies, the estate duty deduction which is allowable by reference to the relevant event is the amount determined under sub-paragraph (2) below.

(2) The amount referred to in sub-paragraph (1) above is that given by the formula—

$$\frac{A \times C}{B}$$

where—

"A" is the chargeable realised development value determined under paragraph 26(1) above or the chargeable realised development value which accrues on the subsequent disposal, whichever is the less;

"B" is the amount taken as the consideration for the DLT disposal referred to in paragraph 26(1) above; and

"C" is the amount of estate duty levied on the principal value of the material interest at the estate rate applicable to the deceased's estate.

SCH. 6

Application of deduction to later DLT disposals

28.—(1) Subject to the provisions of this paragraph, where paragraphs 25 to 27 above have had effect in relation to a DLT disposal falling within paragraph 25(1)(*c*) above (in the following provisions of this Part of this Schedule referred to as " the first relevant DLT disposal ") no estate duty deduction shall be allowable by reference to the relevant event on any later disposal of the material interest.

(2) Subject to paragraph 30 below, in any case where—

(*a*) the first relevant DLT disposal was a part disposal only, and

(*b*) in relation to the first relevant DLT disposal, " A " in the formula specified in paragraph 27(2) above was the chargeable realised development value which accrued on that disposal, and

(*c*) within the period of six years referred to in paragraph 25(1)(*c*) above, the person who made the first relevant DLT disposal or a person claiming through him for DLT purposes makes a later material DLT disposal, and

(*d*) paragraph 25 above applies in relation to the later material DLT disposal referred to in paragraph (*c*) above,

sub-paragraph (1) above shall not apply but paragraphs 26 and 27 above shall have effect in relation to that later material DLT disposal subject to sub-paragraph (3) below.

(3) Sub-paragraphs (3) to (6) of paragraph 21 above shall have effect for the purposes of this paragraph as they have effect for the purposes of that, but subject to the following modifications:—

(*a*) for any reference to paragraph 19(1) or paragraph 20(2) above there shall be substituted a reference to paragraph 26(1) or paragraph 27(2) above respectively, and

(*b*) for any reference to capital transfer tax deduction there shall be substituted a reference to estate duty deduction, and

(*c*) any reference to the later relevant DLT disposal shall be construed as a reference to the later material DLT disposal referred to in sub-paragraph (2) above and

(*d*) any reference to the subsequent disposal shall be construed in accordance with paragraph 25(1)(*c*) above.

Assembly of interests after relevant event

29.—(1) In any case where—

(*a*) the conditions in paragraphs (*a*) and (*b*) of sub-paragraph (1) of paragraph 25 above are fulfilled, and

(*b*) within the period of six years referred to in paragraph (*c*) of that sub-paragraph there is a DLT disposal which is one to which Part I of Schedule 2 to this Act applies, and

(*c*) for the purposes of Part I of Schedule 2 to this Act, the material interest is, in relation to the DLT disposal referred to in paragraph (*b*) above, a part of the interest which is the subject matter of that disposal,

the DLT disposal shall be treated as falling within paragraph (*c*) of sub-paragraph (1) of paragraph 25 above, notwithstanding that it is a disposal of an interest greater than the material interest.

(2) If, in a case where paragraph 25 above applies by virtue of sub-paragraph (1) above, there is more than one event— Sch. 6

(*a*) on the occasion of which a person acquires an interest in land which for the purposes of Part I of Schedule 2 to this Act is, in relation to the subsequent disposal, a part of the interest which is the subject matter of that disposal, and

(*b*) which is capable of constituting the relevant event in relation to the subsequent disposal,

paragraphs 26 and 27 above shall have effect subject to the following provisions of this paragraph ; and in those provisions and paragraph 30 below the events falling within paragraphs (*a*) and (*b*) above are referred to as " the material events ".

(3) Subject to sub-paragraph (4) below, where sub-paragraph (2) above applies,—

(*a*) paragraphs 26 and 27(2) above shall be applied separately in relation to each of the material events, and

(*b*) sub-paragraph (1) of paragraph 27 above shall have effect as if the reference therein to the amount determined under sub-paragraph (2) of that paragraph were a reference to the aggregate of the amounts so determined.

(4) If the aggregate of the amounts of chargeable realised development value determined under paragraph 26(1) above in relation to each of the material events is greater than the chargeable realised development value which accrues on the subsequent disposal then, for the purpose of paragraph 27(2) above (as applied by sub-paragraph (3) above), each of those amounts of chargeable realised development value shall be treated as reduced proportionately so that the aggregate of them is equal to the chargeable realised development value which accrues on the subsequent disposal.

Part disposals out of assemblies

30.—(1) In a case falling within sub-paragraph (2) of paragraph 29 above, sub-paragraphs (2) and (3) of paragraph 28 above shall not apply, but if, in such a case—

(*a*) the subsequent disposal was a part disposal only, and

(*b*) sub-paragraph (4) of paragraph 29 above applies, and

(*c*) within the period of six years beginning on the date of the first of the material events, the person who made the first relevant DLT disposal or a person claiming through him for DLT purposes makes a later DLT disposal, and

(*d*) that later DLT disposal is a material disposal, as defined in paragraph 21(3) above, as that paragraph has effect by virtue of paragraph 28(3) above, and

(*e*) paragraph 25 above applies in relation to that later DLT disposal,

there shall be determined the amount (in this paragraph referred to as " the balance carried forward ") by which the gross deduction determined under sub-paragraph (2) below exceeds the amount which was the estate duty deduction in relation to the first relevant DLT disposal.

SCH. 6

(2) The gross deduction referred to in sub-paragraph (1) above is the amount which would have been the estate duty deduction in relation to the first relevant DLT disposal if, in paragraph 29 above, sub-paragraph (4) (and the reference thereto in sub-paragraph (3)) were omitted.

(3) Sub-paragraphs (3) to (6) of paragraph 23 above shall have effect where sub-paragraph (1) above applies as they have effect where sub-paragraph (1) of that paragraph applies, but subject to the following modifications:—

(*a*) any reference to sub-paragraph (1) of that paragraph shall be construed as a reference to sub-paragraph (1) of this paragraph;

(*b*) for the reference to paragraphs 19 and 20 above there shall be substituted a reference to paragraphs 26 and 27 above and for the reference to paragraph 22(4) above there shall be substituted a reference to paragraph 29(4) above;

(*c*) for any reference to capital transfer tax deduction there shall be substituted a reference to estate duty deduction; and

(*d*) any reference to the first relevant DLT disposal or the balance carried forward shall be construed as if that reference were in this paragraph.

Section 39.

SCHEDULE 7

SUPPLEMENTARY PROVISIONS RELATING TO DISPOSALS WHERE DEVELOPMENT LAND TAX DEDUCTED FROM CONSIDERATION

1.—(1) In any case where the consideration for the material disposal exceeds 110 per cent. of the acquiring authority's estimate of the value which, for the purposes of this Act, is the current use value of the relevant interest at the time of their acquisition, the acquiring authority shall give notice to the Board in the prescribed form (in this Schedule referred to as a "notice of acquisition"); and in this Schedule, in relation to the material disposal,—

(*a*) "the acquiring authority" means the exempt body to whom the disposal is made;

(*b*) "prescribed" means prescribed by the Board; and

(*c*) "the relevant interest" means the interest in land which is acquired by that authority.

(2) Subject to sub-paragraphs (3) and (7) below, where a notice of acquisition is required to be given under sub-paragraph (1) above it shall be given at the time of the material disposal or, if—

(*a*) the acquiring authority acquire the relevant interest compulsorily, and

(*b*) the time of acquisition of the relevant interest precedes the time (in this sub-paragraph referred to as "the operative time") at which the compensation for the acquisition is agreed or otherwise determined (variations on appeal being disregarded for this purpose),

at the operative time.

(3) Subject to sub-paragraph (7) below, where a notice of acquisition is required to be given under sub-paragraph (1) above and the acquiring authority acquire the relevant interest— Sch. 7

(a) in England, Scotland or Wales by virtue of a general vesting declaration, within the meaning of Schedule 3 to the Town and Country Planning Act 1968 or, as the case may be, Schedule 24 to the Town and Country Planning (Scotland) Act 1972, or 1968 c. 72. 1972 c. 52.

(b) in Northern Ireland by way of a vesting order,

the notice shall be given at the time at which the compensation for the acquisition is agreed or otherwise determined (variations on appeal being disregarded for this purpose).

(4) Without prejudice to their obligation to give any other notice under this paragraph, in a case falling within sub-paragraph (1) above the acquiring authority—

(a) may give provisional notice to the Board in the prescribed form (in this Schedule referred to as a " provisional notice of acquisition ") at any time after the time at which the amount of the consideration for the material disposal is agreed but before that disposal takes place, and

(b) shall give a provisional notice of acquisition if requested to do so at any such time by the person by whom the material disposal is to be made.

(5) If,—

(a) in relation to their acquisition of the relevant interest, the acquiring authority are required by section 52 of the Land Compensation Act 1973, section 48 of the Land Compensation (Scotland) Act 1973 or Article 49 of the Land Acquisition and Compensation (Northern Ireland) Order 1973 (advance payment of compensation) to make a payment in respect of an amount determined in accordance with subsection (3) of that section or, as the case may be, paragraph (3) of that Article (agreement or estimation of amount of compensation payable), and 1973 c. 26. 1973 c. 56. S.I. 1973/1896 (N.I. 21).

(b) the amount referred to in paragraph (a) above exceeds 110 per cent. of the acquiring authority's estimate of the value which, for the purposes of this Act, is the current use value of the relevant interest at the time of their acquisition,

the acquiring authority shall, at the time at which that amount is so determined, give notice to the Board in the prescribed form (in this Schedule referred to as a " notice of advance payment ").

(6) In any case where sub-paragraph (1) above does not apply on the material disposal of an interest in land but—

(a) subsection (2) of section 22 of the Community Land Act 1975 (value of land developed where planning permission suspended) applies in determining the value of that land for the purposes of compensation, or 1975 c. 77.

SCH. 7

(*b*) development has been carried out on that land without planning permission, and, on the date of the material disposal, planning permission covering that development has not been granted as mentioned in subsection (3) of that section,

the acquiring authority shall give a notice of acquisition and may give a provisional notice of acquisition as if sub-paragraph (1) above did apply.

(7) If the acquiring authority acquire the relevant interest compulsorily and, by reason only of the variation at any time of an amount which was previously agreed or determined to be the compensation for the acquisition, they would, apart from this sub-paragraph, be required to give notice of acquisition at an earlier time, sub-paragraphs (2) and (3) above shall not apply and the notice of acquisition shall be given at the time of the variation.

(8) If it comes to the attention of an acquiring authority that a notice which they have given under the preceding provisions of this paragraph was incorrect or should not have been given, the authority shall forthwith give notice in writing to the Board of the correction required or, as the case may be, of the withdrawal of the notice previously given.

(9) Where, in relation to a material disposal, an acquiring authority give a notice to the Board under the preceding provisions of this paragraph, the authority shall give a copy of the notice to the chargeable person.

(10) A notice of acquisition, provisional notice of acquisition or notice of advance payment shall contain such information as the Board may reasonably require for the purposes of this Act.

2.—(1) Subject to sub-paragraph (2) below, in any case where—

(*a*) the Board receive a notice under paragraph 1 above relating to a material disposal, and

(*b*) it appears to them that that disposal does not or will not give rise to any liability for development land tax, and

(*c*) where the notice referred to in paragraph (*a*) above is a provisional notice of acquisition, the person by whom the material disposal is or is to be made agrees that the Board should act under this paragraph,

they shall, as soon as practicable, notify the acquiring authority by whom the notice was given that it appears to them that there is no such liability in respect of the disposal and, accordingly, that no DLT deduction should be made from the consideration for the disposal.

(2) If, after the Board have notified the acquiring authority as mentioned in sub-paragraph (1) above,—

(*a*) the Board receive a further notice under paragraph 1 above relating to the same material disposal, and

(*b*) the Board remain of the opinion that the material disposal does not give rise to any liability for development land tax,

the Board shall be under no obligation to send a further notification under sub-paragraph (1) above.

3.—(1) If, in a case where paragraph 2 above does not apply, the Board receive a notice of acquisition relating to a material disposal and (before or after the receipt of that notice) an assessment to development land tax is made in respect of that disposal, then, in accordance with sub-paragraph (3) below, the Board shall— SCH. 7

(*a*) furnish to the acquiring authority the particulars relating to that assessment which are specified in sub-paragraph (2) below ; and

(*b*) where any provision of paragraph 4 below so requires notify the acquiring authority of the amount of the specific deduction which in accordance with that paragraph is applicable to the material disposal.

(2) The particulars relating to an assessment which are referred to in sub-paragraph (1)(*a*) above are—

(*a*) the name and address of the person assessed ;

(*b*) the amount of development land tax charged by the assessment ;

(*c*) the date of issue of the notice of assessment ;

(*d*) the date which is the reckonable date in relation to the liability for the development land tax charged by the assessment ; and

(*e*) whether the amount referred to in paragraph (*b*) above has been agreed by the person assessed or the assessment has become final in the absence of an appeal and, if notice of appeal has been given, the amount (if any) which has become due and payable under the Taxes Management Act 1970. 1970 c. 9.

(3) The obligation under sub-paragraph (1) above to furnish particulars of an assessment and, where paragraph 4 below so requires, to notify the amount of a specific deduction shall be complied with—

(*a*) in the case of an assessment of which notice was issued before the expiry of the period of twenty-one days beginning with the date of the receipt of the notice of acquisition, not later than the end of that period ; and

(*b*) in the case of any other assessment, at the same time as the notice of assessment is issued.

(4) The preceding provisions of this paragraph shall have effect, with any necessary modifications, in relation to a variation under the Taxes Management Act 1970 in the amount of development land tax charged by an assessment to which sub-paragraph (1) above applies or in any such amount as is referred to in sub-paragraph (2)(*e*) above as they apply where such an assessment is made.

(5) If, in a case where paragraph 2 above does not apply,—

(*a*) the Board receive a provisional notice of acquisition or notice of advance payment relating to a material disposal, or

SCH. 7

(*b*) the Board receive a notice of acquisition relating to a material disposal but no obligation arises or, as the case may be, has yet arisen under sub-paragraph (1)(*b*) above,

the Board may, with the agreement of the person by whom the material disposal is or is to be made, notify the acquiring authority of the amount of the specific deduction which, in accordance with paragraph 4(5) below, is applicable to the material disposal.

Notification of specific deduction

4.—(1) If, by virtue of the receipt of a notice of acquisition and the making of an assessment to development land tax (in this paragraph referred to as " the relevant assessment ") the Board are under the obligation to furnish particulars of the relevant assessment as mentioned in paragraph (*a*) of sub-paragraph (1) of paragraph 3 above, the obligation to notify the acquiring authority as mentioned in paragraph (*b*) of that sub-paragraph shall arise in any case where, at the time the particulars of the relevant assessment are so furnished, any of the conditions in sub-paragraph (2) below is fulfilled.

(2) The conditions referred to in sub-paragraph (1) above are—

(*a*) that the liability for development land tax in respect of the material disposal has been agreed or determined in the amount charged by the relevant assessment ;

(*b*) that the period of thirty days beginning on the date of issue of the notice of the relevant assessment has expired without a notice of appeal having been given against the relevant assessment ;

(*c*) that notice of appeal has been given against the relevant assessment and an amount of development land tax has become due and payable under the Taxes Management Act 1970 ; and

1970 c. 9.

(*d*) that notice of appeal has been given against the relevant assessment but no amount of development land tax has become due and payable under the Taxes Management Act 1970 and the amount of tax charged by the relevant assessment is less than the amount of the formula deduction, within the meaning of paragraph 5 below, which would be applicable to a payment of the whole of the consideration for the material disposal.

(3) Where the obligation of the Board to notify the acquiring authority of the amount of the specific deduction applicable to the material disposal arises by reason of the fulfilment of any condition in sub-paragraph (2) above, then—

(*a*) if the condition fulfilled is that in paragraph (*c*) of that sub-paragraph, the amount of the specific deduction shall be equal to the amount of tax referred to in that paragraph ; and

(*b*) in any other case, the amount of the specific deduction shall be equal to the amount of tax charged by the relevant assessment.

(4) Where sub-paragraph (4) of paragraph 3 above applies, the Board shall be under the obligation specified in sub-paragraph (1)(*b*) of that paragraph and in such a case the amount of the specific deduction applicable to the material disposal shall be equal to the amount of development land tax which, taking account of the variation referred to in sub-paragraph (4) of that paragraph, is charged by the assessment concerned or, as the case may be, has become due and payable under the Taxes Management Act 1970. — SCH. 7 — 1970 c. 9.

(5) In relation to the exercise by the Board of their power to notify the acquiring authority as mentioned in sub-paragraph (5) of paragraph 3 above, the amount of the specific deduction applicable to the material disposal concerned shall be such as may be agreed between the Board and the person referred to in that sub-paragraph to represent—

(*a*) the amount of his liability or prospective liability for development land tax in respect of that material disposal ; or

(*b*) so much of the development land tax for which he is or will be liable in respect of that material disposal as is not in dispute.

The formula deduction

5.—(1) Subject to paragraphs 7 and 8 below if, at a time when a payment of consideration falls to be made in respect of a material disposal to which paragraph 1(1) above applies, the acquiring authority have not received—

(*a*) a notification under paragraph 2(1) above, or

(*b*) a notification under paragraph 3 above stating the amount of the specific DLT deduction applicable to the disposal,

the acquiring authority shall deduct from that payment a DLT deduction of an amount determined in accordance with this paragraph (in the following provisions of this Schedule referred to as a " formula deduction ").

(2) In relation to a formula deduction " the relevant payment " means the payment of consideration from which the deduction falls to be made by virtue of sub-paragraph (1) above ; and any reference in this paragraph to the amount of the relevant payment is a reference to the amount of that payment before the formula deduction is made, but exclusive of any interest payable by the acquiring authority.

(3) If the amount of the consideration for the material disposal does not exceed the aggregate of—

(*a*) 110 per cent. of the acquiring authority's estimate of the value which, for the purposes of this Act, is the current use value of the relevant interest at the time of their acquisition, and

(*b*) £10,000,

the amount of the formula deduction shall be nil ; and in relation to a material disposal the aggregate amount determined under this sub-paragraph is referred to as " the exempt amount ".

SCH. 7

(4) If sub-paragraph (3) above does not apply and the material disposal occurs in an interim financial year, then, subject to sub-paragraphs (5) and (8) and paragraph 7(3) below, the formula deduction shall be whichever is the less of the following amounts, namely,—

(*a*) 50 per cent. of the amount of the relevant payment; and

(*b*) 66⅔ per cent. of the amount by which the consideration for the disposal exceeds the exempt amount.

(5) If, in a case where sub-paragraph (4) above applies, the consideration for the material disposal exceeds the exempt amount by more than £150,000, that sub-paragraph and sub-paragraph (8) below shall have effect as if for paragraph (*b*) of sub-paragraph (4) above there were substituted the following paragraph:—

" (*b*) £100,000 plus 80 per cent. of the amount by which the consideration for the disposal exceeds the aggregate of the exempt amount and £150,000 ".

(6) If sub-paragraph (3) above does not apply and the material disposal occurs after 31st March 1979, then, subject to sub-paragraph (8) and paragraph 7(3) below, the formula deduction shall be whichever is the less of the following amounts, namely,—

(*a*) the appropriate percentage of the amount of the relevant payment; and

(*b*) 80 per cent. of the amount by which the consideration for the disposal exceeds the exempt amount.

(7) In sub-paragraph (6)(*a*) above " the appropriate percentage " means such percentage as may be specified by the Board by regulations made by statutory instrument; but no such regulations shall be made unless a draft of the regulations has been laid before and approved by a resolution of the Commons House of Parliament.

(8) If, before the time at which the relevant payment falls to be made in respect of a material disposal, a previous payment of consideration has been made in respect of that disposal, then, in calculating the formula deduction, the amount determined under sub-paragraph (4)(*b*) or, as the case may be, sub-paragraph (6)(*b*) above shall be reduced by the amount of the DLT deduction made from that previous payment or, if there has been more than one such payment, by the aggregate of the DLT deductions made from those payments.

Amount of DLT deduction where specific deduction notified

6.—(1) Subject to the provisions of this paragraph and paragraph 8 below, if a payment of consideration falls to be made in respect of a material disposal after the time at which an acquiring authority receive a notification under paragraph 3 above of the amount of the specific deduction applicable to that disposal, the acquiring authority shall deduct from that payment a DLT deduction equal to the specific deduction applicable to the disposal, less the amount of the DLT deduction deducted from any previous payment of consideration made in respect of that disposal or, where there has been more than one such previous payment, less the aggregate amount of the DLT deductions made from those payments. SCH. 7

(2) Subject to paragraphs 7 and 8 below, where a payment of consideration which falls to be made as mentioned in sub-paragraph (1) above is neither the only nor the last payment of consideration which falls to be made in respect of the material disposal concerned, there shall be determined, as at the time immediately before the payment is made,—

(*a*) the total amount of consideration which remains to be paid in respect of the disposal, and

(*b*) the amount of the specific deduction applicable to the disposal, less the amount of the DLT deduction deducted from any previous payment of consideration made in respect of that disposal or, where there has been more than one such previous payment, less the aggregate amount of the DLT deductions made from those payments,

and the amount of the DLT deduction to be made from that payment of consideration shall be equal to that proportion of the amount referred to in paragraph (*b*) above which the amount of that payment bears to the total amount referred to in paragraph (*a*) above.

(3) In any case where, apart from this sub-paragraph, the amount of the DLT deduction to be made by virtue of sub-paragraph (1) or sub-paragraph (2) above from a payment of consideration would exceed the amount of that payment, that DLT deduction shall be of an amount equal to the amount of that payment.

(4) Any reference in this paragraph to the amount of any consideration or of any payment of consideration is a reference to the amount of that consideration or payment before any DLT deduction is made from it, but exclusive of any interest payable by the acquiring authority.

(5) If an acquiring authority receive more than one notification under paragraph 3 above of the amount of the specific deduction applicable to a material disposal, the later or latest notification shall be taken to supersede any earlier notification ; but the receipt of a second or subsequent notification shall not require the re-determination of the amount of the DLT deduction applicable to a payment of consideration made before the receipt of that notification.

Advance payments of compensation

7.—(1) In their application to a payment of consideration which consists of such a payment as is referred to in paragraph 1(5)(*a*) above (in this paragraph referred to as an " advance payment of compensation ") paragraphs 5 and 6 above shall have effect subject to the provisions of this paragraph.

(2) In relation to an advance payment of compensation made in connection with a material disposal, any reference in paragraph 5 above or in the following provisions of this paragraph to the consideration for that material disposal shall be construed as a reference to an amount equal to ten-ninths of the amount of that advance payment.

SCH. 7

(3) In a case where the relevant payment, within the meaning of paragraph 5 above, is an advance payment of compensation, the formula deduction applicable to that advance payment shall be calculated as if the reference in sub-paragraphs (4)(*a*) and (6)(*a*) of that paragraph to the amount of the relevant payment were a reference to the amount of the consideration for the material disposal.

(4) If, apart from this sub-paragraph, the DLT deduction to be made from an advance payment of compensation would, by virtue of paragraph 5(1) above, be a formula deduction, then—

(*a*) if the formula deduction applicable to the advance payment does not exceed 10 per cent. of the consideration for the material disposal concerned, no DLT deduction shall be made by virtue of that paragraph from that advance payment ; and

(*b*) in any other case the DLT deduction to be made by virtue of paragraph 5(1) above from the advance payment shall be the amount by which the formula deduction applicable to that advance payment exceeds 10 per cent. of the consideration for the material disposal concerned.

(5) In its application to an advance payment of compensation, paragraph 6 above shall have effect with the omission of sub-paragraph (2).

DLT deduction not to exceed balance remaining after discharge of pre-12th May 1976 mortgage or charge

8.—(1) Subject to sub-paragraphs (3) and (4) below, in the case of a material disposal where—

(*a*) immediately before the time of the transfer of the relevant interest to the acquiring authority (in this paragraph referred to as " the material time ") a mortgage or charge entered into or or before 11th May 1976 subsists in the relevant land ; and

(*b*) by virtue of the material disposal the mortgage or charge is to be discharged at or before the material time and falls to be so discharged, in whole or in part, out of the consideration for that disposal ; and

(*c*) the cost of redemption of the mortgage or charge exceeds the amount which would remain after deducting from the consideration for the disposal the amount which, apart from this paragraph, would be the DLT deduction,

the DLT deduction relevant to the material disposal shall be the amount (if any) by which the consideration for that disposal exceeds the cost of redemption of the mortgage or charge.

(2) In this paragraph " the relevant land " means the land in which the relevant interest subsists immediately after its transfer to the acquiring authority, and in any case where the mortgage or charge

referred to in paragraph (*a*) of sub-paragraph (1) above subsists in other land, as well as the relevant land,— SCH. 7

(*a*) the references in paragraph (*b*) of that sub-paragraph to the discharge of the mortgage or charge shall be construed as references to the discharge of the mortgage or charge so far as it relates to the relevant land ; and

(*b*) the reference in paragraph (*c*) of that sub-paragraph to the cost of redemption of the mortgage or charge shall be construed as a reference to that proportion of that cost which is properly attributable to the relevant land.

(3) No DLT deduction shall be made from the consideration for the material disposal if, by reference to a mortgage or charge entered into on or before 11th May 1976, that consideration is agreed or determined under any of the following enactments,—

(*a*) section 15(1) of the Compulsory Purchase Act 1965, section 101 of the Lands Clauses Consolidation (Scotland) Act 1845 or, in Northern Ireland, section 110 of the Lands Clauses Consolidation Act 1845 (debt secured on land exceeds the value of the land) ; or 1965 c. 56. 1845 c. 19. 1845 c. 18.

(*b*) section 16(1) of the Compulsory Purchase Act 1965, section 103 of the Lands Clauses Consolidation (Scotland) Act 1845 or, in Northern Ireland, section 112 of the Lands Clauses Consolidation Act 1845 (acquisition of part of land subject to mortgage or charge).

(4) Nothing in this paragraph shall impose on an acquiring authority an obligation to make a DLT deduction limited to the amount referred to in sub-paragraph (1) above unless, before the material time, the creditor under the mortgage or charge informs the acquiring authority of the cost of redemption of the mortgage or charge and furnishes to them any other information which the authority might reasonably require from him for the purpose of determining the amount of that DLT deduction.

(5) In this paragraph " mortgage or charge " means an interest falling within paragraph (*a*) or paragraph (*b*) of subsection (2) of section 46 of this Act and for the purposes of this paragraph—

(*a*) a mortgage or charge shall be taken to be entered into on or before 11th May 1976 if it was entered into after that date in pursuance of an offer which was accepted before that date ; and

(*b*) the cost of redemption of a mortgage or charge means the amount required to discharge the mortgage or charge at the date of the material disposal, less the amount of the principal of any further advance made after 11th May 1976, otherwise than in pursuance of such an offer as is referred to in paragraph (*a*) above.

(6) Any question arising under sub-paragraph (2)(*b*) above as to the proportion of the cost of redemption of a mortgage or charge which is properly attributable to any land shall be determined by agreement between the chargeable person, the creditor under the

SCH. 7 mortgage or charge and the acquiring authority or, in default of agreement, by the Lands Tribunal, the Lands Tribunal for Scotland or the Lands Tribunal for Northern Ireland, according to the location of the land.

Compulsory purchase : sums paid into court or deposited

1965 c. 56. 9.—(1) In the application of section 9 of the Compulsory Purchase Act 1965 (refusal to convey, failure to make title, etc.) to a material disposal in connection with which the acquiring authority are required to make a deduction under section 39 of this Act,—

(*a*) any reference in the said section 9 to the compensation agreed or awarded to be paid or the compensation payable in respect of the relevant interest shall be construed as a reference to the amount of the compensation so agreed or awarded less the amount of the deduction required to be made therefrom under section 39 of this Act ; and

(*b*) the reference in subsection (1) of the said section 9 to the tender of the compensation shall be construed as including a reference to the giving of an undertaking to furnish an appropriate statement under subsection (4) of section 39 of this Act.

(2) Where sub-paragraph (1) above has effect in relation to an amount of compensation paid into court under section 9(1) of the Compulsory Purchase Act 1965, section 39 of this Act and the preceding provisions of this Schedule shall apply as if that amount were being paid direct to the chargeable person by way of consideration for the disposal.

(3) Sub-paragraphs (1) and (2) above shall apply in relation to Scotland subject to the following modifications:—

(*a*) for any reference to section 9 or subsection (1) of section 9 of the Compulsory Purchase Act 1965 there shall be substituted a reference to section 75 of the Lands Clauses Consolidation (Scotland) Act 1845 ; and (1845 c. 19.)

(*b*) for any reference to compensation there shall be substituted a reference to purchase-money or compensation ; and

(*c*) in sub-paragraph (2) above for the words " paid into court " there shall be substituted the word " deposited ".

(4) Sub-paragraphs (1) and (2) above shall apply in relation to Northern Ireland subject to the following modifications:—

(*a*) for any reference to section 9 or subsection (1) of section 9 of the Compulsory Purchase Act 1965 there shall be substituted a reference to section 76 of the Lands Clauses Consolidation Act 1845 ; and (1845 c. 18.)

(*b*) for any reference to compensation there shall be substituted a reference to purchase money or compensation ; and

(*c*) in sub-paragraph (2) above for the words " paid into court " there shall be substituted the word " deposited ".

(5) Without prejudice to the operation of subsection (5) of section 39 of this Act, in determining whether the condition of a bond given under the enactment permitting entry on the giving of security has been performed, nothing in that section shall authorise the making of a deduction from any amount required to be paid into court or deposited under that enactment. SCH. 7

(6) In sub-paragraph (5) above, " the enactment permitting entry on the giving of security " means—

(*a*) In England and Wales, Schedule 3 to the Compulsory Purchase Act 1965 ; 1965 c. 56.

(*b*) in Scotland, section 84 of the Lands Clauses Consolidation (Scotland) Act 1845 ; and 1845 c. 19.

(*c*) in Northern Ireland, section 85 of the Lands Clauses Consolidation Act 1845. 1845 c. 18.

Procedure subsequent to making of DLT deduction

10.—(1) Where, in connection with a material disposal, the acquiring authority makes a payment of consideration from which they deduct a DLT deduction, the authority shall forthwith furnish to the Board a certificate giving the particulars contained in the statement required to be furnished under section 39(4) of this Act and such other information as may be appropriate to identify the transaction concerned.

(2) If, after the receipt of a certificate under sub-paragraph (1) above, the Board notify the acquiring authority by whom the certificate was furnished that the amount of the DLT deduction in respect of the material disposal concerned exceeds the amount of development land tax for which the chargeable person is liable in respect of that disposal,—

(*a*) the amount of the excess shall be payable by the acquiring authority to the Board ; and

(*b*) the Board shall account to the chargeable person for the amount of the excess as an amount of development land tax paid in excess of his liability ; and

(*c*) sections 65 to 68 and 70 of the Taxes Management Act 1970 (proceedings for recovery of tax) shall have effect as if the amount of the excess were an amount of tax, within the meaning of that Act, due from the acquiring authority. 1970 c. 9.

(3) In so far as the liability of the chargeable person for development land tax in respect of a material disposal exceeds the amount of the DLT deduction in respect of that disposal, the amount of the excess shall be due and payable to the Board in like manner as an amount of development land tax for which the chargeable person is liable in respect of a disposal which is not a material disposal.

(4) A certificate under sub-paragraph (1) above shall be either in a form prescribed by the Board or in a form authorised by them for use in substitution for the form prescribed and containing a statement that it has been so authorised.

SCH. 7

Interest on DLT deductions made before reckonable date

11.—(1) In any case where—

(*a*) in connection with a material disposal the acquiring authority make a payment of consideration from which they deduct a DLT deduction, and

(*b*) that payment is made before the date which is the reckonable date in relation to the chargeable person's liability for development land tax in respect of that disposal,

then, subject to sub-paragraph (2) below, the chargeable person shall be credited with interest on the amount of that DLT deduction for the period beginning on the date on which the payment is made and ending on the reckonable date.

(2) If a sum representing the whole or any part of a DLT deduction is paid to the chargeable person before the reckonable date, he shall not be credited with interest on that sum beyond the date of payment.

(3) Interest with which a person is credited under this paragraph—

(*a*) shall be calculated at the rate which is for the time being the prescribed rate for the purposes of section 86A of the Taxes Management Act 1970 (interest on unpaid development land tax);

1970 c. 9.

(*b*) shall not be income of that person for any tax purposes; and

(*c*) shall be treated for all purposes as an amount of development land tax paid by that person to the Board in respect of the material disposal referred to in sub-paragraph (1)(*a*) above;

and subsection (7) of section 39 of this Act shall apply in relation to any amount treated as having been paid to the Board by virtue of paragraph (*c*) above as it applies to an amount so treated by virtue of subsection (5)(*b*) of that section.

Exclusion of provisions as to interest on unpaid tax

12. Notwithstanding that a payment of consideration from which a DLT deduction is deducted may be made after the reckonable date, section 86A of the Taxes Management Act 1970 (interest on unpaid development land tax) shall not apply to any development land tax which a person is treated as having paid to the Board by virtue of section 39(5)(*b*) of this Act.

Inspection of books, accounts, etc.

13. Whenever called upon to do so by an officer authorised in that behalf by the Board, an exempt body shall produce to that officer for inspection, at its principal office or place of business, all, or such as may be specified by that officer of, the books, accounts and other documents and records in the possession or under the control of that body and relating to—

(*a*) amounts paid by way of consideration for material disposals by which interests in land were acquired by that body; and

(*b*) any DLT deductions made in connection with such material disposals.

SCHEDULE 8

Section 41.

Administration of Development Land Tax

Part I

Amendments of the Taxes Management Act 1970

1970 c. 9.

1. In section 1 (taxes under the care and management of the Board), in subsection (1) after the words " corporation tax " there shall be inserted the words " development land tax ".

2.—(1) In section 29 (assessing procedure) after subsection (1) there shall be inserted the following subsection:—

" (1A) All assessments to development land tax shall be made by the Board and,—

(*a*) if they are satisfied from a notice given or any information or documents furnished under Part II of Schedule 8 to the Development Land Tax Act 1976 or such an instrument as is referred to in paragraph 35(2) of that Schedule that they have been afforded correct and complete information concerning the profits which accrue to a person on the disposal of an interest in land or on which he is otherwise liable to development land tax, they shall make an assessment accordingly ; and

(*b*) in any other case, they may make an assessment to the best of their judgment ".

(2) In subsection (8) of that section (meaning of " profits ") after paragraph (*c*) there shall be inserted the following paragraph:—

" (*d*) in relation to development land tax, means realised development value ".

3.—(1) In section 31 (right of appeal), at the beginning of subsection (3) (certain appeals to lie to the Special Commissioners) there shall be inserted the words " Subject to subsection (3A) below ".

(2) After the said subsection (3) there shall be inserted the following subsection:—

" (3A) Subsection (3) above shall not apply to an appeal if the only question in dispute on the appeal is whether any realised development value is excluded from the charge to development land tax by virtue of section 14 or section 15 of the Development Land Tax Act 1976."

4. In section 32 (relief for double assessment), in subsection (1) after the words " chargeable period " there shall be inserted the words " or, in the case of an assessment to development land tax, on the same amount of realised development value ".

5.—(1) In section 33 (excessive assessment due to error or mistake) after subsection (4) there shall be inserted the following subsection:—

" (4A) In relation to an assessment to development land tax,—

(*a*) subsection (1) above shall have effect as if for the word ' return ' there were substituted the words ' notice given or in any information or document furnished

SCH. 8

under Part II of Schedule 8 to the Development Land Tax Act 1976 or in such an instrument as is referred to in paragraph 35(2) of that Schedule ; and as if for the words ' year of assessment ' there were substituted the words ' financial year ' ;

(*b*) subsection (2) above shall have effect as if for the words from ' return was in fact ' to the end of that subsection there were substituted the words ' notice, information, document or instrument concerned was in fact given, furnished or made on the basis or in accordance with the practice generally prevailing at the time when it was so given, furnished or made ' ; and

(*c*) subsection (3) above shall have effect as if for the words ' chargeable periods other than that ' there were substituted the words " profits other than those ."

(2) At the end of subsection (5) of that section (meaning of " profits ") there shall be added the following paragraph:—

" (*d*) in relation to development land tax, means realised development value ".

6. In section 34 (ordinary time limit for assessments), at the end of subsection (1) there shall be added the words " or, if the assessment is to development land tax, after the end of the financial year in which occurred the disposal or other event giving rise to the liability for that tax ".

7. At the end of section 37 (assessments to tax where there is fraud, wilful default or neglect) there shall be added the following subsection:—

" (10) In the application of the preceding provisions of this section in relation to development land tax—

(*a*) references to an assessment to tax for any year are references to an assessment to development land tax the liability for which arose in any financial year ;

(*b*) references to a year of assessment are references to a financial year ;

(*c*) in subsection (5) above, for the words ' tax for a year ' there shall be substituted the words ' development land tax the liability for which arose in a financial year ' ;

(*d*) in subsection (6) above, for the words ' years for which those assessments were made ' there shall be substituted the words ' financial years in which arose the liabilities giving rise to those assessments ' ;

(*e*) in subsection (8) above the words ' for any year ' and ' for that year ' shall be omitted ; and

(*f*) subsection (9) above shall be omitted ".

8. In section 38 (modification of section 37 in relation to partnerships), in subsection (3) (assessment on person who was a partner and carried on the business in the year for which the assessment is

made) for the words " subsection (5) " there shall be substituted the words " subsections (3A) and (5) " and at the end of that subsection there shall be added the following subsection:—

" (3A) In its application to an assessment to development land tax, subsection (3) above shall have effect as if—

(*a*) for the words ' the profits or gains ' there were substituted the words ' realised development value accruing in the course ' ; and

(*b*) for the words ' year for which the assessment is made ' there were substituted the words ' financial year in which arose the liability giving rise to the assessment '."

9.—(1) In section 40 (assessment on personal representatives) in subsection (3) (definition of " tax " for the purposes of the section) for the words " this section " there shall be substituted the words " subsections (1) and (2) above ".

(2) After the said subsection (3) there shall be inserted the following subsections:—

" (4) For the purpose of the charge of development land tax on the executors or administrators of a deceased person in respect of a liability to development land tax which arose before his death, the time allowed by section 34 or 36 above shall in no case extend beyond the end of the third year next following the financial year in which the deceased died.

(5) Subject to section 41 below, for the purpose of making good to the Crown any loss of development land tax attributable to the fraud, wilful default or neglect of a person who has died, an assessment on his personal representatives to development land tax where the liability for that tax arose in a financial year ending not earlier than six years before his death may be made at any time before the end of the third year next following the financial year in which he died."

10. At the end of section 41 (leave required for certain assessments) there shall be inserted the following subsection:—

" (3) In its application to an assessment to development land tax, paragraph (*b*) of subsection (1) above shall have effect as if for the words ' for a period ' there were substituted the words ' where the liability for the tax arose in a financial year '. "

11. In section 42 (procedure for making claim), at the end of subsection (11) (meaning of " profits ") there shall be added the words—

" (*d*) in relation to development land tax, means realised development value ".

12.—(1) In section 43 (time limit for making claims) at the end of subsection (1) there shall be inserted the words " or, if it relates to an amount of development land tax, the end of the financial year in which the liability for that tax arose (or would arise but for the claim) ".

SCH. 8

(2) After subsection (2) of that section there shall be added the following subsection:—

"(3) A claim (including a supplementary claim) which could not have been allowed but for the making of an assessment to development land tax after the end of the financial year in which arose the liability for the tax to which the claim relates may be made at any time before the end of the financial year following that in which the assessment was made".

13. After section 47 there shall be inserted the following section:—

"Special jurisdiction relating to development land tax.

47A. If and so far as the question in dispute on any appeal against an assessment to development land tax or against a decision on a claim relating to development land tax is a question of the value of an interest in land or of any other rights relating to land or an interest in it or a question as to how much of any expenditure on improvements is expenditure on relevant improvements in relation to an interest in land, then,—

(*a*) if the land is in England or Wales the question shall be determined on a reference to the Lands Tribunal, and

(*b*) if the land is in Scotland the question shall be determined on a reference to the Lands Tribunal for Scotland, and

(*c*) if the land is in Northern Ireland the question shall be determined on a reference to the Lands Tribunal for Northern Ireland".

14. In section 55 (recovery of tax not postponed on appeal), at the end of subsection (1) there shall be added the words—

"(*f*) an assessment to development land tax".

15. In subsection (9) of section 56 (statement of case for opinion of the High Court) and subsection (6) of section 59 (election for county court in Northern Ireland) after the word "inspector" where it appears in paragraph (*b*) of the proviso to each of those subsections there shall be added the words "or other officer of the Board".

16. After section 57 there shall be inserted the following:—

"*Development land tax*

Regulations about appeals.

57A.—(1) The Board may make regulations—

(*a*) as respects the conduct of appeals against assessments to development land tax and decisions on claims relating to development land tax,

(*b*) entitling persons, in addition to those who would be so entitled apart from the regulations, to appear on such appeals,

(*c*) regulating the time within which such appeals or claims may be brought or made, (*d*) where the consideration for a particular disposal or acquisition of an interest in land, or the market value or current use value of an interest in land on a particular date, or an apportionment or any other matter may affect the liability to development land tax of two or more persons, enabling any of those persons to have the matter determined by the tribunal having jurisdiction to determine that matter if arising on an appeal against an assesssment, and prescribing a procedure by which the matter is not determined differently on different occasions,

(*e*) authorising an inspector or other officer of the Board, notwithstanding the obligation as to secrecy imposed by virtue of this or any other Act,—

(i) to disclose to a person entitled to appear on such an appeal the consideration for the disposal or acquisition, the market value, or the current use value of an interest in land, as determined for the purposes of an assessment or decision on a claim ; or

(ii) to disclose to a person whose liability to development land tax may be affected by the determination of any such consideration, of any such value on a particular date, or an apportionment or any other matter, any decision on the matter made by an inspector or other officer of the Board.

(2) Regulations under this section may contain such supplemental and incidental provisions as appear to the Board to be expedient, including in particular provisions authorising the giving of conditional decisions where, under section 47A of this Act, questions on an appeal against an assessment or decision on a claim may go partly to one tribunal and partly to another.

(3) Regulations under this section—

(*a*) shall be made by statutory instrument subject to annulment in pursuance of a resolution of the House of Commons, and

(*b*) shall have effect notwithstanding anything in this Act."

17. At the end of section 62 (priority of claim for tax) there shall be added the following subsection:—

"(3) In their application to development land tax, the preceding provisions of this section shall have effect as if—

(*a*) in subsection (1) for the words 'which are payable for the year' there were substituted the words 'for which the liability arose in the financial year';

SCH. 8

(*b*) in the proviso to subsection (1) for the words 'for more than one year' there were substituted the words 'in respect of liabilities arising in more than one financial year'; and

(*c*) in the proviso to subsection (1) and in subsection (2) for the words 'for one whole year' there were substituted the words 'in respect of liabilities which arose in any one financial year'."

18. At the end of section 64 (priority of claim for tax in Scotland) there shall be added the following subsection:—

"(3) In their application to development land tax, the preceding provisions of this section shall have effect as if—

(*a*) in the proviso to subsection (1) for the words 'for more than one year' there were substituted the words 'in respect of liabilities arising in more than one financial year'; and

(*b*) in the proviso to subsection (1) and in subsection (2) for the words 'for one whole year' there were substituted the words 'in respect of liabilities which arose in any one financial year'."

19. After section 77 there shall be inserted the following:—

"*Development land tax*

Application of Part VII to development land tax.

77A.—(1) This Part of this Act (except section 76 above) shall apply in relation to development land tax as it applies in relation to income tax, and subject to any necessary modifications.

(2) This Part of this Act as applied by this section shall not affect the question of who is the person to whom realised development value accrues, or who is chargeable to development land tax, so far as that question is relevant for the purposes of determining the amount of development land tax which is chargeable."

20. After section 85 there shall be inserted the following:—

"*Development land tax*

Non-residents chargeable to development land tax.

85A.—(1) Where a non-resident person is chargeable to an amount of development land tax, he shall be assessable and chargeable to that amount in the name of any such trustee, guardian, tutor, curator or committee as is mentioned in section 72 of this Act, or of any branch or agent, whether or not the branch or agent has the receipt of any consideration for the disposal of an interest in land which accrues to that person.

(2) The person in whose name the non-resident person is chargeable shall be answerable for all matters required to be done under the enactments relating to development land tax for the purpose of assessment and payment of that tax.

(3) A person who has been charged under this section in respect of any non-resident person may retain, out of money coming into his hands on behalf of any such person, so much thereof from time to time as is sufficient to pay the tax charged, and shall be indemnified for all such payments made in pursuance of the enactments relating to development land tax. SCH. 8

(4) In this section 'non-resident person' means a person whose usual place of abode is outside the United Kingdom."

21. After section 86 there shall be inserted the following:—

"Development land tax

Interest on development land tax unpaid on reckonable date.

86A.—(1) Where a person becomes liable for an amount of development land tax then, except as provided by paragraph 12 of Schedule 7 to the Development Land Tax Act 1976, that amount shall, until payment, carry interest at the prescribed rate calculated, subject to sub-paragraphs (2) and (3) below, from the reckonable date, within the meaning of that Act.

(2) If, after the disposal of an interest in land,—

(*a*) a contingent liability which was assumed by any person and was not taken into account in determining the consideration for the disposal becomes enforceable and is enforced on any date, and

(*b*) by virtue of the enforcement of that liability, the development land tax for which a person is liable on that disposal is increased by an amount,

the amount referred to in paragraph (*b*) above shall carry interest only from the date referred to in paragraph (*a*) above.

(3) Where tax is payable by instalments under any of the provisions of paragraphs 44 to 49 of Schedule 8 to the Development Land Tax Act 1976, each instalment or other part of that tax which becomes payable in accordance with those provisions on a particular date shall carry interest only from that date.

(4) Development land tax shall carry interest from a date ascertained in accordance with this section even if that date is a non-business day within the meaning of section 92 of the Bills of Exchange Act 1882. 1882 c. 61.

(5) Where an amount of interest payable under this section on the development land tax for which a person is liable on the disposal of an interest in land or other event does not exceed £10, that amount of interest may, if the Board thinks fit, be remitted."

22.—(1) In section 88 (interest on tax recovered to make good loss due to taxpayer's fault), in subsection (3), after " 85 " there shall be inserted the words " or section 86A ".

SCH. 8

(2) At the end of subsection (5) of that section (meaning of reference to date when tax ought to have been paid) there shall be added the following paragraph:—

"(*f*) in the case of development land tax, the date which, in relation to the liability of the person concerned for that tax, is the reckonable date, within the meaning of the Development Land Tax Act 1976".

23. In section 89 (prescribed rate of interest), in subsection (1), after "86", in both places where it occurs, there shall be inserted "86A".

24. In section 91 (effect on interest of reliefs) in subsection (2) (relief by way of repayment may be applied in discharge of other tax) after the word "tax", in the first place where it occurs, there shall be inserted the words "(other than development land tax)".

25. After section 91 there shall be inserted the following:—

"*Development land tax*

Reliefs etc.: effect on interest on development land tax.

91A. In any case where—

(*a*) interest is payable under section 86A of this Act on an amount of development land tax to which a person is assessed, and

(*b*) all or any of the tax charged by the assessment is discharged by way of relief or other adjustment,

such adjustment shall be made of the amount of the interest referred to in paragraph (*a*) above, and such repayment shall be made of any amounts of interest previously paid under that section in relation to the tax referred to in that paragraph, as are necessary to secure that the total sum, if any, paid or payable under that section in relation to the amount of tax assessed is the same as it would have been if the tax discharged had never been charged".

26.—(1) In section 100 (procedure for recovery of penalties) at the beginning of each of subsections (3) and (4) there shall be inserted the words "Subject to subsection (10) below".

(2) At the end of that section there shall be added the following subsection:—

"(10) In the application of this section to proceedings for the recovery of any penalty relating to development land tax,—

(*a*) subsection (3) above shall have effect with the omission of the words 'either' and 'General or'; and

(*b*) subsection (4) above shall be omitted".

27. In section 101 (evidence of profits for purposes of provisions of Part X) after the words "chargeable gains" there shall be inserted the words "or realised development value" and after the words "were received" there shall be inserted the words "or accrued".

28.—(1) In section 103 (time limit for recovery of penalties) in subsection (3) (time limit for penalty determined by reference to tax charged in an assessment for a chargeable period) after the word " tax ", in the first place where it occurs, there shall be inserted the words " other than development land tax ". SCH. 8

(2) After the said subsection (3) there shall be inserted the following subsection:—

" (3A) Where the amount of any penalty to which a person is liable under the Taxes Acts is determined by reference to development land tax charged in an assessment made not later than six years after the end of the financial year in which the liability for that tax arose, proceedings for the recovery of the penalty may be commenced within three years of the final determination of the amount of that tax."

(3) In subsection (4) of that section after the words " subsection (3) " there shall be inserted the words " or subsection (3A) ".

29. At the end of section 108 (responsibility of company officers) there shall be added the following subsection:—

" (4) Subsection (2) above shall apply in relation to development land tax as it applies in relation to corporation tax."

30. In section 111 (valuation of assets: power to inspect) after subsection (1) there shall be inserted the following subsection:—

" (1A) If for the purposes of the Development Land Tax Act 1976 the Board authorise an officer of the Board to inspect any land for the purpose of ascertaining any value of an interest therein, any person in possession or occupation of the land shall permit the officer so authorised to inspect it at such reasonable times as the Board may consider necessary ".

31. In section 112 (loss, destruction or damage to assessments, etc.) after subsection (1) there shall be inserted the following subsection:—

" (1A) The proviso to subsection (1) above shall have effect, in its application to a charge to development land tax, as if for the words from ' for the same chargeable period ' to ' in respect of and on ' there were substituted the words ' in respect of the realised development value on or in respect of '."

32. In section 118(1) (interpretation)—

(*a*) at the end of the definition of " company " there shall be added the words " or, in relation to development land tax, the meaning given by section 47 of the Development Land Tax Act 1976 ";

(*b*) after the definition of " the principal Act " there shall be inserted the following definition:—

" ' realised development value ' has the same meaning as in the Development Land Tax Act 1976 ";

SCH. 8

(c) in the definition of "tax" after the words "corporation tax" there shall be inserted the words "nor development land tax"; and

(d) at the end of the definition of "the Taxes Acts" there shall be added the words "and

(c) the Development Land Tax Act 1976 and any other enactment relating to development land tax".

33. At the end of section 119 (commencement and construction) there shall be added the following subsection:—

"(5) This Act, so far as it relates to realised development value, shall be construed as one with the Development Land Tax Act 1976".

34. In Schedule 3 (rules for assigning proceedings to Commissioners), after Rule 5 there shall be inserted the following Rule:—

"5A. An appeal against an assessment to development land tax.	The place where the land to which the assessment relates is situated".

PART II

NOTIFICATION

Notice of principal disposals

35.—(1) Subject to the provisions of this Part of this Schedule if, on the disposal, other than a deemed disposal, of an interest in land,—

(a) realised development value accrues to the chargeable person, and

(b) the consideration for the disposal exceeds £10,000 or, if the whole of that consideration is not payable before the expiry of the period of seven years beginning with the date of the disposal, so much of that consideration as is payable before the expiry of that period exceeds £10,000,

the chargeable person shall, not later than one year after the date of the disposal, give notice of the disposal to the Board.

(2) Sub-paragraph (1) above shall not apply in relation to a disposal if, not later than one year after the date of the disposal, an instrument to which the chargeable person is a party has been signed or executed for giving effect to the disposal and that instrument—

1931 c. 28.

(a) is required to be produced to the Board in accordance with section 28 of the Finance Act 1931 or would be so required but for subsection (2) of that section (leases in same terms as agreements for leases already produced) or any regulations made under section 35(x) of that Act (exemption for certain instruments in Scotland where particulars are obtained through any register of sasines); or

1936 c. 33 (N.I.)

(b) is required to be produced to the Board in accordance with section 9 of the Finance Act (Northern Ireland) 1936.

(3) Sub-paragraph (1) above shall not apply in relation to a disposal if— Sch. 8

(*a*) the disposal is a material disposal within the meaning of section 39 of this Act; and

(*b*) before the expiry of the period for giving notice of the disposal under sub-paragraph (1) above, the body to whom the disposal is made makes, in connection with the disposal, a payment of consideration from which it deducts a DLT deduction, within the meaning of that section.

(4) Notice of a disposal under sub-paragraph (1) above shall contain such information as the Board may reasonably require for the purposes of this Act and shall be in such form as they may prescribe.

(5) In the case of a disposal which consists of the grant of a lease, paragraphs 26 to 28 of Schedule 2 to this Act shall not apply to determine whether the condition in sub-paragraph (1)(*b*) above is fulfilled.

Notice of commencement of project

36.—(1) Subject to sub-paragraph (3) below, a person who, having a major interest in any land, begins or causes or permits any other person to begin to carry out a project of material development of that land or any part of it shall—

(*a*) not earlier than sixty days before the date on which the project is begun, and

(*b*) not later than thirty days after that date,

give notice of the project to the Board.

(2) Notice of a project under sub-paragraph (1) above shall contain such information as the Board may reasonably require for the purposes of this Act and shall be in such form as they may prescribe.

(3) A person shall not be required to give notice of a project under sub-paragraph (1) above if some other person falling within that sub-paragraph has previously given notice of the project in accordance with that sub-paragraph (and sub-paragraph (2) above).

(4) For the purposes of Part I of Schedule 1 to this Act, notice of a project under sub-paragraph (1) above is an operative notice if, in relation to the project,—

(*a*) it is the only notice given under that sub-paragraph, or

(*b*) it is the first such notice to be given and no subsequent notice differs from that first notice in its specification of the nature and scope of the project or of the land comprised in it.

(5) If, in relation to a project of material development, more than one notice is given under sub-paragraph (1) above and no such notice is an operative notice for the purposes of that Part, the

SCH. 8 Board shall, after consulting such persons as appear to them to be appropriate, determine what should be taken to be—

(a) the nature and scope of the project, and

(b) the land comprised in the project, and

(c) the date on which the project is begun,

and shall serve notice of their determination on each person who, in relation to that project, gave notice under sub-paragraph (1) above.

(6) On an appeal against an assessment to development land tax, the Special Commissioners shall have jurisdiction to review a determination made by the Board under sub-paragraph (5) above.

(7) For the purposes of paragraph 4(3) of Schedule 1 to this Act a person who began or caused or permitted any other person to begin to carry out a project of material development may give notice to the Board that he no longer intends to carry out or to cause or permit any other person to carry out a part of the material development comprised in the project ; but such a notice shall be of no effect for the purposes of that paragraph unless—

(a) it contains such information relating to the variation as the Board may reasonably require for the purposes of this Act ; and

(b) it is in such form as the Board may prescribe for the purposes of this sub-paragraph.

Notice of additional development

37.—(1) Where a project of material development (in this paragraph referred to as " the original project ") is carried out so as to include material development (in this paragraph referred to as " the additional development ") which, disregarding paragraph 6 of Schedule 1 above, is not comprised in the project in accordance with Part I of that Schedule, then,—

(a) in any case where, if the additional development were comprised in a separate project of material development, that project would be taken to be begun not less than three years after the time at which the original project began, this Part of this Schedule shall have effect as if the additional development were so comprised ; and

(b) in any other case, a person who has a major interest in any land comprised in the original project or in any other land to which the additional development relates and who carried out or caused or permitted any other person to carry out any of the additional development shall, subject to sub-paragraph (3) below, give notice in writing of the additional development to the Board.

(2) Notice of the additional development under sub-paragraph (1) above—

(a) shall contain such information relating to the additional development as the Board may reasonably require for the purposes of this Act ; and (*b*) shall be in such form as the Board may prescribe for the purposes of this sub-paragraph ; and SCH. 8

(*c*) shall be given not more than thirty days after the date on which, if the additional development had been comprised in a separate project of material development, that separate project would have been taken to have been begun.

(3) A person shall not be required to give notice of the additional development under sub-paragraph (1) above if some other person falling within paragraph (*b*) of that sub-paragraph has previously given notice of the additional development in accordance with that sub-paragraph (and sub-paragraph (2) above).

(4) For the purposes of Part I of Schedule 1 to this Act, notice of the additional development under sub-paragraph (1) above is an operative notice if—

(*a*) in relation to that development, it is the only notice given under that sub-paragraph, or

(*b*) it is the first such notice to be given and no subsequent notice differs from that first notice in its specification of the nature and scope of the additional development or of the land to which that development relates.

(5) If, in relation to the additional development, more than one notice is given under sub-paragraph (1) above and no such notice is an operative notice for the purposes of that Part, the Board shall, after consulting such persons as appear to them to be appropriate, determine what should be taken to be—

(*a*) the nature and scope of the additional development, and

(*b*) the land to which that development relates,

and shall serve notice of their determination on each person who gave notice of the additional development under sub-paragraph (1) above.

(6) On an appeal against an assessment to development land tax, the Special Commissioners shall have jurisdiction to review a determination made by the Board under sub-paragraph (5) above.

Notice of other disposals and of events giving rise to a liability for development land tax

38.—(1) Subject to sub-paragraphs (2) and (3) below, if a person is chargeable to development land tax by virtue of the disposal of an interest in land and—

(*a*) the disposal is neither one in respect of which notice has been given under sub-paragraph (1) of paragraph 35 above nor one in relation to which that sub-paragraph does not apply by reason of sub-paragraph (2) or sub-paragraph (3) of that paragraph, and

(*b*) the disposal is not a deemed disposal occasioned by the start of a project of material development of which he has reasonable grounds for believing that notice has been given under paragraph 36 above,

the chargeable person shall, not later than the end of the financial year following that in which the disposal occurred, give notice of it to the Board.

SCH. 8

(2) Nothing in sub-paragraph (1) above shall require notice to be given of a disposal if—

(*a*) it consists of the disposal of an interest in land which comprises a dwelling-house with or without land occupied with the dwelling-house ; and

(*b*) the aggregate of the area of the site of the dwelling-house and of the land occupied together with it does not exceed one acre ; and

(*c*) the disposal is not a part disposal ; and

(*d*) the consideration for the disposal does not exceed £25,000.

(3) Nothing in sub-paragraph (1) above shall require a person to give notice of a disposal if—

(*a*) in the financial year in which the disposal is made, no other disposal of an interest in land is made by that person ; and

(*b*) so much of the consideration for the disposal as is payable before the expiry of the period of seven years beginning with the date of the disposal does not exceed £10,000.

(4) In the case of a disposal which consists of the grant of a lease, paragraphs 26 to 28 of Schedule 2 to this Act shall not apply to determine whether the condition in sub-paragraph (3)(*b*) above is fulfilled.

39.—(1) A person who becomes chargeable to development land tax by virtue of the occurrence of an event which is not a disposal of an interest in land but which, by virtue of any provision of this Act, is treated as such for the purposes of section 27 of this Act shall, not later than the end of the financial year following that in which that event occurs, give notice to the Board that he is so chargeable.

(2) Where, for the purposes of this Act, the consideration for the disposal of an interest in land—

(*a*) is determined, in the first instance, on the basis that a contingent liability assumed by any person is left out of account, and

(*b*) subsequently, by virtue of that liability being or having been enforced, falls to be determined on the basis that it is brought into account,

and the amount of the consideration determined on the basis referred to in paragraph (*b*) above would exceed that amount determined on the basis referred to in paragraph (*a*) above, the chargeable person shall, if he is chargeable to development land tax by virtue of the disposal, give notice of the enforcement of that liability to the Board.

(3) A notice under sub-paragraph (2) above shall be given not later than the end of the financial year following that in which the contingent liability is enforced.

(4) If at any time a body ceases to be a charity and, as a result, becomes chargeable to development land tax on an amount of realised development value which is treated as accruing to it by

virtue of section 24(6) of this Act, the body shall, not later than the end of the financial year following that in which it ceases to be a charity, give notice to the Board that it is so chargeable. SCH. 8

Information as to interests in land and disposals etc.

40.—(1) If it appears to the Board that there has been a disposal of an interest in land on which realised development value has or may have accrued to any person, they may by notice in writing require any person who appears to them to hold or to have held an interest in that land to furnish to them within such time, being not less than thirty days, as may be specified in the notice—

(*a*) a statement in writing as to the matters specified in sub-paragraph (2) below, or

(*b*) such information and documents which are in his possession or power as may be specified in the notice and as may be required by the Board for the purpose of determining any of the matters specified in sub-paragraph (3) below,

or both such a statement and such information and documents.

(2) The matters about which the Board may by notice require a person to furnish a statement in writing under sub-paragraph (1)(*a*) above are—

(*a*) whether he holds an interest in the land specified in the notice from the Board and, if so, the nature of that interest, and

(*b*) the name and address of any other person known or believed by him to hold an interest in that land.

(3) The matters about which the Board may by notice require a person to furnish information and documents under paragraph (*b*) of sub-paragraph (1) above where it appears to them that there has been such a disposal of an interest in land as is referred to in that sub-paragraph are—

(*a*) whether any interest in that land has been disposed of and whether any realised development value has accrued on the disposal ; and

(*b*) whether any realised development value which has accrued on that disposal is chargeable to development land tax or whether any liability to tax on that value is deferred by virtue of any provision of this Act ; and

(*c*) if any realised development value which has accrued on that disposal is chargeable to development land tax, the amount of that tax and the person or persons who may be liable for that tax ; and

(*d*) whether any disposal or other event has occurred which might be the occasion of a charge to development land tax by virtue of section 27 of this Act or which might affect the amount or time of payment of any instalment of development land tax.

SCH. 8

Penalties

41.—(1) Subject to sub-paragraph (4) below, if any person—

(*a*) fails to give a notice which he is required to give under paragraph 35(1) or paragraph 39 above, or

(*b*) fails to comply with a notice under paragraph 40 above,

he shall be liable to a penalty not exceeding £50 and, if the failure continues after it has been declared by the court or Commissioners before whom proceedings for the penalty have been commenced, to a further penalty not exceeding £10 for each day on which the failure so continues.

(2) Subject to the following provisions of this paragraph, if any person fails to give a notice which he is required to give under sub-paragraph (1) of paragraph 36 or sub-paragraph (1)(*b*) of paragraph 37 above, he shall be liable—

(*a*) to a penalty not exceeding £500 or the overriding maximum penalty, whichever is the less, or

(*b*) if the failure continues after the end of the period of six months beginning on the last day on which the notice might have been given in accordance with that paragraph, to a penalty not exceeding £5,000 or the overriding maximum penalty, whichever is the less,

and, if the failure continues after it has been declared by the court or Commissioners before whom proceedings for the penalty have been commenced, to a further penalty not exceeding £50 for each day on which the failure so continues.

(3) Subject to sub-paragraph (4) below, if any person fails to give a notice which he is required to give under paragraph 38 above, he shall be liable to a penalty not exceeding £100.

(4) Except in a case falling within sub-paragraph (2)(*b*) above, a person shall not be liable to a penalty for any such failure as is mentioned in sub-paragraphs (1) to (3) above if the failure is remedied before proceedings for the recovery of the penalty are commenced.

(5) The overriding maximum penalty referred to in sub-paragraph (2) above is—

(*a*) in the case of a person assessed to an amount of development land tax in respect of the material event, the aggregate of £50 and the amount of development land tax to which he is finally so assessed ; and

(*b*) in the case of a person who is shown not to be liable for development land tax in respect of the material event, £50 ;

and in any case where proceedings for the recovery from any person of a penalty for a failure to give such a notice as is referred to in sub-paragraph (2) above are begun before the overriding maximum penalty is established in his case and that limit has still not been established when a penalty comes to be awarded in those proceedings, that sub-paragraph shall have effect with the omission of any reference to the overriding maximum penalty.

(6) If, after a penalty has been awarded against any person by virtue of paragraph (*a*) or paragraph (*b*) of sub-paragraph (2) above,— Sch. 8

(*a*) an assessment on him to development land tax in respect of the material event becomes final or it is proved to the satisfaction of the Board that he has no liability for development land tax in respect of that event, and

(*b*) the penalty so awarded exceeds the aggregate of £50 and the amount of development land tax (if any) to which he is so assessed,

the penalty so awarded shall be treated as reduced to the aggregate referred to in paragraph (*b*) above and, if the penalty has already been paid, the amount of the excess shall be remitted to him by the Board.

(7) Any reference in sub-paragraph (5) or sub-paragraph (6) above to the material event shall be construed by reference to the nature of the failure which gives rise to the proceedings under sub-paragraph (2) above so that—

(*a*) if the failure is a failure to give notice of a project of material development, the material event is the deemed disposal of any interest in land which is occasioned by the beginning of that project; and

(*b*) if the failure is a failure to give notice of the additional development, as defined in paragraph 37(1) above, the material event is the deemed disposal of any interest in land which is occasioned by the start of the project of material development in which the additional development is comprised.

(8) For the purposes of this paragraph, an assessment to development land tax becomes final when it can no longer be varied by any Commissioners on appeal or by order of any court.

42.—(1) If a person liable for development land tax on the disposal of an interest in land fraudulently or negligently gives, makes or furnishes any incorrect notice, statement, information or document which, by virtue of the preceding provisions of this Part of this Schedule, he is required or permitted to give, make or furnish in connection with that disposal or with any project of material development the start of which is the occasion of that disposal, he shall be liable,—

(*a*) in the case of fraud, to a penalty not exceeding £500 or the aggregate of £50 and twice the difference mentioned in sub-paragraph (2) below, whichever is the greater, and

(*b*) in the case of negligence, to a penalty not exceeding £250 or the aggregate of £50 and the difference mentioned in sub-paragraph (2) below, whichever is the greater.

(2) The difference referred to in sub-paragraph (1) above is the amount by which the tax for which the person concerned is liable as mentioned in that sub-paragraph exceeds what would be the amount of that tax if the facts were as shown in the notice, statement, information or document.

SCH. 8

(3) If a person who is not liable for development land tax as mentioned in sub-paragraph (1) above fraudulently or negligently gives, makes or furnishes any incorrect notice, statement, information or document which, by virtue of the preceding provisions of this Part of this Schedule, he is required to give, make or furnish, he shall be liable,—

(*a*) in the case of fraud, to a penalty not exceeding £500, and

(*b*) in the case of negligence, to a penalty not exceeding £250.

(4) If after any notice, statement, information or document has been given, made or furnished by any person (in pursuance of the preceding provisions of this Part of this Schedule) without fraud or negligence, it comes to his notice (or, if he has died, to the notice of his personal representatives) that it was incorrect in any material respect, it shall be treated for the purposes of this paragraph as having been negligently given, made or furnished by him unless the error is remedied without unreasonable delay.

(5) Any person who assists in or induces the giving, making or furnishing in pursuance of the preceding provisions of this Part of this Schedule of any notice, statement, information or document which he knows to be incorrect shall be liable to a penalty not exceeding £500.

PART III

PAYMENT

Date for payment of tax

43. Subject to the provisions of this Part of this Schedule, development land tax assessed on any person in respect of the disposal of an interest in land or other event shall be payable by that person not later than—

(*a*) the reckonable date, or

(*b*) the expiry of the period of thirty days beginning with the date of issue of the notice of assessment,

whichever is the later.

Right to elect to pay tax by instalments in certain cases

44.—(1) Where a person is liable to development land tax—

(*a*) on the disposal of an interest in land to which, by virtue of sub-paragraph (2) below, this sub-paragraph applies, or

(*b*) on the occurrence of an event to which, by virtue of sub-paragraph (3) below, this sub-paragraph applies,

the tax may, if he so elects, be paid by instalments which, according to his election, shall be yearly or half-yearly.

(2) Sub-paragraph (1) above applies to the disposal of an interest in land which is—

(*a*) a deemed disposal, or

(*b*) a part disposal consisting of the grant of a lease under which rent is payable and, on the first date on which it is payable, the rent does not exceed the commercial rent on that date.

(3) Sub-paragraph (1) above applies to an event— Sch. 8

(*a*) which is not a disposal of an interest in land but which, by virtue of any provision of this Act, is treated as such for the purposes of section 27 of this Act ; and

(*b*) where the project of material development the start of which was the occasion of the deemed disposal referred to in subsection (1) of that section comprised material development authorised by planning permission granted for a limited period, which occurs before the expiry of the relevant period.

(4) If, in a case where section 27 of this Act has effect, the operative disposal or, as the case may be, a further disposal falling within subsection (5) of that section is such a disposal as is mentioned in sub-paragraph (2)(*b*) above, this Part of this Schedule (other than this sub-paragraph) shall have effect as if—

(*a*) at the time of that disposal there occurred an event falling within paragraph (*a*) of sub-paragraph (3) above, and

(*b*) any liability arising at the time of that disposal for development land tax on any of the accrued development value arose on that event and not on that disposal,

and in this sub-paragraph " the operative disposal " and " the accrued development value " have the same meaning as in section 27 of this Act.

Dates and frequency of instalments : normal rules

45.—(1) Where the development land tax for which a person is liable on a disposal of an interest in land or on the occurrence of an event to which sub-paragraph (1) of paragraph 44 above applies is payable by instalments by virtue of an election under that sub-paragraph the provisions of this paragraph shall have effect, subject to paragraphs 47 and 48 below, to determine the number of the yearly or half-yearly instalments referred to in that sub-paragraph and the dates on which those instalments fall due.

(2) Subject to the following provisions of this paragraph—

(*a*) the first instalment shall fall due at the expiry of the period of twelve months beginning with the date of the disposal or, as the case may be, the event referred to in sub-paragraph (1) above ; and

(*b*) the number of yearly instalments shall be eight and the number of half-yearly instalments shall be sixteen.

(3) In any case where—

(*a*) the liability referred to in sub-paragraph (1) above arises on the deemed disposal of an interest in land, and

(*b*) the relevant project comprises material development authorised by planning permission granted for a limited period, and

(*c*) the last day of the relevant period falls within the period of eight years beginning with the date on which the relevant project was begun,

the number of yearly or half-yearly instalments shall be such that they all fall due before the expiry of the relevant period.

SCH. 8

(4) In any case where—

(*a*) the liability referred to in sub-paragraph (1) above arises on the occurrence of an event to which sub-paragraph (1) of paragraph 44 above applies, and

(*b*) the condition in sub-paragraph (3)(*b*) of that paragraph is fulfilled,

the number of yearly or half-yearly instalments shall be such that they all fall due before the expiry of the relevant period referred to in sub-paragraph (3)(*b*) of that paragraph.

(5) If the liability referred to in sub-paragraph (1) above arises on a part disposal consisting of the grant of a lease and the presumed expiry date of the lease, for the purposes of section 44(2) of this Act, falls within the period of eight years beginning with the date of the disposal, the number of yearly or half-yearly instalments shall be such that they all fall due before the presumed expiry date.

(6) If the liability referred to in sub-paragraph (1) above arises on the deemed disposal of an interest in land, then, at the option of the person referred to in that sub-paragraph, sub-paragraph (7) below shall apply in any case where—

(*a*) that interest is an interest in reversion on one or more leases, and

(*b*) the relevant project was begun by a person other than the landlord, and

(*c*) the rent or the aggregate of the rents and of any premium or premiums to which, under or by virtue of the lease or leases, the landlord is entitled does not reflect the value or any part of the value of the development comprised in the relevant project, and

(*d*) the rent or the aggregate of the rents and of any premium or premiums to which, under or by virtue of the lease or any of the leases, the landlord is entitled can be made to reflect that value or part of it from a date on which the lease in question provides for a review of any rent or premium payable under it ;

and in this sub-paragraph " the landlord " means the person who was the chargeable person in relation to the deemed disposal.

(7) Where this sub-paragraph applies—

(*a*) the first instalment shall fall due at the expiry of the period of twelve months beginning with the review date ; and

(*b*) the number of yearly or half-yearly instalments of tax shall be such that they all fall due before the expiry of the period of eight years beginning with the review date ;

and in this sub-paragraph " the review date " means the date referred to in sub-paragraph (6)(*d*) above or, if there is more than one such date, the first of those dates.

(8) If, in a case where this paragraph applies, an instalment of tax would, apart from this sub-paragraph, fall due before the first date on which, if the tax were not payable by instalments, tax of an amount not less than the amount mentioned in sub-paragraph (9) below would become payable under paragraph 43 above, that instalment shall not fall due until that date; but nothing in this sub-paragraph shall affect— SCH. 8

(*a*) the determination of the number of any instalments of tax; or

(*b*) the date on which falls due any instalment to which this sub-paragraph does not apply; or

(*c*) the date on which any instalment is to be taken to fall due for the purposes of section 86A of the Taxes Management Act 1970. 1970 c. 9.

(9) The amount referred to in sub-paragraph (8) above in relation to an instalment of tax is the aggregate of—

(*a*) the amount of the instalment, and

(*b*) the amount of any instalment which has previously fallen due, and

(*c*) the amount of any other instalment which, apart from sub-paragraph (8) above, would have fallen due before the instalment referred to in paragraph (*a*) above.

(10) In this Part of this Schedule, " the relevant project ", in relation to the deemed disposal of an interest in land, means the project of material development the start of which is the occasion of that disposal.

Amount of instalments

46.—(1) Where the development land tax for which a person is liable as mentioned in sub-paragraph (1) of paragraph 44 above (in this paragraph referred to as " the tax ") is payable by instalments by virtue of an election under that sub-paragraph, the provisions of this paragraph shall have effect, subject to paragraph 48(2) below, to determine the amount of the instalments referred to in that sub-paragraph; and in this Part of this Schedule references to the relevant tax at any time are references to the amount of the tax which, if the tax were not payable by instalments, would have become payable at or before that time.

(2) Subject to the following provisions of this paragraph—

(*a*) the instalments shall be of equal amounts, and

(*b*) in the first instance, the instalments shall be calculated by reference to the relevant tax immediately before the date on which the first instalment falls due.

(3) If, at any time after an instalment has fallen due, there is an alteration in the amount of the relevant tax,—

(*a*) the amount of the instalments (including any instalments which have fallen due) shall be recalculated by reference to the relevant tax immediately after that time; and

SCH. 8

(*b*) if the recalculated amount of an instalment falling due before that time exceeds the amount which was previously calculated to be the amount ot that instalment, then, the amount of the excess—

(i) shall be payable forthwith, and

1970 c. 9. (ii) for the purposes only of section 86A of the Taxes Management Act 1970, shall be taken to have become payable on the date on which the instalment fell due.

(4) Where the liability for the tax arises on a part disposal consisting of the grant of a lease and, on a date before the whole of the tax has become payable, an amount is paid by way of premium in respect of the lease,—

(*a*) the relevant fraction of the relevant tax on that date shall be payable on that date, and

(*b*) the amount of any instalments becoming payable after that date shall be recalculated accordingly.

(5) The reference in sub-paragraph (4) above to the liability for the tax arising on a part disposal consisting of the grant of a lease includes a reference to the case where—

(*a*) by virtue of paragraph 44(4)(*b*) above, the liability for the tax is treated as arising on an event ; and

(*b*) the disposal which under paragraph 44(4)(*a*) above determines the time of that event is a part disposal consisting of the grant of a lease.

(6) If, in a case where the liability referred to in sub-paragraph (1) above arises on a deemed disposal and sub-paragraph (7) of paragraph 45 above applies, an amount which reflects the value or any part of the value of the development comprised in the relevant project is paid—

(*a*) by way of premium in respect of a lease mentioned in sub-paragraph (6)(*a*) of that paragraph, and

(*b*) before the whole of the tax has become payable,

the relevant fraction of the relevant tax on that date shall be payable on that date and the amount of any instalments becoming payable after that date shall be recalculated accordingly.

(7) For the purposes of sub-paragraph (4) or sub-paragraph (6) above, the relevant fraction on any date is—

(*a*) that of which the numerator is the amount of the premium referred to in sub-paragraph (4) or, as the case may be, sub-paragraph (6) above and the denominator is the net proceeds of the disposal, or

(*b*) that fraction of the relevant tax on that date which has not become payable before that date,

whichever is the smaller.

Payment of balance in certain cases

47.—(1) In any case where—

(*a*) the development land tax for which a person is liable on the disposal of an interest in land or other event is payable by instalments by virtue of an election under paragraph 44(1) above, and

(*b*) on any date after that disposal or event, this paragraph applies by virtue of any provision of sub-paragraphs (2) to (6) below,

so much of the relevant tax on that date as has not previously become payable shall be payable on that date ; and if, after that date, the relevant tax is increased by an amount, that amount shall be payable forthwith.

(2) Where the liability referred to in sub-paragraph (1)(*a*) above arises on a part disposal consisting of the grant of a lease, this paragraph applies on any date after that disposal on which—

(*a*) rent payable under the lease exceeds the commercial rent on that date ; or

(*b*) there is a further disposal for which consideration is given and as a result of which the rights of the landlord under the lease become vested, in whole or in part, in another person.

(3) Where the liability referred to in sub-paragraph (1)(*a*) above arises on the occurrence of an event to which paragraph 44(1) above applies and that event is connected with the grant of a lease, this paragraph applies on any date after that event on which—

(*a*) rent payable under the lease exceeds the commercial rent on that date ; or

(*b*) there is a material disposal of the interest which was the retained interest in relation to the part disposal consisting of the grant of that lease.

(4) Where the liability referred to in sub-paragraph (1)(*a*) above arises on the occurrence of an event to which paragraph 44(1) above applies and that event is not connected with the grant of a lease, this paragraph applies on any date after that event on which there is a material disposal of the interest which, for the purposes of section 27 of this Act, was treated as being disposed of on that event.

(5) For the purposes of this paragraph there is a material disposal of an interest in land if—

(*a*) there is a disposal either of that interest or of an interest of which it is a part for the purposes of Part I of Schedule 2 to this Act ; and

(*b*) the disposal referred to in paragraph (*a*) above is neither a deemed disposal nor a part disposal consisting of the grant of a lease under which, on the first date on which rent is payable, the rent does not exceed the commercial rent on that date.

SCH. 8

(6) In any case where—

(*a*) there is a part disposal of an interest in land consisting of the grant of a lease, and

(*b*) if sub-paragraph (5)(*b*) above had not been enacted that disposal would be a material disposal of the interest referred to in sub-paragraph (3)(*b*) or sub-paragraph (4) above,

this paragraph applies on any date on which—

(i) rent payable under that lease exceeds the commercial rent on that date ; or

(ii) there is a material disposal of the interest which was the retained interest in relation to that part disposal.

(7) If, after a part disposal which falls within paragraphs (*a*) and (*b*) of sub-paragraph (6) above there is a disposal of the retained interest referred to in paragraph (ii) of that sub-paragraph and that disposal—

(*a*) is not a material disposal, but

(*b*) consists of the grant of a further lease,

sub-paragraph (6) above shall again have effect as if that retained interest were itself the interest referred to in sub-paragraph (3)(*b*) or, as the case may be, sub-paragraph (4) above.

(8) For the purposes of this paragraph an event is connected with the grant of a lease if, by virtue of paragraph 44(4) above, that event is treated as occurring at the time of the disposal consisting of the grant of the lease.

Effect of disposals after a project of material development

48.—(1) In any case where—

(*a*) by virtue of an election under paragraph 44(1) above the development land tax for which a person is liable on the disposal of an interest in land (in this paragraph referred to as " the relevant disposal ") is payable by instalments, and

(*b*) the relevant disposal is the deemed disposal of an interest in land (in this paragraph referred to as " the relevant interest "), and

(*c*) after the relevant disposal there is a disposal, other than a deemed disposal, of the relevant interest or of the balance of the relevant interest (in this paragraph and paragraph 49 below referred to as a " subsequent disposal "), and

(*d*) the whole or part of the amount which is the relevant tax on the date of a subsequent disposal (excluding for this purpose any amount of the tax which on that date is already payable by instalments under paragraph 49(1) below) has not become payable before that date,

this paragraph shall apply on the occasion of that subsequent disposal, and in the following provisions of this paragraph and paragraph 49 below the tax which has not become payable as mentioned in paragraph (*d*) above is referred to as " the unpaid tax ".

(2) Subject to paragraph 49(1) below, where this paragraph applies on the occasion of a subsequent disposal, the unpaid tax shall be payable on the date of that disposal or, if that disposal is a part disposal and the fraction determined under sub-paragraph (3) below is less than unity,— Sch. 8

(*a*) that fraction of the unpaid tax shall be payable on that date ; and

(*b*) the amount of any instalments of tax payable in accordance with the preceding provisions of this Part of this Schedule and becoming so payable after the subsequent disposal shall be recalculated accordingly.

(3) The fraction referred to in sub-paragraph (2) above is that of which—

(*a*) the numerator is the adjusted net proceeds of the subsequent disposal, and

(*b*) the denominator is the net proceeds of the relevant disposal.

(4) If at any time after the date of a subsequent disposal, the relevant tax would, apart from this sub-paragraph, be increased by an amount (in this sub-paragraph and sub-paragraph (5) below referred to as " the added amount "), then, subject to sub-paragraph (5) below, paragraph 44(1) above shall not apply to the added amount.

(5) If, in a case falling within sub-paragraph (4) above,—

(*a*) the subsequent disposal is a part disposal, and

(*b*) at the time referred to in that sub-paragraph, any instalments of tax provided for by paragraph 45 above have not yet become payable,

then, notwithstanding anything in sub-paragraph (4) above, paragraph 44(1) above shall apply to that part of the added amount which remains after deducting therefrom the fraction of that amount determined under sub-paragraph (6) below.

(6) The fraction referred to in sub-paragraph (5) above is that of which the numerator is—

(*a*) the adjusted net proceeds of the subsequent disposal, or

(*b*) if there has previously been a subsequent disposal or disposals, the aggregate of the adjusted net proceeds of each subsequent disposal,

and the denominator is the net proceeds of the relevant disposal.

(7) In this paragraph, references to the adjusted net proceeds of a disposal of an interest in land are references to the amount of the net proceeds of that disposal less the amount which, for the purpose of determining the relevant base value of that interest on that disposal, is the amount of expenditure on improvements.

SCH. 8

(8) For the purposes of this paragraph, a disposal of the balance of the relevant interest means—

(*a*) a disposal of the interest which was the retained interest in relation to the disposal of the relevant interest referred to in sub-paragraph (1)(*c*) above, or

(*b*) a disposal which would fall within paragraph (*a*) above if, in the period beginning immediately after the disposal of the relevant interest referred to in sub-paragraph (1)(*c*) above and ending immediately before the disposal in question, no disposal had occurred which falls within either paragraph (*a*) above or this paragraph.

(9) For the purpose of determining whether there is a disposal of the relevant interest or of the balance of the relevant interest, a disposal to which Part I of Schedule 2 to this Act applies shall be regarded also as a separate disposal of each interest which is, within the meaning of that Part, a part of the interest disposed of.

49.—(1) In any case where—

(*a*) paragraph 48 above applies on the occasion of a subsequent disposal, and

(*b*) that disposal is a part disposal consisting of the grant of a lease under which rent is payable, and

(*c*) on the first date on which rent is payable under the lease it does not exceed the commercial rent on that date,

then, notwithstanding anything in sub-paragraph (2) of paragraph 48 above, the unpaid tax or part thereof which would otherwise be payable on the date of the subsequent disposal in accordance with that sub-paragraph may, at the option of the person liable to pay it, be paid by instalments in accordance with the provisions of this paragraph.

(2) Where an amount of tax (in the following provisions of this paragraph referred to as " the material tax ") is payable by instalments under sub-paragraph (1) above then, subject to the following provisions of this paragraph,—

(*a*) that tax shall be paid by equal instalments ; and

(*b*) an instalment shall fall due on each date after the date of the disposal referred to in sub-paragraph (1) above on which an instalment of tax provided for by the preceding provisions of this Part of this Schedule falls due or would have fallen due but for paragraph 48(2) above.

(3) If, on a date before the whole of the material tax has become payable, an amount is paid by way of premium in respect of the lease referred to in sub-paragraph (1) above, then,—

(*a*) the relevant fraction of the material tax shall be payable on that date, and

(*b*) the amount of any instalments payable in accordance with sub-paragraph (2) above and becoming so payable after that date shall be recalculated accordingly.

(4) Where the material tax is payable by instalments and there is on any date a disposal— Sch. 8

(*a*) for which consideration is given, and

(*b*) as a result of which the rights of the landlord under the lease referred to in sub-paragraph (1) above become vested, in whole or in part, in another person,

so much of the material tax has not previously become payable shall be payable on that date.

(5) If rent payable on any date under the lease referred to in sub-paragraph (1) above exceeds the commercial rent on that date, so much of the material tax as has not previously become payable shall be payable on that date.

(6) For the purposes of sub-paragraph (3) above, the relevant fraction on the date referred to in that sub-paragraph is—

(*a*) that of which the numerator is the amount of the premium referred to in that sub-paragraph and the denominator is the net proceeds of the disposal referred to in sub-paragraph (1) above, or

(*b*) that fraction of the material tax which has not become payable before that date,

whichever is the smaller.

Payment of tax by instalments in other cases where consideration payable by instalments

50.—(1) In any case where—

(*a*) a person is liable for development land tax on the disposal of an interest in land to which sub-paragraph (1) of paragraph 44 above does not apply, and

(*b*) in accordance with the terms of the disposal the consideration or part of the consideration for the disposal is payable by instalments over a period which ends more than eighteen months after the date of the disposal, and

(*c*) that person satisfies the Board that he would otherwise suffer undue hardship,

the tax may, at his option, be paid by such instalments as the Board may allow over a period which ends not later than eight years after the reckonable date or, if it is earlier, the date on which the last of the instalments mentioned in paragraph (*b*) of this sub-paragraph is payable.

(2) In any case where—

(*a*) on the date of the disposal of an interest in land which is a subsequent disposal for the purposes of paragraph 48 above an amount of development land tax which had not previously become payable would, apart from this sub-paragraph, become payable on that date in accordance with sub-paragraph (2) of that paragraph, and

(*b*) that amount could, at the option of the person liable to pay it, have been paid by instalments by virtue of sub-paragraph

SCH. 8

(1) of paragraph 49 above if paragraph (*c*) of that sub-paragraph had not been enacted, and

(*c*) the person liable to pay that amount satisfies the Board that he would otherwise suffer undue hardship,

then, notwithstanding anything in paragraph 48(2) above, that amount of tax may, at his option, be paid by such instalments as the Board may allow.

(3) In any case where—

(*a*) on any date an amount of development land tax which had not previously become payable would, apart from this sub-paragraph, become payable under—

(i) sub-paragraph (1) of paragraph 47 above, by virtue of any of sub-paragraphs (2)(*a*), (3)(*a*) and (6)(i) of that paragraph, or

(ii) sub-paragraph (5) of paragraph 49 above, and

(*b*) the person liable to pay that amount satisfies the Board that he would otherwise suffer undue hardship,

then, notwithstanding anything in those sub-paragraphs, that amount of tax may, at his option, be paid by such instalments as the Board may allow.

(4) Where an amount of tax is payable by instalments in accordance with sub-paragraph (2) or sub-paragraph (3) above, the last instalment shall fall due not later than the expiry of the period of eight years beginning with the date which is the reckonable date in relation to the liability for that tax.

51. Notwithstanding that a person has opted to pay an amount of tax by instalments under the preceding provisions of this Part of this Schedule, the tax for the time being unpaid, together with any interest which has accrued before the time of payment, may be paid at any time.

Postponement of tax on incorporation disposal

52.—(1) This paragraph applies where—

(*a*) as part of the transfer of his business to a company a person disposes of an interest in land to the company, and

(*b*) on that disposal (in this paragraph referred to as " the incorporation disposal ") the chargeable person becomes liable for an amount of development land tax (whether in respect of realised development value accruing on that disposal or by virtue of section 27 of this Act), and

(*c*) the transfer of the business is one where, for the purposes of Part III of the Finance Act 1965 (capital gains tax), paragraph 15 of Schedule 19 to the Finance Act 1969 applies (special rules on transfer of business as a going concern to a company).

1965 c. 25.
1969 c. 32.

(2) Where this paragraph applies, so much of the development land tax referred to in sub-paragraph (1)(*b*) above as appears to the Board or, on an appeal, to the Commissioners concerned to be just

and reasonable shall not become payable until such time as may be determined in accordance with sub-paragraphs (4) to (6) below; and in the following provisions of this paragraph the amount of tax which does not become payable until that time is referred to as "the postponed tax". SCH. 8

(3) In determining under sub-paragraph (2) above the amount of the development land tax referred to in sub-paragraph (1)(*b*) above which is to be the postponed tax, the Board or, as the case may require, the Commissioners concerned shall have regard to the proportion of the consideration for the transfer of the business referred to in sub-paragraph (1)(*a*) above which consists of shares.

(4) If at any time within the period of eight years beginning on the date of the incorporation disposal there is a disposal—

(*a*) of any of the shares comprised in the consideration for the transfer of the business concerned, or

(*b*) of the interest referred to in sub-paragraph (1)(*a*) above or of any other interest in land which is derived, directly or indirectly, from that interest,

so much of the postponed tax as may be determined by the Board under sub-paragraph (5) below shall become payable at the time of that disposal.

(5) In making a determination under sub-paragraph (4) above in relation to a disposal of shares or an interest in land, the Board shall have regard—

(*a*) to the proportion of the consideration for the transfer of the business or, as the case may be, the proportion of the value of the interest referred to in sub-paragraph (1)(*a*) above which is represented by the shares or interest disposed of; and

(*b*) in the case of a disposal of an interest in land which is a deemed disposal, to the extent to which liability for development land tax on any realised development value which accrues or might accrue on that deemed disposal is or would be deferred under any provision of this Act.

(6) At the expiry of the period of eight years beginning on the date of the incorporation disposal, there shall become payable so much of the postponed tax as has not previously become payable by virtue of sub-paragraph (4) above.

(7) In this paragraph "shares" includes stock.

Interpretation

53.—(1) In this Part of this Schedule—

"planning permission granted for a limited period" has the same meaning as in the relevant planning enactment and, in relation to such permission, "the relevant period" means the period specified in the condition by virtue of which the permission is planning permission granted for a limited period;

SCH. 8

"premium" has the same meaning as in Part III of Schedule 1 to this Act;

"the relevant project" shall be construed in accordance with paragraph 45(10) above; and

"the relevant tax" shall be construed in accordance with paragraph 46(1) above.

(2) In determining for the purposes of this Part of this Schedule whether rent payable in respect of a lease on any date exceeds the commercial rent on that date, "commercial rent" means the rent which might have been expected to be paid on that date under a lease negotiated in the open market at the time at which the actual lease was granted and which (except as to rent) is identical to the actual lease and provides for rent payable—

(*a*) at the same intervals as those provided for under the actual lease; and

(*b*) at a uniform rate or, if the rent payable under the actual lease is rent at a progressive rate (and such that the amount of rent payable for any year is never less than the amount payable for any previous year), a rate which progresses by gradations proportionate to those provided by the actual lease.

PART IV

OTHER ADMINISTRATIVE PROVISIONS

Liability of trustees and personal representatives

54. Development land tax chargeable in respect of realised development value accruing to the trustees of a settlement or due from the personal representatives of a deceased person may be assessed and charged on and in the name of any one or more of those trustees or personal representatives.

Recovery from beneficiary of tax assessed on trustees or personal representatives

55.—(1) In any case where—

(*a*) development land tax assessed on any one or more trustees of a settlement or personal representatives in respect of realised development value accruing to the trustees or personal representatives on the disposal of an interest in land (in this paragraph referred to as "the material disposal") is not paid within the period of six months beginning on the date on which it becomes payable, and

(*b*) before or after the expiry of that period of six months any part of the consideration for the material disposal or, as the case may be, an interest relevant to the material disposal is transferred by the trustees or personal representatives to a person who is absolutely entitled to it as against them,

then, subject to sub-paragraph (3) below, the person referred to in paragraph (*b*) above may at any time within the period of two years beginning with the date when the tax became payable be assessed and charged (in the name of the trustees or personal representatives) to all or any part of that tax. SCH. 8

(2) For the purposes of this paragraph, an interest in land is relevant to the material disposal if,—

(*a*) in a case where that disposal is a deemed disposal followed by a deemed reacquisition, it is the interest reacquired or an interest derived from it ; and

(*b*) in a case where that disposal is a part disposal, it is the retained interest or an interest derived from it.

(3) If, in a case falling within sub-paragraph (1) above,—

(*a*) part only of the consideration for the material disposal, or

(*b*) an interest relevant to the material disposal but having an open market value less than the consideration for the material disposal,

was transferred as mentioned in paragraph (*b*) of that sub-paragraph, the maximum amount of development land tax to which the person concerned may be assessed and charged by virtue of that sub-paragraph shall be reduced proportionately.

(4) The reference in sub-paragraph (3)(*b*) above to the open market value of an interest which was transferred as mentioned in sub-paragraph (1) (*b*) above is a reference to the consideration which that interest might reasonably have been expected to fetch on a sale in the open market at the time of the transfer.

(5) For the purposes of this paragraph, a person is absolutely entitled as against trustees or personal representatives to any consideration or to an interest in land if that person has the exclusive right, subject only to satisfying any outstanding charge, lien or other right of the trustees or personal representatives to resort to the consideration or interest for payment of duty, taxes, costs or other outgoings, to direct how that consideration or interest shall be dealt with.

(6) Subsection (4) of section 28 of this Act shall have effect for the construction of any reference in this paragraph to a person absolutely entitled as against the trustees or personal representatives as if this paragraph were included in that section and as if the reference in that subsection to trustees included a reference to personal representatives.

Recovery of tax assessed on one member of a group from another member

56.—(1) If, on the disposal of an interest in land at any time, realised development value accrues to a company which is then a member of a group of companies and any of the development land tax assessed on the company in respect of the disposal is not paid within the period of six months beginning on the date when it becomes payable by the company, then a company—

(*a*) which was the principal company of the group at the time of the disposal, or

SCH. 8

(*b*) which in any part of the period of two years ending on the date of the disposal was a member of the group and owned either the interest disposed of or an interest which, on the disposal, was a part of that interest for the purposes of Part I of Schedule 2 to this Act,

may at any time within the period of two years beginning with the date on which the tax became payable be assessed and charged (in the name of the company to which the realised development value accrued) to all or any part of that tax.

(2) A company paying an amount of development land tax under sub-paragraph (1) above shall be entitled to recover a sum equal to the aggregate of that amount and of any interest charged thereon

1970 c. 9. under Part IX of the Taxes Management Act 1970—

(*a*) from the company to which the realised development value accrued, or

(*b*) if that company is not the company which was the principal company of the group at the time of the disposal, from that principal company.

(3) A company paying any amount under sub-paragraph (2)(*b*) above shall be entitled to recover a sum of that amount from the company to which the realised development value accrued and, so far as it is not so recovered, to recover from any company which—

(*a*) is for the time being a member of the group, and

(*b*) has while a member of the group owned the interest disposed of or any other interest falling within sub-paragraph (1)(*b*) above,

such proportion of the amount unrecovered as is just, having regard to the value of the interest disposed of (or of the rights which subsequently made up that interest) at the time when that company disposed of the interest owned by it as mentioned in paragraph (*b*) above.

(4) If at any time a company which is a member of a group (in this sub-paragraph referred to as " the chargeable company ") becomes liable for an amount of development land tax by virtue of section 27 of this Act and any of the development land tax assessed on the chargeable company by virtue of that liability is not paid within the period of six months beginning with the date on which it becomes payable by the chargeable company, then a company which was the principle company of the group at the time the liability arose may, at any time within the period of two years beginning with the date on which the tax became payable, be assessed and charged (in the name of the chargeable company) to all or any part of that tax, and a company paying any amount of tax under this sub-paragraph shall be entitled to recover from the chargeable company a sum equal to the aggregate of that amount and of any interest charged thereon under Part IX of the Taxes Management Act 1970.

(5) If, in a case where section 21 of this Act applies, any of the development land tax assessed on the chargeable company in consequence of that section is not paid within the period of six months

beginning with the date on which it becomes payable by that company, then a company— SCH. 8

(*a*) which on that date, or immediately after the time of severance, was the principal company of the group referred to in subsection (1) of that section, or

(*b*) which on that date owned the relevant interest,

may at any time within the period of two years beginning with the date on which the tax became payable be assessed and charged (in the name of the chargeable company) to all or any part of that tax; and a company paying any amount of tax under this sub-paragraph shall be entitled to recover from the chargeable company a sum equal to the aggregate of that amount and of any interest charged thereon under Part IX of the Taxes Management Act 1970. 1970 c. 9.

(6) In sub-paragraph (5) above "the chargeable company", "the time of severance" and "the relevant interest" have the same meaning as in section 21 of this Act.

57.—(1) This paragraph applies in any case where—

(*a*) a company (in this paragraph referred to as "the chargeable company") becomes liable for an amount of development land tax in respect of the disposal of an interest in land or other event; and

(*b*) a person who is connected with the chargeable company for the purposes of Part III of the Finance Act 1965 (capital gains tax) receives or becomes entitled to receive in respect of shares in the chargeable company any capital distribution from the company, other than a capital distribution representing a reduction of capital; and 1965 c. 25.

(*c*) either the capital so distributed derives from or the distribution constitutes the disposal or other event referred to in paragraph (*a*) above.

(2) If, in a case where this paragraph applies, any of the development land tax assessed on the chargeable company by virtue of the liability referred to in paragraph (*a*) of sub-paragraph (1) above is not paid within the period of six months beginning with the date when it becomes payable by the chargeable company, the person referred to in paragraph (*b*) of that sub-paragraph may, at any time within the period of two years beginning with the date on which the tax became payable, be assessed and charged (in the name of the chargeable company) to an amount of that development land tax—

(*a*) not exceeding the amount or value of the capital distribution which that person has received or become entitled to receive; and

(*b*) not exceeding the proportion of that tax which that person's share of the capital distribution bears to the whole of that distribution.

(3) A person paying an amount of tax under sub-paragraph (2) above shall be entitled to recover from the chargeable company a sum equal to the aggregate of that amount and of any interest charged thereon under Part IX of the Taxes Management Act 1970.

SCH. 8

(4) In this paragraph " capital distribution " means any distribution from a company, including a distribution, in the course of dissolving or winding up the company, in money or money's worth, except a distribution which in the hands of the recipient constitutes income for the purposes of income tax.

Advance payments

58.—(1) Where a person who is liable for development land tax in respect of the disposal of an interest in land or other event makes a payment on account of that tax before an assessment is made in respect of that liability, so much of the development land tax for which he is so liable as is equal to the amount of the payment on account shall not carry interest under any provision of Part IX

1970 c. 9. of the Taxes Management Act 1970 in respect of any time—

(*a*) after the date of the payment, or

(*b*) if he is required to give notice under any of paragraphs 35 to 39 above with respect to the disposal, project or other event concerned and the notice is not given before the payment on account is made, after the date on which he gives the notice.

(2) If any amount paid on account of any development land tax for which a person is liable as is mentioned in sub-paragraph (1) above exceeds the amount for which that person is assessed as being so liable, the excess shall be repaid to him.

Interest on repayments

59.—(1) Any repayment of an amount paid in excess of a liability for, or for interest on, development land tax shall carry interest from the reckonable date or the date of payment, whichever is the later, at the rate which is for the time being the prescribed rate for the purposes of section 86A of the Taxes Management Act 1970.

(2) Interest paid to any person under this paragraph shall not be income of that person for any tax purposes.

Fair Employment (Northern Ireland) Act 1976

1976 CHAPTER 25

An Act to establish an Agency with the duties of promoting equality of opportunity in employments and occupations in Northern Ireland between people of different religious beliefs and of working for the elimination of discrimination which is unlawful by virtue of the Act; to render unlawful, in connection with such employments and occupations, certain kinds of discrimination on the ground of religious belief or political opinion; and for connected purposes. [22nd July 1976]

BE IT ENACTED by the Queen's most Excellent Majesty, by and with the advice and consent of the Lords Spiritual and Temporal, and Commons, in this present Parliament assembled, and by the authority of the same, as follows:—

PART I

THE FAIR EMPLOYMENT AGENCY FOR NORTHERN IRELAND

Constitution and general duties of the Agency.

1.—(1) There shall be a body named the Fair Employment Agency for Northern Ireland (" the Agency "), consisting of a chairman and at least five but not more than eleven other members all appointed by the head of the Department of Manpower Services for Northern Ireland (" the Department "), which shall have the duties of—

(*a*) promoting equality of opportunity in Northern Ireland ; and

PART I

(*b*) working for the elimination of discrimination which is unlawful by virtue of this Act,

and for the purposes of discharging those duties shall have the functions conferred on it by this Act.

(2) Schedule 1 shall have effect with respect to the Agency and its affairs.

Educational functions.

2.—(1) In order to assist the Agency in discharging its duties the Agency may—

(*a*) establish services for giving advice on matters connected with equality of opportunity;

(*b*) provide training courses;

(*c*) hold conferences;

(*d*) undertake research which appears to the Agency to be necessary or expedient for purposes of its functions; and

(*e*) disseminate (subject to the safeguard in Schedule 5, paragraph 12(4)) information about the Agency's activities or anything to which those activities relate;

or it may arrange for, or assist (financially or otherwise), any of those things to be done.

(2) The Agency may make charges for training or other facilities or services made available by it.

PART II

EQUALITY OF OPPORTUNITY

General

Meaning of " equality of opportunity ".

3.—(1) In this Act " equality of opportunity " means equality of opportunity between persons of different religious beliefs.

(2) For the purposes of this Act a person of any religious belief has equality of opportunity with a person of any other religious belief if, being—

(*a*) a person who is seeking employment or in employment, or

(*b*) a person who is seeking to become engaged in, or is engaged in, any occupation,

he has in any circumstances the same opportunity of a kind mentioned in subsection (3) as that other person has or would have in those circumstances, due allowance being made for any material difference in their suitability.

PART II

(3) The kinds of opportunity referred to in subsection (2) are—

(*a*) in relation to an employment, the opportunity to be considered, and to be submitted for consideration, for the employment, and to have and hold it on any terms, with access to all benefits connected with it and without being subjected to any detriment; and

(*b*) in relation to an employment or an occupation,—

(i) the opportunity to become, and be, on any terms a member of any vocational organisation which exists for purposes of the employment or the occupation (or for purposes of employments or occupations of any class which includes the employment or occupation), with access to all the benefits of membership and without being subjected to any detriment, and

(ii) where services in connection with training for the employment are provided by a person other than the employer, or where services in connection with training for the occupation are provided by any person, the opportunity to have those services on any terms, with access to all benefits connected with them, and

(iii) the opportunity to have conferred on him, and to hold, on any terms any qualification which is needed for, or facilitates, his engagement in the employment or the occupation.

The Fair Employment Appeals Board.

4.—(1) There shall be a body named the Fair Employment Appeals Board (" the Appeals Board "), consisting of a chairman and two other members all appointed by the head of the Department, which shall have the functions of hearing and determining the appeals which are authorised by this Part to be made to the Appeals Board.

(2) At least one of the members of the Appeals Board shall be a barrister or solicitor of not less than seven years' standing.

(3) Schedule 2 shall have effect with respect to the Appeals Board and its affairs.

Encouragement of commitment to standards and principle of equality of opportunity

Guide to manpower policy and practice.

5.—(1) The Department, after consultation with the Standing Advisory Commission on Human Rights and the Agency, with such organisations appearing to it to be representative of employers, of organisations of workers, and of persons engaged in occupations in Northern Ireland as it thinks fit, and with such

PART II

other persons as it thinks fit, shall prepare and cause to be published a guide to good manpower policy and practice containing recommendations as to policies and practices which, if adopted by employers and vocational organisations, would, in the opinion of the Department, promote equality of opportunity.

(2) The Department shall take such steps as it considers necessary to publicise the guide and to encourage employers and vocational organisations in Northern Ireland to adopt the policies and practices recommended in it.

(3) The Department shall keep the contents of the guide under review and, when necessary, revise it and cause it to be published in its revised form.

(4) In carrying out its functions under this Act, the Agency, when considering whether equality of opportunity is or is not being afforded, shall have such regard to the recommendations contained in the guide as it considers proper in all the circumstances.

Declaration of commitment to, and intent to implement, principle of equality of opportunity.

6.—(1) As soon as reasonably practicable after the commencement of this Act the Agency shall invite such organisations as appear to it to be representative of employers, of organisations of workers, and of persons engaged in occupations in Northern Ireland to subscribe to a declaration of commitment to the principle of equality of opportunity, to be known as " the Declaration of Principle and Intent ", and to encourage their members to subscribe to it.

(2) The Agency shall also use its best endeavours to encourage all employers and all vocational organisations to subscribe to the Declaration.

(3) The Declaration shall be in the form set out in Schedule 3 or in such other form to the like effect as the Agency specifies as being appropriate for any particular declarant.

The Register of Equal Opportunity Employers and Organisations.

7.—(1) The Agency shall keep a register of those who have subscribed to the Declaration of Principle and Intent ; and each employer or organisation whose name is for the time being on the register shall be entitled to receive from the Agency, and to hold, a certificate describing him or it as an " Equal Opportunity Employer " or, as the case may be, an " Equal Opportunity Organisation ", and so to describe himself or itself.

(2) The power of the Agency to keep the register includes power to fix its form and to rectify it ; and in particular the Agency may—

(*a*) require a declarant, as a condition of remaining on the register, to reaffirm, at such intervals and in such manner as the Agency may determine, his intention to adhere to the Declaration ;

PART II

(*b*) remove from the register the name of any declarant who—

(i) fails to comply with a requirement imposed under paragraph (*a*), or

(ii) has declared that he no longer adheres to the Declaration, or

(iii) is found by the Agency in consequence of an investigation under section 12 or section 24 to have acted in a manner inconsistent with adhering to the Declaration ; and

(*c*) restore to the register the name of any declarant which has been removed, where the declarant reaffirms his intention to adhere to the Declaration and it appears to the Agency that he is likely to do so.

(3) When the Agency removes the name of any declarant from the register for any of the reasons mentioned in subsection (2)(*b*), it shall serve on him notice of the fact, stating the reason and requiring him to return to the Agency the certificate issued under subsection (1).

(4) Where a name is removed from the register under subsection (2)(*b*)(i) or (iii), the notice under subsection (3) shall inform the declarant of the right of appeal conferred by section 8.

(5) The register shall be open to public inspection during normal office hours free of charge ; and any person shall be entitled to obtain from the Agency a copy of the register, or of any entry in it, upon payment of such reasonable fee as the Agency may fix.

Appeal against removal of name from, or refusal to restore name to, the register in certain circumstances.

8.—(1) A declarant aggrieved—

(*a*) by the removal of his name from the register under section 7(2)(*b*)(i) or (iii), or

(*b*) by the Agency's refusal to restore his name to the register upon his reaffirming the intention mentioned in section 7(2)(*c*),

may appeal to the Appeals Board against the removal or refusal.

(2) An appeal against the removal of a declarant's name from the register under section 7(2)(*b*)(i) may be made on the ground that in all the circumstances it was unreasonable of the Agency to require the declarant to reaffirm his intention to adhere to the Declaration of Principle and Intent, or to do so after any particular interval or in any particular manner.

(3) Schedule 4 shall have effect with respect to the conduct of an appeal under this section.

(4) Where, on an appeal under this section, the question arises whether a person has acted in a manner inconsistent with

PART II

adhering to the Declaration of Principle and Intent, the Appeals Board shall have such regard as it considers proper in all the circumstances to the recommendations contained in the guide to good manpower policy and practice prepared by the Department under section 5.

(5) The Appeals Board may give such directions for the rectification of the register as it considers necessary for giving effect to its decision.

Publication of names of Equal Opportunity Employers and Organisations.

9.—(1) The Agency shall take such steps as it considers necessary to publicise the names of employers and organisations on the register, and in particular the Agency shall, within six months from the commencement of this Act and thereafter at yearly intervals, notify the public authorities mentioned in subsection (2) of the names of employers' currently on the register.

(2) The public authorities referred to in subsection (1) are—

(*a*) every authority and body listed in the following enactments (as for the time being in force)—

1969 c. 10 (N.I.).

(i) the Parliamentary Commissioner Act (Northern Ireland) 1969, Schedule 1, and

1969 c. 25 (N.I.).

(ii) the Commissioner for Complaints Act (Northern Ireland) 1969, Schedule 1;

1967 c. 13.

(*b*) such of the authorities or bodies listed in the Parliamentary Commissioner Act 1967, Schedule 2, (as for the time being in force) as the Agency considers appropriate;

(*c*) the Police Authority for Northern Ireland; and

(*d*) the Post Office.

(3) When any employer's name is removed from the register, the Agency shall, as soon as reasonably practicable, notify each of those public authorities of the fact.

(4) Where a public authority notified of an employer's name under subsection (1) is of the opinion that the employer has acted in the course of performing a contract entered into with the authority in a manner inconsistent with the terms of the Declaration of Principle and Intent and his name has not already been removed from the register, the authority shall forthwith inform the Agency of the opinion, stating the reasons for it.

Offences in relation to s. 7.

10.—(1) If—

(*a*) any employer who is not the holder of a certificate under section 7(1) for the time being in force describes himself or causes or permits himself to be described, or (*b*) any person acting on behalf of—

(i) such an employer, or

(ii) an organisation which is not the holder of such a certificate,

describes that employer or organisation, or causes or permits him or it to be described,

as an Equal Opportunity Employer or an Equal Opportunity Organisation or by any other words calculated to give the impression that the employer or organisation has subscribed to the Declaration of Principle and Intent or is registered under section 7, that employer or, as the case may be, that person shall be guilty of an offence.

(2) Where an individual or a body corporate is required by a notice under section 7(3) to return a certificate to the Agency and fails without reasonable excuse to do so, he or it shall be guilty of an offence.

(3) Where an unincorporated body is required by a notice under section 7(3) to return a certificate to the Agency, the proper officer of the body shall be under a duty to ensure that the certificate is duly returned, and, if he fails without reasonable excuse to do so, he shall be guilty of an offence.

(4) An offence under subsection (1), (2) or (3) shall be punishable on summary conviction by a fine not exceeding £100.

(5) In any proceedings for any offence under this section a document purporting to be a certificate or other document issued by the Agency and to be signed by a duly authorised officer of the Agency which states—

(*a*) that a particular name was removed from the register on a particular day, or

(*b*) that a particular name was not for the time being registered in the register on a particular day,

shall, until the contrary is proved, be deemed to be such a certificate or document and to be properly issued and shall be evidence of the facts stated in it.

Identification of patterns and trends of employment, etc.

Survey of employment, etc., patterns.

11. It shall be the duty of the Agency to identify and keep under review patterns and trends of employment in Northern Ireland and of occupations in Northern Ireland for the purposes of—

(*a*) considering whether they reveal the existence or absence of equality of opportunity; and

(*b*) assisting the Agency in forming an opinion about—

(i) the manner in which equality of opportunity can best be achieved, or

(ii) where such equality is absent, the reasons for its absence.

PART II

Investigation and remedying of practices which fail to afford equality of opportunity

Investigation of employment, etc., practices.

12.—(1) For the purpose of assisting the Agency in—

(*a*) ascertaining the existence, nature and extent of failures to afford equality of opportunity; and

(*b*) considering what action, if any, for promoting equality of opportunity ought to be taken by any of the following persons (" the person concerned "), that is to say,—

(i) any employer, or

(ii) any person who is empowered by virtue of an enactment to select or nominate another person for employment by a third person, or

(iii) any employment agency, or

(iv) any vocational organisation, or

(v) any person who provides services in connection with training for employment in any capacity, or for any particular employment, (not being services provided by the employer of a person who is seeking to obtain or is receiving those services) or any person who provides services in connection with training for a particular occupation, or

(vi) any person who has power to confer a qualification which is needed for, or facilitates, engagement in employment in any capacity, or in a particular employment or occupation,

the Agency may conduct the investigations mentioned in subsection (2).

(2) Those investigations are investigations—

(*a*) into the composition, by reference to religious beliefs, of any of the following classes of person (or of any class of person within such a class), that is to say,—

(i) the employees of, or other persons who have applied for employment by, any employer or employers of any class, or

(ii) the persons who have applied for or obtained the services of any employment agency, or

(iii) the members of, or other persons who have applied for membership of, any vocational organisation or the members of such organisations of any class, or

(iv) the persons who have sought (or on whose behalf there have been sought) or who have obtained the services of a person such as is mentioned in subsection (1)(*b*)(v), or

PART II

(v) the persons who have applied to have, or have had, conferred on them any qualification such as is mentioned in subsection (1)(*b*)(vi); and

(*b*) into practices—

(i) affecting the recruitment, admission to membership or access to benefits or services of persons belonging to any class referred to in paragraph (*a*), or the terms of employment or membership or provision of services applicable to such persons, or

(ii) involving any detriment to such persons, or

(iii) affecting the conferring or holding of any qualification such as is mentioned in subsection (1)(*b*)(vi),

including practices discontinued before the time of the investigation so far as relevant for explaining the composition of the class of person in question at that time.

(3) Schedule 5 shall have effect with respect to the conduct of investigations under this section.

Undertaking or directions for remedying of certain practices.

13.—(1) Where, following an investigation under section 12, the Agency is of the opinion that the person concerned has failed to afford equality of opportunity, either generally or in relation to any class of person, the Agency shall use its best endeavours—

(*a*) to ensure that he takes such action for promoting equality of opportunity as is, in all the circumstances, reasonable and appropriate; and

(*b*) where appropriate, to secure a satisfactory written undertaking by him that such action will be taken.

(2) Where the Agency asks the person concerned for an undertaking such as is mentioned in subsection (1)(*b*), but—

(*a*) the undertaking is not given, or

(*b*) the undertaking, although given, is not complied with,

the Agency, unless it decides that no further action by it is appropriate,—

(i) where paragraph (*a*) applies, shall serve on the person concerned a notice containing directions such as are mentioned in subsection (3), or

(ii) where paragraph (*b*) applies, shall either serve on him such a notice (whose directions shall supersede the undertaking) or make an application to the county court under section 15 for enforcement of the undertaking.

PART II

(3) The directions contained in a notice served under subsection (2) (i) or (ii) shall be those which the Agency considers to be, in all the circumstances, reasonable and appropriate for promoting equality of opportunity, and the directions may in particular include—

(*a*) directions for the abandonment, or for the modification in accordance with any instructions given in the directions, of any practice which results or may result in failure to afford equality of opportunity, or for the substitution or adoption of new practices specified by the Agency ; and

(*b*) such directions as the Agency considers necessary to ensure that other directions are duly carried out ;

but the terms of directions contained in a notice served under subsection (2)(ii) which supersede an undertaking shall be such as, in the opinion of the Agency, are not more onerous than the terms of the undertaking.

(4) A notice served under subsection (2)(i) or (ii) shall inform the person concerned of the right of appeal against the directions which is conferred by section 14.

(5) The Agency, on the written application of the person concerned, may—

(*a*) revoke all of the directions ; or

(*b*) modify the directions in accordance with the application—

(i) by revoking any of them, or

(ii) by substituting new directions for all or any of them ;

and, in substitution for any directions which are revoked under paragraph (*a*), may accept from that person an undertaking such as is mentioned in subsection (1)(*b*).

(6) The Agency shall serve notice of the revocation or modification on the person concerned.

(7) Any reference in the succeeding provisions of this Act to directions given by the Agency—

(*a*) does not include directions revoked under subsection (5)(*a*) ; and

(*b*) where the directions have been modified under subsection (5)(*b*), is to them as so modified.

(8) The directions shall be binding on the person concerned (except to the extent that they are quashed, or other directions are substituted for them, by the Appeals Board under section 14) and shall be enforceable only in accordance with section 15.

Appeals and legal proceedings in relation to the remedying of practices

PART II

Appeal to Appeals Board against directions under s. 13.

14.—(1) Where, under section 13, the Agency serves on the person concerned a notice containing directions (not being directions substituted for others in accordance with an application made by him under section 13(5)), he may, within 21 days from the date of service, appeal to the Appeals Board against the directions.

(2) The appeal may be brought on any of the following grounds—

(*a*) that in all the circumstances it is unreasonable to expect the appellant to comply with the directions;

(*b*) that in all the circumstances the directions are not appropriate for promoting equality of opportunity; or

(*c*) that the appellant is already affording equality of opportunity, and the directions are, therefore, unnecessary.

(3) Schedule 4 shall have effect with respect to the conduct of the appeal.

(4) On hearing the appeal the Appeals Board may—

(*a*) dismiss the appeal; or

(*b*) quash the directions or any of them; or

(*c*) substitute for the directions or any of them such other directions (of a kind that the Agency could have given) as the Appeals Board considers reasonable and appropriate in all the circumstances.

(5) Directions substituted under subsection (4)(*c*) shall be binding on the person concerned and shall be enforceable only in accordance with section 15.

(6) In coming to its decision the Appeals Board shall have such regard as it considers proper in all the circumstances to the recommendations contained in the guide to good manpower policy and practice prepared by the Department under section 5.

Enforcement by county court of undertaking or directions.

15.—(1) Where, within such period as the Agency considers reasonable,—

(*a*) an undertaking to take action for promoting equality of opportunity—

(i) which has been given to the Agency under section 13(1) and has not been superseded by directions given by the Agency, or

(ii) which has been given to the Agency under section 13(5),

has not been complied with; or

PART II

(*b*) directions given by the Agency have not been complied with,

or steps have not been taken to the Agency's satisfaction to comply with it or them, the Agency may, subject to subsection (2), make an application to the county court under this section for enforcement of the undertaking or the directions.

(2) Notice of an application for the enforcement of directions shall not be given—

(*a*) until the expiration of the period allowed by section 14(1) for an appeal to the Appeals Board against the directions ; or

(*b*) if notice of such an appeal is served within that period—

(i) unless the appeal is abandoned or dismissed, or

(ii) where the Appeals Board quashes, or makes substitutions for, some only of the directions, except in relation to directions which have not been quashed or for which no substitution has been made.

(3) On such an application the court shall have power to make an order (to which section 46 shall apply) directing the person concerned to do any act which he ought to do in order to fulfil all or any of his commitments under the undertaking or comply with all or any of his obligations under the directions.

(4) This section (except subsection (2)) applies also to directions substituted by the Appeals Board under section 14(4)(*c*) for directions given by the Agency.

PART III

UNLAWFUL DISCRIMINATION

General

Meaning of " discrimination " and " unlawful discrimination ".

16.—(1) In this Act " discrimination " means—

(*a*) discrimination on the ground of religious belief or political opinion ; or

(*b*) discrimination by way of victimisation ;

and " discriminate " shall be construed accordingly.

(2) For the purposes of this Act a person discriminates against another person on the ground of religious belief or political opinion if, on either of those grounds, he treats that other person less favourably in any circumstances than he treats or would treat any other person in those circumstances.

(3) For the purposes of this Act a person discriminates against another person (" the person victimised ") by way of victimisation if he treats that other person less favourably in any circumstances

than he treats or would treat any other person in those circumstances, and does so by reason that the person victimised has—

(*a*) made a complaint against him or any other person under this Act of unlawful discrimination, or

(*b*) given evidence or information in connection with any such complaint or any investigation, legal proceedings or appeal under this Act, or

(*c*) alleged that he or any other person has committed an act which (whether or not the allegation so states) would amount to a contravention of this Act, or

(*d*) otherwise done anything under or by reference to this Act in relation to him or any other person,

or by reason that he knows the person victimised intends to do any of these things, or that he suspects the person victimised has done, or intends to do any of them.

(4) Subsection (3) does not apply to treatment of a person by reason of any allegation made by him if the allegation was false and not made in good faith.

(5) For the purposes of this Act a person commits unlawful discrimination against another if he does an act in relation to that other which is unlawful by virtue of this Part, or if he is treated by virtue of any provision of Part IV as doing such an act.

Acts of unlawful discrimination

Discrimination by employers.

17. It shall be unlawful for an employer to discriminate against a person, in relation to employment in Northern Ireland,—

(*a*) where that person is seeking employment—

(i) in the arrangements the employer makes for the purpose of determining who should be offered employment, or

(ii) by refusing or deliberately omitting to offer that person employment for which he applies, or

(iii) in the terms on which he offers him employment; or

(*b*) where that person is employed by him—

(i) in the terms of employment which he affords him, or

(ii) in the way he affords him access to benefits or by refusing or deliberately omitting to afford him access to them, or

(iii) by dismissing him, or

(iv) by subjecting him to any other detriment.

PART III

Discrimination against contract workers.

18.—(1) This section applies to any work for a person (" the principal ") which is available to be done by individuals (" contract workers ")—

(*a*) who are employed not by the principal himself but by another person, who supplies them under a contract made with the principal, and

(*b*) who, if they were instead employed by the principal to do that work, would be in his employment in Northern Ireland.

(2) It shall be unlawful for the principal, in relation to work to which this section applies, to discriminate against a contract worker—

(*a*) in the terms on which he allows him to do that work, or

(*b*) by not allowing him to do it or continue to do it, or

(*c*) in the way he affords him access to benefits or by refusing or deliberately omitting to afford him access to them, or

(*d*) by subjecting him to any other detriment.

Discrimination by persons with statutory power to select employees for others.

19. It shall be unlawful for a person who is empowered by virtue of an enactment to select or nominate another person for employment by a third person to discriminate against a person, in relation to employment in Northern Ireland,—

(*a*) by refusing or deliberately omitting to select or nominate him for employment, or

(*b*) where candidates are selected or nominated in order of preference, by selecting or nominating him lower in order than any other who is selected or nominated.

Discrimination by employment agencies.

20.—(1) It shall be unlawful for an employment agency to discriminate against a person, in relation to employment in Northern Ireland,—

(*a*) in the terms on which the agency offers to provide any of its services, or

(*b*) by refusing or deliberately omitting to provide any of its services, or

(*c*) in the way it provides any of its services.

(2) References in subsection (1) to the services of an employment agency include guidance on careers and any other services related to employment.

(3) This section does not apply if the discrimination only concerns employment which the employer could lawfully refuse to offer the person concerned.

PART III

(4) An employment agency shall not be subject to any liability under this section if it proves—

(*a*) that it acted in reliance on a statement made to it by the employer to the effect that, by reason of the operation of subsection (3), its action would not be unlawful, and

(*b*) that it was reasonable for it to rely on the statement.

(5) A person who knowingly or recklessly makes a statement such as is referred to in subsection (4)(*a*) which in a material respect is false or misleading shall be guilty of an offence, and shall be liable on summary conviction to a fine not exceeding £400.

Discrimination by vocational organisations.

21. It shall be unlawful for a vocational organisation to discriminate against a person who is employed or is seeking employment in Northern Ireland, or who is engaged or is seeking to become engaged in an occupation in Northern Ireland,—

(*a*) where that person is not a member of the organisation—

(i) by refusing or deliberately omitting to accept his application for membership, or

(ii) in the terms on which it is prepared to admit him to membership ; or

(*b*) where that person is a member of the organisation—

(i) in the way it affords him access to benefits or by refusing or deliberately omitting to afford him access to them, or

(ii) by depriving him of membership, or varying the terms on which he is a member, or

(iii) by subjecting him to any other detriment.

Discrimination by persons providing training services.

22.—(1) It shall be unlawful for a person who provides services in connection with the training of persons for employment in any capacity, or for a particular employment or occupation, in Northern Ireland to discriminate against another person—

(*a*) where that other person is seeking to obtain those services or they are sought to be obtained on his behalf—

(i) by refusing or deliberately omitting to provide those services, or

(ii) in the terms on which the person offers to provide those services ; or

(*b*) where that other person is receiving those services—

(i) in the way the person provides those services, or

(ii) in the way he affords him access to benefits connected with the services or by refusing or

PART III

deliberately omitting to afford him access to them, or

(iii) by withdrawing those services from him or varying the terms on which they are provided, or

(iv) by subjecting him to any other detriment.

(2) In subsection (1) " services ", in relation to training for employment, means services provided otherwise than by the employer of the person who is seeking to obtain or is receiving the services.

Discrimination by persons with power to confer qualifications.

23. It shall be unlawful for a person who has power to confer on another a qualification which is needed for, or facilitates, his engagement in employment in any capacity, or in a particular employment or occupation, in Northern Ireland to discriminate against him—

(*a*) by refusing or deliberately omitting to confer that qualification on him on his application, or

(*b*) in the terms on which the person is prepared to confer it, or

(*c*) by withdrawing it from him or varying the terms on which he holds it.

Complaints of unlawful discrimination

Investigation of complaint of unlawful discrimination.

24.—(1) Subject to the provisions of this section, where a person makes a complaint in writing to the Agency alleging that unlawful discrimination has been committed against him by another person (" the respondent "), the Agency shall investigate the complaint (unless it considers that the complaint is frivolous).

(2) Where a person against whom unlawful discrimination is alleged to have been committed has died or is for any reason unable to act for himself, the complaint may be made by his personal representative or by a member of his family or other individual suitable to represent him ; and where a person who has made or continued a complaint dies or becomes unable to act, the complaint may be continued by the personal representative, or a member of the family, of the person against whom the discrimination is alleged to have been committed, or by such other individual as aforesaid.

(3) A complaint must be made before the expiration of—

(*a*) two months from the day on which the complainant first had knowledge, or might reasonably be expected first to have had knowledge, of the act complained of ; or

(*b*) six months from the day on which the act was done, whichever first occurs ; but the Agency may, if it thinks fit, investigate a complaint made after the expiration of that period, if of the opinion that there are special circumstances which make it proper to do so.

(4) For the purposes of this section—

(*a*) where the inclusion of any term in a contract renders the making of the contract an unlawful act, that act shall be treated as extending throughout the duration of the contract, and

(*b*) any act extending over a period shall be treated as done at the end of that period, and

(*c*) a deliberate omission shall be treated as done when the person in question does an act inconsistent with doing the omitted act or, if he has done no such inconsistent act, when the period expires within which he might reasonably have been expected to do the omitted act if it were to be done.

(5) The Agency shall not consider a complaint relating to an act which is unlawful by virtue of section 23, if the act is one in respect of which an appeal, or proceedings in the nature of an appeal, may be brought to a court under any enactment.

(6) Without prejudice to subsection (5), where the Agency is satisfied that the subject-matter of a complaint has been or is being considered by some other statutory body or by a person holding a statutory office, the Agency shall not be obliged to investigate the complaint; but it may do so, after consultation with that other body or person, if it thinks fit.

(7) Schedule 5 shall have effect with respect to the conduct of investigations under this section.

(8) Where the Agency is of the opinion that, by virtue of any provision of Part V, it is precluded from investigating, or continuing the investigation, of a complaint, the Agency shall serve on the complainant and the respondent a notice stating the opinion.

Finding following investigation; attempts at conciliation.

25.—(1) On completing its investigation of a complaint the Agency shall—

(*a*) form an opinion (its " finding ") whether or not unlawful discrimination has been committed by the respondent against the complainant; and

(*b*) use its best endeavours—

(i) to secure a settlement of any difference between the complainant and the respondent which was disclosed by the complaint, and

PART III

(ii) where the finding is that unlawful discrimination has been committed, to secure, if it is appropriate to do so, a satisfactory written undertaking by the respondent to comply with the terms of the settlement.

(2) As soon as reasonably practicable after arriving at its finding, the Agency shall serve on the complainant and the respondent a notice stating the finding and the reasons for it; and, if the finding is that unlawful discrimination has been committed, as soon as reasonably practicable thereafter the Agency shall serve on the complainant a notice stating whether or not the Agency has secured a settlement, or a settlement and undertaking, as mentioned in subsection (1)(*b*), and if so on what terms.

(3) A notice under subsection (2) stating the Agency's finding shall inform the complainant and the respondent of the right of appeal against the finding which is conferred by section 28.

(4) A finding that unlawful discrimination has been committed by the respondent against the complainant—

(*a*) shall not be questioned in any legal proceedings under this Act, except by appeal under section 28; and

(*b*) in any such proceedings, except on such an appeal, shall be evidence that the unlawful discrimination was committed.

Further attempts at conciliation: recommendations.

26.—(1) If the Agency's finding is that unlawful discrimination has been committed by the respondent against the complainant, and if a settlement and, where appropriate, a satisfactory undertaking have not been secured, then, unless the Agency decides that no further action by it is appropriate, it shall serve on the complainant and the respondent a notice containing recommendations as to the action to be taken by the respondent to dispose of the difference disclosed by the complaint.

(2) The recommendations may be contained in a notice served under section 25(2) or in a subsequent notice.

(3) Where such an undertaking has already been secured but has not been complied with, the Agency, unless it decides that no further action by it is appropriate, shall either—

(*a*) serve on the complainant and the respondent a notice such as is mentioned in subsection (1); or

(*b*) proceed to institute an action under section 30 by way of a claim in tort in respect of the unlawful discrimination.

(4) Without prejudice to the Agency's power to make any relevant recommendation, the recommendations may include a

recommendation for the submission for consideration for employment, or for the employment, re-employment, admission to membership or reinstatement, of, or for the provision of any service for, the affording of access to any benefit to, the removal of any detriment from, or the conferment of any qualification on, the person against whom the unlawful discrimination was committed, and may also include a recommendation for the payment by the respondent of compensation such as is mentioned in section 31(1) (including compensation payable only in the event of some other recommendation not being complied with). PART III

(5) The Agency, on the respondent's written application, may—

(*a*) revoke all of the recommendations ; or

(*b*) modify the recommendations in accordance with the application—

(i) by revoking any of them, or

(ii) by substituting new recommendations for all or any of them ;

and, in substitution for any recommendations which are revoked under paragraph (*a*), may accept from the respondent a satisfactory written undertaking to comply with the terms of any settlement which may have been reached in order to dispose of the difference disclosed by the complaint.

(6) The Agency shall serve on the complainant and the respondent notice of any revocation or modification of the recommendations under subsection (5), and shall serve on the complainant notice of the terms of any undertaking accepted under that subsection.

(7) Any reference in the succeeding provisions of this Act to recommendations made by the Agency—

(*a*) does not include recommendations revoked under subsection (5)(*a*) ; and

(*b*) where the recommendations have been modified under subsection (5)(*b*), is to them as so modified.

(8) Where—

(*a*) a settlement such as is mentioned in section 25 or this section, or

(*b*) a recommendation under subsection (1) or (5),

provides for the payment of any sum by the respondent to the complainant, then, if the Agency has made any payment to the complainant in respect of expenses or allowances as mentioned in Schedule 5, paragraph 11, a sum equal to the amount of that payment shall be a first charge for the benefit of the Agency on

PART III

the sum so provided for, unless the Agency in any particular case waives that charge.

Remedying of practices excluding equality of opportunity which are disclosed on investigation of complaint.

27. Where, following its investigation of a complaint, the Agency (whether or not its finding is that unlawful discrimination has been committed by the respondent against the complainant) is of the opinion that the respondent has failed to afford equality of opportunity in relation to persons of any class, the Agency shall use its best endeavours to ensure that action such as is mentioned in section 13(1) is taken and that, where appropriate, an undertaking is given as there mentioned, and, without prejudice to the operation of any provision of this Part in consequence of the Agency's finding, the provisions of this Act shall have effect as if the Agency had formed that opinion following an investigation under section 12.

Appeal against finding following complaint of unlawful discrimination

Appeal to county court against Agency's finding on complaint of unlawful discrimination.

28.—(1) This section has effect where, following a complaint of unlawful discrimination, the Agency serves a notice under section 25(2) on the complainant and the respondent stating the Agency's finding.

(2) If the finding is that unlawful discrimination has been committed, the respondent may appeal against the finding.

(3) If the finding is that such discrimination has not been committed, the complainant may appeal against the finding.

(4) An appeal under this section shall lie to the county court and notice of the appeal must be given within 21 days from the date of service of the notice stating the finding.

(5) In an appeal under subsection (2) the parties shall be the respondent and the Agency, and in an appeal under subsection (3) the parties shall be the complainant and the respondent.

Supplementary provisions as to appeal under s. 28.

29.—(1) On an appeal under section 28—

(*a*) if the court agrees with the Agency's finding, it shall dismiss the appeal ; or

(*b*) if the court disagrees with the Agency's finding, then,—

(i) if the court decides that unlawful discrimination has been committed by the respondent against the complainant it shall remit the case to the Agency and thereupon section 25(1)(*b*) and, if appropriate, section 26 shall have effect as if that were the Agency's finding ; or

PART III

(ii) if the court decides that such discrimination has not been committed, the court shall quash the complaint.

(2) Where the court disagrees with the Agency's finding it shall state the reasons for its decision.

(3) Where the court on an appeal under section 28 disagrees with the Agency's finding and decides that unlawful discrimination has been committed by the respondent against the complainant, the court's decree shall be evidence that the unlawful discrimination was committed, if it would not be such evidence apart from this provision, and shall not be questioned, in any legal proceedings under this Act.

Legal proceedings to secure compensation for, or the remedying of, unlawful discrimination

Action in county court following breakdown of attempts at conciliation.

30.—(1) Where, within such period as the Agency considers reasonable,—

(*a*) an undertaking to comply with the terms of a settlement such as is mentioned in section 25(1)(*b*), or an undertaking accepted by the Agency under section 26(5) in substitution for revoked recommendations, has not been complied with ; or

(*b*) recommendations made by the Agency have not been complied with,

the Agency, on behalf of the injured person (that is to say, the person against whom the unlawful discrimination was committed or, where that person is dead, his personal representative) may institute an action in the county court against the respondent by way of a claim in tort in respect of the unlawful discrimination.

(2) Such an action shall not be instituted in consequence of failure to comply with recommendations—

(*a*) until the expiration of the period allowed by section 28 for an appeal against the finding which led to the recommendations ; or

(*b*) if notice of such an appeal is given within that period, unless the appeal is abandoned or dismissed ;

but this subsection does not apply to anything done after a case has been remitted by the court to the Agency under section 29(1)(*b*)(i).

(3) Subsection (4) of section 24 (time when certain acts are to be treated as done) shall have effect for determining, for the purposes of the Statute of Limitations (Northern Ireland) 1958, when a cause or right of action under subsection (1) of this section accrued. 1958 c. 10 (N.I.).

PART III

(4) In an action under this section the court shall have power by its decree—

(*a*) to award damages ; or

(*b*) to grant an injunction ; or

(*c*) to award damages and grant an injunction,

in accordance with the provisions of section 31, or sections 31 and 46 ; and the damages may be awarded to the Agency as if it were the injured person, and it shall be for the Agency to take steps to recover the damages and, subject to section 31(6), to account to the injured person for any damages recovered.

(5) The court shall state the reasons for its decree.

Powers of court as to damages and injunctions.

31.—(1) In an action under section 30, the amount of any damages awarded shall be such as the court considers just in all the circumstances to compensate the injured person for any loss or injury he has suffered in consequence of the act of unlawful discrimination in question, including (without prejudice to the generality of the foregoing provision of this subsection)—

(*a*) compensation for expenses reasonably incurred by the injured person in connection with the subject-matter of the complaint which led to the action (which for the purposes of this section shall be taken to include compensation for loss of his time) ; and

(*b*) compensation for loss of opportunity, that is to say for loss of any employment, occupation or benefit which the injured person might reasonably be expected to have had but for the unlawful discrimination ;

but—

(i) any award of damages for loss of opportunity shall be subject to the application of the same rule concerning the duty of a person to mitigate his loss as applies in relation to damages recoverable at common law ; and

(ii) compensation shall not be awarded for the same loss both by way of damages under this Act and by way of damages under any other enactment or at common law.

(2) Where the undertaking or any of the recommendations mentioned in section 30(1) includes provision for the injured person to be given a benefit of any kind by the respondent, and that provision has not been complied with,—

(*a*) if the court finds that the reason why the provision was not complied with was that the injured person refused an offer of benefit on the terms stated in that provision, and the court considers that he acted unreasonably in doing so, the court may reduce the assessment of his loss ; or (*b*) if the court finds that the reason why the provision was not complied with was that the respondent refused or failed to make such an offer, and the court considers that he acted unreasonably in doing so, the court may increase that assessment,

to such extent (in either case) as in all the circumstances the court considers just and equitable.

(3) Where it appears to the court in an action under section 30 that justice can be done to the injured person only by directing the defendant in the action to do, or refrain from doing, any particular act or acts, the court, if satisfied that in all the circumstances it is reasonable to do so, may make an order (to which section 46 shall apply) containing such a direction.

(4) The powers conferred on the county court by subsections (1) and (2) may be exercised by that court notwithstanding anything to the contrary in any enactment which imposes limitations on the jurisdiction of a county court by reference to an amount claimed.

(5) Where the injured person is the personal representative of the person (" the victim ") against whom the unlawful discrimination was committed, the reference in subsection (1) to any loss or injury the injured person has suffered shall be construed—

(*a*) in relation to any item of damages which compensates for the expenses mentioned in subsection (1)(*a*), as including a reference to the victim, and

(*b*) in relation to any item of damages which compensates for the loss mentioned in subsection (1)(*b*), as a reference to the victim.

(6) An award of damages for expenses incurred as mentioned in paragraph (*a*) of subsection (1) (including that paragraph as modified by subsection (5)) may include compensation for expenses so incurred which have been defrayed by sums paid by the Agency under Schedule 5, paragraph 11; and so much of the damages as compensates for expenses so defrayed shall be identified by the court's decree as a separate item of damages and shall be retained by the Agency and applied for its benefit.

(7) Section 26(8) shall apply to sums payable under a compromise or settlement arrived at to avoid or bring an end to an action under section 30 as it applies to a settlement such as is mentioned in section 25 or 26.

Power of court to revise contracts.

32.—(1) Where a term is included in or omitted from a contract in contravention of any provision of this Part or in consequence of such a contravention, then, notwithstanding that the making of the contract is an unlawful act, neither the contract nor any part of it is unenforceable by reason only of the contravention; but in an action under section 30—

(*a*) the Agency on behalf of the injured person; or

(*b*) the defendant,

may apply to the court to revise the contract or any of its terms.

(2) On such an application the court may make such order as it considers just in all the circumstances revising the contract or any of its terms so as to secure that, as from the date of the order, the contract in no way contravenes, or has any effect in consequence of a contravention of, any provision of this Part.

(3) Where the court makes an order under this section, every party to the contract, whether or not a party in the action, shall be bound by the order; but the court shall not make such an order which affects a party to the contract who is not a party in the action without giving him an opportunity of being heard.

PART IV

OTHER UNLAWFUL ACTS

Discriminatory advertisements.

33.—(1) It shall be unlawful to publish in Northern Ireland, or cause to be published there, an advertisement which indicates, or could reasonably be understood as indicating, an intention by a person to do an act which is unlawful by virtue of Part III.

(2) Subsection (1) does not apply if the intended act would be prevented from being unlawful by any provision of Part V.

(3) The publisher of an advertisement which is unlawful by virtue of subsection (1) shall not be subject to any liability under that subsection in respect of the publication of the advertisement if he proves—

(*a*) that the advertisement was published in reliance on a statement made to him by the person who caused it to be published to the effect that, by reason of the operation of subsection (2), the publication would not be unlawful, and

(*b*) that it was reasonable for him to rely on the statement.

(4) A person who knowingly or recklessly makes a statement such as is referred to in subsection (3)(*a*) which in a material respect is false or misleading shall be guilty of an offence, and shall be liable on summary conviction to a fine not exceeding £400.

Accessories and incitement.

34.—(1) Any person who—

(*a*) knowingly aids or incites, or

(*b*) directs, procures or induces,

another to do an act which is unlawful by virtue of Part III or section 33 shall be treated for the purposes of this Act as if he, as well as that other, had done that act.

(2) For the purposes of subsection (1) an employee or agent for whose act the employer or principal is liable under section 35 (or would be so liable but for section 35(3)) shall be deemed to aid the doing of the act by the employer or principal.

(3) A person does not under this section knowingly aid another to do an unlawful act if—

(*a*) he acts in reliance on a statement made to him by that other person that, by reason of any provision of this Act, the act which he aids would not be unlawful, and

(*b*) it is reasonable for him to rely on the statement.

(4) A person who knowingly or recklessly makes a statement such as is referred to in subsection (3) (*a*) which in a material respect is false or misleading shall be guilty of an offence, and shall be liable on summary conviction to a fine not exceeding £400.

(5) An inducement consisting of an offer of benefit or a threat of detriment is not prevented from falling within subsection (1) because the offer or threat was not made directly to the person in question.

Liability of employers and principals.

35.—(1) Anything done by a person in the course of his employment shall be treated for the purposes of this Act as done by his employer as well as by him, whether or not it was done with the employer's knowledge or approval.

(2) Anything done by a person as agent for another person with the authority (whether express or implied and whether precedent or subsequent) of that other person shall be treated for the purposes of this Act as done by that other person as well as by him.

(3) In proceedings brought under this Act against any person in respect of an act alleged to have been done by an employee of his it shall be a defence for that person to prove that he took such steps as were reasonably practicable to prevent the employee from doing that act or from doing in the course of his employment acts of the same description.

Enforcement of s. 33.

36.—(1) If it appears to the Agency—

(*a*) that a person has done an act which by virtue of section 33 was unlawful, and

(*b*) that unless restrained he is likely to do further acts which by virtue of that section are unlawful,

the Agency may apply to the county court for an order restraining him from doing such acts; and the court, if satisfied that the

PART IV

application is well-founded and that in all the circumstances it is reasonable to do so, may make the order (to which section 46 shall apply).

(2) Where the act mentioned in subsection (1)(*a*) is a continuing act, the reference in subsection (1)(*b*) to further acts shall include a reference to the continuance of that act.

PART V

EXCEPTIONS

Excepted employments, etc.

37.—(1) Parts II to IV shall not apply to or in relation to—

(*a*) any employment or occupation as a clergyman or minister of a religious denomination ;

(*b*) employment for the purposes of a private household ; or

(*c*) employment as a teacher in a school.

(2) Part II shall not apply to or in relation to any employment or occupation, other than one mentioned in subsection (1), where the essential nature of the job requires it to be done by a person holding, or not holding, a particular religious belief.

(3) Parts III and IV, so far as they relate to discrimination on the ground of religious belief, shall not apply to or in relation to any employment or occupation, other than one mentioned in subsection (1), where the essential nature of the job requires it to be done by a person holding, or not holding, a particular religious belief ; nor, so far as they relate to discrimination on the ground of political opinion, shall they apply to or in relation to an employment or occupation where the essential nature of the job requires it to be done by a person holding, or not holding, a particular political opinion.

(4) No provision of Parts II to IV shall apply—

(*a*) during the two years beginning with the commencement of this Act, to, or to employment by, an employer who employs not more than 25 persons in addition to any employed for the purposes of his private household ; and

(*b*) during the year following those two years, to, or to employment by, an employer who employs not more than 10 persons in addition to any employed for the purposes of his private household.

(5) Subsection (1) is subject to the power conferred by section 39 to remove or limit the exception made by paragraph (*c*) of that subsection.

PART V

Review of exception of school-teachers.

38.—(1) The Agency shall keep under review the exception contained in section 37(1)(*c*) relating to the employment of teachers in schools, with a view to considering whether, in the Agency's opinion, it is appropriate that any steps should be taken to further equality of opportunity in the employment of such teachers.

(2) For the purpose of assisting it in the discharge of its duty under subsection (1), the Agency may conduct investigations—

(*a*) into the composition, by reference to religious beliefs, of the staff employed as teachers, or teachers of any class, in schools generally, schools of any class or particular schools; and

(*b*) into practices—

(i) affecting the recruitment or access to benefits of, or the terms of employment applicable to, such staff, or

(ii) involving any detriment to such staff,

including practices discontinued before the time of the investigation so far as relevant for explaining the composition of the staff at that time.

(3) The Agency may from time to time, and shall whenever the Secretary of State so directs, report to the Secretary of State upon the exercise of its functions under this section; and a report under this subsection may make recommendations as to any action which the Agency considers ought to be taken to further equality of opportunity in the employment of teachers, or teachers of any class, in schools, or in schools of any class (including action by way of the exercise of the power conferred by section 39 to remove or limit the exception contained in section 37(1)(*c*)).

(4) Schedule 5 shall have effect with respect to the conduct of investigations under this section.

Power to remove or limit exception of school-teachers.

39.—(1) The Secretary of State may by order provide that section 37(1)(*c*)—

(*a*) shall cease to have effect; or

(*b*) shall, on and after such day or days as may be specified in the order, have effect only in relation to particular classes of teachers or particular classes of schools or for particular purposes of this Act.

(2) An order under subsection (1) may make all or any of the provisions mentioned in paragraph (*b*) of that subsection, and may do so by way of exception or otherwise.

(3) An order under subsection (1) may include transitional provisions.

PART V

(4) The power to make an order under subsection (1)(*b*) includes power to vary or revoke the order.

(5) The Secretary of State shall not make an order under subsection (1) unless a draft of the order has been laid before, and has been approved by, both Houses of Parliament.

Charities.

40.—(1) Nothing in this Act shall—

(*a*) be construed as affecting a provision to which this subsection applies, or

(*b*) render unlawful an act which is done in order to give effect to such a provision.

(2) Subsection (1) applies to a provision for conferring benefits on persons of a particular religious belief or a particular political opinion (disregarding any benefits to persons not of that belief or opinion which are exceptional or are relatively insignificant), being a provision—

(*a*) which is contained in an enactment or instrument, and

(*b*) which has been enacted or made for purposes which are exclusively charitable according to the law of Northern Ireland.

(3) In subsection (2) " enactment " includes an enactment contained in a local or personal Act (including an Act of the Parliament of Northern Ireland).

Acts done under statutory authority.

41.—(1) Nothing in this Act shall render unlawful anything done in order to comply with a requirement—

(*a*) of an enactment enacted before the passing of this Act; or

(*b*) of an instrument made or approved (whether before or after the passing of this Act) under an enactment enacted before the passing of this Act.

(2) Where an enactment enacted after the passing of this Act re-enacts (with or without modification) a provision of an enactment enacted before the passing of this Act, subsection (1) shall apply to that provision as re-enacted as if it continued to be contained in an enactment enacted before the passing of this Act.

Acts done to safeguard national security, etc.

42.—(1) This Act shall not apply to an act done for the purpose of safeguarding national security or of protecting public safety or public order.

(2) A certificate signed by or on behalf of the Secretary of State and certifying that an act specified in the certificate was done for a purpose mentioned in subsection (1) shall be conclusive evidence that it was done for that purpose.

(3) A document purporting to be a certificate such as is mentioned in subsection (2) shall be received in evidence and, unless the contrary is proved, shall be deemed to be such a certificate.

Part VI
Miscellaneous
Restriction on proceedings

Restriction on proceedings for contravention of Act.

43.—(1) Except as provided by this Act, no proceedings, whether civil or criminal, shall be brought against any person in respect of an act by reason that the act is unlawful by virtue of a provision of this Act.

(2) Nothing in subsection (1) prevents the making of an application for an order of certiorari, mandamus or prohibition.

Supplementary provisions as to the county court

Jurisdiction as to acts done on ships, etc.

44. Without prejudice to any jurisdiction exercisable by the county court by virtue of section 45 or any other enactment, the county court shall have jurisdiction to hear and determine an application, appeal or action under this Act with respect to an act done or to be done on a ship, aircraft or hovercraft outside the division for which the court sits, including such an act done or to be done outside Northern Ireland.

County court rules and orders.

1959 c. 25 (N.I.).

45. County court rules and county court orders made under section 146 of the County Courts Act (Northern Ireland) 1959 may make such provision as appears to the authority having for the time being power to make those rules and orders to be necessary for regulating the practice and procedure of county courts in the exercise of the jurisdiction conferred by this Act, and (without prejudice to the generality of any power to make such rules or orders) those rules or orders may in particular provide for—

(*a*) an application made under section 15 to be made to a county court sitting for the division in which the person concerned carried on business or, as the case may be, had an office at the time when the undertaking sought to be enforced was given or the notice containing the direction sought to be enforced was served;

(*b*) an appeal under section 28 or an action under section 30 to be brought in a county court sitting for the division in which the person alleged to have been injured by the act of unlawful discrimination is resident, or was resident at the time when the act was done;

(*c*) the service of process on persons outside Northern Ireland.

PART VI

Powers of county court as to injunctions.

46.—(1) For the purposes of an order under section 15(3), section 31(3) or section 36 the county court shall have the like jurisdiction as the High Court to grant any mandatory or other injunction.

1959 c. 25 (N.I.).

(2) Section 141(4) of the County Courts Act (Northern Ireland) 1959 (enforcement by committal) applies to the enforcement of an order made in exercise of the jurisdiction conferred by any of the provisions mentioned in subsection (1) in conjunction with this section.

(3) Where an application is made for such an order (including an application in the course of an action under section 30) the court may make the order in the terms applied for or in more limited terms.

Execution of order for damages or costs.

47. Where in an action under section 30 the county court, in exercise of the jurisdiction conferred on it by virtue of this Act, makes an order for the payment of a sum in respect of damages or costs, or both damages and costs, by a person who was domiciled in England and Wales or in Scotland at the time of the commencement of the action, that sum shall be recoverable under the Inferior Courts Judgments Extension Act 1882 notwithstanding that the whole cause of action had not arisen, or the obligation to which the order relates had not been due to be fulfilled, within the division for which the court sits, or that the civil bill commencing the action had not been served upon the defendant personally within that division; and section 9 of that Act (saving as to limits of local jurisdiction) shall not apply to such an order.

1882 c. 31.

Appeal from county court.

1964 c. 3 (N.I.).

48. Without prejudice to section 2 of the County Court Appeals Act (Northern Ireland) 1964 (appeal to Court of Appeal in Northern Ireland on point of law) and section 7 of that Act (different modes of appeal to be exclusive), the Agency or the respondent, if dissatisfied with a decree of the county court in an action under section 30, may appeal from that decree, notwithstanding that damages have been claimed or awarded in excess of the amount that could have been claimed or awarded apart from section 31(4), as if the decree had been made in exercise of the jurisdiction conferred by Part III of the County Courts Act (Northern Ireland) 1959 and the appeal were brought under section 1 of that Act of 1964.

Construction of references to employment or occupation in Northern Ireland

Meaning of "employment in Northern Ireland" and "occupation in Northern Ireland".

49.—(1) For the purposes of this Act, employment is to be regarded as being employment in Northern Ireland unless the employee does his work wholly or mainly outside Northern Ireland.

(2) Subsection (1) does not apply to—

(*a*) employment on board a ship registered at a port of registry in Northern Ireland, or

(*b*) employment on an aircraft or hovercraft operated by a person who has his principal place of business, or is ordinarily resident, in Northern Ireland;

but for the purposes of this Act such employment is to be regarded as being employment in Northern Ireland unless the employee does his work wholly outside Northern Ireland.

(3) In relation to employment concerned with the exploration of the sea bed or subsoil or the exploitation of their natural resources, the Department may by order provide that subsections (1) and (2) shall each have effect as if the last reference to Northern Ireland included any area for the time being designated under section 1(7) of the Continental Shelf Act 1964, or any part of such an area, in which the law of Northern Ireland applies. 1964 c. 29.

(4) An order under subsection (3) may provide that, in relation to employment to which the order applies or any class of such employment, this Act is to have effect with such modifications as are specified in the order.

(5) The power to make an order under subsection (3) includes power to vary or revoke the order.

(6) The Department shall not make an order under subsection (3) unless a draft of the order has been laid before, and has been approved by, the Northern Ireland Assembly.

(7) During the interim period subsection (6) shall not apply, but an order under subsection (3) shall be subject to annulment in pursuance of a resolution of either House of Parliament in like manner as a statutory instrument, and section 5 of the Statutory Instruments Act 1946 shall apply accordingly. 1946 c. 36.

(8) In this section references to the work an employee does include, in relation to a person who is seeking employment or a person who has ceased to be in employment, references to, respectively, the work he would do if employed or the work he did when employed.

(9) This section has effect for construing references in this Act to a person's being engaged, or seeking to become engaged, in an occupation in Northern Ireland as if references in this section to employment were references to an occupation and references to an employee were to a person engaged, or seeking to become engaged, in an occupation.

PART VI

Application to the Crown, police and public bodies

Application of Act to the Crown.

50.—(1) Subject to sections 51 to 54, this Act applies—

(*a*) to an act done by or for purposes of a Minister of the Crown or a government department, or

(*b*) to an act done on behalf of the Crown by a statutory body or a person holding a statutory office, or

(*c*) to an act done by a member of Her Majesty's forces acting as such,

as it applies to an act done by a private person.

(2) For the purposes of subsection (1), in this Act—

(*a*) references to employment include references to—

(i) service for purposes of a Minister of the Crown or government department, other than service of a person holding a statutory office, and

(ii) service on behalf of the Crown for purposes of a person holding a statutory office or purposes of a statutory body, and

(iii) service as a member of Her Majesty's forces;

(*b*) references to a contract of employment include references to the terms of such service;

(*c*) references to an employee include references to a person who is seeking to become engaged in such service, who is in such service or who has ceased to be in such service; and

(*d*) references to an employer, in relation to an employee, include references to (as the case requires) the authority with power to appoint him, to fix his terms of service, to afford him any benefit, to dismiss him or to subject him to any detriment.

(3) Subsection (2) of section 49 (or that subsection as it has effect by virtue of an order under subsection (3) of that section) shall have effect in relation to any ship, aircraft or hovercraft belonging to or possessed by Her Majesty in right of the Government of Northern Ireland as it has effect in relation to a ship, aircraft or hovercraft mentioned in paragraph (*a*) or (*b*) of that subsection; and that subsection shall not have effect in relation to any ship, aircraft or hovercraft belonging to or possessed by Her Majesty in right of the Government of the United Kingdom.

(4) In this section and sections 51, 52 and 54 references to the Crown include it both in right of the Government of the United Kingdom and in right of the Government of Northern Ireland; and—

(*a*) in this section and section 54 references to Her Majesty's forces are references to—

(i) the naval, military or air forces of the Crown, and

PART VI

(ii) any women's service administered by the Defence Council,

but do not include references to any cadet training corps for the time being administered by the Ministry of Defence ; and

(*b*) in this section service " for purposes of " a Minister of the Crown or government department does not include service in any office in Schedule 2 (Ministerial offices) to the House of Commons Disqualification Act 1975 as for the time being in force. 1975 c. 24.

Proceedings against Crown for unlawful discrimination. 1947 c. 44.

51. The provisions of Parts II to IV of the Crown Proceedings Act 1947 shall apply to proceedings against the Crown under section 30 as they apply to proceedings in Northern Ireland which by virtue of section 23 of that Act are treated for the purposes of Part II of that Act as civil proceedings by or against the Crown, except that in their application to proceedings under section 30—

(*a*) section 20 of that Act (removal of proceedings from county court to High Court) shall not apply ; and

(*b*) section 28 of that Act (discovery) shall have effect subject to section 52(2) of this Act.

Disclosure of information by Crown for purposes of investigation or proceedings.

52.—(1) Subject to subsection (2), any obligation to maintain secrecy or other restriction upon the disclosure of information obtained by or furnished to persons in the service of the Crown, whether imposed by any enactment or by any rule of law, shall not apply to the disclosure of information for the purposes of any investigation, appeal or proceedings under this Act ; and the Crown shall not be entitled in relation to any such investigation, appeal or proceedings to any such privilege in respect of the production of documents or the giving of evidence as is allowed to the Crown alone by law in legal proceedings.

(2) A Minister of the Crown or the head of a Northern Ireland department may by a certificate in writing, with respect to any document or information specified in the certificate, or documents or information of any class so specified, certify that in his opinion the disclosure of that document or information or of documents or information of that class would be prejudicial to the safety of the United Kingdom or any part of it or otherwise contrary to the public interest ; and where such a certificate is given nothing in this Act shall be construed as authorising or requiring the communication to any person or for any purpose of any document or information specified in the certificate, or any document or information of a class so specified.

PART VI

(3) A document purporting to be a certificate such as is mentioned in subsection (2) shall be received in evidence and, unless the contrary is proved, shall be deemed to be such a certificate.

1911 c. 28.

(4) Where, in consequence of the enactment of subsection (1), any information is disclosed to persons not in the service of the Crown, those persons shall, without prejudice to subsections (1) and (2) and subject to subsection (5), be subject to the same restrictions upon the disclosure of the information as if they were in that service, and, in particular, the Official Secrets Act 1911 shall have effect in relation to them as if they were persons holding office under Her Majesty.

(5) Where a person to whom subsection (4) applies is a member, officer or servant of the Agency or of the Appeals Board, or a person whose services have been made available for purposes of the Appeals Board, that subsection shall not preclude his disclosing the information in question to any other person so far as such disclosure is necessary—

(*a*) for the purpose of communicating in accordance with the provisions of this Act—

(i) the Agency's finding following an investigation and the reasons for it, or

(ii) the Appeals Board's decision on an appeal and the reasons for it; or

(*b*) for the purposes of any criminal proceedings or to comply with the order of a court.

(6) Any reference in subsection (2) to a Minister of the Crown includes a reference to the Commissioners of Customs and Excise and the Commissioners of Inland Revenue.

Application of Act to the police.

53.—(1) For the purposes of this Act the holding of the office of constable shall be treated as employment—

(*a*) by the chief officer of police as respects any act done by him in relation to a constable or that office;

(*b*) by the police authority as respects any act done by them in relation to a constable or that office.

(2) There shall be defrayed as expenses of the police authority—

(*a*) any damages or costs awarded against a chief officer of police in any proceedings under this Act, any costs incurred by him in any such proceedings so far as not recovered by him in the proceedings, and any costs incurred by him in connection with any investigation

PART VI

under this Act so far as not defrayed by sums paid by the Agency under Schedule 5, paragraph 11 ; and

(*b*) any sum required by a chief officer of police in connection with the settlement of any complaint made or action brought against him under this Act, if the settlement is approved by the police authority.

(3) Any proceedings under this Act which, by virtue of subsection (1), would lie against a chief officer of police shall be brought against the chief officer of police for the time being or, in the case of a vacancy in that office, against the person for the time being performing the functions of that office ; and references in subsections (2) and (4) to the chief officer of police shall be construed accordingly.

(4) The police authority may make arrangements for the legal representation of the chief officer of police in any investigation or proceedings under this Act.

(5) This section applies to a police cadet and appointment as a police cadet as it applies to a constable and the office of constable.

(6) In this section—

" chief officer of police "—

(*a*) in relation to a person appointed, or an appointment falling to be made, to the police force or as a police cadet in relation to that force, means the Chief Constable of the Royal Ulster Constabulary,

(*b*) in relation to any other person or appointment means the officer who has the direction and control of the body of constables or cadets in question ;

" police authority "—

(*a*) in relation to a person appointed, or an appointment falling to be made, to the police force or as a police cadet in relation to that force, means the Police Authority for Northern Ireland,

(*b*) in relation to any other person or appointment, means the authority by whom the person in question is, or on appointment would be, paid ;

" police cadet " means any person appointed to undergo training with a view to becoming a constable ;

" police force " has the same meaning as in the Police Act (Northern Ireland) 1970. 1970 c. 9 (N.I.).

PART VI

Procedure following investigation under s. 12 of Minister, government department, certain statutory bodies or statutory officers and police.

54.—(1) This section applies where, following an investigation under section 12, the Agency is of the opinion that there has been a failure to afford equality of opportunity by any of the following authorities, namely,—

(*a*) a Minister of the Crown or a government department or a person acting for purposes of such a Minister or department; or

(*b*) a member of Her Majesty's forces acting as such; or

(*c*) any other person acting on behalf of the Crown, being a statutory body or a person holding a statutory office; or

(*d*) the Police Authority for Northern Ireland or the Chief Constable of the Royal Ulster Constabulary;

and, accordingly, section 13(2) to (8) and sections 14 and 15 shall not have effect in relation to any such authority.

(2) Where the Agency asks for an undertaking such as is mentioned in section 13(1)(*b*), but—

(*a*) the undertaking is not given, or

(*b*) the undertaking, although given, is not complied with,

the Agency shall, subject to subsection (4), send a report of the results of its investigation and of the opinion it has formed in relation to the subject-matter of the investigation (including any recommendations the Agency considers appropriate for action on the part of the authority concerned)—

(i) where the investigation related to a Minister of the Crown, to that Minister;

(ii) where the investigation related to a government department, to the Minister of the Crown in charge of the department, or in the case of a Northern Ireland department to the head of the department, or

(iii) where the investigation related to any other authority, to the Minister of the Crown or the head of the Northern Ireland department generally responsible for matters falling within the scope of the functions of that authority.

(3) Where the report is sent to a Minister of the Crown he shall lay it before Parliament; and where the report is sent to the head of a Northern Ireland department he shall lay it before the Northern Ireland Assembly.

(4) During the interim period any report which is required by subsections (2) and (3) to be sent to the head of a Northern Ireland department and laid before the Northern Ireland Assembly shall, instead, be sent to the Secretary of State and laid by him before Parliament.

PART VI

(5) A person who is not in the service of the Crown shall not be regarded as within subsection (1)(*a*) by reason only of his acting in pursuance of a contract entered into with a Minister of the Crown or a government department.

General

Service of documents.

55.—(1) Any notice or other document which is required or permitted by this Act to be served on a person may—

(*a*) if that person is an individual, be served on him—

(i) by delivering it to him, or

(ii) by sending it to him by post, addressed to him at his usual or last-known place of residence or business, or

(iii) by leaving it for him at that place ; or

(*b*) if that person is a body corporate or unincorporate, be served on the body—

(i) by sending it by post to the proper officer of the body at its registered or principal office, or at its principal office in Northern Ireland, or

(ii) by addressing it to the proper officer of the body and leaving it at any such office.

(2) Subsection (1) does not prejudice any other lawful method of service.

Orders and reports.

56.—(1) Any power of the Secretary of State to make an order under section 39(1) or section 59(5) shall be exercisable by statutory instrument.

(2) An order made by the Department under section 49(3) shall be made by statutory rule for the purposes of the Statutory Rules Act (Northern Ireland) 1958. 1958 c. 18 (N.I.).

(3) For the purpose of laying before the Northern Ireland Assembly—

(*a*) a draft of an order under section 49(3) ; or

(*b*) a report under section 54(2) ; or

(*c*) the Agency's annual report,

section 41(3) of the Interpretation Act (Northern Ireland) 1954 (laying of statutory documents) shall have effect as if the draft order and the reports were statutory documents within the meaning of that Act. 1954 c. 33 (N.I.).

General interpretation.

57.—(1) In this Act, unless the context otherwise requires,—

" access " shall be construed in accordance with subsection (7) ;

PART VI

"act" includes a deliberate omission, and any reference to an act, action or other thing done shall be construed accordingly;

"advertisement" includes every form of advertisement, whether to the public or not, and whether in a newspaper or other publication, by television or radio, by display or circulation of notices or circulars, by exhibition of pictures, models or films or in any other way, and references to the publishing of advertisements shall be construed accordingly;

"the Agency" means the Fair Employment Agency for Northern Ireland;

"the Appeals Board" means the Fair Employment Appeals Board;

"benefits" includes all opportunities, services and facilities, and, in particular, includes opportunities for training, transfer or promotion, for betterment of any kind (including more attractive times or conditions of work) or for any financial advantage (including bonuses, advances of money and preferential terms for acquiring property of any kind);

"the commencement of this Act" shall be construed in accordance with section 59(6);

"complainant" means a person making a complaint that unlawful discrimination has been committed against him or, in relation to a complaint made or continued under section 24(2), means—

(*a*) subject to paragraph (*b*) below, in relation to any act which, under this Act, must or may be done by, to or in relation to the complainant, the person making or for the time being continuing the complaint; and

(*b*) in relation to the complainant's having, or being expected to have had, knowledge of anything, the person making the complaint or the person against whom the unlawful discrimination is alleged to have been committed, whichever of them first had, or might reasonably be expected to have had, that knowledge; and

(*c*) in any other connection, the person against whom the unlawful discrimination is alleged to have been committed;

"complaint" means a complaint of unlawful discrimination made to the Agency under section 24;

"confer", in relation to a qualification, includes renew and extend;

PART VI

" contract " includes any contract, whether in writing or oral, express or implied ;

" contravention ", in relation to any provision, includes a failure to comply with that provision ;

" costs " includes expenses ;

" the county court ", in relation to any proceedings, means a county court sitting for the county court division in Northern Ireland in which those proceedings may be taken by virtue of rules of court ;

" the Declaration of Principle and Intent " has the meaning given by section 6(1) ;

" the Department " means the Department of Manpower Services for Northern Ireland ;

" the Department of Finance " means the Department of Finance for Northern Ireland ;

" discrimination " and " discriminate " shall be construed in accordance with section 16(1) to (4) ;

" employer " means—

(*a*) in relation to a person who is seeking employment, anybody who has employment available ;

(*b*) in relation to a person employed under a contract of service or of apprenticeship or a contract personally to execute any work or labour, the person entitled to the benefit of that contract ;

(*c*) in relation to a person who has ceased to be in employment, his former employer ;

and " employee ", correspondingly, means such a person as is first mentioned in paragraph (*a*), (*b*) or (*c*) of this definition ;

" employment " means employment under a contract of service or apprenticeship or a contract personally to execute any work or labour, and, without prejudice to the definitions of "employer " and " employee " above, related expressions shall be construed accordingly ;

" employment agency " means a person who, for profit or not, provides services for the purpose of finding employment for workers or supplying employers with workers ;

" employment in Northern Ireland " shall be construed in accordance with section 49 ;

" enactment " includes an enactment contained in an Act of the Parliament of Northern Ireland or an Order in Council made under the Northern Ireland (Temporary Provisions) Act 1972, or in a Measure of the Northern Ireland Assembly ; 1972 c. 22.

PART VI

" equality of opportunity " shall be construed in accordance with section 3 ;

" financial year " means a year ending on 31st March ;

" finding ", in relation to the investigation of a complaint, has the meaning given by section 25(1) ;

" government department " includes a Northern Ireland department ;

" the High Court " means the High Court of Justice in Northern Ireland ;

" the injured person ", in relation to an action under section 30, has the meaning given by section 30(1) ;

" the interim period " has the meaning given by section
1974 c. 28. 1(4) of the Northern Ireland Act 1974 for purposes of that Act ;

" member ", in relation to a vocational organisation, includes (except in section 21) a person seeking to become a member and a person who has ceased to be a member, and in relation to such an organisation (other than an organisation of workers or employers) also includes any person belonging to a class of person recognised by the organisation as having any particular status in connection with an employment or occupation for the purposes of which the organisation exists, including students and associates, and " membership " shall be construed accordingly ;

" Northern Ireland " includes such of the territorial waters of the United Kingdom as are adjacent to Northern Ireland ;

" notice " means a notice in writing ;

" occupation " includes any trade, business, profession or vocation, but not any employment ;

" occupation in Northern Ireland " shall be construed in accordance with section 49 ;

" organisation " includes any society or association whether corporate or unincorporate ;

" the person concerned ", in relation to an investigation under section 12, has the meaning given by subsection (1)(*b*) of that section ;

" practices " includes procedures and arrangements ;

" proper officer ", in relation to any body corporate or unincorporate, means the secretary or other executive officer charged with the conduct of the general affairs of the body ;

PART VI

" qualification " includes authorisation, recognition, registration, enrolment, approval and certification;

" the register " means the Register of Equal Opportunity Employers and Equal Opportunity Organisations;

" the respondent ", in relation to a complaint, has the meaning given by section 24(1);

" satisfactory ", in relation to an undertaking, means appearing to the Agency to be satisfactory, having regard to all the circumstances;

" school " has the same meaning as in the Education and Libraries (Northern Ireland) Order 1972; S.I. 1972/1263 (N.I.12).

" the Standing Advisory Commission on Human Rights " means the commission constituted by that name under section 20 of the Northern Ireland Constitution Act 1973; 1973 c. 36.

" statutory body " means a body set up by or in pursuance of an enactment, and " statutory office " means an office so set up;

" training " includes any form of education or instruction, except that in sections 3(3)(*b*)(ii), 12(1)(*b*)(v) and 22 it does not include education in—

(*a*) a school, or

(*b*) an institution of further education within the meaning of the Education and Libraries (Northern Ireland) Order 1972 or an institution in respect of which contributions are paid by an Education and Library Board under Article 23(3) of that Order, or

(*c*) an institution which is maintained in pursuance of arrangements made by the Department of Education for Northern Ireland under Article 55(1) of that Order of 1972, or in respect of which grants are paid by that Department under Article 55(2) of that Order, or

(*d*) the Ulster College, or

(*e*) a university;

" unlawful discrimination " shall be construed in accordance with section 16(5);

" vocational organisation " means—

(*a*) an organisation of workers, or

(*b*) an organisation of employers, or

(*c*) any other organisation of persons engaged in a particular employment or occupation, or employments or occupations of any class, for the purposes of which the organisation exists.

PART VI

(2) In this Act references to a person's religious belief or political opinion include references to his supposed religious belief or political opinion and to the absence or supposed absence of any, or any particular, religious belief or political opinion.

(3) In this Act any reference to a person's political opinion does not include an opinion which consists of or includes approval or acceptance of the use of violence for political ends connected with Northern Irish affairs (including the use of violence for the purpose of putting the public or any section of the public in fear).

(4) In this Act any reference to failure to afford equality of opportunity includes a reference to unintentional failure.

(5) For the purposes of this Act a person is seeking employment if he is available for employment, whether or not he is aware of the existence of an opportunity for any particular employment.

(6) References in this Act to submitting a person for consideration for employment include references to making available to an employer in any way relevant particulars relating to him.

(7) References in this Act to the affording by any person of access to benefits are not limited to benefits provided by him alone, but include any means by which it is in his power to facilitate access to benefits provided by others.

(8) Without prejudice to any provision of section 49 or any order under subsection (3) of that section and subject to any other provision of this Act which is limited by its express terms to acts done in Northern Ireland, references (however expressed) in this Act to acts done or to power to do any acts, other than references to acts which may be the subject of criminal proceedings under this Act, include references to acts done or power to do the acts outside Northern Ireland; and references to a contract include references to a contract the proper law of which is not the law of Northern Ireland.

(9) In this Act any reference to a declarant is a reference to an employer who, or an organisation which, subscribes, or (as the context requires) proposes to subscribe or has subscribed, to the Declaration of Principle and Intent.

(10) For the purposes of this Act an undertaking is not complied with unless the whole of it is complied with, and directions or recommendations are not complied with unless they are all complied with.

(11) Except so far as the context otherwise requires, any reference in this Act to an enactment shall be construed as a reference

to that enactment as amended or extended by or under any other enactment, including this Act. PART VI

(12) In this Act, except where otherwise indicated,—

(*a*) a reference to a numbered Part, section or Schedule is a reference to the Part or section of, or the Schedule to, this Act so numbered, and

(*b*) a reference in a section to a numbered subsection is a reference to the subsection of that section so numbered, and

(*c*) a reference in a section, subsection or Schedule to a numbered paragraph is a reference to the paragraph of that section, subsection or Schedule so numbered, and

(*d*) a reference in a paragraph of a section, subsection or Schedule to a numbered sub-paragraph is a reference to the sub-paragraph of that paragraph so numbered.

Amendments and extension of enactments, and repeal.

58.—(1) The enactments mentioned in Schedule 6 shall have effect subject to the respective amendments there specified (being amendments consequential on the provisions of this Act).

(2) The following enactments, namely,—

(*a*) section 5(2)(*a*) of the Parliamentary Commissioner Act 1967; 1967 c. 13.

(*b*) section 5(2)(*a*) of the Parliamentary Commissioner Act (Northern Ireland) 1969; and 1969 c. 10 (N.I.).

(*c*) section 5(3)(*a*) of the Commissioner for Complaints Act (Northern Ireland) 1969, 1969 c. 25 (N.I.).

shall have effect in relation to the right of a person to make a complaint of unlawful discrimination under this Act as if it were such a right of appeal, reference or review as is mentioned in those enactments.

(3) Section 20(1)(*b*) of the Northern Ireland Constitution Act 1973 is hereby repealed. 1973 c. 36.

Short title, extent and commencement.

59.—(1) This Act may be cited as the Fair Employment (Northern Ireland) Act 1976.

(2) Subject to subsections (3) and (4) and without prejudice to section 57(8) or to the application by virtue of Schedule 4, paragraph 7, or Schedule 5, paragraph 8, of any enactment which extends to the whole of the United Kingdom, this Act extends to Northern Ireland only.

(3) The amendments, extension and repeal of enactments which are made by section 58(1), (2)(*a*) and (3) and Schedule 6 have the same extent as the enactments that are so amended, extended or repealed.

PART VI

(4) Sections 47 and 52 and so much of section 57 as applies for the interpretation of those sections extend to the whole of the United Kingdom.

(5) This Act shall come into operation on such day as the Secretary of State may by order appoint.

(6) An order under subsection (5)—

(*a*) may appoint different days for different provisions of this Act or for different purposes of the same provision; and

(*b*) may be revoked or varied by a subsequent order under that subsection;

and any reference in a provision of this Act to the commencement of this Act shall be construed—

(i) where different days are appointed for different provisions, as a reference to the day appointed for the coming into operation of that provision; or

(ii) where different days are appointed for different purposes of that provision, as a reference, in relation to each such purpose, to the day appointed for that purpose.

SCHEDULES

SCHEDULE 1

Section 1(2), Sch. 5 para. 12(1)(*a*).

THE FAIR EMPLOYMENT AGENCY FOR NORTHERN IRELAND

Incorporation and status

1. On the appointment of the first members of the Agency, the Agency shall come into existence as a body corporate.

2.—(1) The Agency is not an emanation of the Crown, and shall not act or be treated as the servant or agent of the Crown.

(2) Accordingly—

(*a*) neither the Agency nor any of its members or members of its staff as such is entitled to any status, immunity, privilege or exemption enjoyed by the Crown ;

(*b*) the members of the Agency and members of its staff as such are not civil servants ; and

(*c*) the Agency's property is not property of, or held on behalf of, the Crown.

Tenure of office of members

3.—(1) A person shall hold and vacate his office as chairman or other member of the Agency in accordance with the terms of his appointment:

Provided that no such appointment shall be for a period exceeding five years in the case of the chairman and three years in the case of another member.

(2) A person may at any time resign office as chairman or other member of the Agency by notice to the Department.

(3) Past service as chairman or other member of the Agency is no bar to re-appointment.

Remuneration of members

4. The Department may pay, or make such payments towards the provision of, such remuneration, allowances (including allowances for expenses), pensions or gratuities to or in respect of the chairman and other members of the Agency, or any of them, as, with the approval of the Department of Finance, it may determine.

Staff

5.—(1) The Agency may with the approval of the Department and the Department of Finance as to numbers and as to remuneration and other terms and conditions of employment—

(*a*) employ such officers and servants as the Agency considers necessary ;

(*b*) employ the services of such other persons as the Agency considers expedient for any particular purpose.

(2) The Agency may, in the case of such persons employed by it as may be determined by the Agency with the approval of the

SCH. 1

Department and the Department of Finance, pay to or in respect of them such allowances (including allowances for expenses), pensions or gratuities, or provide and maintain for them such pension schemes (whether contributory or not), or contributory or other pension arrangements, as may be so determined.

Proceedings

6.—(1) Without prejudice to any provision of Schedule 5, the Agency may regulate its own procedure and business including the formalities for affixing its common seal to any document and, subject to sub-paragraph (2), its quorum.

(2) The quorum for meetings of the Agency shall, in the first instance, be determined by a meeting of the Agency attended by not less than five members.

7. The validity of any proceedings of the Agency shall not be affected by any vacancy in the office of chairman or other member of the Agency or by any defect in the appointment of the chairman or any other member.

Instruments

8. A document purporting to be duly executed under the common seal of the Agency shall be received in evidence and shall, unless the contrary is proved, be deemed to be so executed.

9. Any contract or instrument which, if entered into or executed by an individual, would not require to be under seal may be entered into or executed on behalf of the Agency by any person generally or specially authorised by the Agency to act for that purpose, and any document purporting to be such a contract or instrument shall be deemed to be such a contract or instrument until the contrary is proved.

Discharge of functions

10.—(1) The Agency may authorise the discharge, under the general direction of the Agency, of its functions in relation to—

(*a*) any complaint or other matter falling to be dealt with by it; or

(*b*) any class of such matters,

by either a member or a group of members of the Agency selected by the chairman.

(2) Anything done by or in relation to a member or group of members in or in connection with the discharge of functions he or they are authorised to discharge under sub-paragraph (1) shall have the same effect as if done by or in relation to the Agency.

(3) A group of members authorised to discharge any functions under sub-paragraph (1) may regulate their own procedure and business, including their quorum.

(4) The validity of any proceedings of a member or group of members so authorised shall not be affected by any defect in his appointment or any of their appointments; and the validity of the

proceedings of any such group shall not be affected by any vacancy in their number. **Sch. 1**

(5) The chairman may select himself as the member, or as one of the group of members, mentioned in this paragraph.

11. The Agency may appoint as assessors, to assist—

(*a*) the Agency ; or

(*b*) any member or group of members authorised to discharge functions under paragraph 10,

in the investigation of any complaint or other matter, persons appearing to the Agency to have special knowledge and experience of the matters to which the investigation relates and of any other circumstances appearing to the Agency to be relevant.

Expenses and accounts

12. All expenditure incurred by or on behalf of the Agency—

(*a*) within the terms of any general authorisation in writing given by the Department and the Department of Finance ; or

(*b*) with the approval of those Departments ;

may be defrayed as expenses of the Department.

13.—(1) The Agency shall keep proper accounts in such form as may be approved by the Department, and proper records in relation to the accounts, and shall prepare in respect of the period ending on 31st March 1977 and in respect of each subsequent financial year a statement of accounts in such form as the Department, with the approval of the Department of Finance may direct.

(2) The accounts of the Agency shall be audited by auditors appointed by the Agency with the approval of the Department and shall be vouched to the satisfaction of the auditors.

(3) The Agency shall, at such time in each year as the Department may direct, transmit to the Department and the Comptroller and Auditor-General copies, certified by the auditors, of the annual statement of accounts.

(4) The Comptroller and Auditor-General—

(*a*) shall examine a copy of each annual statement of accounts of the Agency ;

(*b*) may, in connection with such examination, examine any accounts kept by the Agency and any records relating to the accounts ; and

(*c*) shall make a report on the copy of each annual statement of accounts and send the report to the Department.

(5) Subject to sub-paragraph (6), a copy of every annual statement of accounts of the Agency and a copy of the Comptroller and Auditor-General's report thereon shall be laid by the head of the Department before the Northern Ireland Assembly.

(6) During the interim period the copies mentioned in sub-paragraph (5) shall, instead, be sent by the Department to the Secretary of State and laid by him before Parliament.

SCH. 1

(7) In this paragraph "the Comptroller and Auditor-General" means the Comptroller and Auditor-General for Northern Ireland.

Annual report

14.—(1) The Agency shall prepare in respect of the period ending on 31st March 1977 and in respect of each subsequent financial year a report on the Agency's activities during that period or year ("the annual report").

(2) The annual report shall include a general survey of developments, during the period to which it relates, in respect of matters falling within the scope of the Agency's functions.

(3) Subject to sub-paragraph (4), the annual report shall be made to the head of the Department and shall be laid by him before the Northern Ireland Assembly.

(4) During the interim period the annual report shall, instead, be made to the Secretary of State and laid by him before Parliament.

(5) The Department, or where sub-paragraph (4) applies the Secretary of State, shall cause the annual report to be published.

Section 4(3).

SCHEDULE 2

THE FAIR EMPLOYMENT APPEALS BOARD

Tenure of office of members

1.—(1) A person shall hold and vacate his office as chairman or other member of the Appeals Board in accordance with the terms of his appointment:

Provided that no such appointment shall be for a period exceeding five years.

(2) A person may at any time resign office as chairman or other member of the Appeals Board by notice to the Department.

(3) Past service as chairman or other member of the Appeals Board is no bar to re-appointment.

Remuneration of members

2. The Department may pay, or make such payments towards the provision of, such remuneration, allowances (including allowances for expenses), pensions or gratuities to or in respect of the chairman and other members of the Appeals Board, or any of them, as, with the approval of the Department of Finance, it may determine.

Staff and accommodation

3.—(1) The Department may, with the approval of the Department of Finance as to numbers and as to remuneration and other terms and conditions of employment, appoint officers and servants to assist the Appeals Board in the execution of its functions or may make the services of members of the Department's staff, and such accommodation or facilities as may be agreed upon between the Department and the Board, available for purposes of the Board.

(2) The remuneration of persons appointed under sub-paragraph (1) shall be paid by the Department, and the Department may also pay to or in respect of such of those persons as may be

determined by it with the approval of the Department of Finance such allowances (including allowances for expenses), pensions or gratuities as may be so determined. SCH. 2

Proceedings

4.—(1) Subject to sub-paragraph (2) and without prejudice to any provision of Schedule 4, the Appeals Board may regulate its own procedure.

(2) Where any member of the Appeals Board is indisposed or is for any other reason unable to act, the chairman of the Board may direct that any particular appeal or appeals of any class may be heard by or continued before, and may be determined by, two members of the Board, and for the purposes of the provisions of this Act relating to appeals to the Board those two members shall constitute the Board.

5. The validity of the proceedings of the Appeals Board shall not be affected by any vacancy in the office of chairman or other member of the Board or by any defect in the appointment of the chairman or any other member.

Expenses of Board

6. Any expenditure incurred in accordance with the provisions of this Act by the Appeals Board, or by the Department for purposes of the Appeals Board, may be defrayed as expenses of the Department.

SCHEDULE 3

Section 6(3).

DECLARATION OF PRINCIPLE AND INTENT

I/We affirm and declare that it is my/our intent to promote and protect equality of opportunity in employment, according to the letter and spirit of the Fair Employment (Northern Ireland) Act 1976 by every means at my/our disposal, and to co-operate to that end with the Fair Employment Agency for Northern Ireland.

I/We further undertake that I/we will use my/our best endeavours to encourage all persons within the range of my/our influence to commit themselves to the same intent."

SCHEDULE 4

Sections 8(3), 14(3), 59(2), Sch. 2 para. 4(1).

CONDUCT OF APPEALS BY THE APPEALS BOARD

Preliminary

1. In this Schedule " the appeal " means an appeal to the Appeals Board brought under section 8 or section 14.

SCH. 4

Notices

2.—(1) The appeal shall be initiated by the appellant serving a notice on the Appeals Board—

(*a*) stating that he is appealing to the Board ;

(*b*) specifying the subject-matter of the appeal ; and

(*c*) setting out the grounds on which the appeal is made.

(2) The appellant shall at the same time serve a copy of the notice on the Agency.

Procedure

3. Both the appellant and the Agency shall be entitled—

(*a*) to appear before the Appeals Board ;

(*b*) to be represented by solicitor or counsel ; and

(*c*) to examine their witnesses and cross-examine each other's.

4. Without prejudice to paragraph 3, the Appeals Board shall afford to every person who appears to the Board to be able to propound evidence relevant to the subject matter of the appeal an opportunity of being heard.

5. The appeal shall be conducted in private.

6. Subject to paragraphs 3 to 5, the Appeals Board may give directions with respect to the practice and procedure to be followed in any proceedings before the Board in connection with the appeal and anything incidental to or consequential on such proceedings ; and such directions may be given with general effect or with respect to cases of any class or any particular case.

Evidence

7.—(1) For the purposes of the appeal, the Appeals Board may require any person who in its opinion is able to furnish information or produce documents relevant to the appeal to furnish any such information or produce any such document.

(2) For those purposes the Appeals Board shall have the same powers as the High Court in respect of—

(*a*) the attendance and examination of witnesses, including the administration of oaths or affirmations and the examination of witnesses abroad ; and

(*b*) the production of documents.

(3) A person shall not be compelled for the purposes of the appeal—

(*a*) to give any information or produce any document which he could not be compelled to give in evidence or produce in civil proceedings before the High Court ; or

(*b*) to give any information or produce any document which discloses, or from which there can be deduced, his religious belief, if he informs the Appeals Board that he objects to doing so ; or (*c*) to attend at any place unless the necessary expenses of his journey to and from that place are paid or tendered to him ;

but head (*a*) above does not prejudice the provisions of section 52(1).

Obstruction and contempt

8.—(1) If any person, without lawful excuse, obstructs the Appeals Board, any member or officer of the Board or any person whose services have been made available for purposes of the Board in the performance of its or his functions in connection with the appeal, or is guilty of any act in relation to the appeal which, if the appeal were a proceeding in the High Court, would constitute contempt of court, the Board may certify the offence to the High Court.

(2) Where an offence is certified under this paragraph, the High Court may inquire into the matter and after hearing—

(*a*) any witnesses who may be produced against or on behalf of the person charged with the offence ; and

(*b*) any statement that may be offered in defence,

may deal with the person charged with the offence in any manner in which the court could deal with him if he had committed the like offence in relation to the court.

Expenses

9. The Appeals Board may, if it thinks fit, pay to the appellant and to any other person (except the Agency or anybody acting on its behalf) who attends at the hearing of, or furnishes evidence for the purposes of, the appeal—

(*a*) sums in respect of expenses properly incurred by him ; and

(*b*) allowances by way of compensation for the loss of his time,

in accordance with such scales and subject to such conditions as the Department with the approval of the Department of Finance may determine.

Notification of decision

10.—(1) Following the hearing of the appeal, the Appeals Board shall serve notice of the Board's decision on both the appellant and the Agency.

(2) The notice shall state the reasons for the decision.

Confidentiality of information

11.—(1) Without prejudice to any provision of section 52, no information supplied to the Appeals Board for the purposes of an appeal shall be disclosed by a member, officer or servant of the Board, or a person whose services have been made available for purposes of the Board, to a person who is not a member of, or in the employment of, the Board or whose services have not been made available as aforesaid, except so far as such disclosure is necessary—

(*a*) for the purposes of the appeal ; or

(*b*) for communicating to any person, in pursuance of paragraph 10, the Board's decision on the appeal and the reasons for the decision ; or

SCH. 4

(*c*) for the purposes of any criminal proceedings or to comply with the order of a court.

(2) If any person discloses any information in contravention of sub-paragraph (1) he shall be guilty of an offence and shall be liable on summary conviction to a fine not exceeding £400.

Sections 2(1)(*e*), 12(3), 24(7), 26(8), 31(6), 38(4), 53(2)(*a*), 59(2), Sch. 1 para. 6(1).

SCHEDULE 5

CONDUCT OF INVESTIGATIONS BY THE AGENCY

Preliminary

1. In this Schedule " the investigation " means—

(*a*) an investigation under section 12 for the purposes of ascertaining the existence, nature and extent of failures to afford equality of opportunity and considering what action, if any, ought to be taken for promoting equality of opportunity ; or

(*b*) an investigation under section 24 following a complaint of unlawful discrimination ; or

(*c*) an investigation under section 38 in relation to teachers in schools.

Notices

2. Where the investigation is to be of the kind mentioned in paragraph 1(*a*) or (*c*), the Agency, before holding the investigation,—

(*a*) shall serve on every person whose practices it is minded to investigate notice of the Agency's intention to hold the investigation, and

(*b*) shall furnish to each such person, in writing, particulars of the scope and purpose of the investigation.

3. Where the investigation is to be of the kind mentioned in paragraph 1(*b*), the Agency, before holding the investigation,—

(*a*) shall serve on the person against whom the complaint is made notice of the Agency's intention to hold the investigation ; and

(*b*) shall furnish to that person, in writing,—

(i) particulars of the allegations made in the complaint so far as they relate to him, and

(ii) a statement of the substance of any evidence which the Agency has reason to believe may be tendered in support of those allegations.

Procedure

4. The Agency shall afford to every person such as is mentioned in paragraph 2(*a*) or 3(*a*) an opportunity to comment on the matters or allegations which are the subject of the investigation and to furnish oral or other evidence respecting them.

5. The investigation shall be conducted in private.

6. Subject to paragraphs 4 and 5, the procedure for conducting the investigation shall be such as the Agency considers appropriate in the circumstances of the case. SCH. 5

Information and evidence

7. For the purposes of the investigation, the Agency may obtain information from such persons and (subject to paragraph 5) in such manner and may make such inquiries and call for such reports (including reports by officers of the Agency on inquiries, interviews or hearings conducted by them on the Agency's behalf) as the Agency thinks fit.

8.—(1) For the purposes of the investigation the Agency may require any person who in its opinion is able to furnish information or produce documents relevant to the investigation to furnish any such information or produce any such document.

(2) For those purposes the Agency shall have the same powers as the High Court in respect of—

(*a*) the attendance and examination of witnesses, including the administration of oaths or affirmations and the examination of witnesses abroad ; and

(*b*) the production of documents.

(3) A person shall not be compelled for the purposes of the investigation—

(*a*) to give any information or produce any document which he could not be compelled to give in evidence or produce in civil proceedings before the High Court ; or

(*b*) to give any information or produce any document which discloses, or from which there can be deduced, his religious belief, if he informs the Agency that he objects to doing so ; or

(*c*) to attend at any place unless the necessary expenses of his journey to and from that place are paid or tendered to him ;

but head (*a*) above does not prejudice the provisions of section 52(1).

9. For the purposes of the investigation the Agency may also require an employer or a vocational organisation to take such reasonable action as the Agency specifies for communicating to his or its employees or members (as the case requires), or to employees or members of any class, any written material provided for the purpose by the Agency.

Obstruction and contempt

10.—(1) If any person, without lawful excuse, obstructs the Agency or any member or officer of the Agency in the performance of its or his functions in connection with the investigation, or is guilty of any act in relation to the investigation which, if the investigation were a proceeding in the High Court, would constitute contempt of court, the Agency may certify the offence to the High Court.

SCH. 5 (2) Where an offence is certified under this paragraph, the High Court may inquire into the matter and after hearing—

(*a*) any witnesses who may be produced against or on behalf of the person charged with the offence ; and

(*b*) any statement that may be offered in defence,

may deal with the person charged with the offence in any manner in which the court could deal with him if he had committed the like offence in relation to the court.

Expenses

11.—(1) Without prejudice to paragraph 8(3)(*c*), the Agency may, if it thinks fit,—

(*a*) where the investigation follows a complaint, pay to the complainant, or

(*b*) in any case, pay to any other person who attends, or furnishes information for the purposes of, the investigation,

sums in respect of expenses properly incurred by him and allowances by way of compensation for the loss of his time in accordance with such scales and subject to such conditions as the Department with the approval of the Department of Finance may determine.

(2) A payment made under this paragraph to a person who, under section 24(2) continues a complaint made or continued by another may also include sums in respect of expenses properly incurred by, or loss of time of, that other or any predecessor of his.

Confidentiality of information

12.—(1) Without prejudice to any provision of section 52, no information supplied to the Agency in the course of the investigation shall be disclosed by a member, officer or servant of the Agency to a person who is not a member of, or in the employment of, the Agency, except so far as such disclosure—

(*a*) is relevant for the purposes of section 2(1), section 38(3), Schedule 1, paragraph 14 or sub-paragraph (2) or (3) ; or

(*b*) is necessary for the purpose of carrying out an investigation into a complaint, or for the purpose of communicating to any person, in accordance with the provisions of this Act, the Agency's finding following such an investigation and the reasons for it ; or

(*c*) is necessary for the purposes of any proceedings under this Act, either before a court or before the Appeals Board ; or

(*d*) is necessary for the purposes of any criminal proceedings or to comply with the order of a court ;

but any such disclosure as is mentioned in head (*a*) above is subject to the safeguard in sub-paragraph (4).

(2) Without prejudice to sub-paragraph (4), where it is necessary or expedient to do so for the proper discharge of the functions of the Agency, a member, officer or servant of the Agency may— SCH. 5

(*a*) disclose to an employer any information in the Agency's possession which relates to his employees or to other persons who have applied for employment by him ;

(*b*) disclose to a principal (within the meaning of section 18) any information in the Agency's possession which relates to contract workers whose services are or have been available to him ;

(*c*) disclose to any person who is empowered by virtue of an enactment to select or nominate another person for employment by a third person any information in the Agency's possession which relates to a person who has applied for the employment in question ;

(*d*) disclose to an employment agency any information in the Agency's possession which relates to a person who has applied for or obtained the services of the agency ;

(*e*) disclose to a vocational organisation any information in the Agency's possession which relates to members of that organisation or other persons who have applied for membership ;

(*f*) disclose to a person who provides services in connection with the training of persons for employment in any capacity, or for a particular employment or occupation, any information in the Agency's possession which relates to a person who has sought, or on whose behalf it has been sought, to obtain those services, or who has obtained those services ; or

(*g*) disclose to a person who has power to confer a qualification such as is mentioned in section 23 any information in the Agency's possession which relates to a person who has applied to have, or has had, that qualification conferred on him.

(3) Without prejudice to sub-paragraph (4), the Agency shall supply to the Department any information in the Agency's possession which the Department requests.

(4) No information in the Agency's possession which discloses, or from which there can be deduced, the religious belief of any identifiable individual shall, without that individual's written consent, be disclosed to any person, except where—

(*a*) it is disclosed to a person employed by the Agency the nature of whose duties renders it reasonable for him to be supplied with the information ; or

(*b*) its disclosure is necessary for a purpose mentioned in sub-paragraph (1)(*b*), (*c*) or (*d*).

(5) If any person discloses any information in contravention of any provision of this paragraph he shall be guilty of an offence and shall be liable on summary conviction to a fine not exceeding £400.

Section 58(1), 59(3).

SCHEDULE 6

Amendments

The Northern Ireland Constitution Act 1973 (*c.* 36)

1. In section 19 of the Northern Ireland Constitution Act 1973 (religious or political discrimination by certain public authorities to be unlawful)—

(*a*) at the beginning of subsection (1) there shall be inserted the words " Subject to subsection (4) below " ; and

(*b*) after subsection (3) there shall be inserted the following subsection—

" (4) This section does not apply to any act or omission which is unlawful by virtue of the Fair Employment (Northern Ireland) Act 1976 or would be unlawful but for some exception made by virtue of Part V of that Act."

2. In section 20(2) of that Act (membership of the Standing Advisory Commission on Human Rights), after paragraph (*d*) there shall be inserted the following paragraph—

" (*dd*) the chairman of the Fair Employment Agency for Northern Ireland ; and " ;

and for " (*d*) " in the second place where it occurs there shall be substituted " (*dd*) ".

The House of Commons Disqualification Act 1975 (*c.* 24)

3. In Part II of Schedule 1 to the House of Commons Disqualification Act 1975 (bodies of which all members are disqualified under that Act) there shall (at the appropriate place in alphabetical order) be inserted the following entries—

" The Fair Employment Agency for Northern Ireland.

The Fair Employment Appeals Board."

The Northern Ireland Assembly Disqualification Act 1975 (*c.* 25)

4. In Part II of Schedule 1 to the Northern Ireland Assembly Disqualification Act 1975 (bodies of which all members are disqualified under that Act) there shall (at the appropriate place in alphabetical order) be inserted the following entries—

" The Fair Employment Agency for Northern Ireland.

The Fair Employment Appeals Board."

Explosives (Age of Purchase &c.) Act 1976

1976 CHAPTER 26

An Act to restrict further the sale to young persons of explosive substances, including fireworks, and to increase the penalties provided by sections 31 and 80 of the Explosives Act 1875. [22nd July, 1976]

BE IT ENACTED by the Queen's most Excellent Majesty, by and with the advice and consent of the Lords Spiritual and Temporal, and Commons, in this present Parliament assembled, and by the authority of the same, as follows:—

Increase of age for purchase of fireworks etc and of certain penalties relating to fireworks etc.

1875 c. 17.

1.—(1) In section 31 of the Explosives Act 1875 (which, as extended by section 39 of that Act, prohibits the sale to children of explosives, including fireworks, and provides that a person who makes a sale in contravention of the said section 31 shall be liable to a penalty not exceeding £20) for the words " any child apparently under the age of thirteen " there shall be substituted the words " any person apparently under the age of sixteen " and for the word " £20 " there shall be substituted the word " £200 ".

(2) In section 80 of that Act (which provides that a person who lets fireworks off in a highway or public place shall be liable to a penalty not exceeding £20) for the word " £20 " there shall be substituted the word " £200 ".

Citation, extent and commencement.

2.—(1) This Act may be cited as the Explosives (Age of Purchase &c.) Act 1976, and this Act and the Explosives Acts 1875 and 1923 may be cited together as the Explosives Acts 1875 to 1976.

(2) This Act shall not extend to Northern Ireland.

(3) This Act shall come into force at the expiration of one month beginning with the date of its passing.

Theatres Trust Act 1976

1976 CHAPTER 27

An Act to establish a Theatres Trust for the better protection of theatres; and for purposes connected therewith. [22nd July, 1976]

BE IT ENACTED by the Queen's most Excellent Majesty, by and with the advice and consent of the Lords Spiritual and Temporal, and Commons, in this present Parliament assembled, and by the authority of the same, as follows:—

Incorporation of Theatres Trust.

1.—(1) On the appointed day there shall be a body known as the Theatres Trust, which shall be a body corporate having perpetual succession and a common seal.

(2) The affairs and property of the Trust shall be managed and administered by the trustees.

(3) The Schedule to this Act shall have effect with respect to the trustees.

Objects of Trust and powers of trustees.

2.—(1) The objects of the Trust are to promote the better protection of theatres for the benefit of the nation.

(2) The trustees shall have power exclusively for the furtherance of the above-mentioned objects—

(*a*) to acquire by purchase, gift or bequest and hold any theatre or any land required for the benefit of any theatre;

(*b*) to contribute towards the acquisition of any theatre or any such land;

(*c*) to maintain or assist in the maintenance of any theatre;

(*d*) subject to the provisions of section 29 of the Charities Act 1960, from time to time to sell, mortgage, charge, let, surrender, exchange or otherwise dispose of any land or any personal estate or property (including moneys secured on mortgage of or charged upon any land) vested in or acquired by the trustees or any part thereof or any easements, rights or privileges to be exercised or enjoyed in, over, upon or under the same or any part thereof, and to do and execute all such acts, deeds, matters and things as may be necessary for effectuating and completing any such sale, mortgage, charge, letting, surrender, exchange or disposition ; 1960 c. 58.

(*e*) to print, publish and sell literature, pictures and photographs and other things relating to the trust property ;

(*f*) to give financial and other assistance to any body whose objects are charitable and similar to those of the Trust and to give such assistance in connection with any function or scheme for a purpose which is both charitable and similar to an object of the Trust ;

(*g*) to co-operate with other persons engaged in activities similar to those of the objects of the Trust and in connection therewith to provide for the interchange of staff ;

(*h*) to accept, receive and retain legacies, gifts, grants, annuities and other benefits and consistently with the objects of the Trust but not otherwise to undertake and perform any services or conditions attached to the receipt thereof ;

(*i*) to raise or borrow money for the purposes of the Trust and secure the same and any interest thereon upon the property of the Trust ;

(*j*) to make appeals, advertise and conduct such other lawful activities of a similar nature as may be necessary to raise funds for the Trust or to make known its existence, purposes or work ;

(*k*) to do all such other things as are incidental to the attainment of the objects of the Trust.

3. The trustees shall have power— Employment of staff.

(*a*) to appoint a director, a secretary and such other officers and servants as the trustees may determine ;

(*b*) to pay to the trustees such travelling and subsistence allowances while attending meetings of the trustees or any committee of the trustees or while on any other business of the trustees as the trustees may determine ;

(*c*) to pay to their officers and servants such remuneration as the trustees may determine;

(*d*) as regards any officers or servants in whose case they may determine to do so—

(i) to pay to, or in respect of them, such pensions and gratuities as the trustees may determine;

(ii) to provide and maintain for them such superannuation schemes (whether contributory or not) as the trustees may determine; or

(iii) to enter into and carry into effect agreements with any insurance company or other association or company for securing to any such officer or servant or his widow, family or dependant such gratuities or pensions as are by this paragraph authorised to be paid.

Saving for powers of Treasury. 1946 c. 58.

4. It shall not be lawful to exercise the powers of borrowing conferred by this Act otherwise than in accordance with the provisions of any order in force under section 1 of the Borrowing (Control and Guarantees) Act 1946.

Interpretation.

5. In this Act—

" the appointed day " means such day as the Secretary of State may by order appoint;

1968 c. 54.

" play " has the same meaning as in the Theatres Act 1968;

" theatre " means any building or part of a building constructed wholly or mainly for the public performance of plays;

" the Trust " means the Theatres Trust constituted by this Act;

" the trustees " means the trustees appointed under the provisions of the Schedule to this Act;

" the trust property " means the stocks, shares and other securities, sums of money and other property for the time being held by the trustees for the purposes of the Trust.

Short title, commencement and extent.

6.—(1) This Act may be cited as the Theatres Trust Act 1976.

(2) This Act shall come into force on such date (not being later than the expiration of the period of six months beginning with the day on which it is passed) as the Secretary of State may by order appoint and different dates may be appointed for different provisions and for different purposes.

(3) The power of the Secretary of State to make orders under this Act shall be exercisable by statutory instrument.

(4) This Act does not extend to Scotland or Northern Ireland.

SCHEDULE

Appointment, Constitution and Functions of the Trustees

1. Subject as hereinafter provided, there shall be fifteen trustees of the Trust appointed by the Secretary of State and the Secretary of State shall appoint one of them to be chairman and one to be deputy chairman of the trustees.

2. In appointing the trustees the Secretary of State shall have regard to the desirability of securing the services of persons with knowledge and experience of—

(*a*) the ownership of theatres;

(*b*) the production of plays;

(*c*) employment in, or in connection with, plays;

(*d*) organisations established for the encouragement of the arts;

(*e*) local government;

(*f*) planning;

(*g*) commercial or financial matters; or

(*h*) safeguarding the interests of the environment.

3. The Secretary of State shall satisfy himself that any person whom he proposes to appoint to be a trustee will have or has, as the case may be, no such financial or other interest as is likely to affect him in the discharge of his functions as a trustee; and any such person shall, whenever requested by the Secretary of State to do so, give the Secretary of State such information as he considers necessary for the performance of his duty under this paragraph.

4. Before appointing a person to be a trustee the Secretary of State shall consult such bodies, if any, as appear to him to be representative of the interests concerned.

5. The term of office of the trustees shall be three years.

6. If a trustee fails throughout a period of two years to attend any meeting of the trustees he shall, unless the failure was due to some reason approved by the trustees, cease to be a trustee:

Provided that attendance at a meeting of the executive committee or any other committee of the trustees to which any functions of the trustees have been delegated shall be deemed for the purposes of this paragraph to be attendance at a meeting of the trustees.

7. A trustee may at any time, by notice in writing addressed to the Secretary of State, resign his office.

8. A person ceasing to be a trustee shall be eligible for reappointment.

9. A person appointed by the Secretary of State to fill a casual vacancy shall hold office until the date upon which the trustee whose vacancy he has filled would have regularly retired.

10. The trustees shall in every year hold an annual meeting and at least one other meeting.

11.—(1) The trustees shall appoint each year at the annual meeting an executive committee and may appoint such other committees composed of the trustees for any such general or special purpose as in the opinion of the trustees would be better regulated and managed by means of a committee and may delegate to the executive committee or such other committee so appointed with or without restrictions as they think fit any functions of the trustees.

(2) The executive committee shall consist of not more than eight trustees and any other committee of the trustees of such number of trustees as the trustees may determine.

12. The powers of the trustees and any committee of the trustees may be exercised notwithstanding any vacancy, and no proceedings of the trustees or of any committee of the trustees shall be invalidated by any defect in the appointment of a trustee.

13. The trustees shall have power from time to time to make, alter and revoke regulations with respect to the management and administration of the trust property, the holding of meetings of the trustees, the executive committee and any other committee of the trustees, the conduct of proceedings at those meetings (including quorum), and for all other purposes necessary for the execution of the Trust.

14. The trustees shall keep proper accounts of all sums received or paid by them and proper records in relation to those accounts, and the accounts for each financial year of the Trust shall be audited by an auditor or auditors appointed by the trustees.

No person shall be qualified to be appointed auditor under this paragraph unless he is a member of one or more of the following bodies:—

the Institute of Chartered Accountants in England and Wales ;

the Institute of Chartered Accountants of Scotland ;

the Association of Certified Accountants ;

the Institute of Chartered Accountants in Ireland ;

any other body of accountants established in the United Kingdom and for the time being recognised for the purposes of paragraph (*a*) of subsection (1) of section 161 of the Companies Act 1948 ; 1948 c. 38.

but a Scottish firm may be so appointed if each of the partners is qualified to be appointed.

Congenital Disabilities (Civil Liability) Act 1976

1976 CHAPTER 28

An Act to make provision as to civil liability in the case of children born disabled in consequence of some person's fault; and to extend the Nuclear Installations Act 1965, so that children so born in consequence of a breach of duty under that Act may claim compensation.
[22nd July 1976]

BE IT ENACTED by the Queen's most Excellent Majesty, by and with the advice and consent of the Lords Spiritual and Temporal, and Commons, in this present Parliament assembled, and by the authority of the same, as follows:—

Civil liability to child born disabled.

1.—(1) If a child is born disabled as the result of such an occurrence before its birth as is mentioned in subsection (2) below, and a person (other than the child's own mother) is under this section answerable to the child in respect of the occurrence, the child's disabilities are to be regarded as damage resulting from the wrongful act of that person and actionable accordingly at the suit of the child.

(2) An occurrence to which this section applies is one which—

(*a*) affected either parent of the child in his or her ability to have a normal, healthy child; or

(*b*) affected the mother during her pregnancy, or affected her or the child in the course of its birth, so that the child is born with disabilities which would not otherwise have been present.

(3) Subject to the following subsections, a person (here referred to as " the defendant ") is answerable to the child if he was liable in tort to the parent or would, if sued in due time, have been so; and it is no answer that there could not have been such liability because the parent suffered no actionable injury, if there was a breach of legal duty which, accompanied by injury, would have given rise to the liability.

(4) In the case of an occurrence preceding the time of conception, the defendant is not answerable to the child if at that time either or both of the parents knew the risk of their child being born disabled (that is to say, the particular risk created by the occurrence); but should it be the child's father who is the defendant, this subsection does not apply if he knew of the risk and the mother did not.

(5) The defendant is not answerable to the child, for anything he did or omitted to do when responsible in a professional capacity for treating or advising the parent, if he took reasonable care having due regard to then received professional opinion applicable to the particular class of case; but this does not mean that he is answerable only because he departed from received opinion.

(6) Liability to the child under this section may be treated as having been excluded or limited by contract made with the parent affected, to the same extent and subject to the same restrictions as liability in the parent's own case; and a contract term which could have been set up by the defendant in an action by the parent, so as to exclude or limit his liability to him or her, operates in the defendant's favour to the same, but no greater, extent in an action under this section by the child.

(7) If in the child's action under this section it is shown that the parent affected shared the responsibility for the child being born disabled, the damages are to be reduced to such extent as the court thinks just and equitable having regard to the extent of the parent's responsibility.

Liability of woman driving when pregnant.

2. A woman driving a motor vehicle when she knows (or ought reasonably to know) herself to be pregnant is to be regarded as being under the same duty to take care for the safety of her unborn child as the law imposes on her with respect to the safety of other people; and if in consequence of her breach of that duty her child is born with disabilities which would not otherwise have been present, those disabilities are to be regarded as damage resulting from her wrongful act and actionable accordingly at the suit of the child.

3.—(1) Section 1 of this Act does not affect the operation of the Nuclear Installations Act 1965 as to liability for, and compensation in respect of, injury or damage caused by occurrences involving nuclear matter or the emission of ionising radiations.

Disabled birth due to radiation.

1965 c. 57.

(2) For the avoidance of doubt anything which—

(*a*) affects a man in his ability to have a normal, healthy child; or

(*b*) affects a woman in that ability, or so affects her when she is pregnant that her child is born with disabilities which would not otherwise have been present,

is an injury for the purposes of that Act.

(3) If a child is born disabled as the result of an injury to either of its parents caused in breach of a duty imposed by any of sections 7 to 11 of that Act (nuclear site licensees and others to secure that nuclear incidents do not cause injury to persons, etc.), the child's disabilities are to be regarded under the subsequent provisions of that Act (compensation and other matters) as injuries caused on the same occasion, and by the same breach of duty, as was the injury to the parent.

(4) As respects compensation to the child, section 13(6) of that Act (contributory fault of person injured by radiation) is to be applied as if the reference there to fault were to the fault of the parent.

(5) Compensation is not payable in the child's case if the injury to the parent preceded the time of the child's conception and at that time either or both of the parents knew the risk of their child being born disabled (that is to say, the particular risk created by the injury).

4.—(1) References in this Act to a child being born disabled or with disabilities are to its being born with any deformity, disease or abnormality, including predisposition (whether or not susceptible of immediate prognosis) to physical or mental defect in the future.

Interpretation and other supplementary provisions.

(2) In this Act—

(*a*) " born " means born alive (the moment of a child's birth being when it first has a life separate from its mother), and " birth " has a corresponding meaning; and

(*b*) " motor vehicle " means a mechanically propelled vehicle intended or adapted for use on roads.

(3) Liability to a child under section 1 or 2 of this Act is to be regarded—

(*a*) as respects all its incidents and any matters arising or to arise out of it; and (*b*) subject to any contrary context or intention, for the purpose of construing references in enactments and documents to personal or bodily injuries and cognate matters,

as liability for personal injuries sustained by the child immediately after its birth.

(4) No damages shall be recoverable under either of those sections in respect of any loss of expectation of life, nor shall any such loss be taken into account in the compensation payable in respect of a child under the Nuclear Installations Act 1965 as extended by section 3, unless (in either case) the child lives for at least 48 hours.

1965 c. 57.

(5) This Act applies in respect of births after (but not before) its passing, and in respect of any such birth it replaces any law in force before its passing, whereby a person could be liable to a child in respect of disabilities with which it might be born; but in section 1(3) of this Act the expression "liable in tort" does not include any reference to liability by virtue of this Act, or to liability by virtue of any such law.

(6) References to the Nuclear Installations Act 1965 are to that Act as amended; and for the purposes of section 28 of that Act (power by Order in Council to extend the Act to territories outside the United Kingdom) section 3 of this Act is to be treated as if it were a provision of that Act.

Crown application.

5. This Act binds the Crown.

Citation and extent.

6.—(1) This Act may be cited as the Congenital Disabilities (Civil Liability) Act 1976.

(2) This Act extends to Northern Ireland but not to Scotland.

Representation of the People (Armed Forces) Act 1976

1976 CHAPTER 29

An Act to make provision for the registration for electoral purposes of members of the armed forces and the wives and husbands of such members. [22nd July 1976]

BE IT ENACTED by the Queen's most Excellent Majesty, by and with the advice and consent of the Lords Spiritual and Temporal, and Commons, in this present Parliament assembled, and by the authority of the same, as follows:—

Change in effect of service declarations by members of the forces, etc.

1.—(1) The rule established by section 2(1) of the Representation of the People Act 1969 that a service declaration shall be made only with a view to registration in the register of electors for a particular year and with reference to the qualifying date for that register shall not apply to members of the forces and their wives and husbands, and that subsection and subsection (2) of that section (time of making, and expiry of, service declaration) shall cease to have effect. 1969 c. 15.

(2) Instead, in section 10 of the Representation of the People Act 1949 (service qualification), after subsection (3) there shall be inserted the following subsections:— 1949 c. 68.

"(3A) A service declaration made by a member of the forces or the wife or husband of such a member shall, if not cancelled, continue in force so long as the declarant has a service qualification, except in so far as regulations provide that the declaration shall cease to be in force on a change in the circumstances giving the service qualification.

(3B) A service declaration made by any other person shall be made with a view to registration in the register of electors for a particular year and with reference to the qualifying date for that register.

(3C) A service declaration made with reference to any qualifying date shall be made during the twelve months ending with that date, but shall not have effect if after it is made and before that date the declarant ceases to have a service qualification or cancels the declaration or, in so far as regulations so provide, if after the declaration is made and before that date there is a change in the circumstances giving the service qualification.".

Change of service qualification. 1949 c. 68.

2. The wife or husband of a member of the forces shall have a service qualification for the purposes of the Representation of the People Act 1949, notwithstanding that she or he does not satisfy the requirement of paragraph (*c*) of section 10(1) of that Act that she or he must be residing outside the United Kingdom to be with that member, and accordingly for that paragraph there shall be substituted the following paragraphs:—

"(*c*) any person who is the wife or husband of a member of the forces;

(*d*) any person who is the wife or husband of a person mentioned in paragraph (*b*) or (*bb*) above and is residing outside the United Kingdom to be with her husband or, as the case may be, his wife,"

and in paragraph (*b*) of that subsection, after the word "who" there shall be inserted the words "(not being such a member)".

Consequential amendments and repeals.

3.—(1) In accordance with sections 1 and 2 above the Representation of the People Act 1949 shall be amended as mentioned in subsections (2) to (6) below.

(2) In the provisos to section 8(1) and (2) (persons with service qualifications not entitled to be registered as electors except in pursuance of a service declaration) for the words from "except in pursuance" to the end of each proviso there shall be substituted the words "except in pursuance of the appropriate service declaration".

(3) After section 8(2) there shall be inserted the following subsection:—

"(3) The appropriate service declaration for a member of the forces or the wife or husband of such a member is a service declaration made in accordance with section 10 of this Act and in force on the qualifying date and in any other case is a service declaration made in accordance with that section with reference to that date.".

(4) For paragraphs (*b*) and (*c*) of section 10(5) there shall be substituted the following paragraphs:—

" (*b*) where the declarant is a member of the forces or the wife or husband of such a member, that on that date the declarant is, or but for the circumstances entitling him to make the declaration would have been, residing in the United Kingdom ;

(*bb*) in the case of any other declarant, that on that date and, unless it is a qualifying date, on the qualifying date next following he is or will be, or but for those circumstances would have been, residing in the United Kingdom ;

(*c*) the address where the declarant is or, as the case may be, will be or would have been residing in the United Kingdom or, if he cannot give any such address, an address at which he has resided in the United Kingdom.".

(5) For section 10(6) there shall be substituted the following subsection:—

" (6) A member of the forces or the wife or husband of such a member whose service declaration is in force on the qualifying date shall be treated for the purposes of registration, and any other person whose service declaration is made with reference to the qualifying date for any register shall be so treated in relation to that register,—

(*a*) as resident on the qualifying date at the address specified in the declaration ;

(*b*) in the case of registration in Northern Ireland, as resident in Northern Ireland during the whole of the period of three months ending on the qualifying date ; and

(*c*) in any case, until the contrary is proved, as being a British subject or a citizen of the Republic of Ireland of the age appearing from the declaration and as not being subject to any legal incapacity except as so appearing.".

(6) In section 10(9) for the words " and made with reference to the same qualifying date " there shall be substituted the words " if, in the case of a service declaration made otherwise than by a member of the forces or the wife or husband of such a member, it is made with reference to the same qualifying date ".

(7) In subsections (2) to (6) above any reference to any provision of the Representation of the People Act 1949 is a refer- 1949 c. 68.

1969 c. 15.

ence to that provision as amended by Schedule 2 to the Representation of the People Act 1969.

(8) In the said Act of 1969 the following are hereby repealed, that is to say—

(*a*) section 2(4) ;

(*b*) in Schedule 2, paragraphs 2(1) and 4(3) and in paragraph 4(1) the words from " and at the end of paragraph (*c*) " onwards ; and

(*c*) in Schedule 4, the entry relating to section 2(1) and (2).

Short title, citation and commencement.

4.—(1) This Act may be cited as the Representation of the People (Armed Forces) Act 1976, and shall be included among the Acts that may be cited as the Representation of the People Acts.

(2) This Act shall come into force on such date as the Secretary of State may by order made by statutory instrument appoint.

Fatal Accidents Act 1976

1976 CHAPTER 30

An Act to consolidate the Fatal Accidents Acts.

[22nd July 1976]

BE IT ENACTED by the Queen's most Excellent Majesty, by and with the advice and consent of the Lords Spiritual and Temporal, and Commons, in this present Parliament assembled, and by the authority of the same, as follows:—

1.—(1) If death is caused by any wrongful act, neglect or default which is such as would (if death had not ensued) have entitled the person injured to maintain an action and recover damages in respect thereof, the person who would have been liable if death had not ensued shall be liable to an action for damages, notwithstanding the death of the person injured.

Right of action for wrongful act causing death.

(2) Every such action shall be for the benefit of the dependants of the person (" the deceased ") whose death has been so caused.

(3) In this Act " dependant " means—

(*a*) the wife or husband of the deceased,

(*b*) any person who is a parent or grandparent of the deceased,

(*c*) any person who is a child or grandchild of the deceased, and

(*d*) any person who is, or is the issue of, a brother, sister, uncle or aunt of the deceased.

(4) In deducing any relationship for the purposes of subsection (3)—

(*a*) any relationship by affinity shall be treated as a relationship by consanguinity, any relationship of that half blood as a relationship of the whole blood, and the stepchild of any person as his child, and

(*b*) an illegitimate person shall be treated as the legitimate child of his mother and reputed father.

(5) Any reference in this Act to injury includes any disease and any impairment of a person's physical or mental condition.

Persons entitled to bring the action.

2.—(1) The action shall be brought by and in the name of the executor or administrator of the deceased.

(2) If—

(*a*) there is no executor or administrator of the deceased, or

(*b*) no action is brought within six months after the death by and in the name of an executor or administrator of the deceased,

the action may be brought by and in the name of all or any of the dependants.

(3) Not more than one action shall lie for and in respect of the same subject matter of complaint.

(4) The plaintiff in the action shall be required to deliver to the defendant or his solicitor full particulars of the dependants for whom and on whose behalf the action is brought, and of the nature of the claim in respect of which damages are sought to be recovered.

Assessment of damages.

3.—(1) In the action such damages may be awarded as are proportioned to the injury resulting from the death to the dependants respectively, and the amount so recovered, after deducting the costs not recovered from the defendant, shall be divided among the dependants in such shares as may be directed.

(2) In assessing damages payable to a widow in respect of the death of her husband in an action under this Act there shall not be taken into account the remarriage of the widow or her prospects of remarriage.

(3) If the dependants have incurred funeral expenses in respect of the deceased, damages may be awarded in respect of those expenses.

(4) Money paid into court in satisfaction of a cause of action under this Act may be in one sum without specifying the dependants' shares.

4.—(1) In assessing damages in respect of a person's death in an action under this Act, there shall not be taken into account any insurance money, benefit, pension or gratuity which has been or will or may be paid as a result of the death.

Assessment of damages: disregard of certain benefits.

(2) In this section—

" benefit " means benefit under the enactments relating to social security, including enactments in force in Northern Ireland, and any payment by a friendly society or trade union for the relief or maintenance of a member's dependants,

" insurance money " includes a return of premiums, and

" pension " includes a return of contributions and any payment of a lump sum in respect of a person's employment.

5. Where any person dies as the result partly of his own fault and partly of the fault of any other person or persons, and accordingly if an action were brought for the benefit of the estate under the Law Reform (Miscellaneous Provisions) Act 1934 the damages recoverable would be reduced under section 1(1) of the Law Reform (Contributory Negligence) Act 1945, any damages recoverable in an action brought for the benefit of the dependants of that person under this Act shall be reduced to a proportionate extent.

Contributory negligence.

1934 c. 41.

1945 c. 28.

6.—(1) Schedule 1 to this Act contains consequential amendments.

Consequential amendments and repeals.

(2) The enactments in Schedule 2 to this Act are repealed to the extent specified in the third column of that Schedule.

7.—(1) This Act may be cited as the Fatal Accidents Act 1976.

Short title, etc.

(2) This Act shall come into force on 1st September 1976, but shall not apply to any cause of action arising on a death before it comes into force.

(3) This Act shall not extend to Scotland or Northern Ireland.

SCHEDULES

Section 6.

SCHEDULE 1

Consequential Amendments

General

1.—(1) Any enactment or other document whatsoever referring to any enactment repealed by this Act shall, unless the contrary intention appears, be construed as referring (or as including a reference) to the corresponding enactment in this Act.

(2) This paragraph applies whether or not the enactment or other document was enacted, made, served or issued before the passing of this Act.

(3) This paragraph is without prejudice to section 38 of the
1889 c. 63. Interpretation Act 1889 (effect of repeals), and the following provisions of this Schedule are without prejudice to the generality of this paragraph.

2.—(1) In the following enactments references to the Fatal
1846 c. 93. Accidents Acts, or to the Fatal Accidents Act 1846, or to section 1 of that Act, include references to this Act.

(2) The said enactments are—

1934 c. 41. section 1(5) of the Law Reform (Miscellaneous Provisions) Act 1934 (cause of action surviving death),

1957 c. 59. section 12(1)(*a*)(iii) of the Coal Mining Subsidence Act 1957 (civil liability under that Act),

1961 c. 27. section 3 of the Carriage by Air Act 1961 (civil liability under Convention implemented by that Act),

1965 c. 36. section 14(2) of the Gas Act 1965 (civil liability under that Act),

1971 c. 22. section 10 of the Animals Act 1971 (civil liability under that Act),

1971 c. 61. section 11(2) of the Mineral Workings (Offshore Installations) Act 1971 (civil liability under that Act),

1972 c. 21. section 2(4) of the Deposit of Poisonous Waste Act 1972 (civil liability under that Act),

1974 c. 40. section 88(4)(*a*) of the Control of Pollution Act 1974 (civil liability under that Act),

1975 c. 16. section 6(1)(*d*) of the Industrial Injuries and Diseases (Old Cases) Act 1975,

1975 c. 74. section 30(1) of the Petroleum and Submarine Pipe-Lines Act 1975 (civil liability under that Act).

1939 c. 21. *Limitation Act 1939*

3. In sections 2B, 2C and 2D of the Limitation Act 1939 (inserted
1975 c. 54. by the Limitation Act 1975)—

(*a*) in section 2D(6) the reference to section 1 of the Fatal Accidents Act 1846 shall be construed as including a reference to section 1(1) of this Act, and (*b*) any other reference to the Fatal Accidents Act 1846 shall be construed as including a reference to this Act. Sch. 1

Carriage by Railway Act 1972 1972 c. 33.

4. In section 3 of the Carriage by Railway Act 1972—

(*a*) the reference to section 3 of the Fatal Accidents Act 1846 includes a reference to section 2(3) of this Act,

(*b*) the reference to section 2 of the Fatal Accidents Act 1959 includes a reference to section 4 of this Act,

(*c*) other references to the Fatal Accidents Act 1846 include references to this Act.

SCHEDULE 2

Section 6.

Repeals

Chapter	Short title	Extent of repeal
9 & 10 Vict. c. 93.	Fatal Accidents Act 1846.	The whole Act.
27 & 28 Vict. c. 95.	Fatal Accidents Act 1864.	The whole Act.
24 & 25 Geo. 5. c. 41.	Law Reform (Miscellaneous Provisions) Act 1934.	Section 2.
8 & 9 Geo. 6. c. 28.	Law Reform (Contributory Negligence) Act 1945.	Section 1(4). In section 4 the definition of "dependant".
7 & 8 Eliz. 2. c. 65.	Fatal Accidents Act 1959.	The whole of section 1 except for subsection (4). Section 2.
1971 c. 43.	Law Reform (Miscellaneous Provisions) Act 1971.	Part II, but not so as to affect a right to make an application under section 5(2).
1973 c. 38.	Social Security Act 1973.	In Schedule 27 paragraph 20.
1975 c. 54.	Limitation Act 1975.	In Schedule 1 paragraph 1.

Legitimacy Act 1976

1976 CHAPTER 31

An Act to consolidate certain enactments relating to legitimacy. [22nd July 1976]

BE IT ENACTED by the Queen's most Excellent Majesty, by and with the advice and consent of the Lords Spiritual and Temporal, and Commons, in this present Parliament assembled, and by the authority of the same, as follows:—

1.—(1) The child of a void marriage, whenever born, shall, subject to subsection (2) below and Schedule 1 to this Act, be treated as the legitimate child of his parents if at the time of the act of intercourse resulting in the birth (or at the time of the celebration of the marriage if later) both or either of the parties reasonably believed that the marriage was valid. Legitimacy of children of certain void marriages.

(2) This section only applies where the father of the child was domiciled in England and Wales at the time of the birth or, if he died before the birth, was so domiciled immediately before his death.

2. Subject to the following provisions of this Act, where the parents of an illegitimate person marry one another, the marriage shall, if the father of the illegitimate person is at the date of marriage domiciled in England and Wales, render that person, if living, legitimate from the date of the marriage. Legitimation by subsequent marriage of parents.

3. Subject to the following provisions of this Act, where the parents of an illegitimate person marry one another and the father of the illegitimate person is not at the time of the marriage domiciled in England and Wales but is domiciled in a country Legitimation by extraneous law.

by the law of which the illegitimate person became legitimated by virtue of such subsequent marriage, that person, if living, shall in England and Wales be recognised as having been so legitimated from the date of the marriage notwithstanding that, at the time of his birth, his father was domiciled in a country the law of which did not permit legitimation by subsequent marriage.

Legitimation of adopted child.

1975 c. 72.

4.—(1) Paragraph 3 of Schedule 1 to the Children Act 1975 does not prevent an adopted child being legitimated under section 2 or 3 above if either natural parent is the sole adoptive parent.

(2) Where an adopted child (with a sole adoptive parent) is legitimated—

(*a*) sub-paragraph (2) of the said paragraph 3 shall not apply after the legitimation to the natural relationship with the other natural parent, and

(*b*) revocation of the adoption order in consequence of the legitimation shall not affect Part II of the said Schedule 1 as it applies to any instrument made before the date of legitimation.

Rights of legitimated persons and others to take interests in property.

5.—(1) Subject to any contrary indication, the rules of construction contained in this section apply to any instrument other than an existing instrument, so far as the instrument contains a disposition of property.

(2) For the purposes of this section, provisions of the law of intestate succession applicable to the estate of a deceased person shall be treated as if contained in an instrument executed by him (while of full capacity) immediately before his death.

(3) A legitimated person, and any other person, shall be entitled to take any interest as if the legitimated person had been born legitimate.

(4) A disposition which depends on the date of birth of a child or children of the parent or parents shall be construed as if—

(*a*) a legitimated child had been born on the date of legitimation,

(*b*) two or more legitimated children legitimated on the same date had been born on that date in the order of their actual births,

but this does not affect any reference to the age of a child.

(5) Examples of phrases in wills on which subsection (4) above can operate are—

1. Children of A " living at my death or born afterwards ".

2. Children of A " living at my death or born afterwards before any one of such children for the time being in existence attains a vested interest, and who attain the age of 21 years ".

3. As in example 1 or 2, but referring to grandchildren of A, instead of children of A.

4. A for life " until he has a child " and then to his child or children.

Note. Subsection (4) above will not affect the reference to the age of 21 years in example 2.

(6) If an illegitimate person or a person adopted by one of his natural parents dies, or has died before the commencement of this Act, and—

(*a*) after his death his parents marry or have married ; and

(*b*) the deceased would, if living at the time of the marriage, have become a legitimated person,

this section shall apply for the construction of the instrument so far as it relates to the taking of interests by, or in successsion to, his spouse, children and remoter issue as if he had been legitimated by virtue of the marriage.

(7) In this section " instrument " includes a private Act settling property, but not any other enactment.

Dispositions depending on date of birth.

6.—(1) Where a disposition depends on the date of birth of a child who was born illegitimate and who is legitimated (or, if deceased, is treated as legitimated), section 5(4) above does not affect entitlement under Part II of the Family Law Reform Act 1969 (illegitimate children). 1969 c. 46.

(2) Where a disposition depends on the date of birth of an adopted child who is legitimated (or, if deceased, is treated as legitimated) section 5(4) above does not affect entitlement by virtue of paragraph 6(2) of Schedule 1 to the Children Act 1975. 1975 c. 72.

(3) This section applies for example where—

(*a*) a testator dies in 1976 bequeathing a legacy to his eldest grandchild living at a specified time,

(*b*) his daughter has an illegitimate child in 1977 who is the first grandchild,

(*c*) his married son has a child in 1978,

(*d*) subsequently the illegitimate child is legitimated,

and in all those cases the daughter's child remains the eldest grandchild of the testator throughout.

Protection of trustees and personal representatives.

7.—(1) A trustee or personal representative is not under a duty, by virtue of the law relating to trusts or the administration of estates, to enquire, before conveying or distributing any property, whether any person is illegitimate or has been adopted by one of his natural parents, and could be legitimated (or if deceased be treated as legitimated), if that fact could affect entitlement to the property.

(2) A trustee or personal representative shall not be liable to any person by reason of a conveyance or distribution of the property made without regard to any such fact if he has not received notice of the fact before the conveyance or distribution.

(3) This section does not prejudice the right of a person to follow the property, or any property representing it, into the hands of another person, other than a purchaser, who has received it.

Personal rights and obligations.

8. A legitimated person shall have the same rights, and shall be under the same obligations in respect of the maintenance and support of himself or of any other person as if he had been born legitimate, and, subject to the provisions of this Act, the provisions of any Act relating to claims for damages, compensation, allowance, benefit or otherwise by or in respect of a legitimate child shall apply in like manner in the case of a legitimated person.

Re-registration of birth of legitimated person.

9.—(1) It shall be the duty of the parents of a legitimated person or, in cases where re-registration can be effected on information furnished by one parent and one of the parents is dead, of the surviving parent to furnish to the Registrar General information with a view to obtaining the re-registration of the birth of that person within 3 months after the date of the marriage by virtue of which he was legitimated.

(2) The failure of the parents or either of them to furnish information as required by subsection (1) above in respect of any legitimated person shall not affect the legitimation of that person.

(3) This section does not apply in relation to a person who was legitimated otherwise than by virtue of the subsequent marriage of his parents.

(4) Any parent who fails to give information as required by this section shall be liable on summary conviction to a fine not exceeding £2.

Interpretation.

10.—(1) In this Act, except where the context otherwise requires,—

" disposition " includes the conferring of a power of appointment and any other disposition of an interest in or right over property ;

"existing", in relation to an instrument, means one made before 1st January 1976;

"legitimated person" means a person legitimated or recognised as legitimated—

(*a*) under section 2 or 3 above; or

(*b*) under section 1 or 8 of the Legitimacy Act 1926; or 1926 c. 60.

(*c*) except in section 8, by a legitimation (whether or not by virtue of the subsequent marriage of his parents) recognised by the law of England and Wales and effected under the law of any other country;

and cognate expressions shall be construed accordingly;

"power of appointment" includes any discretionary power to transfer a beneficial interest in property without the furnishing of valuable consideration;

"void marriage" means a marriage, not being voidable only, in respect of which the High Court has or had jurisdiction to grant a decree of nullity, or would have or would have had such jurisdiction if the parties were domiciled in England and Wales.

(2) For the purposes of this Act "legitimated person" includes, where the context admits, a person legitimated, or recognised as legitimated, before the passing of the Children Act 1975. 1975 c. 72.

(3) For the purpose of this Act, except where the context otherwise requires,—

(*a*) the death of the testator is the date at which a will or codicil is to be regarded as made;

(*b*) an oral disposition of property shall be deemed to be contained in an instrument made when the disposition was made.

(4) It is hereby declared that references in this Act to dispositions of property include references to a disposition by the creation of an entailed interest.

(5) Except in so far as the context otherwise requires, any reference in this Act to an enactment shall be construed as a reference to that enactment as amended by or under any other enactment, including this Act.

Savings, amendments and repeals.

11.—(1) Schedule 1 to this Act, which contains savings and amendments to enactments consequential upon the provisions of this Act, shall have effect.

(2) The enactments mentioned in Schedule 2 to this Act are hereby repealed to the extent specified in column 3 of that Schedule.

Short title, commencement and extent.

12.—(1) This Act may be cited as the Legitimacy Act 1976.

(2) This Act shall come into force at the end of the period of one month beginning with the date on which it is passed.

(3) This Act does not extend to Scotland or to Northern Ireland.

SCHEDULES

Section 11.

SCHEDULE 1

SAVINGS AND CONSEQUENTIAL AMENDMENTS

SAVINGS

1.—(1) Notwithstanding the repeal by this Act of sections 1 and 8 of the Legitimacy Act 1926 persons legitimated or recognised as legitimated under that Act shall continue to be legitimated or recognised as legitimated by virtue of section 1 or, as the case may be, section 8 of that Act. 1926 c. 60.

(2) In any enactment whether passed before or after this Act references to persons legitimated or recognised as legitimated under section 1 or section 8 of the Legitimacy Act 1926 or under section 2 or section 3 of this Act shall be construed as including references to persons legitimated or recognised as legitimated under section 2 or section 3 of this Act or under section 1 or section 8 of the said Act of 1926 respectively.

2.—(1) The enactments repealed by Part II of Schedule 4 to the Children Act 1975 (which are superseded by section 5 of this Act) shall, notwithstanding those repeals, continue to have effect as respects existing instruments. 1975 c. 72.

In this sub-paragraph " instrument " has the same meaning as in section 5 of this Act.

(2) Subject to paragraph (3)(*b*) below, nothing in this Act or in the Legitimacy Act 1926 (in so far as the effect of that Act is preserved by sub-paragraph (1) above) shall affect the operation or construction of any disposition coming into operation before 1st January 1927 or affect any rights under the intestacy of a person dying before that date.

(3) Sub-paragraph (2) above shall apply in relation to a person to whom the said Act of 1926 applied by virtue of section 1(1) of the Legitimacy Act 1959 with the substitution for " 1st January 1927 " of " 29th October 1959 ". 1959 c. 73.

3. Section 1 does not—

(*a*) affect any rights under the intestacy of a person who died before 29th October 1959, or

(*b*) affect the operation or construction of any disposition coming into operation before 29th October 1959 except so far as may be necessary to avoid the severance from a dignity or title of honour of property limited (expressly or not) to devolve (as nearly as the law permits) along with the dignity or title of honour.

4.—(1) Section 1 of this Act, so far as it affects the succession to a dignity or title of honour, or the devolution of property limited as aforesaid, only applies to children born after 28th October 1959.

(2) Apart from section 1, nothing in this Act shall affect the succession to any dignity or title of honour or render any person capable of succeeding to or transmitting a right to succeed to any such dignity or title.

SCH. 1

(3) Apart from section 1, nothing in this Act shall affect the devolution of any property limited (expressly or not) to devolve (as nearly as the law permits) along with any dignity or title of honour.

This sub-paragraph applies only if and so far as a contrary intention is not expressed in the instrument, and shall have effect subject to the instrument.

5. It is hereby declared that nothing in this Act affects the Succession to the Throne.

CONSEQUENTIAL AMENDMENTS

Births and Deaths Registration Act 1953 (*c.20*)

6. In section 14 of the Births and Deaths Registration Act 1953 the following subsection is added at the end—

"(5) This section shall apply and be deemed always to have applied in relation to all persons recognised by the law of England and Wales as having been legitimated by the subsequent marriage of their parents whether or not their legitimation or the recognition thereof was effected under any enactment."

Children Act 1975 (*c.72*)

7. In paragraph 1(4) of Schedule 1 to the Children Act 1975 for the words "These definitions of adoption and legitimation include" and "those effected" there are substituted respectively the words "This definition of adoption includes" and "an adoption effected".

Section 11.

SCHEDULE 2

ENACTMENTS REPEALED

Chapter	Short Title	Extent of Repeal
16 & 17 Geo. 5. c. 60.	Legitimacy Act 1926.	Sections 1(1) and (4). Sections 6, 7 and 8. Sections 10, 11 and 12. The Schedule.
5 & 6 Eliz. 2. c. 39.	Legitimation (Re-registration of Birth) Act 1957.	Section 1(1). Section 2.
7 & 8 Eliz. 2. c. 73.	Legitimacy Act 1959.	Section 1. In section 2, subsections (1) to (5). Section 6(4).
1969 c. 46.	Family Law Reform Act 1969.	Section 16(2).
1975 c. 72.	Children Act 1975.	In section 8(9) the words from "and related" to the end. In Schedule 1, paragraphs 1(3), 12 and 13; in paragraph 14, sub-paragraphs (1)(*b*) and (2), and words "or is legitimated" in sub-paragraph (3)(*d*); and paragraph 15(1)(*b*).

Lotteries and Amusements Act 1976

1976 CHAPTER 32

An Act to consolidate certain enactments relating to lotteries, prize competitions and amusements with prizes. [22nd July 1976]

BE IT ENACTED by the Queen's most Excellent Majesty, by and with the advice and consent of the Lords Spiritual and Temporal, and Commons, in this present Parliament assembled, and by the authority of the same, as follows:—

PART I

LEGAL AND ILLEGAL LOTTERIES

General illegality of lotteries

1.—All lotteries which do not constitute gaming are unlawful, except as provided by this Act. Illegality of lotteries.

2.—(1) Subject to the provisions of this section, every person who in connection with any lottery promoted or proposed to be promoted either in Great Britain or elsewhere— General lottery offences.

(*a*) prints any tickets for use in the lottery ; or

(*b*) sells or distributes, or offers or advertises for sale or distribution, or has in his possession for the purpose of sale or distribution, any tickets or chances in the lottery ; or

(*c*) prints, publishes or distributes, or has in his possession for the purpose of publication or distribution—

(i) any advertisement of the lottery ; or

PART I

(ii) any list, whether complete or not, of prize winners or winning tickets in the lottery; or

(iii) any such matter descriptive of the drawing or intended drawing of the lottery, or otherwise relating to the lottery, as is calculated to act as an inducement to persons to participate in that lottery or in other lotteries; or

(*d*) brings, or invites any person to send, into Great Britain for the purpose of sale or distribution any ticket in, or advertisement of, the lottery; or

(*e*) sends or attempts to send out of Great Britain any money or valuable thing received in respect of the sale or distribution, or any document recording the sale or distribution, or the identity of the holder, of any ticket or chance in the lottery; or

(*f*) uses any premises, or causes or knowingly permits any premises to be used, for purposes connected with the promotion or conduct of the lottery; or

(*g*) causes, procures or attempts to procure any person to do any of the above-mentioned acts,

shall be guilty of an offence.

(2) In any proceedings instituted under subsection (1) above, it shall be a defence to prove either—

(*a*) that the lottery to which the proceedings relate was a lottery declared not to be unlawful by section 3, 4 or 25(6) below, and that at the date of the alleged offence the person charged believed, and had reasonable ground for believing, that none of the conditions required by the relevant enactment to be observed in connection with the promotion and conduct of the lottery had been broken; or

(*b*) that the lottery to which the proceedings relate was a society's lottery or a local lottery, and that at the date of the alleged offence the person charged believed, and had reasonable ground for believing, that it was being conducted in accordance with the requirements of this Act; or

(*c*) that the lottery to which the proceedings relate was not promoted wholly or partly outside Great Britain and constituted gaming as well as a lottery.

(3) In England and Wales, proceedings under subsection (1)(*c*)(iii) above in respect of any matter published in a newspaper shall not be instituted except by, or by direction of, the Director of Public Prosecutions.

PART I

Exceptions

Small lotteries incidental to exempt entertainments.

3.—(1) In this Act " exempt entertainment " means a bazaar, sale of work, fete, dinner, dance, sporting or athletic event or other entertainment of a similar character, whether limited to one day or extending over two or more days.

(2) Where a lottery is promoted as an incident of an exempt entertainment, that lottery is not unlawful, but the conditions set out in subsection (3) below shall be observed in connection with its promotion and conduct and, if any of those conditions is contravened, every person concerned in the promotion or conduct of the lottery shall be guilty of an offence unless he proves that the contravention occurred without his consent or connivance and that he exercised all due diligence to prevent it.

(3) The conditions referred to in subsection (2) above are that—

(a) the whole proceeds of the entertainment (including the proceeds of the lottery) after deducting—

(i) the expenses of the entertainment, excluding expenses incurred in connection with the lottery ; and

(ii) the expenses incurred in printing tickets in the lottery ; and

(iii) such sum, if any, not exceeding £50 or such other sum as may be specified in an order made by the Secretary of State, as the promoters of the lottery think fit to appropriate on account of any expenses incurred by them in purchasing prizes in the lottery,

shall be devoted to purposes other than private gain ;

(b) none of the prizes in the lottery shall be money prizes ;

(c) tickets or chances in the lottery shall not be sold or issued, nor shall the result of the lottery be declared, except on the premises on which the entertainment takes place and during the progress of the entertainment ; and

(d) the facilities for participating in lotteries under this section, or those facilities together with any other facilities for participating in lotteries or gaming, shall not be the only, or the only substantial, inducement to persons to attend the entertainment.

Private lotteries.

4.—(1) In this Act " private lottery " means a lottery in Great Britain which is promoted for, and in which the sale of tickets or chances by the promoters is confined to, either—

(a) members of one society established and conducted for purposes not connected with gaming, betting or lotteries ; or

PART I

(*b*) persons all of whom work on the same premises; or

(*c*) persons all of whom reside on the same premises,

and which is promoted by persons each of whom is a person to whom under the foregoing provisions of this subsection tickets or chances may be sold by the promoters and, in the case of a lottery promoted for the members of a society, is a person authorised in writing by the governing body of the society to promote the lottery.

(2) For the purposes of this section, each local or affiliated branch or section of a society shall be regarded as a separate and distinct society.

(3) A private lottery is not unlawful, but the following conditions shall be observed in connection with its promotion and conduct, that is to say—

(*a*) the whole proceeds, after deducting only expenses incurred for printing and stationery, shall be devoted to the provision of prizes for purchasers of tickets or chances, or, in the case of a lottery promoted for the members of a society, shall be devoted either—

(i) to the provision of prizes as aforesaid; or

(ii) to purposes which are purposes of the society; or

(iii) as to part to the provision of prizes as aforesaid and as to the remainder to such purposes as aforesaid;

(*b*) there shall not be exhibited, published or distributed any written notice or advertisement of the lottery other than—

(i) a notice of it exhibited on the premises of the society for whose members it is promoted or, as the case may be, on the premises on which the persons for whom it is promoted work or reside; and

(ii) such announcement or advertisement of it as is contained in the tickets, if any;

(*c*) the price of every ticket or chance shall be the same, and the price of any ticket shall be stated on the ticket;

(*d*) every ticket shall bear upon the face of it the name and address of each of the promoters and a statement of the persons to whom the sale of tickets or chances by the promoters is restricted, and a statement that no prize won in the lottery shall be paid or delivered by the promoters to any person other than the person to whom the winning ticket or chance was sold by them, and no prize shall be paid or delivered except in accordance with that statement;

PART I

(*e*) no ticket or chance shall be issued or allotted by the promoters except by way of sale and upon receipt of its full price, and no money or valuable thing so received by a promoter shall in any circumstances be returned; and

(*f*) no tickets in the lottery shall be sent through the post.

(4) Subject to subsection (5) below, if any of the conditions set out in subsection (3) above is contravened, each of the promoters of the lottery, and, where the person by whom the condition is broken is not one of the promoters, that person also, shall be guilty of an offence.

(5) It shall be a defence for a person charged with an offence under subsection (4) above only by reason of his being a promoter of the lottery to prove that the contravention occurred without his consent or connivance and that he exercised all due diligence to prevent it.

Societies' lotteries.

5.—(1) In this Act "society's lottery" means a lottery promoted on behalf of a society which is established and conducted wholly or mainly for one or more of the following purposes, that is to say—

(*a*) charitable purposes;

(*b*) participation in or support of athletic sports or games or cultural activities;

(*c*) purposes which are not described in paragraph (*a*) or (*b*) above but are neither purposes of private gain nor purposes of any commercial undertaking.

(2) Any purpose for which a society is established and conducted and which is calculated to benefit the society as a whole shall not be held to be a purpose of private gain by reason only that action in its fulfilment would result in benefit to any person as an individual.

(3) Subject to the provisions of this Act, a society's lottery is not unlawful if—

(*a*) it is promoted in Great Britain; and

(*b*) the society is for the time being registered under Schedule 1 to this Act; and

(*c*) it is promoted in accordance with a scheme approved by the society; and

(*d*) either—

(i) the total value of tickets or chances to be sold is £5,000 or less; or

(ii) the scheme is registered with the Board before any tickets or chances are sold.

PART I

(4) The whole proceeds of a society's lottery, after deducting sums lawfully appropriated on account of expenses or for the provision of prizes, shall be applied to purposes of the society such as are described in subsection (1) above.

(5) Schedule 1 to this Act shall have effect.

Local lotteries.

6.—(1) In this Act " local lottery " means a lottery promoted by a local authority.

(2) Subject to the provisions of this Act, a local lottery is not unlawful if—

(*a*) it is promoted in Great Britain ; and

(*b*) it is promoted in accordance with a scheme approved by the local authority ; and

(*c*) the scheme is registered with the Board before any tickets or chances are sold.

(3) The functions of local authorities for the discharge of which arrangements may be made under section 101 of the Local Government Act 1972 or section 56 of the Local Government (Scotland) Act 1973 (arrangements for the discharge of a local authority's functions by a committee, a sub-committee or an officer of the authority, or by another local authority) do not include the approval of schemes for local lotteries.

1972 c. 70.
1973 c. 65.

PART II

PROVISIONS RELATING TO SOCIETIES' LOTTERIES AND LOCAL LOTTERIES

Provisions relating to local lotteries

Purposes of a local lottery.

7.—(1) A local authority may promote a local lottery for any purpose for which they have power to incur expenditure under any enactment, including, without prejudice to the generality of this subsection, section 137 of the Local Government Act 1972 and section 83 of the Local Government (Scotland) Act 1973 (power of local authorities to incur expenditure for certain purposes not otherwise authorised).

(2) It shall be the duty of a local authority—

(*a*) to give such publicity to the object of a local lottery as will be likely to bring it to the attention of persons purchasing tickets or chances ; and

(*b*) subject to the following provisions of this section, to apply money accruing from a local lottery only to the object of the lottery.

(3) In this section " object " means the particular purpose or purposes for which a local authority promote a local lottery.

PART II

(4) The Secretary of State, upon receipt of an application from a local authority for his consent to the use of money accruing from a local lottery for a purpose suggested by the local authority other than the object of the lottery, may give that consent if and only if he is satisfied—

(*a*) that the object of the lottery, in whole or in part—

(i) has been as far as may be fulfilled ; or

(ii) cannot be carried out ; or

(*b*) that the object provides a use for part only of the money accruing from the lottery ; or

(*c*) that the money accruing from the lottery and other money applicable for similar purposes can be more effectively used in conjunction, and to that end can suitably be made applicable to common purposes ; or

(*d*) that the object was specified by reference to an area which was, when the object was specified, but has since ceased to be, a unit for some other purpose, or by reference to a class of persons or to an area which has for any reason since ceased to be suitable ; or

(*e*) that the object, in whole or in part, has since it was specified—

(i) been adequately provided for by other means ; or

(ii) ceased in any other way to provide a suitable and effective method of using money accruing from the lottery.

(5) If the Secretary of State consents to the use of money accruing from a local lottery for a purpose other than its object, it shall be the duty of the local authority to use it only for the purpose for which the consent is given.

Proceeds of local lotteries.

8.—(1) A local authority shall pay the whole proceeds of a local lottery, after deducting the expenses of promoting it and the sums required for prizes, into a fund (in this section referred to as a " lottery fund "), and any money in such a fund shall be invested by the local authority and any income arising from such investment shall be credited to the fund.

(2) It shall be the duty of a local authority to maintain a separate lottery fund for each local lottery which they promote.

(3) The payment by a local authority out of their rate fund, within the meaning of subsection (7) of section 1 of the Local Government Act 1974, of money accruing from a local lottery 1974 c. 7.

PART II

shall not be relevant expenditure within the meaning of subsection (4) of that section.

Provisions relating to societies' lotteries and local lotteries

Schemes for societies' lotteries and local lotteries.

9. Schedule 2 to this Act shall have effect.

Frequency of lotteries.

10.—(1) No society or local authority shall hold more than 52 lotteries under section 5 or 6 above in any period of 12 months, but—

(*a*) when the date of two or more society's lotteries promoted on behalf of one society is the same and the total value of the tickets or chances to be sold in those lotteries does not exceed £10,000, all those lotteries shall be treated as one; and

(*b*) when the date of two or more lotteries promoted by one local authority is the same and the total value of the tickets or chances to be sold in those lotteries does not exceed £10,000, all those lotteries shall be treated as one.

(2) The date of any lottery promoted on behalf of a society shall be not less than seven days after the date of any previous lottery promoted on behalf of that society, except that the date of a lottery promoted for the purpose of selling tickets or chances wholly or mainly to persons attending a particular athletic or sporting event may be less than seven days after the date of a previous lottery promoted on behalf of the society.

(3) The date of any lottery promoted by a local authority shall be not less than seven days after the date of any previous lottery promoted by that authority.

Rules for authorised lotteries.

11.—(1) In the case of a society's lottery—

(*a*) the promoter of the lottery shall be a member of the society authorised in writing by the governing body of the society to act as the promoter; and

(*b*) every ticket and every notice or advertisement of the lottery lawfully exhibited, distributed or published shall specify the name of the society, the name and address of the promoter and the date of the lottery.

(2) No ticket or chance in a society's lottery or a local lottery shall be sold at a price exceeding 25p.

(3) The price of every ticket or chance shall be the same, and the price of any ticket shall be stated on the ticket.

Part II

(4) No person shall be admitted to participate in a society's lottery or a local lottery in respect of a ticket or chance except after payment to the society or authority of the whole price of the ticket or chance; and no money received for or on account of a ticket or chance shall in any circumstances be returned.

(5) No prize in a society's lottery which satisfies the condition specified in section 5(3)(*d*)(i) above shall exceed £1,000 in amount or value.

(6) No prize—

(*a*) in a society's lottery which satisfies the condition specified in section 5(3)(*d*)(ii) above, or

(*b*) in a local lottery,

shall exceed in amount or value the sum which is specified in subsection (7) below as the appropriate sum in relation to that lottery.

(7) The appropriate sum is—

(*a*) £1,000, for a short-term lottery,

(*b*) £1,500, for a medium-term lottery, and

(*c*) £2,000, for any other lottery.

(8) The total value of the tickets or chances sold—

(*a*) in a society's lottery which satisfies the condition specified in section 5(3)(*d*)(ii) above, or

(*b*) in a local lottery,

shall not exceed the sum which is specified in subsection (9) below as the appropriate sum in relation to that lottery.

(9) The appropriate sum is—

(*a*) £10,000, for a short-term lottery,

(*b*) £20,000, for a medium-term lottery, and

(*c*) £40,000, for any other lottery.

(10) For the purposes of subsections (7) and (9) above—

(*a*) a lottery is a short-term lottery if less than one month has passed between the date of that lottery and the date of a previous lottery promoted on behalf of the same society or by the same authority; and

(*b*) a lottery is a medium-term lottery if less than three months but not less than one month has passed between the date of that lottery and the date of a previous lottery promoted on behalf of the same society or by the same authority.

(11) The amount of the proceeds of a society's lottery or a local lottery appropriated for the provision of prizes shall not exceed one half of the whole proceeds of the lottery.

PART II

(12) The amount of the proceeds of a society's lottery or a local lottery appropriated on account of expenses (exclusive of prizes) shall not exceed whichever is the less of—

(*a*) the expenses actually incurred ; and

(*b*) whichever of the amounts specified in subsection (13) below applies.

(13) The amounts referred to in subsection (12)(*b*) above are—

(*a*) where the whole proceeds of the lottery do not exceed £5,000, 25 per cent. of those proceeds ; or

(*b*) where the whole proceeds of the lottery exceed £5,000, 15 per cent. of those proceeds or such larger percentage, not exceeding 25 per cent., as the Board may authorise in the case of a particular lottery.

Regulations.

12.—(1) The Secretary of State may by regulations prescribe provisions to be included in—

(*a*) any scheme approved by a society for the promotion of a society's lottery ; and

(*b*) any scheme approved by a local authority for the promotion of a local lottery.

(2) The Secretary of State may by regulations make such provision with respect to the promotion of society's lotteries or local lotteries as he may consider necessary or expedient.

(3) Without prejudice to the generality of subsection (2) above, the Secretary of State may by regulations impose requirements or restrictions with respect to all or any of the following matters—

(*a*) the persons to whom and by whom tickets or chances in a lottery may or may not be sold ;

(*b*) the circumstances in which tickets or chances may be sold and in which persons may be invited to purchase tickets or chances ;

(*c*) the minimum age at which any person may buy a ticket or chance ;

(*d*) any information which must, or must not, appear on a ticket ;

(*e*) the manner in which a lottery may be advertised ;

(*f*) the use of postal services in connection with lotteries ;

(*g*) the matters in respect of which expenses in a lottery may be incurred.

(4) Any power to make regulations under this section may be exercised so as to make different provision in relation to different cases or different circumstances.

(5) It shall be the duty of the Secretary of State before making any regulations under this section to consult— PART II

(*a*) the Board, and

(*b*) such associations of local authorities as appear to him to be concerned.

Offences relating to societies' lotteries and local lotteries.

13.—(1) If any requirement of this Act or of any regulations made under it in respect of a society's lottery or a local lottery is contravened, the promoter of that lottery and any other person who is party to the contravention shall be guilty of an offence.

(2) It shall be a defence for a person charged with any such offence only by reason of his being the promoter to prove that the contravention occurred without his consent or connivance and that he exercised all due diligence to prevent it.

(3) It shall be a defence for any person charged with an offence in respect of an appropriation made in contravention of section 11(11) or (12) above to prove—

(*a*) that the proceeds of the lottery fell short of the sum reasonably estimated; and

(*b*) that the appropriation was made in order to fulfil an unconditional undertaking as to prizes given in connection with the sale of the relevant tickets or chances, or in respect of expenses actually incurred; and

(*c*) that the total amounts appropriated in respect of prizes or expenses did not exceed the amounts which could lawfully have been appropriated out of the proceeds of the lottery under the said subsections if the proceeds had amounted to the sum reasonably estimated.

(4) It shall be a defence for any person charged with an offence in respect of a contravention of section 10 above or of section 11(6) or (8) above to prove that the date of a lottery was later than he had expected for reasons which he could not foresee.

PART III

COMPETITIONS AND AMUSEMENTS

Newspaper and other competitions

Prize competitions.

14.—(1) Subject to subsection (2) below, it shall be unlawful to conduct in or through any newspaper, or in connection with any trade or business or the sale of any article to the public—

(*a*) any competition in which prizes are offered for forecasts of the result either—

(i) of a future event; or

(ii) of a past event the result of which is not yet ascertained, or not yet generally known;

PART III (*b*) any other competition in which success does not depend to a substantial degree on the exercise of skill.

(2) Nothing in subsection (1) above with respect to the conducting of competitions in connection with a trade or business shall apply in relation to sponsored pool betting or in relation to pool betting operations carried on by a person whose only trade or business is that of a bookmaker.

(3) Any person who contravenes this section shall, without prejudice to any liability to be proceeded against under section 2 above, be guilty of an offence.

(4) In this section "bookmaker", "pool betting" and "sponsored pool betting" have the meanings assigned to them
1963 c. 2. by section 55 of the Betting, Gaming and Lotteries Act 1963.

Amusements with prizes

Provision of amusements with prizes at exempt entertainments.

15.—(1) This section applies to the provision at any exempt entertainment of any amusement with prizes which constitutes a lottery or gaming or both but does not constitute—

1968 c. 65. (*a*) gaming to which Part II of the Gaming Act 1968 applies, or

(*b*) gaming by means of a machine to which Part III of that Act applies.

(2) Where any such amusement constitutes a lottery, nothing in section 1 or 2 above shall apply to it.

(3) In relation to any such amusement (whether it constitutes a lottery or not) the conditions set out in subsection (4) below shall be observed, and if either of those conditions is contravened every person concerned in the provision or conduct of that amusement shall be guilty of an offence unless he proves that the contravention occurred without his consent or connivance and that he exercised all due diligence to prevent it.

(4) The conditions referred to in subsection (3) above are—

(*a*) that the whole proceeds of the entertainment, after deducting the expenses of the entertainment, shall be devoted to purposes other than private gain; and

(*b*) that the facilities for winning prizes at amusements to which this section applies, or those facilities together with any other facilities for participating in lotteries or gaming, shall not be the only, or the only substantial, inducement to persons to attend the entertainment.

(5) Where any payment falls to be made—

(*a*) by way of a hiring, maintenance or other charge in
1968 c. 65. respect of a machine to which Part III of the Gaming Act 1968 applies, or

PART III

(*b*) in respect of any equipment for holding a lottery or gaming at any entertainment,

then if, but only if, the amount of that charge falls to be determined wholly or partly by reference to the extent to which that or some other such machine or equipment is used for the purposes of lotteries or gaming, that payment shall be held to be an application of the proceeds of the entertainment for the purposes of private gain.

(6) The reference to expenses in subsection (4)(*a*) above shall accordingly not include a reference to any charge mentioned in subsection (5) above and falling to be determined as there mentioned.

Provision of amusements with prizes at certain commercial entertainments. 1968 c. 65.

16.—(1) This section shall have effect for the purpose of permitting the provision of amusements with prizes where those amusements constitute a lottery or gaming or both but do not constitute gaming to which Part II of the Gaming Act 1968 applies or gaming by means of a machine to which Part III applies, and they are provided—

(*a*) on any premises in respect of which a permit under this section has been granted in accordance with Schedule 3 to this Act and is for the time being in force, or

(*b*) on any premises used mainly for the purposes of amusements by means of machines to which Part III of the Gaming Act 1968 applies, being premises in respect of which a permit granted under section 34 of that Act is for the time being in force, or

(*c*) at a pleasure fair consisting wholly or mainly of amusements provided by travelling showmen which is held on any day of the year on premises not previously used in that year on more than 27 days for the holding of such a pleasure fair.

(2) Nothing in section 1 or 2 above shall apply in relation to amusements falling within subsection (1) above, but in relation to any such amusement the conditions set out in subsection (3) below shall be observed, and if any of those conditions is contravened every person concerned in the provision or conduct of that amusement shall be guilty of an offence unless he proves that the contravention occurred without his consent or connivance and that he exercised all due diligence to prevent it.

(3) The conditions referred to in subsection (2) above are—

(*a*) that the amount paid by any person for any one chance to win a prize does not exceed 10p, and

(*b*) that the aggregate amount taken by way of the sale of chances in any one determination of winners, if any, of prizes does not exceed £5, and that the sale of those

PART III

chances and the declaration of the result take place on the same day and on the premises on which, and during the time when, the amusement is provided, and

(*c*) that no money prize is distributed or offered which exceeds 10p, and

(*d*) that the winning of, or the purchase of a chance to win, a prize does not entitle any person, whether or not subject to a further payment by him, to any further opportunity to win money or money's worth by taking part in any amusement with prizes or in any gaming or lottery, and

(*e*) in the case of such a pleasure fair as is mentioned in subsection (1)(*c*) above, that the opportunity to win prizes at amusements to which this subsection applies is not the only, or the only substantial, inducement to persons to attend the fair.

(4) Schedule 3 to this Act shall have effect.

Restriction on grant and provisions as to duration and forfeiture of permits.

1968 c. 65.

17.—(1) No permit under section 16 above shall be granted in respect of any premises where a licence under the Gaming Act 1968 is for the time being in force in respect of them or where a club or a miners' welfare institute is for the time being registered in respect of them under Part II of that Act; and, where such a licence is granted or a club or a miners' welfare institute is so registered in respect of any premises, and a permit under section 16 above is then in force in respect of those premises, the permit shall thereupon cease to have effect.

(2) The court by or before which the holder of a permit under section 16 above is convicted of an offence under that section in connection with the premises to which the permit relates may, if the court thinks fit, order that the permit shall be forfeited and cancelled.

(3) An order under subsection (2) above shall be deemed for the purposes of any appeal to be part of the sentence for the offence ; and the permit shall not be forfeited or cancelled under that order—

(*a*) until the date of expiry of the period within which notice of appeal against the conviction or sentence may be given, nor

(*b*) if notice of appeal against the conviction or sentence is duly given within that period, until the date of the determination or abandonment of the appeal.

(4) Subsection (3) above shall not apply to Scotland, but the holder of a permit in respect of which an order under subsection (2) above is made by a court in Scotland may, without prejudice to any other form of appeal under any rule of law, appeal

against the order in the same manner as against a conviction; and a permit shall not be forfeited or cancelled under an order so made—

(a) until the expiry of the period of 14 days commencing with the date on which the order was made, nor

(b) if an appeal against the order or the conviction which gave rise to it is taken within that period, until the date when that appeal is determined or abandoned or deemed to have been abandoned.

PART IV
SUPPLEMENTARY

Powers of Secretary of State as to monetary limits, fees etc.

18.—(1) The Secretary of State may by order—

(a) vary the figure of £5,000 in section 5(3)(d)(i) above and in paragraph 2 of Schedule 2 below;

(b) vary any monetary limit in section 10(1) or 11 above;

(c) direct that any provision of section 16 above which is specified in the order and which specifies a sum shall have effect as if for that sum there were substituted such other sum as may be specified in the order;

(d) vary the fee payable under paragraph 3 or 9 of Schedule 1 below;

(e) prescribe the fees to be payable under paragraph 7 of Schedule 2 below; and

(f) vary the fee payable under paragraph 18 of Schedule 3 below, or provide that it shall cease to be payable.

(2) An order made by virtue of subsection (1)(e) above may, instead of specifying the amount of any fee, authorise the Board to determine the amount subject to such limit, or in accordance with such provisions, as may be prescribed by the order.

Search warrants.

19. If—

(a) in England or Wales, a justice of the peace, or

(b) in Scotland, a justice of the peace or sheriff,

is satisfied on information on oath that there is reasonable ground for suspecting that an offence under this Act is being, has been or is about to be commiued on any premises, he may issue a warrant in writing authorising any constable to enter those premises, if necessary by force, at any time within 14 days from the time of the issue of the warrant and search them; and any constable who enters the premises under the authority of the warrant may—

(a) seize and remove any document, money or valuable thing, instrument or other thing whatsoever found on

PART IV

the premises which he has reasonable cause to believe may be required as evidence for the purposes of proceedings in respect of any such offence, and

(*b*) arrest and search any person found on the premises whom he has reasonable cause to believe to be committing or to have committed any such offence.

Penalties and forfeitures.

20.—(1) A person guilty of an offence under this Act shall be liable—

(*a*) on summary conviction, to a fine not exceeding £400; or

(*b*) on conviction on indictment, to imprisonment for a term not exceeding two years or a fine, or both.

(2) The court by or before which a person is convicted of any offence under this Act may order anything produced to the court and shown to the satisfaction of the court to relate to the offence to be forfeited and either destroyed or dealt with in such other manner as the court may order.

Offences by bodies corporate.

21.—(1) Where an offence under this Act committed by a body corporate is proved to have been committed with the consent or connivance of, or to have been attributable to any neglect on the part of, any director, manager, secretary or other similar officer of the body corporate or any person who was purporting to act in any such capacity, he, as well as the body corporate, shall be guilty of that offence and be liable to be proceeded against and punished accordingly.

(2) In subsection (1) above, except as it applies for the purposes of section 13 above, " director ", in relation to a body corporate established by or under any enactment for the purpose of carrying on under national ownership any industry or part of an industry or undertaking, being a body corporate whose affairs are managed by its members, means a member of that body corporate.

Meaning of " private gain " in relation to proceeds of entertainments, lotteries and gaming promoted on behalf of certain societies.

22.—(1) For the purposes of this Act proceeds of any entertainment, lottery or gaming promoted on behalf of a society to which this subsection extends which are applied for any purpose calculated to benefit the society as a whole shall not be held to be applied for purposes of private gain by reason only that their application for that purpose results in benefit to any person as an individual.

(2) Subsection (1) above extends to any society which is established and conducted either—

(*a*) wholly for purposes other than purposes of any commercial undertaking; or (*b*) wholly or mainly for the purpose of participation in or support of athletic sports or athletic games. PART IV

23.—(1) In this Act, except where the context otherwise requires— Interpretation.

" the Board " means the Gaming Board for Great Britain ;

" contravention ", in relation to any requirement, includes a failure to comply with that requirement, and cognate expressions shall be construed accordingly ;

" date ", in relation to a lottery, means the date on which the winners in that lottery are ascertained ;

" distribute ", in relation to documents or other matters, includes distribution to persons or places within or outside Great Britain, and " distribution " shall be construed accordingly ;

" exempt entertainment " has the meaning assigned to it by section 3(1) above ;

" gaming " has the same meaning as in the Gaming Act 1968 ; 1968 c. 65.

" local authority " means—

(*a*) in England, a county council, the Greater London Council, a district council, a London borough council, the Common Council of the City of London, the Council of the Isles of Scilly and a parish council ;

(*b*) in Wales, a county council, a district council and a community council ; and

(*c*) in Scotland, a regional council, an islands council and a district council ;

" local lottery " has the meaning assigned to it by section 6(1) above ;

" money " includes a cheque, banknote, postal order or money order ;

" newspaper " includes any journal, magazine or other periodical publication ;

" premises " includes any place ;

" printing " includes writing and other modes of reproducing words in a visible form ;

" private lottery " has the meaning assigned to it by section 4(1) above ;

" society " includes any club, institution, organisation or association of persons, by whatever name called, and any separate branch or section of such a club, institution, organisation or association ;

PART IV

"society's lottery" has the meaning assigned to it by section 5(1) above;

"ticket", in relation to any lottery, includes any document evidencing the claim of a person to participate in the chances of the lottery.

(2) In this Act, unless the context otherwise requires, a reference to the promotion of a society's lottery or a local lottery includes a reference to the conduct of that lottery, and "promote" shall be construed accordingly.

Orders and regulations.

24.—(1) Any power to make an order or regulations under this Act shall be exercisable by statutory instrument subject, except in the case of an order under section 25(7) below, to annulment in pursuance of a resolution of either House of Parliament.

(2) Any power conferred by this Act to make an order includes power to vary or revoke the order by a subsequent order.

Citation, etc.

25.—(1) This Act may be cited as the Lotteries and Amusements Act 1976.

(2) The amendments specified in Schedule 4 to this Act shall have effect.

(3) The enactments specified in Schedule 5 to this Act are repealed to the extent specified in column 3 of that Schedule.

(4) In so far as any instrument made or any other thing whatsoever done under any enactment repealed by this Act could have been made or done under a corresponding enactment in this Act, it shall not be invalidated by the repeal of that enactment but shall have effect as if made or done under that corresponding enactment; and for the purposes of this provision anything which under section 57(3) of the Betting, Gaming and Lotteries Act 1963 had effect as if done under any enactment in that Act shall, so far as may be necessary for the continuity of the law, be treated as done under the corresponding enactment in this Act.

1963 c. 2.

(5) Any enactment or other document referring to an enactment repealed by this Act or by the Betting, Gaming and Lotteries Act 1963 shall, so far as may be necessary for preserving its effect, be construed as referring, or as including a reference, to the corresponding enactment in this Act.

1846 c. 48.

(6) Nothing in this Act shall affect the operation of the Art Unions Act 1846, and a lottery promoted and conducted in accordance with that Act shall not be unlawful.

1960 c. 60.

(7) Where any provision contained in any local Act passed before the Betting and Gaming Act 1960 appears to the Secretary

of State to have been superseded by, or to be inconsistent with, section 15 or 16 above, the Secretary of State may by order, a draft of which shall be laid before Parliament, specify that provision for the purposes of this subsection; and, without prejudice to the operation of any rule of law relating to the effect on any such provision of the relevant enactment in the said Act of 1960, any provision so specified is hereby repealed as from the date of the making of the order. PART IV

(8) Section 254(2)(*c*) of the Local Government Act 1972 (power of Secretary of State to amend, etc., enactments by order) shall apply to this Act as if it had been passed before 1st April 1974. 1972 c. 70.

(9) This Act shall come into force immediately after the coming into force of the Lotteries Act 1975, or, if the provisions of that Act come into force on different dates, immediately after the coming into force of the last of them; but 1975 c. 58.

(*a*) nothing in this subsection shall be taken as prejudicing the exercise, by virtue of section 37 of the Interpretation Act 1889 (exercise of statutory powers between passing and commencing of Act) of any powers under the Lotteries Act 1975 or this Act in respect of the registration of schemes for societies' lotteries or local lotteries; and 1889 c. 63.

(*b*) nothing in this Act shall be taken as prejudicing the operation of section 38 of that Act (which relates to the effect of repeals).

(10) This Act does not extend to Northern Ireland.

SCHEDULES

Section 5.

SCHEDULE 1

REGISTRATION OF SOCIETIES

PART I

REGISTRATION

1.—(1) An application for the registration of a society for the purposes of section 5 above shall be made to the registration authority.

(2) In this Schedule " registration authority ", in relation to any society, means—

(*a*) in England, a London borough council, a district council, the Common Council of the City of London, or the Council of the Isles of Scilly ;

(*b*) in Wales, a district council ;

(*c*) in Scotland, an islands or district council,

being the authority within whose area the office or head office of the society is situated.

2. Any such application shall specify the purposes for which the society is established and conducted.

3. Subject to the provisions of this Schedule, upon application being duly made on behalf of a society and upon payment of a fee of £10, the registration authority shall register the society in a register to be kept for the purposes of section 5 above and notify the society in writing that they have done so.

4.—(1) The registration authority may, after giving the society an opportunity of being heard, refuse or revoke the registration of the society under this Part of this Schedule if it appears to the authority—

(*a*) that any person has been convicted of an offence to which this paragraph applies committed in connection with a lottery promoted or proposed to be promoted on behalf of the society ; or

(*b*) that the society does not satisfy or has ceased to satisfy the conditions specified in section 5(1) above.

(2) This paragraph applies to any of the following offences, namely—

(*a*) an offence under section 2 or 13 above ;

1963 c. 2.

(*b*) an offence under paragraph 14 below or paragraph 12 of Schedule 7 to the Betting, Gaming and Lotteries Act 1963 ;

(*c*) an offence under section 42 or 45 of that Act ; and

(*d*) an offence involving fraud or dishonesty.

5. Where the registration of any society has been refused or revoked under paragraph 4 above by a registration authority in England or Wales, that authority shall forthwith notify the society of the refusal

or revocation and the society may appeal to the Crown Court, and any such appeal shall be commenced by giving notice to the appropriate officer of the Crown Court and to the registration authority within 21 days of the day on which notice of the refusal or revocation is given to the society. SCH. 1

6. Where the registration of any society has been refused or revoked under paragraph 4 of this Schedule by a registration authority in Scotland, that authority shall forthwith notify the society of the refusal or revocation, and the society may appeal, within such time, and in accordance with such rules, as may be prescribed by the Court of Session by act of sederunt, to the sheriff having jurisdiction in the registration authority's area, and on any such appeal the decision of the sheriff shall be final and may include such order as to the expenses of the appeal as he thinks proper.

7. Where the registration authority revoke a registration under paragraph 4 above, then, until the time within which notice of appeal under paragraph 5 or 6 above may be given has expired and, if such notice is duly given, until the determination or abandonment of the appeal, the registration shall be deemed to continue in force, and if the Crown Court or, as the case may be, the sheriff confirms the decision of the registration authority, the Court or the sheriff may, if it or he thinks fit, order that the registration shall continue in force for a further period not exceeding two months from the date of the order.

8. A society which is for the time being registered under this Part of this Schedule may at any time apply to the registration authority for the cancellation of the registration; and in any such case the authority shall cancel the registration accordingly.

9. Every society which is registered under this Part of this Schedule shall pay to the registration authority on 1st January in each year while it is registered a fee of £5, and any such fee which remains unpaid after the date on which it becomes payable may be recovered by the authority as a debt.

10. Subject to the provisions of this Schedule, the registration of any society under Schedule 7 to the Betting, Gaming and Lotteries Act 1963 shall have effect as registration under this Schedule. 1963 c. 2.

PART II

RETURNS

11. Subject to paragraph 12 below, the promoter of a society's lottery shall, not later than the end of the third month after the date of the lottery, send to the registration authority a return certified by two other members of the society, being persons of full age appointed in writing by the governing body of the society, showing—

(a) a copy of the scheme under which the lottery was promoted;

(b) the whole proceeds of the lottery;

(c) the sums appropriated out of those proceeds on account of expenses and on account of prizes respectively;

SCH. 1

(*d*) the particular purpose or purposes to which proceeds of the lottery were applied in pursuance of section 5(4) above, and the amount applied for that purpose, or for each of those purposes, as the case may be ; and

(*e*) the date of the lottery.

12. Paragraph 11 above shall not apply to a society's lottery promoted in accordance with a scheme registered with the Board.

13. The registration authority shall preserve any return sent to them under paragraph 11 above for a period of at least 18 months, and during that period shall keep it deposited at their office and permit any member of the public to inspect it during office hours free of charge.

14. Any person who fails to send a return in accordance with the provisions of this Part of this Schedule, or who knowingly gives in any such return sent by him any information which is false in a material particular, or who certifies any such return knowing it to contain such information, shall be guilty of an offence.

Section 9.

SCHEDULE 2

REGISTRATION OF SCHEMES

1. A local authority shall submit to the Board any scheme approved by the authority under section 6(2)(*b*) above.

2. A society shall submit to the Board any scheme approved by the society under section 5(3)(*c*) above if the total value of tickets or chances to be sold in any lottery promoted in accordance with that scheme exceeds £5,000.

3.—(1) The Board shall register a scheme submitted to them under this Schedule unless—

(*a*) in the case of a scheme submitted by a society, that society is not registered under Schedule 1 above ; or

(*b*) the scheme is contrary to law ; or

(*c*) except where the Secretary of State otherwise directs, the Board is not satisfied either—

(i) that all lotteries promoted by or on behalf of the applicant within the last five years have been properly conducted ; or

(ii) that all fees payable under this Act have been paid ; or

(iii) that all the requirements of the Board under paragraph 6 below have been complied with ; or

(*d*) except where the Secretary of State otherwise directs, it appears to the Board that an unsuitable person will be employed for reward in connection with the promotion of a lottery under the scheme. Sch. 2

(2) In this paragraph and in paragraph 4 below "unsuitable person" means a person who has been convicted of—

(*a*) an offence under section 2 or 13 above;

(*b*) an offence under paragraph 14 of Schedule 1 above or paragraph 12 of Schedule 7 to the Betting, Gaming and Lotteries Act 1963; 1963 c. 2.

(*c*) an offence under section 42 or 45 of that Act; or

(*d*) an offence involving fraud or dishonesty.

4.—(1) The Board shall have power to revoke the registration of any scheme on any of the grounds (*a*), (*b*), (*c*) or (*d*) specified in paragraph 3(1) above.

(2) The Board shall also have power to revoke the registration of any scheme where it appears to them that an unsuitable person has been employed for reward in connection with the promotion of any lottery under that scheme.

(3) The revocation of the registration of any scheme under this paragraph shall not have effect in relation to any lottery in respect of which any tickets or chances have already been sold at the date of revocation.

5.—(1) The Secretary of State may direct the Board to restore any registration which, in pursuance of paragraph 4 above, the Board have revoked on any of the grounds specified in paragraph 3(1)(*c*) or (*d*) above or paragraph 4(2) above, and the Board shall give effect to any such direction.

(2) The restoration of any registration under sub-paragraph (1) above shall have effect from the date of revocation or such later date as may be specified in the direction.

6. The Board shall have power to require the provision of accounts in relation to any lottery promoted under a scheme registered by them, and any other information which they may require in respect of any lottery promoted or to be promoted under a scheme registered by them or submitted to them for registration.

7.—(1) The following fees shall be payable to the Board—

(*a*) a prescribed fee on an application for the registration of a scheme; and

(*b*) where more than one lottery is to be promoted under a scheme registered by the Board, a further prescribed fee for each lottery promoted under that scheme.

(2) Any such fees received by the Board shall be paid into the Consolidated Fund.

8. Any person who, in pursuance of a requirement under paragraph 6 above, knowingly or recklessly gives to the Board any information which is false in a material particular shall be guilty of an offence.

Section 16.

SCHEDULE 3

Permits for Commercial Provision of Amusements With Prizes

Interpretation

1.—(1) In this Schedule "the appropriate authority " means—

(*a*) in relation to any premises in England or Wales in respect of which a justices' on-licence (other than a Part IV licence) is for the time being in force, the licensing justices for the licensing district in which the premises are situated ;

(*b*) in relation to any other premises in England or Wales, the local authority within whose area the premises are situated ;

(*c*) in relation to any premises in Scotland in respect of which a hotel certificate or a public house certificate is for the time being in force, the licensing court for the licensing area in which the premises are situated ;

(*d*) in relation to any other premises in Scotland, the local authority within whose area the premises are situated.

(2) In this Schedule—

1964 c. 26. " justices' on-licence ", licensing district " and " Part IV licence " have the same meanings as in the Licensing Act 1964 ;

1959 c. 51. " hotel certificate ", " licensing area " and " public house certificate " have the same meanings as in the Licensing (Scotland) Act 1959 ;

" local authority " means—

(*a*) in England, a district council, a London borough council and the Common Council of the City of London ;

(*b*) in Wales, a district council ; and

(*c*) in Scotland, an islands council and a district council ; and

" permit " means a permit under section 16 above.

Resolution by local authority as to grant or renewal of permits

2. Any local authority may pass either of the following resolutions, that is to say—

(*a*) that (subject to paragraph 3 below) the authority will not grant any permits in respect of premises of a class specified in the resolution ; or

(*b*) that (subject to paragraph 3 below) the authority will neither grant nor renew any permit in respect of premises of a class specified in the resolution.

3.—(1) No resolution under paragraph 2 above shall have effect in relation to the grant or renewal of permits in respect of premises to which this paragraph applies.

(2) This paragraph applies to any premises used or to be used wholly or mainly for the purposes of a pleasure fair consisting wholly or mainly of amusements. Sch. 3

Application for grant or renewal of permit

4.—(1) An application to the appropriate authority for the grant of a permit in respect of any premises may be made—

(*a*) by the holder of the licence or certificate, in the case of premises such as are mentioned in paragraph 1(1)(*a*) or (*c*) above, and

(*b*) in any other case, by the person who is, or by any person who proposes if the permit is granted to become, the occupier of the premises.

(2) The holder of a permit may apply from time to time for the renewal of the permit.

5. The appropriate authority shall not refuse to grant or renew a permit without affording to the applicant or a person acting for him an opportunity of appearing before, and being heard by, the appropriate authority or (where that authority is a local authority) a committee of the local authority.

Grounds for refusal to grant or renew permit

6.—(1) Where an application for the grant or renewal of a permit is made to a local authority, then if—

(*a*) there is for the time being in force a resolution passed by that authority in accordance with paragraph 2 above which is applicable to the premises to which the application relates, and

(*b*) the permit could not be granted or renewed without contravening that resolution,

it shall be the duty of the authority to refuse to grant or renew the permit.

(2) The grant or renewal of a permit shall not be invalidated by any failure to comply with this paragraph, and no duty of a local authority to comply with this paragraph shall be enforceable by legal proceedings.

7.—(1) In the case of premises to which paragraph 3 above applies—

(*a*) the grant of a permit shall be at the discretion of the appropriate authority ; but

(*b*) the appropriate authority shall not refuse to renew a permit except either on the grounds that they or their authorised representatives have been refused reasonable facilities to inspect the premises or by reason of the conditions in which amusements with prizes have been provided on the premises, or the manner in which any such amusements have been conducted, while the permit has been in force.

SCH. 3 (2) In the case of premises other than premises to which paragraph 3 above applies, the grant or renewal of a permit shall (subject to paragraph 6 above) be at the discretion of the appropriate authority; and in particular, and without prejudice to the generality of that discretion, the appropriate authority may refuse to grant or renew any such permit on the grounds that, by reason of the purposes for which, or the persons by whom, or any circumstances in which, the premises are or are to be used, it is undesirable that amusements with prizes should be provided on those premises.

(3) The preceding provisions of this paragraph shall have effect subject to section 17(1) above.

(4) In this paragraph any reference to amusements with prizes includes any amusements provided by means of a machine to which Part III of the Gaming Act 1968 applies. 1968 c. 65.

Appeal in England or Wales against decision of appropriate authority

8.—(1) Where on an application under this Schedule in England or Wales the appropriate authority refuse to grant or renew a permit, or grant or renew it subject to a condition, the authority shall forthwith give to the applicant notice of their decision and of the grounds on which it is made.

(2) Where such a notice has been given, the applicant may, by notice to the clerk to the appropriate authority, appeal against the decision to the Crown Court.

(3) As soon as practicable after receiving notice of appeal against a decision of the appropriate authority, the clerk to the authority shall send the notice to the appropriate officer of the Crown Court together with a statement of the decision against which the appeal is brought and of the name and last-known residence or place of business of the appellant, and on receipt of the notice, that officer shall enter the appeal and give to the appellant and to the appropriate authority not less than seven days' notice in writing of the date, time and place appointed for the hearing of the appeal.

(4) A justice shall not act in the hearing or determination of an appeal under this paragraph from any decision in which he took part.

9. The Court shall not allow an appeal under this Schedule if satisfied that, by virtue of paragraph 6 above, it was the duty of the appropriate authority to refuse to grant or renew the permit.

10. Subject to paragraph 9 above, on any such appeal the Court may by its order allow or dismiss the appeal, or reverse or vary any part of the decision of the appropriate authority, and may deal with the application as if it had been made to the Court in the first instance; and the judgment of the Court on the appeal shall be final.

11. Where the appropriate authority is the licensing justices for a licensing district and the Court—

(*a*) has allowed an appeal, or

(b) has awarded the licensing justices any costs and is satisfied that the licensing justices cannot recover those costs, Sch. 3

the Court shall order payment out of central funds of such sums as appear to the Court sufficient to indemnify the licensing justices from all costs and charges whatever to which they have been put in consequence of the appellant's having served notice of appeal.

Appeal in Scotland against decision of appropriate authority

12. Where on an application under this Schedule in Scotland the appropriate authority refuse to grant or renew a permit, or grant or renew it subject to a condition, the authority shall forthwith give to the applicant notice of their decision and of the grounds on which it is made; and the applicant may, within such time, and in accordance with such rules, as may be prescribed by the Court of Session by act of sederunt, appeal against the decision to the sheriff having jurisdiction in the authority's area.

13. The sheriff shall not allow an appeal under this Schedule if satisfied that, by virtue of paragraph 6 above, it was the duty of the appropriate authority to refuse to grant or renew the permit.

14.—(1) Subject to paragraph 13 above, on any such appeal the sheriff may allow or dismiss the appeal, or reverse or vary any part of the decision of the appropriate authority, and may deal with the application as if it had been made to him in the first instance.

(2) The decision of the sheriff on the appeal shall be final and may include such order as to the expenses of the appeal as he thinks proper.

Duration of permit

15. Subject to the following provisions of this Schedule, and without prejudice to the cancellation of any permit under section 17(2) above, a permit—

(a) if not renewed, shall cease to have effect on such date, not being less than three years beginning with the date on which it was granted, as may be specified in the permit, or

(b) if renewed, shall, unless further renewed, cease to have effect on such date, not being less than three years beginning with the date on which it was renewed or last renewed, as the case may be, as may be specified in the decision to renew it.

16.—(1) Where an application for the renewal of a permit is made not less than one month before the date on which it is due to expire, the permit shall not cease to have effect by virtue of paragraph 15 above before the appropriate authority have determined the application or the application has been withdrawn.

(2) Where, on such an application, the appropriate authority refuse to renew the permit, it shall not cease to have effect by

SCH. 3 virtue of paragraph 15 above before the time within which the applicant can appeal against the refusal has expired, and, if he so appeals, shall not cease to have effect by virtue of that paragraph until the appeal has been determined or abandoned.

17.—(1) A permit shall not be transferable, and, subject to the following provisions of this paragraph, shall cease to have effect if—

(*a*) in the case of premises falling within paragraph 1(1)(*a*) or (*c*) above, the holder of the permit ceases to be the holder of the licence or certificate in respect of the premises, or

(*b*) in the case of any other premises, the holder of the permit ceases to be the occupier of the premises.

(2) If the holder of a permit dies while the permit is in force—

(*a*) the permit shall not cease to have effect by virtue of paragraph 15 above or by virtue of the preceding sub-paragraph before the end of the period of six months beginning with the date of his death, and

(*b*) except for the purposes of a renewal of the permit, his personal representatives shall be deemed to be the holder of the permit;

and the appropriate authority may from time to time on the application of those personal representatives, extend or further extend the period for which the permit continues to have effect by virtue of this sub-paragraph if satisfied that the extension is necessary for the purpose of winding up the estate of the deceased and that no other circumstances make it undesirable.

Payment of fees

18. Notwithstanding anything in the preceding provisions of this Schedule, no permit shall be granted or renewed except on payment by the applicant to the appropriate authority or their clerk of a fee of £2·50.

Section 25.

SCHEDULE 4

CONSEQUENTIAL AMENDMENTS

1968 c. 65.

Gaming Act 1968

1. In section 1(2)(*c*) of the Gaming Act 1968 (gaming to which Part I of that Act applies) for the words from the first " in " to " 1963 " there shall be substituted the words " as mentioned in section 15(1) or 16(1) of the Lotteries and Amusements Act 1976 ".

2. In section 34(1)(*c*) of that Act (uses of machines) for the words " section 49 of the Act of 1963 " there shall be substituted the words " section 16 of the Lotteries and Amusements Act 1976 ".

3. In section 41(1)(*c*) of that Act (gaming at entertainments not held for private gain) for the words from the first " in " to " 1963 " there shall be substituted the words " as mentioned in section 15(1) or 16(1) of the Lotteries and Amusements Act 1976 ".

SCH. 4

4. In section 42(2)(*d*) of that Act (restrictions on advertisements relating to gaming) for the words from " 4 " to " 49 " there shall be substituted the words " 3 of Schedule 3 to the Lotteries and Amusements Act 1976 applies and in respect of which a permit under section 16 ".

5. The following section shall be added after section 51 of that Act:—

" Meaning of " private gain " in relation to non-commercial entertainments.

51A.—(1) In construing sections 33 and 41 of this Act, proceeds of any entertainment, lottery or gaming promoted on behalf of a society to which this subsection extends which are applied for any purpose calculated to benefit the society as a whole shall not be held to be applied for purposes of private gain by reason only that their application for that purpose results in benefit to any person as an individual.

(2) Subsection (1) above extends to any society which is established and conducted either—

(*a*) wholly for purposes other than purposes of any commercial undertaking ; or

(*b*) wholly or mainly for the purpose of participation in or support of athletic sports or athletic games ;

and in this section " society " includes any club, institution, organisation or association of persons, by whatever name called, and any separate branch or section of such a club, institution, organisation or association.

(3) For the purposes of sections 33 and 41 of this Act, where any payment falls to be made by way of a hiring, maintenance or other charge in respect of a machine to which Part III of this Act applies or in respect of any equipment for holding a lottery or gaming at any entertainment, then if, but only if, the amount of that charge falls to be determined wholly or partly by reference to the extent to which that or some other machine or equipment is used for the purposes of lotteries or gaming, that payment shall be held to be an application of the proceeds of the entertainment for the purposes of private gain.".

6.—(1) In subsection (1) of section 52 of that Act (interpretation) after the definition of " machine " there shall be inserted the following definition:—

" newspaper " includes any journal, magazine or other periodical publication ;

(2) In subsection (3)(*a*) of that section for the words from " section 43(1) " to the end of the sub-paragraph there shall be substituted the words " section 3 (small lotteries incidental to certain entertainment), 4 (private lotteries), 5 (societies' lotteries) or 6 (local lotteries) of the Lotteries and Amusements Act 1976 and ".

SCH. 4

Pool Competitions Act 1971

1971 c. 57. 7.—(1) In section 2(5) of the Pool Competitions Act 1971 (licence to promote competitions) at the end of paragraph (*c*) there shall be inserted—

" and

(*d*) the Lotteries and Amusements Act 1976 ".

(2) In section 6(1) of that Act (offences for which consent to prosecute is required)—

(*a*) in paragraph (*a*), for the words " section 42 or section 47 of the Betting, Gaming and Lotteries Act 1963 " there shall be substituted the words " section 2 or section 14 of the Lotteries and Amusements Act 1976 " ;

(*b*) in paragraph (*b*), for the words " that Act " there shall be substituted the words " the Betting, Gaming and Lotteries Act 1963 ".

1972 c. 25.

Betting and Gaming Duties Act 1972

8.—(1) In section 6 of the Betting and Gaming Duties Act 1972 (pool betting duty), for paragraph (*b*) of subsection (3) there shall be substituted the following paragraph:—

" (*b*) " bet " does not include the taking of a ticket or chance—

(i) in any lottery which is declared by section 3, 4 or 25(6) of the Lotteries and Amusements Act 1976 not to be unlawful ; or

(ii) in any society's lottery or local lottery within the meaning of section 5 or 6 of that Act, in which the relevant monetary limits are not exceeded (disregarding any variation of those limits made by order under section 18 of that Act)."

1975 c. 58. (2) For subsection (4) of that section (which was added by paragraph 3(*b*) of Schedule 3 to the Lotteries Act 1975) there shall be substituted the following subsection:—

"(4) In subsection (3) above " relevant monetary limits " means the limits referred to in section 5(4)(*a*) and subsections (2), (5) (6) and (8) of section 11 of the said Act of 1976.".

1974 c. 7.

Local Government Act 1974

9. In section 1(4) of the Local Government Act 1974 (relevant expenditure for purposes of rate support grant) for the words " and section 5(3) of the Lotteries Act 1975 " (which were inserted by that Act) there shall be substituted the words " and section 8(3) of the Lotteries and Amusements Act 1976 ".

SCHEDULE 5

Section 25.

Repeals

Chapter	Short title	Extent of Repeal
1963 c. 2.	The Betting, Gaming and Lotteries Act 1963.	Parts III and IV. Section 52(1A). Section 54. In section 55, the definition of " newspaper " in subsection (1), and subsection (2). Schedule 6.
1966 c. 42.	The Local Government Act 1966.	In Part II of Schedule 3, in paragraph 23 the words " paragraph 16 of Schedule 6 ".
1966 c. 51.	The Local Government (Scotland) Act 1966.	In Part II of Schedule 4, in paragraph 26 the words " paragraph 16 of Schedule 6 ".
1968 c. 65.	The Gaming Act 1968.	Section 33(6). Section 41(11). In section 53, in subsection (1) the words in paragraph (*a*) from " and the Schedule " onwards. In Schedule 11, in Part I the entries relating to sections 41, 42, 48, 49 and 54 of the Betting, Gaming and Lotteries Act 1963, and Part II.
1971 c. 23.	The Courts Act 1971.	In Schedule 9, in the entry relating to the Betting, Gaming and Lotteries Act 1963, the words " Schedule VI, 8 to 11 " and the words " Schedule VII, 5 ".
1971 c. 57.	The Pool Competitions Act 1971.	Section 2(5)(*b*).
1973 c. 65.	The Local Government (Scotland) Act 1973.	In Schedule 24, paragraphs 28 and 29.
1975 c. 58.	The Lotteries Act 1975.	The whole Act, except section 20(1) and (3) and paragraph 6 of Schedule 4.

Restrictive Practices Court Act 1976

1976 CHAPTER 33

An Act to consolidate certain enactments relating to the Restrictive Practices Court. [22nd July 1976]

BE IT ENACTED by the Queen's most Excellent Majesty, by and with the advice and consent of the Lords Spiritual and Temporal, and Commons, in this present Parliament assembled, and by the authority of the same, as follows:—

The Court. 1956 c. 68.

1.—(1) The Restrictive Practices Court (" the Court ") established by the Restrictive Trade Practices Act 1956 shall continue in being by that name as a superior court of record.

(2) The Court shall consist of the following members—

(*a*) five nominated judges ; and

(*b*) not more than ten appointed members.

(3) Of the nominated judges one, to be selected by the Lord Chancellor, shall be President of the Court.

(4) The Court shall have an official seal which shall be judicially noticed.

Judges of the Court.

2.—(1) The nominated judges of the Court shall be—

(*a*) three puisne judges of the High Court nominated by the Lord Chancellor ;

(*b*) one judge of the Court of Session nominated by the Lord President of that Court ;

(c) one judge of the Supreme Court of Northern Ireland nominated by the Lord Chief Justice of Northern Ireland.

(2) A judge of any court who is nominated under this section shall not be required to sit in any place outside the jurisdiction of that court, and shall be required to perform his duties as a judge of that court only when his attendance on the Restrictive Practices Court is not required.

(3) In the case of the temporary absence or inability to act of a nominated judge, the Lord Chancellor, the Lord President of the Court of Session, or the Lord Chief Justice of Northern Ireland (as the case may be) may nominate another judge of the same court to act temporarily in his place, and a judge so nominated shall, when so acting, have all the functions of the judge in whose place he acts.

(4) No judge shall be nominated under this section except with his consent.

Non-judicial members.

3.—(1) The other members of the Court (" appointed members ") may be appointed by Her Majesty on the recommendation of the Lord Chancellor, and any person recommended for appointment shall be a person appearing to the Lord Chancellor to be qualified by virtue of his knowledge of or experience in industry, commerce or public affairs.

(2) An appointed member shall hold office for such period (not less than three years) as may be determined at the time of his appointment, and shall be eligible for reappointment, but—

(a) he may at any time by notice in writing to the Lord Chancellor resign his office ;

(b) the Lord Chancellor may, if he thinks fit, remove any appointed member for inability or misbehaviour, or on the ground of any employment or interest which appears to the Lord Chancellor incompatible with the functions of a member of the Court.

(3) In the case of the temporary absence or inability to act of an appointed member, the Lord Chancellor may appoint a temporary member, being a person appearing to him to be qualified as provided in subsection (1) above, to act in place of that member ; and a temporary member shall, when so acting, have all the functions of an appointed member.

Provision for additional judges or members.

4.—(1) The Lord Chancellor may—

(a) after consultation with the Lord President of the Court of Session and the Lord Chief Justice of Northern Ireland, by order increase the number of nominated judges of the Court ;

(*b*) with the approval of the Minister for the Civil Service, by order increase the maximum number of appointed members ;

and sections 1 to 3 above, as to the number of judges and members, have effect subject to any order in force under this section.

(2) Orders under this section shall be made by statutory instrument ; and an order shall be of no effect until it is approved by resolution of each House of Parliament.

Pay and pensions of non-judicial members.

5.—(1) There may be paid to the appointed members of the Court, and to any temporary member, such remuneration as the Lord Chancellor may, with the approval of the Minister for the Civil Service, determine.

(2) In the case of any such holder of the office of appointed member as may be determined by the Lord Chancellor acting with that approval, there shall be paid such pension, allowance or gratuity to or in respect of him on his retirement or death, or such contributions or other payments towards provision for such a pension, allowance or gratuity as may be so determined.

(3) As soon as may be after the making of any determination under subsection (2) above the Lord Chancellor shall lay before each House of Parliament a statement of the amount of the pension, allowance or gratuity or contributions or other payments, as the case may be, payable in pursuance of the determination.

Administration.

6.—(1) The Lord Chancellor may appoint such officers and servants of the Court as he may, with the approval of the Minister for the Civil Service as to numbers and conditions of service, determine.

(2) The principal civil service pension scheme within the meaning of section 2 of the Superannuation Act 1972 and for the time being in force applies, with the necessary adaptations, to officers and servants of the Court as to other persons employed in the civil service of the State.

1972 c. 11.

(3) The central office of the Court shall be in London.

(4) Subject to its rules, the Court may sit at such times and in such place or places in any part of the United Kingdom as may be most convenient for the determination of proceedings before it.

(5) When sitting in public in London, the Court shall sit at the Royal Courts of Justice or at such other place as the Lord Chancellor may appoint.

(6) The Court may sit either as a single court or in two or more divisions concurrently and either in private or in public.

7.—(1) For the hearing of any proceedings the Court shall consist of a presiding judge and at least two other members, except that in the case of proceedings involving only issues of law the Court may instead consist of a single member being a judge.

Hearing and judgment.

(2) On the hearing of any proceedings, the opinion of the judge or judges sitting as members of the Court upon any question of law shall prevail; but subject to this the decision of the Court shall be taken by all the members sitting, or, in the event of a difference of opinion, by the votes of the majority of the members.

In the event of an equality of votes, the presiding judge shall be entitled to a second or casting vote.

(3) The judgment of the Court in any proceedings shall be delivered by the presiding judge.

8.—(1) Every person who has the right of audience at the trial of an action in the High Court or in the Court of Session, or in proceedings preliminary to such a trial, shall have the like right at the hearing of any application to the Court, whether sitting in England and Wales or in Scotland, or in proceedings preliminary to such a hearing, as the case may be.

Right of audience.

(2) Every person who has the right of audience at the trial of an action in the High Court of Northern Ireland, or in proceedings preliminary to such trial, shall have the like right at the hearing of any application to the Court when sitting in Northern Ireland, or in proceedings preliminary to such a hearing, as the case may be.

9.—(1) The procedure in or in connection with any proceedings before the Court and, subject to the approval of the Treasury, the fees chargeable in respect of such proceedings, shall be such as may be determined by rules made by the Lord Chancellor.

Procedure.

Rules under this section shall be made by statutory instrument subject to annulment in pursuance of a resolution of either House of Parliament.

(2) Without prejudice to the generality of subsection (1) above, rules made under that subsection may provide—

(*a*) with respect to the persons to be made respondents to any application to the Court;

(*b*) with respect to the place at which the Court is to sit for the purposes of any proceedings ;

(*c*) with respect to the evidence which may be required or admitted in any proceedings ;

(*d*) for securing, by means of preliminary statements of facts and contentions, and by the production of documents, the administration of interrogatories and other methods of discovery, that all material facts and considerations are brought before the Court by all parties to any proceedings, including the Director General of Fair Trading.

(3) In relation to the attendance and examination of witnesses, the production and inspection of documents, the enforcement of its orders, and all other matters incidental to its jurisdiction, the Court shall have the like powers, rights, privileges and authority—

(*a*) in England and Wales, as the High Court ;

(*b*) in Scotland, as the Court of Session ; and

(*c*) in Northern Ireland, as the High Court of Northern Ireland.

(4) No person shall be punished for contempt of the Court except by or with the consent of a judge who is a member of the Court.

Appeal.

10.—(1) Subject to and in accordance with this section, an appeal lies from any decision or order of the Court—

(*a*) in the case of proceedings in England and Wales, to the Court of Appeal ;

(*b*) in the case of proceedings in Scotland, to the Court of Session ; and

(*c*) in the case of proceedings in Northern Ireland, to the Court of Appeal in Northern Ireland.

1973 c. 41.

(2) In proceedings under Part III of the Fair Trading Act 1973 (consumer protection) the appeal lies on a question of fact or on a question of law.

(3) In proceedings other than those referred to in subsection (2) above—

(*a*) the appeal lies on a question of law only and the Court's decision on a question of fact is final ; and

(*b*) the appeal—

(i) to the Court of Appeal, or to the Court of Appeal in Northern Ireland, is by way of case stated ; and

(ii) to the Court of Session, is by way of stated case.

11.—(1) In paragraph (*e*) of subsection (4) of section 3 of the Superannuation (Miscellaneous Provisions) Act 1967 for " 4(1) of the Restrictive Trade Practices Act 1956 " substitute " 3(1) of the Restrictive Practices Court Act 1976 ". Consequential amendment, savings and repeals. 1967 c. 28.

(2) In so far as anything done under an enactment repealed by this Act could have been done under a corresponding provision of this Act, it is not invalidated by the repeal but has effect as if done under that provision.

(3) The enactments mentioned in the Schedule to this Act are hereby repealed to the extent specified in the third column of that Schedule.

12.—(1) This Act may be cited as the Restrictive Practices Court Act 1976. Short title, extent and commencement.

(2) This Act extends to Northern Ireland.

(3) This Act shall come into operation on such day as the Lord Chancellor may appoint by order made by statutory instrument.

Section 11

SCHEDULE

REPEALS

Chapter	Short Title	Extent of Repeal
4 & 5 Eliz. 2. c. 68.	The Restrictive Trade Practices Act 1956.	Sections 2 to 5. In section 23, subsection (1); in subsection (2), from the beginning of that subsection to the end of paragraph (*a*); subsection (3). In the Schedule, paragraphs 1 to 8 and 10 to 12.
1972 c. 11.	The Superannuation Act 1972.	In Schedule 6, paragraph 35.
1973 c. 41.	The Fair Trading Act 1973.	In Schedule 12, the entries so far as they relate to section 23 of the Restrictive Trade Practices Act 1956 and the Schedule to that Act.

Restrictive Trade Practices Act 1976

1976 CHAPTER 34

An Act to consolidate the enactments relating to restrictive trade practices. [22nd July, 1976]

BE IT ENACTED by the Queen's most Excellent Majesty, by and with the advice and consent of the Lords Spiritual and Temporal, and Commons, in this present Parliament assembled, and by the authority of the same, as follows:—

PART I

REGISTRATION AND JUDICIAL INVESTIGATION OF RESTRICTIVE AGREEMENTS

Registration of agreements and Court's jurisdiction.

1.—(1) Every agreement to which this Act applies by virtue of—

(*a*) section 6 below (restrictive agreements as to goods);

(*b*) an order under section 7 below (information agreements as to goods);

(*c*) an order under section 11 below (restrictive agreements as to services);

(*d*) an order under section 12 below (information agreements as to services);

is subject to registration under this Act.

(2) The Director General of Fair Trading (" the Director ") continues charged with the duty—

(*a*) of compiling and maintaining a register of agreements subject to registration under this Act;

(*b*) of entering or filing in the register such particulars as may be prescribed by regulations made under section 27 below of any such agreement, being—

(i) particulars duly furnished to him under this Act by parties to the agreement; or

PART I

(ii) documents or information obtained by him under this Act;

(*c*) of taking proceedings before the Restrictive Practices Court (" the Court ") in respect of the agreements of which particulars are from time to time entered or filed in the register; but this paragraph is subject to—

(i) such directions as may be given by the Secretary of State as to the order in which those proceedings are to be taken;

(ii) section 21 below (Director's duties as to proceedings for investigation).

(3) The Court has jurisdiction, on the Director's application in respect of an agreement of which particulars are for the time being registered under this Act, to declare whether or not any restrictions or information provisions by virtue of which this Act applies to the agreement are contrary to the public interest; but this jurisdiction is subject to paragraphs 6(2) and 9(2) of Schedule 3 to this Act.

Restrictions against public interest and consequent Court orders.

2.—(1) Where under section 1(3) above any restrictions or information provisions by virtue of which this Act applies to an agreement are found by the Court to be contrary to the public interest, the agreement shall be void in respect of those restrictions or those information provisions.

(2) Without prejudice to subsection (1) above, the Court may, on the Director's application, make such order as appears to the Court to be proper for restraining all or any of those mentioned in subsection (3) below—

(*a*) from giving effect to, or enforcing or purporting to enforce, the agreement in respect of those restrictions or those information provisions;

(*b*) from making any other agreement (whether with the same parties or with other parties) to the like effect; or

(*c*) where such an agreement as is mentioned in paragraph (*b*) above has already been made, from giving effect to that agreement or enforcing or purporting to enforce it.

(3) Those who may be restrained by an order of the Court under subsection (2) above are—

(*a*) the persons party to the agreement who carry on business within the United Kingdom;

(*b*) a trade association or a services supply association of which any such person is a member; or

(*c*) any person acting on behalf of any such association.

(4) Where any of the parties to an agreement against whom an order under subsection (2) is made is a member of a trade association or of a services supply association, the order may include provisions for restraining the association and any person acting on behalf of the association from procuring or assisting any such party to do anything which would be a contravention of the order in its application to him.

(5) Where—

(*a*) any restriction accepted under a term implied by virtue of section 8(2) below in an agreement for the constitution of a trade association;

(*b*) any information provision made under a term implied by virtue of section 8(4) below in an agreement for the constitution of a trade association;

(*c*) any restriction accepted under a term implied by virtue of section 16(3) below in an agreement for the constitution of a services supply association;

(*d*) any information provision made under a term implied by virtue of section 16(5) below in an agreement for the constitution of a services supply association;

is found by the Court to be contrary to the public interest, the Court may (without prejudice to its powers under this section) make such order as appears to the Court to be proper for restraining the association or any person acting on behalf of the association from making any recommendation to which that term would apply.

(6) The powers of the Court under this and the preceding section are not affected by the determination of an agreement effected after the commencement of the proceedings, and where an agreement is varied after the commencement of the proceedings, the Court may make a declaration and, if it thinks fit, an order under subsection (2) or subsection (5) above, either in respect of the agreement as at the commencement of the proceedings or in respect of the agreement as varied, or both.

Interim orders of the Court.

3.—(1) Where the Director has made an application under section 1(3) above, he may apply to the Court for an interim order under this section—

(*a*) at any time before the Court has made an order under section 2(2) above in respect of the agreement, and

(*b*) whether before or after the Court has made a declaration under section 1(3) in respect of the agreement.

PART I

(2) An application under this section shall specify the restrictions or information provisions which appear to the Director, in relation to the agreement to which the application relates—

(*a*) to be restrictions or information provisions such as are mentioned in section 1(3), and

(*b*) to be contrary to the public interest, and

(*c*) to be restrictions or information provisions in respect of which, in accordance with the following provisions of this section, it would be appropriate for an interim order to be made.

(3) If on an application under this section the Court is satisfied that the following conditions are fulfilled in relation to all or any of the restrictions or information provisions specified in the application—

(*a*) that they are restrictions or information provisions such as are mentioned in section 1(3);

(*b*) that they could not reasonably be expected to be shown to fall within any of paragraphs (*a*) to (*h*) of section 10(1) below or any of paragraphs (*a*) to (*h*) of section 19(1) below, as the case may be; and

(*c*) that the operation of the restrictions or information provisions, during the period likely to elapse before an order can be made in respect of them under section 2(2), is likely to cause material detriment to the public or a section of the public generally, or to a particular person who is not a party to the agreement;

the Court may, if it thinks fit, make an interim order specifying the restrictions or information provisions in relation to which the Court is satisfied that those conditions are fulfilled.

(4) Any such interim order may exercise, in respect of the restrictions or information provisions specified in the order, any powers which could be exercised in respect of them by an order under section 2(2) if those restrictions or those information provisions had been found by the Court to be contrary to the public interest.

(5) At any time when any such interim order is in force the Court, on the application of the Director or of any person who is subject to or entitled to the benefit of any restriction or information provision specified in the order, may discharge the order and substitute for it any interim order which could have been made on the original application under this section.

(6) An interim order made under this section in respect of an agreement ceases to have effect on the occurrence of whichever of the following first occurs—

(*a*) the termination of such period, or the happening of such event, as may be specified for that purpose in the order;

(b) the discharge of the order by the Court;

(c) a declaration by the Court that the restrictions or information provisions specified in the interim order are not contrary to the public interest;

(d) the final determination by the Court of an application under section 2(2) in respect of that agreement.

Variation of the Court's decisions.

4.—(1) The Court, upon application made in accordance with this section, may—

(a) discharge any previous declaration of the Court in respect of any restriction or information provision, and any order made by the Court in pursuance of that declaration, and

(b) substitute such other declaration, and make such order in pursuance of that declaration,

as appears to the Court to be proper at the time of the hearing of the application.

(2) The provisions of section 10 below or of section 19 below, as the case may be, apply with the necessary modifications in relation to proceedings on an application under this section as they apply in relation to the proceedings mentioned in those sections.

(3) An application under this section may be made by the Director or by any person who is, or was at the time of the previous determination of the Court, subject to or entitled to the benefit of the restriction or information provision in question.

(4) No application shall be made under this section except with the leave of the Court, and such leave shall not be granted except upon prima facie evidence of a material change in the relevant circumstances.

(5) Notwithstanding anything in subsection (4) above, leave to make an application under this section for the discharge of a declaration or order of the Court made before the commencement of the Restrictive Trade Practices Act 1968 (25th November 1968) may, if the applicant proposes to rely on paragraph (h) of section 10(1) below, be granted upon prima facie evidence of the relevance of that paragraph to the application. 1968 c. 66.

(6) This section does not apply in relation to any order made under section 3 above.

The European Communities.

5.—(1) This Act applies to an agreement notwithstanding that it is or may be void by reason of any directly applicable Community provision, or is expressly authorised by or under any such provision; but this subsection is subject to subsection (2) and section 34 below.

PART I

(2) The Court—

(*a*) may decline or postpone the exercise of its jurisdiction under sections 1 and 2 above, or

(*b*) may, notwithstanding subsection (2) of section 4 above, exercise its jurisdiction under that section,

if and in so far as it appears to the Court right so to do having regard to the operation of any directly applicable Community provision or to the purpose and effect of any authorisation or exemption granted in relation to such a provision.

PART II

GOODS

Restrictive agreements as to goods.

6.—(1) This Act applies to agreements (whenever made) between two or more persons carrying on business within the United Kingdom in the production or supply of goods, or in the application to goods of any process of manufacture, whether with or without other parties, being agreements under which restrictions are accepted by two or more parties in respect of any of the following matters—

(*a*) the prices to be charged, quoted or paid for goods supplied, offered or acquired, or for the application of any process of manufacture to goods;

(*b*) the prices to be recommended or suggested as the prices to be charged or quoted in respect of the resale of goods supplied;

(*c*) the terms or conditions on or subject to which goods are to be supplied or acquired or any such process is to be applied to goods;

(*d*) the quantities or descriptions of goods to be produced, supplied or acquired;

(*e*) the processes of manufacture to be applied to any goods, or the quantities or descriptions of goods to which any such process is to be applied; or

(*f*) the persons or classes of persons to, for or from whom, or the areas or places in or from which, goods are to be supplied or acquired, or any such process applied.

(2) For the purposes of subsection (1) above it is immaterial—

(*a*) whether any restrictions accepted by parties to an agreement relate to the same or different matters specified in that subsection, or have the same or different effect in relation to any matter so specified, and

(*b*) whether the parties accepting any restrictions carry on the same class or different classes of business.

PART II

(3) For the purposes of this Part of this Act an agreement which—

(*a*) confers privileges or benefits only upon such parties as comply with conditions as to any such matters as are described in subsection (1)(*a*) to (*f*) above ; or

(*b*) imposes obligations upon parties who do not comply with such conditions ;

shall be treated as an agreement under which restrictions are accepted by each of the parties in respect of those matters.

(4) Without prejudice to subsection (3) above, an obligation on the part of any party to an agreement to make payments calculated by reference—

(*a*) to the quantity of goods produced or supplied by him, or to which any process of manufacture is applied by him ; or

(*b*) to the quantity of materials acquired or used by him for the purpose of or in the production of any goods or the application of any such process to goods ;

being payments calculated, or calculated at an increased rate, in respect of quantities of goods or materials exceeding any quantity specified in or ascertained in accordance with the agreement, shall be treated for the purposes of this Act as a restriction in respect of the quantities of those goods to be produced or supplied, or to which that process is to be applied.

This subsection does not apply to any obligation on the part of any person to make payments to a trade association of which he is a member, if the payments are to consist only of bona fide subscriptions for membership of the association.

Information agreements as to goods.

7.—(1) The Secretary of State may by statutory instrument make an order directing that this Act shall apply to information agreements (whenever made) of any class described in the order ; and in this section " information agreement " means an agreement between two or more persons carrying on within the United Kingdom any such business as is described in section 6(1) above, whether with or without other parties, being an agreement under which provision is made for or in relation to the furnishing by two or more parties to each other or to other persons (whether parties or not) of information in respect of any of the following matters—

(*a*) the prices charged, quoted or paid or to be charged, quoted or paid for goods which have been or are to be supplied, offered or acquired or for the application of any process of manufacture to goods ;

PART II

(*b*) the prices to be recommended or suggested as the prices to be charged or quoted in respect of the resale of goods supplied;

(*c*) the terms or conditions on or subject to which goods have been or are to be supplied or acquired or any such process has been or is to be applied to goods;

(*d*) the quantities or descriptions of goods produced, supplied or acquired or to be produced, supplied or acquired;

(*e*) the costs incurred or to be incurred in producing, supplying or acquiring goods or in applying any such process to goods;

(*f*) the processes of manufacture which have been or are to be applied to any goods or the quantities or descriptions of goods to which any such process has been or is to be applied;

(*g*) the persons or classes of persons to or for whom goods have been or are to be supplied, or from or for whom goods have been or are to be acquired, or for whom any such process has been or is to be applied;

(*h*) the areas or places in or from which goods have been or are to be supplied or acquired or in which any such process has been or is to be applied to goods.

(2) For the purposes of subsection (1) above it is immaterial—

(*a*) whether any information provisions made by the parties to an agreement relate to the same or different matters specified in that subsection, or have the same or different effect in relation to any matter so specified, and

(*b*) whether the parties by whom any information is to be furnished carry on the same class or different classes of business.

(3) An order under this section may describe the classes of information agreements to which it applies by reference to one or more of the following matters—

(*a*) the trade or industry in which the persons to whom the information provision made by the agreement applies are engaged, or the class of business carried on by such persons;

(*b*) the character of the information provision made by the agreement, or the goods, processes, transactions, areas, places or other matters with respect to which that provision relates;

(*c*) any other features which appear to the Secretary of State to be expedient.

(4) No order shall be made under this section unless a draft of the order has been laid before, and approved by resolution of, each House of Parliament.

PART II

(5) The Secretary of State shall, before laying before Parliament the draft of an order under this section for applying this Act in relation to information agreements of any class, publish in such manner as he thinks appropriate a notice—

(*a*) describing the classes of agreements to which the proposed order would apply ; and

(*b*) specifying a period (not being less than 28 days) within which representations with respect to the proposed order may be made to the Secretary of State ;

and in settling the draft to be laid before Parliament shall take into consideration any such representations received by him within that period.

Trade associations.

8.—(1) This Act has effect in relation to an agreement made by a trade association as if the agreement were made between all persons who are members of the association or are represented on it by such members and, where any restriction is accepted or information provision made in the agreement on the part of the association, as if the like restriction or the like information provision were accepted or made by each of those persons.

(2) Where—

(*a*) specific recommendations (whether express or implied) are made by or on behalf of an association to its members, or to any class of its members, and

(*b*) those recommendations are as to the action to be taken or not to be taken by them in relation to any particular class of goods or process of manufacture in respect of any matters described in section 6(1) above,

this Act has effect in relation to the agreement for the constitution of the association (notwithstanding any provision in the agreement to the contrary) as if that agreement contained the term mentioned in subsection (3) below.

(3) The term referred to in subsection (2) above is one by which each such member, and any person represented on the association by any such member, agrees to comply with those recommendations and with any subsequent recommendations made to them by or on behalf of the association as to the action to be taken by them in relation to the same class of goods or process of manufacture and in respect of the same matters.

(4) In the case of an order under section 7 above, where—

(*a*) specific recommendations (whether express or implied) are made by or on behalf of an association to its members, or to any class of its members, and

PART II

(*b*) those recommendations are as to the furnishing of information in relation to any particular class of goods or process of manufacture in respect of any matters described in subsection (1) of that section,

this Act has effect in relation to the agreement for the constitution of the association (notwithstanding any provision in the agreement to the contrary) as if that agreement contained the term mentioned in subsection (5) below.

(5) The term referred to in subsection (4) above is one by which each such member, and any person represented on the association by any such member, agrees to comply with those recommendations and with any subsequent recommendations made to them by or on behalf of the association as to the furnishing of information in relation to the same class of goods or process of manufacture and in respect of the same matters.

Provisions to be disregarded under Part II.

9.—(1) In determining whether an agreement is an agreement to which this Act applies by virtue of this Part, where—

(*a*) the parties to the agreement are or include two or more bodies to which this subsection applies, and

(*b*) restrictions or information provisions relating to coal or steel, or relating to both coal and steel, are accepted or made, as the case may be, under the agreement by two or more such bodies, whether the restrictions so accepted or the information provisions so made by those bodies are the same restrictions or different restrictions or are the same information provisions or different information provisions,

no account shall be taken of any such restriction or information provision which is accepted or made under the agreement by a body to which this subsection applies, whether that restriction or information provision is also accepted or made by any other party to the agreement or not.

(2) Subsection (1) above applies to any body which, in accordance with Article 80 of the E.C.S.C. Treaty, constitutes an undertaking for the purposes of Articles 65 and 66 of that Treaty, and in that subsection " coal " and " steel " have the meanings assigned to them respectively by Annex I to that Treaty.

(3) In determining whether an agreement for the supply of goods or for the application of any process of manufacture to goods is an agreement to which this Act applies by virtue of this Part, no account shall be taken of any term which relates exclusively to the goods supplied, or to which the process is applied, in pursuance of the agreement.

PART II

(4) Where any such restrictions as are described in section 6(1) above are accepted or any such information provisions as are described in section 7(1) above are made as between two or more persons by whom, or two or more persons to or for whom, goods are to be supplied, or the process applied, in pursuance of the agreement, subsection (3) above shall not apply to those restrictions or to those information provisions unless accepted or made in pursuance of a previous agreement—

(*a*) in respect of which particulars have been registered under this Act ; or

(*b*) which is exempt from registration by virtue of an order under section 29 (agreements important to the national economy) or section 30 (agreements holding down prices) below.

(5) In determining whether an agreement is an agreement to which this Act applies by virtue of this Part, no account shall be taken of any term by which the parties or any of them agree to comply with or apply, in respect of the production, supply or acquisition of any goods or the application to goods of any process of manufacture—

(*a*) standards of dimension, design, quality or performance, or

(*b*) arrangements as to the provision of information or advice to purchasers, consumers or users,

being either standards or arrangements for the time being approved by the British Standards Institution or standards or arrangements prescribed or adopted by any trade association or other body and for the time being approved by order of the Secretary of State made by statutory instrument.

(6) In determining whether an agreement is an agreement to which this Act applies by virtue of this Part, no account shall be taken of any restriction or information provision which affects or otherwise relates to the workers to be employed or not employed by any person, or as to the remuneration, conditions of employment, hours of work or working conditions of such workers.

In this subsection " worker " means a person who has entered into or works under a contract with an employer whether the contract be by way of manual labour, clerical work, or otherwise, be express or implied, oral or in writing, and whether it be a contract of service or of apprenticeship or a contract personally to execute any work or labour.

(7) Any reference in Schedule 3 to this Act to—

(*a*) such restrictions as are described in section 6(1) above, or

PART II

(*b*) such information provisions as are described in section 7(1) above,

shall be construed, in relation to any agreement, as not including references to restrictions or information provisions of which, by virtue of any provision of this section, account cannot be taken in determining whether the agreement is one to which this Act applies by virtue of this Part, or of restrictions accepted or information provisions made by any term of which account cannot be so taken.

Presumption under Part II as to the public interest.

10.—(1) For the purposes of any proceedings before the Court under Part I of this Act, a restriction accepted or information provision made in pursuance of an agreement to which this Act applies by virtue of this Part shall be deemed to be contrary to the public interest unless the Court is satisfied of any one or more of the following circumstances—

(*a*) that the restriction or information provision is reasonably necessary, having regard to the character of the goods to which it applies, to protect the public against injury (whether to persons or to premises) in connection with the consumption, installation or use of those goods;

(*b*) that the removal of the restriction or information provision would deny to the public as purchasers, consumers or users of any goods other specific and substantial benefits or advantages enjoyed or likely to be enjoyed by them as such, whether by virtue of the restriction or information provision itself or of any arrangements or operations resulting therefrom;

(*c*) that the restriction or information provision is reasonably necessary to counteract measures taken by any one person not party to the agreement with a view to preventing or restricting competition in or in relation to the trade or business in which the persons party thereto are engaged;

(*d*) that the restriction or information provision is reasonably necessary to enable the persons party to the agreement to negotiate fair terms for the supply of goods to, or the acquisition of goods from, any one person not party thereto who controls a preponderant part of the trade or business of acquiring or supplying such goods, or for the supply of goods to any person not party to the agreement and not carrying on such a trade or business who, either alone or in combination with any other such person, controls a preponderant part of the market for such goods;

(*e*) that, having regard to the conditions actually obtaining or reasonably foreseen at the time of the application, the removal of the restriction or information provision would be likely to have a serious and persistent adverse effect on the general level of unemployment in an area, or in areas taken together, in which a substantial proportion of the trade or industry to which the agreement relates is situated ;

(*f*) that, having regard to the conditions actually obtaining or reasonably foreseen at the time of the application, the removal of the restriction or information provision would be likely to cause a reduction in the volume or earnings of the export business which is substantial either in relation to the whole export business of the United Kingdom or in relation to the whole business (including export business) of the said trade or industry ;

(*g*) that the restriction or information provision is reasonably required for purposes connected with the maintenance of any other restriction accepted or information provision made by the parties, whether under the same agreement or under any other agreement between them, being a restriction or information provision which is found by the Court not to be contrary to the public interest upon grounds other than those specified in this paragraph, or has been so found in previous proceedings before the Court ; or

(*h*) that the restriction or information provision does not directly or indirectly restrict or discourage competition to any material degree in any relevant trade or industry and is not likely to do so ;

and is further satisfied (in any such case) that the restriction or information provision is not unreasonable having regard to the balance between those circumstances and any detriment to the public or to persons not parties to the agreement (being purchasers, consumers or users of goods produced or sold by such parties, or persons engaged or seeking to become engaged in the trade or business of selling such goods or of producing or selling similar goods) resulting or likely to result from the operation of the restriction or the information provision.

(2) In this section—

(*a*) " purchasers ", " consumers " and " users " include persons purchasing, consuming or using for the purpose or in the course of trade or business or for public purposes ; and

(*b*) references to any one person include references to any two or more persons being interconnected bodies corporate or individuals carrying on business in partnership with each other.

PART III

SERVICES

Restrictive agreements as to services.

11.—(1) The Secretary of State may by statutory instrument make an order in respect of a class of services described in the order (in this Act referred to, in relation to an order under this section, as "services brought under control by the order") and direct by the order that this Act shall apply to agreements (whenever made) which—

(*a*) are agreements between two or more persons carrying on business within the United Kingdom in the supply of services brought under control by the order, or between two or more such persons together with one or more other parties; and

(*b*) are agreements under which restrictions, in respect of matters specified in the order for the purposes of this paragraph, are accepted by two or more parties.

(2) The matters which may be specified in such an order for the purposes of subsection (1)(*b*) above are any of the following—

(*a*) the charges to be made, quoted or paid for designated services supplied, offered or obtained;

(*b*) the terms or conditions on or subject to which designated services are to be supplied or obtained;

(*c*) the extent (if any) to which, or the scale (if any) on which, designated services are to be made available, supplied or obtained;

(*d*) the form or manner in which designated services are to be made available, supplied or obtained;

(*e*) the persons or classes of persons for whom or from whom, or the areas or places in or from which, designated services are to be made available or supplied or are to be obtained.

Information agreements as to services.

12.—(1) The Secretary of State may by statutory instrument make an order in respect of a class of services described in the order (in this Act referred to, in relation to an order under this section, as "services brought under control by the order") and direct by the order that this Act shall apply to agreements (whenever made) which—

(*a*) are agreements between two or more persons carrying on business within the United Kingdom in the supply of services brought under control by the order, or between two or more such persons together with one or more other parties; and

(*b*) are agreements under which provision is made for or in relation to the furnishing by two or more parties to

PART III

each other or to other persons (whether parties or not) of information with respect to matters specified in the order for the purposes of this paragraph.

(2) The matters which may be specified in such an order for the purposes of subsection (1)(*b*) above are any of the following—

(*a*) the charges made, quoted or paid or to be made, quoted or paid for designated services which have been or are to be supplied, offered or obtained;

(*b*) the terms or conditions on or subject to which designated services have been or are to be supplied or obtained;

(*c*) the extent (if any) to which, or the scale (if any) on which, designated services have been or are to be made available, supplied or obtained;

(*d*) the form or manner in which designated services have been or are to be made available, supplied or obtained;

(*e*) the costs incurred or to be incurred in making available, supplying or obtaining designated services;

(*f*) the persons or classes of persons for whom or from whom, or the areas or places in or from which, designated services have been or are to be made available or supplied or have been or are to be obtained.

Designated services.

13.—(1) In relation to any order made under section 11 or section 12 above, " designated services " in this Act means services of any class described in the order as being designated services.

(2) Subject to subsection (3) below, a class of services described in any such order as being designated services may consist wholly or partly of services brought under control by the order or wholly or partly of other services, and may be described so as to consist—

(*a*) of services of one or more descriptions specified in that behalf in the order, or

(*b*) of all services except services of one or more descriptions so specified,

and different classes of services may be so described in relation to different matters specified in the order for the purposes of section 11(1)(*b*) or section 12(1)(*b*) above, as the case may be.

(3) A class of services described in such an order as being designated services shall not include any of the services specified in Schedule 1 to this Act.

PART III

Supplementary provisions as to orders under Part III.

14.—(1) A class of services described in an order under section 11 or section 12 above as being the services brought under control by the order may consist—

(*a*) of services of one or more descriptions specified in that behalf in the order; or

(*b*) of all services except services of one or more descriptions so specified; or

(*c*) of all services without exception.

(2) An order under section 11 or section 12 may limit the operation of the order to agreements fulfilling such conditions (in addition to those mentioned in section 11 or section 12, as the case may be) as may be specified in the order.

(3) In particular, but without prejudice to the generality of subsection (2) above, an order under section 12 may limit the operation of the order to agreements under which the provision for the furnishing of information (as mentioned in subsection (1)(*b*) of that section) is provision of a kind specified in the order or provides for the furnishing of information of a kind so specified.

(4) Subject to subsection (2) above—

(*a*) for the purposes of any order under section 11 it is immaterial whether any restrictions accepted by parties to an agreement relate to the same or to different matters specified in the order for the purposes of subsection (1)(*b*) of that section, or have the same or a different effect in relation to any matter so specified, and

(*b*) for the purposes of any order under section 12 it is immaterial whether any information provision made by an agreement relates to the same or to different matters specified in the order for the purposes of subsection (1)(*b*) of that section,

and it is immaterial for those purposes whether the parties accepting any restrictions, or the parties by whom any information is to be furnished, as the case may be, carry on the same class or different classes of business.

(5) Where, at a time when an order under section 11 or section 12 (in this subsection referred to as " the earlier order ") is in force, another order (in this subsection referred to as " the subsequent order ") is made under the same section, the subsequent order may provide that—

(*a*) for the purposes of the earlier order; or

(*b*) for the purposes of the subsequent order; or

(*c*) for the purposes of both orders;

the condition specified in section 11(1)(*a*) or in section 12(1)(*a*).

as the case may be, shall be treated as fufilled in relation to an agreement if it is an agreement to which the parties are or include one person carrying on business in the United Kingdom in the supply of services brought under control by the earlier order and one person carrying on business within the United Kingdom in the supply of services brought under control by the subsequent order.

This subsection has effect without prejudice to any power to vary any order made under section 11 or section 12.

(6) In the following provisions of this Part of this Act " the relevant provisions ", in relation to an order under section 11 or section 12 above, means the provisions of this Act as they have effect in relation to that order.

Procedure as to orders under Part III.

15.—(1) No order shall be made under section 11 or section 12 above unless a draft of the order has been laid before Parliament and approved by a resolution of each House of Parliament.

(2) Before laying before Parliament a draft of any such order, the Secretary of State shall publish in such manner as he thinks appropriate a notice—

(*a*) describing the classes of services which, if the order is made, will be services brought under control by the order and will be designated services in relation to the order respectively;

(*b*) indicating the nature of any limitation to be imposed by the order under section 14(2) or (3) above; and

(*c*) specifying a period (not being less than 28 days) within which representations with respect to the proposed order may be made to the Secretary of State.

(3) In settling the draft to be laid before Parliament the Secretary of State shall take into consideration any representations with respect to the proposed order which may be received by him within the period specified in the notice in accordance with subsection (2)(*c*) above.

Services supply associations.

16.—(1) For the purposes of any order made under section 11 or section 12 above, and for the purposes of the relevant provisions, subsections (2) to (6) below have effect in relation to any association (whether incorporated or not) if—

(*a*) its membership consists wholly or mainly of persons (in this subsection referred to as " members affected by the order ") who are either engaged in the supply of services brought under control by the order or are employed by or represent persons so engaged; and

PART III

(*b*) its objects or activities include the promotion of the interests of persons engaged in the supply of those services who are either members affected by the order or are persons represented by such members.

(2) The relevant provisions have effect in relation to any agreement made by an association described in subsection (1) above (" services supply association ")—

(*a*) as if the agreement were made between all persons who are members of the associaton or are represented on it by members of the association, and

(*b*) where any restriction is accepted under the agreement by the association, or any information provision is made in the agreement by the association, as if the like restriction were accepted by, or (as the case may be) the like provision were made by, each of the persons who are members of the association or are so represented.

(3) In the case of an order under section 11, where—

(*a*) specific recommendations (whether express or implied) are made by or on behalf of the association to its members, or to any class of its members, and

(*b*) those recommendations are as to the action to be taken or not to be taken by them in relation to any particular class of services in respect of any matters specified in the order for the purposes of subsection (1)(*b*) of that section,

the relevant provisions have effect in relation to the agreement for the constitution of the association (notwithstanding any provision in the agreement to the contrary) as if that agreement contained the term mentioned in subsection (4) below.

(4) The term referred to in subsection (3) above is one by which each such member, and any person represented on the association by any such member, agrees to comply with those recommendations and with any subsequent recommendations made to them by or on behalf of the association as to the action to be taken by them in relation to the same class of services and in respect of the same matters.

(5) In the case of an order under section 12 above, where—

(*a*) specific recommendations (whether express or implied) are made by or on behalf of the association to its members, or to any class of its members, and

(*b*) those recommendations are as to the furnishing of information in relation to any particular class of services in respect of any matters specified in the order for the purposes of subsection (1)(*b*) of that section, the relevant provisions have effect in relation to the agreement for the constitution of the association (notwithstanding any provision in the agreement to the contrary) as if that agreement contained the term mentioned in subsection (6) below.

(6) The term referred to in subsection (5) above is one by which each such member, and any person represented on the association by any such member, agrees to comply with those recommendations and with any subsequent recommendations made to them by or on behalf of the association as to the furnishing of information in relation to the same class of services and in respect of the same matters.

Matters equivalent to restrictions for purposes of s. 11.

17.—(1) For the purposes of any order made under section 11 above, and for the purposes of the relevant provisions, an agreement which—

(*a*) any designated services are made available or supplied comply with conditions as to any such matters as are mentioned in subsection (2) of that section ; or

(*b*) imposes obligations upon parties who do not comply with such conditions ;

shall be treated as an agreement under which restrictions are accepted by each of the parties in respect of those matters.

(2) Without prejudice to subsection (1) above, an obligation on the part of any party to an agreement to make payments calculated by reference to the extent to which, or the scale on which—

(*a*) any designated services are made available or supplied by him ; or

(*b*) any services are obtained by him for the purpose of making available or supplying any designated services ;

if the payments are calculated, or calculated at an increased rate, in respect of an extent or scale exceeding an extent or scale specified in or ascertained in accordance with the agreement, shall be treated for the purposes mentioned in subsection (1) as a restriction in respect of the extent or scale of the designated services to be made available or supplied.

This subsection does not apply to any obligation on the part of any person to make payments to a services supply association of which he is a member, if the payments are to consist only of bona fide subscriptions for membership of the association.

Provisions to be disregarded under Part III.

18.—(1) The following provisions of this section have effect for the purpose of determining whether an agreement is one to which this Act applies by virtue of an order under section 11 or section 12 above.

PART III

(2) Subject to subsections (3) and (4) below, no account shall for that purpose be taken of any term which relates exclusively to the services supplied in pursuance of the agreement in question.

(3) Where—

(*a*) the order referred to in subsection (1) above is an order under section 11, and

(*b*) any of the restrictions accepted as mentioned in subsection (1)(*b*) of that section are accepted as between two or more persons by whom, or two or more persons for whom, designated services are to be supplied in pursuance of the agreement,

subsection (2) above does not apply to any term of the agreement which imposes those restrictions unless they are accepted in pursuance of a previous agreement in respect of which particulars have been registered under this Act by virtue of this Part.

(4) Where—

(*a*) the order referred to in subsection (1) is an order under section 12, and

(*b*) the term referred to in subsection (2) is one by which provision is made for the furnishing of information as mentioned in subsection (1)(*b*) of that section by two or more persons by whom, or two or more persons for whom, designated services are to be supplied in pursuance of the agreement,

subsection (2) does not apply to that term unless it is included in the agreement in pursuance of a previous agreement of which particulars have been registered under this Act by virtue of this Part.

(5) For the purpose mentioned in subsection (1) no account shall be taken of any term by which the parties or any of them agree to comply with or apply, in respect of making available, supplying or obtaining any designated services—

(*a*) any standards (whether being standards of performance in the provision of the services or standards of dimension, design, quality or performance in respect of goods used in providing them) which are either standards approved for the time being by the British Standards Institution or standards prescribed or adopted by an association or other body and for the time being approved by an order made by the Secretary of State by statutory instrument ; or

(*b*) any arrangements either approved by the British Standards Institution, or prescribed or adopted and approved by an order of the Secretary of State, as mentioned in the preceding paragraph, as to the provision of information or advice to persons for whom designated services are supplied or agreed to be supplied. PART III

(6) For the purpose mentioned in subsection (1) no account shall be taken of any restriction which affects or relates to any of the matters mentioned in section 9(6) above (which relates to employment and to terms and conditions of employment) or of any information provision with respect to any of those matters.

(7) Any reference in Schedule 3 to this Act—

(*a*) to restrictions accepted in respect of matters specified in an order under section 11 for the purposes of subsection (1)(*b*) of that section ; or

(*b*) to information provisions made with respect to matters specified in an order under section 12 for the purposes of subsection (1)(*b*) of that section ;

shall be construed, in relation to any agreement, as not including anything of which, by virtue of this section, account cannot be taken for the purpose mentioned in subsection (1).

Presumption under Part III as to the public interest.

19.—(1) For the purposes of any proceedings before the Court under Part I of this Act, a restriction accepted or information provision made in pursuance of an agreement to which this Act applies by virtue of this Part shall be deemed to be contrary to the public interest unless the Court is satisfied of any one or more of the following circumstances—

(*a*) that the restriction or information provision is reasonably necessary having regard to the character of the services to which it applies, to protect the public against injury (whether to persons or to premises) in connection with the use of those services or in connection with the consumption, installation or use of goods in relation to which those services are supplied ;

(*b*) that the removal of the restriction or information provision would deny to the public as users of any services, or as purchasers, consumers or users of any goods in relation to which any services are supplied, other specific and substantial benefits or advantages enjoyed or likely to be enjoyed by them as such, whether by virtue of the restriction or information provision itself or of any arrangements or operations resulting therefrom ;

(*c*) that the restriction or information provision is reasonably necessary to counteract measures taken by any one person not party to the agreement with a view to preventing or restricting competition in or in relation to the trade or business in which the person party thereto are engaged ;

(*d*) that the restriction or information provision is reasonably necessary to enable the persons party to the

PART III

agreement to negotiate fair terms for the supply of services to, or for obtaining services from, any one person not party thereto who controls a preponderant part of the trade or business of supplying such services, or for the supply of services to any person not party to the agreement and not carrying on such a trade or business who, either alone or in combination with any other such person, controls a preponderant part of the market for such services;

(*e*) that, having regard to the conditions actually obtaining or reasonably foreseen at the time of the application, the removal of the restriction or information provision would be likely to have a serious and persistent adverse effect on the general level of unemployment in an area, or in areas taken together, in which a substantial proportion of the trade or industry to which the agreement relates is situated;

(*f*) that, having regard to the conditions actually obtaining or reasonably foreseen at the time of the application, the removal of the restriction or information provision would be likely to cause a reduction in the volume or earnings of the export business which is substantial either in relation to the whole export business of the United Kingdom or in relation to the whole business (including export business) of the said trade or industry;

(*g*) that the restriction or information provision is reasonably required for purposes connected with the maintenance of any other restriction accepted or information provision made by the parties, whether under the same agreement or under any other agreement between them, being a restriction or information provision which is found by the Court not to be contrary to the public interest upon grounds other than those specified in this paragraph, or has been so found in previous proceedings before the Court; or

(*h*) that the restriction or information provision does not directly or indirectly restrict or discourage competition to any material degree in any relevant trade or industry and is not likely to do so;

and is further satisfied (in any such case) that the restriction or information provision is not unreasonable having regard to the balance between those circumstances and any detriment to the public or to persons not parties to the agreement (being users of services supplied by such parties, or persons engaged or seeking to become engaged in any business of supplying such services or of making available or supplying similar services, or being purchasers, consumers or users of goods in relation to which any such services or similar services are supplied) resulting or likely to result from the operation of the restriction or information provision.

(2) In this section—

(*a*) " purchasers ", " consumers " and " users " include persons purchasing, consuming or using for the purpose or in the course of trade or business or for public purposes ; and

(*b*) references to any one person include references to any two or more persons being interconnected bodies corporate or individuals carrying on business in partnership with each other.

Interpretation of Part III.

20. In this Part of this Act—

" business " includes a professional practice ;

" the relevant provisions " has the meaning given by section 14(6) above ;

" scale " (where the reference is to the scale on which any services are, or are to be, made available, supplied or obtained) means scale measured in terms of money or money's worth or in any other manner ;

" services "—

(*a*) does not include the application to goods of any process of manufacture or any services rendered to an employer under a contract of employment (that is, a contract of service or of apprenticeship, whether it is express or implied, and, if it is express, whether it is oral or in writing), but, with those exceptions,

(*b*) includes engagements (whether professional or other) which for gain or reward are undertaken and performed for any matter other than the production or supply of goods,

and any reference to the supply of services or to supplying, obtaining or offering services or to making services available shall be construed accordingly.

PART IV

GENERAL

Proceedings

Director's duties as to proceedings for investigation.

21.—(1) The Director may refrain from taking proceedings before the Court—

(*a*) in respect of an agreement if and for so long as he thinks it appropriate so to do having regard to the

PART IV

operation of any directly applicable Community provision and to the purpose and effect of any authorisation or exemption granted in relation to such a provision;

(*b*) where an agreement—

(i) of which particulars are entered or filed in the register pursuant to this Act has been determined (whether by effluxion of time or otherwise); or

(ii) has been so determined in respect of all restrictions accepted or information provisions made under that agreement.

(2) If it appears to the Secretary of State, upon the Director's representation, that the restrictions accepted or information provisions made under an agreement of which particulars are so entered or filed are not of such significance as to call for investigation by the Court, the Secretary of State may give directions discharging the Director from taking proceedings in the Court in respect of that agreement during the continuance in force of the directions.

(3) The Secretary of State may at any time upon the Director's representation withdraw any directions given by him under subsection (2) above if satisfied that there has been a material change of circumstances since the directions were given.

Rules of procedure. 1976 c. 33.

22.—(1) Without prejudice to the generality of section 9(1) of the Restrictive Practices Court Act 1976, rules made under that subsection may provide—

(*a*) for enabling a single application to be made to the Court in respect of a number of related agreements, or separate applications made in respect of related agreements to be heard together;

(*b*) for enabling the Court to determine in a summary way any issue arising in relation to an agreement where it appears to the Court that the relevant provisions of the agreement and the circumstances of the case are substantially similar to the provisions and circumstances considered, in relation to any other agreement, in any previous proceedings before the Court;

(*c*) for enabling the Court to make an order for the payment by any party to proceedings under sections 1, 2 and 4 above of costs in respect of proceedings in which he is guilty of unreasonable delay, or in respect of any improper, vexatious, prolix or unnecessary proceedings or any other unreasonable conduct on his part.

(2) The Court—

(*a*) does not have power to order the payment of costs by any party to proceedings under sections 1, 2 and

PART IV

4 above except so far as may be provided by rules made in pursuance of subsection (1)(*c*) above; but

(*b*) without prejudice to section 9(3) of the Restrictive Practices Court Act 1976, the Court has power in exercise of its jurisdiction under sections 26, 35 and 37 below to order the payment of costs by any party to proceedings before the Court. 1976 c. 33.

Registration

General provisions as to the register.

23.—(1) The register for the purposes of this Act shall be kept by the Director—

(*a*) at such premises within the United Kingdom; and

(*b*) in such form;

as he may determine.

(2) The Director shall cause notice of—

(*a*) any declaration made under section 1(3) above;

(*b*) any order made under section 2 above;

to be entered in the register.

(3) Regulations made under section 27 below shall provide for the maintenance of a special section of the register, and for the entry or filing in that section of such particulars as the Secretary of State may direct, being—

(*a*) particulars containing information the publication of which would in the Secretary of State's opinion be contrary to the public interest;

(*b*) particulars containing information as to any secret process of manufacture (or, in relation to Part III of this Act, any secret process) or as to the presence, absence or situation of any mineral or other deposits or as to any other similar matter, being information the publication of which in the Secretary of State's opinion would substantially damage the legitimate business interests of any person.

(4) The register, other than the special section, shall be open to public inspection during such hours and subject to payment of such fee as may be prescribed by regulations made under section 27.

(5) Any person may, upon payment of such fee as may be prescribed by regulations made under section 27, require the Director to supply to him a copy of or extract from any particulars entered or filed in the register, other than the special section, certified by the Director to be a true copy or extract.

(6) No process for compelling the production of the register or of any other document kept by the Director shall issue from

PART IV

any court except with the leave of the court, and any such process if issued shall bear a statement that it is issued with the leave of the court.

(7) A copy of or extract from any document entered or filed in the register, certified under the hand of the Director or an officer authorised to act on his behalf (whose official position it shall not be necessary to prove), shall in all legal proceedings be admissible in evidence as of equal validity with the original.

Particulars and time for registration.

24.—(1) In respect of every agreement which is subject to registration under this Act the following particulars shall be furnished to the Director—

(*a*) the names and addresses of the persons who are parties to the agreement ; and

(*b*) the whole of the terms of the agreement, whether or not relating to any such restriction or information provision as is described in this Act.

(2) The additional provisions contained in Schedule 2 to this Act have effect as to the particulars to be furnished in respect of—

(*a*) an agreement which is subject to registration under this Act ; and

(*b*) the variation or determination of such an agreement ;

and such particulars shall in the cases specified in the first column of the Table in paragraph 5(1) of that Schedule be furnished within the time specified in the second column of that Table.

(3) In relation to an agreement to which this Act—

(*a*) has effect by virtue of section 8 above as if it were an agreement between members of a trade association, or persons represented on the trade association by such members ;

(*b*) has effect by virtue of section 16 above as if it were an agreement between members of a services supply association, or persons represented on the services supply association by such members ;

references in this section and Schedule 2 to the parties to the agreement include references to those members or persons, and in relation to an agreement in which a term is implied by virtue of section 8(2) or (4) above, or section 16(3) or (5) above, as the case may be, the reference in this section to the terms of the agreement includes a reference to that term, and references in this section and Schedule 2 to an agreement shall be construed accordingly. PART IV

Particulars of export agreements.

25. Section 24 above has effect in relation to an agreement which is or becomes one to which this Act would apply but for—

(*a*) paragraph 6(1) of Schedule 3 to this Act, where the agreement relates to exports from the United Kingdom, or

(*b*) paragraph 9(1) of that Schedule,

as if that agreement were subject to registration under this Act.

Court's power to rectify the register, etc.

26.—(1) The Court may, on the application of any person aggrieved, order the register to be rectified by the variation or removal of particulars included in the register in respect of any agreement.

(2) The Court may, on the application of—

(*a*) any person party to an agreement; or

(*b*) the Director, in respect of an agreement of which particulars have been furnished to him under this Act;

declare whether or not the agreement is one to which this Act applies, and if so whether or not it is subject to registration under this Act.

(3) Where application is made under subsection (2) above by a party to an agreement before the expiry of the time within which, if the agreement is subject to registration under this Act, particulars are required to be furnished under section 24 above, then—

(*a*) if particulars of the agreement have not been so furnished before the commencement of the proceedings, that time shall be extended by a time equal to the time during which the proceedings and any appeal therein are pending, and such further time, if any, as the Court may direct; and

(*b*) if particulars have been so furnished, the Director shall not enter or file particulars of the agreement in the register during the time during which the proceedings and any appeal therein are pending.

PART IV

(4) Notice of an application to the Court under this section shall be served, in accordance with rules of court—

(*a*) in the case of an application by a person other than the Director, on the Director;

(*b*) in the case of an application by the Director, on the parties to the agreement or such of them as may be prescribed or determined by or under the rules;

and a party on whom notice is so served shall be entitled, in accordance with such rules, to appear and be heard on the application.

Regulations for registration.

27.—(1) Subject to the provisions of this Act, the Director may make regulations for the purposes of registration under this Act and for purposes connected therewith, and in particular, but without prejudice to the generality of the foregoing provision—

(*a*) for requiring that—

(i) in respect of an agreement he is furnished with information as to any steps taken, or decision given, under or for the purpose of any directly applicable Community provision affecting the agreement; and

(ii) the information so given or such part, if any of it, as may be provided by the regulations is included in the particulars to be entered or filed in the register under section 1(2)(*b*) above;

(*b*) for regulating the procedure to be followed in connection with the furnishing of particulars, information and documents under section 24 above and section 36 below;

(*c*) for excluding from the particulars to be furnished or from the particulars to be entered in the register under this Act—

(i) such details as to parties or other persons, prices (or, in relation to Part III of this Act, charges) terms or other matters as are material for the purpose only of defining the particular application of continuing restrictions accepted or information provisions made under agreements of which particulars are so entered;

(ii) particulars of such variations as may be specified in the regulations, being variations the registration of which is in the Director's opinion unnecessary for the purposes of this Act;

(*d*) for prescribing the form of any notice, certificate or other document to be given, made or furnished under the provisions of this Act;

PART IV

(e) for regulating the inspection of the register or of any document kept by the Director;

(f) for prescribing anything authorised or required by this Act to be prescribed by regulations made under this section.

(2) Nothing in regulations made by virtue of subsection (1)(c) above shall affect the Director's power under section 36(3) to require the furnishing of further documents or information by any such person as is mentioned in section 36(3).

(3) Any regulations made under this section prescribing a fee for inspection of the register or for the supply of copies of or extracts from particulars entered or filed in the register, shall be made with the approval of the Treasury.

(4) The Director's power to make regulations under this section is exercisable by statutory instrument, and the Statutory Instruments Act 1946 shall apply to such regulations as it applies to regulations made by a Minister of the Crown within the meaning of that Act. 1946 c. 36.

Exemptions

Excepted agreements.

28. This Act does not apply to the agreements described in Schedule 3 to this Act.

Agreements important to the national economy.

29.—(1) If it appears to the Secretary of State, on consideration of an agreement proposed to be made by any parties, that the conditions set out in subsection (2) below are complied with in respect of the proposed agreement, he may, by order made on or before the conclusion of the agreement, approve the agreement for the purposes of this section; and any agreement so approved shall be exempt from registration under this Act during the continuance in force of the order.

(2) The conditions for the making of an order under subsection (1) above in respect of an agreement (in this section referred to as the conditions of exemption) are—

(a) that the agreement is calculated to promote the carrying out of an industrial or commercial project or scheme of substantial importance to the national economy;

(b) that its object or main object is to promote efficiency in a trade or industry or to create or improve productive capacity in an industry;

(c) that the object cannot be achieved or achieved within a reasonable time except by means of the agreement or of an agreement for similar purposes;

PART IV

(*d*) that no restrictions are accepted or information provisions made under the agreement other than such as are reasonably necessary to achieve that object; and

(*e*) that the agreement is on balance expedient in the national interest.

(3) In considering the national interest for the purposes of subsection (2)(*e*) above the Secretary of State shall take into account any effects which an agreement is likely to have on persons not parties thereto as purchasers, consumers or users of any relevant goods or, in relation to an agreement to which this Act applies by virtue of an order under section 11 or section 12 above, as users of any relevant services.

(4) An order under this section shall continue in force for such period as may be specified therein, which may be extended by subsequent order of the Secretary of State: but the period so specified or extended shall not exceed the period which appears to the Secretary of State sufficient for the purposes for which the order was made.

(5) An order under this section approving an agreement may be revoked by order of the Secretary of State at any time after the expiry of one year from the day on which the first-mentioned order was made if it appears to him—

(*a*) that the object or main object of the agreement has not been or is not likely to be achieved, or that any other condition or exemption is no longer satisfied in respect of the agreement; or

(*b*) that the agreement is used for purposes other than those for which it was approved;

and may be so revoked at any time if the Secretary of State becomes aware of circumstances by reason of which, if known to him at the material time, the agreement would not have been approved.

The Secretary of State shall not make an order by virtue of paragraph (*a*) or paragraph (*b*) of this subsection unless he has given to each of the parties at least 28 days' notice of his intention to make the order.

(6) The Secretary of State shall—

(*a*) lay before each House of Parliament a copy of any order made under this section and of the agreement to which the order relates; and

(*b*) make available for public inspection a copy of any such agreement.

(7) Subsection (6) above shall not apply—

(*a*) to an agreement which varies an agreement previously approved under this section; or

(*b*) to an order approving such an agreement;

if in the Secretary of State's opinion the variation does not substantially affect the operation of restrictions accepted or information provisions made under the agreement previously approved.

Agreements holding down prices.

30.—(1) A competent authority may by order approve for the purposes of this section any agreement made at the request of the competent authority, or any term included at their request in any agreement, being an agreement or term which relates exclusively—

(*a*) to the prices to be charged in connection with transactions of any description and is designed either to prevent or restrict increases or to secure reductions in those prices; or

(*b*) in relation to an agreement to which this Act applies by virtue of an order under section 11 or section 12 above, to the charges to be made in connection with transactions of any description and is designed either to prevent or restrict increases or to secure reductions in those charges.

(2) Where an agreement is approved by order under this section, the agreement shall be exempt from registration under this Act during the continuance in force of the order; and where a term of an agreement is so approved, that term, and any restrictions accepted or information provisions made thereunder, shall during the continuance in force of the order be disregarded for all purposes in determining whether this Act applies to the agreement.

(3) An order under this section shall continue in force for such period as may be specified therein, which may be extended by subsequent order of the competent authority: but the period so specified shall not exceed two years, and shall not be extended by more than two years at a time.

(4) An order under this section may at any time be revoked by order of the competent authority if it appears to that authority that the relevant agreement or term is used for purposes other than those for which it was approved.

(5) A competent authority shall make available for public inspection a copy of any agreement or term of an agreement approved by order under this section.

PART IV

(6) The competent authorities for the purposes of this section are the Secretary of State, and the Minister of Agriculture, Fisheries and Food.

Supplementary provisions for ss. 29 and 30.

31.—(1) Sections 29 and 30 above apply, with the necessary modifications, in relation to any recommendation made by or on behalf of a trade association or a services supply association as they apply in relation to an agreement; and where any such recommendation is approved by order under either of those sections—

(*a*) subsection (2) or subsection (4) of section 8 above;

(*b*) subsection (3) or subsection (5) of section 16 above;

shall not apply in relation to the recommendation during the continuance in force of the order.

(2) In the case of an order under section 29 approving a recommendation by or on behalf of a trade association or of a services supply association, as the case may be—

(*a*) the requirement of subsection (5) of that section as to the giving of notice of intention to revoke the order shall be treated as a requirement to give such notice as is there mentioned to the association; and

(*b*) any notice under that subsection which is required to be given to a trade association or to a services supply association or to each of the members of such an association shall be treated as duly so given if it is given either—

(i) to the association; or

(ii) to the secretary, manager or other similar officer of the association.

(3) An order under section 29 or section 30 made before the conclusion of the agreement or issue of the recommendation to which it relates may be made subject to conditions—

(*a*) as to the time within which the agreement is to be concluded or the recommendation issued; and

(*b*) as to the furnishing of copies of the agreement or recommendation to the Secretary of State or other competent authority.

(4) There may be omitted from the copies of any agreement, term of an agreement or recommendation to be laid before Parliament under section 29, and to be made available for public inspection under that section or section 30, the particulars mentioned in subsection (5) below.

PART IV

(5) The particulars referred to in subsection (4) above are such as would, in the opinion of the Secretary of State or other competent authority, fall to be entered in the special section of the register referred to in section 23(3) above if the relevant agreement were subject to registration under this Act.

(6) If any agreement, term of an agreement or recommendation approved by order under secton 29 or section 30 is subsequently varied, the order shall cease to have effect unless the variation is also approved by order under section 29 or section 30, as the case may be ; and a variation may be so approved if (and only if) the agreement, term or recommendation could be so approved as varied.

(7) The approval by order under section 29 or section 30 of an agreement or recommendation made by or on behalf of a trade association or a services supply association shall not be affected by any change in the persons who are members of the association or are represented on the association by such members, but without prejudice to the power of the Secretary of State or other competent authority to revoke the order under section 29 or section 30.

(8) No order made by the Court in proceedings under this Act for restraining any person from making an agreement or recommendation, and no corresponding undertaking given to the Court in such proceedings, shall be construed as extending to an agreement or recommendation which is exempt from registration by virtue of an order under section 29 or section 30.

(9) In any proceedings before the Court under sections 1 and 2 above in respect of an agreement, the fact that the agreement has or has not at any time been the subject of an order under section 29 or section 30 shall not be treated as relevant to the question whether any restrictions accepted or information provisions made under the agreement are contrary to the public interest.

Wholesale co-operative societies.

32.—(1) The Secretary of State may approve under this section any industrial and provident society which in his opinion fulfils the following conditions—

(*a*) that it carries on business in the production or supply of goods or in the supply of services or in the application to goods of any process of manufacture ;

(*b*) that its shares are wholly or mainly held by industrial and provident societies ; and

(*c*) that those societies are retail societies or societies whose shares are wholly or mainly held by retail societies ;

and a society which is for the time being so approved shall not be treated as a trade association or a services supply association.

PART IV

(2) An approval given in respect of a society under this section (if it has not been previously withdrawn) expires at the end of the period of two years beginning with the date on which it was given or, if that period is extended (once or more than once) under subsection (3) below, at the end of that period as so extended, or further extended, as the case may be.

(3) The Secretary of State may extend or, if it has already been extended under this subsection, may further extend the period of two years referred to in subsection (2) above by such period, not exceeding two years, as he may specify.

(4) The Secretary of State may at any time withdraw an approval given in respect of a society under this section if it appears to him—

(*a*) that the society has made an agreement which would have been subject to registration under this Act if the approval had not been given, or that such a recommendation as is mentioned in section 8(2) or (4) above has been made by or on behalf of the society ; and

(*b*) that the agreement or recommendation has such adverse effects on competition that it should not be precluded from being investigated by the Court under the provisions of this Act.

(5) In relation to a society which is for the time being approved under this section but which, in consequence of an order made under section 11 or section 12 above, is a society to which the provisions of section 16 above would apply if it were not so approved, subsection (4) above has effect as if in that subsection—

(*a*) any reference to an agreement which would have been subject to registration under this Act if the approval had not been given included a reference to an agreement which would in those circumstances have been subject to such registration by virtue of the order ; and

(*b*) any reference to such a recommendation as is mentioned in section 8(2) or (4) included a reference to such a recommendation as is mentioned in section 16(3) or (5).

(6) On the expiry or withdrawal of an approval given in respect of a society under this section, the provisions of this Act shall have effect in relation to agreements and recommendations made by the society during the currency of the approval as if the society had not been approved under this section.

(7) In this section—

" industrial and provident society " means a society registered or deemed to be registered under the Indus-

PART IV

trial and Provident Societies Acts 1965 to 1975 or under the Industrial and Provident Societies Act (Northern Ireland) 1969 ; 1969 c. 24 (N.I.).

"retail society" means a society which carries on business in the sale by retail of goods for the domestic or personal use of individuals dealing with the society, or in the provision of services for such individuals.

Agricultural and forestry associations, and fisheries associations.

33.—(1) Subject to the provisions of this section, this Act does not apply to an agreement between members of an association to which this section applies, or between such an association and any other person, whether a member of the association or not, by reason only of any restriction accepted or treated as accepted, or any information provision made or treated as made, by the association, or by members of the association or of any constituent association, for the purposes of or in connection with—

(*a*) the marketing or preparation for market by the association of produce produced by members of the association on land occcupied by them and used for agriculture or forestry (with or without similar produce not so produced) ; or

(*b*) the marketing or preparation for market by the association of fish or shellfish caught or taken by members of the association in the course of their business (with or without fish or shellfish not so caught or taken) ; or

(*c*) the supply by the association to the members of goods required for the production of that produce on that land, or for the catching or taking of fish or shellfish in the course of that business, as the case may be ; or

(*d*) the production of produce or the catching or taking of fish or shellfish, as the case may be, by members of the association ; or

(*e*) the supply of produce, or the supply of fish or shellfish, as the case may be, by members of the association ;

and in determining whether any such agreement is an agreement to which this Act applies, no account shall be taken of any such restriction or information provision.

(2) This section applies—

(*a*) to any association in the case of which the conditions specified in subsection (3) below are satisfied where the association is—

(i) of persons occupying land used for agriculture or forestry or both ;

(ii) of persons engaged in the business of catching or taking fish or shellfish ;

PART IV

(*b*) to any association of the associations referred to in paragraph (*a*) above which—

(i) satisfies the condition specified in paragraph (*a*) of subsection (3) below; and

(ii) would satisfy the condition specified in paragraph (*c*) of subsection (3) if references in that paragraph to members of the association included references to members of constituent associations;

(*c*) to any co-operative association (whether or not the conditions specified in paragraphs (*a*) to (*c*) of subsection (3) are satisfied) which has as its object or primary object to assist its members—

(i) in the carrying on of the businesses of agriculture or forestry or both on land occupied by them; or

(ii) in the carrying on of businesses consisting in the catching or taking of fish or shellfish.

(3) The conditions referred to in subsection (2) above are that—

(*a*) the association is or is deemed to be registered under the Industrial and Provident Societies Acts 1965 to 1975 or, being a company within the meaning of the
1948 c. 38. Companies Act 1948, contains in its memorandum or articles of association such provisions as may be prescribed by order of the Ministers with respect to the number of members, numbers of shares held by members, distribution of profits, voting rights or other matters;

(*b*) at least 90 per cent. of the voting power is attached to shares held by persons occupying land used for agriculture or forestry or both, or by persons engaged in the business of catching or taking fish or shellfish, as the case may be; and

(*c*) the only business, or the principal business, carried on by the association is one or more of the following—

(i) the marketing or preparation for market of produce produced by members of the association on land occupied by them and used for agriculture or forestry or both (with or without similar produce not so produced);

(ii) the marketing or preparation for market of fish or shellfish caught or taken by members of the association in the course of their business (with or without fish or shellfish not so caught or taken);

(iii) the supply to the members of goods required for the production of that produce on that land, or for the catching or taking of fish or shellfish in the course of that business, as the case may be; PART IV

(iv) in the case of an association of persons occupying land for forestry, the carrying out of forestry operations for the members on that land.

References in this subsection to the Industrial and Provident Societies Acts 1965 to 1975, and the Companies Act 1948, include references respectively to the Industrial and Provident Societies Act (Northern Ireland) 1969 and the Companies Act (Northern Ireland) 1960. 1948 c. 38. 1969 c. 24 (N.I.). 1960 c. 22 (N.I.).

(4) The Ministers may by order made by statutory instrument direct that the exemption provided by subsection (1) shall not apply—

(*a*) in relation to agreements of such classes as may be prescribed by the order ; or

(*b*) in relation to agreements, or agreements of any class, made by associations of such classes as may be so prescribed ;

and any such order may apply to agreements made before as well as after the coming into force of the order.

(5) In this section—

" agriculture " has the meaning given by the Agriculture Act 1947 and the Agriculture (Scotland) Act 1948 ; 1947 c. 48. 1948 c. 45.

" co-operative association " has the meaning given by section 340(8) and (9) of the Income and Corporation Taxes Act 1970, and references to members of a co-operative association include references to members of any such association which is a member of that association ; 1970 c. 10.

" forestry " includes the processing of wood for sale, but not the manufacture of articles of wood ;

" the Ministers " means—

(*a*) the Minister of Agriculture, Fisheries and Food and the Secretaries of State respectively concerned with agriculture in Scotland and Northern Ireland, acting jointly ; but

(*b*) in the case of functions exercisable in relation to associations falling within paragraph (*c*) of subsection (2) above and concerned only with forestry in Wales " Secretary of State " shall be substituted for " Minister of Agriculture, Fisheries and Food " ;

" produce " means anything (whether live or dead) produced in the course of agriculture or forestry.

(6) Without prejudice to the responsibilities of the Secretaries of State respectively concerned with agriculture in Scotland and

PART IV

Northern Ireland, the discharge of any functions as functions exercisable by virtue of subsection (5) above by the Secretary of State shall belong to the Secretary of State for Wales; but nothing in this subsection shall be taken—

(*a*) to prejudice any powers exercisable in relation to the functions of Ministers of the Crown and government departments by virtue of Her Majesty's prerogative, or

(*b*) to affect the power of any Secretary of State to perform any functions of that office in place of the Secretary of State entrusted with the discharge of those functions.

Authorisations for purposes of E.C.S.C. Treaty.

34. An agreement is exempt from registration under this Act so long as there is in force in relation to that agreement an authorisation given for the purpose of any provision of the E.C.S.C. Treaty relating to restrictive trade practices.

Enforcement

Failure to register.

35.—(1) If particulars of an agreement which is subject to registration under this Act are not duly furnished within the time required by section 24 above, or within such further time as the Director may, upon application made within that time, allow—

(*a*) the agreement is void in respect of all restrictions accepted or information provisions made thereunder; and

(*b*) it is unlawful for any person party to the agreement who carries on business within the United Kingdom to give effect to, or enforce or purport to enforce, the agreement in respect of any such restrictions or information provisions.

(2) No criminal proceedings lie against any person on account of a contravention of subsection (1)(*b*) above; but the obligation to comply with that paragraph is a duty owed to any person who may be affected by a contravention of it and any breach of that duty is actionable accordingly subject to the defences and other incidents applying to actions for breach of statutory duty.

(3) Without prejudice to any right which any person may have by virtue of subsection (2) above to bring civil proceedings in respect of an agreement affected by subsection (1)(*b*), the Court may, upon the Director's application, make such order as appears to the Court to be proper for restraining all or any of those mentioned in subsection (4) below from giving effect to, or enforcing or purporting to enforce—

(*a*) the agreement in respect of any restrictions or information provisions;

(*b*) other agreements in contravention of subsection (1) above;

and nothing in subsection (2) prevents the enforcement of any such order by appropriate proceedings.

(4) Those who may be restrained by an order of the Court under subsection (3) above are—

(*a*) any person party to the agreement who carries on business within the United Kingdom;

(*b*) a trade association or a services supply association of which any such person is a member; or

(*c*) any person acting on behalf of any such association.

(5) Where an order is made under subsection (3) against any party to an agreement and that party is a member of a trade association or a services supply association, the order may include provisions for restraining the association, and any person acting on its behalf, from procuring or assisting that party to do anything which would be a contravention of the order in its application to him.

(6) In relation to an agreement for the constitution of a trade association or a services supply association which is subject to registration in consequence of the making of a recommendation to which—

(*a*) subsection (2) or subsection (4) of section 8 above;

(*b*) subsection (3) or subsection (5) of section 16 above;

applies, the Court's power under subsection (3) includes power to make such order as appears to the Court to be proper for restraining the association or any person acting on its behalf from making other such recommendations

(7) Where any issue, whether of law or of fact or partly of law and partly of fact, has been finally determined on an application under subsection (3) above in respect of an agreement, then in any proceedings brought in respect of that agreement by virtue of subsection (2) above in which the same issue arises—

(*a*) any finding of fact relevant to that issue which was made on the application shall be evidence (and in Scotland sufficient evidence) of that fact; and

(*b*) any decision on a question of law relevant to that issue which was given on the application shall be binding on the court in so far as the material facts found in those proceedings are the same as were found on the application.

(8) Where an agreement which is subject to registration under this Act is varied so as to extend or add to the restrictions

PART IV

accepted or information provisions made under the agreement, the provisions of this section apply, with the necessary modifications, in relation to the variation as they apply in relation to an original agreement which is subject to registration under this Act.

Director's power to obtain information.

36.—(1) If the Director has reasonable cause to believe that a person being—

(*a*) a person carrying on within the United Kingdom any such business as is described in section 6(1) above; or

(*b*) a trade association, the members of which consist of or include persons carrying on business as so described, or representatives of such persons; or

(*c*) a person carrying on within the United Kingdom any business of supplying services brought under control by an order under section 11 or section 12 above; or

(*d*) an association which, in relation to such an order, is a services supply association;

is or may be party to an agreement subject to registration under this Act, he may give to that person such notice as is described in subsection (2) below.

(2) The notice referred to in subsection (1) above may require any person mentioned in paragraphs (*a*) to (*d*) of that subsection to notify the Director (within such time as may be specified in the notice) whether that person is party to any agreement relating to—

(*a*) any such matters as are described in paragraphs (*a*) to (*f*) of section 6(1); or

(*b*) any such matters as are described in paragraphs (*a*) to (*h*) of section 7(1) above; or

(*c*) matters specified in the relevant order for the purposes of section 11(1)(*b*) above; or

(*d*) matters specified in the relevant order for the purposes of section 12(1)(*b*) above;

and if so to furnish to the Director such particulars of the agreement as may be specified in the notice.

(3) The Director may give notice to any person by whom particulars are furnished under section 24 above in respect of an agreement, or to any other person being party to the agreement, requiring him to furnish such further documents or information in his possession or control as the Director considers expedient for the purposes of or in connection with the registration of the agreement.

(4) In the case of—

(*a*) any such trade association as is mentioned in subsection (1)(*b*) above ; or

(*b*) any such services supply association as is mentioned in subsection (1)(*d*) above ;

a notice may be given under subsection (1) by the Director either to the association or to the secretary, manager or other similar officer of the association.

For the purposes of this section any such trade association or services supply association shall be treated as party to any agreement to which members of the association, or persons represented on the association by such members, are parties as such.

(5) In subsection (1) the reference to an agreement subject to registration under this Act shall, in relation to Part II, be construed as including a reference to any agreement which—

(*a*) relates to exports from the United Kingdom ; and

(*b*) would, but for paragraph 6(1) of Schedule 3 to this Act, be an agreement subject to registration under this Act.

(6) In subsection (1) the reference to an agreement subject to registration under this Act shall, in relation to Part III, be construed as including a reference to any agreement which would, but for paragraph 9(1) of Schedule 3, be an agreement subject to registration under this Act.

Court's power to order examination on oath.

37.—(1) In any case in which the Director has given notice to any person under section 36 above the Court may on the Director's application order that person to attend and be examined on oath in accordance with this section concerning the matters in respect of which the Director has given notice to him under that section.

(2) Where an order is made under this section for the attendance and examination of any person—

(*a*) the Director shall take part in the examination and for that purpose may be represented by solicitor or counsel ;

(*b*) the person examined shall answer all such questions as the Court may put or allow to be put to him, but may at his own cost employ a solicitor with or without counsel, who shall be at liberty to put to him such questions as the Court may deem just for the purpose of enabling him to explain or qualify any answers given by him ;

(*c*) notes of the examination shall be taken down in writing and shall be read over to or by, and signed by, the

PART IV

person examined, and may thereafter be used in evidence against him;

(*d*) the Court may require the person examined to produce any such particulars, documents or information in his possession or control as may be specified in the notice given by the Director as aforesaid.

(3) Where notice under section 36 has been given to a body corporate, an order may be made under this section for the attendance and examination—

(*a*) of any director, manager, secretary or other officer of that body corporate; or

(*b*) of any other person who is employed by the body corporate and appears to the Court to be likely to have particular knowledge of any of the matters in respect of which the notice was given.

(4) In any case referred to in subsection (3) above—

(*a*) the reference in subsection (1) above to matters in respect of which the Director has given notice to the person examined shall be construed as a reference to matters in respect of which notice was given to the body corporate; and

(*b*) in paragraph (*d*) of subsection (2) above and in paragraph (*c*) so far as it relates to evidence, references to the person examined shall include references to the body corporate.

(5) The provisions of subsections (3) and (4) above have effect—

(*a*) in relation to a trade association which is not incorporated;

(*b*) in relation to a services supply association which is not incorporated;

as those provisions have effect in relation to a body corporate.

(6) Nothing in this section shall be taken to compel the disclosure by a barrister, advocate or solicitor of any privileged communication made by or to him in that capacity, or the production by him of any document containing any such communication.

Offences in connection with registration.

38.—(1) A person who fails without reasonable excuse to comply with a notice duly given to him under section 36 above is guilty of an offence and liable on summary conviction to a fine not exceeding £100.

(2) If a person who furnishes or is required to furnish any particulars, documents or information under this Act— PART IV

(*a*) makes any statement, or furnishes any document, which he knows to be false in a material particular; or

(*b*) recklessly makes any statement, or furnishes any document, which is false in a material particular; or

(*c*) wilfully alters, suppresses or destroys any document which he is required to furnish as aforesaid;

he is guilty of an offence under this section.

(3) A person guilty of an offence mentioned in subsection (2) above is liable—

(*a*) on summary conviction to imprisonment for a term not exceeding three months or to a fine not exceeding £100, or to both such imprisonment and such a fine; or

(*b*) on conviction on indictment to imprisonment for a term not exceeding two years or to a fine, or to both such imprisonment and a fine.

(4) If any default in respect of which a person is convicted of an offence under subsection (1) above continues after the conviction, that person is guilty of a further offence and liable on summary conviction to a fine—

(*a*) not exceeding £100; or

(*b*) not exceeding £10 for every day on which the default continues within the three months next following his conviction for the first-mentioned offence;

whichever is the greater.

(5) For the purposes of subsection (4) above a default in respect of the furnishing of any particulars, documents or information shall be deemed to continue until the particulars, documents or information have been furnished.

(6) Where an offence under this section committed by a body corporate is proved to have been committed with the consent or connivance of, or to be attributable to any neglect on the part of, any director, manager, secretary or other similar officer of the body corporate or any person who was purporting to act in any such capacity, he as well as the body corporate is guilty of that offence and liable to be proceeded against and punished accordingly.

(7) In this section " director ", in relation to a body corporate established by or under any enactment for the purpose of carrying on under national ownership any industry or part of an industry or undertaking, being a body corporate whose affairs are managed by its members, means a member of that body corporate.

PART IV

Proceedings and venue in respect of offences.

39.—(1) No proceedings for an offence under the preceding provisions of this Act shall be instituted—

(*a*) in England and Wales except by or with the consent of the Director of Public Prosecutions or the Director;

(*b*) in Northern Ireland except by or with the consent of the Attorney General for Northern Ireland or the Director.

(2) Any information relating to an offence under the preceding provisions of this Act may be tried by a magistrates' court or by a court of summary jurisdiction in Northern Ireland, if it is laid at any time—

(*a*) within three years after the commission of the offence; and

(*b*) within twelve months after the date on which evidence sufficient in the opinion of the Director of Public Prosecutions, the Attorney General for Northern Ireland or the Director, as the case may be, to justify the proceedings comes to his knowledge;

1952 c. 55. 1964 c. 21 (N.I.).

notwithstanding anything in section 104 of the Magistrates' Courts Act 1952 or in section 34 of the Magistrates' Courts Act (Northern Ireland) 1964.

(3) Proceedings in Scotland for an offence against the preceding provisions of this Act may be commenced at any time—

(*a*) within three years after the commission of the offence; and

(*b*) within twelve months after the date on which evidence sufficient in the Director's opinion to justify a report to the Lord Advocate with a view to consideration of the question of proceedings comes to the Director's knowledge;

1954 c. 48.

notwithstanding anything in section 23 of the Summary Jurisdiction (Scotland) Act 1954.

(4) For the purposes of subsections (2) and (3) above, a certificate of the Director of Public Prosecutions, the Attorney General for Northern Ireland or the Director, as the case may be, as to the date on which such evidence as aforesaid came to his knowledge shall be conclusive evidence.

(5) An offence under section 38 above may be tried by a court having jurisdiction either in the county or place in which the offence was actually committed or in any county or place in which the alleged offender carries on business.

S.I. 1972/538 (N.I. 1).

(6) For the purposes of article 7(2) of the Prosecution of Offences (Northern Ireland) Order 1972 (which relates to consents to prosecutions by the Director of Public Prosecutions for

Northern Ireland) subsections (1) and (2) above shall be treated as if they were in force before the coming into operation of that order.

PART V

MISCELLANEOUS AND SUPPLEMENTAL

Order under s. 56 of Fair Trading Act 1973.

40.—(1) The Court may, upon application made by any person who desires to make an agreement—

(*a*) which, if made, would be an agreement to which this Act applies, and

(*b*) is one the making of which is unlawful by virtue of any order in force under section 56 of the Fair Trading Act 1973 or having effect as if made under that section, 1973 c. 41.

declare whether or not any restrictions or information provisions by virtue of which this Act would apply to the agreement (not being such restrictions or information provisions as are described in paragraphs (*b*) to (*d*) of paragraph 6(1) of Schedule 3 to this Act) are contrary to the public interest.

(2) The provisions of section 2(1) to (4) above apply with the necessary modifications in relation to any such declaration as they apply in relation to a finding under that section.

(3) Where an application is made to the Court under subsection (1) above and—

(*a*) on that application the Court makes a declaration under that subsection in relation to a restriction proposed to be accepted or an information provision proposed to be made under an agreement, and

(*b*) by virtue of an order under section 56 of the 1973 Act which is for the time being in force, the making or carrying out of an agreement under which that restriction was accepted or that information provision was made would be unlawful,

the order under section 56 of the 1973 Act shall cease to have effect in so far as it renders unlawful the making or carrying out of an agreement under which that restriction is accepted or that information provision is made.

(4) The Director shall be the respondent to any application made under this section; and the provisions of section 10 or section 19 above apply with the necessary modifications in relation to proceedings on any such application as they apply in relation to the proceedings mentioned in that section.

PART V

Disclosure of information.

41.—(1) Subject to subsection (2) below, no information with respect to any particular business which has been obtained under or by virtue of the provisions of this Act shall, so long as that business continues to be carried on, be disclosed without the consent of the person for the time being carrying on that business; but this subsection does not apply to any disclosure of information which is made—

(*a*) for the purpose of facilitating the performance of any functions of the Director, the Monopolies and Mergers Commission, the Secretary of State or any other Minister under this Act or the Fair Trading Act 1973;

1973 c. 41.

(*b*) in pursuance of a Community obligation;

(*c*) for the purposes of any proceedings before the Court or of any other legal proceedings, whether civil or criminal, under this Act or the Fair Trading Act 1973.

(2) Nothing in subsection (1) above shall be construed—

(*a*) as limiting the particulars which may be entered or filed in, or made public as part of, the register under this Act; or

(*b*) as applying to any information which has been made public as part of that register.

(3) Any person who discloses any information in contravention of this section is guilty of an offence and liable—

(*a*) on summary conviction, to a fine not exceeding £400;

(*b*) on conviction on indictment, to imprisonment for a term not exceeding two years or to a fine or to both.

(4) No prosecution for an offence under this section shall be commenced after the expiry of three years from the commission of the offence or one year from its discovery by the prosecutor, whichever is the earlier.

1952 c. 55.

(5) Notwithstanding anything in section 104 of the Magistrates' Courts Act 1952, a magistrates' court may try an information for an offence under this section if the information was laid within twelve months from the commission of the offence.

1954 c. 48.

(6) Notwithstanding anything in section 23 of the Summary Jurisdiction (Scotland) Act 1954, summary proceedings in Scotland for an offence under this section may be commenced within twelve months from the commission of the offence, and subsection (2) of the said section 23 applies for the purposes of this subsection as it applies for the purposes of that section.

(7) In the application of this section to Northern Ireland, for the references in subsection (5) above to section 104 of the

PART V

Magistrates' Courts Act 1952 and to the trial and laying of an information there shall be substituted respectively references to section 34 of the Magistrates' Courts Act (Northern Ireland) 1964 and to the hearing and determination and making of a complaint. 1952 c. 55. 1964 c. 21 (N.I.).

Orders and regulations.

42.—(1) Any statutory instrument by which—

(*a*) an order is made under section 18(5) or section 33(4) above ; or

(*b*) regulations are made under section 27(1) above ;

is subject to annulment in pursuance of a resolution of either House of Parliament.

(2) Any power conferred by a preceding provision of this Act to make an order by statutory instrument includes power to revoke or vary that order by a subsequent order made under that provision.

Interpretation and construction.

43.—(1) In this Act—

" agreement " includes any agreement or arrangement, whether or not it is or is intended to be enforceable (apart from any provision of this Act) by legal proceedings, and references in this Act to restrictions accepted or information provisions made under an agreement shall be construed accordingly;

" the Court " means the Restrictive Practices Court ;

" designated services " has the meaning given by section 13(1) above ;

" the Director " means the Director General of Fair Trading appointed under the Fair Trading Act 1973 ; 1973 c. 41.

" goods " includes ships and aircraft, minerals, substances and animals (including fish), and references to the production of goods include references to the getting of minerals and the taking of such animals ;

" information provision " includes a provision for or in relation to the furnishing of information ;

" interconnected bodies corporate " means bodies corporate which are members of the same group, and for the purposes of this definition " group " means a body corporate and all other bodies corporate which are its subsidiaries—

(*a*) within the meaning of section 154 of the Companies Act 1948 (or for companies in Northern Ireland, section 148 of the Companies Act (Northern Ireland) 1960) ; or 1948 c. 38. 1960 c. 22 (N.I.).

(*b*) in the case of an industrial and provident society, within the meaning of section 15 of the Friendly and Industrial and Provident Societies Act 1968 c. 55.

PART V

1968 (or for industrial and provident societies in Northern Ireland, section 47 of the Industrial and Provident Societies Act (Northern Ireland) 1969);

1969 c. 24 (N.I.).

" price " includes a charge of any description;

" restriction " includes a negative obligation, whether express or implied and whether absolute or not;

" services supply association " means such an association as is described in section 16(1) above;

" supply " includes supply by way of lease or hire, and " acquire " shall be construed accordingly;

" trade association " means a body of persons (whether incorporated or not) which is formed for the purpose of furthering the trade interests of its members, or of persons represented by its members.

(2) For the purposes of—

(*a*) sections 6 to 9 above, and Schedule 3 to this Act except for paragraph 5(4) to (8) of that Schedule;

(*b*) Part III of this Act except as is provided by section 19(2) above;

any two or more interconnected bodies corporate, or any two or more individuals carrying on business in partnership with each other, shall be treated as a single person.

(3) This Act applies to the construction or carrying out of buildings, structures and other works by contractors, as it applies to the supply of goods, and for the purposes of this Act any buildings, structures or other works so constructed or carried out shall be deemed to be delivered at the place where they are constructed or carried out.

(4) For the purposes of this Act a person shall not be deemed to carry on a business within the United Kingdom by reason only of the fact that he is represented for the purposes of that business by an agent within the United Kingdom.

(5) Any reference in this Act to any other enactment is a reference to that enactment as amended, or extended or applied by or under any other enactment, including this Act.

Consequential amendments, repeals and transitional provisions.

44. The provisions of Schedule 4 to this Act have effect; and subject to the transitional provisions and savings contained in that Schedule—

(*a*) the enactments specified in Schedule 5 to this Act have effect subject to the amendments (being amendments consequent on the provisions of this Act) specified in that Schedule, and (*b*) the enactments specified in Schedule 6 to this Act are hereby repealed to the extent specified in the third column of that Schedule, PART V

but nothing in this Act shall be taken as prejudicing the operation of section 38 of the Interpretation Act 1889 (which relates to the operation of repeals). 1889 c. 63.

45.—(1) This Act may be cited as the Restrictive Trade Practices Act 1976. Short title, extent and commencement.

(2) This Act extends to Northern Ireland.

(3) This Act shall come into operation on such day as the Secretary of State may by order made by statutory instrument appoint.

SCHEDULES

Section 13.

SCHEDULE 1

SERVICES EXCLUDED FROM SECTION 13 (DESIGNATED SERVICES)

1. Legal services (that is to say, the services of barristers, advocates or solicitors in their capacity as such).

2. Medical services (that is to say, the provision of medical or surgical advice or attendance and the performance of surgical operations).

1957 c. 28.

3. Dental services (that is to say, any services falling within the practice of dentistry within the meaning of the Dentists Act 1957).

4. Ophthalmic services (that is to say, the testing of sight).

1966 c. 36.

5. Veterinary services (that is to say, any services which constitute veterinary surgery within the meaning of the Veterinary Surgeons Act 1966).

1957 c. 15.
1951 c. 55.
1970 c. 11 (N.I.).

6. Nursing services (that is to say, any services which constitute nursing within the meaning of the Nurses Act 1957, the Nurses (Scotland) Act 1951 or the Nurses and Midwives Act (Northern Ireland) 1970).

7. The services of midwives, physiotherapists or chiropodists in their capacity as such.

8. The services of architects in their capacity as such.

9. Accounting and auditing services (that is to say, the making or preparation of accounts or accounting records and the examination, verification and auditing of financial statements).

1949 c. 87.

10. The services of patent agents (within the meaning of the Patents Act 1949), in their capacity as such.

11. The services of parliamentary agents entered in the register in either House of Parliament as agents entitled to practise both in promoting and in opposing Bills, in their capacity as such parliamentary agents.

12. The services of surveyors (that is to say, of surveyors of land, of quantity surveyors, of surveyors of buildings or other structures and of surveyors of ships) in their capacity as such surveyors.

13. The services of professional engineers or technologists (that is to say, of persons practising or employed as consultants in the field of—

(*a*) civil engineering ;

(*b*) mechanical, aeronautical, marine, electrical or electronic engineering ;

(*c*) mining, quarrying. soil analysis or other forms of mineralogy or geology ;

(*d*) agronomy, forestry, livestock rearing or ecology ;

(*e*) metallurgy, chemistry, biochemistry or physics ; or

SCH. 1

(*f*) any other form of engineering or technology analogous to those mentioned in the preceding sub-paragraphs) ;

in their capacity as such engineers or technologists.

14. Services consisting of the provision—

(*a*) of primary, secondary or further education within the meaning of the Education Act 1944, the Education (Scotland) Acts 1939 to 1971 or the Education and Libraries (Northern Ireland) Order 1972, or 1944 c. 31. 1972/1263 (N.I. 12).

(*b*) of university or other higher education not falling within the preceding sub-paragraph.

15. The services of ministers of religion in their capacity as such ministers.

SCHEDULE 2

Section 24.

FURNISHING OF PARTICULARS OF AGREEMENTS

1.—(1) Subject to paragraph 2 below, the duty to furnish particulars in respect of an agreement which at any time is subject to registration shall not be affected by any subsequent variation or determination of the agreement.

(2) If at any time after an agreement has become subject to registration it is varied (whether in respect of the parties or in respect of the terms) or determined otherwise than by effluxion of time, particulars of the variation or determination shall be furnished to the Director.

2.—(1) The following provisions of this paragraph apply where an agreement becomes subject to registration after it is made.

(2) If, before the expiry of the time within which, apart from this paragraph, particulars would be required to be furnished in respect of the agreement, and before particulars have been so furnished, the agreement is determined (whether by effluxion of time or otherwise), section 24(1) above and paragraph 1 above shall cease to apply to the agreement.

(3) If, before the expiry of that time and before particulars have been furnished in respect of the agreement, the agreement is varied, the particulars to be furnished under section 24 shall be particulars of the agreement as varied, and paragraph 1 above shall not apply in relation to the variation.

3. Particulars of an agreement shall—

(*a*) in so far as the agreement, or any variation or determination of it, is made by an instrument in writing, be furnished by the production of the original or a true copy of the instrument ;

(*b*) in so far as the agreement, or any variation or determination of it, is not made by an instrument in writing, be furnished by the production of a memorandum in writing signed by the person by whom the particulars are furnished.

SCH. 2

4.—(1) Particulars may be furnished by or on behalf of any person who is party to the agreement or, as the case may be, was party thereto immediately before its determination.

(2) Where such particulars are duly furnished by or on behalf of any such person the provisions of section 24 and this Schedule shall be deemed to be complied with on the part of all such persons.

5.—(1) The following Table shows the time within which particulars of agreements and any variation or determination of an agreement, are to be furnished under section 24 and this Schedule:—

TABLE

Description of agreement	*Time for registering particulars*
(*a*) Agreement made on or after 25th November 1968, other than an agreement to which (*b*) to (*j*) below apply.	Before the date on which any restriction accepted or information provision made under the agreement takes effect, and in any case within 3 months from the day on which the agreement is made.
(*b*) Agreement approved by order under section 29 or section 30 above which becomes subject to registration by virtue of the expiry or revocation of that order.	Within 1 month from the day on which the agreement becomes so subject.
(*c*) Agreement which becomes subject to registration by virtue of the revocation of an order under section 9(5) above.	Within 1 month from the day on which the agreement becomes so subject.
(*d*) Agreement which becomes subject to registration by virtue of an order under section 7 above coming into force after the making of the agreement.	Within 3 months from the day on which the agreement becomes so subject.
(*e*) Agreement which becomes subject to registration by virtue of an order under section 11 or section 12 above coming into force after the making of the agreement.	Within 3 months from the day on which the agreement becomes so subject.
(*f*) Agreement whether made before on or after 25th November 1968 which becomes subject to registration by virtue of a variation on or after that date.	Within the time which would apply under (*a*) above if the agreement were made on the day on which it becomes so subject.
(*g*) Agreement which becomes subject to registration by virtue of the expiry or withdrawal of an approval given under section 32 above.	Within 3 months from the day on which the agreement becomes so subject.

SCH. 2

Description of agreement	*Time for registering particulars*
(*h*) Agreement which was subject to registration on 25th November 1968, of which particulars had not been duly furnished.	Within 3 months from 25th November 1968.
(*i*) Variation on or after 25th November 1968 of an agreement (whether made before or after that date) being a variation which extends or adds to the restrictions accepted or information provisions made under the agreement.	Within the time which would apply under (*a*) above in the case of an agreement made on the day of the variation.
(*j*) Any other variation of an agreement, and the determination of an agreement.	Within 3 months from the day of the variation or determination.

(2) Any reference in the second column of the Table in this paragraph to a period calculated from a specified day is a reference to the period in question inclusive of that day.

SCHEDULE 3

Section 28.

EXCEPTED AGREEMENTS

Agreements for statutory purposes

1.—(1) This Act does not apply to an agreement which is expressly authorised by an enactment, or by any scheme, order or other instrument made under an enactment.

(2) This Act does not apply to an agreement which constitutes or forms part of a scheme certified by the Secretary of State under Chapter V of Part XIV of the Income and Corporation Taxes Act 1970 (which relates to schemes for rationalising industry). 1970 c. 10.

(3) Sub-paragraphs (1) and (2) above have effect in relation to any agreement notwithstanding any order under section 11 or section 12 above.

Exclusive dealing

2. This Act does not apply to an agreement for the supply of goods between two persons, neither of whom is a trade association, being an agreement to which no other person is party and under which no such restrictions as are described in section 6(1) above are accepted or no such information provisions as are described in section 7(1) above are made other than restrictions accepted or provision made for the furnishing of information—

(*a*) by the party supplying the goods, in respect of the supply of goods of the same description to other persons ; or

(*b*) by the party acquiring the goods, in respect of the sale, or acquisition for sale, of other goods of the same description.

SCH. 3

Know-how about goods

3. This Act does not apply to an agreement between two persons (neither of whom is a trade association) for the exchange of information relating to the operation of processes of manufacture (whether patented or not) where—

(*a*) no other person is party to the agreement ; and

(*b*) no such restrictions as are described in section 6(1) above are accepted or no such information provisions as are described in section 7(1) above are made under the agreement except in respect of the descriptions of goods to be produced by those processes or to which those processes are to be applied.

Trade marks

4.—(1) This Act does not apply to an agreement made in accordance with regulations approved by the Secretary of State under section 37 of the Trade Marks Act 1938 (which makes provision as to certification trade marks) authorising the use of such a trade mark, being an agreement under which no such restrictions as are described in section 6(1) above are accepted or no such information provisions as are described in section 7(1) above are made other than restrictions or information provisions permitted by those regulations.

1938 c. 22.

(2) This Act does not apply to an agreement—

(*a*) between the registered proprietor of a trade mark (other than a certification trade mark) and a person authorised by the agreement to use the mark subject to registration as a registered user under section 28 of the Trade Marks Act 1938 (which makes provision as to registered users) ; and

(*b*) under which no such restrictions as are described in section 6(1) are accepted or no such information provisions as are described in section 7(1) are made except in respect of—

(i) the descriptions of goods bearing the mark which are to be produced or supplied ; or

(ii) the processes of manufacture to be applied to such goods or to goods to which the mark is to be applied.

Patents and registered designs

5.—(1) Subject to sub-paragraphs (4) to (8) below, this Act does not apply—

(*a*) to a licence granted by the proprietor or a licensee of a patent or registered design, or by a person who has applied for a patent or for the registration of a design ;

(*b*) to an assignment of a patent or registered design, or of the right to apply for a patent or for the registration of a design ; or

(*c*) to an agreement for such a licence or assignment ;

being a licence, assignment or agreement such as is described in sub-paragraph (2) or sub-paragraph (3) below.

(2) The licence, assignment or agreement referred to in sub-paragraph (1) above is in relation to Part II of this Act one under which no such restrictions as are described in section 6(1) above are accepted or no such information provisions as are described in section 7(1) above are made except in respect of—

(*a*) the invention to which the patent or application for a patent relates, or articles made by the use of that invention ; or

(*b*) articles in respect of which the design is or is proposed to be registered and to which it is applied ;

as the case may be.

(3) The licence, assignment or agreement referred to in sub-paragraph (1) above is in relation to Part III of this Act one under which—

(*a*) in the case of an order under section 11 above, no restrictions in respect of matters specified in the order for the purposes of subsection (1)(*b*) of that section are accepted except in respect of the invention to which the patent or application for a patent relates ; or

(*b*) in the case of an order under section 12 above, no information provision with respect to matters specified in the order for the purposes of subsection (1)(*b*) of that section is made except in respect of that invention.

(4) No licence, assignment or agreement is by virtue of sub-paragraph (1) above precluded from being an agreement to which this Act applies if—

(*a*) it is a patent or design pooling agreement ; or

(*b*) it is a licence, assignment or agreement granted or made in pursuance (directly or indirectly) of a patent or design pooling agreement.

(5) In this paragraph, subject to sub-paragraph (8) below, " patent or design pooling agreement " means an agreement—

(*a*) to which the parties are or include at least three persons (in this and the following sub-paragraph the " principal parties ") each of whom has an interest in one or more patents or registered designs, and

(*b*) by which each of the principal parties agrees, in respect of patents or registered designs in which he has an interest, or in respect of patents or registered designs in which he has or may during the currency of the agreement acquire an interest, to grant such an interest as is mentioned in sub-paragraph (6) below.

(6) The grant referred to in sub-paragraph (5) above is—

(*a*) of an interest in one or more such patents or registered designs to one or more of the other principal parties, or to one or more of those parties and to other persons ; or

(*b*) of an interest in at least one such patent or registered design to a third person for the purpose of enabling that person to grant an interest in it to one or more of the other

SCH. 3

principal parties, or to one or more of those parties and to other persons ;

and " interest ", in relation to a patent or registered design, means an interest as proprietor or licensee of the patent or registered design or an interest consisting of such rights as a person has by virtue of having applied for a patent or for the registration of a design or by virtue of having acquired the right to apply for a patent or for the registration of a design.

(7) For the purposes of sub-paragraphs (4) to (6) above, a licence, assignment or agreement—

(*a*) shall be taken to be granted or made directly in pursuance of a patent or design pooling agreement if it is granted or made in pursuance of provisions of that agreement such as are mentioned in sub-paragraph (6)(*a*) ; and

(*b*) shall be taken to be granted or made indirectly in pursuance of a patent or design pooling agreement if it is granted or made by a third person to whom an interest has been granted in pursuance of provisions of that agreement such as are mentioned in sub-paragraph (6)(*b*).

(8) In relation to any interest held by or granted to any two or more persons jointly, sub-paragraphs (5) and (6) apply as if those persons were one person by whom the interest is held or to whom it is granted, and accordingly those persons shall be treated for the purposes of those sub-paragraphs as together constituting one party.

(9) In this paragraph, references—

(*a*) to an assignment mean, in relation to Scotland, an assignation ;

(*b*) to the registration of designs have effect only in relation to Part II.

Agreements as to goods with overseas operation

6.—(1) This Act does not apply to an agreement in the case of which all such restrictions as are described in section 6(1) above, or all such information provisions as are described in section 7(1) above, relate exclusively—

(*a*) to the supply of goods by export from the United Kingdom ;

(*b*) to the production of goods, or the application of any process of manufacture to goods, outside the United Kingdom ;

(*c*) to the acquisition of goods to be delivered outside the United Kingdom and not imported into the United Kingdom for entry for home use ; or

(*d*) to the supply of goods to be delivered outside the United Kingdom otherwise than by export from the United Kingdom ;

and subsections (2) and (4) of section 8 above do not apply in relation to recommendations relating exclusively to those matters.

(2) The Court's jurisdiction mentioned in section 1(3) above does not extend to restrictions or to information provisions in respect of

matters described in paragraphs (*b*) to (*d*) of sub-paragraph (1) above. SCH. 3

Exclusive supply of services

7. This Act does not apply to an agreement to which there are no parties other than one person who agrees to supply services and another person for whom they are to be supplied, where neither of those persons is, in relation to any order under Part III of this Act, a services supply association and, except in respect of the supply of services of the same description to, or obtaining services of the same description from, other persons—

(*a*) in the case of an order under section 11 above, no restrictions are accepted under the agreement by those parties in respect of matters specified in the order for the purposes of subsection (1)(*b*) of that section ; or

(*b*) in the case of an order under section 12 above, no information provision is made under the agreement with respect to matters specified in the order for the purposes of subsection (1)(*b*) of that section.

Know-how about services

8. This Act does not apply to an agreement between two persons (neither of whom is a services supply association) for the exchange of information relating to techniques or processes to be applied in the provision of designated services where—

(*a*) no other person is party to the agreement ; and

(*b*) all such restrictions as are mentioned in section 11(1)(*b*) above which are accepted under the agreement relate exclusively to the form or manner in which services incorporating those techniques or processes are to be made available or supplied.

Agreements for supplying services with overseas operation

9.—(1) This Act does not apply to an agreement where—

(*a*) in the case of an order under section 11 above, all such restrictions as are accepted under the agreement in respect of matters specified in the order for the purposes of subsection (1)(*b*) of that section (or, in a case falling within section 16(3) above, all the recommendations referred to in that subsection) relate to the supply of services outside the United Kingdom or to the supply of services to persons or in relation to property (of any description, whether movable or immovable) outside the United Kingdom ; or

(*b*) in the case of an order under section 12 above, all such provision as is made under the agreement for or in relation to the furnishing of information with respect to matters specified in the order for the purposes of subsection (1)(*b*) of that section (or, in a case falling within section 16(5), every such recommendation as is referred to in that subsection) relates to the supply of services as mentioned in paragraph (*a*) above.

SCH. 3

(2) The Court's jurisdiction mentioned in section 1(3) above does not extend to restrictions or to information provisions—

(*a*) in respect of the supply of services outside the United Kingdom ; or

(*b*) in respect of the supply of services to persons or in relation to property (of any description, whether movable or immovable) outside the United Kingdom.

Section 44.

SCHEDULE 4

TRANSITIONAL PROVISIONS AND SAVINGS

General provisions

1.—(1) In so far as anything done under an enactment repealed by this Act could have been done under a corresponding provision of this Act it shall not be invalidated by the repeal but shall have effect as if done under that provision.

(2) Without prejudice to sub-paragraph (1) above, any reference in this Act (whether express or implied) to a thing done or required or authorised to be done, or omitted to be done, or to an event which has occurred, under or for the purposes of or by reference to or in contravention of any provisions of this Act shall, except where the context otherwise requires, be construed as including a reference to the corresponding thing done or required or authorised to be done, or omitted, or to the corresponding event which occurred, as the case may be, under or for the purposes of or by reference to or in contravention of any corresponding provisions of the repealed enactments.

2. Where a document refers expressly or by implication to an enactment repealed by this Act the reference shall (except where the context otherwise requires) be construed as a reference to the corresponding provision of this Act.

3. Where any period of time specified in an enactment repealed by this Act is current at the commencement of this Act, and there is a corresponding provision in this Act, this Act shall have effect as if that corresponding provision had been in force when that period began to run.

Insignificant agreements under the Restrictive Trade Practices Act 1956, *s.* 12.

1956 c. 68.

4.—(1) Directions under section 12 of the Restrictive Trade Practices Act 1956 in force at the commencement of this Act for the removal from the register of particulars of such agreements as appeared to be of no substantial economic significance continue to have effect by virtue of this paragraph.

(2) Sub-paragraph (1) above does not affect the operation in relation to the agreement of paragraph 1 of Schedule 2 to this Act ;

and where any such agreement is varied as mentioned in that paragraph— **Sch. 4**

(*a*) the particulars to be furnished thereunder shall include all such particulars as would be required in the case of an original agreement in the terms of the agreement as varied ;

(*b*) the directions referred to in sub-paragraph (1) shall cease to have effect, but without prejudice to the Secretary of State's power to give further directions under section 21(2) above.

Section 18(2) *of the Restrictive Trade Practices Act* 1956

5. Nothing in this Act affects the right of a person to make an application to the Court in a case where an order is in force against that person under section 18(2) of the Restrictive Trade Practices Act 1956. 1956 c. 68.

Disclosure of information

6. Section 41 above applies in relation to information obtained under or by virtue of—

(*a*) the Restrictive Trade Practices Act 1956 ;

(*b*) the Restrictive Trade Practices Act 1968 ; 1968 c. 66.

as that section applies in relation to information obtained under or by virtue of this Act.

Particulars of certain export agreements

7. Any particulars furnished to the Board of Trade or to the Secretary of State under section 31(1) of the Restrictive Trade Practices Act 1956 shall be treated as if they had been furnished to the Director under sections 24 and 25 above.

Restrictive Trade Practices Act 1968, *s.* 11

8. An agreement which—

(*a*) was made before the commencement of this Act by a society at a time when it was approved for the purposes of section 11 of the Restrictive Trade Practices Act 1968 (wholesale co-operative societies), and

(*b*) by virtue of that approval was not subject to registration under Part I of the Restrictive Trade Practices Act 1956,

shall, notwithstanding the repeal of that section (by the Fair Trading Act 1973), not be subject to registration under this Act. 1973 c. 41.

SCHEDULE 5

Section 44.

Consequential Amendments

Restrictive Trade Practices Act 1956 *c.*68

In section 25(3) of the Restrictive Trade Practices Act 1956 for " Part I of this Act " substitute " the Restrictive Trade Practices Act 1976 ".

Sch. 5

Northern Ireland Act 1962 c.30

In Part I of Schedule 1 to the Northern Ireland Act 1962 for " The Restrictive Trade Practices Act, 1956 " substitute " The Restrictive Trade Practices Act 1976 " ; and in the adjoining entry for " Section thirteen " substitute " Section twenty-six ".

Plant Varieties and Seeds Act 1964 c.14

In section 8 of the Plant Varieties and Seeds Act 1964 for " Part I of the Restrictive Trade Practices Act 1956 " substitute " The Restrictive Trade Practices Act 1976 ".

Cereals Marketing Act 1965 c.14

In paragraph 3 of Schedule 1 to the Cereals Marketing Act 1965 for " Restrictive Trade Practices Act 1956 " substitute " Restrictive Trade Practices Act 1976 " and for " section 6(8) " substitute " section 43(1) ".

Agriculture Act 1967 c.22

In section 9(11) of the Agriculture Act 1967 for " Part I of the Restrictive Trade Practices Act 1956 " substitute " the Restrictive Trade Practices Act 1976 ".

Livestock Marketing Commission Act (*Northern Ireland*) 1967 c. 21

In section 2(6) of the Livestock Marketing Commission Act (Northern Ireland) 1967 for " Part I of the Restrictive Trade Practices Act 1956 " substitute " the Restrictive Trade Practices Act 1976 ".

Agriculture (*Miscellaneous Provisions*) *Act* 1968 c.34

In section 45 of the Agriculture (Miscellaneous Provisions) Act 1968—

(*a*) in subsection (1)—

(i) for " Restrictive Trade Practices Act 1956 " substitute " Restrictive Trade Practices Act 1976 " ; and

(ii) for " section 6(8) " substitute " section 43(1) " ;

(*b*) in subsection (2) for " Part I of the said Act of 1956 " substitute " the said Act of 1976 " ;

(*c*) in subsection (3)—

(i) for " Part I of the said Act of 1956 " substitute " the said Act of 1976 " ; and

(ii) for " said Part I " substitute " said Act of 1976 " ;

(*d*) in subsection (5)—

(i) for " Part I of the said Act of 1956 " substitute " the said Act of 1976 " ;

(ii) for " section 6 " substitute " section 43(1) " ; and

(iii) for " Part I " substitute " Act of 1976 " ;

(*e*) in subsection (7)—

(i) for "Part I of the Restrictive Trade Practices Act 1956" substitute "Restrictive Trade Practices Act 1976";

(ii) for "said Part I" substitute "said Act of 1976".

Agriculture Act 1970 *c.*40

In the Agriculture Act 1970—

(*a*) in section 7(2) for "Part I of the Restrictive Trade Practices Act 1956" substitute "the Restrictive Trade Practices Act 1976"; and

(*b*) in paragraph 3 of Schedule 1 for "Restrictive Trade Practices Act 1956" substitute "Restrictive Trade Practices Act 1976"; and for "section 6(8)" substitute "section 43(1)".

Fair Trading Act 1973 *c.*41

In the Fair Trading Act 1973—

(*a*) in

(i) section 10(2);

(ii) section 54(5)(*b*); and

(iii) section 78(3);

for "Part I of the Act of 1956" substitute "the Act of 1976";

(*b*) in section 133, in subsection (2)(*a*) and in subsection (3) for "Act of 1956 or the Act of 1968" substitute "Restrictive Trade Practices Act 1956 or the Restrictive Trade Practices Act 1968";

(*c*) in section 137(1) for '"the Act of 1956" means the Restrictive Trade Practices Act 1956' substitute '"the Act of 1976" means the Restrictive Trade Practices Act 1976';

(*d*) in subparagraphs (1) and (2) of paragraph 3 of Schedule 8 for "Part I of the Act of 1956" substitute "the Act of 1976";

Section 44.

SCHEDULE 6

REPEALS

Chapter	Short Title	Extent of Repeal
4 & 5 Eliz. 2. c. 68.	The Restrictive Trade Practices Act 1956.	Section 1. Sections 6 to 17. Sections 19 to 22. In section 23, in subsection (2), paragraphs (*b*) to (*d*). Section 30. In the Schedule, paragraph 9.
1962 c. 29.	The Agricultural and Forestry Associations Act 1962.	The whole Act.
1968 c. 34.	The Agriculture (Miscellaneous Provisions) Act 1968.	Section 44.
1968 c. 66.	The Restrictive Trade Practices Act 1968.	The whole Act, except sections 12, 14, 15, 16(3)(*b*), 17(1) and Schedule 1.
1972 c. 68.	The European Communities Act 1972.	Section 10.
1973 c. 41.	The Fair Trading Act 1973.	In section 54(5), the words " Part I of " where they appear before the words " that Act ". In section 94(2) the words " the Act of 1956 " and the words " and the Act of 1968 ". Sections 95 to 106. Part X. Section 128. In section 133, in subsection (1), the words " or under or by virtue of the Act of 1956 or the Act of 1968 "; and in subsection (4), paragraph (*b*). In section 137, in subsection (1), the reference to the " the Act of 1968 "; in subsection (2), the words " except in Part X "; in subsection (3), the words " other than Part X (and without prejudice to the construction of that Part in accordance with section 117 of this Act) " and the words " with that exception "; in subsection (4), the words " except Part X "; and in subsection (5) the words " other than Part X ".

SCH. 6

Chapter	Short Title	Extent of Repeal
1973 c. 41.—*cont.*	The Fair Trading Act 1973—*cont.*	In section 140, subsection (2). Schedule 10. In Schedule 11, paragraphs 12 and 13. In Schedule 12, the entries relating to— (*a*) the Restrictive Trade Practices Act 1956 (except so far as they relate to section 23 of that Act and to the Schedule to that Act); (*b*) the Restrictive Trade Practices Act 1968 (except so far as they relate to section 12 of that Act); and (*c*) the European Communities Act 1972.

Police Pensions Act 1976

1976 CHAPTER 35

An Act to consolidate the Police Pensions Act 1948 and certain other enactments relating to the pensions to be paid to and in respect of members of police forces.
[22nd July 1976]

BE IT ENACTED by the Queen's most Excellent Majesty, by and with the advice and consent of the Lords Spiritual and Temporal, and Commons, in this present Parliament assembled, and by the authority of the same, as follows:—

1.—(1) Regulations to be made by the Secretary of State, with the consent of the Minister for the Civil Service and after consultation with the Police Council for the United Kingdom, shall make provision— **Police pensions regulations.**

(*a*) as to the pensions which are to be paid to and in respect of members of police forces, whether as of right or otherwise ;

(*b*) as to the contributions in respect of pension rights which are to be made by members of police forces ; and

(*c*) as to the times at which and the circumstances in which members of police forces are or may be required to retire otherwise than on the ground of misconduct.

(2) Without prejudice to the generality of the provisions of subsection (1) above, any such regulations shall provide for the payment subject to the regulations—

(*a*) of pensions to and in respect of persons who cease to be members of a police force after having served for such period as may be prescribed by the regulations ;

(*b*) of pensions to and in respect of persons who cease to be members of a police force after such shorter period as may be prescribed by the regulations by reason of infirmity of mind or body;

(*c*) of pensions to and in respect of persons who cease to be members of a police force by reason of injury received in the execution of their duty;

(*d*) of pensions to and in respect of persons who cease to be members of a police force on the ground of age; and

(*e*) of pensions in respect of persons who die while serving as members of police forces.

(3) Regulations made under this section may contain such consequential or incidental provisions as appear to the Secretary of State to be necessary or expedient, including, in particular, provision as to the cases in which pensions are to be—

(*a*) varied, suspended, terminated or forfeited; or

(*b*) applied otherwise than by being paid to the persons to whom they were awarded;

and may provide for a pension to be forfeited wholly or in part and for the forfeiture to be permanent or temporary.

(4) Without prejudice to the generality of subsection (3) above, the provision which may be made by regulations under this section with respect to forfeiture shall include provision by reference not only to the fact that a person to whom a pension has been awarded has committed and been convicted of an offence as specified in the regulations but also to the fact that the offence in question has been certified by a Minister of the Crown either to have been gravely injurious to the State or to be liable to lead to serious loss of confidence in the public service.

(5) Regulations made under this section may be framed so as to have effect as from a date earlier than the making of the regulations.

(6) The power to make regulations under this section shall be exercisable by statutory instrument which shall be subject to annulment in pursuance of a resolution of either House of Parliament.

Application of regulations to existing members.

2.—(1) Any regulations made under section 1 above shall be so framed as to secure, for existing members of police forces, the results—

(*a*) as to compulsory age of retirement, and

(*b*) as to scale of pensions payable under the regulations,

specified respectively in subsections (2) and (3) below.

(2) The result as to compulsory age of retirement referred to in subsection (1) above is that the times at which an existing member of a police force is or may be required under the regulations to retire on the ground of age do not, unless he at any time elects otherwise, differ from those which would have been applicable in his case if the regulations in question had not come into force.

(3) The result as to scale of pensions referred to in subsection (1) above is that the scale of pensions payable under the regulations to an existing member of a police force who ceases to be a member of that police force either—

(*a*) after having served for any period prescribed by the regulations in question, or

(*b*) by reason of infirmity of mind or body (not being due to injury received in the execution of his duty) after having served for any shorter period so prescribed,

is not, unless he elects otherwise within such time and in such manner as may be so prescribed, less favourable than the scale applicable in his case immediately before the coming into force of the regulations.

(4) Regulations made under section 1 above shall not be invalid by reason that in fact they do not secure the results specified in subsections (2) and (3) above, but if the Secretary of State is satisfied, or it is held by the High Court or by the Court of Session, that any such regulations have failed to secure those results, the Secretary of State shall so soon as may be make under section 1 the necessary amending regulations, and any such amending regulations shall have effect as from the date of the coming into force of the regulations which they amend.

(5) In this section, "existing member", in relation to any police force, means a person who is serving in that police force at the date when the regulations in question come into force.

Application of regulations to former members.

3.—(1) Subject to the following provisions of this section, any regulations made under section 1 above may be framed—

(*a*) so as to apply in relation to the pensions which are being paid or may become payable under the regulations to or in respect of persons who, having served as members of police forces, have ceased so to serve or died before the regulations come into force; or

(*b*) so as to require or authorise the payment of pensions to or in respect of such persons.

(2) No provision shall be made by regulations under section 1 above by virtue of subsection (1) above unless any person who is placed in a worse position than he would have been in if the

provision had not applied in relation to any pension which is being paid or may become payable to him is by the regulations given an opportunity to elect that the provision shall not so apply.

(3) No provision with respect to the forfeiture of pensions included in regulations made under section 1 above shall apply in relation to pensions granted under any of the enactments, rules and regulations specified in paragraph 3 of Schedule 1 to this Act; and that Schedule shall have effect—

- (*a*) for the purpose of excluding entirely certain pensions to or in respect of former members of police forces from the operation of regulations made under section 1; and
- (*b*) with respect to the forfeiture of pensions so granted and appeals against forfeiture in certain cases.

Transfers.

4.—(1) Without prejudice to the generality of section 1 above, regulations made under that section may contain such provision as appears to the Secretary of State to be necessary or expedient in relation to a person who transfers or has transferred from or to service in a police force to or from other service or employment, whether in a police force or not.

(2) Regulations made by virtue of subsection (1) above may include provisions enabling the other service or employment in question to be reckoned in whole or in part as service in a police force and provisions authorising or requiring payments to be made by or to the person or into or out of the fund out of which a pension may become or might have become payable to or in respect of the person in question as a member of a police force including—

- (*a*) payments of contributions;
- (*b*) payments of transfer values;
- (*c*) payments towards the burden of a pension payable by another person or out of another fund; or
- (*d*) other payments directed to the creation or preservation of pension rights of the person in question.

(3) Regulations made by virtue of subsection (1) above, in so far as they apply in relation to persons who have ceased to be members of a police force before the date on which the regulations come into force,—

- (*a*) may authorise, but shall not require, such payments as are mentioned in subsection (2) above; and
- (*b*) shall not affect any pension payable to or in respect of any person as a person who ceased to be a member of a police force before that date.

5.—(1) Without prejudice to the generality of section 1 above, regulations made under that section may provide that where a person is a member of a police force immediately before— **Servicemen.**

(*a*) he undertakes compulsory national service;

(*b*) he undertakes any other service of a description specified in Schedule 1 to the Reserve and Auxiliary Forces (Protection of Civil Interests) Act 1951; or **1951 c. 65.**

(*c*) he attends for hourly instruction as defined in section 42 of that Act;

the period of that service or attendance and such further period, if any, as may be specified in the regulations may be treated, in such manner, to such extent and on such conditions as to contributions or otherwise as may be so specified, as a period of service as a member of a police force.

(2) A person who, before 5th July 1948, had ceased to be a member of a police force in order to undertake—

(*a*) any service by virtue of which he was at that date a person to whom section 1 of the Police and Firemen (War Service) Act 1939 applied; or **1939 c. 103.**

(*b*) compulsory national service;

shall, in such circumstances and to such extent as may be provided by regulations made under section 1 above, be treated as if he had been still a member of a police force at that date.

(3) In this section, " compulsory national service " means service in any of the armed forces of the Crown undertaken by virtue of an enlistment notice or a training notice served under the National Service Acts 1939 to 1947 or under Part I of the National Service Act 1948 (as the case may require), or work or training in pursuance of an order made or direction given under Part I of the said Act of 1948 as respects a conditionally registered conscientious objector. **1948 c. 64.**

6.—(1) Subject to the following provisions of this section, regulations made under section 1 above shall make provision as to the court or other person by whom appeals are to be heard and determined in the case of any person who is aggrieved— **Appeals.**

(*a*) by the refusal of the police authority to admit a claim to receive as of right a pension, or a larger pension than that granted, under regulations made under that section; or

(*b*) by the forfeiture of any pension granted to him thereunder.

(2) No provision made in the regulations by virtue of subsection (1) above shall confer a right of appeal against anything done by the police authority in the exercise of any power which

is conferred on them by the regulations and is expressly declared by the regulations to be a power which they are to exercise in their discretion.

(3) The regulations may provide, in relation to questions arising thereunder, for the reference of any such matter as is prescribed, either by the policy authority or by the court, to a medical practitioner whose decision thereon shall, subject to such rights of appeal as may be provided by the regulations to such tribunal as may be constituted thereunder, be final on the matter so referred.

Payment of pensions and contributions.

7.—(1) Regulations made under section 1 above shall specify the persons by and to whom and the funds into or out of which pensions and contributions in respect of pension rights are to be payable, may provide for the establishment or continuance of special funds for the purpose, and, subject to the provisions of subsection (2) below, may provide for payments of contributions or pensions, and such other payments as are mentioned in section 4(2) above, being made into the Consolidated Fund or out of moneys provided by Parliament.

(2) No regulations made by virtue of this section shall provide for payments into the Consolidated Fund or out of moneys provided by Parliament except in relation to a person who is or has been—

(*a*) such a person as is mentioned in section 1(1) of the Police (Overseas Service) Act 1945; (1945 c. 17.)

(*b*) an officer to whom the Overseas Service Act 1958 applies or applied, whose service as such an officer is or was for the time being service in respect of which the provisions of section 5 of that Act have or had effect; (1958 c. 14.)

(*c*) an inspector or assistant inspector of constabulary; or

(*d*) a person engaged on central service;

or any other person whose salary or remuneration is or was wholly or partly payable out of moneys provided by Parliament or who is or may become entitled to or eligible for a pension so payable.

(3) For the purposes of subsection (2) above regulations shall not be treated as providing for payments out of moneys provided by Parliament by reason only that, as a result of the making of the regulations, an increased sum may be payable out of moneys provided by way of a grant towards the expenses of a police force.

Consolidation of regulations.

8.—(1) Regulations made under section 1 above which revoke regulations previously so made, either wholly or as respects cases or matters of any description, shall contain provisions having the same effect as the provisions they revoke, except for any change (whether by way of alteration or omission) made in accordance with this Act.

(2) Subsection (4) of section 2 above shall have effect as if the reference to subsections (2) and (3) of that section included a reference to subsection (1) above.

Assignment etc. of pension to be void.

9. Every assignment of or charge on a pension granted under the regulations made under section 1 above, and every agreement to assign or charge such a pension shall, except so far as it is made for the benefit of a dependant of the pensioner, be void; and on the bankruptcy of the pensioner such a pension shall not pass to any trustee or other person acting on behalf of the creditors.

Obtaining pension by self-inflicted injury etc.

10. If any person obtains or attempts to obtain for himself or any other person any pension under any regulations made under section 1 above by maiming or injuring himself, or causing himself to be maimed or injured, or otherwise producing disease or infirmity, he shall be liable—

(*a*) on conviction on indictment, to imprisonment for a term not exceeding two years; or

(*b*) on summary conviction, to imprisonment for a term not exceeding three months or to a fine not exceeding £25.

Interpretation.

11.—(1) This Act shall have effect as if any reference (however expressed) to membership of a police force or to service or employment in a police force included a reference to—

(*a*) service as an officer to whom the Overseas Service Act 1958 applies, being service in respect of which the provisions of section 5 of that Act have effect; 1958 c. 14.

(*b*) service as an inspector or assistant inspector of constabulary appointed on or after 1st August 1964; and

(*c*) central service in respect of which the provisions of section 43 of the Police Act 1964 or (as the case may be) of section 38 of the Police (Scotland) Act 1967 have effect. 1964 c. 48. 1967 c. 77.

(2) In this Act " police authority " means any police authority within the meaning of the Police Act 1964 or the Police (Scotland) Act 1967, except that—

(*a*) in relation to any regulations made under the Police (Overseas Service) Act 1945 and any service such as is mentioned in subsection (1)(*a*) above, it means the Secretary of State or the Minister of Overseas Development; and 9 & 10 Geo. 6. c. 17.

(*b*) in relation to any service such as is mentioned in subsection (1)(*b*) or (*c*) above, it means the Secretary of State.

(3) In this Act, except so far as the context otherwise requires, " police force " means any police force within the meaning of the Police Act 1964 or the Police (Scotland) Act 1967, and, in respect of—

1964 c. 48.
1967 c. 77.

(*a*) any person such as is mentioned in section 1(1) of the Police (Overseas Service) Act 1945 ; and

9 & 10 Geo. 6. c. 17.

(*b*) any person engaged or employed in any service such as is mentioned in subsection (1)(*a*), (*b*) or (*c*) above ;

any body in which that person is serving.

(4) This Act shall have effect—

(*a*) as if commissioners and assistant commissioners of the metropolitan police force and commissioners of the City of London police force were members of those forces respectively ; and

(*b*) in relation to any person who on 5th July 1948 was or had been the surgeon of the City of London police force or a clerk or other person employed in or in connection with that force, as if such surgeons, clerks or other persons employed in or in connection with that force were members of that force ;

and references in this Act to membership of a police force shall be construed accordingly.

(5) Except so far as the context otherwise requires, in this Act—

" central service " has the meaning given in section 43(5) of the Police Act 1964 or section 38(5) of the Police (Scotland) Act 1967 (as the case may require) ;

" injury " includes disease ;

" pension ", in relation to a person, means a pension, whether contributory or not, of any kind whatsoever payable to or in respect of him, and includes a lump sum or a gratuity so payable and a return of contributions ; and

" pension rights " includes, in relation to any person, all forms of right to, or eligibility for, the present or future payment of a pension to or in respect of that person.

Savings and transitional provisions.

12.—(1) Nothing in any repeal made by this Act shall affect any regulations made or other thing done under any enactment repealed by this Act, and any such regulations or thing, if in force, existing or effective at the passing of this Act shall, subject to the provisions of this Act, remain in force, existence or effect, and be deemed to have been made or done under the corresponding provision of this Act.

(2) In so far as, by virtue of section 15(4) of the Superannuation Act 1972, the provisions of sections 4(1) and (2) and 5(1) and (5) of the Police Pensions Act 1948, as in force immediately before 25th March 1972, continued to apply, immediately before the passing of this Act, in relation to pensions granted under regulations made under section 1 of the said Act of 1948, those provisions shall be deemed to have effect as if they were provisions of regulations made under section 1 of this Act, and may be revoked accordingly. 1972 c. 11. 1948 c. 24.

(3) Any reference in any document (including an enactment) to any enactment repealed by this Act, whether a specific reference or a reference to provisions of a description which includes, or apart from any repeal made by this Act includes, the enactment so repealed shall be construed as, or, as the case may require, as including, a reference to the corresponding enactment in this Act.

(4) Nothing in this section, in section 13 below or in Schedule 2 to this Act shall be taken as prejudicing the operation of section 38 of the Interpretation Act 1889 (which relates to the effect of repeals). 1889 c. 63.

Consequential amendments and repeals.

13.—(1) The enactments specified in Schedule 2 to this Act shall have effect subject to the amendments set out in that Schedule, being amendments consequential on the preceding provisions of this Act.

(2) The enactments specified in Schedule 3 to this Act (which include enactments which were spent before the passing of this Act) are hereby repealed to the extent specified in the third column of that Schedule.

Short title and extent.

14.—(1) This Act may be cited as the Police Pensions Act 1976.

(2) This Act shall not extend to Northern Ireland; but this subsection shall not be construed as preventing any regulations such as are referred to in section 4 above from requiring payments to be made to a person or into a fund in Northern Ireland.

SCHEDULES

Section 3(3).

SCHEDULE 1

Pensions Under Repealed Enactments

Pensions excluded from the operation of regulations under this Act

1.—(1) Nothing in regulations made under section 1 of this Act shall—

(*a*) affect any pension granted by virtue of section 4(3) of the Police and Firemen (War Service) Act 1939, if the period (or last period, if more than one) which, by virtue of section 2(1) of that Act, is treated as a period of approved service in the case of the person in question, ended before 5th July 1948 ; or

1939 c. 103.

(*b*) apply to any pension to or in respect of a person to whom the National Fire Service (Preservation of Pensions) (Police Firemen) Regulations 1941 apply ; or

S.I. 1941/1271.

(*c*) apply to any pension to any person who, having formerly been a member of a police force, was on 5th July 1948 serving in any capacity mentioned in section 10(1)(i) of the Police Pensions Act 1921, and has not since and does not after the passing of this Act again become a member of a police force.

1921 c. 31.

(2) Except so far as relates to the forfeiture of any such pension as is mentioned in sub-paragraph (1) above, nothing in this Act shall be taken as affecting the application in relation to any such pension of the pensions enactments applicable thereto immediately before the passing of this Act.

Forfeiture of pensions under repealed enactments

2.—(1) Every pension (whether described as a pension or as an allowance) granted under any of the enactments specified in paragraph 3(1) below (which reproduces so far as relevant Part I of Schedule 1 to the Police Pensions Act 1948) shall be deemed to have been granted only upon condition that it may be forfeited by the police authority in any of the cases mentioned in sub-paragraph (2) below.

1948 c. 24.

(2) The cases referred to in sub-paragraph (1) above are any of the following, that is to say, if the grantee—

(*a*) is convicted of any offence and is sentenced to preventive detention or corrective training or to imprisonment for a term exceeding twelve months ; or

(*b*) enters into or continues to carry on any business, occupation or employment which is illegal, or in which the grantee has made use of the fact of former employment in a police force in a manner which is discreditable or improper ; or (*c*) supplies to any person or publishes in a manner which is discreditable or improper any information which the grantee had obtained in the course of employment in a police force; or SCH. 1

(*d*) solicits or, without the consent of the police authority, accepts directly or indirectly any testimonial or gift having any pecuniary value on retirement from the police force or otherwise in connection with his service in a police force; or

(*e*) enters into or continues in any business, occupation or employment as a private detective, after the police authority have given him notice in writing requiring him on any reasonable grounds not to do so.

(3) A pension shall not be forfeited under sub-paragraph (2)(*b*) above unless reasonable warning has previously been given in writing by the police authority.

(4) A forfeiture under this paragraph may affect the pension wholly or in part, and may be permanent or temporary as the police authority may determine.

(5) Without prejudice to the validity of any forfeiture before the passing of this Act, a pension to which this paragraph applies shall not be capable of being forfeited otherwise than in accordance with the provisions of this paragraph.

(6) This paragraph shall apply in relation to the rules and regulations specified in sub-paragraph (2) of paragraph 3 below (which reproduces so far as relevant Part II of Schedule 1 to the Police Pensions Act 1948) as it applies in relation to the enactments 1948 c. 24. specified in sub-paragraph (1) of that paragraph, subject, however, to any necessary adaptations.

3.—(1) The enactments referred to in paragraph 2(1) above are—

The Metropolitan Police Act 1829; 1829 c. 44.

The County and Borough Police Act 1859; 1859 c. 32.

The Police Superannuation Act 1865; 1865 c. 35.

The Police (Pensions) Act 1918; 1918 c. 51.

The Police Pensions Act 1921; 1921 c. 31.

The Police and Firemen (War Service) Act 1939; 1939 c. 103.

The Police (Overseas Service) Act 1945; 9 & 10 Geo. 6. c. 17.

The Police Act 1946; 1946 c. 46.

The Police (Scotland) Act 1946. 1946 c. 71.

(2) The rules and regulations referred to in paragraph 2(6) above are—

The Women's Auxiliary Police Corps Rules 1945;

The Women's Auxiliary Police Corps (Scotland) Rules 1945;

The Police (Overseas Service) (Germany) Regulations 1947;

The Police (Overseas Service) (Austria) Regulations 1947;

The Police (Overseas Service) (Greece) Regulations 1948.

SCH. 1

4.—(1) If any person is aggrieved by the forfeiture under paragraph 2 above of any pension granted to him under any of the enactments specified in paragraph 3(1) above, he may appeal to the Crown Court and that Court, after enquiring into the case, may make such order in the matter as appears to the Court to be just.

(2) In the application of sub-paragraph (1) above to Scotland, for the reference therein to the Crown Court there shall be substituted a reference to the sheriff having jurisdiction in the place where the person concerned last served as a member of a police force.

Section 13(1).

SCHEDULE 2

CONSEQUENTIAL AMENDMENTS

9 & 10 Geo. 6. c. 17.

1. The reference in section 2(1) of the Police (Overseas Service) Act 1945 to a pension, allowance or gratuity becoming payable to a person out of moneys provided by Parliament by virtue of regulations made under that Act shall be construed as including a reference to a pension (as defined for the purposes of this Act) payable by virtue of regulations made under this Act, being a pension which becomes payable in such circumstances as may be specified for the purposes of this paragraph by the last mentioned regulations.

1951 c. 65.

2. In section 63 of the Reserve and Auxiliary Forces (Protection of Civil Interests) Act 1951, for the words from "Police Pensions Act 1948" to "of this Act" there shall be substituted the words "Police Pensions Act 1976".

1961 c. 35.

3. In section 1 of the Police Pensions Act 1961—

(*a*) in subsection (2), for the words "the said section one" in the first place where they occur there shall be substituted the words "section one of the Police Pensions Act 1976"; and

(*b*) in subsection (3), for the words from the beginning to "principal" in the second place where it occurs there shall be substituted the words "Subsection (4) of section 2 of the said Act of 1976 (which provides for regulations not to be invalid by reason only of their failure to secure the results specified in subsections (2) and (3) of that section but requires their amendment to secure those results) shall have effect as if the reference to the said subsections (2) and (3) included a reference to subsection (2) of this section and as if the references to regulations or amending regulations under section one of that".

4. In section 2 of the Police Pensions Act 1961—

(*a*) in subsection (1), the words from "and this" to the end shall be omitted; and (*b*) in subsection (2), the words from the beginning to " in Northern Ireland " shall be omitted. Sch. 2

5. In sections 43(1) and 58(4) of the Police Act 1964, for the words " Police Pensions Act 1948 " there shall be substituted the words " Police Pensions Act 1976. " 1964 c. 48.

6. In the Police (Scotland) Act 1967— 1967 c. 77

(*a*) for the words " Police Pensions Act 1948 " in section 38(1); and

(*b*) for those words in both places where they occur in subsection (4) of section 23 (as substituted by section 146(8) of the Local Government (Scotland) Act 1973); 1973 c. 65.

there shall be substituted the words " Police Pensions Act 1976 ".

7. In section 4(5) of the Police Act 1969 the words preceding paragraph (*a*) shall be omitted, and for the words " that Council " in that paragraph there shall be substituted the words " the Police Council for the United Kingdom ". 1969 c. 63.

8. In Schedule 2 to the Pensions (Increase) Act 1971— 1971 c. 56.

(*a*) in paragraph 15, for the words " Police Pensions Act 1948 " there shall be substituted the words " Police Pensions Act 1976 "; and

(*b*) in paragraph 43, for the words from the beginning of sub-paragraph (*a*) to " that Act " there shall be substituted the words " the Police Pensions Act 1976, or any enactment repealed by the Police Pensions Act 1948 ".

9. In Schedule 1 to the Tribunals and Inquiries Act 1971, in paragraphs 23(*c*) and 43(*c*), for the words " Police Pensions Act 1948 (c. 24) " there shall be substituted the words " Police Pensions Act 1976 ". 1971 c. 62.

10. In section 24(1)(*a*) of the Superannuation Act 1972, for the words " Police Pensions Act 1948 " there shall be substituted the words " Police Pensions Act 1976 ". 1972 c. 11.

11. In paragraph 8(3) of Schedule 2 to the Social Security Pensions Act 1975, for the words " the Police Pensions Act 1948 " there shall be substituted the words " the Police Pensions Act 1976 ". 1975 c. 60.

SCHEDULE 3

Section 13(2).

Enactments Repealed

Chapter	Short title	Extent of repeal
11 & 12 Geo. 6. c. 24.	The Police Pensions Act 1948.	The whole Act.
11 & 12 Geo. 6. c. 58.	The Criminal Justice Act 1948.	In Schedule 9, the entry relating to the Police Pensions Act 1948.

SCH. 3

Chapter	Short title	Extent of repeal
12, 13 & 14 Geo. 6. c. 94.	The Criminal Justice (Scotland) Act 1949.	In Schedule 11, the entry relating to the Police Pensions Act 1948.
14 & 15 Geo. 6. c. 65.	The Reserve and Auxiliary Forces (Protection of Civil Interests) Act 1951.	Section 43. In section 44(1), the words from " and any regulations " to " police force ".
6 & 7 Eliz. 2. c. 14.	The Overseas Service Act 1958.	Section 5(3). Schedule 2.
9 & 10 Eliz. 2. c. 35.	The Police Pensions Act 1961.	Section 1(1) and (4). In section 2, in subsection (1) the words from " and this " to the end, and in subsection (2) the words from the beginning to " in Northern Ireland ".
1964 c. 48.	The Police Act 1964.	Section 40. Section 43(4). Schedule 6. In Schedule 9, the entries relating to the Police Pensions Act 1948.
1967 c. 28.	The Superannuation (Miscellaneous Provisions) Act 1967.	Section 11(7).
1967 c. 77.	The Police (Scotland) Act 1967.	Section 35. Section 38(4). In Schedule 4, the entry relating to the Police Pensions Act 1948.
1969 c. 63.	The Police Act 1969.	In section 4(5), the words preceding paragraph (*a*).
1972 c. 11.	The Superannuation Act 1972.	In section 15, subsections (1) to (4) and in subsection (5), paragraph (*a*). In Schedule 6, paragraph 23.

Adoption Act 1976

1976 CHAPTER 36

An Act to consolidate the enactments having effect in England and Wales in relation to adoption.

[22nd July 1976]

BE IT ENACTED by the Queen's most Excellent Majesty, by and with the advice and consent of the Lords Spiritual and Temporal, and Commons, in this present Parliament assembled, and by the authority of the same, as follows:—

PART I

THE ADOPTION SERVICE

The Adoption Service

1.—(1) It is the duty of every local authority to establish and maintain within their area a service designed to meet the needs, in relation to adoption, of— Establishment of Adoption Service.

(*a*) children who have been or may be adopted,

(*b*) parents and guardians of such children, and

(*c*) persons who have adopted or may adopt a child,

and for that purpose to provide the requisite facilities, or secure that they are provided by approved adoption societies.

(2) The facilities to be provided as part of the service maintained under subsection (1) include—

(*a*) temporary board and lodging where needed by pregnant women, mothers or children;

PART I

(*b*) arrangements for assessing children and prospective adopters, and placing children for adoption;

(*c*) counselling for persons with problems relating to adoption.

(3) The facilities of the service maintained under subsection (1) shall be provided in conjunction with the local authority's other social services and with approved adoption societies in their area, so that help may be given in a co-ordinated manner without duplication, omission or avoidable delay.

(4) The services maintained by local authorities under subsection (1) may be collectively referred to as "the Adoption Service", and a local authority or approved adoption society may be referred to as an adoption agency.

Local authorities' social services.

2. The social services referred to in section 1(3) are the functions of a local authority which stand referred to the authority's social services committee, including, in particular but without prejudice to the generality of the foregoing, a local authority's functions relating to—

(*a*) the promotion of the welfare of children by diminishing the need to receive children into care or keep them in care, including (in exceptional circumstances) the giving of assistance in cash;

(*b*) the welfare of children in the care of a local authority;

(*c*) the welfare of children who are foster children within the meaning of the Children Act 1958; 1958 c. 65.

(*d*) children who are subject to supervision orders made in matrimonial proceedings;

(*e*) the provision of residential accommodation for expectant mothers and young children and of day-care facilities.

(*f*) the regulation and inspection of nurseries and child minders;

(*g*) care and other treatment of children through court proceedings.

Adoption societies

Approval of adoption societies.

3.—(1) Subject to regulations under section 9(1), a body desiring to act as an adoption society or, if it is already an adoption society, desiring to continue to act as such may, in the manner specified by regulations made by the Secretary of State, apply to the Secretary of State for his approval to its doing so.

(2) On an application under subsection (1), the Secretary of State shall take into account the matters relating to the applicant specified in subsections (3) to (5) and any other relevant considerations, and if, but only if, he is satisfied that the applicant

is likely to make, or, if the applicant is an approved adoption society, is making, an effective contribution to the Adoption Service he shall by notice to the applicant give his approval, which shall be operative from a date specified in the notice or, in the case of a renewal of approval, from the date of the notice.

(3) In considering the application, the Secretary of State shall have regard, in relation to the period for which approval is sought, to the following—

(*a*) the applicant's adoption programme, including, in particular, its ability to make provision for children who are free for adoption,

(*b*) the number and qualifications of its staff,

(*c*) its financial resources, and

(*d*) the organisation and control of its operations.

(4) Where it appears to the Secretary of State that the applicant is likely to operate extensively within the area of a particular local authority he shall ask the authority whether they support the application, and shall take account of any views about it put to him by the authority.

(5) Where the applicant is already an approved adoption society or, whether before or after the passing of this Act, previously acted as an adoption society, the Secretary of State, in considering the application, shall also have regard to the record and reputation of the applicant in the adoption field, and the areas within which and the scale on which it is currently operating or has operated in the past.

(6) If after considering the application the Secretary of State is not satisfied that the applicant is likely to make or, as the case may be, is making an effective contribution to the Adoption Service, the Secretary of State shall, subject to section 5(1) and (2), by notice inform the applicant that its application is refused.

(7) If not withdrawn earlier under section 4, approval given under this section shall last for a period of three years from the date on which it becomes operative, and shall then expire or, in the case of an approved adoption society whose further application for approval is pending at that time, shall expire on the date that application is granted or, as the case may be, refused.

Withdrawal of approval.

4.—(1) If, while approval of a body under section 3 is operative, it appears to the Secretary of State that the body is not making an effective contribution to the Adoption Service he shall, subject to section 5(3) and (4), by notice to the body withdraw the approval from a date specified in the notice.

PART I

(2) If an approved adoption society fails to provide the Secretary of State with information required by him for the purpose of carrying out his functions under subsection (1), or fails to verify such information in the manner required by him, he may by notice to the society withdraw the approval from a date specified in the notice.

(3) Where approval is withdrawn under subsection (1) or (2) or expires the Secretary of State may direct the body concerned to make such arrangements as to children who are in its care and other transitional matters as seem to him expedient.

Procedure on refusal to approve, or withdrawal of approval from, adoption societies.

5.—(1) Before notifying a body which has applied for approval that the application is refused in accordance with section 3(6) the Secretary of State shall serve on the applicant a notice—

(*a*) setting out the reasons why he proposes to refuse the application ;

(*b*) informing the applicant that it may make representations in writing to the Secretary of State within 28 days of the date of service of the notice.

(2) If any representations are made by the applicant in accordance with subsection (1), the Secretary of State shall give further consideration to the application taking into account those representations.

(3) The Secretary of State shall, before withdrawing approval of an adoption society in accordance with section 4(1), serve on the society a notice—

(*a*) setting out the reasons why he proposes to withdraw the approval ; and

(*b*) informing the society that it may make representations in writing to the Secretary of State within 28 days of the date of service of the notice.

(4) If any representations are made by the society in accordance with subsection (3), the Secretary of State shall give further consideration to the withdrawal of approval under section 4(1) taking into account those representations.

(5) This section does not apply where the Secretary of State, after having considered any representations made by the applicant in accordance with this section, proposes to refuse approval or, as the case may be, to withdraw approval for reasons which have already been communicated to the applicant in a notice under this section.

Welfare of children

Duty to promote welfare of child.

6. In reaching any decision relating to the adoption of a child a court or adoption agency shall have regard to all the circumstances, first consideration being given to the need to safeguard and promote the welfare of the child throughout his childhood; and shall so far as practicable ascertain the wishes and feelings of the child regarding the decision and give due consideration to them, having regard to his age and understanding.

Religious upbringing of adopted child.

7. An adoption agency shall in placing a child for adoption have regard (so far as is practicable) to any wishes of a child's parents and guardians as to the religious upbringing of the child.

Supplemental

Inactive or defunct adoption societies.

8.—(1) If it appears to the Secretary of State that an approved adoption society, or one in relation to which approval has been withdrawn under section 4 or has expired, is inactive or defunct he may, in relation to any child who is or was in the care of the society, direct what appears to him to be the appropriate local authority to take any such action as might have been taken by the society or by the society jointly with the authority; and if apart from this section the authority would not be entitled to take that action, or would not be entitled to take it without joining the society in the action, it shall be entitled to do so.

(2) Before giving a direction under subsection (1) the Secretary of State shall, if practicable, consult both the society and the authority.

Regulation of adoption agencies.

9.—(1) The Secretary of State may by regulations prohibit unincorporated bodies from applying for approval under section 3; and he shall not approve any unincorporated body whose application is contrary to regulations made under this subsection.

(2) The Secretary of State may make regulations for any purpose relating to the exercise of its functions by an approved adoption society.

(3) The Secretary of State may make regulations with respect to the exercise by local authorities of their functions of making or participating in arrangements for the adoption of children.

(4) Any person who contravenes or fails to comply with regulations made under subsection (2) shall be guilty of an offence and liable on summary conviction to a fine not exceeding £400.

Inspection of books, etc., of approved adoption societies.

10.—(1) A local authority may at any time give notice in writing to an approved adoption society, or to any officer of such a society, requiring that society or officer to produce to the authority such books, accounts and other documents relating to the performance by the society of the function of making arrangements for the adoption of children as the authority may

PART I

consider necessary for its own information or that of the Secretary of State.

(2) Any such notice may contain a requirement that any information to be furnished in accordance with the notice shall be verified in a manner specified in the notice.

(3) Any person who fails to comply with the requirements of a notice under this section shall be guilty of an offence and liable on summary conviction to imprisonment for a term not exceeding 3 months or to a fine not exceeding £50 or to both.

Restriction on arranging adoptions and placing of children.

11.—(1) A person other than an adoption agency shall not make arrangements for the adoption of a child, or place a child for adoption, unless—

(*a*) the proposed adopter is a relative of the child, or

(*b*) he is acting in pursuance of an order of the High Court.

(2) An adoption society approved as respects Scotland under section 4 of the Children Act 1975, but which is not approved under section 3 of this Act, shall not act as an adoption society in England and Wales except to the extent that the society considers it necessary to do so in the interests of a person mentioned in section 1 of that Act.

1975 c. 72.

(3) A person who—

(*a*) takes part in the management or control of a body of persons which exists wholly or partly for the purpose of making arrangements for the adoption of children and which is not an adoption agency; or

(*b*) contravenes subsection (1); or

(*c*) receives a child placed with him in contravention of subsection (1),

shall be guilty of an offence and liable on summary conviction to imprisonment for a term not exceeding 3 months or to a fine not exceeding £400 or to both.

(4) In any proceedings for an offence under paragraph (*a*) of subsection (3), proof of things done or of words written, spoken or published (whether or not in the presence of any party to the proceedings) by any person taking part in the management or control of a body of persons, or in making arrangements for the adoption of children on behalf of the body, shall be admissible as evidence of the purpose for which that body exists.

(5) Section 26 shall apply where a person is convicted of a contravention of subsection (1) as it applies where an application for an adoption order is refused.

Part II

Adoption Orders

The making of adoption orders

12.—(1) An adoption order is an order vesting the parental rights and duties relating to a child in the adopters, made on their application by an authorised court. Adoption orders.

(2) The order does not affect the parental rights and duties so far as they relate to any period before the making of the order.

(3) The making of an adoption order operates to extinguish—

(*a*) any parental right or duty relating to the child which—

(i) is vested in a person (not being one of the adopters) who was the parent or guardian of the child immediately before the making of the order, or

(ii) is vested in any other person by virtue of the order of any court; and

(*b*) any duty arising by virtue of an agreement or the order of a court to make payments, so far as the payments are in respect of the child's maintenance for any period after the making of the order or any other matter comprised in the parental duties and relating to such a period.

(4) Subsection (3)(*b*) does not apply to a duty arising by virtue of an agreement—

(*a*) which constitutes a trust, or

(*b*) which expressly provides that the duty is not to be extinguished by the making of an adoption order.

(5) An adoption order may not be made in relation to a child who is or has been married.

(6) An adoption order may contain such terms and conditions as the court thinks fit.

(7) An adoption order may be made notwithstanding that the child is already an adopted child.

13.—(1) Where— Child to live with adopters before order made.

(*a*) the applicant, or one of the applicants, is a parent, step-parent or relative of the child, or

(*b*) the child was placed with the applicants by an adoption agency or in pursuance of an order of the High Court,

an adoption order shall not be made unless the child is at least 19 weeks old and at all times during the preceding 13 weeks had his home with the applicants or one of them.

PART II

(2) Where subsection (1) does not apply, an adoption order shall not be made unless the child is at least 12 months old and at all times during the preceding 12 months had his home with the applicants or one of them.

(3) An adoption order shall not be made unless the court is satisfied that sufficient opportunities to see the child with the applicant, or, in the case of an application by a married couple, both applicants together in the home environment have been afforded—

(*a*) where the child was placed with the applicant by an adoption agency, to that agency, or

(*b*) in any other case, to the local authority within whose area the home is.

Adoption by married couple.
1975 c. 72.

14.—(1) Subject to section 37(1) of the Children Act 1975 (which provides for the making of a custodianship order instead of an adoption order in certain cases) an adoption order may be made on the application of a married couple where each has attained the age of 21 years but an adoption order shall not otherwise be made on the application of more than one person.

(2) An adoption order shall not be made on the application of a married couple unless—

(*a*) at least one of them is domiciled in a part of the United Kingdom, or in the Channel Islands or the Isle of Man, or

(*b*) the application is for a Convention adoption order and section 17 is complied with.

(3) If the married couple consist of a parent and step-parent of the child, the court shall dismiss the application if it considers the matter would be better dealt with under section 42 (orders for custody etc.) of the Matrimonial Causes Act 1973.

1973 c. 18.

Adoption by one person.

15.—(1) Subject to section 37(1) of the Children Act 1975 (which provides for the making of a custodianship order instead of an adoption order in certain cases) an adoption order may be made on the application of one person where he has attained the age of 21 years and—

(*a*) is not married, or

(*b*) is married and the court is satisfied that—

(i) his spouse cannot be found, or

(ii) the spouses have separated and are living apart, and the separation is likely to be permanent, or

(iii) his spouse is by reason of ill-health, whether physical or mental, incapable of making an application for an adoption order.

(2) An adoption order shall not be made on the application of one person unless—

(*a*) he is domiciled in a part of the United Kingdom, or in the Channel Islands or the Isle of Man, or

(*b*) the application is for a Convention adoption order and section 17 is complied with.

(3) An adoption order shall not be made on the application of the mother or father of the child alone unless the court is satisfied that—

(*a*) the other natural parent is dead or cannot be found, or

(*b*) there is some other reason justifying the exclusion of the other natural parent,

and where such an order is made the reason justifying the exclusion of the other natural parent shall be recorded by the court.

(4) If the applicant is a step-parent of the child, the court shall dismiss the application if it considers the matter would be better dealt with under section 42 (orders for custody etc.) of the Matrimonial Causes Act 1973. 1973 c. 18.

Parental agreement.

16.—(1) An adoption order shall not be made unless—

(*a*) the child is free for adoption by virtue of an order made in England and Wales under section 18 or made in Scotland under section 14 of the Children Act 1975 (freeing children for adoption in Scotland); or 1975 c. 72.

(*b*) in the case of each parent or guardian of the child the court is satisfied that—

(i) he freely, and with full understanding of what is involved, agrees unconditionally to the making of an adoption order (whether or not he knows the identity of the applicants), or

(ii) his agreement to the making of the adoption order should be dispensed with on a ground specified in subsection (2).

(2) The grounds mentioned in subsection (1)(*b*)(ii) are that the parent or guardian—

(*a*) cannot be found or is incapable of giving agreement;

(*b*) is withholding his agreement unreasonably;

(*c*) has persistently failed without reasonable cause to discharge the parental duties in relation to the child;

(*d*) has abandoned or neglected the child;

PART II

(*e*) has persistently ill-treated the child;

(*f*) has seriously ill-treated the child (subject to subsection (5)).

(3) Subsection (1) does not apply in any case where the child is not a United Kingdom national and the application for the adoption order is for a Convention adoption order.

(4) Agreement is ineffective for the purposes of subsection (1)(*b*)(i) if given by the mother less than six weeks after the child's birth.

(5) Subsection (2)(*f*) does not apply unless (because of the ill-treatment or for other reasons) the rehabilitation of the child within the household of the parent or guardian is unlikely.

Convention adoption orders.

17.—(1) An adoption order shall be made as a Convention adoption order if the application is for a Convention adoption order and the following conditions are satisfied both at the time of the application and when the order is made.

(2) The child—

(*a*) must be a United Kingdom national or a national of a Convention country, and

(*b*) must habitually reside in British territory or a Convention country.

(3) The applicant or applicants and the child must not all be United Kingdom nationals living in British territory.

(4) If the application is by a married couple, either—

(*a*) each must be a United Kingdom national or a national of a Convention country, and both must habitually reside in Great Britain, or

(*b*) both must be United Kingdom nationals, and each must habitually reside in British territory or a Convention country,

and if the applicants are nationals of the same Convention country the adoption must not be prohibited by a specified provision (as defined in subsection (8)) of the internal law of that country.

(5) If the application is by one person, either—

(*a*) he must be a national of a Convention country, and must habitually reside in Great Britain, or

(*b*) he must be a United Kingdom national and must habitually reside in British territory or a Convention country, and if he is a national of a Convention country the adoption must not be prohibited by a specified provision (as defined in subsection (8)) of the internal law of that country. PART II

(6) If the child is not a United Kingdom national the order shall not be made—

(*a*) except in accordance with the provisions, if any, relating to consents and consultations of the internal law relating to adoption of the Convention country of which the child is a national, and

(*b*) unless the court is satisfied that each person who consents to the order in accordance with that internal law does so with full understanding of what is involved.

(7) The reference to consents and consultations in subsection (6) does not include a reference to consent by and consultation with the applicant and members of the applicant's family (including his or her spouse), and for the purposes of subsection (6) consents may be proved in the manner prescribed by rules and the court shall be treated as the authority by whom, under the law mentioned in subsection (6), consents may be dispensed with and the adoption in question may be effected; and where the provisions there mentioned require the attendance before that authority of any person who does not reside in Great Britain, that requirement shall be treated as satisfied for the purposes of subsection (6) if—

(*a*) that person has been given a reasonable opportunity of communicating his opinion on the adoption in question to the proper officer or clerk of the court, or to an appropriate authority of the country in question, for transmission to the court; and

(*b*) where he has availed himself of that opportunity, his opinion has been transmitted to the court.

(8) In subsections (4) and (5) " specified provision " means a provision specified in an order of the Secretary of State as one notified to the Government of the United Kingdom in pursuance of the provisions of the Convention which relate to prohibitions on an adoption contained in the national law of the Convention country in question.

Freeing for adoption

Freeing child for adoption.

18.—(1) Where, on an application by an adoption agency, an authorised court is satisfied in the case of each parent or guardian of the child that—

(*a*) he freely, and with full understanding of what is involved, agrees generally and unconditionally to the making of an adoption order, or

PART II

(*b*) his agreement to the making of an adoption order should be dispensed with on a ground specified in section 16(2),

the court shall make an order declaring the child free for adoption.

(2) No application shall be made under subsection (1) unless—

(*a*) it is made with the consent of a parent or guardian of a child, or

(*b*) the adoption agency is applying for dispensation under subsection (1)(*b*) of the agreement of each parent or guardian of the child, and the child is in the care of the adoption agency.

(3) No agreement required under subsection (1)(*a*) shall be dispensed with under subsection (1)(*b*) unless the child is already placed for adoption or the court is satisfied that it is likely that the child will be placed for adoption.

(4) An agreement by the mother of the child is ineffective for the purposes of this section if given less than 6 weeks after the child's birth.

(5) On the making of an order under this section, the parental rights and duties relating to the child vest in the adoption agency, and subsections (2) and (3) of section 12 apply as if the order were an adoption order and the agency were the adopters.

(6) Before making an order under this section, the court shall satisfy itself, in relation to each parent or guardian who agrees to the adoption of the child, that he has been given an opportunity of making, if he so wishes, a declaration that he prefers not to be involved in future questions concerning the adoption of the child; and any such declaration shall be recorded by the court.

(7) Before making an order under this section in the case of an illegitimate child whose father is not its guardian, the court shall satisfy itself in relation to any person claiming to be the father that either—

(*a*) he has no intention of applying for custody of the child under section 9 of the Guardianship of Minors Act 1971, or [1971 c. 3.]

(*b*) if he did apply for custody under that section the application would be likely to be refused.

Progress reports to former parent.

19.—(1) This section and section 20 apply to any person (" the former parent ") who was required to be given an opportunity of making a declaration under section 18(6) but did not do so.

PART II

(2) Within the 14 days following the date 12 months after the making of the order under section 18 the adoption agency in which the parental rights and duties were vested on the making of the order, unless it has previously by notice to the former parent informed him that an adoption order has been made in respect of the child, shall by notice to the former parent inform him—

(*a*) whether an adoption order has been made in respect of the child, and (if not)

(*b*) whether the child has his home with a person with whom he has been placed for adoption.

(3) If at the time when the former parent is given notice under subsection (2) an adoption order has not been made in respect of the child, it is thereafter the duty of the adoption agency to give notice to the former parent of the making of an adoption order (if and when made), and meanwhile to give the former parent notice whenever the child is placed for adoption or ceases to have his home with a person with whom he has been placed for adoption.

(4) If at any time the former parent by notice makes a declaration to the adoption agency that he prefers not to be involved in future questions concerning the adoption of the child—

(*a*) the agency shall secure that the declaration is recorded by the court which made the order under section 18, and

(*b*) the agency is released from the duty of complying further with subsection (3) as respects that former parent.

20.—(1) The former parent, at any time more than 12 months after the making of the order under section 18 when— Revocation of s. 18 order.

(*a*) no adoption order has been made in respect of the child, and

(*b*) the child does not have his home with a person with whom he has been placed for adoption,

may apply to the court which made the order for a further order revoking it on the ground that he wishes to resume the parental rights and duties.

(2) While the application is pending the adoption agency having the parental rights and duties shall not place the child for adoption without the leave of the court.

(3) Where an order freeing a child for adoption is revoked under this section—

(*a*) the parental rights and duties relating to the child are vested in the individual or, as the case may be, the individuals in whom they vested immediately before that order was made ;

PART II

(*b*) if the parental rights and duties, or any of them, vested in a local authority or voluntary organisation immediately before the order freeing the child for adoption was made, those rights and duties are vested in the individual, or as the case may be, the individuals in whom they vested immediately before they were vested in the authority or organisation; and

(*c*) any duty extinguished by virtue of section 12(3)(*b*) is forthwith revived,

but the revocation does not affect any right or duty so far as it relates to any period before the date of the revocation.

(4) Subject to subsection (5), if the application is dismissed on the ground that to allow it would contravene the principle embodied in section 6—

(*a*) the former parent who made the application shall not be entitled to make any further application under subsection (1) in respect of the child, and

(*b*) the adoption agency is released from the duty of complying further with section 19(3) as respects that parent.

(5) Subsection (4)(*a*) shall not apply where the court which dismissed the application gives leave to the former parent to make a further application under subsection (1), but such leave shall not be given unless it appears to the court that because of a change in circumstances or for any other reason it is proper to allow the application to be made.

Transfer of parental rights and duties between adoption agencies. 1975 c. 72.

21. On the joint application of an adoption agency in which the parental rights and duties relating to a child who is in England or Wales are vested under section 18(5) or this section or under Part I of the Children Act 1975 (adoption in Scotland), and any other adoption agency, an authorised court may if it thinks fit by order transfer the parental rights and duties to the latter agency.

Supplemental

Notification to local authority of adoption application.

22.—(1) An adoption order shall not be made in respect of a child who was not placed with the applicant by an adoption agency unless the applicant has, at least 3 months before the date of the order, given notice to the local authority within whose area he has his home of his intention to apply for the adoption order.

(2) On receipt of such a notice the local authority shall investigate the matter and submit to the court a report of their investigation.

(3) Under subsection (2), the local authority shall in particular investigate,—

(*a*) so far as is practicable, the suitability of the applicant, and any other matters relevant to the operation of section 6 in relation to the application; and

PART II

(*b*) whether the child was placed with the applicant in contravention of section 11.

(4) A local authority which receives notice under subsection (1) in respect of a child whom the authority know to be in the care of another local authority shall, not more than 7 days after the receipt of the notice, inform that other local authority in writing, that they have received the notice.

Reports where child placed by agency.

23. Where an application for an adoption order relates to a child placed by an adoption agency, the agency shall submit to the court a report on the suitability of the applicants and any other matters relevant to the operation of section 6, and shall assist the court in any manner the court may direct.

Restrictions on making adoption orders.

24.—(1) The court shall not proceed to hear an application for an adoption order in relation to a child where a previous application for a British adoption order made in relation to the child by the same persons was refused by any court unless—

(*a*) in refusing the previous application the court directed that this subsection should not apply, or

(*b*) it appears to the court that because of a change in circumstances or for any other reason it is proper to proceed with the application.

(2) The court shall not make an adoption order in relation to a child unless it is satisfied that the applicants have not, as respects the child, made any payment or given any reward to a person in contravention of section 57.

Interim orders.

25.—(1) Where on an application for an adoption order the requirements of sections 16(1) and 22(1) are complied with, the court may postpone the determination of the application and make an order vesting the legal custody of the child in the applicants for a probationary period not exceeding 2 years upon such terms for the maintenance of the child and otherwise as the court thinks fit.

(2) Where the probationary period specified in an order under subsection (1) is less than 2 years, the court may by a further order extend the period to a duration not exceeding 2 years in all.

Care etc. of child on refusal of adoption order.

26.—(1) Where on an application for an adoption order in relation to a child under the age of 16 years the court refuses to make the adoption order then—

(*a*) if it appears to the court that there are exceptional circumstances making it desirable that the child should be under the supervision of an independent person, the

PART II

court may order that the child shall be under the supervision of a specified local authority or under the supervision of a probation officer;

(*b*) if it appears to the court that there are exceptional circumstances making it impracticable or undesirable for the child to be entrusted to either of the parents or to any other individual, the court may by order commit the child to the care of a specified local authority.

(2) Where the court makes an order under subsection (1)(*b*) the order may require the payment by either parent to the local authority, while it has the care of the child, of such weekly or other periodical sum towards the maintenance of the child as the court thinks reasonable.

1973 c. 29.

(3) Sections 3 and 4 of the Guardianship Act 1973 (which contain supplementary provisions relating to children who are subject to supervision, or in the care of local authorities, by virtue of orders made under section 2 of that Act) apply in relation to an order under this section as they apply in relation to an order under section 2 of that Act.

PART III

CARE AND PROTECTION OF CHILDREN AWAITING ADOPTION

Restrictions on removal of children

Restrictions on removal where adoption agreed or application made under s. 18.

27.—(1) While an application for an adoption order is pending in a case where a parent or guardian of the child has agreed to the making of the adoption order (whether or not he knows the identity of the applicant), the parent or guardian is not entitled, against the will of the person with whom the child has his home, to remove the child from the custody of that person except with the leave of the court.

(2) While an application is pending for an order freeing a child for adoption and—

(*a*) the child is in the care of the adoption agency making the application, and

(*b*) the application was not made with the consent of each parent or guardian of the child,

no parent or guardian of the child is entitled, against the will of the person with whom the child has his home, to remove the child from the custody of that person except with the leave of the court.

(3) Any person who contravenes subsection (1) or (2) shall be guilty of an offence and liable on summary conviction to imprisonment for a term not exceeding 3 months or a fine not exceeding £400 or both.

PART III

(4) This section, except subsection (3), applies notwithstanding that the child is in Scotland at the time he is removed.

(5) Any person who removes a child from the custody of any other person while the child is in England or Wales, contrary to section 34 of the Adoption Act 1958 (which makes for Scotland provision similar to this section), shall be guilty of an offence and liable on summary conviction to imprisonment for a term not exceeding 3 months or a fine not exceeding £400 or both.

1958 c. 5 (7 & 8 Eliz. 2)

Restrictions on removal where applicant has provided home for 5 years.

28.—(1) While an application for an adoption order in respect of a child made by the person with whom the child has had his home for the 5 years preceding the application is pending, no person is entitled, against the will of the applicant, to remove the child from the applicant's custody except with the leave of the court or under authority conferred by any enactment or on the arrest of the child.

(2) Where a person (" the prospective adopter ") gives notice to the local authority within whose area he has his home that he intends to apply for an adoption order in respect of a child who for the preceding 5 years has had his home with the prospective adopter, no person is entitled, against the will of the prospective adopter, to remove the child from the prospective adopter's custody, except with the leave of a court or under authority conferred by any enactment or on the arrest of the child, before—

(*a*) the prospective adopter applies for the adoption order, or

(*b*) the period of 3 months from the receipt of the notice by the local authority expires,

whichever occurs first.

(3) In any case where subsection (1) or (2) applies and—

(*a*) the child was in the care of a local authority before he began to have his home with the applicant or, as the case may be, the prospective adopter, and

(*b*) the child remains in the care of the local authority,

the authority shall not remove the child from the actual custody of the applicant or of the prospective adopter except in accordance with section 30 or 31 or with leave of a court.

(4) In subsections (2) and (3) " a court " means a court with jurisdiction to make adoption orders.

(5) A local authority which receives such notice as is mentioned in subsection (2) in respect of a child whom the authority know to be in the care of another local authority or of a voluntary organisation shall, not more than 7 days after

PART III

the receipt of the notice, inform that other authority or the organisation, in writing, that they have received the notice.

(6) Subsection (2) does not apply to any further notice served by the prospective adopter on any local authority in respect of the same child during the period referred to in paragraph (*b*) of that subsection or within 28 days after its expiry.

(7) Any person who contravenes subsection (1) or (2) shall be guilty of an offence and liable on summary conviction to imprisonment for a term not exceeding 3 months or a fine not exceeding £400 or both.

(8) This section, except subsection (6), applies notwithstanding that the child is in Scotland at the time he is removed.

(9) Any person who removes a child from the custody of any other person while the child is in England or Wales, contrary to section 34A of the Adoption Act 1958 (which makes for Scotland provision similar to this section), shall be guilty of an offence and liable on summary conviction to imprisonment for a term not exceeding 3 months or a fine not exceeding £400 or both.

1958 c. 5 (7 & 8 Eliz. 2).

(10) The Secretary of State may by order amend subsection (1) or (2) to substitute a different period for the period of 5 years mentioned in that subsection (or the period which, by a previous order under this subsection, was substituted for that period).

Return of child taken away in breach of s. 27 or 28.

29.—(1) An authorised court may on the application of a person from whose custody a child has been removed in breach of section 27 or 28 order the person who has so removed the child to return the child to the applicant.

(2) An authorised court may on the application of a person who has reasonable grounds for believing that another person is intending to remove a child from the applicant's custody in breach of section 27 or 28 by order direct that other person not to remove the child from the applicant's custody in breach of section 27 or 28.

(3) If, in the case of an order made by the High Court under subsection (1), the High Court or, in the case of an order made by a county court under subsection (1), a county court is satisfied that the child has not been returned to the applicant, the court may make an order authorising an officer of the court to search such premises as may be specified in the order for the child and, if the officer finds the child, to return the child to the applicant.

(4) If a justice of the peace is satisfied by information on oath that there are reasonable grounds for believing that a child to whom an order under subsection (1) relates is in premises specified in the information, he may issue a search warrant authorising a constable to search the premises for the child;

and if a constable acting in pursuance of a warrant under this section finds the child, he shall return the child to the person on whose application the order under subsection (1) was made. PART III

(5) An order under subsection (3) may be enforced in like manner as a warrant for committal.

Return of children placed for adoption by adoption agencies.

30.—(1) Subject to subsection (2), at any time after a child has been delivered into the actual custody of any person in pursuance of arrangements made by an adoption agency for the adoption of the child by that person, and before an adoption order has been made on the application of that person in respect of the child,—

(*a*) that person may give notice to the agency of his intention not to retain the custody of the child ; or

(*b*) the agency may cause notice to be given to that person of their intention not to allow the child to remain in his custody.

(2) No notice under paragraph (*b*) of subsection (1) shall be given in respect of a child in relation to whom an application has been made for an adoption order except with the leave of the court to which the application has been made.

(3) Where a notice is given to an adoption agency by any person or by an adoption agency to any person under subsection (1), or where an application for an adoption order made by any person in respect of a child placed in his actual custody by an adoption agency is refused by the court or withdrawn, that person shall, within 7 days after the date on which notice was given or the application refused or withdrawn, as the case may be, cause the child to be returned to the agency, who shall receive the child.

(4) Where the period specified in an interim order made under section 25 (whether as originally made or as extended under subsection (2) of that section) expires without an adoption order having been made in respect of the child, subsection (3) shall apply as if the application for an adoption order upon which the interim order was made, had been refused at the expiration of that period.

(5) It shall be sufficient compliance with the requirements of subsection (3) if the child is delivered to, and is received by, a suitable person nominated for the purpose by the adoption agency.

(6) Where an application for an adoption order is refused the court may, if it thinks fit at any time before the expiry of the period of 7 days mentioned in subsection (3), order that period to be extended to a duration, not exceeding 6 weeks, specified in the order.

PART III

(7) Any person who contravenes the provisions of this section shall be guilty of an offence and liable on summary conviction to imprisonment for a term not exceeding 3 months or to a fine not exceeding £400 or to both; and the court by which the offender is convicted may order the child in respect of whom the offence is committed to be returned to his parent or guardian or to the adoption agency which made the arrangements referred to in subsection (1).

Application of s. 30 where child not placed for adoption.

31.—(1) Where a person gives notice in pursuance of section 22(1) to the local authority within whose area he has his home of his intention to apply for an adoption order in respect of a child who is for the time being in the care of a local authority, not being a child who was delivered into the actual custody of that person in pursuance of such arrangements as are mentioned in section 30(1), that section shall apply as if the child had been so delivered, except that where the application is refused by the court or withdrawn the child need not be returned to the local authority in whose care he is unless that authority so require.

(2) Where notice of intention is given as aforesaid in respect of any child who is for the time being in the care of a local authority then, until the application for an adoption order has been made and disposed of, any right of the local authority to require the child to be returned to them otherwise than in pursuance of section 30 shall be suspended.

1933 c. 12.

(3) While the child remains in the actual custody of the person by whom the notice is given no contribution shall be payable (whether under a contribution order or otherwise) in respect of the child by any person liable under section 86 of the Children and the Young Persons Act 1933 to make contributions in respect of him (but without prejudice to the recovery of any sum due at the time the notice is given), unless 12 weeks have elapsed since the giving of the notice without the application being made or the application has been refused by the court or withdrawn.

Protected children

Meaning of "protected child".

32.—(1) Where a person gives notice in pursuance of section 22(1) to the local authority within whose area he lives of his intention to apply for an adoption order in respect of a child, the child is for the purposes of this Part a protected child while he has his home with that person.

1958 c. 5 (7 & 8 Eliz. 2).

(2) A child shall be deemed to be a protected child for the purposes of this Part if he is a protected child within the meaning of section 37 of the Adoption Act 1958.

PART III

(3) A child is not a protected child by reason of any such notice as is mentioned in subsection (1) while—

(*a*) he is in the care of any person in any such school, home or institution as is mentioned in subsection (3) or (5) of section 2 of the Children Act 1958; or 1958 c. 65.

(*b*) he is resident in a residential home for mentally disordered persons as defined by section 19 of the Mental Health Act 1959; or 1959 c. 72.

(*c*) he is liable to be detained or subject to guardianship under the said Act of 1959.

(4) A protected child ceases to be a protected child—

(*a*) on the appointment of a guardian for him under the Guardianship of Minors Act 1971; 1971 c. 3.

(*b*) on the notification to the local authority for the area where the child has his home that the application for an adoption order has been withdrawn;

(*c*) on the making of any of the following orders in respect of the child—

(i) an adoption order;

(ii) an order under section 26;

(iii) a custodianship order;

(iv) an order under section 42, 43 or 44 of the Matrimonial Causes Act 1973; or 1973 c. 18.

(*d*) on his attaining the age of 18 years,

whichever first occurs.

Duty of local authorities to secure well-being of protected children.

33.—(1) It shall be the duty of every local authority to secure that protected children within their area are visited from time to time by officers of the authority, who shall satisfy themselves as to the well-being of the children and give such advice as to their care and maintenance as may appear to be needed.

(2) Any officer of a local authority authorised to visit protected children may, after producing, if asked to do so, some duly authenticated document showing that he is so authorised, inspect any premises in the area of the authority in which such children are to be or are being kept.

Removal of protected children from unsuitable surroundings.

34.—(1) If a juvenile court is satisfied, on the complaint of a local authority, that a protected child is being kept or is about to be received by any person who is unfit to have his care or in any premises or any environment detrimental or likely to be detrimental to him, the court may make an order for his removal to a place of safety until he can be restored to a parent, relative or guardian of his, or until other arrangements can be made with respect to him; and on proof that there is imminent danger to the health or well-being of the child the power to make

PART III

an order under this section may be exercised by a justice of the peace acting on the application of a person authorised to visit protected children.

(2) An order under this section may be executed by any person authorised to visit protected children or by any constable.

1948 c. 43.

(3) A local authority may receive into their care under section 1 of the Children Act 1948 any child removed under this section, whether or not the circumstances of the child are such that they fall within paragraphs (*a*) to (*c*) of subsection (1) of that section and notwithstanding that he may appear to the local authority to be over the age of 17 years.

(4) Where a child is removed under this section the local authority shall, if practicable, inform a parent or guardian of the child, or any person who acts as his guardian.

Notices and information to be given to local authorities.

35.—(1) Where a person who has a protected child in his actual custody changes his permanent address he shall, not less than 2 weeks before the change, or, if the change is made in an emergency, not later than one week after the change, give notice specifying the new address to the local authority in whose area his permanent address is before the change, and if the new address is in the area of another local authority, the authority to whom the notice is given shall inform that other local authority and give them such of the following particulars as are known to them, that is to say—

(*a*) the name, sex and date and place of birth of the child;

(*b*) the name and address of every person who is a parent or guardian or acts as a guardian of the child or from whom the child was received.

(2) If a protected child dies, the person in whose actual custody he was at his death shall within 48 hours give notice of the child's death to the local authority.

Offences relating to protected children.

36.—(1) A person shall be guilty of an offence if—

(*a*) being required, under section 35 to give any notice or information, he fails to give the notice within the time specified in that provision or fails to give the information within a reasonable time, or knowingly makes or causes or procures another person to make any false or misleading statement in the notice of information;

(*b*) he refuses to allow the visiting of a protected child by a duly authorised officer of a local authority or the inspection, under the power conferred by section 33(2) of any premises;

(*c*) he refuses to comply with an order under section 34 for the removal of any child or obstructs any person in the execution of such an order.

(2) A person guilty of an offence under this section shall be liable on summary conviction to imprisonment for a term not exceeding 3 months or a fine not exceeding £400 or both.

Miscellaneous provisions relating to protected children. 1933 c. 12.

37.—(1) For the purposes of section 40 of the Children and Young Persons Act 1933, under which a warrant authorising the search for and removal of a child may be issued on suspicion of unnecessary suffering caused to, or certain offences committed against, the child, any refusal to allow the visiting of a protected child or the inspection of any premises by a person authorised to do so under section 33 shall be treated as giving reasonable cause for such a suspicion.

(2) A person who maintains a protected child shall be deemed for the purposes of the Life Assurance Act 1774 to have no interest in the life of the child. 1774 c. 48.

(3) An appeal shall lie to the Crown Court against any order made under section 34 by a juvenile court or a justice of the peace.

(4) Subsection (2) of section 47 of the Children and Young Persons Act 1933 (which restricts the time and place at which a sitting of a juvenile court may be held and the persons who may be present at such a sitting) shall not apply to any sitting of a juvenile court in any proceedings under section 34. 1933 c. 12.

PART IV

STATUS OF ADOPTED CHILDREN

Meaning of "adoption" in Part IV.

38.—(1) In this Part " adoption " means adoption—

(*a*) by an adoption order;

(*b*) by an order made under the Children Act 1975, the Adoption Act 1958, the Adoption Act 1950 or any enactment repealed by the Adoption Act 1950; 1975 c. 72. 1958 c. 5 (7 & 8 Eliz. 2).

(*c*) by an order made in Scotland, Northern Ireland, the Isle of Man or in any of the Channel Islands; 1950 c. 26.

(*d*) which is an overseas adoption; or

(*e*) which is an adoption recognised by the law of England and Wales and effected under the law of any other country,

and cognate expressions shall be construed accordingly.

(2) The definition of adoption includes, where the context admits, an adoption effected before the passing of the Children Act 1975, and the date of an adoption effected by an order is the date of the making of the order.

PART IV

Status conferred by adoption.

39.—(1) An adopted child shall be treated in law—

(*a*) where the adopters are a married couple, as if he had been born as a child of the marriage (whether or not he was in fact born after the marriage was solemnized) ;

(*b*) in any other case, as if he had been born to the adopter in wedlock (but not as a child of any actual marriage of the adopter).

(2) An adopted child shall, subject to subsection (3), be treated in law as if he were not the child of any person other than the adopters or adopter.

(3) In the case of a child adopted by one of its natural parents as sole adoptive parent, subsection (2) has no effect as respects entitlement to property depending on relationship to that parent, or as respects anything else depending on that relationship.

(4) It is hereby declared that this section prevents an adopted child from being illegitimate.

(5) This section has effect—

(*a*) in the case of an adoption before 1st January 1976, from that date, and

(*b*) in the case of any other adoption, from the date of the adoption.

(6) Subject to the provisions of this Part, this section—

(*a*) applies for the construction of enactments or instruments passed or made before the adoption or later, and so applies subject to any contrary indication ; and

(*b*) has effect as respects things done, or events occurring, after the adoption, or after 31st December 1975, whichever is the later.

Citizenship.

40.—(1) Where an adoption order is made in relation to a child who is not a citizen of the United Kingdom and Colonies, but the adopter or, in the case of a joint adoption, the adoptive father is a citizen of the United Kingdom and Colonies, the child shall be a citizen of the United Kingdom and Colonies as from the date of the adoption.

(2) In subsection (1) the reference to an adoption order includes a reference to an order authorising the adoption of a child in Scotland, Northern Ireland, the Isle of Man or in any of the Channel Islands.

(3) Where a Convention adoption order, or a specified order ceases to have effect, either on annulment or otherwise, the cesser shall not affect the status as a citizen of the United Kingdom and Colonies of any person who, by virtue of this section or section 19 of the Adoption Act 1958, became such a citizen in consequence of the order.

1958 c. 5 (7 & 8 Eliz. 2).

PART IV

Adoptive relatives.

41. A relationship existing by virtue of section 39 may be referred to as an adoptive relationship, and—

(*a*) a male adopter may be referred to as the adoptive father;

(*b*) a female adopter may be referred to as the adoptive mother;

(*c*) any other relative of any degree under an adoptive relationship may be referred to as an adoptive relative of that degree,

but this section does not prevent the term " parent ", or any other term not qualified by the word " adoptive " being treated as including an adoptive relative.

Rules of construction for instruments concerning property.

42.—(1) Subject to any contrary indication, the rules of construction contained in this section apply to any instrument, other than an existing instrument, so far as it contains a disposition of property.

(2) In applying section 39(1) to a disposition which depends on the date of birth of a child or children of the adoptive parent or parents, the disposition shall be construed as if—

(*a*) the adopted child had been born on the date of adoption,

(*b*) two or more children adopted on the same date had been born on that date in the order of their actual births,

but this does not affect any reference to the age of a child.

(3) Examples of phrases in wills on which subsection (2) can operate are—

1. Children of A " living at my death or born afterwards ".

2. Children of A " living at my death or born afterwards before any one of such children for the time being in existence attains a vested interest and who attain the age of 21 years ".

3. As in example 1 or 2, but referring to grandchildren of A instead of children of A.

4. A for life " until he has a child ", and then to his child or children.

Note. Subsection (2) will not affect the reference to the age of 21 years in example 2.

(4) Section 39(2) does not prejudice any interest vested in possession in the adopted child before the adoption, or any interest expectant (whether immediately or not) upon an interest so vested.

PART IV

(5) Where it is necessary to determine for the purposes of a disposition of property effected by an instrument whether a woman can have a child, it shall be presumed that once a woman has attained the age of 55 years she will not adopt a child after execution of the instrument, and, notwithstanding section 39, if she does so that child shall not be treated as her child or as the child of her spouse (if any) for the purposes of the instrument.

(6) In this section, "instrument" includes a private Act settling property, but not any other enactment.

Dispositions depending on date of birth.

1969 c. 46.

43.—(1) Where a disposition depends on the date of birth of a child who was born illegitimate and who is adopted by one of the natural parents as sole adoptive parent, section 42(2) does not affect entitlement under Part II of the Family Law Reform Act 1969 (illegitimate children).

(2) Subsection (1) applies for example where—

(*a*) a testator dies in 1976 bequeathing a legacy to his eldest grandchild living at a specified time,

(*b*) his daughter has an illegitimate child in 1977 who is the first grandchild,

(*c*) his married son has a child in 1978,

(*d*) subsequently the illegitimate child is adopted by the mother as sole adoptive parent,

and in all those cases the daughter's child remains the eldest grandchild of the testator throughout.

Property devolving with peerages etc.

44.—(1) An adoption does not affect the descent of any peerage or dignity or title of honour.

(2) An adoption shall not affect the devolution of any property limited (expressly or not) to devolve (as nearly as the law permits) along with any peerage or dignity or title of honour.

(3) Subsection (2) applies only if and so far as a contrary intention is not expressed in the instrument, and shall have effect subject to the terms of the instrument.

Protection of trustees and personal representatives.

45.—(1) A trustee or personal representative is not under a duty, by virtue of the law relating to trusts or the administration of estates, to enquire, before conveying or distributing any property, whether any adoption has been effected or revoked if that fact could affect entitlement to the property.

(2) A trustee or personal representative shall not be liable to any person by reason of a conveyance or distribution of the property made without regard to any such fact if he has not received notice of the fact before the conveyance or distribution.

(3) This section does not prejudice the right of a person to follow the property, or any property representing it, into the hands of another person, other than a purchaser, who has received it. PART IV

46.—(1) In this Part, unless the context otherwise requires,— Meaning of " disposition ".

" disposition " includes the conferring of a power of appointment and any other disposition of an interest in or right over property;

" power of appointment " includes any discretionary power to transfer a beneficial interest in property without the furnishing of valuable consideration.

(2) This Part applies to an oral disposition as if contained in an instrument made when the disposition was made.

(3) For the purposes of this Part, the death of the testator is the date at which a will or codicil is to be regarded as made.

(4) For the purposes of this Part, provisions of the law of intestate succession applicable to the estate of a deceased person shall be treated as if contained in an instrument executed by him (while of full capacity) immediately before his death.

(5) It is hereby declared that references in this Part to dispositions of property include references to a disposition by the creation of an entailed interest.

47.—(1) Section 39 does not apply for the purposes of the table of kindred and affinity in Schedule 1 to the Marriage Act 1949 or sections 10 and 11 (incest) of the Sexual Offences Act 1956. Miscellaneous enactments. 1949 c. 76. 1956 c. 69.

(2) Without prejudice to section 40, section 39 does not apply for the purposes of any provision of—

(*a*) the British Nationality Acts 1948 to 1965,

(*b*) the Immigration Act 1971, 1971 c. 77.

(*c*) any instrument having effect under an enactment within paragraph (*a*) or (*b*), or

(*d*) any other provision of the law for the time being in force which determines citizenship of the United Kingdom and Colonies.

(3) Section 39 shall not prevent a person being treated as a near relative of a deceased person for the purposes of section 32 of the Social Security Act 1975 (payment of death grant), if apart from section 39 he would be so treated. 1975 c. 14.

(4) Section 39 does not apply for the purposes of section 70(3)(*b*) or section 73(2) of the Social Security Act 1975 (payment of industrial death benefit to or in respect of an illegitimate child of the deceased and the child's mother).

PART IV

1975 c. 14. (5) Subject to regulations made under section 72 of the Social Security Act 1975 (entitlement of certain relatives of deceased to industrial death benefit), section 39 shall not affect the entitlement to an industrial death benefit of a person who would, apart from section 39, be treated as a relative of a deceased person for the purposes of the said section 72.

Pensions. **48.** Section 39(2) does not affect entitlement to a pension which is payable to or for the benefit of a child and is in payment at the time of his adoption.

Insurance. **49.** Where a child is adopted whose natural parent has effected an insurance with a friendly society or a collecting society or an industrial insurance company for the payment on the death of the child of money for funeral expenses, the rights and liabilities under the policy shall by virtue of the adoption be transferred to the adoptive parents who shall for the purposes of the enactments relating to such societies and companies be treated as the person who took out the policy.

PART V

REGISTRATION AND REVOCATION OF ADOPTION ORDERS AND CONVENTION ADOPTIONS

Adopted Children Register. **50.**—(1) The Registrar General shall maintain at the General Register Office a register, to be called the Adopted Children Register, in which shall be made such entries as may be directed to be made therein by adoption orders, but no other entries.

(2) A certified copy of an entry in the Adopted Children Register, if purporting to be sealed or stamped with the seal of the General Register Office, shall, without any further or other proof of that entry, be received as evidence of the adoption to which it relates and, where the entry contains a record of the date of the birth or the country or the district and sub-district of the birth of the adopted person, shall also be received as aforesaid as evidence of that date or country or district and sub-district in all respects as if the copy were a certified copy of an entry in the Registers of Births.

(3) The Registrar General shall cause an index of the Adopted Children Register to be made and kept in the General Register Office; and every person shall be entitled to search that index and to have a certified copy of any entry in the Adopted Children Register in all respects upon and subject to the same terms, conditions and regulations as to payment of fees and otherwise as are applicable under the Births and Deaths Registration Act 1953, and the Registration Service Act 1953, in respect of searches in other indexes kept in the General

1953 c. 20.
1953 c. 37.

Register Office and in respect of the supply from that office of certified copies of entries in the certified copies of the Registers of Births and Deaths. PART V

(4) The Registrar General shall, in addition to the Adopted Children Register and the index thereof, keep such other registers and books, and make such entries therein, as may be necessary to record and make traceable the connection between any entry in the Registers of Births which has been marked "Adopted" and any corresponding entry in the Adopted Children Register.

(5) The registers and books kept under subsection (4) shall not be, nor shall any index thereof be, open to public inspection or search, and the Registrar General shall not furnish any person with any information contained in or with any copy or extract from any such registers or books except in accordance with section 51 or under an order of any of the following courts, that is to say—

(*a*) the High Court;

(*b*) the Westminster County Court or such other county court as may be prescribed; and

(*c*) the court by which an adoption order was made in respect of the person to whom the information, copy or extract relates.

(6) In relation to an adoption order made by a magistrates' court, the reference in paragraph (*c*) of subsection (5) to the court by which the order was made includes a reference to a court acting for the same petty sessions area.

(7) Schedule 1 to this Act, which, among other things, provides for the registration of adoptions and the amendment of adoption orders, shall have effect.

Disclosure of birth records of adopted children.

51.—(1) Subject to subsections (4) and (6), the Registrar General shall on an application made in the prescribed manner by an adopted person a record of whose birth is kept by the Registrar General and who has attained the age of 18 years supply to that person on payment of the prescribed fee (if any) such information as is necessary to enable that person to obtain a certified copy of the record of his birth.

(2) On an application made in the prescribed manner by an adopted person under the age of 18 years, a record of whose birth is kept by the Registrar General and who is intending to be married in England or Wales, and on payment of the prescribed fee (if any), the Registrar General shall inform the applicant whether or not it appears from information contained in the registers of live births or other records that the applicant and the person whom he intends to marry may be within the

PART V

1949 c. 76. prohibited degrees of relationship for the purposes of the Marriage Act 1949.

(3) It shall be the duty of the Registrar General and each local authority and approved adoption society to provide counselling for adopted persons who apply for information under subsection (1).

(4) Before supplying any information to an applicant under subsection (1) the Registrar General shall inform the applicant that counselling services are available to him—

(*a*) at the General Register Office; or

(*b*) from the local authority for the area where the applicant is at the time the application is made; or

(*c*) from the local authority for the area where the court sat which made the adoption order relating to the applicant; or

(*d*) if the applicant's adoption was arranged by an adoption society which is approved under section 3 of this Act or under section 4 of the Children Act 1975, from that society.

1975 c. 72.

(5) If the applicant chooses to receive counselling from a local authority or an adoption society under subsection (4) the Registrar General shall send to the authority or society of the applicant's choice the information to which the applicant is entitled under subsection (1).

(6) The Registrar General shall not supply a person who was adopted before 12th November 1975 with any information under subsection (1) unless that person has attended an interview with a counsellor either at the General Register Office or in pursuance of arrangements made by the local authority or adoption society from whom the applicant is entitled to receive counselling in accordance with subsection (4).

(7) In this section, " prescribed " means prescribed by regulations made by the Registrar General.

Revocation of adoptions on legitimation.

52.—(1) Where any person adopted by his father or mother alone has subsequently become a legitimated person on the marriage of his father and mother, the court by which the adoption order was made may, on the application of any of the parties concerned, revoke that order.

1959 c. 73. (2) Where any person legitimated by virtue of section 1 of the Legitimacy Act 1959, had been adopted by his father and mother before the commencement of that Act, the court by which the adoption order was made may, on the application of any of the parties concerned, revoke that order.

(3) Where a person adopted by his father or mother alone by virtue of a regulated adoption has subsequently become a

legitimated person on the marriage of his father and mother, the High Court may, upon an application under this subsection by the parties concerned, by order revoke the adoption. PART V

(4) In relation to an adoption order made by a magistrates' court, the reference in subsections (1) and (2) to the court by which the order was made includes a reference to a court acting for the same petty sessions area.

Annulment etc. of overseas adoptions.

53.—(1) The High Court may, upon an application under this subsection, by order annul a regulated adoption—

(*a*) on the ground that at the relevant time the adoption was prohibited by a notified provision, if under the internal law then in force in the country of which the adopter was then a national or the adopters were then nationals the adoption could have been impugned on that ground;

(*b*) on the ground that at the relevant time the adoption contravened provisions relating to consents of the internal law relating to adoption of the country of which the adopted person was then a national, if under that law the adoption could then have been impugned on that ground;

(*c*) on any other ground on which the adoption can be impugned under the law for the time being in force in the country in which the adoption was effected.

(2) The High Court may, upon an application under this subsection—

(*a*) order that an overseas adoption or a determination shall cease to be valid in Great Britain on the ground that the adoption or determination is contrary to public policy or that the authority which purported to authorise the adoption or make the determination was not competent to entertain the case;

(*b*) decide the extent, if any, to which a determination has been affected by a subsequent determination.

(3) Any court in Great Britain may, in any proceedings in that court, decide that an overseas adoption or a determination shall, for the purposes of those proceedings, be treated as invalid in Great Britain on either of the grounds mentioned in subsection (2).

(4) An order or decision of the Court of Session on an application under subsection (3) of section 6 of the Adoption Act 1968 shall be recognised and have effect as if it were an order or decision of the High Court on an application under subsection (3) of this section. 1968 c. 53.

(5) Except as provided by this section and section 52(3) the validity of an overseas adoption or a determination shall not

PART V

be impugned in England and Wales in proceedings in any court.

Provisions supplementary to ss. 52(3) and 53.

54.—(1) Any application for an order under section 52(3) or 53 or a decision under section 53(3) shall be made in the prescribed manner and within such period, if any, as may be prescribed.

(2) No application shall be made under section 52(3) or section 53(1) in respect of an adoption unless immediately before the application is made the person adopted or the adopter habitually resides in England and Wales or, as the case may be, both adopters habitually reside there.

(3) In deciding in pursuance of section 53 whether such an authority as is mentioned in section 59 was competent to entertain a particular case, a court shall be bound by any finding of fact made by the authority and stated by the authority to be so made for the purpose of determining whether the authority was competent to entertain the case.

(4) In section 53—

" determination " means such a determination as is mentioned in section 59 of this Act;

" notified provision " means a provision specified in an order of the Secretary of State as one in respect of which a notification to or by the Government of the United Kingdom was in force at the relevant time in pursuance of the provisions of the Convention relating to prohibitions contained in the national law of the adopter; and

" relevant time " means the time when the adoption in question purported to take effect under the law of the country in which it purports to have been effected.

PART VI

MISCELLANEOUS AND SUPPLEMENTAL

Adoption of children abroad.

55.—(1) Where on an application made in relation to a child by a person who is not domiciled in England and Wales or Scotland an authorised court is satisfied that he intends to adopt the child under the law of or within the country in which the applicant is domiciled, the court may, subject to the following provisions of this section, make an order vesting in him the parental rights and duties relating to the child.

(2) The provisions of Part II relating to adoption orders, except sections 12(1), 14(2), 15(2), 17 to 21 and 25, shall apply in relation to orders under this section as they apply in relation to adoption orders subject to the modification that in section 13(1) for " 19 " and " 13 " there are substituted " 32 " and " 26 " respectively.

PART VI

(3) Sections 50 and 51 and paragraphs 1 and 2(1) of Schedule 1 shall apply in relation to an order under this section as they apply in relation to an adoption order except that any entry in the Registers of Births, or the Adopted Children Register which is required to be marked in consequence of the making of an order under this section shall, in lieu of being marked with the word " Adopted " or " Re-adopted " (with or without the addition of the word " (Scotland) "), be marked with the words " Proposed foreign adoption " or " Proposed foreign re-adoption ", as the case may require.

(4) References in sections 27, 28, 30, 31 and 32 to an adoption order include references to an order under this section or under section 25 of the Children Act 1975 (orders in Scotland authorising adoption abroad). 1975 c. 72.

Restriction on removal of children for adoption outside Great Britain.

56.—(1) Except under the authority of an order under section 55, or under section 25 of the Children Act 1975 (orders in Scotland authorising adoption abroad) it shall not be lawful for any person to take or send a child who is a British subject or a citizen of the Republic of Ireland out of Great Britain to any place outside the British Islands with a view to the adoption of the child by any person not being a parent or guardian or relative of the child; and any person who takes or sends a child out of Great Britain to any place in contravention of this subsection, or makes or takes part in any arrangements for transferring the actual custody of a child to any person for that purpose, shall be guilty of an offence and liable on summary conviction to imprisonment for a term not exceeding 3 months or to a fine not exceeding £400 or to both.

(2) In any proceedings under this section, a report by a British consular officer or a deposition made before a British consular officer and authenticated under the signature of that officer shall, upon proof that the officer or the deponent cannot be found in the United Kingdom, be admissible as evidence of the matters stated therein, and it shall not be necessary to prove the signature or official character of the person who appears to have signed any such report or deposition.

(3) A person shall be deemed to take part in arrangements for transferring the actual custody of a child to a person for the purpose referred to in subsection (1) if—

(*a*) he facilitates the placing of the child in the actual custody of that person; or

(*b*) he initiates or takes part in any negotiations of which the purpose or effect is the conclusion of any agreement or the making of any arrangement therefor, and if he causes another person to do so.

PART VI

Prohibition on certain payments.

57.—(1) Subject to the provisions of this section, it shall not be lawful to make or give to any person any payment or reward for or in consideration of—

(*a*) the adoption by that person of a child;

(*b*) the grant by that person of any agreement or consent required in connection with the adoption of a child;

(*c*) the transfer by that person of the actual custody of a child with a view to the adoption of the child; or

(*d*) the making by that person of any arrangements for the adoption of a child.

(2) Any person who makes or gives, or agrees or offers to make or give, any payment or reward prohibited by this section, or who receives or agrees to receive or attempts to obtain any such payment or reward, shall be guilty of an offence and liable on summary conviction to imprisonment for a term not exceeding 3 months or to a fine not exceeding £400 or to both; and the court may order any child in respect of whom the offence was committed to be removed to a place of safety until he can be restored to his parents or guardian or until other arrangements can be made for him.

(3) This section does not apply to any payment made to an adoption agency by a parent or guardian of a child or by a person who adopts or proposes to adopt a child, being a payment in respect of expenses reasonably incurred by the agency in connection with the adoption of the child, or to any payment or reward authorised by the court to which an application for an adoption order in respect of a child is made.

(4) If an adoption agency submits to the Secretary of State a scheme for the payment by the agency of allowances to persons who have adopted or intend to adopt a child where arrangements for the adoption were made, or are to be made, by that agency, and the Secretary of State approves the scheme, this section shall not apply to any payment made in accordance with the scheme.

(5) The Secretary of State, in the case of a scheme approved by him under subsection (4), may at any time—

(*a*) make, or approve the making by the agency of, alterations to the scheme;

(*b*) revoke the scheme.

1975 c. 72.

(6) The Secretary of State shall, within seven years of the date on which section 32 of the Children Act 1975 came into force and, thereafter, every five years, publish a report on the operation of the schemes since that date or since the publication of the last report.

(7) Subject to the following subsection, subsection (4) of this section shall expire on the seventh anniversary of the date on which section 32 of the Children Act 1975 came into force.

(8) The Secretary of State may by order made by statutory instrument at any time before the said anniversary repeal subsection (7) of this section.

(9) An order under subsection (8) of this section shall not be made unless a report has been published under subsection (6) of this section.

(10) Notwithstanding the expiry of subsection (4) of this section or the revocation of a scheme approved under this section, subsection (1) of this section shall not apply in relation to any payment made, whether before or after the expiry of subsection (4) or the revocation of the scheme, in accordance with a scheme which was approved under this section to a person to whom such payments were made—

(*a*) where the scheme was not revoked, before the expiry of subsection (4), or

(*b*) if the scheme was revoked, before the date of its revocation.

Restriction on advertisements.

58.—(1) It shall not be lawful for any advertisement to be published indicating—

(*a*) that the parent or guardian of a child desires to cause a child to be adopted ; or

(*b*) that a person desires to adopt a child ; or

(*c*) that any person (not being an adoption agency) is willing to make arrangements for the adoption of a child.

(2) Any person who causes to be published or knowingly publishes an advertisement in contravention of the provisions of this section shall be guilty of an offence and liable on summary conviction to a fine not exceeding £400.

Effect of determination and orders made in Scotland and overseas in adoption proceedings.

59.—(1) Where an authority of a Convention country or any British territory other than Great Britain having power under the law of that country or territory—

(*a*) to authorise or review the authorisation of a regulated adoption or a specified order ; or

(*b*) to give or review a decision revoking or annulling a regulated adoption, a specified order or a Convention adoption order,

makes a determination in the exercise of that power, then, subject to sections 52(3) and 53 and any subsequent determination having effect under this subsection, the determination shall have effect in England and Wales for the purpose of effecting, confirming or terminating the adoption in question or confirming its termination, as the case may be.

(2) Subsections (2) and (3) of section 12 shall apply in relation to an order under section 14 of the Children Act 1975 (freeing 1975 c. 72.

PART VI

children for adoption in Scotland) as if the order were an adoption order; and, on the revocation of the order under section 16 of that Act, any duty extinguished by section 12(3)(*b*) is forthwith revived but the revival does not have the effect as respects anything done or not done before the revival.

(3) Sections 12(3) and (4) and 49 apply in relation to a child who is the subject of an order which is similar to an order under section 55 and is made (whether before or after this Act has effect) in Scotland, Northern Ireland, the Isle of Man or any of the Channel Islands, as they apply in relation to a child who is the subject of an adoption order.

Evidence of adoption in Scotland and Northern Ireland.

60. Any document which is receivable as evidence of any matter—

(*a*) in Scotland under section 22(2) of the Adoption Act 1958; or

1958 c. 5 (7 & 8 Eliz. 2).

1967 c. 35 (N.I.).

(*b*) in Northern Ireland under section 23(4) of the Adoption Act (Northern Ireland) 1967 or any corresponding provision contained in a Measure of the Northern Ireland Assembly for the time being in force,

shall also be so receivable in England and Wales.

Evidence of agreement and consent.

61.—(1) Any agreement or consent which is required by this Act to be given to the making of an order or application for an order (other than an order to which section 17(6) applies) may be given in writing, and, if the document signifying the agreement or consent is witnessed in accordance with rules, it shall be admissible in evidence without further proof of the signature of the person by whom it was executed.

(2) A document signifying such agreement or consent which purports to be witnessed in accordance with rules shall be presumed to be so witnessed, and to have been executed and witnessed on the date and at the place specified in the document, unless the contrary is proved.

Courts.

62.—(1) In this Act, "authorised court", as respects an application for an order relating to a child, shall be construed as follows.

(2) Subject to subsections (4) to (6), if the child is in England or Wales when the application is made, the following are authorised courts—

(*a*) the High Court;

(*b*) the county court within whose district the child is, and, in the case of an application for an order freeing a child for adoption, any county court within whose district a parent or guardian of the child is;

PART VI

(c) any other county court prescribed by rules made under section 102 of the County Courts Act 1959; 1959 c. 22.

(d) a magistrates' court within whose area the child is, and, in the case of an application for an order freeing the child for adoption, a magistrates' court within whose area a parent or guardian of the child is.

(3) If, in the case of an application for an adoption order or for an order freeing a child for adoption, the child is not in Great Britain when the application is made, the High Court is the authorised court.

(4) In the case of an application for a Convention adoption order, paragraphs (b), (c) and (d) of subsection (2) do not apply.

(5) Subsection (2) does not apply in the case of an application under section 29 but for the purposes of such an application the following are authorised courts—

(a) if there is pending in respect of the child an application for an adoption order or an order freeing him for adoption, the court in which that application is pending;

(b) if paragraph (a) does not apply and there is no application for an order under section 8 or 14 of the Children Act 1975 (which make provision in Scotland for adoption orders and orders freeing children for adoption pending in respect of the child), the High Court, the county court within whose district the applicant lives and the magistrates' court within whose area the applicant lives. 1975 c. 72.

(6) In the case of an order under section 55, paragraph (d) of subsection (2) does not apply.

Appeals etc.

63.—(1) Subject to subsection (4), where any application has been made under this Act to a county court, the High Court may, at the instance of any party to the application, order the application to be removed to the High Court and there proceeded with on such terms as to costs as it thinks proper.

(2) Subject to subsections (3) and (4), where on an application to a magistrates' court under this Act the court makes or refuses to make an order, an appeal shall lie to the High Court.

(3) Subject to subsection (4), where an application is made to a magistrates' court under this Act, and the court considers that the matter is one which would more conveniently be dealt with by the High Court, the magistrates' court shall refuse to make an order, and in that case no appeal shall lie to the High Court.

(4) This section does not apply in relation to an application for leave of the court to remove a child from a person's custody

PART VI

under section 27 or 28 or to serve a notice under section 30(1) or in relation to an appeal against an order made under section 34.

Proceedings to be in private.

64. Proceedings under Part II, section 29 or section 55—

(*a*) in the High Court, may be disposed of in chambers;

(*b*) in a county court, shall be heard and determined in camera;

(*c*) in a magistrates' court, shall be domestic proceedings for the purposes of the Magistrates' Courts Act 1952, but section 57(2)(*d*) of that Act shall not apply in relation thereto.

1952 c. 55.

Guardians ad litem and reporting officers.

65.—(1) For the purpose of any application for an adoption order or an order freeing a child for adoption or an order under section 20 or 55 rules shall provide for the appointment, in such cases as are prescribed—

(*a*) of a person to act as guardian ad litem of the child upon the hearing of the application, with the duty of safeguarding the interests of the child in the prescribed manner;

(*b*) of a person to act as reporting officer for the purpose of witnessing agreements to adoption and performing such other duties as the rules may prescribe.

(2) A person who is employed—

(*a*) in the case of an application for an adoption order, by the adoption agency by whom the child was placed; or

(*b*) in the case of an application for an order freeing a child for adoption, by the adoption agency by whom the application was made; or

(*c*) in the case of an application under section 20, by the adoption agency with the parental rights and duties relating to the child,

shall not be appointed to act as guardian ad litem or reporting officer for the purposes of the application but, subject to that, the same person may if the court thinks fit be both guardian ad litem and reporting officer.

Rules of procedure.

66.—(1) Rules in regard to any matter to be prescribed under this Act and dealing generally with all matters of procedure and incidental matters arising out of this Act and for carrying this Act into effect shall be made by the Lord Chancellor.

(2) Subsection (1) does not apply in relation to proceedings before magistrates' courts, but the power to make rules conferred by section 15 of the Justices of the Peace Act 1949, shall include power to make provision as to any of the matters mentioned in that subsection.

1949 c. 101.

PART VI

(3) In the case of—

(*a*) an application for an adoption order in relation to a child who is not free for adoption;

(*b*) an application for an order freeing a child for adoption,

rules shall require every person who can be found and whose agreement or consent to the making of the order is required under this Act to be notified of a date and place where he will be heard on the application and of the fact that, unless he wishes or the court requires, he need not attend.

(4) In the case of an application under section 55, rules shall require every parent and guardian of the child who can be found to be notified as aforesaid.

(5) Rules made as respects magistrates' courts may provide for enabling any fact tending to establish the identity of a child with a child to whom a document relates to be proved by affidavit and for excluding or restricting in relation to any facts that may be so proved the power of a justice of the peace to compel the attendance of witnesses.

(6) This section does not apply in relation to sections 9, 10, 11 and 32 to 37.

Orders, rules and regulations.

67.—(1) Any power to make orders, rules or regulations conferred by this Act on the Secretary of State, the Lord Chancellor or the Registrar General shall be exercisable by statutory instrument.

(2) A statutory instrument containing rules or regulations made under any provision of this Act, except section 3(1), shall be subject to annulment in pursuance of a resolution of either House of Parliament.

(3) An order under section 28(10) or 57(8) shall not be made unless a draft of the order has been approved by resolution of each House of Parliament.

(4) An order made under any provision of this Act, except section 74, may be revoked or varied by a subsequent order under that provision.

(5) Orders and regulations made under this Act may make different provision in relation to different cases or classes of cases and may exclude certain cases or classes of cases.

(6) The Registrar General shall not make regulations under section 51 or paragraph 1(1) of Schedule 1 except with the approval of the Secretary of State.

Offences by bodies corporate.

68. Where an offence under this Act committed by a body corporate is proved to have been committed with the consent or connivance of or to be attributable to any neglect on the part

PART VI

of, any director, manager, member of the committee, secretary or other officer of the body, he as well as the body shall be deemed to be guilty of that offence and shall be liable to be proceeded against and punished accordingly.

Service of notices etc.

69. Any notice or information required to be given under this Act may be given by post.

Nationality.

70.—(1) If the Secretary of State by order declares that a description of persons specified in the order has, in pursuance of the Convention, been notified to the Government of the United Kingdom as the description of persons who are deemed to possess the nationality of a particular Convention country, persons of that description shall, subject to the following provisions of this section, be treated for the purposes of this Act as nationals of that country.

(2) Subject to section 54(3) and subsection (3) of this section, where it appears to the court in any proceedings under this Act, or to any court by which a decision in pursuance of section 53(3) falls to be given, that a person is or was at a particular time a national of two or more countries, then—

(*a*) if it appears to the said court that he is or was then a United Kingdom national, he shall be treated for the purposes of those proceedings or that decision as if he were or had then been a United Kingdom national only;

(*b*) if, in a case not falling within paragraph (*a*), it appears to the said court that one only of those countries is or was then a Convention country, he shall be treated for those purposes as if he were or had then been a national of that country only;

(*c*) if, in a case not falling within paragraph (*a*), it appears to the said court that two or more of those countries are or were then Convention countries, he shall be treated for those purposes as if he were or had then been a national of such one only of those Convention countries as the said court considers is the country with which he is or was then most closely connected;

(*d*) in any other case, he shall be treated for those purposes as if he were or had then been a national of such one only of those countries as the said court considers is the country with which he is or was then most closely connected.

(3) A court in which proceedings are brought in pursuance of section 17, 52(3) or 53 shall be entitled to disregard the provisions of subsection (2) in so far as it appears to that court appropriate to do so for the purposes of those proceedings; but

nothing in this subsection shall be construed as prejudicing the provisions of section 54(3). PART VI

(4) Where, after such inquiries as the court in question considers appropriate, it appears to the court in any proceedings under this Act, or to any court by which such a decision as aforesaid falls to be given, that a person has no nationality or no ascertainable nationality, he shall be treated for the purposes of those proceedings or that decision as a national of the country in which he resides or, where that country is one of two or more countries having the same law of nationality, as a national of those countries.

Internal law of a country.

71.—(1) In this Act " internal law " in relation to any country means the law applicable in a case where no question arises as to the law in force in any other country.

(2) In any case where the internal law of a country falls to be ascertained for the purposes of this Act by any court and there are in force in that country two or more systems of internal law, the relevant system shall be ascertained in accordance with any rule in force throughout that country indicating which of the systems is relevant in the case in question or, if there is no such rule, shall be the system appearing to that court to be most closely connected with the case.

Interpretation.

72.—(1) In this Act, unless the context otherwise requires—

" adoption agency " in sections 11, 13, 18 to 23 and 27 to 31 includes an adoption agency within the meaning of section 1 of the Children Act 1975 (adoption agencies in Scotland); 1975 c. 72.

" adoption order " means an order under section 12(1) and, in sections 12(3) and (4), 18 to 21 and 30 to 32 includes an order under section 8 of the Children Act 1975 (adoption orders in Scotland);

" adoption society " means a body of persons whose functions consist of or include the making of arrangements for the adoption of children;

" approved adoption society " means an adoption society approved under Part I;

" authorised court " shall be construed in accordance with section 62;

" body of persons " means any body of persons, whether incorporated or unincorporated;

" British adoption order " means an adoption order, an order under section 8 of the Children Act 1975 (adoption orders in Scotland), or any provision for the adoption of a child effected under the law of Northern Ireland or any British territory outside the United Kingdom;

PART VI

" British territory " means, for the purposes of any provision of this Act, any of the following countries, that is to say, Great Britain, Northern Ireland, the Channel Islands, the Isle of Man and a colony, being a country designated for the purposes of that provision by order of the Secretary of State or, if no country is so designated, any of those countries ;

" child ", except where used to express a relationship, means a person who has not attained the age of 18 years ;

" the Convention " means the Convention relating to the adoption of children concluded at the Hague on 15th November 1965 and signed on behalf of the United Kingdom on that date ;

" Convention adoption order " means an adoption order made in accordance with section 17(1) ;

" Convention country " means any country outside British territory, being a country for the time being designated by an order of the Secretary of State as a country in which, in his opinion, the Convention is in force ;

" existing ", in relation to an enactment or other instrument, means one passed or made at any time before 1st January 1976 ;

" guardian " means—

(*a*) a person appointed by deed or will in accordance with the provisions of the Guardianship of
1971 c. 3. Infants Acts 1886 and 1925 or the Guardianship of Minors Act 1971 or by a court of competent jurisdiction to be the guardian of the child, and

(*b*) in the case of an illegitimate child, includes the father where he has custody of the child by virtue of an order under section 9 of the Guardianship of Minors Act 1971, or under section 2 of the
1930 c. 33. Illegitimate Children (Scotland) Act 1930 ;

" internal law " has the meaning assigned by section 71 ;

" local authority " means the council of a county (other than a metropolitan county), a metropolitan district, a London borough or the Common Council of the City of London and, in sections 13, 22, 28 to 31, 35(1) and 51, includes a regional or islands council ;

" notice " means a notice in writing ;

" order freeing a child for adoption " means an order under section 18 ;

" overseas adoption " has the meaning assigned by subsection (2) ;

PART VI

"place of safety" means a community home provided by a local authority, a controlled community home, police station, or any hospital, surgery or other suitable place the occupier of which is willing temporarily to receive a child;

"prescribed" means prescribed by rules;

"regulated adoption" means an overseas adoption of a description designated by an order under subsection (2) as that of an adoption regulated by the Convention;

"relative" in relation to a child means a grandparent, brother, sister, uncle or aunt, whether of the full blood or half-blood or by affinity and includes, where the child is illegitimate, the father of the child and any person who would be a relative within the meaning of this definition if the child were the legitimate child of his mother and father;

"rules" means rules made under section 66(1) or made by virtue of section 66(2) under section 15 of the Justices of the Peace Act 1949; 1949 c. 101.

"specified order" means any provision for the adoption of a child effected under enactments similar to section 12(1) and 17 in force in Northern Ireland or any British territory outside the United Kingdom;

"United Kingdom national" means, for the purposes of any provision of this Act, a citizen of the United Kingdom and colonies satisfying such conditions, if any, as the Secretary of State may by order specify for the purposes of that provision;

"voluntary organisation" means a body other than a public or local authority the activities of which are not carried on for profit.

(2) In this Act "overseas adoption" means an adoption of such a description as the Secretary of State may by order specify, being a description of adoptions of children appearing to him to be effected under the law of any country outside Great Britain; and an order under this subsection may contain provision as to the manner in which evidence of an overseas adoption may be given.

(3) For the purposes of this Act, a person shall be deemed to make arrangements for the adoption of a child if he enters into or makes any agreement or arrangement for, or for facilitating, the adoption of the child by any other person, whether the

PART VI

adoption is effected, or is intended to be effected, in Great Britain or elsewhere, or if he initiates or takes part in any negotiations of which the purpose or effect is the conclusion of any agreement or the making of any arrangement therefor, and if he causes another person to do so.

(4) Except so far as the context otherwise requires, any reference in this Act to an enactment shall be construed as a reference to that enactment as amended by or under any other enactment, including this Act.

(5) In this Act, except where otherwise indicated—

(*a*) a reference to a numbered Part, section or Schedule is a reference to the Part or section of, or the Schedule to, this Act so numbered, and

(*b*) a reference in a section to a numbered subsection is a reference to the subsection of that section so numbered, and

(*c*) a reference in a section, subsection or Schedule to a numbered paragraph is a reference to the paragraph of that section, subsection or Schedule so numbered.

Transitional provisions, amendments and repeals.

73.—(1) The transitional provisions contained in Schedule 2 shall have effect.

(2) The enactments specified in Schedule 3 shall have effect subject to the amendments specified in that Schedule, being amendments consequential upon the provisions of this Act.

(3) The enactments specified in Schedule 4 are hereby repealed to the extent specified in column 3 of that Schedule.

Short title, commencement and extent.

74.—(1) This Act may be cited as the Adoption Act 1976.

(2) This Act shall come into force on such date as the Secretary of State may by order appoint and different dates may be appointed for different provisions.

(3) This Act, except sections 22, 23, 51 and 73(2), this section and Part II of Schedule 3, shall not extend to Scotland and the said Part II shall not extend to England and Wales.

1958 c. 5 (7 & 8 Eliz. 2). 1964 c. 57. 1968 c. 53.

(4) This Act, except section 40 and Schedule 4 so far as it repeals section 19 of the Adoption Act 1958, section 1(3) of the Adoption Act 1964 and sections 9(5) and 14 of the Adoption Act 1968, shall not extend to Northern Ireland.

SCHEDULES

SCHEDULE 1

Section 50.

Registration of Adoptions

Registration of adoption orders

1.—(1) Every adoption order shall contain a direction to the Registrar General to make in the Adopted Children Register an entry in such form as the Registrar General may by regulations specify.

(2) The direction contained in a Convention adoption order in pursuance of this paragraph shall include an instruction that the entry made in that register in consequence of the order shall be marked with the words " Convention order ".

(3) Where on an application to a court for an adoption order in respect of a child (not being a child who has previously been the subject of an adoption order made by a court in England or Wales under this Act or any enactment at the time in force) there is proved to the satisfaction of the court the identity of the child with a child to whom an entry in the Registers of Births relates, any adoption order made in pursuance of the application shall contain a direction to the Registrar General to cause the entry in the Registers of Births to be marked with the word " Adopted ".

(4) Where an adoption order is made in respect of a child who has previously been the subject of an adoption order made by a court in England or Wales under this Act or any enactment at the time in force, the order shall contain a direction to the Registrar General to cause the previous entry in the Adopted Children Register to be marked with the word " Re-adopted ".

(5) Where an adoption order is made, the prescribed officer of the court which made the order shall cause the order to be communicated in the prescribed manner to the Registrar General, and upon receipt of the communication the Registrar General shall cause compliance to be made with the directions contained in the order.

Registration of adoptions in Scotland, Northern Ireland, the Isle of Man and the Channel Islands

2.—(1) Where the Registrar General is notified by the Registrar General for Scotland that an adoption order has been made by a court in Scotland in respect of a child to whom an entry in the Registers of Births or the Adopted Children Register relates, the Registrar General shall cause the entry to be marked " Adopted (Scotland) " or, as the case may be, " Re-adopted (Scotland) " ; and where, after an entry has been so marked, the Registrar General is notified as aforesaid that the adoption order has been quashed, or that an appeal against the adoption order has been allowed, he shall cause the marking to be cancelled.

(2) Where the Registrar General is notified by the authority maintaining a register of adoptions in Northern Ireland, the Isle of Man or any of the Channel Islands that an order has been made

SCH. 1 in that country authorising the adoption of a child to whom an entry in the Registers of Births or the Adopted Children Register relates, he shall cause the entry to be marked with the word "Adopted" or "Re-adopted", as the case may require, followed by the name, in brackets, of the country in which the order was made.

(3) Where, after an entry has been so marked, the Registrar General is notified as aforesaid that the order has been quashed, that an appeal against the order has been allowed or that the order has been revoked, he shall cause the marking to be cancelled; and a copy or extract of an entry in any register, being an entry the marking of which is cancelled under this sub-paragraph, shall be deemed to be an accurate copy if and only if both the marking and the cancellation are omitted therefrom.

(4) The preceding provisions of this paragraph shall apply in relation to orders corresponding to orders under section 55 as they apply in relation to orders authorising the adoption of a child; but any marking of an entry required by virtue of this sub-paragraph shall consist of the words "proposed foreign adoption" or as the case may require, "proposed foreign re-adoption" followed by the name in brackets of the country in which the order was made.

(5) Without prejudice to sub-paragraphs (2) and (3) where, after an entry in the Registers of Births has been marked in accordance with this paragraph, the birth is re-registered under section 14 of the Births and Deaths Registration Act 1953 (re-registration of births of legitimated children) the entry made on the re-registration shall be marked in the like manner.

1953 c. 20.

Registration of overseas adoptions

3. If the Registrar General is satisfied that an entry in the Registers of Births relates to a person adopted under an overseas adoption and that he has sufficient particulars relating to that person to enable an entry, in the form specified for the purposes of this sub-paragraph in regulations made under paragraph 1(1), to be made in the Adopted Children Register in respect of that person, he shall—

- (*a*) make such an entry in the Adopted Children Register; and
- (*b*) if there is a previous entry in respect of that person in that register, mark the entry (or if there is more than one such entry the last of them) with the word "Re-adopted" followed by the name in brackets of the country in which the adoption was effected; and
- (*c*) unless the entry in the Registers of Births is already marked with the word "Adopted" (whether or not followed by other words), mark the entry with that word followed by the name in brackets of the country aforesaid.

Amendment of orders and rectification of Registers.

4.—(1) The court by which an adoption order has been made may, on the application of the adopter or of the adopted person, amend the order by the correction of any error in the particulars contained therein, and may— Sch. 1

(*a*) if satisfied on the application of the adopter or the adopted person that within one year beginning with the date of the order any new name has been given to the adopted person (whether in baptism or otherwise), or taken by him, either in lieu of or in addition to a name specified in the particulars required to be entered in the Adopted Children Register in pursuance of the order, amend the order by substituting or adding that name in those particulars, as the case may require ;

(*b*) if satisfied on the application of any person concerned that a direction for the marking of an entry in the Registers of Births or the Adopted Children Register included in the order in pursuance of sub-paragraph (3) or (4) of paragraph 1 was wrongly so included, revoke that direction.

(2) Where an adoption order is amended or a direction revoked under sub-paragraph (1), the prescribed officer of the court shall cause the amendment to be communicated in the prescribed manner to the Registrar General who shall as the case may require—

(*a*) cause the entry in the Adopted Children Register to be amended accordingly ; or

(*b*) cause the marking of the entry in the Registers of Births or the Adopted Children Register to be cancelled.

(3) Where an adoption order is quashed or an appeal against an adoption order allowed by any court, the court shall give directions to the Registrar General to cancel any entry in the Adopted Children Register, and any marking of an entry in that Register, or the Registers of Births as the case may be, which was effected in pursuance of the order.

(4) Where an adoption order has been amended, any certified copy of the relevant entry in the Adopted Children Register which may be issued pursuant to subsection (3) of section 50 shall be a copy of the entry as amended, without the reproduction of any note or marking relating to the amendment or of any matter cancelled pursuant thereto ; and a copy or extract of an entry in any register, being an entry the marking of which has been cancelled, shall be deemed to be an accurate copy if and only if both the marking and the cancellation are omitted therefrom.

(5) If the Registrar General is satisfied—

(*a*) that a Convention adoption order or an overseas adoption has ceased to have effect, whether on annulment or otherwise ; or

(*b*) that any entry or mark was erroneously made in pursuance of paragraph 3 in any register mentioned in that paragraph,

he may cause such alterations to be made in any such register as he considers are required in consequence of the cesser or to correct the error ; and where an entry in such a register is amended in pursuance of this sub-paragraph, any copy or extract of the entry shall

SCH. 1 be deemed to be accurate if and only if it shows the entry as amended but without indicating that it has been amended.

(6) In relation to an adoption order made by a magistrates' court, the reference in sub-paragraph (1) to the court by which the order has been made includes a reference to a court acting for the same petty sessions area.

Marking of entries on re-registration of birth on legitimation

5.—(1) Without prejudice to section 52, where, after an entry in the Registers of Births has been marked with the word "Adopted" (with or without the addition of the word "(Scotland)"), the birth is re-registered under section 14 of the Births and Deaths Registration Act 1953 (re-registration of births of legitimated persons) the entry made on the re-registration shall be marked in the like manner.

1953 c. 20.

(2) Without prejudice to paragraph 4(5), where an entry in the Registers of Births is marked in pursuance of paragraph 3 and the birth in question is subsequently re-registered under the said section 14, the entry made on re-registration shall be marked in the like manner.

Cancellations in Registers on legitimation

6. Where an adoption order, other than a Convention adoption order, is revoked under section 52(1) or (2) the prescribed officer of the court shall cause the revocation to be communicated in the prescribed manner to the Registrar General who shall cause to be cancelled—

- (*a*) the entry in the Adopted Children Register relating to the adopted person; and
- (*b*) the marking with the word "Adopted" (or, as the case may be, with that word and the word "(Scotland)") of any entry relating to him in the Registers of Births;

and a copy or extract of an entry in any register, being an entry the marking of which is cancelled under this section, shall be deemed to be an accurate copy if and only if both the marking and the cancellation are omitted therefrom.

Section 73.

SCHEDULE 2

TRANSITIONAL PROVISIONS AND SAVINGS

General

1. In so far as anything done under an enactment repealed by this Act could have been done under a corresponding provision of this Act it shall not be invalidated by the repeal but shall have effect as if done under that provision.

2. Where any period of time specified in an enactment repealed by this Act is current at the commencement of this Act, this Act shall have effect as if the corresponding provision thereof had been in force when that period began to run.

3. Nothing in this Act shall affect the enactments repealed by this Act in their operation in relation to offences committed before the commencement of this Act.

4. Any reference in any document, whether express or implied, to any enactment repealed by this Act shall, unless the context otherwise requires, be construed as a reference to the corresponding enactment of this Act. SCH. 2

Existing adoption orders

5.—(1) Without prejudice to paragraph 1, an adoption order made under an enactment at any time before this Act comes into force shall not cease to have effect by virtue only of a repeal effected by this Act.

(2) Paragraph 4(1) and (2) of Schedule 1 shall apply in relation to an adoption order made before this Act came into force as if the order had been made under section 12, but as if, in sub-paragraph (1)(*b*) of the said paragraph 4, there were substituted for the reference to paragraph 1(3) and (4) a reference—

(*a*) in the case of an order under the Adoption of Children Act 1926, to section 12(3) and (4) of the Adoption of Children Act 1949, 1926 c. 29. 1949 c. 98.

(*b*) in the case of an order under the Adoption Act 1950, to section 18(3) and (4) of that Act, 1950 c. 26.

(*c*) in the case of an order under the Adoption Act 1958, to section 21(4) and (5) of that Act. 1958 c. 5 (7 & 8 Eliz. 2).

(3) The power of the court under the said paragraph 4(1) to amend an order includes power, in relation to an order made before 1st April 1959, to make on the application of the adoptor or adopted person any such amendment of the particulars contained in the order as appears to be required to bring the order into the form in which it would have been made if paragraph 1 of Schedule 1 had applied to the order.

(4) Section 52(1) and paragraph 6 of Schedule 1 shall apply in relation to an adoption order made under an enactment at any time before this Act came into force as they apply in relation to an adoption order made under this Act.

Rights relating to property

6.—(1) Section 39—

(*a*) does not apply to an existing instrument or enactment in so far as it contains a disposition of property, and

(*b*) does not apply to any public general Act in its application to any disposition of property in an existing instrument or enactment.

(2) Sections 16 and 17 of the Adoption Act 1958, and provisions containing references to those sections shall continue to apply in relation to dispositions of property effected by existing instruments notwithstanding the repeal of those sections, and such provisions, by the Children Act 1975. 1975 c. 72.

(3) Section 46 shall apply in relation to this paragraph as if it were contained in Part IV.

Sch. 2

Payments relating to adoptions

7. Section 57(7), (8) and (9) shall not have effect if, immediately before section 57 comes into force, there is in force in England and Wales an order under section 50(8) of the Adoption Act 1958.

1958 c. 5 (7 & 8 Eliz. 2).

Registers of adoptions

8. Any register, or index to a register kept under the Adoption Act 1958, or any register or index deemed to be part of such a register, shall be deemed to be part of the register kept under section 50.

Section 73.

SCHEDULE 3

Consequential Amendments

Part I

Amendments Extending Only to England and Wales

Children Act 1948 (*c.* 43)

1. In section 2 of the Children Act 1948—

(*a*) in subsection (8)(*b*), after the words " section 14 or 25 of the Children Act 1975 " there are added the words " section 18 or 55 of the Adoption Act 1976 " ;

(*b*) in subsection (11), for the words " section 14 of the Children Act 1975 " and " section 25 " there are substituted respectively the words " section 18 of the Adoption Act 1976 " and " section 55 ".

2. In section 43(1) of the said Act of 1948, for the words from " Adoption Act 1958 " to the end there are substituted the words " the Children Act 1975 and the Adoption Act 1976 ".

3. In section 51(1) of the said Act of 1948, for the words " Part IV of the Adoption Act 1958 " there are substituted the words " section 34 of the Adoption Act 1976 ".

Magistrates' Courts Act 1952 (*c.* 55)

4. In section 56(1) of the Magistrates' Courts Act 1952, for paragraph (*f*) there is substituted the following paragraph—

" (*f*) under Part II of the Children Act 1975 or under the provisions (other than section 34) of the Adoption Act 1976."

Children Act 1958 (*c.* 65)

5. In section 2(4A) of the Children Act 1958, for the words from " by such " to the end there are substituted the words " by an adoption agency within the meaning of section 1 of the Adoption Act 1976 or section 1 of the Children Act 1975 or while he is a protected child within the meaning of Part III of the said Act of 1976.".

6. In section 6(1) of the said Act of 1958, in paragraph (*f*), after the words " section 43 of the Adoption Act 1958 " there are added the words " or section 34 of the Adoption Act 1976 ". Sch. 3

County Courts Act 1959 (c. 22)

7. In section 109(2) of the County Courts Act 1959, after paragraph (*h*) there is added the following paragraph—

" (*i*) any proceedings under Part II or section 29 or 55 of the Adoption Act 1976.".

Children and Young Persons Act 1963 (c. 37)

8. In section 23(1)(*c*) of the Children and Young Persons Act 1963 for the words " section 43 of the Adoption Act 1958 " there are substituted the words " section 34 of the Adoption Act 1976 ".

Health Services and Public Health Act 1968 (c. 46)

9. In section 64(3)(*a*) of the Health Services and Public Health Act 1968 there is added at the end the following paragraph—

" (xviii) the Adoption Act 1976."

10. In section 65(3)(*b*) of the said Act of 1968 there is added at the end the following paragraph—

" (xix) the Adoption Act 1976 ".

Children and Young Persons Act 1969 (c. 54)

11. In section 21A of the Children and Young Persons Act 1969 for the references to sections 14 and 25 of the Children Act 1975 there are substituted references to section 18 and 55 respectively of this Act.

12. In section 58(1) of the said Act 1969—

(*a*) in paragraph (*bb*) after the words " Children Act 1975 " there are inserted the words " or section 1 of the Adoption Act 1976 " ;

(*b*) in paragraph (*e*) for the words " Part IV of the Adoption Act 1958 " there are substituted the words " Part III of the Adoption Act 1976 ".

13. In section 63(6) of the said Act of 1969 at the end there is added the following paragraph—

" (*j*) the Adoption Act 1976.".

Administration of Justice Act 1970 (c. 31)

14. In Schedule 1 to the Administration of Justice Act 1970 for the words " Adoption Acts 1958 and 1968 " there are substituted the words " Adoption Act 1976 ", and at the end of that Schedule there is added the following paragraph—

" Proceedings on appeal under Part II or section 29 or 55 of the Adoption Act 1976.".

SCH. 3

Local Authority Social Services Act 1970 (*c*. 42)

15. In Schedule 1 to the Local Authority Social Services Act 1970, the following is added at the end—

" Adoption Act 1976 (*c*. 36)	Maintenance of Adoption Service; functions of local authority as adoption agency; applications for orders freeing children for adoption; inquiries carried out by local authorities in adoption cases; care, possession and supervision of children awaiting adoption.".

Guardianship of Minors Act 1971 (*c*. 3)

16. In section 9(6) of the Guardianship of Minors Act 1971, for the words from " (within " to the end there are substituted the following words " by virtue of an order under section 18 of the Adoption Act 1976 (orders in England and Wales) or section 14 of the Children Act 1975 (orders in Scotland) ".

Immigration Act 1971 (*c*. 77)

17. In section 33(1) of the Immigration Act 1971, in the definition of " legally adopted ", for the words " section 4 of the Adoption Act 1968 " there are substituted the words " section 72(2) of the Adoption Act 1976 ".

Legal Aid Act 1974 (*c*. 4)

18. In Schedule 1 to the Legal Aid Act 1974 in paragraph 3(*d*) for the words " Part I of the Children Act 1975 " there are substituted the words " Part II or section 29 or 55 of the Adoption Act 1976 ".

Children Act 1975 (*c*. 72)

19. In section 37(1) of the Children Act 1975 for the words " section 12 " and " section 24(6) " there are substituted respectively the words " section 16 of the Adoption Act 1976 " and " section 17(6) of that Act ".

20. In section 60(6) of the said Act of 1975 after the words " section 14 " and " section 25 " there are added the words " section 18 of the Adoption Act 1976 " and " section 55 of that Act " respectively.

21. In section 98(1)(*b*) of the said Act of 1975 at the end there are added the words " within the meaning of section 1 of the Adoption Act 1976 ".

22. In section 103(1)(*a*) of the said Act of 1975 for paragraph (i) there is substituted the following paragraph—

" (i) section 65 of the Adoption Act 1976 ; ".

Legitimacy Act 1976 (*c*. 31)

23. In section 4 of the Legitimacy Act 1976,

(*a*) in subsection (1), for the words " Paragraph 3 of Schedule 1 to the Children Act 1975 " there are substituted the words " Section 39 of the Adoption Act 1976 " ;

(*b*) in subsection (2)(*a*), for the words " sub-paragraph (2) of the said paragraph 3 " there are substituted the words " subsection (2) of the said section 39 " ;

(*c*) in subsection (2)(*b*), for the words " Part II of the said Schedule I " there are substituted the words " section 39, 41 or 42 of the Adoption Act 1976 ".

24. In section 6(2) of the said Act of 1976, for the words " paragraph 6(2) of Schedule 1 to the Children Act 1975 " there are substituted the words " section 42(2) of the Adoption Act 1976 ".

Part II

Amendments Extending Only to Scotland

Children Act 1958 (6 & 7 *Eliz.* 2 *c.* 65)

25. In section 2(4A) of the Children Act 1958, after the words " Children Act 1975 " there are inserted the words " or in Part I of the Adoption Act 1976 ".

26. In section 6(1) of the said Act of 1958, in paragraph (*f*), after the words " section 43 of the Adoption Act 1958 " there are added the words " or section 34 of the Adoption Act 1976 ".

Adoption Act 1958 (7 & 8 *Eliz.* 2 *c.* 5)

27. In section 22(4A) of the Adoption Act 1958, in paragraph (*b*) after the word " 1975 " there are inserted the words " or under section 3 of the Adoption Act 1976 ".

28. In section 29(2) of the said Act of 1958 after the word " 1975 " there are inserted the words " or the Adoption Act 1976 ".

29. In section 34 of the said Act of 1958 the following subsections are added after subsection (3)—

" (4) This section, except subsection (3), applies notwithstanding that the child is in England or Wales at the time he is removed.

(5) Any person who removes a child from the custody of any other person while the child is in Scotland, contrary to section 27 of the Adoption Act 1976, shall be guilty of an offence and liable on summary conviction to imprisonment for a term not exceeding 3 months or a fine not exceeding £400 or both."

30. In section 34A of the said Act of 1958 the following subsections are inserted after subsection (6)—

" (6A) This section, except subsection (6), applies notwithstanding that the child is in England or Wales at the time he is removed.

(6B) Any person who removes a child from the custody of any other person while the child is in Scotland, contrary to section 28 of the Adoption Act 1976, shall be guilty of an offence and liable on summary conviction to imprisonment for a term not exceeding 3 months or a fine not exceeding £400 or both."

SCH. 3

31. In section 37 of the said Act of 1958, the following subsection is inserted after subsection (1)—

"(2) A child shall be deemed to be a protected child within the meaning of this Part of this Act if he is a protected child within the meaning of section 32(1) of the Adoption Act 1976."

32. In section 52(1) of the said Act of 1958, after the word "1975" there are inserted the words "or section 55 of the Adoption Act 1976".

33. In section 57 of the said Act of 1958 the following subsection is inserted after subsection (1A)—

"(1B) In sections 22, 29, 34 to 37 and 40(4) of this Act—

(*a*) "adoption agency" includes an adoption agency within the meaning of section 1 of the Adoption Act 1976,

(*b*) except in sections 34 and 34A "adoption order" includes an order under section 12 of the Adoption Act 1976,

(*c*) "local authority" includes the council of a county (other than a metropolitan county), a metropolitan district, a London borough or the Common Council of the City of London.

Social Work (Scotland) Act 1968 (*c.* 49)

34. In section 16(3) and (11)(*b*) of the Social Work (Scotland) Act 1968, after the words "Children Act 1975" there are added the words "or under section 18 or 55 of the Adoption Act 1976".

Adoption Act 1968 (*c.* 53)

35. In section 6 of the Adoption Act 1968 the following subsection is inserted after subsection (4)—

"(4A) Any order or decision of the High Court on an application under subsection (2) of section 53 of the Adoption Act 1976 shall be recognised and have effect as if it were an order or decision of the Court of Session on an application under subsection (3) of this section."

36. In section 11(1) of the said Act of 1968, in the definition of "the court", the words "the High Court or" shall cease to have effect.

Children Act 1975 (*c.* 72)

37. In section 8(3) of the Children Act 1975, for the words "the order" in the first place where they occur there are substituted the words "the adoption order".

38. In section 12(1) of the said Act of 1975, after paragraph (*a*) there is inserted the following paragraph—

"(*aa*) he is the subject of an order under section 18 of the Adoption Act 1976; or"

39. In section 16(3)(*c*) after the words " section 8(3)(*b*) " there are inserted the words " or section 12(3)(*b*) of the Adoption Act 1976 ".

40. In section 23 of the said Act of 1975, after the words " this section " there are inserted the words " or under Part II of the Adoption Act 1976 ".

41. In section 25(4) of the said Act of 1975 after the words " this section " there are inserted the words " or under section 55 of the Adoption Act 1976 ".

42. In section 100(9)(*a*)(ii) after the words " section 14 " there are added the words " or under section 18 of the Adoption Act 1976 ".

43. In section 107 of the said Act of 1975—

(*a*) in subsection (1), in the definition of " British Adoption Order " after the words " an adoption order " there are inserted the words " an order under section 12 of the Adoption Act 1976 " ; and

(*b*) the following subsection is inserted after subsection (2)—

" (2A) In this Act—

(*a*) in sections 9, 14 to 16, 18, 22 and 23, " adoption agency " includes an adoption agency within the meaning of section 1 of the Adoption Act 1976 (adoption agencies in England and Wales) ;

(*b*) in sections 8(3) and (4), 14 to 16, 23 and 100(9), " adoption order " includes an order under section 12 of the Adoption Act 1976 (adoption orders in England and Wales) ;

(*c*) in sections 9 and 18, " local authority " includes the council of a county (other than metropolitan county), a metropolitan district, a London borough or the Common Council of the City of London ;

(*d*) in section 14(6) the reference to an order under that section shall be construed as including an order under section 18 of the Adoption Act 1976 ".

44. In paragraph 7 of Schedule 2 to the said Act of 1975, in sub-paragraph (*c*), after the word " in " there are inserted the words " England, Wales,".

SCHEDULE 4

Repeals

Chapter	Short title	Extent of Repeal
1958 c. 5 (7 & 8 Eliz. 2).	Adoption Act 1958.	The whole Act so far as unrepealed.
1959 c. 72.	Mental Health Act 1959.	In section 19(3), the words " or a protected child within the meaning of Part IV of the Adoption Act 1958 ".
1960 c. 59.	Adoption Act 1960.	The whole Act.
1964 c. 57.	Adoption Act 1964.	The whole Act.
1968 c. 46.	Health Services and Public Health Act 1968.	In section 64(3)(*a*), paragraphs (v) and (xii). In section 65(3)(*b*), paragraphs (v) and (xiii).
1968 c. 53.	Adoption Act 1968.	The whole Act.
1969 c. 54.	Children and Young Persons Act 1969.	In Schedule 5, paragraphs 33 to 36.
1970 c. 31.	Administration of Justice Act 1970.	In Schedule 1, the paragraph relating to appeals under section 10 of the Adoption Act 1958.
1970 c. 42.	Local Authorities Social Services Act 1970.	In Schedule 1, the paragraphs relating to the Adoption Act 1958 and Part I of the Children Act 1975.
1971 c. 3.	Guardianship of Minors Act 1971.	In Schedule 1, the paragraph relating to the Adoption Act 1958.
1972 c. 70.	Local Government Act 1972.	In Schedule 23, paragraph 8.
1975 c. 72.	Children Act 1975.	Part I. Section 100(4), (5) and (6). In section 102(1), the words " Part I except section 24(6) or " and paragraph (*a*). In section 107(1), the definitions of " adoption order ", " adoption society ", " approved adoption society ", " British adoption order ", " British territory ", " the Convention ", " Convention adoption order ", " Convention country " and " United Kingdom national ", and, in the definition of " guardian ", paragraph (*b*). Schedules 1 and 2. In Schedule 3, paragraphs 6, 16(*b*), 17, 21 to 40, 44, 45, 61 to 65, and 74(*a*).
1976 c. 31.	Legitimacy Act 1976.	In Schedule 1, paragraph 7.

Food and Drugs (Control of Food Premises) Act 1976

1976 CHAPTER 37

An Act to amend the Food and Drugs Act 1955 by prohibiting the sale, etc., of food in certain circumstances. [22nd July 1976]

BE IT ENACTED by the Queen's most Excellent Majesty, by and with the advice and consent of the Lords Spiritual and Temporal, and Commons, in this present Parliament assembled, and by the authority of the same, as follows:—

Closure of food premises or stalls dangerous to health.

1.—(1) Subject to subsection (2) below, where on an information laid by a local authority a person is convicted of an offence under regulations made under section 13 of the Food and Drugs Act 1955 and the offence includes— 1955 c. 16.

(*a*) the carrying on of a food business at any insanitary premises or at any premises the condition, situation or construction of which is such that food is exposed to the risk of contamination; or

(*b*) the carrying on of a food business on, at or from a stall which is insanitary, or which is so situated or constructed, or is in such a condition, that the food is exposed to the risk of contamination,

then, if the court is satisfied that—

(i) food continues or is likely to continue to be prepared, stored, sold or offered or exposed for sale at those premises or on, at or from that stall; and

(ii) by reason of the situation, construction or insanitary or defective condition of the premises or stall or the insanitary or defective condition of the fittings or fixtures or equipment or the infestation of vermin or the accumulation of refuse, the carrying on of a food business at those premises or on, at or from that stall would be dangerous to health,

the court may on the application of the local authority, whether or not it makes any other order, by order (hereinafter referred to as " a closure order ") prohibit the preparation, storage, sale or offer or exposure for sale at those premises or on, at or from that stall of food until the local authority certifies under subsection (4) below that such specified measures as the court considers necessary to remove the danger to health have been carried out.

(2) A closure order shall not be made unless the local authority have, not less than fourteen days before the trial of the information, given—

(*a*) the person against whom the information was laid, and

(*b*) if he is not that person, the owner of the premises or stall (unless the local authority are unable after reasonable inquiry to ascertain his identity),

written notice of their intention to apply for the order.

(3) The local authority shall in any notice under subsection (2) above specify the measures which, in their opinion, should be taken to remove any danger to health.

(4) Any person who wishes to carry on a food business at any premises or on, at or from any stall with respect to which a closure order is in force may make application to the local authority who, if satisfied that the measures specified by the closure order have been carried out, shall as soon as practicable and in not more than fourteen days give to the applicant a certificate to that effect, and such certificate shall be conclusive evidence of the matters therein stated.

Emergency order for closing food premises or stalls where imminent risk of danger to health.

2.—(1) Subject to subsection (2) below, where an information is, or has been, laid by a local authority in relation to an offence described in section 1(1) above and application is made by the local authority for an order under this section, the court may, if satisfied—

(*a*) by evidence tendered by the local authority; and

(*b*) after affording, if he appears, the person against whom the information is or was laid and, if he is not that person, the owner of the premises or stall an opportunity to be heard and tender evidence,

that the use of the premises or stall for the preparation, storage, sale or offer or exposure for sale of food involves imminent risk of danger to health, make an order (hereinafter referred to as " an emergency order ") prohibiting, either absolutely or subject to conditions, the use of those premises or that stall for those purposes until the determination of the proceedings to which the information gave rise or the issue of a certificate by the local authority under subsection (6) below, whichever is the earlier.

(2) The court shall not consider an application under this section unless it is satisfied that at least three clear days' notice in writing of intention to make that application and of the time at which it would be made has been given to the person against whom the information is or was laid and, if he is not that person, to the owner of the premises or stall.

(3) The local authority shall in any notice under subsection (2) above specify the measures which, in their opinion, should be taken to remove any danger to health.

(4) Notice for the purpose of subsection (2) above may be served in any way, except by post, authorised by rules made under section 15 of the Justices of the Peace Act 1949 for the service of a summons issued by a justice of the peace or by leaving it for him with some person who appears to be employed at the premises or stall to which the information relates. 1949 c. 101.

(5) The local authority shall serve a copy of an emergency order made under this section as soon as may be after the order has been made on the person against whom the information was laid and, if he is not that person, on the owner of the premises or stall, and shall affix a copy of it in a conspicuous position on the premises or, if practicable, on the stall.

(6) Any person who wishes to carry on a food business at any premises or on, at or from any stall, with respect to which an emergency order is in force, may make application to the local authority who, if satisfied there is no longer any risk of danger to health, shall as soon as practicable and in not more than fourteen days issue a certificate to that effect.

Right to compensation.

3.—(1) If on the trial of an information relating to an offence described in section 1(1) above the court, on the application of an interested person—

(*a*) determines that at the date of any emergency order the use of the premises or stall did not involve imminent risk of danger to health; and

(*b*) is satisfied that loss has been occasioned by the emergency order,

the court may order the local authority to pay to that person compensation of such amount as the court thinks proper.

(2) The following are interested persons for the purposes of subsection (1) above and section 4(2) below, namely—

(*a*) the person against whom the information was laid;

(*b*) the owner of the premises or stall;

(*c*) any person (not falling within paragraph (*a*) or (*b*) above) who at the time when the emergency order was made was carrying on a food business at those premises or on, at or from that stall.

Right of appeal.

4.—(1) Where an application for a closure order is refused or granted—

(*a*) if the application is refused, the local authority by whom the application was made may appeal to the Crown Court;

(*b*) if the application is granted, any person to whom notice of the application was given under section 1(2) above may appeal as aforesaid.

(2) Where an application for an order under section 3 above for the payment of compensation is granted or refused, the following persons may appeal to the Crown Court—

(*a*) the local authority by whom the application for the emergency order in question was made; or

(*b*) any interested person who applied for the payment of compensation under that section in respect of that order.

(3) Where a person applies for a certificate under section 1(4) or 2(6) above, and the local authority refuses or fails to give it, the applicant may appeal to a magistrates' court who may, if satisfied that it is proper to do so, direct the authority to give such certificate.

1955 c. 16.

(4) Section 117 of the Food and Drugs Act 1955 (appeals to magistrates' courts) shall apply in relation to appeals under subsection (3) above as it applies in relation to appeals under that Act.

Penalties.

5.—(1) A person who contravenes a closure order or an emergency order shall be liable on summary conviction to a fine not exceeding £400.

(2) Section 113 of the Food and Drugs Act 1955 (contravention due to default of some other person) shall apply in relation to proceedings under this section as it applies in relation to proceedings under that Act.

Interpretation.

6.—(1) In the application of this Act in connection with an offence under any such regulations as are mentioned in section 1(1) above—

(*a*) any expression to which a meaning is assigned by the regulations in question shall, unless the context otherwise requires, have the same meaning in this Act as in those regulations; and (*b*) sections 1 to 5 above shall have effect as if the references to premises included places which are not premises within the meaning of those regulations.

(2) In this Act " local authority " means a district council, a London borough council, the Common Council of the City of London, the Sub-Treasurer of the Inner Temple or the Under Treasurer of the Middle Temple.

Power to make corresponding provision in relation to ships.

7.—(1) The following subsection applies to any offence under regulations made under section 13 of the Food and Drugs Act 1955 which includes the carrying on of a food business in any insanitary ship or in any ship the condition, situation or construction of which is such that food is exposed to the risk of contamination.

1955 c. 16.

(2) In relation to an offence to which this subsection applies the Secretary of State may make regulations containing provisions corresponding, with such additions, omissions or other modifications as he thinks fit, to the provisions of sections 1 to 6 above.

(3) The penalty provided for by any provision in the regulations corresponding to section 5(1) above shall be the same as in that subsection.

(4) The power to make regulations under this section shall be exercisable by statutory instrument subject to annulment in pursuance of a resolution of either House of Parliament.

Short title, commencement and extent.

8.—(1) This Act may be cited as the Food and Drugs (Control of Food Premises) Act 1976.

(2) This Act shall come into force at the end of the period of two months beginning with the date on which it is passed.

(3) This Act shall not apply to Scotland or Northern Ireland.

Dangerous Wild Animals Act 1976

1976 CHAPTER 38

An Act to regulate the keeping of certain kinds of dangerous wild animals. [22nd July 1976]

BE IT ENACTED by the Queen's most Excellent Majesty, by and with the advice and consent of the Lords Spiritual and Temporal, and Commons, in this present Parliament assembled, and by the authority of the same, as follows:—

1.—(1) Subject to section 5 of this Act, no person shall keep any dangerous wild animal except under the authority of a licence granted in accordance with the provisions of this Act by a local authority. Licences.

(2) A local authority shall not grant a licence under this Act unless an application for it—

(*a*) specifies the species (whether one or more) of animal, and the number of animals of each species, proposed to be kept under the authority of the licence;

(*b*) specifies the premises where any animal concerned will normally be held;

(*c*) is made to the local authority in whose area those premises are situated;

(*d*) is made by a person who is neither under the age of 18 nor disqualified under this Act from keeping any dangerous wild animal; and

(*e*) is accompanied by such fee as the authority may stipulate (being a fee which is in the authority's opinion sufficient to meet the direct and indirect costs which it may incur as a result of the application).

(3) A local authority shall not grant a licence under this Act unless it is satisfied that—

(*a*) it is not contrary to the public interest on the grounds of safety, nuisance or otherwise to grant the licence;

(*b*) the applicant for the licence is a suitable person to hold a licence under this Act ;

(*c*) any animal concerned will at all times of its being kept only under the authority of the licence—

(i) be held in accommodation which secures that the animal will not escape, which is suitable as regards construction, size, temperature, lighting, ventilation, drainage and cleanliness and which is suitable for the number of animals proposed to be held in the accommodation, and

(ii) be supplied with adequate and suitable food, drink and bedding material and be visited at suitable intervals ;

(*d*) appropriate steps will at all such times be taken for the protection of any animal concerned in case of fire or other emergency ;

(*e*) all reasonable precautions will be taken at all such times to prevent and control the spread of infectious diseases ;

(*f*) while any animal concerned is at the premises where it will normally be held, its accommodation is such that it can take adequate exercise.

(4) A local authority shall not grant a licence under this Act unless the application for it is made by a person who both owns and possesses, or proposes both to own and to possess, any animal concerned, except where the circumstances are in the authority's opinion exceptional.

(5) A local authority shall not grant a licence under this Act unless a veterinary surgeon or veterinary practitioner authorised by the authority to do so under section 3 of this Act has inspected the premises where any animal will normally be held in pursuance of the licence and the authority has received and considered a report by the surgeon or practitioner, containing such particulars as in the authority's opinion enable it to decide whether the premises are such that any animal proposed to be kept under the authority of the licence may suitably be held there, and describing the condition of the premises and of any animal or other thing found there.

(6) Subject to subsections (2) to (5) of this section, a local authority may grant or refuse a licence under this Act as it thinks fit, but where it decides to grant such a licence it shall specify as conditions of the licence—

(*a*) conditions that, while any animal concerned is being kept only under the authority of the licence,—

(i) the animal shall be kept by no person other than such person or persons as is or are specified (whether by name or description) in the licence ;

(ii) the animal shall normally be held at such premises as are specified in the licence;

(iii) the animal shall not be moved from those premises or shall only be moved from them in such circumstances as are specified in the licence;

(iv) the person to whom the licence is granted shall hold a current insurance policy which insures him and any other person entitled to keep the animal under the authority of the licence against liability for any damage which may be caused by the animal; and

(v) the terms of any such policy shall be satisfactory in the opinion of the authority;

(*b*) conditions restricting the species (whether one or more) of animal, and number of animals of each species, which may be kept under the authority of the licence;

(*c*) a condition that the person to whom the licence is granted shall at all reasonable times make available a copy of the licence to any person entitled to keep any animal under the authority of the licence;

(*d*) such other conditions as in the opinion of the authority are necessary or desirable for the purpose of securing the objects specified in paragraphs (*c*) to (*f*) of subsection (3) of this section.

(7) Subject to subsection (6) of this section, a local authority may, in granting a licence under this Act, specify such conditions of the licence as it thinks fit.

(8) Where a local authority proposes to insert in a licence under this Act a provision permitting any animal to be, for any continuous period exceeding 72 hours, at premises outside the area of the authority, the authority shall consult the local authority in whose area those premises are situated.

(9) A local authority which grants a licence under this Act may at any time vary the licence by specifying any new condition of the licence or varying or revoking any condition of it (including any condition specified, or previously varied, under this subsection); but any condition of a licence specified by virtue of subsection (6) of this section may not be revoked and any condition specified by virtue of paragraph (*a*)(ii) of that subsection may not be varied.

(10) Where a local authority varies a licence under subsection (9) of this section, then—

(*a*) if the variation was requested by the person to whom the licence was granted, the variation shall take effect immediately after the authority decides to make it;

(*b*) in any other case, the variation shall not take effect until the person to whom the licence was granted has become aware of the variation and had a reasonable time to comply with it.

Provisions supplementary to section 1.

2.—(1) Where—

(*a*) a person is aggrieved by the refusal of a local authority to grant a licence under this Act, or

(*b*) a person to whom such a licence has been granted is aggrieved by a condition of the licence (whether specified at the time the licence is granted or later) or by the variation or revocation of any condition of the licence,

he may appeal to a magistrates' court; and the court may on such appeal give such directions with respect to the grant of a licence or, as the case may be, with respect to the conditions of the licence as it thinks proper, having regard to the provisions of this Act.

(2) Any licence under this Act shall (according to the applicant's requirements) relate to the calendar year in which it is granted or to the next following year.

In the former case, the licence shall come into force at the beginning of the day on which it is granted, and in the latter case it shall come into force at the beginning of the next following year.

(3) Subject to the provisions hereinafter contained with respect to cancellation, any licence under this Act shall remain in force until the end of the year to which it relates and shall then expire:

Provided that if application is made for a further licence before the said date of expiry the licence shall be deemed to be still in force pending the grant or refusal of the said application, and if it is granted the new licence shall commence from the date of the expiry of the last licence.

(4) In the event of the death of anyone to whom a licence has been granted under this Act the said licence shall continue in force for a period of twenty-eight days as if it had been granted to the personal representatives of the deceased and if application is made for a new licence within the said period the said licence shall be deemed to be still in force pending the grant or refusal of that application.

(5) Any person who contravenes the provisions of section 1(1) of this Act shall be guilty of an offence.

(6) If any condition of a licence under this Act is contravened or not complied with, then,—

(*a*) the person to whom the licence was granted, and

(*b*) any other person who is entitled to keep any animal under the authority of the licence and who was primarily responsible for the contravention or failure to comply,

shall, subject to subsection (7) of this section, be guilty of an offence.

(7) In any proceedings for an offence under subsection (6) of this section, it shall be a defence for the person charged to prove that he took all reasonable precautions and exercised all due diligence to avoid the commission of such an offence.

(8) In the application of this section to Scotland, in subsection (1) for any reference to a magistrates' court there shall be substituted a reference to the sheriff.

Inspection by local authority.

3.—(1) Subject to subsection (2) of this section, a local authority to which an application has been made for a licence under this Act, or which has granted such a licence, may authorise in writing any veterinary surgeon or veterinary practitioner or such other person as it may deem competent to do so to inspect any premises where any animal is proposed to be held in pursuance of a licence for which an application has been made under this Act, or where any animal is or may be held in pursuance of a licence which has been granted under this Act; and any persons authorised under this section may, on producing their authority if so required, enter any such premises at all reasonable times and inspect them and any animal or other thing found there, for the purpose of ascertaining whether or not a licence should be granted or varied or whether an offence has been or is being committed against this Act.

(2) A local authority shall not give an authority under subsection (1) of this section to inspect premises situated outside its area unless it has obtained the approval of the local authority in whose area those premises are situated.

(3) The local authority may require the person who has applied for a licence under this Act or, as the case may be, to whom the licence concerned has been granted under this Act to pay the local authority the reasonable costs of the inspection.

(4) Any person who wilfully obstructs or delays any person in the exercise of his power of entry or inspection under this section shall be guilty of an offence.

Power to seize and to dispose of animals without. compensation.

4.—(1) Where—

(*a*) an animal is being kept contrary to section 1(1) of this Act, or

(*b*) any condition of a licence under this Act is contravened or not complied with,

the local authority in whose area any animal concerned is for the time being may seize the animal, and either retain it in the authority's possession or destroy or otherwise dispose of it, and shall not be liable to pay compensation to any person in respect of the exercise of its powers under this subsection.

(2) A local authority which incurs any expenditure in exercising its powers under subsection (1)(*a*) of this section shall be entitled to recover the amount of the expenditure summarily as a civil debt from any person who was at the time of the seizure a keeper of the animal concerned.

(3) A local authority which incurs any expenditure in exercising its powers under subsection (1)(*b*) of this section shall be entitled to recover the amount of the expenditure summarily as a civil debt from the person to whom the licence concerned was granted.

Exemptions.

5. The provisions of this Act shall not apply to any dangerous wild animal kept in:—

(1) a zoological garden;

(2) a circus;

1951 c. 35. (3) premises licensed as a pet shop under the Pet Animals Act 1951;

1876 c. 77. (4) a place registered pursuant to the Cruelty to Animals Act 1876 for the purpose of performing experiments.

Penalties.

6.—(1) Any person guilty of an offence under any provision of this Act shall be liable on summary conviction to a fine not exceeding £400.

1963 c. 43. 1964 c. 70. 1970 c. 32. 1973 c. 60.

(2) Where a person is convicted of any offence under this Act or of any offence under the Protection of Animals Acts 1911 to 1964, the Protection of Animals (Scotland) Acts 1912 to 1964, the Pet Animals Act 1951, the Animal Boarding Establishments Act 1963, the Riding Establishments Acts 1964 and 1970, or the Breeding of Dogs Act 1973, the court by which he is convicted may cancel any licence held by him under this Act, and may, whether or not he is the holder of such a licence, disqualify him from keeping any dangerous wild animal for such period as the court thinks fit.

(3) A court which has ordered the cancellation of a person's licence, or his disqualification, in pursuance of the last foregoing subsection may, if it thinks fit, suspend the operation of the order pending an appeal.

Interpretation.

7.—(1) Subject to subsection (2) of this section, for the purposes of this Act a person is a keeper of an animal if he has it in his possession; and if at any time an animal ceases to be in the possession of a person, any person who immediately before that time was a keeper thereof by virtue of the preceding provisions of this subsection continues to be a keeper of the animal until another person becomes a keeper thereof by virtue of those provisions.

(2) Where an animal is in the possession of any person for the purpose of—

(*a*) preventing it from causing damage,

(*b*) restoring it to its owner,

(*c*) undergoing veterinary treatment, or

(*d*) being transported on behalf of another person,

the person having such possession shall not by virtue only of that possession be treated for the purposes of this Act as a keeper of the animal.

(3) In this Act expressions cognate with " keeper " shall be construed in accordance with subsections (1) and (2) of this section.

(4) In this Act, unless the context otherwise requires, the following expressions have the meanings hereby respectively assigned to them, that is to say—

" circus " includes any place where animals are kept or introduced wholly or mainly for the purpose of performing tricks or manœuvres;

" damage " includes the death of, or injury to, any person;

" dangerous wild animal " means any animal of a kind for the time being specified in the first column of the Schedule to this Act;

" local authority " means in relation to England and Wales a district council, a London borough council or the Common Council of the City of London, and, in relation to Scotland, an islands council or a district council;

" premises " includes any place;

" veterinary practitioner " means a person who is for the time being registered in the supplementary veterinary register;

" veterinary surgeon " means a person who is for the time being registered in the register of veterinary surgeons;

" zoological garden " means any place, other than a circus or deer-park, where wild animals not living in their natural surroundings are kept for the purpose of being regularly exhibited to members of the public for gain; and in this definition " deer-park " means any enclosure where deer of a species indigenous to or feral in the United Kingdom are kept.

(5) The second column of the Schedule to this Act is included by way of explanation only; in the event of any dispute or proceedings, only the first column is to be taken into account.

Power of Secretary of State to modify the Schedule.

8.—(1) If the Secretary of State is satisfied that the scope of this Act should be extended so as to include animals of a kind not for the time being specified in the Schedule to this Act or diminished so as to exclude animals of a kind for the time being specified in that Schedule, he may by order make the necessary modifications to that Schedule and any such order may be revoked by a subsequent order under this subsection.

(2) The power conferred by the foregoing subsection on the Secretary of State shall be exercisable by statutory instrument which shall be subject to annulment in pursuance of a resolution of either House of Parliament.

Protection of existing keepers.

9. Notwithstanding anything in this Act, a person who immediately before the date of the commencement of this Act was keeping a dangerous wild animal at any premises and who is not disqualified as mentioned in section 6(2) of this Act, shall be entitled to keep such animal at those premises without a licence under this Act—

(*a*) for the period of 90 days beginning with that date; and

(*b*) if before the expiration of that period he applies for a licence under this Act, until the licence is granted or finally refused or the application is withdrawn.

Short title, commencement and extent.

10.—(1) This Act may be cited as the Dangerous Wild Animals Act 1976.

(2) This Act shall come into operation at the expiration of a period of three months beginning with the date on which it is passed.

(3) This Act does not extend to Northern Ireland.

SCHEDULE

Section 7.

Kinds of Dangerous Wild Animals

NOTE: see section 7(5) of this Act for the effect of the second column of this Schedule.

Scientific name of kind	*Common name or names*
Canidae, except the species Canis familiaris and Vulpes vulpes	This kind includes the wild dog, wolf, jackal, coyote, fennec and fox, except that the domestic dog and the common red fox are specifically excluded.
Casuariidae	Cassowary
Cercopithecidae	Old World monkey (including langur, colobus, macaque, guenon, patas, mangabey, baboon and mandrill)
Crocodylia	This kind includes the alligator, crocodile, gharial, false gharial and caiman.
Dromaiidae	Emu
Elapidae (including Hydrophiidae)	This kind includes the cobra, krait, mamba, coral snake and sea snake, and all Australian poisonous snakes (including the death adder).
Felidae, except the species Felis catus	This kind includes the lynx, caracal, serval, bobcat, cheetah, lion, tiger, leopard, panther, jaguar, puma, cougar and ocelot, except that the domestic cat is specifically excluded.
Helodermatidae	Gila monster and Mexican beaded lizard
Hylobatidae	Gibbon
Pongidae	Anthropoid ape (including orang utan, gorilla and chimpanzee)
Rheidae	Rhea
Struthionidae	Ostrich
Ursidae	This kind includes the polar bear, brown bear and grizzly bear.
Viperidae (including Crotalidae)	This kind includes— (*a*) most snakes known as vipers and adders, and (*b*) the rattlesnake, bushmaster, fer-de-lance, water moccasin and copperhead.

Divorce (Scotland) Act 1976

1976 CHAPTER 39

An Act to amend the law of Scotland relating to divorce and separation; to facilitate reconciliation of the parties in consistorial causes; to amend the law as to the power of the court to make orders relating to financial provision arising out of divorce and to settlements and other dealings by a party to the marriage, and as to the power of the court to award aliment to spouses in actions for aliment; to abolish the oath of calumny; and for purposes connected with the matters aforesaid. [22nd July 1976]

BE IT ENACTED by the Queen's most Excellent Majesty, by and with the advice and consent of the Lords Spiritual and Temporal, and Commons, in this present Parliament assembled, and by the authority of the same, as follows:—

Divorce

Irretrievable breakdown of marriage to be sole ground of divorce.

1.—(1) In an action for divorce the court may grant decree of divorce if, but only if, it is established in accordance with the following provisions of this Act that the marriage has broken down irretrievably.

References in this Act (other than in sections 5(1) and 13 of this Act) to an action for divorce are to be construed as references to such an action brought after the commencement of this Act.

(2) The irretrievable breakdown of a marriage shall, subject to the following provisions of this Act, be taken to be established in an action for divorce if—

(*a*) since the date of the marriage the defender has committed adultery; or

(*b*) since the date of the marriage the defender has at any time behaved (whether or not as a result of mental abnormality and whether such behaviour has been active or passive) in such a way that the pursuer cannot reasonably be expected to cohabit with the defender; or

(*c*) the defender has wilfully and without reasonable cause deserted the pursuer; and during a continuous period of two years immediately succeeding the defender's desertion—

(i) there has been no cohabitation between the parties, and

(ii) the pursuer has not refused a genuine and reasonable offer by the defender to adhere; or

(*d*) there has been no cohabitation between the parties at any time during a continuous period of two years after the date of the marriage and immediately preceding the bringing of the action and the defender consents to the granting of decree of divorce; or

(*e*) there has been no cohabitation between the parties at any time during a continuous period of five years after the date of the marriage and immediately preceding the bringing of the action.

(3) The irretrievable breakdown of a marriage shall not be taken to be established in an action for divorce by reason of subsection (2)(*a*) of this section if the adultery mentioned in the said subsection (2)(*a*) has been connived at in such a way as to raise the defence of *lenocinium* or has been condoned by the pursuer's cohabitation with the defender in the knowledge or belief that the defender has committed the adultery.

(4) Provision shall be made by act of sederunt—

(*a*) for the purpose of ensuring that, where in an action for divorce to which subsection (2)(*d*) of this section relates the defender consents to the granting of decree, he has been given such information as will enable him to understand—

(i) the consequences to him of his consenting as aforesaid; and

(ii) the steps which he must take to indicate his consent; and

(*b*) prescribing the manner in which the defender in such an action shall indicate his consent, and any withdrawal of such consent, to the granting of decree;

and where the defender has indicated (and not withdrawn) his consent in the prescribed manner, such indication shall be sufficient evidence of such consent.

(5) Nowithstanding that irretrievable breakdown of a marriage has been established in an action for divorce by reason of subsection (2)(*e*) of this section, the court shall not be bound to grant

decree in that action if in the opinion of the court the grant of decree would result in grave financial hardship to the defender.

For the purposes of this subsection, hardship shall include the loss of the chance of acquiring any benefit.

(6) In an action for divorce the standard of proof required to establish the ground of the action shall be on balance of probability.

Encouragement of reconciliation.

2.—(1) At any time before granting decree in an action for divorce, if it appears to the court that there is a reasonable prospect of a reconciliation between the parties, it shall continue, or further continue, the action for such period as it thinks proper to enable attempts to be made to effect such a reconciliation; and if during any such continuation the parties cohabit with one another, no account shall be taken of such cohabitation for the purposes of that action.

(2) Adultery shall not be held to have been condoned within the meaning of section 1(3) of this Act by reason only of the fact that after the commission of the adultery the pursuer has continued or resumed cohabitation with the defender, provided that the pursuer has not cohabited with the defender at any time after the end of the period of three months from the date on which such cohabitation as is referred to in the said section 1(3) was continued or resumed as aforesaid.

(3) The irretrievable breakdown of a marriage shall not be taken to be established in an action for divorce by reason of section 1(2)(*c*) of this Act if, after the expiry of the period mentioned in the said section 1(2)(*c*), the pursuer has resumed cohabitation with the defender and has cohabited with the defender at any time after the end of the period of three months from the date on which the cohabitation was resumed as aforesaid.

(4) In considering whether any period mentioned in paragraph (*c*), (*d*), or (*e*) of section 1(2) of this Act has been continuous no account shall be taken of any period or periods not exceeding six months in all during which the parties cohabited with one another; but no such period or periods during which the parties cohabited with one another shall count as part of the period of non-cohabitation required by any of those paragraphs.

Action for divorce following on decree of separation.

3.—(1) The court may grant decree in an action for divorce notwithstanding that decree of separation has previously been granted to the pursuer on the same, or substantially the same, facts as those averred in support of the action for divorce; and in any such action (other than an action for divorce by reason of section 1(2)(*a*) of this Act) the court may treat an extract decree of separation lodged in process as sufficient proof of the facts upon which such decree was granted.

(2) Nothing in this section shall entitle the court to grant decree of divorce without receiving evidence from the pursuer.

Actions for separation

Actions for separation.

4.—(1) Sections 1, 2 and 11 of this Act shall apply to an action for separation or separation and aliment brought after the commencement of this Act and decree in such action as those sections apply to an action for divorce and decree therein subject to—

(*a*) the modification that any reference to irretrievable breakdown of a marriage shall be construed as a reference to grounds justifying decree of separation of the parties to a marriage ; and

(*b*) all other necessary modifications.

(2) In an action for separation or separation and aliment brought after the commencement of this Act, decree of separation shall not be pronounced except in accordance with the provisions of this section.

Financial provision for spouses and children

Orders for financial provision.

5.—(1) In an action for divorce (whether brought before or after the commencement of this Act), either party to the marriage may, at any time prior to decree being granted, apply to the court for any one or more of the following orders—

(*a*) an order for the payment to him or for his benefit by the other party to the marriage of a periodical allowance ;

(*b*) an order for the payment to him or for his benefit by the other party to the marriage of a capital sum ;

(*c*) an order varying the terms of any settlement made in contemplation of or during the marriage so far as taking effect on or after the termination of the marriage:

Provided that any reference in this subsection to payment by the other party to the marriage shall include a reference to payment out of any estate belonging to that party or held for his benefit.

(2) Where an application under the foregoing subsection has been made in an action, the court, on granting decree in that action, shall make with respect to the application such order, if any, as it thinks fit, having regard to the respective means of the parties to the marriage and to all the circumstances of the case, including any settlement or other arrangements made for financial provision for any child of the marriage.

(3) Where an application for an order for the payment of a periodical allowance under subsection (1)(*a*) of this section has been withdrawn or refused, or where no such application has been made, either party to the marriage may apply to the court for such an order after the date of the granting of decree of divorce if since that date there has been a change in the circumstances of either of the parties to the marriage; and the court shall make with respect to that application such order, if any, as it thinks fit, having regard to the factors mentioned in subsection (2) of this section.

(4) Any order made under this section relating to the payment of a periodical allowance may, on an application by or on behalf of either party to the marriage (or his executor) on a change of circumstances, be varied or recalled by a subsequent order.

(5) Any order made under this section relating to payment of a periodical allowance—

(*a*) shall, on the death of the person by whom the periodical allowance is payable, continue to operate against that person's estate, but without prejudice to the making of an order under the last foregoing subsection;

(*b*) shall cease to have effect on the remarriage or death of the person to whom or for whose benefit the periodical allowance is payable, except in relation to any arrears due under it on the date of such remarriage or death.

(6) Provision shall be made by act of sederunt to impose upon the pursuer in an action for divorce to which section 1(2)(*d*) or 1(2)(*e*) of this Act relates a duty to inform the defender of his right to apply for—

(*a*) financial provision under this Act,

(*b*) an order providing for the custody, maintenance and education of any child of the marriage under section 9 of the Conjugal Rights (Scotland) Amendment Act 1861, **1861 c. 86.**

in such form and manner as the act of sederunt may require, and, for the purposes of this subsection, where the pursuer alleges that the address of the defender is unknown to him, he shall satisfy the court that all reasonable steps have been taken to ascertain it.

(7) Any reference in this section to a settlement shall be construed as including a settlement by way of a policy of assurance to which section 2 of the Married Women's Policies of Assurance (Scotland) Act 1880 relates. **1880 c. 26.**

Orders relating to settlements and other dealings.

6.—(1) Where a claim has been made, being—

(*a*) an application under subsection (1)(*a*) or (1)(*b*) or (3) or (4) of section 5 of this Act which has been made by either party to the marriage, or

(*b*) an action for separation and aliment, adherence and aliment or interim aliment which has been brought by either party to the marriage, or

(*c*) an application for variation of an award of aliment (other than an interim award) in such an action which has been made by the party of the marriage who has brought that action,

that party may, at any time before the expiration of a period of one year from the disposal of the said claim, apply to the court for an order—

(i) reducing or varying any settlement or disposition of property belonging to the other party to the marriage made by him in favour of any third party at any time after the date occurring three years before the making of the said claim ; or

(ii) interdicting the other party to the marriage from making any such settlement or disposition, or transferring out of the jurisdiction of the court, or otherwise dealing with, any property belonging to him.

(2) On an application for an order under the foregoing subsection the court may make such an order if it is shown to its satisfaction that the settlement or disposition was made or is about to be made, or that the property is about to be transferred or otherwise dealt with, wholly or partly for the purpose of defeating in whole or in part any claim referred to in the foregoing subsection which has been made or might be made:

Provided that an order under this subsection shall not prejudice the rights (if any) in that property of any third party who has in good faith acquired it or any of it for value, or who derives title to the property or any of it from any person who has done so.

Power of court to award aliment.

7.—(1) Without prejudice to its other powers to award aliment, it shall be competent for the court, in an action for interim aliment brought after the commencement of this Act, to grant decree therein if it is satisfied that—

(*a*) the pursuer and the defender are not cohabiting with one another, and

(*b*) the pursuer is unwilling to cohabit with the defender whether or not the pursuer has reasonable cause for not so cohabiting by virtue of the circumstances set out in paragraph (*a*), (*b*) or (*c*) of section 1(2) of this Act:

Provided that, where the pursuer does not have reasonable cause for not cohabiting as aforesaid, the court shall not grant decree if it is satisfied that the defender is willing to cohabit with the pursuer.

(2) In determining the amount of aliment, if any, to be awarded in a decree of separation and aliment, adherence and aliment or interim aliment, the court shall have regard to the factors mentioned in section 5(2) of this Act.

This subsection shall apply to actions brought before the commencement of this Act as well as to actions brought after such commencement.

8. Section 3 of the Sheriff Courts (Civil Jurisdiction and Procedure) (Scotland) Act 1963 is amended as follows— Amendment of Sheriff Courts (Civil Jurisdiction and Procedure) (Scotland) Act 1963. 1963 c. 22.

(*a*) For subsection (1) there shall be substituted the following subsection—

" (1) An action of interim aliment by one party to a marriage against the other may competently be brought before the sheriff as a summary cause if the aliment claimed in the action does not exceed—

(i) the sum of £25 per week in respect of the pursuer ; and

(ii) the sum of £7·50 in respect of each child (if any) of the marriage ;

and any provision in any enactment limiting the jurisdiction of the sheriff in a summary cause by reference to any amount, or limiting the period for which a decree granted by him shall have effect, shall not apply in relation to such an action of interim aliment as is described in this subsection."

(*b*) In subsection (2) for the words " in the small debt court " there shall be substituted the words " as a summary cause ".

(*c*) After subsection (2) there shall be added the following subsections—

" (2A) The Lord Advocate may by order vary the amounts prescribed in paragraphs (i) and (ii) of subsection (1) above.

(2B) The power to make an order under the last foregoing subsection shall be exercisable by statutory instrument subject to annulment in pursuance of a resolution of either House of Parliament, and shall include power to vary or revoke any order made thereunder.".

(*d*) Subsection (3) is hereby repealed,

and this section shall come into force on 1st September 1976.

Supplemental

Abolition of oath of calumny.

9. In a consistorial action (whether brought before or after the commencement of this Act) the oath of calumny shall not be administered to the pursuer, and accordingly that oath is hereby abolished, but nothing in this section shall affect any rule of law relating to collusion.

Right of husband to cite paramour as a co-defender and to sue for damages abolished.

10.—(1) After the commencement of this Act the following rights of a husband shall be abolished, that is to say—

(*a*) the right to cite a paramour of his wife as a co-defender in an action for divorce, and

(*b*) the right to claim or to obtain damages (including solatium) from a paramour by way of reparation.

(2) Nothing in the provisions of the foregoing subsection shall preclude the court from awarding the expenses of the action for or against the paramour or alleged paramour in accordance with the practice of the court.

1861 c. 86.

(3) Section 7 of the Conjugal Rights (Scotland) Amendment Act 1861 (citation of a co-defender in an action for divorce and decree for expenses against him) shall cease to have effect.

Curator *ad litem* to be appointed in certain cases.

11. Provision shall be made by act of sederunt for the purpose of securing that, where in an action for divorce the defender is suffering from mental illness, the court shall appoint a curator *ad litem* to the defender.

Amendments, repeals and transitional provisions.

12.—(1) The enactments described in Schedule 1 to this Act shall have effect subject to the amendments specified therein in relation to them respectively.

(2) The enactments specified in columns 1 and 2 of Schedule 2 to this Act are hereby repealed to the extent specified in relation to them respectively in column 3 of that Schedule.

1889 c. 63.

(3) Subject to the following provisions of this section and without prejudice to the operation of section 38 of the Interpretation Act 1889 (effect of repeals), nothing in this section shall affect any proceedings brought, anything done, or the operation of any order made, under any enactment repealed by this section; nor shall anything in this Act be taken to revive any rule of law superseded by any enactment repealed by this section.

1938 c. 50.
1964 c. 41.

(4) Anything which, prior to the commencement of this Act, could have been done under section 2 of the Divorce (Scotland) Act 1938 or section 26 or 27 of the Succession (Scotland) Act 1964 may, after the commencement of this Act, be done under the corresponding provision of section 5 or 6 of this Act.

(5) An order under section 2 of the Divorce (Scotland) Act 1938 for the payment of an annual or periodical allowance to or for the behoof of a child of the marriage may, after the commencement of this Act, be varied or recalled by a subsequent order under subsection (2) of that section as if that section had not been repealed by this Act. 1938 c. 50.

(6) Subsection (5) of section 5 of this Act shall apply in relation to an order for the payment of an annual or periodical allowance under section 2 of the Divorce (Scotland) Act 1938 or of a periodical allowance under section 26 of the Succession (Scotland) Act 1964 as it applies in relation to an order for the payment of a periodical allowance under the said section 5. 1964 c. 41.

Interpretation.

13.—(1) In this Act, unless the context otherwise requires—

" action for divorce " has the meaning assigned to it by section 1(1) of this Act;

" the court " means—

(*a*) in relation to an action for divorce or an order under section 5 or 6 of this Act, the Court of Session;

(*b*) in relation to any other action, the Court of Session or the sheriff, as the case may require.

(2) For the purposes of this Act, the parties to a marriage shall be held to cohabit with one another only when they are in fact living together as man and wife; and " cohabitation " shall be construed accordingly.

(3) References in this Act to any enactment are references to that enactment as amended, and include references thereto as applied, by any other enactment, including, except where the context otherwise requires, this Act.

Citation, commencement and extent.

14.—(1) This Act may be cited as the Divorce (Scotland) Act 1976.

(2) This Act except section 8 shall come into operation on 1st January 1977.

(3) So much of section 12 of, and Schedule 1 to, this Act as affects the operation of section 16 of the Maintenance Orders Act 1950 shall extend to England and Wales and to Northern Ireland as well as Scotland, but save as aforesaid this Act shall extend to Scotland only. 1950 c. 37.

SCHEDULES

Section 12(1)

SCHEDULE 1

Enactments Amended

1950 c. 37. 1. In section 16(2)(*b*)(i) of the Maintenance Orders Act 1950, for the words " under section 26 of the Succession (Scotland) Act 1964 " there shall be substituted the words " an order for the payment of a periodical allowance under section 26 of the Succession (Scotland) Act 1964 or section 5 of the Divorce (Scotland) Act 1976.".

1964 c. 41. 2. In section 33(2) of the Succession (Scotland) Act 1964 there shall be added at the end the words " or section 5 of the Divorce (Scotland) Act 1976 ".

1966 c. 19. 3. In section 8(1) of the Law Reform (Miscellaneous Provisions) (Scotland) Act 1966, at the end of paragraph (*c*), there shall be added the words " or under section 5 of the Divorce (Scotland) Act 1976 ".

1968 c. 70. 4. In section 11(4) of the Law Reform (Miscellaneous Provisions) (Scotland) Act 1968, for the words from " administering " to the end of the subsection there shall be substituted the words " receiving evidence from the pursuer ".

1973 c. 45. 5. In Schedule 2 to the Domicile and Matrimonial Proceedings Act 1973, after paragraph 12 there shall be inserted the following paragraph—

> " 12A. Section 5 (orders for financial provision) and section 6 (orders relating to settlements and other dealings) of the Divorce (Scotland) Act 1976."

SCHEDULE 2

Section 12(2).

Enactments Repealed

Chapter	Short Title	Extent of Repeal
6 Geo. 4. c. 120.	The Court of Session Act 1825.	In section 28 the words " or adultery ".
11 Geo. 4 & 1 Will. 4. c. 69.	The Court of Session Act 1830.	In section 36 the words from the beginning to " to the pursuer; and ".
24 & 25 Vict. c. 86.	Conjugal Rights (Scotland) Amendment Act 1861.	Section 7.
3 Edw. 7. c. 25.	The Licensing (Scotland) Act 1903.	Section 73.
1 & 2 Geo. 6. c. 50.	The Divorce (Scotland) Act 1938.	The whole Act, except sections 5, 6(1) and 8.
6 & 7 Eliz. 2. c. 54.	The Divorce (Insanity and Desertion) Act 1958.	The whole Act.
8 & 9 Eliz. 2. c. 61.	The Mental Health (Scotland) Act 1960.	In Schedule 4 the paragraph relating to the Divorce (Scotland) Act 1938.
1964 c. 41.	The Succession (Scotland) Act 1964.	Section 25. Section 26. Section 27.
1964 c. 91.	The Divorce (Scotland) Act 1964.	The whole Act.
1966 c. 19.	The Law Reform (Miscellaneous Provisions) (Scotland) Act 1966.	Section 8(5).

Finance Act 1976

1976 CHAPTER 40

An Act to grant certain duties, to alter other duties, and to amend the law relating to the National Debt and the Public Revenue, and to make further provision in connection with Finance. [29th July 1976]

Most Gracious Sovereign,

WE, Your Majesty's most dutiful and loyal subjects, the Commons of the United Kingdom in Parliament assembled, towards raising the necessary supplies to defray Your Majesty's public expenses, and making an addition to the public revenue, have freely and voluntarily resolved to give and grant unto Your Majesty the several duties hereinafter mentioned; and do therefore most humbly beseech Your Majesty that it may be enacted, and be it enacted by the Queen's most Excellent Majesty, by and with the advice and consent of the Lords Spiritual and Temporal, and Commons, in this present Parliament assembled, and by the authority of the same, as follows:—

PART I

CUSTOMS AND EXCISE

Duties on alcoholic beverages

Increase of duties on spirits, beer, wine and made-wine.

1.—(1) In the Table in section 9 of the Finance (No. 2) Act 1975 (excise duty on spirits) for " 22·0900 " and " 22·1650 " there shall be substituted " 24·6300 " and " 24·7050 " respectively.

1975 c. 45.

(2) In section 10(1) of that Act (excise duty on beer) for " £13·6800 " and " £0·4560 " there shall be substituted " £15·8400 " and " £0·5280 " respectively.

PART I

(3) For the provisions of Schedule 4 to that Act (rates of excise duty on wine) there shall be substituted the provisions of Schedule 1 to this Act.

(4) For the provisions of Schedule 5 to that Act (rates of excise duty on made-wine) there shall be substituted the provisions of Schedule 2 to this Act.

(5) This section shall be deemed to have come into force on 7th April 1976.

Excise duty on cider.

2.—(1) As from 6th September 1976 there shall be charged on cider—

(*a*) imported into the United Kingdom ; or

(*b*) made in the United Kingdom by a person who is required by subsection (2) below to be registered as a maker of cider,

a duty of excise at the rate of £0·22 a gallon.

(2) Subject to subsection (3) below, a person who, on any premises in the United Kingdom, makes cider for sale must be registered with the Commissioners in respect of those premises.

(3) The Treasury may by order made by statutory instrument provide for exempting from subsection (2) above makers of cider whose production does not exceed such limit as is specified in the order and who comply with such other conditions as may be so specified ; and any order under this subsection may be varied or revoked by a subsequent order.

(4) If any person who is required by subsection (2) above to be registered in respect of any premises makes cider on those premises without being registered in respect of them, he shall be liable to a penalty of £500 and the cider and all vessels, utensils and materials for making cider found in his possession shall be liable to forfeiture.

(5) The Commissioners may with a view to managing the duty imposed by this section on cider made in the United Kingdom make regulations—

(*a*) regulating the making of cider for sale and the registration and cancellation of registration of makers of cider ;

(*b*) for determining the duty and the rate thereof and in that connection prescribing the method of charging the duty ;

(*c*) for securing and collecting the duty ;

(*d*) for relieving cider from the duty in such circumstances and to such extent as may be prescribed in the regulations.

(6) If any person fails to comply with any regulation made under subsection (5) above, he shall be liable to a penalty of £50 and any article in respect of which the offence was committed shall be liable to forfeiture. PART I

(7) As from 6th September 1976 the enactments mentioned in Schedule 3 to this Act shall have effect subject to the amendments there specified, being amendments consequential on this section.

(8) In this section "cider" means cider (or perry) of a strength less than 8·7 per cent. of alcohol by volume (at a temperature of 20°C) obtained from the fermentation of apple or pear juice without the addition at any time of any alcoholic liquor or of any liquor or substance which communicates colour or flavour other than such as the Commissioners may allow as appearing to them to be necessary to make cider (or perry).

Relaxation of prohibition on retail sales at distilleries. 1952 c. 44.

3.—(1) Subsection (1) of section 105 of the Customs and Excise Act 1952 (restriction on carrying on of other trades by distillers and rectifiers) shall cease to apply to the trade of retailer of spirits; and after that subsection there shall be inserted—

"(1A) Save with the permission of the Commissioners and subject to compliance with such conditions as they see fit to impose, a distiller or rectifier shall not—

(*a*) carry on upon his premises the trade of a retailer of spirits; or

(*b*) carry on the trade of a distiller or, as the case may be, rectifier on any premises communicating otherwise than by a public roadway with other premises on which the trade of retailer of spirits is carried on."

(2) Subsection (1) of section 160 of that Act (which precludes a dealer in or retailer of spirits from carrying on his business on premises communicating otherwise than by a public roadway with premises entered or used by a distiller or rectifier) shall cease to apply to a retailer of spirits; and for subsection (2) of that section (which precludes a retailer of spirits from being concerned or interested in the business of a distiller or rectifier carried on within two miles of his premises) there shall be substituted—

"(2) Save with the permission of the Commissioners and subject to compliance with such conditions as they see fit to impose, a retailer of spirits shall not—

PART I

(*a*) carry on his business on any premises which are entered or used by a distiller or rectifier or which communicate otherwise than by a public roadway with any such premises; or

(*b*) be concerned or interested in the business of a distiller or rectifier carried on upon any premises within two miles of any premises at which he sells spirits by retail."

(3) In subsection (3) of the said section 160 (penalties) after the words " provisions of this section " there shall be inserted the words " or any condition imposed thereunder ".

Tobacco products duty

Charge and administration.

4.—(1) As from 10th May 1976 there shall be charged on tobacco products imported into or manufactured in the United Kingdom a duty of excise at the rates shown in the following Table—

TABLE

1. Cigarettes	An amount equal to 20 per cent. of the retail price.
2. Cigars	£2·765 per pound.
3. Hand-rolling tobacco	£2·400 per pound.
4. Other smoking tobacco and chewing tobacco.	£1·550 per pound.

(2) Subject to such conditions as they see fit to impose, the Commissioners shall remit or repay the duty charged by this section where it is shown to their satisfaction that the products in question have been—

(*a*) exported or shipped as stores; or

(*b*) used solely for the purposes of research or experiment;

and the Commissioners may by regulations provide for the remission or repayment of the duty in such other cases as may be specified in the regulations and subject to such conditions as they see fit to impose.

(3) The Commissioners may with a view to managing the duty charged by this section make regulations—

(*a*) prescribing the method of charging the duty and for securing and collecting the duty;

(*b*) for the registration of premises for the safe storage of tobacco products and for requiring the deposit of such products in, and regulating their treatment in and removal from, premises so registered;

(*c*) for requiring the keeping and preservation of such records, and the making of such returns, as may be specified in the regulations ; and

(*d*) for the inspection of goods, documents and premises.

(4) If any person fails to comply with any regulation made under this section he shall be liable to a penalty of £200 and any article in respect of which, or found on premises in respect of which, the offence was committed shall be liable to forfeiture.

(5) In subsection (1) above " hand-rolling tobacco " means tobacco—

(*a*) which is sold or advertised by the importer or manufacturer as suitable for making into cigarettes ; or

(*b*) of which more than 25 per cent. by weight of the tobacco particles have a width of less than 0·6 mm.

(6) In this section and the other provisions of this Part of this Act relating to tobacco " tobacco products " means any of the products mentioned in the Table in subsection (1) above which are manufactured wholly or partly from tobacco or any substance used as a substitute for tobacco but does not include products commonly known as herbal cigarettes or herbal smoking mixtures.

Retail price of cigarettes.

5.—(1) For the purposes of the duty chargeable at any time under section 4 above in respect of cigarettes of any description, the retail price of the cigarettes shall be taken to be—

(*a*) in a case in which paragraph (*b*) below does not apply, the highest price at which cigarettes of that description are normally sold by retail at that time in the United Kingdom ;

(*b*) in any case where—

(i) there is a price recommended by the importer or manufacturer for the sale by retail at that time in the United Kingdom of cigarettes of that description ; and

(ii) duty is tendered and accepted by reference to that price,

the price so recommended.

(2) The duty in respect of any number of cigarettes shall be charged by reference to the price which, in accordance with subsection (1) above, is applicable to cigarettes sold in packets of twenty or of such other number as the Commissioners may determine in relation to cigarettes of the description in question ; and the whole of the price of a packet shall be regarded as referable to the cigarettes it contains notwithstanding that it also contains a coupon, token, card or other additional item.

PART I

(3) In any case in which duty is chargeable in accordance with paragraph (*a*) of subsection (1) above—

(*a*) the question as to what price is applicable under that paragraph shall, subject to subsection (4) below, be determined by the Commissioners ; and

(*b*) the Commissioners may require security (by deposit of money or otherwise to their satisfaction) for the payment of duty to be given pending their determination.

(4) Any person who has paid duty in accordance with a determination of the Commissioners under subsection (3)(*a*) above and is dissatisfied with their determination may require the question of what price was applicable under subsection (1)(*a*) above to be referred to the arbitration of a referee appointed by the Lord Chancellor, not being an official of any government department ; and if the referee determines that the price was lower than that determined by the Commissioners, they shall repay the duty overpaid, together with interest thereon from the date of the overpayment at such rate as the referee may determine.

(5) The procedure on any reference to a referee under subsection (4) above shall be such as may be determined by the referee ; and the referee's decision on any such reference shall be final and conclusive.

Alteration of rates of duty.

6.—(1) The Treasury may by order increase or decrease any of the rates of duty for the time being in force under the Table in section 4(1) above by such percentage thereof, not exceeding ten per cent., as may be specified in the order, but any such order shall cease to be in force at the expiration of a period of one year from the date on which it takes effect unless continued in force by a further order under this section.

(2) Any order under this section may be varied or revoked by a subsequent order ; and in relation to any order to continue, vary or replace a previous order, the reference in subsection (1) above to the rate for the time being in force is a reference to the rate that would be in force if no order under this section had been made.

(3) The power to make orders under this section shall be exercisable by statutory instrument.

(4) Any order under this section increasing the rate in force at the time of making an order shall be laid before the House of Commons after being made ; and unless it is approved by that House before the expiration of twenty-eight days beginning

PART I

with the date on which it was made, it shall cease to have effect on the expiration of that period, but without prejudice to anything previously done thereunder or to the making of a new order.

In reckoning any such period no account shall be taken of any time during which Parliament is dissolved or prorogued or during which the House of Commons is adjourned for more than four days.

(5) Any order under this section to which subsection (4) above does not apply shall be subject to annulment in pursuance of a resolution of the House of Commons.

(6) Section 9 of the Finance Act 1961 (surcharges and rebates in respect of revenue duties) shall not apply to duty charged under section 4 above. 1961 c. 36.

Charge in cases of default.

7.—(1) Where the records or returns kept or made by any person in pursuance of regulations under section 4 above show that any tobacco products or materials for their manufacture are or have been in his possession or under his control, the Commissioners may from time to time require him to account for those products or materials and unless he proves—

(*a*) that duty has been paid or secured under that section in respect of the products or, as the case may be, products manufactured from the materials ; or

(*b*) that the products or materials are being or have been otherwise dealt with in accordance with the regulations,

the Commissioners may require him to pay duty under that section in respect of those products or, as the case may be, in respect of such products as in their opinion might reasonably be expected to be manufactured from those materials.

(2) Where a person has failed to keep or make any records or returns required by regulations under section 4 above or it appears to the Commissioners that any such records or returns are inaccurate or incomplete they may require him to pay any duty under that section which they consider would have been shown to be due if proper records or returns had been kept or made.

Existing tobacco duties

Reduction of tobacco duties.

8.—(1) As from 10th May 1976 the rates of the duties of customs and excise chargeable on tobacco under the provisions mentioned in subsection (2) below shall each be reduced by £1·855 per pound ; and as respects tobacco on which there have been paid duties of customs and excise at the said reduced rates, the rates of drawback allowable under those provisions shall each be reduced by the like amount per pound.

PART I

(2) The provisions mentioned in subsection (1) above are the provisions of—

1964 c. 49. 1973 c. 51. 1974 c. 30. 1975 c. 45.

(*a*) section 4 of the Finance Act 1964, Schedule 5 to the Finance Act 1973, section 1(6) of the Finance Act 1974 and section 1(6) of the Finance (No. 2) Act 1975; and

(*b*) any order made before the said 10th May under section 1(4) of the said Act of 1973.

(3) In section 1(4) of the said Act of 1973 for paragraphs (*a*) and (*b*) there shall be substituted the words " the rates of the duty of customs and of drawback in respect of tobacco "; and subsection (1) above is without prejudice to the powers conferred on the Treasury by the said section 1(4).

(4) The Commissioners may make regulations for the repayment of any amounts of duty paid, and the recovery of any amounts of drawback allowed, in the period beginning with the said 10th May and ending with the passing of this Act which would not have been payable or allowable if this Act had been passed on that date; and the regulations may provide for setting off against any such repayment any amount due for that period by way of duty under section 4 above.

(5) If it is shown to the satisfaction of the Commissioners that any tobacco which has borne duty before the said 10th May under the provisions mentioned in subsection (2) above has been or will be used in the manufacture of tobacco products chargeable with duty under section 4 above, they shall make a repayment at the rate of £1·855 per pound in respect of the duty borne by that tobacco as aforesaid; and the rate per pound at which drawback is allowable on tobacco in respect of which a repayment has been made under this subsection shall be reduced by £1·855.

Hydrocarbon oil duty

Increase of duty on hydrocarbon oil etc.

9.—(1) In section 11 of the Finance (No. 2) Act 1975 (excise duty on hydrocarbon oil etc.) for the words " £0·2250 a gallon " there shall be substituted the words " £0·3000 a gallon ".

(2) This section shall be deemed to have come into force at 6 o'clock in the evening of 9th April 1976.

Use of rebated heavy oil. 1971 c. 12.

10.—(1) In paragraphs 2(*b*) and 3(*b*) of Schedule 1 to the Hydrocarbon Oil (Customs & Excise) Act 1971 (vehicles in which heavy oil may be used without repayment of rebate) for the words " or mowing machine " there shall be substituted the words " , mowing machine or fisherman's tractor ".

PART I

(2) In paragraphs 3 and 5 of that Schedule (which contain references to provisions of the Vehicles (Excise) Act (Northern Ireland) 1954 now consolidated in the Vehicles (Excise) Act (Northern Ireland) 1972), for " section 7(1)(*h*) ", " section 7(5) ", " section 4(2)(*a*), (*b*), (*c*), or (*d*) of ", " section 20 " and " 1954 " wherever it occurs there shall be substituted " section 4(1)(*h*) ", " section 7(1) ", " Schedule 3 to ", " section 23 " and " 1972 " respectively.

1972 c. 10 (N.I.).

Vehicles excise duty

Information about goods vehicles and registration of trailers.

1971 c. 10.

11.—(1) The power to make regulations under the Vehicles (Excise) Act 1971 as to the declaration to be made and particulars to be furnished by a person applying for a licence under that Act shall, in the case of applications for licences for goods vehicles, include power to require the declaration and particulars to extend to any matter specified in subsection (2) below as to which the Secretary of State may require information with a view to an alteration in the basis on which duty is chargeable under that Act in respect of such vehicles.

(2) The matters referred to in subsection (1) above are—

(*a*) the construction of the vehicle;

(*b*) the plated weights of the vehicle under Part II of the Road Traffic Act 1972; 1972 c. 20.

(*c*) if the vehicle has no such plated weights, the weight, when laden with the maximum load which it is constructed or adapted to carry, of the vehicle or, if it falls within paragraph 6 of Schedule 4 to the said Act of 1971, of the single vehicle of which it is treated as forming part;

(*d*) the use to which the vehicle has been or is likely to be put.

(3) In section 23(*d*) of the said Act of 1971 (and subsection (3) of the section 23 set out in paragraph 20 of Part I of Schedule 7 to that Act) references to mechanically propelled vehicles in respect of which duty is not chargeable under that Act shall include references to trailers.

(4) In this section " goods vehicle " and " trailer " have the same meaning as in Schedule 4 to the said Act of 1971.

(5) This section shall apply to Northern Ireland with the substitution for references to the said Act of 1971 of references to the Vehicles (Excise) Act (Northern Ireland) 1972 (and, in subsection (3), for the reference to Schedule 7 of a reference to Schedule 9) and with the substitution for the reference to Part II of the Road Traffic Act 1972 of a reference to any corresponding provisions for the time being in force in Northern Ireland.

PART I

Charges on request for registration number.
1971 c. 10.

12.—(1) Regulations under the Vehicles (Excise) Act 1971 may provide for a prescribed charge to be made in cases where by request a particular registration mark is assigned to a vehicle (whether on its first registration or later), having previously been assigned to another vehicle.

(2) The regulations may—

(*a*) require the vehicle to which a mark is requested to be assigned, and also in prescribed cases the other vehicle, to be made available for inspection either at a place designated by or under the regulations, or elsewhere;

(*b*) provide for a prescribed charge to be made for the inspection, and for the whole or part of this charge to be retained whether or not the mark is assigned as requested.

(3) Charges prescribed for the purposes of this section may be of any amount approved by the Treasury, and need not be related to the costs of making the assignment or (as the case may be) of arranging for any vehicle to be inspected.

(4) The first regulations under the Vehicles (Excise) Act 1971 prescribing the amount of any charge by virtue of this section shall not be made unless a draft of a statutory instrument containing them has been laid before Parliament and approved by a resolution of each House; and those regulations shall not then be subject to annulment as otherwise provided for regulations under the Act.

(5) The Vehicles (Excise) Act 1971 and this section shall be construed as if this section (without this subsection) were contained in that Act; and this section shall apply to Northern Ireland with the substitution for references to that Act of references to the Vehicles (Excise) Act (Northern Ireland) 1972.

1972 c. 10 (N.I.).

Restriction of exemption for disabled persons.
1971 c. 68.

13.—(1) Subject to subsection (2) below, a vehicle shall not be exempt from duty by virtue of section 7 of the Finance Act 1971 for any period after 6th April 1976 for which the person in whose name the vehicle is registered is entitled to a mobility allowance.

(2) Where a person—

(*a*) has before the said 6th April obtained, in pursuance of regulations made under the Vehicles (Excise) Act 1971, a document in the form of a licence in respect of a vehicle exempt under the said section 7; or

(*b*) has since the beginning of 1976 and before that date applied for the certificate required by the regulations for obtaining such a document, the vehicle shall not cease to be exempt by virtue of this section before the expiration of the period of validity of the document obtained by him before that date or, as the case may be, the first such document obtained by him after that date by virtue of the certificate. PART I

(3) This section shall apply to Northern Ireland with the substitution for any reference to the said section 7 of a reference to section 7(2A) of the Vehicles (Excise) Act (Northern Ireland) 1972 and for the reference to the Vehicles (Excise) Act 1971 of a reference to the said Act of 1972. 1972 c. 10. (N.I.). 1971 c. 10.

Fishermen's tractors.

14.—(1) The Vehicles (Excise) Act 1971 shall be amended in accordance with subsections (2) to (4) below.

(2) After paragraph 5 of Part I of Schedule 3 there shall be inserted—

"5A. In this Schedule "fisherman's tractor" means a tractor registered under this Act in the name of a person engaged in the business of sea fishing for food and not used on public roads for hauling anything except—

(*a*) a fishing boat, and anything (including the catch) carried in it, which belongs to that person or to him and other persons engaged in that business in the same locality;

(*b*) fishing tackle or other equipment required by the crew, or for the operation, of any such boat;

(*c*) fishing tackle or other equipment required for, and the catch resulting from, fishing operations carried out with the tractor."

(3) In paragraph 1 in column 1 of Part II of that Schedule after the words "mowing machines" there shall be inserted the words "fishermen's tractors".

(4) In Part I of Schedule 4, in paragraph 3(*c*) for the words "or works truck" there shall be substituted the words ", works truck or fisherman's tractor" and in paragraph 9(1) after the definition of "farmer's goods vehicle" there shall be inserted—

"'fisherman's tractor' has the same meaning as in Schedule 3 to this Act;".

(5) In section 6(1) of the Finance Act 1971 (definition of "tractor") after the words "paragraph 2" there shall be inserted the words "or of 'fisherman's tractor' in paragraph 5A". 1971 c. 68.

(6) Subsections (2) to (4) above shall also have effect in relation to the Vehicles (Excise) Act (Northern Ireland) 1972; and in paragraph 2(2) of Schedule 3 to that Act, after the words "sub-paragraph (1)" there shall be inserted the words "and 'fisherman's tractor' in paragraph 5A".

PART I

Miscellaneous

Deferred payment of customs duty.

15.—(1) The Commissioners may by regulations provide for the payment of customs duty to be deferred in such cases as may be specified by the regulations and subject to such conditions as may be imposed by or under the regulations; and duty of which payment is deferred under the regulations shall be treated, for such purposes as may be specified thereby, as if it had been paid.

(2) Regulations under this section may make different provision for goods of different descriptions or for goods of the same description in different circumstances.

1952 c. 44. 1975 c. 45.

(3) Section 34 (1A) of the Customs and Excise Act 1952 and section 16(6) of the Finance (No. 2) Act 1975 (which are superseded by this section) shall cease to have effect on the coming into force of the first regulations under this section.

Continuation of powers under Finance Act 1961 s. 9. 1961 c. 36.

16. The period after which orders of the Treasury under section 9 of the Finance Act 1961 may not be made or continue in force (which, by section 7 of the Finance (No. 2) Act 1975, was extended until the end of August 1976) shall extend until the end of August 1977 or such later date as Parliament may hereafter determine.

PART II

VALUE ADDED TAX

Reduction of higher rate.

17.—(1) In section 17(1) of the Finance (No. 2) Act 1975 (higher rate) for the words "25 per cent." there shall be substituted the words "12½ per cent.".

(2) This section shall be deemed to have come into force on 12th April 1976.

Annual adjustments of input tax. 1972 c. 41.

18. In section 3(4) of the Finance Act 1972 (regulations for attributing input tax where not all supplies are taxable) for paragraphs (*a*) and (*b*) there shall be substituted—

"(*a*) determining a proportion of supplies in any prescribed accounting period which is to be taken as consisting of taxable supplies and provisionally attributing input tax for that period in accordance with the proportion so determined; and

(*b*) adjusting, in accordance with a proportion determined in like manner for any longer period comprising two or more prescribed accounting periods or parts thereof, the provisional attribution for any of those prescribed accounting periods; and

PART II

(*c*) dispensing with an adjustment where the amounts of input tax deductible for any such longer period in accordance with the provisional and adjusted attributions do not differ by more than—

(i) an amount equal to such percentage (not exceeding 10 per cent.) of the input tax for that period as may be specified in the regulations ; or

(ii) such an amount (not exceeding £10) as may be so specified,

whichever is the greater ; ".

Effect on value of surcharges and rebates in respect of revenue duties. 1972 c. 41. 1961 c. 36.

19. For the purposes of section 11(*b*) and 27(2)(*b*) of the Finance Act 1972 (value of imported goods and of supply of goods in warehouse to include duty) the amount of any duty shall be taken to be the amount with any addition or deduction falling to be made under section 9 of the Finance Act 1961 (surcharges and rebates in respect of revenue duties).

Credit and discounts.

20.—(1) Paragraph 3 of Schedule 3 to the Finance Act 1972 (goods supplied pursuant to agreement subject to Hire-Purchase Acts to be treated as supplied for cash price) shall cease to have effect.

(2) For paragraph 4 of that Schedule (consideration in cases where reduction is allowed for immediate payment etc.) there shall be substituted—

" 4.—(1) Where goods or services are supplied for a consideration in money and on terms allowing a discount for prompt payment, the consideration shall be taken for the purposes of this Part of this Act as reduced by the discount whether or not payment is made in accordance with those terms.

(2) This paragraph does not apply where the terms include any provision for payment by instalments."

(3) This section shall come into force on the day appointed under section 192(4) of the Consumer Credit Act 1974 for the repeal of section 7 of the Hire-Purchase Act 1965, section 7 of the Hire-Purchase (Scotland) Act 1965 and section 7 of the Hire-Purchase Act (Northern Ireland) 1966.

1974 c. 39. 1965 c. 66. 1965 c. 67. 1966 c. 42 (N.I.).

Assessments.

21.—(1) In subsection (1) of section 31 of the Finance Act 1972 (power to assess tax where taxable person has failed to make returns etc.) the word " taxable " shall be omitted.

(2) Where the person failing to make a return, or making a return which appears to the Commissioners to be incomplete or incorrect, was required to make the return as a personal representative, trustee in bankruptcy, receiver, liquidator or person otherwise acting in a representative capacity in relation to

PART II

another person, subsection (1) of the said section 31 shall apply as if the reference to tax due from him included a reference to tax due from that other person.

(3) For the purposes of the said section 31 notification to a personal representative, trustee in bankruptcy, receiver, liquidator or person otherwise acting as aforesaid shall be treated as notification to the person in relation to whom he so acts.

Priority in bankruptcy etc.

1972 c. 41.

22. For the avoidance of doubt it is hereby declared that in section 41 of the Finance Act 1972 (priority in bankruptcy etc.)—

(*a*) the reference to tax due at the relevant date is a reference to tax which is then unpaid (whether payable before or after that date); and

(*b*) references to tax which has become due within the twelve months next before that date are references to tax (whether payable before or after that date) which is attributable to any prescribed accounting period falling—

(i) wholly within those twelve months; or

(ii) subject to apportionment in accordance with subsection (2) of that section, partly within and partly outside those twelve months,

including such tax assessed (whether before or after that date) under section 31 of that Act.

Failure of resolution under Provisional Collection of Taxes Act 1968.

1968 c. 2.

23.—(1) Where—

(*a*) by virtue of a resolution having effect under the Provisional Collection of Taxes Act 1968 value added tax has been paid at a rate specified in the resolution on the supply of any goods or services by reference to a value determined under section 10(2) of the Finance Act 1972, and

(*b*) by virtue of section 1(6) or (7) or 5(3) of the said Act of 1968 any of that tax is repayable in consequence of the restoration in relation to that supply of a lower rate,

the amount repayable shall be the difference between the tax paid by reference to that value at the rate specified in the resolution and the tax that would have been payable by reference to that value at the lower rate.

(2) Where—

(*a*) by virtue of such a resolution value added tax is chargeable at a rate specified in the resolution on the supply of any goods or services by reference to a value determined under the said section 10(2), but

(b) before the tax is paid it ceases to be chargeable at that rate in consequence of the restoration in relation to that supply of a lower rate,

the tax chargeable at the lower rate shall be charged by reference to the same value as that by reference to which tax would have been chargeable at the rate specified in the resolution.

(3) The tax that may be deducted as input tax under section 3(1) of the Finance Act 1972 or refunded under section 15 or 15A of that Act does not include tax that has been repaid by virtue of any of the provisions mentioned in subsecton (1)(b) above or that would be repayable by virtue of any of those provisions if it had been paid.

1972 c. 41.

PART III

INCOME TAX, CORPORATION TAX AND CAPITAL GAINS TAX

CHAPTER I

GENERAL

Charge of income tax for 1976–77.

24. Income tax for the year 1976-77 shall be charged at the basic rate of 35 per cent. ; and

(a) in respect of so much of an individual's total income as exceeds £5,000 at such higher rates as are specified in the Table below ; and

(b) in respect of so much of the investment income included in an individual's total income as exceeds £1,000 at the additional rates of 10 per cent. for the first £1,000 of the excess and 15 per cent. for the remainder ;

except that, in the case of an individual who shows that, at any time within that year, his age or that of his wife living with him was sixty-five years or more, income tax at the additional rate of 10 per cent. shall not be charged in respect of the first £500 of the excess mentioned in paragraph (b) above.

TABLE

Part of excess over £5,000	*Higher rate*
The first £500	40 per cent
The next £1,000	45 per cent
The next £1,000	50 per cent
The next £1,000	55 per cent
The next £1,500	60 per cent
The next £2,000	65 per cent
The next £3,000	70 per cent
The next £5,000	75 per cent
The remainder	83 per cent

PART III

Charge of corporation tax for financial year 1975.

25. Corporation tax shall be charged for the financial year 1975 at the rate of 52 per cent.

Rate of advance corporation tax for financial year 1976.

26. The rate of advance corporation tax for the financial year 1976 shall be thirty-five sixty-fifths.

Corporation tax: other rates and fractions.

1972 c. 41.

1975 c. 45.

27.—(1) The fraction by which, under section 93(2) of the Finance Act 1972, chargeable gains are to be reduced before they are for the purposes of corporation tax included in the profits of an authorised unit trust or investment trust shall, as from 1st April 1975, be sixty-nine one-hundred-and-fourths (instead of the fraction specified in section 27(1) of the Finance (No. 2) Act 1975).

(2) The small companies rate for the financial year 1975 shall be 42 per cent., and for that year the fraction mentioned in subsection (2) of section 95 of the Finance Act 1972 (marginal relief for small companies) shall be three-twentieths

(3) For the financial year 1975 and subsequent financial years subsection (3) of the said section 95 shall have effect with the substitution for any reference to £25,000 of a reference to £30,000 and with the substitution for any reference to £40,000 of a reference to £50,000.

(4) Where by virtue of subsection (3) above the said section 95 has effect with different relevant amounts in relation to different parts of the same accounting period, those parts shall be treated for the purposes of that section as if they were separate accounting periods, and the profits and income of the company for that period (as defined in that section) shall be apportioned between those parts.

Relief for interest: limit for 1976–77.

1974 c. 30.

28. In paragraph 5(1) of Schedule 1 to the Finance Act 1974 (limit on relief for interest on certain loans for purchase or improvement of land used as an only or main residence) the references to £25,000 shall have effect for the year 1976-77 as well as for the years 1974-75 and 1975-76.

Alteration of personal reliefs.

29.—(1) In section 8 of the Taxes Act (personal reliefs)—

(*a*) in subsection (1)(*a*) (married) for " £955 " there shall be substituted " £1,085 " ;

(*b*) in subsections (1)(*b*) (single) and (2) (wife's earned income relief) for " £675 " there shall be substituted " £735 " ;

(*c*) in subsections (1A) and (1B) (age allowance) for " £1,425 ", " £950 " and " £3,000 " there shall be substituted " £1,555 ", " £1,010 " and " £3,250 " respectively.

PART III

(2) In the year 1976-77 only, the allowances set out in section 10(3) of the Taxes Act (children) shall be amended as follows—

(*a*) in paragraph (*a*) (child over 16) for " £305 " there shall be substituted " £365 ";

(*b*) in paragraph (*b*) (child over 11 but not over 16) for " £275 " there shall be substituted " £335 ";

(*c*) in paragraph (*c*) (child not over 11) for " £240 " there shall be substituted " £300 ".

(3) In section 10(5) of that Act (restriction of relief where child has income exceeding £115) for " £115 " there shall be substituted " £350 " and at the end of the proviso there shall be inserted the words " and that in the case of a child who—

(*a*) is under the age of eighteen at the end of the year of assessment and is unmarried throughout that year; and

(*b*) either has no earned income or has earned income not exceeding £235,

this subsection shall have effect with the substitution for the words " income exceeding £350 " of the words " investment income (that is to say, income other than earned income) exceeding £115 ".

(4) In section 14(2) and (3) of that Act (additional relief for widows and others in respect of children) for " £280 " there shall be substituted " £350 ".

(5) In section 14(2)(*a*) of that Act (relief available only for claimant entitled to relief under section 10 in respect of a child resident with him) after the words " resident with him " there shall be inserted the words " or would be so entitled apart from subsection (5) of that section ".

Retirement annuities.

30.—(1) Sections 227 and 228 of the Taxes Act (which prescribe limits subject to which relief is available for premiums paid under approved retirement annuity contracts etc.) shall be amended as follows—

(*a*) in subsections (1A) and (1C) of section 227 and subsections (1) and (4) of section 228 for " £1,500 ", wherever it occurs, there shall be substituted " £2,250 ";

(*b*) in subsections (1B) and (1C) of section 227 for " £500 ", wherever it occurs, there shall be substituted " £750 "; and

(*c*) in the Table in subsection (4) of section 228 for " £1,600 ", " £1,700 ", " £1,800 ", " £1,900 ", and " £2,000 " there shall be substituted respectively

PART III

"£2,400", "£2,550", "£2,700", "£2,850" and "£3,000".

(2) In section 226(2)(*b*) and (10) and section 226A(1)(*b*) and (3)(*b*) (upper age limit in relation to approval of contracts etc.) for references to the age of 70 there shall be substituted references to the age of 75.

(3) This section does not affect relief for any year of assessment before the year 1976-77.

War widows.

31. For the purposes of calculating taxable income, the first 50 per cent. of war widow's pension shall be exempt.

Child benefit.

32.—(1) The Income Tax Acts shall have effect with the following amendments, being amendments which—

(*a*) apply to child benefit the provisions applying to family allowances; and

(*b*) make other changes in those provisions.

(2) In section 8(2)(*b*) of the Taxes Act (wife's earned income relief) for the words "on account of an allowance under the Family Allowances Act 1965 or the Family Allowances Act (Northern Ireland) 1966" there shall be substituted the words "of child benefit".

(3) In section 24 of that Act (reduction of reliefs on account of family allowances)—

(*a*) in subsection (1) for the words "on account of an allowance under the Family Allowances Act 1965 or the Family Allowances Act (Northern Ireland) 1966" there shall be substituted the words "of child benefit in respect of one child" and for the words from "on account of two or more allowances" onwards there shall be substituted the words "of child benefit in respect of two or more children the appropriate reduction shall be made under the preceding provisions of this subsection in respect of the child benefit in respect of each child";

(*b*) subsection (2) shall be omitted;

(*c*) in subsection (3)(*a*) for the words "or child's special allowance" there shall be substituted the words ", child's special allowance or invalid care allowance";

(*d*) after subsection (3) there shall be inserted—

"(3A) The said subsection (1) shall not apply to payments of child benefit in respect of a child in respect of which the individual to whom the payments are made is entitled to a guardian's allowance under the Social Security Act 1975 or the Social Security (Northern Ireland) Act 1975."

PART III

(4) In section 219(1)(*b*) of that Act (benefits chargeable to tax under Schedule E) for the words " on account of allowances under the Family Allowances Act 1965 or the Family Allowances Act (Northern Ireland) 1966 " there shall be substituted the words " of child benefit ".

(5) In section 530(2)(*c*) of that Act (meaning of " earned income ") for the words " family allowances " there shall be substituted the words " child benefit ".

(6) In paragraph 1(*b*) of Schedule 4 to the Finance Act 1971 (separate taxation of wife's earnings) for the words " on account of an allowance under the Family Allowances Acts 1965 to 1969 or the Family Allowances Acts (Northern Ireland) 1966 to 1969 " there shall be substituted the words " of child benefit ". 1971 c. 68.

(7) Section 32 of the Finance (No. 2) Act 1975 (interim benefit for unmarried or separated parents with children) shall cease to have effect. 1975 c. 45.

(8) The provisions of subsections (2) to (7) above (other than subsection (3)(*c*)) do not affect the operation of any of the enactments there mentioned in relation to any allowance or benefit payable in respect of a period before the appointed day for the purposes of the Child Benefit Act 1975 and the Child Benefit (Northern Ireland) Order 1975. 1975 c. 61. 1975/1504.

Certification of life insurance policies. 1975 c. 7.

33.—(1) Until such day as the Treasury may by order made by statutory instrument appoint, paragraph 1(1) of Schedule 2 to the Finance Act 1975 (which requires qualifying policies to be certified or to conform with a form certified by the Board) shall not apply to a policy issued in respect of an insurance made before 1st April 1976 which is varied on or after that date.

(2) In relation to the variation before the day appointed under subsection (1) above of any such policy as is there mentioned paragraph 11(2) of Schedule 1 to the Taxes Act (which was amended by the said Schedule 2 so as to transfer the function of certification from the body issuing the policy to the Board) shall have effect as originally enacted and not as so amended.

Relief on life policies etc.

34. For the year 1979-80 and subsequent years of assessment sections 19 to 21 of the Taxes Act and the other enactments mentioned in Schedule 4 to this Act shall have effect subject to the provisions of that Schedule.

Loan annuity contracts by the elderly.

35. Paragraph 16(1) and (2) of Schedule 2 to the Finance Act 1975 (charge in connection with contract for life annuity where money is lent to the annuitant etc.) shall not apply in relation to a contract if and to the extent that interest on the

PART III

1972 c. 41.

1974 c. 30.

sum lent is eligible for relief under section 75 of the Finance Act 1972 by virtue of paragraph 24 of Schedule 1 to the Finance Act 1974 (loan to elderly person for purchase of life annuity).

Husband and wife: income tax.

36.—(1) The Income Tax Acts shall have effect with the following amendments, being amendments which—

(*a*) in general preclude a wife's income from aggregation with her husband's until the beginning of the year of assessment following their marriage ; and

(*b*) make other changes in provisions applying to husbands and wives.

(2) In section 37(1) of the Taxes Act (aggregation of wife's income with husband's) for the words " so far as it is income for a year of assessment or part of a year of assessment during which she is a married woman living with her husband " there shall be substituted the words " so far as it is income for—

(*a*) a year of assessment ; or

(*b*) any part of a year of assessment, being a part beginning with 6th April,

during which she is a married woman living with her husband ".

(3) In section 38(1) of that Act (options for separate assessment) after the words " any year of assessment " there shall be inserted the words " for which his income would include any of hers " and the proviso shall be omitted.

(4) In section 14 of that Act—

(*a*) in subsection (2) for the words " Subject to subsection (3) below " there shall be substituted the words " Subject to subsections (3) and (4) below " ; and

(*b*) after subsection (3) there shall be inserted—

" (4) A person to whom this section applies by virtue of subsection (1)(*a*) above shall not be entitled to relief under this section for a year of assessment during any part of which that person is married and living with his or her spouse unless the child in connection with which the relief is claimed is resident with that person during a part of the year in which that person is not married and living with his or her spouse."

(5) In section 19 of that Act (life insurance relief)—

(*a*) in subsection (2)(*b*) for the word " wife " there shall be substituted the word " spouse " ; and

(*b*) in subsection (7) after the word " Where " there shall be inserted the words " in any year of assessment for which her husband's income includes or, if there were any, would include any of hers ".

(6) After section 21(1) of that Act (life insurance premium relief not to exceed one-sixth of a person's total income) there shall be inserted— PART III

" (1A) In relation to a year of assessment in which a woman is married and living with her husband but for which his income does not or, if there were any, would not include any of hers, subsection (1) above shall apply to each of them as if the maximum there specified were increased by an amount equal to the difference between—

(*a*) one-sixth of the other's total income; and

(*b*) the premiums or other sums in respect of which relief is given to the other."

(7) Where during any part of a year of assessment a husband and wife are living together but his income for that year does not or, if there were any, would not include any of hers, then, if either of them—

(*a*) would, if he or she had sufficient income for that year, be entitled to have any amount deducted from or set off against it under a provision to which this subsection applies; and

(*b*) makes a claim in that behalf,

that amount or, as the case may be, so much of it as cannot be deducted from or set off against his or her own income for that year shall instead be deducted from and set off against the income for that year of the other spouse.

(8) Subsection (7) above applies—

(*a*) in the case of the husband, to any provision of Chapter II of Part I of the Taxes Act (personal reliefs) and section 75 of the Finance Act 1972 (relief for payment of interest); 1972 c. 41.

(*b*) in the case of the wife, to—

(i) any provision of that Chapter except sections 8(1)(*b*) and (1A)(*b*), 12, 13 and 14; and

(ii) the said section 75 so far as applicable to interest paid in the part of the year of assessment mentioned in subsection (7) above.

(9) For the purposes of section 168 of the Taxes Act and section 71 of the Capital Allowances Act 1968 (set-off of losses and capital allowances against general income), section 37(1)(*b*) of the Taxes Act shall have effect as if the words " being a part beginning with 6th April " were omitted. 1968 c. 3.

(10) In section 23(2) and (4) of the Finance Act 1971 (election for separate taxation of wife's earnings to be made or revoked 1971 c. 68.

PART III

within six months after the end of the year of assessment) for the words " six months after " there shall be substituted the words " twelve months after ".

Relief for increase in stock values.

37. Schedule 5 to this Act shall have effect for affording relief for increases in the value of trading stock and work in progress in any period of account.

Restriction of relief for payments of interest.

38.—(1) Relief shall not be given to any person under any provision of the Tax Acts in respect of any payment of interest if a scheme has been effected or arrangements have been made (whether before or after the time when the payment is made) such that the sole or main benefit that might be expected to accrue to that person from the transaction under which the interest is paid was the obtaining of a reduction in tax liability by means of such relief as aforesaid.

(2) In this section " relief " means relief by way of deduction in computing profits or gains or deduction or set off against income or total profits.

(3) Where the relief is claimed by virtue of section 259(6) of the Taxes Act (group relief) any question under this section as to what benefit might be expected to accrue from the transaction in question shall be determined by reference to the claimant company and the surrendering company taken together.

(4) This section applies—

(*a*) where the payment is after 8th June 1976 ; and

(*b*) as respects relief—

(i) under section 248 or 259(6) of the Taxes Act in relation to the total profits for an accounting period beginning after that date or for any part falling after that date of an accounting period beginning earlier ; or

1972 c. 41.

(ii) under section 75 of the Finance Act 1972 in relation to income for the part of the year 1976-77 falling after that date,

where the payment is on or before that date.

(5) For the purposes of subsection (4)(*b*) above—

(*a*) the total profits for part of an accounting period shall be so much of the total profits for the whole period (reduced by any relief otherwise than in respect of the payment or payments in question) as is apportioned to that part ;

(*b*) the income for part of a year of assessment shall be so much of the income for the whole year (reduced by any relief otherwise than as aforesaid and otherwise than under Chapter II of Part I of the Taxes Act) as is apportioned to that part;

and any apportionment for the purposes of this subsection shall be made on a time basis.

Capital allowances: writing-down allowances.

39.—(1) Notwithstanding section 40 of the Finance Act 1971 and section 68(1) of the Finance Act 1972 (which exclude from the system of capital allowances introduced in 1971 expenditure incurred before 27th October 1970 and certain expenditure incurred later), the expenditure to which subsection (4)(*a*) of section 44 of the said Act of 1971 applies in the case of a person's first new chargeable period shall include the amount still unallowed, at the beginning of that period or its basis period, of any eligible expenditure incurred by him on the provision for the purposes of his trade of machinery or plant which then—

1971 c. 68.
1972 c. 41.

(*a*) belongs to him; and

(*b*) is or has been used for those purposes; and

(*c*) has not permanently ceased to be so used;

and elsewhere in the said section 44 references to capital expenditure shall include references to such eligible expenditure as aforesaid.

(2) In the case of such eligible expenditure as is mentioned in subsection (1) above no allowances or charges shall be made under Chapter II of Part I of the Capital Allowances Act 1968 for any new chargeable period; and in the case of other expenditure section 20(1) of that Act (normal method of calculating writing-down allowances) shall have effect for any such period with the substitution for the words " a percentage " of the words " 25 per cent.".

1968 c. 3.

(3) In this section " eligible expenditure " means, subject to subsection (4) below, expenditure in respect of which an allowance or allowances have been (or, if claimed, could have been) made under the said Chapter II; and in subsection (1) above the reference to the amount of any such expenditure still unallowed shall be construed in accordance with section 41 in that Chapter.

(4) The following is not eligible expenditure—

(*a*) expenditure on the provision of a new ship within the meaning of section 31 of the said Act of 1968;

(*b*) expenditure in respect of which an allowance or allowances have been (or, if claimed, could have been) made by virtue of or in accordance with the following provisions of the said Act of 1968—

(i) section 18(5) or 28 (assets used partly for trade and partly for other purposes);

PART III

(ii) section 18(6) or 29 (subsidies for wear and tear) ;

(iii) section 32 (cars) ; or

(iv) section 42 or 43 (lessors or lessees) ;

(*c*) expenditure in respect of which an allowance or allowances have been made in accordance with section 21 of the said Act of 1968 (alternative method of calculating writing-down allowances) ;

(*d*) expenditure incurred by a person under a contract which provides that he shall or may become the owner of the machinery or plant on the performance of the contract and which has not been performed before the beginning of his first new chargeable period or its basis period ;

(*e*) expenditure to which the person by whom it was incurred elects that subsection (1) above shall not apply.

(5) Any election under subsection (4)(*e*) above shall be made by notice in writing to the inspector given within two years from the end of the first new chargeable period of the person concerned.

(6) In this section " new chargeable period " means—

(*a*) where the chargeable period is a company's accounting period, an accounting period ending after 5th April 1976 ;

(*b*) where the chargeable period is a year of assessment, a year of assessment the basis period for which ends after that date.

(7) This section shall be construed as if contained in Chapter I of Part III of the said Act of 1971.

Capital allowances: disposal value.

1971 c. 68.

40.—(1) After subsection (6) of section 44 of the Finance Act 1971 (calculation of disposal value for purposes of writing-down allowances and balancing adjustments) there shall be inserted—

" (7) Where the person mentioned in the proviso to subsection (6) above has acquired the machinery or plant as a result of a transaction which was, or of a series of transactions each of which was, between connected persons within the meaning of section 533 of the Taxes Act, that proviso shall have effect as if it referred to the capital expenditure on the provision of the machinery or plant incurred by whichever party to that transaction, or to any of those transactions, incurred the greatest such expenditure."

1972 c. 41.

(2) Section 68(2) of the Finance Act 1972 (which is superseded by this section) shall cease to have effect.

PART III

(3) This section does not affect any case in which the event by reason of which the disposal value of the machinery or plant falls to be taken into account is before 16th April 1976.

Capital allowances: restriction of set-off against general income.

41.—(1) Relief shall not be given to an individual under section 168 of the Taxes Act (set-off against general income) by reference to a first-year allowance made to him in respect of expenditure incurred on the provision of machinery or plant for leasing in the course of a trade if—

(*a*) at the time when the expenditure was incurred the trade was carried on by him in partnership with a company (with or without other partners); or

(*b*) a scheme has been effected or arrangements have been made (whether before or after that time) with a view to the trade being carried on by him as aforesaid.

(2) Relief shall not be given to an individual under the said section 168 by reference to a first-year allowance if—

(*a*) the allowance is made in connection with—

(i) a trade which at the time when the expenditure was incurred was carried on by him in partnership or which has subsequently been carried on by him in partnership or transferred to a person who was connected with him within the meaning of section 533 of the Taxes Act; or

(ii) an asset which after that time has been transferred by him to a person who was connected with him as aforesaid or, at a price lower than that which it would have fetched if sold in the open market, to any other person; and

(*b*) a scheme has been effected or arrangements have been made (whether before or after that time) such that the sole or main benefit that might be expected to accrue to the individual from the transaction under which the expenditure was incurred was the obtaining of a reduction in tax liability by means of such relief as aforesaid.

(3) Where relief has been given in a case to which subsection (1) or (2) above applies it shall be withdrawn by the making of an assessment under Case VI of Schedule D.

(4) For the purposes of subsection (1) above letting a ship on charter shall be regarded as leasing it if, apart from this provision, it would not be so regarded.

(5) In this section " first-year allowance " means a first-year allowance under Chapter I of Part III of the Finance Act 1971, " trade " includes any activity in connection with which 1971 c. 68.

PART III

a first-year allowance can be given and any expression defined in section 50 of the said Act of 1971 has the meaning given in that section.

1968 c. 3.

(6) This section applies to relief under the proviso to section 71(1) of the Capital Allowances Act 1968 as it applies to relief under the said section 168.

(7) Subsections (1) and (2) above apply where the expenditure in respect of which the allowance is made to the individual in question was incurred by him after the commencement date and otherwise than under a contract entered into by him on or before that date; and " the commencement date " is, in relation to subsection (1), 15th December 1975 and, in relation to subsection (2), 6th April 1976.

Capital allowances: subsidies and contributions.

42.—(1) After subsection (1) of section 85 of the Capital Allowances Act 1968 (allowances in respect of contributions to capital expenditure) there shall be inserted—

" (1A) Subsection (1) above shall not apply where the person making the contribution and the person receiving it are connected persons within the meaning of section 533 of the principal Act.".

(2) This section applies in relation to contributions made after 8th July 1976.

Capital allowances: motor cars. 1971 c. 68.

43.—(1) In paragraphs 10 to 12 of Schedule 8 to the Finance Act 1971 (special capital allowances rules for motor cars) for any reference to £4,000 or £1,000 there shall be substituted a reference to £5,000 or £1,250 respectively.

(2) This section applies in relation to expenditure incurred after 6th April 1976; and section 50(4) of the said Act of 1971 applies for the purposes of this subsection.

Close companies: loans to participators.

44.—(1) In relation to any claim made after the passing of this Act under subsection (5) of section 286 of the Taxes Act (relief where loan to participator is repaid) that subsection shall have effect with the substitution for the words " year of assessment " of the words " financial year ".

(2) After section 287 of that Act there shall be inserted—

" Extension of s. 286 to loans by controlled companies.

287A.—(1) Subject to subsection (4) below, where a company which is controlled by a close company makes a loan which, apart from this section does not give rise to a charge under subsection (1) of section 286 above, that section shall apply as if the loan had been made by the close company.

(2) Subject to subsection (4) below, where a company which is not controlled by a close company

makes a loan which, apart from this section does not give rise to a charge under subsection (1) of section 286 above, and a close company subsequently acquires control of it, that section shall apply as if the loan had been made by the close company immediately after the time when it acquired control. PART III

(3) Where two or more close companies together control the company that makes or has made the loan, subsections (1) and (2) above shall have effect—

(*a*) as if each of them controlled that company; and

(*b*) as if the loan had been made by each of those close companies;

but the loan shall be apportioned between those close companies in such proportion as may be appropriate having regard to the nature and amount of their respective interests in the company that makes or has made the loan.

(4) Subsections (1) and (2) above do not apply if it is shown that no person has made any arrangements (otherwise than in the ordinary course of a business carried on by him) as a result of which there is a connection—

(*a*) between the making of the loan and the acquisition of control; or

(*b*) between the making of the loan and the provision by the close company of funds for the company making the loan;

and the close company shall be regarded as providing funds as aforesaid if it directly or indirectly makes any payment or transfers any property to, or releases or satisfies (in whole or in part) a liability of, the company making the loan.

(5) Where, by virtue of this section, section 286 above has effect as if a loan made by one company had been made by another any question under that section or section 287 above whether—

(*a*) the company making the loan did so otherwise than in the ordinary course of a business carried on by it which includes the lending of money;

(*b*) the loan or any part of it has been repaid to the company;

PART III

(*c*) the company has released or written off the whole or part of the debt in respect of the loan,

shall be determined by reference to the company that made the loan.

(6) This section shall be construed as one with section 286 above, and in this section " loan " includes advance, and references to a company making a loan include references to cases in which the company is, or if it were a close company would be, regarded as making a loan by virtue of subsection (2) of that section.

1972 c. 41.

(3) In paragraph 19(5) of Schedule 16 to the Finance Act 1972 (information powers) for the words " sections 286 and 287 of the Taxes Act " there shall be substituted the words " sections 286, 287 and 287A of the Taxes Act ".

(4) Subsection (2) above has effect as respects loans made or debts incurred or assigned after 15th April 1976.

Close companies: notice of liability.

45. In paragraph 6(2) of Schedule 16 to the Finance Act 1972 (which requires a notice of liability to be served on a close company if a participator does not pay the tax assessed in respect of a sum apportioned to him) for the words " shall be served " there shall be substituted the words " may be served " and for the words " shall thereupon be payable by the company " there shall be substituted the words " shall be payable by the company upon service of the notice ".

Effect of advance corporation tax on preference dividends etc.

46.—(1) In paragraph 18(1) of Schedule 23 to the Finance Act 1972 (dividends etc., at gross rate or of gross amount; transitional provisions on introduction of advance corporation tax), the reference to " the rate of advance corporation tax in force on that date " is to the rate in force on 6th April 1973.

This subsection shall be deemed always to have had effect.

(2) Where in the case of shares not carrying cumulative rights, a company, relying on the alternative view of paragraph 18, has reduced any dividend to which the paragraph applies below what it would have been according to the original view, the deficiency may be made up by means of supplementary dividend payable to shareholders registered on a given date; and—

(*a*) this has effect notwithstanding any restriction, of whatsoever nature, on the company's power to pay dividends, except that which requires dividends to be paid only out of profits and reserves;

(b) the date mentioned above is either the date of declaration of the supplementary dividend or such other date (but not earlier than two months before the due date for its payment) as may be appointed by the company.

(3) In the case of shares carrying cumulative rights, the obligation arising from this section to make good any underpayment of dividend made in reliance on the alternative view shall be carried forward to subsequent periods of account in the same way as with any other underpayment.

(4) In the case of shares carrying both non-cumulative and cumulative rights, subsections (2) and (3) above apply respectively according as dividend is payable by reference to the one category of rights or the other.

(5) Subject to subsections (3) and (4) above, this section does not invalidate anything done with reliance in good faith either on the original or on the alternative view of paragraph 18; nor does it give rise to any liability or increased liability on any person for acting, or omitting to act, in a particular way where he did so with reliance in good faith on the one or on the other view.

(6) In this section—

(a) "dividend" includes any other distribution;

(b) "share" includes stock, and any other interest of a member in a company, and any securities within the meaning of Part X of the Taxes Act; and

(c) "paragraph 18" means paragraph 18 of Schedule 23 to the Finance Act 1972; 1972 c. 41.

and for the purposes of subsections (2) to (5) the original view of paragraph 18 is that it has, and always had, the meaning given to it by subsection (1) above, and the alternative view is that the rate of advance corporation tax referred to in the paragraph is the rate in force from time to time.

Relief for levies on insurance companies.

47. For the purposes of section 304 of the Taxes Act as applied by section 305 of that Act (expenses of management of insurance companies), any sums paid by a company, whether before or after the passing of this Act, under a long term business levy imposed by virtue of the Policyholders Protection Act 1975 shall be treated as part of its expenses of management. 1975 c. 75.

Friendly societies.

48.—(1) In section 332 of the Taxes Act (registered friendly societies) after subsection (9) there shall be inserted—

"(10) Where at any time a registered friendly society ceases by virtue of section 84 of the Friendly Societies Act

PART III

1974 (conversion into company) to be registered under that Act, any part of its life or endowment business consisting of business which—

(*a*) relates to contracts made before that time; and

(*b*) immediately before that time was tax exempt life or endowment business,

shall thereafter continue to be tax exempt life or endowment business for the purposes of this Chapter.

(11) Where a registered friendly society—

(*a*) at any time ceases by virtue of section 84 of the said Act of 1974 to be registered under that Act; and

(*b*) immediately before that time was exempt from income tax or corporation tax on profits arising from any business carried on by it other than life or endowment business,

the company into which the society is converted shall be so exempt on its profits arising from any part of that business which relates to contracts made before that time so long as there is no increase in the scale of benefits which it undertakes to provide in the course of carrying on that part of its business.

(12) For the purposes of the Corporation Tax Acts any part of a company's business—

(*a*) which continues to be tax exempt life or endowment business by virtue of subsection (10) above; or

(*b*) in respect of the profits from which the company is exempt by virtue of subsection (11) above,

shall be treated as a separate business from any other business carried on by the company."

(2) In the definition of " tax exempt life or endowment business " in section 337(3) of the Taxes Act for the words " subject to section 332(6) to (9) " there shall be substituted the words " subject to section 332(6) to (10) ".

1974 c. 46.

(3) The amendment of section 337(5)(*b*) of the Taxes Act made by paragraph 23(*b*) of Schedule 9 of the Friendly Societies Act 1974 shall extend to Northern Ireland.

New double taxation arrangements with Ireland.

49.—(1) If in the year 1976 Her Majesty by Order in Council under section 497 of the Taxes Act declares, with respect to arrangements made between Her Government in the United Kingdom and the Government of the Republic of Ireland with a view to affording relief from double taxation, that it is expedient that those arrangements should have effect, then the following provisions of this section (going to the implementation of those arrangements or required in consequence of them) shall come into force with the Order (or, in the case of the Order in Council having come into force before this Act is passed, shall be deemed to have done so). PART III

(2) The following enactments (giving effect to, or consequent on, arrangements made between the two countries in the years up to 1975) are hereby repealed, that is to say—

(*a*) in the Taxes Act—

section 315(7) and (8) (Republic of Ireland included with United Kingdom for purposes of provisions about foreign life assurance funds),

section 473(2) (exception of Irish residents from certain United Kingdom measures about transactions in securities),

in section 498(1), the proviso (excluding unilateral relief in the case of Irish tax),

section 513 and, in Schedule 12 (which by virtue of the section saves the effect of the former Agreements up to and including that of 1960 and provides for their implementation), Parts I and II and paragraphs 1, 3(1) and (2), 4 and 5 of Part III;

(*b*) in the Finance Act 1973, section 42 and Schedule 17 (implementation of 1973 Agreement); and 1973 c. 51.

(*c*) in the Finance (No. 2) Act 1975, section 65 and Schedule 11 (implementation of 1975 Agreement). 1975 c. 45.

(3) In Part III of Schedule 12 to the Taxes Act (provisions already operating so as to give effect to double taxation arrangements with Ireland), paragraphs 2, 3(3) and 6 continue in force by virtue of this section and not, as previously, by virtue of section 513 of that Act.

(4) In Part III of Schedule 12 to the Taxes Act (provisions in force before 1976 for giving effect to double taxation arrangements with Ireland and continued by this section), the following is added at the end of paragraph 2—

"(3) In charging any income which is excluded from sub-paragraph (1) above by sub-paragraph (2)(*a*), the same deductions shall be made, and there shall be the same limitation on reliefs, as under section 23(3) and (4) of the Finance Act 1974 (method of charging income from trade, etc. carried on abroad) in the case of income computed by virtue of that section in accordance with the rules applicable to Cases I and II of Schedule D.".

(5) In section 75 of the Finance Act 1972 (relief for payment of interest) the following is substituted for subsection (6)— 1972 c. 41.

PART III

"(6) This section has effect as if references to the United Kingdom included references to the Republic of Ireland.".

1974 c. 30.

(6) In section 22(1) of the Finance Act 1974 (foreign pensions etc.) the reference to a pension which would have fallen under section 122(2)(*c*) of the Taxes Act (remittance basis) includes any which would have so fallen but for paragraph 2 of Part III of Schedule 12 to the Taxes Act.

(7) The repeals in subsection (2) above, and the amendments made by subsections (4) to (6), take effect from 6th April 1976, subject however to so much of the new Agreement as retains any former Agreement in force for years of assessment ending on or before 5th April 1977.

(8) In this section "the new Agreement" means any Convention between the Governments of the United Kingdom and the Republic of Ireland relating to avoidance of double taxation and entering into force in the year 1976; and the "former Agreements" are those set out in Part I of Schedule 12 to the
1973 c. 51. Taxes Act, Schedule 17 to the Finance Act 1973 and Schedule 11
1975 c. 45. to the Finance (No. 2) Act 1975.

Other provisions relating to double taxation.

50.—(1) In the case of a person not resident in the United Kingdom who carries on in the United Kingdom a banking business, an insurance business or a business consisting wholly or partly in dealing in securities, receipts of interest or dividend which have been treated as tax-exempt under double taxation arrangements are not to be excluded from trading income or profits of the business so as to give rise to losses to be set off (under section 177 or 312 of the Taxes Act) against income or profits arising on or after 15th April 1976.

In this subsection "double taxation arrangements" means arrangements having effect by virtue of section 497 of the Taxes Act; and "securities" includes stocks and shares.

(2) In section 497 of the Taxes Act, in subsection (3) (foreign tax treated as paid though not payable)—

(*a*) the words (in the second paragraph of the subsection) from "to any relief" onwards shall become paragraph (*a*); and

(*b*) after that paragraph there shall be added—

"and

(*b*) to any relief provided under and in accordance with the arrangements, where the latter expressly contemplate that the relief is to fall within this subsection".

PART III

(3) In section 506 of the Taxes Act (computation of underlying tax on foreign company profits), the following shall be inserted after subsection (1)—

" (1A) Where under the foreign tax law the dividend has been increased for tax purposes by an amount to be set off against the recipient's own tax under that law or, to the extent that it exceeds his own tax thereunder, paid to him, then from the amount of the underlying tax to be taken into account under subsection (1) above there is to be subtracted the amount of that increase.".

This subsection has effect as from 1st April 1976.

Capital gains: small disposals. 1971 c. 68.

51.—(1) In section 57(1) and (2) of the Finance Act 1971 (small disposals) for " £500 " there shall be substituted " £1,000 ".

(2) This section applies for the year 1975-76 and subsequent years of assessment.

Capital gains: husband and wife.

52.—(1) The enactments relating to capital gains tax shall have effect with the following amendments, being amendments corresponding to or consequential on the amendments made by section 36 above.

1965 c. 25.

(2) In section 21(4) of the Finance Act 1965 (capital gains chargeable on income tax basis) after the words " a married woman who in the year of assessment is a married woman living with her husband " there shall be inserted the words " and whose income for, or for any part of, that year is included in his by virtue of section 37(1) of the Income and Corporation Taxes Act 1970 ".

(3) In paragraph 3(1) of Schedule 10 to that Act (married woman's chargeable gains to be assessed on her husband) for the words " in a year of assessment, or part of a year of assessment, during which she is a married woman living with her husband " there shall be substituted the words " in—

(*a*) a year of assessment ; or

(*b*) any part of a year of assessment, being a part beginning with 6th April,

during which she is a married woman living with her husband ".

(4) After section 57(3) of the Finance Act 1971 (small disposals) there shall be inserted—

" (3A) Subsection (3) above applies only to disposals made in a year of assessment for which, by virtue of section 37(1) of the Income and Corporation Taxes Act 1970, the husband's income includes or, if there were any, would include, any of the wife's."

PART III

Capital gains: compensation stock.

53.—(1) This section has effect where gilt-edged securities are exchanged for shares in pursuance of any enactment (including an enactment passed after this Act) which provides for the compulsory acquisition of any shares and the issue of gilt-edged securities instead.

1965 c. 25.

(2) The exchange shall not constitute a conversion of securities within paragraph 5 of Schedule 7 to the Finance Act 1965 (which has the effect that compensation securities are treated as the same asset as the original shares) and accordingly the gilt-edged securities shall not be treated as having been acquired on any date earlier than that on which they were issued or for any consideration other than the value of the shares as determined for the purposes of the exchange.

(3) The exchange shall be treated as not involving any disposal of the shares by the person from whom they were compulsorily acquired but—

(*a*) there shall be calculated the gain or loss that would have accrued to him if he had then disposed of the shares for a consideration equal to the value mentioned in subsection (2) above ; and

(*b*) on a subsequent disposal of the whole or part of the gilt-edged securities by the person to whom they were issued—

(i) there shall be deemed to accrue to him (in addition to any gain or loss that actually accrues) the whole or a corresponding part of the gain or loss mentioned in paragraph (*a*) above ; and

1969 c. 32.

(ii) if the disposal is within section 41 of the Finance Act 1969 (exemption for gilt-edged securities) that section shall have effect only in relation to any gain or loss that actually accrues and not in relation to any gain or loss that is deemed to accrue as aforesaid.

(4) Where a person to whom gilt-edged securities of any kind were issued as mentioned in subsection (1) above disposes of securities of that kind, the securities of which he disposes—

(*a*) shall, so far as possible, be identified with any securities of that kind which he has acquired otherwise than as mentioned in subsection (1) above within the twelve months preceding the disposal ; and

1971 c. 68.

(*b*) so far as they cannot be identified as aforesaid, shall be identified (without regard to paragraphs 6, 7(3) and 8 of Schedule 10 to the Finance Act 1971) with securities which were issued to him as mentioned in that sub-section, taking those issued earlier before those issued later.

PART III

(5) Subsection (3)(*b*) above shall not apply to any disposal falling within the provisions of—

(*a*) section 24(7) of the Finance Act 1965 (disposals by personal representatives to legatees); or 1965 c. 25.

(*b*) paragraph 20(1) of Schedule 7 to that Act (disposals between husband and wife); or

(*c*) section 273(1) of the Taxes Act (disposals within a group of companies);

but a person who has acquired the securities on a disposal falling within those provisions (and without there having been a previous disposal not falling within those provisions or a devolution on death) shall be treated for the purposes of subsections (3)(*b*) and (4) above as if the securities had been issued to him.

(6) Where the gilt-edged securities to be exchanged for any shares are not issued until after the date on which the shares are compulsorily acquired but on that date a right to the securities is granted, this section shall have effect as if the exchange had taken place on that date, as if references to the issue of the securities and the person to whom they were issued were references to the grant of the right and the person to whom it was granted and references to the disposal of the securities included references to disposals of the rights.

(7) In this section—

"gilt-edged securities" means specified securities within the meaning of section 41 of the Finance Act 1969; 1969 c. 32.

"shares" includes securities within the meaning of paragraph 5 of Schedule 7 to the Finance Act 1965.

(8) This section has effect where the compulsory acquisition is after 6th April 1976.

Capital gains: compulsory acquisition of aircraft and shipbuilding shares.

54.—(1) This section has effect where, in pursuance of any enactment to which this subsection applies, gilt-edged securities are exchanged for shares in a company and, immediately before the exchange, those shares are owned by another company—

(*a*) which is a member of the same group of companies as the first-mentioned company; or

(*b*) which is a member of a consortium by which the first-mentioned company is owned.

(2) Subsection (1) above applies to any enactment providing for the compulsory acquisition of shares in companies engaged in manufacturing aircraft or guided weapons or in shipbuilding or allied industries.

PART III

(3) In any case in which this section has effect the company owning the shares immediately before the exchange may by notice in writing given to the inspector within four years after the exchange, elect—

(*a*) that section 53(3) above shall not apply to the exchange; and

1965 c. 25.

(*b*) that section 33 of the Finance Act 1965 (replacement of business assets) shall have effect in relation to the disposal on the occasion of the exchange as if the shares were assets falling within the classes listed in that section and had, throughout the period of ownership, been used and used only for the purposes of a trade carried on by that company.

(4) For the purposes of this section—

(*a*) two companies shall be deemed to be members of a group of companies if one is the 75 per cent. subsidiary of the other or both are 75 per cent. subsidiaries of a third company;

(*b*) a company is owned by a consortium if all of the ordinary share capital of that company is directly and beneficially owned between them by five or fewer companies, and those companies are called the members of the consortium.

(5) Subsections (6) and (7) of section 53 above shall apply in relation to this section as they apply in relation to that section.

Capital gains: maintenance funds for historic buildings.

55.—(1) This section applies where after 2nd May 1976 a person disposes of an asset to trustees in circumstances such that the disposal is a transfer of value which by virtue of section 84 below is an exempt transfer.

(2) The person making the disposal and the person acquiring the asset on the disposal shall be treated for all the purposes of Part III of the Finance Act 1965 (capital gains tax) as if the asset was acquired from the one making the disposal for a consideration of such an amount as would secure that on the disposal neither a gain nor a loss would accrue to the one making the disposal.

Capital gains: disposals on trust for benefit of employees.

56.—(1) Where a close company within the meaning of section 90 below or an individual disposes of an asset to trustees in circumstances such that the disposal is a disposition which by virtue of that section is not a transfer of value for the purposes of capital transfer tax, Part III of the Finance Act 1965 (capital gains tax) shall have effect in relation to the disposal in accordance with subsections (2) and (3) below.

PART III

(2) Section 22(4) of that Act (consideration deemed to be equal to market value) shall not apply to the disposal; and if the disposal is by way of gift or is for a consideration not exceeding the sums allowable as a deduction under paragraph 4 of Schedule 6 to that Act—

(*a*) the disposal, and the acquisition by the trustees, shall be treated for the purposes of Part III (but not for the purposes of section 57 of the Finance Act 1971) as 1971 c. 68. being made for such consideration as to secure that neither a gain nor a loss accrues on the disposal; and

(*b*) where the trustees dispose of the asset, its acquisition by the company or individual shall be treated as its acquisition by the trustees.

(3) Where the disposal is by a close company, paragraph 18(1) of Schedule 7 to the said Act of 1965 (assets disposed of for less than market value) shall apply to the disposal as if for the reference to market value there were substituted a reference to market value or the sums allowable as a deduction under paragraph 4 of Schedule 6 to that Act, whichever is the less.

(4) Subject to subsection (5) below, Part III of the said Act of 1965 shall also have effect in accordance with subsection (2) above in relation to any disposal made after 6th April 1976 by a company other than such a close company as aforesaid if—

(*a*) the disposal is made to trustees otherwise than under a bargain made at arm's length; and

(*b*) the property disposed of is to be held by them on trusts of the description specified in paragraph 17(1) of Schedule 5 to the Finance Act 1975 (that is to say, 1975 c. 7. those in relation to which the said section 90 has effect) and the persons for whose benefit the trusts permit the property to be applied include all or most of either—

(i) the persons employed by or holding office with the company; or

(ii) the persons employed by or holding office with the company or any one or more subsidiaries of the company.

(5) Subsection (4) above does not apply if the trusts permit any of the property to be applied at any time (whether during any such period as is referred to in the said paragraph 17(1) or later) for the benefit of—

(*a*) a person who is a participator in the company ("the donor company"); or

(*b*) any other person who is a participator in any other company that has made a disposal of property to be

PART III

held on the same trusts as the property disposed of by the donor company, being a disposal in relation to which the said Part III has had effect in accordance with subsection (2) above ; or

(*c*) any other person who has been a participator in the donor company or any such company as is mentioned in paragraph (*b*) above at any time after, or during the ten years before, the disposal made by that company ; or

(*d*) any person who is connected with a person within paragraph (*a*), (*b*) or (*c*) above.

(6) The participators in a company who are referred to in subsection (5) above do not include any participator who on a winding-up of the company would not be entitled to 5 per cent. or more of its assets ; and in determining whether the trusts permit property to be applied as mentioned in that subsection, no account shall be taken of any power to make a payment which is the income of any person for any of the purposes of income tax, or would be the income for any of those purposes of a person not resident in the United Kingdom if he were so resident.

1948 c. 38.

(7) In subsection (4) above " subsidiary " has the same meaning as in the Companies Act 1948 and in subsections (5) and (6) above " participator " has the meaning given in section 303(1) of the Taxes Act, except that it does not include a loan creditor.

Investigatory powers.
1970 c. 9.

57.—(1) For section 20 of the Taxes Management Act 1970 (power to call for documents relating to business profits and tax liability thereon) there shall be substituted the sections 20, 20A, 20B, 20C and 20D set out in Schedule 6 to this Act.

(2) In section 118(1) of that Act (interpretation), in the definition of " tax ", after the words " those taxes " there are inserted the words " except that in sections 20, 20A, 20B, 20C and 20D it does not include development land tax ".

Recovery of tax in sheriff court.

58.—(1) Section 67(1) of the Taxes Management Act 1970 (recovery of tax in sheriff court) shall be amended as follows—

1971 c. 58.

(*a*) for the words " does not exceed £250 " there shall be substituted the words " does not exceed the sum for the time being specified in section 35(1)(*a*) of the Sheriff Courts (Scotland) Act 1971 " ;

(*b*) the words " or in the sheriff's small debt court, whichever is appropriate " shall be omitted.

(2) This section shall come into force on 1st September 1976.

59. After section 131(3) of the Finance Act 1972 (power of Treasury to make order fixing time-limit for applications for repayment of post-war credits) there shall be inserted— PART III Post-war credits.

" (3A) An order under subsection (3) above may make different provision for different cases or classes of case and may provide that no amount shall be ascertained, recorded or notified under section 7 of the Finance Act 1941 after any such time as may be specified in the order." 1972 c. 41. 1941 c. 30.

CHAPTER II

BENEFITS DERIVED BY COMPANY DIRECTORS AND OTHERS FROM THEIR EMPLOYMENT

60.—(1) Subject to the provisions of this Chapter, where in any year a person is employed in director's or higher-paid employment and by reason of his employment there are paid to him in respect of expenses any sums which, apart from this section, are not chargeable to tax as his income, those sums are to be treated as emoluments of the employment and accordingly chargeable to income tax under Schedule E. Payments by way of expenses.

(2) Subsection (1) above is without prejudice to any claim for deductions under section 189, 192 or 194(3) of the Taxes Act (relief for necessary expenses, etc.).

(3) The reference in that subsection to sums paid in respect of expenses includes any sums put at the employee's disposal by reason of his employment and paid away by him.

(4) This section has effect for the year 1977-78 and subsequent years.

61.—(1) Where in any year a person is employed in director's or higher-paid employment and— General provision charging benefits.

(*a*) by reason of his employment there is provided for him, or for others being members of his family or household, any benefit to which this section applies ; and

(*b*) the cost of providing the benefit is not (apart from this section) chargeable to tax as his income,

there is to be treated as emoluments of the employment, and accordingly chargeable to income tax under Schedule E, an amount equal to whatever is the cash equivalent of the benefit.

(2) The benefits to which this section applies are living or other accommodation, entertainment, domestic or other services, and other benefits and facilities of whatsoever nature (whether or not similar to any of those mentioned above in this sub-

PART III

section), excluding however those taxable under sections 64 to 68 below in this Chapter, and subject to the exceptions provided for by the next following section.

(3) For the purposes of this section and sections 62 and 63 below, the persons providing a benefit are those at whose cost the provision is made.

(4) This section has effect for the year 1977-78 and for subsequent years.

Exceptions from general charge.

62.—(1) Without prejudice to its generality, section 61 above applies where by reason of the person's employment a car is made available (without any transfer of the property in it) either to himself or to others being members of his family or household, and it is made available for his or their private use, but applies only where in the relevant year either—

(*a*) the car is not used for the employee's business travel ; or

(*b*) its use for such travel is insubstantial compared with the private use that is made of it.

(2) That section applies to benefits in connection with a car made available as mentioned in subsection (1) above, but only for a year in which either paragraph (*a*) or paragraph (*b*) of that subsection is the case ; and, for a year in which neither paragraph is the case, the section applies only to benefits in connection with the provision of a driver for the car.

(3) Section 61 above does not apply where the benefit consists in provision for the employee, in premises occupied by the employer or others providing it, of accommodation, supplies or services used by the employee solely in performing the duties of his employment.

(4) That section does not apply where the benefit consists in the provision of living accommodation and—

(*a*) the person providing it is the employee's employer, and it is provided in part of premises occupied by him ; and

(*b*) the employee is required by the terms of his employment to reside in the accommodation provided, and it is necessary for him to reside on the premises for the proper performance of his duties.

(5) But subsection (4) above does not operate where the accommodation is provided by a company and either—

(*a*) the employee is a director of that company ; or

(*b*) he is a director of another company over which it has control, or which has control over it, or which is under the control of a person who also has control over the company first mentioned.

(6) Section 61 above does not apply to a benefit consisting in the provision by the employee's employer for the employee himself, or for the spouse, children or dependants of the employee, of any pension, annuity, lump sum, gratuity or other like benefit to be given on the employee's death or retirement.

(7) Section 61 does not apply to a benefit consisting in the provision by the employee's employer of meals in any canteen in which meals are provided for the staff generally.

Cash equivalent of benefits charged under s. 61.

63.—(1) The cash equivalent of any benefit chargeable to tax under section 61 above is an amount equal to the cost of the benefit, less so much (if any) of it as is made good by the employee to those providing the benefit.

(2) Subject to the following subsections, the cost of a benefit is the amount of any expense incurred in or in connection with its provision, and (here and in those subsections) includes a proper proportion of any expense relating partly to the benefit and partly to other matters.

(3) Where the benefit consists in the transfer of an asset by any person, and since that person acquired or produced the asset it has been used or has depreciated, the cost of the benefit is deemed to be the market value of the asset at the time of transfer.

(4) Where the benefit consists in an asset being placed at the employee's disposal, or at the disposal of others being members of his family or household, for his or their use (without any transfer of the property in the asset), or of its being used wholly or partly for his or their purposes, then the cost of the benefit in any year is deemed to be—

(*a*) the annual value of the use of the asset, ascertained under subsection (5) below, plus

(*b*) the total of any expense incurred in or in connection with the provision of the benefit (excluding however the expense of acquiring or producing it incurred by the person to whom the asset belongs).

(5) The annual value of the use of the asset, for the purposes of subsection (4) above—

(*a*) in the case of land, is its annual value determined in accordance with section 531 of the Taxes Act; and

(*b*) in the case of a car to which section 62(1)(*a*) or (*b*) applies in that year, is 20 per cent. of its original market value or 10 per cent. if at the end of the year its age exceeds 4 years; and

(*c*) in any other case is 10 per cent of its market value at the time when it was first applied (by those providing the benefit in question) in the provision of

PART III

any benefit for a person, or for members of his family or household, by reason of his employment.

(6) But where there is payable, by those providing the benefit, any sum by way of rent or hire-charge for the asset, the following applies—

(*a*) if the annual amount of the rent or hire-charge is equal to, or greater than, the annual value of the use of the asset as ascertained under subsection (5) above, that amount is to be substituted for the annual value in subsection (4)(*a*); and

(*b*) if that amount is less than the annual value as so ascertained, the amount is to be left out of account under paragraph (*b*) of that subsection as expense incurred in or in connection with the provision of the benefit.

(7) Where the benefit consists in the provision of accommodation for the employee, or members of his family or household, in premises in whose case there is an amount to be treated under section 185(1) of the Taxes Act as his emoluments, then any expense incurred in or in connection with the provision of the benefit is to be treated as reduced by that amount; and if the amount is greater than the total of that expense, the benefit is to be disregarded for the purposes of any charge to income tax under section 61 above.

(8) From the cash equivalent there are deductible in each case under section 189, 192, or 194(3) of the Taxes Act (necessary expenses etc.) such amounts (if any) as would have been so deductible if the cost of the benefit had been incurred by the employee out of his emoluments.

Cars available for private use.

64.—(1) Where in any year in the case of a person employed in director's or higher-paid employment, a car is made available (without any transfer of the property in it) either to himself or to others being members of his family or household, and—

(*a*) it is so made available by reason of his employment and it is in that year available for his or their private use; and

(*b*) the benefit of the car is not (apart from this section) chargeable to tax as the employee's income,

there is to be treated as emoluments of the employment, and accordingly chargeable to income tax under Schedule E, an amount equal to whatever is the cash equivalent of that benefit in that year.

(2) Subject to the provisions of this section, the cash equivalent of that benefit is to be ascertained—

(*a*) from Tables A and B in Part I of Schedule 7 to this Act, in the case of cars with an original market value up to £6,000; and (*b*) from Table C in that Part of that Schedule in the case of cars with an original market value more than that amount, PART III

the equivalent in each case being shown in the second or third column of the applicable Table by reference to the age of the car at the end of the relevant year of assessment.

(3) This section has effect for the year 1977-78 and subsequent years.

(4) The Treasury may by order taking effect from the beginning of any year beginning after it is made (but not of any year earlier than 1978-79)—

(*a*) increase (or further increase) the money sum specified in subsection (2)(*a*) above ;

(*b*) with or without such an increase, substitute for any of the three Tables a different Table of cash equivalents.

Orders under this subsection shall be made by statutory instrument subject to annulment in pursuance of a resolution of the House of Commons ; and any such order may revoke a previous order thereunder.

(5) Part II of Schedule 7 to this Act has effect—

(*a*) with respect to the application of the Tables in Part I ; and

(*b*) for reduction of the cash equivalent under this section in cases where the car has not been available for the whole of the relevant year, or the use of it has been preponderantly business use, or the employee makes any payment for the use of it.

65.—(1) This section applies to any car in whose case the inspector is satisfied (whether on a claim under this section or otherwise) that it has for any year been included in a car pool for the use of the employees of one or more employers. Pooled cars.

(2) A car is to be treated as having been so included for a year if—

(*a*) in that year it was made available to, and actually used by, more than one of those employees and, in the case of each of them, it was made available to him by reason of his employment but it was not in that year ordinarily used by any one of them to the exclusion of the others ; and

(*b*) in the case of each of them any private use of the car made by him in that year was merely incidental to his other use of it in the year ; and

PART III

(*c*) it was in that year not normally kept overnight on or in the vicinity of any residential premises where any of the employees was residing, except while being kept overnight on premises occupied by the person making the car available to them.

(3) Where this section applies to a car, then for the year in question the car is to be treated under sections 61 and 64 of this Act as not having been available for the private use of any of the employees.

(4) A claim under this section in respect of a car for any year may be made by any one of the employees mentioned in subsection (2)(*a*) above (they being referred to below in this section as " the employees concerned ") or by the employer on behalf of all of them.

(5) On an appeal against the decision of the inspector on a claim under this section all the employees concerned may take part in the proceedings, and the determination of the body of Commissioners or county court appealed to shall be binding on all those employees, whether or not they have taken part in the proceedings.

(6) Where an appeal against the decision of the inspector on a claim under this section has been determined, no appeal against the inspector's decision on any other such claim in respect of the same car and the same year shall be entertained.

Beneficial loan arrangements.

66.—(1) Where in the case of a person employed in director's or higher-paid employment there is outstanding for the whole or part of a year a loan (whether to the employee himself or a relative of his) of which the benefit is obtained by reason of his employment and—

(*a*) no interest is paid on the loan for that year ; or

(*b*) the amount of interest paid on it for the year is less than interest at the official rate,

there is to be treated as emoluments of the employment, and accordingly chargeable to income tax under Schedule E, an amount equal to whatever is the cash equivalent of the benefit of the loan for that year.

(2) There is no charge to tax under subsection (1) if the cash equivalent does not exceed £50 or (for a year in which there are two or more loans outstanding) the total of all the cash equivalents does not exceed that amount.

(3) Where in the case of a person employed in director's or higher-paid employment there is in any year released or written off the whole or part of a loan (whether to the employee himself or a relative of his, and whether or not such a loan as is

mentioned in subsection (1)), the benefit of which was obtained by reason of his employment, then, subject to subsection (5) below, there is to be treated as emoluments of the employment, and accordingly chargeable to income tax under Schedule E, an amount equal to that which is released or written off. PART III

(4) If the employee shows that he derived no benefit from a loan made to a relative of his, subsections (1) and (3) shall not apply to that loan.

(5) Subsection (3) does not apply where the amount released or written off is chargeable to income tax as income of the employee apart from this section, except—

(*a*) where it is chargeable only by virtue of section 187 of the Taxes Act (payments on retirement or removal from employment) ; or

(*b*) to the extent that the amount exceeds the sums previously falling to be treated as the employee's income under section 451 of the Taxes Act (sums paid to settlor otherwise than as income).

(6) Where there was outstanding at any time when a person was in director's or higher-paid employment the whole or part of a loan to him (or to a relative of his) the benefit of which was obtained by reason of his employment, and that director's or higher-paid employment has terminated, whether on the employee ceasing to be employed or ceasing to be employed in director's or higher-paid employment, subsection (3) applies as if it had not terminated.

(7) But on the employee's death—

(*a*) a loan within subsection (1) ceases to be outstanding for the purposes of the operation of that subsection; and

(*b*) no charge arises under subsection (3) by reference to any release or writing-off which takes effect on or after the death.

(8) Part I of Schedule 8 to this Act has effect as to what is meant by the benefit of a loan obtained by reason of a person's employment ; the cash equivalent of the benefit is to be ascertained in accordance with Part II of that Schedule ; and Part III of that Schedule has effect for excluding from the operation of subsection (1) of this section loans on which interest is eligible for relief under section 75 of the Finance Act 1972. 1972 c. 41

(9) In this section, section 67 below and Schedule 8—

(*a*) " loan " includes any form of credit ;

(*b*) references to a loan include references to any other loan applied directly or indirectly towards the replacement of the first-mentioned loan ;

PART III

(*c*) references to making a loan include arranging, guaranteeing or in any way facilitating a loan (related expressions being construed accordingly) ; and

(*d*) references to the official rate of interest are to the rate prescribed from time to time by the Treasury by order in a statutory instrument subject to annulment in pursuance of a resolution of the House of Commons.

(10) For the purposes of this section, a person is a relative of another person if he or she is—

(*a*) the spouse of that other ; or

(*b*) a parent or remoter forebear, child or remoter issue, or brother or sister of that other or of the spouse of that other ; or

(*c*) the spouse of a person falling within paragraph (*b*) above.

(11) This section applies to loans whether made before or after this Act is passed ; and—

(*a*) subsection (1) has effect for the year 1978-79 and subsequent years ; but for that year and 1979-80 the cash equivalent under that subsection instead of being the amount arrived at by applying Part II of Schedule 8 is that amount reduced by half ; and

(*b*) subsection (3) has effect for the year 1976-77 and subsequent years, except that it does not apply to benefits received in pursuance of arrangements made at any time with a view to protecting the holder of shares acquired before 6th April 1976 from a fall in their market value.

Employee shareholdings.

67.—(1) Subsections (2) to (6) of this section apply where after 6th April 1976—

(*a*) a person employed or about to be employed in director's or higher-paid employment (" the employee "), or a person connected with him, acquires shares in a company (whether the employing company or not) ; and

(*b*) the shares are acquired at an under-value in pursuance of a right or opportunity available by reason of the employment.

(2) " At an under-value " means the shares being acquired either without payment for them at the time or being acquired for an amount then paid which is less than the market value of fully paid up shares of that class (in either case with or without obligation to make payment or further payment at some later time).

(3) In the circumstances specified above, section 66(1) of this Act, with Schedule 8, applies as if the employee had the benefit of an interest-free loan obtained by reason of his employment; and this is "the notional loan" referred to in the following subsections.

(4) The amount initially outstanding of the notional loan is so much of the under-value on acquisition (that is, the market value referred to in subsection (2) less any payment then made for the shares) as is not chargeable to tax as an emolument of the employee; and—

(*a*) the loan remains outstanding until terminated under subsection (5) below; and

(*b*) payments or further payments made for the shares after the initial acquisition go to reduce the amount outstanding of the notional loan.

(5) The notional loan terminates on the occurrence of any of the following events—

(*a*) the whole amount of it outstanding is made good by means of payments or further payments made for the shares; or

(*b*) the case being one in which the shares were not at the time of acquisition fully paid up, any outstanding or contingent obligation to pay for them is released, transferred or adjusted so as no longer to bind the employee or any person connected with him; or

(*c*) the shares are so disposed of by surrender or otherwise that neither he nor any such person any longer has a beneficial interest in the shares; or

(*d*) the employee dies.

(6) If the notional loan terminates as mentioned in subsection (5)(*b*) or (*c*) above, there is then for the year in which the event in question occurs the same charge to income tax on the employee, under section 66(3) of this Act, as if an amount equal to the then outstanding amount of the notional loan had been released or written off from a loan within that section.

(7) Where after 6th April 1976 shares are acquired, whether or not at an under-value but otherwise as mentioned in subsection (1) above, and —

(*a*) the shares are subsequently disposed of by surrender or otherwise so that neither the employee nor any person connected with him any longer has a beneficial interest in them; and

(*b*) the disposal is for a consideration which exceeds the then market value of the shares,

PART III

then for the year in which the disposal is effected the amount of the excess is treated as emoluments of the employee's employment and accordingly chargeable to income tax under Schedule E.

(8) If at the time of the event giving rise to a charge by virtue of subsection (6) or (7) above the person who is " the employee " under this section by reference to his employment in director's or higher-paid employment mentioned in subsection (1)(*a*) has ceased to be employed in that employment, subsections (6) and (7) apply as if he had not so ceased.

(9) But no charge arises under subsection (7) by reference to any disposal effected after the death of the employee, whether by his personal representatives or otherwise.

(10) This section applies in relation to acquisition and disposal of an interest in shares less than full beneficial ownership (including an interest in the proceeds of sale of part of the shares but not including a share option) as it applies in relation to the acquisition and disposal of shares, and in those cases—

(*a*) for references to the shares acquired substitute references to the interest in shares acquired ;

(*b*) for the reference to the market value of the shares acquired substitute a reference to the proportion corresponding to the size of the interest of the market value of the shares in which the interest subsists ;

(*c*) for the reference to shares of the same class as those acquired substitute references to shares of the same class as those in which the interest subsists ; and

(*d*) for the reference to the market value of fully paid up shares of that class substitute a reference to the proportion of that value corresponding to the size of the interest.

(11) In this section—

(*a*) " shares " includes stock and also includes securities as defined in section 237(5) of the Taxes Act ;

(*b*) " acquisition ", in relation to shares, includes receipt by way of allotment or assignment, or otherwise howsoever ;

(*c*) any reference to payment for shares includes giving any consideration in money or money's worth or making any subscription, whether in pursuance of a legal liability or not ;

1965 c. 25.

(*d*) " market value " has the same meaning as, for the purposes of Part III of the Finance Act 1965, it has by virtue of section 44 of that Act ;

and section 533 of the Taxes Act (connected persons) applies for the purposes of this section. PART III

(12) In respect of any shares or interest in shares this section only operates to include an amount in emoluments so far as any amount corresponding to it, and representing the same benefit, does not otherwise fall to be so included under the Tax Acts.

(13) Where an amount is chargeable to tax by virtue of subsection (6) above in respect of shares or an interest in shares, then—

(*a*) on a disposal of the shares or interest, where that is the event giving rise to the charge ; or

(*b*) in any other case on the first disposal of the shares or interest after the event,

paragraph 4(1)(*a*) of Schedule 6 to the Finance Act 1965 (expenditure allowable in computation of chargeable gains) applies as if a sum equal to the amount chargeable had formed part of the consideration given by the person making the disposal for his acquisition of the shares or interest. 1965 c. 25.

(14) This section has effect for the year 1976-77 and subsequent years.

Medical insurance.

68.—(1) Where in the case of a person employed in any employment (whether or not director's or higher-paid)—

(*a*) expense is incurred by his employer or others in or in connection with the provision for him, and for others being members of his family or household, of insurance against the cost of medical treatment ; and

(*b*) that provision is made by reason of his employment and, apart from this Chapter, the expense would not be chargeable to tax as his income,

there is to be treated as emoluments of the employment, and accordingly chargeable to tax under Schedule E, an amount equal to that of the expenditure (disregarding so much of it, if any, as is made good by him to those incurring it).

(2) Where the provision is made for a group or class to which the employees or the others in question belong, then the amount to be taken into account under subsection (1) above in respect of him is such proportion of the total expenses for all the members of the group or class as is just and reasonable.

(3) This section does not apply to expense incurred wholly in or in connection with the provision for the employee of insurance against the cost of medical treatment outside the United Kingdom, the need for which arises while the employee is outside the United Kingdom for the purpose of performing the duties of his employment.

PART III

(4) For the purposes of this section, medical treatment includes all forms of treatment for, and all procedures for diagnosing, any physical or mental ailment, infirmity or defect; and the cost of medical treatment includes the cost of being an in-patient, whether or not in a private room, for the purpose of medical treatment.

(5) This section has effect for the year 1976-77 and subsequent years.

Employments subject to ss. 60 to 67.

69.—(1) In this Chapter "director's or higher-paid employment" means—

(*a*) employment as a director of a company (but excluding, if he does not have a material interest in the company, employment as a full-time working director); or

(*b*) employment with emoluments at the rate of £5,000 a year or more.

(2) For this purpose emoluments are to be calculated—

(*a*) on the basis that they include all such amounts as come into charge under this Chapter in the case of those in director's or higher-paid employment or under section 68, or under section 36 or 37 of the Finance (No. 2) Act 1975 (cash or other vouchers); and

1975 c. 45.

(*b*) without any deduction under section 189, 192 or 194(3) of the Taxes Act (necessary expenses of employment, etc.).

(3) But where a person is employed in two or more employments by the same employer, and the total of the emoluments of those employments (applying this section) is at the rate of £5,000 a year or more, all the employments are to be treated as director's or higher-paid.

(4) All employees of a partnership or body over which an individual or another partnership or body has control are to be treated for the purposes of this section (but not for any other purpose) as if the employment were an employment by the individual or by that other partnership or body, as the case may be.

Notice of nil liability under this Chapter.

70.—(1) If a person furnishes to the inspector a statement of the cases and circumstances in which payments of a particular character are made, or benefits or facilities of a particular kind are provided, for any employees (whether his own or those of anyone else), and the inspector is satisfied that no additional tax is payable under this Chapter by reference to the payments, benefits or facilities mentioned in the statement, the inspector shall notify the person accordingly; and then nothing in this

Chapter applies to those payments, or to the provision of those benefits or facilities, or otherwise for imposing any additional charge to income tax. PART III

(2) The inspector may, if in his opinion there is reason to do so, by notice in writing served on the person to whom notification under subsection (1) above was given, revoke the notification, either as from the date of its making or as from such later date as may be specified in the notice under this subsection; and then all such income tax becomes chargeable, and all such returns are to be made by that person and by the employees in question, as would have been chargeable or would have had to be made in the first instance if the notification under subsection (1) had never been given or, as the case may be, it had ceased to have effect on the specified date.

Cash vouchers. 1975 c. 45.

71.—(1) Section 37 of the Finance (No. 2) Act 1975 (taxation of cash vouchers for year 1976-77 and subsequent years of assessment) shall not have effect for the year 1976-77 and accordingly—

(*a*) in subsection (6) of that section the words " and subsection (6) " shall be omitted ; and

(*b*) after that subsection there shall be inserted—

" (7) This section has effect for the year 1977-78 and subsequent years of assessment."

(2) In subsection (5) of that section for the words from " income tax " onwards there shall be substituted the words " income tax in respect of all payments made in exchange for vouchers issued under the scheme to be deducted in accordance with regulations under section 204 of the Taxes Act ".

Interpretation of this Chapter; supplementary.

72.—(1) The following provisions of this section apply for the interpretation of expressions used in sections 60 to 71 above, and Schedules 7 and 8.

(2) " Employment " means an office or employment whose emoluments fall to be assessed under Schedule E; and related expressions are to be construed accordingly.

(3) For the purposes of this Chapter, all sums paid to an employee by his employer in respect of expenses, and all such provision as is mentioned in this Chapter which is made for an employee, or for members of his family or household, by his employer, are deemed to be paid to or made for him or them by reason of his employment.

But this does not apply to any such payment or provision made by the employer, being an individual, as can be shown to have been made in the normal course of his domestic, family or personal relationships.

PART III

(4) References to members of a person's family or household are to his spouse, his sons and daughters and their spouses, his parents and his servants, dependants and guests.

(5) As respects cars, the following definitions apply—

(*a*) " car " means any mechanically propelled road vehicle except—

(i) a vehicle of a construction primarily suited for the conveyance of goods or burden of any description,

(ii) a vehicle of a type not commonly used as a private vehicle and unsuitable to be so used,

1972 c. 20. (iii) a motor cycle as defined in section 190(4) of the Road Traffic Act 1972, and

(iv) an invalid carriage as defined in section 190(5) of that Act;

(*b*) the age of a car at any time is the interval between the date of its first registration and that time;

(*c*) " business travel " means travelling which a person is necessarily obliged to do in the performance of the duties of his employment;

(*d*) the date of a car's first registration is the date on which it was first registered—

1971 c. 10. (i) in Great Britain, under the Vehicles (Excise) Act 1971 or corresponding earlier legislation, or

(ii) elsewhere, under the corresponding legislation of any country or territory;

(*e*) the original market value of a car is the inclusive price which it might reasonably have been expected to fetch if sold in the United Kingdom singly in a retail sale in the open market immediately before the date of its first registration (" inclusive price " meaning the price inclusive of customs or excise duty, of any tax chargeable as if it were a duty of customs, and of car tax); and

(*f*) " private use ", in relation to a car made available to any person, or to others being members of his family or household, means any use otherwise than for his business travel.

(6) For the purposes of this Chapter—

(*a*) a car made available in any year to an employee, or to others being members of his family or household, by reason of his employment is deemed to be available in that year for his or their private use unless the terms on which the car is made available prohibits such use and no such use is made of the car in that year;

PART III

(*b*) a car made available to an employee, or to others being members of his family or household, by his employer is deemed to be made available to him or them by reason of his employment (unless the employer is an individual and it can be shown that the car was made so available in the normal course of his domestic, family or personal relationships).

(7) For the purposes of section 63, the market value of an asset at any time is the price which it might reasonably have been expected to fetch on a sale in the open market at that time.

(8) " Director " means—

(*a*) in relation to a company whose affairs are managed by a board of directors or similar body, a member of that board or similar body ;

(*b*) in relation to a company whose affairs are managed by a single director or similar person, that director or person ; and

(*c*) in relation to a company whose affairs are managed by the members themselves, a member of the company,

and includes any person in accordance with whose directions or instructions the directors of the company (defined as above) are accustomed to act.

But a person is not under this subsection to be deemed a person in accordance with whose directions or instructions the directors of the company are accustomed to act by reason only that the directors act on advice given by him in a professional capacity.

(9) " Full-time working director " means a director who is required to devote substantially the whole of his time to the service of the company in a managerial or technical capacity.

(10) A person shall be treated as having a material interest in a company—

(*a*) if he, either on his own or with any one or more of his associates, or if any associate of his with or without such other associates, is the beneficial owner of, or able, directly or through the medium of other companies or by any other indirect means, to control, more than 5 per cent. of the ordinary share capital of the company, or

(*b*) if, in the case of a close company, on an amount equal to the whole distributable income of the company falling to be apportioned under Chapter III of Part XI of the Taxes Act for the purpose of computing total income, more than 5 per cent. of that amount could be apportioned to him together with his associates (if any), or to any associate of his, or any such associates taken together.

PART III

In this subsection " associate " has the same meaning as in section 303(3) of the Taxes Act, except that for this purpose " relative " in that subsection has the same meaning as in this Chapter.

(11) " Control ", in relation to a body corporate or partnership, has the meaning given to it by section 534 of the Taxes Act; and the definition of " control " in that section applies (with the necessary modifications) in relation to an unincorporated association as it applies in relation to a body corporate.

(12) " Year " means year of assessment (except where the expression is used with reference to the age of a car).

(13) The enactments specified in Schedule 9 to this Act shall be amended as there specified (which are amendments consequential on the replacement by this Chapter of Chapter II of Part VIII of the Taxes Act and other provisions); Part I of that Schedule substitutes a new section for section 15 of the Taxes Management Act 1970, and contains consequential amendments; Part II contains other amendments.

1970 c. 9.

PART IV

CAPITAL TRANSFER TAX

Relief for business and agricultural property and woodlands

Relief for business property.

73. Schedule 10 to this Act shall have effect for reducing, in the cases mentioned therein,—

(*a*) the value transferred by a transfer of value; and

(*b*) the amount of a distribution payment made, or capital distribution treated as made.

Relief for agricultural property.
1975 c. 7.

74.—(1) Schedule 8 to the Finance Act 1975 shall be amended as follows.

(2) In sub-paragraph (1) of paragraph 1, paragraph (*a*) shall be omitted and for the words " so computed " there shall be substituted the words " computed in accordance with paragraph 2 below ".

(3) In sub-paragraph (2) of paragraph 1, after the words " transfer of value " in paragraph (*a*) there shall be inserted the words " and either that transfer or the current transfer was or would have been a transfer made on death " and at the end of paragraph (*d*) there shall be added the words " and

(*e*) the agricultural property became, through the earlier transfer, the property of the person or of the spouse of the person who is the transferor in relation to the current transfer.

PART IV

(2A) Where, by virtue of sub-paragraph (2) above, the conditions stated in paragraph 3 below are deemed to be satisfied but, under the earlier transfer mentioned in that sub-paragraph, the amount of the value transferred which was attributable to the agricultural property was part only of the value of that property, a like part of its agricultural value shall be substituted for the agricultural value of the property in ascertaining the part eligible for relief under paragraph 2 below ".

(4) In paragraph 2 for the words from " reduced " to the end there shall be substituted the words " reduced by one half ".

(5) After sub-paragraph (*b*) of paragraph 4 there shall be inserted the following sub-paragraph:

" (*bb*) where the value of the shares or debentures is taken, by virtue of paragraph 9A of Schedule 10 to this Act, to be less than their value as previously determined, they would have been sufficient, without any other property, to give the transferor control as mentioned in sub-paragraph (*b*) above ; and ".

(6) At the end of paragraph 5(2) there shall be added " and

(*c*) the area of any rough grazing land shall be counted as one-sixth of its actual area.

(2A) The Board may consult the Minister of Agriculture, Fisheries and Food or, as the case may require, the Secretary of State or the Department of Agriculture for Northern Ireland on any question arising under this paragraph whether any land is rough grazing land ; and paragraph 7(4) of Schedule 4 to this Act shall apply in relation to any such question as if it were a question as to the value of the land."

(7) The preceding provisions of this section have effect as follows:—

(*a*) subsections (1), (2) and (4) to (6), in relation to chargeable transfers made after 6th April 1976 ; and

(*b*) subsection (3) in relation to chargeable transfers made after the passing of this Act.

Relief for woodlands. 1975 c. 7.

75. In Schedule 9 to the Finance Act 1975, in paragraph 6(2)(*b*) (expenses allowable under the Schedule to include those incurred in replanting within three years of a disposal) after the word " disposal " there shall be inserted the words " (or such longer time as the Board may allow) ".

PART IV

Relief for works of art, historic buildings etc.

Conditionally exempt transfers.

76.—(1) Subject to the provisions of this section, a transfer of value made after 6th April 1976 is an exempt transfer to the extent that the value transferred by it is attributable to property—

(*a*) which, on a claim made for the purpose, is designated by the Treasury under section 77 below; and

(*b*) with respect to which the requisite undertaking described in that section is given by such person as the Treasury think appropriate in the circumstances of the case.

(2) A transfer of value exempt as aforesaid with respect to any property is hereafter referred to as a conditionally exempt transfer of that property.

1975 c. 7.

(3) Subsection (1) above does not apply to a transfer of value other than one which under section 22 of the Finance Act 1975 a person makes on his death unless—

(*a*) the transferor or his spouse, or the transferor and his spouse between them, have been beneficially entitled to the property throughout the six years ending with the transfer; or

1930 c. 28.
1931 c. 24 (N.I.).

(*b*) the transferor acquired the property on a death and either there was under the said section 22 a transfer of value on the occasion of the death which was itself a conditionally exempt transfer of the property or the value of the property was, under section 31 or 34 of the said Act of 1975, section 40 of the Finance Act 1930 or section 2 of the Finance Act (Northern Ireland) 1931 left out of account for the purposes of the capital transfer tax or estate duty chargeable on the death.

(4) Subsection (1) above does not apply to a transfer of value to the extent to which it is an exempt transfer under paragraph 1 or 10 of Schedule 6 to the said Act of 1975 (gifts to spouses or charities).

(5) As from 7th April 1976 the enactments mentioned in Schedule 11 to this Act shall have effect subject to the amendments there specified, being amendments consequential on the provisions of this section and sections 77 to 84 below.

Designation and undertakings.

77.—(1) The Treasury may designate under this section

(*a*) any pictures, prints, books, manuscripts, works of art, scientific collections or other things not yielding income which appear to the Treasury to be of national, scientific, historic or artistic interest;

(*b*) any land which in the opinion of the Treasury is of outstanding scenic or historic or scientific interest;

PART IV

(c) any building for the preservation of which special steps should in the opinion of the Treasury be taken by reason of its outstanding historic or architectural interest ;

(d) any land which adjoins such a building as is mentioned in paragraph (c) above and which in the opinion of the Treasury is essential for the protection of the character and amenities of the building ;

(e) any object which in the opinion of the Treasury is historically associated with such a building as is mentioned in paragraph (c) above.

(2) In the case of property within subsection (1)(a) above, the requisite undertaking is that, until the person beneficially entitled to the property dies or the property is disposed of, whether by sale or gift or otherwise—

(a) the property will be kept permanently in the United Kingdom and will not leave it temporarily except for a purpose and a period approved by the Treasury ; and

(b) reasonable steps will be taken for the preservation of the property and for securing reasonable access to the public.

(3) If it appears to the Treasury, on a claim made for the purpose, that any documents which are designated or to be designated under subsection (1)(a) above contain information which for personal or other reasons ought to be treated as confidential, they may exclude those documents, either altogether or to such extent as they think fit, from so much of an undertaking given or to be given under subsection (2)(b) above as relates to public access.

(4) In the case of other property within subsection (1) above, the requisite undertaking is that, until the person beneficially entitled to the property dies or the property is disposed of, whether by sale or gift or otherwise, reasonable steps will be taken—

(a) in the case of land falling within subsection (1)(b) above, for the maintenance of the land and the preservation of its character ; and

(b) in the case of any other property, for the maintenance, repair and preservation of the property and, if it is an object falling with subsection (1)(e) above, for keeping it associated with the building concerned ;

and for securing reasonable access to the public.

(5) In this section " national interest " includes interest within any part of the United Kingdom.

PART IV

Chargeable events.

78.—(1) Where there has been a conditionally exempt transfer of any property, tax shall be charged under this section on the first occurrence after the transfer of an event which under this section is a chargeable event with respect to the property.

(2) If the Treasury are satisfied that at any time an undertaking given with respect to the property under section 76 above or subsection (5)(*b*) below has not been observed in a material respect, the failure to observe the undertaking is a chargeable event with respect to the property; and the person liable for the tax chargeable by reference to that event is the person who, if the property were sold at the time the tax becomes chargeable, would be entitled to receive (whether for his benefit or not) the proceeds of sale or any income arising from them.

(3) If—

(*a*) the person beneficially entitled to the property dies; or

(*b*) the property is disposed of, whether by sale or gift or otherwise,

the death or disposal is, subject to subsections (4) and (5) below, a chargeable event with respect to the property; and the person liable for the tax chargeable by reference to the event is, in a case within paragraph (*a*), the person who, if the property were sold immediately after the death would be entitled to receive (whether for his own benefit or not) the proceeds of sale or any income arising from them and, in a case within paragraph (*b*), the person for whose benefit the property is disposed of.

(4) A death or disposal is not a chargeable event with respect to any property if the personal representatives of the deceased (or, in the case of settled property, the trustees or the person next entitled) within three years of the death make or, as the case may be, the disposal is—

(*a*) a disposal of the property by sale by private treaty to a body mentioned in paragraph 12 of Schedule 6 to the Finance Act 1975 (museums etc.) or a disposal of it to such a body otherwise than by sale; or

1975 c. 7.

(*b*) a disposal to the Board in pursuance of paragraph 17 of Schedule 4 to that Act or in accordance with directions given by the Treasury under section 50 or 51 of the Finance Act 1946 (acceptance of property in satisfaction of tax);

1946 c. 64.

and a death or disposal of the property after such a disposal as is mentioned in paragraph (*a*) or (*b*) above is not a chargeable event with respect to the property unless there has again been a conditionally exempt transfer of it after that disposal.

PART IV

(5) A death or disposal otherwise than by sale is not a chargeable event with respect to any property if—

(*a*) the transfer of value made on the death or the disposal is itself a conditionally exempt transfer of the property ; or

(*b*) the undertaking previously given with respect to the property under section 76 above (or any undertaking previously given with respect to the property under this paragraph) is replaced by a corresponding undertaking given by such person as the Treasury think appropriate in the circumstances of the case.

(6) Where tax is chargeable under this section with respect to any property within section 77(1)(*c*), (*d*) or (*e*) above, tax shall also be chargeable with respect to any property associated with it ; but the Treasury may direct that the foregoing provisions of this subsection shall not apply if it appears to them that the entity consisting of the building, land and objects concerned has not been materially affected.

(7) For the purposes of subsection (6) above two or more properties are associated with each other if one of them is a building falling within subsection (1)(*c*) of section 77 above and the other or others such land or objects as, in relation to that building, fall within subsection (1)(*d*) or (*e*) of that section.

Amount of charge under s. 78.

79.—(1) Subject to the provisions of this section, tax chargeable in respect of any property under section 78 above by reference to a chargeable event shall be charged—

(*a*) on an amount equal to the value of the property at the time of the chargeable event ; and

(*b*) at the following rate or rates—

(i) if the relevant transferor is alive, the rate or rates that would be applicable to that amount under the second Table in section 37 of the Finance Act 1975 if it were the value transferred by a chargeable transfer made by the relevant transferor at that time ; 1975 c. 7.

(ii) if the relevant transferor is dead, the rate or rates that would have applied to that amount under the appropriate Table in that section if it had been added to the value transferred on his death and had formed the highest part of that value.

(2) For the purposes of subsection (1)(*b*)(ii) above the appropriate Table is, if the conditonally exempt transfer by the relevant transferor was made on death, the first Table and, if not, the second.

PART IV

(3) Where the chargeable event is a disposal on sale and—

(*a*) the sale was not intended to confer any gratuitous benefit on any person; and

(*b*) was either a transaction at arm's length between persons not connected with each other or a transaction such as might be expected to be made at arm's length between persons not connected with each other,

the value of the property at the time of the chargeable event shall be taken for the purposes of subsection (1)(*a*) above to be equal to the proceeds of the sale.

(4) Where by virtue of section 76(4) above the conditionally exempt transfer extended only to part of the property, the amount mentioned in subsection (1)(*a*) above shall be proportionately reduced.

(5) The relevant transferor in relation to the tax chargeable on the occasion of a chargeable event in respect of any property is—

(*a*) if there has been only one conditionally exempt transfer of the property before the event, the person who made that transfer;

(*b*) if there have been two or more such transfers and the last was before, or only one of them was within, the period of thirty years ending with the event, the person who made the last of those transfers;

(*c*) if there have been two or more such transfers within that period, the person who made whichever of those transfers the Board may select.

(6) The conditionally exempt transfers to be taken into account for the purpose of subsection (5) above in relation to a chargeable event do not include transfers made before any previous chargeable event in respect of the same property or before any event which apart from section 78(4) above would have been such a chargeable event.

(7) Where after a conditionally exempt transfer of any property there is a chargeable transfer the value transferred by which is wholly or partly attributable to that property, any tax charged on that value so far as attributable to that property shall be allowed as a credit—

(*a*) if the chargeable transfer is a chargeable event with respect to the property, against the tax chargeable in accordance with this section by reference to that event;

(*b*) if the chargeable transfer is not such a chargeable event, against the tax chargeable in accordance with this section by reference to the next chargeable event with respect to the property.

PART IV

Reinstatement of transferor's cumulative total.

80.—(1) Where tax has become chargeable under section 78 above by reference to a chargeable event in respect of any property (" the relevant event ") the rate or rates of tax applicable to any subsequent chargeable transfer made by the person who made the last conditionally exempt transfer of the property before the relevant event shall be determined as if the amount on which tax has become chargeable as aforesaid were value transferred by a chargeable transfer made by him at the time of the relevant event.

(2) Where the person who made the last conditionally exempt transfer of the property before the relevant event—

(*a*) is dead ; and

(*b*) is the relevant transferor in relation to a subsequent chargeable event,

section 79(1)(*b*)(ii) above shall have effect as if the value transferred on his death were increased by the amount on which tax has become chargeable on the occasion of the relevant event.

(3) If—

(*a*) the person who made the last conditionally exempt transfer of the property before the relevant event is not the relevant transferor in relation to that event ; and

(*b*) at the time of that event or within the previous five years the property is or has been comprised in a settlement made not more than thirty years before that event ; and

(*c*) a person who is the settlor in relation to the settlement has made a conditionally exempt transfer of the property within those thirty years,

subsections (1) and (2) above shall have effect with the substitution for references to the person who made the last conditionally exempt transfer before the relevant event of a reference to any such person as is mentioned in paragraph (*c*) above.

(4) The conditionally exempt transfers to be taken into account for the purposes of subsection (3)(*c*) above in relation to the relevant event do not include transfers made before any previous chargeable event in respect of the same property or before any event which apart from section 78(4) above would have been such a chargeable event.

Conditionally exempt distributions.

1975 c. 7.

81.—(1) A transfer of property or other event shall not constitute or give rise to a distribution payment or capital distribution under any provision of Schedule 5 to the Finance Act 1975 (settled property) other than paragraph 12 if the property by reference to which the amount of the distribution payment or capital distribution would fall to be determined has been com-

PART IV prised in the settlement throughout the six years ending with the transfer or event, and—

(*a*) the property is, on a claim made for the purpose, designated by the Treasury under section 77 above; and

(*b*) the requisite undertaking described in that section is given with respect to the property by such person as the Treasury think appropriate in the circumstances of the case.

(2) A transfer or event which by virtue of subsection (1) above does not constitute or give rise to a distribution payment or capital distribution is hereafter referred to as a conditionally exempt distribution of the property in question.

(3) Subject to the following provisions of this section, sections 78, 79 and 80 above shall have effect as if—

(*a*) references to a conditionally exempt transfer included references to a conditionally exempt distribution;

(*b*) references to a disposal otherwise than by sale included references to any event on the occurrence of which a capital distribution or distribution payment is treated as made under any provision of the said Schedule 5 other than paragraph 12; and

(*c*) references to an undertaking given under section 76 above included references to an undertaking given under this section.

(4) Where the relevant transferor for the purposes of section 79 above falls to be determined by reference to a conditionally exempt distribution, paragraph (*b*) of subsection (1) of that section shall not apply and the rate or rates at which the tax is charged on the amount mentioned in paragraph (*a*) of that section shall be—

(*a*) if the settlement is still in existence at the time of the chargeable event, the rate or rates that would be applicable (under paragraph 7 or, as the case may be, paragraph 8 of the said Schedule 5) to that amount if a capital distribution of that amount were made at that time out of the property comprised in the settlement;

(*b*) if the settlement has then ceased to exist—

(i) subject to sub-paragraph (ii) below, the rate or rates that would be applicable as mentioned in paragraph (*a*) above but by reference to a capital distribution made on the occasion on which the settlement ceased to exist;

(ii) if a capital distribution was made or treated as made on that occasion, the rate or rates that would have been applicable to that amount if it had been included in the amount of that distribution and had formed the highest part of it.

(5) Where tax has become chargeable as mentioned in section 80 above by reference to a chargeable event ("the relevant event") and the person to whom that section applies falls to be determined by reference to a conditionally exempt distribution, the following provisions shall have effect instead of subsections (1) and (2) of that section—

(*a*) the rate or rates of tax applicable to any subsequent capital distribution out of the property comprised in the settlement shall be determined as if the amount on which tax has become chargeable had been the amount of a distribution payment made at the time of the relevant event; and

(*b*) where the settlement has ceased to exist and the tax chargeable on the occasion of a subsequent chargeable event falls to be calculated in accordance with paragraph (i) or (ii) of subsection (4)(*b*) above, that paragraph shall have effect as if the amount of the capital distribution mentioned in that paragraph were increased by the amount on which tax has become chargeable on the occasion of the relevant event.

Exemption from periodic charge.

82.—(1) Where property is comprised in a settlement and there has been a conditionally exempt transfer of the property on or before the occasion on which it became comprised in the settlement, paragraph 12 of Schedule 5 to the Finance Act 1975 (periodic charge to tax where there is no interest in possession) shall not have effect in relation to the property on any relevant date (whether a relevant anniversary or, in a case within subparagraph (2) of that paragagh, the end of a year) falling before the first occurrence after the transfer of a chargeable event with respect to the property. 1975 c. 7.

(2) Where property is comprised in a settlement and there has been, on or before the occasion on which it became comprised in the settlement, a disposal of the property in relation to which subsection (4) of section 31 of the Finance Act 1965 (capital gains tax relief for works of art etc.) had effect, the said paragraph 12 shall not have effect in relation to the property on any relevant date falling before the first occurrence after the disposal of an event on the happening of which the property is treated as sold under subsection (5) of that section. 1965 c. 25.

(3) Where property is comprised in a settlement and there has been no such transfer or disposal of the property as is mentioned in subsection (1) or (2) above on or before the occasion on which it became comprised in the settlement, then, if—

(*a*) the property has, on a claim made for the purpose, been designated by the Treasury under section 77 above; and

PART IV

(*b*) the requisite undertaking described in that section has been given by such person as the Treasury think appropriate in the circumstances of the case,

tax which would otherwise be chargeable under the said paragraph 12 in respect of the property on a relevant date shall be deferred until the first occurrence of an event which, if there had been a conditionally exempt transfer of the property when the claim was made and the undertaking had been given under section 76 above, would be a chargeable event with respect to the property.

(4) Where any deferred tax becomes chargeable on the occurrence of a chargeable event, it shall be charged—

(*a*) subject to subsection (5) below, on an amount equal to the value of the property at the time of the chargeable event; and

(*b*) at the rate at which it would be chargeable if the relevant date had fallen at that time.

(5) If more than one relevant date has passed and, accordingly, more than one deferred tax becomes chargeable—

(*a*) the second deferred tax shall be charged on the value mentioned in subsection (4)(*a*) above less the amount of the first deferred tax; and

(*b*) the third deferred tax (if any) shall be charged on the amount found under paragraph (*a*) above less the amount of the second deferred tax,

and so on.

(6) In its application to a capital distribution made after the chargeable event, paragraph 13(1) of the said Schedule 5 (tax credit for periodic charge) shall have effect as if the reference to tax charged at a relevant anniversary included a reference to tax deferred from a relevant anniversary and charged under subsection (4) above.

(7) The persons liable for any deferred tax shall be those who would have been liable but for the deferment.

Transfers on or before 6th April 1976.

83.—(1) Section 31 to 34 of the Finance Act 1975 (conditional exemption for certain objects, land etc. on death) shall not apply to any death after 6th April 1976.

1975 c. 7.

(2) Where tax is chargeable after that date under subsection (3) of section 33 or subsection (8) of section 34 of the said Act of 1975 by reason of a sale, so much of paragraph (*b*) of that subsection as provides for the value of the object or property to be treated as equal to the proceeds of sale shall not apply unless the sale was—

(*a*) not intended to confer any gratuitous benefit on any person; and (*b*) was either a transaction at arm's length between persons not connected with each other or a transaction such as might be expected to be made at arm's length between persons not connected with each other. PART IV

(3) Where there has been a transfer of value in relation to which the value of any property has been left out of account under the provisions of sections 31 to 34 of the said Act of 1975 and, before any tax has become chargeable in respect of that property under those provisions, there is a conditionally exempt transfer of that property, then, on the occurrence of a chargeable event in respect of that property—

(*a*) if there has been no conditionally exempt transfer of the property on death, tax shall be chargeable either under section 78 above or under those provisions as the Board may elect; and

(*b*) if there has been such a conditionally exempt transfer, tax shall be chargeable under that section and not under those provisions.

(4) In sections 79(7) and 82 above references to a conditionally exempt transfer of any property include references to a transfer of value in relation to which the value of any property has been left out of account under the provisions of the said sections 31 to 34 and, in relation to such property, references to a chargeable event or to the tax chargeable in accordance with section 79 above by reference to a chargeable event include references to an event on the occurrence of which tax becomes chargeable under those provisions or to the tax so chargeable.

(5) In paragraph 19(1)(*c*) of Schedule 4 to the Finance Act 1975 (interest on unpaid tax) after " section 32 " there shall be inserted " or 34 ". 1975 c. 7.

(6) In its application to a sale on any date after 6th April 1976 which does not satisfy the requirements of subsection (2)(*a*) and (*b*) above, subsection (2) of section 40 of the Finance Act 1930 shall have effect as if the reference to the proceeds of sale were a reference to the value of the objects on that date. 1930 c. 28.

(7) Subsections (3) and (4) above shall apply to a death in relation to which the value of any property has been left out of account under the said section 40 as they apply to such a transfer of value as is there mentioned, taking references to tax becoming chargeable under the provisions there mentioned as references to estate duty becoming chargeable under that section or section 48 of the Finance Act 1950. 1950 c. 15.

(8) In determining for the purposes of subsection (2) of the said section 40 what is the last death on which the objects passed there shall be disregarded any death after 6th April 1976.

PART IV

1930 c. 28. 1950 c. 15. 1931 c. 24. (N.I.). 1972/1100 (N.I.).

(9) In the application of this section to Northern Ireland for references to section 40 of the Finance Act 1930 and section 48 of the Finance Act 1950 there shall be substituted references to section 2 of the Finance Act (Northern Ireland) 1931 and Article 6 of the Finance (Northern Ireland) Order 1972 respectively.

Maintenance funds for historic buildings. 1975 c. 7.

84.—(1) Subject to the provisions of Part II of Schedule 6 to the Finance Act 1975 as applied by this section, a transfer of value made after 2nd May 1976 is an exempt transfer to the extent that—

(*a*) the value transferred by it is attributable to property which becomes comprised in a settlement; and

(*b*) the Treasury so direct (whether before or after the time of the transfer);

and paragraphs 6 to 12 of Schedule 5 to that Act shall not apply in relation to property comprised in a settlement by virtue of a transfer of value exempt under this section.

(2) The Treasury shall, on a claim made for the purpose, give a direction under subsection (1) above if—

(*a*) they are satisfied that—

(i) the settlement complies with the requirements of subsection (3) below; and

(ii) the property is of a character and amount appropriate for the purposes of the settlement; and

(*b*) the trustees include a custodian trustee and are approved by the Treasury.

(3) The requirements referred to in subsection (2)(*a*) above are—

(*a*) that during the continuance of the settlement none of the property comprised in it can be applied otherwise than—

(i) for the maintenance, repair or preservation of, or making provision for public access to, a building or land which is for the time being a qualifying building or qualifying land as defined in subsection (5) below; or

(ii) as respects income not so applied and not accumulated, for the benefit of a body mentioned in paragraph 12 of Schedule 6 to the said Act of 1975 (museums etc.) or of a qualifying charity as defined in subsection (7) below; and

(*b*) that on the termination of the settlement none of the property comprised in it can devolve otherwise than on any such body or charity as aforesaid.

(4) Where property is comprised in a settlement by virtue of a transfer of value exempt under this section the trustees shall from time to time furnish the Treasury with such accounts and other information relating to the settlement as the Treasury may reasonably require. PART IV

(5) A building or land is a qualifying building or qualifying land for the purposes of subsection (3)(*a*) above if—

(*a*) it has been designated under section 34(1)(*b*) or (*c*) of the Finance Act 1975 or section 77(1)(*c*) or (*d*) above; and 1975 c. 7.

(*b*) the requisite undertaking has been given with respect to it under the said section 34 or under section 76, 78(5)(*b*) or 82(3) above; and

(*c*) tax has not (since the last occasion on which such an undertaking was given) become chargeable with respect to it under the said section 34 or under section 78 or 82(3) above.

(6) If it appears to the Treasury that provision is, or is to be, made by a settlement for the maintenance, repair or preservation of any such property as is mentioned in subsection (1)(*c*) or (*d*) of section 77 above, they may, on a claim made for the purpose—

(*a*) designate that property under this subsection; and

(*b*) accept with respect to it an undertaking such as is described in subsection (4) of that section;

and, if they do so, subsection (5) above shall have effect as if the designation were under that section and the undertaking under section 76 above and as if the reference to tax becoming chargeable were a reference to the occurrence of an event on which tax would become chargeable under section 78 above if there had been a conditionally exempt transfer of the property when the claim was made and the undertaking had been given under the said section 76.

(7) A charity is a qualifying charity for the purposes of subsection (3) above if it exists wholly or mainly for maintaining, repairing or preserving for the public benefit buildings of historic or architectural interest, land of scenic, historic or scientific interest or objects of national, scientific, historic or artistic interest.

In this subsection " national interest " includes interest within any part of the United Kingdom.

(8) In paragraph 15(1), (2) and (3) of Schedule 6 to the said Act of 1975 after the words " to 13 above " there shall be inserted the words " and section 84 of the Finance Act 1976 ".

PART IV

(9) In the application of this section to Scotland for the reference in subsection (2)(*b*) above to a custodian trustee there shall be substituted a reference to any such body or charity as is mentioned in subsection (3) above or any other body approved by the Treasury for the purposes of this subsection.

1906 c. 55.
1933 c. 16 (N.I.).

(10) For the purposes of the application of this section to Northern Ireland, section 4(2) and (3) of the Public Trustee Act 1906 (custodian trustees) shall extend to Northern Ireland as if a trust corporation within the meaning of the Probates and Letters of Administration Act (Northern Ireland) 1933 were a body corporate entitled by rules made under the said Act of 1906 to act as a custodian trustee.

Gifts for public benefit. 1975 c. 7.

85. In Schedule 6 to the Finance Act 1975, in paragraph 13(2)(*f*), for the words " or historic or scientific " there shall be substituted the words " scientific, historic or artistic ".

Mutual and voidable transfers

Mutual transfers: exemption for donee's gift.

86.—(1) This section and section 87 below have effect where—

(*a*) a person (" the donor ") makes a chargeable transfer (" the donor's transfer ") which increases the estate of another person (" the donee ") ; and

(*b*) the donee subsequently makes a transfer of value (" the donee's transfer ") which either—

(i) is made in the donor's life-time and increases the value of the estate of the donor or his spouse ; or

(ii) is made within two years after the donor's death and increases the value of the estate of the donor's widow or widower.

(2) The donee's transfer shall be an exempt transfer to the extent to which the value thereby transferred does not exceed—

(*a*) the amount by which his estate was increased by the donor's transfer ; or

(*b*) if there has been a previous donee's transfer, so much of that amount as has not been taken into account under this subsection for exempting that transfer.

(3) In subsection (1) above references to a transfer are references to a transfer (whether made before or after the passing of this Act) that is a disposition between individuals, including any disposition treated as made by virtue of section 20(7) of the Finance Act 1975 but not anything else that is treated as a disposition for the purposes of capital transfer tax.

(4) Subsection (1)(*b*) above has effect in relation to a person as the donor's spouse, widow or widower only if at the relevant time both the donor and that person were, or neither of them

was, domiciled in the United Kingdom ; and for that purpose the relevant time is, in the case of a spouse, the time of the donee's transfer and, in the case of a widow or widower, the time of the donor's death. PART IV

(5) Where the donor has died before 1st April 1975 subsection (1)(*b*)(ii) above shall have effect with the substitution for the reference to his death of a reference to that date.

Mutual transfers: relief for donor's gift.

87.—(1) The donor may, within six years after the donee's transfer, claim that for the purposes of this section the value transferred by the donor's transfer shall be treated as cancelled by the donee's transfer to the extent specified in subsection (3) below ; and thereupon—

(*a*) tax on the cancelled value paid or payable (whether or not by the claimant) shall be repaid to him by the Board or, as the case may be, shall not be payable ; and

(*b*) the rate or rates of tax applicable to any chargeable transfer made by the donor after the claim shall be determined as if the values previously transferred by chargeable transfers made by the donor were reduced by the cancelled value.

(2) Where the donor has died, then—

(*a*) if the case falls within section 86(1)(*b*)(i) above, a claim may be made under subsection (1) above by the donor's personal representatives and paragraph (*b*) of that subsection shall apply as if for the reference to any chargeable transfer made by the donor after the claim there were substituted a reference to the chargeable transfer made by him on his death ;

(*b*) if the case falls within section 86(1)(*b*)(ii) above, a claim may be made under subsection (1) above by the donor's widow or widower.

(3) The amount of the value transferred to be treated as cancelled by a donee's transfer shall be such amount thereof as, after deduction of the tax charged on it, is equal—

(*a*) if paragraph (*b*) below does not apply, to the value restored by the transfer ;

(*b*) if more than twelve months have elapsed between the donor's transfer and the donee's, to the value so restored reduced by 4 per cent. for every twelve months that have so elapsed ;

and where the cancelled amount is less than the whole of the value transferred it shall be treated as the highest part of that value.

PART IV

(4) As between two or more donor's transfers made by the same donor to the same donee value transferred by a later transfer shall be treated as cancelled rather than value transferred by an earlier one; and where there has been a claim in respect of a previous donee's transfer references in the foregoing provisions of this section to the value transferred shall be construed as references to the part of that value not treated as cancelled by that transfer.

(5) For the purposes of subsection (3) above the value restored by the donee's transfer is so much of the value thereby transferred as does not exceed—

(*a*) the amount by which the donee's estate was increased by the donor's transfer; or

(*b*) if there has been a previous donee's transfer, so much of that amount as was not taken into account as the value restored by that transfer.

(6) In paragraph (*a*) of subsection (1) above the reference to tax includes a reference to interest on tax.

(7) Tax repayable on a claim under this section shall carry interest (which shall not constitute income for any tax purposes) at the rate for the time being applicable under paragraph 19(1)(ii) of Schedule 4 to the Finance Act 1975 from the date on which the claim is made.

1975 c. 7.

(8) For the purposes of liability to additional tax by reason of the donor's death within three years after the donor's transfer, the value thereby transferred which is treated as cancelled by a donee's transfer made before the death shall include any value that would be so treated if subsection (3)(*b*) above had not applied.

(9) Where the donee's transfer has increased the estate of the spouse, widow or widower of another person any value thereby transferred which can (or if a claim were made could) be taken into account as value restored in relation to a transfer made by the spouse, widow or widower shall not be so taken into account in relation to a transfer made by that other person.

Voidable transfers.

88.—(1) Where on a claim made for the purpose it is shown that the whole or any part of a chargeable transfer (" the relevant transfer ") has by virtue of any enactment or rule of law been set aside as voidable or otherwise defeasible—

(*a*) tax paid or payable by the claimant (in respect of the relevant transfer or any other chargeable transfer made before the claim) that would not have been payable if

PART IV

the relevant transfer had been void ab initio shall be repaid to him by the Board, or as the case may be, shall not be payable ; and

(*b*) the rate or rates of tax applicable to any chargeable transfer made after the claim by the person who made the relevant transfer shall be determined as if that transfer or that part of it had been void as aforesaid.

(2) In subsection (1)(*a*) above " tax " includes interest on tax.

(3) Tax repayable on a claim under subsection (1) above shall carry interest (which shall not constitute income for any tax purposes) at the rate for the time being applicable under paragraph 19(1)(ii) of Schedule 4 to the Finance Act 1975 from the date on which the claim is made. 1975 c. 7.

(4) This section applies in relation to transfers before as well as after the passing of this Act.

Dispositions that are not transfers of value

Dispositions allowable for income tax or conferring retirement benefits.

89.—(1) A disposition made by any person is not a transfer of value if it is allowable in computing that person's profits or gains for the purposes of income tax or corporation tax or would be so allowable if those profits or gains were sufficient and fell to be so computed.

(2) Without prejudice to subsection (1) above, a disposition made by any person is not a transfer of value if—

(*a*) it is a contribution to a retirement benefits scheme which is approved by the Board for the purposes of Chapter II of Part II of the Finance Act 1970 (occupational pension schemes) and provides benefits in respect of service which is or includes service as an employee (as defined in that Chapter) of that person ; or 1970 c. 24.

(*b*) it is made so as to provide—

(i) benefits on or after retirement for a person not connected with him who is or has been in his employ ; or

(ii) benefits on or after the death of such a person for his widow or dependants,

and does not result in the recipient receiving benefits which, having regard to their form and amount, are greater than what could be provided under a scheme approved as aforesaid.

(3) Where a person makes dispositions of the kinds described in both paragraph (*a*) and paragraph (*b*) of subsection (2) above in respect of service by the same person, they shall be regarded

PART IV

as satisfying the conditions of that subsection only to the extent to which the benefits they provide do not exceed what could be provided by a disposition of the kind described in either of those paragraphs.

(4) For the purposes of subsection (2)(*b*) above, the right to occupy a dwelling rent-free or at a rent less than might be expected to be obtained in a transaction at arm's length between persons not connected with each other shall be regarded as equivalent to a pension at a rate equal to the rent or additional rent that might be expected to be obtained as aforesaid.

(5) Where a disposition satisfies the conditions of the preceding provisions of this section to a limited extent only, so much of it as satisfies them and so much of it as does not satisfy them shall be treated as separate dispositions.

1975 c. 7.

(6) Paragraph 9 of Schedule 6 to the Finance Act 1975 (which is superseded by subsection (1) above) shall cease to have effect.

(7) This section applies to dispositions before as well as after the passing of this Act.

Dispositions on trust for benefit of employees.

90.—(1) Subject to subsection (3) below, a disposition of property made to trustees by a close company whereby the property is to be held on trusts of the description specified in paragraph 17(1) of Schedule 5 to the Finance Act 1975 is not a transfer of value if the persons for whose benefit the trusts permit the property to be applied include all or most of either—

(*a*) the persons employed by or holding office with the company; or

(*b*) the persons employed by or holding office with the company or any one or more subsidiaries of the company.

(2) Subject to subsection (3) below, a disposition of property made to trustees by an individual beneficially entitled to shares in a company whereby the property is to be held on trusts of the said description is not a transfer of value if—

(*a*) the property consists of all the shares and securities of the company to which he is beneficially entitled; and

(*b*) immediately after the disposition there are no shares or securities of the company to which his spouse is beneficially entitled; and

(*c*) as a result of the disposition and of any other dispositions made on the same occasion, the trustees—

(i) hold all or substantially all of the ordinary shares in the company, and

PART IV

(ii) have powers of voting on all questions affecting the company as a whole which if exercised would yield a majority of the votes capable of being exercised thereon ; and

(*d*) the persons for whose benefit the trusts permit the property to be applied include all or most of the persons employed by or holding office with the company.

(3) Subject to subsection (4) below, subsections (1) and (2) above do not apply if the trusts permit any of the property to be applied at any time (whether during any such period as is referred to in the said paragraph 17(1) or later) for the benefit of—

(*a*) a person who is a participator in the company making the disposition or, as the case may be, the company whose shares are disposed of ; or

(*b*) any other person who is a participator in any close company that has made a disposition whereby property became comprised in the same settlement, being a disposition which but for this section would have been a transfer of value ; or

(*c*) any other person who has been a participator in any such company as is mentioned in paragraph (*a*) or (*b*) above at any time after, or during the ten years before, the disposition made by that company or, as the case may be, the disposition of its shares ; or

(*d*) any person who is connected with any person within paragraph (*a*), (*b*) or (*c*) above.

(4) The participators in a company who are referred to in subsection (3) above do not include any participator who on a winding-up of the company would not be entitled to 5 per cent. or more of its assets ; and in determining whether the trusts permit property to be applied as mentioned in that subsection, no account shall be taken of any power to make a payment which is the income of any person for any of the purposes of income tax, or would be the income for any of those purposes of a person not resident in the United Kingdom if he was so resident.

(5) In this section—

" close company " and " participator " have the same meanings as in section 39 of the Finance Act 1975 ; 1975 c. 7.

" ordinary shares " means shares which carry either—

(*a*) a right to dividends not restricted to dividends at a fixed rate, or

(*b*) a right to conversion into shares carrying such a right as is mentioned in paragraph (*a*) above ;

" subsidiary " has the same meaning as in the Companies Act 1948 ; 1948 c. 38.

PART IV

and references in subsections (3) and (4) above to a participator in a company shall, in the case of a company which is not a close company, be construed as references to a person who would be a participator in the company if it were a close company.

(6) This section applies to dispositions made after 6th April 1976.

Waiver of remuneration.

91.—(1) Subject to subsection (2) below, the waiver or repayment of an amount of remuneration shall not be a transfer of value if, apart from the waiver or repayment, that amount would be assessable to income tax under Schedule E.

(2) Where, apart from the waiver or repayment, the amount of the remuneration would be allowable as a deduction in computing for the purposes of income tax or corporation tax the profits or gains or losses of the person by whom it is payable or paid, this section applies only if, by reason of the waiver or repayment, it is not so allowed or is otherwise brought into charge in computing those profits or gains or losses.

(3) This section applies to waivers or repayments before as well as after the passing of this Act.

Waiver of dividends.

92.—(1) A person who waives any dividend on shares of a company within twelve months before any right to the dividend has accrued does not by reason of the waiver make a transfer of value.

(2) This section applies to waivers before as well as after the passing of this Act.

Other exemptions and reliefs

Exemption for transfers under £2,000. 1975 c. 7.

93.—(1) In paragraph 2 of Schedule 6 to the Finance Act 1975 (exemption for transfers of value under £1,000) for " £1,000 " wherever it occurs there shall be substituted " £2,000 ".

(2) This section does not affect the operation of paragraph 2 in relation to transfers of value made before 6th April 1976 or the amount which, under sub-paragraph (2) of that paragraph, may be carried forward to the year beginning on that date.

Transfers between spouses.

94.—(1) In relation to transfers of value made after 6th April 1976, paragraph 1 of Schedule 6 to the Finance Act 1975 shall have effect with the following amendments.

(2) In sub-paragraph (1), for the words " the value of the estate of the transferor's spouse is increased " there shall be substituted the words " the value transferred is attributable

to property which becomes comprised in the estate of the transferor's spouse or, so far as the value transferred is not so attributable, to the extent that that estate is increased ". PART IV

(3) In sub-paragraph (2)—

(*a*) for the words from " transfer is exempt " to " does not " there shall be substituted the words " value in respect of which the transfer is exempt (calculated as a value on which no tax is payable) shall not ";

(*b*) for the words " less any increase " there shall be substituted the words " less any amount ".

95.—(1) Paragraph 15 of Schedule 6 to the Finance Act 1975 shall be amended as follows. Exempt transfers: modification of exceptions. 1975 c. 7.

(2) In sub-paragraph (3), in paragraph (*b*) the words " is given subject to an interest reserved or created by the donor or " shall be omitted and after that paragraph there shall be inserted—

" (*ba*) the property is an interest in possession in settled property and the settlement does not come to an end in relation to that settled property on the making of the transfer ; or

(*bb*) the property is land or a building and is given subject to an interest reserved or created by the donor which entitles him, his spouse or a person connected with him to possession of, or to occupy, the whole or any part of the land or building rent-free or at a rent less than might be expected to be obtained in a transaction at arm's length between persons not connected with each other ; or

(*bc*) the property is not land or a building and is given subject to an interest reserved or created by the donor other than—

(i) an interest created by him for full consideration in money or money's worth ; or

(ii) an interest which does not substantially affect the enjoyment of the property by the person or body to whom it is given ; or ".

(3) After sub-paragraph (4) there shall be inserted—

" (4A) Where a person or body acquires a reversionary interest in any settled property for a consideration in money or money's worth, paragraphs 1 and 10 to 13 above do not apply in relation to the property when it becomes the property of that person or body on the termination of the interest on which the reversionary interest is expectant."

(4) Subsection (2) above applies in relation to transfers of value made after 15th April 1976 and subsection (3) applies where the acquisition of the reversionary interest is after that date.

PART IV

Exempt transfers: modification of supplementary provisions.

96.—(1) In relation to transfers of value made after 6th April 1976, Part III of Schedule 6 to the Finance Act 1975 shall have effect with the amendments set out in subsections (2) to (6) below.

1975 c. 7.

(2) In paragraph 16, for sub-paragraph (*b*) there shall be substituted—

"(*b*) paragraph 22 shall have effect as respects the burden of tax."

(3) For sub-paragraph (1) of paragraph 19 there shall be substituted—

"(1) Such part of the value transferred shall be attributable to specific gifts as corresponds to the value of the gifts; but if or to the extent that the gifts—

(*a*) are not gifts with respect to which the transfer is exempt or are outside the limit up to which the transfer is exempt, and

(*b*) do not bear their own tax,

the amount corresponding to the value of the gifts shall be taken to be the amount arrived at in accordance with sub-paragraphs (3) to (3B) below".

(4) For sub-paragraph (3) of paragraph 19 there shall be substituted—

"(3) Where the only gifts with respect to which the transfer is or might be chargeable are specific gifts which do not bear their own tax, the amount referred to in sub-paragraph (1) above is the aggregate of—

(*a*) the sum of the value of those gifts, and

(*b*) the amount of tax which would be chargeable if the value transferred equalled that aggregate.

(3A) Where the specific gifts not bearing their own tax are not the only gifts with respect to which the transfer is or might be chargeable, the amount referred to in sub-paragraph (1) above is such amount as, after deduction of tax at the assumed rate specified in sub-paragraph (3B) below, would be equal to the sum of the value of those gifts.

(3B) For the purposes of sub-paragraph (3A) above—

(*a*) the assumed rate is the rate found by dividing the assumed amount of tax by that part of the value transferred with respect to which the transfer would be chargeable on the hypothesis that—

(i) the amount corresponding to the value of specific gifts not bearing their own tax is equal to the aggregate referred to in sub-paragraph (3) above, and

PART IV

(ii) the parts of the value transferred attributable to specific gifts and to gifts of residue or shares in residue are determined accordingly; and

(*b*) the assumed amount of tax is the amount that would be charged on the value transferred on the hypothesis mentioned in paragraph (*a*) above."

(5) For paragraph 22 there shall be substituted—

" *Burden of tax*

22. Notwithstanding the terms of any disposition—

(*a*) none of the tax on the value transferred shall fall on any specific gift if or to the extent that the transfer is exempt with respect to the gift; and

(*b*) none of the tax attributable to the value of property comprised in residue shall fall on any gift of a share of residue if or to the extent that the transfer is exempt with respect to the gift."

(6) At the end of paragraph 23 there shall be added—

" (3) Where—

(*a*) the whole or part of the value transferred by a transfer of value is attributable to property which is the subject of two or more gifts, and

(*b*) the aggregate of the values of the property given by each of those gifts is less than the value transferred or, as the case may be, that part of it,

then for the purposes of this Part of this Schedule (and notwithstanding the definition of a gift in sub-paragraph (1) above) the value of each gift shall be taken to be the relevant proportion of the value transferred or, as the case may be, that part of it; and the relevant proportion in relation to any gift is the proportion which the value of the property given by it bears to the said aggregate."

(7) After paragraph 22 of Schedule 6 to the Finance Act 1975 there shall be inserted the following paragraph— 1975 c. 7.

" *Legal rights in Scotland*

22A.—(1) Where on the death of a person legal rights are claimed by a person entitled to claim such rights, those rights shall be treated as a specific gift which bears its own tax.

(2) In determining the value of legal rights mentioned in sub-paragraph (1) above, any capital transfer tax repayable on the estate of the deceased shall be left out of account.

(3) In the case of any death occurring after 13th March 1975 and before the passing of the Finance Act 1976, the

PART IV

executors of the deceased may elect that this paragraph shall apply to the estate of the deceased.

(4) This paragraph extends to Scotland only ".

Relief for successive charges.

1975 c. 7.

97.—(1) Section 30 of the Finance Act 1975 shall have effect, and be deemed always to have had effect, as if for subsection (3) there were substituted—

" (3) Where the value of a person's estate was increased—

(*a*) on a death on which estate duty was payable ; or

(*b*) in consequence of—

(i) a gift inter vivos ; or

(ii) a disposition or determination of a beneficial interest in possession in any property comprised in a settlement,

where, by reason of the gift or interest, estate duty or capital transfer tax under section 22(5) of this Act was payable on a subsequent death,

the preceding provisions of this section shall apply with the necessary modifications and, in particular, as if the increase had been by a chargeable transfer on the occasion of the death and, in a case where estate duty was payable, that duty had been tax on the value transferred thereby."

(2) Paragraph 5 of Schedule 5 to the said Act of 1975 shall have effect, and be deemed always to have had effect, as if for sub-paragraph (2) there were substituted—

" (2) Where the transferor became entitled to the interest—

(*a*) on a death on which estate duty was payable in respect of the settled property ; or

(*b*) in consequence of—

(i) a gift inter vivos ; or

(ii) a disposition or determination of a beneficial interest in possession in any property comprised in a settlement,

where, by reason of the gift or interest, estate duty or capital transfer tax under section 22(5) of this Act was payable on a subsequent death in respect of the settled property,

sub-paragraph (1) above shall apply as if the period referred to therein were the period between the death and the chargeable transfer."

Gifts to spouses—relief from transitional charge.

98. For the purpose of determining in relation to a death after 6th April 1976 whether any increase is to be made in the deceased's estate by virtue of section 22(5) of the Finance Act 1975 (which provides for such an increase in certain cases where, by reason of a gift or an interest in possession under a settlement, property would have been within the charge to estate duty), section 121(1)(*c*) of the Finance Act 1972 (relief from estate duty for gifts etc. to the deceased's widow or widower) shall have effect as if the reference to a widow or widower included a reference to a spouse who died before the deceased. PART IV 1972 c. 41.

Transfers within three years before death.

99.—(1) Subject to the following provisions, this section applies where additional tax becomes chargeable in respect of the value transferred by a chargeable transfer because of the transferor's death within three years of the transfer and all or part of the value transferred is attributable to the value of property (" the transferred property ") which—

(*a*) is, at the date of the death, the property of the person (" the transferee ") whose property it became on the transfer or of his spouse, or

(*b*) has, before that date, been sold by the transferee or his spouse by a qualifying sale ;

and in the following provisions of this section " the relevant date " means, in a case within sub-paragraph (*a*) above, the date of the death, and in a case within sub-paragraph (*b*), the date of the qualifying sale.

(2) If the market value of the transferred property at the time of the chargeable transfer exceeds its market value on the relevant date, the additional tax shall be calculated as if the value transferred were reduced by the amount of the excess.

(3) This section shall not apply unless—

(*a*) the transferor's death occurs after 6th April 1976, and

(*b*) a claim is made by a person liable to pay the whole or part of the additional tax.

(4) This section shall not apply if the transferred property is tangible movable property that is a wasting asset, and in other cases shall apply subject to the provisions of Schedule 12 to this Act.

(5) For the purposes of this section the market value at any time of any property is the price which the property might reasonably be expected to fetch if sold in the open market at the time ; but—

(*a*) that price shall not be assumed to be reduced on the ground that the whole property is on the market at one and the same time ; and

(*b*) paragraph 13 of Schedule 10 to the Finance Act 1975 shall apply as it applies for determining the value of unquoted shares and securities for the purposes of tax. 1975 c. 7

PART IV

(6) A sale is a qualifying sale for the purposes of this section if—

(*a*) it is at arm's length for a price freely negotiated at the time of the sale; and

(*b*) no person concerned as vendor (or as having an interest in the proceeds of the sale) is the same as or connected with any person concerned as purchaser (or as having an interest in the purchase); and

(*c*) no provision is made, in or in connection with the agreement for the sale, that the vendor (or any person having an interest in the proceeds of sale) is to have any right to acquire some or all of the property sold or some interest in or created out of it.

(7) The transferred property is a wasting asset for the purposes of this section if, immediately before the chargeable transfer, it had a predictable useful life not exceeding fifty years, having regard to the purpose for which it was held by the transferor; and plant and machinery shall in every case be regarded as having a predictable useful life of less than fifty years.

Valuation

Liability for tax not in fact paid.
1975 c. 7.

100.—(1) In paragraph 9 of Schedule 10 to the Finance Act 1975 after sub-paragraph (2) there shall be inserted—

"(2A) If in determining the value of a person's estate immediately before his death a liability for tax is taken into account, then, if that tax or any part of it is not in the event paid out of the estate, the value of the estate immediately before his death shall be treated as increased by an amount equal to that tax or so much of it is not so paid."

(2) This section has effect in relation to deaths occurring after 15th April 1976.

Falls in value of land after death.

101.—(1) At the end of paragraph 9 of Schedule 10 to the Finance Act 1975 there shall be added—

"(4) Part III of this Schedule shall apply with respect to the valuation of interests in land which are comprised in a person's estate immediately before his death and are sold by the appropriate person (as defined in that Part) within the period of three years immediately following the date of the death."

(2) After Part II of the said Schedule there shall be added the provisions set out in Schedule 13 to this Act.

(3) This section has effect in relation to deaths occurring after 6th April 1976.

PART IV

Sales of related property after a death.
1975 c. 7.

102.—(1) After paragraph 9 of Schedule 10 to the Finance Act 1975 there shall be inserted—

" 9A.—(1) This paragraph has effect where, within three years after the death of any person, there is a qualifying sale of any property (" the relevant property ") comprised in his estate immediately before his death and valued for the purposes of tax—

(*a*) in accordance with paragraph 7 above, or

(*b*) in conjunction with property which was also comprised in the estate but has not at any time since the death been vested in the vendors.

(2) If a claim is made for relief under this paragraph then, subject to sub-paragraphs (4) and (5) below, the value of the relevant property immediately before the death shall be taken to be what it would have been if it had not been determined as mentioned in sub-paragraph (1) above.

(3) For the purposes of sub-paragraph (1) above a sale is a qualifying sale if—

(*a*) the vendors are the persons in whom the relevant property vested immediately after the death or the deceased's personal representatives; and

(*b*) it is at arm's length for a price freely negotiated at the time of the sale and is not made in conjunction with a sale of any of the related property taken into account as mentioned in sub-paragraph (1)(*a*) above or any of the property mentioned in sub-paragraph (1)(*b*) above; and

(*c*) no person concerned as vendor (or as having an interest in the proceeds of sale) is the same as or connected with any person concerned as purchaser (or as having an interest in the purchase); and

(*d*) neither the vendors nor any other person having an interest in the proceeds of sale obtain in connection with the sale a right to acquire the property sold or any interest in or created out of it.

(4) Sub-paragraph (2) above shall not apply unless the price obtained on the sale, with any adjustment needed to take account of any difference in circumstances at the date of the sale and at the date of the death, is less than the value which, apart from this paragraph and apart from Part III of this Schedule, would be the value of the relevant property determined as mentioned in sub-paragraph (1) above.

(5) Where the relevant property consists of shares in or securities of a close company, sub-paragraph (2) above shall

PART IV

not apply if at any time between the death and the qualifying sale the value of the shares or securities is reduced by more than 5 per cent. as a result of an alteration in the company's share or loan capital or in any rights attaching to shares in or securities of the company; and for the purposes of this sub-paragraph—

"alteration" includes extinguishment, and

"close company" has the same meaning as in section 39 of this Act."

(2) This section has effect in relation to deaths occurring after 6th April 1976.

Related property: property given to charities etc.
1975 c. 7.

103.—(1) In paragraph 7 of Schedule 10 to the Finance Act 1975, at the end of sub-paragraph (2) there shall be added "or

(*c*) it is or has within the preceding five years been—

(i) the property of a charity, or held on trust for charitable purposes only, or

(ii) the property of a body mentioned in paragraph 11, 12 or 13 of Schedule 6 to this Act,

and became so on a transfer of value which was made by him or his spouse after 15th April 1976 and was exempt to the extent that the value transferred was attributable to the property".

(2) This section has effect in relation to transfers of value before as well as after the passing of this Act.

Sales of certain securities within twelve months after a death.

104. Where the estate of a person who dies after 6th April 1976 comprises shares or securities in respect of which quotation on a recognised stock exchange is suspended at the date of the death, the shares or securities shall be qualifying investments for the purposes of Part II of Schedule 10 to the Finance Act 1975 if they are again quoted on a recognised stock exchange at the time when they are sold as mentioned in paragraph 15 or exchanged as mentioned in paragraph 24 of that Schedule.

Settled property

Survivorship clauses.

105.—(1) Schedule 5 to the Finance Act 1975 shall have effect, and subject to subsections (2) and (3) below shall be deemed always to have had effect, as if paragraph 6(7) were omitted and the following paragraph inserted after paragraph 22—

"*Survivorship clauses*

22A.—(1) Where under the terms of a will or otherwise property is held for any person on condition that he survives another for a specified period of not more than six months, this Part of this Act shall apply as if the dispositions taking effect at the end of the period or, if he does not

PART IV

survive until then, on his death (including any such disposition which has effect by operation of law or is a separate disposition of the income from the property) had had effect from the beginning of the period.

(2) Sub-paragraph (1) above does not affect the application of this Part of this Act in relation to any distribution or application of property occurring before the dispositions there mentioned take effect.

(3) Where the death with which the period mentioned in sub-paragraph (1) above begins occurred before 13th March 1975, that sub-paragraph shall not apply in relation to any property if or to the extent that, by virtue of section 121(1)(*c*) of the Finance Act 1972 (relief for property given to a surviving spouse), the value attributable to it was disregarded for the purposes of estate duty chargeable on that death." 1972 c. 41.

(2) Subsection (1) above shall not have effect in a case where the period there mentioned ended before 7th April 1976 if the application at the end of the period of sub-paragraph (2) of paragraph 6 of the said Schedule 5 was excluded by sub-paragraph (7) of that paragraph.

(3) Where the person for whom property was held as mentioned in subsection (1) above—

(*a*) was the spouse of the other person there mentioned, and

(*b*) died before the end of 1976 and during the period there mentioned,

that subsection shall not have effect if the persons mentioned in subsection (4) below so elect by written notice given to the Board within twelve months of the second death or such longer time as the Board may allow.

(4) The persons referred to in subsection (3) above are the personal representatives of each spouse and the trustees of every settlement in which either of the spouses had an interest in possession immediately before his death.

Accumulation and maintenance settlements.

1975 c. 7.

106.—(1) In paragraph 15 of Schedule 5 to the Finance Act 1975, at the end of sub-paragraph (1) there shall be added the words " and

(*c*) either—

(i) not more than twenty-five years have elapsed since the day on which the settlement was made or, if it was later, since the time (or latest time) when the conditions stated in paragraphs (*a*) and (*b*) above became satisfied with respect to the property or part ; or

PART IV

(ii) all the persons who are or have been beneficiaries are or were either grandchildren of a common grandparent or children, widows or widowers of such grandchildren who were themselves beneficiaries but died before the time when, had they survived, they would have become entitled as mentioned in paragraph (*a*) above."

(2) For sub-paragraphs (4) and (5) of the said paragraph 15 there shall be substituted—

" (4) Where the conditions stated in paragraphs (*a*) and (*b*) of sub-paragraph (1) above were satisfied on 15th April 1976 with respect to any property comprised in a settlement made before that day, paragraph (*c*)(i) of that sub-paragraph shall have effect with the substitution of a reference to that day for the reference to the day on which the settlement was made, and the condition stated in paragraph (*c*)(ii) shall be treated as satisfied if—

(*a*) it is satisfied in respect of the period beginning with 15th April 1976 ; or

(*b*) it is satisfied in respect of the period beginning with 1st April 1977 and either there was no beneficiary living on 15th April 1976 or the beneficiaries on 1st April 1977 include a living beneficiary ; or

(*c*) there is no power under the terms of the settlement whereby it could have become satisfied in respect of the period beginning with 1st April 1977, and the trusts of the settlement have not been varied at any time after 15th April 1976.

(5) In sub-paragraph (1) above " persons " includes unborn persons ; but the conditions stated in paragraphs (*a*) and (*b*) of that sub-paragraph shall be treated as not satisfied unless there is or has been a living beneficiary.

(6) Paragraph 11 above shall apply for the interpretation of this paragraph as it applies for the interpretation of paragraphs 6 to 10 ; and for the purposes of this paragraph a person's children shall be taken to include his illegitimate children, his adopted children and his step-children."

(3) In paragraph 14(5)(*b*) of the said Schedule 5, after the word " therein " there shall be inserted the words " living at the time of the capital distribution ".

Employee trusts.
1975 c. 7.

107.—(1) Paragraph 17 of Schedule 5 to the Finance Act 1975 shall be amended as follows.

(2) After sub-paragraph (4) there shall be inserted—

" (4A) Where any property to which this paragraph applies ceases to be comprised in a settlement and, either immediately or not more than one month later, the whole of it becomes comprised in another settlement, then, if this paragraph again applies to it when it becomes comprised in the second settlement, it shall be treated for all the purposes of this Part of this Act as if it had remained comprised in the first settlement." PART IV

(3) At the end of sub-paragraph (6) there shall be added the words " except that if more than one relevant anniversary has passed and, accordingly, more than one deferred tax becomes chargeable—

(*a*) the second deferred tax shall be charged on that value less the amount of the first deferred tax; and

(*b*) the third deferred tax (if any) shall be charged on the amount found under paragraph (*a*) above less the amount of the second deferred tax;

and so on."

(4) In sub-paragraph (9)(*b*) for the words " is chargeable " there shall be substituted the words " would, apart from sub-paragraph (7)(*b*) above, be chargeable ".

(5) This section shall be deemed to have come into force on 7th April 1976.

108.—(1) The following paragraph shall be inserted after paragraph 17 of Schedule 5 to the Finance Act 1975— Newspaper trusts. 1975 c. 7.

" 17A.—(1) In relation to property comprised in a settlement to which this paragraph applies, paragraph 17 above shall have effect as if newspaper publishing companies were included among the persons within paragraphs (*a*) to (*c*) of sub-paragraph (1) of that paragraph.

(2) This paragraph applies to a settlement if shares in a newspaper publishing company or a newspaper holding company are the only or principal property comprised in the settlement.

(3) In this paragraph—

" newspaper publishing company " means a company whose business consists wholly or mainly in the publication of newspapers in the United Kingdom; and

" newspaper holding company " means a company which—

(*a*) has as its only or principal asset shares in a newspaper publishing company, and

(*b*) has powers of voting on all or most questions affecting the publishing company as a whole which if exercised would yield a majority of the votes capable of being exercised thereon;

PART IV

and for the purposes of this paragraph shares shall be treated as the principal property comprised in a settlement or the principal asset of a company if the remaining property comprised in the settlement or the remaining assets of the company are such as may be reasonably required to enable the trustees or the company to secure the operation of the newspaper publishing company concerned."

(2) This section shall be deemed to have come into force on 7th April 1976.

Remuneration of trustees.
1975 c. 7.

109. After paragraph 19 of Schedule 5 to the Finance Act 1975 there shall be inserted—

"*Trustees' annuities etc.*

19A. Where under the terms of a settlement a person is entitled by way of remuneration for his services as trustee to an interest in possession in property comprised in the settlement, then, except to the extent that the interest represents more than a reasonable amount of remuneration,—

(*a*) the interest shall be left out of account in determining for the purposes of this Part of this Act the value of his estate immediately before his death, and

(*b*) tax shall not be charged under paragraph 4(2) above when the interest comes to an end."

Settlor's widow.

110.—(1) At the end of section 22(3) of the Finance Act 1975 there shall be added—

"The references in this subsection to the settlor's spouse include, in a case where the settlor died less than two years before the deceased or the deceased died before 1st April 1977, references to the settlor's widow or widower."

(2) In paragraph 4 of Schedule 5 to that Act, at the end of sub-paragraph (6) there shall be added—

"The references in this sub-paragraph to the settlor's spouse include, in a case where the settlor has died less than two years before the interest comes to an end or the interest comes to an end before 1st April 1977, references to the settlor's widow or widower."

(3) In paragraph 6 of that Schedule, at the end of sub-paragraph (6) there shall be added—

"The references in this sub-paragraph to the settlor's spouse include, in the case of a distribution payment made less than two years after the settlor's death or made before 1st April 1977, references to the settlor's widow or widower".

PART IV

(4) This section shall be deemed always to have had effect.

Distributions to charities etc.

1975 c. 7.

111.—(1) For sub-paragraph (2) of paragraph 10 of Schedule 6 to the Finance Act 1975 there shall be substituted—

" (2) Subject to the provisions of Part II of this Schedule, where property comprised in a settlement is given to a charity, the payment or transfer of the property out of the settlement shall not be a distribution payment for the purposes of Schedule 5 to this Act."

(2) In paragraph 11 of the said Schedule 6, after sub-paragraph (1) there shall be inserted—

" (1A) Subject to the provisions of Part II of this Schedule, where property comprised in a settlement becomes the property of a political party qualifying for exemption under this paragraph, the payment or transfer of the property out of the settlement shall not be a distribution payment for the purposes of Schedule 5 to this Act."

(3) At the end of paragraph 12 of the said Schedule 6 there shall be added—

" (2) Subject to the provisions of Part II of this Schedule, where property comprised in a settlement becomes the property of a body mentioned in sub-paragraph (1) above, the payment or transfer of the property out of the settlement shall not be a distribution payment for the purposes of Schedule 5 to this Act."

(4) In paragraph 13 of the said Schedule 6, after sub-paragraph (1) there shall be inserted—

" (1A) Subject to the provisions of Part II of this Schedule, where—

(*a*) property comprised in a settlement becomes at any time the property of a body not established or conducted for profit, and

(*b*) the Treasury so direct (whether before or after that time),

the payment or transfer of the property out of the settlement shall not be a distribution payment for the purposes of Schedule 5 to this Act." ;

in sub-paragraphs (3) and (4) for the words " sub-paragraph (1) above " there shall be substituted the words " this paragraph " ; and at the end of sub-paragraph (7) there shall be added the words " or if both become the property of the same body or the making of the same payment or transfer out of a settlement ".

PART IV

(5) At the end of paragraph 15 of the said Schedule 6 there shall be added—

"(6) In a case where property is given by a payment or transfer out of a settlement this paragraph shall have effect as if—

(*a*) any reference to a transfer of value were a reference to the payment or transfer, and

(*b*) paragraphs (*b*) to (*bc*) of sub-paragraph (3) above were omitted."

(6) This section shall be deemed to have come into force on 7th April 1976.

Settled property: other amendments.

112. Schedule 14 to this Act (which makes further amendments in relation to settled property) shall have effect.

Application of tax rates

Chargeable transfers made on same day. 1975 c. 7.

113.—(1) At the end of section 43 of the Finance Act 1975 there shall be added—

"(3) Subject to subsection (2) above, the rate at which tax is charged on the values transferred by two or more chargeable transfers made by the same person on the same day shall be the effective rate at which tax would have been charged if those transfers had been a single chargeable transfer of the same total value.

(4) The chargeable transfers referred to in subsections (2) and (3) above do not include a transfer made on the death of the transferor.

(5) For the purposes of subsections (2) and (3) above, capital distributions shall be treated as made by the same person if they are made out of property comprised in the same settlement."

(2) This section has effect in relation to chargeable transfers made after 15th April 1976.

Transfers reported late.

114.—(1) This section has effect where a person has made a transfer of value ("the earlier transfer") which—

(*a*) is not notified to the Board in an account under paragraph 2, or by information furnished under paragraph 5, of Schedule 4 to the Finance Act 1975 before the expiration of the period specified in paragraph 2 for the delivery of accounts; and

(*b*) is not discovered until after payment has been accepted by the Board in full satisfaction of the tax on the value transferred by another transfer of value ("the later transfer") made by him on or after the day on which he made the earlier transfer.

(2) For the purposes of section 37 of the Finance Act 1975 (except so much of that section as determines the appropriate Table) the earlier transfer shall be treated as if it had been made on the date on which it was discovered or, if the later transfer is made on death, immediately before the later transfer. PART IV 1975 c. 7.

(3) Where the later transfer is the relevant transfer for the purposes of paragraph 7 of Schedule 5 to the said Act of 1975, the earlier transfer shall not by virtue of subsection (2) above be treated for those purposes as made after the late transfer.

(4) Subsection (2) above shall not increase the amount in respect of which interest is payable under paragraph 19 of Schedule 4 to the said Act of 1975 in relation to the earlier transfer in respect of any period falling before the expiration of six months from the date on which it was discovered.

(5) Where, apart from this subsection, the earlier transfer would be wholly or partly exempt by reason of some or all of the value thereby transferred falling within a limit applicable to an exemption, then, if tax has been accepted as mentioned in subsection (1)(*b*) above on the basis that the later transfer is partly exempt by reason of part of the value thereby transferred falling within that limit—

(*a*) tax shall not be chargeable on that part of the value transferred by the later transfer; but

(*b*) a corresponding part of the value transferred by the earlier transfer shall be treated as falling outside that limit.

(6) Subsection (1)(*b*) above shall apply to a transfer in respect of which no tax is chargeable because the rate of tax applicable under the said section 37 is nil as if payment had been accepted when the transfer was notified in an account under paragraph 2 of the said Schedule 4.

(7) For the purposes of this section a transfer is discovered—

(*a*) if it is notified under the provisions mentioned in subsection (1)(*a*) above after the expiration of the period there mentioned, on the date on which it is so notified;

(*b*) in any other case, on the date on which the Board give notice of a determination in respect of the transfer under paragraph 6 of the said Schedule 4.

(8) This section shall apply to distribution payments as defined in paragraph 11 of the said Schedule 5 and to capital distributions as it applies to transfers of value; and for the purposes of this section such payments or distributions shall be treated as made by the same person if they are made out of property comprised in the same settlement.

PART IV

Loans

Free loans etc.

115.—(1) Where an individual (" the lender ") allows another person (" the borrower ") the use of money or other property in any year, then, subject to the provisions of this section and section 116 below, the lender shall be treated as making a disposition as a result of which the value of his estate is reduced by the amount (if any) by which any consideration for the use falls short of the cost to him of allowing it (determined in accordance with section 116 below).

(2) The disposition under subsection(1) above shall be treated as made at the end of the year or, if earlier, at the time when the use comes to an end.

(3) Where the use of the property is allowed for a period specified in advance, or where in any other case the lender has no right to terminate the use immediately after it begins, subsection (1) above shall not apply in relation to use before the expiration of the specified period or, as the case may be, before the earliest time when the lender could terminate the use if he exercised his right to do so at the earliest opportunity.

(4) Subsection (1) above shall not apply in relation to any use of property allowed to the borrower at a time when it is mainly used by the lender or the lender's spouse.

(5) Subsection (1) above shall not apply in relation to the use of property for a period which is less than twelve months unless that period falls within a period of twenty-four months during which the lender allows the borrower the use of that property or similar property for periods which amount in aggregate to twelve months or more; and in calculating that aggregate no account shall be taken of—

(*a*) use to which, by virtue of subsection (3) or (4) above, subsection (1) does not apply, or

(*b*) use to which (apart from this subsection) subsection (1) above does apply, if the disposition under that subsection is not a transfer of value.

(6) Subsection (1) above shall not apply in relation to the use of property where the borrower is a body corporate if—

(*a*) it is not a close company; or

(*b*) not less than 90 per cent. in nominal value of its issued ordinary shares are shares to which the lender or his spouse is beneficially entitled; or

(*c*) it is not an investment company and either—

(i) the lender or his spouse is a participator in the company or its holding company or has been such a participator at any time during the year or either of the two preceding years; or

PART IV

(ii) the lender's spouse died during the year or either of the two preceding years and was at any time during the three years ending with the year in which he died a participator in the company or its holding company.

(7) Subsection (1) above shall not apply in relation to the use of property where the borrower is a firm if—

(*a*) the lender or his spouse is a partner or has been a partner at any time during the year or either of the two preceding years ; or

(*b*) the lender's spouse died during the year or either of the two preceding years and was a partner at any time during the three years ending with the year in which he died.

(8) Subsection (1) above shall not apply in relation to a loan in respect of which any person is chargeable to income tax under Schedule E by virtue of section 66(1) above.

(9) For the purposes of this section an individual who makes a revocable gift of any property to another person shall, so long as the gift continues revocable, be taken to allow him the use of that property.

(10) In this section—

" close company " and " participator " have the same meanings as in section 39 of the Finance Act 1975 ; 1975 c. 7.

" firm " has the same meaning as in the Partnership Act 1890 ; 1890 c. 39.

" holding company " has the same meaning as in section 154 of the Companies Act 1948 ; 1948 c. 38.

" investment company " means a company falling within paragraph (*a*) of paragraph 16(3) of Schedule 4 to the Finance Act 1975 and not falling also within paragraph (*b*) or (*c*) of that paragraph ;

" ordinary shares " has the same meaning as in paragraph 13 of that Schedule ;

" year " means period of twelve months beginning with 6th April.

(11) This section has effect, in place of section 41 of the Finance Act 1975, in relation to the year beginning 6th April 1976 and subsequent years.

Free loans etc.: value transferred.

116.—(1) The cost to the lender of allowing the use of money or land shall be taken to be equal to the consideration which might be expected in a transaction on the same terms as those on which the use is allowed (apart from terms as to consideration) made at arm's length between persons not connected with each other.

PART IV

(2) The cost to the lender of allowing the use of property other than money or land shall be taken to be equal to the aggregate of—

(*a*) the annual value of the use of the property or, if the use does not continue throughout the year, a proportionate part of that annual value, and

(*b*) any expense incurred by the lender in connection with property during the year or, if the use does not continue throughout the year, a proportionate part of that expense, but excluding expense incurred in the acquisition or production of the property and excluding any hire charges;

except that if the property is hired by the lender and the annual amount of the hire charges is greater than the annual value of the use of the property, paragraph (*a*) above shall have effect as if it referred to that annual amount instead of to that annual value.

(3) If the property is money or land, the amount arrived at under section 115(1) above shall be reduced by the income tax which would be chargeable in respect of that amount (after taking account in the case of land of any deductions which might be made for the purposes of Schedule A) if it were the highest part of the lender's total income; and in calculating that income there shall be disregarded any such sum as is mentioned in paragraphs (*a*) to (*c*) of section 529 of the Taxes Act.

Modification of exemptions for loans.
1975 c. 7.

117.—(1) Schedule 6 to the Finance Act 1975 shall apply with the following modifications to—

(*a*) any transfer of value which is a disposition under section 115 above, and

(*b*) any other transfer of value, whether made before or after the passing of this Act, if or to the extent that it is a disposition whereby the use of money or other property is allowed by one person (" the lender ") to another (" the borrower ").

(2) For the purposes of paragraph 1 (transfers between spouses) the borrower's estate shall be treated as increased by an amount equal to the value transferred.

(3) For the purposes of paragraphs 4 (small gifts) and 6 (gifts in consideration of marriage) the transfer of value shall be treated as made by outright gift.

(4) Paragraph 5(1) (normal expenditure out of income) shall apply as if for the conditions stated in paragraphs (*a*) and (*b*) there were substituted the condition that the transfer was a normal one on the part of the transferor.

PART IV

(5) Paragraphs 10 and 11 (gifts to charities and to political parties) shall apply without sub-paragraph (1)(*b*) (£100,000 limit for transfers within one year of death); and for the purposes of those paragraphs and paragraphs 12 and 13 (gifts for national purposes and for public benefit)—

(*a*) the value transferred shall be treated as attributable to the property of which the borrower is allowed the use, and

(*b*) that property shall be treated as given to, or as becoming the property of, the borrower unless the use allowed includes use for purposes other than charitable purposes or those of a body mentioned in paragraph 11, 12 or 13.

(6) Part II (exceptions) shall not apply.

Miscellaneous

Close companies. 1975 c. 7.

118.—(1) In section 39 of the Finance Act 1975 the following subsections shall be inserted after subsections (6) and (8) respectively:—

" (6A) In determining for the purposes of this section whether a disposition made by a close company is a transfer of value or what value is transferred by such a transfer no account shall be taken of the surrender by the company, in pursuance of section 258 of the Taxes Act or of section 92 of the Finance Act 1972, of any relief or of the benefit of any amount of advance corporation tax paid by it.

(8A) Where part of a close company's share capital consists of preference shares (within the meaning of section 234(3) of the Taxes Act) and a transfer of value made by that or any other close company has only a small effect on the value of those shares, compared with its effect on the value of other parts of the company's share capital, the preference shares shall be left out of account in determining the respective rights and interests of the participators for the purposes of this section.

(8B) Where a close company (in this subsection and subsection (8C) below referred to as the transferor company) is a member, but not the principal member, of a group; and—

(*a*) a disposal by the transferor company of any asset is a disposal to which section 273(1) of the Taxes Act applies and is also a transfer of value; and

(*b*) the transfer of value has only a small effect on the value of the minority participators' rights and

PART IV

interests in that company compared with its effect on the value of the other participators' rights and interests in the company;

the rights and interests of the minority participators shall be left out of account in determining the respective rights and interests of the transferor company's participators for the purpose of apportioning the value transferred under this section.

(8C) For the purposes of subsection (8B) above—

(*a*) the principal member of a group is the member of which all the other members are 75 per cent. subsidiaries; and

(*b*) a minority participator is a participator of the transferor company who is not, and is not a person connected with, a participator of the principal member of the group or of any of the principal member's participators;

and in that subsection and this subsection " group " and " 75 per cent. subsidiary " have the same meanings as in section 272 of the Taxes Act.

(8D) Where the value of the estate of a company (in this subsection referred to as the transferee company) is increased as the result of a transfer of value made by a close company (in this subsection referred to as the transferor company) and an individual to whom part of the value transferred is apportioned under this section has an interest in the transferee company (or in a company which is a participator of the transferee company or any of its participators, and so on), then, in computing for the purposes of this section the amount to be offset, that is to say, the amount by which the value of his estate is more than it would be but for the transfer,—

(*a*) the increase in the value of the transferee company's estate shall be taken to be such part of the value transferred as accounts for the increase; and

(*b*) the increase so computed shall be apportioned among the transferee company's participators according to their respective rights and interests in the company immediately before the transfer (and, where necessary, further apportioned among their participators, and so on), and the amount so apportioned to the individual shall be taken to be the amount to be offset.".

1975 c. 7.

(2) Where, by virtue of section 39(5) of the Finance Act 1975, an alteration in a close company's share or loan capital or of

any rights attaching to shares in or debentures of a close company is treated as a disposition made by the participators, and— PART IV

(*a*) a person is a participator in his capacity as trustee of a settlement; and

(*b*) the disposition would, if the trustee were beneficially entitled to the settled property, be a transfer of value made by him;

subsection (3) below shall apply if at the time of the alteration an individual is beneficially entitled to an interest in possession in the whole or part of so much of the settled property as consists of shares in or securities of the close company which are not quoted on a recognised stock exchange, and subsection (4) below shall apply unless at that time an individual is beneficially entitled to an interest in possession in the whole of so much of the settled property as consists of such shares or securities.

(3) Where this subsection applies such part of the individual's interest shall be deemed for the purposes of paragraph 4 of Schedule 5 to the Finance Act 1975 to come to an end at the time of the alteration as corresponds to the relevant decrease of the value of the property in which the interest subsists, that is to say the decrease caused by the alteration. 1975 c. 7.

(4) Where this subsection applies, a capital distribution shall be deemed to be made at the time of the alteration out of so much of the settled property as—

(*a*) consists of shares in or securities of the close company which are not quoted on a recognised stock exchange; and

(*b*) is not a part in which at the time of the alteration an interest in possession subsists to which an individual is beneficially entitled;

and the amount of the capital distribution shall be taken to be the amount by which the value of the property out of which it is treated as being made is less than it would be but for the alteration, and that amount shall for the purposes of paragraphs 7 to 9 of Schedule 5 to the Finance Act 1975 be deemed to be a distribution payment made out of that property; and paragraph 6(4)(*a*) of that Schedule shall have effect, in relation to a capital distribution treated as made under this subsection as if the words " less the tax payable on it " were omitted.

(5) In paragraph 24(1)(*b*) of Schedule 5 to the Finance Act 1975 for the words " subsection (4) " there shall be substituted the words " subsections (4) and (8D) ".

(6) In section 39(2)(*a*) of the Finance Act 1975 after the words " corporation tax " there shall be inserted the words " or would fall to be so taken into account but for section 239 of the Taxes Act ".

PART IV

1975 c. 7.

(7) At the end of section 39(5) of the Finance Act 1975 there shall be added the words " and shall not be taken to have affected the value immediately before that time of the shares or debentures not so quoted ".

(8) At the end of paragraph 8 of Schedule 6 to the Finance Act 1975 there shall be added the words " but references in paragraph 2 above to transfers of value made by a transferor and to the values transferred by them (calculated as there mentioned) include references to apportionments made to a person under section 39 of this Act and the amounts for the tax on which (if charged) he would be liable ".

(9) In paragraph 9(2) of Schedule 10 to the Finance Act 1975 after the words " an increase or decrease of the value of any property so comprised " there shall be inserted the words " other than a decrease resulting from such an alteration as is mentioned in section 39(5) of this Act ".

(10) The preceding provisions of this section have effect as follows:—

(*a*) subsections (1), (5), (6) and (8) in relation to transfers of value or dispositions made after 15th April 1976; and

(*b*) subsections (2) to (4), (7) and (9) in relation to alterations made or deaths occurring after 27th May 1976.

Liability for tax in respect of transfer by spouse.

119.—(1) Section 25(8) of the Finance Act 1975 (which makes the transferor's spouse liable for tax in respect of a chargeable transfer to the extent of the value of property acquired by the spouse on another transfer made by the transferor) shall have effect as if for the reference to the value of the property (" the transferred property ") at the time of the other transfer there mentioned (" the spouse transfer ") there were substituted a reference to the market value of the property at that time or, in a case where subsection (2) below applies, to the lower market value mentioned in paragraph (*c*) of that subsection.

(2) This subsection applies where—

(*a*) the chargeable transfer is made after the spouse transfer; and

(*b*) the transferred property either remains the property of the transferor's spouse (" the transferee ") at the date of the chargeable transfer, or has before that date been sold by the transferee by a qualifying sale; and

(*c*) the market value of the transferred property on the relevant date (that is to say, the date of the chargeable transfer or, as the case may be, of the qualifying sale) is lower than its market value at the time of the spouse transfer; and (*d*) the transferred property is not tangible movable property. PART IV

(3) In this section " market value " and " qualifying sale " have the same meanings as in section 99 above; and, subject to subsection (4) below, Schedule 12 to this Act shall have effect for the purposes of this section as it has effect for the purposes of that section.

(4) In its application by virtue of subsection (3) above Schedule 12 to this Act shall have effect as if—

(*a*) references to the chargeable transfer were references to the spouse transfer; and

(*b*) references to the transferee's spouse were omitted; and

(*c*) references to section 99 above were references to this section.

Excluded property: reversionary interests.

120.—(1) In section 24(3) of the Finance Act 1975, after paragraph (*a*) there shall be inserted— 1975 c. 7.

" (*aa*) it is one to which either the settlor or his spouse is beneficially entitled; or ".

(2) This section shall be deemed to have come into force on 16th April 1976, but shall not apply in relation to a reversionary interest under a settlement made before that date.

Deeds of family arrangement etc.

121.—(1) In section 47 of the Finance Act 1975, after section (1) there shall be inserted—

" (1A) Where property comprised in a person's estate immediately before his death is settled by his will and, within the period of two years after his death and before any interest in possession has subsisted in the property, a distribution payment (within the meaning of paragraph 6 of Schedule 5 to this Act) is made out of the property or an event occurs on the happening of which a capital distribution would (apart from this subsection) be treated as so made under paragraphs 6(2) or 15(3) of that Schedule, then—

(*a*) the making of the distribution payment shall not be a capital distribution, and paragraphs 6(2) and 15(3) shall have effect on the happening of the event as if the references in them to a capital distribution were references to a distribution payment, and

(*b*) this Part of this Act shall apply as if the will had provided that on the testator's death the property should be applied or held as it is applied by the distribution payment or held after the happening of the event.

PART IV

(1B) Where a testator expresses a wish that property bequeathed by his will should be transferred by the legatee to other persons, and the legatee transfers any of the property in accordance with that wish within the period of two years after the death of the testator—

(*a*) the transfer shall not be a transfer of value, and

(*b*) this Part of this Act shall have effect as if the property transferred had been bequeathed by the will to the transferee.".

(2) Subsection (1) above applies in relation to deaths before as well as after the passing of this Act, and shall have effect in relation to a death occurring after 9th December 1972 but before 13th March 1975 as if the references to the period of two years after the death were references to the period ending with 13th March 1977.

Inheritance (Provision for Family and Dependants) Act 1975.
1975 c. 63.

122.—(1) Where an order is made under section 2 of the Inheritance (Provision for Family and Dependants) Act 1975 in relation to any property forming part of the net estate of a deceased person, then, without prejudice to section 19(1) of that Act, the property shall for the purposes of capital transfer tax be treated as if it had on his death devolved subject to the provisions of the order.

(2) Where an order is made under section 10 of the said Act of 1975 requiring a person to provide any money or other property by reason of a disposition made by the deceased, then—

(*a*) if that disposition was a chargeable transfer and the personal representatives of the deceased make a claim for the purpose—

(i) tax paid or payable on the value transferred by that chargeable transfer (whether or not by the claimants) shall be repaid to them by the Board or, as the case may be, shall not be payable ; and

(ii) the rate or rates of tax applicable to the transfer of value made by the deceased on his death shall be determined as if the values previously transferred by chargeable transfers made by him were reduced by that value ;

(*b*) the money or property shall be included in the deceased's estate for the purpose of the transfer of value made by him on his death.

(3) Where the money or other property ordered to be provided under the said section 10 is less than the maximum permitted by that section subsection (2)(*a*) above shall have effect in relation to such part of the value there mentioned as is appropriate.

(4) The adjustment in consequence of the provisions of this section or of section 19(1) of the said Act of 1975 of the tax payable in respect of the transfer of value made by the deceased on his death shall not affect— PART IV

(*a*) the amount of any deduction to be made under section 8 of that Act in respect of tax borne by the person mentioned in subsection (3) of that section ; or

(*b*) the amount of tax to which regard is to be had under section 9(2) of that Act ;

and where a person is ordered under that Act to make a payment or transfer property by reason of his holding property treated as part of the deceased's net estate under section 8 or 9 and tax borne by him is taken into account for the purposes of the order, any repayment of that tax shall be made to the personal representatives of the deceased and not to that person.

(5) Tax repaid under paragraph (*a*)(i) of subsection (2) above shall be included in the deceased's estate for the purposes of the transfer of value made by him on his death ; and tax repaid under that paragraph or under subsection (4) above shall form part of the deceased's net estate for the purposes of the said Act of 1975.

(6) A distribution payment made in compliance with an order under the said Act of 1975 shall not be a capital distribution ; and where an order under that Act provides for property to be settled or for the variation of a settlement and, apart from this subsection—

(*a*) tax would be charged under paragraph 4(2) of Schedule 5 to the Finance Act 1975 on the coming into force of the order ; or 1975 c. 7.

(*b*) a capital distribution would be treated as made on that occasion under any other provision of the said Schedule 5,

the said paragraph 4(2) shall not apply and any such provision as is mentioned in paragraph (*b*) above shall apply as if it referred to a distribution payment instead of a capital distribution.

(7) In subsections (2)(*a*) and (5) above " tax " includes interest on tax.

(8) Tax overpaid or underpaid in consequence of subsection (1) above or of the said section 19(1) shall not carry interest for any period before the order there mentioned is made ; and tax repayable on a claim under subsection (2) above shall carry interest (which shall not constitute income for any tax purposes) at the rate for the time being applicable under paragraph 19(1)(ii) of Schedule 4 to the Finance Act 1975 from the date on which the claim is made.

PART IV

(9) This section applies in relation to deaths after 6th April 1976.

Legitim.

123.—(1) Where a testator dies leaving a surviving spouse and a person under the age of 18 entitled to claim legitim, and provision is made in his will or other testamentary document for a disposition to his spouse which, if it could take effect, would leave insufficient property in the estate to satisfy the entitlement of that person in respect of legitim, the following provisions of this section shall apply.

(2) Subject to subsections (3) and (4) below, tax shall be charged at the testator's death as if the disposition to the spouse did not include any amount in respect of legitim, but if within the period mentioned in subsection (8) below the person or persons concerned renounce their claim to legitim, tax shall be repaid to the estate calculated on the basis that the disposition to the spouse did include the amount renounced, and the tax to be repaid shall carry interest at the rate for the time being set out in paragraph 19(1)(*c*)(i) of Schedule 4 to the Finance Act 1975 from the date on which the tax was paid.

1975 c. 7.

(3) The executors or judicial factor of the testator may, in accordance with the provisions of this section, elect that subsection (2) above shall not apply but that subsection (4) below shall apply.

(4) Tax shall be charged at the testator's death as if the disposition to the spouse had taken effect, but where the person or persons concerned claim legitim within the period mentioned in subsection (8) below, tax shall be charged on the amount so claimed calculated on the basis that the legitim fund had been paid out in full at the testator's death (excluding any part of the fund renounced before any claim has been made) and the tax chargeable thereon had been apportioned rateably among the persons entitled to claim legitim (excluding any who have renounced as aforesaid) and the amount of tax charged shall carry interest at the rate mentioned in subsection (2) above as if paragraph 19(1)(*b*) of Schedule 4 to the Finance Act 1975 had applied.

1894 c. 30.

(5) Section 8(3) and (4) of the Finance Act 1894 and section 25(5)(*a*) of the Finance Act 1975 shall not apply in relation to tax charged by virtue of subsection (4) above but the person liable in respect of that tax shall be the person who claims legitim and any person mentioned in section 25(5)(*c*) of that Act, and section 27(1) of that Act shall apply in relation to the person who claims legitim as it applies in relation to the personal representatives of a deceased person.

(6) Where within the period mentioned in subsection (8) below a person renounces his claim to legitim, that shall not be a transfer of value. **Part IV**

(7) Where the executors or judicial factor of the testator decide to make an election under subsection (3) above they shall give notice in writing of that election to the Board within two years from the date of death of the testator or such longer period as the Board may permit.

(8) For the purposes of subsections (2) and (4) above, a person shall be treated as having claimed legitim unless he has renounced his claim before attaining the age of 18 or he renounces his claim within two years of his attaining that age or such longer period as the Board may permit.

(9) Where a person dies before attaining the age of 18 or before making a renunciation under subsection (8) above the provisions of this section shall apply in relation to that person's executors or judicial factor as they would have applied in relation to that person if that person had attained the age of 18 with the substitution of the date of death of that person for the date on which a person attained that age, but where the executors or factor renounce a claim to legitim in respect of a person the amount renounced shall not be treated as part of that person's estate.

(10) Where subsection (2) above applies in relation to any estate, then notwithstanding anything in paragraph 24 of Schedule 4 to the Finance Act 1975 the Board may repay tax under that subsection without limit of time. 1975 c. 7.

(11) Where subsection (4) above applies in relation to any estate, then notwithstanding anything in section 11 of the Finance Act 1894 or paragraph 25 of Schedule 4 to the Finance Act 1975 a certificate of discharge may be given under the said section 11 or the said paragraph 25 in respect of the whole estate, and notwithstanding anything in section 8(7) of the Finance Act 1894 or paragraph 23 of Schedule 4 to the Finance Act 1975 the giving of the certificate shall not preclude the Board from claiming tax under subsection (4) above without limit of time. 1894 c. 30.

(12) In the case of a testator who died before 13th March 1975, any reference in this section to tax includes a reference to estate duty.

(13) This section has effect in relation to the estate of any testator who died after 12th November 1974 and extends to Scotland only.

PART IV

Acceptance of property in satisfaction of tax.
1975 c. 7.

124. In Schedule 4 to the Finance Act 1975, in paragraph 17(4), for paragraphs (*a*) and (*b*) there shall be substituted—

"(*a*) any picture, print, book, manuscript, work of art, scientific object or other thing which the Treasury are satisfied is pre-eminent for its national, scientific, historic or artistic interest;".

Double taxation relief.

125.—(1) For paragraph 8 of Schedule 7 to the Finance Act 1975 (unilateral double taxation relief) there shall be substituted—

"8.—(1) Where the Board are satisfied that in any territory outside the United Kingdom (an "overseas territory") any amount of tax imposed by reason of any disposition or other event is attributable to the value of any property, then, if—

(*a*) that tax is of a character similar to that of capital transfer tax or is chargeable on or by reference to death or gifts inter vivos; and

(*b*) any capital transfer tax chargeable by reference to the same disposition or other event is also attributable to the value of that property,

they shall allow a credit in respect of that amount ("the overseas tax") against that capital transfer tax in accordance with the following provisions.

(2) Where the property is situated in the overseas territory and not in the United Kingdom, the credit shall be of an amount equal to the overseas tax.

(3) Where the property—

(*a*) is situated neither in the United Kingdom nor in the overseas territory; or

(*b*) is situated both in the United Kingdom and in the overseas territory,

the credit shall be of an amount calculated in accordance with the following formula—

$$\frac{A}{A + B} \times C$$

where A is the amount of the capital transfer tax, B is the overseas tax and C is whichever of A and B is the smaller.

(4) Where tax is imposed in two or more overseas territories in respect of property which—

(*a*) is situated neither in the United Kingdom nor in any of those territories; or

(*b*) is situated both in the United Kingdom and in each of those territories, sub-paragraph (3) above shall apply as if, in the formula there set out, B were the aggregate of the overseas tax imposed in each of those territories and C were the aggregate of all, except the largest, of A and the overseas tax imposed in each of them.

(5) Where credit is allowed under sub-paragraph (2) above or paragraph 7 above in respect of overseas tax imposed in one overseas territory, any credit under sub-paragraph (3) above in respect of overseas tax imposed in another shall be calculated as if the capital transfer tax were reduced by the credit allowed under sub-paragraph (2) or paragraph 7; and where, in the case of any overseas territory mentioned in sub-paragraph (3) or (4) above, credit is allowed against the overseas tax for tax charged in a territory in which the property is situated, the overseas tax shall be treated for the purposes of those paragraphs as reduced by the credit.

(6) In this paragraph references to tax imposed in an overseas territory are references to tax chargeable under the law of that territory and paid by the person liable to pay it.

(7) Where relief can be given both under this paragraph and paragraph 7 above, relief shall be given under whichever paragraph provides the greater relief."

(2) This section has effect in relation to dispositions and other events after 6th April 1976.

PART V

MISCELLANEOUS AND SUPPLEMENTARY

Stamp duty: exemption for transfers of loan capital.

126.—(1) Subject to subsections (2) and (3) below, stamp duty shall not be chargeable on any transfer of loan capital.

(2) Subsection (1) above does not apply to loan capital which, at the time when it is transferred, carries a right (exercisable then or later) of conversion into shares or other securities or to the acquisition of shares or other securities, including loan capital of the same description.

(3) Subsection (1) above does not apply to loan capital which, at the time when it is transferred or at any earlier time, carries or has carried—

(*a*) a right to interest the amount of which—

(i) exceeds a reasonable commercial return on the nominal amount of the capital; or

PART V

(ii) falls or has fallen to be determined to any extent by reference to the results of, or of any part of, a business or to the value of any property; or

(*b*) a right on repayment to an amount which exceeds the nominal amount of the capital and is not reasonably comparable with what is generally repayable (in respect of a similar nominal amount of capital) under the terms of issue of loan capital listed in the Official List of The Stock Exchange.

1891 c. 39. 1939 c. 41. 1971 c. 68. 1972/1100 (N.I.).

(4) Section 115 of the Stamp Act 1891, section 37 of the Finance Act 1939, section 65 of the Finance Act 1971 and Article 11 of the Finance (Northern Ireland) Order 1972 (composition for stamp duty on transfers of loan capital etc.) shall cease to have effect.

(5) In this section " loan capital " means—

(*a*) any debenture stock, corporation stock or funded debt (by whatever name known) issued by any body corporate or other body of persons formed or established in the United Kingdom or any capital raised by any such body, being capital which is borrowed, or has the character of borrowed money, whether it is in the form of stock or any other form; and

(*b*) stock or marketable securities issued by the government of any country or territory within the commonwealth outside the United Kingdom.

(6) This section shall be construed as one with the said Act of 1891.

(7) This section shall be deemed to have come into force on 17th May 1976.

Stamp duty: stock exchange transfers.

127.—(1) Stamp duty shall not be chargeable on any transfer to a stock exchange nominee which is executed for the purposes of a stock exchange transaction.

(2) A transfer otherwise than on sale from a stock exchange nominee to a jobber or his nominee shall be regarded for the purposes of stamp duty as a transfer on sale for a consideration equal to the value of the stock or marketable securities thereby transferred.

1920 c. 18.

(3) For the purposes of section 42 of the Finance Act 1920 (jobbers' transfers) a transfer by a jobber or his nominee to a stock exchange nominee shall be regarded as a transfer to a bona fide purchaser.

Part V

(4) In section 33(1) of the Finance Act 1970 (composition by Stock Exchange in respect of transfer duty) after the words " the heading " Conveyance or Transfer on Sale " " there shall be inserted the words " or " Conveyance or Transfer of any kind not hereinbefore described " " and the words " being instruments executed for the purposes of stock exchange transactions as defined in section 4(1) of the Stock Transfer Act 1963 " shall be omitted. 1970 c. 24.

(5) This section shall be construed as one with the Stamp Act 1891 and in this section— 1891 c. 39.

" jobber " means a member of The Stock Exchange who is recognised by the Council thereof as carrying on the business of a jobber and carries on that business in the United Kingdom ;

" stock exchange nominee " means any person designated for the purposes of this section as a nominee of The Stock Exchange by an order made by the Secretary of State ;

" stock exchange transaction " has the meaning given in section 4 of the Stock Transfer Act 1963. 1963 c. 18.

(6) The power to make an order under subsection (5) above shall be exercisable by statutory instrument and includes power to vary or revoke a previous order.

(7) Section 33 of the Finance Act 1970 shall extend to Northern Ireland ; and in the application of that section and this section to Northern Ireland for any reference to the Stock Transfer Act 1963 there shall be substituted a reference to the Stock Transfer Act (Northern Ireland) 1963. 1963 c. 24 (N.I.).

Stamp duty: chargeable transactions in respect of capital companies. 1973 c. 51. 1973/1323 (N.I.).

128. In paragraph 10 of Schedule 19 to the Finance Act 1973 and paragraph 10 of Schedule 2 to the Finance (Miscellaneous Provisions) (Northern Ireland) Order 1973 (exemption from duty in cases of mergers etc.) after sub-paragraph (5) there shall be inserted—

" (6) This paragraph applies also where the acquired company is a corporation or body of persons which is not a capital company for the purposes of this Schedule but which is treated as such in another member State ; and paragraph 3(1) above shall apply for the interpretation of this sub-paragraph as it applies for the interpretation of paragraph 1 above."

Development gains. 1974 c. 30.

129.—(1) Section 39 of the Finance Act 1974 (exemption or relief for small disposals) shall have effect, and be deemed always to have had effect, with the following amendments.

PART V

(2) For subsections (1) to (3) there shall be substituted—

" (1) Where the amount of chargeable gains that would, apart from this subsection, be a person's development gains for any chargeable period does not exceed—

(*a*) in the case of an individual or the personal representatives of a deceased person as such, £10,000; or

(*b*) in the case of a company or the trustees of a settlement, £1,000,

no part of those chargeable gains shall be development gains; and where that amount exceeds the limit applicable to that person under paragraph (*a*) or (*b*) above only so much of that amount as exceeds the limit shall be development gains.

(2) For the purposes of this section a man and his wife living with him shall be treated as one individual."

(3) In subsection (4)(*c*) for the words " subsections (1) and (2) above " there shall be substituted the words " subsection (1) above."

(4) Subsection (5) shall be omitted.

Petroleum revenue tax.
1975 c. 22.

130.—(1) Schedule 2 to the Oil Taxation Act 1975 (management and collection) shall be amended as follows.

(2) In paragraph 12(1), after paragraph (*c*) there shall be inserted " or

(*d*) that for any chargeable period they ought to have made an assessment to tax instead of a determination of loss or a determination of loss instead of an assessment to tax ; "

and for the words " adjustments in assessments or determinations " there shall be substituted the words " assessments or determinations or amendments of assessments or determinations ".

(3) After paragraph 12(2) there shall be inserted—

" (3) Where under this paragraph the Board make an assessment or determination or amend an assessment or determination they shall give notice thereof to the participator concerned; and sub-paragraphs (4), (5) and (6) of paragraph 10 above shall apply in relation to any such assessment, determination or amendment as they apply in relation to an assessment or determination under that paragraph."

PART V

(4) In paragraph 14(1) after the words " an assessment or determination " there shall be inserted the words " or an amendment of an assessment or determination " and at the end there shall be inserted the words " or of the notice of the amendment ".

(5) In paragraph 14(9), in paragraph (*a*), for the words " or determination " there shall be substituted the words " , determination or amendment " and for the words from " on the adjustments " onwards there shall be substituted the words " on how the assessment, determination, amendment or decision should be varied or on what assessment or determination should be substituted in relation to the chargeable period in question, the same consequences shall ensue as if the Commissioners had determined the appeal to that effect."

(6) For paragraph 14(10) there shall be substituted—

" (10) If, on the appeal, it appears to a majority of the Commissioners present at the hearing that the assessment, determination or amendment is wrong—

(*a*) because no, or a smaller, assessable profit or a, or a larger, allowable loss has accrued for the chargeable period in question ; or

(*b*) because a, or a larger, assessable profit or no, or a smaller, allowable loss has accrued for that period,

the Commissioners shall vary the assessment, determination or amendment in such manner, or substitute such assessment or determination, as may be required ; and it shall be for the participator to satisfy the Commissioners as to any matter within paragraph (*a*) above."

(7) In paragraph 14(11) for the words " the determination of the Special Commissioners in any proceedings " there shall be substituted the words " the determination by the Special Commissioners of any appeal ".

Inter-American Development Bank.

131.—(1) The following provisions of this section shall have effect on the United Kingdom's becoming a member of the Inter-American Development Bank (" the Bank ").

(2) A person not resident in the United Kingdom shall not be liable to income tax in respect of income from any security issued by the Bank if he would not be liable but for the fact that—

(*a*) the security or income is issued, made payable or paid in the United Kingdom or in sterling ; or

(*b*) the Bank maintains an office or other place of business in the United Kingdom ;

and such a security shall be taken for the purposes of capital transfer tax and capital gains tax to be situated outside the United Kingdom.

PART V

1891 c. 39. (3) No stamp duty shall be chargeable under the heading " Bearer Instrument " in Schedule 1 to the Stamp Act 1891 on the issue of any instrument by the Bank or on the transfer of the stock constituted by, or transferable by means of, any instrument issued by the Bank.

Citation, interpretation, construction and repeals.

132.—(1) This Act may be cited as the Finance Act 1976.

1970 c. 10. (2) In this Act " the Taxes Act " means the Income and Corporation Taxes Act 1970.

(3) In this Act—

1952 c. 44. (*a*) Part I (except sections 11 to 14) shall be construed as one with the Customs and Excise Act 1952 ;

1972 c. 41. (*b*) Part II shall be construed as one with Part I of the Finance Act 1972 ;

1965 c. 25. (*c*) Part III, so far as it relates to income tax, shall be construed as one with the Income Tax Acts, so far as it relates to corporation tax shall be construed as one with the Corporation Tax Acts and, so far as it relates to capital gains tax, shall be construed as one with Part III of the Finance Act 1965 ;

1975 c. 7. (*d*) Part IV shall be construed as one with Part III of the Finance Act 1975.

(4) Except so far as the context otherwise requires, any reference in this Act to any enactment shall be construed as a reference to that enactment as amended, and as including a reference to that enactment as applied, by or under any other enactment, including this Act.

(5) The enactments mentioned in Schedule 15 to this Act (which include spent enactments) are hereby repealed to the extent specified in the third column of that Schedule, but subject to any provision at the end of any Part of that Schedule.

SCHEDULES

SCHEDULE 1

Section 1(3).

WINE: RATES OF DUTY

Description of wine (in strengths measured by reference to the following percentages of alcohol by volume at a temperature of 20° C.)	Rates of duty (per gallon)
	£
Wine of an alcoholic strength—	
not exceeding 15 per cent.	2·9550
exceeding 15 but not exceeding 18 per cent. ...	3·4100
exceeding 18 but not exceeding 22 per cent. ...	4·0150
exceeding 22 per cent.	4·0150 plus £0·4300 for every 1 per cent. or part of 1 per cent. in excess of 22 per cent.;
	each of the above rates of duty being, in the case of sparkling wine, increased by £0·6500 per gallon.

SCHEDULE 2

Section 1(4).

MADE-WINE: RATES OF DUTY

Description of made-wine (in strengths measured by reference to the following percentages of alcohol by volume at a temperature of 20° C.)	Rates of duty (per gallon)
	£
Made-wine of an alcoholic strength—	
not exceeding 10 per cent.	1·9200
exceeding 10 but not exceeding 15 per cent. ...	2·8750
exceeding 15 but not exceeding 18 per cent. ...	3·1600
exceeding 18 per cent.	3·1600 plus £0·4300 for every 1 per cent. or part of 1 per cent. in excess of 18 per cent.;
	each of the above rates of duty being, in the case of sparkling made-wine, increased by £0·3000 per gallon.

Section 2(7).

SCHEDULE 3

Cider: Consequential Amendments

1952 c. 44.

The Customs and Excise Act 1952

1. In section 172(6) of the Customs and Excise Act 1952 for the words " wine or made-wine ", in both places, there shall be substituted the words " wine, made-wine or cider ".

2. In section 248(2) of that Act for the words " or producer of wine or made-wine " there shall be substituted the words " producer of wine or made-wine or maker of cider ".

3. In section 249(5) of that Act for the words " and producers of wine or made-wine " there shall be substituted the words " producers of wine or made-wine and makers of cider ".

4. In section 253(3) of that Act for the words " or licensed producer of wine or made-wine " there shall be substituted the words " licensed producer of wine or made-wine or registered maker of cider ".

5. In section 263(4) of that Act—

(*a*) for the words " wine or made-wine ", wherever they occur, there shall be substituted the words " wine, made-wine or cider " ;

(*b*) for the words " or, as the case may be, licensed producer of wine or of made-wine " there shall be substituted the words " licensed producer of wine or made-wine or registered maker of cider, as the case may be " ;

(*c*) for the words " or producer " there shall be substituted the words " producer or maker ".

6. In section 295(2) of that Act for the words " or producer of wine or of made-wine " there shall be substituted the words " producer of wine or of made-wine or maker of cider ".

7. In section 307 of that Act—

(*a*) for the definition of " cider " there shall be substituted the definition in section 2(8) of this Act ;

(*b*) in the definition of " made-wine " for the words " non-excisable cider " there shall be substituted the word " cider " ;

(*c*) the definition of " non-excisable cider " shall be omitted.

1964 c. 49.

The Finance Act 1964

8. In section 8(2)(*b*) of the Finance Act 1964 for the words " and made-wine " there shall be substituted the words " made-wine and cider ".

The Finance (*No.* 2) *Act* 1975 Sch. 3

9. In section 15 of the Finance (No. 2) Act 1975— 1975 c. 45.

(*a*) in subsection (4)(*b*) for the words " non-excisable cider " there shall be substituted the word " cider " ;

(*b*) in subsection (6), in the definition of " made-wine " for the words " non-excisable cider " there shall be substituted the word " cider " and the definition of " non-excisable cider " shall be omitted.

SCHEDULE 4

Section 34.

Life Policies, Etc.

Preliminary

1. In this Schedule references to any sections not otherwise identified are to sections of the Taxes Act and " Schedule 1 " means Schedule 1 to that Act.

Short-term assurances

2. A policy which secures a capital sum payable only on death or payable either on death or on earlier disability shall not be a qualifying policy within the meaning of Schedule 1 if the capital sum is payable only if the event in question happens before the expiry of a specified term ending less than one year after the making of the insurance.

Relief by deduction from premiums

3.—(1) In section 19(1) for the words " if the claimant " to the end there shall be substituted the words " an individual who pays any such premium as is specified in subsection (2) below shall (without making any claim) be entitled to relief under this section, and Schedule 4 to the Finance Act 1976 shall apply with respect to that relief."

(2) In section 19(2)—

(*a*) for the words from " by the claimant " to " (ii) with underwriters " there shall be substituted the words " by an individual under a policy of insurance or contract for a deferred annuity, where—

(*a*) the payments are made to—

(i) any insurance company legally established in the United Kingdom or any branch in the United Kingdom of an insurance company lawfully carrying on in the United Kingdom life assurance business (as defined in section 323(2) of this Act) ; or

(ii) underwriters ; "

(*b*) in sub-paragraphs (iii) and (iv) of paragraph (*a*) the word " with " shall be omitted ;

SCH. 4

(*c*) in paragraph (*b*) for the word " claimant " there shall be substituted the word " individual " ; and

(*d*) at the end of paragraph (*c*) there shall be added the words " or his spouse ".

4.—(1) Relief under section 19 in respect of any premiums paid by an individual in a year of assessment shall be given by making good to the person to whom they are paid any deficiency arising from the deductions authorised under paragraph 5 below.

(2) Where the individual is not resident in the United Kingdom but is entitled to relief by virtue of subsection (2) of section 27, sub-paragraph (1) above shall not apply but (subject to the proviso to that subsection) the like relief shall be given to him under paragraph 15 below.

5. Subject to the following provisions of this Schedule,—

(*a*) an individual resident in the United Kingdom who is entitled to relief under section 19 in respect of any premium may deduct from any payment in respect of the premium and retain an amount equal to 17½ per cent. thereof ; and

(*b*) the person to whom the payment is made shall accept the amount paid after the deduction in discharge of the individual's liability to the same extent as if the deduction had not been made and may recover the deficiency from the Board.

Limit on deductions authorised under paragraph 5

6.—(1) Where the premiums payable in any year in respect of any policy or contract exceed £1,500 the percentage mentioned in paragraph 5(*a*) above is a percentage of such part only of any payment as bears to the whole thereof the same proportion as £1,500 bears to the total amount of the premiums so payable ; but without prejudice to the operation of paragraph 15 below in any case where by virtue of this paragraph the relief given under section 19 is reduced below the limit specified in section 21.

(2) In this paragraph " year " means the twelve months beginning with the making of the assurance or contract and any subsequent period of twelve months.

Husband and wife

7. Subsection (7) of section 19 shall be omitted.

8. The references in section 19 to an individual's spouse shall include any person who was that individual's spouse at the time the insurance or contract was made, unless the marriage was dissolved before 6th April 1979.

1971 c. 68.

9. Where an election under section 23 of the Finance Act 1971 is in force, the relief to which either the husband or the wife is entitled under section 19 in respect of an insurance or contract on the life of the other or made by the other shall not be affected by paragraph 3 of Schedule 4 to that Act (which requires relief to be determined as if the husband and the wife were not married).

10. Where, throughout a year of assessment, a woman is a married woman living with her husband, then— SCH. 4

(*a*) if no election under section 38 is in force, section 21 and paragraph 15 below shall apply as if any relief to which the wife is entitled under section 19 were relief to which the husband is entitled ; and

(*b*) if an election under section 38 is in force, section 21 and paragraph 15 below shall apply separately to the amounts paid by each of them, but as if for the limit specified in section 21 there were substituted, in relation to each of them, a limit of £750 or one-twelfth of their total income, whichever is the greater, plus any amount by which the payments in respect of which relief can be given to the other fall short of the limit so substituted.

Industrial assurance policies

11.—(1) This paragraph applies to—

(*a*) a policy issued in the course of an industrial assurance business as defined in section 1(2) of the Industrial Assurance Act 1923 or the Industrial Assurance Act (Northern Ireland) 1924 ; and 1923 c. 8. 1924 c. 21 (N.I.).

(*b*) a policy issued by a registered friendly society in the course of tax exempt life or endowment business (as defined in section 337(3)).

(2) If a policy to which this paragraph applies was issued before the passing of this Act section 19 shall have effect in relation to it as if subsections (2)(*b*), (3) and (4) were omitted ; and if a policy to which this paragraph applies was issued after the passing of this Act, paragraph (*b*) of section 19(2) shall have effect in relation to it as if it permitted the insurance to be on the life of the individual's parent or grandparent or, subject to sub-paragraph (3) below, on the life of the individual's child or grandchild.

(3) Relief may be given in respect of premiums under a policy of insurance on the life of an individual's child or grandchild which is issued after the passing of this Act as if paragraph (*b*) of section 19(3) were omitted, but may be given only if the annual amount of the premiums, together with that of any relevant premiums, does not exceed £52 ; and for this purpose a relevant premium, in relation to an insurance made at any time on the life of an individual's child or grandchild, is any premium under a policy of insurance on the same life, where the insurance is made at the same time or earlier, whether it is made by the individual or any other person.

(4) In this paragraph " child " has the same meaning as in section 10 and " grandchild ", " parent " and " grandparent " have corresponding meanings.

12. In paragraph 4(1) of Schedule 1, sub-paragraph (iii) of paragraph (*d*) shall be omitted, together with the " and " preceding it, and after paragraph (*d*) there shall be inserted the words " or if the policy was issued before 6th April 1976, or was issued before 6th April 1979 and is in substantially the same form as policies so issued before 6th April 1976.".

SCH. 4

Premiums payable to friendly societies and industrial assurance companies

13.—(1) Where a policy is issued by a registered friendly society or a policy to which paragraph 11 above applies is issued by an industrial assurance company, paragraphs 4 and 5 above shall apply in relation to premiums payable under the policy subject to the following modifications.

(2) References to the deductions authorised under paragraph 5 shall be construed as including references to any amount retained by or refunded to the person paying the premium under any scheme made by the society or company in accordance with regulations made under this paragraph.

(3) The appropriate authority may make regulations authorising—

(*a*) the adoption by registered friendly societies and industrial assurance companies of any prescribed scheme for securing that in the case of policies or contracts to which the scheme applies amounts equal to 17½ per cent. of the premiums payable are retained by or refunded to the person paying the premiums or that, in the case of such policies or contracts issued or made before 6th April 1979, the amounts expressed as the amounts of the premiums payable are treated as amounts arrived at by deducting 17½ per cent. from the amounts payable and that the amounts of the capital sums assured or guaranteed are treated as correspondingly increased ; or

(*b*) the adoption by any such society or company of any special scheme for that purpose which may, in such circumstances as may be prescribed, be approved by the appropriate authority.

(4) Increases treated as made in pursuance of regulations under this paragraph shall not be treated as variations of a policy or contract and shall be disregarded for the purposes of section 332 of and paragraph 4 of Schedule 1 to the Taxes Act and section 7(6)
1975 c. 7. of the Finance Act 1975 ; and the regulations may include such adaptations and modifications of the enactments relating to friendly societies or industrial assurance companies and such other incidental and supplementary provisions as appear to the appropriate authority necessary or expedient for the purpose of enabling such societies or companies to adopt the schemes authorised by the regulations.

1969 c. 19. (5) Subsections (4), (5) and (7) to (11) of section 6 of the Decimal Currency Act 1969 shall, with the necessary modifications, apply in relation to regulations made under this paragraph.

Supplementary provisions as to relief under section 19

14. Where it appears to the Board that the relief (if any) to which a person is entitled under section 19 has been exceeded or might be exceeded unless the premiums payable by him under any policy were paid in full, they may by notice in writing to that person and to the person to whom the payments are made exclude the application

of paragraph 5 above in relation to any payments due or made after such date as may be specified in the notice and before such date as may be specified in a further notice in writing to those persons. SCH. 4

15.—(1) Where in any year of assessment the relief to which a person is entitled under section 19 has not been fully given in accordance with the preceding provisions of this Schedule, he may claim relief for the difference, and relief for the difference shall then be given by a payment made by the Board or by discharge or repayment of tax or partly in one such manner and partly in another; and where the relief given to any person in accordance with the preceding provisions of this Schedule exceeds that to which he is entitled under section 19, he shall be liable to make good the excess and an inspector may make such assessments as may in his judgment be required for recovering the excess.

(2) The Taxes Management Act 1970 shall apply to any assessment under this paragraph as if it were an assessment to tax for the year of assessment in which the relief was given and as if— 1970 c. 9.

(*a*) the assessment were among those specified in sections 55(1) (recovery of tax not postponed) and 86(2) (interest on overdue tax) of that Act; and

(*b*) the sum charged by the assessment were tax specified in paragraph 3 of the Table in section 86(4) of that Act (reckonable date).

16.—(1) The Board may make regulations for carrying the preceding provisions of this Schedule into effect.

(2) Without prejudice to the generality of sub-paragraph (1) above, regulations under this paragraph may provide—

(*a*) for the manner in which claims for the recovery of any sum under paragraph 5(*b*) above may be made;

(*b*) for the furnishing of such information by persons by or to whom premiums are payable as appears to the Board necessary for deciding such claims and for exercising their powers under paragraph 14 or paragraph 15 above; and

(*c*) for requiring persons to whom premiums are paid to make available for inspection by an officer authorised by the Board such books and other documents in their possession or under their control as may reasonably be required for the purpose of determining whether any information given by those persons for the purposes of this Schedule is correct and complete.

(3) In section 98 of the Taxes Management Act 1970 (penalty for failure to furnish information etc.) the following shall be added in the second column of the Table:

" Regulations under paragraph 16 of Schedule 4 to the Finance Act 1976 ".

(4) The following provisions of the Taxes Management Act 1970, that is to say—

(*a*) section 29(3)(*c*) (excessive relief);

SCH. 4

(*b*) section 30 (recovery of tax repaid in consequence of fraud or negligence);

(*c*) section 88 (interest); and

(*d*) section 95 (incorrect return or accounts);

shall apply in relation to the payment of a sum claimed under paragraph 5(*b*) above to which the claimant was not entitled as if it had been income tax repaid as a relief which was not due.

1970 c. 9.

17. A notice given to a person under section 8 of the Taxes Management Act 1970 may require him to include in the return of his income particulars of premiums paid by him or his wife living with him under policies of life insurance or contracts for deferred annuities and of deductions made from the premiums payable.

Consequential amendments

18.—(1) In section 5 after the words " who makes a claim in that behalf " there shall be inserted the words " (or, in the case of relief under section 19 below, who satisfies the conditions of that section) ".

(2) In section 25(2) the words " section 19 or " shall be omitted.

(3) The proviso to section 27(2) shall have effect as if the amount of any relief to which an individual is entitled under section 19 were an amount by which his liability to income tax is reduced.

(4) In section 39(1)(*c*) the words " 19 or " shall be omitted.

1975 c. 7.

19.—(1) In section 7(5) of the Finance Act 1975 for the words " the basic rate of income tax in force " there shall be substituted the words " the percentage found by doubling that mentioned in paragraph 5(*a*) of Schedule 4 to the Finance Act 1976 as in force ".

(2) In section 8(2) of the Finance Act 1975 for the words " one half of the basic rate of income tax in force " there shall be substituted the words " that mentioned in paragraph 5(*a*) of Schedule 4 to the Finance Act 1976 as in force ".

(3) In paragraph (*b*) of section 9(4) of the Finance Act 1975 for the words from " income tax " where they first occur to " liability " there shall be substituted " section 19 of the Taxes Act as a sum paid by that person in satisfaction of his liability " and in the words following the paragraph the words " increase in " shall be omitted.

(4) In paragraph 7(1) of Schedule 2 to the Finance Act 1975 there shall be substituted—

(*a*) for the words " the conditions of paragraphs (a) and (*d*)(iii) of that sub-paragraph are satisfied " the words " the condition of paragraph (*a*) of that sub-paragraph is satisfied ";

(*b*) for the words " they are not " the words " it is not "; and

(*c*) for the words " those conditions " the words " that condition ".

20. In section 20 the following shall be omitted:—

(*a*) in subsection (1), paragraph (*a*) and the words " on the amount of the premium paid by him or ";

(*b*) subsection (2);

(*c*) in subsection (4), the words " premiums or other ";

(*d*) in subsection (5), the words " premiums or " and the proviso; and

(*e*) subsection (6).

21.—(1) Section 21 shall be amended as follows.

(2) In subsection (1) for the words " sections 19 and 20 " there shall be substituted the words " section 19 " and for the words " one-sixth of that person's total income " there shall be substituted the words " £1,500 in any year of assessment or one-sixth of that person's total income, whichever is the greater ".

(3) Subsection (1A) shall be omitted.

(4) In subsection (3) for the words " the said sections " there shall be substituted the words " sections 19 and 20 above ".

(5) In subsection (4) for the words " one-half of the basic rate " there shall be substituted " 17½ per cent." and the words " premiums or " in paragraph (*b*) and the words following that paragraph shall be omitted.

SCHEDULE 5

Section 37.

Relief for Increase in Value of Trading Stock and Work in Progress

Part I

Income Tax

Entitlement to relief

1.—(1) Where a person carries on a trade in respect of which he is within the charge to income tax under Case I of Schedule D and—

(*a*) the value of his trading stock at the end of a period of account (the " closing stock value ") exceeds

(*b*) the value of his trading stock at the beginning of that period (the " opening stock value "),

he shall, subject to the provisions of this Schedule, be entitled to relief under this paragraph by reference to the amount of that excess (the " increase in stock value ").

(2) The amount of relief to which a person is entitled under this paragraph for any trade in respect of any period of account is the amount of the increase in stock value in that period less 15% of the relevant income of that trade for that period.

(3) A person shall not be entitled to relief under this paragraph in respect of any period of account unless a claim for the relief is made within two years after the end of the year of assessment in which that period of account ends.

SCH. 5

Charge by way of recovery of relief

2.—(1) Where a person carries on a trade in respect of which he is within the charge to income tax under Case I of Schedule D and in a period of account his closing stock value is less than his opening stock value, then, subject to the provisions of this Schedule, a charge by way of recovery of relief shall be made on him, on whichever is the lesser of—

(*a*) the whole amount of the reduction in stock value in that period ; or

(*b*) the amount of unrecovered past relief allowed to him for that trade.

(2) Where during or at the end of a period of account a person carrying on a trade ceases to do so, or ceases to be within the charge to income tax under Case I of Schedule D in respect of the trade, he is not entitled to relief or liable to a charge in respect of that period under the foregoing provisions of this Part, but a final charge by way of recovery of relief shall be made on him on an amount equal to the unrecovered past relief allowed to him for that trade.

This sub-paragraph is subject to paragraphs 20 and 21 below (which provide for continuity in the case of certain successions).

(3) Where during or at the end of a period of account a person carrying on a trade ceases (by virtue of ceasing to be resident in the United Kingdom) to be within the charge to income tax under Case I of Schedule D in respect of a part of the trade, he shall be treated for the purposes of this Schedule as if that part were a separate trade carried on by him in that period ; and all necessary apportionments between the two parts of the trade (including the apportionment of unrecovered past relief allowed for that trade) shall be made by reference to the respective values of the trading stock of each part immediately after that event.

Method of giving effect to relief or charge

3.—(1) Relief under paragraph 1 above in respect of any period of account shall be given as a deduction in charging the profits or gains of the trade to income tax for the relevant year of assessment.

The relief shall be deducted before any deduction is made for capital allowances.

(2) A charge under paragraph 2 above in respect of any period of account shall be made by means of an assessment to income tax on the profits or gains of the trade—

(*a*) in the case of a charge under paragraph 2(1), for the relevant year of assessment ; and

(*b*) in the case of a charge under paragraph 2(2) for the year of assessment in which the discontinuance or other event takes place.

Any such assessment is in addition to any other assessment falling to be made on the profits or gains of the trade for the year of assessment in question.

Top-slicing

4.—(1) Where a trade has been carried on by a person for more than one year before the discontinuance or other event on which a charge under paragraph 2(2) above falls to be made on him, then his liability to tax for the year of assessment for which the charge is made shall, on a claim made by him within two years of the end of that year of assessment, be reduced in accordance with the following provisions of this paragraph.

(2) The reduction is the amount of the difference between—

(*a*) the tax on the whole amount on which the charge is made (the " chargeable amount "), calculated on the basis set out in sub-paragraph (4) below ; and

(*b*) the tax (if any) on the appropriate fraction of the chargeable amount, calculated on the same basis, and multiplied by the reciprocal of the appropriate fraction.

(3) The " appropriate fraction " depends on the period for which the trade has been carried on before the discontinuance or other event and is—

(*a*) one-half if the trade has been so carried on for more than one but less than two years ;

(*b*) one-third if it has been so carried on for two years or more.

(4) The amounts of tax referred to in sub-paragraph (2) are to be calculated on the following assumptions—

(*a*) that the person's total income does not include any amount in respect of which he is chargeable to tax under section 80, 81 or 82 of the Taxes Act (premiums, etc. treated as rent), section 187 of that Act (payments on retirement or removal from office) or section 399(1)(*a*) of that Act (gains from life policies, etc) ;

(*b*) that deductions to be made in computing the tax are so far as possible set against sums other than the chargeable amount (or the fraction of it) ;

(*c*) that the chargeable amount (or fraction), after any deductions remaining to be made after applying paragraph (*b*), is the highest part of the person's total income (notwithstanding any other provisions of the Income Tax Acts directing any other income to be so treated).

(5) Where a claim under this paragraph for any year of assessment is made in respect of more than one trade, the paragraph applies to each chargeable amount individually as if there were only one charge in that year.

(6) For the purposes of section 400, paragaphs 3 and 4 of Schedule 3 and paragraph 8 of Schedule 8 of the Taxes Act (other top-slicing provisions) a person's total income shall not be treated as including any amount as a result of a charge under paragraph 2(2).

SCH. 5

Meaning of " relevant year of assessment " and " basis period "

5.—(1) This paragraph provides for ascertaining the relevant year of assessment in relation to a period of account for the purposes of this Part of this Schedule.

(2) In this Part of this Schedule—

(*a*) the " basis period " for any year of assessment means the period on the profits or gains of which income tax for that year falls to be finally computed under Case I of Schedule D in respect of the trade in question, or, where, by virtue of any provision of section 115 of the Taxes Act, the profits or gains of any other period are to be taken as the profits or gains of the said period, that other period ; and

(*b*) references to a period of account entering into a basis period are to the period of account, or any part of it, falling within or coinciding with that basis period.

(3) Where a period of account enters into the basis period for only one year of assessment, that year is the relevant year of assessment in relation to that period of account.

(4) Where a period of account enters into the basis period for more than one year of assessment, then—

(*a*) if this is by virtue of section 116 or 117 of the Taxes Act (commencement of trade), the relevant year of assessment in relation to that period of account is the first year of assessment into whose basis period the period of account enters ; and

(*b*) in any other case, the relevant year of assessment is the last such year of assessment.

(5) Where a period of account does not enter into the basis period for any year of assessment, the relevant year of assessment in relation to that period of account is that following the year of assessment in which the period of account ends.

Right to set unused relief against general income

6.—(1) Subject to the provisions of this paragraph, a claim made under section 168 of the Taxes Act (set-off of losses against general income) for relief in respect of a loss sustained by the claimant in a trade in any year of assessment (the " year of loss ") may require the amount of that loss to be determined as if an amount equal to the relief to which he is entitled under this Part of this Schedule for the year of assessment for which the year of loss is the basis year were to be deducted in computing the profits or gains or losses of the trade in the year of loss.

(2) A claim may be made under the said section 168 for relief in respect of a loss sustained by the claimant in any trade in any year of assessment notwithstanding that—

(*a*) unless relief under this Part of this Schedule is brought into account ; or (*b*) unless there are brought into account both that relief and capital allowances (by virtue of section 169 of the Taxes Act), Sch. 5

the claimant will not have sustained a loss in the trade in that year.

(3) Relief for any year of assessment shall be taken into account by virtue of this paragraph only if and so far as it is not required to offset any charge for that year under paragraph 2; and for the purposes of this sub-paragraph the relief for a year of assessment shall be treated as required to offset the charge for a year up to the amount on which the charge falls to be made after deducting from it the amount (if any) of relief for earlier years which is carried forward to that year and would, if not set against the charge, be unused in that year.

(4) Where the relief taken into account by virtue of this paragraph is that for the year of assessment for which the claim is made or for the preceding year (the year of loss being the basis year for that year itself, or the claim being made by way of carry forward of the loss by virtue of section 168(2) of the Taxes Act), effect shall not be given to that relief in respect of an amount greater than the amount unused in the year for which the claim is made, or, in the case of relief for the preceding year, the amount unused in both years.

(5) For the purposes of this paragraph—

(*a*) where the end of the basis period for a year of assessment falls in, or coincides with the end of any year of assessment, that year is the basis year for the first mentioned year of assessment, but so that, if a year of assessment would under the foregoing provision be the basis year both for that year itself and for another year of assessment, it shall be the basis year for the year itself and not for the other year,

(*b*) any reference to the relief or charge for a year of assessment shall be construed as a reference to the relief or charge falling to be given effect in that year (excluding, in the case of relief, any part of the relief for an earlier year carried forward under paragraph 7 below),

(*c*) any reference to an amount of relief unused in a year shall be construed as referring to the amount by which, by reason of an insufficiency of profits or gains, effect cannot be given in that year, and

(*d*) effect shall be deemed to be given to relief carried forward from an earlier year before it is given to relief for a later year.

(6) Where, on a claim made by virtue of this paragraph, relief is not given under section 168 of the Taxes Act for the full amount of the loss determined as mentioned in sub-paragraph (1) above, the relief under that section shall be attributed to the loss sustained by the claimant in the trade rather than to the relief under this Schedule in respect of that trade, but shall be attributed to relief

SCH. 5 under this Schedule rather than to the capital allowances in respect of the trade brought into account by virtue of section 169 of the Taxes Act.

(7) Where a claim is made under the said section 168 by a person who, since the end of the year for which the claim is made, has carried on the trade in question in partnership, then effect shall be given to this paragraph in relation to that claim only with the consent in writing of every other person engaged in carrying on the trade between the end of that year and the making of the claim, except that where the claim is for a loss sustained before an event treated as the permanent discontinuance of the trade, the consent is not required of a person so engaged only since the discontinuance.

(8) If a person whose consent is required under sub-paragraph (7) has died, the consent in writing of his personal representatives is required instead.

Carry forward of unused relief

7.—(1) Where, in any year of assessment, full effect cannot be given to any relief falling to be allowed under this Part of this Schedule owing to there being no profits or gains of the trade chargeable for that year, or owing to the profits or gains chargeable being less than the amount of the relief, the relief or part of the relief to which effect has not been given, as the case may be, shall be carried forward and, for the purpose of making the assessment to income tax for the following year, be added to the amount of relief for that year and be deemed to be part of that relief, or, if no relief falls to be allowed for that year, be deemed to be relief for that year, and so on for succeeding years.

(2) This paragraph has effect subject to paragraph 6 above.

Social security contributions

1975 c. 14. 8. In computing for the purposes of Schedule 2 to the Social Security Act 1975 the amount of the profits or gains of a trade in respect of which Class 4 contributions are payable—

(*a*) deductions or additions shall be made under paragraph 2 of that Schedule for any relief or charge under this Part of this Schedule which falls to be made in charging profits or gains to income tax under Case I of Schedule D; and

(*b*) paragraphs 6 and 7 above shall be included among the relief provisions to which paragraph 3(1) of that Schedule applies.

PART II

CORPORATION TAX

Entitlement to relief

9.—(1) Where a company carries on a trade in respect of which it is within the charge to corporation tax under Case I of Schedule D and—

(*a*) the value of its trading stock at the end of a period of account (the " closing stock value ") exceeds (*b*) the value of its trading stock at the beginning of that period (the " opening stock value "),

the company shall, subject to the provisions of this Schedule, be entitled to relief under this paragraph by reference to the amount of that excess (the " increase in stock value ").

(2) The amount of relief to which a company is entitled under this paragraph for any trade in respect of any period of account is the amount of the increase in stock value in that period less 15% of the relevant income of that trade for that period.

(3) A company shall not be entitled to relief under this paragraph unless a claim for the relief is made within two years after the end of the period of account in respect of which the relief is claimed.

Charge by way of recovery of relief

10.—(1) Where a company carries on a trade in respect of which it is within the charge to corporation tax under Case I of Schedule D and in a period of account its closing stock value is less than its opening stock value, then, subject to the provisions of this Schedule, a charge by way of recovery of relief shall be made on the company, on whichever is the lesser of—

(*a*) the whole amount of the reduction in stock value in that period ; or

(*b*) the amount of unrecovered past relief allowed to the company for that trade.

(2) Where during or at the end of a period of account a company carrying on a trade ceases to do so, or ceases to be within the charge to corporation tax under Case I of Schedule D in respect of the trade, it is not entitled to relief or liable to a charge in respect of that period under the foregoing provisions of this Part, but a final charge by way of recovery of relief shall be made on the company on an amount equal to the unrecovered past relief allowed to it for that trade.

This sub-paragraph is subject to paragraphs 20 and 21 below (which provide for continuity in the case of certain successions).

(3) Where during or at the end of a period of account a company carrying on a trade ceases (by virtue of ceasing to be resident in the United Kingdom) to be within the charge to corporation tax in respect of a part of the trade, it shall be treated for the purposes of this Schedule as if that part were a separate trade carried on by it in that period ; and all necessary apportionments between the two parts of the trade (including the apportionment of unrecovered past relief allowed for that trade) shall be made by reference to the respective values of the trading stock of each part immediately after that event.

11.—(1) Where there is a change of ownership of a company and section 483 of the Taxes Act applies so as to restrict the carrying forward of losses incurred before the change, then relief to which those disallowed losses are attributable shall, although unrecovered

Sch. 5

in periods of account ending before the change of ownership nevertheless be disregarded in ascertaining the amount of unrecovered past relief in later periods of account.

(2) Relief to which disallowed losses are attributable is that which was not given effect in the period of account or base period for which it was allowed or in a subsequent period of account.

(3) For the purposes of sub-paragraph (2) relief is assumed to be given effect before capital allowances and profits or gains are assumed to be set against losses attributable to relief before other losses.

Section 483(5) of the Taxes Act has effect subject to this sub-paragraph.

(4) For the purpose of ascertaining the extent to which relief to which disallowed losses are attributable has been recovered in periods of account ending before the change of ownership, it shall be assumed—

(*a*) that relief is recovered from earlier periods before later periods ; and

(*b*) that effect is given to relief from earlier periods before later periods.

Method of giving effect to relief or charge

12.—(1) Relief under paragraph 9 above in respect of any period of account shall, subject to the provisions of this paragraph, be given effect by treating the amount of the relief as a trading expense of the trade in that period.

(2) A charge under paragraph 10 above in respect of any period of account shall, subject to the provisions of this paragraph, be given effect by treating the amount on which the charge is to be made as a trading receipt of the trade in that period.

(3) Where a trade is set up and commenced by a company during a period of account, any amount which in accordance with this paragraph falls to be treated as an expense or receipt of the trade in that period, shall be brought into account only in respect of the accounting period, or periods, beginning with or after that commencement.

(4) Where during a period of account a company carrying on a trade ceases to do so, or ceases in respect of it to be within the charge to corporation tax under Case I of Schedule D, any relief or charge which in accordance with this paragraph falls to be treated as an expense or receipt of the trade in that period, shall be brought into account only in respect of the accounting period, or periods, ending on or before that discontinuance or other event.

Part III

Sch. 5

Link With Previous Stock Relief Provisions

Interpretation

13. In this Part of this Schedule, " Schedule 10 " means Schedule 10 to the Finance (No. 2) Act 1975, " Schedule 10 relief " means relief under that Schedule and " base period " means a base period (including a further base period) as defined in that Schedule. 1975 c. 45.

Entry into operation of Parts I and II

14.—(1) The provisions of this paragraph indicate the periods of account to which Parts I and II of this Schedule apply (being, in most cases, the periods of account falling after the base period for which Schedule 10 relief was given).

(2) The periods of account in respect of which entitlement is relief or liability to charge may arise under Part I of this Schedule are, subject to sub-paragraph (3) below, those falling after the following—

(*a*) the last period of account ending in the year 1974-75 ; or

(*b*) if no period of account ended in that year, the first period of account ending after 5th April 1975.

(3) Where a trade was set up and commenced after 5th April 1974 and there is no period of account ending in the year 1974-75, such entitlement or liability may arise in respect of any period of account the whole or part of which falls after that commencement.

(4) The periods of account in respect of which entitlement to relief or liability to charge may arise under Part II of this Schedule are, subject to sub-paragraph (5) below, those falling after the following—

(*a*) the last period of account ending in the financial year 1974 ; or

(*b*) if no period of account ended in that year, the first period of account ending after 31st March 1975.

(5) Where a trade was set up and commenced after 31st March 1974 and there is no period of account ending in the financial year 1974, such entitlement or liability may arise in respect of any period of account the whole or part of which falls after that commencement.

Transitional relief

15.—(1) The provisions of this paragraph apply for supplementing Schedule 10 relief in the case of persons whose base period ended after 5th April 1975, or, in the case of a company, 31st March 1975 (the relief having been proportionately reduced in those cases).

(2) There is entitlement to transitional relief under this paragraph—

(*a*) where the base period of a person other than a company ended after 5th April 1975 and a claim for relief is made before 6th April 1978 ;

SCH. 5

(*b*) where a company's base period ended after 31st March 1975 and a claim for relief is made within two years after the end of the base period.

(3) In either case the amount of transitional relief is given by the formula

$$(B-I) \times \frac{M}{N}$$

where—

B is the base period increase, as defined in paragraph 1(1) or 6(1) of Schedule 10,

I is 15 per cent. of the relevant income for the base period, computed in accordance with this Schedule,

M is, in the case of a person other than a company, the lesser of 12 or the number of months in the base period in excess of 24, and, in the case of a company, is the number of months between the end of the accounting period ending in the financial year 1974 and the end of the base period, and

N is the number of months in the base period.

(4) Where a base period consists of a number of complete months and a fraction of a month or consists only of a fraction of a month, references in this paragraph to the number of months in that period shall be construed as including that fraction, or as a reference to that fraction, as the case may be.

(5) Transitional relief to which a person other than a company is entitled shall be given as a deduction in charging the profits or gains of the trade to income tax for the last year of assessment in the basis period for which (as defined in paragraph 5 above) there falls the whole or any part of the period of account whose end also marks the end of the base period.

(6) Transitional relief to which a company is entitled shall be given effect by treating the amount of the relief as a trading expense of the trade in the accounting period whose end also marks the end of the base period.

(7) Any claim, or adjustment of a claim, for any other relief which falls to be made in consequence of a claim for transitional relief may be made at any time when a claim for transitional relief could be made, notwithstanding that it would otherwise be out of time.

(8) All such adjustments shall be made in any assessments to tax as are necessary to give effect to the provisions of this paragraph.

Succession during or at end of base period

16.—(1) In this paragraph " succession " means such a succession in the persons engaged in carrying on a trade as is mentioned in paragraph 13 of Schedule 10, and " predecessor " and " successor " mean the persons so engaged before and after a succession.

(2) Where there was a succession within the 12 months before the end of the base period and— Sch. 5

(*a*) the predecessor was an individual, a partnership or a company ; and

(*b*) the successor was a company,

the inspector may, on an application by the successor, notwithstanding anything in Schedule 10, apportion the relief falling to be given under that Schedule as seems to him just between the predecessor and successor.

(3) Where there was a succession at the end of the base period, the successor may elect that the predecessor's closing stock value at the end of the base period be reduced in accordance with Schedule 10, notwithstanding anything in paragraphs 5, 11 and 12 of that Schedule (change of persons engaged in carrying on a trade to be treated as cessation of that trade).

(4) An application or election under this paragraph must be made by notice in writing to the inspector by 1st January 1977 or after that date but within two years after the end of the base period.

(5) Any claim, or adjustment of a claim, for other relief which falls to be made in consequence of an application or election under this paragraph may be made at any time when the application or election could be made, notwithstanding that it would otherwise be out of time.

(6) All such adjustments shall be made in any assessments to tax as are necessary to give effect to the provisions of this paragraph.

Time limit for claiming Schedule 10 *relief*

17. A claim by a company for Schedule 10 relief may be made at any time before 1st January 1977 notwithstanding that the time limit imposed by paragraph 6(3) of that Schedule has expired.

Recovery of Schedule 10 relief

18.—(1) The provisions of this paragraph apply for making Schedule 10 relief and relief under this Part recoverable in the same way as relief under Part I or II of this Schedule.

(2) The reference in paragraph 26 below (meaning of " past relief " for purposes of recovery of relief) to the amount of Schedule 10 relief allowed to any person in respect of a trade is to—

(*a*) the amount by which his closing stock value at the end of the base period was reduced in accordance with paragraph 1(2)(*a*)(i) or 6(2)(*a*)(i) of Schedule 10 ; together with

(*b*) the amount of any relief to which he is entitled under this Part.

(3) In ascertaining the amount of Schedule 10 relief no account is to be taken of any diminution directed by paragraph 8(3) of that Schedule in the case where the end of the base period coincided with the end of the reference period for relief under section 18 of the Finance Act 1975. 1975 c. 7.

SCH. 5

(4) For the purpose of ascertaining at any time the amount of unrecovered past relief allowed to any person in respect of a trade, relief given to a predecessor by virtue of paragraph 16 above shall be treated as if given to the successor.

(5) In consequence of the foregoing provisions of this paragraph paragraph 1(2)(*b*) and paragraph 6(2)(*b*) of Schedule 10 are repealed and shall be deemed never to have had effect; and no account shall be taken for any of the purposes of this Schedule of any reduction in the value of trading stock under section 18(4) of the Finance Act 1975.

1975 c. 7.

PART IV

GENERAL

Partnerships

19.—(1) Where a trade is carried on by persons in partnership, entitlement to relief or liability to charge under this Schedule is a joint entitlement or liability, and any claim for relief under this Schedule shall be a single claim made in the partnership name.

(2) Where none of those persons is a company, entitlement to relief and liability to charge under this Schedule shall be ascertained and given effect as if the trade were carried on by an individual.

(3) Where any of those persons is a company, entitlement to relief and liability to charge under this Schedule shall be ascertained as if the partnership were a company and shall be given effect in accordance with the following provisions of this paragraph.

(4) A company's share in any such entitlement or liability in any accounting period of the partnership shall be determined according to the interests of the partners during that period, and shall be given effect as if the share derived from a trade carried on by the company alone in its corresponding accounting period or periods.

In this sub-paragraph "corresponding accounting period or periods" means the accounting period or periods of the company comprising or together comprising the accounting period of the partnership, and any necessary apportionment shall be made between corresponding accounting periods if more than one.

(5) The share in any such entitlement or liability of the partner or partners other than companies shall be given effect as if that share derived from a trade carried on by him, or, as the case may be, by them in partnership, otherwise than in partnership with a company.

Successions

20.—(1) The provisions of this paragraph apply—

(*a*) where the whole or part of a trade carried on by one company ("the predecessor") is transferred to another company ("the successor") and section 252 of the Taxes Act (company reconstructions) has effect in relation to that event; or

(b) where the whole of a trade carried on by an individual or by persons in partnership (" the predecessor ") is transferred to a company resident in the United Kingdom (" the successor ") and at the date of the transfer not less than three-quarters of the ordinary share capital of the company is held by that individual or those persons, Sch. 5

and, in either case, the trading stock is transferred at cost or at market value.

(2) Where the whole of a trade is transferred and the predecessor and successor so elect, then, for the purposes of this Schedule—

(a) the trading stock transferred shall be treated both as forming part of the predecessor's closing stock in his period of account which ends with or includes the date of transfer, and as forming part of the successor's opening stock in his period of account which begins with or includes the date of transfer ; and

(b) in ascertaining in that or any later period of account the amount of unrecovered past relief allowed to a person in respect of the trade, the successor shall be treated as having carried on the trade since the predecessor began (or is himself treated, by virtue of this sub-paragraph or of any other provision of this Schedule, as having begun) to do so.

(3) Where part of a trade is transferred and the predecessor and successor so elect, then, for the purposes of this Schedule, the predecessor shall be treated as having carried on in the period of account during or at the end of which the transfer occurs a separate trade consisting of the part transferred ; and all necessary apportionments between the two parts of the trade (including the apportionment of unrecovered past relief allowed for the trade) shall be made by reference to the respective values of the trading stock of each part immediately after the transfer.

(4) An election under this paragraph shall be by notice in writing signed by both the predecessor and the successor and sent to the inspector within two years after the date of the transfer.

21.—(1) Subject to the provisions of this paragraph, where there is a change in the persons engaged in carrying on a trade, this Schedule applies as if the trade had been permanently discontinued at the date of the change and a new trade had been then set up and commenced.

For the purposes of this paragraph, a change in the personal representatives of any person, or in the trustees of any trust, shall not be treated as a change in the persons carrying on any trade carried on by those personal representatives or trustees as such.

(2) Where there is a change of persons but—

(a) a person engaged in carrying on the trade immediately before the change continues to be so engaged immediately after the change ; and

(b) the trading stock of the trade immediately before the change is the trading stock immediately after the change,

an election may be made to the effect that sub-paragraph (1) shall not apply to the change.

SCH. 5 (3) An election under this paragraph must be made by all the persons engaged in carrying on the trade before the change (" the predecessors ") and all those so engaged immediately after the change (" the successors "), and be signed by them and sent to the inspector within two years after the date of the change.

Where those persons have elected under section 154(2) of the Taxes Act that the trade be treated as continuing for income tax purposes, they shall be treated as having also made an election under this paragraph.

(4) In ascertaining for the purposes of this Schedule the amount of unrecovered past relief allowed to a person in respect of a trade where at an earlier date a change in the persons carrying on that trade has been the subject of an election under this paragraph, the successors (in relation to that change) shall be treated as having carried on the trade since the predecessors began (or are themselves treated, by virtue of this sub-paragraph or of any other provision of this Schedule, as having begun) to do so.

(5) Where during a period of account there is a change in the persons engaged in carrying on a trade, and—

(*a*) an election is made under this paragraph ; but

(*b*) no election is made under section 154(2) of the Taxes Act in relation to that change,

any relief or charge under this Schedule in respect of that period of account shall be apportioned between the precedessors and successors according to the respective lengths of the parts of the period falling before and after the change, and for the purpose of giving effect to that relief or charge each of those parts shall be treated as if it were a separate period of account.

Adjustment for special circumstances

22.—(1) Where any arrangements have been effected by a person carrying on a trade, or by him and other persons acting together, such as, in particular, the following—

(*a*) any acquisition or disposal of trading stock otherwise than in the normal course of the trade in question ; or

(*b*) any change in the normal pattern or method of carrying on the trade ; or

(*c*) any change in the date to which the accounts of the trade are made up ; or

(*d*) any increase in the value of a person's trading stock which is associated with a decrease in the trading stock of another person connected with him (within the meaning of section 533(5) or (6) of the Taxes Act),

and it appears that the sole or main benefit which, but for this paragraph, might have been expected to accrue to that person was the obtaining of relief or the reduction of the amount of a charge under this Schedule, an adjustment shall be made under this paragraph.

(2) The adjustment is to substitute, for the purposes of this Schedule, for any opening or closing value of trading stock in any period of account which appears to have been affected by the arrangements, the value which it appears there would have been had those arrangements not been made.

Valuation of stock in certain cases

23.—(1) For the purposes of this Schedule in ascertaining the entitlement of a person to relief, or his liability to a charge, in respect of any period of account—

(*a*) in a case where at any time during the twelve months preceding the beginning of that period of account he was not carrying on the trade in question ; or

(*b*) in a case where during that period of account there was a major alteration in the conduct of the trade in question which resulted in an exceptional increase in his trading stock,

he shall be treated as having at the beginning of that period of account trading stock of such value as may be attributed in accordance with this paragraph.

(2) If for any of the purposes of this Schedule there falls to be ascertained the value of any trading stock at a date other than the beginning or end of a period of account and when no value was in fact determined, that value shall be such as may be attributed in accordance with this paragraph.

(3) The value to be attributed is such value as is reasonable and just having regard to all the relevant circumstances of the case, and in particular—

(*a*) to the opening and closing values of trading stock of the trade for that period of account ;

(*b*) to movements during that period of account in the costs of items of a kind comprised in the person's trading stock during the period ; and

(*c*) to changes during that period in the volume of the trade carried on by that person.

Discontinuity in stock values

24.—(1) Where a person's closing stock value in a period of account is not calculated on the same basis as that used for the calculation of the opening stock value in that period, he shall be treated, for the purposes of this Schedule, as having at the beginning of that period trading stock of the amount he would have had if the basis of calculation had been that used for the closing stock value.

(2) Where a person's opening stock value in a period of account (including a value he is treated as having by virtue of sub-paragraph (1) above or of any other provision of this Schedule) is less than the amount of unrecovered past relief allowed to him for that trade, he shall be treated, for the purposes of this Schedule, as having at the beginning of that period trading stock of an amount equal to the amount of unrecovered past relief.

SCH. 5

Farm animals

25.—(1) Animals treated as trading stock under Schedule 6 to the Taxes Act (farm animals etc.) shall, subject to the provisions of this paragraph, be so treated for the purposes of this Schedule.

(2) Where a person makes an election for the herd basis under that Schedule which takes effect during a period of account, animals forming part of a herd with respect to which the election has effect shall be treated for the purposes of this Schedule as not having been trading stock of that person at any time during that period.

(3) Where a person makes an election for the herd basis under that Schedule then at the end of the last period of account not affected by the election (hereafter referred to as " the point of election ") the unrecovered past relief allowed to him for the farming or other trade in question (including the relief in respect of that period of account) shall be apportioned between the herd and the rest of his trading stock by reference to their respective values at the point of election, and in subsequent periods of account that part attributed to the herd is recoverable in accordance with the following provisions of this paragraph.

(4) A charge by way of recovery of relief shall be made where in a period of account for which the election has effect there is a reduction of the number of animals in the herd and—

(*a*) in the case of the first period in respect of which such a charge arises, the number at the end of that period is less than the number of animals in the herd at the point of election (that difference being referred to hereafter as " the relevant number ") ; or

(*b*) in the case of any subsequent period in respect of which such a charge arises, the number at the end of that period is less than the number of animals in the herd at the end of the last preceding period of account in respect of which such a charge arose (that difference being referred to hereafter as " the relevant number ").

This paragraph also applies (subject to sub-paragraph (6) below) where the person ceases to keep the herd and the first-mentioned number in paragraph (*a*) or (*b*) above is accordingly nil.

(5) The amount on which the charge to be made is the amount which bears to the whole amount of unrecovered past relief attributed to the herd at the point of election, the same proportion as the relevant number of animals in relation to the period of account in question bears to the number of animals in the herd at the point of election.

(6) Where a herd is sold as a whole and another production herd of the same class is acquired, this paragraph applies as if those herds were the same herd.

(7) A charge under this paragraph shall be treated for all purposes as if it were a charge by way of recovery of relief under paragraph 2 or 10 above falling to be made for the farming or other trade in question, and shall be given effect accordingly.

(8) In this paragraph "herd" and "production herd" have the same meaning as in Schedule 6 to the Taxes Act, and this paragraph applies (as does that Schedule), with the necessary adaptations, to animals or other creatures kept singly as it applies in relation to herds.

Meaning of "past relief"

26.—(1) References in this Schedule to "past relief", in relation to a trade carried on by any person in any period of account, are to the aggregate amount of the following reliefs allowed to him (or treated as allowed to him)—

(*a*) Schedule 10 relief (as defined in paragraph 18 above) allowed for that trade; and

(*b*) relief under Part I or Part II of this Schedule allowed for that trade in respect of earlier periods of account.

(2) The amount of unrecovered past relief in any period of account is that aggregate amount less the aggregate of the amounts on which charges by way of recovery of relief have been made on that person for that trade in respect of earlier periods of account.

Application to professions and foreign trades etc.

27.—(1) The foregoing provisions of this Schedule have effect, with the necessary modifications, in relation to professions and vocations chargeable under Case II of Schedule D as they have effect in relation to trades chargeable under Case I of that Schedule.

(2) The foregoing provisions of this Schedule (including sub-paragraph (1) of this paragraph) have effect, with the necessary modifications, in relation to trades, professions and vocations carried on outside the United Kingdom and chargeable under Case V of Schedule D otherwise than on a remittance basis as they have effect in relation to trades, professions and vocations chargeable under Case I or Case II of that Schedule, except that where, in charging the income from that trade, profession or vocation, a deduction of one quarter of the amount of that income falls to be allowed under section 23(3) of the Finance Act 1974 (income charged to income tax otherwise than on remittance basis) the amount of relief under this Schedule shall be confined to three-quarters of the amount which would have been applicable had the trade, profession or vocation been chargeable under the said Case I or Case II. 1974 c. 30.

Interpretation

28.—(1) In this Schedule "period of account" means a period for which an account is made up in relation to the trade, profession or vocation in question.

(2) For the purposes of this Schedule a source of income is "within the charge to" income tax or corporation tax if that tax is chargeable on the income arising from it, or would be so chargeable if there were any such income, and references to a person or to profits or gains, being within the charge to tax shall be similarly construed.

Sch. 5

29.—(1) Subject to the provisions of this paragraph, in this Schedule " trading stock " means property of any description, whether real or personal, being either—

(*a*) property such as is sold in the ordinary course of the trade, profession or vocation in question, or would be so sold if it were mature or if its manufacture, preparation or construction were complete ; or

(*b*) materials such as are used in the manufacture, preparation or construction of any such property as is referred to in paragraph (*a*) above,

and includes work in progress.

(2) Sub-paragraph (1) above does not apply to—

(*a*) securities, which for this purpose includes stocks and shares ; or

(*b*) land, other than such as is ordinarily sold in the course of the trade, profession or vocation only—

(i) after being developed by the person carrying on the trade, profession or vocation, or

(ii) in the case of a company which is a member of a group, for the purpose of being developed by another company in that group ; or

(*c*) goods which the person carrying on the trade, profession or vocation has let on hire or hire-purchase.

(3) In sub-paragraph (2) above, references to development are references to the construction or substantial reconstruction of buildings on the land in question and " group " shall be construed in accordance with section 272 of the Taxes Act.

(4) For the purposes of this Schedule the value of a person's trading stock at any time shall be reduced to the extent to which payments on account have been made at or before that time in respect of that stock.

(5) References in this Schedule to trading stock are to the trading stock brought into account in computing the profits or gains of a trade, profession or vocation in accordance with Case I or, as the case may be, Case II of Schedule D.

(6) Where a person not resident in the United Kingdom carries on a trade partly within the United Kingdom and partly abroad, references in this Schedule to his trading stock are to the stock attributable to that part of the trade within the charge to United Kingdom tax.

30. In this Schedule " work in progress " means—

(*a*) any services performed in the ordinary course of the trade, profession or vocation, the performance of which was partly completed at the material time and for which it would be reasonable to expect that a charge will subsequently be made ; and

(*b*) any article produced, and any such material as is used, in the performance of any such services.

31.—(1) In this Schedule "relevant income" in relation to a person carrying on a trade, profession or vocation, means the income from that trade, profession or vocation computed in accordance with the rules applicable to Case I or, as the case may be, Case II of Schedule D.

(2) In computing, for the purposes of this Schedule, the relevant income for any period of account—

(*a*) no account shall be taken of any set-off or reduction of income by virtue of section 168, 171, 174, 177 or 178 of the Taxes Act, in respect of losses;

(*b*) no deduction or addition shall be made by virtue of any provision of this Schedule, in respect of any relief or charge; and

(*c*) no account shall be taken of any reduction in the value of trading stock directed by section 18 of the Finance Act 1975 or Schedule 10 to the Finance (No. 2) Act 1975

1975 c. 7.
1975 c. 45.

but there shall be taken into account any deduction or addition in respect of capital allowances and balancing charges referable to that period of account.

(3) In a case falling within Part I of this Schedule, the capital allowances and balancing charges referable to a period of account are—

(*a*) the first year and initial allowances claimed for expenditure incurred in that period;

(*b*) balancing allowances and charges on disposals in that period; and

(*c*) the appropriate fraction of the writing down allowances for the year which in relation to that period of account is the relevant year of assessment for the purposes of the said Part I.

(4) The appropriate fraction mentioned in sub-paragraph (3)(*c*) is the fraction of which the denominator is the number of months during which the trade was carried on in the relevant year of assessment and the numerator is the number of months during which the trade was carried on in the period of account.

For the purposes of this sub-paragraph fractions of a month shall be disregarded.

(5) In a case falling within Part II of this Schedule the capital allowances referable to a period of account are the allowances (less any balancing charges) for the accounting period or periods constituting that period of account.

(6) In a case falling within Part III of this Schedule the relevant income for the base period there referred to is the aggregate amount of the relevant income for each of the periods of account comprising that period, and the capital allowances and balancing charges referable to each such period of account shall be ascertained as if those periods were periods to which Part I or, as the case may be, Part II of this Schedule applied.

SCH. 5

32. Any reference in this Schedule to a period ending in another period includes a reference to a period ending on the same day as the other period.

Section 57.

1970 c. 9.

SCHEDULE 6

SECTIONS TO BE SUBSTITUTED FOR SECTION 20 OF TAXES MANAGEMENT ACT 1970

Power to call for documents of taxpayer and others.

20.—(1) Subject to this section, an inspector may by notice in writing require a person to deliver to him such documents as are in the person's possession or power and as (in the inspector's reasonable opinion) contain, or may contain, information relevant to any tax liability to which the person is or may be subject, or to the amount of any such liability.

(2) Subject to this section, the Board may by notice in writing require a person to deliver, to a named officer of theirs, such documents as are in the person's possession or power and as (in the Board's reasonable opinion) contain, or may contain, information relevant to any tax liability to which he is or may be subject, or to the amount of any such liability.

(3) Subject to this section, an inspector may, for the purpose of enquiring into the tax liability of any person (" the taxpayer "), by notice in writing require any of the persons who in relation to the taxpayer are subject to this subsection to deliver to the inspector or, if the person to whom the notice is given so elects, to make available for inspection by a named officer of the Board, such documents as are in his possession or power and as (in the inspector's reasonable opinion) contain, or may contain, information relevant to any tax liability to which the taxpayer is or may be, or may have been, subject, or to the amount of any such liability.

(4) The persons so subject are—

(*a*) the taxpayer's spouse, and any son or daughter of his ;

(*b*) in so far as the inspector's enquiries relate to liability of the taxpayer in respect of income, profits or gains that were, or may have been, derived from—

(i) any business (past or present) carried on by the taxpayer or his spouse, or

(ii) any business (past or present) with whose management either of them was concerned at a material time,

any person who is carrying on a business, or was doing so at a material time, and any company whether carrying on a business or not.

(5) For the purposes of subsection (4) above, every director of a company is to be taken as being concerned with the management of any business carried on by the company ; and a material time is any time which (in the inspector's reasonable opinion) is, or may have been, material in the ascertainment of any past or present tax liability of the taxpayer.

(6) The persons who may be treated as " the taxpayer " under subsections (3) and (4) include a company which has ceased to exist and an individual who has died ; and in relation to such an individual the references in subsection (4) to the spouse are then instead to the widow or widower (the circumstance that she or he may have re-married being immaterial for the purposes of those subsections).

(7) Notices under this section are not to be given by an inspector unless he is authorised by the Board for its purposes ; and—

(*a*) a notice is not to be given by him except with the consent of a General or Special Commissioner ; and

(*b*) the Commissioner is to give his consent only on being satisfied that in all the circumstances the inspector is justified in proceeding under this section.

(8) The references in subsections (1), (2) and (3) above to documents are to those specified or described in the notice in question ; and—

(*a*) the notice shall require them to be delivered or (as the case may be) made available within such time as may be there specified ; and

(*b*) the person to whom they are delivered or made available may take copies of, or extracts from them ;

and a notice under subsection (3) shall name the taxpayer with whose liability the inspector (or, as the case may be, the Board) is concerned.

(9) To the extent specified in section 20B below, the above provisions are subject to the restrictions of that section.

Power to call for papers of tax accountant.

20A.—(1) Where after the passing of the Finance Act 1976 a person—

(*a*) is convicted of an offence in relation to tax (whenever committed) by or before any court in the United Kingdom ; or

(*b*) has awarded against him a penalty incurred by him (whether before or after the passing of that Act) under section 99 of this Act,

SCH. 6

and he has stood in relation to others as tax accountant, an inspector authorised by the Board for the purpose of this section may by notice in writing require the person to deliver to him such documents as are in his possession or power and as (in the inspector's reasonable opinion) contain information relevant to any tax liability to which any client of his is or has been, or may be or have been, subject, or to the amount of any such liability.

For this purpose section 20(8) above applies, substituting " the client " for " the taxpayer."

(2) Subsection (1) above does not have effect in relation to a person convicted or penalised as there mentioned for so long as an appeal is pending against the conviction or award ; and—

(*a*) for this purpose an appeal is to be treated as pending (where one is competent but has not been brought) until the expiration of the time for bringing it or, in the case of a conviction in Scotland, until the expiration of 28 days from the date of conviction ; and

(*b*) references here to appeal include further appeal but, in relation to the award of a penalty, do not include appeal against the amount of the penalty.

(3) A notice is not to be given to any person under this section unless with the consent of the appropriate judicial authority ; and that authority is to give his consent only on being satisfied that in all the circumstances the inspector is justified in so proceeding.

(4) The power to give a notice under this section, by reference to a person's conviction or the award against him of a penalty, ceases at the expiration of the period of 12 months beginning with the date on which it was first exercisable in his case by virtue of that conviction or award.

(5) To the extent specified in section 20B below, the above provisions are subject to the restrictions of that section.

Restrictions on powers under ss. 20 and 2A.

20B.—(1) Before a notice is given to a person by an inspector under section 20(1) or (3), or under section 20A, the person must have been given a reasonable opportunity to deliver (or, in the case of section 20(3), to deliver or make available) the documents in question ; and the inspector must not apply for consent under section 20(7) or, as the case may be, section 20A(3), until the person has been given that opportunity.

(2) A notice under section 20(1) does not oblige a person to deliver documents relating to the conduct of any pending appeal by him ; a notice under section 20(3) does

not oblige a person to deliver or make available documents relating to the conduct of a pending appeal by the taxpayer ; and a notice under section 20A does not oblige a person to deliver documents relating to the conduct of a pending appeal by the client. Sch. 6

" Appeal " means appeal relating to tax.

(3) An inspector cannot under section 20(1) or (3), or under section 20A(1), give notice to a barrister, advocate or solicitor, but the notice must in any such case be given (if at all) by the Board ; and accordingly in relation to a barrister, advocate or solicitor for references in section 20(3) and (4) and section 20A to the inspector there are substituted references to the Board.

(4) To comply with a notice under section 20(1) or section 20A(1), and as an alternative to delivering documents to comply with a notice under section 20(3), copies of documents may be delivered instead of the originals ; but—

(*a*) the copies must be photographic or otherwise by way of facsimile ; and

(*b*) if so required by the inspector (or, as the case may be, the Board) in the case of any documents specified in the requirement, the originals must be made available for inspection by a named officer of the Board (failure to comply with this requirement counting as failure to comply with the notice).

(5) A notice under section 20(3), if given to a person who is carrying on a business or was doing so at any time material to the subject matter of the inspector's (or the Board's) enquiries, or if given to a company (whether carrying on a business or not), does not oblige the person or company to deliver or make available any document the whole of which originates more than 6 years before the date of the notice.

(6) But subsection (5) does not apply where the notice is so expressed as to exclude the restrictions of that subsection ; and it can only be so expressed where—

(*a*) the notice being given by an inspector with consent under section 20(7), the Commissioner giving consent has also given approval to the exclusion ;

(*b*) the notice being given by the Board, they have applied to a General or Special Commissioner for, and obtained, that approval.

For this purpose the Commissioner gives approval only if satisfied, on the inspector's or the Board's application, that there is reasonable ground for believing that tax

SCH. 6

has, or may have been, lost to the Crown owing to the fraud of the taxpayer.

(7) A notice under section 20(3) in relation to a taxpayer who has died cannot be given to a person by virtue of her or his being the taxpayer's widow, widower, son or daughter if more than 6 years have elapsed since the death.

(8) A notice under section 20(3) or section 20A(1) does not oblige a barrister, advocate or a solicitor to deliver or make available, without his client's consent, any document with respect to which a claim to professional privilege could be maintained.

(9) A notice under section 20(3) does not, in the case of a person who (in the course of a business carried on by him) has stood in relation to another as tax accountant, oblige that person to deliver or make available documents which are his (the accountant's) property and originate as working papers of that relationship.

Entry with warrant to obtain documents.

20C.—(1) If the appropriate judicial authority is satisfied on information on oath given by an officer of the Board that—

(*a*) there is reasonable ground for suspecting that an offence involving any form of fraud in connection with, or in relation to, tax has been committed and that evidence of it is to be found on premises specified in the information; and

(*b*) in applying under this section, the officer acts with the approval of the Board given in relation to the particular case,

the authority may issue a warrant in writing authorising an officer of the Board to enter the premises, if necessary by force, at any time within 14 days from the time of issue of the warrant, and search them.

(2) Section 4A of the Inland Revenue Regulation Act 1890 (Board's functions to be exercisable by an officer acting under their authority) does not apply to the giving of Board approval under this section.

(3) On entering the premises with a warrant under this section, the officer may seize and remove any things whatsoever found there which he has reasonable cause to believe may be required as evidence for the purposes of proceedings in respect of such an offence as is mentioned in subsection (1) above.

But this does not authorise the seizure and removal of documents in the possession of a barrister, advocate or solicitor with respect to which a claim to professional privilege could be maintained.

(4) Where entry to premises has been made with a warrant under this section, and the officer making the

entry has seized any things under the authority of the warrant, he shall, if so requested by a person showing himself either—

(*a*) to be the occupier of the premises ; or

(*b*) to have had the possession or custody of those things immediately before the seizure,

provide that person with a list of them.

(5) Where documents are seized which relate to any business, and it is shown that access to them is required for the continued conduct of the business, the officer who has seized them shall afford reasonable access to the documents to the person carrying on the business.

Interpretation of ss. 20 to 20C.

20D.—(1) For the purposes of section 20A and 20C above, " the appropriate judicial authority " is—

(*a*) in England and Wales, a Circuit judge ;

(*b*) in Scotland, a sheriff ; and

(*c*) in Northern Ireland, a county court judge.

(2) For the purposes of sections 20 and 20A, a person stands in relation to another as tax accountant at any time when he assists the other in the preparation of returns or accounts to be made or delivered by the other for any purpose of tax ; and his clients are all those to whom he stands or has stood in that relationship.

(3) In sections 20 and 20C above " business " includes trade, profession and vocation ; and in those sections and in section 20B " documents " includes books, accounts and other documents or records whatsoever.

Section 64.

SCHEDULE 7

TAXATION OF DIRECTORS AND OTHERS IN RESPECT OF CARS

PART I

TABLES OF FLAT RATE CASH EQUIVALENTS

TABLE A

CARS WITH ORIGINAL MARKET VALUE UP TO £6,000 AND HAVING A CYLINDER CAPACITY

Cylinder capacity of car in cubic centimetres	Age of car at end of relevant year of assessment	
	Under 4 years	4 years or more
1,300 or less	£175	£120
More than 1,300, but not more than 1,800	£225	£150
More than 1,800	£350	£235

TABLE B

CARS WITH ORIGINAL MARKET VALUE UP TO £6,000 AND NOT HAVING A CYLINDER CAPACITY

Original market value of car	Age of car at end of relevant year of assessment	
	Under 4 years	4 years or more
Less than £2,000	£175	£120
£2,000 or more, but less than £3,000 ...	£225	£150
£3,000 or more, but not more than £6,000	£350	£235

SCH. 7

TABLE C

CARS WITH ORIGINAL MARKET VALUE MORE THAN £6,000

Original market value of car	Age of car at end of relevant year of assessment	
	Under 4 years	4 years or more
More than £6,000, but not more than £10,000	£500	£335
More than £10,000	£800	£535

PART II

SUPPLEMENTARY PROVISIONS

Application of Tables A and B

1.—(1) In the case of cars with an original market value of £6,000 or less, Table A applies to those having an internal combustion engine with one or more reciprocating pistons, and Table B applies to other cars.

(2) A car's cylinder capacity is the cylinder capacity of its engine calculated as for the purposes of the Vehicles (Excise) Act 1971 or the Vehicles (Excise) Act (Northern Ireland) Act 1972. 1971 c. 10. 1972 c. 10 (N.I.).

Reduction for periods when car not available for use

2.—(1) If for any part of the relevant year the car was unavailable, the cash equivalent is to be reduced by an amount which bears to the full amount of the equivalent (ascertained under Part I of this Schedule) the same proportion as the number of days in the year on which the car was unavailable bears to 365.

(2) The car is to be treated as having been unavailable on any day if—

(*a*) it was not made available to the employee until after that day, or it had ceased before that day to be available to him ; or

(*b*) it was incapable of being used at all throughout a period of not less than 30 consecutive days of which that day was one.

Car used preponderantly for business purposes

3.—(1) The cash equivalent derived from Table A, B or C is to be reduced (or, where paragraph 2 applies, further reduced) by half if it is shown to the inspector's satisfaction that the employee was required by the nature of his employment to make, and made

SCH. 7 use of the car preponderantly for business travel, which means that such travel must have amounted to at least 25,000 miles in the relevant year.

(2) In relation to a car which for part of the year was unavailable in the sense of paragraph 2 above, the figure of 25,000 miles above mentioned is proportionately reduced.

Reduction for employee paying for use of car

4. If in the relevant year the employee was required, as a condition of the car being available for his private use, to pay any amount of money (whether by way of deduction from his emoluments or otherwise) for that use, the cash equivalent—

(*a*) is to be reduced (or, if already reduced under the foregoing paragraphs, further reduced) by the amount so paid by the employee in or in respect of the year, or

(*b*) if that amount exceeds the equivalent shown in the applicable Table in Part I of this Schedule, is nil.

Section 66.

SCHEDULE 8

TAXATION OF BENEFIT FROM LOANS OBTAINED BY REASON OF EMPLOYMENT

PART I

MEANING OF " OBTAINED BY REASON OF EMPLOYMENT "

1.—(1) The benefit of a loan is obtained by reason of a person's employment if it was made by his employer.

(2) But this does not apply to a loan made by the employer, being an individual, and shown to have been made in the normal course of his domestic, family or personal relationships.

2. That benefit is so obtained if the loan was made by a company—

(*a*) over which the employer had control,

(*b*) by which the employer (being a company) was controlled, or

(*c*) which was controlled by a person by whom the employer (being a company) was controlled.

3. That benefit is so obtained if—

(*a*) the employer was or had control over, or was controlled by, a close company, and

(*b*) the loan was made by a person having a material interest in the close company or, the close company being controlled by another company, in that other company.

4. In this Part of this Schedule—

(*a*) references to a loan being made by any person include references to his assuming the rights and liabilities of the person who originally made the loan and to his arranging, guaranteeing or in any way facilitating the continuation of a loan already in existence;

(*b*) " employer " includes a prospective employer ; and

(*c*) " company ", except as part of the expression " close company ", includes a partnership.

PART II

CALCULATION OF CASH EQUIVALENT OF LOAN BENEFIT

General

5.—(1) The cash equivalent for any year of the benefit obtained from a loan is—

(*a*) the amount of interest (calculated in accordance with paragraph 6 or 7 below) which would have been payable for that year had interest at the official rate been payable on the loan ; less

(*b*) the amount of interest actually paid on the loan for that year.

(2) Where an assessment for any year in respect of a loan has been made or determined on the footing that the whole or part of the interest payable on the loan for that year was not in fact paid, but it is subsequently paid, then, on a claim in that behalf, the cash equivalent for that year shall be recalculated so as to take that payment into account and the assessment shall be adjusted accordingly.

(3) All the loans between the same lender and borrower for which a cash equivalent falls to be ascertained and which are outstanding at any time, as to any amount, in any year are to be treated for the purposes of this Schedule as a single loan.

Normal method of calculation (averaging)

6. In the absence of a requirement or election that paragraph 7 below should apply, the amount of interest at the official rate payable on a loan for any year (" the relevant year ") shall be ascertained as follows:

(*a*) take half the aggregate of—

(i) the maximum amount of the loan outstanding on 5th April preceding the relevant year or, if it was made in that year, on the date on which it was made, and

(ii) the maximum amount of the loan outstanding on 5th April in the relevant year or, if the loan was discharged in that year, the date of discharge ;

Sch. 8

(*b*) multiply that figure by the number of whole months during which the loan was outstanding in that year, and divide by 12;

(*c*) multiply the result by the official rate of interest in force during the period when the loan was outstanding in that year or, if the official rate changed during that period, the average rate during that period ascertained by reference to the number of days in the period and the number of days for which each rate was in force.

For the purposes of this paragraph, months begin on the sixth day of the calendar month.

Election for alternative method of calculation

7.—(1) For any year of assessment ("the relevant year") the alternative method of calculation set out in this paragraph applies if—

(*a*) the inspector so requires, by notice in writing given to the employee, for the purpose of any assessment to income tax (or the adjustment of any such assessment in consequence of an appeal); or

(*b*) the employee so elects, by notice in writing given to the inspector within the time allowed by sub-paragraph (2) below.

(2) An election by the employee must be made—

(*a*) in a case where an assessment including the emoluments in question has been made on the basis of the normal method of calculation, within the time allowed for appealing against that assessment or such further time as the inspector may allow;

(*b*) where no such assessment has been made, within 6 years after the end of the relevant year of assessment.

(3) The alternative method of calculating the amount of interest at the official rate payable on a loan for the relevant year is as follows—

(*a*) take each period in the relevant year during which the official rate of interest remains the same;

(*b*) for each such period take for each day in the period the maximum amount outstanding of the loan on that day, and add those amounts together;

(*c*) multiply that sum by the official rate in force during the period divided by 365; and

(*d*) add together the resulting figures for each period in the relevant year.

Part III

Exceptions Where Interest Eligible for Relief

8.—(1) In this Part of this Schedule "eligible for relief", in relation to interest, means eligible for relief under section 75 of the

1972 c. 41. Finance Act 1972.

SCH. 8

(2) In determining for the purposes of this Part of this Schedule whether interest is eligible for relief there shall be disregarded the restriction imposed by section 75(3) of the Finance Act 1972 (which provides, in relation to certain loans taken out before 27th March 1974, that the first £35 of interest paid in any year is not eligible for relief). 1972 c. 41.

9. Section 66(1) does not apply to a loan in any year—

(*a*) for which interest is paid on the loan and the whole of that interest is eligible for relief, or

(*b*) for which no interest is paid on the loan but had interest been paid on it at the official rate the whole of that interest would have been eligible for relief.

10. Where for any year interest is paid on a loan and part of that interest is eligible for relief, the calculation of the cash equivalent under Part II of this Schedule is modified as follows:—

(*a*) where paragraph 6 applies, the maximum amounts referred to in paragraph 6(*a*)(i) and (ii) shall be proportionately reduced by reference to the proportion which so much of the interest paid for that year as is not eligible for relief bears to the whole of the interest so paid ;

(*b*) where paragraph 7 applies, the maximum amounts referred to in paragraph 7(3)(*b*) shall be proportionally reduced by reference to the proportion which so much of the interest paid on each such amount for the day in question as is not eligible for relief bears to the whole of the interest so paid ; and

(*c*) the amount of interest eligible for relief shall be left out of account in ascertaining for the purposes of paragraph 5(1)(*b*) above the amount of interest paid for that year.

11.—(1) Where for any year no interest is paid on a loan but had interest been paid on it at the official rate part of that interest would have been eligible for relief, the calculation of the cash equivalent under Part II of this Schedule shall be modified as provided by paragraph 10(*a*) or (*b*) above with the substitution for the references to the amounts of interest paid or not eligible for relief of references to the amounts (ascertained in accordance with the following provisions of this paragraph) which would have been paid or would not have been eligible for relief.

(2) For the purposes of paragraph 10(*a*) as applied by this paragraph, the whole amount of interest at the official rate which would have been paid for any year shall be taken to be the amount payable for that year calculated in accordance with paragraph 6 (disregarding paragraph 10) ; and the amount of that interest which would not have been eligible for relief shall be ascertained—

(*a*) by finding that amount on the assumption that the amount referred to in paragraph 6(*a*)(i) was the amount outstanding for the whole year ;

SCH. 8

(*b*) by finding that amount on the assumption that the amount referred to in paragraph 6(*a*)(ii) was the amount outstanding for the whole year ; and

(*c*) by adding together the resulting figures and dividing by 2.

(3) For the purposes of paragraph 10(*b*) as applied by this paragraph, the amount of interest which would have been paid and the amount of it which would not have been eligible for relief shall be ascertained on the assumption that interest at the official rate was paid daily throughout the year on the maximum amount outstanding on each day.

Section 72.

SCHEDULE 9

AMENDMENTS OF TAX ACTS CONSEQUENT ON PART III, CHAPTER II

PART 1

REPLACEMENT OF SECTION 15 OF THE TAXES MANAGEMENT ACT 1970 (c. 9)

Taxes Management Act 1970 (*c*. 9)

1. For section 15 of the Taxes Management Act 1970 (return of employees' emoluments, etc.) there shall be substituted the following section—

" Return of employees emoluments, etc.

15.—(1) Every employer, when required to do so by notice from an inspector, shall, within the time limited by the notice, prepare and deliver to the inspector a return relating to persons who are or have been employed by him, containing the information required under the following provisions of this section.

(2) An employer shall not be required to include in his return information relating to a year of assessment beginning more than six years before the year of assessment in which the notice is given.

(3) A notice under subsection (1)—

(*a*) shall specify the employees for whom a return is to be made and may, in particular, specify individuals (by name or otherwise) or all employees of an employer or all his employees who are in director's or higher-paid employment ; and

(*b*) shall specify the years of assessment or other periods with respect to which the information is to be provided.

(4) A notice under subsection (1) may require the return to state the name and place of residence of an employee to whom it relates. SCH. 9

(5) A notice under subsection (1) may require the return to contain, in respect of an employee to whom it relates, particulars of the payments made to him in respect of his employment including—

(*a*) payments to him in respect of expenses (including sums put at his disposal and paid away by him),

(*b*) payments made on his behalf and not repaid, and

(*c*) payments to him for services rendered in connection with a trade or business, whether the services were rendered in the course of his employment or not.

(6) Where, for the purposes of his return, an employer apportions expenses incurred partly in or in connection with a particular matter and partly in or in connection with other matters—

(*a*) the return shall contain a statement that the sum included in the return is the result of such an apportionment; and

(*b*) if required to do so by notice from the inspector, he shall prepare and deliver to the inspector, within the time limited by the notice, a return containing full particulars as to the amount apportioned and the manner in which, and the grounds on which, the apportionment has been made.

(7) A notice under subsection (1) may require the return—

(*a*) to state in respect of an employee to whom it relates whether any benefits are or have been provided for him (or for any other person) by reason of his employment, such as may give rise to charges to tax under section 196 of the principal Act, section 36 or 37 of the Finance (No. 2) Act 1975 or sections 61 to 68 of the Finance Act 1976 (miscellaneous benefits in cash or in kind); and

(*b*) if such benefits are or have been provided, to contain such particulars of those benefits as may be specified in the notice.

(8) Where such benefits are provided the notice may, without prejudice to subsection (7)(*b*), require the return to contain the following particulars—

(*a*) where the benefits are or have been provided by the employer, particulars of the cost of providing them; and

SCH. 9

(*b*) where the benefits are or have been provided otherwise than by the employer himself, the name and business address of any person who has (either by arrangement with the employer, or to his knowledge) provided them.

(9) Where it appears to an inspector that a person has, in any year of assessment, been concerned in providing benefits to or in respect of employees of another, the inspector may at any time up to 6 years after the end of that year of assessment by notice require him to deliver to the inspector, within the time limited by the notice, such particulars of those benefits as may be specified in the notice (so far as known to him) and to include with those particulars the names and addresses (so far as known to him) of the employees concerned.

(10) Where the employer is a body of persons, the secretary of the body or other officer (by whatever name called) performing the duties of secretary shall be treated as the employer for the purposes of this section.

Provided that, where the employer is a body corporate, that body corporate, as well as the secretary or other officer, shall be liable to a penalty for failure to comply with this section.

(11) In this section—

(*a*) " employee " means an office holder or employee whose emoluments fall to be assessed under Schedule E, and related expressions are to be construed accordingly ; and

(*b*) " director's or higher-paid employment " has the same meaning as in Chapter II of Part III of the Finance Act 1976.".

2. For the year 1976-77 the section substituted by paragraph 1 above has effect as if the provisions of sections 64 and 68 of, and Schedule 7 to, this Act were in operation for that year.

1970 c. 9. 3. In section 98(3) of the Taxes Management Act 1970, the reference in the Table to section 200 of the Taxes Act shall be omitted.

Income and Corporation Taxes Act 1970 (*c*. 10)

4. The following provisions and passages in the Taxes Act are hereby repealed—

(*a*) in section 195, subsection (2) ;

(*b*) in section 196(1), the words " and section 15 of the Taxes Management Act 1970 " ;

(*c*) section 200.

Finance Act 1974 (*c*. 30)

5. In section 24 of the Finance Act 1974 (returns relating to persons treated as employees) for the words from " except paragraph (*b*) " to " are performed ; " there shall be substituted the words " shall apply as if the person for whose benefit the duties were

performed were the employer, but only so as to require him to make a return of the name and place of residence of the person performing the duties ; ". Sch. 9

Savings

6. Nothing in this Part of this Act shall prejudice the validity of anything done before the passing of this Act for the purposes of section 15 of the Taxes Management Act 1970 or section 200 of the Taxes Act, including any notice given, return made or proceedings taken, and anything so done shall be complied with and proceeded with, and proceedings for failure to comply with those sections may be instituted or continued, as if this Part of this Act had not been passed. 1970 c. 9.

PART II

OTHER AMENDMENTS

7. The amendments set out in this Part of this Schedule have effect for 1977-78 and subsequent years.

Capital Allowances Act 1968 (*c.* 3)

8. In section 33 of the Capital Allowances Act 1968 (balancing allowances and charges), in paragraph (*b*) of the proviso to subsection (2) for the words " Part VIII " to the end there shall be substituted the words " Part III of the Finance Act 1976 ".

9. In section 34 of that Act (notional sales), in subsection (3), for the words " Part VIII of the principal Act " there shall be substituted the words " Part III of the Finance Act 1976 ".

Taxes Management Act 1970 (*c.* 9)

10.—(1) In section 35(2) of the Taxes Management Act 1970, paragraph (*a*) shall be omitted.

(2) Sub-paragraph (1) has effect in relation to income assessable for 1977-78 and subsequent years.

11. In Schedule 3 to that Act (rules for assigning proceedings to Commissioners), after paragraph 5A there shall be inserted—

" 5B. An appeal against the decision of an inspector under section 65 of the Finance Act 1976.	The place where the employees concerned (or most of them) are employed."

Income and Corporation Taxes Act 1970 (*c.* 10)

12. In section 75 of the Taxes Act (sporting rights), in subsection (2), for the words from " section 196 " to the end there shall be substituted the words " section 61 of the Finance Act 1976 ".

SCH. 9

13. In section 185 of that Act (accommodation occupied by holder of office or employment), in subsection (4) for the words " 198(1) below " there shall be substituted the words " Chapter II of Part III of the Finance Act 1976 ".

14.—(1) Sections 195 to 199 and 201 to 203 of that Act are hereby repealed.

(2) Where there was in force under section 199 a notification that an inspector was satisfied that certain payments or other benefits provided by an employer would not result in additional tax liability under Chapter II of Part VIII of that Act, that notification shall, subject to the following provisions of this paragraph, continue in force as if made under section 70 of this Act in relation to tax liability under Chapter II of Part III of this Act.

(3) Such a notification does not continue in force so far as it relates to benefits or facilities chargeable to tax under sections 64 to 68 of this Act.

(4) The inspector may, if in his opinion there is reason to do so, by notice in writing served on the persons to whom the notification was given, revoke a notification continued in force by this paragraph, either from the date of its original making or as from such later date as may be specified in the notice; and then all such income tax becomes chargeable (whether under Chapter II of Part VII of the Taxes Act or Chapter II of Part III of this Act), and all such returns are to be made by that person and by the employees for whom the benefits or facilities are provided, as would have been chargeable or would have had to be made in the first instance if the notification had never been given or, as the case may be, it had ceased to have effect on the specified date.

15. In section 284(2) of the Taxes Act (close company distributions), for the proviso there shall be substituted—

" Provided that this subsection shall not apply to expense incurred in or in connection with the provision—

(*a*) for a person employed in director's or higher-paid employment (within Chapter II of Part III of the Finance Act 1976) of such benefits as are mentioned in any of sections 61 to 68 of that Act; or

(*b*) for the spouse, children or dependants of a person employed by the company of any pension, annuity on that person's death or retirement.".

16. In that section of that Act, for subsection (3) there shall be substituted the following subsection—

" (3) The amount of the expense to be taken into account under subsection (2) above as a distribution shall be the same as would under Chapter II of Part III of the Finance Act 1976 be the cash equivalent of the resultant benefit to the participator.".

SCHEDULE 10

Section 73.

Relief for Business Property

Preliminary

1. In this Schedule " transfer of value " includes a distribution payment made and a capital distribution treated as made, and references to the amount transferred by a transfer of value and to a transferor shall be construed as including respectively the amount of such a payment or distribution and the trustees of the settlement concerned.

Nature of relief

2.—(1) Where the whole or part of the value transferred by a transfer of value is attributable to the value of any relevant business property and the transfer is made after 6th April 1976, the whole or that part of the value transferred shall be treated as reduced by 30 per cent., but subject to the following provisions of this Schedule.

(2) For the purposes of this paragraph, the value transferred by a transfer of value shall be calculated as a value on which no tax is chargeable.

Relevant business property

3.—(1) Subject to the following provisions of this paragraph and to paragraphs 4, 5 and 8(3) below, in this Schedule " relevant business property " means, in relation to any transfer of value,—

(*a*) property consisting of a business or interest in a business ;

(*b*) shares in or securities of a company which (either by themselves or together with other such shares or securities owned by the transferor) gave the transferor control of the company immediately before the transfer ; and

(*c*) any land or building, machinery or plant which, immediately before the transfer, was used wholly or mainly for the purposes of a business carried on by a company of which the transferor then had control or by a partnership of which he then was a partner ;

and " business " includes a business carried on in the exercise of a profession or vocation, but does not include a business carried on otherwise than for gain.

(2) Subject to sub-paragraph (3) below, a business or interest in a business, or shares in or securities of a company are not relevant business property, if the business or, as the case may be, the business carried on by the company, consists wholly or mainly of one or more of the following, that is to say, dealing in securities, stocks or shares, land or buildings or making or holding investments.

(3) Sub-paragraph (2) above—

(*a*) does not apply to any property if the business concerned is that of a jobber (as defined in section 477 of the Taxes Act) or discount house and is carried on in the United Kingdom, and

SCH. 10

(*b*) does not apply to shares in or securities of a company if the business of the company consists wholly or mainly in being a holding company of one or more companies whose business does not fall within that sub-paragraph.

(4) Where any property would be relevant business property in relation to a transfer of value but a binding contract for its sale has been entered into at the time of the transfer, it is not relevant business property in relation to the transfer unless—

(*a*) the property is a business or interest in a business and the sale is to a company which is to carry on the business and is made in consideration wholly or mainly of shares in or securities of that company ; or

(*b*) the property is shares in or securities of a company and the sale is made for the purpose of reconstruction or amalgamation.

(5) Shares in or securities of a company are not relevant business property in relation to a transfer of value if at the time of the transfer a winding-up order has been made in respect of the company or the company has passed a resolution for voluntary winding-up or is otherwise in process of liquidation, unless the business of the company is to continue to be carried on after a reconstruction or amalgamation and the reconstruction or amalgamation either is the purpose of the winding-up or liquidation or takes place not later than one year after the transfer of value.

(6) Land, a building, machinery or plant owned by the transferor and used wholly or mainly for the purposes of a business carried on as mentioned in sub-paragraph (1)(*c*) above is not relevant business property in relation to a transfer of value, unless the transferor's interest in the business is or, as the case may be, shares or securities of the company carrying on the business immediately before the transfer are, relevant business property in relation to the transfer.

Minimum period of ownership

4.—(1) Property is not relevant business property in relation to a transfer of value unless—

(*a*) it was owned by the transferor throughout the two years immediately preceding the transfer ; or

(*b*) it replaced other property and it, the other property and any property directly or indirectly replaced by the other property were owned by the transferor for periods which together comprised at least two years falling within the five years immediately preceding the transfer of value ;

and, in the case of paragraph (*b*) above, any other property concerned was such that, had the transfer of value been made immediately before the property was replaced, that property would (apart from this paragraph) have been relevant business property in relation to the transfer.

(2) Subject to sub-paragraph (3) below, in a case falling within sub-paragraph (1)(*b*) above relief under this Schedule shall not exceed what it would have been had the replacement or any one or more of the replacements not been made.

(3) For the purposes of sub-paragraph (2) above changes resulting from the formation, alteration or dissolution of a partnership or from the acquisition of a business by a company controlled by the former owner of the business shall be disregarded. SCH. 10

(4) For the purposes of this paragraph, where the transferor became entitled to any property on the death of another person—

(*a*) he shall be deemed to have owned it from the date of the death; and

(*b*) if that other person was his spouse he shall also be deemed to have owned it for any period during which the spouse owned it.

5.—(1) Where—

(*a*) the whole or part of the value transferred by a transfer of value (in this paragraph referred to as the earlier transfer) was eligible for relief under this Schedule (or would have been so eligible if such relief had been capable of being given in respect of transfers of value made at that time); and

(*b*) the whole or part of the property which, in relation to the earlier transfer, was relevant business property became, through the earlier transfer, the property of the person or of the spouse of the person who is the transferor in relation to a subsequent transfer of value; and

(*c*) that property or part, or any property directly or indirectly replacing it would (apart from paragraph 4 above) have been relevant business property in relation to the subsequent transfer of value; and

(*d*) either the earlier transfer was, or the subsequent transfer of value is, a transfer made on the death of the transferor;

the property which would have been relevant business property but for paragraph 4 above shall be relevant business property notwithstanding that paragraph.

(2) Where the property which, by virtue of sub-paragraph (1) above, is relevant business property replaced the property or part referred to in paragraph (*c*) of that sub-paragraph, relief under this Schedule shall not exceed what it would have been had the replacement or any one or more of the replacements not been made, but paragraph 4(3) above shall apply with the necessary modifications for the purposes of this sub-paragraph.

(3) Where, under the earlier transfer, the amount of the value transferred which was attributable to the property or part referred to in sub-paragraph (1)(*c*) above was part only of its value, a like part only of the value which (apart from this sub-paragraph) would fall to be reduced under this Schedule by virtue of this paragraph shall be so reduced.

Value of business

6. For the purposes of this Schedule the value of a business or of an interest in a business shall be taken to be the value which would be its net value if determined under paragraph 14(2) of Schedule 4 to the Finance Act 1975. 1975 c. 7.

SCH. 10

Value of shares in or securities of certain companies

7. Where a company is a member of a group and the business of any other company which is a member of the group falls within paragraph 3(2) above, then, unless either—

(*a*) that business also falls within paragraph 3(3) above, or

(*b*) that business consists wholly or mainly in the holding of land or buildings wholly or mainly occupied by members of the group whose business either does not fall within paragraph 3(2) above or falls within both that paragraph and paragraph 3(3) above,

the value of shares in or securities of the company shall be taken for the purposes of this Schedule to be what it would be if that other company were not a member of the group.

Exclusion of value of excepted assets

8.—(1) In determining for the purposes of this Schedule what part of the value transferred by a transfer of value is attributable to the value of any relevant business property so much of the last-mentioned value as is attributable to any excepted assets within the meaning of sub-paragraph (2) below shall be left out of account.

(2) An asset is an excepted asset in relation to any relevant business property if it was not either used wholly or mainly for the purposes of the business concerned throughout the whole or the last two years of the relevant period defined in sub-paragraph (5) below, or required at the time of the transfer for future use for those purposes; but where the business concerned is carried on by a company which is a member of a group, the use of an asset for the purposes of a business carried on by another company which at the time of the use and immediately before the transfer was also a member of that group shall be treated as use for the purposes of the business concerned, unless that other company's membership of the group falls to be disregarded under paragraph 7 above.

(3) Sub-paragraph (2) above does not apply in relation to an asset which is relevant business property by virtue only of paragraph 3(1)(*c*) above, but an asset is not relevant business property by virtue only of that paragraph unless either—

(*a*) it was used as mentioned in that paragraph throughout the two years immediately preceding the transfer of value ; or

(*b*) it replaced another asset so used and it and the other asset and any asset directly or indirectly replaced by that other asset were so used for periods which together comprised at least two years falling within the five years immediately preceding the transfer of value ;

but in a case where paragraph 5 above applies this condition shall be treated as satisfied if the asset (or it and the asset or assets replaced by it) was or were so used throughout the period between the earlier and the subsequent transfer mentioned in that paragraph (or throughout the part of that period during which it or they were owned by the transferor or the transferor's spouse).

(4) Where part but not the whole of any land or building is used exclusively for the purposes of any business and the land or building would, but for this sub-paragraph, be an excepted asset, or, as the case may be, prevented by sub-paragraph (3) above from being relevant business property, the part so used and the remainder shall for the purposes of this paragraph be treated as separate assets, and the value of the part so used shall (if it would otherwise be less) be taken to be such proportion of the value of the whole as may be just. Sch. 10

(5) For the purposes of this paragraph the relevant period, in relation to any asset, is the period immediately preceding the transfer of value during which the asset (or, if the relevant business property is an interest in a business, a corresponding interest in the asset) was owned by the transferor or, if the business concerned is that of a company, was owned by that company or any other company which immediately before the transfer of value was a member of the same group.

(6) For the purposes of this paragraph an asset shall be deemed not to have been used wholly or mainly for the purposes of the business concerned at any time when it was used wholly or mainly for the personal benefit of the transferor or of a person connected with him.

Avoidance of double relief

9. So much of the value transferred by a transfer of value as is attributable to shares in or securities of a company which would not have been sufficient, without any other property, to give the transferor control of the company immediately before the transfer shall not be reduced under this Schedule, if the value of the shares or securities is taken, by virtue of paragraph 9A of Schedule 10 to the Finance Act 1975, to be less than the value previously determined. 1975 c. 7.

10. Where any part of the value transferred by a transfer of value is reduced under Schedule 8 to the Finance Act 1975 by reference to the agricultural value of any property, or would be so reduced but for paragraph 1(2A) thereof, such part of the value transferred as is or would be so reduced under that Schedule shall not be reduced under this Schedule.

11. Where the value transferred by a transfer of value is reduced under paragraph 4 of Schedule 9 to the Finance Act 1975 by reference to the tax chargeable on the disposal of any trees or underwood, the value to be reduced under paragraph 2 above shall be the value as reduced under the said paragraph 4 (but subject to paragraph 2(2) above).

12. Where, under section 22(5) of the Finance Act 1975, any value is included in the value of a person's estate immediately before his death, the value so included shall not be reduced under this Schedule.

Meaning of " group ", " holding company ", " subsidiary " and " control "

13.—(1) For the purposes of this Schedule a company and all its subsidiaries are members of a group, and " holding company " and " subsidiary " have the same meanings as in section 154 of the Companies Act 1948. 1948 c. 38.

SCH. 10 — (2) Paragraph 13(7) of Schedule 4 to the Finance Act 1975 (control of company) applies for the purposes of this Schedule.

1975 c. 7.

Section 76.

SCHEDULE 11

WORKS OF ART, HISTORIC BUILDINGS ETC.: CONSEQUENTIAL AMENDMENTS

1965 c. 25.

The Finance Act 1965

1.—(1) For sections 31 and 32 of the Finance Act 1965 there shall be substituted

"Works of art etc.

31.—(1) A gain accruing on the disposal of an asset by way of gift shall not be a chargeable gain if the asset is property falling within sub-paragraph (2) of paragraph 13 of Schedule 6 to the Finance Act 1975 (gifts for public benefit) and the Treasury give a direction in relation to it under sub-paragraph (1) of that paragraph.

(2) A gain shall not be a chargeable gain if it accrues on the disposal of an asset with respect to which a capital transfer tax undertaking or an undertaking under the following provisions of this section has been given and—

(*a*) the disposal is by way of sale by private treaty to a body mentioned in paragraph 12 of the said Schedule 6 (museums, etc) or is to such a body otherwise than by sale; or

(*b*) the disposal is to the Board in pursuance of paragraph 17 of Schedule 4 to the said Act of 1975 or in accordance with directions given by the Treasury under section 50 or 51 of the Finance Act 1946 (acceptance of property in satisfaction of tax).

(3) Subsection (4) below shall have effect in respect of the disposal of any asset which is property which has been or could be designated under section 77 of the Finance Act 1976, being—

(*a*) a disposal by way of gift, including a gift in settlement; or

(*b*) a disposal of settled property by the trustee on an occasion when, under section 25(3) or (4) of this Act, the trustee is deemed to dispose of and immediately re-acquire settled property,

if the requisite undertaking described in the said section 77 (maintenance, preservation and access) is given by such person as the Treasury think appropriate in the circumstances of the case.

(4) The person making a disposal to which subsection (3) above applies and the person acquiring the asset on the disposal shall be treated for all the purposes of this Part of this Act as if the asset was acquired from the

one making the disposal for a consideration of such an amount as would secure that on the disposal neither a gain nor a loss would accrue to the one making the disposal. Sch. 11

(5) If—

(*a*) there is a sale of the asset and capital transfer tax is chargeable under section 78 of the Finance Act 1976 (or would be chargeable if a capital transfer tax undertaking as well as an undertaking under this section had been given) ; or

(*b*) the Treasury are satisfied that at any time during the period for which any such undertaking was given it has not been observed in a material respect,

the person selling that asset or, as the case may be, the owner of the asset shall be treated for the purposes of this Part of this Act as having sold the asset for a consideration equal to its market value, and, in the case of a failure to comply with the undertaking, having immediately re-acquired it for a consideration equal to its market value.

(6) The period for which an undertaking under this section is given shall be until the person beneficially entitled to the asset dies or it is disposed of, whether by sale or gift or otherwise ; and if the asset subject to the undertaking is disposed of—

(*a*) otherwise than on sale ; and

(*b*) without a further undertaking being given under this section,

subsection (5) above shall apply as if the asset had been sold to an individual.

References in this subsection to a disposal shall be construed without regard to any provision of this Part of this Act under which an asset is deemed to be disposed of.

(7) Where under subsection (5) above a person is treated as having sold for a consideration equal to its market value any asset within section 77(1)(*c*), (*d*) or (*e*) of the Finance Act 1976, he shall also be treated as having sold and immediately re-acquired for a consideration equal to its market value any asset associated with it ; but the Treasury may direct that the foregoing provisions of this subsection shall not have effect in any case in which it appears to them that the entity consisting of the asset and any assets associated with it has not been materially affected.

For the purposes of this subsection two or more assets are associated with each other if one of them is a building falling within the said section 77(1)(*c*) and the

Sch. 11

other or others such land or objects as, in relation to that building, fall within the said section 77(1)(*d*) or (*e*).

(8) If in pursuance of subsection (5) above a person is treated as having on any occasion sold an asset and capital transfer tax becomes chargeable on the same occasion, then, in determining the value of the asset for the purposes of that tax, an allowance shall be made for the capital gains tax chargeable on any chargeable gain accruing on that occasion.

(9) In this section " capital transfer tax undertaking " means an undertaking under sections 76 to 81 of the Finance Act 1976 or section 31 or 34 of the Finance Act 1975."

(2) This paragraph does not affect the continued operation of sections 31 and 32 of the said Act of 1965, in the form in which they were before 13th March 1975, in relation to estate duty in respect of deaths occurring before that date.

1975 c. 7.

The Finance Act 1975

2. In section 26(2) of the Finance Act 1975 after the words " of this Act " (where they first occur) there shall be inserted the words " or section 78 of the Finance Act 1976 ".

3. In paragraphs 2(7), 12(4) and 19(1)(*c*) of Schedule 4 to that Act after the words " of this Act " there shall be inserted the words " or section 78 of the Finance Act 1976 ".

4. In paragraph 11(2) of Schedule 5 to that Act after the words " this Act " (in both places where they occur) there shall be inserted the words " or section 76 of the Finance Act 1976 ".

5. In paragraph 16 of Schedule 6 to that Act after the words " paragraphs 1 and 10 to 13 above " there shall be inserted the words " and sections 76 and 84 of the Finance Act 1976."

1975 c. 45.

The Finance (*No.* 2) *Act* 1975

6. Section 56 shall be omitted.

Sections 99 and 119.

SCHEDULE 12

Transfers Within Three Years Before Death

Interpretation

1. In this Schedule—

" close company " has the same meaning as in section 39 of the Finance Act 1975 ; 1975 c. 7.

" interest in land " does not include any estate, interest or right by way of mortgage or other security ;

" shares " includes securities ;

" the principal section " means section 99 of this Act ;

and expressions used in the principal section have the same meanings as in that section.

Shares—capital receipts

2.—(1) If the transferred property consists of shares and at any time before the relevant date the transferee or his spouse becomes entitled to a capital payment in respect of them, then for the purposes of the principal section the market value of the transferred property on the relevant date shall (except where apart from this paragraph it reflects a right to the payment) be taken to be increased by an amount equal to the payment.

(2) If at any time before the relevant date the transferee or his spouse receives or becomes entitled to receive in respect of the transferred property a provisional allotment of shares and disposes of the rights, the amount of the consideration for the disposal shall be treated for the purposes of this paragraph as a capital payment in respect of the transferred property.

(3) In this paragraph " capital payment " means any money or money's worth which does not constitute income for the purposes of income tax.

Payments of calls

3. If the transferred property consists of shares and at any time before the relevant date the transferee or his spouse becomes liable to make a payment in pursuance of a call in respect of them, then for the purposes of the principal section the market value of the transferred property on the relevant date shall (except where apart from this paragraph it reflects the liability) be taken to be reduced by an amount equal to the payment.

Reorganisation of share capital etc.

4.—(1) This paragraph has effect where the transferred property consists of shares in relation to which there occurs before the relevant date a transaction to which paragraph 4 of Schedule 7 to the Finance Act 1965 applies or would apply but for section 53 of this Act, that is to say— 1965 c. 25.

(*a*) a reorganisation, within the meaning of that paragraph, or reduction of the share capital of a company ; or

(*b*) the conversion of securities within the meaning of paragraph 5 of that Schedule ; or

(*c*) the issue by a company of shares in exchange for shares in another company in such circumstances that paragraph 6 of that Schedule applies ; or

(*d*) the issue by a company of shares under such an arrangement as is referred to in paragraph 7 of that Schedule ;

or any transaction relating to a unit trust scheme which corresponds to any of the transactions referred to in paragraphs (*a*) to (*d*) above and to which paragraph 4 of that Schedule applies by virtue of section 45(8) of the Finance Act 1965.

(2) In the following provisions of this paragraph " the original shares " and " the new holding " shall be construed in accordance with the said paragraph 4.

Sch. 12

(3) Where this paragraph has effect the original shares and the new holding shall be treated as the same property for the purposes of the principal section and this Schedule.

(4) Where this paragraph has effect and, as part of or in connection with the transaction concerned, the transferee or his spouse becomes liable to give any consideration for the new holding or any part of it, then for the purposes of the principal section the market value of the transferred property on the relevant date shall (except where apart from this paragraph it reflects the liability) be taken to be reduced by an amount equal to that consideration.

(5) For the purposes of sub-paragraph (4) above, there shall not be treated as consideration given for the new holding or any part of it—

(*a*) any surrender, cancellation or other alteration of any of the original shares or of the rights attached thereto, or

(*b*) any consideration consisting of any application, in paying up the new holding or any part of it, of assets of the company concerned or of any dividend or other distribution declared out of those assets but not made.

Transfers of value etc. by close companies

5.—(1) This paragraph applies where the transferred property consists of shares in a close company and at any time after the chargeable transfer and before the relevant date there is a relevant transaction in relation to the shares; and for this purpose "relevant transaction" means a transaction which is—

(*a*) the making of a transfer of value by the company, or

(*b*) an alteration in so much of the company's share or loan capital as does not consist of shares quoted on a recognised stock exchange or an alteration in any rights attaching to shares in or debentures of the company which are not so quoted,

but which does not give rise to an adjustment, under any of the preceding paragraphs of this Schedule, in the market value of the transferred property on the relevant date.

(2) Subject to sub-paragraphs (3) and (4) below, where this paragraph applies the market value of the transferred property on the relevant date shall for the purposes of the principal section be taken to be increased by an amount equal to the difference between—

(*a*) the market value of the transferred property at the time of the chargeable transfer, and

(*b*) what that value would have been if the relevant transaction had occurred before rather than after that time.

(3) Where the relevant transaction is the making by the company of a transfer of value by which the value of the estate of the person who made the chargeable transfer or, if his spouse is domiciled in the United Kingdom, his spouse is increased by any amount, the increase provided for by sub-paragraph (2) above shall be reduced by that amount'.

(4) Where the market value of the transferred property at the time of the chargeable transfer is less than it would have been as mentioned in sub-paragraph (2) above, that sub-paragraph shall apply as if, instead of providing for an increase, it provided for the market value on the relevant date to be reduced to what it would have been if the relevant transaction had not occurred.

Interests in land

6.—(1) Where the transferred property is an interest in land in relation to which the conditions mentioned in sub-paragraph (2) below are not satisfied, then, subject to sub-paragraphs (3) and (4) below, the market value of the transferred property on the relevant date shall for the purposes of the principal section be taken to be increased by an amount equal to the difference between—

(*a*) the market value of the interest at the time of the chargeable transfer, and

(*b*) what that market value would have been if the circumstances prevailing on the relevant date and by reason of which the conditions are not satisfied had prevailed at the time of the chargeable transfer.

(2) The conditions referred to in sub-paragraph (1) above are—

(*a*) that the interest was the same in all respects and with the same incidents at the time of the chargeable transfer and on the relevant date, and

(*b*) that the land in which the interest subsists was in the same state and with the same incidents at the time of the chargeable transfer and on the relevant date.

(3) If after the date of the chargeable transfer but before the relevant date compensation becomes payable under any enactment to the transferee or his spouse—

(*a*) because of the imposition of a restriction on the use or development of the land in which the interest subsists, or

(*b*) because the value of the interest is reduced for any other reason,

the imposition of the restriction or the other cause of the reduction in value shall be ignored for the purposes of sub-paragraphs (1) and (2) above, but the market value of the interest on the relevant date shall be taken to be increased by an amount equal to the amount of the compensation.

(4) Where the market value of the interest at the time of the chargeable transfer is less than it would have been as mentioned in sub-paragraph (1) above, that sub-paragraph shall apply as if, instead of providing for an increase, it provided for the market value on the relevant date to be reduced to what it would have been if the change in circumstances by reason of which the conditions mentioned in sub-paragraph (2) above are not satisfied had not occurred.

SCH. 12

Leases

7.—(1) Where the transferred property is the interest of a lessee under a lease the duration of which at the time of the chargeable transfer does not exceed fifty years, then for the purposes of the principal section the market value of the interest on the relevant date shall be taken to be increased by an amount equal to the appropriate fraction of the market value of the interest at the time of the chargeable transfer.

(2) In sub-paragraph (1) above, "the appropriate fraction" means the fraction—

$$\frac{P(1) - P(2)}{P(1)}$$

where

1965 c. 25. P(1) is the percentage that would be derived from the Table in paragraph 1 of Schedule 8 to the Finance Act 1965 (capital gains: leases) for the duration of the lease at the time of the chargeable transfer, and

P(2) is the percentage that would be so derived for the duration of the lease on the relevant date.

Other property

8.—(1) Where the transferred property is neither shares nor an interest in land and the condition mentioned in sub-paragraph (2) below is not satisfied in relation to it, then, subject to sub-paragraph (3) and paragraph 9 below, the market value of the property on the relevant date shall for the purposes of the principal section be taken to be increased by an amount equal to the difference between—

(*a*) the market value of the property at the time of the chargeable transfer, and

(*b*) what that value would have been if the circumstances prevailing at the relevant date and by reason of which the condition is not satisfied had prevailed at the time of the chargeable transfer.

(2) The condition referred to in sub-paragraph (1) above is that the transferred property was the same in all respects at the time of the chargeable transfer and on the relevant date.

(3) Where the market value of the transferred property at the time of the chargeable transfer is less than it would have been as mentioned in sub-paragraph (1) above, that sub-paragraph shall apply as if, instead of providing for an increase, it provided for the market value on the relevant date to be reduced to what it would have been if the property had remained the same in all respects as it was at the time of the chargeable transfer.

9. Where the transferred property is neither shares nor an interest in land and during the period between the time of the chargeable transfer and the relevant date benefits in money or money's worth are derived from it which exceed a reasonable return on its market value at the time of the chargeable transfer, then—

(*a*) any effect of the benefits on the transferred property shall be ignored for the purposes of paragraph 8 above ; but

(*b*) the market value of the transferred property on the relevant date shall be taken for the purposes of the principal section to be increased by an amount equal to the said excess.

SCHEDULE 13

Section 101.

Falls in Value of Land After Death [Provisions Added to Schedule 10 to Finance Act 1975]

" Part III

Valuation of Interests in Land Sold Within Three Years of Death

Interpretation

31.—(1) In this Part of this Schedule—

" the appropriate person ", in relation to any interest in land comprised in a person's estate immediately before his death, means the person liable for tax attributable to the value of that interest or, if there is more than one such person and one of them is in fact paying the tax, that person ;

" interest in land " does not include any estate, interest or right by way of mortgage or other security ;

" sale price ", in relation to any interest in land, means the price for which it is sold or, if greater, the best consideration that could reasonably have been obtained for it at the time of the sale ;

" sale value ", in relation to any interest in land, means its sale price as increased or reduced under the following provisions of this Part of this Schedule ;

" value on death ", in relation to any interest in land comprised in a person's estate immediately before his death, means the value which, apart from this Part of this Schedule (and apart from paragraph 9A above) would be its value as part of that estate for the purposes of tax.

(2) For the purposes of this Part of this Schedule—

(*a*) the personal representatives of the deceased, and

(*b*) the trustees of a settlement,

shall each be treated as a single and continuing body of persons (distinct from the persons who may from time to time be the personal representatives or trustees).

The relief

32.—(1) Where—

(*a*) an interest in land is comprised in a person's estate immediately before his death and is sold by the appropriate

SCH. 13

person within the period of three years immediately following the date of the death, and

(*b*) the appropriate person makes a claim under this paragraph stating the capacity in which he makes it,

the value for the purposes of tax of that interest and of any other interest in land comprised in that estate and sold within that period by the person making the claim acting in the same capacity shall, subject to the following provisions of this Part of this Schedule, be its sale value.

(2) Sub-paragraph (1) above shall not apply to an interest if its sale value would differ from its value on death by less than the lower of—

(*a*) £1,000, and

(*b*) 5 per cent. of its value on death.

(3) Sub-paragraph (1) above shall not apply to an interest if its sale is—

(*a*) a sale by a personal representative or trustee to—

(i) a person who, at any time between the death and the sale, has been beneficially entitled to, or to an interest in possession in, property comprising the interest sold, or

(ii) the spouse or a child or remoter descendant of a person within sub-paragraph (i) above, or

(iii) trustees of a settlement under which a person within sub-paragraph (i) or (ii) above has an interest in possession in property comprising the interest sold ; or

(*b*) a sale in connection with which the vendor or any person within sub-paragraph (i), (ii) or (iii) of paragraph (*a*) above obtains a right to acquire the interest sold or any other interest in the same land ;

and for the purposes of this sub-paragraph a person shall be treated as having in the property comprised in an unadministered estate (within the meaning of paragraph 22(2) of Schedule 5 to this Act) the same interest as he would have if the administration of the estate had been completed.

(4) In the following provisions of this Part of this Schedule, any reference to the interests to which a claim relates is a reference to the interests to which this paragraph applies by virtue of the claim.

Adjustment for changes between death and sale

33.—(1) Where the conditions mentioned in sub-paragraph (2) below are not satisfied in relation to any interest to which the claim relates then, subject to sub-paragraphs (3) and (4) below, an addition shall be made to the sale price of the interest ; and the amount of the addition shall be equal to the difference between—

(*a*) the value on death of the interest, and

(*b*) what that value would have been if the circumstances prevailing at the date of the sale and by reason of which the conditions are not satisfied had prevailed immediately before the death. Sch. 13

(2) The conditions referred to in sub-paragraph (1) above are—

(*a*) that the interest was the same in all respects and with the same incidents at the date of the death and at the date of the sale ; and

(*b*) that the land in which the interest subsists was in the same state and with the same incidents at the date of the death and at the date of the sale.

(3) If after the date of the death but before the date of the sale compensation becomes payable under any enactment to the appropriate person or any other person liable for tax attributable to the value of the interest—

(*a*) because of the imposition of a restriction on the use or development of the land in which the interest subsists, or

(*b*) because the value of the interest is reduced for any other reason,

the imposition of the restriction or the other cause of the reduction in value shall be ignored for the purposes of sub-paragraphs (1) and (2) above, but there shall be added to the sale price of the interest an amount equal to the amount of compensation.

(4) Where the value on death of an interest is less than it would have been as mentioned in sub-paragraph (1) above, that sub-paragraph shall apply as if, instead of providing for an addition to be made to the sale price, it provided for that price to be reduced to what it would have been if the change in circumstances by reason of which the conditions mentioned in sub-paragraph (2) above are not satisfied had not occurred.

Leases

34.—(1) Where the claim relates to an interest which is the interest of a lessee under a lease the duration of which at the date of the death does not exceed fifty years, an addition shall be made to the sale price of the interest ; and the amount of the addition shall be equal to the appropriate fraction of the value on death of the interest.

(2) In sub-paragraph (1) above, " the appropriate fraction " means the fraction—

$$\frac{P(1)-P(2)}{P(1)}$$

where—

P(1) is the percentage that would be derived from the Table in paragraph 1 of Schedule 8 to the Finance Act 1965 (capital gains : leases) for the duration of the lease at the date of the death, and 1965 c. 25.

P(2) is the percentage that would be so derived for the duration of the lease at the date of the sale.

Adjustment for valuation by reference to other interests

35. If in determining the value on death of any interest to which the claim relates, any other interests, whether in the same or other

SCH. 13 land, were taken into account, an addition shall be made to the sale price of the interest; and the amount of the addition shall be equal to the difference between the value on death of the interest and the value which would have been the value on death if no other interests had been taken into account.

Adjustment for certain sales and exchanges

36.—(1) This paragraph applies where a person who makes a claim under paragraph 32 above, acting in the same capacity as that in which he makes the claim—

(*a*) sells an interest to which paragraph 32 would apply but for sub-paragraph (3) of that paragraph, or

(*b*) within the period of three years immediately following the date of the death exchanges (with or without any payment by way of equality of exchange) any interest in land which was comprised in the deceased's estate immediately before his death,

and the sale price of the interest, or in the case of an exchange its market value at the date of the exchange, exceeds its value on death.

(2) Where this paragraph applies, an addition shall be made to the sale price of any interest to which the claim relates; and the amount of the addition—

(*a*) if the claim relates to one interest only, shall be equal to the excess referred to in sub-paragraph (1) above, and

(*b*) if the claim relates to more than one interest, shall be equal to the appropriate fraction of that excess.

(3) In sub-paragraph (2) above "the appropriate fraction" in relation to any interest to which this claim relates is the fraction of which—

(*a*) the numerator is the difference between the value on death of that interest and its sale price as adjusted under paragraphs 33 to 35 above, and

(*b*) the denominator is the aggregate of that difference and the corresponding differences for all the other interests to which the claim relates;

and the aggregate referred to in paragraph (*b*) above shall be calculated without regard to which is the greater, in the case of any particular interest, of its value on death and its sale price.

Adjustment for purchases

37.—(1) This paragraph applies where a claim is made under paragraph 32 above and, at any time during the period beginning on the date of the death and ending four months after the last of the sales referred to in sub-paragraph (1) of that paragraph, the person making the claim purchases any interests in land in the same capacity as that in which he makes the claim.

(2) If the aggregate of the purchase prices of all the interests purchased as mentioned in sub-paragraph (1) above equals or

exceeds the aggregate of the sale prices, as adjusted under paragraphs 33 to 35 above, of all the interests to which the claim relates, this Part of this Schedule shall not apply in relation to the claim; but otherwise sub-paragraph (3) below shall have effect, and in that sub-paragraph " the appropriate fraction " means the fraction of which— SCH. 13

(*a*) the numerator is the aggregate of the said purchase prices, and

(*b*) the denominator is the aggregate of the said sale prices.

(3) Subject to sub-paragraph (4) below, where this sub-paragraph has effect an addition shall be made to the sale price of every interest to which the claim relates; and the amount of the addition shall be equal to the appropriate fraction of the difference between the value on death of the interest and its sale price as adjusted under paragraphs 33 to 36 above.

(4) Where the value on death of an interest is less than its sale price as adjusted under paragraphs 33 to 36 above, sub-paragraph (3) above shall apply as if it provided for a reduction instead of an increase in the sale price.

Compulsory acquisition more than three years after death

38.—(1) If after the end of the period of three years immediately following the date of the death an interest in land is acquired from the appropriate person in pursuance of a notice to treat served before the death or within that period by an authority possessing powers of compulsory acquisition, then, subject to the following sub-paragraphs, this Part of this Schedule shall apply in relation to the interest as it applies in relation to interests sold within that period.

(2) Sub-paragraph (1) above shall not have effect in relation to an interest if its sale value would exceed its value on death.

(3) In determining the period referred to in paragraph 37(1) above, no account shall be taken of the sale of an interest in relation to which sub-paragraph (1) above has effect; and if the claim relates only to such interests, paragraph 37 shall not apply in relation to the claim.

Supplementary

39. In any case where, for the purposes of this Part of this Schedule, it is necessary to determine the price at which any interest was purchased or sold or the best consideration that could reasonably have been obtained on the sale of any interest, no account shall be taken of expenses (whether by way of commission, stamp duty or otherwise) which are incidental to the sale or purchase.

40.—(1) Subject to the following sub-paragraphs, the date on which an interest in land is sold or purchased by the appropriate person shall for the purposes of this Part of this Schedule be taken to be the date on which he enters into a contract to sell or purchase it.

(2) If the sale or purchase of any interest by the appropriate person results from the exercise (whether by him or by any other person) of an option granted not more than six months earlier, the date on

Sch. 13 which the interest is sold or purchased shall be taken to be the date on which the option was granted.

(3) If an interest is acquired from the appropriate person in pursuance of a notice to treat served by an authority possessing powers of compulsory acquisition, the date on which the interest is sold shall, subject to sub-paragraph (4) below, be taken to be the date on which compensation for the acquisition is agreed or otherwise determined (variations on appeal being disregarded for this purpose) or, if earlier, the date when the authority enter on the land in pursuance of their powers.

(4) If an interest in land is acquired from the appropriate person—

(*a*) in England, Scotland or Wales by virtue of a general vesting
1968 c. 72. declaration within the meaning of Schedule 3 to the Town and Country Planning Act 1968 or, in Scotland, Schedule
1972 c. 52. 24 to the Town and Country Planning (Scotland) Act 1972, or

(*b*) in Northern Ireland, by way of a vesting order,

the date on which it is sold by the appropriate person shall be taken to be the last day of the period specified in the declaration or, in Northern Ireland, the date on which the vesting order becomes operative."

Section 112.

SCHEDULE 14

Settled Property

Interpretation

1. References in the following provisions of this Schedule to sections or Schedules are, except where otherwise indicated, references
1975 c. 7. to sections of or Schedules to the Finance Act 1975.

Capital distributions

2. In section 51(1), after the definition of " the Board " there shall be inserted—

" " capital distribution " has the same meaning as in Schedule 5 to this Act, and includes a capital distribution treated as made by virtue of any provision of that Schedule ; ".

3. After subsection (2) of section 51 there shall be inserted—

" (2A) Subsection (2) above shall not have effect in relation to capital distributions ; but, except where the context otherwise requires, references in this Part of this Act to chargeable transfers or to the values transferred by them shall be construed as including references to capital distributions or to the amounts on which tax is chargeable in respect of them."

4. In paragraph 2(1) of Schedule 4, after paragraph (*b*) there shall be inserted the words " or

(*c*) is liable as trustee of a settlement for tax on a capital distribution, or would be so liable if tax were chargeable on it ; ".

5. At the end of paragraph 6 of Schedule 4 there shall be added—

" (6) References in this paragraph to transfers of value or to the values transferred by them shall be construed as including references to capital distributions or to the amounts on which tax is chargeable in respect of them." Sch. 14

6.—(1) Paragraph 16 of Schedule 4 shall be amended as follows.

(2) In sub-paragraph (5), for the words " transfer of value " there shall be substituted the words " chargeable transfer ".

(3) For sub-paragraph (6) there shall be substituted—

" (6) The reference in sub-paragraph (5) above to any previous chargeable transfer made by the same transferor means, in relation to a chargeable transfer which is a capital distribution, any previous capital distribution made out of property comprised in the same settlement other than a capital distribution treated as made under paragraph 12 of Schedule 5 to this Act."

(4) In sub-paragraph (7), after the word " day " there shall be inserted the words " and capital distributions made out of property comprised in the same settlement on the same day ".

7. At the end of paragraph 25 of Schedule 4 there shall be added—

" (5) References in this paragraph to a transfer of value, or to the value transferred by a transfer of value, shall be construed as including references to a capital distribution or to the amount on which tax is chargeable in respect of a capital distribution."

8.—(1) In paragraph 12(3) of Schedule 5, for the words " next capital distribution " onwards there shall be substituted the words " next capital distribution made out of the property or, as the case may be, out of the part concerned, not being a capital distribution treated as made under that sub-paragraph."

(2) At the end of paragraph 13(1) of Schedule 5 there shall be added the words " not being a capital distribution treated as made under paragraph 12 above ".

9. At the end of paragraph 11 of Schedule 10, there shall be added—

" (5) References in this paragraph to a transfer of value shall be construed as including references to a capital distribution."

Interests in possession in Scotland

10. In paragraph 1(9) of Schedule 5, for the word " Schedule " there shall be substituted the words " Part of this Act " and for the words from " actually " to " that interest " there shall be substituted the words " by virtue of which the person in right of that interest is entitled to the enjoyment of the property or would be so entitled if the property were capable of enjoyment ".

Charge on capital distributions

11. In paragraph 6(5) of Schedule 5, for the words " ; and in relation " onwards there shall be substituted the words " or, in the case of a capital distribution treated as made under sub-paragraph (2) above or paragraph 15(3) below, any tax which is payable out of the property whose value is taken as the amount of the capital distribution ; and in relation to a capital distribution treated as made

SCH. 14 under sub-paragraph (3) above or paragraph 12 or 24(2) below, sub-paragraph (4)(*a*) above shall have effect as if the words " less the tax payable on it " were omitted ".

Settlor etc. becoming entitled to interest in possession

12.—(1) Paragraph 6 of Schedule 5 shall have effect, and shall be deemed always to have had effect, as if after sub-paragraph (6) there were inserted—

" (6A) Where the person referred to in sub-paragraph (2) above is the settlor, the settlor's spouse or, if the settlor has died less than two years before the time there referred to, the settlor's widow or widower, and is domiciled in the United Kingdom at that time, that sub-paragraph shall have effect as if the reference in it to a capital distribution were a reference to a distribution payment to the settlor or, as the case may be, the settlor's spouse, widow or widower ".

(2) Paragraph 11(8) of Schedule 5 shall have effect, and shall be deemed always to have had effect, as if after the words " this sub-paragraph " in each place where they occur there were inserted the words " or paragraph 6(6A) above ".

Non-resident beneficiaries

13. The following provisions shall cease to have effect—

(*a*) in section 22(3)(*a*), the words from " and resident " to " occurred " ;

(*b*) in paragraph 4(6) of Schedule 5, the words from " and resident " to " end " ;

(*c*) in paragraph 6(6) of Schedule 5, the words from " and resident " to the end ;

(*d*) in paragraph 14(5) of Schedule 5, the words from " and resident " to the end.

Distribution payments made on same day

14.—(1) After paragraph 10 of Schedule 5 there shall be inserted—

" 10A. Where a capital distribution is made on the same day and out of property comprised in the same settlement as a distribution payment that is not a capital distribution, the capital distribution shall for the purpose of paragraphs 7 to 9 above be treated as made before the distribution payment.".

(2) This paragraph has effect in relation to distribution payments made after 15th April 1976.

Settlements of excluded property

15.—(1) In determining for the purposes of any provision of Schedule 5 whether there has been a transfer of value which satisfies the conditions stated in sub-paragraph (2) of paragraph 11 of that Schedule or what is the relevant transfer within the meaning of that sub-paragraph in relation to any settlement, the fact that any property is excluded property shall be ignored.

(2) This paragraph shall be deemed to have come into force on 16th April 1976.

Partially exempt transfers into settlement

16. In paragraph 11(2) of Schedule 5, after the words " where it was not a chargeable transfer " there shall be inserted the words " (or was a chargeable transfer of some only of the value transferred by it) ".

Periodic charge to tax

17. For paragraph 12(7) of Schedule 5 there shall be substituted—

" (7) Paragraph 11 above shall apply for the interpretation of this paragraph as it applies for the interpretation of paragraphs 6 to 10, except that paragraph 11(4) shall be disregarded in determining in relation to any settled property whether the trustees are resident in the United Kingdom."

Superannuation schemes

18. Paragraph 16(1) of Schedule 5 shall have effect, and shall be deemed always to have had effect, as if after the words " that Act applies " there were inserted the words " to any scheme approved under section 226 or 226A of that Act ".

Protective trusts

19.—(1) In paragraph 18 of Schedule 5, for paragraph (*a*) of sub-paragraph (2) there shall be substituted—

" (*a*) tax shall not be charged under paragraph 4(2) above on the coming to an end of the principal beneficiary's interest in the property if the property is then held on discretionary trusts to the like effect as those specified in paragraph (ii) of the said section 33(1) ".

(2) This paragraph shall be deemed to have come into force on 16th April 1976.

Liability of settlor

20. Section 25(3)(*d*) (which imposes liability for tax on the settlor where the trustees are non-resident) shall not apply, and shall be deemed never to have applied, in relation to a settlement made before 11th December 1974 if—

(*a*) the trustees were resident in the United Kingdom when the settlement was made, and

(*b*) in the case of a chargeable transfer made after 10th December 1974, the trustees have not been resident in the United Kingdom at any time during the period between that date and the time of the transfer.

Section 132.

SCHEDULE 15

REPEALS

PART I

CUSTOMS AND EXCISE

Chapter	Short title	Extent of repeal
15 & 16 Geo. 6 & 1 Eliz. 2 c. 44.	The Customs and Excise Act 1952.	Section 34(1A). In section 105(1) the word " spirits " where it first occurs. In section 160(1) the words " or retailer of ". In section 307 the definition of " non-excisable cider ".
1967 c. 54.	The Finance Act 1967.	In Schedule 6, paragraph 2.
1971 c. 12.	The Hydrocarbon Oil (Customs & Excise) Act 1971.	In Schedule 1, paragraph 6.
1972 c. 68.	The European Communities Act 1972.	In Schedule 4, paragraph 2(2).
1973 c. 51.	The Finance Act 1973.	In section 1, in subsection (4) the words from " or any obligation " onwards and in subsection (5)(*b*) the words "the Hydrocarbon Oil (Customs & Excise) Act 1971 and " and " and substitute for any relief under the Act of 1971 such relief as may be specified in the order ".
1975 c. 45.	The Finance (No. 2) Act 1975.	Section 7. In section 15(6) the definition of " non-excisable cider ". Section 16(6). In Schedule 3, in paragraph 44(*d*)(i) the words " and of " non-excisable cider " ".

1. The repeals in section 307 of the Customs and Excise Act 1952 and section 15 of and Schedule 3 to the Finance (No. 2) Act 1975 take effect on 6th September 1976.

2. The repeals in section 34 of the Customs and Excise Act 1952, in the European Communities Act 1972 and in section 16 of the Finance (No. 2) Act 1975 take effect on the coming into force of the first regulations under section 15 of this Act.

PART II

VALUE ADDED TAX

Chapter	Short title	Extent of repeal
1972 c. 41.	The Finance Act 1972.	In section 31(1), the word " taxable ". In Schedule 3, paragraph 3.

The repeal in Schedule 3 to the Finance Act 1972 takes effect on the day referred to in section 20(3) of this Act.

PART III

INCOME TAX, CORPORATION TAX AND CAPITAL GAINS TAX

Chapter	Short title	Extent of repeal
1968 c. 3.	The Capital Allowances Act 1968.	Section 20(2) to (5). In section 24, in subsection (2), the words " by virtue of section 20(3), or ", in subsection (3) the words " section 20(4) or " and in subsection (4) the words " section 20(7) or, as the case may be ". In section 26(6) the words " section 20(4) or ". In section 31(1) the words " determined in accordance with the subsequent provisions of the said section 20 ". In Schedule 4— in paragraph 1, in sub-paragraph (2) the words " section 20(3) or " (in both places), " or under that subsection " and " as the case may be ", in sub-paragraph (3) the words " section 20(4) or ", " section 281 or ", " the said section 20(4) or " and " as the case may be ", and sub-paragraph (4); in paragraph 2, sub-paragraph (2), in sub-paragraph (4) the words " section 20(4) or, as the case may be " and " (2) or ", in sub-paragraph (5)(*a*) the words " section 20(3) or ", in sub-paragraph (5)(*b*) the words " (2) or ", " section 20(3) or ", " as the case may be " (where next occurring) and " sub-paragraph (2)(*c*) or, as the case may be ";

SCH. 15

Chapter	Short title	Extent of repeal
1968 c. 3.—*cont.*	The Capital Allowances Act 1968—*cont.*	in paragraph 3, in sub-paragraph (1) the words " section 281(2) or, as the case may be ", in sub-paragraph (2) the words " 281 or " and in sub-paragraph (3) the words " section 20(1) or, as the case may be,".
1970 c. 9.	The Taxes Management Act 1970.	In section 35(2), paragraph (*a*). In section 67(1) the words " or in the sheriff's small debt court, whichever is appropriate ". In the Table in section 98(3), in the first column, the reference to section 200 of the Taxes Act.
1970 c. 10.	The Income and Corporation Taxes Act 1970.	Section 24(2). In section 38(1), the proviso. Sections 195 to 203. Section 315(7) and (8). Section 473(2). In section 498(1), the proviso. Section 513. In Schedule 12, Parts I and II and, in Part III, paragraphs 1, 3(1) and (2), 4 and 5.
1972 c. 41.	The Finance Act 1972.	Section 68(2).
1973 c. 51.	The Finance Act 1973.	Section 42. Schedule 17.
1974 c. 30.	The Finance Act 1974.	Section 18.
1975 c. 7.	The Finance Act 1975.	In Schedule 12, paragraphs 14 and 15.
1975 c. 45.	The Finance (No. 2) Act 1975.	Section 30(1) and (2). Section 32. Section 35. In section 37(6) the words " and subsection (6).". Section 56. Section 65. In Schedule 10, paragraphs 1(2)(*b*) and 6(2)(*b*). Schedule 11.

1. The repeals in the Capital Allowances Act 1968 have effect for any new chargeable period within the meaning of section 39 of this Act.

2. The repeal in section 67(1) of the Taxes Management Act 1970 comes into force on 1st September 1976.

3. The following repeals have effect for 1977–78 and subsequent years—

(*a*) the repeal in section 35(2) of the Taxes Management Act 1970;

(*b*) the repeal of sections 195 to 199 of the Taxes Act (except the repeals mentioned in paragraph 4(*a*) and (*b*) of Schedule 9 to this Act); and

(*c*) the repeal of sections 201 to 203 of the Taxes Act.

4. In the case of the enactments mentioned in paragraphs 3, 4 and 14 of Schedule 9 to this Act, their repeal is subject as mentioned in paragraphs 6 and 14 of that Schedule.

5. In the case of the enactments mentioned in section 49(2)(*a*) to (*c*) of this Act, their repeal is subject as mentioned in section 49(7).

6. The repeal of section 68(2) of the Finance Act 1972 has effect as respects disposals after 15th April 1976.

7. The repeals in Schedule 12 to the Finance Act 1975 and of section 56 of the Finance (No. 2) Act 1975 come into force on 7th April 1976.

8. The repeal of section 24(2) of the Income and Corporation Taxes Act 1970 and section 32 of the Finance (No. 2) Act 1975 does not affect the operation of those provisions in relation to any allowance or benefit payable in respect of a period before the appointed day for the purposes of the Child Benefit Act 1975 and the Child Benefit (Northern Ireland) Order 1975.

9. The repeal of section 35 of the Finance (No. 2) Act 1975 has effect from 6th April 1976.

PART IV
LIFE POLICIES

Chapter	Short title	Extent of repeal
1970 c. 10.	The Income and Corporation Taxes Act 1970.	In section 19, in subsection (2)(*a*)(iii) and (iv) the word " with "; and subsection (7). In section 20, in subsection (1), paragraph (*a*) and the words " on the amount of the premium paid by him or "; subsection (2); in subsection (4), the words " premiums or other "; in subsection (5), the words " premium or " and the proviso; and subsection (6). In section 21, in subsection (4), the words " premiums or " and the words following paragraph (*b*). In section 25, in subsection (2), the words " section 19 or ". In section 230(7)(*b*) the words " from income tax ". In section 39(1)(*c*) the words " 19 or ". In Schedule 1, paragraph 4(1)(*d*)(iii), and the word " and " preceding it.
1971 c. 68.	The Finance Act 1971.	Section 33(3)(*e*).
1975 c. 7.	The Finance Act 1975.	In section 9, in subsection (4), the words " increase in " in the second place where they occur.

These repeals have effect for the year 1979–80 and subsequent years.

SCH. 15

PART V

CAPITAL TRANSFER TAX

Chapter	Short title	Extent of repeal

1975 c. 7.	The Finance Act 1975.	In section 22(3)(*a*), the words from " and resident " to " occurred ".
		Section 39(7).
		Section 41.
		In Schedule 5—
		in paragraph 4(6), the words from " and resident " to " end ";
		in paragraph 6(6), the words from " and resident " to the end;
		paragraph 6(7);
		paragraph 12(8);
		in paragraph 14(5), the words from " and resident " to the end.
		In Schedule 6, paragraph 9 and in paragraph 15(3)(*b*) the words " is given subject to an interest reserved or created by the donor or ".
		In Schedule 8, paragraphs 1(1)(*a*) and 9 and, in paragraph 10, the words from " and the multiplied " to the end.

The repeals in Schedule 8 to the Finance Act 1975 have effect in relation to chargeable transfers made after 6th April 1976.

PART VI

STAMP DUTY

Chapter	Short title	Extent of repeal
54 & 55 Vict. c. 39.	The Stamp Act 1891.	Section 115. Schedule 2.
10 & 11 Geo. 5. c. 18.	The Finance Act 1920.	Section 37(3).
2 & 3 Geo. 6. c. 41.	The Finance Act 1939.	Section 37.
9 & 10 Geo. 6. c. 64.	The Finance Act 1946.	Section 54(5).
10 & 11 Geo. 6. c. 17 (N.I.).	The Finance (No. 2) Act (Northern Ireland) 1946.	Section 25(5).
1963 c. 25.	The Finance Act 1963.	Section 58(1) and (3). Section 62(3).
1967 c. 54.	The Finance Act 1967.	Section 29(5)(*a*).

Sch. 15

Chapter	Short title	Extent of repeal
1970 c. 24.	The Finance Act 1970.	In section 33, in subsection (1) the words " being instruments executed for the purposes of stock exchange transactions as defined in section 4(1) of the Stock Transfer Act 1963 ". and subsection (3).
1970 c. 21 (N.I.).	The Finance Act (Northern Ireland) 1970.	Section 8.
1971 c. 68.	The Finance Act 1971.	Section 65.
S.I. 1972 No. 1100 (N.I. 11).	The Finance (Northern Ireland) Order 1972.	Article 11.
1974 c. 30.	The Finance Act 1974.	In Schedule 11, paragraphs 6, 7, 8, 16 and 17.

Part VII

Miscellaneous

Chapter	Short Title	Extent of Repeal
17 & 18 Geo. 5. c. 10.	The Finance Act 1927.	Section 53.
6 & 7 Geo. 6. c. 20 (N.I.).	The Finance (No. 2) Act (Northern Ireland) 1942.	Section 2.
1961 c. 10 (N.I.).	The Finance Act (Northern Ireland) 1961.	Section 13.
1968 c. 17 (N.I.).	The Finance Act (Northern Ireland) 1968.	Section 22.
1972 c. 41.	The Finance Act 1972.	In section 119(2)(*a*) the words " or section 39 of the Finance Act 1974 ".
1974 c. 30.	The Finance Act 1974.	Section 39(5). In section 44(2) the words " (subject to Schedule 5 to this Act) ". Schedule 5. In Schedule 6, paragraph 8(2).

Iron and Steel (Amendment) Act 1976

1976 CHAPTER 41

An Act to make provision with respect to the limit on the sums borrowed by, or paid by the Secretary of State to, the British Steel Corporation and the publicly-owned companies, with respect to the powers of the Corporation to lend and borrow and the powers of those companies to borrow and with respect to the Corporation's accounts; and for connected purposes.

[29th July 1976]

BE IT ENACTED by the Queen's most Excellent Majesty, by and with the advice and consent of the Lords Spiritual and Temporal, and Commons, in this present Parliament assembled, and by the authority of the same, as follows:—

Preliminary. 1975 c. 64.

1.—(1) The Iron and Steel Act 1975 shall be amended in accordance with the following provisions of this Act, and in this Act a reference to a section is a reference to a section of that Act.

(2) In this Act " the Corporation " means the British Steel Corporation and " publicly-owned company " has the same meaning as in the Iron and Steel Act 1975.

Increase in borrowing powers of Corporation, etc.

2.—(1) Section 19 (aggregate of money borrowed by the Corporation and the publicly-owned companies and of money invested in Corporation by Secretary of State limited to £2,000 million) shall be re-numbered as subsection (1) of that section, and in that subsection for " £2,000 million " there shall be substituted " the limit imposed by or by virtue of subsection (2) below ".

(2) The following subsection shall be inserted at the end of section 19(1)—

" (2) The said limit is £3,000 million or such greater sum not exceeding £4,000 million as the Secretary of State may specify by order made with the consent of the Treasury."

(3) Accordingly, in section 36 (regulations, orders and rules)—

(*a*) the following subsection shall be inserted after subsection (3)—

" (3A) No order shall be made under section 19(2) of this Act unless a draft of the order has been laid before, and approved by a resolution of, the House of Commons." ; and

(*b*) in subsection (5) (power to vary or revoke orders) after " 6(3) " there shall be inserted " 19(2) ".

Amounts of loans from a publicly-owned company to Corporation or another such company not to be limited.

3. In section 19(1)—

(*a*) at the end of paragraph (*a*) (aggregate subject to the limit includes money borrowed by Corporation, other than money borrowed by them for certain purposes) there shall be inserted " and other than money borrowed by them from a publicly-owned company " ; and

(*b*) in paragraph (*c*) (aggregate includes money borrowed under section 16 by the publicly-owned companies other than from Corporation) for the words from " under section 16 " to the end there shall be substituted " by any publicly-owned company, other than money borrowed from the Corporation or another publicly-owned company ".

Borrowing by publicly-owned companies.

4.—(1) A publicly-owned company shall have, and have only, such power to borrow as it would have apart from subsections (4) and (5) of section 16 (powers of, and restrictions on, borrowing of publicly-owned companies), and accordingly—

(*a*) subsection (4) shall be omitted, and

(*b*) in subsection (5) for " neither the Corporation nor a publicly-owned company shall " there shall be substituted " the Corporation shall not ".

(2) Without prejudice to section 3(5) (Corporation's powers, including power to lend), the Corporation shall have power to lend to a publicly-owned company such sums as that company has power to borrow.

(3) After section 16(5) there shall be inserted the following subsection—

" (6) The Corporation shall secure that no publicly-owned company borrows money otherwise than from the Corporation or from another publicly-owned company except with the consent of the Secretary of State and the approval of the Treasury.

Borrowing by Corporation from publicly-owned companies.

5. The following new subsection shall be inserted in section 16 (in place of the subsection omitted by this Act)—

" (4) Without prejudice to the preceding provisions of this section, the Corporation may, without obtaining the consent of the Secretary of State or the approval of the Treasury under this section,—

(*a*) borrow temporarily, by way of overdraft or otherwise, from a publicly-owned company such sums in any currency as the Corporation may require for—

(i) meeting their obligations or exercising and performing their functions under this Act ; or

(ii) lending money temporarily to another publicly-owned company ;

(*b*) borrow (otherwise than by way of temporary loan) from a publicly-owned company such sums in any currency as the Corporation may require for all or any of the purposes mentioned in subsection (2) above.".

Corporation's accounts.

6.—(1) In section 24(1) (Corporation to prepare certain statements of accounts in respect of each financial year)—

(*a*) in paragraph (*b*) (Corporation to prepare a statement dealing with Corporation and the publicly-owned companies as a whole) for " and the publicly-owned companies as a whole " there shall be substituted " and their subsidiaries or, if the Secretary of State so directs in respect of any financial year, of the Corporation and their subsidiaries other than any subsidiary (not being a publicly-owned company) specified in the direction " ; and

(*b*) in paragraph (*c*) (where Secretary of State so directs, Corporation to prepare a statement dealing with Corporation and, according as may be specified in the direction, their subsidiaries or specified subsidiaries) for the words from " and (according " to the end there shall be substituted " and the publicly-owned companies as a whole ".

(2) The first financial year in respect of which section 24(1) is to have effect as amended by this Act is that ending with 3rd April 1976.

Short title and Schedule

7.—(1) This Act may be cited as the Iron and Steel (Amendment) Act 1976.

(2) Sections 16, 19 and 24(1) as amended by this Act are set out in the Schedule to this Act.

SCHEDULE

Section 7(2).

SECTIONS 16, 19 AND 24(1) REPRINTED WITH AMENDMENTS

Borrowing powers of the Corporation and publicly-owned companies.

16.—(1) The Corporation may borrow temporarily, by way of overdraft or otherwise, either from the Secretary of State or, with the consent of the Secretary of State and the approval of the Treasury, from any other person, such sums in sterling as the Corporation may require for—

(*a*) meeting their obligations or exercising and performing their functions under this Act ; or

(*b*) lending money temporarily to a publicly-owned company.

(2) The Corporation may borrow (otherwise than by way of temporary loan) from the Secretary of State, or, with his consent and the approval of the Treasury, from the Commission of the European Communities or the European Investment Bank, such sums in sterling as they may require for all or any of the following purposes—

(*a*) the provision of money for meeting any expenses incurred by the Corporation or a publicly-owned company in connection with any works the cost of which is properly chargeable to capital ;

(*b*) the provision of working capital required by the Corporation or a publicly-owned company ;

(*c*) the acquisition under section 3 of this Act of any interests in, or property or rights of, a company or the formation under that section of a company ;

(*d*) the lending of money to a publicly-owned company (otherwise than by way of temporary loan) ;

(*e*) the repayment of any money borrowed by the Corporation ;

(*f*) any other purpose for which capital moneys are properly applicable.

(3) The Corporation may, with the consent of the Secretary of State (which shall require the approval of the Treasury), borrow any sum in a currency other than sterling which they have power to borrow in sterling from the Secretary of State.

(4) Without prejudice to the preceding provisions of this section, the Corporation may, without obtaining the consent of the Secretary of State or the approval of the Treasury under this section,—

(*a*) borrow temporarily, by way of overdraft or otherwise, from a publicly-owned company such sums in any currency as the Corporation may require for—

(i) meeting their obligations or exercising and performing their functions under this Act ; or

(ii) lending money temporarily to another publicly-owned company ;

(*b*) borrow (otherwise than by way of temporary loan) from a publicly-owned company such sums in any currency as the Corporation may require for all or any of the purposes mentioned in subsection (2) above.

(5) A power to borrow any sum under this section is subject to the limit imposed by section 19 of this Act, and the Corporation shall not have power to borrow money except in accordance with this section.

(6) The Corporation shall secure that no publicly-owned company borrows money otherwise than from the Corporation or from another publicly-owned company except with the consent of the Secretary of State and the approval of the Treasury.

Limit on borrowing by, and investment in the Corporation.

19.—(1) The aggregate of the following shall not at any time exceed the limit imposed by or by virtue of subsection (2) below—

(*a*) the amount outstanding in respect of the principal of any money borrowed under section 16 of this Act by the Corporation, other than money borrowed by them for the payment off of any part of their commencing capital debt, being the debt of £133,988,359·20 which the Corporation were treated as having assumed on 28th July 1967 and other than money borrowed by them from a publicly-owned company ;

(*b*) any sums paid by the Secretary of State to the Corporation under subsection (1) of section 18 of this Act (but not any sums deemed to have been so paid by virtue of subsection (3) or (4) of that section) ; and

(*c*) the amount outstanding in respect of the principal of any money borrowed by any publicly-owned company, other than money borrowed from the Corporation or another publicly-owned company.

(2) The said limit is £3,000 million or such greater sum not exceeding £4,000 million as the Secretary of State may specify by order made with the consent of the Treasury.

Accounts of the Corporation and audit.

24.—(1) The Corporation shall keep proper accounts and other records and shall prepare in such form as the Secretary of State may, with the approval of the Treasury, direct—

(*a*) in respect of each financial year, a statement of the accounts of the Corporation ;

(*b*) in respect of each financial year, a consolidated statement of accounts dealing with the state of affairs and profit or loss of the Corporation and their subsidiaries or, if the Secretary of State so directs in respect of any financial year, of the Corporation and their subsidiaries other than any subsidiary (not being a publicly-owned company) specified in the direction ; and

(*c*) in respect of a financial year as to which the Secretary of State, with the approval of the Treasury, directs that this paragraph shall have effect, a consolidated statement of accounts realing with the state of affairs and profit or loss of the Corporation and the publicly-owned companies as a whole.

Protection of Birds (Amendment) Act 1976

1976 CHAPTER 42

An Act to amend further the Protection of Birds Act 1954. [29th July 1976]

BE IT ENACTED by the Queen's most Excellent Majesty, by and with the advice and consent of the Lords Spiritual and Temporal, and Commons, in this present Parliament assembled, and by the authority of the same, as follows:—

Amendment of Protection of Birds Act 1954.
1954 c. 30.

1. Section 12(2) of the Protection of Birds Act 1954 shall be amended as follows:—

(*a*) in paragraph (*a*), for the words " twenty-five pounds " there shall be substituted the words " one hundred pounds "; and

(*b*) in paragraph (*b*) for the words " five pounds " there shall be substituted the words " twenty pounds ".

Short title and citation.

2.—(1) This Act may be cited as the Protection of Birds (Amendment) Act 1976.

(2) The Protection of Birds Acts 1954 to 1967 and this Act may be cited together as the Protection of Birds Acts 1954 to 1976.

Appropriation Act 1976

1976 CHAPTER 43

An Act to apply a sum out of the Consolidated Fund to the service of the year ending on 31st March 1977, to appropriate the supplies granted in this Session of Parliament, and to repeal certain Consolidated Fund and Appropriation Acts. [6th August 1976]

Most Gracious Sovereign,

WE, Your Majesty's most dutiful and loyal subjects the Commons of the United Kingdom in Parliament assembled, towards making good the supply which we have cheerfully granted to Your Majesty in this Session of Parliament, have resolved to grant unto Your Majesty the sum hereinafter mentioned; and do therefore most humbly beseech Your Majesty that it may be enacted, and be it enacted by the Queen's Most Excellent Majesty, by and with the advice and consent of the Lords Spiritual and Temporal, and Commons, in this present Parliament assembled, and by the authority of the same, as follows:—

Grant out of Consolidated Fund

Issue out of the Consolidated Fund for the year ending 31st March 1977.

1. The Treasury may issue out of the Consolidated Fund of the United Kingdom and apply towards making good the supply granted to Her Majesty for the service of the year ending on 31st March 1977 the sum of £21,625,001,000.

Appropriation of Grants

Appropriation of sums voted for supply services.

2. All sums granted by this Act and the other Acts mentioned in Schedule (A) annexed to this Act out of the said Consolidated Fund towards making good the supply granted to Her Majesty amounting, as appears by the said schedule, in the aggregate, to the sum of £39,593,883,351·80 are appropriated, and shall be deemed to have been appropriated as from the date of the passing of the Acts mentioned in the said Schedule (A), for the services and purposes expressed in Schedule (B) annexed hereto.

The abstract of schedules and schedules annexed hereto, with the notes (if any) to such schedules, shall be deemed to be part of this Act in the same manner as if they had been contained in the body thereof.

1891 c. 24.

In addition to the said sums granted out of the Consolidated Fund, there may be applied out of any money directed, under section 2 of the Public Accounts and Charges Act 1891, to be applied as appropriations in aid of the grants for the services and purposes specified in Schedule (B) annexed hereto the sums respectively set forth in the last column of the said schedule.

Sanction for application of surpluses on certain votes.

3. Whereas, in the year ending on 31st March 1975, surpluses arising on certain Votes were applied towards making good deficits on other Votes in that year as shown in the statement set out in Schedule (C) to this Act:

It is enacted that the application of those surpluses as shown in the said statement is hereby sanctioned.

Repeals.

4. The enactments mentioned in Schedule (D) annexed to this Act are hereby repealed.

Short title.

5. This Act may be cited as the Appropriation Act 1976.

ABSTRACT

OF

SCHEDULES (A) and (B) to which this Act refers

SCHEDULE (A)

Section 2.

Grants out of the Consolidated Fund - £39,593,883,351·80

SCHEDULE (B)—Appropriation of Grants

Section 2.

	Supply Grants	Appropriations in Aid
	£	£
1974–75 and 1975–76		
Part 1. Defence (Excesses), 1974–75	1,876,684·44	**−1,000,871·79*
Part 2. Civil (Excesses), 1974–75	10,860,667·36	82,752,853·16
Part 3. Defence (Supplementary), 1975–76	541,622,000·00	91,153,500·00
Part 4. Civil Departments (Supplementary), 1975–76	3,569,781,000·00	292,437,960·00
	£4,124,140,351·80	£465,343,441·37

* Deficit.

SCHEDULE (B)—Appropriation of Grants—*continued*

	Supply Grants	Appropriations in Aid
	£	£
1976–77		
Part 5. Defence, Class I	5,604,379,000·00	696,366,000·00
Part 6. Civil, Class II	824,589,000·00	25,705,185·00
Part 7. Civil, Class III	889,878,000·00	332,401,000·00
Part 8. Civil, Class IV	3,192,243,000·00	298,707,881·00
Part 9. Civil, Class VI	1,305,500,000·00	30,849,650·00
Part 10. Civil, Class VII	2,089,362,000·00	502,030·00
Part 11. Civil, Class VIII	226,249,000·00	31,563,060·00
Part 12. Civil, Class IX	990,686,000·00	71,304,010·00
Part 13. Civil, Class X	1,446,738,000·00	2,614,000·00
Part 14. Civil, Class XI	5,207,068,000·00	608,638,540·00
Part 15. Civil, Class XII	4,100,294,000·00	415,149,000·00
Part 16. Civil, Class XIII	948,252,000·00	108,502,150·00
Part 17. Civil, Class XIV	890,920,000·00	270,370,010·00
Part 18. Civil, Class XV	526,042,000·00	4,384,300·00
Part 19. Civil, Class XVII	7,227,543,000·00	471,812,000·00
Total, Defence and Civil	£35,469,743,000·00	£3,368,868,816·00
Grand Total	£39,593,883,351·80	£3,834,212,257·37

SCHEDULE (A)

GRANTS OUT OF THE CONSOLIDATED FUND

	£
For the service of the year ended 31st March 1975—	
Under Act 1976 c. 2 - - - - - -	12,737,351·80
For the service of the year ended 31st March 1976—	
Under Act 1975 c. 79 - - - - - -	3,159,885,000·00
Under Act 1976 c. 2 - - - - - -	951,518,000·00
For the service of the year ending on 31st March 1977—	
Under Act 1975 c. 79 - - - - - -	13,844,742,000·00
Under this Act - - - - - -	21,625,001,000·00
TOTAL - - - - -	£39,593,883,351·80

Defence (Excesses), 1974–75.

SCHEDULE (B)—PART 1

DEFENCE (EXCESSES), 1974–75

SUMS granted, and sums which may be applied as appropriations in aid in addition thereto, to make good excesses on certain grants for Defence Services for the year ended 31st March 1975, viz.:—

Vote	Supply Grants	Appropriations in Aid
CLASS I	£	£
6. PAY, &c., OF CIVILIANS - -	1,876,684·44	*−*1,000,871·79*
TOTAL, DEFENCE (EXCESSES), 1974-75 - - - -£	1,876,684·44	*−*1,000,871·79*

* Deficit.

SCHEDULE (B)—Part 2

Civil (Excesses), 1974–75.

Civil (Excesses), 1974–75

Sums granted, and sums which may be applied as appropriations in aid in addition thereto, to make good excesses on certain grants for Civil Services for the year ended 31st March 1975, viz.:—

Vote	Supply Grants	Appropriations in Aid
	£	£
Class II		
3A. Overseas Information: Broadcasting - - - -	10·00	—
7. Overseas Aid For expenditure by the Ministry of Overseas Development on the official United Kingdom aid programme, for certain subscriptions to International Organisations, and for certain payments under the Commonwealth Scholarship and Fellowship Plan, including grants in aid and assistance to the Crown Agents - - - - -	10·00	84,999,990·00
8. Overseas Aid Administration -	256,298·90	**–*20,937·20*
Class IV		
3. Industrial Innovation: General Industrial Research and Development -	664,815·69	**–*161,422·54*
Class VI		
3. Transport Industries - -	10·00	14,427·90
4. Roads and Transport (Scottish Development Department) - - - - - -	548,285·37	**–*46,213·58*
7. Shipping Services - - - -	10·00	*2,353·19*
Class VIII		
3. Environmental Research -	1,090,844·25	**–*367,258·97*

* Deficit

Vote	Supply Grants	Appropriations in Aid
	£	£
CLASS VIII—*continued*		
7. CENTRAL ADMINISTRATION (DEPARTMENT OF THE ENVIRONMENT) - - - -	1,348,420·41	**—657,237·96*
CLASS IX		
2. ADMINISTRATION OF JUSTICE, SCOTLAND - - - -	18,029·00	86,664·28
7. ADMINISTRATION OF JUSTICE: SUPREME COURT OF JUDICATURE, NORTHERN IRELAND -	10·00	2,418·48
8. TREATMENT OF OFFENDERS, ENGLAND AND WALES - -	2,984,857·25	**—405,316·55*
9. GENERAL PROTECTIVE SERVICES, ENGLAND AND WALES - -	1,308,811·14	69,910·18
13. CENTRAL AND MISCELLANEOUS SERVICES (HOME OFFICE) -	461,931·87	**—7,288·56*
CLASS X		
21. NATIONAL PORTRAIT GALLERY -	19,476·49	—
CLASS XIII		
22. OTHER SERVICES: CABINET OFFICE	24,242·33	272·62
27. OTHER SERVICES: PUBLIC TRUSTEE	10,040·59	9,420·17
CLASS XIV		
3. STATIONERY AND PRINTING -	2,124,564·07	**—766,928·30*
TOTAL, CIVIL (EXCESSES) 1974–75 - - - -£	10,860,667·36	82,752,853·16

* Deficit.

SCHEDULE (B).—PART 3

DEFENCE (SUPPLEMENTARY), 1975–76

Defence, (Supplementary) 1975–76.

SCHEDULE OF SUPPLEMENTARY SUMS granted, and of the sums which may be applied as appropriations in aid in addition thereto, to defray the charges for the Defence Services herein particularly mentioned for the year ended 31st March, 1976, viz.:—

	Supply Grants	Appropriations in Aid
	£	£
CLASS I		
Vote		
1. For expenditure by the Ministry of Defence on pay, allowances &c., of the Royal Navy, the Royal Marines, the Royal Naval Reserve, the Royal Fleet Reserve and Cadet Forces &c.	11,800,000	181,000
2. For expenditure by the Ministry of Defence on pay, allowances &c., of the Army, the Regular Reserve, the Territorial and Army Volunteer Reserve, the Ulster Defence Regiment and Cadet Forces - - - -	46,500,000	3,300,000
3. For expenditure by the Ministry of Defence on pay, allowances &c., of the Royal Air Force, Royal Air Force Reserves, Royal Auxiliary Air Force and Cadet Forces - - - -	12,940,000	935,000
4. For expenditure by the Ministry of Defence on retired pay, pensions &c. and related non-recurrent payments and for the Royal Hospital, Chelsea	27,950,000	3,000,000
5. For expenditure by the Ministry of Defence on movements; certain stores; plant and machinery; charter and contract repair of ships; supplies and services; certain research; lands and buildings; sundry grants; payments abroad including contributions and subscriptions to international organisations; grants in aid; and the expenses of the Referendum on the European Economic Community -	62,697,000	38,959,500
6. For expenditure by the Ministry of Defence on pay &c. of Defence Ministers and of certain civilian staff employed by the Ministry of Defence	99,500,000	2,575,000

	Supply Grants	Appropriations in Aid
	£	£
CLASS I—*continued*		
Vote		
7. For expenditure by the Procurement Executive of the Ministry of Defence in operating its Headquarters and Establishments and for its other common services, for research &c. by contract, and for sundry other Procurement Executive services, including those on repayment terms to non-Exchequer customers - - -	38,000,000	8,990,000
8. For expenditure by the Ministry of Defence on development by contract, production, repair, &c., and purchases for sale abroad of sea systems, and for a grant - - - - -	41,000,000	—
9. For expenditure by the Ministry of Defence on development by contract, production, repair, &c., reservation of capacity for, and purchases for sale abroad of, land systems - - -	53,000,000	* *−3,000,000*
10. For expenditure by the Ministry of Defence on development by contract, production, repair, &c., and purchases for sale abroad of air systems - -	104,000,000	33,428,000
11. For expenditure including loans by the Property Services Agency of the Department of the Environment on public building work and certain accommodation services, &c., for defence purposes - - - -	44,235,000	2,785,000
TOTAL, DEFENCE (SUPPLEMENTARY), 1975–76 - - - - -£	541,622,000	91,153,500

* Deficit.

SCHEDULE (B).—PART 4

Civil Departments (Supplementary) 1975–76.

CIVIL DEPARTMENTS (SUPPLEMENTARY), 1975–76

SCHEDULE OF SUPPLEMENTARY SUMS granted, and of the sums which may be applied as appropriations in aid in addition thereto, to defray the charges for the Civil Services herein particularly mentioned for the year ended 31st March, 1976, viz.:—

	Supply Grants	Appropriations in Aid
	£	£
CLASS II		
Vote		
1. For expenditure by the Foreign and Commonwealth Office on the salaries and expenses of Her Majesty's Diplomatic Service and sundry other services - - - - - -	6,906,000	3,906,000
2. For expenditure by the Property Services Agency of the Department of the Environment on public building work and accommodation services &c. for civil purposes overseas -	1,000	19,000
3. For expenditure by the Foreign and Commonwealth Office on official information services, promotion of cultural and information exchanges (including a subscription to an international organisation and certain grants in aid), external broadcasting and monitoring and for a grant in aid of and a loan to the British Council -	2,460,000	7,000
4. For expenditure by the Home Office on grants in aid to the British Broadcasting Corporation for external broadcasting and monitoring - -	2,025,000	207,000
5. For expenditure by the Foreign and Commonwealth Office on subscriptions &c. to certain international organisations, military aid, certain grants in aid and sundry other grants and services - - - - - -	8,751,000	475,290
6. For a grant in aid of the Commonwealth War Graves Commission and certain other expenses - - - - -	855,000	—
7. For Her Majesty's foreign and other secret services - - - - -	4,500,000	—

	Supply Grants	Appropriations in Aid
	£	£
CLASS II—*continued*		
Vote		
8. For expenditure by the Ministry of Overseas Development on the official United Kingdom aid programme, for certain subscriptions to International Organisations, and for certain payments under the Commonwealth Scholarship and Fellowship Plan, including grants in aid - - -	18,759,000	2,800,000
9. For expenditure by the Ministry of Overseas Development on administration, including the costs of the Fay Committee of Inquiry - - - -	1,730,000	60,000
10. For expenditure by the Ministry of Overseas Development on pensions and supplements to pensions in respect of overseas services and for sundry services and expenses - -	4,778,000	502,000
CLASS III		
1. For expenditure by the Ministry of Agriculture, Fisheries and Food in England and Wales on price guarantees, production grants and subsidies, grants and loans for capital and other improvements, support for agriculture in special areas and certain other services; and for certain of these services, in the United Kingdom -	5,779,000	17,038,000
2. For expenditure by the Department of Agriculture and Fisheries for Scotland on price guarantees, production grants and subsidies, grants and loans for capital and other improvements, support for agriculture in special areas and certain other services - -	5,247,000	—
3. For expenditure by the Intervention Board for Agricultural Produce on carrying out the obligations of the United Kingdom under the Common Agricultural Policy of the European Economic Community in connection with arrangements for import and export, support for certain agricultural and other products, including fish, assistance to producers, and arrangements for food aid; and for certain other services - - -	78,591,000	21,450,000

Vote	Supply Grants	Appropriations in Aid
	£	£
CLASS III—*continued*		
4. For expenditure by the Ministry of Agriculture, Fisheries and Food on educational, advisory, research and development services, livestock services and pest control, food services and assistance to marketing, including grants in aid - - - - -	84,459,000	490,000
5. For the expenditure of the Department of Prices and Consumer Protection on implementation of certain food subsidies - - - - -	40,500,000	—
6. For expenditure by the Department of Agriculture and Fisheries for Scotland on educational, advisory, research and development services, livestock services and pest control, assistance to marketing, administration, land management and land settlement, the Royal Botanic and associated Gardens, assistance to crofters and certain other services, including grants in aid	2,013,000	*–*100,000*
7. For expenditure by the Ministry of Agriculture, Fisheries and Food on central administration including land management and smallholdings, Royal Botanic Gardens, land drainage and flood protection and certain other services including a grant in aid and subscriptions to certain international organisations - - - - -	4,931,000	—
8. For expenditure by the Ministry of Agriculture, Fisheries and Food on assistance to the fishing industry, research and development, administration and other services including a grant in aid and subscriptions to certain international organisations -	2,781,000	11,000
9. For expenditure by the Department of Agriculture and Fisheries for Scotland on assistance to the Scottish fishing industry and the United Kingdom herring industry, research and development and protective and certain other services including a grant in aid	1,250,000	50,000
10. For a grant in aid of the Forestry Fund	5,150,000	—

* Deficit.

	Supply Grants	Appropriations in Aid
	£	£
CLASS IV		
Vote		
1. For expenditure by the Department of Industry on regional development grants, provision of land and buildings, selective assistance to industry in assisted areas, assistance for publicity and certain other services, including grants in aid - - -	111,196,000	*—*4,000*
3. For expenditure by the Department of Industry on the Industrial Research Establishments of the Department, the Computer Aided Design Centre, on contracts, grants and other support for industrial research and development and loans and grants to the National Research Development Corporation, including grants in aid -	2,934,000	9,000
4. For expenditure of the Department of Industry on technological and industrial sponsorship, including subscriptions to international organisations and a grant in aid - - -	1,000	*—*620,000*
5. For the expenditure of the Department of Industry on civil aerospace research and development, the support of development and production of civil aircraft and associated equipment, contributions to international organisations, loans, the purchase of certain assets of companies and sundry other items - - - - - -	127,794,000	*—*22,998,000*
6. For the expenditure by the United Kingdom Atomic Energy Authority and the Department of Energy in connection with nuclear energy and related research and development, including the purchase of nuclear materials, subscriptions and contributions to international organisations and projects, a grant in aid, loans, grants, guarantees, expenditure arising from the reorganisation of the nuclear industry including the purchase of shares &c., and for sundry other services - - - - - -	23,406,000	3,322,000

* Deficit.

	Supply Grants	Appropriations in Aid
	£	£
CLASS IV—*continued*		
Vote		
7. For expenditure of the Department of Industry on selective assistance to industry, support for the shipbuilding industry, investment grants, certain other services and support for the Steel Industry - - - -	183,817,000	17,152,000
8. For expenditure by the Department of Energy in connection with the energy industries, including certain financial assistance to the nationalised industries, oil storage and certain other services including a grant in aid -	2,000	2,910,000
9. For expenditure by the Department of Energy in connection with compensation to nationalised industries for the consequences of price restraint -	12,600,000	—
11. For expenditure by the Department of Trade on promotion of tourism, export promotion, trade co-operation, protection of innovation, regulation of trading practices, central and miscellaneous services and certain other services, including grants in aid and international subscriptions - -	1,000	—
12. For expenditure incurred by the Export Credits Guarantee Department in connection with export credits guarantees including an international subscription, performance bond guarantees, pre-shipment finance guarantees, refinancing arrangements made for facilitating trade with other countries and assistance towards the cost of financing export credits, the purchase of securities, overseas investment insurance and cost escalation guarantees - - - - - -	131,374,000	2,757,000
13. For expenditure by the Office of Fair Trading - - - - -	911,000	*−*660,000*
14. For expenditure by the Registry of Friendly Societies - - - - -	15,000	—

* Deficit.

	Supply Grants	Appropriations in Aid
	£	£
CLASS IV—*continued*		
Vote		
15. For expenditure by the Department of Employment on grants in aid to the Manpower Services Commission, the Health and Safety Commission and the Advisory, Conciliation and Arbitration Service; on a Royal Commission on the Distribution of Income and Wealth, an Advisory, Conciliation and Arbitration Service, and on industrial relations, other labour market services including provision for a loan to the National Dock Labour Board, services for seriously disabled people and sundry other services including provision for agency payments on behalf of the European Economic Community and an international subscription - - -	49,005,000	5,660,000
16. For the expenditure of the Department of Industry on central and miscellaneous services, international subscriptions and Post Office civil defence - - - - - -	1,659,000	210,700
17. For expenditure by the Scottish Economic Planning Department on grants in aid to the Scottish Development Agency and to the Highlands and Islands Development Board, on provision of land and buildings, on selective assistance to industry, on the promotion of tourism, on financial assistance to nationalised industries, and on sundry other services in connection with trade and industry including grants in aid - - -	4,610,000	*−*98,000*
17A. For expenditure by the Welsh Office on the provision of land and buildings, selective assistance to industry in assisted areas, on the promotion of tourism, on assistance for publicity and on the Welsh Development Agency including grants in aid- -	4,462,000	41,000
18. For expenditure by the Department of Prices and Consumer Protection on prices, consumer protection, standards and quality assurance and central and miscellaneous services, including a grant to the Price Commission, grants in aid and international subscriptions	1,750,000	17,000

* Deficit.

	Supply Grants	Appropriations in Aid
	£	£
CLASS VI		
Vote		
1. For expenditure by the Department of the Environment on roads and certain associated services, including lorry areas, lighting and road safety - -	59,621,000	264,000
2. For expenditure by the Department of the Environment on assistance to local transport &c. - - -	8,460,000	—
3. For expenditure by the Department of the Environment on support to nationalised transport industries, assistance to ports, services in connection with a Channel Tunnel and certain other transport services, including a grant in aid and international subscriptions - - -	38,172,000	*−*475,000*
5. For expenditure by the Scottish Economic Planning Department on support for transport services in the Highlands and Islands and on piers and harbours - - - - -	1,860,000	800,000
6. For expenditure by the Welsh Office on roads and certain associated services including lorry areas, lighting and road safety, and on assistance to public surface transport - - - -	7,058,000	—
7. For expenditure by the Department of Trade on services connected with shipping, including a grant in aid -	1,887,000	*−*427,000*
8. For the expenditure by the Department of Trade on civil aviation services, including a grant in aid of the Civil Aviation Authority, certain payments of Regional Employment Premium and international subscriptions -	11,723,000	*−*714,000*

* Deficit.

Vote	Supply Grants	Appropriations in Aid
	£	£
CLASS VII		
2. For expenditure by the Scottish Development Department on subsidies, the option mortgage scheme, improvements, rent registration and sundry other housing services - - -	15,496,000	—
3. For expenditure by the Scottish Economic Planning Department on grants to New Town Development Corporations in connection with housing and other services - - - -	4,393,000	—
4. For expenditure by the Welsh Office on subsidies, the option mortgage scheme, improvements, the rent officer service and sundry other housing services -	15,976,000	—
CLASS VIII		
1. For expenditure by the Department of the Environment on water supply, sewerage, town and country planning (including compensation), recreation and other environmental services, including grants in aid and international subscriptions, on a grant in aid to the Development Fund, on grants for rate rebates and domestic rate relief, and on sundry other services - - - - - -	2,000	88,000
2. For expenditure by the Department of the Environment on Royal Palaces, Royal Parks, historic buildings and ancient monuments, on certain public buildings and accommodation services, on assistance to the Zoological Society of London, including grants in aid and a special purchase for display at the Tower of London -	1,722,000	571,000
3. For expenditure by the Department of the Environment on research, including grants in aid and an international subscription - - - - -	2,762,000	231,000

Vote	Supply Grants	Appropriations in Aid
	£	£
CLASS VIII—*continued*		
4. For expenditure by the Scottish Development Department in connection with water supply, sewerage, land drainage and flood protection, town and country planning (including compensation), recreation, historic buildings, acquisition of land, domestic rate relief and other environmental services, including a grant in aid - -	1,200,000	38,990
5. For expenditure by the Welsh Office in connection with water supply, sewerage, town and country planning (including compensation), recreation, historic buildings and other environmental services, the promotion of tourism, and with primary and secondary education, on grants for rate rebates and domestic rate relief and on sundry other services, including grants in aid and an international subscription - - - - - -	1,000	—
6. For expenditure by the Department of the Environment on central administration and certain other services -	6,650,000	*—*66,000*
CLASS IX		
1. For expenditure by the Lord Chancellor's Department on court services, the Law Commission and certain other legal services - - - - -	1,000	5,645,000
2. For expenditure by the Scottish Courts Administration on court services, the Scottish Law Commission and certain other legal services, including a grant in aid - - - - - - -	917,000	251,000
3. For grants to the Legal Aid Fund and to Law Centres - - - - -	2,703,000	—
4. For expenditure by the Departments of the Director of Public Prosecutions, the Law Officers and the Treasury Solicitor on Crown prosecutions and other legal services and on legal services for Government Departments	1,052,000	92,000

* Deficit.

Vote	Supply Grants	Appropriations in Aid
	£	£
CLASS IX—*continued*		
5. For expenditure by the Queen's and Lord Treasurer's Remembrancer on Crown prosecutions, legal services for Government Departments and certain other legal services	799,000	—
6. For expenditure by the Home Office on court services, Crown prosecutions, legal aid and other services related to crime, including a grant in aid	9,069,000	304,000
7. For expenditure by the Home Office on prisons, probation, after-care and other services for the treatment of offenders, including a grant in aid	21,696,000	152,000
8. For expenditure by the Home Office on police, fire, control of immigration and nationality and of gaming, and other protective services, including grants in aid and an international subscription	88,907,000	555,000
9. For expenditure by the Home Office on civil defence	1,133,000	195,000
10. For expenditure by the Ministry of Agriculture, Fisheries and Food on emergency food services and strategic reserves	82,000	37,000
11. For expenditure by the Home Office on community relations, the urban programme and assistance towards certain voluntary services, including grants in aid	431,000	2,993,970
12. For expenditure by the Home Office on central administration and certain other services, including expenses of the Referendum on the European Economic Community	1,271,000	*—*12,000*

* Deficit.

	Supply Grants	Appropriations in Aid
	£	£
CLASS IX—*continued*		
Vote		
13. For expenditure by the Scottish Home and Health Department on legal aid, services related to crime, prisons, other services for the treatment of offenders, police, fire services, civil defence and certain other services, including a grant in aid and expenses of the Referendum on the European Economic Community - - -	13,039,000	*–*136,000*
CLASS X		
1. For expenditure by the Department of Education and Science on schools, the University Grants Committee, universities and certain other institutions, further education, teacher training and student awards, including grants in aid and a subscription to an international organisation - -	63,881,000	108,000
2. For expenditure by the Scottish Education Department on schools, higher and further education, libraries, miscellaneous educational services, research and administration, sport and certain grants in aid - - -	8,470,000	—
3. For grants in aid to the British Library and certain other institutions - -	2,202,000	—
4. For the expenditure of the National Library of Scotland, including a purchase grant in aid - - - -	145,000	—
5. For grants in aid of the National Library of Wales and the National Museum of Wales and a grant to the Council of Museums in Wales - - - -	378,000	—
6. For expenditure by the Department of Education and Science on miscellaneous educational services, research and administration, including grants in aid, international subscriptions and compensation payments for redundant staff at Colleges of Education - -	4,198,000	259,000

*** Deficit.**

	Supply Grants	Appropriations in Aid
	£	£
CLASS X—*continued*		
Vote		
7. For grants in aid of the Social Science Research Council, including a subscription to an international organisation - - - - - -	818,000	—
8. For grants in aid of the Science Research Council, including subscriptions to certain international organisations -	10,010,000	—
9. For a grant in aid of the Natural Environment Research Council -	2,071,000	—
10. For grants in aid of the Medical Research Council, including subscriptions to certain international organisations -	5,070,000	—
11. For a grant in aid of the Agricultural Research Council - - - -	1,963,000	—
12. For the expenditure of the British Museum (Natural History), including a purchase grant in aid - - -	172,000	—
13. For a grant in aid of the Royal Society	31,000	—
14. For the expenditure of the British Museum including a purchase grant in aid - - - - - -	520,000	—
15. For the expenditure of the Science Museum including purchase grants in aid - - - - - -	432,000	—
16. For the expenditure of the Victoria and Albert Museum, including purchase grants in aid - - - - -	567,000	—
17. For the expenditure of the Imperial War Museum, including a purchase grant in aid - - - - - -	148,000	—
19. For the expenditure of the National Gallery, including a purchase grant in aid - - - - - -	205,000	—
20. For the expenditure of the National Maritime Museum, including a purcase grant in aid - - - -	183,000	—
21. For the expenditure of the National Portrait Gallery, including purchase grants in aid - - - - -	50,000	—

Vote		Supply Grants	Appropriations in Aid
		£	£
	CLASS X—*continued*		
22.	For the expenditure of the Tate Gallery, including a purchase grant in aid and the payment of an indemnity claim from the Nordrhein Westfalen Collection - - - - -	139,000	—
23.	For the expenditure of the Wallace Collection - - - - - -	52,000	—
24.	For the expenditure of the National Gallery of Scotland, the Scottish National Gallery of Modern Art and the Scottish National Portrait Gallery, including purchase grants in aid -	243,000	—
25.	For the expenditure of the National Museum of Antiquities of Scotland, including a purchase grant in aid -	37,000	—
26.	For expenditure by the Scottish Education Department on the Royal Scottish Museum and certain grants for the arts, including purchase grants in aid - - - - - - -	557,000	—
27.	For grants in aid to the Arts Council and certain other institutions and for other grants for the Arts - - -	3,768,000	—
	CLASS XI		
1.	For expenditure by the Department of Health and Social Security on the provision of services under the National Health Service in England, on other health and personal social services including certain services in relation to Wales, and on research, services for the disabled, welfare food and certain other services; including grants in aid, international subscriptions and grants under section 8 of the Industry Act 1972 - - -	382,127,000	41,615,490
2.	For expenditure by the Scottish Home and Health Department on the provision of services under the National Health Service in Scotland, on other health services and on research, services for the disabled, welfare food and certain other services - -	41,270,000	4,270,000

	Supply Grants	Appropriations in Aid
	£	£
CLASS XI—*continued*		
Vote		
3. For expenditure by the Scottish Education Department in connection with social work and the urban programme	841,000	—
4. For expenditure by the Welsh Office on the provision of services under the National Health Service in Wales, on other health and personal social services, and on research, services for the disabled, welfare food and certain other services - - - - -	27,164,000	2,202,000
CLASS XII		
1. For sums payable out of the Consolidated Fund to the National Insurance Fund - - - - - - -	93,000,000	—
2. For expenditure by the Department of Health and Social Security on pensions, &c., for disablement or death arising out of war or service in the Armed Forces after 2 September 1939 and on certain associated services, on attendance allowances, old persons' retirement pensions, non-contributory invalidity pensions and mobility allowance, &c. - - - -	9,000,000	—
3. For expenditure by the Department of Health and Social Security on supplementary pensions and allowances and lump sum payments for pensioners, &c., and repayments to Local Authorities - - - - -	150,019,000	9,000,000
5. For expenditure by the Department of Health and Social Security on administration, certain Selective Employment Refunds, selective butter subsidy, and certain other services, including an international subscription - -	13,857,000	40,964 000

	Supply Grants	Appropriations in Aid
	£	£
CLASS XIII		
Vote		
1. For the expenditure of the House of Lords - - - - - -	392,000	1,000
2. For the expenditure of the House of Commons, including a grant in aid -	3,623,000	11,000
4. For expenditure by the Treasury on the management of the economy, the Paymaster General's Office and certain other services, including grants in aid to certain Parliamentary bodies and others - - - - - -	1,809,000	* *−234,980*
5. For the expenditure of the Department of the Comptroller and Auditor General - - - - -	700,000	130,000
6. For expenditure by the Customs and Excise Department, including the expenses of Value Added Tax Tribunals and an international subscription -	1,905,000	945,000
7. For the expenditure of the Inland Revenue Department - - -	16,862,000	2,727,000
8. For expenditure by the Department of the Environment in connection with driver and motor vehicle registration and licensing and the collection of revenue - - - - -	11,740,000	101,000
9. For expenditure of the National Debt Office and Pensions Commutation Board - - - - - -	1,000	27,790
10. For the expenditure of the Public Works Loan Commission - - - -	1,000	29,000
11. For the expenditure of the Department for National Savings - - -	1,569,000	3,744,000
12. For the expenditure by the Civil Service Department on the central management of the civil service, on Royal Commissions, Committees, special enquiries, the Office of the Parliamentary Counsel, and certain other services, including grants in aid to the Government Hospitality Fund and other bodies - - - - -	1,518,000	192,000

* Deficit.

	Supply Grants	Appropriations in Aid
	£	£
CLASS XIII—*continued*		
Vote		
13. For the expenditure of the Public Record Office	225,000	—
14. For the expenditure of the Scottish Record Office; and on certain other services including grants in aid	64,000	20,000
18. For the expenditure of the Department of the Registers of Scotland	1,000	284,000
19. For the expenditure of the Charity Commission for England and Wales	108,000	—
21. For the expenditure of the Cabinet Office, including the salary of the Chancellor of the Duchy of Lancaster, expenses of the Referendum on the European Economic Community, and subscriptions to international organisations	402,000	—
22. For expenditure by the Scottish Office on central administration	2,579,000	297,000
23. For expenditure by the Welsh Office on central administration	639,000	104,000
24. For expenditure by the Home Office on grants to the British Broadcasting Corporation for home broadcasting, and civil defence, central administration, wireless telegraphy and sundry other services	1,000	196,000
26. For the expenditure of the Office of the Public Trustee	1,000	328,000
CLASS XIV		
1. For expenditure by the Property Services Agency of the Department of the Environment on public building work and accommodation services, &c., for civil purposes in the United Kingdom, transport services and sundry other services	1,700,000	17,700,000
3. For the expenditure of Her Majesty's Stationery Office on the procurement and production of stationery and printing, on publishing, and on certain other services	15,172,000	8,479,000

	Supply Grants	Appropriations in Aid
	£	£
CLASS XIV—*continued*		
Vote		
4. For expenditure by the Central Computer Agency (Civil Service Department) in connection with computers and general telecommunications including an international subscription	2,038,000	1,671,000
5. For expenditure by the Central Office of Information on home and overseas publicity - - - - - -	3,700,000	*—*500,000*
6. For expenditure by the Assistant Paymaster General on the superannuation of civil servants, pensions, &c., in respect of former members of the Royal Irish Constabulary and other pensions and non-recurrent payments; and for certain other services - -	24,500,000	18,300,000
7. For the expenditure of the Rating of Government Property Department; for rates and contributions in lieu of rates for property occupied by the Crown and premises occupied by representatives of Commonwealth and foreign countries and international organisations; and for certain sewerage, &c., charges - - - - -	1,695,000	235,000
9. For the expenditure of the Civil Service Catering Organisation (Civil Service Department) in connection with the provision of catering services - -	85,000	1,175,000
CLASS XV		
1. For expenditure by the Ministry of Agriculture, Fisheries and Food on certain services in Northern Ireland, including price guarantees, production grants and subsidies, grants and loans for capital and other improvements, support for agriculture in special areas, educational and livestock services, food services and assistance to marketing, land management, special assistance to agriculture in Northern Ireland, assistance to the fishing industry and administration by the Department of Agriculture for Northern Ireland - - - - - -	335,000	*—*78,000*

* Deficit.

	Supply Grants	Appropriations in Aid
CLASS XV—*continued*	£	£
Vote		
2. For expenditure by the Northern Ireland Office on Court Services, Crown prosecutions, legal aid, Commissioners and Appeal Tribunal and Office of the Advisers, other services related to crime, compensation for criminal injuries, prisons, probation and after-care, young offenders, police, home defence, central and miscellaneous services, accommodation services in respect of prisons and courts and legal services for Government departments including grants in aid - - - - - -	16,631,000	63,000
3. For expenditure by the Northern Ireland Office on the Supreme Court of Judicature and Court of Criminal Appeal of Northern Ireland and on certain other legal services in Northern Ireland - - - - - -	1,000	19,000
4. For expenditure by the Northern Ireland Office on election expenses, including expenses of the Referendum on the European Economic Community, central administration, transfers to the Northern Ireland Consolidated Fund, including a grant in aid and accommodation services in respect of the Department's Offices in Northern Ireland - - - - - -	170,960,000	7,861,710
CLASS XVII		
1. For rate support grants to local authorities in England and Wales, for National Parks supplementary grants to County Councils, and for supplementary grants for transport purposes to County Councils and the Greater London Council - - - -	1,078,701,000	—
2. For rate support grants, equalisation grants and rate rebates grants to local authorities in Scotland - - -	129,920,000	—
3. For expenditure by the Department of Her Majesty's Secretary of State for Education and Science on superannuation allowances and gratuities, &c., in respect of teachers, and the widows, children and dependants of deceased teachers - - - -	3,000	21,114,000

	Supply Grants	Appropriations in Aid
	£	£
CLASS XVII—*continued*		
Vote		
4. For the expenditure by the Scottish Home and Health Department on superannuation allowances and gratuities, &c., in respect of teachers, and the widows and dependants of deceased teachers - - - -	1,000	2,165,000
5. For expenditure by the Department of Health and Social Security on pensions, allowances, gratuities, &c., to or in respect of persons engaged in health services or in other approved employment - - - - -	2,000	37,648,000
6. For expenditure by the Scottish Home and Health Department on pensions, allowances, gratuities, &c., to or in respect of persons engaged in health services or in other approved employment - - - - - -	2,000	2,844,000
7. For payment of pensions, &c., to persons who contributed to the United Kingdom Atomic Energy Authority's Superannuation Schemes and other related expenditure - - -	1,000	1,419,000
9. For salaries and expenses of the Crown Estate Office - - - - -	20,000	—
10. For transitional relief under the Finance Acts 1965 and 1972, for companies with an overseas source of trading income - - - - - -	1,500,000	—
TOTAL, CIVIL DEPARTMENTS (SUPPLEMENTARY), 1975–76 £	3,569,781,000	292,437,960

Defence, Class I, 1976–77.

SCHEDULE (B).—Part 5

DEFENCE.—Class I

Schedule of Sums granted, and of the sums which may be applied as appropriations in aid in addition thereto, to defray the charges of the several Defence Services herein particularly mentioned, which will come in course of payment during the year ending on 31st March 1977, including provision for numbers of personnel as set out hereunder, viz.:—

	Supply Grants	Appropriations in Aid
	£	£
Vote		
1. For expenditure by the Ministry of Defence on pay, allowances, &c., of the Royal Navy, the Royal Marines (including provision for Naval Service to a number not exceeding 78,000), the Royal Naval Reserve, the Royal Fleet Reserve and Cadet Forces, &c. -	298,035,000	3,763,000
2. For expenditure by the Ministry of Defence on pay, allowances, &c., of the Army (including provision for Army Service to a number not exceeding 189,500), the Regular Reserve (to a number not exceeding 65,000), the Territorial and Army Volunteer Reserve (to a number not exceeding 86,500), the Ulster Defence Regiment (to a number not exceeding 10,000), and Cadet Forces - - - - -	637,527,000	26,992,000
3. For expenditure by the Ministry of Defence on pay, allowances, &c., of the Royal Air Force (including provision for Air Force Service to a number not exceeding 93,800), RAF Reserves (to a number not exceeding 10,600), Royal Auxiliary Air Force (to a number not exceeding 400), and Cadet Forces -	356,296,000	5,957,000
4. For expenditure by the Ministry of Defence on retired pay, pensions, &c., and related non-recurrent payments and for the Royal Hospital, Chelsea -	299,033,000	5,191,000

SCHEDULE (B).—PART 5—*continued*

Defence, Class I, 1976–77.

Vote	Supply Grants	Appropriations in Aid
	£	£
5. For expenditure by the Ministry of Defence on movements; certain stores; supplies and services; plant and machinery; charter and contract repair of ships; certain research; lands and buildings; sundry grants; payments abroad including contributions and subscriptions to international organisations; and grants in aid (including a Supplementary sum of £81,000) - - - - - -	569,389,000	204,667,000
6. For expenditure by the Ministry of Defence on pay &c., of Defence Ministers and of certain civilian staff employed by the Ministry of Defence	651,418,000	18,916,000
7. For expenditure by the Procurement Executive of the Ministry of Defence in operating its Headquarters and Establishments and for its other common services, for research &c. by contract, and for sundry other Procurement Executive services including those on repayment terms to non-Exchequer customers - -	399,163,000	50,002,000
8. For expenditure by the Ministry of Defence on development by contract, production, repair &c. and purchases for sale abroad of sea systems, and for a grant - - - - - - -	482,825,000	57,650,000
9. For expenditure by the Ministry of Defence on development by contract, production, repair &c., reservation of capacity for, and purchases for sale abroad of, land systems - - -	437,200,000	130,600,000
10. For expenditure by the Ministry of Defence on development by contract, production, repair &c. and purchases for sale abroad of air systems - -	840,169,000	136,690,000
11. For expenditure including loans by the Property Services Agency of the Department of the Environment on public building work and certain accommodation services &c. for defence purposes - - - - -	409,430,000	50,675,000

Defence, Class I, 1976–77.

SCHEDULE (B).—PART 5—*continued*

	Supply Grants	Appropriations in Aid
	£	£
Vote 12. For operating the Royal Dockyards and for the repair of ships by contract including work undertaken on repayment terms for Exchequer and non-Exchequer customers - - -	223,894,000	5,263,000
TOTAL, DEFENCE, CLASS I - -£	5,604,379,000	696,366,000

SCHEDULE (B).—Part 6

Civil, Class II, 1976–77.

CIVIL.—Class II

Schedule of Sums granted, and of the sums which may be applied as appropriations in aid in addition thereto, to defray the charges of the several Civil Services herein particularly mentioned, which will come in course of payment during the year ending on 31st March, 1977, viz.:—

Vote	Supply Grants	Appropriations in Aid
	£	£
1. For expenditure by the Foreign and Commonwealth Office on the salaries and expenses of Her Majesty's Diplomatic Service and sundry other services - - - - - - -	113,226,000	16,098,000
2. For expenditure by the Property Services Agency of the Department of the Environment on public building work and accommodation services &c. for civil purposes overseas - - - -	25,950,000	3,100,000
3. For expenditure by the Foreign and Commonwealth Office on official information services, promotion of cultural and information exchanges (including a subscription to an international organisation and certain grants in aid), external broadcasting and monitoring and for a grant in aid of and a loan to the British Council (including a Supplementary sum of £23,000) - - - -	22,738,000	49,550
4. For expenditure by the Home Office on grants in aid to the British Broadcasting Corporation for external broadcasting and monitoring - -	26,679,000	1,578,000
5. For expenditure by the Foreign and Commonwealth Office on subscriptions &c., to certain international organisations, military aid, certain grants in aid and sundry other grants and services (including a Supplementary sum of £1,842,000) - - -	26,033,000	583,635
For a grant in aid of the Commonwealth War Graves Commission and certain other expenses - - - - -	4,065,000	—

Civil, Class II, 1976–77.

SCHEDULE (B).—Part 6—*continued*

	Supply Grants	Appropriations in Aid
	£	£
Vote		
7. For Her Majesty's foreign and other secret services - - - -	28,000,000	—
8. For expenditure by the Ministry of Overseas Development on the official United Kingdom aid programme and certain aid administration expenses, for certain subscriptions to International Organisations, and for certain payments under the Commonwealth Scholarship and Fellowship Plan, including grants in aid (including a Supplementary sum of £7,761,000) - - - - -	501,531,000	4,100,000
9. For expenditure by the Ministry of Overseas Development on administration, including the costs of the Fay Committee of Inquiry - - -	9,652,000	180,000
10. For expenditure by the Ministry of Overseas Development on pensions and supplements to pensions in respect of overseas service and for sundry services and expenses - -	66,715,000	16,000
Total, Civil, Class II - -£	824,589,000	25,705,185

SCHEDULE (B).—PART 7

Civil, Class III, 1976–77.

CIVIL.—CLASS III

SCHEDULE OF SUMS granted, and of the sums which may be applied as appropriations in aid in addition thereto, to defray the charges of the several Civil Services herein particularly mentioned, which will come in course of payment during the year ending on 31st March, 1977, viz.:—

	Supply Grants	Appropriations in Aid
	£	£
Vote		
1. For expenditure by the Ministry of Agriculture, Fisheries and Food in England and Wales on price guarantees, production grants and subsidies, grants and loans for capital and other improvements, support for agriculture in special areas and certain other services; and, for certain of these services, in the United Kingdom (including a Supplementary sum of £1,000) - - - - - -	101,946,000	214,380,000
2. For expenditure by the Department of Agriculture and Fisheries for Scotland on price guarantees, production grants and subsidies, grants and loans for capital and other improvements, support for agriculture in special areas and certain other services (including a Supplementary sum of £500,000) - - - - - -	44,285,000	783,000
3. For expenditure by the Intervention Board for Agricultural Produce on carrying out the obligations of the United Kingdom under the Common Agricultural Policy of the European Economic Community in connection with arrangements for import and export, support for certain agricultural and other products including fish, assistance to producers, and arrangements for food aid; and for certain other services (including a Supplementary sum of £32,416,000)	43,929,000	101,200,000
4. For expenditure by the Ministry of Agriculture, Fisheries and Food on educational, advisory, research and development services, livestock services and pest control, food services and assistance to marketing, including grants in aid - - - -	91,264,000	5,278,000

Civil, Class III, 1976–77.

SCHEDULE (B).—PART 7—*continued*

Vote	Supply Grants	Appropriations in Aid
	£	£
5. For the expenditure of the Department of Prices and Consumer Protection on implementation of certain food subsidies - - - - -	400,400,000	—
6. For expenditure by the Department of Agriculture and Fisheries for Scotland on educational, advisory, research and development services, livestock services and pest control, assistance to marketing, administration, land management and land settlement, the Royal Botanic and associated Gardens, assistance to crofters and certain other services, including grants in aid - - - - -	26,982,000	4,618,000
7. For expenditure by the Ministry of Agriculture, Fisheries and Food on central administration including land management and smallholdings, Royal Botanic Gardens, land drainage and flood protection and certain other services including subscriptions to certain international organisations (Revised sum) - - - -	129,418,000	5,903,000
8. For expenditure by the Ministry of Agriculture, Fisheries and Food on assistance to the fishing industry, research and development, administration and other services including a grant in aid and subscriptions to certain international organisations (including a Supplementary sum of £2,730,000) - - - - -	18,081,000	91,000
9. For expenditure by the Department of Agriculture and Fisheries for Scotland on assistance to the Scottish fishing industry and the United Kingdom herring industry, research and development and protective and certain other services including a grant in aid	5,943,000	148,000
10. For a grant in aid of the Forestry Fund	27,630,000	—
TOTAL, CIVIL, CLASS III - -£	889,878,000	332,401,000

SCHEDULE (B).—PART 8

Civil, Class IV, 1976–77.

CIVIL.—CLASS IV

SCHEDULE OF SUMS granted, and of the sums which may be applied as appropriations in aid in addition thereto, to defray the charges of the several Civil Services herein particularly mentioned, which will come in course of payment during the year ending on 31st March, 1977, viz.:—

	Supply Grants	Appropriations in Aid
	£	£
Vote		
1. For expenditure by the Department of Industry on regional development grants, provision of land and buildings, selective assistance to industry in assisted areas, assistance for publicity and certain other services, including grants in aid (including a Supplementary sum of £1,000) -	419,565,000	815,000
2. For payments by the Department of Employment to certain employers in Development Areas; and residual payments of refunds of Selective Employment Tax - - - - -	212,550,000	11,000
3. For expenditure by the Department of Industry on the Industrial Research Establishments of the Department, the Computer Aided Design Centre and on contracts, grants and other support for industrial research and development, including grants in aid -	36,640,000	7,452,000
4. For expenditure of the Department of Industry on technological and industrial sponsorship including subscriptions to international organisations, a grant to the National Research Development Corporation and a grant in aid - - - - - -	8,462,000	1,226,000
5. For the expenditure of the Department of Industry on civil aerospace research and development, the support of development and production of civil aircraft and associated equipment, contributions to international organisations, loans, the purchase of certain assets of companies and sundry other items - - - - - - -	79,849,000	54,628,00

Civil, Class IV, 1976–77.

SCHEDULE (B).—PART 8—*continued*

Vote	Supply Grants	Appropriations in Aid
	£	£
6. For the expenditure by the United Kingdom Atomic Energy Authority and the Department of Energy in connection with nuclear energy and related research and development, including the purchase of nuclear materials, subscriptions and contributions to international organisations and projects, a grant in aid, loans, grants, guarantees, expenditure arising from the reorganisation of the nuclear industry including the purchase of shares &c., and for sundry other services - - -	122,418,000	61,507,010
7. For expenditure by the Department of Industry on selective assistance to industry, support for the shipbuilding industry, investment grants, certain other services and support for the Steel Industry (including a Supplementary sum of £2,350,000) - -	819,795,000	400,000
8. For expenditure by the Department of Energy in connection with the energy industries, including certain financial assistance to the nationalised industries, oil storage and certain other services including a grant in aid (including a Supplementary sum of £14,500,000) - - - - -	98,340,000	9,656,000
9. For expenditure by the Department of Energy in connection with compensation to nationalised industries for the consequences of price restraint (including a Supplementary sum of £8,000,000) - - - - -	19,500,000	—
10. For expenditure by the Department of Industry in connection with compensation to nationalised industries for the consequences of price restraint -	1,300,000	—
11. For expenditure by the Department of Trade on promotion of tourism, export promotion, trade co-operation, protection of innovation, regulation of trading practices, central and miscellaneous services and certain other services including grants in aid and international subscriptions (including a Supplementary sum of £2,055,000) -	40,056,000	31,349,851

SCHEDULE (B).—PART 8—*continued*

Civil, Class IV, 1976–77.

Vote	Supply Grants	Appropriations in Aid
	£	£
12. For expenditure incurred by the Export Credits Guarantee Department in connection with export credits guarantees including an international subscription, payments to minimise loss under guarantees, performance bond guarantees, pre-shipment finance guarantees, refinancing arrangements made for facilitating trade with other countries and assistance towards the cost of financing export credits, the purchase of securities, overseas investment insurance and cost escalation guarantees (including a Supplementary sum of £135,700,000) - - -	507,336,000	73,715,020
13. For expenditure by the Office of Fair Trading - - - - - -	1,000	2,083,000
14. For the salaries and expenses of the Registry of Friendly Societies - -	469,000	70,000
15. For expenditure by the Department of Employment on grants in aid to the Manpower Services Commission, the Health and Safety Commission and the Advisory, Conciliation and Arbitration Service; on a Royal Commission on the Distribution of Income and Wealth and on industrial relations, other labour market services, including provision for a loan to the National Dock Labour Board, services for seriously disabled people and sundry other services including provision for agency payments on behalf of the European Economic Community and an international subscription (including a Supplementary sum of £112,563,000) - - - -	636,084,000	54,933,000
16. For the expenditure of the Department of Industry on central and miscellaneous services, international subscriptions, and Post Office civil defence - - - - -	36,543,000	606,000

Civil, Class IV, 1976–77.

SCHEDULE (B).—PART 8—*continued*

Vote	Supply Grants	Appropriations in Aid
	£	£
17. For expenditure by the Scottish Economic Planning Department on grants in aid to the Scottish Development Agency and to the Highlands and Islands Development Board, on selective assistance to industry, on the promotion of tourism, on financial assistance to nationalised industries, and on sundry other services in connection with trade and industry including grants in aid (including a Supplementary sum of £57,000,000) -	113,353,000	—
18. For expenditure by the Welsh Office on selective assistance to industry in assisted areas, on the promotion of tourism and on the Welsh Development Agency including grants in aid	25,473,000	—
19. For expenditure by the Department of Prices and Consumer Protection on prices, consumer protection, standards and quality assurance and central and miscellaneous services, including a grant to the Price Commission, grants in aid and international subscriptions (including a Supplementary sum of £10,000) - - - - -	14,509,000	256,000
TOTAL, CIVIL, CLASS IV - -£	3,192,243,000	298,707,881

SCHEDULE (B).—PART 9

Civil, Class VI, 1976–77.

CIVIL.—CLASS VI

SCHEDULE OF SUMS granted, and of the sums which may be applied as appropriations in aid in addition thereto, to defray the charges of the several Civil Services herein particularly mentioned, which will come in course of payment during the year ending on 31st March, 1977, viz.:—

	Supply Grants	Appropriations in Aid
	£	£
Vote		
1. For expenditure by the Department of the Environment on roads and certain associated services including lorry areas, lighting and road safety - -	457,475,000	5,275,000
2. For expenditure by the Department of the Environment on assistance to local transport, town and country planning (including compensation), recreation, and on sundry other services including an international subscription (Revised sum) - - -	106,218,000	13,050
3. For expenditure by the Department of the Environment on support to nationalised transport industries, assistance to ports, services in connection with a Channel Tunnel and certain other transport services, including a grant in aid and international subscriptions (including a Supplementary sum of £34,400,000) - -	511,662,000	15,157,000
4. For expenditure by the Scottish Development Department on roads and certain associated services, including lighting and road safety, on assistance to local transport and on certain other transport services (including a Supplementary sum of £42,000) - - -	78,994,000	97,600
5. For expenditure by the Scottish Economic Planning Department on support for transport services in the Highlands and Islands and on piers and harbours - - - -	4,341,000	4,560,000
6. For expenditure by the Welsh Office on roads and certain associated services including lorry areas, lighting and road safety, and on assistance to public surface transport - - -	61,961,000	176,000

Civil, Class VI, 1976–77.

SCHEDULE (B).—PART 9—*continued*

Vote	Supply Grants	Appropriations in Aid
	£	£
7. For expenditure by the Department of Trade on services connected with shipping including a grant in aid	9,355,000	2,497,000
8. For the expenditure by the Department of Trade on civil aviation services including a grant in aid of the Civil Aviation Authority, certain payments of Regional Employment Premium and international subscriptions (including a Supplementary sum of £4,000,000)	75,494,000	3,074,000
TOTAL, CIVIL, CLASS VI £	1,305,500,000	30,849,650

SCHEDULE (B).—Part 10

Civil, Class VII, 1976–77.

CIVIL.—Class VII

Schedule of Sums granted, and of the sums which may be applied as appropriations in aid in addition thereto, to defray the charges of the several Civil Services herein particularly mentioned, which will come in course of payment during the year ending on 31st March, 1977, viz.:—

	Supply Grants	Appropriations in Aid
	£	£
Vote		
1. For expenditure by the Department of the Environment on subsidies, the option mortgage scheme, improvements, the rent officer service and sundry other housing services - -	1,778,622,000	502,000
2. For expenditure by the Scottish Development Department on subsidies, the option mortgage scheme, improvements, rent registration, capital grants to housing associations and sundry other housing services - - -	205,714,000	—
3. For expenditure by the Scottish Economic Planning Department on grants to New Town Development Corporations in connection with housing and other services - - - -	17,967,000	—
4. For expenditure by the Welsh Office on subsidies, the option mortgage scheme, improvements, the rent officer service and sundry other housing services -	87,059,000	30
Total, Civil, Class VII - - £	2,089,362,000	502,030

Civil, Class VIII, 1976–77.

SCHEDULE (B).—Part 11

CIVIL.—Class VIII

Schedule of Sums granted, and of the sums which may be applied as appropriations in aid in addition thereto, to defray the charges of the several Civil Services herein particularly mentioned, which will come in course of payment during the year ending on 31st March, 1977, viz.:—

	Supply Grants	Appropriations in Aid
	£	£
Vote		
1. For expenditure by the Department of the Environment on water supply, sewerage, town and country planning, recreation and other environmental services including grants in aid and international subscriptions, on a grant in aid to the Development Fund, and on sundry other services (Revised sum) - - - - - - -	56,281,000	47,040
2. For expenditure by the Department of the Environment on Royal Palaces, Royal Parks, historic buildings and ancient monuments, on certain public buildings and accommodation services, on assistance to the Zoological Society of London, including grants in aid (including a Supplementary sum of £1,000) - - - - - - -	33,972,000	8,076,000
3. For expenditure by the Department of the Environment on research, including grants in aid and an international subscription - - - - - -	36,708,000	2,801,000
4. For expenditure by the Scottish Development Department in connection with water supply, sewerage, land drainage and flood protection, town and country planning (including compensation), recreation, historic buildings, acquisition of land, domestic rate relief, urban programme and other environmental services including a grant in aid - - - -	16,950,000	22,010

SCHEDULE (B).—PART 11—*continued*

Civil, Class VIII, 1976–77.

Vote	Supply Grants	Appropriations in Aid
	£	£
5. For expenditure by the Welsh Office in connection with water supply, sewerage, town and country planning (including compensation), recreation, historic buildings and other environmental services, and with primary and secondary education, on grants for rate rebates and domestic rate relief and on sundry other services including grants in aid - - - - -	11,591,000	7,010
6. For expenditure by the Department of the Environment on central administration and certain other services -	70,747,000	20,610,000
TOTAL, CIVIL, CLASS VIII - £	226,249,000	31,563,060

Civil, Class IX, 1976–77.

SCHEDULE (B).—Part 12

CIVIL.—Class IX

Schedule of Sums granted, and of the sums which may be applied as appropriations in aid in addition thereto, to defray the charges of the several Civil Services herein particularly mentioned, which will come in course of payment during the year ending on 31st March, 1977, viz.:—

	Supply Grants	Appropriations in Aid
	£	£
Vote		
1. For expenditure by the Lord Chancellor's Department on court services, the Law Commission and certain other legal services - - -	20,108,000	32,386,000
2. For expenditure by the Scottish Courts Administration on court services, the Scottish Law Commission and certain other legal services, including a grant in aid - - - - - -	1,483,000	2,411,000
3. For grants to the Legal Aid Fund and to Law Centres - - - - -	50,055,000	—
4. For expenditure by the Departments of the Director of Public Prosecutions, the Law Officers and the Treasury Solicitor on Crown prosecutions and other legal services and on legal services for Government Departments	6,380,000	394,000
5. For expenditure by the Queen's and Lord Treasurer's Remembrancer on Crown prosecutions, legal services for Government Departments and certain other legal services - - - -	3,901,000	3,000
6. For expenditure by the Home Office on court services, Crown prosecutions, legal aid and other services related to crime, including a grant in aid -	82,135,000	2,916,000
7. For expenditure by the Home Office on prisons, probation, after-care and other services for the treatment of offenders, including a grant in aid -	222,981,000	13,077,000

SCHEDULE (B).—PART 12—*continued*

Civil, Class IX, 1976–77.

Vote	Supply Grants	Appropriations in Aid
	£	£
8. For expenditure by the Home Office on police, fire, control of immigration and nationality and of gaming, and other protective services, including grants in aid and an international subscription - - - - -	462,973,000	9,339,000
9. For expenditure by the Home Office on civil defence - - - - -	7,250,000	875,000
10. For expenditure by the Ministry of Agriculture, Fisheries and Food on emergency food services and strategic reserves - - - - - -	7,822,000	368,000
11. For expenditure by the Home Office on community relations, the urban programme and assistance towards certain voluntary services, including grants in aid - - - - -	38,865,000	7,076,000
12. For expenditure by the Home Office on central administration and certain other services including expenses of the Referendum on the European Economic Community - - -	15,183,000	74,000
13. For expenditure by the Scottish Home and Health Department on legal aid, services related to crime, prisons, other services for the treatment of offenders, police, fire services, civil defence and certain other services, including a grant in aid and expenses of the Referendum on the European Economic Community - - -	71,550,000	2,385,010
TOTAL, CIVIL, CLASS IX - - £	990,686,000	71,304,010

Civil, Class X, 1976–77.

SCHEDULE (B).—PART 13

CIVIL.—CLASS X

SCHEDULE OF SUMS granted, and of the sums which may be applied as appropriations in aid in addition thereto, to defray the charges of the several Civil Services herein particularly mentioned, which will come in course of payment during the year ending on 31st March, 1977, viz.:—

	Supply Grants	Appropriations in Aid
	£	£
Vote		
1. For expenditure by the Department of Education and Science on schools, the University Grants Committee, universities and certain other institutions, further education, teacher training and student awards, including grants in aid and a subscription to an international organisation (including a Supplementary sum of £40,316,000) - - -	1,026,690,000	1,162,000
2. For expenditure by the Scottish Education Department on schools, higher and further education, libraries, miscellaneous educational services, research and administration, sport, and certain grants in aid - - -	86,306,000	46,000
3. For grants in aid to the British Library and certain other institutions - -	19,285,000	—
4. For the expenditure of the National Library of Scotland, including a purchase grant in aid - - - -	904,000	37,000
5. For grants in aid of the National Library of Wales and the National Museum of Wales and a grant to the Council of Museums in Wales - - - -	3,376,000	—
6. For expenditure by the Department of Education and Science on miscellaneous educational services, research and administration, including grants in aid and international subscriptions and compensation payments for redundant staff at Colleges of Education	27,824,000	1,369,000
7. For a grant in aid of the Agricultural Research Council - - - -	18,329,000	—
8. For grants in aid of the Medical Research Council including subscriptions to certain international organisations - - - -	37,357,000	—

SCHEDULE (B).—PART 13—*continued*

Civil, Class X, 1976–77.

Vote	Supply Grants	Appropriations in Aid
	£	£
9. For a grant in aid of the Natural Environment Research Council -	26,047,000	—
10. For grants in aid of the Science Research Council including subscriptions to certain international organisations -	117,186,000	—
11. For grants in aid of the Social Science Research Council including a subscription to an international organisation - - - - - - -	11,184,000	—
12. For the expenditure of the British Museum (Natural History), including a purchase grant in aid - - - -	3,771,000	—
13. For a grant in aid of the Royal Society -	1,980,000	—
14. For the expenditure of the British Museum including a purchase grant in aid - - - - - - -	5,030,000	—
15. For the expenditure of the Science Museum including purchase grants in aid - - - - - - -	2,729,000	—
16. For the expenditure of the Victoria and Albert Museum including purchase grants in aid - - - - - -	4,131,000	—
17. For the expenditure of the Imperial War Museum including a purchase grant in aid - - - - - - -	1,269,000	—
18. For the expenditure of the National Gallery, including a purchase grant in aid - - - - - - -	2,202,000	—
19. For the expenditure of the National Maritime Museum, including a purchase grant in aid - - - -	1,701,000	—
20. For the expenditure of the National Portrait Gallery including a purchase grant in aid - - - - - -	631,000	—
21. For the expenditure of the Tate Gallery including a purchase grant in aid -	2,010,000	—

Civil, Class X, 1976–77.

SCHEDULE (B).—PART 13—*continued*

Vote	Supply Grants	Appropriations in Aid
	£	£
22. For the expenditure of the Wallace Collection - - - - - -	340,000	—
23. For the expenditure of the National Gallery of Scotland, the Scottish National Gallery of Modern Art and the Scottish National Portrait Gallery, including purchase grants in aid -	781,000	—
24. For the expenditure of the National Museum of Antiquities of Scotland, including a purchase grant in aid -	302,000	—
25. For expenditure by the Scottish Education Department on the Royal Scottish Museum and certain grants for the arts including purchase grants in aid - - - - - - -	1,394,000	—
26. For grants in aid to the Arts Council and certain other institutions and for other grants for the Arts (including a Supplementary sum of £300,000) -	43,979,000	—
TOTAL, CIVIL, CLASS X - -£	1,446,738,000	2,614,000

SCHEDULE (B).—Part 14

Civil, Class XI, 1976–77.

CIVIL.—Class XI

Schedule of Sums granted, and of the sums which may be applied as appropriations in aid in addition thereto, to defray the charges of the several Civil Services herein particularly mentioned, which will come in course of payment during the year ending on 31st March, 1977, viz.:—

	Supply Grants	Appropriations in Aid
	£	£
Vote 1. For expenditure by the Department of Health and Social Security on the provision of services under the National Health Service in England, on other health and personal social services including certain services in relation to Wales, and on research, services for the disabled, welfare food and certain other services; including grants in aid, international subscriptions and grants under section 8 of the Industry Act 1972 (including a Supplementary sum of £283,000,000) -	4,361,071,000	528,222,020
2. For expenditure by the Scottish Home and Health Department on the provision of services under the National Health Service in Scotland, on other health services and on research, services for the disabled, welfare food and certain other services - -	570,837,000	52,983,010
3. For expenditure by the Scottish Education Department in connection with social work - - - - - -	4,690,000	9,010
4. For expenditure by the Welsh Office on the provision of services under the National Health Service in Wales, on other health and personal social services, and on research, services for the disabled, welfare food and certain other services (including a Supplementary sum of £17,155,000) - -	270,470,000	27,424,500
Total, Civil, Class XI - -£	5,207,068,000	608,638,540

Civil, Class XII, 1976–77.

SCHEDULE (B).—PART 15

CIVIL.—CLASS XII

SCHEDULE OF SUMS granted, and of the sums which may be applied as appropriations in aid in addition thereto, to defray the charges of the several Civil Services herein particularly mentioned, which will come in course of payment during the year ending on 31st March, 1977, viz.:—

	Supply Grants	Appropriations in Aid
	£	£
Vote		
1. For sums payable out of the Consolidated Fund to the National Insurance Fund - - - - - -	1,303,000,000	—
2. For expenditure by the Department of Health and Social Security on pensions, &c., for disablement or death arising out of war or service in the Armed Forces after 2 September 1939 and on certain associated services, on attendance allowances, invalid care allowance, old persons' retirement pensions, non-contributory invalidity pensions and mobility allowance, &c. (including a Supplementary sum of £23,000,000) - - - - -	500,925,000	75,000
3. For expenditure by the Department of Health and Social Security on supplementary pensions and allowances and lump sum payments for pensioners, &c., and repayments to Local Authorities (including a Supplementary sum of £58,000,000) - - -	1,508,000,000	182,000,000
4. For expenditure by the Department of Health and Social Security on family allowances, child interim benefit and family income supplements - -	557,888,000	112,000
5. For expenditure by the Department of Health and Social Security on administration and certain other services including an international subscription (including a Supplementary sum of £18,000,000) - - - - -	230,481,000	232,962,000
TOTAL, CIVIL, CLASS XII - -£	4,100,294,000	415,149,000

SCHEDULE (B).—PART 16

Civil, Class XIII, 1976–77.

CIVIL.—CLASS XIII

SCHEDULE OF SUMS granted, and of the sums which may be applied as appropriations in aid in addition thereto, to defray the charges of the several Civil Services herein particularly mentioned, which will come in course of payment during the year ending on 31st March, 1977, viz.:—

	Supply Grants	Appropriations in Aid
	£	£
Vote		
1. For the expenditure of the House of Lords - - - - - -	1,719,000	26,000
2. For the expenditure of the House of Commons, including a grant in aid -	13,653,000	68,000
3. For the expenditure of the Department of Her Majesty's Most Honourable Privy Council - - - -	264,000	3,000
4. For expenditure by the Treasury on the management of the economy, the Paymaster General's Office and certain other services including grants in aid to certain Parliamentary bodies and others (including a Supplementary sum of £18,000) - - - -	37,231,000	1,784,000
5. For the expenditure of the Department of the Comptroller and Auditor General - - - - -	3,326,000	625,000
6. For expenditure by the Customs and Excise Department including the expenses of Value Added Tax Tribunals and an international subscription - - - - -	140,610,000	4,615,000
7. For the expenditure of the Inland Revenue Department (including a Supplementary sum of £28,500,000) -	325,840,000	15,073,000
8. For expenditure by the Department of the Environment in connection with driver and motor vehicle registration and licensing and the collection of revenue - - - - - -	49,144,000	563,000

Civil, Class XIII, 1976–77.

SCHEDULE (B).—PART 16—*continued*

Vote	Supply Grants	Appropriations in Aid
	£	£
9. For the expenditure of the National Debt Office and Pensions Commutation Board - - - - - -	1,000	307,000
10. For the expenditure of the Public Works Loan Commission - - - -	1,000	185,000
11. For the expenditure of the Department for National Savings (including a Supplementary sum of £4,000,000) -	38,406,000	44,105,000
12. For the expenditure by the Civil Service Department on the central management of the civil service, on Royal Commissions, Committees, special enquiries, the Office of the Parliamentary Counsel, and certain other services, including grants in aid to the Government Hospitality Fund and other bodies - - - - - - -	21,011,000	871,000
13. For the expenditure of the Public Record Office - - - - - - -	1,389,000	260,000
14. For the expenditure of the Scottish Record Office including a grant in aid	421,000	109,000
15. For the expenditure of the Office of Population Censuses and Surveys, including a grant in aid - - -	8,260,000	2,959,000
16. For the expenditure of the Department of the Registrar General of Births, Deaths and Marriages in Scotland -	1,140,000	340,000
17. For the expenditure of the Land Registry	1,000	20,794,000
18. For the expenditure of the Department of the Registers of Scotland - -	1,000	1,517,000
19. For the expenditure of the Charity Commission for England and Wales -	1,505,000	200
20. For expenditure by the Ordnance Survey on the survey of Great Britain and other mapping services (including a Supplementary sum of £700,000) -	12,870,000	9,848,000
21. For the expenditure of the Cabinet Office and subscriptions to international organisations - - -	4,256,000	35,850

SCHEDULE (B).—PART 16—*continued*

Civil, Class XIII, 1976–77.

	Supply Grants	Appropriations in Aid
	£	£
Vote		
22. For expenditure by the Scottish Office on central administration and certain other services - - - -	36,841,000	734,000
23. For the expenditure by the Welsh Office on central administration - -	8,284,000	427,000
24. For expenditure by the Home Office on grants to the British Broadcasting Corporation for home broadcasting, and civil defence, central administration, wireless telegraphy and sundry other services - - - - -	239,443,000	1,377,000
25. For the expenditure of the Office of the Parliamentary Commissioner for Administration and the Health Service Commissioners for England, Scotland and Wales - - - - - -	597,000	—
26. For the expenditure of the Office of the Public Trustee - - - -	1,000	1,876,000
27. For charges in connection with land purchases in Northern Ireland, and the expenses of management of guaranteed stocks and bonds issued for the purpose of Irish land purchases	297,000	100
28. For transitional payments to certain charities - - - - - -	1,300,000	—
29. To repay to the Contingencies Fund certain miscellaneous advances -	440,000	—
TOTAL, CIVIL, CLASS XIII - -£	948,252,000	108,502,150

Civil, Class XIV, 1976–77.

SCHEDULE (B).—PART 17

CIVIL.—CLASS XIV

SCHEDULE OF SUMS granted, and of the sums which may be applied as appropriations in aid in addition thereto, to defray the charges of the several Civil Services herein particularly mentioned, which will come in course of payment during the year ending on 31st March, 1977, viz.:—

	Supply Grants	Appropriations in Aid
	£	£
Vote		
1. For expenditure by the Property Services Agency of the Department of the Environment on public building work and accommodation services, &c., for civil purposes in the United Kingdom, transport services and sundry other services (including a Supplementary sum of £1,400,000) - - -	342,465,000	80,543,010
3. For the expenditure of Her Majesty's Stationery Office on the procurement and production of stationery and printing, on publishing, and on certain other services - - - -	88,549,000	74,342,000
4. For expenditure by the Central Computer Agency (Civil Service Department) in connection with computers and general telecommunications including an international subscription.	37,003,000	24,686,000
5. For expenditure by the Central Office of Information on home and overseas publicity - - - - -	23,601,000	4,755,000
6. For expenditure by the Assistant Paymaster General on the superannuation of civil servants, pensions, &c., in respect of former members of the Royal Irish Constabulary and other pensions and non-recurrent payments; and for certain other services - -	276,160,000	67,090,000

SCHEDULE (B).—PART 17—*continued*

Civil,
Class XIV,
1976–77.

Vote	Supply Grants	Appropriations in Aid
	£	£
7. For rates and contributions in lieu of rates paid by the Rating of Government Property Department in respect of property occupied by the Crown and premises occupied by representatives of Commonwealth and foreign countries and international organisations; and for certain sewerage, &c., charges - - - - - -	121,870,000	10,000,000
8. For the expenditure of the Department of the Government Actuary - -	255,000	204,000
9. For the expenditure of the Civil Service Catering Organisation (Civil Service Department) in connection with the provision of catering services - -	1,017,000	8,750,000
TOTAL, CIVIL, CLASS XIV - -£	890,920,000	270,370,010

Civil, Class XV, 1976–77.

SCHEDULE (B).—PART 18

CIVIL.—CLASS XV

SCHEDULE OF SUMS granted, and of the sums which may be applied as appropriations in aid in addition thereto, to defray the charges of the several Civil Services herein particularly mentioned, which will come in course of payment during the year ending on 31st March, 1977, viz.:—

	Supply Grants	Appropriations in Aid
	£	£
Vote		
1. For expenditure by the Ministry of Agriculture, Fisheries and Food on certain services in Northern Ireland, including price guarantees, production grants and subsidies, grants and loans for capital and other improvements, support for agriculture in special areas, educational and livestock services, food services and assistance to marketing, land management, special assistance to agriculture in Northern Ireland, assistance to the fishing industry and administration by the Department of Agriculture for Northern Ireland - - - - -	24,240,000	281,080
2. For expenditure by the Northern Ireland Office on court services, Crown prosecutions, legal aid, Office of the Advisers, other services related to crime, compensation for criminal injuries, prisons, probation and after-care, young offenders, police, home defence, central and miscellaneous services, accommodation services in respect of prisons and courts and legal services for Government Departments including grants in aid - -	167,781,000	316,200
3. For expenditure by the Northern Ireland Office on the Supreme Court of Judicature and Court of Criminal Appeal of Northern Ireland and on certain other legal services in Northern Ireland - - - - -	192,000	277,000

SCHEDULE (B).—PART 18—*continued*

Civil, Class XV, 1976–77.

	Supply Grants	Appropriations in Aid
	£	£
Vote 4. For expenditure by the Northern Ireland Office on election expenses, central administration, transfers to the Northern Ireland Consolidated Fund, including a grant in aid, and accommodation services in respect of the Department's Offices in Northern Ireland - - - - -	333,829,000	3,510,020
TOTAL, CIVIL, CLASS XV - £	526,042,000	4,384,300

Civil, Class XVII, 1976–77.

SCHEDULE (B).— PART 19

CIVIL.—CLASS XVII

SCHEDULE OF SUMS granted, and of the sums which may be applied as appropriations in aid in addition thereto, to defray the charges of the several Civil Services herein particularly mentioned, which will come in course of payment during the year ending on 31st March, 1977, viz.:—

	Supply Grants	Appropriations in Aid
	£	£
Vote		
1. For rate support grants to local authorities in England and Wales, for National Parks supplementary grants to County Councils, for supplementary grants for transport purposes to County Councils and the Greater London Council and for rate rebate and domestic rate relief grants to local authorities in England (Revised sum)	6,313,151,000	—
2. For rate support grants, equalisation grants and rate rebates grants to local authorities in Scotland - - - -	841,700,000	—
3. For expenditure by the Department of Education and Science on superannuation allowances and gratuities, &c., in respect of teachers, and the widows, children and dependants of deceased teachers. - - - - -	1,000	250,474,000
4. For the expenditure by the Scottish Home and Health Department on superannuation allowances and gratuities, &c., in respect of teachers, and the widows and dependants of deceased teachers - - - - -	1,000	37,876,000
5. For expenditure by the Department of Health and Social Security on pensions, allowances, gratuities, &c., to or in respect of persons engaged in health services or in other approved employment - - - - - -	1,000	155,750,000
6. For expenditure by the Scottish Home and Health Department on pensions, allowances, gratuities, &c., to or in respect of persons engaged in health services or in other approved employment - - - - - -	1,000	21,018,000

SCHEDULE (B).—PART 19—*continued*

Civil, Class XVII, 1976–77.

	Supply Grants	Appropriations in Aid
	£	£
Vote		
7. For payment of pensions, &c., to persons who contributed to the Authority's Superannuation Schemes and other related expenditure - - -	1,000	6,694,000
8. For payment to the Trustees of the Post Office Pensions Fund in respect of former civil servants - - -	45,000,000	—
9. For the salaries and expenses of the Crown Estate Office - - -	687,000	—
10. For transitional relief under the Finance Acts 1965 and 1972 for companies with an overseas source of trading income - - - - - -	27,000,000	—
TOTAL, CIVIL, CLASS XVII - - £	7,227,543,000	471,812,000

Section 3.

SCHEDULE (C)

Surpluses and Deficits on certain Votes in year ending 31*st March* 1975

Class and Vote			Surpluses £	Deficits £
II,	3A	Overseas Information: Broadcasting - - - - -		4,372,000
IV,	7	General Support to Industry -	9,000,000	
IV,	10	Department of Trade [formerly Trade and Consumer Affairs]		11,600,000
IV,	16	Central and Miscellaneous Services (Department of Industry)	5,300,000	
IV,	18	Department of Prices and Consumer Protection - -		2,700,000
IX,	12	Community Services (Home Office) - - - - -		980,000
IX,	13	Community Services (Civil Service Department) [Estimate withdrawn] - -	1,000,000	
IX,	13	Central and Miscellaneous Services (Home Office) [renumbered from IX, 14] -		20,000
XIII,	25	Other Services: Broadcasting, Posts and Telecommunications - - - - -	69,103,000	
XIII,	25A	Other Services: Home Broadcasting and Wireless Telegraphy - - - - -		53,481,000
XVII,	7A	Department of Industry (Post Office Pensions Fund) -		11,250,000
			£84,403,000	£84,403,000

SCHEDULE (D)

Section 4.

Enactments Repealed

Chapter	Short Title
1974 c. 1	Consolidated Fund Act 1974.
1974 c. 2	Appropriation Act 1974.
1974 c. 12	Consolidated Fund (No. 2) Act 1974.
1974 c. 15	Consolidated Fund (No. 3) Act 1974.
1974 c. 31	Appropriation (No. 2) Act 1974.
1974 c. 57	Consolidated Fund (No. 4) Act 1974.

Drought Act 1976

1976 CHAPTER 44

An Act to confer fresh powers to meet deficiencies in the supply of water due to exceptional shortage of rain and for connected purposes. [6th August 1976]

BE IT ENACTED by the Queen's most Excellent Majesty, by and with the advice and consent of the Lords Spiritual and Temporal, and Commons, in this present Parliament assembled, and by the authority of the same, as follows:—

Provision for meeting water shortages —general.

1.—(1) If the Secretary of State is satisfied that, by reason of an exceptional shortage of rain, a serious deficiency of supplies of water in any area exists or is threatened then, subject to the provisions of this section, he may by order make such provision authorised by this section as appears to him to be expedient with a view to meeting the deficiency.

(2) Subject to subsection (6) below, the power to make an order under this section in relation to any area shall only be exercisable where an application is made to the Secretary of State by a water authority or statutory water company who supply water in that area and in this section " the authority " means the water authority or statutory water company on whose application an order is made under this section.

(3) An order under this section may contain any of the following provisions, that is to say—

(*a*) provision authorising the authority (or persons authorised to do so by the authority) to take water from any source specified in the order subject to any conditions or restrictions so specified;

(*b*) provision authorising the authority to prohibit or limit the use of water for any purpose specified in the order being a purpose for the time being prescribed by the Secretary of State in a direction given to water authorities and statutory water companies generally as a purpose which may be specified by virtue of this paragraph in any order under this section;

(*c*) provision authorising the authority (or persons authorised to do so by the authority) to discharge water to any place specified in the order subject to any conditions or restrictions so specified;

(*d*) provision authorising the authority to prohibit or limit the taking by any person (including other water authorities or statutory water companies) of water from a source specified in the order if the authority is satisfied that the taking of water from that source seriously affects the supplies available to the authority;

(*e*) provision suspending or modifying, subject to any conditions specified in the order, any restriction or obligation to which the authority or any person are or is subject as respects—

(i) the taking of water from any source;

(ii) the discharge of water;

(iii) the supply of water (whether in point of quantity, pressure, quality, means of supply or otherwise); or

(iv) the filtration or other treatment of water;

(*f*) provision authorising the authority to suspend, vary or attach conditions to, any consent specified in the order for the discharge within the authority's area (whether by the authority or any other person) of sewage effluent or trade effluent;

and may also contain such supplemental, incidental and consequential provisions as appear to the Secretary of State to be expedient.

(4) An order under this section which contains a provision authorising the authority to prohibit or limit the use of water may authorise the authority to prohibit or limit its use by consumers generally or a class of consumer specified in the order and where the order specifies a class of consumer it may authorise the authority to apply the prohibition or limitation to any particular consumer within that class.

(5) Nothing in an order under this section shall affect the right of the authority, in the event of an interruption or diminution of the supply of water, to raise, charge and levy any water rate or minimum charge which might have been raised, charged and levied if there had been no such interruption or diminution.

(6) The Secretary of State may revoke or vary any direction given by him under subsection (3)(*b*) above by a further direction under that paragraph, but where any purpose which is prescribed under that paragraph will cease, by virtue of the variation or revocation, to be one which may be specified in an order under this section the Secretary of State shall (if he does not exercise his power of revocation) exercise his power to vary orders under this section as respects all orders which will be affected by the variation or revocation of the direction so as to make them conform to the variation or reflect the revocation and may do so without an application being made to him.

(7) The revocation or variation of a direction under subsection (6) above shall not affect the validity of anything done in pursuance of an order before the giving of the further direction or any obligation or liability accrued or incurred before the giving of the further direction.

(8) Subject to section 5(6) of this Act, no authorisation given, no prohibition or limitation imposed and no suspension or modification effected by or under an order under this section shall have effect for a period longer than six months beginning with the day on which the order came into operation.

(9) Schedule 1 to this Act shall have effect in relation to the procedure to be followed in connection with the making of orders under this section on the application of water authorities or statutory water companies.

(10) Part I of Schedule 2 to this Act shall have effect with respect to the payment of compensation by the authority to persons affected by orders under this section.

(11) Except as provided by Part I of the said Schedule 2, the authority shall not incur any liability to any person for damage suffered by reason of any thing done or omitted in pursuance of an order under this section.

Provision for meeting water shortages in an emergency.

2.—(1) If the Secretary of State is satisfied that, by reason of an exceptional shortage of rain, a serious deficiency of supplies of water in any area exists or is threatened and is further satisfied that the deficiency is such as to be likely to impair the economic or social well-being of persons in the area then, subject to the provisions of this section, he may by order make such provision authorised by this section as appears to him to be expedient with a view to meeting the deficiency.

(2) The power to make an order under this section in relation to any area shall only be exercisable where an application is made to the Secretary of State by a water authority or statutory water company who supply water in that area and in this section "the authority" means the water authority or statutory water company on whose application an order is made under this section.

(3) An order under this section may contain any of the following provisions, that is to say—

(*a*) any provision which could be included under this Act in an order under section 1 except one authorised by subsection (3)(*b*) of that section;

(*b*) provision authorising the authority to prohibit or limit the use of water for such purposes as the authority think fit;

(*c*) provision authorising the authority to supply water in their area or in any place within their area by means of stand-pipes or water tanks, and to erect or set up and maintain stand-pipes or water tanks in any street in that area;

and may also contain such supplemental, incidental and consequential provisions as appear to the Secretary of State to be expedient.

(4) The Secretary of State may give such directions as he considers necessary or expedient to an authority on whom powers have been conferred by an order under this section as to the manner in which or the circumstances in which any power is or is not to be exercised.

(5) The following provisions apply where an order under this section contains a provision authorising the authority to prohibit or limit the use of water, that is to say—

(*a*) the power may be exercised in relation to consumers generally, a class of consumer or a particular consumer;

(*b*) the authority shall take such steps as they think appropriate for bringing the prohibition or limitation to the attention of the persons to whom the prohibition or limitation will apply and, in particular, shall—

(i) cause notice of the prohibition or limitation to be published in one or more local newspapers circulating within that part of the authority's area which would be affected by the provision of the order, or

(ii) send notice of the prohibition or limitation to the persons to whom the prohibition or limitation will apply,

as the authority think appropriate;

(*c*) the prohibition or limitation shall not come into operation until the expiration of the period of 72 hours beginning with the day on which the notice is published or sent to the person in question, as the case may be.

(6) It shall be the duty of an authority to whom any direction has been given under subsection (4) above to comply with the direction.

(7) The giving of a direction under subsection (4) above in relation to any power shall not affect the validity of anything

done in the exercise of that power before the giving of the direction or any obligation or liability incurred before the giving of the direction.

(8) Subsection (5) of section 1 of this Act shall apply in relation to an order under this section as it applies in relation to an order under that section.

(9) Any works to be carried out under the authority of an order under this section shall be included in the definition of emergency works in section 39(1) of the Public Utilities Street Works Act 1950. 1950 c. 39.

(10) Subject to section 5(6) of this Act, no authorisation given, no prohibition or limitation imposed and no suspension or modification of any restriction or obligation effected by or under an order under this section shall have effect for a period longer than three months beginning with the day on which the order came into operation.

(11) Schedule 1 to this Act shall have effect in relation to the procedure to be followed in connection with the making of orders under this section.

(12) Part II of Schedule 2 to this Act shall have effect with respect to the payment of compensation by the authority to persons affected by orders under this section.

(13) Except as provided by Part II of the said Schedule 2, the authority shall not incur any liability to any person for damage suffered by reason of any thing done or omitted in pursuance of an order under this section.

Supplementary provisions as to the powers conferred under section 1 or 2.

3.—(1) This section has effect in relation to orders under section 1 or 2 of this Act and in it " the authority " has the same meaning as it has in those sections.

(2) In an order—

(*a*) authorising the taking of water from a source from which water is supplied to an inland navigation ; or

(*b*) suspending or modifying—

(i) a restriction as respects the taking of water from a source from which water is supplied to an inland navigation ; or

(ii) an obligation to discharge compensation water into a canal or into any river or stream which forms part of, or from which water is supplied to, an inland navigation ;

the Secretary of State may include provision for prohibiting or imposing limitations on the taking of water from the inland navigation or for the suspension or modification of any obligation to which the navigation authority are subject as respects the discharge of water from the inland navigation.

(3) A prohibition or limitation on the taking of water from any source may be imposed so as to have effect in relation to a source from which a person to whom the prohibition or limitation applies has a right to take water whether by virtue of an enactment or instrument, an agreement or the ownership of land.

(4) An order may authorise the authority, subject to any conditions and restrictions specified in the order, to execute any works required for the discharge of their functions under the order and—

(*a*) may authorise the authority for that purpose to enter upon any land specified in the order and to occupy and use the land to such extent and in such manner as may be requisite for the execution and maintenance of the works ; and

(*b*) may apply in relation to the execution of the works such of the provisions of the waterworks code as appear to the Secretary of State to be appropriate, subject to such modifications and adaptations as may be specified in the order.

(5) In an order which authorises the authority to enter on land the Secretary of State shall include provisions requiring the authority to give to the occupier of the land and to such other persons concerned with the land as may be specified in the order not less than 7 days' notice of their intended entry on the land.

(6) The Secretary of State may require an authority on whom powers have been conferred by an order to furnish him with such information relating to the exercise by the authority of any of those powers as he considers necessary to enable him to discharge his functions under this Act.

Offences.

4.—(1) If any person—

(*a*) takes or uses water in contravention of a prohibition or limitation imposed by or under an order under section 1 or 2 of this Act or takes or uses water otherwise than in accordance with any condition or restriction so imposed ; or

(*b*) discharges water otherwise than in accordance with any condition or restriction imposed by or under such an order ;

he shall be guilty of an offence under this section.

(2) If any person—

(*a*) fails to construct or maintain in good order a gauge, weir or other apparatus for measuring the flow of water which he was required to construct or maintain by an order under section 1 or 2 of this Act ; or (*b*) fails to allow some person authorised for the purpose by or under any such order to inspect and examine any such apparatus or any records made thereby or kept by that person in connection therewith or to take copies of any such records;

he shall be guilty of an offence under this section.

(3) In any proceedings for an offence under this section it shall be a defence for the accused person to prove that he took all reasonable precautions and exercised all due diligence to avoid the commission of such an offence.

(4) A person who is guilty of an offence under this section shall be liable—

(*a*) on summary conviction, to a fine not exceeding £400;

(*b*) on conviction on indictment, to a fine.

(5) Where an offence under this section which has been committed by a body corporate is proved to have been committed with the consent or connivance of, or to be attributable to any neglect on the part of, any director, manager, secretary or other similar officer of the body corporate or any person who was purporting to act in any such capacity, he as well as the body corporate shall be guilty of that offence and be liable to be proceeded against and punished accordingly.

Where the affairs of a body corporate are managed by its members the preceding provisions of this subsection shall apply in relation to the acts and defaults of the member in connection with his functions of management as if he were a director of the body corporate.

5.—(1) In this Act, except where the context otherwise requires— General.

"compensation water" means water which any water authority or statutory water company are under an obligation to discharge into a river, stream, brook or other running water or into a canal as a condition of carrying on their undertaking;

"drainage authority" means a water authority or internal drainage board;

"inland navigation" includes any canal or navigable river;

"obligation" includes an obligation imposed by an enactment, instrument or agreement and "restriction" has a corresponding meaning;

"take", in relation to water, includes the collection, impounding, diversion and appropriation of water;

"trade effluent" has the same meaning as it has in the Control of Pollution Act 1974; 1974 c. 40.

1945 c. 42. "the waterworks code" means Schedule 3 to the Water Act 1945;

and any other expression which is used in this Act and is defined in section 59 of the Water Act 1945 shall have the same meaning in this Act as it is given in that section.

(2) Any reference in this Act to the area of an authority is, where the authority is a statutory water company, a reference to the limits of supply of the company and, where the authority is an internal drainage board, a reference to the district of the board.

(3) Any reference in this Act to an enactment shall be construed as a reference to that enactment as amended, applied or extended by or under any other enactment.

(4) The power to make an order under section 1 or 2 of this Act shall be exercisable by statutory instrument.

(5) The Secretary of State may by order in a statutory instrument revoke any order made by him under the said section 1 or 2.

(6) The power to make an order under section 1 or 2 of this Act includes power—

(*a*) from time to time to extend a period specified in a previous order, but not so as to extend beyond a year the period mentioned in section 1(8) of this Act or beyond 5 months the period mentioned in section 2(10) of this Act;

(*b*) to vary a previous order in any other respect.

1958 c. 67. (7) The Water Act 1958 (which is superseded by this Act) is hereby repealed except in its application to Scotland subject, however, to the transitional and saving provisions contained in Schedule 3 to this Act.

(8) Any reference in any enactment to the Water Act 1958 in its application to England and Wales or to any provision of that Act shall be construed as a reference to this Act or, as the case may be, to the corresponding provision of this Act.

Short title and extent.

6.—(1) This Act may be cited as the Drought Act 1976.

(2) This Act does not extend to Scotland or Northern Ireland.

SCHEDULES

SCHEDULE 1

Sections 1(9), 2(11).

Procedure for Making Orders

1.—(1) The authority who are applying for an order under section 1 or 2 of this Act shall cause notice in writing of the application to be served on the persons specified in the following Table—

All orders	Every local authority and every water authority or statutory water company whose area would be affected by the order.
Orders which suspend or modify an enactment.	Such persons (if any) as are specified by name in the enactment as being persons for whose protection it was enacted.
Orders concerning the taking of water from a source or the discharge of water or effluent to a place.	(*a*) Every local authority and every drainage authority (other than the applicants) in whose area the source, or the place at which water or effluent is to be discharged, is situated. (*b*) Every navigation authority exercising functions over any watercourse affected by the order. (*c*) If the order concerns any consent relating to the discharge of sewage effluent or trade effluent, the person to whom the consent was given.
Orders which authorise the execution of any works.	(*a*) Every local authority within whose area the works are situated. (*b*) If the order authorises the execution of works in, under or over a watercourse every drainage authority (other than the applicants) within whose area the works, or any part of the works, are situated.
Orders which authorise the occupation and use of land.	Every owner, lessee and occupier of the land.
Orders which prohibit or limit the taking of water.	Every named person to whom the prohibition or limitation applies.

(2) The authority shall also cause a notice of the application to be published—

(*a*) in one or more local newspapers circulating within that part of the area of the authority which would be affected by the order,

Sch. 1

(*b*) in one or more local newspapers circulating within that part of the area of any other water authority or statutory water company which would be affected by the order, and

(*c*) where the application is for an order concerning the taking of water from a source or the discharge of water or effluent to a place, in one or more local newspapers circulating within the area of every local authority within whose area the source or the place at which the water or effluent is to be discharged is situated.

(3) The authority shall in addition to the notices specified in sub-paragraph (2) above cause a notice of the application to be published in the London Gazette.

(4) A notice under this paragraph—

(*a*) shall state the general effect of the application, and

(*b*) shall specify a place within that part of the area of the authority which would be affected by the order where a copy of any relevant map or plan may be inspected by any person free of charge at all reasonable hours within a period of 7 days from the date on which it is served or, in the case of publication of a notice in pursuance of any of the foregoing provisions of this paragraph, from the date of the publication, and

(*c*) shall state that objections to the application may be made to the Secretary of State within 7 days from the date on which it is served or, in the case of publication of a notice in pursuance of any of the foregoing provisions of this paragraph, from the date of the publication, and

(*d*) in the case of an application for an order authorising the occupation and use of land, shall specify the land to which the application relates.

2. A notice which is required under this Schedule to be served on any person may be served either—

(*a*) by delivering it to the person on whom it is to be served, or

(*b*) by leaving it, or sending it in a pre-paid letter addressed to that person, at his usual or last-known residence, or

(*c*) in the case of an incorporated company or body, by delivering it to their clerk or secretary at their registered or principal office, or by sending it in a pre-paid letter addressed to him at that office, or

(*d*) in the case of a notice to be served on a person as being the owner of any land by virtue of the fact that he receives the rack rent thereof as an agent for another, or would so receive it if the land was let at a rack rent, by leaving it, or sending it in a pre-paid letter addressed to him, at his place of business, or

(*e*) in the case of a notice to be served on the owner, lessee or occupier of any land, if it is not practicable after reasonable inquiry to ascertain the name and address of the person on whom it should be served, or if the land is unoccupied, by addressing it to the person concerned by the description of " owner ", " lessee " or " occupier " of the land (describing it) to which it relates, and delivering it to some person on the land, or if there is no person on the land to whom it can be delivered, by fixing it, or a copy of it, to some conspicuous part of the land. SCH. 1

A notice sent in a letter in pursuance of paragraph (*b*), (*c*) or (*d*) above shall not be treated as having been properly served unless the sender takes such steps as are for the time being required to secure that the letter is transmitted in priority to letters of other descriptions.

3.—(1) If any objection is duly made with respect to the application and is not withdrawn, then, subject to the provisions of this paragraph, the Secretary of State shall before making the order either cause a public local inquiry to be held or afford to any person by whom any objections have been duly made and not withdrawn an opportunity of appearing before and being heard by a person appointed by the Secretary of State for the purpose, and if any person by whom an objection has been made avails himself of the opportunity to be heard, the Secretary of State shall afford to the authority applying for the order, and to any other persons to whom it appears to the Secretary of State expedient to afford it, an opportunity of being heard on the same occasion.

(2) Where it appears to the Secretary of State that the order is required to be made urgently if it is to enable the authority effectively to meet the deficiency of supplies of water in their area he may direct that the requirements of sub-paragraph (1) of this paragraph shall be dispensed with in relation to the application:

Provided that nothing in this sub-paragraph shall authorise the Secretary of State to disregard any objection which has been duly made and not withdrawn.

(3) Notwithstanding anything in sub-paragraph (1) of this paragraph, the Secretary of State may require any person who has made an objection to state in writing the grounds thereof, and may disregard the objection for the purposes of this paragraph if the Secretary of State is satisfied—

(*a*) that the objection relates exclusively to matters which can be dealt with on a reference under Schedule 2 to this Act or by any person by whom compensation is to be assessed, or

(*b*) in a case where the order is one confined to the extension of a period specified in a previous order, that the objection is one that has in substance been made with respect to the application for that previous order.

(4) Subject to the requirements of this paragraph, the Secretary of State, upon being satisfied that the proper notices have been published and served, may, if he thinks fit, make the order in respect of which the application is made with or without modifications.

(5) The Secretary of State may hold a public local inquiry on any application for an order under this Act notwithstanding that he is not required to do so by this paragraph and the provisions of section 250 of the Local Government Act 1972 shall extend to any local inquiry held by virtue of this paragraph subject to the modification that the reference in subsection (4) to a local authority shall 1972 c. 70.

SCH. 1 be taken to include a reference to any water authority or statutory water company concerned in the inquiry.

4. After an order under this Act has been made, the authority on whose application it was made shall cause to be published (in the manner in which notice of the application was required under sub-paragraphs (2) and (3) of paragraph 1 of this Schedule to be published) a notice stating that the order has been made and naming a place where a copy thereof may be inspected.

Sections 1(10) and 2(12).

SCHEDULE 2

COMPENSATION

PART I

SECTION 1 ORDERS

1. The following provisions of this Part of this Schedule have effect for providing compensation to persons who suffer damage by reason of things done or omitted in pursuance of an order under section 1 of this Act.

2.—(1) Compensation in respect of the taking of water from a source or its taking from a source otherwise than in accordance with a restriction or obligation which has been suspended or modified shall be made by the authority to the owners of and all other persons interested in the source of water or injuriously affected by the taking of the water for damage sustained by any of those persons by reason of the taking of the water.

(2) In assessing the compensation to be made under this paragraph, the Lands Tribunal may, if it thinks fit, have regard to the amount of water which, on an equitable apportionment of the water available from the source between the claimant, the authority and other persons taking water from the source, may fairly be apportioned to the claimant.

3.—(1) Compensation in respect of water's being discharged or not discharged to any place or its being discharged otherwise than in accordance with a restriction or obligation (whether relating to the treatment or discharge of the water) which has been suspended or modified shall be made by the authority to the owners of and all other persons interested in the place of discharge or injuriously affected by the discharge or lack of discharge for damage sustained by reason of the water being discharged or not discharged or being discharged otherwise than in accordance with the restriction or obligation.

(2) In assessing the compensation to be made under this paragraph in respect of the lack of discharge of compensation water, the Lands Tribunal may, if it thinks fit, have regard to the amount of water which, under the conditions existing by reason of the shortage of rain, would have been available to the claimant during the period during which the deficiency of supplies of water is continued, if the authority in relation to whom the obligation was imposed had never carried on their undertaking.

4. Compensation in respect of the imposition of a prohibition or limitation on the taking of water from a source shall be made by the authority to any persons to whom the prohibition or limitation applies for damage sustained by reason of the prohibition or limitation. Sch. 2

5. Compensation in respect of the discharge of sewage effluent or trade effluent otherwise than in accordance with any consent relating to its discharge shall be made by the authority to the person to whom the consent was given for damage sustained by that person by reason of the suspension or variation of the consent or the attachment of conditions to the consent.

6. Compensation in respect of the entry upon or occupation or use of land shall be made by the authority to the owners and occupiers of and all other persons interested in the land or injuriously affected by the entry upon, occupation or use of the land for damage sustained by reason of the entry upon, occupation or use of the land.

7.—(1) A claim for compensation under this Part of this Schedule shall be made by serving upon the authority a notice in writing stating the grounds of the claim and the amount claimed.

(2) A claim for compensation under this Part of this Schedule may be made at any time not later than six months after the end of the period for which the order authorises—

(*a*) the taking or discharge of water,

(*b*) the imposition of a prohibition or limitation on the taking of water,

(*c*) the suspension or modification of any restriction or obligation, or

(*d*) the suspension or variation of or attachment of conditions to any consent relating to the discharge of sewage effluent or trade effluent,

as the case may be.

(3) Any question as to the right of a claimant to recover compensation, or as to the amount of compensation recoverable, shall in default of agreement be referred to, and determined by, the Lands Tribunal.

(4) Where a claim is made during the continuance of an order, the Lands Tribunal may, if it thinks fit, award a sum representing the damage which is likely to be sustained by the claimant in respect of each day on which—

(*a*) water is taken or discharged,

(*b*) water is not discharged or is discharged otherwise than in accordance with an obligation or restriction, or

(*c*) sewage effluent or trade effluent is discharged otherwise than in accordance with a consent originally given,

as the case may be.

Part II

Section 2 Orders

8. The following provisions of this Part of this Schedule have effect for providing compensation to persons who suffer damage by reason of things done or omitted in pursuance of an order under section 2 of this Act.

SCH. 2

9. Compensation in respect of the entry upon or occupation or use of land shall be made by the authority to the owners and occupiers of and all other persons interested in the land or injuriously affected by the entry upon, occupation or use of the land for damage sustained by reason of the entry upon, occupation or use of the land.

10.—(1) A claim for compensation under this Part of this Schedule shall be made by serving upon the authority a notice in writing stating the grounds of the claim and the amount claimed.

(2) Any question as to the right of a claimant to recover compensation, or as to the amount of compensation recoverable, shall in default of agreement be referred to, and determined by, the Lands Tribunal.

Section 5(7).

SCHEDULE 3

TRANSITIONAL AND SAVING PROVISIONS

1958 c. 67.

1.—(1) The repeal by this Act of the Water Act 1958 in its application to England and Wales shall not affect the validity of an order under that Act which was in force immediately before the repeal took effect and—

(*a*) the order may be varied by a subsequent order made under and in accordance with that Act as if that Act were still in force in relation to England and Wales ;

(*b*) any thing done or omitted after the repeal took effect which would have constituted an offence under that Act if that Act had remained in force shall constitute an offence under that Act and be punishable accordingly.

(2) Sub-paragraph (1) above applies also to an order which has been made under the Water Act 1958 but has not come into operation when the repeal takes effect.

2.—(1) Where an application for an order under the Water Act 1958 is pending when the repeal of that Act in its application to England and Wales by this Act takes effect then the application shall, according as it is an application for an order under section 1 or 2 of that Act, be deemed to be an application for an order under section 1 or 2 of this Act.

(2) Any thing duly done before the repeal takes effect for the purposes of the application under the Water Act 1958 shall be deemed to have been duly done for the purposes of an application under this Act and the proceedings on the application shall be continued accordingly.

Rating (Charity Shops) Act 1976

1976 CHAPTER 45

An Act to amend section 40 of the General Rate Act 1967 and section 4 of the Local Government (Financial Provisions etc.) (Scotland) Act 1962 as respects charity shops. [6th August 1976]

BE IT ENACTED by the Queen's most Excellent Majesty, by and with the advice and consent of the Lords Spiritual and Temporal, and Commons, in this present Parliament assembled, and by the authority of the same, as follows:—

Rating relief for charity shops.

1967 c. 9.

1.—(1) In section 40 of the General Rate Act 1967 (relief for charitable and other organisations) after subsection (9) there shall be inserted the following subsection—

" (9A) Without prejudice to the meaning of the expression " wholly or mainly used for charitable purposes ", a hereditament shall be treated as so used, for the purposes of subsection (1) of this section, if—

(*a*) it is used wholly or mainly for the sale of goods donated to a charity; and

(*b*) the proceeds of sale (after any deduction of expenses) are applied for the purposes of a charity.".

1962 c. 9.

(2) At the end of section 4 of the Local Government (Financial Provisions etc.) (Scotland) Act 1962 (relief for charitable and other organisations), there shall be added the following subsection—

" (11) Without prejudice to the meaning of the expression " wholly or mainly used for charitable purposes ", lands and heritages shall be treated as so used, for the purposes of subsection (2) of this section, if—

(*a*) they are used wholly or mainly for the sale of goods donated to a charity; and

(*b*) the proceeds of sale (after any deduction of expenses) are applied for the purposes of a charity.".

(3) In subsection (2) of the said section 4 the words " not later than the thirtieth day of June in any year ", so far as relating to such lands and heritages as are referred to in subsection (11) of that section, shall not apply in respect of the financial year 1976–77.

Short title and extent.

2.—(1) This Act may be cited as the Rating (Charity Shops) Act 1976.

(2) This Act does not extend to Northern Ireland.

Police Act 1976

1976 CHAPTER 46

An Act to Establish a Police Complaints Board with functions relating to complaints from the public against members of police forces in England and Wales; to amend the law relating to the discipline of those forces; and for connected purposes. [6 August 1976] A.D. 1976

BE IT ENACTED by the Queen's most Excellent Majesty, by and with the advice and consent of the Lords Spiritual and Temporal, and Commons, in this present Parliament assembled, and by the authority of the same, as follows:—

PART I

COMPLAINTS AGAINST THE POLICE

The Police Complaints Board.

1.—(1) For the purposes of this Part of this Act there shall be a board known as the Police Complaints Board consisting of not less than nine members appointed by the Prime Minister.

(2) The members of the Board shall not include any person who is or has been a constable in any part of the United Kingdom.

(3) Persons may be appointed as whole-time or part-time members of the Board.

(4) The Prime Minister shall appoint—

(*a*) one of the members of the Board to be chairman; and

(*b*) either one or two members of the Board (as he may decide) to be deputy chairman or deputy chairmen.

PART I

(5) The Schedule to this Act shall have effect with respect to the Board.

Reference to Board of complaint reports.

1964 c. 48.

2.—(1) Where a chief officer of police receives the report of an investigation into a complaint under section 49 of the Police Act 1964 (complaints by members of the public against the police) he shall, subject to subsection (2) and section 5 below, send to the Police Complaints Board a copy of the report together with—

(*a*) a copy of the complaint; and

(*b*) a memorandum signed by him stating—

(i) his opinion on the merits of the complaint;

(ii) whether he has preferred disciplinary charges in respect of the matter or matters complained of and, if not, his reasons for not doing so; and

(iii) if he has preferred such disciplinary charges, particulars of the charges and of any exceptional circumstances affecting the case by reason of which he considers that section 4 below should apply to the hearing of them.

(2) Subsection (1) above shall not apply—

(*a*) where disciplinary charges have been preferred in respect of the matter or matters complained of and the accused has admitted the charges and not withdrawn his admission; or

(*b*) where, in accordance with regulations made by the Secretary of State under section 6 below, the complaint has been withdrawn or the complainant has indicated that he does not wish any further steps to be taken; or

(*c*) where the complaint is against an officer holding a rank above superintendent and, in accordance with regulations made by the Secretary of State under section 33 of the Police Act 1964, any disciplinary charges would be drawn up by a solicitor and heard by a person selected from a list of persons nominated by the Lord Chancellor.

(3) Where, by virtue of subsection (2)(*a*) above, subsection (1) above does not apply in relation to a complaint, the chief officer of police shall, after the conclusion of the disciplinary proceedings (including any appeal to the Secretary of State), send to the Board—

(*a*) a copy of the complaint and of the report of the investigation under the said section 49; and

(*b*) particulars of the disciplinary charges preferred and of any punishment imposed.

PART I

(4) Where in the case of any complaint the documents mentioned in subsection (1) above are not sent to the Board before the expiration of such period as may be prescribed by regulations made by the Secretary of State under section 6 below (whether because the investigation has not been completed or for any other reason) the chief officer of police shall send to the Board—

(*a*) as soon as possible after the expiration of that period, a copy of the complaint; and

(*b*) when he sends that copy and, in accordance with any provision made by the regulations, from time to time thereafter, information as to the stage reached in dealing with the complaint;

but the obligations imposed by this subsection shall apply only if and so long as the case is one to which subsection (1) above applies or could apply, and where a copy of the complaint is sent to the Board under this subsection no further copy need be sent under that subsection.

(5) References in this section to a copy of the complaint shall in the case of a complaint made orally, be construed as references to a copy of the record of the complaint.

Powers of Board as to disciplinary charges.

3.—(1) Where the report of an investigation into a complaint is sent to the Police Complaints Board under section 2(1) above the following provisions shall have effect in relation to disciplinary charges in respect of the matter or matters complained of; and for the purpose of discharging their functions under those provisions the Board may request the chief officer of police to furnish them with such additional information as they may reasonably require.

(2) Where the chief officer of police has not preferred disciplinary charges the Board may, if they disagree with his decision, make recommendations to him as to the charges which they consider should be preferred; and if, after the Board have made such recommendations and consulted the chief officer, he is still unwilling to prefer such charges as the Board consider appropriate they may direct him to prefer such charges as they may specify.

(3) Where the Board give a chief officer a direction under subsection (2) above they shall furnish him with a written statement of their reasons for doing so.

(4) Where disciplinary charges have been or are preferred they shall not be withdrawn except with the leave of the Board.

(5) Where disciplinary charges have been or are preferred (otherwise than in pursuance of a direction under subsection (2) above) the Board may direct that section 4 below shall apply

PART I to the hearing of the charges if they consider that to be desirable by reason of any exceptional circumstances affecting the case; and that section shall also apply to the hearing of any charges preferred in pursuance of a direction under that subsection.

(6) Notwithstanding subsection (5) above, section 4 below shall not apply in any case in which the accused admits the charges and does not withdraw his admission before the beginning of the hearing.

(7) A chief officer of police shall comply with any direction given to him under subsection (2) above and, subject to any regulations made by the Secretary of State under section 6 below, with any request under subsection (1) above.

(8) In discharging their functions under subsections (2) and (4) above the Board shall have regard to any guidance given to them by the Secretary of State with respect to such matters affecting the preferring and withdrawing of disciplinary charges as are for the time being the subject of guidance by him to chief officers of police, including in particular the principles to be applied in cases that involve any question of criminal proceedings and are not governed by section 11 below.

Disciplinary tribunals.

4.—(1) Where this section applies to the hearing of a disciplinary charge—

(*a*) the function of determining whether the accused is guilty of the charge shall be discharged by a tribunal consisting of—

(i) a chairman who shall, subject to subsection (2) below, be the chief officer of police by whom that function would fall to be discharged apart from this section; and

(ii) two members of the Police Complaints Board nominated by the Board, being members who were not concerned with the case under section 3 above; and

(*b*) the function of determining what punishment is to be imposed if the accused is found guilty shall, subject to subsection (4) below, be discharged by the chairman after consulting the other members of the tribunal.

(2) Where the accused is a member of the metropolitan police force and the function mentioned in subsection (1)(*a*) above would, apart from this section, fall to be discharged by a person or persons other than a chief officer of police (whether the Commissioner of Police or the chief officer of another police force) the chairman of the tribunal shall be—

(*a*) a person nominated by the Commissioner, being either an Assistant Commissioner of Police of the Metropolis or an officer of the metropolitan police force of such rank as may be prescribed by regulations under section 6 below; or

(*b*) in default of any nomination, the Commissioner himself.

(3) The decision of the tribunal in discharging the function mentioned in subsection (1)(*a*) above may be a majority decision.

(4) Where the chairman of the tribunal is not the chief officer of police of the police force to which the accused belongs (and that chief officer is neither interested in the case otherwise than in his capacity as such nor a material witness) the function mentioned in subsection (1)(*b*) above shall be discharged by that chief officer after considering any recommendation as to punishment made by the chairman, and before making any recommendation the chairman shall consult the other members of the tribunal.

(5) Where by virtue of section 3(5) above this section applies to the hearing of any disciplinary charge and there is another disciplinary charge against the accused which, in the opinion of the chief officer of police of the police force to which he belongs, can conveniently and fairly be determined at the same time, the chief officer may direct that this section shall apply also to the hearing of the other charge.

Complaints that may involve criminal proceedings.

5.—(1) Where the report of an investigation into a complaint is sent to the Director of Public Prosecutions in pursuance of section 49(3) of the Police Act 1964 (cases where criminal offences may have been committed) section 2(1) above shall not apply to the complaint until the question of criminal proceedings has been dealt with by the Director.

1964 c. 48.

(2) Where it appears to the Police Complaints Board that any information furnished to them under section 2 or 3 above—

(*a*) may be relevant to the question of criminal proceedings against the member of a police force against whom the complaint in question is made; but

(*b*) has not been furnished to the Director of Public Prosecutions,

the Board may request the chief officer of that force to transmit that information to the Director; and the chief officer shall transmit that information accordingly unless it has already been furnished to the Director or the chief officer is satisfied that it cannot be relevant as aforesaid.

PART I

(3) A chief officer of police who is requested under subsection (2) above to transmit any information to the Director shall notify the Board whether he has transmitted it and, if not, his reasons for not doing so.

Complaints regulations.

6.—(1) The Secretary of State may make regulations—

(*a*) as to the procedure to be followed by chief officers of police and the Police Complaints Board in relation to complaints from members of the public against members of police forces;

(*b*) without prejudice to paragraph (*a*) above—

(i) for requiring a chief officer of police to furnish a member of his police force against whom such a complaint is made with a copy of, or of the record of, the complaint;

(ii) for requiring the Board to transmit any such complaint received by them to the chief officer of the police force concerned;

(*c*) for requiring any action or decision of the Board to be notified to the persons concerned and, in connection therewith, for enabling the Board to furnish those persons with any relevant information;

(*d*) for requiring chief officers of police to furnish the Board with information and documents relating to such complaints;

(*e*) as to the procedure to be followed by disciplinary tribunals under section 4 above;

(*f*) for dispensing with any requirements of section 49 of the Police Act 1964 where a complaint is withdrawn or the complainant indicates that he does not wish any further steps to be taken;

1964 c. 48.

(*g*) for enabling the Board to dispense with any requirements of that section or of the foregoing provisions of this Part of this Act in circumstances other than those mentioned in paragraph (*f*) above;

(*h*) for enabling chief officers of police to delegate any function under the said section 49, under section 2, 3, 4(5) or 5(2) and (3) above or under the regulations;

(*i*) generally for carrying the foregoing provisions of this Part of this Act into effect.

(2) Regulations under this section may make different provision for different circumstances and may authorise the Secretary of State to make provision for any purposes specified in the regulations.

PART I

(3) Section 46(3) of the said Act of 1964 (which requires the Secretary of State to consult the Police Advisory Board for England and Wales about regulations under that Act) shall apply also to regulations under this section.

(4) The power to make regulations under this section shall be exercisable by statutory instrument.

(5) Regulations containing any such provision as is mentioned in subsection (1)(*g*) above shall not be made unless a draft of them has been approved by resolution of each House of Parliament; and other regulations under this section shall be subject to annulment in pursuance of a resolution of either House of Parliament.

Constabularies maintained by authorities other than police authorities.

7.—(1) The Police Complaints Board may, with the approval of the Secretary of State, make arrangements with any authority maintaining a body of constables, not being a police authority, for the discharge by the Board in relation to those constables of functions corresponding to any of those conferred on the Board by the foregoing provisions of this Part of this Act; and any such arrangements may, with the like approval, be varied or terminated.

(2) If in the case of any body of constables the Board have not within six months after the coming into force of this section made such arrangements as are mentioned in subsection (1) above, the Secretary of State may, if he thinks fit and after consulting the Board and the authority in question, by order make such arrangements as aforesaid.

(3) The power to make orders under this section includes power to vary or revoke a previous order and shall be exercisable by statutory instrument; and any statutory instrument containing such an order shall be subject to annulment in pursuance of a resolution of either House of Parliament.

(4) Any such authority as aforesaid shall, if it would not otherwise do so, have power to enter into and carry into effect any such arrangements as are mentioned in subsection (1) above.

(5) The Board shall not under any such arrangements exercise functions in relation to anything done by a constable outside England and Wales.

Reports.

8.—(1) The Police Complaints Board shall, at the request of the Secretary of State, report to him on such matters relating generally to complaints to which this Part of this Act applies as the Secretary of State may specify; and the Board may for that purpose carry out research into any such matters.

PART I

(2) The Board may make to the Secretary of State a report on any matters coming to their notice to which they consider that his attention should be drawn by reason of their gravity or of other exceptional circumstances; and the Board shall send a copy of any such report to the police authority and the chief officer of police of any police force which appears to the Board to be concerned or, if the report concerns any such body of constables as is mentioned in section 7 above, to the authority maintaining, and the officer having the direction and control of, that body of constables.

(3) As soon as practicable after the end of each calendar year the Board shall make to the Secretary of State a report on the discharge by the Board in that year of their functions under the foregoing provisions of this Part of this Act, and the report shall contain a statement of any guidance given to them in that year under section 3(8) above.

(4) The Secretary of State shall lay before Parliament a copy of every report received by him under subsection (3) above and shall cause every such report to be published.

(5) The Board shall send to every police authority—

(*a*) a copy of every report made by the Board under subsection (3) above; and

(*b*) any statistical or other general information relating to the year dealt with by the report and the area of that authority which the Board consider should be brought to the authority's attention in connection with their functions under section 50 of the Police Act 1964.

1964 c. 48.

(6) The Board shall keep under review the working of this Part of this Act and make to the Secretary of State a report thereon at least once in every three years after the coming into force of this section.

Restriction on disclosure of information.

9.—(1) No information received by the Police Complaints Board in connection with any complaint shall be disclosed by any person who is or has been a member, officer or servant of the Board except—

(*a*) to the Secretary of State or any other member, officer or servant of the Board or, so far as may be necessary for the proper discharge of the functions of the Board, to other persons;

(*b*) for the purposes of any criminal, civil or disciplinary proceedings; or

(*c*) in the form of a summary or other general statement made by the Board which does not identify the person from whom the information was received or to whom it relates. PART I

(2) Any person who discloses information in contravention of this section shall be guilty of an offence and liable on summary conviction to a fine not exceeding £400.

PART II

AMENDMENTS OF DISCIPLINE PROVISIONS

10.—(1) Regulations under section 33(2)(*e*) of the Police Act 1964 (discipline regulations) shall provide— Discipline regulations. 1964 c. 48.

(*a*) for the determination of questions whether offences against discipline have been committed; and

(*b*) for members of police forces who are found to have committed such offences to be punished by way of dismissal, requirement to resign, reduction in rank, reduction in rate of pay, fine, reprimand or caution.

(2) In the case of a police force maintained under section 1 of that Act (county or combined police force) the regulations shall provide for the functions mentioned in subsection (1)(*a*) or (*b*) above to be discharged—

(*a*) in relation to the chief constable, deputy chief constable and any assistant chief constable, by the police authority;

(*b*) in relation to any other member of the police force, by the chief constable,

but subject, in a case within paragraph (*b*) above, to section 4 above and subsections (3) and (4) below.

(3) If in a case within subsection (2)(*b*) above the chief constable—

(*a*) is interested in the case otherwise than in his capacity as such; or

(*b*) is a material witness,

the regulations shall provide for the functions mentioned in subsection (1)(*a*) and (*b*) above to be discharged by another chief officer of police.

(4) Without prejudice to subsection (3) above, the regulations may, as respects any case within subsection (2)(*b*) above, provide—

(*a*) for enabling a chief constable, where he considers it appropriate to do so, to direct that his function under subsection (1)(*a*) above shall be discharged by another chief officer of police; and

PART II

(*b*) where such a direction is given, for the function mentioned in subsection (1)(*b*) above to be discharged by the chief constable after considering any recommendation as to punishment made by the other chief officer of police.

(5) Subsections (2) to (4) above shall apply in the case of the City of London police force as they apply in the case of a police force maintained under section 1 of the said Act of 1964 but with the substitution—

(*a*) for the reference in subsection (2)(*a*) to the officers there mentioned of a reference to an assistant commissioner of police for the City of London and any officer holding a rank appearing to the Secretary of State to correspond to that of assistant chief constable in a force maintained under that section; and

(*b*) for the references to the chief constable in subsections (2)(*b*), (3) and (4) of references to the Commissioner of Police for the City of London.

(6) Section 33(3) of the said Act of 1964 (which is superseded by the foregoing provisions) is hereby repealed.

Disciplinary charges in criminal cases.

11.—(1) Where a member of a police force has been acquitted or convicted of a criminal offence he shall not be liable to be charged with any offence against discipline which is in substance the same as the offence of which he has been acquitted or convicted.

(2) Subsection (1) above shall not be construed as applying to a charge in respect of an offence against discipline which consists of having been found guilty of a criminal offence.

Disciplinary appeals.
1964 c. 48.

12.—(1) In subsection (2)(*c*) of section 37 of the Police Act 1964 (power of Secretary of State to substitute some other punishment (whether more or less severe) where a person appeals to him under that section) for the words " some other punishment (whether more or less severe) " there shall be substituted the words " some other punishment appearing to him to be less severe ".

(2) Subsection (4) of the said section 37 (which precludes a member of the metropolitan police force from appealing to the Secretary of State until he has exercised any right of appeal to the Commissioner) shall apply also in relation to any right of appeal to an Assistant Commissioner and accordingly after the word " Commissioner ", in both places where it occurs in that subsection, there shall be inserted the words " or an Assistant Commissioner ".

(3) For paragraph 2 of Schedule 5 to that Act (respondent in disciplinary appeals) there shall be substituted— Part II

" 2.—(1) On any appeal under the principal section against the decision of a police authority the respondent shall be that authority.

(2) On any other appeal under that section the respondent shall be the chief officer of police of the police force to which the appellant belongs or such other person as the Secretary of State may direct; and the Secretary of State may direct any respondent under this sub-paragraph to act in relation to the appeal in consultation with such other person or persons as the Secretary of State may specify.".

(4) For paragraph 3(1) of that Schedule (inquiries) there shall be substituted—

" 3.—(1) The Secretary of State may in any case appoint one or more persons (one at least of whom shall be a person engaged or experienced in police administration) to hold an inquiry and report to him and shall do so where it appears to him that the case cannot be properly determined without taking evidence.

(1A) The Secretary of State may require any person or persons appointed under this paragraph to deal in the report with any particular matter specified by him.".

(5) In paragraph 3(4) of that Schedule (reference for further consideration by the disciplinary authority) for the words " the disciplinary authority " there shall be substituted the words " the person or persons whose decision is the subject of the appeal ".

(6) In sub-paragraph (1) of paragraph 5 of that Schedule (rules) after paragraph (*b*) there shall be inserted—

" (*c*) providing for the person or persons holding an inquiry to receive evidence or representations in writing instead of holding a hearing " ;

and in sub-paragraph (2) of that paragraph for the words " provide for giving to the appellant the right to appear at an inquiry " there shall be substituted the words " where there is a hearing in the course of an inquiry, provide for giving to the appellant the right to appear ".

Part III

Supplementary

Commencement.

13.—(1) This Act shall come into force on such day as the Secretary of State may by order appoint, and different days may be appointed for different provisions and for different purposes.

PART III

(2) An order under this section may make such transitional provision as appears to the Secretary of State to be necessary or expedient in connection with the provisions thereby brought into operation.

(3) The power to make orders under this section shall be exercisable by statutory instrument; and any such order appointing a day for the coming into force of any provisions may be varied or revoked before that day.

Short title and extent.

14.—(1) This Act may be cited as the Police Act 1976.

(2) Paragraphs 6, 8(1) and 9 of the Schedule to this Act have the same extent as the enactments to which they refer but, save as aforesaid, this Act extends to England and Wales only.

SCHEDULE

The Police Complaints Board

Section 1(5).

Incorporation and status

1. The Police Complaints Board shall be a body corporate.

2. The Board shall not be regarded as the servant or agent of the Crown or as enjoying any status, privilege or immunity of the Crown; and the Board's property shall not be regarded as property of or property held on behalf of the Crown.

Members

3.—(1) Subject to the following provisions of this Schedule, a person shall hold office as a member or as chairman or deputy chairman of the Board in accordance with the terms of his appointment.

(2) A person shall not be appointed as a member of the Board for more than three years at a time.

(3) A person may at any time resign his office as a member or as chairman or deputy chairman.

(4) The Prime Minister may at any time remove a person from office as a member if satisfied that—

(*a*) he has without reasonable excuse failed to carry out his duties for a continuous period of three months beginning not earlier than six months before that time; or

(*b*) he has been convicted of a criminal offence; or

(*c*) he has become bankrupt or made an arrangement with his creditors; or

(*d*) he is incapacitated by physical or mental illness; or

(*e*) he is otherwise unable or unfit to perform his duties.

(5) If a person who is chairman or deputy chairman ceases to be a member of the Board he shall also cease to be chairman or deputy chairman.

4. The Secretary of State may pay, or make such payments towards the provision of, such remuneration, pensions, allowances or gratuities to or in respect of members of the Board or any of them as, with the consent of the Minister for the Civil Service, he may determine.

5. Where a person ceases to be a member of the Board otherwise than on the expiry of his term of office, and it appears to the Secretary of State that there are special circumstances which make it right for that person to receive compensation, the Secretary of State may with the consent of the Minister for the Civil Service direct the Board to make to that person a payment of such amount

as, with the consent of that Minister, the Secretary of State may determine.

1975 c. 24. 1975 c. 25. 6. In Part II of Schedule 1 to the House of Commons Disqualification Act 1975 and Part II of Schedule 1 to the Northern Ireland Assembly Disqualification Act 1975 (bodies of which all members are disqualified under those Acts) there shall be inserted at the appropriate place in alphabetical order—

"The Police Complaints Board".

Staff

7. The Board may, after consultation with the Secretary of State, appoint such officers and servants as they think fit, subject to the approval of the Minister for the Civil Service as to numbers and as to remuneration and other terms and conditions of service.

8.—(1) Employment by the Board shall be included among the kinds of employment to which a superannuation scheme under section
1972 c. 11. 1 of the Superannuation Act 1972 can apply, and accordingly in Schedule 1 to that Act, at the end of the list of "Other Bodies" there shall be inserted—

"Police Complaints Board".

(2) Where a person who is employed by the Board and is by reference to that employment a participant in a scheme under section 1 of the said Act of 1972 becomes a member of the Board, the Minister for the Civil Service may determine that his service as a member shall be treated for the purposes of the scheme as service as an employee of the Board; and his rights under the scheme shall not be affected by paragraph 4 above.

1969 c. 57. 9. The Employers' Liability (Compulsory Insurance) Act 1969 shall not require insurance to be effected by the Board.

Proceedings

10.—(1) Subject to the provisions of this Act, the arrangements for the proceedings of the Board (including the quorum for meetings) shall be such as the Board may determine.

(2) The arrangements may, with the approval of the Secretary of State, provide for the discharge, under the general direction of the Board, of any of the Board's functions by a committee or by one or more of the members, officers or servants of the Board.

11. The validity of any proceedings of the Board shall not be affected by any defect in the appointment of a member or by any vacancy among the members or in the office of chairman or deputy chairman.

Finance

12. The Secretary of State shall pay to the Board expenses incurred or to be incurred by the Board under paragraphs 5 and 7 above and, with the consent of the Minister for the Civil Service and the Treasury, shall pay to the Board such sums as the Secretary of State thinks fit for enabling the Board to meet other expenses.

13.—(1) It shall be the duty of the Board—

(*a*) to keep proper accounts and proper records in relation to the accounts ;

(*b*) to prepare in respect of each financial year of the Board a statement of accounts in such form as the Secretary of State may direct with the approval of the Treasury ; and

(*c*) to send copies of the statement to the Secretary of State and the Comptroller and Auditor General before the end of the month of November next following the financial year to which the statement relates.

(2) The Comptroller and Auditor General shall examine, certify and report on each statement received by him in pursuance of this paragraph and shall lay copies of each statement and of his report before Parliament.

(3) The financial year of the Board shall be the twelve months ending on 31st March.

14. Any sums required by the Secretary of State for making payments under this Schedule shall be defrayed out of moneys provided by Parliament.

Stock Exchange (Completion of Bargains) Act 1976

1976 CHAPTER 47

An Act to amend and clarify the law relating to the transfer of securities and to companies, trustees and personal representatives with a view to simplifying the activities connected with the periodic completion of bargains made on stock exchanges; and for purposes connected therewith. [12th October 1976]

BE IT ENACTED by the Queen's most Excellent Majesty, by and with the advice and consent of the Lords Spiritual and Temporal, and Commons, in this present Parliament assembled, and by the authority of the same, as follows:—

Exemption from obligation to prepare share certificates etc.

1. A company of which shares or debentures are allotted or debenture stock is allotted to a stock exchange nominee, or with which a transfer is lodged for transferring any shares, debentures or debenture stock of the company to a stock exchange nominee, shall not be required in consequence of the allotment or the lodging of the transfer to complete and have ready for delivery, in pursuance of section 80(1) of the Companies Act 1948, the certificates of the shares or the debentures or the certificates of the debenture stock, as the case may be.

1948 c. 38.

Official seals for sealing share certificates etc.

2.—(1) A company may have, for use for sealing securities issued by the company and for sealing documents creating or evidencing securities so issued, an official seal which is a facsimile of the common seal of the company with the addition on its face of the word " Securities ".

(2) A company which was incorporated before the date when this Act comes into force and which has such an official seal as is mentioned in the preceding subsection may use the seal

for sealing such securities and documents as are there mentioned notwithstanding anything in any instrument constituting or regulating the company or in any instrument made before that date which relates to any securities issued by the company; and any provision of such an instrument which requires any such securities or documents to be signed shall not apply to the securities or documents if they are sealed with that seal.

(3) In section 81 of the Companies Act 1948 (which provides for share certificates under the common seal of a company to be evidence of title) after the word " company " there shall be inserted the words " or the seal kept by the company by virtue of section 2 of the Stock Exchange (Completion of Bargains) Act 1976 "; and in regulation 8 of Part I of Table A in Schedule 1 to the Companies Act 1948 (which among other things provides for share certificates to be under the common seal of the company) after the word " seal " there shall be inserted the words " or under the official seal kept by the company by virtue of section 2 of the Stock Exchange (Completion of Bargains) Act 1976 ". 1948 c. 38.

Use of computers etc for certain company records.

3.—(1) It is hereby declared that the power conferred on a company by section 436(1) of the Companies Act 1948 to keep a register or other record by recording the matters in question otherwise than by making entries in bound books includes power to keep the register or other record by recording the matters in question otherwise than in a legible form so long as the recording is capable of being reproduced in a legible form.

(2) Any provision of an instrument made by a company before the date when this Act comes into force which requires a register of holders of debentures of the company to be kept in a legible form shall be construed as requiring the register to be kept in a legible or non-legible form.

(3) If any such register or other record of a company as is mentioned in the said section 436(1) or a register of holders of debentures of a company is kept by the company by recording the matters in question otherwise than in a legible form, any duty imposed on the company by virtue of the Companies Acts 1948 to 1967 to allow inspection of, or to furnish a copy of, the register or other record or any part of it shall be treated as a duty to allow inspection of, or to furnish, a reproduction of the recording or of the relevant part of it in a legible form.

(4) The Secretary of State may, by regulations made by statutory instrument, make such provision in addition to the preceding subsection as he considers appropriate in connection with such registers or other records as are mentioned in that subsection and are kept as there mentioned, and the regulations may make modifications of provisions of the Companies Acts

1948 to 1967 relating to such registers or other records as are mentioned in that subsection.

(5) Any statutory instrument made by virtue of the preceding subsection shall be subject to annulment in pursuance of a resolution of either House of Parliament.

Application of ss. 1 to 3 to unregistered companies. 1948 c. 38.

4.—(1) Section 435 of the Companies Act 1948 (which enables certain enactments to be extended to unregistered companies) shall have effect as if sections 1 to 3 of this Act were among the sections mentioned in Schedule 14 to that Act with an entry in column 3 of that Schedule to the effect that those sections are to apply so far only as may be specified by regulations under the said section 435 and to such bodies corporate as may be so specified.

(2) In relation to sections 1 to 3 of this Act the power to make adaptations and modifications conferred by subsection (1) of the said section 435 shall be construed as a power to make additions, omissions and amendments.

Acquisition and disposal of securities by trustees and personal representatives.

5. A trustee or personal representative shall not be chargeable with breach of trust or, as the case may be, with default in administering the estate by reason only of the fact that—

(*a*) he has, for the purpose of acquiring securities which he has power to acquire in connection with the trust or estate, paid for the securities under arrangements which provide for them to be transferred to him from a stock exchange nominee but not to be so transferred until after payment of the price ; or

(*b*) he has, for the purpose of disposing of securities which he has power to dispose of in connection with the trust or estate, transferred the securities to a stock exchange nominee under arrangements which provide that the price is not to be paid to him until after the transfer is made.

Forms for transfer of securities. 1963 c. 18.

6.—(1) In section 3 of the Stock Transfer Act 1963 (which among other things provides that the Treasury may by order amend the Schedules to that Act by altering the transfer forms set out in those Schedules or substituting different forms for those forms or adding forms for use as alternatives to those forms) after subsection (4) there shall be inserted the following subsection—

(5) An order under subsection (2) of this section may—

(*a*) provide for forms on which some of the particulars mentioned in subsection (1) of section 1 of this Act are not required to be specified ;

(*b*) provide for that section to have effect, in relation to such forms as are mentioned in the preceding paragraph or other forms specified in the order, subject to such amendments as are so specified (which may include an amendment of the reference in subsection (1) of that section to an instrument under hand);

(*c*) provide for all or any of the provisions of the order to have effect in such cases only as are specified in the order.

(2) The subsection (5) inserted in the said section 3 by the preceding subsection shall extend to Northern Ireland in accordance with the provisions of section 5(1) and (2) of the said Act of 1963.

7.—(1) This Act may be cited as the Stock Exchange (Completion of Bargains) Act 1976. Short title, interpretation, commencement and extent.

(2) In this Act " stock exchange nominee " means any person whom the Secretary of State designates by order as a nominee of The Stock Exchange for the purposes of this Act; and the Secretary of State may by order vary or revoke any previous order made in pursuance of this subsection.

The powers to make orders conferred by this subsection shall be exercisable by statutory instrument.

(3) In this Act any expression to which a meaning is assigned by section 455(1) of the Companies Act 1948 has the same meaning as in that Act except where the context requires otherwise; and any reference in this Act to an enactment is a reference to it as amended by or under any other enactment. 1948 c. 38.

(4) This Act shall come into force on such date as the Secretary of State may appoint by an order made by statutory instrument.

(5) Except as provided by section 6(2) of this Act, this Act does not extend to Northern Ireland.

Parliamentary and other Pensions and Salaries Act 1976

1976 CHAPTER 48

An Act to amend the Parliamentary and other Pensions Act 1972; to make further provision with respect to the salaries and pensions payable to or in respect of the Comptroller and Auditor General, the Parliamentary Commissioner for Administration and the Health Service Commissioners; and for connected purposes. [12th October 1976]

BE IT ENACTED by the Queen's most Excellent Majesty, by and with the advice and consent of the Lords Spiritual and Temporal, and Commons, in this present Parliament assembled, and by the authority of the same, as follows:—

Pensions of Members and office-holders

Member's pensionable salary. 1972 c. 48.

1.—(1) For section 3(6) (meaning of " a Member's ordinary salary ") of the Parliamentary and other Pensions Act 1972 (" the Act of 1972 ") there shall be substituted the following subsections—

" (6) In this Part of this Act " a Member's pensionable salary ", in relation to a resolution of the House of Commons relating to the remuneration of Members, means a Member's ordinary salary or, if the resolution provides for a Members' ordinary salary to be regarded for pension purposes as being at a higher rate, a notional yearly salary at that higher rate ; and for this purpose " a Member's ordinary salary "—

(*a*) if the resolution provides for salary to be paid at a rate higher than one or more other rates specified in the resolution to Members other than those who are holders of an office, or in receipt of a salary as holders of an office, or in receipt of a pension as former holders of an office, of a kind specified or described in the resolution, means a Member's yearly salary at that higher rate, and

(*b*) in any other case, means a Member's yearly salary at the rate specified in the resolution.

(7) Any reference in this Part of this Act to a resolution of the House of Commons relating to the remuneration of Members shall be construed, where there are two or more such resolutions for the time being in force, as a reference those resolutions taken together."

(2) For the words " a Member's ordinary salary ", in each other place where they occur in Part I of the Act of 1972, that is to say in sections 3(2), 4(3), 7(5) (twice), 10(2) and (6) (twice), 16(3) and 25(1), there shall be substituted the words " a Member's pensionable salary ".

(3) In section 229(1) of the Income and Corporation Taxes Act 1970 as substituted by section 32(1) of the Act of 1972 (annuity premiums of Ministers and other office-holders), for the words " a Member's ordinary salary ", in both places where they occur, there shall be substituted the words " a Member's pensionable salary ". 1970 c. 10.

(4) This section shall be deemed to have come into operation on 13th June 1975.

Power to increase contributions from office-holders.

2. In section 4 of the Act of 1972 (contributions from participants in office-holders' scheme) after subsection (3) there shall be inserted the following subsection—

" (3A) Her Majesty may from time to time by Order in Council direct that any salary specified in the Order shall be regarded for the purposes of subsection (2) or, as the case may be, subsection (3) of this section as being payable at such higher rate as may be so specified; but no recommendation shall be made to Her Majesty to make an Order under this subsection unless a draft of the Order has been approved by resolution of each House of Parliament or, if it relates only to salaries payable in respect of the offices of Chairman of Ways and Means and Deputy Chairman of Ways and Means, by resolution of the House of Commons.

An Order in Council made under this subsection may be varied or revoked by a subsequent Order so made."

Additional qualifying office.

3.—(1) In section 2(1)(*c*) of the Act of 1972 (qualifying offices) for the words " and Chairman of Committees of the House of Lords " there shall be substituted the words " Chairman of Committees of the House of Lords and Deputy Chairman of Committees of the House of Lords ".

(2) This section shall be deemed to have come into operation on 2nd May 1974.

Other amendments of Part I of the Act of 1972.

4.—(1) The following provisions of Part I of the Act of 1972 shall have effect, and shall be deemed always to have had effect, as if they were amended as follows.

(2) In section 7(4) (early retirement of Members) for the words " the date on which he ceased to be a Member of the House of Commons " and the words " the date on which he ceased to be a Member " there shall be substituted the words " the date of his application or, if later, such other date as may be there specified ".

(3) In section 10(4) (early retirement of office-holders) for the words " the date on which he ceased to hold the qualifying office in question " and the words " the date on which he ceased to hold that office " there shall be substituted the words " the date of his application or, if later, such other date as may be there specified ".

(4) In section 18(3)(*c*) (conditions for refund of contributions) for the words " does not exceed " there shall be substituted the words " is less than ".

(5) In section 25 (interpretation of Part I) there shall be inserted after subsection (2) the following subsection—

> " (3) For the purposes of this Part of this Act a person shall be treated as a Member of the House of Commons at any time if, at that time, a salary is or was payable to him pursuant to any resolution of the House of Commons relating to the remuneration of Members for the time being in force."

Pensions of Prime Minister, Speaker and Lord Chancellor

Power to increase pensions.

5. In section 29 of the Act of 1972 (preservation of ratio between salary and pension) after subsection (2) there shall be inserted the following subsection—

> " (2A) Her Majesty may from time to time by Order in Council direct that any increased salary specified in the Order shall be regarded for the purposes of subsection (2) of this section as being payable at such higher rate as may be so specified; but no recommendation shall be made to Her Majesty to make an Order under this subsection unless a draft of the Order has been approved by resolution of each House of Parliament or, if it relates only to an increased salary payable in respect of the office of Speaker of the House of Commons, by resolution of that House.
>
> An Order in Council made under this subsection may be varied or revoked by a subsequent Order so made."

Salaries and pensions of Comptroller, Parliamentary Commissioner and Health Service Commissioners

6.—(1) Section 1 of the Exchequer and Audit Departments Act 1957 (salary of Comptroller and Auditor General) and section 2 of the Parliamentary Commissioner Act 1967 (salary and pension of Parliamentary Commissioner) shall be amended as follows.

Comptroller and Parliamentary Commissioner.

1957 c. 45.
1967 c. 13.

(2) For subsections (1) and (2) of the said section 1 there shall be substituted the following subsections—

"(1) There shall be paid to the holder of the office of Comptroller and Auditor General the same salary as if he were employed in the civil service of the State in such appointment as the House of Commons may by resolution from time to time determine; and a resolution under this subsection may take effect from the date on which it is passed or from such other date as may be specified in the resolution.

(2) In relation to any time before the first resolution under subsection (1) above takes effect, the salary payable to the holder of the office of Comptroller and Auditor General shall be the same salary as if he were employed in the civil service of the State as a Permanent Secretary.";

and those subsections shall also be substituted for subsections (1) and (2) of the said section 2 but modified for that purpose by the substitution of references to the Commissioner for references to the Comptroller and Auditor General.

(3) For subsection (3) of the said section 1 there shall be substituted the following subsections—

"(3) The salary payable to a holder of the office of Comptroller and Auditor General shall be abated by the amount of any pension payable to him in respect of any public office in the United Kingdom or elsewhere to which he had previously been appointed or elected.

(3A) In computing the salary of a former holder of the office of Comptroller and Auditor General for the purposes of section 13 of the Superannuation Act 1972 (pension of Comptroller and Auditor General)—

(*a*) any abatement of that salary under subsection (3) above,

(*b*) any temporary abatement of that salary in the national interest, and

(*c*) any voluntary surrender of that salary in whole or in part,

shall be disregarded."

(4) In subsection (4) of the said section 2 the words from " but any such abatement " to the end shall be omitted and after that subsection there shall be inserted the following subsection—

" (4A) In computing the salary of a former holder of the office of Commissioner for the purposes of the said Schedule 1—

(*a*) any abatement of that salary under subsection (4) above,

(*b*) any temporary abatement of that salary in the national interest, and

(*c*) any voluntary surrender of that salary in whole or in part,

shall be disregarded."

(5) This section shall be deemed to have come into operation on 1st January 1975.

Health Service Commissioners.
1973 c. 32.
1972 c. 58.

7.—(1) Section 32 of the National Health Service Reorganisation Act 1973 and section 43 of the National Health Service (Scotland) Act 1972 (salaries and pensions of Health Service Commissioners) shall be amended as follows.

(2) In subsection (1) of each section for the words " such salary " there shall be substituted the words " the same salary as if he were employed in the civil service of the State in such appointment ".

(3) In subsection (3) of each section the words from " but any such abatement " to the end shall be omitted and after that subsection there shall be inserted the following subsection—

" (3A) In computing the salary of a former holder of the office of Commissioner for the purposes of the said Schedule 1—

(*a*) any abatement of that salary under subsection (3) above,

(*b*) any temporary abatement of that salary in the national interest, and

(*c*) any voluntary surrender of that salary in whole or in part,

shall be disregarded."

Supplemental

Financial provisions.

8. There shall be paid out of money provided by Parliament, or paid into or out of the Consolidated Fund, any increase attributable to this Act in the sums so payable under any other Act.

9.—(1) This Act may be cited as the Parliamentary and other Pensions and Salaries Act 1976. Short title, etc.

(2) The enactments specified in the Schedule to this Act are hereby repealed to the extent specified in the third column of that Schedule.

Section 9(2).

SCHEDULE

Repeals

Chapter	Short title	Extent of repeal
1967 c. 13.	The Parliamentary Commissioner Act 1967.	In section 2(4), the words from " but any such abatement " to the end.
1972 c. 11.	The Superannuation Act 1972.	Section 13(4).
1972 c. 58.	The National Health Service (Scotland) Act 1972.	In section 43(3), the words from " but any such abatement " to the end.
1973 c. 32.	The National Health Reorganisation Act 1973.	In section 32(3), the words from " but any such abatement " to the end.

Chronically Sick and Disabled Persons (Amendment) Act 1976

1976 CHAPTER 49

An Act to amend the Chronically Sick and Disabled Persons Act 1970; and to provide access and parking facilities for disabled persons at newly provided places of employment in order to improve employment opportunities for disabled persons.

[26th October 1976]

BE IT ENACTED by the Queen's most Excellent Majesty, by and with the advice and consent of the Lords Spiritual and Temporal, and Commons, in this present Parliament assembled, and by the authority of the same, as follows:—

Amendment of Chronically Sick and Disabled Persons Act 1970. 1970 c. 44.

1. In section 4(2) of the Chronically Sick and Disabled Persons Act 1970, after the words " of section 8 " there shall be inserted the words " or in subsection (2) of section 8A".

Access to, and facilities at, offices and other premises.

2. After section 8 of the said Act there shall be inserted the following section:

"Access to, and facilities at, offices and other premises.

8A.—(1) Any person undertaking the provision of premises mentioned in subsection (2) below shall in the means of access both to and within the premises, and in the parking facilities and sanitary conveniences to be available (if any), make provision, in so far as it is in the circumstances both practicable and reasonable, for the needs of persons using the premises who are disabled.

(2) Premises to which this section applies are:—

(*a*) office premises, shop premises and railway premises to which the Offices, Shops and Railway Premises Act 1963 applies;

(*b*) premises which are deemed to be such premises for the purposes of that Act, and

(*c*) factories as defined by section 175 of the Factories Act 1961,

being (in each case) premises in which persons are employed to work."

Short title.

3. This Act may be cited as the Chronically Sick and Disabled Persons (Amendment) Act 1976.

Domestic Violence and Matrimonial Proceedings Act 1976

1976 CHAPTER 50

An Act to amend the law relating to matrimonial injunction; to provide the police with powers of arrest for the breach of injunction in cases of domestic violence; to amend section 1(2) of the Matrimonial Homes Act 1967; to make provision for varying rights of occupation where both spouses have the same rights in the matrimonial home; and for purposes connected therewith. [26th October 1976]

BE IT ENACTED by the Queen's most Excellent Majesty, by and with the advice and consent of the Lords Spiritual and Temporal, and Commons, in this present Parliament assembled, and by the authority of the same, as follows:—

1.—(1) Without prejudice to the jurisdiction of the High Court, on an application by a party to a marriage a county court shall have jurisdiction to grant an injunction containing one or more of the following provisions, namely,— Matrimonial injunctions in the county court.

(*a*) a provision restraining the other party to the marriage from molesting the applicant;

(*b*) a provision restraining the other party from molesting a child living with the applicant;

(*c*) a provision excluding the other party from the matrimonial home or a part of the matrimonial home or from a specified area in which the matrimonial home is included;

(*d*) a provision requiring the other party to permit the applicant to enter and remain in the matrimonial home or a part of the matrimonial home;

whether or not any other relief is sought in the proceedings.

(2) Subsection (1) above shall apply to a man and a woman who are living with each other in the same household as husband and wife as it applies to the parties to a marriage and any reference to the matrimonial home shall be construed accordingly.

Arrest for breach of injunction.

2.—(1) Where, on an application by a party to a marriage, a judge grants an injunction containing a provision (in whatever terms)—

(*a*) restraining the other party to the marriage from using violence against the applicant, or

(*b*) restraining the other party from using violence against a child living with the applicant, or

(*c*) excluding the other party from the matrimonial home or from a specified area in which the matrimonial home is included,

the judge may, if he is satisfied that the other party has caused actual bodily harm to the applicant or, as the case may be, to the child concerned and considers that he is likely to do so again, attach a power of arrest to the injunction.

(2) References in subsection (1) above to the parties to a marriage include references to a man and a woman who are living with each other in the same household as husband and wife and any reference in that subsection to the matrimonial home shall be construed accordingly.

(3) If, by virtue of subsection (1) above, a power of arrest is attached to an injunction, a constable may arrest without warrant a person whom he has reasonable cause for suspecting of being in breach of such a provision of that injunction as falls within paragraphs (*a*) to (*c*) of subsection (1) above by reason of that person's use of violence or, as the case may be, of his entry into any premises or area.

(4) Where a power of arrest is attached to an injunction and a person to whom the injunction is addressed is arrested under subsection (3) above,—

(*a*) he shall be brought before a judge within the period of 24 hours beginning at the time of his arrest, and

(*b*) he shall not be released within that period except on the direction of the judge,

but nothing in this section shall authorise his detention at any time after the expiry of that period.

(5) Where, by virtue of a power of arrest attached to an injunction, a constable arrests any person under subsection (3) above, the constable shall forthwith seek the directions—

(*a*) in a case where the injunction was granted by the High Court, of that court, and

(*b*) in any other case, of a county court,

as to the time and place at which that person is to be brought before a judge.

Amendment of Matrimonial Homes Act 1967. 1967 c. 75.

3. In section 1(2) of the Matrimonial Homes Act 1967 (which provides for applications for orders of the court declaring, enforcing, restricting or terminating rights of occupation under the Act or regulating the exercise by either spouse of the right to occupy the dwelling-house),—

(*a*) for the word " regulating " there shall be substituted the words " prohibiting, suspending or restricting "; and

(*b*) at the end of the subsection there shall be added the words " or requiring either spouse to permit the exercise by the other of that right ".

Order restricting occupation of matrimonial home.

4.—(1) Where each of two spouses is entitled, by virtue of a legal estate vested in them jointly, to occupy a dwelling-house in which they have or at any time have had a matrimonial home, either of them may apply to the court, with respect to the exercise during the subsistence of the marriage of the right to occupy the dwelling-house, for an order prohibiting, suspending or restricting its exercise by the other or requiring the other to permit its exercise by the applicant.

(2) In relation to orders under this section, section 1(3), (4) and (6) of the Matrimonial Homes Act 1967 (which relate to the considerations relevant to and the contents of, and to the jurisdiction to make, orders under that section) shall apply as they apply in relation to orders under that section; and in this section " dwelling-house " has the same meaning as in that Act.

(3) Where each of two spouses is entitled to occupy a dwelling-house by virtue of a contract, or by virtue of any enactment giving them the right to remain in occupation, this section shall apply as it applies where they are entitled by virtue of a legal estate vested in them jointly.

Short title, commencement and extent.

5.—(1) This Act may be cited as the Domestic Violence and Matrimonial Proceedings Act 1976.

(2) This Act shall come into force on such day as the Lord Chancellor may appoint by order made by statutory instrument, and different days may be so appointed for different provisions of this Act:

Provided that if any provisions of this Act are not in force on 1st April 1977, the Lord Chancellor shall then make an order by statutory instrument bringing such provisions into force.

(3) This Act shall not extend to Northern Ireland or Scotland.

Maplin Development Authority (Dissolution) Act 1976

1976 CHAPTER 51

An Act to dissolve the Maplin Development Authority; and for purposes connected therewith.

[26th October 1976]

BE IT ENACTED by the Queen's most Excellent Majesty, by and with the advice and consent of the Lords Spiritual and Temporal, and Commons, in this present Parliament assembled, and by the authority of the same, as follows:—

Transfer of property and dissolution of Maplin Development Authority.

1.—(1) On such day as the Secretary of State may by order appoint (" the transfer date ") all property, rights and liabilities to which the Maplin Development Authority was entitled or subject immediately before that day shall by virtue of this section vest in the Secretary of State.

(2) At the expiration of the period of one month beginning with the transfer date, or at such later time as the Secretary of State may by order appoint, the Authority shall cease to exist.

(3) Any power to make an order under this section shall be exercisable by statutory instrument, which shall be laid before Parliament after being made.

Financial provisions.

2.—(1) In consequence of section 1(1) above, the assets of the National Loans Fund shall on the transfer date be reduced by an amount equal to the aggregate amount owed by the Authority immediately before that date in respect of the principal of and

1973 c. 64. interest on the initial debt under section 13 of the Maplin Development Act 1973 and loans made by the Secretary of State in pursuance of section 14(2) of that Act.

(2) The last accounting year of the Authority shall be the period between the end of March 1975 and the transfer date.

(3) Any expenses incurred by the Authority on or after the transfer date shall be defrayed by the Secretary of State.

Short title and repeals.

3.—(1) This Act may be cited as the Maplin Development Authority (Dissolution) Act 1976.

(2) The enactments specified in the Schedule to this Act are, to the extent specified in the third column of that Schedule, hereby repealed with effect from the time when the Authority ceases to exist.

SCHEDULE

Section 3.

Enactments Repealed

Chapter	Short title	Extent of repeal
1930 c. 44.	The Land Drainage Act 1930.	In section 61(1), paragraph (*i*).
1973 c. 64.	The Maplin Development Act 1973.	The whole Act.
1974 c. 8.	The Statutory Corporations (Financial Provisions) Act 1974.	In Schedule 2, the entry relating to the Maplin Development Authority.
1975 c. 24.	The House of Commons Disqualification Act 1975.	In Part II of Schedule 1, the words " The Maplin Development Authority ".

Armed Forces Act 1976

1976 CHAPTER 52

An Act to continue the Army Act 1955, the Air Force Act 1955 and the Naval Discipline Act 1957; to amend those Acts and other enactments relating to the armed forces; to authorise the establishment of courts for the trial outside the United Kingdom of civilians subject to Part II of the Army Act 1955 or Part II of the Air Force Act 1955; to make provision for the powers of the courts so authorised in relation to such civilians; to make further provision for the powers of courts-martial in relation to such civilians and to civilians subject to Parts I and II of the Naval Discipline Act 1957; to make further provision as to the disqualification of members of the forces for membership of the House of Commons or the Northern Ireland Assembly; to make further provision for Greenwich Hospital; and for connected purposes.

[26th October 1976]

BE IT ENACTED by the Queen's most Excellent Majesty, by and with the advice and consent of the Lords Spiritual and Temporal, and Commons, in this present Parliament assembled, and by the authority of the same, as follows:—

PART I

GENERAL

Duration of Army Act, Air Force Act and Naval Discipline Act

1.—(1) The Army Act 1955, the Air Force Act 1955 and the Naval Discipline Act 1957 shall, instead of expiring at the end of the year 1976, continue in force until 31st August 1977, and shall then expire unless continued in force in accordance with the following provisions of this section.

Duration of Services Acts. 1955 c. 18. 1955 c. 19. 1957 c. 53.

PART I

(2) Subject to subsection (3) below, Her Majesty may from time to time by Order in Council provide for any of the said Acts to continue in force for a period not exceeding twelve months beyond the day on which it would otherwise expire.

(3) No Order in Council shall be made under subsection (2) above so as to continue any of the said Acts beyond the end of the year 1981.

(4) No recommendation shall be made to Her Majesty in Council to make an order under subsection (2) above unless a draft thereof has been laid before Parliament and approved by resolution of each House of Parliament.

1971 c. 33.

(5) Section 1 of the Armed Forces Act 1971 shall be repealed at the end of the year 1976.

Service in and constitution of forces

Regulations as to variation of term of service.
1966 c. 45.

2. In section 2(1)(*f*) of the Armed Forces Act 1966 (regulations enabling a person to extend full-time or reserve service) after the word "extend" there shall be inserted the words "or reduce".

Royal Marines.

3.—(1) The amendments specified in Part I of Schedule 1 to this Act shall have effect for the purpose of applying certain enactments to the Royal Marines.

(2) The amendments specified in Part II of that Schedule shall have effect for the purpose of applying certain enactments to warrant officers of the Royal Marines.

QARNNS and WRNS.
1957 c. 53.

4. The amendments of the Naval Discipline Act 1957 specified in Schedule 2 to this Act shall have effect for the purpose of including Queen Alexandra's Royal Naval Nursing Service and the Women's Royal Naval Service in Her Majesty's naval forces for the purposes of that Act.

PART II

TRIAL AND PUNISHMENT OF OFFENCES

Summary punishment

Increased powers of summary punishment.
1955 c. 18.
1955 c. 19.

5.—(1) The maximum period of detention that may be awarded to a soldier or airman by his commanding officer under section 78 of the Army Act 1955 or section 78 of the Air Force Act 1955 shall be 60 days; and accordingly, in subsection (3)(*a*) of section 78 of each Act, for the word "twenty-eight" there shall be substituted the word "60".

PART II

(2) The maximum amount of a fine that may be awarded for an offence, whether or not committed on active service,—

(a) by virtue of section 78 of the Army Act 1955 or section 78 of the Air Force Act 1955 (without prejudice to paragraph (b) of the second proviso to subsection (3) of each section (fines for civil offences)), or 1955 c. 18. 1955 c. 19.

(b) to an officer (below the rank of lieutenant-colonel or wing-commander), or to a warrant officer, by virtue of section 79 of either Act (under which there is the same maximum),

shall not exceed the amount of the offender's pay for 28 days.

Civilians

Establishment of Standing Civilian Courts.

6.—(1) Courts may be established for the trial outside the United Kingdom of persons (in this section and section 7 below referred to as " civilians ") to whom Part II of the Army Act 1955 or Part II of the Air Force Act 1955 is applied by section 209 of either Act (including persons to whom Part II of either Act applies by virtue of section 131 (persons treated as continuing to be subject to Part II for purposes of trial and punishment of offences)).

(2) Courts established under this section shall be known as Standing Civilian Courts.

(3) The Secretary of State, with the approval of the Lord Chancellor, may by order direct that any area specified in the order shall be an area for which trials may be directed to be held before Standing Civilian Courts for offences committed in that area or elsewhere.

(4) The Lord Chancellor shall appoint such number of the assistants to the Judge Advocate General appointed under section 30 of the Courts-Martial (Appeals) Act 1951 as he considers necessary to sit as magistrates in Standing Civilian Courts. 1951 c. 46.

(5) Subject to subsections (12) and (13) below, a trial held by virtue of this section shall be before such a magistrate.

(6) The Secretary of State may direct such authority as appears to him to be appropriate in relation to an area for which trials may be directed to be held before Standing Civilian Courts to draw up and from time to time add to a panel of persons whom the authority considers suitable to act as assessors in trials before such courts under subsection (12) below.

(7) If the Secretary of State is satisfied, after consultation with the Lord Chancellor, that there are in any area for which trials may be directed to be held before Standing Civilian Courts

PART II

sufficient persons suitably qualified by training and experience to sit as members of Standing Civilian Courts, he may by order direct that subsection (13) below shall have effect in relation to trials before Standing Civilian Courts for that area.

(8) If an order is made under subsection (7) above, the Secretary of State, with the approval of the Lord Chancellor, shall draw up and from time to time add to a panel of persons qualified as mentioned in that subsection to sit as members of Standing Civilian Courts for the area specified in the order.

(9) Each member of a panel under subsection (6) or (8) above shall be—

(*a*) a civilian, or

1955 c. 18.
1955 c. 19.

(*b*) an officer of the Royal Navy, the regular forces or the regular air force (as defined respectively in the Army Act 1955 and the Air Force Act 1955), Queen Alexandra's Royal Naval Nursing Service, or the Women's Royal Naval Service.

(10) A person shall cease to be a member of such a panel if he ceases—

(*a*) to be a person such as is mentioned in subsection (9) above, or

(*b*) to reside in the area for which the panel is drawn up.

(11) The Secretary of State may, if he thinks fit, remove a member of a panel under subsection (6) or (8) above from that panel on the ground of incapacity or misbehaviour, but shall not exercise the power conferred by this subsection in relation to a member of a panel under subsection (8) above without the approval of the Lord Chancellor.

(12) For a trial where the person, or every person to be tried was under 17 years of age at the date of the alleged commission of the offence for which he is to be tried, and in relation to which subsection (13) below does not have effect, not more than two members of the appropriate panel under subsection (6) above may sit with the magistrate as assessors.

(13) If this subsection applies, the court for such a trial shall consist of a magistrate and not more than two members of the appropriate panel under subsection (8) above.

(14) The magistrate for any sitting or succession of sittings of a Standing Civilian Court shall be specified by or on behalf of the Judge Advocate General.

(15) The persons to sit as assessors or members of the court under subsection (12) or (13) above shall be specified for a trial or succession of trials by the authority who directs the trial or trials to be held.

PART II

(16) Any power to make an order under this section shall be exercisable by statutory instrument, which shall be subject to annulment in pursuance of a resolution of either House of Parliament.

(17) Schedule 3 to this Act shall have effect.

Jurisdiction of Standing Civilian Courts.

7.—(1) The offences for which a civilian may be tried by a Standing Civilian Court are offences committed outside the United Kingdom for which a court-martial may try a civilian, other than—

(*a*) any offence under section 57 of the Army Act 1955 or the Air Force Act 1955 (offences in relation to courts), and 1955 c. 18. 1955 c. 19.

(*b*) any offence under section 70 of either of those Acts constituted by the commission of an offence which, if the person charged were alleged to have committed it in England or Wales, a magistrates' court would be unable to try.

(2) No person may be tried by a Standing Civilian Court if he or any person jointly charged with him elects to be tried by court-martial in accordance with the provisions of this Act or of any order made under this Act.

(3) Subject to subsection (4) below, no person shall be tried by a Standing Civilian Court unless the trial is begun within three years after the alleged commission of the offence with which he is charged.

(4) No person shall be tried for an offence under section 70 of the Army Act 1955 or section 70 of the Air Force Act 1955 in any case where proceedings for the corresponding civil offence must be brought within a limited time, unless the trial is begun within that time.

Powers of courts in relation to civilians.

8.—(1) Subject to subsection (3) below and to section 71A of the Army Act 1955 and section 71A of the Air Force Act 1955, the punishments which may be awarded by sentence of a Standing Civilian Court are—

(*a*) imprisonment for a term not exceeding six months ; and

(*b*) a fine not exceeding £400.

(2) Such a court may award consecutive terms of imprisonment, provided that their aggregate does not exceed 12 months.

(3) Where a person is found guilty by a Standing Civilian Court of an offence under section 70 of the Army Act 1955 or of the Air Force Act 1955 (civil offences) the court may not

PART II

award a term of imprisonment or impose a fine which a magistrates' court in England or Wales could not award or impose for the corresponding civil offence.

1955 c. 18.
1955 c. 19.
1957 c. 53.

(4) Without prejudice to any of the other powers of a court-martial under the Army Act 1955, the Air Force Act 1955 or the Naval Discipline Act 1957 or of a Standing Civilian Court under this section—

(*a*) on the trial of a person to whom the Schedule inserted in the Army Act 1955 and the Air Force Act 1955 by Schedule 4 below applies, a court-martial or Standing Civilian Court shall have the powers specified in the Schedule so inserted ; and

(*b*) on the trial of a person to whom that Schedule as inserted in the Naval Discipline Act 1957 by Schedule 4 below applies, a court-martial shall have the powers specified in the Schedule as so inserted.

Constitution of courts-martial for civilians.

9.—(1) After paragraph (*f*) of section 209(3) of the Army Act 1955 and section 209(3) of the Air Force Act 1955 (modifications of Acts in relation to civilians) there shall be inserted the following paragraphs:—

" (*fa*) a court-martial for the trial of any such person as is mentioned in subsection (1) or (2) above may include in place of the corresponding number of officers—

(i) if it is a general court-martial constituted under section 87 above, not more than two persons who are in the service of the Crown and are persons such as are mentioned in subsection (1) or (2) above, and

(ii) if it is a district court-martial constituted under section 88 above, not more than one person who is in the service of the Crown and is himself a person such as is mentioned in either of those subsections,

but a person who is a member of a court-martial by virtue of this paragraph shall not be appointed the president of the court-martial ;

(*fb*) the reference to an officer under instruction in section 93(1) above shall include a reference to a person under instruction who is qualified for membership of courts-martial under paragraph (*fa*) above ; ".

(2) After section 118(3) of the Naval Discipline Act 1957 there shall be inserted the following subsection:—

" (3A) A court-martial for the trial of any such person may include in place of the corresponding number of officers not more than two persons who are in the service of the Crown and are persons to whom this Act applies by virtue of this section, but a person who is a member of a court-martial by virtue of this subsection shall not be appointed the president of the court-martial.". PART II

Juveniles

10.—(1) The following section shall be inserted after section 71 of the Army Act 1955 and section 71 of the Air Force Act 1955:— Powers of courts in relation to juveniles. 1955 c. 18. 1955 c. 19.

"Juveniles. 71A.—(1) A person under 17 years of age shall not be sentenced to imprisonment.

(2) A person under 21 years of age shall not be sentenced to imprisonment unless the court is of opinion that no other method of dealing with him is appropriate; and for the purpose of determining whether any other method of dealing with any such person is appropriate the court shall obtain and consider information about the circumstances, and shall take into account any information before the court which is relevant to his character and his physical and mental condition.

(3) A person convicted of murder who was under 18 years of age when the offence was committed shall not be sentenced to imprisonment for life, nor shall sentence of death be pronounced on or recorded against a person convicted of any offence who was under 18 years of age when the offence was committed; but in lieu thereof the court shall (notwithstanding anything in this or any other Act) sentence him to be detained during Her Majesty's pleasure, and if so sentenced he shall be liable to be detained in such place and under such conditions as the Secretary of State may direct.

(4) A person under 17 years of age found guilty of a civil offence (other than one the sentence for which is fixed) which is punishable by a civil court in England or Wales on indictment by, in the case of an adult, a term of imprisonment for 14 years or more, may be sentenced by the court, if it is of opinion that none of the other methods in which the case may be legally dealt with is suitable, to be detained for such period, not exceeding the maximum term of imprisonment with which the offence is punishable by such a civil court in the case of an adult, as may be specified in the sentence; and where such a sentence has been passed, the person on whom it is passed shall during that period be liable to be detained in such place and on such conditions as the Secretary of State may direct.

PART II

(5) A sentence of detention under subsection (3) or (4) above shall be treated for the purposes of this Part of this Act as a punishment provided by this Act involving the same degree of punishment as a sentence of imprisonment; and section 71(3) and (4) above shall apply to such a sentence of detention as they apply to a sentence of imprisonment.

(6) A person detained pursuant to the directions of the Secretary of State under this section shall, while so detained, be deemed to be in legal custody.".

1957 c. 53.

(2) The said section shall also be inserted after section 43 of the Naval Discipline Act 1957, and shall have effect as section 43A of that Act but with substitution in subsection (5)—

(*a*) of the word " authorised " for the word " provided ", and

(*b*) of the words " 43(3) and (4) " for the words " 71(3) and (4) ".

(3) Accordingly—

1955 c. 18.
1955 c. 19.

(*a*) in section 70(3) of the Army Act 1955 and section 70(3) of the Air Force Act 1955 (civil offences), there shall be inserted at the beginning the words " Subject to section 71A below,";

(*b*) in section 71(1) of each of those Acts (punishments available to courts-martial) after the word " section " there shall be inserted the words " and section 71A below ";

(*c*) in section 42(1) of the Naval Discipline Act 1957 (civil offences), after the word " shall " there shall be inserted the words " subject to section 43A below "; and

(*d*) in section 43(1) of that Act (punishments which may be awarded) after the word " section " there shall be inserted the words " and section 43A below ".

Court-martial procedure

Proof at courts-martial by written statement.

11. The amendments specified in Schedule 5 to this Act shall have effect for the purpose of rendering admissible as evidence at courts-martial under the Army Act 1955 and the Air Force Act 1955 written statements made by the persons mentioned in that Schedule.

Exemption of certain persons from duty to take oath at court-martial.

12.—(1) In section 93(1) of the Army Act 1955 and section 93(1) of the Air Force Act 1955 (administration of oaths):—

(*a*) after the word " person " there shall be inserted the words " , other than an exempted person,"; and

(*b*) the words " shorthand writer " shall cease to have effect.

(2) The following subsection shall be added after each of those subsections:— PART II

"(1A) In subsection (1) above "exempted person" means any person appointed under section 30 of the Courts-Martial (Appeals) Act 1951 (assistants to Judge Advocate General) who is acting as judge advocate at the court-martial and was appointed so to act either by or on behalf of the Judge Advocate General or by the convening officer.".

(3) In section 60(1) of the Naval Discipline Act 1957 (administration of oaths) the words "for the purpose of reporting or transcribing the proceedings or" shall cease to have effect. 1957 c. 53.

Powers of court-martial etc.

Imprisonment in default of payment of fines. 1955 c. 18. 1955 c. 19.

13. The amendments specified in Schedule 6 to this Act shall have effect for the purpose of enabling a court-martial which imposes a fine on a person convicted of an offence under the Army Act 1955, the Air Force Act 1955 or the Naval Discipline Act 1957 to impose, in certain circumstances, a term of imprisonment not exceeding 12 months in default of payment of that fine.

Restitution and compensation.

14. The amendments specified in Schedule 7 to this Act shall have effect for the purpose of enabling orders for restitution or compensation under the Army Act 1955, the Air Force Act 1955 and the Naval Discipline Act 1957 to be made in relation to offences taken into consideration and of removing the limit on the amount of compensation imposed by section 76 of the said Act of 1957.

Naval Offences

Territorial scope of certain offences.

15.—(1) In sections 93 and 94 of the Naval Discipline Act 1957 (offences by civilians of spying and seduction from duty in ships or naval establishments outside Her Majesty's Dominions) for the words "Her Majesty's Dominions" there shall be substituted the words "the United Kingdom and Colonies".

(2) In sections 96, 97(1) and 98(1) of that Act (offences relating to desertion etc. and to purchase of naval property) for the words "Her Majesty's Dominions" there shall be substituted the words "the United Kingdom".

Powers of civil courts

Enforcement by civil courts of financial penalties awarded under Services Acts.

16. Schedule 8 to this Act shall have effect for the purpose of enabling financial penalties awarded under the Army Act 1955, the Air Force Act 1955 and the Naval Discipline Act 1957 to be enforced by certain civil courts in the United Kingdom.

PART II

Rehabilitation

Rehabilitation of civilians found guilty in service disciplinary proceedings.

17.—(1) In the application of section 2 of the Rehabilitation of Offenders Act 1974 (by virtue of which that Act extends to persons found guilty in Service disciplinary proceedings) to persons to whom Part II of the Army Act 1955 or the Air Force Act 1955 is applied by section 209 of either of those Acts, or to whom Parts I and II of the Naval Discipline Act 1957 are applied by section 118 of that Act, subsections (2) to (4) shall be omitted.

(2) Subject to subsection (1) above, the said section shall have effect in relation to persons found guilty in proceedings before Standing Civilian Courts and in relation to orders made under Schedule 5A to the Army Act 1955 or the Air Force Act 1955 or under Schedule 4A to the Naval Discipline Act 1957.

1974 c. 53.
1955 c. 18.
1955 c. 19.
1957 c. 53.

PART III

MISCELLANEOUS AND SUPPLEMENTARY

Deductions for maintenance of children.

18.—(1) In subsections (1) and (5) of section 151 of the Army Act 1955 and in subsections (1) and (5) of section 151 of the Air Force Act 1955 (power to order deductions from pay for maintenance of wife or child, qualified, in relation to children, by reference to the age of sixteeen) for the word " sixteen " wherever it occurs, there shall be substituted the word " seventeen ".

(2) In subsection (1) of each of those sections after the word " seventeen " inserted by subsection (1) above there shall be inserted the words " or that such a child of his is in care ".

(3) The following subsection shall be added after each of those subsections:—

" (1A) A child is in care for the purposes of this section at any time when by virtue of any enactment (including an enactment of the Parliament of Northern Ireland or a Measure of the Northern Ireland Assembly)—

(*a*) he is in the care of a local authority in England or Wales ; or

(*b*) he is subject to a supervision requirement to which Part VI of the Social Work (Scotland) Act 1968 applies ; or

(*c*) he is in the care—

(i) of the managers of a training school in Northern Ireland, or

(ii) of a fit person in Northern Ireland, or

(iii) of the Department of Health and Social Services for Northern Ireland.".

19. Nothing in section 144(2) of the Air Force Act 1955 (penal deductions) shall apply to deductions from pensions; and accordingly, after the word "deduction", in the first place where it occurs in that subsection, there shall be inserted the words "from such pay".

PART III
Deductions from RAF pensions.
1955 c. 19.

20. In section 1 of the House of Commons Disqualification Act 1975 and section 1 of the Northern Ireland Assembly Disqualification Act 1975 (each of which disqualifies holders of certain offices and places)—

(*a*) the words "or the Ulster Defence Regiment" shall be added at the end of subsection (1)(*c*), and

(*b*) the following definition shall be substituted for the definition of "regular armed forces of the Crown" in subsection (3) of the former section and subsection (2) of the latter, namely—

"" regular armed forces of the Crown" means the Royal Navy, the regular forces as defined by section 225 of the Army Act 1955, the regular air force as defined by section 223 of the Air Force Act 1955, Queen Alexandra's Royal Naval Nursing Service and the Women's Royal Naval Service.".

Disqualification of members of forces for House of Commons and Northern Ireland Assembly.
1975 c. 24.
1975 c. 25.

21.—(1) The Secretary of State shall continue to apply the income of the Travers Foundation property, after deducting the necessary and proper expenses of management, in granting such pensions to qualified officers, and under such conditions, as Her Majesty may from time to time by Order in Council direct; and all such pensions shall continue to be distinguished as Travers pensions.

Greenwich Hospital.

(2) Subject to subsection (1) above, the Secretary of State shall apply the income of the Travers Foundation property for the general purposes of the Greenwich Hospital Acts 1865 to 1967.

(3) The Greenwich Hospital Acts 1865 to 1967 shall have effect as if the said property were property which vested in the Admiralty by virtue of the Greenwich Hospital Act 1865, and the capital and revenue of the property were capital and revenue of Greenwich Hospital, except that the accounts of the property shall be kept distinct from the general accounts of Greenwich Hospital, and be shown separately in any statement rendered to Parliament under the Greenwich Hospital Acts 1865 to 1967.

1865 c. 89.

(4) The rents and profits of the lands which vested in the Admiralty by virtue of the Greenwich Hospital Act 1865 and the Naval Knights of Windsor (Dissolution) Act 1892 shall

1892 c. 34.

PART III continue to be paid, either with or without deductions of the necessary and proper expenses of management of those lands, and of other necessary and proper outgoings in respect of them, into the Bank of England to the cash account of Her Majesty's Paymaster General, who shall carry them to the Greenwich Hospital Income Account and to the account mentioned in subsection (3) above respectively.

(5) In this section—

"qualified officers" means retired officers of the rank of lieutenant in the Navy, or officers of the Navy who have retired from the active list of lieutenants with the rank of commander in the Navy; and

"the Travers Foundation property" means the property which was transferred to the Admiralty by the Naval
1892 c. 34. Knights of Windsor (Dissolution) Act 1892 and from them to the Secretary of State by the Defence (Transfer
1964 c. 15. of Functions) Act 1964.

Citation etc.

22.—(1) This Act may be cited as the Armed Forces Act 1976.

(2) Section 21 above may be cited together with the Greenwich Hospital Acts 1865 to 1967 as the Greenwich Hospital Acts 1865 to 1976.

(3) Except so far as the context otherwise requires, any reference in this Act to any other enactment is a reference to that enactment as amended by or under any subsequent enactment, including an enactment contained in this Act.

(4) Any power to make an order conferred by any provision of this Act shall include power to make an order varying or revoking any order previously made under that provision.

(5) The minor and consequential amendments specified in Schedule 9 to this Act shall have effect.

(6) The enactments specified in Schedule 10 to this Act (which include enactments which were obsolete or unnecessary before the passing of this Act) are repealed to the extent specified in the third column of that Schedule.

(7) The following provisions of this Act shall come into force on the day this Act is passed, namely—

section 1;
section 10;
section 17(1);
section 20(*a*);
section 21;
subsections (1) to (4) and (7) to (9) of this section;

subsection (5) of this section so far as it relates to paragraphs 4, 11 and 20(2), (4) and (5) of Schedule 9 ; and PART III

subsection (6) of this section so far as it relates to the repeal of the following, namely—

the Naval Knights of Windsor (Dissolution) Act 1892, 1892 c. 34.

section 1 of the Armed Forces Act 1971, 1971 c. 33.

section 10(4) of the House of Commons Disqualification Act 1975, and 1975 c. 24.

section 5(3) of the Northern Ireland Assembly Disqualification Act 1975. 1975 c. 25.

(8) Subject to subsection (7) above, this Act shall come into force on such day as the Secretary of State may by order made by statutory instrument appoint.

(9) An order under subsection (8) above—

(*a*) may appoint different days for different provisions and for different purposes ; and

(*b*) may make savings from the effect of any provision which it brings into force.

SCHEDULES

Section 3.

SCHEDULE 1

ROYAL MARINES

PART I

ROYAL MARINES—GENERAL

1955 c. 18.

1. In paragraph 6 of Schedule 7 to the Army Act 1955 (exclusion of certain provisions of Parts I and II from application to marines) the words " sections fourteen and seventeen " shall cease to have effect.

2. For paragraph 19 of that Schedule (deductions from pay) there shall be substituted the following paragraph:—

> " 19. Except to the extent that they are applied by paragraph 22 below, sections 150 and 151 shall not apply to officers, warrant officers, non-commissioned officers and marines of the Royal Marines, the Royal Marine Forces Volunteer Reserve or the Royal Fleet Reserve.".

PART II

ROYAL MARINES WARRANT OFFICERS

3. The following sub-paragraphs shall be inserted after paragraph 5(2) of that Schedule (discharge of marines and transfer to the Royal Fleet Reserve):—

> " (2A) Where a marine enlisted in the United Kingdom is, when entitled to be discharged, serving out of the United Kingdom, then—
>
> (*a*) if he requires to be discharged in the United Kingdom, he shall be sent there free of cost with all convenient speed and shall be discharged on his arrival there or, if he consents to his discharge being delayed, within six months from his arrival ; but
>
> (*b*) if at his request he is discharged at the place where he is serving he shall have no claim to be sent to the United Kingdom or elsewhere.
>
> (2B) A marine who is discharged in the United Kingdom shall be entitled to be conveyed free of cost from the place where he is discharged to the place stated in his attestation paper to be the place where he was attested or to any place at which he intends to reside and to which he can be conveyed with no greater cost.
>
> (2C) Where a marine, when falling to be transferred to the Royal Fleet Reserve, is serving out of the United Kingdom, he shall be sent to the United Kingdom free of cost with all convenient speed and shall be transferred to the Reserve on his arrival there, or if he consents to his transfer being delayed, within six months from his arrival:

Provided that if he so requests he may be transferred to the Reserve without being required to return to the United Kingdom. SCH. 1

(2D) A marine who is transferred to the Reserve in the United Kingdom shall be entitled to be conveyed free of cost from the place where he is transferred to the place stated in his attestation paper to be the place where he was attested or to any place at which he intends to reside and to which he can be conveyed with no greater cost:

Provided that he shall not be entitled to be conveyed to any place outside the United Kingdom.".

4. In paragraph 11 of Schedule 6 to the Air Force Act 1955 (application of Act to members of Royal Marines attached to Royal Air Force) after the words "In relation to officers," there shall be inserted the words "warrant officers,". 1955 c. 19.

SCHEDULE 2

Section 4.

QARNNS AND WRNS

1. For section 54(2) of the Naval Discipline Act 1957 (officers qualified for appointment as members of courts-martial) there shall be substituted the following subsection:— 1957 c. 53.

"(2) No officer shall be appointed a member of a court-martial except an officer who for a period of not less than 3 years or periods amounting in the aggregate to not less than 3 years has held a commission in any of the armed forces of the Crown or been an officer in Queen Alexandra's Royal Naval Nursing Service or the Women's Royal Naval Service or in any reserve of either of those services.".

2. The following subsections shall be substituted for section 111(1) and (2) of that Act (which list certain persons subject to it):—

"(1) Every officer on the active list, and every rating, of the Royal Navy, Queen Alexandra's Royal Naval Nursing Service and the Women's Royal Naval Service is subject to this Act at all times.

(2) Any officer on any retired or emergency list of officers of the Royal Navy or of Queen Alexandra's Royal Naval Nursing Service or the Women's Royal Naval Service is subject to this Act when ordered on any duty or service for which such an officer is liable, and is so subject from the time appointed to report or attend for that purpose until duly released or discharged.".

3. Section 113(3) of that Act (which prevents women members of Her Majesty's military or air forces attached to Her Majesty's naval forces being subject to the Act) shall cease to have effect.

4. In section 132(5) of that Act (which defines Her Majesty's naval forces) after the words "Royal Navy" there shall be inserted the words ", Queen Alexandra's Royal Naval Nursing Service, the Women's Royal Naval Service,".

Section 6.

SCHEDULE 3

Standing Civilian Courts

Interpretation

1.—(1) In this Schedule—

"civilian" means a person who may be tried by a Standing Civilian Court;

"the court" means a Standing Civilian Court;

"the directing officer" means, in relation to a civilian sent for trial by the court, the higher authority who sent him or any officer for the time being discharging the functions of that authority;

"prescribed" means prescribed by an order under paragraph 12 below; and

"sentence" includes any order made by the court on finding a person guilty.

1955 c. 18. 1955 c. 19. (2) Any reference in this Schedule to a provision of the Army Act 1955 includes a reference to the corresponding provision of the Air Force Act 1955.

Sittings of the Court

2.—(1) Subject to sub-paragraphs (2) and (3) below, the court shall sit at such places in its area as the directing officer may, after consultation with the Judge Advocate General or his deputy, direct.

(2) The court shall adjourn from one such place to another if so directed by the directing officer and may so adjourn without any such direction if it appears to the court expedient in the interests of justice to sit at that other place.

(3) If the directing officer thinks it expedient in the interests of justice, he may, after consultation with the Judge Advocate General or his deputy, direct the court to sit at such place outside its area and outside the United Kingdom for such purpose and upon such terms, if any, as he thinks fit.

Court to sit in public

3.—(1) Subject to the provisions of this paragraph, the court shall sit in open court and in the presence of the accused.

(2) The court may exclude members of the public from the trial of a person under 17 years of age or direct that the trial of such a person shall only be reported to such extent as may be specified in the direction.

(3) The court may sit in camera on the ground that it is necessary or expedient in the interests of the administration of justice to do so; and without prejudice to that power the court may order that, subject to any exceptions the court may specify, the public shall be excluded from all or any part of the proceedings of the court if it appears to the court that any evidence to be given or statements to be made

in the course of the proceedings or that part, as the case may be, might otherwise lead to the disclosure of any information which would or might be directly or indirectly useful to an enemy. Sch. 3

(4) The court may sit in closed court while deliberating on its finding or sentence or during any other deliberation among its members, but finding and sentence shall in all cases be announced in open court and in the presence of the accused.

Right to court-martial

4.—(1) An accused person has a right to elect, before the court commences his trial, that the charges on which he is to be tried shall be tried by court-martial instead of by the court.

(2) Before the court commences a trial, it shall inform the accused in the prescribed manner of the right conferred by sub-paragraph (1) above, whether or not he has already been informed of it.

(3) The court shall proceed with the case unless the accused or, if more than one person is jointly charged, any of the accused, exercises the right so conferred.

(4) If the accused, or any of the accused, exercises that right, the court shall adjourn, and report to the directing officer in the prescribed manner the fact that the election for trial by court-martial has been made.

(5) The directing officer shall thereupon—

(*a*) exercise any power conferred on higher authority by section 80 of the Army Act 1955 ; or 1955 c. 18.

(*b*) take the prescribed steps with a view to the accused being tried by court-martial.

Assessors

5. The function of assessors at a trial shall be to advise the magistrate on matters, other than questions of law, arising at any stage during it.

Accused unfit

6.—(1) Where it appears to the court that a person—

(*a*) is unfit to stand his trial, or

(*b*) committed the acts or omissions constituting the offence with which he is charged, but was insane at the time when he committed them,

the court shall adjourn the hearing and report the matter in the prescribed manner to the directing officer.

(2) The directing officer shall—

(*a*) exercise any power conferred on higher authority by section 80 of the Army Act 1955 ; or

(*b*) take the prescribed steps with a view to his being tried by court-martial ; or

SCH. 3

(c) where the hearing was adjourned by virtue of sub-paragraph (1)(a) above and it appears to the directing officer that the person in question is fit to stand his trial, refer the charge back to the court to continue the hearing.

(3) For purposes of this paragraph " unfit to stand his trial " means under any disability such as apart from the Criminal Procedure (Insanity) Act 1964 would constitute a bar to a trial on indictment in England or Wales.

1964 c. 84.

Re-trial in interests of administration of justice

7. The directing officer may direct a re-trial before a Standing Civilian Court in any case where, after the commencement of a trial before such a court, it appears to him necessary or expedient in the interests of the administration of justice.

Re-trial where court ceases to be properly constituted

8.—(1) Without prejudice to the generality of paragraph 7 above, the directing officer may in the prescribed manner direct a re-trial if after the commencement of a trial before a magistrate sitting alone the magistrate dies or is otherwise unable to attend.

(2) Where the court for a trial to which section 6(13) above applies has two members in addition to the magistrate, the directing officer may in the prescribed manner direct a re-trial—

(a) if after the commencement of the trial the magistrate dies or is otherwise unable to attend, or

(b) if after its commencement both the other members of the court die or are otherwise unable to attend.

(3) Where the court for a trial to which section 6(13) above applies has one member in addition to the magistrate, the directing officer may in the prescribed manner direct a re-trial if after the commencement of the trial either of them dies or is otherwise unable to attend.

(4) An assessor's death or inability to attend after the commencement of a trial shall not preclude the trial continuing.

Decisions of the Court etc.

9.—(1) Subject to the provisions of this paragraph, every question to be determined by the court shall be determined—

(a) by the magistrate, if he is sitting alone or with assessors, and

(b) where section 6(13) above applies, by a majority of the votes of the members of the court.

(2) For a trial where section 6(13) above applies, the magistrate shall preside over the court and give rulings on any questions of law.

(3) In case of an equality of votes on a finding, the court shall acquit the accused.

(4) In case of an equality of votes on the sentence, or on any other question before the court, except a question of law or the finding, the magistrate shall have a second or casting vote.

Privilege of witnesses and others Sch. 3

10. A witness before the court or any other person whose duty it is to attend on or before the court shall be entitled to the same immunities and privileges as a witness before a magistrates' court in England or Wales.

Rules of evidence

11.—(1) Subject to the provisions of any order made under paragraph 12 below, the rules as to the admissibility of evidence to be observed in proceedings before Standing Civilian Courts shall be the same as those observed in magistrates' courts in England and Wales, and no person shall be required in proceedings before a Standing Civilian Court to answer any question or to produce any document which he could not be required to answer or produce in similar proceedings before a magistrates' court in England or Wales.

(2) A Standing Civilian Court shall take judicial notice of all matters of notoriety and of all other matters of which judicial notice would be taken in a magistrates' court in England or Wales.

Procedure etc. of court

12.—(1) The Secretary of State may by order made by statutory instrument make provision with respect to all or any of the following matters, namely—

(*a*) the trial of offences by Standing Civilian Courts ;

(*b*) the awarding of sentences by such courts ;

(*c*) the review of findings and sentences of such courts ; and

(*d*) appeals from such courts,

and to such other matters relating to Standing Civilian Courts as he considers necessary or expedient.

(2) An order under this paragraph shall confer a right on a person charged to elect to be tried by court-martial instead of by a Standing Civilian Court.

(3) Any such order may apply, with or without exceptions or modifications, any provision of the Army Act 1955 or the Air Force Act 1955, and any enactment not contained in either of those Acts but relating to courts-martial. 1955 c. 18. 1955 c. 19.

(4) Without prejudice to the generality of sub-paragraphs (1) and (3) above, an order under this paragraph may make provision with respect to all or any of the following matters, namely—

(*a*) the procedure to be observed in the bringing of charges before a Standing Civilian Court (including the manner of election for trial by court-martial) ;

(*b*) requiring any person appointed a magistrate under subsection (4) of section 6 above or a member of a panel under subsection (6) or (8) of that section to take an oath upon his appointment in a prescribed form and manner ;

(*c*) the exercise of their functions by assessors and their rights in relation to trials at which they sit ;

(*d*) the sittings of Standing Civilian Courts ;

SCH. 3

(*e*) the procedure to be observed in trials before them;

(*f*) the representation of the accused at such trials;

(*g*) procuring the attendance of witnesses;

(*h*) empowering the court and the directing officer in such cases and to such extent as may be prescribed to amend a charge which is being tried by the court;

(*j*) empowering the court, where the particulars proved or admitted at a trial differ from those alleged in the charge but are sufficient to support a finding of guilty of the like offence as that charged, to make a finding of guilty subject to exceptions or variations specified in the finding if it appears to the court that the difference is not so material as to have prejudiced the accused in his defence;

(*k*) determining the cases in which and the extent to which the court, in sentencing any person for an offence, may take into consideration at his request other offences against the Army Act 1955 or the Air Force Act 1955 committed by him;

1955 c. 18.
1955 c. 19.

(*l*) applying section 99A of the Army Act 1955 (proof at courts-martial by written statement), section 1AAA of the Perjury Act (Northern Ireland) 1946 (false written statements at courts-martial) and sections 10 and 11 of the Criminal Justice Act 1967 (formal admission and notice of alibi) subject to any exceptions or modifications that appear to the Secretary of State to be necessary or proper for the purpose of the operation of those sections in relation to proceedings before Standing Civilian Courts;

1946 c. 13 (N.I.).
1967 c. 80.

(*m*) directing that the powers conferred by section 7 of the Bankers' Books Evidence Act 1879 (which enables orders to be made for the inspection of bankers' books for the purposes of legal proceedings) may be exercised, for the purposes of any trial before a Standing Civilian Court, either by the court or the directing officer;

1879 c. 11.

(*n*) the transfer of cases to courts-martial;

(*o*) the procedure to be observed in bringing appeals from Standing Civilian Courts;

(*p*) the forms of orders and other documents to be made for the purposes of any provision of this Schedule or of the order; and

(*q*) any matter which by this Schedule is required or authorised to be prescribed.

(5) The Secretary of State shall secure that any power to amend charges conferred by an order under this paragraph shall not be exercisable in circumstances substantially different from those in which charges which are being tried by court-martial may be amended.

(6) The power to make an order conferred by this paragraph includes power to make provision for specified cases or classes of cases, and to make different provision for different classes of cases, and for the purposes of any such order classes of cases may be defined by reference to any circumstances specified in the order.

(7) An order under this paragraph shall be subject to annulment in pursuance of a resolution of either House of Parliament.

Duration of sentences etc. SCH. 3

13. Where any sentence of the court is limited by reference to a period of time, that period shall begin to run from the beginning of the day on which the sentence is passed, except in a case where it is suspended under paragraph 20(4) below.

14. Where the court passes any such sentence and the period of any previous sentence passed on the same person has not expired, the court may order that the new sentence shall begin to run from the expiry of the period.

Supplementary

15.—(1) Section 57(1) of the Army Act 1955 (offences) shall have effect in relation to a Standing Civilian Court as it has effect in relation to a court-martial. 1955 c. 18.

(2) The magistrate sitting in such a court may direct the arrest of any person for an alleged offence under that section.

(3) A person arrested by virtue of sub-paragraph (2) above may be released by the magistrate, if he thinks fit; and no further proceedings shall be taken in the matter in relation to a person so released.

16. Sections 133 and 134(1) and (2) of the Army Act 1955 (safeguards against repeated trial for the same offence) shall have effect, with any necessary modifications, as if any reference to a court-martial included a reference to a Standing Civilian Court.

17. Section 138 of that Act (restitution or compensation for theft, etc.) shall have effect as if—

(*a*) the reference to a court-martial in subsection (1) included a reference to a Standing Civilian Court; and

(*b*) the following subsection were substituted for subsection (9):—

"(9) The operation of an order under this section made by a Standing Civilian Court shall be suspended—

(*a*) in any case until the end of the period within which notice of appeal may be given; and

(*b*) if such notice is given, until the appeal is determined or abandoned.".

Appeals

18.—(1) Subject to the provisions of this paragraph and to paragraphs 5(4) and 14(8) of Schedule 5A to the Army Act 1955 and Schedule 5A to the Air Force Act 1955 (no appeal from absolute and conditional discharges, community supervision orders and recognisances entered into by parents or guardians), a person found guilty by the court may appeal to a court-martial— 1955 c. 19.

(*a*) if he pleaded guilty, against his sentence;

(*b*) if he did not, against his conviction or sentence or both.

(2) A person sentenced by the court for an offence in respect of which an order for conditional discharge or a community supervision

Sch. 3

1955 c. 18.
1955 c. 19.
1957 c. 53.

order has been previously made under Schedule 5A to the Army Act 1955, Schedule 5A to the Air Force Act 1955 or Schedule 4A to the Naval Discipline Act 1957 may appeal to a court-martial against the sentence.

(3) The right of appeal conferred by this paragraph shall not be exercisable unless within 21 days of the date of the court's sentence the accused lodges with the prescribed person a notice in the prescribed form and addressed to the directing officer stating his intention to appeal against his conviction or sentence or both.

(4) When the directing officer receives a notice of appeal lodged under sub-paragraph (3) above, he shall take the steps specified in Rules of Procedure under section 103 of the Army Act 1955 with a view to the appeal being heard by a court-martial.

(5) An appeal against conviction on any charge shall take the form of a rehearing of that charge.

(6) An appeal against sentence alone shall not take the form of a rehearing of the charge in respect of which the sentence was imposed.

(7) The term of any sentence passed by a court-martial on such an appeal shall, unless the court otherwise directs, begin to run from the time from which it would have begun to run if it had been passed in the proceedings from which the appeal was brought; and section 118 of the Army Act 1955 (commencement of sentences) shall accordingly not apply to any such sentence.

(8) Subject to sub-paragraph (7) above, a sentence passed on such an appeal shall be treated for the purposes of any enactment as if it had been a sentence passed on a trial by court-martial.

(9) Subject to sub-paragraphs (10) and (11) below, and to any order under paragraph 12 above, the provisions of the Army Act 1955 or the Air Force Act 1955 relating to courts-martial shall apply to appeals under this paragraph.

(10) A person who sat in the Standing Civilian Court on the trial shall not attend the court-martial as a member thereof or as judge advocate.

(11) Whether the appeal is against sentence or against conviction, the court-martial may only award a sentence which a Standing Civilian Court could award.

Review

19. At any time after a Standing Civilian Court has sentenced a person, but not later than the end of the prescribed period, he may present to the prescribed person a petition against finding or sentence or both in the prescribed form and addressed to a reviewing authority.

20.—(1) A finding or sentence of a Standing Civilian Court may at any time be reviewed by a reviewing authority; and if a petition against finding or sentence is duly presented under paragraph 19 above, or notice is given of an appeal against a finding or sentence, the finding or sentence shall be reviewed by the reviewing authority as soon as may be after the presentation of the petition or notice and after consideration of the matters alleged in it. SCH. 3

(2) On a review the reviewing authority may—

(a) in so far as the review is of a finding, quash the finding, and if the sentence relates only to the finding quashed, the sentence ; and

(b) in so far as the review is of a sentence, quash the sentence ; and

(c) in any case, subject to sub-paragraph (3) below, exercise the like powers of substituting findings, substituting sentences and remitting or commuting punishments as are conferred on a confirming officer in relation to the findings and sentences of courts-martial by subsections (2) to (4) of section 110 of the Army Act 1955 ; 1955 c. 18.

and any substituted finding or sentence, or sentence having effect after the remission or commutation of punishment, shall be treated for all purposes as a finding or sentence of the court.

(3) Neither the power to substitute a different sentence for a sentence imposed by the court nor the power to commute such a sentence shall be exercisable so as to impose a sentence which the court could not have imposed.

(4) Where a person is in custody under a sentence which falls to be reviewed in accordance with this paragraph, the reviewing authority may suspend the sentence.

(5) Where the sentence of a person in custody is suspended under sub-paragraph (4) above, he shall thereupon be released.

(6) Where, while any sentence is so suspended the person sentenced is sentenced by a Standing Civilian Court or a court-martial under the Army Act 1955, the Air Force Act 1955 or the Naval Discipline Act 1957 for a fresh offence, the suspension of the earlier sentence may be determined— 1955 c. 19. 1857 c. 53.

(a) by order of any such court on awarding the later sentence, or

(b) by order of the appropriate authority on the review of that sentence.

(7) In sub-paragraph (6) above, " the appropriate authority " means—

(a) where the later sentence was awarded by a Standing Civilian Court, the reviewing authority, or

(b) where the later sentence was awarded by a court-martial, the authority conducting its review.

(8) A sentence which has been suspended shall, unless the suspension has been sooner determined, be remitted by virtue of this sub-paragraph at the expiry of one year from the date on which the suspension took effect.

(9) The reviewing authorities for the purposes of this paragraph and paragraph 19 above shall be the directing officer and any superior officer or authority.

Section 8.

SCHEDULE 4

ORDERS THAT MAY BE MADE ON TRIAL OF CIVILIANS

1955 c. 18. 1. The following Schedule shall be inserted after Schedule 5 to the Army Act 1955.

" SCHEDULE 5A

POWERS OF COURT ON TRIAL OF CIVILIAN

General

1. The powers conferred by this Schedule shall be exercisable on the trial of a person (in this Schedule referred to as a " civilian ") to whom Part II of this Act is applied by section 209 above.

2.—(1) In this Schedule—

" community supervision order " has the meaning assigned to it by paragraph 4(2) below ;

" compensation order " has the meaning assigned to it by paragraph 11(1) below ;

" the court " means a court-martial or a Standing Civilian Court ;

" custodial order " has the meaning assigned to it by paragraph 10(1) below ;

" local authority in England or Wales " means the council of a non-metropolitan county, a metropolitan district or a London borough or the Common Council of the City of London ;

" local authority in Scotland " means a regional or islands council ;

" order for absolute discharge " means an order under paragraph 3 below discharging a person absolutely ;

" order for conditional discharge " means an order under that paragraph discharging a person subject to a condition ;

" period of conditional discharge " means the period specified in an order for conditional discharge ;

" prescribed " means prescribed by regulations under paragraph 17 below ;

" reception order " has the meaning assigned to it by paragraph 6(1) below ;

" the Services Acts " means this Act, the Air Force Act 1955 and the Naval Discipline Act 1957 ; and

" supervision period " and " supervisor " have the meanings assigned to them by paragraph 4(2) below.

(2) A parent or guardian is a service parent or guardian for the purposes of this Schedule if—

(*a*) he is subject to service law, or

(*b*) Part II of this Act is applied to him by section 209 above, or

(c) Part II of the Air Force Act 1955 is applied to him by section 209 of that Act, or Sch. 4

(d) Parts I and II of the Naval Discipline Act 1957 are applied to him by section 118 of that Act.

Absolute and conditional discharge

3.—(1) The court by which a civilian is found guilty of an offence (not being an offence the sentence for which is fixed by law) may make an order discharging him absolutely, or, if the court thinks fit, discharging him subject to the condition that, during such period, not exceeding 3 years from the date of the order, as may be specified in the order, he commits no offence that may be tried by court-martial under any of the Services Acts or by a Standing Civilian Court.

(2) If a court-martial under any of the Services Acts finds a person in whose case an order for conditional discharge has been made guilty of an offence committed during the period of conditional discharge, the court-martial may deal with him for the offence for which the order was made in any manner in which the court which made the order could deal with him if it had just found him guilty of that offence.

(3) If a Standing Civilian Court finds such a person guilty of an offence committed during the period of conditional discharge, the Standing Civilian Court may deal with him for the offence for which the order was made in any manner in which such a court could deal with him if it had just found him guilty of that offence.

(4) Before making an order for conditional discharge the court shall explain to the offender in ordinary language that if he commits another offence during the period of conditional discharge he will be liable to be sentenced for the original offence.

Community supervision orders

4.—(1) Subject to sub-paragraph (4) below, where a civilian under 21 years of age is found guilty of an offence and the court is of opinion that, having regard to the circumstances, including the nature of the offence and the character of the offender, it is expedient that he should undergo a period of supervision, the court may make an order directing him to comply during a specified period not exceeding 12 months with the reasonable requirements of a specified person nominated in the prescribed manner.

(2) In this Schedule—

"community supervision order" means an order under this paragraph;

"supervision period" means the period specified in a community supervision order; and

"supervisor" means a person with whose requirements a community supervision order for the time being requires compliance on the part of the person subject to it.

Sch. 4

(3) The court making a community supervision order may include in it directions to the person who is to be subject to it to comply during the whole or any specified part of the supervision period with such requirements of any prescribed description as the court, having regard to the circumstances, considers will be beneficial for him.

(4) Before making a community supervision order the court—

(*a*) shall explain in ordinary language to the person who is to be subject to it the effect of such an order and the consequences under sub-paragraphs (6) to 10) below of breach of any requirement imposed by virtue of sub-paragraph (1) or (3) above, and

(*b*) shall obtain his consent and, if he is under 17 years of age, the consent of his parent or guardian, to the making of the order and to the inclusion in it of any requirement by virtue of sub-paragraph (3) above.

(5) If the court makes a community supervision order against any person on finding him guilty of an offence, it may not make any other order except a compensation order in respect of his conviction for that offence.

(6) If a person subject to a community supervision order fails without reasonable excuse to comply with any requirement reasonably imposed by his supervisor or with any requirement included in the order by virtue of sub-paragraph (3) above, he shall be guilty of an offence triable by court-martial.

(7) Any such offence shall be treated as if it were an offence against a provision of Part II of this Act.

(8) If a court-martial under any of the Services Acts finds a person guilty of any offence (including an offence under sub-paragraph (6) above) committed during a supervision period, the court-martial may deal with him for the offence for which the community supervision order was made in any manner in which the court which made the order could deal with him if it had just found him guilty of that offence.

(9) If a Standing Civilian Court finds a person guilty of any offence (including an offence under sub-paragraph (6) above) committed during a supervision period, the Standing Civilian Court may deal with him for the offence for which the community supervision order was made in any manner in which such a court could deal with him if it had just found him guilty of it.

(10) If the court finds a person guilty of an offence under sub-paragraph (6) above, it may, instead of dealing with him for the offence for which the community supervision order was made, impose a fine not exceeding £50 upon him.

(11) An officer authorised by the Defence Council—

(*a*) may discharge a community supervision order or modify such an order in any way which in his opinion does not increase its severity, and (*b*) may replace a supervisor by specifying a new supervisor nominated in the prescribed manner. SCH. 4

(12) The powers conferred by sub-paragraph (11)(*a*) above are without prejudice to any of the powers of a confirming officer or reviewing authority.

Absolute and conditional discharge and community supervision orders—supplementary

5.—(1) If upon finding a person guilty of an offence the court makes in respect of that offence—

(*a*) an order for his absolute discharge, or

(*b*) an order for his conditional discharge, or

(*c*) a community supervision order,

he shall be deemed not to have been convicted of the offence except—

(i) where the order was an order for conditional discharge or a community supervision order, for the purposes of paragraph 3(2) or (3) or 4(8) or (9) above, as the case may be, and

(ii) in all cases, for the purposes specified in sub-paragraph (2) below.

(2) The purposes mentioned in sub-paragraph (1)(ii) above are the purposes—

(*a*) of the proceedings in which the order is made,

(*b*) of any confirmation, revision or review of those proceedings,

(*c*) of any appeal against conviction in those proceedings, and

(*d*) of the Rehabilitation of Offenders Act 1974.

(3) Sub-paragraph (1) above shall not affect—

(*a*) any right of a person in respect of whom an order for absolute or conditional discharge or a community supervision order was made to rely on his conviction in bar of any subsequent proceedings for the same offence ; or

(*b*) the restoration of any property in consequence of the conviction.

(4) No appeal shall lie against any such order.

(5) If a person is dealt with for an offence for which an order for conditional discharge or a community supervision order was made, the original order shall cease to have effect.

(6) The powers conferred by paragraphs 3(2) and (3) and 4(8) and (9) above to deal with an offence for which an order for conditional discharge or a community supervision order has been made are without prejudice to any power of the court to deal with an offence, whenever committed, other than the offence for which the order in question was made.

SCH. 4

Reception orders and committal into care—general

6.—(1) Where a civilian under 17 years of age is found guilty of an offence punishable under this Act with imprisonment, the court may make an order (in this Schedule referred to as a "reception order") declaring that the Secretary of State may authorise any local authority in England or Wales to receive him into their care, and the Secretary of State may authorise any such authority accordingly.

(2) Before making a reception order, the court shall consider any report made in respect of the offender by or on behalf of the Secretary of State.

(3) The court shall give a copy of any such report to the offender or any person representing him.

(4) The Secretary of State may at any time revoke an authorisation under this paragraph.

(5) A reception order shall continue to have effect while the person named in it—

(*a*) is in the care of a local authority in England or Wales under this paragraph or paragraph 7 below ; or

(*b*) is subject to a supervision requirement of a children's hearing in Scotland following a reference under paragraph 8 below, or

(*c*) is in care in Northern Ireland by virtue of paragraph 9 below.

(6) A reception order shall be sufficient authority for the detention of the person named in it by the Secretary of State until he is received into the care of a local authority in England or Wales whom the Secretary of State has authorised to receive him.

(7) A reception order shall be sufficient authority for the detention of the person to whom it relates by any local authority in England or Wales, or by any constable, for the purpose of his transfer to the care of a local authority in England or Wales who are to receive him or his transfer to Scotland or Northern Ireland under paragraph 8 or 9 below.

Committal into care—England and Wales

7.—(1) Without prejudice to the generality of sub-paragraph (4) of paragraph 6 above, the Secretary of State may revoke an authorisation under that paragraph and authorise another local authority in England or Wales to receive the person named in the reception order into their care.

(2) When the Secretary of State informs a local authority that he has revoked an authorisation in accordance with sub-paragraph (1) above, they shall ensure the transfer of the person named in the reception order to the local authority named in the new authorisation.

(3) A person in the care of a local authority in England or Wales by virtue of this paragraph or paragraph 6 above shall be deemed, subject to sub-paragraph (4) below, to be the subject of a care order as defined in section 20 of the Children and

Young Persons Act 1969 (not being an interim order as so defined) committing him to the care of that authority. SCH. 4

(4) The Children and Young Persons Act 1969 shall apply to such a person as if sections 20(3) (care order ceasing to have effect), 21(5) (appeals) and 25(2) (transfer of responsibility to Northern Ireland) were omitted.

(5) An authorisation under this paragraph or paragraph 6 above shall cease to have effect—

(*a*) when the Secretary of State informs the local authority that he has revoked it or that the reception order has been discharged on appeal or review ; or

(*b*) when the case is disposed of under paragraph 8 below, or the person named in it is received into care under paragraph 9 below ; or

(*c*) when the person named in it attains—

(i) 19 years of age if he had attained 16 years of age when the reception order naming him was originally made ; or

(ii) 18 years of age in any other case.

Committal into care—transfer to Scotland

8.—(1) Where a local authority in England or Wales for the time being having the care of a person by virtue of an authorisation under paragraph 6 or 7 above are satisfied that the person's welfare would be best served by his being subject to compulsory measures of care in Scotland, the authority may refer the case to the reporter of the local authority in Scotland which they consider relevant, and if the case is so referred the reporter shall arrange a children's hearing for the consideration and determination of the case under Part III of the Social Work (Scotland) Act 1968, as if the reference under this sub-paragraph were a reference under Part V of that Act in respect of a care order within the meaning of the Children and Young Persons Act 1969.

(2) Any such reference shall include particulars of the authorisation by virtue of which the local authority in England or Wales has the care of the person in question ; and for the purposes of any children's hearing arranged pursuant to the reference those particulars shall be conclusive of the existence of that authorisation in relation to the person.

(3) Where a children's hearing is arranged under this paragraph it shall be the duty of the authority who make the reference as aforesaid to ensure the transfer of the person to the place notified to them by the reporter.

Committal into care—transfer to Northern Ireland

9.—(1) If it appears to the Secretary of State, on the application of a local authority in England or Wales for the time being having the care of a person by virtue of an authorisation under paragraph 6 or 7 above, that the person's welfare would be best served by a transfer to care in Northern Ireland, the Secretary of State may make an order committing him to the care of the managers of a training school in Northern Ireland or to the care

SCH. 4

of the Department of Health and Social Services for Northern Ireland; and the provisions of the Children and Young Persons Act (Northern Ireland) 1968 (except sections 88(3), 90 and 91(3)) shall apply to an order under this sub-paragraph as if it were a training school order under that Act made on the date of the order under this sub-paragraph or, if the case so requires, a fit person order under that Act made on that date.

(2) An order under this paragraph shall, unless it is discharged earlier, cease to have effect on the date when the authorisation would have ceased by effluxion of time to have effect, or

(*a*) if the person to whom the order relates is committed by it to the care of the said Department and will attain 18 years of age before that date, on the date when he attains that age;

(*b*) if the order has effect as a training school order under the said Act and the period of supervision under that Act following the release from detention of the person to whom it applies expires before that date, on the date when that period expires.

Custodial orders

10.—(1) Where a civilian who has attained 17 years of age but is under 21 years of age is found guilty of an offence punishable under this Act with imprisonment, the court shall have power, instead of so punishing him, to make an order (in this Schedule referred to as a "custodial order") committing him to be detained in accordance with the provisions of this paragraph for a maximum period to be specified in the order of not more than two years, if the order is made by a court-martial, or than six months if it is made by a Standing Civilian Court.

(2) Before making a custodial order, the court shall consider any report made in respect of the offender by or on behalf of the Secretary of State.

(3) The court shall give a copy of any such report to the offender or any person representing him.

(4) A person in respect of whom such an order is made shall as soon as practicable be removed to the United Kingdom and shall be detained there in such appropriate institution as the Secretary of State may direct, and any enactment applying to persons detained in any such institution shall apply to a person so detained under this paragraph.

(5) A custodial order shall be sufficient authority for the detention of the person subject to it in service custody until he is received into the institution specified in the Secretary of State's direction.

(6) In this paragraph "appropriate institution" means—

(*a*) where the offender is removed to England or Wales—

(i) if the maximum period specified in the order exceeds six months, a borstal institution, and

(ii) in any other case, a detention centre;

(b) where the offender is removed to Scotland, a young offenders' institution ; Sch. 4

(c) where the offender is removed to Northern Ireland—

(i) if the maximum period specified in the order exceeds six months or there is no accommodation available in a young offenders' centre, a borstal institution, and

(ii) if the maximum period so specified does not exceed six months and accommodation is available in a young offenders' centre, such a centre ;

and in sub-paragraph (4) above "enactment", in relation to an offender who is removed to Northern Ireland, includes an enactment of the Parliament of Northern Ireland and a Measure of the Northern Ireland Assembly.

Compensation orders

11.—(1) The court, on finding a civilian guilty of an offence, may, on application or otherwise (and whether or not it makes any other order), make an order (in this Schedule referred to as a "compensation order") requiring him to pay such sum as appears to the court to be just as or towards compensation for any loss or damage, other than personal injury, resulting from the offence or any other offence taken into consideration in determining sentence.

(2) The sum specified in a compensation order made by a Standing Civilian Court shall not exceed £400.

(3) In the case of an offence of unlawfully obtaining any property (whether by stealing it, handling it or otherwise), where the property in question is recovered, any damage to the property occurring while it was out of the owner's possession shall be treated for the purposes of this paragraph as having resulted from the offence, however and by whomsoever the damage was caused.

(4) No compensation order shall be made in respect of loss suffered by the dependants of a person in consequence of his death, and no such order shall be made in respect of loss or damage due to an accident arising out of the presence of a motor vehicle on a road, except such damage as is treated by sub-paragraph (3) above as resulting from an offence of unlawfully obtaining any property.

(5) In determining whether to make a compensation order against any person, and in determining the amount to be paid by any person under such an order, the court shall have regard to his means so far as they appear or are known to the court.

12.—(1) The operation of a compensation order made by a court-martial shall be suspended—

(a) in any case until the end of the period specified under Part II of the Courts-Martial (Appeals) Act 1968 as the period within which an application for leave to appeal must be lodged ; and

SCH. 4

(*b*) if such an application is duly lodged, until either the application is finally refused or it is withdrawn or the appeal is determined or abandoned.

(2) The operation of a compensation order made by a Standing Civilian Court shall be suspended—

(*a*) in any case until the end of the period within which notice of appeal may be given; and

(*b*) if such notice is given, until the appeal is determined or abandoned.

(3) Where a compensation order has been made against any person in respect of an offence taken into consideration in determining his sentence—

(*a*) the order shall cease to have effect if he successfully petitions or appeals against his conviction of the offence or all the offences of which he was convicted in the proceedings in which the order was made; and

(*b*) he may petition or appeal against the order as if it were part of the sentence imposed for the offence in respect of which it was made.

Imposition of fines on and making of compensation orders against parents and guardians

13.—(1) Subject to sub-paragraph (2) below, where a civilian under 17 years of age is found guilty of any offence, the court, instead of imposing a fine on or making a compensation order against him, may impose a fine on or make a compensation order against any parent or guardian of his who is a service parent or guardian, but shall not do so without giving the parent or guardian an opportunity of being heard unless—

(*a*) he has been required in the manner prescribed by Rules of Procedure under section 103 above or, as the case may be, by an order under paragraph 12 of Schedule 3 to the Armed Forces Act 1976 to attend the court, and

(*b*) he has failed to do so.

(2) The power conferred by sub-paragraph (1) above shall not be exercisable in any case where the court is satisfied that the parent or guardian cannot be found or that he has not conduced to the commission of the offence by neglecting to exercise due care or control of the person found guilty of it.

(3) A parent or guardian may petition or (notwithstanding any other enactment) appeal against a fine imposed on him or order made against him under this paragraph.

(4) If a parent or guardian against whom a fine is so imposed or an order so made—

(*a*) is a member of the regular forces, or

(*b*) is a member of the regular air force, as defined by section 223(1) of the Air Force Act 1955, or SCH. 4

(*c*) is subject to the Naval Discipline Act 1957,

any sum which he is liable to pay, in so far as not otherwise paid by him, may be deducted from his pay.

Orders requiring parents or guardians to enter into recognisance

14.—(1) Subject to sub-paragraph (2) below, where a civilian under 17 years of age is found guilty of any offence, the court may make an order requiring any parent or guardian of his who is a service parent or guardian to enter into a recognisance for an amount not exceeding £50 for a period not exceeding one year to exercise proper control over him.

(2) The power conferred by sub-paragraph (1) above shall not be exercisable unless the parent or guardian consents.

(3) Before making an order in the exercise of that power the court .shall explain to the parent or guardian in ordinary language that if the offender is found guilty by court-martial under any of the Services Acts or by a Standing Civilian Court of another offence committed during the period specified in the order, his recognisance may be forfeited under sub-paragraph (4) below.

(4) If a person whose parent or guardian has entered into a recognisance under this paragraph is found guilty by court-martial under any of the Services Acts or by a Standing Civilian Court of any offence committed within the period specified in the order, the recognisance or any part of it may in the prescribed manner be declared to be forfeited (without prejudice to any power of the court to punish the offender or to make any other order against him or an order against his parent or guardian under this paragraph or paragraph 13 above) and the person bound by it adjudged, subject to sub-paragraphs (5) and (6) below, to pay the sum in which he is bound or any lesser sum.

(5) No declaration may be made except against a person who is a service parent or guardian when it is made.

(6) No declaration may be made against any person without giving him an opportunity of being heard unless—

(*a*) he has been required in the manner prescribed by Rules of Procedure under section 103 above or, as the case may be, by an order under paragraph 12 of Schedule 3 to the Armed Forces Act 1976 to attend the court, and

(*b*) he has failed to do so.

(7) Payment of any sum adjudged to be paid under this paragraph shall be enforceable as if it were a fine imposed for an offence against section 70 above.

(8) No appeal shall lie from an order or declaration under this paragraph.

SCH. 4

Scale of punishments and orders

15.—(1) In their application to civilians, references in this Act to any punishment provided by this Act are, subject to sub-paragraphs (4) to (7) below and to the limitation imposed in any particular case by the addition of the word " less ", references to any one or more of the punishments that may be awarded to civilians under this Act or of the orders that may be made against them under it.

(2) For the purposes of Part II of this Act—

(*a*) a punishment or order specified in any paragraph of one of the columns in the Table below shall be treated as less than any punishments or orders specified in the paragraphs preceding that paragraph and greater than those specified in the paragraphs following it ; and

(*b*) a fine on or compensation order against an offender's parent or guardian shall be treated as involving the same degree of punishment as a fine of the same amount on the offender or, as the case may be, a compensation order of the same amount against him.

(3) In the Table—

(*a*) the first column applies in the case of a person who at the date of his conviction had attained 21 years of age ;

(*b*) the second column applies in the case of a person who at the date of his conviction had attained 17 years of age but was under 21 years of age ; and

(*c*) the third column applies in the case of a person who at the date of his conviction was under 17 years of age.

TABLE

GRADING OF PUNISHMENTS AND ORDERS

Offender 21 *or over*	*Offender* 17 *or over but under* 21	*Offender under* 17
1. Death.	1. Death.	1. Detention as the Secretary of State may direct.
2. Imprisonment.	2. Imprisonment.	2. Reception order.
3. Fine.	3. Custodial order.	3. Fine.
4. Compensation order.	4. Fine.	4. Community supervision order.
5. Order for conditional discharge.	5. Community supervision order.	5. Compensation order.
6. Order for absolute discharge.	6. Compensation order.	6. Order binding over parent.
	7. Order for conditional discharge.	7. Order for conditional discharge.
	8. Order for absolute discharge.	8. Order for absolute discharge.

NOTE. In the application of the above Table—

(*a*) to a person convicted of murder who was under 18 years of age when the offence was committed, or (*b*) to a person convicted of any offence who was under 18 years of age when the offence was committed and would be sentenced to death but for section 71A(3) above, Sch. 4

the references to death shall be omitted from the first and second columns, and a reference to detention during Her Majesty's pleasure shall be substituted—

(i) for the reference to imprisonment in the second column, and

(ii) for the reference to detention as the Secretary of State may direct in the third column.

(4) No order requiring the giving of a consent or the making of an explanation may be made on any confirmation, review or revision of a sentence or any appeal against a sentence without the consent being given or the explanation made.

(5) If a community supervision order is made on any such confirmation, review, revision or appeal, no other order may be made except a compensation order.

(6) Where an order under paragraph 13 or 14 above was made at the trial, no other order under either of those paragraphs may be substituted for it on any such confirmation, review, revision or appeal.

(7) Where—

(*a*) on the trial of any person an order might have been made against his parent or guardian under paragraph 13 or 14 above, and

(*b*) there is power, on confirmation, review, revision or appeal, to substitute a fine or compensation order for the order made on the trial,

that power shall include—

(i) power to substitute a fine or compensation order of an equal or smaller amount under paragraph 13 above, and

(ii) power to make an order under paragraph 14 above which is not of greater severity, in the opinion of the person to whom it falls to exercise the power, than the order made on the trial.

Indemnity for persons carrying out orders under Schedule

16. No action shall lie in respect of anything done by any person in pursuance of an order under this Schedule if the doing thereof would have been lawful but for a defect in any instrument made for the purposes of that order.

Regulations

17.—(1) The Secretary of State may by regulations make provision supplementary or incidental to the provisions of this Schedule.

Sch. 4

(2) The power to make regulations conferred by this paragraph includes power to make provision for specified cases or classes of cases, and for the purpose of any such orders classes of cases may be defined by reference to any circumstances specified in the regulations.

(3) The power to make such regulations shall be exercisable by statutory instrument which shall be subject to annulment in pursuance of a resolution of either House of Parliament.".

2.—(1) The said Schedule shall also be inserted, with the modifications specified in sub-paragraphs (2) and (3) below, after Schedule 5 to the Air Force Act 1955.

1955 c. 19.

(2) In paragraph 2 for the words " Air Force " there shall be substituted the word " Army "—

(*a*) in the definition of " the Services Acts " in sub-paragraph (1), and

(*b*) in sub-paragraph (2)(*c*).

(3) The following paragraphs shall be substituted for paragraphs 13(4)(*a*) and (*b*):—

" (*a*) is a member of the regular air force, or

(*b*) is a member of the regular forces, as defined by section 225(1) of the Army Act 1955, or ".

3.—(1) The said Schedule shall also be inserted, with the modifications specified in sub-paragraphs (2) to (10) below, after Schedule 4 to the Naval Discipline Act 1957, where it shall have effect as Schedule 4A to that Act.

1957 c. 53.

(2) In paragraph 1 for the words " Part II of this Act is applied by section 209 above " there shall be substituted the words " Parts I and II of this Act are applied by section 118 above ".

(3) In paragraph 2(1) the following definitions shall be substituted for the definitions of " the court " and " the Services Acts ":—

" the court " means a court-martial ;

" the Services Acts " means this Act, the Army Act 1955 and the Air Force Act 1955 ;.

(4) The following definition shall be inserted in that sub-paragraph after the definition of " the Services Acts ":—

" Standing Civilian Court " means a Standing Civilian Court established under the Armed Forces Act 1976.

(5) The following sub-paragraph shall be substituted for paragraph 2(2):—

" (2) A parent or guardian is a service parent or guardian for the purposes of this Schedule if—

(*a*) he is subject to service law, or

(*b*) Parts I and II of this Act are applied to him by section 118 above, or

(*c*) Part II of the Army Act 1955 is applied to him by section 209 of that Act, or

SCH. 4

(*d*) Part II of the Air Force Act 1955 is applied to him by section 209 of that Act.".

(6) There shall be omitted—

(*a*) from paragraph 10(1) the words from " if the order " to the end ;

(*b*) paragraph 11(2) ; and

(*c*) paragraph 12(2).

(7) In paragraphs 13(1)(*a*) and 14(6)(*a*), for the words from " Rules " to " 1976 " there shall be substituted the words " General Orders under section 58 above ".

(8) The following paragraphs shall be substituted for paragraphs 13(4)(*a*), (*b*) and (*c*):—

" (*a*) is subject to this Act, or

(*b*) is a member of the regular forces, as defined by section 225(1) of the Army Act 1955, or

(*c*) is a member of the regular air force, as defined by section 223(1) of the Air Force Act 1955,".

(9) In paragraph 14(7) for the word " 70 " there shall be substituted the words " 42 ".

(10) In paragraph 15, there shall be substituted—

(*a*) in sub-paragraph (1), for the word " provided " the word " authorised " ;

(*b*) in sub-paragraph (2), for the word " II " the word " I " ; and

(*c*) in paragraph (*b*) of the Note appended to the Table in sub-paragraph (3), for the words " section 71A(3) " the words " section 43A(3) ".

SCHEDULE 5

Section 11.

PROOF AT COURTS-MARTIAL BY WRITTEN STATEMENT

1955 c. 18.

1. After section 99 of the Army Act 1955 (rules of evidence at courts-martial) there shall be inserted the following section:—

" **Proof at courts-martial by written statement.**

99A.—(1) Section 9 of the Criminal Justice Act 1967 (proof by written statement) shall apply subject to subsection (2) below and to service modifications, for the purposes of proceedings before courts-martial (whether held in the United Kingdom or not) as it applies to proceedings on indictment.

(2) The statements rendered admissible by this section are statements made—

(*a*) in the United Kingdom by any person, and

(*b*) outside the United Kingdom by any person who at the time of making the statement was—

(i) a person subject to service law, or

(ii) a person to whom Part II of this Act or Part II of the Air Force Act 1955 is applied by section 208A or section 209 of this Act or that Act respectively, or to whom Parts I and II of the Naval Discipline Act 1957 are applied by section 117 or section 118 of that Act ;

SCH. 5 and the persons mentioned in this paragraph include persons to whom section 131 of this Act, section 131 of the Air Force Act 1955 or section 119 of the Naval Discipline Act 1957 apply.

(3) In subsection (1) above " service modifications " means—

(*a*) modifications made by any regulations under section 12 of the Criminal Justice Act 1967 in force on the coming into force of this section, and

(*b*) such modifications in the said section 9, as applied by subsection (1) above, as the Secretary of State may by regulations made by statutory instrument prescribe thereafter, being modifications which appear to him to be necessary or proper for the purpose of the operation of that section in relation to proceedings before a court-martial.

(4) Regulations under subsection (3)(*b*) above shall be subject to annulment in pursuance of a resolution of either House of Parliament.

(5) Section 89 of the said Act of 1967 (punishment of making false statements tendered under section 9) shall apply to any statement rendered admissible by this section.".

1955 c. 19. 2. The said section shall also be inserted after section 99 of the Air Force Act 1955, but with the substitution throughout of the word " Army " for the words " Air Force ".

3. Accordingly—

1955 c. 18. (*a*) in section 99(1) of the Army Act 1955 and section 99(1) of the Air Force Act 1955 (rules of evidence) after the word " shall ", in the first place where it occurs, there shall be inserted the words " , subject to section 99A below," ; and

1967 c. 80. (*b*) in section 12 of the Criminal Justice Act 1967 (application of provisions about evidence to courts-martial) for the words " the three last foregoing sections shall apply to such proceedings " there shall be substituted the following paragraphs :—

" (*a*) sections 10 and 11 above shall apply to proceedings before courts-martial under the Army Act 1955 and the Air Force Act 1955, and

(*b*) sections 9 to 11 above shall apply to proceedings before courts-martial under the Naval Discipline Act 1957,".

SCHEDULE 6

Section 13.

Imprisonment in Default

1. The following section shall be inserted after section 71A of the Army Act 1955 and section 71A of the Air Force Act 1955:— 1955 c. 18. 1955 c. 19.

"Power to impose imprisonment for default in payment of fines.

71B.—(1) Subject to the provisions of this section, if a court-martial imposes a fine on a person found guilty of any offence—

(*a*) who is sentenced to imprisonment on the same occasion for the same or another offence or,

(*b*) who is already serving or otherwise liable to serve a term of imprisonment,

it may make an order fixing a further consecutive term of imprisonment such as is specified in subsection (2) below which the said person is to undergo if any part of the fine is not duly paid or recovered on or before the date on which he could otherwise be released.

(2) The further term of imprisonment shall be such term, not exceeding 12 months, as the court in all the circumstances thinks fit.

(3) Where the whole amount of the said fine is paid or recovered in the prescribed manner the order under subsection (1) above shall cease to have effect, and the person subject to it shall be released unless he is in custody for some other cause.

(4) Where part of the said amount is paid or recovered in the prescribed manner, the period of the further term of imprisonment specified under subsection (1) above shall be reduced by such number of days as bears to the total number of days in that period less one day the same proportion as the amount so paid or recovered bears to the amount of the said fine.

(5) In calculating the reduction required under the last preceding subsection any fraction of a day shall be left out of account.

(6) In this section, references to the due recovery of any amount include references to deductions from pay under Part III of this Act, but do not include references to amounts forfeited under the said Part III.".

2. The said section shall also be inserted after section 43A of the Naval Discipline Act 1957, and shall have effect as section 43B of that Act, but with the substitution— 1957 c. 53.

(*a*) in subsection (4) of the words " such manner as may be prescribed by regulations of the Defence Council " for the words " the prescribed manner "; and

(*b*) in subsection (6) of " IV " for " III " in both places where it occurs.

Section 14.

SCHEDULE 7

Restitution and Compensation

Army Act 1955 *and Air Force Act* 1955

1955 c. 18.
1955 c. 19.

1.—(1) At the end of section 138(1) of the Army Act 1955 and section 138(1) of the Air Force Act 1955 (restitution or compensation for theft, etc.) there shall be added the words " or where a person has been convicted of any offence by a court-martial and the court has taken such an offence of unlawfully obtaining property into consideration in sentencing him.".

(2) In subsection (9)(*a*) of the said section 138, for the words " the conviction " there shall be substituted the words " a relevant conviction ".

(3) The following subsection shall be added after subsection (11):—

" (12) In this section " relevant conviction " means—

(*a*) where an order under this section was made as a result of a conviction of such an offence of unlawfully obtaining property as is mentioned in subsection (1) above, that conviction ; or

(*b*) where an order under this section was made as a result of such an offence of unlawfully obtaining property having been taken into consideration in determining sentence, the conviction or, if more than one, each conviction in respect of which the sentence fell to be determined.".

Naval Discipline Act 1957

1957 c. 53.

2. At the end of section 58(2)(*aa*) of the Naval Discipline Act 1957 (General Orders as to procedure of court-martial) there shall be added the words " and for conferring on the court taking one or more offences into consideration power to direct the making of such deductions from the offender's pay as the court would have had power to direct if he had been found guilty of the offence or offences taken into consideration as well as the offence of which he was in fact found guilty ; ".

3.—(1) After subsection (1) of section 76 of that Act (restitution or compensation on conviction of certain offences) there shall be inserted the following subsection:—

" (1A) The Defence Council may also exercise the powers conferred by subsection (1) above where the court has taken an offence mentioned in that subsection into consideration in determining sentence.".

(2) Subsection (5) of that section shall cease to have effect.

4.—(1) In section 77(1)(*a*) and (2) of that Act (effect of appeal against conviction on order for restitution or compensation) for the words " the conviction ", in both places where they occur, there shall be substituted the words " a relevant conviction ".

(2) The following subsection shall be added after subsection (4) of that section:— SCH. 7

" (5) In this section " relevant conviction " means—

(*a*) where an order under section 76 above was made as a result of a conviction of such an offence of unlawfully obtaining property as is mentioned in subsection (1) of that section, that conviction ; or

(*b*) where an order under that section was made as a result of such an offence of unlawfully obtaining property having been taken into consideration in determining sentence, the conviction or, if more than one, each conviction in respect of which the said sentence fell to be determined.".

SCHEDULE 8

FINANCIAL PENALTY ENFORCEMENT ORDERS

Section 16.

1. The following section shall be inserted after section 133 of the Army Act 1955:— 1955 c. 18.

" Financial penalty enforcement orders.

133A.—(1) If—

(*a*) a financial penalty has been awarded against any person under this Act, and

(*b*) it was awarded against him on his being convicted of a qualifying offence or as the parent or guardian of a person convicted of such an offence, and

(*c*) no term of imprisonment was imposed in default of payment, and

(*d*) no appeal is outstanding and the time provided for the giving of notice of appeal against the award has expired, and

(*e*) the whole or any part of the penalty remains unpaid or unrecovered, and

(*f*) the person against whom the award was made is a person to whom this section applies,

the Defence Council or an officer authorised by them may make an order (in this section referred to as a " financial penalty enforcement order ") for the registration of the penalty by the relevant court.

(2) This section applies to a person who is, or would be but for section 131 above, neither subject to service law nor a civilian to whom Part II of this Act is applied by section 209 below, Part II of the Air Force Act 1955 is applied by section 209 of that Act or Parts I and II of the Naval Discipline Act 1957 are applied by section 118 of that Act.

(3) In this section " qualifying offence " means

(*a*) an offence under section 36 above committed outside the United Kingdom and consisting of or including acts or omissions that would constitute

Sch. 8

a comparable foreign offence or a local road traffic offence;

(*b*) an offence under section 70 above;

(*c*) an offence under any provision of this Act other than section 70 above consisting of or including acts or omissions which would also constitute an offence under section 70 above;

and for the purposes of this definition—

"comparable foreign offence" means an offence under the civil law of any place outside the United Kingdom which is comparable to an offence under the law of England and Wales; and

"local road traffic offence" means an offence under the civil law of any place outside the United Kingdom relating to road traffic.

(4) A financial penalty enforcement order shall contain a certificate issued on behalf of the Defence Council or by an officer authorised by them and stating—

(*a*) that a financial penalty has been awarded against the person named in the order;

(*b*) that the conditions specified in paragraphs (*b*) to (*f*) of subsection (1) above are satisfied;

(*c*) the nature and amount of the penalty;

(*d*) the date on which and the charge or charges in respect of which it was awarded;

(*e*) if it was awarded against the person named in the order as the parent or guardian of some other person, the fact that it was so awarded and the name of that other person;

(*f*) sufficient particulars of the case (including particulars of any offences taken into consideration at the trial);

(*g*) the date of any payment or recovery of a sum on account of the penalty;

(*h*) the sum outstanding; and

(*j*) the authority to whom and address to which any stoppages or compensation included in the penalty will fall, on recovery, to be remitted under subsection (7) below.

(5) A document purporting to be a financial penalty enforcement order and to be signed on behalf of the Defence Council or by an officer authorised by them shall be deemed to be such an order unless the contrary is proved, and a certificate under subsection (4) above shall be evidence of the matters stated.

(6) Subject to subsection (7) below, upon registration of a financial penalty enforcement order—

(*a*) service enforcement procedures shall cease to be available for the recovery of the sum certified as outstanding, and (*b*) that sum shall be treated for all purposes as if it had been a fine imposed upon a conviction by the relevant court. **Sch. 8**

(7) Stoppages or compensation recovered under this section shall be remitted to the authority at the address specified in the certificate under subsection (4) above.

(8) Where it appears from a financial penalty enforcement order that the penalty was imposed in respect of more than one offence, it shall be deemed for the purposes of enforcement to be a single penalty only.

(9) Where—

(*a*) a financial penalty enforcement order has been made against any person, and

(*b*) he ceases to be a person to whom this section applies at a time when the whole or any part of the certified sum is still outstanding,

service enforcement procedures shall apply to the amount outstanding as if it were a sum payable by way of a fine imposed by a civil court.

(10) In this section—

" financial penalty " means—

(*a*) a fine, including a fine imposed by virtue of paragraph 13 of Schedule 5A below ;

(*b*) stoppages ;

(*c*) a compensation order imposed by virtue of paragraph 11 or 13 of Schedule 5A below ; or

(*d*) a fine together with stoppages or a compensation order ;

" the relevant court " means—

(*a*) the magistrates' court in England or Wales,

(*b*) the sheriff court in Scotland, or

(*c*) the court of summary jurisdiction in Northern Ireland,

within whose jurisdiction the person against whom a financial penalty enforcement order is made appears to the Defence Council or an officer authorised by them to reside or to be likely to reside ;

" service enforcement procedures " means any procedure available by virtue of any of the following enactments, namely—

(*a*) sections 144, 146 and 209(4) and (4A) below and sections 144, 146 and 209(4) and (4A) of the Air Force Act 1955, and

(*b*) sections 128A and 128B of the Naval Discipline Act 1957 ; and

Sch. 8

"stoppages" does not include sums awarded by virtue of section 147 or 148 below.".

1955 c. 19. 2. The said section shall also be inserted after section 133 of the Air Force Act 1955, but with the substitution of the word "Army" for the words "Air Force" wherever occurring.

1957 c. 53. 3.—(1) The said section shall also be inserted after section 128E of the Naval Discipline Act 1957 and shall have effect as section 128F of that Act but with the modifications specified in sub-paragraphs (2) and (3) below.

(2) The following subsections shall be substituted for subsections (2) and (3):—

"(2) This section applies to a person who is, or would be but for section 119 above, neither subject to service law nor a civilian to whom Parts I and II of this Act are applied by section 118 above, Part II of the Army Act 1955 is applied by section 209 of that Act or Part II of the Air Force Act 1955 is applied by section 209 of that Act.

(3) In this section "qualifying offence" means—

(*a*) an offence under section 14A above committed outside the United Kingdom and consisting of or including acts or omissions that would constitute a comparable foreign offence or a local road traffic offence;

(*b*) an offence under section 42 above;

(*c*) an offence under any provision of this Act other than section 42 above consisting of or including acts or omissions which would also constitute an offence under section 42 above;

and for the purposes of this definition—

"comparable foreign offence" means an offence under the civil law of any place outside the United Kingdom which is comparable to an offence under the law of England and Wales; and

"local road traffic offence" means an offence under the civil law of any place outside the United Kingdom relating to road traffic.".

(3) The following definitions shall be substituted for the definitions of "financial penalty", "service enforcement procedures" and "stoppages" in subsection (10), namely—

"financial penalty" means—

(*a*) a fine, including a fine imposed by virtue of paragraph 13 of Schedule 4A below;

(*b*) stoppages;

(*c*) a compensation order imposed by virtue of paragraph 11 or 13 of Schedule 4A below; or

(*d*) a fine together with stoppages or a compensation order;

"service enforcement procedures" means any procedure available by virtue of any of the following enactments, namely—

(*a*) section 128A and section 128B above; and

(*b*) sections 144, 146 and 209(4) and (4A) of the Army Act 1955 and the Air Force Act 1955 ; SCH. 8

" stoppages " has the meaning assigned to it by section 43(1)(*l*) above except that it does not include sums awarded by virtue of section 128C above.

4.—(1) The following subsections shall be inserted after section 215(5) of the Army Act 1955— 1955 c. 18.

" (5A) Where a financial penalty enforcement order has been registered under section 133A above by a court of summary jurisdiction in Northern Ireland in respect of any person, a justice of the peace may issue a summons to that person requiring him to appear before the court which registered that penalty or a warrant for the arrest of that person.

(5B) Where a person appears before a court of summary jurisdiction in Northern Ireland in pursuance of a summons or warrant issued under subsection (5A) above, the court may exercise the like powers as are conferred on it by Part X of the Magistrates' Courts Act (Northern Ireland) 1964 (satisfaction and enforcement of orders).

(5C) A financial penalty enforcement order shall be registered in Northern Ireland under section 133A above in accordance with Magistrates' Courts Rules.".".

(2) The said subsections shall also be inserted after section 213(5) of the Air Force Act 1955. 1955 c. 19.

(3) The said subsections shall also be inserted, as subsections (6A) to (6C), after section 124(6) of the Naval Discipline Act 1957, but with the substitution— 1957 c. 53.

(*a*) of the words " 128F below " for the words " 133A above " (wherever they occur); and

(*b*) of the words " (6A) " for the words " (5A) " in subsection (5B).

SCHEDULE 9

Section 22.

MISCELLANEOUS AMENDMENTS

Criminal Evidence Act 1898

1. In section 6(1) of the Criminal Evidence Act 1898 after the words " 1957 " there shall be inserted the words " and in Standing Civilian Courts established under the Armed Forces Act 1976 ". 1898 c. 36.

The Perjury Act (*Northern Ireland*) 1946

2. The following section shall be inserted after section 1AA of the Perjury Act (Northern Ireland) 1946:— 1946 c. 13 (N.I.).

" False written statements tendered in evidence in courts-martial.

1AAA.—(1) If any person in a written statement tendered in evidence in proceedings before a court-martial by virtue of section 9 of the Criminal Justice Act 1967 as extended by section 12 of that Act or by section 99A of the Army Act 1955 or section 99A of the Air Force Act 1955 wilfully makes a statement material in those proceedings which he knows to be false, or does not believe to be true, he shall be guilty of an offence.

Sch. 9

(2) A person guilty of an offence under this section shall be liable on conviction on indictment to imprisonment for a term not exceeding two years, or to a fine, or to both.

(3) This section is without prejudice to section 1, and subsection (1) of this section applies whether the written statement is made in Northern Ireland or elsewhere.".

Army Act 1955 *and Air Force Act* 1955

1955 c. 18. 1955 c. 19. 1971 c. 33.

3. In section 86 of the Army Act 1955 and section 86 of the Air Force Act 1955 (officers having power to convene courts-martial) subsection (4) (which is inconsistent with amendments made to subsection (1) by the Armed Forces Act 1971) shall cease to have effect.

4. The following section shall be inserted after section 198 of each of those Acts:—

"Provision as to age.

198A. Where the age of any person at any time is material for the purposes of any provision of this Act regulating the powers of a court-martial, his age at the material time shall be deemed to be or to have been that which appears to the court, after considering any available evidence, to be or to have been his age at that time.".

5. The following paragraphs shall be substituted for paragraph (*a*) of subsection (3) of section 209 of each of those Acts (application to civilians):—

"(*a*) on a trial—

(i) a court-martial may award the punishments specified in paragraphs (*a*), (*b*) and (*h*) of section 71(1) above, except that section 71(5)(*a*) above shall not apply to the amount of a fine;

(ii) a Standing Civilian Court established under the Armed Forces Act 1976 may award any punishment authorised for such courts by section 8 of that Act; and

(iii) a court-martial or Standing Civilian Court may make any order authorised by Schedule 5A below;

(*aa*) any such order shall be treated as a punishment for the purposes of this Act;

(*ab*) paragraph 15 of Schedule 5A below shall have effect in substitution for the words in section 71(1) above from "and references in this Act" to the end;".

6. The following subsection shall be inserted after subsection (3) of each of those sections:—

"(3A) In their application to any area for which Standing Civilian Courts are established under the Armed Forces Act 1976—

(*a*) section 75(2) above shall have effect as if references to the assembling of a court-martial for a person's trial included references to his being brought before a Standing Civilian Court; Sch. 9

(*b*) section 103(1) above shall have effect—

(i) as if the words " with respect to the hearing by courts-martial of appeals pursuant to paragraph 18 of Schedule 3 to the Armed Forces Act 1976 against finding and sentences of Standing Civilian Courts established under that Act " were inserted after the word " authorities "; and

(ii) as if the words " and may prescribe modifications of sections 76, 77, 79 and 80 above in relation to charges which may be tried by Standing Civilian Courts and which are brought against persons whom such courts may try " were added at the end; and

(*c*) subsection (3) above shall have effect in relation to charges which may be tried by Standing Civilian Courts and which are brought against persons whom such courts may try, but without prejudice to its effect in relation to other charges, as if the following paragraph were substituted for paragraph (*e*):—

" (*e*) sections 76, 77, 79 and 80 above shall apply as they apply to officers and warrant officers, subject to such modifications consequential on the establishment of Standing Civilian Courts as may be prescribed by Rules of Procedure and by any order under paragraph 12 of Schedule 3 to the Armed Forces Act 1976; ".".

7. The following subsections shall be substituted for subsection (4) of each of those sections:—

" (4) A fine awarded against any person by virtue of this section by a court-martial, a Standing Civilian Court or the appropriate superior authority, and a sum which an order under paragraph 11 of Schedule 5A below requires any person to pay shall be recoverable, in the United Kingdom or any colony, as a debt due to Her Majesty.

(4A) The registration of a financial penalty enforcement order under section 133A above shall not affect the power of recovery in a colony conferred by subsection (4) above.

(4B) Section 199 above shall apply to persons such as are mentioned in subsection (1) or (2) above, as it applies to persons subject to military law.".

8. Section 215 of the Army Act 1955 and section 213 of the Air Force Act 1955 (application to Northern Ireland) shall have effect subject to the following amendments:— 1955 c. 18. 1955 c. 19.

(*a*) in subsection (7), for the words " Minister of Home Affairs " there shall be substituted the words " Department of Health and Social Services " and for the words from " county inspector " onwards there shall be substituted the words " chief superintendent of the Royal Ulster Constabulary or

SCH. 9

any other officer having a rank equivalent to chief superintendent"; and

(*b*) in subsection (8) for the words from "six" onwards there shall be substituted the words "75 of the Road Traffic Act (Northern Ireland) 1970 or any corresponding enactment for the time being in force in Northern Ireland".

1955 c. 18. 1955 c. 19. 9. In section 225(1) of the Army Act 1955 and section 223(1) of the Air Force Act 1955 in the definition of "Her Majesty's naval forces" after those words there shall be inserted the words "(which includes Queen Alexandra's Royal Naval Nursing Service, the Women's Royal Naval Service and reserves of those services)".

Naval Discipline Act 1957

1957 c. 53. 10. The following subsection shall be inserted after section 118(3A) of the Naval Discipline Act 1957 (application to civilians):—

"(3B) On the trial of such a person a court-martial may make an order authorised by Schedule 4A below, and any such order shall be treated as a punishment for the purposes of this Act.".

11. The following section shall be inserted after section 129D of that Act:—

"Provision as to age. 129E. Where the age of any person at any time is material for the purposes of any provision of this Act regulating the powers of a court-martial, his age at the material time shall be deemed to be or to have been that which appears to the court, after considering any available evidence, to be or to have been his age at that time.".

12. The following subsection shall be substituted for section 132(8) of that Act:—

"(8) In this Act "naval reserve forces" means—

(*a*) the Royal Naval Reserve, including officers of reserve to the Royal Navy and including the Royal Fleet Reserve, and

(*b*) any reserve of Queen Alexandra's Royal Naval Nursing Service or the Women's Royal Naval Service.".

13. In Schedule 3 to that Act (classes of civilians subject to Act) the heading (which is inconsistent with amendments made to section
1966 c. 45. 118(2) by the Armed Forces Act 1966) shall be changed to "Persons subject to Act outside the United Kingdom".

14. In Schedule 4 to that Act (application of Act to civilians subject to it)—

(*a*) in paragraph 1 for the words from "and paragraphs" to the end there shall be substituted the words "and in relation to such persons—

(i) paragraphs (*e*) to (*m*) of section 43(1) above shall be omitted; and

(ii) paragraph 15 of Schedule 4A below shall have effect in substitution for the words in that subsection from "and references in this Act" to the end."; and (*b*) the following paragraph shall be added after paragraph 4:— Sch. 9

"5. Section 129B above shall apply to a person to whom this Act applies by virtue of section 118 above, as it applies to a person subject to this Act.".

Criminal Justice Act 1967

15. In section 89(1) of the Criminal Justice Act 1967 (false written statements tendered in evidence) after the word "Act" there shall be inserted the words "or in proceedings before a court-martial by virtue of the said section 9 as extended by section 12 above or by section 99A of the Army Act 1955 or section 99A of the Air Force Act 1955". 1967 c. 80.

Courts-Martial (*Appeals*) *Act* 1968

16. The following subsection shall be inserted after section 8(1) of the Courts-Martial (Appeals) Act 1968 (right of appeal):— 1968 c. 20.

"(1A) An appeal may also be brought, with the leave of the Appeal Court,—

(*a*) by a person convicted by a court-martial, against an order under paragraph 6, 10 or 11 of Schedule 5A to the Army Act, Schedule 5A to the Air Force Act or Schedule 4A to the Naval Discipline Act (reception orders, custodial orders and compensation orders), and

(*b*) by a person on whom a fine is imposed or against whom a compensation order is made under paragraph 13 of any of those Schedules (parents and guardians subject to service jurisdiction).".

17. The following section shall be inserted after section 17 of that Act:—

"Appeals by civilians—supplementary. 17A. Any reference to a sentence in section 13, 14, 15, 16A or 17 above includes a reference to an order under Schedule 5A to the Army Act, Schedule 5A to the Air Force Act or Schedule 4A to the Naval Discipline Act, but the exercise of the power conferred by sections 13, 14, 15 and 16A above shall be subject to the restrictions contained in paragraph 15 of each of those Schedules.".

Treatment of Offenders Act (*Northern Ireland*) 1968

18. In section 33(4)(*b*) of the Treatment of Offenders Act (Northern Ireland) 1968 after the words "court-martial" there shall be inserted the words "or a Standing Civilian Court established under the Armed Forces Act 1976". 1968 c. 29 (N.I.).

Representation of the People Act 1969

19. In section 4(2)(*a*) of the Representation of the People Act 1969 (convicted persons disfranchised while in penal institutions) after "1957", in the second place where it occurs, there shall be inserted the words "or by a Standing Civilian Court established under the Armed Forces Act 1976". 1969 c. 15.

SCH. 9

Rehabilitation of Offenders Act 1974

1974 c. 53.

20.—(1) In subsection (1) of section 2 of the Rehabilitation of Offenders Act 1974 after the word " awarded " there shall be inserted the words " or order made by virtue of Schedule 5A to the Army Act 1955 or to the Air Force Act 1955 or Schedule 4A to the Naval Discipline Act 1957 ".

(2) In subsection (2) of that section after the word " applies ", in the first place where it occurs, there shall be inserted the words " , subject to section 17 of the Armed Forces Act 1976 (rehabilitation of civilians),".

(3) The following paragraph shall be inserted after subsection (5)(*b*) of that section:—

"(*bb*) any proceedings before a Standing Civilian Court established under the Armed Forces Act 1976 ; ".

(4) In paragraph (*d*) of section 5(1) of that Act (sentences excluded from rehabilitation) at the end of the paragraph there shall be inserted the words " or a corresponding court-martial punishment ".

(5) The following subsection shall be inserted after that subsection:—

" (1A) In subsection (1)(*d*) above " corresponding court martial punishment " means a punishment awarded under section 71A(3) or (4) of the Army Act 1955, section 71A(3) or (4) of the Air Force Act 1955 or section 43A(3) or (4) of the Naval Discipline Act 1957.".

21.—(1) The following entries shall be made in Table B in subsection (2) of section 5 of that Act (rehabilitation periods for particular sentences):—

(*a*) after the entry relating to a sentence of Borstal training—

" A custodial order under Schedule 5A to the Army Act 1955 or the Air Force Act 1955, or under Schedule 4A to the Naval Discipline Act 1957, where the maximum period of detention specified in the order is more than six months.	Seven years." ;

(*b*) after the entry relating to an order for detention in a detention centre:—

" A custodial order under any of the Schedules to the said Acts of 1955 and 1957 mentioned above, where the maximum period of detention specified in the order is six months or less.	Three years.".

(2) The following paragraphs shall be added after subsection (5)(*f*) of that section:—

" (*g*) a community supervision order under Schedule 5A to the Army Act 1955 or the Air Force Act 1955, or under Schedule 4A to the Naval Discipline Act 1957 ;

(*h*) a reception order under any of those Schedules ; ".

(3) The following subsection shall be inserted after subsection (10) of that section:— Sch. 9

"(10A) The reference in subsection (5) above to the period during which a reception order has effect includes a reference to any subsequent period during which by virtue of the order having been made the Social Work (Scotland) Act 1968 or the Children and Young Persons Act (Northern Ireland) 1968 has effect in relation to the person in respect of whom the order was made and subsection (10) above shall accordingly have effect in relation to any such subsequent period.".

Treatment of Offenders (Northern Ireland) Order 1976

22. In Article 2(2) of the Treatment of Offenders (Northern Ireland) Order 1976, in the definition of "court" after the words "court-martial" there shall be inserted the words "or a Standing Civilian Court established under the Armed Forces Act 1976". S.I. 1976 No. 226 (N.I. 4).

Section 22.

SCHEDULE 10

Repeals

Chapter	Short Title	Extent of Repeal
55 & 56 Vict. c. 34.	The Naval Knights of Windsor (Dissolution) Act 1892.	The whole Act.
3 & 4 Eliz. 2. c. 18.	The Army Act 1955.	In section 17(2), the words " (except those relating to discharge by purchase) ". In section 78(3), in the second proviso, in paragraph (*a*), the words " fourteen days or, where the offence was committed on active service," and in paragraph (*b*)(i), the words " fourteen days or, where the civil offence constituting the offence against that section was committed on active service,". Section 86(4). In section 93(1), the words " shorthand writer ". In section 225(1), in the definition of " Her Majesty's forces ", the words " 37 and ". In Schedule 7, in paragraph 1, the words from " 10 " to " and ", in the second place where it occurs, paragraph 5A, and in paragraph 6, the words " sections fourteen and seventeen ".
3 & 4 Eliz. 2. c. 19.	The Air Force Act 1955.	In section 17(2), the words " (except those relating to discharge by purchase) ". In section 78(3), in the second proviso, in paragraph (*a*), the words " fourteen days or, where the offence was committed on active service," and in paragraph (*b*)(i), the words " fourteen days or, where the civil offence constituting the offence against that section was committed on active service,". Section 86(4). In section 93(1), the words " shorthand writer ". In section 223(1), in the definition of " Her Majesty's forces ", the words " 37 and ".

Sch. 10

Chapter	Short Title	Extent of Repeal
5 & 6 Eliz. 2. c. 53.	The Naval Discipline Act 1957.	In section 60(1), the words " for the purpose of reporting or transcribing the proceedings or ". Section 76(5). Section 111(5)(*a*) and (*b*). Section 113(3).
1966 c. 45.	The Armed Forces Act 1966.	In section 13(1), the words from " and in place " to the end of the subsection. In Schedule 3, paragraph 2.
1971 c. 33.	The Armed Forces Act 1971.	Section 1. In section 67(3), the words from the beginning of the subsection to " have effect and ". In Schedule 1, paragraph 2(8). In Schedule 3, in paragraph 5(3), the words " and (8) ".
1974 c. 23.	The Juries Act 1974.	In Part III of Schedule 1 the words " or any Voluntary Aid Detachment serving with the Royal Navy ".
1975 c. 24.	The House of Commons Disqualification Act 1975.	Section 10(4).
1975 c. 25.	The Northern Ireland Assembly Disqualification Act 1975.	Section 5(3).

INDEX

TO THE

Public General Acts

AND

GENERAL SYNOD MEASURES 1976

A

B

E

F

FAIR EMPLOYMENT (NORTHERN IRELAND) ACT—*continued*

FINANCE ACT—*continued*

CHAPTER II

BENEFITS DERIVED BY COMPANY DIRECTORS AND OTHERS FROM THEIR EMPLOYMENT

PART IV

CAPITAL TRANSFER TAX

Relief for business and agricultural property and woodlands

Relief for works of art, historic buildings etc.

Mutual and voidable transfers

Dispositions that are not transfers of value

Other exemptions and reliefs

Valuation

G

H

LICENSING (SCOTLAND) ACT—*continued*

PART IV

NEW TOWNS

PART V

THE PERMITTED HOURS

PART VI

OFFENCES

O

P

R

RACE RELATIONS ACT—*continued*